36th Annual Edition

GUNS
ILLUSTRATED®
2004

Edited by
Ken Ramage

Manuscripts, contributions and inquiries, including first class return postage, should be sent to the GUNS ILLUSTRATED Editorial Offices, Krause Publications, 700 E. State Street, Iola, WI 54990-0001. All materials received will receive reasonable care, but we will not be responsible for their safe return. Material accepted is subject to our requirements for editing and revisions. Author payment covers all rights and title to the accepted material, including photos, drawings and other illustrations. Payment is at our current rates.

CAUTION: Technical data presented here, particularly technical data on the handloading and on firearms adjustment and alteration, inevitably reflects individual experience with particular equipment and components under specific circumstances the reader cannot duplicate exactly. Such data presentations therefore should be used for guidance only and with caution. Krause Publications, Inc., accepts no responsibility for results obtained using this data.

Published by

krause publications
An F&W Publications Company

700 East State Street • Iola, WI 54990-0001
715-445-2214 • 888-457-2873
www.krause.com

Please call or write for our free catalog of publications.
Our toll-free number to place an order or obtain a free catalog is 800-258-0929 or please use our regular business telephone, 715-445-2214.

Library of Congress Catalog Number: 69-11342
ISBN: 0-87349-648-5

Edited by Ken Ramage
Designed by Ethel Thulien, Patsy Howell and Thomas Nelsen

—GUNS ILLUSTRATED STAFF—

EDITOR
Ken Ramage

CONTRIBUTING EDITORS
Holt Bodinson   John Haviland   Layne Simpson

Doc Carlson   John Malloy   John Taffin

Editorial Comments and Suggestions

We're always looking for feedback on our books. Please let us know what you like about this edition. If you have suggestions for articles you'd like to see in future editions, please contact.

Ken Ramage/Guns Illustrated
700 East State St.
Iola, WI 54990
email: ramagek@krause.com

About Our Covers...

This is the year of *really* big handguns chambered for *really* big cartridges. It is the year to celebrate the 50th anniversary of one of our favorite single-action revolvers and to welcome yet another source for the venerable 1911 autoloading pistol.

S&W M500

Ruger
Bisley
Hunter

The Front Cover

THE TERM "BIG" has been redefined by Smith & Wesson. The new stainless steel Model 500 is so large that it required a new, larger frame. Why? So the revolver can handle the also-new 500 S&W Magnum cartridge. There are presently two models; the one shown on the cover is the standard version that weighs about 4-1/2 pounds and launches several different weights of 50-caliber bullets to deliver up to 2500 fpe. The Custom Shop version has a longer barrel, additional features...and a sling.

The Bisley Hunter model is new this year from Sturm, Ruger & Co. Following on the heels of last year's introduction of the Super Blackhawk Hunter, this new stainless steel revolver is also chambered for the popular 44 Magnum cartridge. Two significant features make this revolver noteworthy to anyone interested in a new hunting handgun: The heavy, ribbed barrel machined to accept the *(furnished)* Ruger scope rings and the Bisley grip frame, which is increasingly regarded as a better design *(than the standard SA design)* for recoil management. Laminated grips round out the package.

The Back Cover

Single-Six
50th Anniversary
Model

S&W's SW1911

NOT MANY FIREARMS are in production for 50 years. This year the Ruger Single Six revolver has reached that prestigious anniversary and the company has created a special issue Single Six to mark the occasion. Called the 50th Anniversary Model, the revolver carries a 4 5/8-inch barrel with the model name rollmarked and gold-filled on the top of the barrel. The cocobolo grips will carry, for the first time, the Ruger eagle medallions with the early red background. An extra cylinder, chambered for the 22 Winchester Magnum rimfire cartridge, accompanies each cased 50th Anniversary Model.

Also new from Smith & Wesson.... the SW1911. Similar enough to the original that some 1911 aftermarket parts interchange, this new S&W stainless steel autoloader is chambered for the 45 ACP and is initially available only with a 5-inch barrel. There is more discussion about each of these handguns within this edition, so please read on.

Guns Illustrated 2004

The Standard Reference for Today's Firearms

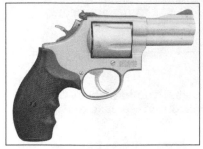

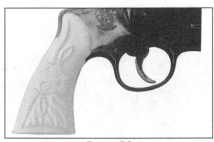

Page 19

Page 50

CONTENTS

About Our Covers 3

FEATURES:

Today's *Really* Big Revolvers
by John Taffin 6

The Shotguns of SIGARMS
by James E. Fender 14

Pocket Pistols — A Hard Look at a Misunderstood Weapon
by Chuck Taylor 18

Handgun News: Autoloading Pistols
by John Malloy 23

Handgun News: Revolvers, Single-Shots & Others
by John Taffin 39

Rifle Report!
by Layne Simpson 51

Shotgun Update
by John Haviland 59

Muzzleloader News
by "Doc" Carlson 65

Ammo Update!
by Holt Bodinson 71

Shooter's Marketplace 79

Page 68

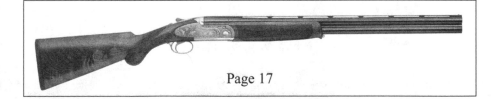

Page 17

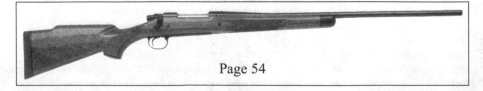

Page 54

Page 70

CATALOG OF TODAY'S FIREARMS

GUNDEX® 87

▨ SEMI-CUSTOM ARMS ▨

HANDGUNS
Autoloaders 95
Revolvers 97
Single Shot 98

RIFLES
Bolt-Action Rifles 99
Autoloaders 103
Double Rifles 104
Single Shot 105

SHOTGUNS 109

▨ COMMERCIAL ARMS ▨

HANDGUNS
Autoloaders 114
Competition 138
Double Action Revolvers 144
Single Action Revolvers 153
Miscellaneous 162

RIFLES
Centerfire Rifles
Autoloaders 165
Lever & Slide 173
Bolt Action 181
Single Shot 208
Drillings, Combination Guns,
Double Rifles 220
Rimfire Rifles
Autoloaders 223
Lever & Slide 227
Bolt Actions & Single Shots 229
Competition Rifles
Centerfire & Rimfire 237

SHOTGUNS
Autoloaders 245
Slide Actions 255
Over/Unders 262
Side-by-Sides 278
Bolt Actions & Single Shots 284
Military & Police 289

BLACKPOWDER
Single Shot Pistols 292
Revolvers 294
Muskets & Rifles 297
Shotguns 309

AIRGUNS
Handguns 310
Long Guns 312

REFERENCE
Directory of the Arms Trade 316

Page 96

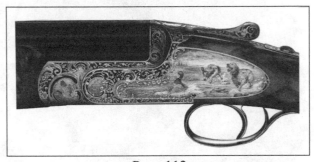

Page 112

Page 118

Page 203

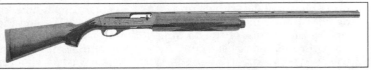

Page 250

Today's REALLY BIG Revolvers

by John Taffin

THE BLAME OR credit, depending on one's viewpoint, goes to the two great handgun sports that really blossomed in the 1970s. Handgun hunting for really large and dangerous game and long-range handgun silhouetting encouraged manufacturers to bring out increasingly powerful cartridges and heavier handguns to handle them. Before the advent of the 44 Magnum, a really heavy six-gun weighed right at 2-1/2 pounds. With the chambering of Smith & Wesson's Model 1950 Target to 44 Magnum it was deemed prudent to add enough weight with a longer cylinder and bull barrel to get it up to an even 3 pounds. Until the time

dedicated handgun hunters and silhouetters really started to put great demands upon revolvers, there was little or no reason to go beyond this standard 3 pounds for 44 Magnum revolvers.

For more than 20 years, six-gunners were well satisfied with the Ruger Super Blackhawk and the Smith & Wesson Model 29 44 Magnums. Both of these were *(and are)* magnificent six-guns—however, a new wave of shooters 30 years ago began to put unanticipated stresses upon these revolvers. For example, Elmer Keith, who had crusaded for the 44 Magnum for 30 years, estimated he fired 600 rounds the first year he had his dream six-gun. That

works out to 12 rounds per week. Twenty years later, it was not all that unusual for handgun hunters and long-range silhouetters to expend Keith's yearly quantity during a week of practice. Factor in the heavier bullets that were beginning to appear, and the resultant beating was more than many revolvers could handle.

Both Smith & Wesson and Ruger added weight to their revolvers. With Ruger it came in the form of a 10 1/2-inch standard barrel, while S&W went for a 10 1/2-inch heavy bull barrel with a special adjustable front sight. Neither of these were enough. Both companies would develop heavier revolvers and S&W

Smith & Wesson added about one-half pound to their 1950 Target to arrive at the Model 29 in the 1950s and then added more weight in the form of a heavy underlug barrel in the 1980s.

would introduce a special endurance package in their six-guns designed to reduce movement of the action parts when the gun was fired. Neither company stopped there; both went on to build heavier, more powerful revolvers. They were not alone. Let's take a look at what has happened—especially in the last decade.

DAN WESSON: The "other" Wesson company, Dan Wesson was the first to really listen to long-range silhouetters. Their 357 Magnum was given special sights and a 10-inch full under-lug barrel. About this time Dan Wesson was also working on the 44 Magnum. There was such a shortage of 44 Magnum double-action revolvers that some Smith & Wessons were actually selling for double the suggested retail price. This would moderate as other makers offered double actions chambered for the big 44.

Dan Wesson had a great advantage as they approached building a revolver for the 44 Magnum. Twenty years earlier Smith & Wesson had chambered an existing revolver and added a half-pound to

the weight. Dan Wesson's only existing revolver was too small so they set about to build a six-gun around the cartridge. The job they did was almost too good! Those first 8-inch heavy-barrel revolvers would not make the 4-pound weight limit IHMSA (International Handgun Metallic Silhouette Association) mandated for a competition revolver. However, the extra weight and the 'user-friendliest' stocks ever offered on a double-action revolver took much of the pain out of shooting a 44 Magnum. Like all Dan Wesson revolvers, they were also exceptionally accurate. Only by judiciously removing

metal from the heavy barrel could this revolver be made legal under IHMSA rules. Factor in a 10-inch barrel and the weight goes even higher–and would be needed for what was to come—the SuperMags.

In the 1970s Elgin Gates, long-time president of IHMSA, decided longer would be better and designed a series of new magnum cartridges. All the new cartridges were dubbed SuperMags by Gates and were 1.610 inches long, or about 0.30-inch longer than standard magnum cartridges, thus a totally new revolver with a longer frame and cylinder. Gates made up SuperMag cartridges in 357-, 375-, 44-, 45-, 50- (remember this one), and 60-caliber. Would anyone really ever build six-guns for these?

The SuperMag series of cartridges did become a reality in the 1980s through the collaborative efforts of Gates and Dan Wesson Firearms. Wesson produced SuperMag revolvers in four stretched Magnum offerings: 357, 375, 414, and 445 SuperMag chamberings. The same bullets that work in the 44 Magnum also work well in the 44 SuperMag *(my preference is for heavier bullets in the 290- to 310-grain weight range)*. The 445 SuperMag is a superbly accurate cartridge in Wesson revolvers, and it picks up about 300-400 fps over 44 Magnum loads with the same bullet weights.

The heavier bullets really make the 445 worthwhile and replacing the 10-inch standard barrel or 8-inch heavy barrel, standard with my early 445 Dan Wesson, with a standard-weight 6-inch barrel makes the 445 handle almost as easily as any 6-inch 44 Magnum. The shorter barrel transforms the big Dan Wesson from a clumsy, heavy competition pistol to a very *packable* hunting pistol.

Ruger started with a standard weight 44 Magnum Blackhawk in 1956, added weight to come up with the Super Blackhawk in 1959, then added more weight with the Hunter Model in the 1990s.

Dan Wesson's Model 15 *(center)* was too small for the 44 Magnum, so Wesson developed the 4 pound-plus Model 44 in 44 Magnum *(top)*, then the even heavier 445 SuperMag *(bottom)*.

Currently Wesson Firearms offers the SuperMags in 357, 414 and 445 SuperMag chamberings, including a compensator-barreled 445 Supermag that adds about 2 inches length, making the 4-inch version about the size of a standard 6-inch 445 SuperMag. This special compensated SuperMag is known as The Alaskan Guide.

Wesson Firearms has also introduced another new cartridge that chambers in their standard large-frame revolver. This is the 360 DW, a stretched 357 Magnum *(longer than the standard 357 Magnum but shorter than the SuperMag version)*, which takes full advantage of the long cylinder of the Dan Wesson revolver.

FREEDOM ARMS: Freedom Arms first began producing the 454 Casull 5-shot revolver in 1983. While other companies were making revolvers more powerful and also heavier, Freedom Arms introduced the most powerful cartridge of the time in a standard-weight revolver. When it comes to really powerful six-guns there are two schools of thought. One prefers the heaviest possible revolver within the bounds of practicality to help fight felt

recoil. The other is more concerned about packing weight, believing if they do have to shoot in a serious situation, recoil will not be a factor. Freedom Arms caters to those in the second group.

When the 357 Magnum arrived in 1935 everyone knew there would never be anything more powerful in a handheld firearm. Twenty years later the 44 Magnum arrived with a bullet more than 50 percent heavier—traveling at the same muzzle velocity. Surely there was no way we could ever pack more power in a pistol! Less than 30 years later the 454 Casull pushed the 44 Magnum into the background with a 300-grain bullet at 1800 fps. Now we had really reached the upper limit—or so we thought.

Even Freedom Arms did not stand still. Their Model 83, already chambered for the 454, was soon chambered for a cartridge heretofore found only in a semi-automatic–the 50 Action Express. Although larger in diameter than the 454, its muzzle energy was quite a bit less. However, for those who placed great stock in large calibers, the 50 AE was what they had been looking for. Freedom Arms had one more step to take.

John Linebaugh's wildcat 475 Linebaugh was made by trimming 45-70 brass to 1.4 inches OAL and using hard cast bullets weighing from 370 to 420 grains. The revolvers were built on Ruger platforms with oversized, five-shot cylinders. Freedom Arms took a good look at

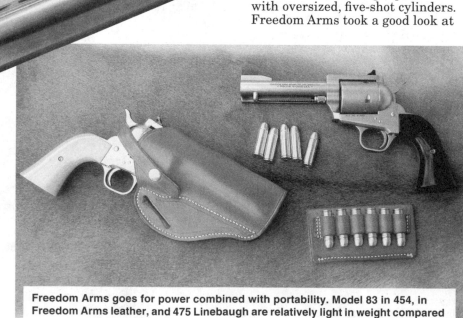

Today Wesson Firearms offers both the 445 SuperMag and this 414 SuperMag model.

Freedom Arms goes for power combined with portability. Model 83 in 454, in Freedom Arms leather, and 475 Linebaugh are relatively light in weight compared to other revolvers at this power level.

the 475; however, the rims of the 45-70 brass were too large to fit in the Model 83 cylinder. Once factory rounds were offered with smaller diameter rims, Freedom Arms chambered their revolver for the 475. Six-gunners are still arguing, in a friendly way of course, as to which is the more practical and most powerful: the 454 Casull or the 475 Linebaugh.

RUGER: Ruger also listened to silhouetters and introduced a totally new revolver— the 357 Maximum. This is, without a doubt, the finest revolver for long-range shooting ever produced by Ruger. Unfortunately, some writers did not understand the concept, applied it the wrong way, and succeeded in killing the revolver. The Maximum *(simply another name for Super-Mag)* was designed to allow silhouette shooters to drive 180- and 200-grain bullets at 357 Magnum velocities. Those that did not understand this instead tried to see how fast they could drive lighter bullets, trying to turn the Maximum into a handgun 220 Swift. Bullets came apart; gas-cutting appeared on the top strap in front of forcing cone. This gun should still be in production—chambered not only for the 357 Maximum but the 414 and 445 SuperMag as well.

Just as Dan Wesson had done, Ruger built a totally new gun around the 44 Magnum, the Redhawk. However, they did not stop there. The Redhawk 44 represented the 44 Magnum of the '80s: big and tough, able to withstand the recoil of not only standard 44 Magnums but the new heavy bullet loads soon demanded by handgun hunters. Handloaders found the durable Redhawk capable of delivering 300-grain cast bullets at 1500 feet per second (fps) from its 7 1/2-inch barrel. Next Ruger brought out an even larger Redhawk, the Super Redhawk.

The Super Redhawk is not simply a Redhawk made bigger, as one might expect. Rather, instead of modifying the Redhawk, Ruger used the GP-100 as the basis for this new 44 Magnum. Three major changes were made. First, the Super Redhawk uses separate springs for the trigger and hammer going back to the hammer spring and strut used in their single-action revolvers, resulting in a much smoother from-the-box trigger pull. Second, the Redhawk grip frame was replaced by the GP-100 stud that accepts the rubberized GP-100 grip panels, as well as felt recoil-reducing rubber grips from Hogue and Pachmayr. The third change was the

Even with 10-inch barrels, both the scoped 454 and silhouette sight-equipped 44 Magnum remain relatively lightweight.

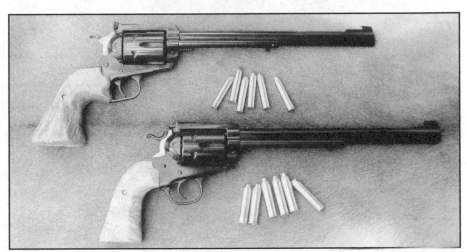

Ruger's 357 Maximum was a superb long-range revolver. It should still be in production along with a companion chambering of 445 as in this Bisley grip frame-equipped custom 445 by Ben Forkin.

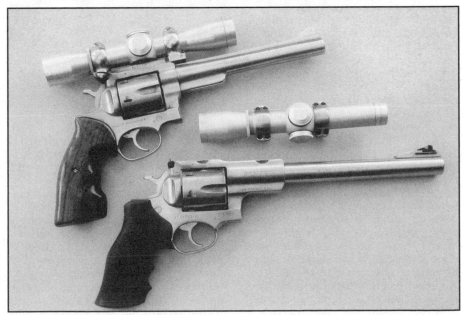

Ruger's first double-action 44 Magnum Redhawk is compared to the even heavier Super Redhawk.

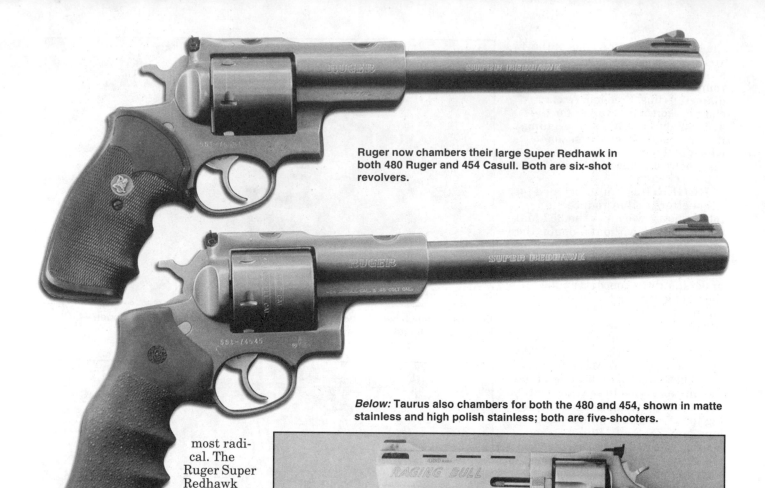

Ruger now chambers their large Super Redhawk in both 480 Ruger and 454 Casull. Both are six-shot revolvers.

Below: Taurus also chambers for both the 480 and 454, shown in matte stainless and high polish stainless; both are five-shooters.

most radical. The Ruger Super Redhawk has a distinctive profile not found on any other revolver. The frame itself was extended forward of the cylinder so that the first 2-1/2 inches of the barrel is actually enclosed by the frame. This feature accomplishes two things: the frame is made heavier and stronger; and also provides for an integral scope mounting system on the frame rather than the barrel. Weight? Remember, heavy six-guns before the 44 Magnum weighed around 39 ounces; the 44 Magnum took it to 48 ounces. With the Redhawk and the Super Redhawk in their longest barrel lengths we were now at 54 and 58 ounces respectively.

Ruger had a large, super-strong revolver chambered in 44 Magnum only— but this was about to change. In 1999 Ruger took a major step forward and chambered the Super Redhawk in 454. Most of us were surprised when this happened. Not because Ruger added the 454 chambering to their lineup but because we expected a five-shot Bisley Model single action, not a six-shot double action. To accomplish this, two major changes had to be made. A higher grade of steel is used *(than in the 44 Magnum Super Redhawk)* and heat-treated differently. The Super Redhawk has been very popular in the 454 Casull chambering.

There is no such thing as a "comfortable-shooting" 44 Magnum or 454 Casull, exactly why handguns have become heavier. With a weight of 58 ounces for the Super Redhawk—plus the added weight of the scope, rings and the soft rubber grips—recoil is much more manageable. Those that shoot heavy-recoil big-bore six-guns more than they pack them will normally opt for the heavier option. The Super Redhawk allows shooting long strings of these powerful cartridges in relative "comfort," and has become very popular with handgun hunters who do not mind the extra weight and do

not buy into the misguided *"scopes do not belong on handguns"* theory. Those espousing this do not understand that handguns can fill more niches than the traditional easy-to-pack and always-ready function.

Ruger did not forget the single-action six-gunners. The Super Blackhawk has been fitted with a 7 1/2-inch heavy ribbed barrel, with "scallops" to accept Ruger scope rings. This Super Blackhawk Hunter Model exceeds the weight of the regular Super Blackhawk by six ounces. Now it is being offered as a Bisley Model Hunter. Without doubt, the Super Blackhawk Hunter

A comparison of cartridges *(l-r)*: 357 Magnum, 44 Magnum, 454 Casull, 480 Ruger, 475 Linebaugh, 357 SuperMag, 414 SuperMag, 445 SuperMag, and 500 S&W.

Model is the # 1 bargain today for handgun hunters and the Bisley version makes it even more so.

TAURUS: The heavier-is-better idea certainly carries over to Taurus six-guns. While Ruger soars high with Redhawks, Taurus runs the Bulls—the Raging Bulls, that is. The Raging Bull was first produced in a 5-shot 454 Casull, as well as a 6-shot version in 44 Magnum. As soon as Hornady started producing 480 Ruger ammunition, Taurus also chambered their Raging Bull in what was then the newest six-gun

cartridge. The Raging Bull is one great-looking revolver. The heavy barrels of all Raging Bulls are of the full under-lug variety with a recess for the ejector rod. Integral to each barrel is a heavy rib with ventilated slots. Barrel, underlug, and the ventilated rib are all machined from one solid piece of steel, as is the ramp for the front sight. This heavy barrel measures 1.650 inches from top to bottom and, when viewed from the front, can be seen to taper from the center to the top of the rib and the bottom of the underlug.

Raging Bulls are heavy sixguns with both the 44 Magnum and the 454 Casull weighing 55 ounces and the 480 Ruger version one ounce lighter; all weights taken with 6 1/2-inch models. The overall weight, ported barrel, and highly functional, pebble-grained black rubber grips with a cushioned red insert along the backstrap area do much to lessen felt recoil. It may not be the easiest revolver to pack but its size and weight make it more pleasant to shoot. Raging Bulls also normally have the smooth actions that

Magnum Research's BFR is offered in a combination 480/475 Linebaugh.

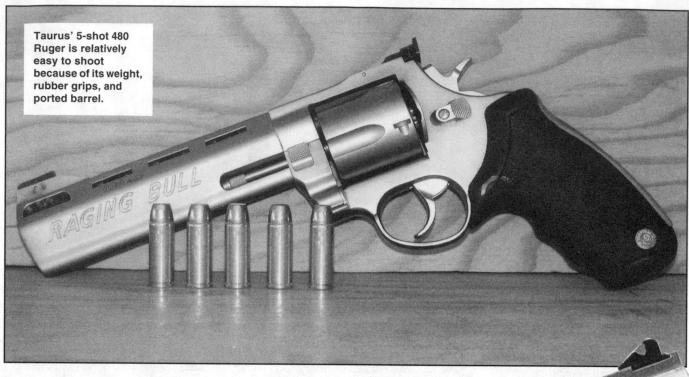

Taurus' 5-shot 480 Ruger is relatively easy to shoot because of its weight, rubber grips, and ported barrel.

Taurus is noted for, and smooth-faced triggers that are kind to trigger fingers.

MAGNUM RESEARCH: Magnum Research's experience with big-bore handguns started with the Israeli Military Industries Desert Eagle semi-automatic pistol chambered in 50 Action Express. The Desert Eagle is a huge handgun. The slide measures approximately 1-3/4 inches in height and 1-1/4 inches in width. The barrel is over one inch in diameter at the rear, with a heavy square rib on top slotted to accept scope rings. The front of the barrel is trapezoidal in shape, with the base being 1-1/4 inches wide. Even the 50-caliber hole does not look large in the massive barrel of the Desert Eagle. It is, of course, not a revolver—however, the weight of 66.5 ounces makes it the heaviest handgun so far. Except for the fact that my stubby fingers have a hard time making it around the grip frame, the Desert Eagle is relatively pleasant to shoot.

Magnum Research started down *Big-Bore Road* with a semi-automatic, but soon found the turn-off marked *Six-Gun Street*. The BFR is an all stainless steel *(except for the sights)* 5-shot revolver looking much like a Ruger Super Blackhawk. The grip frame is definitely Ruger Super Blackhawk size as grips from my Ruger Super Blackhawk also fit the BFR *(Biggest Finest Revolver)*. The BFR has a feature that is usually only found on custom single actions, namely, the cylinder will rotate either clockwise or counter-clockwise when the loading gate is opened. This is always helpful on hard-kickin' six-guns should a bullet jump the crimp, protrude from the case, and lock up the cylinder. With a free-wheeling cylinder, one simply rotates it backwards until the problem round can be removed with the ejector rod.

The BFR comes in two versions. The standard-length cylinder is available in 454 Casull and 480/475, while the long-cylinder version is offered in 444 Marlin, 45-70, and a special 45 Colt version that also accepts .410 shotgun shells. When compared to the Desert Eagle, the standard-cylinder versions are relative lightweights at 56 ounces; the long-cylinder BFR is the heaviest revolver—at 64 ounces—discussed thus far. Both weights are well appreciated when shooting the 475 Linebaugh and 45-70. After extensive testing of both 480 Ruger and 475 Linebaugh reloads and factory ammunition in the BFR, I have found the 480/475 BFR to be an exceptionally accurate revolver.

SMITH & WESSON: For nearly 50 years, from 1935 to 1983, Smith & Wesson was definitely *King of the Magnum Handguns*, having intro-

New this year from Ruger is the Bisley Hunter model in 44 Magnum, developed by fitting the Bisley grip frame, hammer, and trigger to the standard Hunter model.

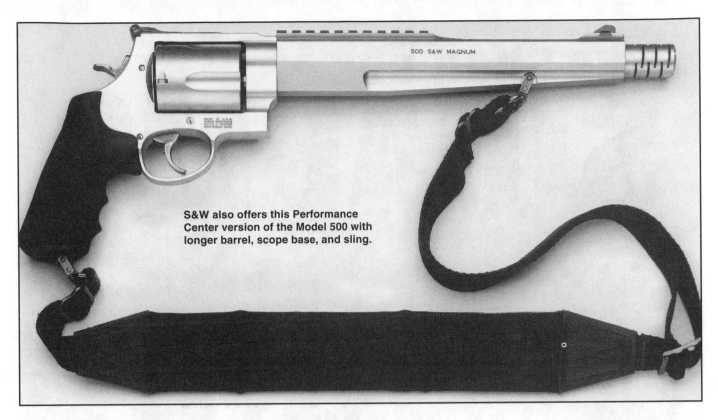

S&W also offers this Performance Center version of the Model 500 with longer barrel, scope base, and sling.

duced the 357 Magnum, the 44 Magnum, and the 41 Magnum. All of this changed in 1983 with the introduction of the new champion cartridge, the 454 Casull. Then came the 475 Linebaugh, and the Smith & Wesson magnums were pushed further down the big-bore handgun ladder. Suddenly, everything changed— today Smith & Wesson leads the pack, and just might do so forever.

Earlier I mentioned the 500 SuperMag, one of the SuperMag cartridges developed by Elgin Gates. John Linebaugh was the first to actually build a revolver chambered in his cartridge, the 500 Linebaugh Long—or 500 Maximum. Linebaugh used Ruger 357 Maximum frames as the basis for his five-shot revolvers. Case length on the 500 Maximum is 1.610 inches; the bullets measure .512-inch. Smith & Wesson now has their version, the 500 S&W, chambered in a totally new revolver.

The new Smith & Wesson Model 500 X-Frame has a heavy under-lugged and ported barrel, and utilizes a stretched frame and cylinder to accommodate the 500 S&W Magnum cartridge with a case length of 1.625 inches. This new cartridge is a true .500-inch and is currently loaded with three different bullets by Cor-Bon. Those loads are a 275-grain Barnes X bullet at 1665 fps, a 400-grain SP at 1675 fps, and a 440-grain Hard Cast traveling at 1625 fps. The muzzle energy of the 440-grain load is approximately 2 1/2 times that of the 44 Magnum and five times that of the 357 Magnum. At 72 ounces with an 8 3/8-inch barrel, it is heavier than any currently manufactured big-bore revolver. A second version *(from the Performance Center)*, the Magnum Hunter Model, will have a 10 1/2-inch barrel with scope-mounting rib for even more recoil-reducing weight.

The original 1847 Colt Walker weighed a massive 4 1/2 pounds (72 ounces), and Colt immediately began downsizing it until they arrived at the lighter (39 ounces) and more powerful 45-caliber Single Action Army in 1873. I have fired the 500 Maximum in a revolver weighing just a little over three pounds and can tell you from that experience that a gun weight of 4-1/2 pounds will be greatly appreciated. Will revolvers continue to get bigger and more powerful? They said *No* in 1935, again in 1955, and again in 1983. Every time *No* has been the wrong answer. Have we finally reached the limit?

Smith & Wesson's 72-ounce king of the mountain, the Model 500 X-Frame in 500 S&W.

The Shotguns of SIGARMS

A 20-gauge TR40 Gold is put through its paces on the Skeet field by SIGARMS' Laura Burgess.

by J. E. Fender

SIGARMS, INCORPORATED, IS more prominently known for its lines of rifles (Blaser, Hammerli, Sauer) and handguns (Hammerli, Mauser, SIG Sauer) rather than shotguns. However, in 1997 the company set out to capture a share of the burgeoning United States market for high-quality, mechanically excellent superposed double shotguns attractive in appearance and price. After visiting the shotgun manufacturing industry centered in the Brescia and Gardone Val Trompia region of northern Italy, Ted Rowe, then president of SIGARMS, and outside consultant Bud Fini, settled upon shotguns manufactured by the firms of Antonio Zoli and Battista Rizzini.

Importation of shotguns designed to appeal to American tastes began in late 1997, with the shotguns, designated as SA (for SIGARMS) 3 and 5, appearing in the 1998 SIGARMS products catalog. The SA 3, in 20 and 12 gauges, was manufactured by Zoli. The SA 5, in 12-gauge only, was manufactured by B. Rizzini. Both models were robust, excellent quality shotguns, but offered little to distinguish them in a highly competitive market. SA 3 and SA 5 sales were, charitably speaking, lackluster. Wesley Lang, a well known and highly skilled sporting clays competitor, was brought into the company as Vice-President of Marketing in early 1998 to develop a shotgun line which would complement

SIGARMS' lines of top quality rifles and handguns—or else eliminate the entire shotgun project.

Lang had previously held key positions at Beretta USA and Seminole Chokes and Gunworks. Knowledge gained in those positions, coupled with his experience as a sporting clays competitor, led to the decision to work exclusively with B. Rizzini. I saw the first 20- and 12-gauge shotguns of the "Apollo" line at the 1999 SHOT Show in Atlanta, and discussed the shotguns with Lang at length. I immediately concluded the line would give Beretta, Browning, Ruger—and the other superposed shotguns in its price range—a real run for their money.

The "Apollo" name was selected because the grade of B. Rizzini shotguns SIGARMS chose to import was sold in Italy under the trade name "Artemis." In Greek mythology Apollo and Artemis were twins, brother and sister, children of Zeus and Leto, so the "Apollo" designation was a logical one. However, Weatherby, Inc., had established prior usage of the "Apollo" trade name, and SIGARMS promptly renamed its shotgun line "Aurora" for the Greek personification of the dawn. The decisions to source its shotgun line exclusively from B. Rizzini and use the trade name Aurora were astute ones for SIGARMS, as we shall see.

SIGARMS, Incorporated, grew from a joint venture between the Swiss gunmaking firm of SIG (*Schweizerische Industrie-Gesellschaft* – Swiss Industry Group) and the German gunmaking firm of J. P. Sauer & Sohn. SIGARMS' first United States location was Herndon, Virginia, but for the last ten years has been located in Exeter, New

Aurora TR20 Field model, this one a .410-bore.

Aurora TR20U Field in 28-gauge, with straight English stock.

Hampshire, where the company is thriving. In late 2000 SIGARMS was purchased by Michael Lüeke and Thomas Ortmeier, two German entrepreneurs headquartered in Emsdetten, who recognized the company's growth potential. The existing SIGARMS management team was left in place, while Lüeke and Ortmeier provided an infusion of funds for product line expansion.

American shotgunners have developed a passion for the superposed shotgun and, rather than abating, the passion is increasing— particularly for over and under shotguns retailing in the $1,500 to $2,600 range. While I have been privy to the yearly production figures of the Ruger Red Label series of over/under shotguns, those figures are, of course, company confidential. However, Sturm, Ruger and Company, in all likelihood could handily sell twice the company's production of superposed double shotguns. A company that can sell a mechanically excellent, well balanced, and attractive superposed double shotgun which offers value far in excess of its cost in this price range will be ideally positioned to capitalize on this demand.

As designed for its import guise, the SIGARMS Aurora line owes its existence to two young men: Wesley Lang and Giorgio Guerini, until recently sales manager for B. Rizzini and a nephew of founder, Battista Rizzini. Lang knew the features that American shotgunners appreciate: a choice of grips, full-pistol, Prince-of-Wales (*the absolute best of the rounded, or semi-pistol grip)*, the superb English straight-hand, a choice of action finishes (*case-colored, coin-finished, or blued*), and a satisfying variety of barrel lengths. The sporting or competition shotguns (designated as Aurora TT) can be purchased in 28-, 30- and 32-inch barrel lengths, while the field shotguns (designated Aurora TR) are available in 26- and 28-inch barrel lengths. Almost the full range of gauges (12, 20, 28 and .410) is being imported by SIGARMS. The superbly efficient 16-gauge is cataloged by B. Rizzini (*fitted to a 12-gauge receiver)*,

but SIGARMS has no plans to add the 16-gauge to its Aurora line. Barrels for the 28-gauge and .410 are fitted onto 20-gauge receivers, not receivers sized specifically to these gauges. Nevertheless, the lines of the sub-gauge Auroras are trim and esthetically very pleasing. Shotgunners interested in the SIGARMS Aurora line have their choice of a basic boxlock or a boxlock fitted with sideplates. Giorgio Guerini knew how to incorporate these features—and quickly—into a high quality machine-made shotgun.

There are a variety of engraving patterns from which to choose. Even though the engravings are photoengraved, they are well executed, although no one will ever mistake them for the superb engravers' art coming from the Pedrettis, the Fricassis, or Creative Art. The Aurora line easily surpasses any other offerings for a machine-made shotgun in its price range.

It is important to note there are many small companies in the northern Italy firearms industry that produce extremely high-quality components on a "cottage industry" basis. There are some shotgun "manufacturers" who actually are "assemblers" since they purchase components and finish them to their standards. Not so B. Rizzini. B. Rizzini shotguns are designed, manufactured and fitted in Rizzini's well-maintained factory in Marcheno.

The Aurora from B. Rizzini is a straightforward boxlock which long has had all extraneous parts and superfluous weight pared away in constant product improvement and safety engineering designs. A fairly recent design change in the trigger system, billed as a "double safety system," ensures sears cannot contact any part of the trigger mechanism while the mechanical tang safety is engaged. The B. Rizzini catalog additionally describes this design as ensuring only a completely closed shotgun can discharge. The trigger mechanism is similar to the original John M. Browning superposed design, with tumblers hinged on the trigger plate and the sears suspended from the receiver's top strap.

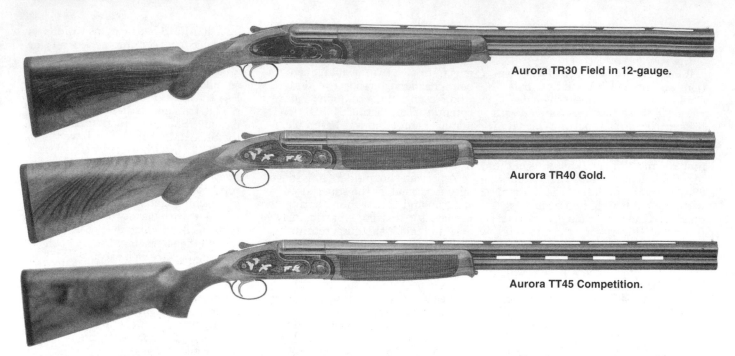

Aurora TR30 Field in 12-gauge.

Aurora TR40 Gold.

Aurora TT45 Competition.

The barrel selector is a button on the tang-mounted safety. The selector is moved approximately 1/16-inch side-to-side to select upper or lower barrel, an innovation originally pioneered by Beretta, but now in wide use by other Italian double shotgun manufacturers.

The receiver sidewalls, after machining, are quite substantial. The trunnions on which the barrels hinge are not machined integral with the sidewalls, but are separate hardened pins attached with Allen screws, and thus readily replaceable should excessive wear ever occur. Ejector actuators and cocking rods are housed in the receiver's bottom. The Aurora action springs are all coil-spring, and the single selective triggers of the line utilize the inertia system.

As do the majority of Italian fine gunmakers, B. Rizzini sources its stock woods from Turkey in the form of varying grades of walnut. The quality of wood is commensurate with the grade of the shotgun. The Aurora line has buttstocks shaped to American tastes, and finished with traditional oil. Buttstocks are attached to their receivers with a standard stock bolt.

The barrels, like the vast majority of machine-made shotguns today, are of monobloc construction, and are struck exceedingly well. Other shotguns in the Aurora line's price ranges

Sorting Out The Rizzinis

There are several firearms manufacturers in the Val Trompia region of Northern Italy near Brescia, who legitimately use the surname "Rizzini" in their companies' trade names, though the practice has occasionally resulted in shotgunners' confusing one "Rizzini" manufacturer's shotguns with another. In actuality, the various Rizzini firearms manufacturers are separate, distinct companies.

The most prestigious is Fratelli Rizzini, Costruttori d'Armi, located in Magno, V.T. Five brothers (fratelli is the Italian word for brothers), Aldo, Allesandro, Amelio, Firmo and Guido founded their company in 1973. The company had earlier manufactured shotguns under the name Zoli and Rizzini. In the late 1960s and early 1970s the venerable New York firm of Abercrombie & Fitch imported Zoli-Rizzini shotguns as the "A&F Knockabout Doubles". Retail prices, circa 1970, ranged from $150 to $300.

Today F.lli Rizzini is world renowned, and deservedly so, for breathtakingly beautiful side-by-side doubles, of which approximately 20 are painstakingly crafted by hand in the course of a year. Depending upon the choice of engraver, a collector desiring one of these incomparable shotguns may have a wait of four or more years between the time an order is placed and the shotgun's delivery.

The other Rizzini firearms' manufacturers are brothers Battista, Emilio and Isidoro, cousins of the men who founded F.lli Rizzini. Battista, Emilio and Isidoro began their respective companies in the mid-1960s or early 1970s as well, though their firearms productions are solely devoted to superposed, or over and under designs. Battista Rizzini is located in Marcheno, V.T., as is Fabbrica Armi Isidoro Rizzini (FAIR, and also known as Tecni-Mec). In 2000 Emilio Rizzini merged into Fausti Stefano, a larger, more diversified shotgun manufacturer

also located in Marcheno. The Emilio Rizzini line manufactured by Fausti Stefano continues the trade name.

In addition to manufacturing the Aurora line of shotguns imported by SIGARMS, a small number of specially finished semi-custom B. Rizzini shotguns are marketed by William Larkin Moore & Company. Similarly, a small number of specially finished semi-custom FAIR or I. Rizzini shotguns are marketed by Bill Hanus Birdguns. Fausti Stefano produced E. Rizzini shotguns are marketed by TriStar and Traditions. These three Rizzini manufacturers produce marvelously precise machine made shotguns that resemble each other externally— and to a marked degree internally—as well. B. Rizzini, E. Rizzini and FAIR manufactured shotguns represent solid value for their owners, but they should not be confused with each other, or with the entirely different side-by-side double shotguns of F.lli Rizzini.

The New Englander shotgun from L. L. Bean.

have thicker barrel walls. The Aurora barrels in field versions, though lighter perhaps only by one or two ounces *(depending on barrel length)* do place the shotgun's balance points well between the hands. Ejectors and their springs are incorporated into the monobloc.

The forends of the Aurora line come with a distinctively European "schnabel," and are attached to the barrels with a reliable Anson-design pushrod that is self-compensating for wear. A cam in the forend cocks the coil-spring powered hammers when the shotgun is opened.

If a schnabel forend is not visually appealing to you, you might consider

selling—one-quarter of B. Rizzini's production. In fact, SIGARMS' Laura Burgess reports substantial backorders of both competition and field guns—which both B. Rizzini and SIGARMS are working assiduously to fill.

What else from B. Rizzini might SIGARMS consider importing? When I visited the B. Rizzini factory in the summer of 2000, Giorgio Guerini proudly showed me shotgun receivers made from aircraft-grade aluminum alloy instead of chromium-nickel-molybdenum alloy steel—B. Rizzini's "Omnium Light" line. A substantial, though still lightweight, titanium insert was fitted

priced in the vicinity of $3,250 - $3,500 would be greeted enthusiastically by American hunters.

Some hunters, thinking of the 30,000—40,000 psi chamber pressure generated by cartridges such as the 30-06, might question whether the single, though massive, transverse underbolt engaging its bite in the monobloc beneath the bottom barrel is sufficiently robust to withstand prolonged firing of high-velocity rifle cartridges. I can respond only that the B. Rizzini Express Rifles, in addition to extensive firing

Aurora TR40 Silver.

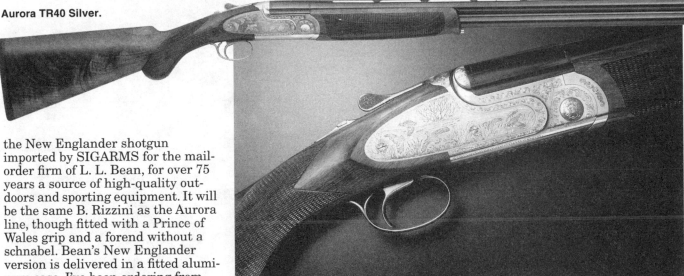

the New Englander shotgun imported by SIGARMS for the mail-order firm of L. L. Bean, for over 75 years a source of high-quality outdoors and sporting equipment. It will be the same B. Rizzini as the Aurora line, though fitted with a Prince of Wales grip and a forend without a schnabel. Bean's New Englander version is delivered in a fitted aluminum case. I've been ordering from Bean for 40 years, and have lived within an hour's drive of the Freeport store for the past 25 years. While I might be wrong, the New Englander is the first shotgun I can recall Bean's selling under its own name. The selection of a B. Rizzini shotgun to bear this cachet is high praise indeed.

SIGARMS also has donated Aurora shotguns to local chapters of the distinguished multi-national waterfowl conservation organization, Ducks Unlimited, for their annual banquets and auctions. The Aurora shotguns have been well received at these local chapter auctions where they generated funds for wetlands conservation and waterfowl habitat improvements.

B. Rizzini's Marcheno Val Trompia factory has a production capacity with its current work force of slightly more than 4,000 shotguns a year. SIGARMS is importing—and

Frame details of the Aurora TR40 Silver showing the hand-inlaid gold images and engraving.

into the breech face around the firing pin holes as a reinforcement plate to counter back-thrust pressures. A shotgun with regular steel barrels assembled on such a receiver can weigh—in 12-gauge—less than six pounds. Such a shotgun would be ideal for the upland bird hunter who walks a lot, frequently in difficult terrain, but fires relatively few shotshells in the course of a day afield.

B. Rizzini manufactures and sells in Europe a highly regarded superposed Express Rifle. This Express Rifle, available in chamberings such as 7x65R, 308 Winchester, 30-06, 9.3x74R, and 444 Marlin, is built on a reinforced 20-gauge receiver—and is, of course, available with a set of 20-gauge barrels. In my opinion, a superposed rifle/ shotgun combination

in the test range on the bottom floor of the factory in Marcheno *(all the shotguns are likewise test-fired)* must pass proof in a *Banco di Prova Nazionale per le Armi Portattili*. The Italian firearms' manufacturers are justifiably proud of the reputations their firearms have earned, and their proof houses guard these reputations zealously.

Wesley Lang and Giorgio Guerini are no longer associated with SIGARMS or B. Rizzini, but they were the catalysts in bringing the Aurora line of shotguns to American shotgunners. SIGARMS and B. Rizzini have, in essence, embarked on a joint venture that affords what well may be the best value in a machine-made shotgun to American shotgunners.

POCKET

A Hard Look at a Misunderstood Weapon

PISTOLS

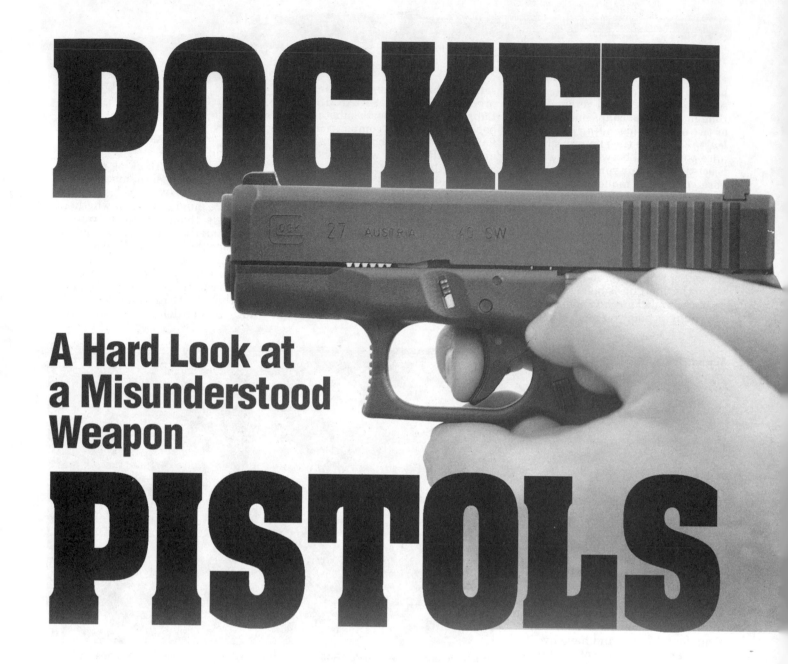

by Chuck Taylor

ALTHOUGH THEY'VE BEEN around in useable form for more than 200 years, the pocket pistol continues to be grossly misunderstood. Perhaps now more than ever, it's the object of repeated attacks from a plethora of handgun experts and gun-writers alike, all loudly proclaiming its worthlessness.

Some say that pocket pistols are no good because they're ultra-compact. *So* compact, in fact, that the shooter cannot obtain a fast, correct grip index on the weapon with the firing hand during rapid presentations.

Others claim that the short grip-frame leaves no place to put the little finger of the firing hand. Thus, the gun feels clumsy in the firing hand, thus subsequently demon-strating less-than-marvelous controllability when fired.

It's also often stated that because they're typically chambered for small cartridges, pocket pistols lack stopping power and *that's* why they're no good. Indeed, statements like, "They're so anemic that you can't even kill time with them!" are often heard.

Still others opine that the pocket pistol's lack of appropriate sights (in some cases, total lack of any sights – period), is why they're useless. "How can you hit anything with a gun with sights so small you can't acquire them quickly—or no sights at all?" they say.

Its barrel is so short that you can't get enough velocity to get a

hollowpoint to expand!" still others cry. "And even if it *has* sights, they're so close together that accurate sighting is impossible!" is yet another complaint often voiced.

And last, some feel that pocket pistols are somehow inaccurate, even to the point where targets are missed at point-blank range, so why bother with them? "You can't hit your hat with one at ten feet, so what good is it?" is one such oft-made statement.

Taken at face value, each of these criticisms seems definitive, even damning. Yes, it's true:

1. Pocket pistols *are* compact and light.

2. They're *often* chambered for small cartridges that, though

entirely lethal, lack the ability to produce quick incapacitation (e.g. "stopping power"), even with properly placed hits.

3. Many examples *do* have tiny sights or no sights at all.

4. Many examples *do* indeed have short grip-frames to make them easier to conceal.

5. Short barrels *do* produce lower bullet velocities, and lower velocities do limit frangible bullet expansion.

6. Short sight radius *does* aggravate alignment errors. Simple geometry proves it.

So, then, if they're *that* poor a choice for self-defense, why bother with them at all? If you believe its critics, we shouldn't. According to them, the pocket pistol is a relic of the past, a handgun with a checkered past and no future, at least in the tactical sense.

Whoa, now. Slow down. Let's wait just a minute before returning

Perhaps the most potent pocket revolver – the S&W M696 44 Special. Compact and light, yet potent, it offers an excellent balance of stopping power and "user-friendliness."

the indictment. Are the criticisms *really* valid? Do they *really* show that the pocket pistol is an inefficient self-defense weapon?

I don't think so.

Though valid in the strict academic sense, criticisms of the pocket pistol are invariably voiced using a general-purpose, rather than specialized, context. In other words, more often than not, it actually amounts to comparing apples to oranges.

Viewed from a general-purpose self-defense context, the inherent characteristics of the pocket pistol do indeed appear deficient. Next to full-sized service handguns designed for a wide variety of tactical missions, they *do* look frail and woefully inadequate.

However, to look at them in such a light is to show ignorance, because pocket pistols have never been intended for general-purpose functions—quite the opposite. Instead, they're highly *specialized* weapons, designed for a limited, yet clearly definable, kind of self-defense situation.

Viewed in *this* context, their small size, low power, lack of high-visibility sights, short sight radius and short barrel is not such a liability; not at all. It's really a matter of defining their *mission*, the purpose for which they were created, that's all.

Because of its far wider tactical mission, a service handgun must be capable of longer ranges, demonstrate better penetration and exhibit decisive target incapacitation. The wearer of a general-purpose handgun might have to shoot through an automobile windshield/bodywork or vegetation to reach his target or engage a target well past point-blank range. He might also be required to engage multiple targets or deliver accurate hits on small, partial or angled targets.

The pocket pistol does not share the same mission.

Instead it is used at *extremely* close range, usually less than seven feet, and often its user is physically struggling with an attacker at the same time. It doesn't *need* great sights because of its intended function.

One of the most prolific sub-compact self-loaders is the Colt Officer's Model 45 ACP. Available with both an aluminum and steel frame, it continues to be a major big-bore pocket pistol contender.

Due in part to its conspicuous presence in the long-running James Bond spy films, the Walther PPK in 22 LR, 32 ACP and 380 ACP has long dominated the self-loader portion of the pocket pistol category.

Colt 25 ACP Pocket Model, a favorite of many women for over five decades. This particular one was successfully used by author's mother back in 1942 to ward off an attacker armed with a butcher knife. She survived intact – he did not.

To a nurse flat on her back in a hospital parking lot with a would-be rapist on top of her, the lack of sights is no handicap. To a woman sitting in her vehicle with a carjacker all over her, its low power isn't especially critical, either. To a gal fending off an attacker in front of her apartment door, the pocket pistol's small size and lack of a place for the pinkie finger of her firing hand means little.

Why? Because of the way the weapon is *used* under such circumstances. In all three, the pocket-pistol wielding victim will quite literally stuff the gun into her assailant's face and repeatedly pull the trigger until something definitive happens. And for such missions, the pocket pistol's inherent characteristics are not a handicap.

Back in 1942, my own mother proved the point. Because of a number of break-ins of the officer's quarters and rapes, the officers' wives on a remote post in Texas were required to be armed at all times. It was June, an extremely hot month along the Tex-Mex border, and closing up all the windows of the house for security was tantamount to turning on the oven and sticking your head inside.

My father was on a field-training problem and thus absent and, per the Commandant's directive, my mother was sitting in the living room of their quarters, reading the newspaper with a Colt Pocket Model 25 ACP in her lap. The front door was open but the screen door was closed and latched and the back door itself closed and locked.

At about nine o'clock, she heard a scratching sound and lowered the newspaper slightly to listen. As she did so, she saw the blade of a butcher knife penetrate the screen and slice it

Easy to conceal and carry, the pocket pistol is an effective weapon if used within its limitations.

downward, cutting a slit of about six inches. The knife was then withdrawn and a hand appeared, unfastening the hook-and-eye latch.

Immediately, she picked up the pistol, but had enough presence of mind to keep the newspaper up in front of her, hiding it from view. A moment later, a man appeared, taking several steps inside the door. She challenged him, advised him to leave and when he responded negatively with remarks about cutting her up and started

toward her, she summarily shot him – six times – with the Pocket Model. As she recalls, the range was about seven feet or so.

Five of the tiny bullets hit him in the torso, while the sixth (clearly the result of mashing the trigger!) struck him in the right thigh, severing the femoral artery. The man dropped the knife, screamed and ran full tilt out the door into the night.

Via telephone, she then summoned the military police, who followed a substantial blood trail for some 200 yards, finding the would-be robber/rapist quite dead in the middle of the parade grounds. There is no doubt that the pistol saved her life, even if it didn't instantly incapacitate her attacker. That it had miniscule sights, was chambered for an anemic cartridge and was a tiny pistol proved to be no liability.

I asked her why she chose such a gun and her response was classic – and typical. She responded that she couldn't handle a larger, heavier, more powerful pistol and decided that the little 25 ACP was better than her fists!

And that brings us to the point of it all. Hits with even a small caliber beat misses with a larger one. Moreover, if the shooter cannot physically hold out a big handgun or manage to control its recoil and muzzle flip, the fact that it's technically a better man-stopper becomes academic. Her story is so typical of how pocket pistols are used, it can honestly be said that it represents the norm.

Generally speaking, pocket pistols are chambered for the 22 LR, 25 ACP, 32 ACP and 380 ACP. However, since the

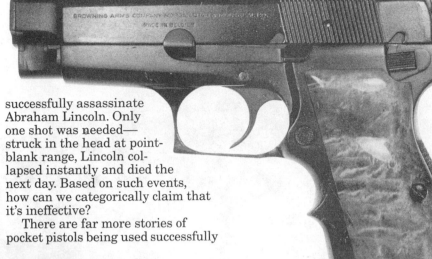

Custom pocket pistols, such as this one made from a Browning P35 Hi-Power, should be viewed with caution, since custom guns of any kind increase their user's civil liability hazard if actually used in self-defense.

1950s, the Smith & Wesson *Chief's Special* and *Bodyguard* series of 38 Spl. snubbies has been available. Based on S&W's J-frame, they're only slightly larger than a 22 or 25 auto and certainly no larger than a 32 ACP or 380 ACP self-loader. This has had the effect of making them immensely popular with the ladies and as a backup gun (which is used exactly the same way the vast majority of the time) with police officers as well.

Beginning in the late 1980s, Colt introduced the Lightweight Officer's Model 45 ACP, subse-

successfully assassinate Abraham Lincoln. Only one shot was needed— struck in the head at point-blank range, Lincoln collapsed instantly and died the next day. Based on such events, how can we categorically claim that it's ineffective?

There are far more stories of pocket pistols being used successfully than unsuccessfully. The trick is to understand that their *mission* is quite different from a general-purpose service handgun and analyze them accordingly. Compared to service handguns, they appear deficient because they *aren't* capable of meeting such broadly-based criteria. But when evaluated using criteria that better illustrates their intended purpose, they obviously perform quite well. For this reason, I regard condemnation of them as being both unfounded and prejudicial.

A hallmark of the pocket pistol – and one the major claims of its critics – is the low-powered cartridge for which it's chambered. Although this makes the pistol easier to shoot, such cartridges have long been noted for their poor stopping power.

quently adding a steel-framed version a short time later. In the mid-1990s, Glock began marketing their highly compact Model 26 9mm and Model 27 40 S&W and the Model 30 45 ACP. By 2000, a slimmer version of the Model 30 featuring a single-column magazine was available.

All of these guns have one thing in common. Though they're small and light, they're chambered for more powerful cartridges, have magazine-mounted extensions for the little finger and high-visibility fixed sights as well. Yes, they are somewhat heavier than a traditional pocket pistol and they still have a short sight radius. But when evaluated intelligently, it becomes clear that they're formidable weapons by *any* criteria.

John Wilkes Booth used a single-shot 41-caliber pocket pistol to

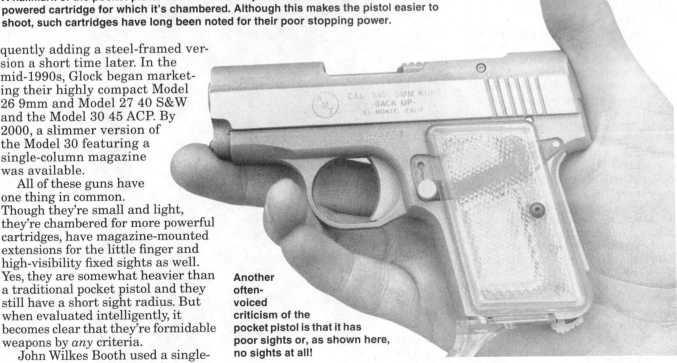

Another often-voiced criticism of the pocket pistol is that it has poor sights or, as shown here, no sights at all!

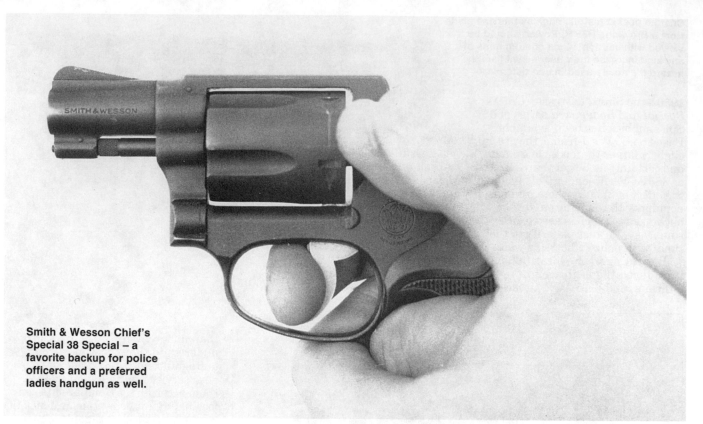

Smith & Wesson Chief's Special 38 Special – a favorite backup for police officers and a preferred ladies handgun as well.

As suggested previously, apples don't compare very well to oranges – the taste preferences of the person eating them tend to override any logic or fact. Thus, to use service-handgun criteria to evaluate pocket pistols is to prove nothing. The fact is that pocket pistols *do* have a place in self-defense and if they're used within their sphere of efficiency, they perform their job well. It's only when they're utilized for purposes outside their mission and capabilities that they appear so inadequate.

History shows us that the pocket pistol has been around for a long, long time, and continues to be popular. No amount of condemnation or rationalization can change that. And history speaks for itself – *if it were as useless as some people would have us believe, it would have disappeared well over 100 years ago.*

That it did not both validates the pocket pistol's claim to legitimacy and guarantees its future.

As a professional weapons and tactics writer, consultant and trainer, I long ago discovered that the dynamics of human confrontations tend to be a repetition of previous events. Based on this well-documented observation, it's my guess that the pocket pistol will remain with us – and rightly so – for at least another hundred years. And why not? For it's intended purpose, it does the job quite well. ●

For many decades, the pocket pistol was generally carried in a purse or pocket; many are now being carried in a holster. If you prefer this mode, ensure the weapon is reasonably secure yet quickly accessible.

HANDGUN NEWS

AUTOLOADERS

by John Malloy

THERE IS SO much going on that it is difficult to quickly summarize the situation as it pertains to autoloading handguns. At the February 2003 SHOT Show, a surprising number of prototypes and pre-production specimens were exhibited. Although there was a great variety of new pistols, the largest number of recent new model introductions have been for the 45 ACP, and most were based on the 1911 design.

It is hard to believe that the 45 ACP (Automatic Colt Pistol) cartridge, introduced in 1905, and the Colt/Browning 1911 pistol design are just a short time shy of their 100th birthdays. Yet, they remain among the most popular cartridge and pistol choices available today.

The big-bore spotlight does not belong exclusively to the 45 ACP, however. Two other new 45-caliber cartridges have been recently introduced. In addition, smaller-caliber bottleneck centerfire pistol cartridges have entered the scene and are gaining recognition. The 22 Long Rifle (22 LR) remains ever popular, and new pistols—and conversion kits to adapt existing centerfire pistols to 22—are offered. The 17-caliber rimfire made an amazing debut in the rifle field last year, and a new 17-caliber cartridge—and new 17-caliber semiautomatic pistols adapted for it —are now being offered.

Autoloading handguns are acquired by ordinary people for personal protection, for competition, for hunting, for plinking and fun and relaxation; and to some degree, for collecting—or just pride of ownership. With the threat of terrorism now never far from our minds, perhaps defense of our families and ourselves plays an even larger role than before. The personal protection aspect is important, and most of the autoloading pistols offered are suitable for such use.

Politics continues to influence the world of autoloading handguns. The elections of November 2002 were encouraging, but did not stanch the flow of anti-gun efforts. Some firearms manufacturers have gone out of business, due in part to restrictive legislation, or to litigation. States such as California, Maryland, Massachusetts and New Jersey make their own rules as to what handguns can and cannot be sold within their borders. Gunmakers must decide whether or not to redesign and retool to conform to these rules. Substantial expense is required to change a pistol design, with no guarantee it will be approved. Some companies just resign themselves to not selling in restrictive states. Nevertheless, more manufacturers are incorporating lock and safety mechanisms into their pistols in an effort to comply with at least some of these restrictions.

Guns have been prominent in the news in the past year or so. The "DC Sniper" killings of October 2002 brought predictable calls for more gun control. However, many people saw, instead, the advantage of ordinary citizens being armed. After a series of murders of women in the Baton Rouge area of Louisiana, the Governor of that state made a public statement that people should become licensed and then carry pistols for personal protection. Airline pilots, after a long uphill fight, were finally authorized by Congress to carry firearms. Or were they? Bureaucratic restrictions were so onerous that at the time of this writing, not a single pilot has been legally armed.

In early 2003, as pressure mounted for war against Iraq, new threats of terrorist activities increased, and the country was put on Orange Alert. Government officials made announcements concerning preparations for a terrorist attack. Although such advice never mentioned firearms (but recommended duct tape), many people read between the lines. They realized they were ultimately responsible for their safety, and that of their loved ones. Another firearm (or a first firearm, for some) seemed like a good idea. Pistols, especially, were favored to be available in case of an emergency.

High-capacity pistols are still being introduced, even though they are limited to 10-round magazines unless sold to police or military. There is a logical reason for this continued interest in high-capacity handguns by people who cannot acquire the high-capacity magazines. Just a short distance down the road lies September 2004. At that time, the so-called "Assault Weapons" law of September 1994 is due to expire. One provision that affected autoloading pistol shooters was the ban on magazines that hold more than 10 rounds. It will be good when this restriction is gone. This provision has created two classes of citizens in the United States—ordinary

Stainless-steel firearms made under the AMT name are no longer available. Galena Industries, the manufacturer, went out of business in 2002. AMT handguns tended to be innovative and eye-catching. Here, Malloy shoots an AMT Long Slide Hardballer, a 1911-style pistol with an impressive 7-inch barrel.

The 22-caliber Beretta U22 Neos pistol is now in production and several variants are available. Malloy tries out one that is equipped with a red-dot sight.

A deluxe version of the 22-caliber NEOS pistol has been added, with optional grip frames and sights. 7 1/2-inch barrels and Inox (stainless) finishes are also available.

The new "Special Duty" specimens of the Beretta 92 and 96 pistols have an integral accessory rail, a heavier "Brigadier" slide and other features.

The new Beretta 92G-SD is an updated version of the original Beretta 92. Here, the new 9mm is fired by Clo Malloy, the writer's sister-in-law.

people who could not be "trusted" with more than 10 shots, and agents of the government who could have more than 10. This provision has driven a wedge between law enforcement and the armed citizen, who is traditionally the greatest ally of the police. This situation should not be allowed to continue. However, anti-gun forces are campaigning to extend the law past its end time.

These are some of the factors influencing the world of autoloading handguns. With all this in mind, let's take a look at what the companies are doing:

AMT

The innovative stainless-steel pistols made under the AMT name are no longer available. The AMT trademark appeared on a number of "firsts" in the firearms industry. The company was the first to make an all-stainless 1911-type pistol, and first to offer a subcompact 380. They marketed semiautomatic pistols in calibers from 22 Long Rifle (22 LR) to 50 Action Express (50 AE). In 1998, Galena Industries acquired the right to produce most of the AMT-developed firearms. Within a few years, the company moved from restrictive California to Sturgis, South Dakota, for a new start. Somehow, it did not work out. The final remaining assets of the company were sold at auction in August 2002. Parts are still available from Numrich Gun Parts and Jack First, but shooters will miss the variety of pistols offered under the AMT name.

Arms Moravia

The on-again, off-again importation of the striking-looking Arms Moravia CZ-G2000 seems to have stabilized. Anderson Arms of Fort Worth, TX will import the pistol. Introduced in 1999, the polymer-frame pistol is now available in all-black or two-tone (nickel slide and black frame) variants. Chambering options are 9mm and 40 S&W. Arms Moravia also makes a nifty little miniature 380 pistol, the ZP 98, which uses a gas-delayed blow-back system. However, it is too small to be imported into the United States under the restrictions of the Gun Control Act of 1968 (GCA 68).

Beretta

The new 22-caliber pistol, the U22 Neos, introduced last year, is now in production. It is the first Beretta pistol 100-percent designed and manufactured in the United States. In case you were wondering, "Neos" is from the Greek, meaning "new." This new Beretta has a replaceable polymer grip frame and comes in 4 1/2-inch and 6-inch barrel lengths.

A deluxe (DLX) version has also been added. Optional grip frames with blue or gray rubber inlays are furnished. Also, black, red and white front sights come with each pistol. Three rear sight blades (color-outlined red and white—as well as black) allow the shooter to mix-and-match the sights to suit his preference. 7 1/2-inch barrels and Inox (stainless) finish are also available on the DLX variants.

All the Neos pistols have their sights set into a mounting rib that allows easy installation of optical or electronic sights.

The modular construction of the U22 pistol has led to speculation that a light carbine, based on the same operating mechanism, might be introduced. Such a carbine is under development, but is not now available.

In the centerfire line, the new models 92- and 96G-SD (92 indicates

▶ The new Bersa Thunder 45 is a compact double-action pistol chambered for the 45 ACP cartridge.

▶ Bond Arms, long-time manufacturer of double derringers, has joined the list of companies making 1911-style 45 pistols. The difference is that this one is designed for a new high-velocity cartridge—the 45 Autobond.

◀ The bullet of the 450 Autobond cartridge *(nearest the cartridge box)* is a light 100-grain fragmenting soft-point pushed to 2300 fps from the Autobond pistol. A 230-grain 45 ACP bullet is shown for comparison.

9mm, 96 indicates 40-caliber) have been introduced. To further break the code, **G** denotes a de-cocker mechanism, and SD represents "Special Duty." The pistols might be seen as a modernized alternative to the original 92. The new SD guns have an accessory rail integral with the frame, a "Brigadier" heavy reinforced slide, and 3-dot tritium night sights. The frame is checkered front and back, and the magazine well is beveled.

Your writer had the opportunity to shoot a new 9mm 92G-SD. Standing at the short-range line of a police range, I faced a standard silhouette target that had been liberally sprinkled by other shooters. Looking for an untouched spot, I chose the left ear. The pistol put nine shots in a cluster on the ear, with only one slightly out of the group. I think it is safe to say that shooters will find the Beretta SD pistols acceptably accurate.

The Beretta B-LOK locking device is being phased in on pistols in the company's line.

Bernardelli

Gone from the handgun scene for some time, the Bernardelli name returned last year, reintroducing much of its previous pistol line. Since then, the company has also added a series of pistols based on the CZ-75 design.

Now, a new design has entered the Bernardelli line. The new pistols are polymer-frame guns using the basic CZ-75 mechanism. To say this is a colorful line is something of an understatement. Frames are available in black, blue, yellow, red, white and purple. Should that array not offer enough choices, slides are available in black or silver finish. The new polymer-frame Bernardelli pistols are designated Model 2000. They entered production in early 2003.

Bersa

The Argentine Bersa firm is noted for their compact blowback pocket pistols. A departure for the company was the introduction of a double-action locked-breech 45-caliber arm in 2003.

The new Bersa, designated the Thunder 45 Ultra Compact, is a nice-looking pistol that feels good in

the hand. It has a conventional double-action trigger mechanism, that is, double-action for the first shot, single-action for succeeding shots. The barrel length is 3.6 inches. The pistol measures 4.9 inches high by 6.7 inches long, which neatly puts it into the compact category (5x7). Weight is 27 ounces. The magazine holds 7 rounds, giving the pistol a 7+1 capacity. Finishes are offered as matte black, Duo-tone and satin nickel. Availability of the Thunder 45 was scheduled for Spring 2003, from Eagle Imports.

Bond

Bond Arms, a long-time maker of double derringers, has entered the semi-auto field with their own 1911-style pistol. The Bond pistol has many of the features in vogue with today's shooters. It is not just a newcomer to the pack, however, as it is designed for its own unique cartridge—the 450 Autobond.

The 450 Autobond round is an interesting concept. Externally of about the same dimensions as the 45 ACP, the Autobond cartridge uses a very light 100-grain bullet pushed to the impressive speed of 2300 feet per second (fps) from a 5-inch barrel. Not since the 1904 appearance of the Danish Schouboe pistol has this approach been tried for a 45-caliber pistol. The Schouboe cartridge used an extremely light 63-grain bullet pushed to 1600 fps, an impressive speed for a handgun of those days. The Schouboe, however, used the light bullet to keep pressures within the capabilities of its blowback action. The Bond pistol was designed for very different circumstances.

The Bond uses the traditional tilting-barrel locking system of the 1911 design. The cartridge case is a reinforced version of the 45 ACP case, and is designed to be used in a fully-supported chamber. Thus, the cartridge is not recommended for use in pistols other than the Bond. The bullet is a frangible one that, in Bond's words, "resists over-penetration." Recoil is reported to be only slightly greater than that of a standard 45 ACP 230-grain load. Those who choose the Bond pistol can make the recoil comparison for themselves. The Autobond can use standard 45 ACP cartridges as well as the special 450 round.

Browning

New for Browning are polymer-frame pistols in 9mm and 40 S&W. The frames of the new PRO-9 and PRO-40 pistols have integral accessory rails and interchangeable backstrap inserts.

Trigger action is conventional double action, with single-action shots after the first. A cocked hammer can be lowered by a decocking lever. In this case, from either side, as the ambidextrous design has a decocking lever on both sides of the frame. The plugged magazines hold, for ordinary Americans, ten rounds of either cartridge.

Browning celebrated its 125th anniversary in 2003, taking the company's history back to 1878, when John M. Browning introduced his famous single-shot rifle. In commemoration, four famous firearms that have carried the Browning

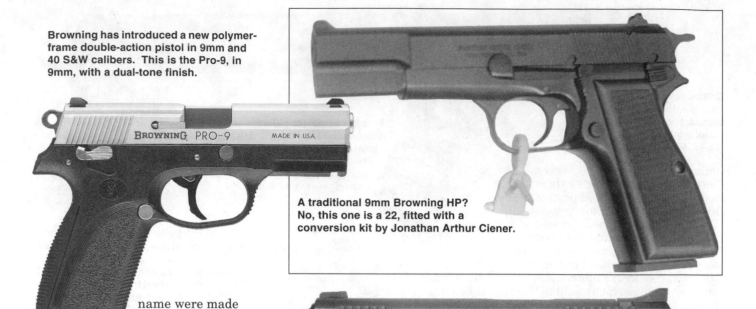

Browning has introduced a new polymer-frame double-action pistol in 9mm and 40 S&W calibers. This is the Pro-9, in 9mm, with a dual-tone finish.

A traditional 9mm Browning HP? No, this one is a 22, fitted with a conversion kit by Jonathan Arthur Ciener.

Charles Daly is offering the new M-5 high-capacity polymer-frame 1911-style pistols, in several variants. Shown here is the Commander version.

name were made as limited editions. The four guns were the Single-Shot, the 22 autoloading rifle, the Superposed shotgun, and—representing the Browning pistols—the 9mm Hi-Power. Only 125 of the Belgian-made commemorative 9mm pistols were to be made. They will have scroll engraving, gold highlights and select walnut grips.

The standard Hi-Power is mysteriously absent from the 2003 Browning master catalog. This situation has led to rumors that Browning has—or plans to—discontinue the Hi-Power. A Browning representative told your writer that this was not so, but was at a loss to explain the absence.

Century

Century International Arms' line of 1911-style 45 pistols, introduced in 2001, has been well-received. The guns are made in the Philippines by SAM (Shooters Arms Manufacturing, Inc.) and include traditional and enhanced variants.

Introduced in 2003 were several new models. The Blue Thunder Commodore is a 4 1/4-inch barrel version of the original striking-looking full-size Blue Thunder. The Commodore 1911 is a 4 1/4-inch enhanced pistol without the distinctive trigger guard and sculptured grip of the Blue Thunder.

The SAM Chief is mechanically the same as the original Blue Thunder, but has a matte finish rather than the original's polished blue. The SAM GI is a more-or-less traditional 1911 design, but with a 4 1/4-inch barrel.

Perhaps the most interesting is the Falcon pistol—a full-size high-capacity pistol *(which now comes with a 10-round magazine)*. It is built with a steel, rather than polymer, frame. Small separate grip panels are attached. The Falcon has a squared trigger guard and extended controls, including an extended magazine release.

Charles Daly

Charles Daly / KBI has discontinued its line of double-action polymer-frame pistols to concentrate on its single-action line. New are the Daly M-5 polymer-frame high-capacity 1911 pistols. Built by BUL in Israel, the pistols feature beavertail grip safeties and ambidextrous manual safeties. Variants are Government, Commander and IPSC models, scheduled for Spring 2003, and the smaller M-5 Ultra-X, coming later.

The newest pistol in the Charles Daly lineup is the Daly HP. Not surprisingly, it is basically a copy of the original Browning HP ("Hi-Power") pistol, a 9mm single-action design. It has the early burr-type hammer spur, but some modern niceties—extended safety lever, ball & bar type express sights, and Uncle Mike's rubber grip panels—have been added. Availability was scheduled for the first quarter of 2003.

Ciener

The 22 Long Rifle (22 LR) conversions of Jonathan Arthur Ciener are especially popular in localities that limit the number of handguns a person may possess. They are not additional firearms, but are kits that may be quickly installed or removed by the shooter. Even without such restrictions, shooters can save ammunition money, get in more practice, and get one gun to serve several purposes. The pistol conversion kits have been available for 1911-type pistols, Beretta and Taurus models, and various Glocks.

Newly introduced is a conversion kit for the Browning Hi-Power and derivative pistols. Availability was scheduled for May 2003.

The kits are available with fixed or adjustable sights, and in matte, high polish or silver finishes. This variety lets shooters match the conversion to the gun's original finish, or create a two-tone effect. Says Ciener, "I don't want to give anyone an excuse to not get a conversion kit."

Cobra

Cobra Enterprises, which took over the defunct Republic, Talon and Davis pistol designs last year, has made improvements and has also added a new line.

It looks like a brand new Colt Model 1911—because it really is. Colt is bringing back the original 1911 design of the World War I period, complete with original markings. This prototype is serial number *1002X*.

Here is a key to the Cobra line: Pistols in the Patriot series are double-action-only (DAO) and have black polymer frames and stainless-steel slide. Chamberings are 45, 9mm and 380. The 45 is the former Republic 45. The 9mm and 380 are improved Talon designs.

The Freedom series comprises 32- and 38-caliber metal-frame pistols. The CA32 and CA380 are modified Davis pistols. New this year are modifications of the old Lorcin design in 32 and 380. Many people liked the Lorcins, and the company sold a lot of guns in years gone by; the design gives Cobra an addition to their line of larger pistols in 32- and 38-calibers.

Many shooters did not like the situation in which misguided legislation and litigation were able to drive legitimate manufacturers out of business. It is good that updates of these affordable designs are again available.

Colt

Colt continues to explore the roots of its semi-auto pistol line. Recall that about two years ago, the company brought out its recreation of the Model 1911A1 as produced at the beginning of World War II. Now it will offer the original Model 1911 as made in the 1918 period. A prototype, serial number 1002X, was displayed at the February 2003 SHOT Show. This will be an authentic 1911, complete to the unrelieved frame, lanyard loop, narrow-slot grip screws and original markings. All required "modern" markings will be on the frame under the grips.

About 3000 of the 1911A1 recreations were made, and it is no longer in production. Note that the serial numbers had a "WMK" prefix *(for Colt's head, Lt. Gen. William M. Keys, who authorized the project)*. The new 1911 pistols will use "WMK" as a serial number suffix. Availability was scheduled for May 2003.

Colt also offers the reproduction of the Series 70 Government Model—a recreation of the pistol produced during the 1970s. The only difference I could spot is the "big diamond" rosewood grips, which the original pistols did not have.

To prove they do not dwell in the past, Colt also has introduced its Gunsite pistol. The pistol was built incorporating ideas from Colt and the Gunsite training facility in Arizona. Features include a "palm swell" beavertail grip safety, Heinie front and Novak rear sights, Wilson extended safety lever, McCormick hammer and sear, and two 8-round Wilson magazines. The gun comes with a $100 coupon good toward training at Gunsite. The Gunsite pistol will be available in blue or stainless-steel finishes.

CZ

Two new CZ pistols are being offered.

The CZ P-01 was accepted last year by the Czech National Police. It has also been rated as a NATO-classified pistol. During testing, the number of stoppages was seven during a total of 15,000 rounds fired. The pistol can probably be considered reliable. The P-01 is chambered for the 9mm Parabellum cartridge. It has an aluminum frame with an integral accessory rail and a lanyard loop. It features a decocker, checkered rubber grips and front-and-rear slide serrations. With a 3.8-inch barrel, the pistol measures 5.3 x 7.2 inches, just a hair over the traditional 5 x 7 measurement for the compact pistol category.

Also new is the CZ 75 Tactical pistol sold with a CZ-logo folding knife. The pistol is a CZ 75B with low-profile sights, checkered rubber grips, a lanyard loop and a green poly-coated frame. Only 1000 Tactical combos were scheduled for production in 2003.

Dan Wesson

The Dan Wesson "Patriot" pistol, introduced last year, is now in full production. Recall that the Patriot is a modification of the 1911 design that uses an external extractor.

In the year 2000, Dan Wesson changed from being a revolver-only company to one that produces revolvers and 45-caliber 1911-type autoloaders. Their line has expanded to cover a number of niches. A special limited-quantity run of 10mm semiautos was scheduled for production in 2003.

DPMS / Panther Arms

Last year, DPMS (Defense Procurement Manufacturing Services) introduced a prototype 1911-type 45 pistol, and production was tentatively scheduled for November 2002.

Latest information from a DPMS representative is that the project has been put on hold. DPMS is a maker of AR-15 style rifles and accessories, and at this time will not add the 45-caliber pistol to their line.

EAA

EAA (European American Armory) is offering two new models in its Witness line.

A polymer-frame Witness will be available with a full-size frame and compact slide. The high-capacity frame will provide a capacity of 10+1. A bull barrel is fitted to this short slide, which carries low-profile sights. The pistol was so new it had

The NATO-classified CZ P-01 pistol was adopted by the Czech National Police and is now offered for commercial sales.

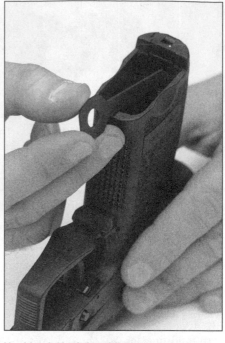

Mike Lott of FNH USA *(left)* points out the operation of the new Hi-Power SFS (Safe Fast Shooting) system to Malloy.

Heckler & Koch is adding a new lockout device to all production pistols.

not yet been given a name at the February 2003 SHOT Show.

Some localities permit a 45-caliber or 10mm pistol for big-game hunting if it is equipped with a barrel of six inches or longer. To fill this niche, the Witness Hunter is made with a 6-inch barrel chambered in 45 ACP and 10mm. It is offered with blue or camo finishes, and a scope rail is available.

All right, EAA also has an item that really isn't a semi-auto pistol, but it is related, and so interesting I must mention it. The "Thor" is a conversion unit that can be mounted on a 1911 frame to form a breakopen single-shot hunting pistol. It is offered in 45-70 only now, with other calibers planned for later.

FNH

Recall that FNH USA is the American subsidiary arm of FN Herstal in Belgium. They offer the HP series, commonly thought of as the "Browning Hi-Power." One new HP pistol has been introduced, the HP-SFS. The last three letters stand for "Safe Fast Shooting" and the mechanism combines features of both single-action and double-action systems. When the hammer is cocked and a shot is not to be made, the hammer can simply be pushed forward. This action engages the manual safety, locks the sear and locks the slide. When the safety is pushed down, the hammer rises to its cocked position, and the pistol is ready to fire again.

A new polymer-frame hammer-fired pistol is the FNP 9. The trigger mechanism is conventional double-action, that is, double-action (DA) for the first shot, then single-action (SA) for succeeding shots. Introduced first in 9mm, a 40-caliber version was also scheduled for late in 2003. With a 4-inch barrel, the pistol is 7 inches long and weighs 25 ounces. Magazine capacity for the 9mm is 16 for law enforcement, 10 for us common folk.

The unusual Five-seveN pistol, introduced last year for the special 5.7 x 28mm cartridge, now has an adjustable-sight model added to the line. The new version has a 10-round magazine and a magazine safety. It will be marketed to individual active-duty police officers. Now that there are two versions, the original version has to be called something to differentiate it, so it is now the "Tactical" version.

Glock

Glock has introduced the new Glock 37, a 45-caliber pistol, but not a 45 ACP. The company's previous offering of the Model 21

The old RamLine polymer pistol is now the Hi-Standard Plinker, offered in both 22 Long Rifle and 17 High Standard calibers.

The new 17 High Standard *(left)* will work in 22 LR Hi-Standard pistols by simply replacing the barrel. For comparison, the 17 Hornady Magnum Rimfire *(with its parent, the 22 Winchester Magnum Rimfire)* was introduced last year in rifles and the Volquartsen Cheetah pistol.

The new Hi-Point 45 pistol has adjustable sights, last round hold-open and an accessory rail on a new contoured polymer frame that has separate polymer grips. A similar 40-caliber version is also offered.

Near a modest-size enlargement of the new 17 High Standard cartridge, Alan Aronstein of High Standard *(left)* points out to Malloy that only a barrel change was necessary to convert this Hi-Standard Citation to the new 17-caliber cartridge.

gave the market a big Glock 45 ACP pistol, and it was subsequently shortened into the 30 and the single-column 36.

Ah—Glock engineers apparently reasoned—it would be possible to produce a full-capacity 45 in the smaller frame size—if only the 45 cartridge were smaller. Accordingly, they created their own cartridge. The new 45 Glock round is smaller than the 45 ACP, with an overall length of 1.10 inches. *(The 45 ACP OAL is 1.28 inches).* Two 45 Glock loads are planned—a 185-grain bullet at 1100 fps, and a 200-grain bullet at 984 fps.

The Glock 37 pistol has a 4-inch barrel, is 1.18 inches wide and weighs 22 ounces (without magazine). The capacity is 10 + 1.

Heckler & Koch

HK has introduced two new pistols. The P 2000 GPM (German Police Model) is a compact (5x7 inches) polymer-frame 9mm pistol designed for the German Police. The trigger mechanism is HK's LEM (Law Enforcement Modification), in which part of the mechanism is pre-cocked by the slide, allowing a light DA pull for most of the trigger motion, then a

short pull of about 7 pounds to fire. In case of a misfire, the trigger has "second snap" capabilities, but the pull is heavy all the way through. The pistol has a 3.62-inch barrel and features ambidextrous slide releases. Interchangeable rear grip inserts are provided to allow the shooter to fit the pistol to his hand. Magazine capacity is 10 rounds, with larger-capacity magazines now available for law enforcement and military users. A 40 S&W variant is also being planned.

The USP Elite is a new longer variant of the popular USP pistol. Chambered for 9mm and 45 ACP, the Elite has a substantially longer 6.2-inch barrel and elongated 9 1/2-inch slide to match. It has the HK O-ring barrel-positioning system and adjustable target sights. The trigger mechanism is conventional DA, and the trigger has a trigger stop. It has a decocker, but can also be carried cocked-and-locked.

A Lock-Out device is being added to all HK production pistols now.

HIGH STANDARD

High Standard's big news is the 17 caliber. Last year, the 17-rimfire cartridge caught on like wildfire, and a number of companies chambered rifles for the new 17 Hornady Magnum Rimfire (17 HMR) cartridge. Only one semi-auto handgun, however, the Volquartsen Cheetah, was able to handle the 17.

Now, that has changed. High Standard Manufacturing Company now has several Hi-Standard semi-automatic pistols chambered for a

new 17-rimfire cartridge—the 17 High Standard!

A similar cartridge was introduced a year or so ago—at least in concept—as the 17 Aguila. Reportedly, no specimens were actually available at the time of introduction. The 17 Aguila was to be based on the 22 LR case necked down to 17 caliber. The concept interested High Standard as a possibility for use in pistols designed for the 22 LR cartridge. Digging into old company history, High Standard's Alan Aronstein was surprised to learn the company had actually developed a 17-caliber cartridge based on the 22 LR back in 1940, and had made at least one pistol in that chambering. World War II apparently stopped developmental work, and the project lay forgotten.

With this background, High Standard and Aguila got together on the project. Reportedly, the 1940 round was only slightly different in dimension from the specifications of the 17 Aguila. Slight modifications were made, and the cartridge was introduced in January 2003 as the 17 High Standard. With a 20-grain bullet, the pressure is balanced to that of the 22 LR, so that any Hi-Standard pistol can be converted to 17 by simply changing the barrel. This swap also works for removable-barrel rifles, such as the AR-7 Explorer.

High Standard now offers all its target pistols in 17 High Standard as well as 22 LR. From an 18-inch test barrel, the cartridge produced a muzzle velocity of 1830 fps. The 10-inch barrel Hi-Standard Citation pistol reportedly tops 1700 fps.

High Standard has also acquired the rights to the discontinued polymer RamLine pistol, and is also planning to offer it—in 22 LR and 17 High Standard—as the Hi-Standard Plinker. Delivery was scheduled for Fall 2003. The new pistol will resurrect the "Plinker" name and will expand the company's offerings.

Lest someone think I am not consistent, let me mention that the new 17 cartridge was introduced on

Kahr Arms' Randall Casseday displays a prototype of the new Thompson Custom 1911 pistol, an enhanced version of the Auto-Ordnance line of 1911-style pistols. This specimen carries serial number 0002.

Kahr's new little 9mm, the polymer-frame PM9, was introduced last year with a two-tone finish. Now the pistol is in full production, and a new all-black variant has been added.

January 20, 2003 as the "17 High Standard," and I have used that nomenclature. However, at the February 2003 SHOT Show, the round was advertised at the Aguila display as "17 Hi-Standard." Both spellings have long been appropriate in different contexts. The company has always been called "High Standard," and the pistol models have been "Hi-Standard." With the predicted popularity of the new 17 cartridge, the terminology should soon become, shall we say, "standardized."

Also, recall that High Standard introduced its own 45-caliber 1911 pistol line in 2000, and offers variants with 4 1/2-, 5- and 6-inch barrels. In 2003, the company introduced a new Custom line of 1911 pistols.

Hi-Point

Without much fanfare, Hi-Point has introduced two new big-bore pistols. The new polymer-frame handguns are a new 45, and a new 40 S&W. In keeping with Hi-Point's concept of phasing in features, the new guns have push-button magazine release, last round hold-open, 3-dot adjustable sights and frame accessory rails. Magazine safeties (the gun won't fire with the magazine out) have also been added. A trigger lock comes with each gun.

The new guns have 4 1/2-inch barrels and weigh 32 ounces. The contoured polymer frame feels good in the hand and, unlike most polymer-frame pistols, the grip panels are separate pieces. The 45 uses a 9-shot maga-

zine, and the 40 variant has a 10-rounder. The magazines are different than those previously used in Hi-Point pistols, and are similar in construction to those used in the company's popular 9mm carbine. It is probably not overly speculative to surmise that Hi-Point, looking to the future, plans 40- and 45-caliber carbines and wants magazines to interchange between their pistols and carbines.

The Hi-Points are simple blowbacks, but are "+P" rated, and have a good reputation for functioning. Repair policy is lifetime, with no questions asked. With a suggested retail price of $169, the new Hi-Points are the least expensive big-bore pistols available.

Kahr

The Kahr PM 9, introduced last year, is in full production, and a new variant has been added. The new Kahr has a blackened stainless-steel slide on a black polymer frame. Availability for this variant is scheduled for May 2003. The PM 9 is Kahr's smallest and lightest 9mm pistol, sporting a 3-inch barrel and weighing less than a pound. Small as it is, it is rated for +P and +P+ ammunition. Two magazines—a six-rounder with a flush base and a 7-round version with a grip extension—are furnished.

The new, larger T9, seen in somewhat different prototype last year, is now a production pistol with two vari-

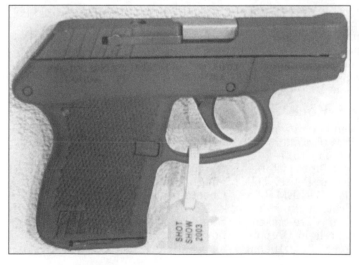

Kel-Tec's Renee Goldman displays the small size of the company's new 38 ACP pistol, the P-3AT. Diagrams showing the pistol's operation are in the background.

Kel-Tec's new offering is the 380 ACP polymer-frame P-3AT. There are very slight dimensional differences, but the little gun is visually indistinguishable from the firm's 32-caliber P-32.

Here is a first peek at Kimber's new 1911 rimfire pistol, introduced at the February 2003 SHOT Show.

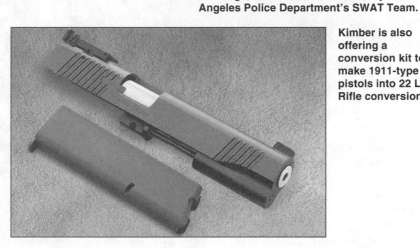

▲ The Kimber TLE (Tactical Law Enforcement) pistol is identical, except for markings, to the sidearm chosen by the Los Angeles Police Department's SWAT Team.

Kimber is also offering a conversion kit to make 1911-type pistols into 22 Long Rifle conversions.

Kimber is now offering 1911 pistols in 22 Long Rifle.

ants. The "Tactical 9" has a 4-inch barrel, and a larger grip frame that accommodates checkered wood grips and an 8-round single-column magazine. The construction of frame and slide is matte-finish stainless steel. The pistol measures about 6 1/2 inches by 5 inches and weighs 28 ounces. Sights are Novak low-profile, with tritium night-sight inserts. The "Target 9" is basically the same pistol with an MMC adjustable rear sight.

Also, a TP 9 was introduced, as a polymer-frame pistol with a 4-inch barrel. This new Kahr did not make it in to the company's 2003 catalog, but has a slightly shorter grip frame than the T9, using a 7-round magazine.

Recall that Kahr also offers the Auto-Ordnance line of 45-caliber pistols, in Standard, Deluxe and WWII Parkerized versions. Now, Kahr is offering a custom 1911. The new Custom pistol will be in stainless steel, with extended safety lever, beveled magazine well, "big diamond" grips, and Chip McCormick trigger and sights.

Kel-Tec

The Florida firm of Kel-Tec comes up with some innovative firearms, both rifles and pistols. The big pistol news is the introduction of their little P-3AT pistol. Sound it out and the name tells its caliber— 38. I had to chuckle out loud when I first read the model number.

The new 380 was developed from the popular P-32 (32 ACP) pistol. The clever design makes the P-3AT almost visually indistinguishable from the P-32. It is only about .080-inch longer, and weighs about a half-ounce more.

Thus, the new 380 is about 3.5 inches high by 5.2 inches long, and weighs about 7.2 ounces. Amazingly, the new gun is still only 3/4 of an inch wide. Mechanically, the internal slide stop has been omitted in the P-3AT, *and (because of the larger-diameter cartridge)* the magazine capacity is reduced to 6 rounds. The nifty little 380 has created a lot of interest, and availability was scheduled for May 2003.

The P-40 pistol has been out of production for a couple of years, and I missed reporting that. A Kel-Tec representative said the pistol worked fine, but the light weight of the gun and the relatively high power of the 40 S&W round could lead to problems when the gun was "limp-wristed" by the shooter.

Kimber

Kimber has been busy in the handgun field. Let's start with the 45-caliber 1911 USA Shooting Team pistol. The distinctive pistol will be used for practice shooting by our rapid-fire pistol team. The gun is offered to the shooting public as the Kimber Team Match II, and for each pistol sold, Kimber is donating $100 to the shooting team. By mid-February 2003, over $50,000 had been raised.

The TLE (Tactical Law Enforcement) pistol is identical to the full-size pistol chosen by the Los Angeles Police Department SWAT team.

Korth has developed a new 45-caliber version of its semiautomatic pistol. Here is a look at prototype 001.

Korth's Silke Musik demonstrates the new Korth 45 ACP prototype to Malloy.

The greatest departure from the traditional Kimber line is the new 1911 in 22 LR. The blowback 22s will be offered in variants of two models—the Rimfire Target (adjustable sights) and the Rimfire Custom (fixed sights). Each model will be available in black or silver finishes. Frames and slides of the rimfire pistols are of aluminum alloy. A conversion kit to convert existing 45-caliber pistols will also be offered.

Korth

The Korth semiautomatic pistol was introduced in 1989 for the 9mm Parabellum cartridge. Since then, it has also been offered in 9x21, 40 S&W and 357 SIG.

At the February 2003 SHOT Show, a new prototype of a Korth pistol in 45 ACP was exhibited. It uses the same basic Korth mechanism, enlarged to handle the dimensions of the 45 cartridge. The magazine is of single-column type and holds 8 rounds. A silenced version of the 45 will be available to law enforcement. As with other Korth pistols, the price is high, but the materials and the workmanship are unsurpassed.

Les Baer

Les Baer Custom was approached by Clint Smith, head of the Thunder Ranch training center in Texas, about a pistol built to his specifications. The result was the Baer 1911 Thunder Ranch Special, a "working" 45 that has features thought desirable by Smith and other shooters. The pistol comes with night sights, extended safety lever and checkered front strap and mainspring housing. The Thunder Ranch logo appears on the slide and grips. For those who like to look at their pistols a lot, a special engraved model with ivory grips is available.

Lone Star

A new series of 1911 pistols has been introduced by Lone Star Armament of Stephenville, Texas. Lone Star makes the slides and frames, then the pistols are assembled by Nowlin Manufacturing, using

The Tactical series is a modified 1911 design with an external extractor. Tactical pistols come in custom (5"), Pro (4") and Ultra (3") variants. A Kimber representative said that, in the future, all Kimber pistols may use the external extractor of the Tactical series.

The Ultra Ten CDP II is a polymer-frame 45 with a machined aluminum insert in the frame. Capacity is 10+1. Kimber Custom Shop features include a "meltdown" treatment *(edges rounded)* and night sights. The new Tactical series extractor and loaded chamber indicator are now standard on Ten II pistols.

Lone Star Armament has introduced a new line of 1911 pistols. This is the Lawman, with a 5-inch barrel.

Wes Ripley proudly exhibits a specimen of Lone Star Armament's new line of 1911-style pistols.

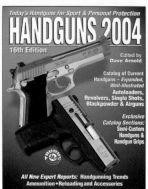
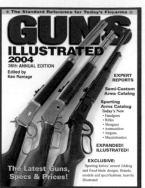
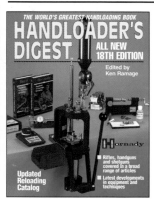

The new polymer-frame SP-21 from IMI is being offered by Magnum Research. Available in 9mm, 40 and 45 calibers, the new pistols use the same magazines as the company's Baby Eagle pistols.

The Mitchell name has returned to the world of 1911-type 45 pistols with the Mitchell Gold Series '03. Here is a look at the first prototype, serial number EXPMA 1.

Mitchell offers restored original Luger pistols as cased sets, with historical information. A reproduction of the Blue Max medal is on the lid of each

This is one of the "Gas Gun" variations offered by NCG (Network Custom Guns). The pistols use forward gas pressure to control rearward recoil. Complete pistols and kits for converting 1911-type pistols are offered.

The pistol has a polymer frame with an integral accessory rail, and the trigger mechanism is conventional double-action. The gun is hammer-fired, and the locking system is tilting-barrel. The barrel has polygonal rifling. Controls comprise an ambidextrous manual safety, a slide release and a decocker on the top of the slide. An internal locking mechanism for times of non-use is included.

The magazine release is reversible for right- or left-hand shooters. The magazines themselves are interchangeable with those of Magnum Research's Baby Eagle pistols—a nice touch. The SP-21 is now offered in 9mm and 40 S&W as well as 45 ACP.

The rear sight is shielded within the raised panel at the rear of the slide. Night sights and adjustable sights are options. A small but important point: there are plenty of grooves at the rear of the slide, and they cover a lot of area. This arrangement makes operating the slide easier, especially under adverse conditions.

Mitchell

It has been a number of years since the Mitchell name has appeared on a 45 automatic. At the February 2003 SHOT Show, three prototypes of a new Mitchell Arms 1911 pistol were exhibited. Pistols numbered EXPMA-1, EXPMA-2 and EXPMA-3 arrived just in time for the opening of the show. Called the Mitchell Gold Series '03 pistols, they are full-size arms with 5-inch barrels. They include some of the niceties today's shooters seem to prefer, such as extended manual safety, beavertail grip safety, skeletonized hammer and trigger and front-and-rear slide serrations. They are cataloged in 40 S&W and 9mm, as well as 45 ACP. Reportedly, the guns will be built by Dan Wesson for Mitchell. Commercial availability was scheduled for Spring 2003.

Mitchell has been doing business as Mitchell's Mausers, and the company has offered rebuilt historical arms. Artisans in Germany are now rebuilding and refinishing original Luger (Parabellum) pistols. Mitchell is offering them, cased, along with the book, *The P08 Luger Pistol* and a History Channel videotape concerning the Luger. Models offered are the Army (4" barrel), Navy (6" barrel) and Artillery (8" barrel) versions.

NCG

NCG (Network Custom Guns) came into our consciousness as a part of KG Industries. KG makes a line of lubrication and cleaning products for firearms owners. Late in 2001, KG became associated with

Nowlin barrels and Chip McCormick parts. Guns are made to shoot inside 1 1/2 inches at 25 yards. The guns are offered in Lawman (5") and Ranger (4") series. "Match" variants with adjustable sights are available in either series.

Magnum Research

Magnum Research displayed a prototype of the IMI (Israeli Military Industries) Barak 45 pistol last year. Now the gun is in production, and has been designated the SP-21.

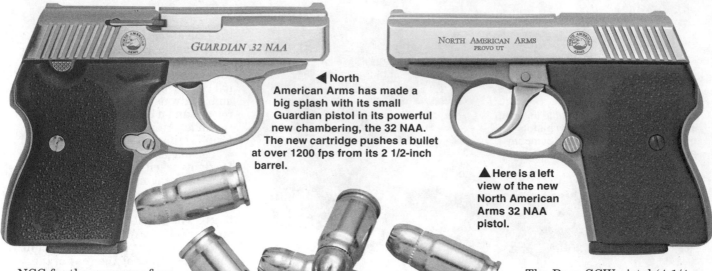

◄ North American Arms has made a big splash with its small Guardian pistol in its powerful new chambering, the 32 NAA. The new cartridge pushes a bullet at over 1200 fps from its 2 1/2-inch barrel.

▲ Here is a left view of the new North American Arms 32 NAA pistol.

▲ The new high-velocity 32 NAA cartridge has now been standardized by the SAAMI.

NCG for the purpose of producing a gas-operated recoil control system for the 1911 design. The design was from NCG's John Adkins, who developed a system that could be added to an existing 1911 pistols. It uses an under-barrel gas piston to retard the rearward movement of the slide. The company now offers conversion kits and complete pistols under the "Gas Gun" tradename.

North American

North American Arms' new Guardian 32 NAA Guardian, introduced last year, has become a hot item in the world of small pocket pistols. Recall that the cartridge case is basically formed by necking a 380 case to 32-caliber. The new cartridge, called appropriately enough the 32 NAA, has been approved by the Sporting Arms & Ammunition Manufacturers Institute (SAAMI). Now that standards have been set, any ammunition manufacturer may decide to produce the cartridges. At present, Cor-Bon makes the ammunition, which pushes a 60-grain bullet out at over 1200 fps from the Guardian's 2 1/2-inch barrel. Consider that the 2-1/2 inches includes the chamber, so the bullet has less than two inches of bore in which to get up to speed. Pretty impressive.

North American never hesitates to hook up with the good ideas of other companies. They have added the Taurus-design key-locking system to the Guardian 32 and 380 pistols. Now the little pocket pistols are California-compliant, as this device is acceptable as a manual safety.

Olympic

Olympic Arms has introduced an eye-catching addition to its 45-caliber 1911 line. The new "Westerner" features a case-color finish on both frame and slide. Various types of

grips can be fitted, but the light-colored ones show the "Westerner" logo well. It is an attractive combination of an Old-West appearance on an up-to-date self-loading pistol.

Para-Ordnance

Para-Ordnance Manufacturing, Inc. has been using the shorter name "Para" more and more lately. Because it uses fewer letters, let's use it here.

The company created quite a stir when it introduced its innovative LDA (Light Double Action) trigger system a few years ago, in 1999. Now, almost all of the Para pistols use this trigger. In February 2003, three new variants were introduced, all in 45 ACP.

The Para CCW pistol (4 1/4-inch barrel) and the Para Companion – Carry Option (3 1/2-inch barrel) are similar except for barrel length and related slide length. They are stainless-steel guns with spurless hammers and the LDA trigger. Capacity is 7+1, and "big diamond" cocobolo grips are fitted. Tritium night sights are standard.

The new Tac-Four is a high-capacity pistol similar to the Para CCW, but with a staggered-column magazine that allows 13+1 capacity. Where legal, the Tac-Four will be shipped with two pre-ban 13-round magazines.

All three of these pistols have traditional (non-extended) safety and slide release levers, and also have a short-tang grip safety—shorter even than the original 1911 Colt part. Para calls this a "bobbed beavertail", reversing the trend to larger and longer beavertail tangs. The result is a more compact, more concealable package to carry for personal protection.

It is a small thing, but Para still cuts slide grooves straight up-and-down, as on the original Colt 1911 and 1911A1 models. Most other companies angle the grooves for appearance. They all seem to work just fine, but the reality of physics is that the more they are slanted, the less purchase the grooves provide for retracting the slide. It is nice that Para is employing the original configuration.

Here is a pre-production specimen of the new Rohrbaugh R-9, a 12-ounce locked-breech 9mm pistol. Type of sights had not been determined when this specimen was exhibited.

Here is a first look at the new Sarsilmaz pistol, which is based on the CZ-75 mechanism. This specimen is serial number 1.

Pardini

The Italian Pardini firm has produced a 45-caliber competition pistol, the Pardini GT 45. The new pistol is available with either a 5- or 6-inch barrel. With a 5-incher, the gun weighs 39 ounces; the 6-inch version tips the scales at 42 ounces. The magazine holds 10 rounds, and the Pardini is suited for IPSC or Practical pistol shooting. Extras, such as a frame-mounted scope base and a German red-dot sight, are also available from the importer, Nygord Precision Products.

Rohrbaugh

Introduced last year, the Rohrbaugh R-9 9mm pistol had its own production facility by February 2003, and deliveries were scheduled for June 2003. Some changes in final production specifications were to be made. Edges will be rounded, and exact types of sights were yet to be determined.

S&W has entered the 1911 market with its new SW1911 pistol. For now, the new pistol is offered only in a 5-inch, stainless steel version.

The little Rohrbaugh pistol claims to be the smallest and lightest 9mm pistol available. There is good evidence for this claim. At 3.6 x 4.9 inches, the pistol will almost hide under a 3x5 index card. Grip choices are polymer, carbon fiber or aluminum. Depending on type of grips, the weight ranges from 12 to 12.7 ounces. The Rohrbaugh pistol uses standard 9mm ammunition, and the capacity is 6+1.

The new company is already looking down the road. Within about 1 1/2 years, they hope to offer a laser-sight option and introduce a 40-caliber version.

Ruger

Sturm, Ruger & Company offered nothing new in their semiauto pistol lines this year. However, developments may be coming soon, as the company is evaluating the need to conform to the requirements of certain restrictive states.

Sarsilmaz

Sarsilmaz, the Turkish company noted for its shotguns, is definitely in the pistol business. Founded in 1880, the company is the only private Turkish armsmaker. Last year, the pistol line was announced, but the pistols themselves were held up in customs. They became available early in 2003. Specimens numbered 01 and 02 were displayed at the 2003 SHOT Show. The Sarsilmaz pistols are based on the CZ-75, and are available in 9mm. Variants are Kilinc (full-size) and Hancer (compact) models.

SIGARMS

Only small changes in the pistol line for SIGARMS, apparently all to their 45-caliber pistols. The full-size P 220 now is available with an accessory rail in the stainless version. Both 7- and 8-shot magazines are available for the P 220.

The downsized P 245 comes with a 6-round magazine, but now an "ErgoGrip" extender can be added to let the smaller pistol use the 8-round magazine. The extender simply snaps over the 8-round magazine. I suspect P 245 owners may want to continue to carry the pistol with the original 6-round magazine, but if a spare is carried, it makes sense to choose the optional 8-rounder.

Smith & Wesson

S&W really introduced a lot of new things at the February 2002 SHOT Show. Without much doubt, the star of their show was a revolver—the big 500 Magnum. That said, you'll have to read about it in the proper place. Here, let us go over the interesting new autoloaders that were almost upstaged by the big revolver.

After years of contending that S&W 45 autos were as good or better than the 1911 design, the company finally entered the fray, and has introduced its own 1911 pistol. The new SW1911 has a few modifications to the original, such as an external extractor. It has an internal drop safety that is disengaged by the grip safety, not the trigger. Other parts interchange, allowing use of 1911 aftermarket parts. However, there may be few that S&W has not already included. The SW1911 uses Wolff springs, Chip McCormick hammer and safety, Wilson beavertail and magazines,

S&W's polymer-frame SW99, previously available in 9mm and 40 S&W, is now offered in 45 ACP.

Novak sights and Briley barrel bushing. The pistol is offered now in only one version, with a 5-inch barrel, and in stainless steel only.

The polymer-frame SW99 is now available in a new chambering—45 ACP. Barrel length of the new, big SW99 is 4 1/4 inches, with a weight of 25.6 ounces. Capacity is 9+1. A more compact variant of the original 9mm and 40-caliber SW99 is now available with a shortened grip frame. Magazine capacity is still 10 rounds for the 9mm, but reduced to 8 for the 40 S&W.

The new Smith & Wesson Model 4040PD is the first scandium-frame semiautomatic pistol. Caliber is 40 S&W. The pistol uses a single-column magazine that holds 7 rounds. With a 3 1/2-inch barrel, the pistol weighs 25.6 ounces.

S&W's Performance Center handguns are now available to all distributors. Thus, limited-edition products such as the Model 945 *(still considered by S&W as the top-of-the-line 45 single-action auto)* and the Model 952 *(the 9mm target pistol)* can be ordered.

Springfield

Springfield made a big splash last year with the introduction of its polymer-frame XD pistol. Now, a new 9mm "Sub-Compact" version, with a 3-inch barrel, is offered. The

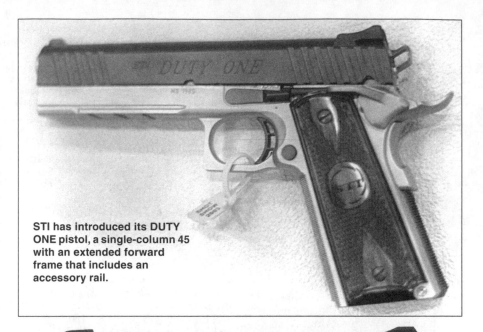

STI has introduced its DUTY ONE pistol, a single-column 45 with an extended forward frame that includes an accessory rail.

Taurus' new Millenium Pro series is an updated version of the original Millenium design. This PT 145 has an all-black finish.

new XD has a shortened grip, but still carries a 10-round magazine made of stainless steel *(two are furnished with each pistol)*. Short as it is, the new XD has a stubby accessory rail at the forward part of its frame, and Springfield has a special XML light to fit. Weight of the small XD is 20-1/2 ounces, and the sights are 3-dot, dovetailed front and rear.

In just a year, the XD has expanded into an entire line of pistols. They are now available with 3-, 4-, and 5-inch barrels, in 9mm, 40S&W and 357 SIG. Frames are black or OD green, and slides are black or silver. Sights may be white dot, several choices of night sights, or fiber optic type. All this presents a lot of possibilities for mixing or matching.

A number of new variants have also been introduced in the 1911-A1 line. One is a 3-inch barrel version with an accessory rail, which will also take the XML light. Two striking-looking pistols are 3-inch and 5-inch pistols made of stainless steel, blackened, then with the sides polished bright. Springfield calls this treatment "Black Stainless."

Steyr

Last year, I reported that Steyr firearms were scheduled to be imported by Dynamit Nobel RWS.

Well, that is half-true. The Nobel firm will import Steyr long guns, but not pistols. By press time, I was unable to learn about the status of the Steyr pistols.

STI

STI International is introducing their "Duty One" pistol, a single-column 45 with an extended frame "dust cover" that carries an accessory rail. The 5-inch bull barrel is ramped, and the chamber fully supported. Delivery was scheduled for third quarter 2003. Finish was planned as flat blue metal, with rosewood grips.

Taurus

The 22-caliber PT 922 introduced last year has changed considerably.

Springfield has introduced a 3-inch barrel version of its new XD polymer-frame pistol. Springfield's Terra Davis displays a specimen in 9mm.

The prototype of 2002 had a metal frame and looked just a bit like a Walther P38. The 2003 version had a polymer frame and looked just a bit like a Colt Woodsman. Even though it was included in the 2003 catalog, Taurus' Eddy Fernandez said it is still under development. This version looked and felt good, and it would be nice to see it finalized.

In the polymer-frame Millenium line, the Millenium "Pro" series has been introduced. This is an updating of the original Millenium design, with pronounced grip checkering, enlarged and smoother-working controls, easier takedown and 3-dot sights. These are some of the

More finish options are offered for Taurus pistols. Here is a dual-tone version of the new Millenium Pro 45-caliber pistol.

Taurus' PT 922, introduced in prototype last year, has already undergone changes in design and appearance. It is now a polymer-frame 22 pistol that is shaped just a bit like the old Colt Woodsman.

subtle, but visible changes. Internally, a captive recoil spring has been added, and the magazine release, trigger pull and internal firing pin lock have been improved.

Tired of all polymer-frame guns having flat black grips? Apparently some people are, for Taurus has brought out the Millenium Deluxe. The new pistols have wood or "pearl" grip inserts added to spruce up the polymer frames.

Valtro

Valtro has added a hard-chrome version to its line of Italian-made 1911-style pistols. The basic pistol is their 1998A1, with many variations made on a custom and semi-custom basis. All Valtro pistols have many of the niceties that modern shooters seem to prefer. The company claims the pistols are machined to the tightest standards in the industry, resulting in accuracy of less than three inches at 50 yards. A Valtro representative said some guns achieve groups of about one inch at that distance, fired from a stationary fixture.

Vektor

Vektor USA, the United States subsidiary of the South African Vektor firm, no longer exists. The only remnant in America is a Vektor Special Projects Office, formed to handle a recall for the Vektor

Linda Moore, Wildey's president, holds one of the big Wildey gas-operated pistols, now available in 44 Auto Mag chambering. The 44 Auto Mag cartridge started the trend to magnum autoloaders.

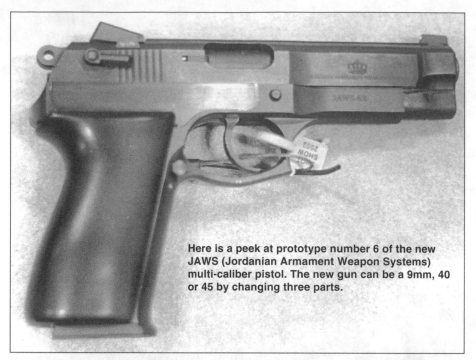

Here is a peek at prototype number 6 of the new JAWS (Jordanian Armament Weapon Systems) multi-caliber pistol. The new gun can be a 9mm, 40 or 45 by changing three parts.

Wildey is now handling the JAWS service pistol, made in Jordan.

demand for a new pistol using this cartridge, and Wildey added it for 2003. It joins the original Wildey chambering, the 45 Winchester Magnum, and the subsequent 45 and 475 Wildey Magnum offerings.

There are lots of hunters who believe that big pistol cartridges are plenty good as ammunition for a handy carbine. For them, Wildey has introduced the Wildey Carbine, based on the pistol mechanism. It has an 18-inch barrel and a skeletonized stock and forearm, both made of walnut. The Wildey Carbine is offered in the same four chamberings as the Wildey pistols.

The company is adding a new line, a big departure for them. Wildey will now also handle a new service-type pistol, chambered for 45 ACP, 40 S&W and 9mm cartridges. The pistol is manufactured in Jordan by Jordanian Armament Weapons Systems, and will be marketed under the logical *(and catchy)* acronym, "JAWS." It is of tilting-barrel locking system, with a conventional double-action trigger mechanism. A special feature is its ability to change calibers simply by changing the barrel, a breechblock in the slide, and an insert in the magazine. JAWS prototype number 6 was exhibited at the February 2003 SHOT Show.

Wilson

Wilson Combat has introduced a Tactical Super Grade Compact pistol. The new handgun is similar to their top-of-the-line 1911-style "Super Grade," but is made with a 4.1-inch barrel. It has many of the features desired today, such as an ambidextrous extended-lever safety, beavertail grip safety and tactical combat sights. Each pistol comes with six magazines *(a nice touch)* and an instructional video, along with other extras. The new pistol has an accuracy guarantee of one inch at 25 yards.

In 2003, Wilson celebrated its 25th year in the custom firearms business. Congratulations!

POSTSCRIPT

It is well to be reminded that antigun forces do not want Americans to possess autoloading handguns. They welcomed the passage of the federal "Assault Weapons" bill of 1994 in part because it also restricted pistol magazine capacity. Now, the law is due to expire in September 2004. There is political agitation to continue the restrictions past the sunset date. It would be wise to contact our Senators and Representatives; we should ask for their support in letting this misguided legislation die at the appointed time. •

CP-1 series of pistols. The recall was scheduled to end in 2003, so owners of such pistols should call 877-831-8313 as soon as possible.

Volquartsen

The Volquartsen Cheetah, the first *(and apparently still the only)* semiautomatic pistol chambered for the 17 HMR (17 Hornady Magnum Rimfire) cartridge, was introduced last year and is now in production. It is also offered in 22 Long Rifle and 22 Winchester Magnum Rimfire.

Wildey

The big Wildey gas-operated pistol is now available in a new chambering, the 44 Auto Mag. Well, the cartridge isn't exactly new, as it was the original magnum semiauto pistol cartridge–designed for the old Auto Mag pistol–and dates back prior to 1970. However, the round has not been commercially chambered in a factory production pistol since the demise of the Auto Mag in the early 1980s. There was a

HANDGUN NEWS

SIX-GUNS AND OTHERS

by John Taffin

WHEN I WAS a kid back in those dinosaur pre-television days, one of the most famous newscasters on radio was a man by the name of Gabriel Heater. He would always come on with the phrase: "Ah, there's good news tonight!" If he were alive he would be the perfect lead-in to announce what is going on in the world of six-guns. There really is good news– and lots of it–for shooters. Dozens of new models are coming out, including those that are entirely original, and others that are simply upgrades-or slightly different versions-of existing six-guns.

Not only do we have new six-guns to talk about, but we also have both the smallest and largest revolver cartridges ever commercially produced being introduced in

◀ Shooters can choose Peacekeepers from AWA with a hard chrome finish and a standard, or Thunderer, grip frame.

▶ AWA's top-of-the-line Peacekeeper, here shown in a 7 1/2-inch 44-40 and 4 3/4-inch 45 Colt, exhibits a deep blue finish, brilliant case colors, and eagle-style rubber grips.

new six-guns this year. Those two cartridges are the 17 HMR (Hornady Magnum Rimfire) and the 500 S&W Magnum. The former is now being chambered in revolvers from Ruger, Smith & Wesson, and Taurus; the latter–at least for now–is found only in the new Model 500 X-Frame from Smith & Wesson.

Competition among the major manufacturers is exceptionally fierce to see who can get there *"fustest with the mostest."* This, of course, is great news for consumers as we reap the benefit of a wide range of both large and small six-guns for virtually any application. Not only in this going to be another great year for handgunners in general, and six-gunners in particular, I speculate that – in the words of the late Al Jolson, that great entertainer from the first half of the 20th century – "You ain't seen nothing yet." If we can continue to hold the anti-gunners at bay, the future will be both exciting and enjoyable. Let us take an alphabetical journey through many of the manufacturers viewing some of the models they are offering.

American Western Arms

American Western Arms (AWA) offers two replica Single-Action Armies known as the Longhorn and the Peacekeeper. The former is their standard-finished Single Action available in 45 Colt, 44-40, 44 Special, 38-40, and 357 Magnum. The Peacekeeper has the same chamberings; however, it is specially tuned, exquisitely finished, and also fitted with checkered rubber grips instead of the one-piece style found on the Longhorn. The Peacekeeper is as beautiful a Single-Action

The Bond Texas Cowboy features easily interchangeable barrel assemblies, shown here are 45 Colt and 32 Magnum barrels.

Army replica as one is ever going to find anywhere. The top-of-the-line model Peacekeeper, in addition to a factory-tuned action, has an 11-degree forcing cone, 1st Generation-style cylinder flutes, and bone/charcoal case-hardened frame.

Both models feature a beveled ejector rod housing to keep the metal from digging into the leather on a tight holster, and both models can be had in nickel finish, while the Peacekeeper can also be ordered with the "blackpowder frame", distinctive because an angled screw in the front of the frame – rather than the spring-loaded cross-pin retainer – holds the cylinder pin in place. It is also available in a satin hard chrome finish that not only looks great, but also cleans up easily for those using blackpowder loads.

American Western Arms cylinders have virtually no end play or side-to-side movement; the one-piece walnut stocks on the Longhorn, and black rubber American Eagle grips on the Peacekeeper are individually fitted with no overlapping of grip or frame. AWA is now fitting their single actions with a coil mainspring. These are more reliable, and give a more even hammer pull and faster hammer fall than the old-style flat mainspring. The coil springs are available in three weights: 15#, 17#, and 19# and can be fitted to older six-guns by filing a small area behind the trigger guard part of the grip frame and using a coil-spring holding shelf that screws into the hole used for the original flat mainspring.

Bond Arms

Several years ago I tested the first Bond Derringer and discovered it was a good, strong two-shooter

with two problems. The trigger pull was very heavy, and the changing of barrel and shims took three hands, or more, to accomplish. That is all past. The Cowboy Derringer is exceptionally easy to use. Changing barrels *(each frame accepts all caliber barrels)* takes about one minute to accomplish, using an Allen wrench of the proper size. On the left side of the frame of the Cowboy Derringer is a spring-loaded camming lever that, when pushed down, unlatches the barrel assembly

allowing it to move upwards to be unloaded and reloaded. Each barrel assembly has its own built-in spring-loaded ejector. The Bond Cowboy Texas Defender Model is stainless steel and comes with grips of an impregnated laminated rosewood that are small, but they nestle comfortably in the hand. The hammer is of the rebounding type and a cross-bolt safety is found on the Bond and should–that is SHOULD–always be applied if the Bond is carried loaded. The Bond Cowboy/Texas Defender Derringer comes in 32 Magnum, 357 Maximum, 9mm, 45ACP, 44 Special/44 Magnum, 40 S&W, 38 Special/357 Magnum, 45 Colt, and 45 Colt/.410.

The Bond Derringer is quality, and unlike some derringers on the market, is easy to operate one-handed. The trigger pull is not overly heavy and the hammer is easy to cock with the thumb of the shooting hand and, for all practical purposes for which such a little gun should be used, point of impact with both barrels is close enough.

Cimarron Firearms

Cimarron is now providing brand-new six-guns in what they call an original finish. This finish is actually what a six-gun would look like after much usage on a daily

Available in either the standard finish *(shown)* or original finish, Cimarron's Wyatt Earp Buntline is an excellent shooter. Shield in the right grip commemorates the presentation of the Buntline Special to Earp.

It is a brand-new six-gun from Cimarron; however this 7 1/2-inch 44-40 looks 125 years old due to its 'original' finish. Period leather is by Will Ghormley.

Cimarron offers both the 45 New Thunderer *(top)*, **and 38 Lightning Model. Custom grips are by Buffalo Brothers.**

▼**Cimarron brings back a short but important time in history with their 1871-72 Open-Top, chambered in 44 Colt. Carved eagle grips are by Buffalo Brothers.**

basis, after hundreds and hundreds of times being drawn and replaced in a leather holster. My original 1879-vintage Colt Frontier Six-Shooter, *(as the early Colts chambered in 44-40 were called)*

with one-piece stocks and a 7 1/2-inch barrel has a finish earned with over 100 years of service. The new 'original' finish of the Cimarron Model P perfectly matches with what is left on my old Six-Shooter. The Cimarron's finish is not simply an in-the- white six-gun with no bluing. Instead it has age marks, blemishes—and even a small spot or two with a brownish patina. The one-piece stocks are also appropriately distressed. CFA also offers the Wyatt Earp Buntline Special 10-inch barrel 45 Colt in either blue/case color or original finish. Either way, it fairly reeks of history and, for most six-gunners, is also easy to shoot well due to the long barrel and great distance between sights.

Cowboy Action Shooting has been responsible for the availability of replicas of most of the great single actions of the past, not only the well known Colt Single-Action Army and Remington Model 1875, but also the Richards Conversion, the Richards-Mason Conversion, and the 1871-72 Open-Top. Cimarron has offered all three of these, and currently offers the Richards-Mason and the Open-Top. While attending Range War in Fredericksburg, Texas I had the opportunity to visit the Cimarron Firearms facility—and came home with a pair of consecutively-numbered 1871-72 Open-Tops, chambered in 44 Colt.

The modern 44 Colt is simply a 44 Special cartridge case that has been slightly shortened, with the diameter of the rim turned down to allow six rounds to fit in the 1860 Army-sized cylinders of the Colt cartridge conversions. Open-Tops, with their connection to the past and mild recoil, are such a pleasure that it seemed reasonable to have them fitted with custom stocks. For grips I called upon Buffalo Brothers. They specialize in molded, antique-looking polymer grips for all the old six-guns, and their replicas. Using old-style patterns and modern coloring techniques, Buffalo Brothers offers ten different shades of historical antique coloring molded into the grip, as well as carvings such as those found on single actions in the middle of the 19th-century. For the Open-Tops I chose ivory grips with a carved Eagle symbol. They really set off these Open-Tops and make them extremely attractive.

Cimarron's newest offering is a Model P in stainless steel. These six-guns are made by Uberti and, as you read this, will be available in both 357 Magnum and 45 Colt in the three standard barrel lengths of 4 3/4, 5 1/2, and 7 1/2 inches. For the first time, those that pack a traditional single action in all kinds of weather will have the advantage of stainless steel's ability to withstand the elements. A bonus, for those shooting blackpowder, is that they are much easier to clean and maintain.

Colt's Manufacturing Company, Inc.

More good news from Colt this year. Two years ago the retail price of the Colt Single Action Army was $1,968. Last year this dropped by $438 to $1,530, and now Colt continues the trend with a new MSRP of $1,380. Some replicas are already running as high as $1,100 or more, so this may cause some six-gunners to take another look at the original Single Action Army. Colt has two advantages over the replicas: First, they are

Jamie Harvey of Cimarron Firearms shows off the new stainless steel Model P 45 Colt.

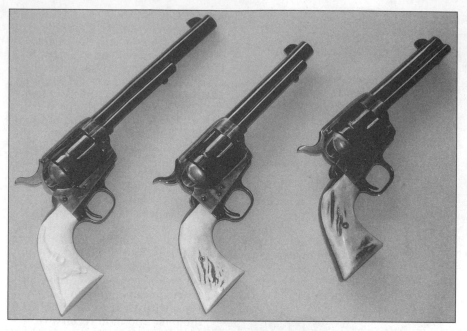

The Classic Colt Single Action Army has not only been lowered in price by nearly $600 over the past two years, it is now offered in all three standard barrel lengths. Custom stocks are extra.

▶ New from EMF this year is the Great Western II, here shown in both the Californian and the satin nickel versions.

◀ ▶ EMF offers both the 1875 Remington and 1890 Remington in 45 Colt. Stocks are by Buffalo Brothers.

genuine Colts—no other single action can make that statement. Second, the Colt Single Action has more than a century and one-half of history behind it. Again, no other single action can make that claim.

A second piece of good news from Colt is that the Single Action Army is once again offered in the original 1873 Cavalry Model 7 1/2-inch barrel length. It has probably been a decade since shooters could have anything except 4 3/4- and 5 1/2-inch Single Actions from Colt. Now all three standard barrel lengths are available in 357 Magnum, 44-40, and 45 Colt. There is a downside, however, as the nickel-plate finish has been dropped from the catalog; now only the standard blued finish with a casehardened frame is offered. Grips are a checkered black composite with the rampant colt emblem at the top and the American Eagle at the bottom.

Colt also continues to offer their answer to Ruger's Vaquero—the Cowboy—in 45 Colt only and a choice of 4 3/4- and 5 1/2-inch barrel lengths. This six-gun is also offered only in the blued/casehardened finish. To round out their six-gun offerings, Colt continues to offer a stainless steel 44 Magnum Anaconda in barrel lengths of 4, 6, and 8 inches, as well as the 357 Python Elite in either of blue or stainless, and a barrel length choice of 4 or 6 inches. All double-action models feature adjustable sights with a red ramp front and white outline rear sight. Anacondas come equipped with finger-grooved rubber grips, while the Python Elite is the only Colt revolver currently offered with wooden stocks (finger-grooved combat-style walnut).

Early & Modern Firearms (EMF)

EMF imports a full line of quality revolvers and offers them under the Hartford label. In the past many of their replica six-guns have been manufactured by Armi San Marco, however

Forty-fours from Freedom Arms: Model 83 *(top)* chambered in 44 Magnum, and the new Model 97 set up for the 44 Special.

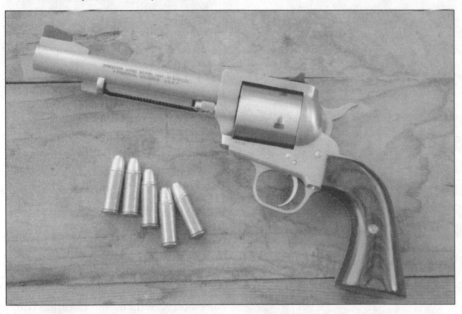

Freedom Arms' newest offering is the mid-framed Model 97, a five-shot 44 Special. This could well be the finest factory-manufactured 44 Special ever.

has a round lanyard ring in the butt. Both six-guns proved to be well above average in the accuracy department for this type of revolver.

Freedom Arms

Freedom Arms full-sized five-shot revolver, the Model 83, continues to be produced in 454 Casull, 44 Magnum, 357 Magnum, 41 Magnum, 475 Linebaugh and 50AE. There is even a 22 LR version. These are simply the finest six-guns ever to come from a factory being, in fact, custom-built. Seven years ago, Freedom Arms introduced their mid-frame six-gun, the Model 97. The Model 97 is built exactly the same way as the larger Model 83, using the same materials and the same strict attention to tight tolerances and precision fitting. Although the Model 83 is available with both a Field Grade and Premier Grade finish, the Model 97 is thus far offered only in Premier Grade. Price-wise, the Model 97 costs about 12 percent less than a comparable Model 83 due to less material being used for the smaller gun, rather than any short-cuts or difference in manufacturing. The cylinders on the little gun are still line-bored as they are on the big gun.

Last year Freedom Arms introduced the Model 97 in 22 Long Rifle with an extra 22 Magnum cylinder. I have now had a chance to thoroughly test this grand little 22 and I can say the Model 97 22/22 Magnum really shoots! The performance of this Model 97 is superb with both cylinders using either 22 Long Rifle or 22 Magnum Rimfire ammunition resulting in groups of less than one-third of an inch for five shots at 25 yards. CCI's Mini-Mag Hollow Points, Remington's Yellow Jackets, and Winchester's High Velocity Hollow Points all came in well under one-third of an inch with the 22 Long Rifle cylinder in place, while CCI's Maxi-Mag Hollow Points delivered the same results with the 22 Magnum cylinder in use.

New for this year is the Model 97 chambered in 44 Special. Most dedicated and knowledgeable six-gunners agree the first 44 Special, the Smith & Wesson 1st Model Hand Ejector of 1907 is not only the finest double-action six-gun ever built, it is also the grandest of 44 Specials. Until now. The old Triple-Lock has met its match with the new Freedom Arms 44 Special.

I've been a connoisseur of 44 Specials since my first Smith & Wesson Model 1950 Target was acquired in 1959. I've had just about every 44 Special ever manufactured: Smith & Wesson Triple-Lock, Model 1926, 1950 Military, 1950 Target, Model 24, and Model 624; Colt New

they have now turned to Pietta to produce a new lineup of single-action six-guns that bear the Great Western name. Although labeled Great Western, these new six-guns are not replicas of the original replica, the Great Western, having the traditional Colt-style firing pin instead of the original frame-mounted firing pin of the original Great Western. Forty years after the demise of the Great Western Frontier Revolver, EMF is offering the Great Western II in nickel, satin nickel, full blue, or blue with a beautifully case-colored frame. Another version, known as The Californian, is offered with a standard finish. I have had the opportunity to test two 4 3/4-inch 45s; one a satin nickel Great Western II with one-piece polymer ivory stocks, the

other a Californian with one-piece wood stocks. The less expensive Californian has the best-looking wooden stocks I have yet to find on any Italian replica. They are perfectly fitted and finished, and performed and shot well.

EMF also offers excellent copies of the Remington single actions. It has been my pleasure to test both a 7 1/2-inch Model 1875 and a 5 1/2-inch Model 1890, both chambered in 45 Colt. Cylinders lock up tightly, and I do mean tightly, and both are timed better than the average Italian replica. Actions are smooth, and mainsprings are also much lighter than found on Remington replicas from two decades ago. The Model 1875 is blued with a case-colored frame and hammer, while the 1890 is fully blued. The Model 1890 also

Freedom Arms is now delivering the Model 97 22LR/22 WMR. This may well be most accurate 22 revolver ever offered to shooters.

Kelly Baker of Freedom Arms displays the new Model 97 44 Special.

Service, Single Action Army, and New Frontier; Great Western Frontier Model; Texas Longhorn Arms South Texas Army and Flat-Top Target; and many custom 44s built on Ruger 357 Magnum Blackhawk Flat-Tops and Three-Screws. None can surpass the Freedom Arms Model 97 for quality, accuracy, and portability. Many cannot understand the deep appreciation for the 44 Special, a cartridge that has been "surpassed" by so many big-bore magnums. For those that do understand, no explanation is necessary; for those that don't, no explanation is possible. It is a spiritual thing with many six-gunners.

Magnum Research

Magnum Research has long been known for the semi-automatic Desert Eagle. However, in recent years they have been offering the BFR *(Biggest Finest Revolver),* an all stainless-steel revolver offered in two frame sizes. The standard frame and cylinder *(they call it the Short Cylinder)* is chambered in 454 Casull, 22 Hornet, and 475 Linebaugh—which also handles the 480 Ruger. The Long Cylinder version handles the 45-70, 444 Marlin, 450 Marlin, or a 45 Colt version that also handles .410 shot shells.

This past year I have been shooting one of the Short Cylinder versions with a 6 1/2–inch barrel chambered in 480/475 Linebaugh. Instead of adjustable sights, it came from the factory fitted with a mounted scope and no iron sights whatsoever. The rubber grips supplied are not pretty but they certainly help in handling felt recoil. With a suggested retail price of $999, the BFR is the most affordable way to own a quality single-action revolver chambered in many large calibers.

The standard BFR rear sight is fully adjustable, and mated with an interchangeable front sight. Barrels are cut-rifled, barrel/cylinder gaps are held to less than 0.005-inch, and cylinders are freewheeling; that is, when the loading gate is

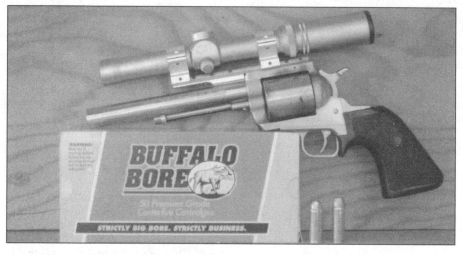

The BFR revolver from Magnum Research has proven to be an extremely accurate six-gun when using either 480 Ruger or 475 Linebaugh ammunition.

Navy Arms is now offering the Schofield Model chambered for 38 Special or 38 Long Colt. Grips are by Buffalo Brothers.

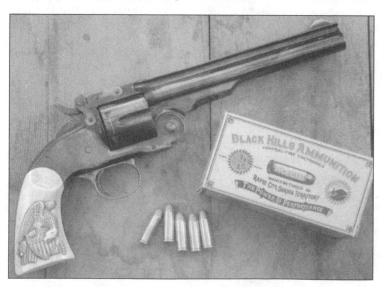

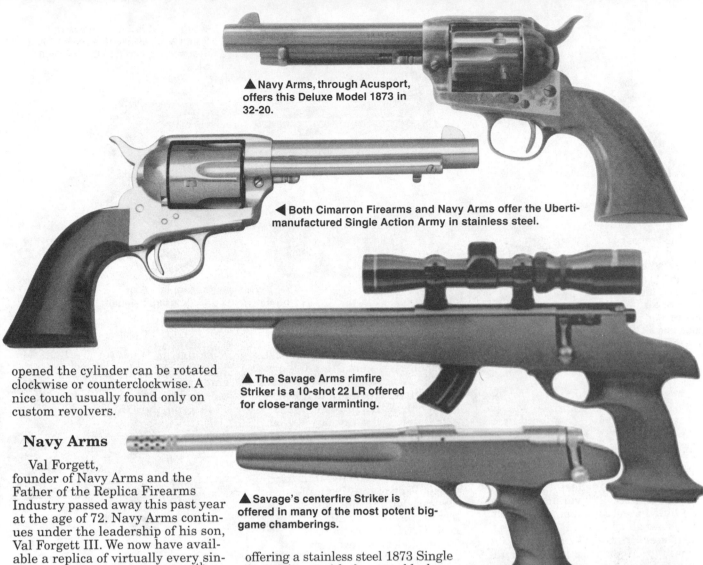

▲ Navy Arms, through Acusport, offers this Deluxe Model 1873 in 32-20.

◀ Both Cimarron Firearms and Navy Arms offer the Uberti-manufactured Single Action Army in stainless steel.

▲ The Savage Arms rimfire Striker is a 10-shot 22 LR offered for close-range varminting.

opened the cylinder can be rotated clockwise or counterclockwise. A nice touch usually found only on custom revolvers.

▲ Savage's centerfire Striker is offered in many of the most potent big-game chamberings.

Navy Arms

Val Forgett, founder of Navy Arms and the Father of the Replica Firearms Industry passed away this past year at the age of 72. Navy Arms continues under the leadership of his son, Val Forgett III. We now have available a replica of virtually every single-action revolver from the 19th century, thanks to the efforts of several individuals. However, it all started back in the 1950s with Forgett introducing a copy of the 1851 Colt Navy. Forgett and Navy Arms were directly responsible for the introduction of Smith & Wesson single actions, beginning with the 1875 Schofield and followed by the Model #3 Russian.

New models from Navy Arms this year include two new Schofields. First is a Founders Model with a color-case-hardened receiver, polymer ivory grips, 7 1/2-inch barrel, and chambered in 45 Colt. The 38 Special Schofield joins the 45 Colt and 44-40 in both the 7 1/2-inch Cavalry and 5 1/2-inch Wells Fargo models.

Those who prefer Colt replicas have not been forgotten. Navy Arms' 1873 Single Actions are now offered as a Gunfighter Series with all standard springs replaced by custom Wolff springs, a nickel-plated back-strap and trigger guard, and black checkered grips. These are offered in the three standard barrel lengths of 4 inches, 5 1/2 inches, and 7 1/2 inches in 357 Magnum, 44-40, and 45 Colt. For the first time, Navy Arms is also

offering a stainless steel 1873 Single Action Army with the same black checkered grips and Wolff springs in all three barrel lengths, chambered in 357 Magnum or 45 Colt.

Finally from Navy Arms comes a Deluxe Model 1873 Single Action Army in 32-20. When the West was wild the most popular chamberings were 45 Colt, 44-40, and 38-40. However, as things began to settle down, around the turn-of-the-century, the 32-20 became very popular so is altogether fitting that Navy Arms would choose this chambering for their Deluxe Model. This version features a color-casehardened receiver and loading gate; charcoal- or fire-blue barrel, cylinder, and grip frame; hand-rubbed walnut stocks, and Wolff springs.

Savage

Savage not only produces some of the finest rifles available, they are also part of the handgunner's world with their Striker bolt-action pistol. All of these superbly accurate handguns have a left-handed bolt and a black ambidextrous synthetic stock, with a finger-groove pistol grip. Centerfire models are

Dale Donough of SIGARMS shows off the new Blaser 93 bolt-action pistol.

◀ Big—that is B-I-G—news from Smith & Wesson is the Model 500 X-Frame chambered in the new 500 S&W.

▶ The lightest 44 Magnum ever offered; the S&W329PD weighs in at 26 ounces. It will pack like a dream and kick like a nightmare.

▶ This year's Mountain Gun offering from S&W is a blued 4-inch Model 29 in 44 Magnum.

offered in both blue and stainless, a magazine capacity of two rounds and chambered in 243 Winchester, 7-08 and 308, while the 223 version is offered in blued steel only. For fanciers of the new short cartridges, a stainless-steel Striker is cataloged, chambered for the 270, 7mm, and 300 WSM. All centerfire Strikers have 14-inch barrels.

For those who prefer to hunt varmints with a rimfire, the Striker is available chambered in 22 WMR and 17 HMR with a 10-inch barrel and five-round magazine, while a 10-shot version can be had for everyone's favorite cartridge for plinking and relaxing, 22 Long Rifle. All Strikers come with scope bases already installed and button-rifled, free-floating barrels.

SIGARMS

No I'm not going to report on any semi-automatics from SIG. John Malloy handles that pleasant chore quite well. However, SIGARMS is offering a handgun that fits into my section. It is the Blaser R93 bolt-action hunting handgun. And a beauty it is! It is a straight-pull, bolt-action pistol built on the same action as the Blaser 93 Rifle, with free-floating interchangeable barrels. Barrels are hammer-forged, 14 inches in length; the stock is beautifully-figured walnut; and the forearm is furnished with a sling swivel for the attachment of a Harris bipod. Chambering options currently

include the 223 Remington, 243 Winchester, 6mm BR, 270 Winchester, 308 Winchester, 30/06, 7-08, 7mm Remington Magnum, and the new 300WSM. With a price tag in the $2650 to $2800 range, only serious handgun hunters need apply.

Smith & Wesson

Smith & Wesson reclaims the title of King of the Magnum Six-guns with the introduction of the 500 S&W Magnum cartridge, and the X-frame Model 500 revolver to handle it. From the 1930s the 1960s it was all Smith & Wesson, as far as magnum chamberings were concerned, as they introduced (in succession) the 357 Magnum, the 44

Magnum, and the 41 Magnum. After that, the game plan changed as other companies and individuals introduced the 454 Casull, the 475 and 500

▲ From the Smith & Wesson Performance Center comes this exceptionally businesslike 2-inch barrel, short-cylinder Model 625 in 45 ACP.

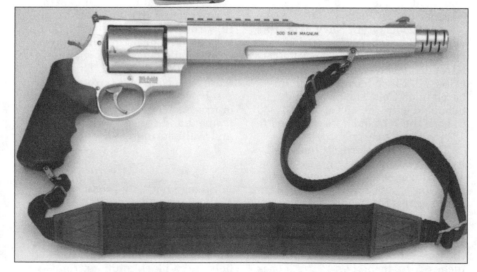

In addition to the standard Model 500, Smith & Wesson also offers this Performance Center model complete with built-in scope mount, sling swivels, and carrying strap.

Shooters now have a choice of six-guns chambered for the largest: 500 S&W, and smallest: 17HMR.

The four big-bore six-gun cartridges introduced by Smith & Wesson: 357 Magnum *(1935)*, 41 Magnum *(1964)*, 44 Magnum *(1955)*, and the 500 S&W *(2003)*.

Jim Rae of the Smith & Wesson Performance Center with a new S&W Model 500 Hunter Model.

Linebaugh, the 357, 375, 445, 475, and 500 Maximums/SuperMags, and the 480 Ruger. Now Smith & Wesson is back on top of the mountain with the 500 Magnum.

When the 357 Magnum was introduced in 1935, there was no way it could ever be surpassed. It was, however, with the 44 Magnum introduction in 1955, which could never be challenged. Then came the 454 in the 1970s, and then the.... Well, you get the picture. With every new cartridge we felt we were at the top. We certainly have reached it now! I cannot see how we could come up with a more powerful cartridge for a handheld six-gun than the 500 that is, by the way, a slightly modified version of John Linebaugh's original 500 Maximum. The latter uses a 1.610-inch cartridge case with a 0.511-inch bullet, while Smith & Wesson's version has a 1.625-inch case and a true 0.500-inch bullet.

The standard Model 500 has an 8 3/8-inch ported barrel,

stretched frame and cylinder to fit the longer cartridge, heavy underlug barrel, felt recoil-reducing rubber grips, stainless-steel finish, and a weight of 4 pounds that will be welcomed by most shooters. The Performance Center will be offering a 10-inch Model 500 with sling swivels and a scope mount base, and Smith & Wesson is at least contemplating an easy-packing 3-inch barrel version. Cor-Bon has three loads for the 500 S&W: a 275-grain Barnes X-Bullet at 1665 fps with a muzzle energy of 1688 ft/lbs; a 400-grain SP at 1675 fps and 2500 ft/lbs; and a 440-grain Hard Cast, 1625 fps and 2580 ft/lbs! This is incredible power in a handheld revolver.

As stout as recoil of the Model 500 will be, it may be overshadowed by the second offering from Smith & Wesson—the 44 Magnum Model 329PD. We are used to titanium and scandium 357 Magnums, now it's time to get ready for light versions in 44 Magnum. The Model 329PD has a scandium frame, titanium cylinder, 4-inch barrel, black matte finish, Hi-Viz front sight, and weighs all of 26 ounces! When I asked Herb Belin of Smith & Wesson why it was equipped with wooden grips, he admitted after he fired it rubber grips were more appropriate. So this Smith & Wesson comes with two pair of grips: Ahrends finger-groove wood and a Hogue rubber Monogrip. One will be able to tell

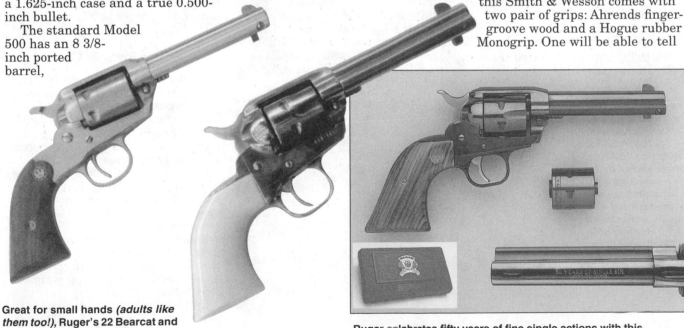

Great for small hands *(adults like them too!)*, Ruger's 22 Bearcat and 32 Single-Six with a short grip frame. One-piece style grips are by Get-A-Grip.

Ruger celebrates fifty years of fine single actions with this Anniversary Model 22 Single-Six 22LR/22WMR.

Ruger's standard model Old Army is now joined by a 5 1/2-inch version. Gunfighter grips are by Eagle grips, auxiliary 45 Colt cylinders are from Taylor's.

what type of loads are being used by which grip is being employed. Recoil will be HEAVY.

Several other revolvers of note: Smith & Wesson is now chambering the 17 HMR in the medium-frame Model 647, with a companion Model 648 in 22 WMR. Both are 6-inch stainless steel six-guns with heavy underlug barrels. From the Performance Center we have the return of the blued Model 29 in a Mountain Gun version with a 4-inch tapered barrel. I have always felt the 357 Magnum Model 27 with a 3 1/2-inch barrel was the most serious-looking double-action revolver around. Now the rather strange-looking Performance Center Model 625, with a two-inch barrel and a shortened cylinder to accommodate the 45 ACP, has surpassed it. Since much of the barrel is in the frame and extends to the front of the cylinder, only a small nub protrudes in front of the frame. Now that six-gun really looks serious!

Sturm, Ruger & Co.

In 1999, Ruger celebrated the 50th anniversary of the founding of

their company by issuing an Anniversary Commemorative Model Red Eagle 22 semi-auto pistol. Now, four years later, it is time for the Ruger Single-Six 50th Anniversary Model. Bill Ruger correctly read the shooting public and resurrected the single-action revolver in 1953. He very wisely maintained the Colt grip shape, while scaling down the rest of the revolver to 22 rimfire size. The price in 1953 was a very affordable $63.25 and a whole box of 22s could be had for well under 50 cents. Single-Sixes have been favored by shooters ever since. The 50th Anniversary Model will feature a New Model Single-Six with a 4 5/8-inch barrel that will be marked "50 Years of Single-Six 1953 to 2003". Grips will be of coco bola and, for the first time ever, will have red eagle medallions. An extra cylinder chambered in 22 MRF will be included.

Last year Ruger reintroduced the 44 Magnum Super Blackhawk Hunter model, which I consider the greatest bargain available to the handgun hunter. With its 7 1/2-inch barrel, stainless-steel construction, and full-length barrel rib cut for the

Ruger scope rings (included), a handgun hunter gets just about everything he needs. Now Ruger has made the Hunter Model even more attractive by providing a Bisley version. Most shooters find the Bisley grip frame handles felt recoil better than any other grip frame configuration. A great bargain just got better.

Ruger's Old Army, which is without doubt the finest cap and ball revolver ever produced, is now being offered in an easier-to-carry 5 1/2-inch version. It should find great favor with cowboy action shooters who prefer blackpowder. Cowboy action shooters will also appreciate that the 4 5/8-inch Bird's Head Vaquero is now offered in 357 Magnum. Last year Ruger introduced several rifles chambered in the new 17 HMR. They are followed with a 6 1/2-inch Single-Six chambered in this smallest of rimfires.

Two six-guns that were announced last year are now coming through regularly. Those two are the Bearcat in 22 rimfire and the Single-Six in 32 Magnum with a shorter grip frame—both in stainless steel. For these two small six-guns I used some of my grandkids as the field-testers and expert panel of judges to report upon their merits. Elyse (17), Laura (16), and Brian John (10), joined me to test the newest Ruger single actions. The Bearcat has a very small grip frame that fits the smallest hands, and the newest 32 Magnum features a grip frame approximately 1/4-inch shorter (top to bottom) than the standard Blackhawk grip frame. The kids liked the way this grip frame fit their relatively small hands. They work pretty well for the rest of us, too.

Taylor's & Co.

Taylor's has producing a line of quality replicas for several years. However, the big news is that Taylor's is now distributing R&D conversion cylinders for both Remington replicas and Ruger Old Army percussion revolvers. I mentioned above the fact Ruger was now offering the Old Army in a 5 1/2-inch version. A pair of these was ordered in stainless steel, along with R&D 45 Colt conversion cylinders from Taylor's. The cylinders are not offered in stainless steel. However, one has a choice of blue or nickel finish, with the latter nicely matching the Ruger stainless-steel finish.

I was very impressed with the quality and workmanship of the cylinders and the fact that they work not only in these two Old Armies,

Taylor's & Co. now offers the R&D 45 Colt Conversion Cylinder for Ruger's Old Army, here shown in the new 5 1/2-inch stainless steel model fitted with Eagle's checkered buffalo horn Gunfighter grips.

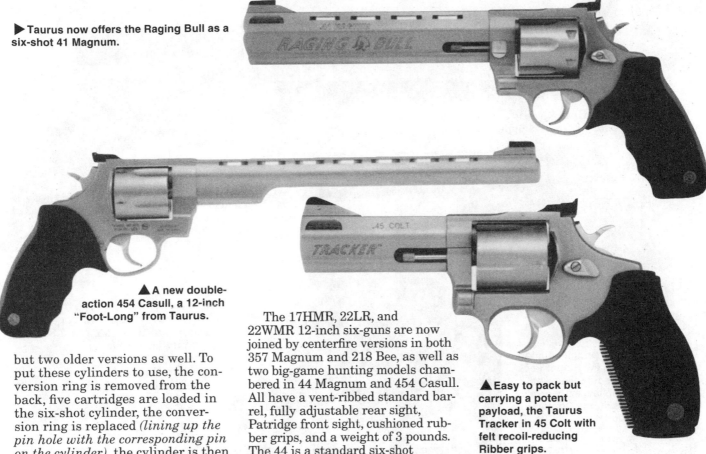

▶ Taurus now offers the Raging Bull as a six-shot 41 Magnum.

▲ A new double-action 454 Casull, a 12-inch "Foot-Long" from Taurus.

▲ Easy to pack but carrying a potent payload, the Taurus Tracker in 45 Colt with felt recoil-reducing Ribber grips.

but two older versions as well. To put these cylinders to use, the conversion ring is removed from the back, five cartridges are loaded in the six-shot cylinder, the conversion ring is replaced *(lining up the pin hole with the corresponding pin on the cylinder)*, the cylinder is then replaced carefully *(with the empty chamber under the hammer)*, and the Ruger Old Army cap-and-ball revolver is converted to use 45 Colt cartridges. I intend to use these guns and cylinders to shoot both Frontier Cartridge and Plainsman in cowboy action shooting matches.

Taurus

This company just continues to amaze—they not let any grass grow under their feet. For the new 17 Hornady Magnum Rimfire they have not only chambered their pump-action rifle, they now are offering shooters 10 six-gun choices. Shooters have a choice of both blue and stainless eight-shooters, or the new Model 17SS12. The "12" of this model number denotes a foot-long barrel. I find myself captivated by these long barrels and I have been shooting both the 22 Long Rifle and 22 Winchester Rimfire Magnum versions since last year. To keep the weight down as much as possible, the long tubes are standard barrels rather than the heavy underlug style. This keeps the weight of the 17HMR version at just two ounces over three pounds. Taurus calls this the "Perfect Gun and Ammunition Match for Coyote, Rabbit, Squirrel, Crow and Other Small Game Hunting." They could well be right and to further ensure this they include a free scope mount base with each foot-long 17.

The 17HMR, 22LR, and 22WMR 12-inch six-guns are now joined by centerfire versions in both 357 Magnum and 218 Bee, as well as two big-game hunting models chambered in 44 Magnum and 454 Casull. All have a vent-ribbed standard barrel, fully adjustable rear sight, Patridge front sight, cushioned rubber grips, and a weight of 3 pounds. The 44 is a standard six-shot revolver, while the 454 is a five-shooter. Taurus also offers an optional arm support that attaches to the grip and wraps around the forearm. It can be bent to give the required tension and has been given the *OK* by ATF.

Taurus' very popular Raging Bull has been offered in 44 Magnum, 454 Casull, and 480 Ruger. The connoisseur's other cartridge, the 41 Magnum has now been added to the line. Raging Bull's feature heavy underlug barrels, four ports on each side of the front sight, fully adjustable rear sight, Patridge front sight, and cushioned rubber grips. Scope mount bases are also offered. The Raging Bulls have now been joined by three other Raging Models, the Raging Hornet (22 Hornet), the Raging Bee (218 Bee), and the Raging Thirty (30 Carbine). These are all eight-shooters weighing two ounces over three pounds with their 10-inch barrels. Scope mounts are also available for these varmint pistols.

For those that are looking for an easy-to-pack but potent six-gun, Taurus offers four 4-inch, five-shot Trackers chambered in 357 Magnum, 41 Magnum, 45 ACP, and 45 Colt. All of these feature heavy underlug barrels and the felt recoil-reducing wraparound "Ribber" grips. All but the 41 are also offered in a 6 1/2-inch vent rib model. This latter version also comes in 17HMR and 218 Bee. Taurus of course continues to offer a full

line of revolvers for concealed carry, including the 2-inch CIA and Protector, in 38 Special and 357 Magnum, including Total Titanium versions in 38. The CIA is a hammerless, DAO five-shooter, while the Protector has just enough of the hammer spur showing to allow cocking for single-action fire. Both models feature finger-grooved rubber grips.

Thompson/Center

T/C's Contender opened up new vistas for the handgun hunter more than three decades ago. The standard Contender frame was replaced last year with the new G2 Contender featuring an easier-to-open action, more room for the hand between the back of the trigger guard and front of the grip, and a hammer-block safety that does not require the action be re-opened if the shooter decides to lower the hammer, and then re-cock. On the old models, once the hammer was lowered, the action had to be opened before it could be re-cocked. The G2 will accept all original Contender barrels; however, the grip frame is different and requires use of the new grip. As of this writing, G2s continue to be in short supply.

The G2 may be in short supply but the Encore is not. This stronger version of the Contender allows the use of high-pressure rifle cartridges above

▼ Dan Wesson's Alaskan Guide is a Teflon-coated, 4-inch ported barrel 445 SuperMag.

▲ Thompson/Center offers the Encore in a full line of centerfire rifle chamberings. Excellent handgun for long-range hunting.

▶ For the serious handgun hunter, Dan Wesson offers the Hunter Pack in several calibers complete with two barrel assemblies, extra grips, all packed in this sturdy Cordura-covered hardwood case.

the level of the 44Magnum/30-30 Contender. The Encore is offered in both 12-inch and 15-inch easy opening models in such chamberings as 454 Casull, 480 Ruger, 22-250 Remington, 25-06, 7-08, 308, 30-06, 45-70, and 450 Marlin and is also used for a whole range of wildcat cartridges from SSK Industries and Reeder Custom Guns. Thompson/Center continues to build the single-shot pistols by which all others are judged.

Wesson Firearms

Dan Wesson has been concentrating on introducing their Pointman series of semi-automatic 45s the past year, however they continue to offer the superbly accurate revolver created by Dan Wesson in 1968. All Dan Wesson revolvers feature easily interchangeable barrels and are offered in several versions—all in stainless steel with fully adjustable sights and finger-grooved rubber grips. The Small Frame is available in 22LR, 32 Magnum, 32-20, and 357 Magnum. Moving up to the Large Frame, we find 360DW, 41 Magnum, 44 Magnum, and 45 Colt. Wesson introduced the SuperMag cartridges

designed by Elgin Gates in the 1980s and their SuperMag revolver is now offered in 445 SuperMag and 357 SuperMag. This revolver is also offered, with special sights, as the Super Ram Silhouette.

The Alaskan Guide Series is a special 445 SuperMag with a compensated 4-inch VH (Vent Heavy) barrel and the entire gun coated in the Teflon-based Yukon Coat to protect it from harsh weather. Other special offerings from Wesson Firearms include ported barrels; The Pistol Pack, featuring a revolver with three or four extra barrel assemblies; The Hunter Pack with two barrel assemblies, one scoped. Both Packs come packaged in a high-quality, foam-lined, Cordura-covered, locking hardwood case.

Carved Ivory Grips

I am one who likes to add a fancy touch to special six-guns in the form of custom grips. There is no better way to do this than with carved ivory.

For great carved ivory grips for single actions, Paul Persinger can be reached at 915-821-7541. Bob Leskovec offers excellent ivories for double actions, single actions, and semi-autos. He is found at 724-449-8360. We earlier mentioned Buffalo Brothers cast polymer grips for virtually every single action ever offered. They are at 480-986-7858 and are also on the web at www.buffalobrothers.net.

Have a great six-gunnin' year. •

▲ Memories of Elmer Keith are stirred with these carved ivory grips by Bob Leskovec, shown on a 44 Special Smith & Wesson.

▲ Beautifully carved ivory grips by Paul Persinger dress up a favorite Colt Single Action Army.

RIFLE REPORT

by Layne Simpson

Anschutz

JULIUS GOTTFERIED ANSCHUTZ started the company back in 1856 and one of his first products was a pocket pistol chambered for a brand new cartridge we now know as the 22 Short. A number of new products have been added to the catalog for 2003. Two are built around the Model 54 action and called 1710KL Monte Carlo and 1712 Silhouette Sporter. Both are in 22 Long Rifle and both are available with stocks classified as semi-fancy and Mastergrade. As you might not have guessed, neither is available in 17 HMR although the 1717D Classic and 1717D KL Monte Carlo are. Same goes for rifles on the Model 64 action; 1517D Classic, 1416D Heavy-Barrel Classic, 1517D Monte Carlo and 1517MPR Multi-Purpose with its heavy 25-1/2 inch barrel, high-comb buttstock and beavertail forearm. A 10-shot group I saw measured about . 400-inch. It was shot at 55 yards with the 17-caliber Model 1517MPR/M-P.

DSA Incorporated

The lineup of civilian versions of the FN/FAL rifle from DSA keeps getting longer. I count fourteen SA58 variations ranging from the Tactical Carbine with a 16 1/4-inch barrel to the Gray Wolf with a 21-inch barrel. Blued carbon steel and stainless steel are available, as are synthetic and wood stocks. Some models come with scope mount and iron sights; others come only with the latter.

Some models are fitted with a carrying handle; others are not. The finish is called Duracoat and it comes in Olive Drab and gray solid colors, as well as camo patterns such as Mossy Oak Breakup, desert, urban, winter twig, underbrush *(my favorite)*, woodland, Belgian and tiger stripe. My favorites? I like the OD stock and handguard with blued steel. I also like the underbrush camo finish over the entire rifle. The type 4140 steel receivers are machined in America in three different styles. The standard receiver is heaviest and stiffest because it has no lightening cuts. Minor lightening cuts in the Type I receiver make it a bit lighter, and additional cuts in the Type II receiver make it lighter still. Standard chamberings are 243 Winchester, 260 Remington, 308 Winchester and believe it or not, 300 WSM.

Les Baer

I never cease to be amazed at how accurate some autoloading rifles designed and built to withstand the hard knocks of war can be when they are fine-tuned for the target range. The civilian version of the M16 is a good example. I have a heavy-barrel AR-15 put together by Les Baer and it will consistently shoot five bullets inside half an inch at 100 yards. It will do it with several handloads and it will do it with Federal Premium ammo loaded with the Nosler 55-grain Ballistic Tip. Upon my suggestion, Les has decided to offer his super-accurate rifle in 6x45mm. The

case is easily formed by necking up 223 brass for 6mm bullets. I have an old Kimber rifle in this caliber. When loaded to 2900 fps with the Nosler 85-grain Partition bullet the 6x45 is quite effective on whitetails out to 200 yards or so and recoil is not enough to notice. Load it to 3300 fps with the 55-grain Ballistic Tip and the 6x45 is not a bad varmint cartridge. The very latest from Baer is a tactical-style rifle called the Thunder Ranch. I have not shot this particular rifle but I have been to the place from which it gets its name and if you haven't you are missing out on a lot of fun.

Benelli

ARGO is short for auto-regulating, gas-operated and it also just happens to be the name a new auto-loading rifle from Benelli goes by in Europe. In America it is called the R1, which also makes sense since it is Benelli's first rifle. To operate the action, propellant gas is tapped from the barrel closer to the chamber than is usually seen on other gas guns. The result, according to a Benelli spokesman, is less residue buildup inside the action. Three locking lugs on the rotating bolt head engage recesses in the barrel extension. The barrel is free-floating, compliments of a receiver-attached forearm. As I write this, two versions should be headed this way on the boat from Italy, one with a blued receiver in 30-06 and 300 Winchester Magnum, the other with its receiver covered with nickel plating and in 30-06 only. Regardless of which way you go, you end up

The SA58 rifle comes in a variety of weights, styles, finishes and calibers, including 300 WSM.

Available in 30-06 and 300 Winchester Magnum, the RI is the first centerfire rifle to be built by Benelli.

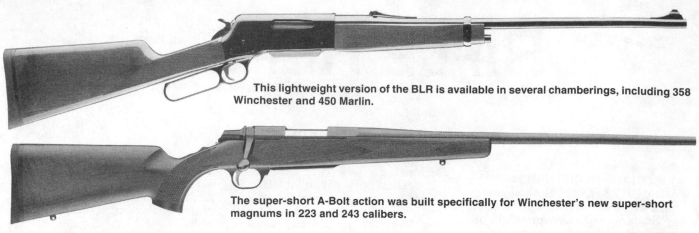

This lightweight version of the BLR is available in several chamberings, including 358 Winchester and 450 Marlin.

The super-short A-Bolt action was built specifically for Winchester's new super-short magnums in 223 and 243 calibers.

with a rifle weighing around 7-1/4 pounds. The receiver is actually two-piece in design. The upper shell houses the bolt and is attached to the barrel. It is also drilled and tapped for scope mounting. The lower receiver houses everything else. The cryogenically treated barrel is 20-1/2 inches long. Shims included with the rifle can be used to adjust drop dimensions of the stock. Two types of detachable magazines are optional; one detaches like the magazine on a Remington Model 7400; the other will remind you of the Browning BAR. I carried a R1 carbine with a 20-inch barrel in 300 Magnum while hunting stag, boar and bear in the Transylvania mountains of Romania. The one issued to me there had the battue-style open sights that are still quite popular among the French, who take shots at driven game. As for me, I'd rather have had a good variable-power scope with either 1X or 1.5X at the lower end of its magnification range. I seldom hunt with autoloading centerfire rifles but if ever I decide to, the R1 might just be the one I will carry.

Blaser

The S2 Safari from Blaser is a double-barrel rifle with a rather unusual locking block. It is available in several elephant-stopping Nitro Express chamberings such as the 470 and 500. A scaled-down version is chambered for an old classic called the 9.3x74mm rimmed.

Browning

The new lightweight version of Browning's BLR leveraction is slated for availability in all the regular chamberings, plus 450 Marlin and 358 Winchester. I am happy to see someone once again offer a rifle chambered for the latter cartridge. I still own a 35-caliber Winchester Model 88 and I would take on any game animal in North America inside 200 yards with it. My favorite handload with either H4895 or IMR-4895 powder pushes the 225-grain Nosler

Partition or Swift A-Frame bullet along at close to 2500 fps. The A-Bolt rifle is now available in a super-short action built especially for the 223 and 224 Winchester super-short magnums it is now chambered for.

Ed Brown

Ed Brown's new Model 702 Denali is a lighter version of the rifle he has been offering for several years. The match-grade barrel is hand-lapped and available in 23-inch lightweight or 22-inch super lightweight configuration. The action is glass-bedded in a McMillan synthetic stock. Available chamberings include all the popular numbers, including Remington's new 7mm and 300 Short Action Ultra Mag. Among other things, the Denali has a steel trigger guard/floorplate assembly, three-position safety and its receiver is drilled and tapped for 8-40 screws. It is rated at 6-3/4 pounds. Even lighter at 6-1/4 pounds is the Ozark. It has a shorter action, a slimmer 21-inch barrel and its synthetic stock is copied after the stock of the Remington Model Seven.

European American Armory

Latest from this importer of economy-grade firearms is a Russian-made single shot with its own decocking system. Also built by Baikal is a combination gun with 22 rimfire barrel up top and a 410-bore barrel below deck.

Cimarron

According to a Cimarron representative, the Sharps Rifle Company built only 36 rifles for the Texas Rangers and the 1863TR is a reproduction thereof. Offered in 45-70 and 50-70, its 22-inch barrel has six-groove rifling with a twist rate of 1:22 inches. Sights consist of a plain-blade front and a windage-adjustable rear.

CZ USA

Sometime back I wrote an article describing how much fun I had been having with a CZ 527 rifle in

7.62x39mm Russian. As luck would have it, CZ management decided to drop that chambering just as my story was published. But not for long. After receiving about a zillion requests from those who read my report, the decision-makers decided to bring back the 30-caliber Russian in 2003. It is a jewel of a little rifle with a miniature Mauser action. They say it will also be available in another of my favorites, the 221 Remington Fire Ball.

Daisy

Since we do not have an air gun editor I don't believe I will be scolded for mentioning that Daisy is bringing back its copy of the Winchester Model 94. It holds 15 of those once-precious golden BBs. As it was for most kids who grew up in the 1950s, my first rifle was a Daisy. Branded on the side of its buttstock were Red Ryder and his sidekick, Little Beaver, both caught in mid-gallop as they headed to the pass to cut off the bad bunch. Like Ralphie's mother in "A Christmas Story" my mom was always warning me about "shooting out your eye with that thing", but I never did. What I did do was make life miserable for every English sparrow in the neighborhood. When combined with just a pinch of childhood imagination the Daisy was also just the ticket for transforming an old tree stump in the yard into a charging grizzly and for bouncing BBs off a tin can that looked for all the world like a ten-point buck.

European American Armory

A problem with the double-barrel rifle is you may not be able to find ammunition that shoots to the correct points of impact for which its barrels were regulated at the factory. According to management at EAA, the engineers at Baikal who designed the MP221 solved that potential problem by making one of its barrels regulation-adjustable. You simply zero the fixed barrel of the rifle with the ammunition you intend to use and then bring bullet point of impact of the other barrel to the same zero by adjusting it in the desired direction. Other features include automatic tang safety, double triggers, adjustable open sights, scope-mounting rail, extractors and walnut stock and forearm. The barrels are chrome-lined for rust resistance.

Also new from EAA is a Baikal single-shot rifle built on a beefed-up shotgun receiver. Among its features are an internal hammer, cocking indicator, hammer-forged and chrome-lined barrel, trigger-block safety, walnut stock and a very interesting decocking system. Chambering options are not available as I write this but my guess is they will at the very least include the 223, 308, 30-06 and several other popular numbers.

Henry Repeating Arms Co.

The name Big Boy sounds more appropriate for a cheeseburger with bacon, lettuce, tomato, onion and all the other trimmings than for a lever-action rifle but that's what somebody at Henry Repeating Arms decided to call the company's latest. Chambered for the 44 Magnum cartridge, it has a 20-inch octagon barrel with 1:38-inch rifling twist, weighs 8-3/4 pounds and measures 38-1/2 inches overall. The receiver, buttplate and barrel band are polished brass while the stock is walnut. Its sights are from Marble: brass-colored bead at the muzzle and a full-adjustable semi buckhorn out back. Come cowboy action-shooting time, I wouldn't be surprised to see a cowpoke or two gallop into town, slide to a screeching halt in a boil of dust and pull one of these from Old Paint's saddle scabbard. Henry has also added the 17 HMR to the list of options for its lever-action rimfire rifle.

High Tech Gun Works

George Vais has introduced a new muzzle brake and while I have not gotten round to giving it a try, he says muzzle blast perceived by the shooter is increased by only three decibels on a rifle in 300 Weatherby Magnum. As I write this, his brakes are available for all calibers up to 30 but larger calibers are in the works. You can contact George by calling 208-323-7674 or by writing to High Tech Gun Works, 182 South Cole Rd., Boise, ID 83708.

Kimber

Biggest news from Kimber for 2003 is the introduction of a scaled-up version of the Model 84M centerfire rifle. Called the Model 8400, it weighs 6-3/4 pounds (a pound heavier than the Model 84M) and is chambered for the 270, 7mm and 300 WSM cartridges. Four variations are available; Classic, Classic Left Hand, SuperAmerica and Montana. All have 24-inch barrels. Kimber's second synthetic-stocked rifle (the Model 84M Longmaster was first), the Model 8400 Montana is rated at six pounds, two ounces. This is about a pound heavier than the Model 82M Montana, which is also new. Both have stainless steel barreled actions, another first for Kimber. The Model 8400 CLH is the first rifle built by Kimber to have a left-hand action and I am sure it will not be the last. Kimber, by the way, is making its own synthetic stocks and I really like the way they look and feel.

Legacy Sports

Seems like everybody who is anybody is chambering rifles for the 300 WSM and Legacy Sports is no exception. This particular company is also offering the 270 and 7mm WSM chamberings. The Howa Model 1500WSM has a 24-inch barrel and is available in blued or stainless steel and with various stock options. Also new from Legacy is the Model 1500 Thumbhole Varminter Supreme in 223, 22-250 and 308 Winchester. In addition to the thumbhole styling the laminated wood stock has a palm swell, a straight, rollover comb and a ventilated forearm. Sure to get your undivided attention with the first squeeze of its trigger is the Brazilian-built Puma Model 92, a lever-action hammer gun in 454 Casull or 480 Ruger. It has a hardwood stock and (let us hope) a very thick and soft recoil pad.

Marlin

I have just about lost count of the number of black bears I have taken through the years but I will never forget the one I bagged on Vancouver Island in June of 2002. That hunt was special for two reasons; I was hunting with good friends and I was hunting with a rifle that brought my bear hunting days back full circle. The first bear I ever killed and one of the best I have taken fell victim during the early 1960s to my old Marlin Model 336 Sporting Carbine in 35 Remington. It wore its original factory iron sights. That bruin weighed 411 pounds on a local farmer's cotton scale and that's big for my neck of the woods. My most recent bear was also taken with a Marlin but it was a 336CB in 38-55 Winchester. I made the hunt even more fun by leaving all my scopes at home and equipping the rifle with a Marble's tang sight sent to me by Frank Brownell. That bear was not quite as large as my first one but it was one of the biggest I have taken. Never in a thousand years will it

happen again but I shot the 38th bear my guide Fred Lackey and I spotted. I'd like to say I shot the bear at 55 yards but the actual truth is, it was 43 yards away when I pulled the trigger. *Brer* bruin dropped in its tracks and never moved again. My handload contained enough Reloder 7 to push the 255-grain Barnes bullet along at just over 1800 fps, which comes close to duplicating the old 38-55 high-velocity loads once offered by Winchester and Remington. Five-shot groups averaged a hair under two inches at 100 yards and five inches at 200. With the rifle zeroed two inches high at 100 yards those big, fat bullets landed dead on my point of aim at 200 yards. Try it sometime and you may rediscover as I did that having to get close before you pull the trigger is as much fun as it used to be.

Remember the Model 336 Marauder sold by Marlin back during the 1960s? It had a straight-grip stock, a 16 1/4-inch barrel and it was available in 30-30 and 35 Remington. A friend of mine by the name of Jimmy Davis owned one in 35-caliber and I really liked it. *(At the time I hunted with a Model 336SC in the same caliber.)* At any rate, Marlin's new Spikehorn variation of America's favorite deer rifle has a 16 1/2-inch barrel and except for its curved grip, it reminds me a lot of my old deer-hunting partner's Marauder. I used to hunt black bear with hounds in some of the steepest, roughest country the mountains in my neck of the woods had to offer and if I were to do it again, the Spikehorn in 35 Remington is the medicine I would carry if I didn't tote a handgun. It weighs a feathery 6-1/2 pounds, and at 34 inches it is not much longer than your arm.

Marlin is now offering the 45 Colt chambering in its Model 1894 Cowboy Competition and, while it obviously is aimed at the cowboy action shooting market, my guess is more will be bought by deer hunters. When handloaded to its true potential the old Colt cartridge is more effective on whitetails at woods ranges than the 44 Magnum, or so say a couple of friends of mine. Both hunt with 45-caliber Ruger Blackhawks in country where deer season is over four months long and there is no bag limit on bucks, so they should know. The 1894CBC has a straight-grip stock, a 20-inch octagon barrel with Ballard-style rifling and its magazine holds 10 rounds. The case-colored receiver really looks nice. Since its action is slicked-up by hand before it leaves the factory the lever travels to and fro like it is riding on oil-suspended roller bearings. The grand old firm of Marble's makes the sights, a fully-adjustable semibuckhorn at the back and a blade up front. Another new Model 1894 variation is called the PG *(which is short for pistol-grip stock?)*. Available in 44 Magnum *(also uses 44 Special ammo)*, its 20-inch barrel has Ballard-style rifling. And if all that isn't enough to make lever-gun fans occupied for the next 12 months, Marlin has also brought back the 41 Magnum chambering in the Model 1894.

I thought the 450 Marlin was a good idea because it is a way for those who do not handload to enjoy the power those of us who do handload have, for many years, been squeezing from the old 45-70 Government cartridge. I consider the 450 an even better idea now that Marlin is offering it in a 22-inch barrel. In addition to its longer barrel, the Model 1895MR has a curved-grip stock carved from a walnut tree, replete with recoil pad.

Back in 1929 Marlin introduced the Model 410 shotgun, a variation of the Model 93 lever-action rifle with a smoothbore barrel chambered for the 2 1/2-inch .410 shotshell. Less than 10,000 were produced before the model was dropped from production in 1932. If you have always wanted a Model 410 but could never find one or you could not afford the one you did find, you need to pay another visit to your local Marlin dealer. There, sitting on his shelf, will be a Model 410 built on the Model 336 action. It will have a 22-inch smoothbore barrel with no choke, or Cylinder Bore as it is commonly called. Like the original Model 410, it is chambered for the 2 1/2-inch shell and its magazine holds four of them. In addition to its cut-checkered walnut stock, the gun has rifle-style sights, fully adjustable rear and a beaded ramp up front replete with a snap-on fiber optic sight. Come September, I will be hunting caribou in the Northwest Territories and plan to take a Model 410 along. Who knows, I might bump into a ptarmigan or something.

Merkel

One of the rifles I would like to have brought home from the SHOT Show was the Merkel single-shot stalking rifle. Both variations are built on the Franz Jager break-open action. The Model K-1 is the standard version with modest checkering on the sides of its boxlock action. Moving up to quite a bit more money is the Model K-2 with octagon barrel, express-style rear sight and ornate engraving on its sideplates. Both models come with scope mounting rings in your choice of one inch or 30mm. Nominal weight is only 5-1/2 pounds. To cock the rifle you simply push its tang safety slide all the way forward, same as the safety on the Krieghoff double-barrel rifle. Pulling the safety to the rear decocks the firing pin and places the rifle on safe. Rifles imported to America will be in 243 Winchester, 270 Winchester, 7x57R, 308 Winchester, 30-06, 7mm Remington Magnum, 300 Winchester Magnum and 9.3x74mm. What a great sheep rifle this one in 270 would make. When fitted out with a lightweight leather carrying sling and a Burris or Leupold 3-9X compact scope, the entire rig would weigh about seven pounds.

M. O. A. Corporation

The M. O. A single-shot pistol with its falling-block action has long been available in a rifle version with buttstock and longer barrel. The tangs on the latest version of the receiver are machined at a different angle and the added beef in the buttstock makes it more resistant to breakage. Through the years I have shot M. O. A. handguns and rifles in various chamberings and all were capable of shooting five bullets inside an inch at 100 yards. Only recently I shot a heavy-barrel gun in 260 Remington and it averaged 0.

72-inch with 45.0 grains of Reloder 19 and the Nosler 120-grain Ballistic Tip. I plan to try the 6.5-284 Norma in this gun. Name a rimfire or centerfire cartridge and chances are good M. O. A. chambers for it. To name but a few more; 17 Remington, 17 HMR, 22 Long Rifle, 220 Swift, 243 Winchester, 25-06, 280 Remington, 308 Winchester, 338-06, 350 Remington Magnum, 375 H&H Magnum and 454 Casull.

Navy Arms

The "Cowboy Combo" from Navy Arms includes two guns, both chambered for the grand old 32-20 Winchester cartridge. One is a single-action revolver and the other is a copy of the Winchester Model 92 lever gun. Buy one of these packages along with a second revolver, a Winchester '97 shotgun and a couple thousand dollars worth of costume and you will be ready to out-cowboy the best of them.

New England Firearms

I recently examined two versions of the Harrington & Richardson single-shot rifle offered by New England Arms and was impressed. The Buffalo Classic is chambered for the 45-70, weighs eight pounds and has a 32-inch barrel. About a half-pound lighter, the Target Model has a 28-inch barrel in 38-55 Winchester. The guns have case-coloring on their receivers and cut checkering on their walnut stocks. Both wear a Williams receiver sight at the rear and a globe-style target sight with eight interchangeable aperture inserts up front. Last but certainly not least from New England, the 7mm-08 Remington chambering is now available in standard and youth versions of the Handi-Rifle. Respective lengths of pull of the hardwood stocks are 14-1/4 and 11-3/4 inches. The stocks wear recoil pads and carrying sling swivels.

Remington

From a distance Remington's new Model 673 Guide Rifle looks a lot like my old Model 600 carbine. Both are

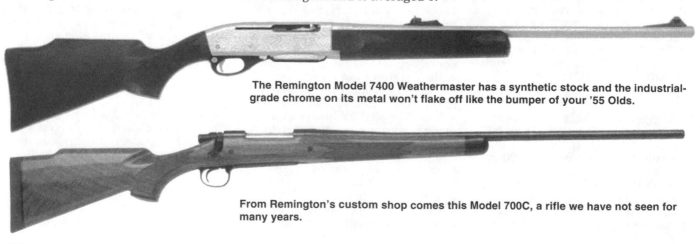

The Remington Model 7400 Weathermaster has a synthetic stock and the industrial-grade chrome on its metal won't flake off like the bumper of your '55 Olds.

From Remington's custom shop comes this Model 700C, a rifle we have not seen for many years.

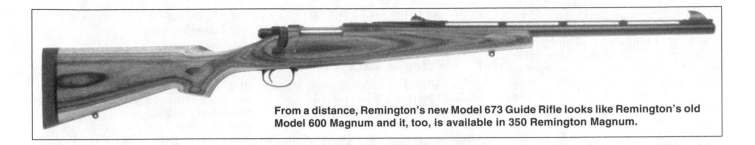

From a distance, Remington's new Model 673 Guide Rifle looks like Remington's old Model 600 Magnum and it, too, is available in 350 Remington Magnum.

The 24-inch barrel of this Remington Model 700 BDL is now chambered to 7mm and 300 Short Action Ultra Mag.

in 350 Remington Magnum, both have laminated wood stocks and both have ventilated ribs replete with fully adjustable sights sitting atop their barrels. The Model 673 has even inherited the shark fin-style front sight of the Model 600. Up close it is easier to see that the Model 673 is built around the Model Seven action, which is basically an improved version of the Model 600 action that was a repeating version of the XP-100 pistol action. Got that straight? Back in August of 2002 I managed to get my hands on the only Model 673 in existence at the time and I was greatly impressed by the quality and workmanship. Wood to metal fit was excellent, as were the wood and metal finishes. With a Burris 3-9X compact scope it weighed exactly 8-3/4 pounds. This compares to 7-1/2 pounds for my Model 600 and its Weaver 1.5X scope. The 22-inch barrel of the Model 673 is 3-1/2 inches longer and it has a heavier contour. This, plus the fact that its barrel rib is steel as opposed to the synthetic rib of the Model 600, explains most of the weight difference. That first Model 673 was not quite as accurate as my old Model 600 but it was accurate enough for shooting a brown bear as far away as should be attempted. My favorite handload for the 350 Magnum—Remington case, Remington 9-1/2 primer, 59.0 grains of W748 and the Nosler 225-grain Partition produced five-shot groups averaging 1.8 inches at 100 yards. Velocity was just over 2700 fps. A few months later I tried Remington's new 200-grain factory load in another Model 673 and, while I did not have an opportunity to check out velocity, it averaged 1.3 inches at 100 yards.

As far as I know, Remington has offered the 300 Savage chambering in more different rifles than any other company. I once owned a Model 722 in that caliber and still own a Model 81. Early on, the Model 760 pump gun was also available in

300 Savage. Add one more to the list as the limited edition Model 700 Classic with a 24-inch barrel will be chambered for the 300 Savage during 2003. The one I shot averaged 1.55 inches overall for five-shot groups at 100 yards with three handloads and five factory loads. Remington's 180-grain roundnose Core-Lokt loading won the factory ammo contest with an average of 1.4 inches at a velocity of 2412 fps. The most accurate handload at 1.1 inches consisted of the Remington case, Remington 9-1/2 primer and 40.0 grains of Reloder 7 pushing the 125-grain Nosler Ballistic Tip along at an average muzzle velocity of 3048 fps. I really like that bullet and powder combination for shooting whitetails and pronghorn antelope at ranges exceeding 100 yards with the 300 Savage. With the charge weight of RL-7 reduced to 38.0 grains my old Savage Model 99 averages 2829 fps and 2.1 inches at 100 yards. That same combination delivers 2862 fps and groups averaging 1.7 inches in my Remington Model 81. Both guns wear iron sights.

Remington's highly successful 7mm and 300 Short Action Ultra Mag chamberings are now available in the Model 700 BDL/SS and the Model 700 Sendero SF. As you may have already correctly guessed, the former is the original Model 700 BDL with a synthetic stock and a stainless steel barreled action. It has a 24-inch barrel. Also a combination of synthetic and stainless steel, the Model 700 Sendero SF has a 26-inch fluted barrel. Both rifles have hinged floorplates and a magazine capacity of three rounds. I shot the Sendero in 300 Short Action Ultra Mag with Remington ammo loaded with the new 150-grain Core-Lokt Ultra bullet and five-shot groups averaged just about dead on an inch at 100 yards.

Remington officials have long refused to chamber a Remington rifle for any cartridge not loaded at its Lonoke, Arkansas ammunition plant so it comes as no surprise to see the

company introduce a 17 HMR factory load along with Model 597 rifles chambered for it. I believe this makes Remington first to offer an autoloading rifle chambered for this close-range varmint cartridge. Called the Model 597 Magnum LS, it weighs six pounds, has a gray laminated wood stock, a 20-inch button-rifled barrel and measures 40 inches overall. Barrel and action have a satin blue finish. The detachable magazine holds eight rounds. I shot one down in Florida and it averaged just under 1-1/4 inches for five shots at 100 yards.

The third annual limited-edition Model 700 Remington is building for the Rocky Mountain Elk Foundation is chambered for the 300 Short Action Ultra Mag. The synthetic stock has the Realtree Hardwoods Gray camo finish with the RMEF logo laser-etched into its right-hand side. All metal is stainless steel, including the 24-inch barrel. This rifle will be available only during 2003 and each will come with a paid membership in the RMEF. Remington also plans to donate a portion of the sales to the foundation.

Considering how popular synthetics and rust-resisting metals have become among American hunters, it comes as no surprise to see the Model 7400 autoloader wearing both. The Model 7400 Weathermaster (great name) has a black synthetic stock and forearm and all metal is covered with an industrial grade nickel that won't chip or flake like the plating did on the bumpers of your old '55 Oldsmobile. For now it is available in the world's two most popular big-game cartridges, 30-06 Springfield and 270 Winchester. The one I shot was in 270 and it averaged less than two inches for five shots with Remington's 130-grain Bronze Point load. Due to its weight of about 8-1/2 pounds (with scope) and its gas-operated action, it was extremely comfortable to shoot. Phyllis enjoys shooting it so well Remington may never get it back. Incidentally, if "Weathermaster" rings a bell to some of you old-timers out there it is because Remington has given other rifles similar names in the past. I still own a Model 81 Woodsmaster in 300 Savage and once owned a Model 141 Gamemaster in 30 Remington. Just thinking about those old names brings back memories of times and places none of us will ever again see.

During the mid-1960s Remington started building a rifle called the Model 700 Custom. It was basically the Model 700 BDL with an oil finish and cut checkering on its stock, all with a price tag of $334. 95. At the time, the standard Model 700 BDL had a plastic finish and impressed checkering on its stock and it sold for $144. 95. I believe the 700C also had a rosewood forend and grip cap. The original Model 700C was discontinued years ago but those clever craftsmen in Remington's custom shop are bringing it back in 2003. Everything the old one had is seen in the new one, including figured walnut with satin finish, cut checkering, rosewood forend and grip cap, and hinged floorplate. Barrel lengths are 26 inches for the Ultra Mags and 24 inches for everything else.

The R3 recoil pad from Remington is darned amazing. As one of Remington's engineers put it, the new recoil pad incorporates a decay time modification system that displaces shock on a broadband spectrum to ensure maximum relief from recoil. In language you and I can better understand, the thing reduces perceived recoil better than any pad I have tried—and I have tried them all. Beginning in 2003 the R3 will be available on eight Remington firearms, all with synthetic stocks; Model 700 BDL/SS, Model 700 BDL/SS/DM, Model 11-87 Special Purpose Synthetic, Model 11-87 Super Magnum SPS, Model 870 SPS, Model 870 Super Magnum SPS, Model SP-10 Magnum Synthetic and Model 1100 Competition Match synthetic. It will also be available as an accessory for retrofitting to various synthetic-stocked versions of the Model 710, Model 700

(ADL and BDL), Model 700 ML, Model 7600, Model 11-87, Model 1100 and Model 870.

Rogue Rifle Co.

The Chipmunk, a lightweight, scaled-down, 2-1/2 pound rifle made just for kids is now available in a number of variations, including walnut or laminated-wood stock and standard-weight or varmint-weight barrel. Its chamberings are 22 Long Rifle, 22 WMR and, new for 2003, the 17 HMR. Santas who buy rifles chambered for the latter cartridge for hiding beneath the Christmas tree should remember to include a few boxes of the equally new Remington and CCI ammunition.

Rossi

The 17 HMR bandwagon becomes even more crowded with the introduction of Rossi's single-shot rifle for this cartridge. One version has a shortened length of pull for kids or anybody else with short arms

Ruger

Ruger is now offering the 17 HMR chambering in two variations of its Model 77 bolt-action rifle, and in the Model 96 lever action as well. The Model 77/17 Varmint has a heavy 24-inch barrel and a black laminated hardwood stock. It weighs seven pounds. The stainless steel barreled action has Ruger's attractive "Target Grey" finish. Weighing a pound less, the standard Model 77/17 has a sporter-weight 22-inch barrel and a synthetic stock. As far as I know, the Model 96/17 is the first lever-action rifle to become available in 17 HMR. An aluminum receiver brings its weight down to a feathery 5-1/4 pounds. The stock is hardwood. All three rifles utilize the same excellent nine-round rotary magazine. Also new from Ruger are the 458 Lott and

405 Winchester chamberings in the No. 1 single-shot rifle.

Savage

Savage rifles have long had a reputation for excellent mechanical accuracy, but poor trigger quality has often made them difficult to shoot to their true potential. The new AccuTrigger being offered on several variations of the Model 110 rifle should take care of that. Using a special tool that comes with the rifle, the trigger is easily adjusted to a pull weight as light as 1-1/2 pounds, yet its design resists accidental discharge should the rifle be jarred or dropped. This is due to the fact that sear travel is blocked until the shooter pulls the AccuRelease lever resting alongside the trigger fingerpiece. Sounds complicated but it is quite simple and should work very well. Savage is also expanded the lineup of chambering options in its Model 110 rifles by adding Remington's short and long Ultra Mags in 7mm and 300 calibers. Savage is also adding the 17 HMR chambering to several of its rimfire rifles, including the Model 93 and Model 30R.

Schuerman Arms Ltd.

Remember how smooth the bolts were on the Colt Sauer or perhaps that old sporterized Krag-Jorgensen you once hunted with? I surely do and sliding the bolt of the Schuerman Arms SA40 to and fro reminded me of those rifles. Like the Colt rifle, the SA40 has pivoting locking lugs but they are located close to the front of the bolt rather than at the rear. Placing the locking lugs up front minimizes receiver stretch and practically eliminates bolt compression during firing. The result is longer case life for the handloader. Other features include a recessed bolt face, firing pin cocking indicator, match-grade trigger, extremely quick lock-time and center-feed detachable magazine. Chambering options

You rainy weather hunters out there can now buy a Weatherby Vanguard with synthetic stock and stainless steel barreled action.

Once sold only at "mart" stores, the Weatherby Vanguard (in a special edition) is now available at your friendly neighborhood gun shop.

range from the 7mm STW to the 416 Remington Magnum.

SIGARMS

The new S2 Safari from SIGARMS is a double-barrel rifle with a manual cocking system. A list of available chamberings is not available as I write this.

Taurus

Taurus has expanded its line of Brazilian-made Winchester Model 62 and Model 63 reproductions. The Model 62 pump gun is available in stainless or blued steel and in 22 Long Rifle, 22 WMR and 17 HMR chamberings. You can also get the carbon steel gun with a blued or case-colored receiver finish. Rifles with 23-inch barrels and carbines with 16 1/2-inch barrels are available. Nominal weights are 4-1/2 pounds for the former and five pounds for the latter. Tubular magazine capacities range from 10 to 13 depending on the cartridge. Button-rifled barrels and fully adjustable sights are standard. Extra-cost options include a folding tang sight, barrel-attached scope mounting base and a plastic carrying case. Then we have the 4-1/2 pound Model 63 autoloader with a 23-inch barrel in the same three chamberings. Like the original built by Winchester from 1933 to 1958, it has a 10-round tubular magazine in its buttstock. Unlike the original, the Taurus rifle has a lock on its bolt that prevents the gun from being fired by anyone except those who hold its key. Taurus offers a folding tang sight for this one as well. Remember the speed loaders used by hawkers at the county fair to fill the magazines of gallery rifles?A plastic version of the old reloading tube is now available from Taurus and it works on any 22 rimfire rifle with a tubular magazine.

Thompson/Center

The 22-caliber autoloader from T/C is now available in a heavy-barrel

As the engraving on its bolt indicates, this Weatherby Mark V is guaranteed to shoot three bullets inside an inch at 100 yards.

version called the Classic Match. Of laminated wood, the stock has a high Monte Carlo-style comb and a beavertail forearm. The 18-inch barrel has a blued finish, as does the receiver. The detachable magazine holds 10 Long Rifle cartridges. Then we have the G2 Contender, a single-shot rifle built on the latest version of the Contender handgun action and with 23-inch interchangeable barrels. Stock and forearm are American walnut and neither is checkered. Optional chamberings for now are 17 HMR, 22 Long Rifle Match, 223 Remington, 30-30 Winchester and 45-70 Government. The 45-caliber muzzleloader barrel uses 209 shotshell primers for ignition. Overall length is a compact 37 inches and weight is less than 5-1/2 pounds. Carbine barrels made for the old Contender will fit this one as well. T/C has also added the 375 Holland & Holland Magnum chambering to the list of options for its Encore rifle line.

Tikka

The T3 rifle from Tikka is now available with a wood or synthetic stock and in stainless or blued steel. Its chamberings include 223, 22-250, 243, 25-06, 7mm Remington Magnum, 270 WSM and 300 WSM.

USRAC

The 17 HMR is now available in two USRAC rifles. One, called the

Model 94/17 is nothing less than the Winchester 94/22 with a smaller diameter hole through its barrel. Another is the neat little Model 1885 Winchester single-shot Low Wall rifle. Quite sometime back USRAC added a transverse safety button to the receiver of the Winchester Model 94 rifle. It has now been replaced by a sliding button on the upper tang. The new safety works great and, while it is more convenient to operate than the old safety, it might not be quite as foolproof. Members of the Rocky Mountain Elk Foundation are excited about a new Model 70 rifle to be built during 2003 just for them. Called the Super Grade Stainless, it is chambered in 300 Winchester Magnum.

Volquartsen

I own three of Tom Volquartsen's incredibly accurate autoloading rifles and all are favorites. One is in 22 Long Rifle, another is in 22 WMR and the other, called the Firefly, is in 22 Short. Last summer I had a ball shooting prairie dogs out to 150 yards or so with the rifle in 22 WMR. It shot inside 3/4-inch at 100 yards with two loads, Remington 33-grain green tip and Federal Premium loaded with the Speer 30-grain TNT hollowpoint. That same rifle is now available with interchangeable barrels in 22 WMR and 17 WMR. I plan to get one, if for no other reason than to once again prove something I discovered years

Weatherby's best buy in varmint rifles is this Mark V SVR with composite stock, Decelerator recoil pad, full adjustable trigger and chrome-moly barrel in 223 or 22-250 for less than a thousand bucks.

The handsome Weatherby Mark V Dangerous Game Rifle is now available in 458 Lott.

The new drop box magazine from Weatherby is easily installed and it increases cartridge capacity of the Mark V rifle to four for the big boys (30-378 through 460 Magnums), five for magnums from 257 Weatherby to 458 Lott and seven for chamberings such as the 270 Winchester and 30-06.

Latest edition of the Weatherby Mark V is the Special Varmint Rifle with a 22-inch, medium-heavy, chrome-moly barrel in 223 or 22-250. Its hand-laminated composite stock consists of Aramid fibers combined with unidirectional graphite and glass fibers and it is finished in black with gray spiderwebbing. The stock also wears a Pachmayr Decelerator recoil pad. While the barrel is free-floating, the action rests in a CNC-machined aluminum bedding block in the stock. Other features include six locking lugs, 54-degree bolt lift and a weight of 7-1/4 pounds.

For many years Weatherby has guaranteed 1-1/2 inch accuracy for three shots at 100 yards with good ammo in its rifles and, while most I have shot did better than that, you can now own a Mark V capable of shooting three bullets into an inch. Accumark and Super VarmintMaster versions of the Mark V are guaranteed to average less than minute-of-angle with specified factory ammo are now available from Weatherby's custom shop. As I explain in my "Testfire" report included elsewhere in this issue of Gun Digest, each rifle will have "Sub-Moa" engraved on its bolt.

Equally new from Weatherby's custom shop is the 458 Lott chambering in the Dangerous Game Rifle. Built around the Mark V action, the DGR in this caliber has a Monte Carlo-style synthetic stock, 25-inch chrome-moly barrel, Decelerator recoil pad, express-style rear sight with gold-filled shallow "V", hooded barrel-band style front sight with large gold bead, black oxide metal finish and front sling swivel post-mounted out on the barrel as it should be on any rifle chambered for a hard-kicking cartridge. Also available in other Weatherby magnum chamberings such as the 375, 416 and 460, the DGR weighs 8-3/4 pounds and comes in black, desert camo and snow camo.

Another great idea from Atascadero is a drop-box magazine that increases the capacity of Mark V rifles chambered for Weatherby's 30-378, 338-378, 416 and 460 Magnum cartridges to four rounds with one in the chamber. The magazine I tried worked without a hitch and you can bet my 416 will soon wear one. Easily retrofitted to both Japanese- and American-built Mark Vs, it increases the capacity of rifles chambered for smaller magnums

such as the 257 Weatherby and 458 Lott to a total of five cartridges. Rifles in standard calibers like the 30-06 and 338-06 will hold a total of seven cartridges, with one up the spout. Suggested retail is $150. From what I see, anyone owning a small wood chisel and having less than 10 thumbs should be able to install the new magazine but those who had rather not do it themselves can have the custom shop do it for an additional $25.

Weatherby Performance Wool Clothing

Since we have no clothing editor I believe it would not be inappropriate for me to mention how impressed I have been with the Performance Wool clothing lineup introduced last year by Weatherby. In lieu of a wool/cotton blend as seen in wool garments from other manufacturers, Wade Krinke, Weatherby's director of soft goods, decided to incorporate a viscose synthetic fiber for increased tear resistance and to make the garments more shrink-resistant during laundering. A hydrophobic synthetic lining traps heat from the body while wicking moisture away from the skin and into the outer wool shell for rapid evaporation and drying. In laymen's terms, the stuff keeps you warm when it is cold without boiling you in your own sweat when the weather warms up at mid-day. Other features include articulated elbows for comfort, two durable layers of fabric at knees and elbows, heavy-duty zippers that work every time and suspenders included with the pants. It all works, too. I wore the parka, double-yoke shirt, cargo pant and ice cap while hunting for bear and stag in the frigid Transylvania mountains of Romania and stayed warm as toast even at an average daily temperature of about 20 degrees Fahrenheit. My only complaint is the clothing can be too good at times. While it is great for sitting or standing still with the thermometer bottomed out, it is a bit too warm for a lot of walking. This is why I am happy to see the same high quality in a lighter 14-ounce fabric ready for a 2003 introduction. The color options are Late Season Gray and High Desert Brown.

Layne's new 325-page book, *Rifles and Cartridges For Large Game,* is in hardback, 8-1/2x11" format and is illustrated with over 150 color photos. Autographed copies are available for $39. 95 plus $5 for shipping and handling from High Country Press, 306 Holly Park Lane, Dept. GD, Simpsonville, SC 29681.

Weatherby's new line of wool clothing proved to be just the ticket for a cold-weather hunt in the Transylvania mountains of Romania.

ago while shooting the 17 Hornet—the 17 HMR is actually inferior to the 22 WMR in the varmint field.

Weatherby

During the past few years the Weatherby Vanguard has been available only in a "mart" version and sold through discount houses across the nation, but real gun shops run by people who know a thing or two about guns now have versions that will be available only from them. They are the Synthetic and Synthetic Stainless versions in a lineup of selected chamberings that includes the 300 WSM. Among other things, the Vanguard has an injection-molded stock made by Butler Creek, forged receiver, 24-inch hammer-forged barrel, hinged floorplate with release button inside the trigger guard, an easy-to-see cocking indicator and fully adjustable trigger. Each rifle comes from the factory with its own three-shot group measuring 1-1/2 inches or less. All of this at a suggested retail price of less than $500 for the Synthetic.

NEW SHOTGUNS

by John Haviland

FOR YEARS WOMEN who hunted birds were given a .410 and patted on the head. Now women, the only growing segment of shotgun shooters, want a shotgun tailored to their needs. My wife is a perfect example. For years, Gail took the only shotgun left in the gun cabinet to shoot clay targets and hunt upland birds. Lately, she said she wanted her own gun, and not a .410 or a clunky 12 gauge.

Proper shotguns for women can be autoloaders, pumps or double guns, as long as they are lightweight. An autoloading shotgun spreads recoil over a longer time to reduce felt recoil, which is a plus for kick-sensitive shooters. Eight-time American and world champion sporting clays shooter Linda Joy shoots an over/under in competition. *"But if I was starting out again I'd go with an autoloader for the lighter kick,"* she says. *"For hunting I'd definitely go with an autoloader because they're so quick to point and light to carry all day,"* she says.

However, many women are put off by an auto's complex operation. Cathy Williams, of Beretta USA, says she shoots an over/under because it is uncomplicated and easy to load. *"I drop in two shells, fire them, open the action and the empties pop out,"* she says.

Pump guns are simple to operate because each back-and-forth cycling of the forearm lets the shooter know when an empty is ejected and a new shell is chambered. Because the shooter works the action, pump-action guns reliably cycle all shells no matter how light the load.

Joy prefers 30-inch barrels on an over/under and a 28-inch barrel on an autoloader. *"You need that length to keep your swing smooth,"* she says. Those barrel lengths also provide an extended sight radius for more precise aim on long shots. A somewhat shorter barrel is better for point-and-shoot shots, like ruffed grouse in a thicket.

Last summer, my wife Gail handled and shot several shotguns in her search for a new grouse gun. She hefted a Remington 870 12-gauge three-inch magnum and immediately put it down. A Remington 870 20-gauge that weighed 6 lbs. 10 oz. felt much better in her hands and she regularly dusted clay pigeons with it, firing Winchester's loading of 3/4-oz. of #7 1/2s. A Browning Gold Hunter autoloader with a 26-inch barrel and rubber butt pad weighed 6 lbs. 11 oz. and took a lot of the sting out of the kick of heavy 1- and 1-1/8 oz. loads. The lighter recoil also permitted a fast second shot. The Gold Hunter was the gun Gail chose for shooting heavy loads at waterfowl and pheasants.

Gail did her best shooting with a Browning and a Beretta over/under. The guns' slender wrists helped Gail control the guns, and the high, full stock combs instantly brought her eye into alignment with the barrel ribs, and then out to the target.

The Browning Feather, with 26-inch barrels and a plastic buttplate, weighed 5 lbs. 10 oz. The Beretta Whitewing with 28-inch barrels and GEL-TEK recoil pad weighed 6 lbs. 2 oz., and was her ultimate choice since the recoil pad with the silicone gel core soaked up a considerable amount of recoil. She knew she would appreciate the light weight on mountain hikes for blue grouse.

During September Gail hunted ruffed grouse in the creek bottoms and blue grouse in the foothills of timbered draws and springs surrounded by mountain maples. Even on the steep uphills the Beretta remained ready in her hands, so when grouse flushed she knocked them down. She's definitely not going back to a clunky old 12 gauge.

Gail must think like a lot of hunters because this year companies have introduced a whole bunch of light, smaller-gauge guns.

Charles Daly

The Field Hunter VR-MC 20-gauge autoloading shotgun is now available in a youth model. The gun has a 22-inch barrel with three interchangeable chokes. The length of pull has also been shortened by 1 5/8 inches, but can be lengthened to full size.

The Field Hunter 12 gauge has also been fully covered with Advantage camouflage. This camo pattern joins several other camo patterns and the black synthetic stock and forearm on other Field Hunter guns.

The 28 gauge has also joined the Field Hunter line. The gun has 24-, 26- or 28-inch ported barrels and screw-in chokes.

Benelli

The Sport II is Benelli's newest all-around competition 12-gauge based on

Light weight and an easy kick are the main features women want in an upland bird gun, like this 20-gauge Beretta Whitewing over/under.

its Inertia System, comprised of a stiff spring between the bolt body and bolt head which begins to compress when the gun moves back during recoil. Benelli states the system is adaptable to almost any sort of ammunition. About the only way to stop a Benelli from cycling is to put the butt against a brick wall, because the shotgun must be free to move back slightly for the bolt spring to compress.

The Sport II traits include cryogenically-treated 28- or 30-inch barrels. Benelli states the cryogenic treatment relieves stresses left over from hammer-forging, and thus delivers a shorter shot string and more evenly distributed patterns. The barrel has a ventilated rib that steps up from the breech. Extralong choke tubes constrict the shot charge more gradually to lessen pellet damage and keep more of pellets in the pattern. Choke tubes include Cylinder, Improved Cylinder, Improved Modified and Full.

The Sport II has a two-piece receiver that rides steel on steel like the Legacy model autoloading shotguns. The sweeping contour of the lower receiver blends into the gun's trigger guard and the checkered walnut stock completes the gun's good looks. Plastic shims supplied with the gun fit between the rear of its receiver and the buttstock wrist to adjust cast, drop of comb and length of pull.

For those who shake like a leaf when a turkey gobbler struts into view, Benelli has added a vertical pistol grip to its Black Eagle and M1 Field turkey guns. The grip allows you to hold a gun more steady while waiting for a gobbler to take those last few steps into sure range, and directs some of the hefty recoil from turkey loads into your hand.

The awesome hitting power—and recoil—of new slug loads like Remington's Copper Solid and Winchester's Partition Gold have convinced many shooters that these 12-gauge loads are too much for deer. The high velocity and good bullets of these sabot slug loads, though, have made the 20 gauge entirely adequate for deer and hogs. In line with that thinking, Benelli's M1 Field Slug Gun is also now available in 20 gauge.

The autoloader comes with a black or Advantage Timber HD camouflage synthetic stock. The gun's 24-inch barrel has a 1:28-inch twist for shooting sabot slugs and is fitted with open sights. The receiver is drilled and tapped to accept scope mounts.

The M1 Practical 12 gauge is ready for you to take out your aggression on bowling pins and the three-gun matches in IPSC shooting. The Practical comes with a 26-inch compensated barrel, oversized

controls and a nine-round magazine. Both ghost ring sights and a Picatinny rail provide a range of sighting options.

The Benelli Nova Pump is also available in 20 gauge with a rifled bore. The Nova has the same stock options, barrel length and rifling twist, sights and scope mounting as the M1 slug gun. My son's friend has been dragging a Nova Pump across the swamps and fields for several years now. Teenagers are known to be a bit hard on equipment, but the Nova has taken everything the young fellow has dished out.

The Nova Pump in 3 1/2-inch 12 gauge is also available in a Tactical version for law enforcement. Sight choices are either open sights or ghost-ring aperture sights.

Beretta

Beretta has upgraded some of its existing autoloader and over/under guns.

The Onyx over/under Pro Series has the X-Tra Wood finish featuring a film and sealant that waterproofs the stock and produces a rich grain pattern. The film is protected by a tough semi-gloss lacquer. The process does partially fill in checkering grooves and covers the sharp points. The Pro Series also comes with a TRUGLO Tru-Bead fiber optic front bead, extended choke tubes, fluted beavertail forearm and Gel-Tek recoil pad. A molded carry case includes five chokes and an assortment of accessories. The gun is chambered for 12, 20, and 28 gauge. A 12-gauge 3 1/2-inch version features a non-reflective matte black finish on the barrels and receiver.

The new White Onyx features a nickel-alloy receiver machined with a Dura-Jewel pattern. A schnabel forearm and "two-point" cut checkering highlight the walnut stock on this 6.8 pound 12-gauge gun. A molded carrying case includes five chokes and an assortment of accessories.

The Silver Pigeon IV over/under is designed for the American market. The black-finish receiver is completely covered in scroll engraving and features gold-filled mallards and pheasants on the 12-gauge model; quail and grouse on the 20- and 28-gauge guns. A gold-filled "three-arrow" Beretta logo rests on the receiver base. A Gel-Tek recoil pad completes the oil-finished walnut stock and beavertail forearm. A TRUGLO fiber-optic bead provides the gun's sight. A hard case and all the chokes and goodies are included.

The side-by-side barrels of the 471 Silver Hawk have been laser-

Gail Haviland with her 20-gauge Beretta and ruffed grouse.

fused to its monoblock. The gun's Optima-Choke tubes have a longer constriction taper to treat pellets kindly and improve patterns. A switch inside the forearm selects either automatic ejection or manual extraction of fired cases. A nickel finish protects the floral engraving.

The 12-gauge Ringneck and 20-gauge Covey join the 686 over/under lineup. The 12 gauge features three gold-filled flushing pheasants to honor the conservation organization Pheasants Forever. The 20 gauge includes a scene on the receiver of flushing quail for the Quail Unlimited conservation organization.

The autoloading AL391 Covey and Ringneck receive the same treatment.

The AL391 Teknys are further refined 391s. The 12- and 20-gauge guns feature a nickel receiver, with polished sides and an anti-glare top. Its TRUGLO fiber-optic front sight comes in two colors. Stocks on the Teknys have been treated with X-Tra Wood to waterproof and improve their appearance. The stock on the 12-gauge model also accepts Beretta's recoil reducer, an 8 1/2-ounce device adapted from the Spring-Mass recoil reduction system on the AL391 Xtremea 3 1/2-inch gun. All 12-gauge guns come standard with Optima-Bore overbored barrels and Optima-Choke Plus tubes. The guns come in a hard case that includes stock adjustment spacers, magazine reducer, grip cap, sling swivels, five choke tubes and wrench and a gas valve disassembly tool.

The AL391 Teknys Gold and Gold Sporting guns include all those features. But select walnut has been used instead of the X-Tra Wood covering. The receiver flats also feature engraved hunting scenes and colored enamel inserts that continue into the grip sides.

The A391 Xtrema 3-1/2 has been in hunters' hands for nearly a year and it is the closest gun yet to an all-around shotgun, if there is such a gun. The Xtrema cycles all my 12-gauge 1 1/8-ounce loads and nearly all my 1-ounce target loads. Plus its in-stock recoil reducer, Gel-Tek recoil pad and rubber inlays in the grip and forearm take a lot of the sting out of 3 1/2-inch magnum shells. I fired 60 magnum shells through it one after another, then a box of target loads at clay pigeons. The gun cycled flawlessly and stood ready for more.

The 3901 is a no-frills autoloading 12- or 20-gauge gun derived from the AL390 Silver Mallard. This year the line has been expanded to include the 3901 Camo with full coverage of Mossy Oak New Break-Up and New Shadowgrass. The 3901 RL (reduced length) in 20 gauge has a shorter 13 1/2-inch length of pull, and a one-inch spacer for when the kids grow up.

Circling ducks will have a more difficult time spotting the ES100 autoloader with its complete covering of Realtree Hardwoods HD camo.

The Sporting version of the EELL Diamond Pigeon 12 gauge has an Optima-Bore and five flush-fitting Optima-Chokes.

Browning

The 28 gauge and .410 bore have been added to the Citori 525 Field, Sporting and Golden Clays over/unders. These smaller gauge guns actually weigh 6 to 12 ounces more than the same model gun in 20 gauge.

A Golden Clays version is now available in the BT-99 single-barrel 12-gauge trap gun. It has an adjustable comb and a GraCoil recoil reduction system. Its engraving is accented with 24-karat gold and there is a brighter finish on its wood.

Browning has also added its Dura-Touch armor-coating finish to the stock and forearm of its Gold and BPS shotguns with Mossy Oak camouflage.

Also standard on Gold and BPS turkey shotguns is the HiViz TriViz fiber-optic sight. The triangular-shaped rear portion of the sight contains two fiber optic beads. The front bead, mounted at the muzzle, aligns between the two rear beads.

EAA Corporation

European American Armory Corporation of Sharpes, Florida,

The 3 1/2-inch, 12-gauge Beretta Extrema has been in the field for a year now and comes close to being the all-around gun.

imports a full line of guns from Russia, from BB guns and target rifles to handguns and shotguns.

A couple of their new guns are the autoloading 12-gauge MP153 SYN with a black synthetic stock and forend, and the IZH18 Sporting single-barrel with a nickel receiver.

EAA's best accessory is rifle barrel inserts for its cowboy IZH43KH side-by-side hammer shotgun. The inserts are chambered in 45-70, 30-06, 308 Winchester, 222 and 223 Remington. The inserts are held in the 12-gauge bore with a lock at the breech, and by the threads of the screw-in chokes at the muzzle. It is a pretty solid gun to contain the pressure of a 308.

FABARM

Gold Lion Mark II has been replaced with the Gold Lion Mark III. The Mark III has a new gas system to reliably cycle all 12-gauge shells—from light target loads to 3-inch goose killers. The Mark III also features nicer walnut in its stock and forearm, as well as scroll engraving and gold inlays on the receiver flats.

The H368 autoloader is now available in a left-hand version. Also added is a polymer stock with a "soft-touch" coating for a sure grip.

Cosmetic changes have been made to several shotguns. Color case-hardening adds a subdued look to the Sporting Clays Max Lion over/under and Lion Elite side-by-side. A black and silver finish highlights the receiver of the Rex Lion autoloader.

New sights grace the FABARM law enforcement shotguns. A ghost ring rear aperture makes for quick sighting. A Picatinny rail accepts scopes and other sights.

Ithaca

Making some internal parts of synthetic material has allowed Ithaca to introduce three lower-cost pump shotguns based on its Model 37. The Deerslayer II Storm has a 24-inch rifled barrel with a 1:35 twist. The gun has open sights and its receiver top is drilled and tapped for scope mounts. The Turkeyslayer Storm 12 gauge has a 24-inch barrel. TRUGLO fiber-optic front and rear sight help aim in low light. Realtree Hardwood Green camo covers the entire gun. The Waterfowler Storm 12 gauge wears a black synthetic stock and forearm with a removable 28-inch barrel and a Raybar front sight. Both bird guns have screw-in choke tubes.

The autoloading 20-gauge Browning Gold was her choice for harder-kicking waterfowl and pheasant loads.

RCBS' *The Grand* shotshell loader.

All three have Parkerized finishes on metal parts. A Sims Limb-Saver recoil pad helps tame recoil.

For Model 37 shotguns with serial numbers above 855,000, Ithaca is offering a Turkey Retro Fit Kit. The Kit includes a camouflaged turkey barrel, stock and forearm and Sims LimbSaver recoil pad. The made-over gun stores in a supplied hard case.

The Ithaca folks say the 16-gauge Model 37 continues to sell very well.

Marlin

Perhaps spurred by the success of Winchester's Model 9410, Marlin now chambers its 1985 lever action in the .410 2 1/2-inch shell and calls it, naturally, the Model 410. This fun little gun has a 22-inch barrel with no choke and a tube magazine that holds four rounds. Sights include an open folding rear, brass-bead front, or a snap-on green fiber-optic front sight. The receiver is ready for scope mounts, in case you want to shoot slugs at chicken-stealing varmints.

Marlin made pretty much the same Model 410 between 1929 and 1932. It was based on the Marlin Model 93 lever action, which was also chambered for the 25-36 Marlin, 30-30, 32 Special, 32-40 and 38-55. What was old is now new.

Mossberg

Mossberg has camouflaged more of its guns and added a few more variations to its Model 500 pump gun.

The new 500 models include the .410 Slugster and .410 Bantam Slugster. Both guns have 24-inch cylinder bore barrels topped with adjustable fiber-optic sights. Both are equipped with black synthetic stocks and forearms and swivel studs to attach slings. The Bantam has a 13-inch length of pull, and a grip contour that places small hands closer to the trigger.

The 500 line now includes the 20-gauge Bantam Turkey with Mossy Oak Treestand-camoed stock and forearm. It also has a 13-inch length of pull, tighter grip and EZ-Reach forearm that brings the pump forend closer to the shooter.

Guns receiving camouflage covering include: SSI-ONE Turkey and Slug with Mossy Oak New Break-Up; Bantam Turkey 20 gauge with Woodlands camo, or Parkerized metal with a Mossy Oak Treestand stock and forearm; 835 Ulti-Mag pump in Realtree Hardwoods HD Green, Mossy Oak New Break-Up, Forest Floor and Shadow Grass. These guns come with a molded hard case and cable lock.

Perazzi

For those who cannot decide whether to drive the Bentley or Hummer to the country estate to hunt woodcock and ruffed grouse, Perazzi has a set of four Game Shotguns. The 12-, 20-, 28-gauge, and .410 over/unders can be made with 26 3/4- to 29 1/2-inch barrels, and a straight- or curved-grip stock of beautifully marbled walnut, plus your choice of several dozen engraving patterns, all meticulously magnificent.

The Model MX8 and MX2000/8 12-gauge competition guns come with an extra set of lighter barrels that accept gauge-reduction tubes.

RCBS' The Grand

Ever since reloading shotshells on RCBS' new The Grand progressive shotshell press, I no longer need to sweep up inadvertently spilled powder and shot because The Grand only dispenses powder and shot when a shell is present to accept it. That's just one of The Grand's features that make loading shotshells easy and fast.

The Grand comes fully assembled, except for the shot and powder hoppers and spent primer catcher. Those require only a couple minutes to install. After weighing the dispensed shot and powder to make sure they were correct, every pull of the handle kicked out a finished shell. All I had to do was insert a hull in the first station and a wad in the fourth station.

The press weighs nearly forty pounds and its heavy frame, steel rod assembly, 1.5-inch diameter ram and compound leverage system make it sturdy and powerful enough to effortlessly load shells. Each pull of the handle completes eight reloading steps from resizing a case to eject a finished shell. On the down stroke, cases rotate to the next reloading step. At every station, cases are easily removed for inspection. In addition to the lockout feature that prevented a mess of spilled powder and shot, the priming system worked flawlessly and the tilt-out wad guide made inserting wads fast and easy. Each station is easily adjusted by loosening a lock nut and screwing the tools up or down to accommodate different style hulls and wads that require varying amounts of pressure to seat primers and wads and crimp the shell mouths. Switching from Federal to Winchester cases took all of one minute.

Changing the powder and shot bushings involved only removing a pin, sliding out the charge bar and inserting bushings. Additional lead shot and powder bushings are available from RCBS. Midway (1-800-243-3220) also lists them at $4.99 each and states Hornady powder bushings are interchangeable. Shot bushings range from 7/8-ounce of #9s to 1 1/2 ounces of #6 lead shot. Bushings for harder nontoxic shots, like steel, are not yet available.

I loaded 100 12-gauge rounds in about 20 minutes. When I finished, I turned the powder and shot hoppers to the "empty" positions and drained the powder and shot back into their containers. Once again, no mess.

The one thing I didn't like about The Grand is the finished shotshells are ejected at the left rear of the press. I had to stretch around to catch each shell as it kicked out or let them pile up on the bench top and then pack them in a box. One solution would be to mount the press on an optional riser stand that raises the press four inches above the bench. Then shells will fall into a container. Also, a three-inch diameter hole can be drilled through the bench top for the shells to fall through into a container beneath the bench, if you don't mind a big hole in your bench. However, letting the shells pile up is a minor inconvenience, considering how smooth and fast The Grand produces shotshells.

The press is available in 12 or 20 gauge. An optional conversion kit switches gauges.

Remington

The 16-gauge Remington Model 870 sold so well during the last year that Remington is back with more models in this middle gauge. Remington calls the 16-gauge Model 1100 Classic Field "the ultimate upland autoloader." The 16-gauge version is based on the 12-gauge receiver with an American walnut stock and forearm. The walnut has white line spacers between the wood and plastic grip cap and buttplate, reminiscent of the 16-gauge 1100 of 30-some years ago. Metal finish is polished blue and a mid-rib aiming bead reminds you to keep your cheek planted on the stock comb. The Synthetic Field has a black plastic stock and black matte finish on its metal. Barrels for both models are 26 or 28 inches, with a ventilated rib and interchangeable chokes.

The Model 1100 Competition Master 12 gauge is Remington's entry for three-gun matches in practical shooting sports. Its stock and forearm are flat-gray synthetic. A Sims R3 recoil pad soaks up recoil. The metal is finished in matte-black. The 22-inch vent-ribbed barrel accepts interchangeable chokes and has a fiber-optic front bead. An eight-round magazine attaches to the barrel and a receiver-mounted ammo carrier holds an extra seven shells. An extended carrier release button and extra large bolt handle helps speed loading.

The Model 1100 Tournament Skeet 12 gauge features American walnut stock and forearm, and polished blued receiver and barrel. The stock dimensions are slightly different from standard models, with a slightly longer 14 3/16-inch length of pull and 1/4-inch less drop at heel compared to Model 1100 Sporting guns. For those who forget what they are doing, "Tournament Skeet" is roll-marked on the barrel. The barrel is 26 inches with a light contour to shave some weight, and a white front bead and mid-rib steel bead. Extended Skeet and Improved Cylinder choke tubes complete the outfit.

Many turkey hunters have found a boxcar full of shot from a 10- or

TRUGLO fiber-optic sights are the hottest sights on shotguns.

12-gauge magnum isn't required to kill a turkey. The three-inch 20 gauge with 1 1/4-ounces of shot is plenty to roll over a gobbler, and the recoil won't knock you out from under your camo cap. Model 870 Express Youth Turkey Camo and Model 1100 Youth Synthetic Turkey Camo 20-gauge guns have been outfitted in Skyline Excel Camouflage. Their 21-inch barrels and 13-inch length of pull are just right for young hunters. The Model 870 SPS-T 20 gauge is made to fit grown-up hunters. It has TRUGLO fiber-optic sights, synthetic stock and forearm, an extended turkey Super Full choke tube and a compete covering of Mossy Oak Break-up camouflage.

The Model 870 Express Turkey Camo gun also has its stock and forearm covered in Skyline Excel Camouflage. The 870 Express Super Magnum Turkey is completely covered in Skyline Excel.

As a tribute to NASCAR legend Dale Earnhardt, Remington has issued a limited edition Model 11-87 Premier Dale Earnhardt. It has a 12-gauge 28-inch light contour barrel and an American walnut stock and forearm. The blued receiver is engraved with Earnhardt's likeness, gold signature and "7 time Winston Cup Champion" banner.

Stevens/Savage

Al Kasper, of Savage/Stevens, says his company has always been associated with value-priced shotguns, like the Savage 330 over/under and Stevens 311 side-by-side. The new Stevens Model 411 Upland Sporter side-by-side in 12, 20 and .410 continues that tradition.

The gun is made in Imz, Russia in a factory that used to supply the Russian military. "But with the Cold War over, the factories had thousands of employees standing around with nothing to do," Kasper says. "Now they're starting to turn their resources to commercial ventures."

When Savage was considering the shotgun, Savage's president, Ron Coburn, traveled to Russia to help the Russians include the fit and features Americans want. Coburn got it right, and at a retail price of $395 for the 12-gauge gun.

A sample gun handled very well with a thin wrist to its checkered grip, one-inch drop between the comb and heel, and nice balance between the stock and splinter forearm of its 26-inch barrels. The 12 gauge weighs 6 3/4 pounds, the 20 gauge and .410 a half-pound less. The gun has chrome-lined bores threaded to accept Full, Modified and Improved Cylinder choke tubes.

The gun also has a single selective trigger, automatic ejectors and a tang-mounted safety that returns to *safe* when the action is opened. Laser engraving shows a dog flushing a duck on one sideplate and a dog flushing a pheasant on the other. Engraving also adorns the trigger guard and forearm iron. A brass middle bead and red fluorescent front bead point the way to the target.

Stoeger

Barrels, a slug gun and a hammerless hinge action are new from Stoeger.

The barrels fit the Model 2000 autoloader. The 26-inch field barrel has a ventilated rib and front white bead. The slug barrel is a 24-inch smooth bore with adjustable sights and screw-in Cylinder choke. Take your pick of black or Advantage Timber HD camo.

The Model 2000 Slug Synthetic has the same barrel with, as the name implies, a black synthetic stock and forearm.

The Single Barrel Hunter is hammerless and its hinge action opens by squeezing the trigger guard up and in. The gun comes in 12, 20 or .410 with four screw-in chokes. The barrel has a ventilated rib and fiber-optic front bead. A youth model in 20 and .410 has a 13-inch length of pull. It's a perfect gun for potting grouse along the trail.

Traditions

Tradition's Fausti Stefano shotguns, produced in Brescia, Italy, have introduced two new models of its Elite side-by-sides and three Field over/unders and Emilio Rizzini side-by-side and over/under guns.

The Fausti Field III 20 has a ventilated rib and 26- or 28-inch barrels, three screw-in chokes, automatic ejectors, single triggers, and gold engraved receiver. Weights are 7 1/4 to 7 1/2 pounds. All that comes packaged in a hard case. The Field Hunter Silver is a slightly plainer version in 12 and 20 gauge. The Sporting Clay III 20 gauge weighs 3/4 of a pound more. Barrels are 28 or 30 inches. Extra features include four chokes, ported barrels, front target bead and 3/8-inch wide rib.

The side-by-side Elite Hunter ST Silver and Elite I DT join the established Elite I ST. The DT has double triggers, fixed chokes and a straight grip. Gauges are 12, 20, 28 and .410 bore. Very retro. But how nice, at 5 3/4 pounds in the 28 gauge, to carry in a ruffed grouse bottom. The ST Silver 12 and 20 have a matte silver receiver and screw-in chokes, single trigger and a curved grip. The

26-inch-barreled 20 gauge weighs 5 3/4 pounds. Very forward thinking.

The 12-gauge Emilio Rizzini over/under Gold Wing includes the III, SL III, II Silver, III Silver and SL III Silver. The Silver grades are made with silver-colored receivers engraved with game birds. The regular Golds have color case-hardened receivers with engraving and gold-filled game birds. All the guns weigh 7 1/2 pounds with a single trigger, 28-inch barrels and screw-in chokes. Walnut stocks have checkered, curved grips and matching forearms.

The Emilion Rizzini Uplander Series includes 12- and 20-gauge side-by-sides in three grades. All the guns have three-inch chambers and 28- or 26-inch ventilated rib barrels, threaded muzzles to accept various choke tubes, and straight-grip stocks and splinter forearms. The Uplander II has double triggers, tang safety and a limited amount of engraving on the receiver. The Uplander III is a step up, with a single trigger and engraved silver receiver featuring a gold-inlayed woodcock. The Uplander V has extended sideplates that, along with the receiver, are completely engraved and include a scene of a gold-inlayed flushing duck.

Tristar

Marty Fajen's father-in-law was Reinhart Fajen, who owned the Fajen gunstock company for decades. After the company was sold Marty decided to open her own company, Tristar, importing shotguns, rifles, revolvers and shooting accessories.

Tristar imports Emilio Rizzini shotguns from Italy. They include over/unders, side-by-sides and semi-auto guns in a wide range of styles, for flying game from geese to quail. Gauges include the 12, 16, 20, 28 and .410 bore. There's even a 12-gauge over/under chambered for the 12-gauge 3 1/2-inch shell, although why anyone would voluntarily take such a sledgehammer blow to the head is a mystery.

Verona

B.C. Outdoors' Verona has brought out new competition, sporting and hunting guns.

The LX980 Top Competition includes the Trap, Sporting and Skeet/Sporting 12 gauge over/unders. All three have 2 3/4-inch chambers; four locking, ported barrels that accept four Briley Spectrum choke tubes, TRUGLO fiber-optic front bead, and plain bead on the middle of the ventilated rib. A hard case protects the Turkish walnut stock from dings and scratches. The Trap model has 32-inch barrels and an adjustable comb. The stock

comb is also adjustable on the Skeet/Sporting, which wears 30-inch barrels. The Sporting wears a standard stock and 30-inch barrels.

The Verona LX692 Gold Competition superposed guns are now available in smaller bores, with two- and three-barrel sets. The LX692GCSK-20/28 is chambered in 20 and 28 with 30-inch barrels, complete with forearms. The LX692GCSK-28/410 comes in 28 and .410 and the LX692GC-Trio in 20, 28 and .410 bore. The 20- and 28-gauge barrels include five screw-in chokes, while the .410 has Skeet and Skeet chokes. All combinations weigh about 6 1/4 pounds and come with a hard case.

Bernardelli in Italy makes the LX801 Sporting and Competition/Sporting semiautomatics. These gas-operated guns include a ported 28- or 30-inch barrel, 9mm-width ventilated rib and TRUGLO front bead and four Trulock screw-in chokes. Stocks have a Monte Carlo hump.

The LX1001 Express Combo is for days when the country holds both furred and feathered game. The over/under has a 28-inch barrel set in 20 gauge. The twin barrels for rifles are chambered for 223, 243, 270, 308 or 30-06. A 30-06/20-gauge set is for grouse and big game during the same hike. Rifle sights are a **V** at the rear on a quarter-rib; at the front a fiber-optic pipe atop a blade. A sling swivel hangs below the bottom rifle barrel.

How did hunters ever kill game without using camouflaged guns? Game won't have an inkling what hit them because the Verona semi-auto 12-gauge SX405 is covered with specific camo patterns for different animals. The SX405 Camo for waterfowl hunters is cloaked with Real Tree Wetland or Hardwood camo. The SX405T Camo for turkey hunters is shrouded in Real Tree Hardwood. The gun has a 24-inch barrel, with front and rear TRUGLO sights. The SX405Slug has a 22-inch rifled barrel and TRUGLO front and rear sights—all hidden under the Hardwood pattern. The SX405 Combo has the same slug barrel, and a 26-inch smoothbore for birds, with a plain black synthetic stock and forearm.

Weatherby

Weatherby's Italian-made Semi-Auto Shotgun (SAS) is decked out in different styles for sporting clays, upland game to waterfowl. Now the SAS is made in a slug gun configuration. The gas-operated 12-gauge, 3-inch gun has a 22-inch rifled barrel with a cantilever scope base that extends back over the receiver. The hump of the Monte Carlo comb says *Weatherby*, and raises the eye to line

up with a scope. Shims fit between the receiver and front of the grip to adjust drop and cast.

Winchester

Winchester had such a hit with its Model 9410 in .410 bore that it has added the Invector-Plus Choke System, with Full, Improved Modified, Modified and Skeet tubes, to its Packer and Packer Compact models. All five 9410 models have the new top tang safety.

The Supreme Select Elegance, Sporting and Field 12-gauge guns are Winchester's next generation of over/under guns. Winchester states balance is their best feature, derived from lighter and slimmer barrels, low-profile receiver and a "well-executed stock." The guns have two locking lugs along the lower sides of the top barrel. The lugs can be adjusted to compensate for wear over the years. A third fixed lug under the barrels reduces wear. Barrels are back-bored and include the Invector-Plus choke tubes.

The Field features a scene of flushing game birds engraved on the receiver flats, and blued barrels to match. Barrel lengths are 26 or 28 inches and come with chrome-plated, three-inch chambers. Its walnut is the plainest of the three models, yet full panels of checkering cover the grip and forearm.

The Elegance is the fancy model and has flushing pheasants engraved on its grayed receiver and Grade III walnut, checkered in a point pattern on the grip and forearm. Barrel choices are 26 or 28 inches, with three-inch chambers. For some reason the butt wears a hard plate.

Probably because the Sporting will be shot more, it has a ribbed recoil pad and ported barrels. A swoop of dark gray on the receiver sides contrasts well with the brushed silver receiver. A trigger shoe easily adjusts length of pull. Barrels are 28 or 30 inches, with 2 3/4-inch chambers.

The Dura-Touch armor coating has been added to more Super X2 shotguns. The coating has a soft feel and provides a sure grip in all the foul weather a waterfowl hunter endures during a season. In addition, the coating protects the finish on the stock and forearm. The finish has been added to the Practical MK II, Signature Red Sporting, Composite, 3 1/2-inch Composite and camouflage models.

The red hardwood stock makes the Super X2 Signature Red Sporting stand out in any rack of guns in the clubhouse. The gun includes shims to adjust the stock's cast and comb height, five choke tubes and two gas pistons that help the gun cycle all sporting loads. ●

BLACK POWDER REVIEW

by Doc Carlson

FOR MANY YEARS, the only folks shooting blackpowder were those interested in traditional muzzle-loading firearms. Hunting was usually done during regular centerfire seasons with the traditional side-hammer flint or percussion firearm. The reproduction guns on the market catered to this interest, and the relative few who were into "reenacting" usually were Civil War re-enactors, or buckskinners who relived the pre-1840 period.

Then the muzzleloading hunting craze hit and the market responded by offering the "in-line" rifle. These guns, while muzzleloaders, duplicated the look and feel of the modern, bolt-action rifle familiar to most hunters. Traditional sidelock guns dwindled in market share.

Then the blackpowder cartridge interest developed, kindled by interest in blackpowder cartridge silhouette, cowboy action shooting and Creedmoor long-range shooting with the old blackpowder cartridge firearms. The marketplace again responded and soon new guns appeared to shoot the blackpowder cartridges of yesteryear. Today, we have a well-balanced market that offers a wide range of all types of blackpowder firearms. There's something for everyone, regardless of the field of interest.

Traditions Performance Firearms

Traditions Performance Firearms is one of the early companies involved in the rebirth of interest in blackpowder. Their first offerings were purely traditional side-hammer guns, but over time their product line expanded to all phases of the blackpowder sport, and now includes modern shotguns as well.

New this year from Traditions are the Evolution and Thunder Bolt series of rifles. These are bolt-action in-line guns. The Evolution features a new, stainless steel bolt system designed to operation smoothly. The striker cocks on lifting of the oversize bolt handle designed to give a firm grip with cold, or gloved fingers. a cocking indicator at the rear of the bolt indicates—by sight or touch— whether the gun is cocked or not. The 24-inch tapered barrel is available in either blued or stainless steel, in 50-caliber with a 1:28-inch twist or 54-caliber with a 1:48-inch spiral. All barrels feature the Positive Alignment System (PAS), a recessed muzzle to ease starting the bullet in perfect alignment with the bore. Projectile alignment is essential to good accuracy and the recessed muzzle eases reloading in the field.

The Evolution rifle is offered in several stock styles including black synthetic, synthetic with a camo finish, beech wood and New X-Wood— which is a coating on a beech stock that looks more like very high-grade walnut than the real thing. The tapered barrel makes these guns balance and shoulder well. Sights are steel fiber optic and the ramrod is aluminum. Ignition is by 209 shotgun primers.

An Evolution LD (Long Distance) is offered with an extended barrel to give more velocity. This one will be available in 45- and 50-caliber, with an internally-ported barrel to handle heavier charges with lower recoil. The Evolution Premier will have all the bells and whistles of the Evolution, plus a ported, fluted barrel.

The Thunder Bolt is a modified, economical version of the Evolution featuring the same bolt system etc., in blued steel only. It is available in 45- or 50-caliber with plastic fiber optic sights and a synthetic ramrod. It is available with either a black or camo synthetic stock and either blued or stainless steel barrel. A youth-size model with black synthetic stock in 50-caliber is available also.

Both the Evolution and Thunder Bolt guns are drilled and tapped for scope mounts and carry sling swivel studs.

Traditions also offers a full line of traditional muzzleloaders—both rifles and pistols—as well as blackpowder cartridge rifles and pistols.

Rossi Firearms

Rossi Firearms is a well recognized as a maker of cartridge pistols, revolvers and rifles. They are now in the muzzle-loading game with a top-break in-line type rifle

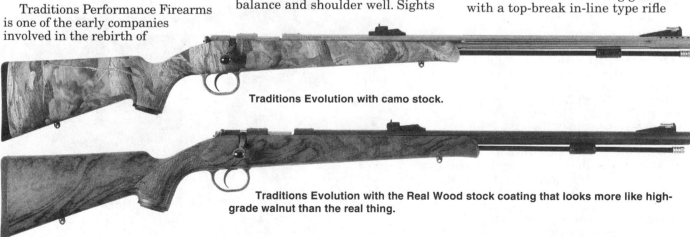

Traditions Evolution with camo stock.

Traditions Evolution with the Real Wood stock coating that looks more like high-grade walnut than the real thing.

that resembles the single-shot shotgun familiar to all. This gun features a center-hung hammer with a hammer-block safety. The easily removable breech plug takes #209 shotgun primers. The 50-caliber barrel is 23 inches long and available in either matte stainless or blued finish. Sights are Tru-Glo fiber optic and a brass and wood collapsible ramrod that tucks under the barrel and into the forend is supplied. The gun is drilled and tapped for scope mounting, if you wish, and a hammer extension is available for ease of cocking under a scope. The stocks are wood and the buttstock is supplied with a rubber recoil pad. A breech plug wrench is included with these rifles, as well as a trigger lock. The Rossi is a good quality rifle at a reasonable price.

The icing on the cake is availability of these rifles in combination sets. The muzzle-loading rifle can be had with interchangeable barrels in

Winchester Firearms/ USRAC

Winchester introduced a bolt-action in-line muzzleloader a couple of years ago and have now added another rifle to the Winchester muzzle-loading line. Called the Apex Magnum, this new offering features a drop-block action. The trigger guard is dropped down, which rotates a breechblock backward and downward to clear the breech plug area of the rifle. A #209 shotgun primer is inserted into the breech plug, the trigger guard is pulled back into position, rotating the breechblock back up behind the breech plug, and the hammer is cocked. When the trigger is pulled, the hammer falls, firing the gun. The dropping block clears the breech plug for ease of installing the #209 primers or removal of the

breech plug for cleaning. When closed, the breechblock provides a weather-tight seal, very important when hunting on a wet, snowy day. These guns feature a typical Monte Carlo stock with palm swell and beavertail forend—in either black fleck or Mossy Oak Break Up synthetic—and are fitted with a magnum recoil pad and sling swivels. Barrel and action finish can be either blue or stainless. Fiber-optic sights are installed on the fluted 30-inch barrel and are guaranteed for life against breakage. Calibers offered are 45 and 50, both with a twist of 1:28 inches and a bullet-guiding, recessed muzzle for loading ease. A synthetic ramrod hangs under the barrel and a sling is included with all guns. Trigger pull is preset at the factory at 3 pounds and the rebounding hammer features a block that keeps the hammer from contact with the firing pin unless the trigger is pulled.

The short, drop-block action on this new Winchester gun allows the use of the 30-inch barrel with no feeling of muzzle-heaviness. The rifle balances and points very well.

Knight Rifles

Knight Rifles continues to add to their line and upgrade their products for the muzzle-loading hunter. Their newest rifle, the Master Hunter Disc Extreme, incorporates the latest upgrades and design advances found in the Knight line, and features the full plastic jacket ignition system that encloses the #209 shotgun

Knight Rifle's Master Hunter Disc Extreme rifle.

20-gauge *(cartridge, with a Modified choke)* and 243 Winchester, or as a three-barrel set with the 50-caliber muzzleloader combined with two of the hottest new cartridges: the 270 Winchester Short Magnum (WSM) and the 17 HMR. These combination sets come with extra forends for their respective barrels and a custom nylon carrying case with a shoulder strap that fits either the carrying case or the guns. A nice set-up, at a very reasonable price, for the all-season hunter and shooter—and a great starter outfit for the beginning shooter.

The Knight Full Plastic Jacket System.

Knight's new disc that takes #11 percussion caps.

primer. The jacket is then slipped on a nipple at the rear of the breech plug and the bolt is closed, sealing the whole system weathertight. The Knight folks have submerged this breech/primer system in water for a full hour with no leakage or failure to fire, so it should work OK in rain or snow, I imagine. The schnabel forend, thumbhole-style stock is made of laminated wood with a high gloss finish. The gun is shipped with a spare synthetic stock that can be used in the hunting field, if one wishes one stock to admire and another one to rattle around in the pickup. Stocks are supplied with recoil pad and sling swivel studs. The fluted stainless barrel is available in 50- or 45-caliber with 1:30 and 1:28 twists, respectively. The stainless barrel is cryogenically accurized by exposure to a controlled heating and freezing process for two days to stabilize the barrel at the molecular level by relieving stresses in the barrel steel. The result is a barrel that has little or no tendency to warp when exposed to the heat of firing, thus delivering superior accuracy, something that the center-fire shooters have known for some time.

The bolt *(and those of all Knight rifles)* has been updated so that it can be disassembled without tools, eliminating the need to carry a special tool afield or to the range. Sights are fiber optic, ramrod is of a synthetic near-unbreakable material and the receiver is, of course, drilled and tapped for scope bases.

Knight has added a modified priming disc, to be used in their standard disc rifles, that takes #11 caps. This allows these guns to be used in states that require the use of percussion caps and ban the #209 shotgun primer.

Rightnour Manufacturing Inc.

Along a more traditional line but with a touch of modern, we have the RMC Accusporter Rifles by Rightnour Manufacturing Inc. This half-stock flintlock rifle *(in either right- or left-hand)* is set into a laminated wood stock (brown or green camo) usually found on a modern in-line action rifle, not a flintlock. The stock style is a shotgun configuration with a flat butt that points and handles recoil well. The 28-inch Green Mountain barrel carries a 1:48 or 1:28 twist for either patched round ball or sabots and bullet-type projectiles. The flintlock itself is made by the L & R Lock Company, well known for quality flint and percussion locks, whose locks are used on many of the custom muzzle-loading guns made by the better-known makers. The rifles are set up for hunting, with fiber-optic sights (standard) and a single trigger. Hardware and barrel are blued. They are available in either right or left hand.

For those with something else in mind, barrel-wise, the lock/stock assembly can also be purchased, *sans* barrel. You can then add any of the standard "drop-in" barrels that fit the T/C Hawken, Lyman Deerstalker or Trade Rifle, Traditions Hawken & Deerhunter, or similar guns. This allows selection of any caliber and barrel length, as long as you stay with 15/16-inch barrels. A nice idea, and not offered anywhere else, to my knowledge.

For those who shoot flint guns because they'd rather—or for those who must, due to game laws in their state—this RMC Accusporter is a well-made, fast-handling little rifle with top quality components.

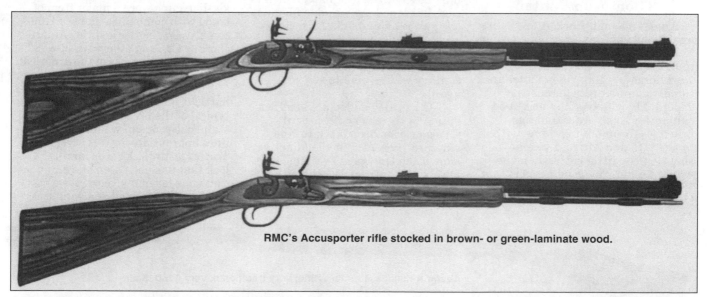

RMC's Accusporter rifle stocked in brown- or green-laminate wood.

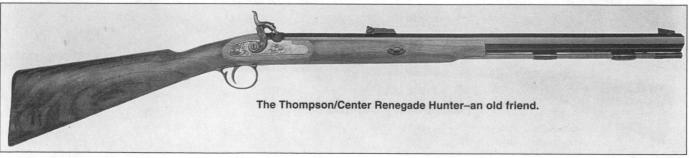

The Thompson/Center Renegade Hunter—an old friend.

The Thompson/Center Renegade is a world-class hunting rifle.

Thompson/Center

An old friend is back. A few years ago Thompson/Center dropped their Renegade series rifles from production. I really missed the little rifle, a workhorse hunting rifle of a traditional, side-hammer percussion design. My wife has had one in 54-caliber for some years and has killed a fair amount of game with it in the U.S. and Africa. I've enjoyed shooting the little rifle–when she would let me. The good news is that T/C has put the Renegade back in the product line.

Available in 50-caliber with a 1-inch, 1:48-inch twist blued barrel, the rifle will handle patched round ball, sabotted bullets or slugs with equal aplomb. The QLA (Quick Load Accurizor) recessed muzzle feature *(eases loading of either patched round ball or conical projectiles)* will be appreciated by hunters everywhere. The reliable percussion lock has the same coil-spring innards found in the well-known T/C Hawken series of rifles.

The Renegade's single hunting trigger is enclosed in a large, roomy trigger guard that is easy to use while wearing gloves. Sights are typical of the T/C bloodline, a fully adjustable rear coupled with a bead front. The sights are fairly coarse; intended for hunting, not precision target shooting. The half-stock is good, close-grained American walnut, with plain forend and recoil pad. All hardware is blued except the lockplate, which is case-hardened. As an added bonus, the gun is available in both right- and left-hand versions.

Welcome back, Renegade. The muzzle-loading hunters of this country will be glad to see you again.

T/C has also added a 45-caliber option to their very successful Omega series drop block in-line rifles. At present, the 45-caliber version of the Omega is available only with a synthetic stock, and either stainless or blued-steel barrel.

Austin & Halleck

The Mountain Rifle, a very traditional half-stock rifle from Austin & Halleck, is available with rifling twists of 1:66 for round ball and 1:28 for bullets. The 32-inch 50-caliber browned barrel of these rifles is 1 inch across the flats and topped with buckhorn rear and silver blade front sights. The sights are fixed *(non-adjustable)*, as were most originals. The double-set, double-throw triggers are enclosed in a scroll trigger guard. All hardware is iron, except the barrel key escutcheons, which appear to be German silver.

The maple stock, a typical southern mountain half-stock style, is available in select grade with a great deal of figure; really beautiful wood. The guns are available in either flintlock or percussion, depending on your preference. These rifles are getting a well-deserved reputation for quality and good looks. They would be equally at home on the hunting trail or at Rendezvous.

Pedersoli/ Dixie Gun Works

Another gun—new this year—undoubtedly of interest to the pre-1830 crowd, is the Indian Trade Gun, made by Pedersoli and imported by Dixie Gun Works. This is a pretty close copy of the trade guns made in the 1700s by many makers: Chance, Barnett, Tryon, Deringer, Lehman and Henry come to mind. These musket-like guns were a major item of trade with companies like the Hudson Bay Co., Northwest Co., American Fur Co., and others who traded for the furs and robes of the American wilderness.

The smoothbore 20-gauge (62-cal.) barrel is just a tad over 36 inches, typical of the breed. The dark-stained, European walnut stock has lines appropriate for this style of gun. The large flintlock is the familiar Lott lock that has been seen on reproduction guns for many years. It's a heavily sprung, good-sparking lock

Austin & Halleck Mountain Rifle; very traditional, very good quality.

Pedersoli/Dixie Indian Trade Gun.

The Gibbs Target Rifle from Dixie.

that can be relied upon to ignite the large pan every time, if the shooter does his part. The large, typical trigger guard and trigger are iron *(browned)* and the wooden ramrod is held under the full-stock forend in brass ferrules. The left side of the stock has the obligatory brass dragon sideplate that carries the lock screws. A brass front sight and brass buttplate complete the picture. There is no rear sight; again, typical of these firearms.Given the interest in the Fur Trade era of American history, I expect Dixie will have a lot of success with this latest offering from Italy.

Over the years there has been a lot of interest in the English rifles, made for hunting and target shooting, by such makers as Manton, Egg, and Gibbs. The English style of rifle is patterned similarly to modern stock styles, although these guns date back to the 1700s. They shoulder, point and handle recoil well. The feel of these guns is similar to a well-fitting, modern shotgun. The Brits definitely knew how to make a rifle. The problem has been that, up to now, the only sources of these fine rifles has been

either an original through the collectors' market or a custom creation—both expensive.

Dixie has again teamed up with Pedersoli to bring one of these fine rifles to the muzzleloader shooter, a copy of an English target rifle made in 1865 by George Gibbs. The pistol grip half-stock is of European walnut, oil-finished and hand-checkered on both pistol grip and forend. It sports a horn buttplate, grip cap and forend tip, as did the original gun. The blued steel barrel is a bit over 35 inches long and goes from an octagon-shaped patent breech area to a tapered round configuration, similar to what is found on most originals. It makes this gun "hang" well for offhand shooting.

The percussion lock is of top quality, as one would expect on a target gun. The trigger mechanism is a simple single trigger with a good let-off. I've always been partial to the English style of gun and this one duplicates the look and feel of the originals pretty well.

The sights supplied with the gun include a precision Creedmoor rear, coupled with a windage-adjustable

front that takes inserts, 18 of which are supplied with the rifle. The Creedmoor rear has adjustment for windage and almost 3 inches of height adjustment. There is an oval escutcheon of German silver *(for the owner's initials)* on the underside of the buttstock, forward of the toe. Sling swivels complete the stock furniture.

The rifle is offered in both 40- and 451-caliber with a twist of 1:23-5/8 inches and 5 lands and grooves. Each rifle is shipped with a sizer to size and lubricate cast bullets to fit the barrel. Dixie carries the correct Pedersoli molds.

This rifle handles and points very well and, while it is called a target rifle, there is certainly no reason it wouldn't perform well in the hunting field. This one definitely deserves a look.

Hodgdon Powder Company

Last year Hodgdon Powder Company brought out their new replica blackpowder called 777. Subsequently, it has made a name for itself among shooters for the absence of fouling and plain water cleanup. There is no sulfur so the "rotten egg" smell is gone, allowing the

Hodgdon's Triple Seven now available in pellets for 50-caliber.

A new blackpowder from Germany– Scheutzen.

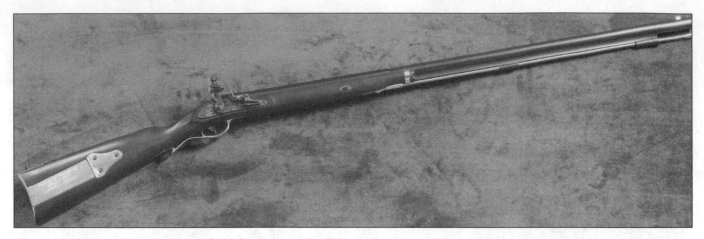

Navy's 1803 Harpers Ferry Lewis and Clark Commemorative Rifle.

blackpowder shooter to mingle in polite society without causing olfactory alarm. New for this year, Hodgdon has figured out how to pelletize Triple Seven, which is now available in 50-grain pellets for 50-caliber in-lines using #209 primers. The maximum load recommended is two of the 50-grain pellets. This new powder is very consistent, and accuracy has been very good in tests.

The new pellets should be well received by hunters since they eliminate the need to carry flasks, measures and the like. Just drop a pellet or two down the barrel, seat a bullet, prime with a #209—and shoot. One of these days someone is going to figure out how to hook a bullet onto these pellets *(maybe even a primer)* and have the complete load in one package.

Petro-Explo, Inc.

Blackpowder shooters and hunters now have another brand of blackpowder to use. Petro-Explo, Inc., the folks that import Elephant and Swiss blackpowder, are bringing in a new powder from Germany called Schuetzen. Manufactured by the Wano Schwartzpulver factory using the much sought-after alder charcoal, this new blackpowder will be available in the standard granulations and should be priced with other powders on the market. The Petro-Explo folks have spent considerable time in the German factory to assure the quality and consistency of this powder is top-notch. German powders have a good reputation and, hopefully, this new powder will enhance it.

American Pioneer Powder Company

American Pioneer Powder Company is marketing a loose, granular powder designed to be a sulfurless blackpowder replacement. It is

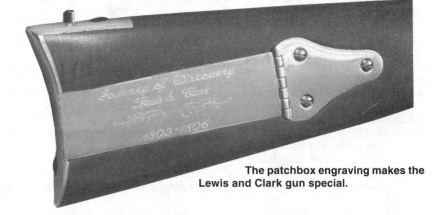

The patchbox engraving makes the Lewis and Clark gun special.

currently available in two granulations—3Fg and 2Fg—and can be used as a volume-for-volume replacement for conventional blackpowder. The manufacturer's published load data show this new powder is slightly hotter than blackpowder, delivering velocities approximately 10 percent above equivalent loads of blackpowder. It is reported to leave little or no fouling in the bore and, according to the manufacturer, requires no wiping between shots or lubrication of the bullet. It cleans up with plain water.

In addition to the loose granulations, the American Pioneer Powder is available in 50-grain equivalent compressed charges for 50-caliber firearms. The compressed charges are square and are simply pushed down the barrel, followed by the bullet. They have no blackpowder "booster charge" added to facilitate ignition, the manufacturer claiming none is needed. Soon to follow are compressed 50-grain equivalent charges for 45-caliber.

The preceding, along with Goex and KIK blackpowder, and Pyrodex and Clean Shot replacement blackpowder, indicate there will be a good supply of fodder to feed your blackpowder firearm. The many choices available in the marketplace should assure the shooter of finding the

right combination of powder and bullet to work best in whatever blackpowder gun is involved, be it muzzleloader or cartridge gun.

Navy Arms Co.

Last year the blackpowder fraternity lost one of its founding fathers, Val Forgett, founder of Navy Arms Co. Navy Arms was one of the first to begin making replica firearms for blackpowder shooters and is, I am happy to say, alive and well and carrying on Val's legacy.

In keeping with the upcoming bicentennial of the Lewis and Clark Expedition, Navy is offering a Model 1803 Harpers Ferry rifle to commemorate the event. The 54-caliber rifle features a half-round, half-octagon browned barrel and an upgraded oil-finished walnut stock. The brass patchbox is engraved "Lewis & Clark Journey of Discovery 1803-1806".Included with each rifle is an exact replica of the Thomas Jefferson Peace Medal or Friendship Medal minted for Lewis & Clark to give to the Indians encountered along the way. This rifle would be a nice memento of the expedition, whether hanging on the wall or being carried afield or to the range.

Enjoy!

AMMO UPDATE

by Holt Bodinson

THE MAGNUMS JUST keep getting shorter. Winchester's launch of the 223 and 243 Super Short Magnums caught us all off guard. There will be more to follow. By whom? That's the question.

Smith & Wesson surprised us a bit as well. The company who has given us the 357, 41, and 44 magnums upped the ante with the release of their 500 S&W Magnum, and a behemoth of a revolver to handle it.

Bonded-core bullets have had a relatively small niche in commercial ammunition and component lines. No longer. Remington has added bonded cores to its Core-Lokt bullet design. Nosler has introduced a new line of bonded-core "Accubond" projectiles, and Hornady has done the same under its "InterBond" label. Think of that. Three new sources of bonded-core bullets in one year. The price of bonded-core hunting bullets is heading down!

Non-toxic projectiles are the rage. We see more signs of "green" bullets in the rifle and handgun ammunition lines each year. This year Lapua brings us the "Naturalis" bullet, naturally.

Lots of great new reloading manuals are out in print, and most include data on the latest short magnums. Look for further information under Hodgdon, Hornady, Lee Precision, Lyman, Nosler, Sierra, and Swift.

Ballistic software is finally becoming more sophisticated and user-friendly. See the latest offerings under Lee Precision, Load from a Disk and Sierra.

It's been an intriguing year in ammunition, ballistics and components.

A-Square Co.

To the many who have asked for the current address of the reconstituted company, it is: A-Square Co., 205 Fairview Ave., Jeffersonville, IN 47130. (812) 283-0577.

Alliant

The focus this year is on shotgun powders and there are two new formulations that fill some gaps in Alliant's lineup. Simply called "410," the new powder is a clean-burning flake powder designed specifically for .410 skeet and field loads. Next,

"E3" powder is being introduced with a burning rate roughly equivalent to 700-X. E3 should prove ideal for 1-1/8 oz. trap and skeet loads in the 12-gauge, light loads in the 10- and 16-gauges, and with possibly some application in handgun cartridges and in reduced lead bullet loads in centerfire calibers. Finally, attention you 223 Remington fans who have found Reloader 10X so useful and accurate. Alliant warns that one of their earlier published loads—34.5 grs. of Reloader 10X with the 45-grain Speer SP bullet—should read, "24.5 grs." of Reloader 10X.
www.alliantpowder.com

Ballistic Products

If you hanker to try your hand at loading Hevi-Shot, send for Ballistic Product's new catalog and their brand new reloading manual on Hevi-Shot that contains extensive data for the 20, 12 and 10 gauges. The company currently stocks Hevi-

Alliant's new "410" powder is a clean-burning flake powder formulated for .410 skeet and field loads.

Shot in shot sizes B, 2,4,6,7.5, and #9-plus they offer a variety of new wads and Mylar wrappers designed specifically for Hevi-Shot. Noting the increasing interest in the 16-gauge, they have designed a Multi-Metal 16-gauge Field wad that can handle any shot type and is provided in an unslit condition with optional Mylar wrappers to protect the bore when slits are cut. Always a proponent of the 10-gauge Magnum for waterfowling, the company has added a new wad for that beloved cannon, the Deci-Max. The Deci-Max is a cushioned wad designed for the smaller shot sizes, such as #4 and #6 in steel or Hevi-Shot. They always seem to have a good supply of Federal 10-gauge 3 1/2-inch, and 12 gauge 3- and 3 1/2-inch hulls in stock and have added a new line of straight-walled, plastic base wad hulls in 12, 16 and .410 from Nobel Sport. See them at www.ballisticproducts.com

Barnes

Barnes is introducing a refined version of their X-Bullet called the "Triple-Shock." Featuring three relief grooves around the shank of the bullet that reportedly reduce pressure and increase accuracy, the Triple-Shock is available in a variety of weights in 6mm, 270, 7mm, and 308 calibers. New, too, is a line of uncoated, super explosive, and competitively priced varmint bullets labeled, "Varmin-A-Tor." The new line is available in 40- and 50-grain .224-inch, 58- and 72-grain 6mm and is available in boxes of 100 or 250 units. www.barnesbullets.com

Berger Bullets

Is the 20-caliber making a comeback? Not since the 5mm Rem. Rimfire Magnum have we seen such interest in this intermediate 0.204-inch bore diameter. Berger has decided to fill the niche with 30-, 35-, 36-, 40-, and 50-grain bullets being offered this year. www.bergerbullets.com

Black Hills Ammunition

A bunch of new loads from the Black Hills of South Dakota. Can the 223 Remington be considered a light

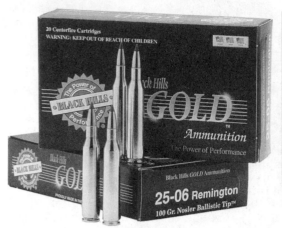

Black Hills has created a true small deer/antelope loading for the 223 Remington featuring a 60-grain Nosler Partition at 3150 fps.

Combining the accuracy of the 100-grain Ballistic Tip and a velocity of 3200 fps, Black Hills' new 25-06 load is suitable for varmints through light big game.

big-game cartridge? Winchester thought so ten years ago and gave us the 64-grain deer bullet loading that also proved adequate for antelope–if all game ranges were kept under 200 yards. This year Black Hills introduces the 223 Remington topped with a 60-grain Nosler Partition at 3150 fps. During load development, this interesting combination produced almost match-level accuracy in even standard twist barrels.

The 38-55 Win. has been a neglected round for many years and typically has been offered with an undersized .375-inch diameter jacketed bullet. No longer. Black Hills has added a proper sized 255-grain lead bullet at 1250 fps to its Cowboy line.

Two perennial favorites are new to the company's Gold line—the 25-06 Rem. with a 115-grain Barnes-X pill at 2975 fps plus a 100-grain Nosler Ballistic Tip at 3200 fps; and the 7mm Rem. Mag. with either a 140-grain Barnes-X or a 140-grain Nosler Ballistic Tip at a respectable 3150 fps. Black Hills has earned an enviable reputation for producing some of the most consistently accurate ammunition being loaded in the industry. Nice folks, too.

Brenneke

Keeping right up with the rifled bores and sabot slugs, Brenneke is fielding a heavy 1-3/8 oz. slug with a muzzle velocity of 1502 fps for the 3-inch 12-gauge. The slug is designed for smoothbores and sports an attractive black coating called "CleanSpeed" that minimizes bore leading. Brenneke claims 2-inch groups at 50 yards and 3-inch groups at 100 yards—from a smoothbore, no less.
www.brennekeusa.com

Loaded with a soft bullet sized to 0.377-inch, Black Hills' 38-55 ammunition will accommodate the variety of bore sizes found in old rifles.

Burgess Bullets

Remember the Littleton Shotmaker? Burgess Bullets has bought the company and improved the product. Capable of turning out 45 pounds of high antimony #6 thru #9 shot per hour from melted wheel weights, the Littleton machine is indeed remarkable. It even produces those hard-to-get shot sizes-- #7 and #8. It's a regular little household shot tower and not expensive.
www.littletonshotmaker.com

Cabela's

Look in their catalog for a new, competitively priced shotgun ammunition line loaded by Federal. Lots of interesting 12-gauge offerings in the turkey and steel shot arenas as well as extra-hard shot upland loads for the 12 and 20.
www.cabelas.com

CCI-SPEER

CCI's extensive, sintered copper/tin, frangible bullet line just got bigger. New this year under the Blazer label is a 140-grain 45 ACP load clocking 1200 fps; a 90-grain 9mm

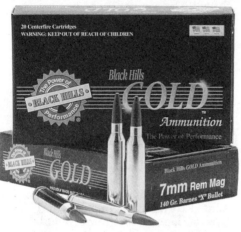

Using a 140-grain Barnes-X bullet, the optimum weight for 7mm, Black Hills has created a fast, deeply penetrating big game load for the 7mm Remington Magnum.

load at 1350 fps; and a 105-grain 40 S&W loading at 1380 fps. Speer is introducing a 250-grain loading for that old stalwart, the 45 Colt, with a respectable velocity of 900 fps. In their component line, Speer has added a 210-grain 44 Magnum Gold Dot HP bullet and 185- and 200-grain Totally Metal Jacket bullets designed for 45 ACP velocities.
www.cci-ammunition.com
www.speer-bullets.com

Cor-Bon

When Smith & Wesson went looking for a new magnum handgun cartridge, Cor-Bon jumped at the chance to design the 500 S&W Magnum cartridge. The brass is being drawn right there in Sturgis, ND by Jamison International and the completed ammunition is being loaded by Cor-Bon. Initially, three different 500 S&W loads are being offered: a 275-grain Barnes X bullet at 1665 fps; a 400-grain SP at 1675 fps; and a wrist-shocking 440-grain gas-checked LBT "wide flat nose" pill at 1625 fps. At the other end of the ballistic scale, Cor-Bon has teamed up with North American Arms (NAA)

500 S&W Magnum

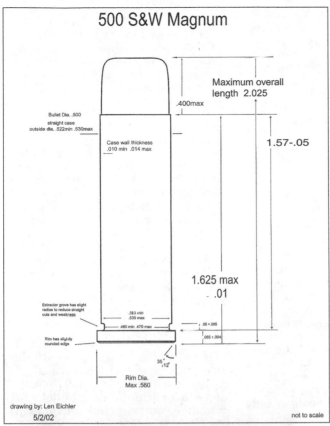

Maximum overall length 2.025

.400 max

Bullet Dia. .500
straight case
outside dia. .522min .530max

1.57-.05

Case wall thickness
.010 min .014 max

1.625 max
- .01

Extractor grove has slight
radius to reduce straight
cuts and weakness

.523 min
.530 max

.460 min .470 max

.05 +.005

.055 ±.004

Rim has slightly
rounded edge

36°
±12°

Rim Dia.
Max .560

drawing by: Len Eichler
5/2/02

not to scale

Smith&Wesson decided to capture the high ground with the release of their 500 S&W Magnum.

◄ **The 1.57-inch case length of S&W's new 500 illustrates how big this new cartridge really is.**

◄ **Hodgdon's pelletized Triple Seven is increasingly being used to load metallic cartridges.**

and created the 32NAA. The 32NAA is a bottlenecked 32-caliber cartridge based on a necked down 380 ACP case that fits in NAA's little pocket automatic, the Guardian. The resulting ballistics from the Guardian's 2.5-inch barrel are impressive. The 32NAA loaded with a 60-grain bullet achieves 1200 fps. Cor-Bon and NAA are now working on the 25NAA that will be a based on a 32ACP case. Stay tuned! www.corbon.com

Environ Metal

Environ Metal is the manufacturer of Hevi-Shot products. New offerings include Hevi-Shot 00 buck (*currently loaded by Remington*) as well as shotguns slugs, 40-caliber

frangible bullets and 30-caliber rifle bullets made from their proprietary, non-toxic alloy. www.hevishot.com

Federal

The 300 Winchester Short Magnum is taking off under the Federal Premium label with a 180-grain Nosler Partition at 2970 fps and a 150-grain Nosler BT at 3300 fps. Priced slightly lower in their Classic cartridge series is a 180-grain Hi-Shok loading at 2970 fps.

Urban geese and other varmints are successfully being taken on with Federal's sub-sonic 12-gauge ammunition. The "Metro Sub-Sonic Tungsten-Iron" 3-inch loading features 1-1/8 oz. of BBs at a lethargic 850 fps, while the 2 3/4-inch "Metro Sub-Sonic Field Load" does slightly better with 1-1/8 oz. of #7-1/2 shot at 900 fps. There are a number of new Trophy Bonded Bear Claw loadings in the Premium centerfire line and a Premium Grand Slam Turkey 2 3/4-inch load with 1-1/2 oz. of copper-plated #4, 5, and 6 shot at 1315 fps. www.federalcartridge.com

GOEX

Clear Shot, Goex's popular, non-corrosive blackpowder replacement, is currently out of production. They hope to get it back on line in the future, but in the meantime, stock up on it. Several of their distributors still have it. www.goexpowder.com

GPA Bullets

North American distribution of this new line of monolithic, copper alloy rifle bullets has been arranged through Rock Enterprise LLC headquartered in Flagstaff, AZ. The line now includes every decimal and metric caliber from 6mm to 600 Nitro. www.rockenterprise.com

Graf & Sons

Great news for everyone who enjoys shooting the military warhorses. Graf has contracted with Hornady to produce Boxer-primed brass and loaded ammunition in 6.5x52 Carcano, 6.5x50 Jap, 7.7x58 Jap, 8x56R Mannlicher, 7.5x54 MAS, 7.65x53 Argentine, 7.5x55 Swiss, and 7.62x54 Russian. Initial headstamps will read "Frontier," later "Graf." Graf also offers a unique 123-grain V-Max bullet for the 7.62x39 and a 160-grain round-nose bullet for the 6.5 Carcano. www.grafs.com

Hodgdon Powder

Good, old slow-burning H870 is gone, but if you've missed Winchester's 540 and 571 series, they're back. Hodgdon is reintroducing them as HS-6 and HS-7, respectfully. Hodgdon offers new loading data—or one can use original 540 and 571 data. Triple Seven, Hodgdon's high energy, blackpowder substitute, has been pelletized as 50-caliber/50-grain charges designed for in-lines with #209 shotshell ignition. The traditional Pyrodex pellet

Muzzleloaders will be pleased with Hodgdon's new 54-caliber Pyrodex pellet.

line has been expanded to include 45-caliber/50-grain, 50-caliber/50-grain, 50-caliber/30-grain, and 54-caliber/60-grain loadings. There's a brand new Pyrodex brochure at your dealer that provides interesting loading data for metallic cartridges and shotshells, as well as muzzleloaders. Speaking about

interesting reloading data, Hodgdon has issued "reduced" loading data for the most popular rifle and shotgun calibers to assist beginning shooters, youths, and informal target shooters. There's a new "annual" reloading manual available that includes data for the latest short magnums plus 5000 other loads and some great articles from the past by Skeeter Skelton and Bob Milek. www.hodgdon.com www.pyrodex.com

Hornady

Bonded bullets are really in this year. Hornady has taken its successful SST design and bonded the jacket and core. Called "InterBond," the new line of bullets retains 90% of its mass, is available in Hornady-brand ammunition as well as components, and will be competitively priced. Initially, the line will feature a 130-grain/270-caliber; 139- and 145-grain/7mm, and 150- and 165-grain/30-caliber bullets. The standard SST design is being introduced in the muzzleloading sabot line. Look for some very streamlined 200-grain 45-caliber, and 250- and 300-grain 50-caliber sabots. Need some 20-caliber bullets for your 20 Squirrel? Look no further. Hornady makes a 33-grain V-Max bullet in .204-inch diameter. There's a lot of fresh loading data available in Hornady's new, two-volume reloading manual for many of the short magnums and other recent cartridge introductions. See Graf and Huntington listings for additional products. www.hornady.com

Huntington

If you need brass, or bullets, or RCBS products, Huntington is the first stop. They are particularly strong in the rare and obsolete caliber department. For example, this year they're adding brass for the 5.6x35R Verling, 280 Ross, 8mm Lebel, 11.2x72 Schuler, 450 NE thin rim, 450 #2, 475 #2, 475 NE, 476 WR, and 500 NE 3-inch. They're the only source for 8mm Nambu bullets and carry the full Woodleigh line. How about 7mm-TCU, 220 Russian, 5.6x61 Vom Hofe, 6mm Remington Benchrest, or 500 Linebaugh brass? Huntington has them—plus they offer a unique service for cartridge collectors and handloaders. They will sell you a single case in every conceivable caliber for a very reasonable price. See their extensive catalog at www.huntington.com

Lapua

Lead-free is in at Lapua with the introduction of their "Naturalis" bullet in 6.5mm, 308 and 9.3mm. It's a monolithic hunting bullet with a plastic point capping a hollow cavity. The new bullet is available in loaded ammunition as well as a component. Under their Aficionado + line of competitive target ammunition are new loadings in 223 Rem. and 308 Win. featuring their highly acclaimed Scenar HPBT match bullets. www.lapua.com www.kaltron.com

Lazzeroni

The father of the short magnums is stretching out in the other direction with the production of the 30-caliber "Battlestar" cartridge. Design characteristics for this super non-belted magnum call for a 180-grain bullet at 3700 fps! New, too, is a proprietary plated, monolithic bullet with relief grooves cut into the shank. Named the "LazerHead," the projectile is available in 120-grain/7mm; 150-grain/30-caliber;

Hornady's two-volume reloading manual contains vital information on their new bullets and cartridge lines.

Hornady new core-bonded bullet is based on the streamlined SST design.

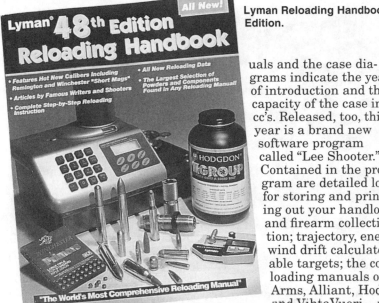

Lyman Reloading Handbook, 48th Edition.

With the popularity of the 300 WSM increasing daily, Norma decided to produce true match quality brass.

and a non-grooved version in 185-grain/338-caliber.
www.lazzeroni.com

Lee Precision

The father of the most affordable and unique reloading equipment line in the world, Richard Lee, has just released the 2nd edition of his book, *Modern Reloading*. This is the most personal and refreshingly written reloading manual in the field. Within its 720 pages is a complete description of the history, theory and practice of reloading that includes original chapters on bullet casting, reduced loads, measuring powder by volume, pressure, and, of course, a full description of the design and function of Lee tools. There is loading data for cartridges not normally covered in other man-

uals and the case diagrams indicate the year of introduction and the capacity of the case in cc's. Released, too, this year is a brand new software program called "Lee Shooter." Contained in the program are detailed logs for storing and printing out your handloading data and firearm collection information; trajectory, energy, recoil, wind drift calculators; printable targets; the complete loading manuals of Accurate Arms, Alliant, Hodgdon, IMR and VihtaVuori—plus the Lee Precision catalog. Priced at only $19.98 plus postage, it's another great Lee bargain.
www.leeprecision.com

Liberty Shooting Supplies

Liberty's a great source for hard-to-find cast bullet designs. Recent introductions include bullets for the 22 WCF, 32 Colt (heeled), 351 Win. and 44 Evans (.423"). Then there are old standbys like 22 Hi-Power, 310 Cadet, 348 Win., 38-55 (.379"), 41 Swiss, and 43 Spanish and Mauser–plus all standard calibers. Many bullets can be custom-sized to order. Liberty bullets are quality products.
www.libertyshootingsupplies.com

Load From A Disk

An upgraded and expanded Version #4 of this popular program is now available.
www.loadammo.com/upgrade.htm

LYMAN

Lyman has just released the 48th Edition of its "*Reloading Handbook*." Advertised as the "world's most comprehensive reloading manual," it lives up to its reputation. Packed with lots of new data and powders and informative articles, the new manual has returned to the practice of indicating the potentially most accurate load. This is a "must have" reloading manual.

Magtech

"Guardian Gold" is the label for Magtech's latest line of jacketed hollowpoint ammunition for law enforcement and personal defense. The new loading is available in 380, 38 Special, 357, 9mm, 40 S&W and 45 Auto. Also new is their "Clean

"Guardian Gold" is the label given Magtech's latest line of JHP ammunition for law enforcement and personal protection.

Range" line—in 380, 38 Special, 9mm and 40 S&W—that features a fully encapsulated bullet and lead-free primer.
www.magtechammunition.com

Norma

With the popularity of the 300 WSM increasing daily, Norma is offering a match-grade case for the new caliber. www.norma.cc

Northern Precision

Imagine a bonded core, spitzer bullet for the 454 Casull that fits in a Freedom Arms cylinder. Northern Precision has them in weights from 300 to 375 grains. A 300-grain/308 bullet short enough to function in standard cases and actions? They've done it by using a powdered tungsten core. There's a new 250-grain, bonded-core bullet for the 356 Win., and a 400-grain/416 Sabre Star bullet designed to open up quickly. Just right for woodchucks. Call for their very unique catalog. (315) 493-1711

Nosler's new .224-inch 77-grain match bullet is designed for AR 15s and 16s with a 1:8 twist.

Nosler's new 728-page reloading manual includes fresh data on the short magnums as well as on the latest Nosler and Combined Technology bullets.

Nosler

Move over Partition. This year Nosler's gone bonded core with a line called "AccuBond". These boattail, polymer-tipped bullets cover the caliber spectrum with a 270/140-grain, 7mm/160-grain, 308/200-grain, 338/225-grain and a 375/260-grain being offered. The 270 WSM, with its attendant higher velocities, has had some influence at Nosler with two, heavier 270-caliber bullets making their appearance—a 140-grain Partition and a 150-grain Ballistic Silvertip. Responding to the almost universal use of the 223 Remington as an

Remington's new AccuTip bullets are designed for sub minute-of-angle accuracy, flat trajectories, and high down-range energy.

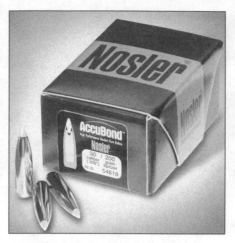

Move over Partition, Nolser's latest AccuBond hunting bullet features a bonded core.

across-the-board match cartridge, Nosler has designed a 77-grain boattail, hollowpoint with a high ballistic coefficient of .340. The new bullet is designed to function through the magazines of semi-automatic service rifles. Finally, Nosler has released a new 728-page reloading manual with lots of new data and new bullets. The graphic displays of loading density, as well as technical footnotes, make this manual a must. www.nosler.com

Old Western Scrounger

What do you do when you have 600,000 rounds of 5mm Rem. Rimfire Magnum back-ordered from your customers? You go make it, right? Well, the Old Western Scrounger has done just that. He's contracted with Aguila to make a run of 2 million rounds. Hold on to your Remington Models 591 and 592. Ammo is on the way. www.ows-ammunition.com

Remington

Did I say bonded core was in? Remington has taken their superb Core-Lokt design and added a bonded core. The new Premier Core-Lokt Ultra bullet design is available in the 243 Win., 270 Win., 7mm Rem. Mag.,

7mm Rem. Ultra Mag., 7mm Rem. SA Ultra Mag., 308 Win., 30-06, 300 Win., 300 Rem. Ultra Mag. and 300 Rem. SA Ultra Mag.

And there's another new rifle bullet at Big Green—a highly accurate, polymer-tipped Premier AccuTip that will be loaded in eight calibers from 243 through 300 Win. Mag. There are three new additions to the metallic cartridge line: the 17 Hornady Magnum Rimfire with a 17-grain V-Max pill; the 454 Casull with a 300-grain bonded-core JHP; and the return of the 350 Rem. Mag. with a 200-grain Core-Lokt SP. Building on their Hevi-Shot relationship, Remington is fielding a Hevi-Shot 00 buckshot loading in the 2 3/4-inch/12-gauge case and much requested Hevi-Shot Magnum Turkey loads in the 3 1/2-inch /10 gauge and 3-inch/20 gauge. Speaking about the 20 gauge, there's a new 260-grain Core-Lokt Ultra Bonded slug for the 2 3/4-inch/20-gauge case with a muzzle velocity of 1900 fps. Accommodating 2 3/4-inch/12-gauge sluggers, Remington has added a BuckHammer Attached-Sabot 1-1/4 oz. soft lead slug to its lineup that is not only accurate but offers tremendous expansion. Finally, going for speed, there's a 7/8 oz. Foster-type rifled slug for the 2 3/4-inch / 12 gauge with a velocity of 1800 fps. www.remington.com

Schroeder Bullets

Here's a small firm that specializes in old and odd size bullets and brass. Need some 22 Cooper Centerfire Magnum or 7.92x33mm *Kurz* brass? Schroeder makes it. His latest creation is 25 Stevens centerfire brass. Interesting catalog. (619) 423-3523

Featuring a 1-1/4 oz. slug with an attached sabot, Remington's Express BuckHammer offers accuracy with tremendous expansion.

Remington's Core-Lokt Ultra Bullets provide controlled 1.8X expansion with deep penetration and 85% weight retention.

Sierra's 5th Edition reloading manual includes the latest cartridges and powders and is bound in a single volume.

The 500 S&W has been wildcatted already as evidenced by SSK's 458/500 and 475/500 Woodswalkers, pictured here with the parent 500.

Sellier & Bellot

NONTOX primers combined with TFMJ bullets are being offered in 9mm and 38 Special this year. www.sb-usa.com

Sierra Bullets

Sierra's 5th Edition *Rifle & Handgun Reloading Manual* has been released and it's better than ever. Lots of new powders and cartridges. The exterior ballistics chapter has been condensed and rewritten so that the whole 1149-page manual now fits in one binder.

Released in concert with the new manual is Sierra's "INFINITY" Version 5.0 exterior ballistics software program. The program has been expanded to include the bullets of all major manufacturers and ammunition companies. A Windows format makes it user-friendly and flexible. No new bullets, but some great Sierra match-grade bullet jackets in 22, 6mm and 30 caliber are now available. www.sierrabullets.com

SSK Industries

What takes 235 grains of 5010 powder and a 1173-grain bullet? J.D. Jones' latest creation—the 14.5mm JDJ. Based on a necked-up and blown-out 50 BMG case, and fired from a 50-caliber rifle, the 14.5mm JDJ was designed for folks who consider the 50 BMG just a bit wimpy. After the appearance of the 500 S&W case, it didn't take JD long to create two new rounds for the Encore. Using the S&W basic case, he's necked it down to form the 475/500 and 458/500 JDJ Woodswalkers. SSK is also busy converting and chambering the AR10T for the 270, 7mm, and 300 WSM. www.sskindustries.com

Starline

Some interesting new brass this year—50 Alaskan, 50 Beowulf, 50-110, 480 Ruger, 41 Colt, 32 S&W and a special run of 475 Wildey–for Wildey. In the planning stages are the 38-55, 45 Auto Rim, some hard-to-find metrics. www.starlinebrass.com

Swift

Kudos to Swift for producing the highest quality handloading manual to date. Swift's hardbound *Reloading Manual Number One* is simply gorgeous. I laid my copy out on our coffee table. It offers extensive coverage of 49 rifle and pistol cartridges loaded with Swift's premium A-Frame and Scirocco bullets. The trajectory charts are adjacent to the loading data, and each cartridge is highlighted with an artist's rendering of a game animal commonly associated with the caliber. It's a real collector's item. (785) 754-3959.

West Coast Bullets

How do you tell duty ammunition from frangible target ammo? West Coast produces non-toxic, sintered iron-tin-copper bullets for all popular handgun calibers–plus the 223 Winchester. To ensure none of their loaded frangible bullets are accidentally carried while an officer is on duty, they color their bullets purple, green; in fact, just about any color you want. www.westcoastbullets.com

Winchester Ammunition

Catching all of us by surprise, Winchester created their new "Super Short Magnum" series in 223 and 243. Designed to equal or exceed the velocities of the 22/250 and 240 Weatherby respectfully, the 223 WSSM and 243 WSSM are being teamed with super short-action Winchester Model 70s and

SSK's 14.5mm JDJ cartridge takes 235 grains of powder and an 1173-grain bullet.

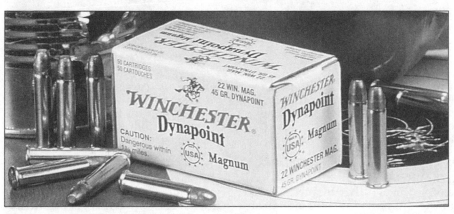

With the success of the Dyna Point design in the LR, Winchester is now loading a new Dyna Point in the 22 Rimfire Magnum.

Winchester's Supreme 20-gauge Platinum Tip slug makes the 20-gauge a serious deer and bear gun.

Sporting clays shooters will find Winchester's new hard shot, high-velocity loads in 28 and .410 gauges ideal.

41 Magnum shooters will be delighted with Winchester's new 240-grain Platinum Tip loading in the handgun line.

Winchester surprised the shooting world with the release of their hot, little 223 and 243 Super Short Magnums.

The 22 WRF is being returned to the Winchester rimfire line.

Browning A Bolts. Having taken several whitetail this past fall using the 223 WSSM loaded with Winchester's 64-grain deer bullet at 3600 fps, I can report that the 223 WSSM is impressive. The 243 WSSM should be spectacular. The 223 WSSM is currently loaded with a 55-grain Ballistic Silvertip (BST) in the Supreme line and a 55-grain soft point and 64-grain Power-Point in the Super-X line. 243 WSSM loadings feature a 55-grain BST and 95-grain BST in the Supreme line and a 100-grain Power-Point in the Super-X. Building on the strength of their existing short magnums, Winchester is giving the 270 WSM a 150-grain BST and Power-Point loading at 3150 fps that should prove ideal on larger big game. Similarly, the 300 WSM is getting a 180-grain BST loading this year. The Supreme Varmint line has been expanded to include 55-grain BST loadings for the 223 Remington and 22-250 Remington.

The old 22 WRF is back in the line, while the 22 Rimfire Magnum sports a new bullet, the 45-grain Dynapoint at 1550 fps. Will 41 Rem. Mag. fans be happy! Winchester is introducing a 240-grain Platinum Tip loading at 1250 fps.

The 28 and .410 gauges are getting the new High Strength AA hull and extra hard shot in the Super Sport line. The 28 gauge will feature 3/4 oz. of #7-1/2 and #8-1/2 while the .410 will carry 1/2 oz. of #8-1/2. All three new loads have a muzzle velocity of 1300 fps. And speaking of shot, #8-1/2 is being brought back to the 12-gauge AA Light and Xtra Lite target lines. There's a new 260-grain Platinum Tip Sabot Slug for the 20-gauge with a velocity of 1700 fps. Even the muzzlestuffers are getting something new this year—a 200-grain Platinum Sabot round for the 45-caliber ML and a 400-grain model for the 54-caliber ML. Finally, controlling the cost of non-toxic waterfowl loads, Winchester is adding a 3-inch/20-gauge steel shot loading of #2 and #4 to its Xpert line.
www.winchester.com   ●

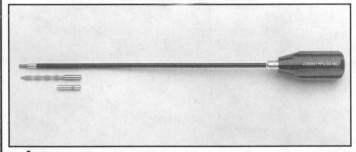

SHOOTER'S MARKETPLACE

FINE GUN STOCKS

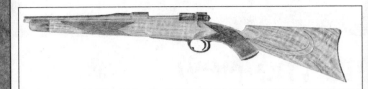

Manufacturing custom and production gunstocks for hundreds of models of rifles and shotguns—made from the finest stock woods and available in all stages of completion.

Visit www.gunstocks.com to view their bargain list of fine custom gunstocks. Each displayed in full color.

GREAT AMERICAN GUNSTOCK COMPANY

3420 Industrial Drive
Yuba City, CA 95993
Phone: 530-671-4570
Fax: 530-671-3906
Gunstock Hotline: 800-784-GUNS (4867)
Web: www.gunstocks.com
E-mail: gunstox@syix.com

BORDER CLASSIC

Gary Reeder Custom Guns, builder of full custom guns including hunting handguns, custom Encores, large caliber hunting rifles and over 20 different series of cowboy guns, including our Border Classic, shown. This beauty is the first ever snubbie Schofield, and can be built on any current Schofield. Fully engraved, round butted, with their Black Chromex finish and a solid silver Mexican coin for the front sight, this one is truly a masterpiece. See them all at their website, or call for a brochure.

GARY REEDER CUSTOM GUNS

2601 E. 7th Avenue, Flagstaff, AZ 86004
Phone: 928-527-4100 or 928-526-3313
Website: www.reedercustomguns.com

NEW CATALOG!

Catalog #25 is Numrich's latest edition! This 1,200 page catalog features more than 500 schematics for use in identifying obsolete and current commercial, military, antique and foreign guns. Edition #25 contains 180,000 items from their inventory of over 650 million parts and accessories and is a necessity for any true gunsmith or hobbyist. It has been the industry's leading reference book for firearm parts and identification for over 50 years!

Order Item #YP-25 $12.95
U.S. Orders: Bulk mail, shipping charges included
Foreign Orders: Air mail, 30-day delivery; or surface, 90-day delivery. Shipping charges additional.

NUMRICH GUN PARTS CORPORATION

226 Williams Lane, P.O. Box 299, West Hurley, NY 12491
Orders Toll-Free: 866-NUMRICH (866-686-7424)
Customer Service: (845) 679-4867
Toll-Free Fax: (877) GUNPART
Web: e-GunParts.com • E-mail: info@gunpartscorp.com

HIGH QUALITY OPTICS

One of the best indicators of quality is a scope's resolution number. The smaller the number, the better. Their scope has a resolution number of 2.8 seconds of angle. This number is about 20% smaller (better) than other well-known scopes costing much more. It means that two .22 caliber bullets can be a hair's breadth apart and edges of each still be clearly seen. With a Shepherd at 800 yards, you will be able to tell a four inch antler from a four inch ear and a burrowing owl from a prairie dog. Bird watchers will be able to distinguish a Tufted Titmouse from a Ticked-Off Field Mouse. Send for free catalog.

SHEPHERD ENTERPRISES, INC.

Box 189, Waterloo, NE 68069
Phone: 402-779-2424 • Fax: 402-779-4010
E-mail: shepherd@shepherdscopes.com • Web: www.shepherdscopes.com

SHOOTER'S MARKETPLACE

PRECISION RIFLE REST

Bald Eagle Precision Machine Co. offers a rifle rest perfect for the serious benchrester or dedicated varminter.

"The Slingshot" or Next Generation has 60° front legs. The rest is constructed of aircraft-quality aluminum or fine grain cast iron and weighs 12 to 20 lbs. The finish is 3 coats of Imron clear. Primary height adjustments are made with a rack and pinion gear. Secondary adjustment uses a mariner wheel with thrust bearings for smooth operation. A hidden fourth leg allows for lateral movement on the bench.

Bald Eagle offers approximately 150 rest combinations to choose from, including windage adjustable, right or left hand, cast aluminum or cast iron.

Prices: $175.00 to $345.00

BALD EAGLE PRECISION MACHINE CO.
101-K Allison Street, Lock Haven, PA 17745
Phone: 570-748-6772 — Fax: 570-748-4443
Web: www.baldeaglemachine.com

FOLDING BIPODS

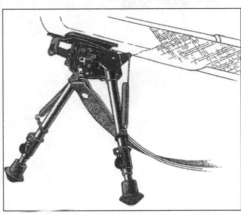

Harris Bipods clamp securely to most stud-equipped bolt-action rifles and are quick-detachable. With adapters, they will fit some other guns. On all models except the Model LM, folding legs have completely adjustable spring-return extensions. The sling swivel attaches to the clamp. This time-proven design is manufactured with heat-treated steel and hard alloys and has a black anodized finish.

Series S Bipods rotate 35° for instant leveling on uneven ground. Hinged base has tension adjustment and buffer springs to eliminate tremor or looseness in crotch area of bipod. They are otherwise similar to non-rotating Series 1A2.

Thirteen models are available from Harris Engineering; literature is free.

HARRIS ENGINEERING INC.
Dept: GD54, Barlow, KY 42024
Phone: 270-334-3633 • Fax: 270-334-3000

6x18x40 VARMINT/TARGET SCOPE

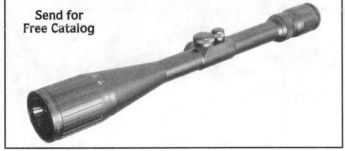

Send for Free Catalog

The Shepherd 6x18x40 Varmint/Target Scope makes long-range varmint and target shooting child's play. Just pick the ranging circle that best fits your target (be it prairie dogs, coyotes or paper varmints) and Shepherd's exclusive, patented Dual Reticle Down Range System does the rest. You won't believe how far you can accurately shoot, even with rimfire rifles.

Shepherd's superior lens coating mean superior light transmission and tack-sharp resolution.

This new shockproof, waterproof scope features 1/4 minute-of-angle clicks on the ranging circles and friction adjustments on the crosshairs that allows fine-tuning to 0.001 MOA. A 40mm adjustable objective provides a 5.5-foot field of view at 100 yards (16x setting). 16.5 FOV @ 6X.

SHEPHERD ENTERPRISES, INC.
Box 189, Waterloo, NE 68069
Phone: 402-779-2424 • Fax: 402-779-4010
Email: shepherd@shepherdscopes.com • Web: www.shepherdscopes.com

CUSTOM RESTORATION/CASE COLORING

Doug Turnbull Restoration continues to offer bone charcoal case hardening work, matching the original case colors produced by Winchester, Colt, Marlin, Parker, L.C. Smith, Fox and other manufacturers. Also available is charcoal blue, known as Carbona or machine blue, a prewar finish used by most makers. "Specializing in the accurate recreation of historical metal finishes on period firearms, from polishing to final finishing. Including Bone Charcoal Color Case Hardening, Charcoal Bluing, Rust Blue, and Nitre Blue".

DOUG TURNBULL RESTORATION
P.O. Box 471, 6680 Rt 5&20, Dept SM2003
Bloomfield, New York 14469 • Phone/Fax: 585-657-6338
E-mail: turnbullrest@mindspring.com
Web: www.turnbullrestoration.com

SHOOTER'S MARKETPLACE

GUNSMITHING SUPPLIES

440 pages! Filled with more than 20,000, top, brand-name accessories to make your rifles, shotguns and handguns look and work better. Plus, 136 of those pages are filled with 9,000, genuine factory parts from 16 factories so you can repair guns to original equipment specs. A huge selection of specialized gunsmithing tools help you install those parts and accessories correctly. Books and videos teach you how to do general gun work and specific repairs, shoot better, identify collectables, reload your own ammo, and buy and sell guns. Full-time tech staff answers your questions. Selection. Service. Satisfaction - 100% guaranteed. Business discounts available.

Call 1-800-741-0015 or order on-line at:
www.brownells.com
Mention Department #AH7
Price of catalog refunded with order. $5.00

FOR THE SERIOUS RELOADER...

Rooster Labs' line of top-quality, innovative products...for individual and commercial reloaders...now includes:
• **ZAMBINI** 220° Pistol Bullet Lubricant (1x4 & 2x6)
• **HVR** 220° High Velocity Rifle Bullet Lube (1x4)
• **ROOSTER JACKET** Waterproof Liquid Bullet Film Lube
• **ROOSTER BRIGHT** Brass Case Polish Media Additive ...Brilliant!
• **CFL-56** Radical Case Forming Lube...for the Wildcatter
• **PDQ-21** Spray Case Sizing Lube...quick, no contamination
• **BP-7 BLACK POWDER** 210°Bullet Lube (1x4 solid)

Rooster LABORATORIES®
P.O. Box 414605, Kansas City, MO 64141
Phone: 816-474-1622 • Fax: 816-474-7622
E-mail: roosterlabs@aol.com
Web: www.roosterlabs.com

CLENZOIL FIELD & RANGE®

This is what museums, collectors, and competitive shooters are switching to in serious numbers.

Clenzoil Field & Range® is a remarkable one-step bore cleaner, lubricant, and long-term protectant that contains absolutely no teflon or silicone, so it never gets gummy or sticky.

A regional favorite for many years, Clenzoil is finally available nationwide. Clenzoil is signing up dealers daily, but your local shop may not carry it yet. If that's the case, you may order 24 hours a day by calling 1-800-OIL-IT-UP. Dealers may join the growing Clenzoil dealer network by calling 440-899-0482.

Clenzoil is a proud supplier to ArmaLite, Inc. and Ithaca Classic Doubles.

THE CLENZOIL CORPORATION
WORLDWIDE

25670 First Street, Westlake, OH 44145
Phone: 440-899-0482 • Fax: 440-899-0483

RUGER 10-22® COMPETITION MATCHED HAMMER AND SEAR KIT

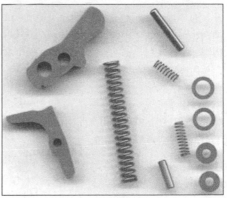

Precision EDM/CNC machined custom hammer and sear for your Ruger 10-22®. Both parts are machined from a solid billet of steel. Case hardened to RC-58-60. These are the highest quality drop in parts available on the market. They will produce a crisp 2-1/2 lbs. trigger pull. They are precision ground with Vapor hand honed engagement surfaces. Includes an Extra Power hammer spring, Extra Power disconnector spring, replacement trigger return spring, 2 hammer shims, and 2 trigger shims.

Price $55.95 plus $3.85 Priority Mail

POWER CUSTOM, INC.
29739 Hwy. J, Dept. KP, Gravois Mills, MO 65037
Phone: 1-573-372-5684 • Fax: 1-573-372-5799
Web: www.powercustom.com • E-mail: rwpowers@laurie.net

2004
GUNS ILLUSTRATED
Complete Compact
CATALOG

GUNDEX® 87

SEMI-CUSTOM ARMS

HANDGUNS
Autoloaders 95
Revolvers 97
Single Shot. 98

RIFLES
Bolt-Action Rifles 99
Autoloaders 103
Double Rifles 104
Single Shot 105

SHOTGUNS 109

COMMERCIAL ARMS

HANDGUNS
Autoloaders 114
Competition 138
Double Action Revolvers 144
Single Action Revolvers 153
Miscellaneous Handguns 162

RIFLES
Centerfire Rifles—
    Autoloaders 165
    Lever & Slide 173
    Bolt Action 181

Single Shot 208
Drillings, Combination Guns,
    Double Rifles 220
Rimfire Rifles—Autoloaders . . . 223
    Lever & Slide 227
    Bolt Actions
    & Single Shots 229
Competition Rifles—
    Centerfire & Rimfire 237

SHOTGUNS
Autoloaders 245
Slide Actions 255
Over/Unders 262
Side-by-Sides 278
Bolt Actions & Single Shots. . . . 284
Military & Police. 289

BLACKPOWDER
Single Shot Pistols 292
Revolvers 294
Muskets & Rifles 297
Shotguns. 309

AIRGUNS
Handguns 310
Long Guns. 312

MANUFACTURERS DIRECTORY
. . . . **316**

A
Accu-Tek Model HC-380 Auto Pistol, 114
Accu-Tek XL-9 Auto Pistol, 114
Airforce Talon Air Rifle, 312
Airforce Talon SS Air Rifle, 312
Airrow Model A-8S1P Stealth Air Gun, 312
Airrow Model A-8SRB Stealth Air Gun, 312
American Derringer DA 38 Model, 162
American Derringer Lady Derringer, 162
American Derringer LM-5 Automatic Pistol, 114
American Derringer Model 1, 162
American Derringer Model 10 Ultra Lightweight, 162
American Derringer Model 4, 162
American Derringer Model 6, 162
American Derringer Model 7 Ultra Lightweight, 162
American Derringer Texas Commemorative, 162
Anschutz 1416D/1516D Classic Rifles, 229
Anschutz 1416D/1516D Walnut Luxus Rifles, 229
Anschutz 1451 Target Rifle, 237
Anschutz 1451R Sporter Target Rifle, 237
Anschutz 1518D Luxus Bolt-Action Rifle, 229
Anschutz 1710D Custom Rifle, 229
Anschutz 1733D Rifle, 181
Anschutz 1740 Monte Carlo Rifle, 181
Anschutz 1743D Bolt-Action Rifle, 181
Anschutz 1808D-RT Super Running Target Rifle, 237
Anschutz 1827 Biathlon Rifle, 237
Anschutz 1827BT Fortner Biathlon Rifle, 237
Anschutz 1903 Match Rifle, 237
Anschutz 1907 Standard Match Rifle, 238
Anschutz 1911 Prone Match Rifle, 238
Anschutz 1912 Sport Rifle, 238
Anschutz 1913 Super Match Rifle, 238
Anschutz 1913 Super Match Rifle, 238
Anschutz 2002 Match Air Rifle, 312
Anschutz 2007 Match Rifle, 237
Anschutz 2012 Sport Rifle, 238
Anschutz 2013 Benchrest Rifle, 237
Anschutz 54.18MS REP Deluxe Silhouette Rifle, 238
Anschutz 64-MS R Silhouette Rifle, 237
Anschutz Model 64P Sport/Target Pistol, 162
Anschutz Super Match Special Model 2013 Rifle, 238
AR-7 Explorer Carbine, 223
Armalite AR-10 (T) Rifle, 239
Armalite AR-10(T), 165
Armalite AR-10A2, 165
Armalite AR-10A4 Special Purpose Rifle, 165
Armalite AR-180B Rifle, 165
Armalite AR-50 Rifle, 208
Armalite M15A2 Carbine, 165
Armalite M15A4 (T) Eagle Eye Rifle, 239
Armalite M15A4 Action Master Rifle, 239
Armoury R140 Hawken Rifle, 297
Armscor M-1600 Auto Rifle, 223
Armscor M-200DC Revolver, 144
Armscor M-20C Auto Carbine, 223
Armscor M-30F Field Pump Shotgun, 255
Armscor Model AK22 Auto Rifle, 223
Armsport 1866 Sharps Rifle, Carbine, 208
Armsport Model 4540 Revolver, 144
Army 1860 Percussion Revolver, 294
Arrieta Sidelock Double Shotguns, 278
ARS Hunting Master AR6 Air Rifle, 312
ARS Hunting Master AR6 Pistol, 310
ARS/Career 707 Air Rifle, 312
Arsenal USA SSR-56, 165
Arsenal USA SSR-74-2, 166
Arsenal USA SSR-85C-2, 166
Aurura TR and TT Shotguns, 262
Austin & Halleck Model 320 LR In-Line Rifle, 297
Austin & Halleck Model 420 LR In-Line Rifle, 297
Austin & Halleck Mountain Rifle, 297
Autauga 32 Auto Pistol, 114
Auto-Ordnance 1911A1 Automatic Pistol, 114
Auto-Ordnance 1927 A-1 Thompson, 166
Auto-Ordnance 1927A1 Commando, 166
Auto-Ordnance Thompson M1/M1-C, 166

GUNDEX

GUNDEX

SEMI-CUSTOM

HANDGUNS

RIFLES

SHOTGUNS

BLACKPOWDER

AIRGUNS

MANUFACTURERS
DIRECTORY

B

Baby Dragoon 1848, 1849 Pocket, Wells Fargo, 294
Baer 1911 Bullseye Wadcutter Pistol, 138
Baer 1911 Custom Carry Auto Pistol, 114
Baer 1911 National Match Hardball Pistol, 138
Baer 1911 Premier II Auto Pistol, 114
Baer 1911 S.R.P. Pistol, 114
Baer 1911 Ultimate Master Combat Pistol, 138
Ballard Model 1885 High Wall Single Shot Rifle, 208
Ballard No. 1 3/4 Far West Rifle, 208
Ballard No. 4 Perfection Rifle, 208
Ballard No. 5 Pacific Single-Shot Rifle, 208
Ballard No. 7 Long Range Rifle, 208
Ballard No. 8 Union Hill Rifle, 208
Ballard Rifle, LLC, 105
Barrett Model 82A-1 Semi-Automatic Rifle, 166
Barrett Model 95 Bolt-Action Rifle, 181
Barrett Model 99 Single Shot Rifle, 208
Beeman Crow Magnum Air Rifle, 312
Beeman HW70A Air Pistol, 310
Beeman Kodiak Air Rifle, 312
Beeman Mako MKII Air Rifle, 312
Beeman P1 Magnum Air Pistol, 310
Beeman P3 Air Pistol, 310
Beeman R1 Air Rifle, 312
Beeman R1 Carbine, 313
Beeman R11 MKII Air Rifle, 312
Beeman R7 Air Rifle, 312
Beeman R9 Air Rifle, 312
Beeman R9 Deluxe Air Rifle, 312
Beeman RX-2 Gas-Spring Magnum Air Rifle, 313
Beeman Super 12 Air Rifle, 312
Beeman/Feinwerkbau 103 Pistol, 310
Beeman/Feinwerkbau 300-S and 300 Junior Mini-Match, 313
Beeman/Feinwerkbau 603 Air Rifle, 313
Beeman/Feinwerkbau P70 and P70 Junior Air Rifle, 313
Beeman/FWB P34 Match Air Pistol, 310
Beeman/HW 97 Air Rifle, 313
Beeman/Webley Hurricane Air Pistol, 310
Beeman/Webley Tempest Air Pistol, 310
Benelli Executive Series Shotguns, 245
Benelli Legacy Shotgun, 245
Benelli M1 Field Shotgun, 245
Benelli M1 Practical, 289
Benelli M1 Tactical Shotgun, 289
Benelli M3 Convertible Shotgun, 289
Benelli Montefeltro Shotgun, 245
Benelli Nova Pump Rifled Slug Gun, 255
Benelli Nova Pump Shotgun, 255
Benelli Nova Pump Slug Gun, 255
Benelli RI Rifle, 166
Benelli Sport II Shotgun, 245
Benelli Super Black Eagle Shotgun, 245
Benelli Super Black Eagle Slug Gun, 245
Benjamin Sheridan Air Rifle, 313
Benjamin Sheridan CO2 Pellet Pistols, 310
Benjamin Sheridan Pneumatic (Pump-Up) Air Rifles, 313
Benjamin Sheridan Pneumatic Pellet Pistols, 310
Beretta 686 Onyx O/U Shotgun, 262
Beretta 686 Silver Pigeon O/U Shotgun, 262
Beretta A391 Xtreme 3.5 Auto Shotguns, 246
Beretta AL391 Urika Auto Shotguns, 245
Beretta AL391 Urika Gold and Gold Sporting Auto Shotguns, 246
Beretta AL391 Urika Parallel Target RL and SL Auto Shotguns, 246
Beretta AL391 Urika Sporting Auto Shotguns, 246
Beretta AL391 Urika Trap Auto Shotguns, 246
Beretta AL391 Urika Youth Shotgun, 246
Beretta DT10 Trident Shotguns, 262
Beretta DT10 Trident Trap Top Single Shotgun, 284
Beretta ES100 Auto Shotguns, 246
Beretta Express Double Rifles, 104
Beretta Express SSO O/U Double Rifles, 220
Beretta Model 1201FP Ghost Ring Auto Shotgun, 289
Beretta Model 21 Bobcat Pistol, 115

Beretta Model 3032 Tomcat Pistol, 115
Beretta Model 455 SxS Express Rifle, 220
Beretta Model 686 Whitewing O/U, 262
Beretta Model 80 Cheetah Series DA Pistols, 115
Beretta Model 8000/8040/8045 Cougar Pistol, 115
Beretta Model 8000/8040/8045 Mini Cougar, 115
Beretta Model 86 Cheetah, 115
Beretta Model 9000S Compact Pistol, 115
Beretta Model 92 Billennium Limited Edition, 115
Beretta Model 92FS Compact and Compact Type M Pistol, 115
Beretta Model 92FS Pistol, 115
Beretta Model 92FS/96 Brigadier Pistols, 115
Beretta Model 96 Pistol, 115
Beretta Model SO5, SO6, SO9 Shotguns, 263
Beretta Model U22 Neos, 116
Beretta Over/Under Field Shotguns, 263
Beretta Premium Grade Shotguns, 109
Beretta S687EL Gold Pigeon Sporting O/U, 263
Beretta Series 682 Gold E Skeet, Trap, Sporting Over/Unders, 262
Beretta Ultralight Deluxe Over/Under Shotgun, 263
Beretta Ultralight Over/Under, 262
Bersa Thunder 380 Auto Pistols, 116
Bersa Thunder 45 Ultra Compact Pistol, 116
BF Classic Hunting Pistol, 138
BF Ultimate Silhouette HB Single Shot Pistol, 138
Blaser R93 Bolt-Action Rifle, 181
Blaser R93 Long Range Rifle, 239
Blue Thunder/Commodore 1911-Style Auto Pistols, 116
Bond Arms Defender Derringer, 163
Bostonian Percussion Rifle, 297
Briley 1911-Style Auto Pistols, 95
BRNO 500 Combination Guns, 220
BRNO 501.2 Over/Under Shotgun, 263
BRNO 98 Bolt-Action Rifle, 181
BRNO Tau-200 Air Rifle, 313
BRNO Tau-7 CO2 Match Pistol, 310
BRNO ZBK 100 Single Barrel Shotgun, 284
BRNO ZBK 110 Single Shot Rifle, 209
BRNO ZH 300 Combination Gun, 220
BRNO ZH 300 Over/Under Shotgun, 263
BRNO ZH Double Rifles, 220
BRNO ZKM 611 Auto Rifle, 223
Brown Classic Single Shot Pistol, 163
Brown Model 97D Single Shot Rifle, 208
Browning 425 Sporting Clays, 265
Browning A-Bolt Classic Hunter, 182
Browning A-Bolt Composite Stalker, 183
Browning A-Bolt Custom Trophy Rifle, 182
Browning A-Bolt Eclipse Hunter, 182
Browning A-Bolt Eclipse M-1000, 182
Browning A-Bolt Medallion Left-Hand, 182
Browning A-Bolt Medallion, 182
Browning A-Bolt Micro Hunter, 182
Browning A-Bolt Rifles, 181
Browning A-Bolt Stainless Stalker, 183
Browning A-Bolt White Gold Medallion, 182
Browning BAR High-Grade Auto Rifles, 167
Browning BAR Mark II Lightweight Semi-Auto, 166
Browning BAR Mark II Safari Rifle in Magnum Calibers, 166
Browning BAR Mark II Safari Semi-Auto Rifle, 166
Browning BAR Mark I, 103
Browning BAR Stalker Auto Rifles, 167
Browning BL-22 Lever-Action Rifle, 227
Browning BPR Pump Rifle, 173
Browning BPS 10 Gauge Camo Pump, 255
Browning BPS 10 Gauge Shotguns, 255
Browning BPS Game Gun Deer Hunter, 256
Browning BPS Game Gun Turkey Special, 256
Browning BPS Micro Pump, 256
Browning BPS NWTF Turkey Series Pump Shotgun, 256
Browning BPS Pump Shotgun, 255
Browning BPS Stalker Pump Shotgun, 256
Browning BPS Waterfowl Camo Pump Shotgun, 256
Browning BT-100 Trap Shotgun, 284
Browning BT-99 Trap Shotgun, 284
Browning Buck Mark 5.5, 117

Browning Buck Mark Bullseye, 117
Browning Buck Mark Bullseye, 139
Browning Buck Mark Camper, 116
Browning Buck Mark Challenge, 116
Browning Buck Mark Field 5.5, 139
Browning Buck Mark Micro, 116
Browning Buck Mark Semi-Auto Rifles, 223
Browning Buck Mark Silhouette, 138
Browning Buck Mark Standard 22 Pistol, 116
Browning Buck Mark Target 5.5, 138
Browning Citori Feather XS Shotguns, 265
Browning Citori High Grade Shotguns, 265
Browning Citori Lightning Feather O/U, 264
Browning Citori O/U Shotguns, 263
Browning Citori Sporting Hunter, 264
Browning Citori Ultra XS Skeet, 264
Browning Citori Ultra XS Sporting, 264
Browning Citori Ultra XS Trap, 264
Browning Citori XT Trap Over/Under, 264
Browning Express Rifles, 104
Browning Gold 10 Auto Shotgun, 248
Browning Gold 10 Gauge Auto Combo, 248
Browning Gold Classic Hunter Auto Shotgun, 247
Browning Gold Classic Stalker, 247
Browning Gold Deer Stalker, 247
Browning Gold Fusion™ Auto Shotgun, 248
Browning Gold Hunter Auto Shotgun, 246
Browning Gold Ladies/Youth Sporting Clays Auto, 247
Browning Gold Light 10 Gauge Auto Shotgun, 248
Browning Gold Micro Auto Shotgun, 247
Browning Gold Mossy Oak® Break-Up Shotguns, 247
Browning Gold Mossy Oak® Shadow Grass Shotguns, 247
Browning Gold NWTF Turkey Series Camo Shotgun, 248
Browning Gold Rifled Deer Hunter Auto Shotgun, 247
Browning Gold Sporting Clays Auto, 247
Browning Gold Sporting Golden Clays, 247
Browning Gold Stalker Auto Shotguns, 247
Browning Gold Turkey/Waterfowl Camo Shotgun, 248
Browning Gold Upland Special Auto Shotgun, 248
Browning Hi-Power 9mm Automatic Pistol, 116
Browning Hi-Power Luxus, 95
Browning Hi-Power Practical Pistol, 116
Browning Light Sporting 802 ES O/U, 265
Browning Lightning BLR Lever-Action Rifle, 173
Browning Lightning BLR Long Action, 173
Browning Lightning Sporting Clays, 265
Browning Micro Citori Lightning, 264
Browning Model 1885 BPCR Rifle, 209
Browning Model 1885 High Wall Single Shot Rifle, 208
Browning Model 1885 Low Wall Rifle, 209
Browning Model 1885 Low Wall Traditional Hunter, 209
Browning Nitra Citori XS Sporting Clays, 265
Browning NWTF Gold Turkey Stalker, 248
Browning Semi-Auto 22 Luxe, 103
Browning Semi-Auto 22 Rifle, 223
Browning Semi-Auto 22, Grade VI, 223
Browning Special Sporting Clays, 265
Browning Superlight Citori Over/Under, 264
Browning Superposed & BSL Shotguns, 111
BSA Magnum Goldstar Magnum Air Rifle, 313
BSA Magnum Supersport™ Air Rifle, 313
BSA Magnum Superstar™ MK2 Magnum Air Rifle, Carbine, 313
BSA Magnum Superten Air Rifle, 313
BSA Meteor MK6 Air Rifle, 313
Buck Mark Commemorative, 117
Bushmaster DCM Competition Rifle, 239
Bushmaster M17S Bullpup Rifle, 167
Bushmaster M4/M4A3 Post-Ban Carbine, 167
Bushmaster Semi-Auto Rifles, 103
Bushmaster Shorty XM15 E2S Carbine, 167
Bushmaster Varminter Rifle, 167
Bushmaster XM15 E25 AK Shorty Carbine, 167
Bushmaster XM15 E2S Dissipator Carbine, 167
Bushmaster XM15 E2S Target Model Rifle, 239
Bushmaster XM15 E2S V-Match Rifle, 240

C

C. Sharps Arms 1875 Classic Sharps, 209
C. Sharps Arms Custom New Model 1877 Long Range Target Rifle, 210
C. Sharps Arms New Model 1874 Old Reliable, 209
C. Sharps Arms New Model 1875 Old Reliable Rifle, 209
C. Sharps Arms New Model 1875 Target & Long Range, 209
C. Sharps Arms New Model 1885 Highwall Rifle, 209
C. Sharps Arms Rifles, 106
Cabanas Espronceda IV Bolt-Action Rifle, 229
Cabanas Laser Rifle, 229
Cabanas Leyre Bolt-Action Rifle, 229
Cabanas Master Bolt-Action Rifle, 229
Cabela's 1858 Henry Replica, 173
Cabela's 1860 Army Snubnose Revolver, 294
Cabela's 1862 Police Snubnose Revolver, 294
Cabela's 1866 Winchester Replica, 173
Cabela's 1873 Winchester Replica, 173
Cabela's Blackpowder Shotguns, 309
Cabela's Blue Ridge Rifle, 297
Cabela's Kodiak Express Double Rifle, 298
Cabela's Millennium Revolver, 153
Cabela's Sharps Basic Rifle, 210
Cabela's Sharps Sporting Rifle, 210
Cabela's Sporterized Hawken Hunter Rifle, 298
Cabela's Traditional Hawken, 297
Carbon One Bolt-Action Rifle, 183
Century Gun Dist. Model 100 Single-action, 153
Charles Daly Diamond DL Double Shotgun, 278
Charles Daly Diamond GTX DL Hunter O/U, 267
Charles Daly Diamond GTX Sporting O/U Shotgun, 266
Charles Daly Diamond GTX Trap AE-MC O/U Shotgun, 266
Charles Daly Diamond Regent DL Double Shotgun, 278
Charles Daly Diamond Regent GTX DL Hunter O/U, 266
Charles Daly Empire Combination Gun, 220
Charles Daly Empire EDL Hunter O/U, 266
Charles Daly Empire Grade Auto Rifle, 224
Charles Daly Empire Grade Rifle, 183
Charles Daly Empire Grade Rifle, 230
Charles Daly Empire Hunter AE-MC Double Shotgun, 278
Charles Daly Empire Magnum Grade Rifle, 229
Charles Daly Empire Sporting O/U, 266
Charles Daly Empire Trap AE MC, 266
Charles Daly Field Grade Auto Rifle, 223
Charles Daly Field Grade Rifle, 229
Charles Daly Field Hunter AE Shotgun, 266
Charles Daly Field Hunter AE-MC, 266
Charles Daly Field Hunter Over/Under Shotgun, 265
Charles Daly Field II, AE-MC Hunter Double Shotgun, 278
Charles Daly M-1911-A1P Auto Loading Pistol, 117
Charles Daly Superior Bolt-Action Rifle, 183
Charles Daly Superior Bolt-Action Rifle, 229
Charles Daly Superior Combination Gun, 220
Charles Daly Superior Hunter AE Shotgun, 266
Charles Daly Superior Hunter and Superior MC Double Shotgun, 278
Charles Daly Superior Magnum Grade Rifle, 229
Charles Daly Superior Sporting O/U, 266
Charles Daly Superior Trap AE MC, 266
Charles Daly True Youth Bolt-Action Rifle, 230
Chipmunk 410 Youth Shotgun, 284
Chipmunk Single Shot Rifle, 230
Chipmunk TM (Target Model), 230
Cimarron 1860 Henry Replica, 173
Cimarron 1866 Winchester Replicas, 174
Cimarron 1872 Open Top Revolver, 154
Cimarron 1873 Long Range Rifle, 174
Cimarron 1873 Short Rifle, 174
Cimarron 1873 Sporting Rifle, 174
Cimarron Billy Dixon 1874 Sharps Sporting Rifle, 210
Cimarron Bisley Model Single-Action Revolvers, 153
Cimarron Flat Top Single-Action Revolvers, 153
Cimarron Lightning SA, 153
Cimarron Model "P" Jr., 153
Cimarron Model 1885 High Wall Rifle, 210
Cimarron Model P, 153

Cimarron Quigley Model 1874 Sharps Sporting Rifle, 210
Cimarron Roughrider Artillery Model Single-Action, 153
Cimarron Silhouette Model 1874 Sharps Sporting Rifle, 210
Cimarron Thunderer Revolver, 154
Cobra Big Bore Derringers, 163
Cobra D-Series Derringers, 163
Cobra Enterprises FS32 Auto Pistol, 117
Cobra Enterprises FS380 Auto Pistol, 117
Cobra Industries CA32, CA380, 117
Cobra Industries Patriot Pistol , 117
Cobra Long-Bore Derringers, 163
Colt 38 Super, 118
Colt Accurized Rifle, 240
Colt Cowboy Single-Action Revolver, 154
Colt Defender, 118
Colt Gold Cup Model O Pistol, 139
Colt Gunsite Pistol, 118
Colt Match Target Competition HBAR II Rifle, 240
Colt Match Target Competition HBAR Rifle, 240
Colt Match Target HBAR Rifle, 240
Colt Match Target Model Rifle, 240
Colt Match Target Rifle, 167
Colt Model 1991 Model O Auto Pistol, 117
Colt Model 1991 Model O Commander Auto Pistol, 117
Colt Series 70, 118
Colt Single-Action Army Revolver, 154
Colt Special Combat Government, 139
Colt XSE Lightweight Commander Auto Pistol, 118
Colt XSE Series Model O Auto Pistols, 117
Comanche I, II, III DA Revolvers, 144
Comanche Super Single Shot Pistol, 163
Competitor Single Shot Pistol, 139
Cook & Brother Confederate Carbine, 298
Cooper Model 57-M Bolt-Action Rifle, 230
Crosman 2260 Air Rifle, 314
Crosman Auto Air II Pistol, 310
Crosman Black Venom Pistol, 310
Crosman Magnum Air Pistols, 310
Crosman Model 1008 Repeat Air, 310
Crosman Model 1077 Repeat Air Rifle, 314
Crosman Model 1377 Air Pistols, 310
Crosman Model 2100 Classic Air Rifle, 314
Crosman Model 2200 Magnum Air Rifle, 314
Crosman Model 2289 Rifle, 314
Crosman Model 66 Powermaster, 313
Crosman Model 760 Pumpmaster, 313
Crosman Semi Auto Air Pistol, 310
Crossfire Shotgun/Rifle, 289
Cumberland Mountain Plateau Rifle, 211
CVA Bobcat Rifle, 298
CVA Eclipse 209 Magnum In-Line Rifle, 298
CVA Firebolt Musketmag Bolt-Action In-Line Rifles, 298
CVA Hawken Pistol, 292
CVA HunterBolt 209 Magnum Rifle, 298
CVA Mountain Rifle, 298
CVA Plainsman Rifle, 298
CVA St. Louis Hawken Rifle, 298
CVA Stag Horn 209 Magnum Rifle, 298
CVA Trapper Percussion Shotgun, 309
CVA Youth Hunter Rifle, 298
CZ 100 Auto Pistol, 119
CZ 452 American Classic Bolt-Action Rifle, 230
CZ 452 M 2E Lux Bolt-Action Rifle, 230
CZ 452 M 2E Varmint Rifle, 230
CZ 511 Auto Rifle, 224
CZ 527 American Classic Bolt-Action Rifle, 183
CZ 527 Lux Bolt-Action Rifle, 183
CZ 550 American Classic Bolt-Action Rifle, 184
CZ 550 Lux Bolt-Action Rifle, 183
CZ 550 Magnum Bolt-Action Rifle, 184
CZ 550 Medium Magnum Bolt-Action Rifle, 184
CZ 581 Solo Over/Under Shotgun, 267
CZ 584 Solo Combination Gun, 220
CZ 589 Stopper Over/Under Gun, 221
CZ 700 M1 Sniper Rifle, 184
CZ 75 Champion Competition Pistol, 139
CZ 75 ST IPSC Auto Pistol, 139
CZ 75/85 Kadet Auto Pistol, 119

CZ 75B Auto Pistol, 118
CZ 75B Compact Auto Pistol, 118
CZ 75B Decocker, 118
CZ 75M IPSC Auto Pistol, 119
CZ 83B Double-Action Pistol, 119
CZ 85 Combat, 119
CZ 85B Auto Pistol, 119
CZ 97B Auto Pistol, 119

D

Daisy 1938 Red Ryder 60th Anniversary Classic, 314
Daisy Model 105 Buck, 314
Daisy Model 7840 Buckmaster, 314
Daisy Model 840 Grizzly, 314
Daisy Model 95 Timberwolf, 314
Daisy/Powerline 1000 Air Rifle, 314
Daisy/Powerline 1170 Pellet Rifle, 314
Daisy/Powerline 1270 CO2 Air Pistol, 311
Daisy/Powerline 45 Air Pistol, 311
Daisy/Powerline 622X Pellet pistol, 311
Daisy/Powerline 645 Air Pistol, 311
Daisy/Powerline 693 Air Pistol, 311
Daisy/Powerline 717 Pellet Pistol, 311
Daisy/Powerline 853, 314
Daisy/Powerline 856 Pump-Up Airgun, 314
Daisy/Powerline 880, 314
Daisy/Powerline 93 Air Pistol, 311
Daisy/Powerline Eagle 7856 Pump-Up Airgun, 314
Daisy/Powerline Model 15XT Air Pistol, 310
Daisy/Youthline Model 105 Air Rifle, 314
Daisy/Youthline Model 95 Air Rifle, 314
Dakota 76 Classic Bolt-Action Rifle, 184
Dakota 76 Rifle, 99
Dakota 76 Safari Bolt-Action Rifle, 184
Dakota 76 Traveler Takedown Rifle, 184
Dakota 97 Lightweight Hunter, 185
Dakota African Grade, 185
Dakota Double Rifle, 221
Dakota Legend/Premier Shotguns, 111
Dakota Long Range Hunter Rifle, 185
Dakota Longbow Tactical E.R. Rifle, 185
Dakota Model 10 Single Shot Rifle, 211
Dakota Model 10, 107
Dakota Premier Grade Shotguns, 279
Dakota The Dakota Legend Shotguns, 279
Dan Wesson 722M Small Frame Revolver, 144
Dan Wesson Firearms Alaskan Guide Special, 145
Dan Wesson Firearms Large Frame Series Revolvers, 145
Dan Wesson Firearms Major Aussie, 120
Dan Wesson Firearms Major Tri-Ops Packs, 120
Dan Wesson Firearms Model 15/715 and 32/732 Revolvers, 144
Dan Wesson Firearms Model 22/722 Revolvers, 144
Dan Wesson Firearms Model 3220/73220 TARGET Revolver, 144
Dan Wesson Firearms Model 360/7360 Revolvers, 145
Dan Wesson Firearms Model 40/740 Revolvers, 144
Dan Wesson Firearms Model 41/741, 44/744 and 45/745 Revolvers, 145
Dan Wesson Firearms Model 414/7414 and 445/7445 SuperMag Revolvers, 144
Dan Wesson Firearms Model 460/7460 Revolvers, 145
Dan Wesson Firearms Model 722 Silhouette Revolver, 144
Dan Wesson Firearms Patriot 1911 Pistol, 120
Dan Wesson Firearms Pointman Dave Pruitt Signature Series, 120
Dan Wesson Firearms Pointman Guardian Auto Pistols, 119
Dan Wesson Firearms Pointman Hi-Cap Auto Pistol, 120
Dan Wesson Firearms Pointman Major Auto Pistol, 119
Dan Wesson Firearms Pointman Minor Auto Pistol, 120
Dan Wesson Firearms Pointman Seven Auto Pistols, 119
Dan Wesson Firearms Standard Silhouette Revolvers, 145
Dan Wesson Firearms Super Ram Silhouette Revolver, 145
Desert Baby Eagle Pistols, 120
Desert Eagle Mark XIX Pistol, 120
Diamond 12 Ga. Pump Shotgun, 256
Diamond Semi-Auto Shotguns, 248

Dixie 1863 Springfield Musket, 298
Dixie 1874 Sharps Blackpowder Silhouette Rifle, 211
Dixie 1874 Sharps Lightweight Hunter/Target Rifle, 211
Dixie Deluxe Cub Rifle, 298
Dixie Early American Jaeger Rifle, 298
Dixie Engraved 1873 Rifle, 174
Dixie Inline Carbine, 299
Dixie Magnum Percussion Shotgun, 309
Dixie Pedersoli 1766 Charleville Musket, 299
Dixie Pedersoli 1857 Mauser Rifle, 299
Dixie Pennsylvania Pistol, 292
Dixie Sharps New Model 1859 Military Rifle, 299
Dixie U.S. Model 1816 Flintlock Musket, 299
Dixie U.S. Model 1861 Springfield, 299
Dixie Wyatt Earp Revolver, 294
Downsizer WSP Single Shot Pistol, 163
DPMS Panther Arms A-15 Rifles, 168
DSA SA58 21" or 24" Bull Barrel Rifle, 169
DSA SA58 Congo, Para Congo, 168
DSA SA58 GI, 168
DSA SA58 Gray Wolf, 168
DSA SA58 Medium Contour, 169
DSA SA58 Mini OSW, 169
DSA SA58 Predator, 168
DSA SA58 T48, 168
DSA SA58 Tactical Carbine, Carbine, 168

E

E.M.F. 1860 Henry Rifle, 174
E.M.F. 1863 Sharps Military Carbine, 299
E.M.F. 1866 Yellowboy Lever Actions, 174
E.M.F. 1874 Metallic Cartridge Sharps Rifle, 211
E.M.F. Hartford Model 1892 Lever-Action Rifle, 174
E.M.F. Hartford Model Cowboy Shotgun, 279
E.M.F. Model 1873 Lever-Action Rifle, 174
EAA Bounty Hunter SA Revolvers, 154
EAA European Model Auto Pistols, 121
EAA IZH-27 Sporting O/U, 267
EAA Standard Grade Revolvers, 145
EAA Witness DA Auto Pistol, 121
EAA Witness Gold Team Auto, 139
EAA Witness Silver Team Auto, 140
EAA/Baikal Bounty Hunter IZH-43K Shotgun, 279
EAA/Baikal Bounty Hunter MP 213 Coach Gun, 279
EAA/Baikal IZH-18 Single Barrel Shotgun, 284
EAA/Baikal IZH-18 Max Single Barrel Shotgun, 284
EAA/Baikal IZH-27 Over/Under Shotgun, 267
EAA/Baikal IZH35 Auto Pistol, 139
EAA/Baikal IZH-43 Bounty Hunter Shotguns, 279
EAA/Baikal IZH-61 Air Rifle, 314
EAA/Baikal IZH-94 Combination Gun, 221
EAA/Baikal IZH-M46 Target Air Pistol, 311
EAA/Baikal IZH MP-532 Air Rifle, 314
EAA/Baikal MP-133 Pump Shotgun, 256
EAA/Baikal MP-153 Auto Shotgun, 248
EAA/Baikal MP-213 Shotgun, 279
EAA/Baikal MP-233 Over/Under Shotgun, 267
EAA/Baikal MP-512 Air Rifle, 314
EAA/Baikal MP-651K Air Pistol/Rifle, 311
EAA/Bul 1911 Auto Pistol, 121
EAA/HW 660 Match Rifle, 241
EAA/Izhmash Biathalon Basic Target Rifle, 241
EAA/Izhmash Biathlon Target Rifle, 241
EAA/Izhmash Ural 5.1 Target Rifle, 241
EAA/Saiga Auto Shotgun, 248
EAA/Saiga Semi-Auto Rifle, 169
Eagle Arms AR-10 Rifle , 169
Eagle Arms M15 Rifle, 169
Ed Brown Class A Limited, 140
Ed Brown Classic Custom and Class A Limited 1911-style Auto Pistols, 95
Ed Brown Classic Custom Pistol, 140
Ed Brown Commander Bobtail, 121
Ed Brown Custom Bolt-Action Rifles, 99
Ed Brown Kobra, Kobra Carry, 121
Ed Brown Model 702 Bushveld, 186
Ed Brown Model 702 Denali, Ozark, 186

Ed Brown Model 702 Light Tactical, 241
Ed Brown Model 702 Savanna, 185
Ed Brown Model 702 Tactical, 241
Ed Brown Model 702 Varmint, 186
Ed Brown Model 702, M40A2 Marine Sniper, 242
EMF 1875 Outlaw Revolver, 155
EMF 1890 Police Revolver, 155
EMF 1894 Bisley Revolver, 154
EMF Hartford Express Single-Action Revolver, 155
EMF Hartford Pinkerton Single-Action Revolver, 154
EMF Hartford Single-Action Revolvers, 154
Entréprise Boxer P500 Auto Pistol, 121
Entréprise Elite P500 Auto Pistol, 121
Entréprise Medalist P500 Auto Pistol, 121
Entréprise Tactical P500 Auto Pistol, 121
Entréprise Tournament Shooter Model I, 140
Erma KGP68 Auto Pistol, 122
Escort Auto Shotgun , 249
Escort Pump Shotgun, 256
Euroarms 1861 Springfield Rifle, 299
Euroarms Volunteer Target Rifle, 299
Excel Industries CP-45, XP-45 Auto Pistol, 140

F

Fabarm Camo Turkey Mag O/U Shotgun, 268
Fabarm Classic Lion Double Shotgun, 280
Fabarm Field Pump Shotgun, 257
Fabarm FP6 Pump Shotgun, 289
Fabarm Gold Lion Mark III Auto Shotgun, 249
Fabarm Max Lion Over/Under Shotguns, 267
Fabarm Max Lion Paradox, 267
Fabarm Monotrap Shotgun, 284
Fabarm Silver Lion Cub Model O/U, 268
Fabarm Silver Lion Over/Under Shotguns, 267
Fabarm Sporting Clays Competition Extra O/U, 268
Fabarm Sporting Clays Extra Auto Shotgun, 249
Fabarm Tactical Semi-Automatic Shotgun, 289
Fabarm Ultra Camo Mag Lion O/U Shotgun, 267
FEG PJK-9HP Auto Pistol, 122
FEG SMC-380 Auto Pistol, 122
Feinwerkebau AW93 Target Pistol, 140
Felk MTF 450 Auto Pistol, 122
Firestorm Auto Pistol, 122
Fox, A.H., Side-By-Side Shotguns, 280
Franchi 48AL Deluxe Shotgun, 249
Franchi 48AL English, 249
Franchi 48AL Short Stock Shotgun, 249
Franchi 48AL Shotgun, 249
Franchi 612 and 620 Shotguns, 249
Franchi 612 Defense Shotgun, 249
Franchi 612 Sporting Shotgun, 249
Franchi 620 Short Stock Shotgun, 249
Franchi 912 Shotgun, 268
Franchi Alcione Field Over/Under Shotgun, 268
Franchi Alcione Sport SL O/U Shotgun, 268
Franchi Alcione SX O/U Shotgun, 268
Franchi Alcione Titanium Over/Under Shotgun, 268
Franchi Model 912, 249
Franchi Veloce English Over/Under Shotgun, 268
Franchi Veloce Over/Under Shotgun, 268
Freedom Arms Model 83 22 Field Grade Silhouette Class, 140
Freedom Arms Model 83 Centerfire Silhouette Models, 140
Freedom Arms Model 83 Field Grade Revolver, 155
Freedom Arms Model 83 Premier Grade Revolver, 155
Freedom Arms Model 83 Varmint Class Revolvers, 155
Freedom Arms Model 97 Premier Grade Revolver, 156
French-Style Dueling Pistol, 292

G

Gamo Auto 45, 311
Gamo Compact Target Pistol, 311
Gamo Delta Air Rifle, 314
Gamo Hunter 440 Air Rifle , 315
Gamo P-23, P-23 Laser Pistol, 311
Gamo PT-80, PT-80 Laser Pistol, 311
Gamo Sporter Air Rifle , 315

Gamo Young Hunter Air Rifle, 314
Garbi Express Double Rifle, 221
Garbi Model 100 Double, 280
Garbi Model 101 Side-by-Side, 280
Garbi Model 103A, B Side-by-Side, 280
Garbi Model 200 Side-by-Side, 280
Gary Reeder Custom Guns Contender and Encore Pistols, 98
Gary Reeder Custom Guns Revolvers, 97
"Gat" Air Pistol, 311
Gaucher GN1 Silhouette Pistol, 163
Gaucher GP Silhouette Pistol, 140
Glock 17 Auto Pistol, 122
Glock 19 Auto Pistol, 122
Glock 20 10mm Auto Pistol, 122
Glock 21 Auto Pistol, 122
Glock 22 Auto Pistol, 123
Glock 23 Auto Pistol, 123
Glock 26, 27 Auto Pistols, 123
Glock 29, 30 Auto Pistols, 123
Glock 31/31C Auto Pistols, 123
Glock 32/32C Auto Pistols, 123
Glock 33 Auto Pistol, 123
Glock 34, 35 Auto Pistols, 123
Glock 36 Auto Pistol, 123
Gonic Model 93 Deluxe M/L Rifle, 300
Gonic Model 93 M/L Rifle, 299
Gonic Model 93 Mountain Thumbhole M/L Rifles, 300

H

Hammerli "Trailside" Target Pistol, 123
Hammerli AP40 Air Pistol, 311
Hammerli AR 50 Air Rifle, 315
Hammerli Model 450 Match Air Rifle, 315
Hammerli SP 20 Target Pistol, 140
Hammerli X-Esse Sport Pistol, 140
Hanus, Bill, Birdgun, 280
Harper's Ferry 1803 Flintlock Rifle, 300
Harper's Ferry 1806 Pistol, 292
Harrington & Richardson 38-55 Target Rifle, 212
Harrington & Richardson Buffalo Classic Rifle, 212
Harrington & Richardson Model 928 Ultra Slug Hunter Deluxe, 285
Harrington & Richardson NWTF Shotguns, 285
Harrington & Richardson SB2-980 Ultra Slug, 285
Harrington & Richardson Tamer Shotgun, 285
Harrington & Richardson Topper Deluxe Model 098, 285
Harrington & Richardson Topper Junior Classic Shotgun, 285
Harrington & Richardson Topper Model 098, 285
Harrington & Richardson Ultra Comp Rifle, 211
Harrington & Richardson Ultra Heavy Barrel 22 Mag Rifle, 230
Harrington & Richardson Ultra Hunter Rifle, 211
Harrington & Richardson Ultra Varmint Rifle, 211
Harris Gunworks Antietam Sharps Rifle, 212
Harris Gunworks Combo M-87 Series 50-Caliber Rifles, 242
Harris Gunworks Long Range Rifle, 242
Harris Gunworks M-86 Sniper Rifle, 242
Harris Gunworks M-89 Sniper Rifle, 242
Harris Gunworks National Match Rifle, 242
Harris Gunworks Signature Alaskan, 186
Harris Gunworks Signature Classic Sporter, 186
Harris Gunworks Signature Classic Stainless Sporter, 186
Harris Gunworks Signature Jr. Long Range Pistol, 140
Harris Gunworks Signature Titanium Mountain Rifle, 187
Harris Gunworks Signature Varminter , 187
Harris Gunworks Talon Safari Rifle, 187
Harris Gunworks Talon Sporter Rifle, 187
Hawken Rifle, 300
Heckler & Koch Elite, 124
Heckler & Koch Mark 23 Special Operations Pistol, 124
Heckler & Koch P2000 GPM Pistol , 125
Heckler & Koch P7M8 Auto Pistol, 124
Heckler & Koch SL8-1 Rifle, 170
Heckler & Koch SLB 2000 Rifle, 170
Heckler & Koch USC Carbine, 170

Heckler & Koch USP Auto Pistol, 123
Heckler & Koch USP Compact Auto Pistol, 124
Heckler & Koch USP Expert Pistol, 124
Heckler & Koch USP45 Auto Pistol, 124
Heckler & Koch USP45 Compact, 124
Heckler & Koch USP45 Tactical Pistol, 124
Henry "Mini" Bolt 22 Rifle, 231
Henry Golden Boy 22 Lever-Action Rifle, 227
Henry Lever-Action 22, 227
Henry Pump-Action 22 Pump Rifle, 227
Henry U.S. Survival Rifle .22, 224
Heritage Rough Rider Revolver, 156
High Standard Trophy Target Pistol, 141
High Standard Victor Target Pistol, 141
Hi-Point 9MM Carbine, 170
Hi-Point Firearms 380 Comp Pistol, 125
Hi-Point Firearms 45 Polymer Frame, 125
Hi-Point Firearms 9mm Comp Pistol, 125
Hi-Point Firearms Model 380 Polymer Pistol, 125
Hi-Point Firearms Model 9mm Compact Pistol, 125
Hoenig Rotary Round Action Combination, 221
Hoenig Rotary Round Action Double Rifle, 221
Hoenig Rotary Round Action Game Gun, 268
Howa Lightning Bolt-Action Rifle, 187
Howa M-1500 Hunter Bolt-Action Rifle, 187
Howa M-1500 Supreme Rifles, 188
Howa M-1500 Ultralight, 188
Howa M-1500 Varmint and Varmint Supreme Rifles, 188

I

IAI M-2000 Pistol, 125
IAI M-333 M1 Garand, 170
IAI M-888 M1 Carbine Semi-Automatic Rifle, 170
IAR Model 1866 Double Derringer, 163
IAR Model 1872 Derringer, 163
IAR Model 1873 Frontier Marshal, 156
IAR Model 1873 Frontier Revolver, 156
IAR Model 1873 Revolver Carbine, 174
IAR Model 1873 Six Shooter, 156
Intrac Arms IAI-65 Rifle, 170
Ithaca Classic Doubles Grade 4E Classic SxS Shotgun, 281
Ithaca Classic Doubles Grade 5E SxS Shotgun, 281
Ithaca Classic Doubles Grade 6E SxS Shotgun, 281
Ithaca Classic Doubles Grade 7E Classic SxS Shotgun, 281
Ithaca Classic Doubles Knickerbocker Trap Gun, 286
Ithaca Classic Doubles Side-By-Side Shotguns, 111
Ithaca Classic Doubles Skeet Grade SxS, 281
Ithaca Classic Doubles Sousa Special Grade SxS Shotgun, 281
Ithaca Ellett Special Model 37 Turkeyslayer, 257
Ithaca Model 37 Deerslayer II Pump Shotgun, 257
Ithaca Model 37 Deerslayer III Pump Shotgun, 257
Ithaca Model 37 Deluxe Pump Shotgun, 257
Ithaca Model 37 Ruffed Grouse Special Edition, 257
Ithaca Model 37 Ultralight Deluxe, 257
Ithaca Model 37 Waterfowl , 257
Ithaca Quad Bore Model 37 Turkeyslayer, 257

J

J.P. Henry Trade Rifle, 300
J.P. Murray 1862-1864 Cavalry Carbine, 300
John Rigby Bolt-Action Rifles, 101
John Rigby Custom African Express Rifle, 101
John Rigby Double Rifles, 104
John Rigby Shotguns, 111

K

Kahr K9 9mm Compact Polymer Pistol, 125
Kahr K9, K40 DA Auto Pistols, 125
Kahr MK9/MK40 Micro Pistol, 125
Kahr PM9 Pistol, 125
Kel-Tec P-11 Auto Pistol, 125
Kel-Tec P-32 Auto Pistol, 126
Kentuckian Rifle, 300
Kentucky Flintlock Pistol, 292
Kentucky Flintlock Rifle, 300

Kentucky Percussion Pistol, 292
Kentucky Percussion Rifle, 300
Kimber 22 Classic Bolt-Action Rifle, 231
Kimber 22 HS (Hunter Silhouette) Bolt-Action Rifle, 231
Kimber 22 SuperAmerica Bolt-Action Rifle, 231
Kimber 22 SVT Bolt-Action Rilfe, 231
Kimber Augusta Shotgun, 268
Kimber CDP II Series Auto Pistol, 127
Kimber Custom II 1911-Style Auto Pistols, 95
Kimber Custom II Auto Pistol, 126
Kimber Custom II Auto Pistol, 126
Kimber Eclipse II Series Auto Pistol, 127
Kimber Gold Combat II Auto Pistol, 127
Kimber Gold Match II Auto Pistol, 126
Kimber Gold Match Ten II Polymer Auto Pistol, 126
Kimber LTP II Polymer Auto Pistol, 127
Kimber Model 84M Bolt-Action Rifle, 188
Kimber Pro Carry II Auto Pistol, 126
Kimber Super Match Auto Pistol, 141
Kimber Super Match II Auto Pistol, 127
Kimber Ten II High Capacity Polymer Pistol, 126
Kimber Ultra Carry II Auto Pistol, 126
Knight 50 Caliber Disc In-Line Rifle, 301
Knight American Knight M/L Rifle, 301
Knight Master Hunter Disc Extreme, 301
Knight Master Hunter II Disc In-Line Rifle, 301
Knight Muzzleloader Disc Extreme, 301
Knight TK2000 Muzzleloading Shotgun (209), 309
Knight Versatile TK2002, 309
Knight Wolverine 209, 301
Kolar AAA Competition Skeet Over/Under Shotgun, 269
Kolar AAA Competition Trap Over/Under Shotgun, 269
Kolar Sporting Clays O/U Shotgun, 269
Korth Combat Revolver, 145
Korth Match Revolver, 141
Korth Pistol, 127
Korth Troja Revolver, 146
Krieghoff Classic Big Five Double Rifle, 221
Krieghoff Classic Double Rifle, 221
Krieghoff Hubertus Single-Shot Rifle, 212
Krieghoff K-20 O/U Shotguns, 269
Krieghoff K-80 O/U Trap Shotgun, 269
Krieghoff K-80 Single Barrel Trap Gun, 286
Krieghoff K-80 Skeet Shotgun, 269
Krieghoff K-80 Sporting Clays O/U, 269
Krieghoff KX-5 Trap Gun, 286

L

L.A.R. Grizzly 50 Big Boar Rifle, 189
Le Mat Revolver, 294
Le Page Percussion Dueling Pistol, 292
Lebeau - Courally Boss-Verees O/U, 269
Lebeau - Courally Boxlock SxS Shotgun, 281
Lebeau - Courally Express Rifle SxS, 221
Lebeau - Courally Sidelock SxS Shotgun, 281
Legacy Sports International M-1500 Custom Rifles, 189
Legacy Sports International Mauser 98 Rifle, 189
Legacy Sports International Texas Safari Rifles, 100
Legacy Sports International Texas Safari Rifles, 189
Les Baer AR 223 Auto Rifles, 103
Les Baer Custom 1911-Style Auto Pistols, 96
Les Baer Custom Ultimate AR 223 Rifles, 171
Linebaugh Custom Sixguns Revolvers, 98
Ljutic LM-6 Super Deluxe O/U Shotgun, 269
Ljutic LTX Pro 3 Deluxe Mono Gun, 286
Ljutic Mono Gun Single Barrel, 286
Llama Max-I Auto Pistols, 128
Llama Micromax 380 Auto Pistol, 127
Llama Minimax Series, 128
Llama Minimax Sub-Compact Auto Pistol, 128
London Armory 1861 Enfield Musketoon, 301
London Armory 2-Band 1858 Enfield, 301
London Armory 3-Band 1853 Enfield, 301
Lone Star Cowboy Action Rifle, 212
Lone Star No. 5 Remington Pattern Rolling Block Rifle, 212
Lone Star Rolling Block Rifles, 107
Lone Star Standard Silhouette Rifle, 212

LR 300 SR Light Sport Rifle, 171
Luger Classic O/U Shotguns, 269
Lyman Deerstalker Rifle, 302
Lyman Great Plains Hunter Rifle, 302
Lyman Great Plains Rifle, 302
Lyman Plains Pistol, 292
Lyman Trade Rifle, 302

M

Magnum Research BFR Revolver, 157
Magnum Research BFR Single-Action Revolver, 156
Magnum Research Magnum Lite Tactical Rifle, 189
Magtech MT 7022 Auto Rifle, 224
Markesbery KM Black Bear M/L Rifle, 302
Markesbery KM Brown Bear M/L Rifle, 303
Markesbery KM Colorado Rocky Mountain M/L Rifle, 302
Markesbery KM Grizzly Bear M/L Rifle, 303
Markesbery KM Polar Bear M/L Rifle, 303
Marksman 2000 Repeater Pistol, 311
Marksman 2005 Laserhawk Special Edition Air Pistol, 311
Marksman 2015 Laserhawk™ BB Repeater Air Rifle, 315
Marksman BB Buddy Air Rifle, 315
Marlin 70PSS Papoose Stainless Rifle, 224
Marlin Model 15YN "Little Buckaroo", 232
Marlin Model 17V Hornady Magnum, 232
Marlin Model 1894 Cowboy Competition Rifle, 176
Marlin Model 1894 Cowboy, 176
Marlin Model 1894 Lever-Action Carbine, 175
Marlin Model 1894C Carbine, 176
Marlin Model 1894PG/1894FG , 176
Marlin Model 1894SS, 176
Marlin Model 1895 Cowboy Lever-Action Rifle, 176
Marlin Model 1895 Lever-Action Rifle, 176
Marlin Model 1895G Guide Gun Lever-Action Rifle, 176
Marlin Model 1895GS Guide Gun, 176
Marlin Model 1895M Lever-Action Rifle, 176
Marlin Model 1897T Rifle, 227
Marlin Model 25MN/25MNC Bolt-Action Rifles, 233
Marlin Model 25N Bolt-Action Repeater, 232
Marlin Model 25NC Bolt-Action Repeater, 232
Marlin Model 336 Cowboy, 175
Marlin Model 336 Y "Spikehorn" , 175
Marlin Model 336A Lever-Action Carbine, 175
Marlin Model 336C Lever-Action Carbine, 175
Marlin Model 336CC Lever-Action Carbine, 175
Marlin Model 336SS Lever-Action Carbine, 175
Marlin Model 336W Lever-Action Rifle, 175
Marlin Model 39A Golden Lever-Action Rifle, 227
Marlin Model 444 Lever-Action Sporter, 175
Marlin Model 444P Outfitter Lever-Action, 175
Marlin Model 60 Auto Rifle, 224
Marlin Model 60SS Self-Loading Rifle, 224
Marlin Model 7000 Auto Rifle, 225
Marlin Model 795 Auto Rifle, 225
Marlin Model 795SS Auto Rifle, 225
Marlin Model 81TS Bolt-Action Rifle, 232
Marlin Model 83TS Bolt-Action Rifle, 233
Marlin Model 880SQ Squirrel Rifle, 232
Marlin Model 880SS Bolt-Action Rifle, 232
Marlin Model 882 Bolt-Action Rifle, 233
Marlin Model 882SS Bolt-Action Rifle, 233
Marlin Model 882SSV Bolt-Action Rifle, 233
Marlin Model 883 Bolt-Action Rifle, 233
Marlin Model 883SS Bolt-Action Rifle, 233
Marocchi Conquista Skeet Over/Under Shotgun, 270
Marocchi Conquista Sporting Clays O/U Shotguns, 270
Marocchi Conquista Trap Over/Under Shotgun, 270
Marocchi Conquista USA Model 92 Sporting Clays O/U
    Shotgun, 270
Marocchi Model 99 Sporting Trap and Skeet, 270
Maximum Single Shot Pistol, 164
MDM Buckwacka In-Line Rifles, 303
MDM M2K In-Line Rifle, 303
Meacham High-Wall Silhouette Rifle, 108
Meacham High Wall Silhouette Rifle, 212
Meacham Low Wall Rifle, 233
Medusa Model 47 Revolver, 146

Merkel Boxlock Double Rifles, 222
Merkel Drillings, 222
Merkel Exhibition, Vintagers Expo and Custom Engraved
    Shotguns, 112
Merkel K-1 Model Lightweight Stalking Rifle, 212
Merkel Model 2001EL O/U Shotgun, 270
Merkel Model 2002 EL O/U Shotgun, 270
Merkel Model 280EL and 360EL Shotguns, 281
Merkel Model 280SL and 360SL Shotguns, 282
Merkel Model 303EL O/U Shotgun, 270
Merkel Model 47E, 147E Side-By-Side Shotguns, 281
Merkel Model 47SL, 147SL Side-By-Sides, 281
Mississippi 1841 Percussion Rifle, 303
Model 1885 High Wall Rifle, 212
Morini 162E Match Air Pistol, 311
Morini Model 84E Free Pistol, 141
Morini Sam K-11 Air Pistol, 311
Mossberg 590DA Double-Action Pump Shotgun, 291
Mossberg Model 500 Bantam Pump, 258
Mossberg Model 500 Camo Pump, 258
Mossberg Model 500 Persuader Security Shotguns, 290
Mossberg Model 500 Persuader/Cruiser Shotguns, 258
Mossberg Model 500 Slugster, 258
Mossberg Model 500 Sporting Pump, 258
Mossberg Model 500, 590 Ghost-Ring Shotguns, 290
Mossberg Model 500, 590 Mariner Pump, 290
Mossberg Model 590 Shotgun, 290
Mossberg Model 590 Special Purpose Shotguns, 258
Mossberg Model 695 Slugster, 286
Mossberg Model 835 Synthetic Stock, 258
Mossberg Model 835 Ulti-Mag Pump, 257
Mossberg Model HS410 Shotgun, 290
Mossberg SSi-One 12 Gauge Slug Shotgun, 286
Mossberg SSi-One Single Shot Rifle, 213
Mossberg SSi-One Turkey Shotgun, 286
Mountain Eagle Magnum Lite Rifle, 190

N

Navy Arms "John Bodine" Rolling Block Rifle, 214
Navy Arms 1763 Charleville, 303
Navy Arms 1836 Paterson Revolver, 294
Navy Arms 1851 Navy Conversion Revolver, 157
Navy Arms 1859 Sharps Cavalry Carbine, 304
Navy Arms 1860 Army Conversion Revolver, 158
Navy Arms 1860 Henry Rifles, 177
Navy Arms 1861 Springfield Rifle, 304
Navy Arms 1863 C.S. Richmond Rifle, 304
Navy Arms 1863 Springfield, 304
Navy Arms 1866 Sporting Yellowboy Rifles, 177
Navy Arms 1866 Yellow Boy Rifle, 177
Navy Arms 1873 Sharps "Quigley", 213
Navy Arms 1873 Sharps No. 2 Creedmoor Rifle, 213
Navy Arms 1873 Single-Action Revolver, 157
Navy Arms 1873 Springfield Cavalry Carbine, 214
Navy Arms 1873 Winchester-style Rifle, 177
Navy Arms 1874 Sharps Buffalo Rifle, 213
Navy Arms 1874 Sharps Cavalry Carbine, 213
Navy Arms 1875 Schofield Revolver, 157
Navy Arms 1885 High Wall Rifle, 213
Navy Arms 1892 Rifle, 177
Navy Arms 1892 Short Rifle, 178
Navy Arms 1892 Stainless Carbine, 177
Navy Arms 1892 Stainless Rifle, 178
Navy Arms Berdan 1859 Sharps Rifle, 304
Navy Arms Bisley Model Single-Action Revolver, 157
Navy Arms Flat Top Target Model Revolver, 157
Navy Arms Iron Frame Henry, 177
Navy Arms Military Henry Rifle, 177
Navy Arms New Model Pocket Revolver, 294
Navy Arms New Model Russian Revolver, 157
Navy Arms Parker-Hale Volunteer Rifle, 303
Navy Arms Parker-Hale Whitworth Military Target Rifle, 304
Navy Arms Rolling Block Rifle, 214
Navy Arms Sharps No. 3 Long Range Rifle, 214
Navy Arms Sharps Plains Rifle, 213
Navy Arms Sharps Sporting Rifle, 213
Navy Arms Smith Carbine, 304

Navy Arms Steel Shot Magnum Shotgun, 309
Navy Arms T&T Shotgun, 309
Navy Model 1851 Percussion Revolver, 295
New England Firearms "Stainless" Huntsman, 305
New England Firearms Camo Turkey Shotguns, 287
New England Firearms Handi-Rifle, 215
New England Firearms Huntsman, 305
New England Firearms Special Purpose Shotguns, 287
New England Firearms Sportster™ Single-Shot Rifles, 233
New England Firearms Standard Pardner, 287
New England Firearms Super Light Rifle, 215
New England Firearms Survivor Rifle, 215
New England Firearms Survivor, 287
New England Firearms Tracker II Slug Gun, 287
New Model 1858 Army Percussion Revolver, 295
New Ultra Light Arms 20RF Bolt-Action Rifle, 233
New Ultra Light Arms Bolt-Action Rifles, 190
North American Arms Guardian Pistol, 128
North American Black Widow Revolver, 158
North American Companion Percussion Revolver, 295
North American Magnum Companion Percussion Revolver,
    295
North American Mini Revolvers, 158
North American Mini-Master, 158

O

Olympic Arms CAR-97 Rifles, 171
Olympic Arms OA-96 AR Pistol, 128
Olympic Arms OA-98 AR Pistol, 128
Olympic Arms PCR-1 Rifle, 242
Olympic Arms PCR-2, PCR-3 Rifles, 243
Olympic Arms PCR-4 Rifle, 171
Olympic Arms PCR-6 Rifle, 171
Olympic Arms PCR-Service Match Rifle, 242

P

Pacific Rifle Big Bore, African Rifles, 305
Pacific Rifle Model 1837 Zephyr, 305
Para-Ordnance C5 45 LDA Para Carry, 128
Para-Ordnance C7 45 LDA Para Companion, 129
Para-Ordnance LDA Auto Pistols, 128
Para-Ordnance LDA Limited Pistols, 128
Para-Ordnance Limited Pistols, 128
Para-Ordnance P-Series Auto Pistols, 128
Pardini GP Rapid Fire Match Pistol, 141
Pardini GT45 Target Pistol, 141
Pardini K22 Free Pistol, 141
Pardini K58 Match Air Pistol, 311
Pardini Model SP, HP Target Pistols, 141
Pardini/Nygord "Master" Target Pistol, 141
Pedersoli Mang Target Pistol, 292
Peifer Model TS-93 Rifle, 305
Perazzi MX10 Over/Under Shotgun, 271
Perazzi MX12 Hunting Over/Under, 271
Perazzi MX20 Hunting Over/Under, 271
Perazzi MX28, MX410 Game O/U Shotguns, 271
Perazzi MX8 Over/Under Shotguns, 270
Perazzi MX8 Special Skeet Over/Under, 271
Perazzi MX8/20 Over/Under Shotgun, 271
Perazzi MX8/MX8 Special Trap, Skeet, 271
Perazzi SCO, SCO Gold, Extra and Extra Gold Shotguns,
    112
Peters Stahl Auto Loading Pistols, 129
Phoenix Arms HP22, HP25 Auto Pistols, 129
Piotti Boss Over/Under Shotgun, 271
Piotti King Extra Side-By-Side, 282
Piotti King No. 1 Side-By-Side, 282
Piotti Lunik Side-By-Side, 282
Piotti Piuma Side-By-Side, 282
Pocket Police 1862 Percussion Revolver, 295
Prairie River Arms PRA Bullpup Rifle, 305
Puma Model 92 Rifles & Carbines, 178

Q

Queen Anne Flintlock Pistol, 293

R

Raptor Bolt-Action Rifle, 190
Remington 40-XB Rangemaster Target Centerfire, 243
Remington 40-XBBR KS, 243
Remington 40-XC KS Target Rifle, 243
Remington 40-XR Custom Sporter, 243
Remington 572 BDL Deluxe Fieldmaster Pump Rifle, 228
Remington 597 Auto Rifle, 225
Remington Custom Shop Auto Shotguns, 113
Remington Custom Shop Over/Under Shotguns, 113
Remington Custom Shop Pump Shotguns, 113
Remington Custom Shop Rolling Block Rifles, 108
Remington Model 1100 Classic Trap Shotgun, 252
Remington Model 1100 LT-20 Synthetic Deer Shotgun, 251
Remington Model 1100 Sporting 12 Shotgun, 252
Remington Model 1100 Sporting 20 Shotgun, 252
Remington Model 1100 Sporting 28, 252
Remington Model 1100 Synthetic Deer Shotgun, 252
Remington Model 1100 Synthetic LT-20 Shotgun, 251
Remington Model 1100 Youth Synthetic Turkey Camo, 251
Remington Model 11-87 Premier Shotgun, 250
Remington Model 11-87 SP and SPS Super Magnum Shotguns, 251
Remington Model 11-87 Special Purpose Magnum, 250
Remington Model 11-87 SPS Cantilever Shotgun, 251
Remington Model 11-87 SPS Special Purpose Synthetic Camo, 250
Remington Model 11-87 SPS-Deer Shotgun, 250
Remington Model 11-87 SPS-T Super Magnum Synthetic Camo, 250
Remington Model 11-87 SPS-T Turkey Camo, 250
Remington Model 11-87 Upland Special Shotgun, 251
Remington Model 332 O/U Shotgun, 271
Remington Model 40-X Custom Shop Target Rifles, 100
Remington Model 552 BDL Deluxe Speedmaster Rifle, 225
Remington Model 673 Guide Rifle, 190
Remington Model 700 ADL Deluxe Rifle, 191
Remington Model 700 ADL Synthetic Youth, 191
Remington Model 700 ADL Synthetic, 191
Remington Model 700 APR African Plains Rifle, 192
Remington Model 700 AWR Alaskan Wilderness Rifle, 192
Remington Model 700 BDL Custom Deluxe Rifle, 191
Remington Model 700 BDL DM Rifle, 191
Remington Model 700 BDL Left Hand Custom Deluxe, 191
Remington Model 700 BDL SS DM Rifle, 191
Remington Model 700 BDL SS Rifle, 191
Remington Model 700 Classic Rifle, 190
Remington Model 700 Custom KS Mountain Rifle, 192
Remington Model 700 Custom Shop Rifles, 100
Remington Model 700 EtronX VSSF Rifle, 193
Remington Model 700 LSS Mountain Rifle, 192
Remington Model 700 LSS Rifle, 192
Remington Model 700 ML, MLS Rifles, 305
Remington Model 700 MTN DM Rifle, 192
Remington Model 700 RMEF, 193
Remington Model 700 Safari Grade, 192
Remington Model 700 Sendero SF Rifle, 193
Remington Model 700 Titanium, 192
Remington Model 700 VLS Varmint Laminated Stock, 192
Remington Model 700 VS SF Rifle, 193
Remington Model 700 VS Varmint Synthetic Rifles, 193
Remington Model 710 Bolt-Action Rifle, 193
Remington Model 7400 Auto Rifle, 171
Remington Model 7600 Pump Action, 178
Remington Model 870 50th Anniversary Classic Trap Shotgun, 259
Remington Model 870 Express Rifle-Sighted Deer Gun, 259
Remington Model 870 Express Super Magnum, 259
Remington Model 870 Express Synthetic 18", 260
Remington Model 870 Express Turkey, 260
Remington Model 870 Express Youth Gun, 259
Remington Model 870 Express, 259
Remington Model 870 Marine Magnum, 259
Remington Model 870 SPS Super Magnum Camo, 260
Remington Model 870 SPS Super Slug Deer Gun, 260
Remington Model 870 SPS-T Synthetic Camo Shotgun, 260

Remington Model 870 Wingmaster LW Small Bore, 259
Remington Model 870 Wingmaster Super Magnum Shotgun, 259
Remington Model 870 Wingmaster , 258
Remington Model Seven Custom KS, 194
Remington Model Seven Custom MS Rifle, 194
Remington Model Seven Custom Shop Rifles, 101
Remington Model Seven LS, 193
Remington Model Seven SS, 193
Remington Model Seven Youth Rifle, 194
Remington Model SP-10 Magnum Camo Shotgun, 253
Remington Model SP-10 Magnum Shotgun, 252
Remington No. 1 Rolling Block Mid-range Sporter, 215
Richmond, C.S., 1863 Musket, 305
Rizzini Artemis Over/Under Shotgun, 272
Rizzini Express 90L Double Rifle, 222
Rizzini S782 Emel Over/Under Shotgun, 272
Rizzini S790 Emel Over/Under Shotgun, 271
Rizzini S792 Emel Over/Under Shotgun, 271
Rizzini Sidelock Side-By-Side, 282
Rizzini Upland EL Over/Under Shotgun, 272
Rock River Arms 1911-Style Auto Pistols, 96
Rock River Arms Standard A2 Rifle, 171
Rock River Arms Standard Match Auto Pistol, 129
Rocky Mountain Arms Patriot Pistol, 129
Rogers & Spencer Percussion Revolver, 295
Rossi Centerfire/Shotgun "Matched Pairs", 216
Rossi Matched Pair Single-Shot Rifle/Shotgun, 233
Rossi Matched Pair Single-Shot Shotgun/Rifle, 287
Rossi Model 351/352 Revolvers, 146
Rossi Model 461/462 Revolvers, 146
Rossi Model 851, 146
Rossi Model 971/972 Revolvers, 146
Rossi Single-Shot Centerfire Rifle, 216
Rossi Single-Shot Shotgun, 287
RPM XL Single-Shot Pistol, 164
Ruger 10/22 Auto Loading Carbine, 225
Ruger 10/22 Deluxe Sporter, 226
Ruger 10/22 International Carbine, 225
Ruger 10/22 Magnum Auto Loading Carbine, 226
Ruger 10/22T Target Rifle, 226
Ruger 22/45 Mark II Pistol, 131
Ruger 77/22 Hornet Bolt-Action Rifle, 194
Ruger 77/22 Rimfire Bolt-Action Rifle, 234
Ruger 77/44 Bolt-Action Rifle, 195
Ruger 77/50 In-Line Percussion Rifle, 305
Ruger Bisley Single-Action Revolver, 159
Ruger Bisley Small Frame Revolver, 160
Ruger Bisley-Vaquero Single-Action Revolver, 159
Ruger Deerfield 99/44 Carbine, 171
Ruger Engraved Red Label O/U Shotguns, 272
Ruger Gold Label Side-By-Side Shotgun, 282
Ruger GP-100 Revolvers, 146
Ruger K10/22RPF All-Weather Rifle, 226
Ruger K77/22 Varmint Rifle, 233
Ruger KP90 Decocker Autoloading Pistol, 130
Ruger KP94 Autoloading Pistol, 130
Ruger KTS-1234-BRE Trap Model Single-Barrel Shotgun, 287
Ruger M77 Mark II All-Weather and Sporter Model Stainless Rifle, 195
Ruger M77 Mark II Compact Rifles, 195
Ruger M77 Mark II Rifle, 195
Ruger M77RL Ultra Light, 195
Ruger M77RSI International Carbine, 195
Ruger M77VT Target Rifle, 196
Ruger Magnum Rifle, 194
Ruger Mark II Bull Barrel, 142
Ruger Mark II Government Target Model, 141
Ruger Mark II Standard Auto Loading Pistol, 130
Ruger Mark II Target Model Auto Loading Pistol, 141
Ruger Mini Thirty Rifle, 172
Ruger Mini-14/5 Auto Loading Rifle, 172
Ruger Model 96 Lever-Action Rifle, 228
Ruger Model 96/44 Lever-Action Rifle, 178
Ruger Model Single-Six Revolver, 159
Ruger New Bearcat Single-Action, 159

Ruger New Model Blackhawk and Blackhawk Convertible, 158
Ruger New Model Single Six Revolver, 158
Ruger New Model Super Blackhawk Hunter, 159
Ruger New Model Super Blackhawk, 159
Ruger No. 1 RSI International, 216
Ruger No. 1A Light Sporter, 216
Ruger NO. 1B Single Shot, 216
Ruger No. 1H Tropical Rifle, 217
Ruger No. 1S Medium Sporter, 217
Ruger No. 1V Varminter, 216
Ruger Old Army Percussion Revolver, 296
Ruger P89 Auto Loading Pistol, 129
Ruger P89 Double-Action-Only Autoloading Pistol, 130
Ruger P89D Decocker Autoloading Pistol, 130
Ruger P90 Manual Safety Model Autoloading Pistol, 130
Ruger P93 Compact Auto Loading Pistol, 130
Ruger P95 Auto Loading Pistol, 130
Ruger P97 Auto Loading Pistol, 130
Ruger PC4, PC9 Carbines, 171
Ruger Red Label O/U Shotgun, 272
Ruger Redhawk, 147
Ruger Single-Six and Super Single-Six Convertible, 160
Ruger SP101 Double-Action-Only Revolver, 146
Ruger SP101 Revolvers, 146
Ruger Sporting Clays O/U Shotgun, 272
Ruger Stainless Competition Model Pistol, 142
Ruger Super Redhawk Revolver, 147
Ruger Vaquero Single-Action Revolver, 159
Ruger Woodside Over/Under Shotgun, 272
RWS 9B/9N Air Pistols, 311
RWS/Diana Model 24 Air Rifle, 315
RWS/Diana Model 34 Air Rifle, 315
RWS/Diana Model 350 Magnum Air Rifle, 315
RWS/Diana Model 36 Air Rifle, 315
RWS/Diana Model 45 Air Rifle, 315
RWS/Diana Model 46 Air Rifle, 315
RWS/Diana Model 52 Air Rifle, 315
RWS/Diana Model 54 Air Rifle, 315
RWS/Diana Model 92/93/94 Air Rifles, 315

S

Safari Arms Big Deuce Pistol, 142
Safari Arms Carrier Pistol, 131
Safari Arms Carry Comp Pistol, 131
Safari Arms Cohort Pistol, 131
Safari Arms Enforcer Pistol, 131
Safari Arms GI Safari Pistol, 131
Safari Arms Matchmaster Pistol, 131
Sako 75 Deluxe Rifle, 196
Sako 75 Finnlight, 234
Sako 75 Hunter Bolt-Action Rifle, 196
Sako 75 Stainless Synthetic Rifle, 196
Sako 75 Varmint Rifle, 197
Sako 75 Varmint Stainless Laminated Rifle, 196
Sako Finnfire Hunter Bolt-Action Rifle, 234
Sako Finnfire Target Rifle, 234
Sako TRG-22 Bolt-Action Rifle, 243
Sako TRG-42 Bolt-Action Rifle, 196
Sako TRG-S Bolt-Action Rifle, 196
Sarsilmaz Over/Under Shotgun, 272
Sarsilmaz Pump Shotgun, 260
Sarsilmaz Semi-Automatic Shotgun, 253
Sauer 202 Bolt-Action Rifle, 197
Savage 24F Predator O/U Combination Gun, 222
Savage Cub G Youth, 236
Savage Mark 30G Stevens "Favorite", 236
Savage Mark I-G Bolt-Action Rifle, 234
Savage Mark II Bolt-Action Rifle, 235
Savage Mark II-FSS Stainless Rifle, 235
Savage Mark II-LV Heavy Barrel Rifle, 235
Savage Model 10/110FP Long Range Rifle, 198
Savage Model 10FCM Scout Ultra Light Rifle, 198
Savage Model 10FM Sierra Ultra Light Rifle, 198
Savage Model 10FP Tactical Rifle, 198
Savage Model 10FP-LE1A Tactical Rifle, 198
Savage Model 10GXP3, 110GXP3 Package Guns, 197

Savage Model 10GY, 200
Savage Model 10ML Muzzleloader Rifle Series, 306
Savage Model 11 Classic Hunter Rifles, Short Action, 199
Savage Model 111 Classic Hunter Rifles, 199
Savage Model 112 Long Range Rifles, 200
Savage Model 114U Ultra Rifle, 200
Savage Model 116 Weather Warriors, 201
Savage Model 116SE Safari Express Rifle, 200
Savage Model 11FXP3, 111FXP3, 111FCXP3, 11FYXP3 (Youth) Package Guns, 197
Savage Model 12 Long Range Rifles, 200
Savage Model 12VSS Varminter Rifle, 200
Savage Model 16FSS Rifle, 201
Savage Model 16FXP3, 116FXP3 SS Action Package Guns, 198
Savage Model 210F Master Shot Slug Gun, 288
Savage Model 64FV Auto Rifle, 226
Savage Model 64G Auto Rifle, 226
Savage Model 93FSS Magnum Rifle, 235
Savage Model 93FVSS Magnum Rifle, 235
Savage Model 93G Magnum Bolt-Action Rifle, 235
Savage Sport Striker Bolt-Action Hunting Handgun, 164
Savage Striker Bolt-Action Hunting Handgun, 164
Second Model Brown Bess Musket, 306
Seecamp LWS 32 Stainless DA Auto, 131
Semmerling LM-4 Slide-Action Pistol, 131
Sheriff Model 1851 Percussion Revolver, 296
Shiloh Rifle Co. Sharps 1874 Long Range Express, 217
Shiloh Rifle Co. Sharps 1874 Montana Roughrider, 218
Shiloh Rifle Co. Sharps 1874 Quigley, 217
Shiloh Rifle Co. Sharps 1874 Saddle Rifle, 217
Shiloh Rifle Co. Sharps Creedmoor Target, 218
SIG Pro Auto Pistol, 132
SIG Sauer P220 Service Auto Pistol, 131
SIG Sauer P220 Sport Auto Pistol, 131
SIG Sauer P226 Service Pistol, 132
SIG Sauer P229 DA Auto Pistol, 132
SIG Sauer P229 Sport Auto Pistol, 132
SIG Sauer P232 Personal Size Pistol, 132
SIG Sauer P239 Pistol, 132
SIG Sauer P245 Compact Auto Pistol, 132
Sigarms SA5 Over/Under Shotgun, 272
Sigarms SHR 970 Synthetic Rifle, 201
Silma Model 70 EJ Standard, 273
Silma Model 70 EJ Superlight, 273
Silma Model 70EJ Deluxe, 273
SKB Model 385 Side-By-Side, 282
SKB Model 385 Sporting Clays, 282
SKB Model 485 Side-By-Side, 282
SKB Model 505 Shotguns, 273
SKB Model 585 Gold Package, 273
SKB Model 585 Over/Under Shotgun, 273
SKB Model 785 Over/Under Shotgun, 273
Smith & Wesson Commemorative Model 2000, 160
Smith & Wesson Commemorative Model 29, 147
Smith & Wesson Enhanced Sigma Series DAO Pistols, 134
Smith & Wesson Model 10 M&P HB Revolver, 147
Smith & Wesson Model 22A Sport Pistol, 132
Smith & Wesson Model 22A Target Pistol, 142
Smith & Wesson Model 22S Sport Pistols, 133
Smith & Wesson Model 22S Target Pistol, 142
Smith & Wesson Model 317 Air Lite, 317 LadySmith Revolvers, 148
Smith & Wesson Model 331, 332 AirLite Ti Revolvers, 149
Smith & Wesson Model 337 Chief's Special AirLite Ti, 149
Smith & Wesson Model 340 PD Centennial, 148
Smith & Wesson Model 342 Centennial AirLite Ti, 149
Smith & Wesson Model 360 PD AirLite Sc Chief's Special, 149
Smith & Wesson Model 36LS, 60LS LadySmith, 147
Smith & Wesson Model 37 Chief's Special & AirWeight, 147
Smith & Wesson Model 386 PD AirLite Sc, 149
Smith & Wesson Model 3913 Traditional Double Action, 133
Smith & Wesson Model 3913-LS LadySmith Auto, 133
Smith & Wesson Model 3913TSW/3953TSW Auto Pistols, 133
Smith & Wesson Model 3953 DAO Pistol, 133
Smith & Wesson Model 4006 TDA Auto, 133

Smith & Wesson Model 4006 TSW, 134
Smith & Wesson Model 4013, 4053 TSW Autos, 133
Smith & Wesson Model 4043, 4046 DA Pistols, 134
Smith & Wesson Model 41 Target, 142
Smith & Wesson Model 410 DA Auto Pistol, 133
Smith & Wesson Model 442 Centennial Airweight, 149
Smith & Wesson Model 4500 Series Autos, 134
Smith & Wesson Model 4513TSW/4553TSW Pistols, 134
Smith & Wesson Model 4566 TSW, 134
Smith & Wesson Model 457 TDA Auto Pistol, 132
Smith & Wesson Model 500, 149
Smith & Wesson Model 5900 Series Auto Pistols, 134
Smith & Wesson Model 60 Chief's Special, 148
Smith & Wesson Model 610 Classic Hunter Revolver, 148
Smith & Wesson Model 617 K-22 Masterpiece, 148
Smith & Wesson Model 625 Revolver, 148
Smith & Wesson Model 629 Classic DX Revolver, 147
Smith & Wesson Model 629 Classic Revolver, 147
Smith & Wesson Model 629 Revolvers, 147
Smith & Wesson Model 637 AirWeight Revolver, 147
Smith & Wesson Model 638 AirWeight Bodyguard, 149
Smith & Wesson Model 64 Stainless M&P, 148
Smith & Wesson Model 640 Centennial DA Only, 148
Smith & Wesson Model 642 Airweight Revolver, 149
Smith & Wesson Model 642LS LadySmith Revolver, 149
Smith & Wesson Model 649 Bodyguard Revolver, 149
Smith & Wesson Model 657 Revolver, 149
Smith & Wesson Model 65LS LadySmith, 148
Smith & Wesson Model 65, 148
Smith & Wesson Model 66 Stainless Combat Magnum, 148
Smith & Wesson Model 67 Combat Masterpiece, 148
Smith & Wesson Model 686 Magnum Plus Revolver, 148
Smith & Wesson Model 696 Revolver, 149
Smith & Wesson Model 908 Auto Pistol, 133
Smith & Wesson Model 910 DA Auto Pistol, 133
Smith & Wesson Model 99, 134
Smith & Wesson Model CS40 Chief's Special Auto, 134
Smith & Wesson Model CS45 Chief's Special Auto, 134
Smith & Wesson Model CS9 Chief's Special Auto, 134
Spiller & Burr Revolver, 296
Springfield M1 Garand Rifle, 172
Springfield M6 Scout Pistol, 164
Springfield, Inc. 1911A1 Bullseye Wadcutter Pistol, 142
Springfield, Inc. 1911A1 Champion Pistol, 135
Springfield, Inc. 1911A1 High Capacity Pistol, 135
Springfield, Inc. 1911A1 N.M. Hardball Pistol, 143
Springfield, Inc. 1911A1 V-Series Ported Pistols, 135
Springfield, Inc. Basic Competition Pistol, 143
Springfield, Inc. Distinguished Pistol, 143
Springfield, Inc. Expert Pistol, 143
Springfield, Inc. Full-Size 1911A1 Auto Pistol, 134
Springfield, Inc. Leatham Legend TGO Series Pistols, 143
Springfield, Inc. Long Slide 1911 A1 Pistol, 135
Springfield, Inc. M-1 Garand American Combat Rifles, 243
Springfield, Inc. M1A Rifle, 172
Springfield, Inc. M1A Super Match, 243
Springfield, Inc. M1A/M-21 Tactical Model Rifle, 243
Springfield, Inc. M6 Scout Rifle/Shotgun, 222
Springfield, Inc. Micro-Compact 1911A1 Pistol, 135
Springfield, Inc. Trophy Match Pistol, 143
Springfield, Inc. TRP Pistols, 135
Springfield, Inc. Ultra Compact Pistol, 135
Springfield, Inc. X-Treme Duty, 135
SSK Industries AR-15 Rifles, 103
SSK Industries Contender and Encore Pistols, 98
Steyr Classic Mannlicher SBS Rifle, 201
Steyr LP 5CP Match Air Pistol, 311
Steyr LP10P Match Pistol, 311
Steyr M & S Series Auto Pistols, 135
Steyr SBS Forester Rifle, 202
Steyr SBS Prohunter Rifle, 202
Steyr Scout Bolt-Action Rifle, 202
Steyr SSG Bolt-Action Rifle, 202
STI Compact Auto Pistols, 96
STI Eagle 5.0, 6.0 Pistol, 143
STI Executive Pistol, 143
STI Trojan, 143
Stoeger Coach Gun Side-By-Side Shotgun, 283

Stoeger Condor Special, 273
Stoeger Model 2000, 253
Stoeger Single-Shot Shotgun, 288
Stoeger Uplander Side-By-Side Shotgun, 283
Stoner SR-15 M-5 Rifle, 172
Stoner SR-15 Match Rifle, 244
Stoner SR-25 Carbine, 172
Stoner SR-25 Match Rifle, 244

T

Tactical Response TR-870 Standard Model Shotgun, 291
Tanner 300 Meter Free Rifle, 244
Tanner 50 Meter Free Rifle, 244
Tanner Standard UIT Rifle, 244
Tar-Hunt DSG (Designated Slug Gun), 113
Tar-Hunt RSG-12 Professional Rifled Slug Gun, 288
Tar-Hunt RSG-20 Mountaineer Slug Gun, 288
Taurus Model 17 "Tracker", 150
Taurus Model 17-12 Target "Silhouette", 150
Taurus Model 17-C Series, 150
Taurus Model 217 Target "Silhouette", 151
Taurus Model 218 Raging Bee, 151
Taurus Model 22H Raging Hornet Revolver, 150
Taurus Model 30C Raging Thirty, 150
Taurus Model 415 Revolver, 151
Taurus Model 425/627 Tracker Revolvers, 151
Taurus Model 44 Revolver, 150
Taurus Model 44 Series Revolver, 151
Taurus Model 444/454/480 Raging Bull Revolvers, 151
Taurus Model 445 Series Revolver, 152
Taurus Model 445, 151
Taurus Model 450 Revolver, 151
Taurus Model 455 "Stellar Tracker", 151
Taurus Model 460 "Tracker", 151
Taurus Model 605 Revolver, 151
Taurus Model 608 Revolver, 151
Taurus Model 617 Revolver, 152
Taurus Model 617ULT Revolver , 152
Taurus Model 62 Pump Rifle, 228
Taurus Model 63 Rifle, 226
Taurus Model 63, 150
Taurus Model 65 Revolver, 150
Taurus Model 650CIA Revolver, 151
Taurus Model 651 CIA Revolver, 151
Taurus Model 66 Revolver, 150
Taurus Model 66 Silhouette Revolver, 150
Taurus Model 72 Pump Rifle, 228
Taurus Model 731 Revolver, 151
Taurus Model 817 Ultra-Lite Revolver, 152
Taurus Model 82 Heavy Barrel Revolver, 150
Taurus Model 85 Revolver, 150
Taurus Model 850 CIA Revolver, 152
Taurus Model 851 CIA Revolver, 152
Taurus Model 905, 405, 455 Pistol Caliber Revolvers, 152
Taurus Model 922 Sport Pistol, 137
Taurus Model 94 Revolver, 150
Taurus Model 94, 941 Revolver, 152
Taurus Model 970/971 Tracker Revolvers, 152
Taurus Model 980/981 Silhouette Revolvers, 152
Taurus Model PT 22/PT 25 Auto Pistols, 136
Taurus Model PT-100/101 Auto Pistol, 136
Taurus Model PT-111 Millennium Pro Auto Pistol, 136
Taurus Model PT-111 Millennium Titanium Pistol, 136
Taurus Model PT24/7, 136
Taurus Model PT-911 Auto Pistol, 136
Taurus Model PT92 Auto Pistol, 136
Taurus Model PT-938 Auto Pistol, 136
Taurus Model PT-940 Auto Pistol, 137
Taurus Model PT-945 Series, 137
Taurus Model PT-957 Auto Pistol, 137
Taurus Model PT99 Auto Pistol, 136
Taurus PT-132 Millenium Pro Auto Pistol, 136
Taurus PT-138 Millenium Pro Series, 136
Taurus PT-140 Millenium Pro Auto Pistol, 136
Taurus PT-145 Millenium Auto Pistol, 136
Taurus Raging Bull Model 416, 152
Taurus Silhouette Revolvers, 150

Tech Force 25 Air Rifle, 315
Tech Force 35 Air Pistol, 311
Tech Force 36 Air Rifle, 315
Tech Force 51 Air Rifle, 315
Tech Force 6 Air Rifle, 315
Tech Force 8 Air Pistol, 311
Tech Force BS4 Olympic Competition Air Rifle, 315
Tech Force S2-1 Air Pistol, 311
Tech Force SS2 Olympic Competition Air Pistol, 311
Texas Paterson 1836 Revolver, 296
Thompson/Center 22 LR Classic Rifle, 226
Thompson/Center Black Diamond Rifle XR, 307
Thompson/Center Encore "Katahdin" Carbine, 218
Thompson/Center Encore 209x50 Magnum Pistol, 293
Thompson/Center Encore 209x50 Magnum, 306
Thompson/Center Encore Pistol, 164
Thompson/Center Encore Rifled Slug Gun, 288
Thompson/Center Encore Rifle, 218
Thompson/Center Encore Turkey Gun, 288
Thompson/Center Fire Storm Rifle, 306
Thompson/Center G2 Contender Pistol, 164
Thompson/Center G2 Contender Rifle, 218
Thompson/Center Hawken Rifle, 307
Thompson/Center Stainless Encore Pistol, 164
Thompson/Center Stainless Encore Rifle, 218
Tikka Continental Long Range Hunting Rifle, 203
Tikka Continental Varmint Rifle, 203
Tikka Target Rifle, 244
Tikka Whitetail Hunter Left-Hand Bolt-Action Rifle, 202
Tikka Whitetail Hunter Stainless Synthetic, 203
Time Precision Bolt-Action Rifles, 101
Traditions 1874 Sharps Deluxe Rifle, 219
Traditions 1874 Sharps Sporting Deluxe Rifle, 219
Traditions 1874 Sharps Standard Rifle, 219
Traditions ALS 2100 Home Security, 253
Traditions ALS 2100 Hunter Combo, 253
Traditions ALS 2100 Series Semi-Automatic Shotguns, 253
Traditions ALS 2100 Slug Hunter, 253
Traditions ALS 2100 Turkey Semi-Automatic Shotgun, 253
Traditions ALS 2100 Waterfowl Semi-Automatic Shotgun, 253
Traditions Buckhunter Pro In-Line Pistol, 293
Traditions Buckhunter Pro Shotgun, 309
Traditions Buckskinner Carbine, 307
Traditions Classic Series O/U Shotguns, 274
Traditions Deerhunter Rifle Series, 307
Traditions E-Bolt 209 Bolt-Action Rifles, 307
Traditions Elite Series Side-By-Side Shotguns, 283
Traditions Hawken Woodsman Rifle, 308
Traditions Kentucky Pistol, 293
Traditions Kentucky Rifle, 308
Traditions Lightning 45 LD Bolt-Action Rifles, 307
Traditions Lightning Lightweight Magnum Bolt-Action Rifles, 307
Traditions Lightning Mag Bolt-Action Muzzleloader, 307
Traditions Mag 350 Series O/U Shotguns, 274
Traditions PA Pellet Flintlock, 308
Traditions Panther Sidelock Rifle, 307
Traditions Pennsylvania Rifle, 308
Traditions Pioneer Pistol, 293
Traditions Rolling Block Sporting Rifle in 30-30 Winchester, 219
Traditions Rolling Block Sporting Rifle, 219
Traditions Shenandoah Rifle, 308
Traditions Tennessee Rifle, 308
Traditions Tracker 209 In-Line Rifles, 308
Traditions Trapper Pistol, 293
Traditions Uplander Series Side-By-Side Shotguns, 283
Traditions Vest-Pocket Derringer, 293
Traditions William Parker Pistol, 293
Tristar CD Diana Auto Shotguns, 253
Tristar Derby Classic Side-By-Side, 283
Tristar Model 1887, 260
Tristar Rota Model 411 Side-By-Side, 283
Tristar Rota Model 411D Side-By-Side, 283
Tristar Rota Model 411F Side-By-Side, 283
Tristar Rota Model 411R Coach Gun Side-By-Side, 283
Tristar Silver II Shotgun, 274

Tristar Silver Sporting O/U, 274
Tristar TR-Class SL Emilio Rizzini O/U, 275
Tristar TR-I, II "Emilio Rizzini" Over/Unders, 275
Tristar TR-Mag "Emilio Rizzini" Over/Under, 275
Tristar TR-Royal "Emilio Rizzini" Over/Under, 274
Tristar TR-SC "Emilio Rizzini" Over/Under, 274
Tristar WS/OU 12 Shotgun, 275
Tristar TR-L "Emilio Rizzini" Over/Under, 275
Tristar/Sharps 1874 Sporting Rifle, 219
Tristar/Uberti 1860 Henry Rifle, 179
Tristar/Uberti 1860 Henry Trapper Carbine, 179
Tristar/Uberti 1866 Sporting Rifle, Carbine, 179
Tristar/Uberti 1873 Sporting Rifle, 178
Tristar/Uberti 1885 Single Shot, 219
Tristar/Uberti Regulator Revolver, 160

U

U.S. Fire-Arms "China Camp" Cowboy Action Revolver, 161
U.S. Fire-Arms Lightning Magazine Rifle , 179
U.S. Fire-Arms Rodeo Cowboy Action Revolver, 161
U.S. Fire-Arms Single Action Army Revolver, 161
U.S. Fire-Arms United States Pre-War, 161
Uberti 1861 Navy Percussion Revolver, 296
Uberti 1873 Buckhorn Single-Action, 160
Uberti 1873 Cattleman Single-Action, 160
Uberti 1875 SA Army Outlaw Revolver, 160
Uberti 1875 Schofield-Style Break-Top Revolver, 161
Uberti 1890 Army Outlaw Revolver, 160
Uberti Baby Rolling Block Carbine, 219
Uberti Bisley Model Flat Top Target Revolver, 161
Uberti Bisley Model Single-Action Revolver, 161
Uberti New Model Russian Revolver, 161
Uberti Rolling Block Target Pistol, 164

V

Vektor Bushveld Bolt-Action Rifle, 203
Vektor H5 Slide-Action Rifle, 179
Vektor Model 98 Bolt-Action Rifle, 203
Verona LX501 Hunting O/U Shotguns, 275
Verona LX680 Competition Trap, 276
Verona LX680 Skeet/Sporting, Trap O/U Shotguns, 276
Verona LX680 Sporting Over/Under Shotguns, 276
Verona LX692 Gold Hunting Over/Under Shotguns, 276
Verona LX692 Gold Sporting Over/Under Shotguns, 276
Verona LX702 Gold Trap Combo, 276
Verona LX702 Skeet/Trap O/U Shotguns, 276
Verona Model SX400 Semi Auto Shotgun, 253
Volquartsen Custom 22 Caliber Auto Pistols, 96
Volquartsen Custom 22 Caliber Auto Rifles, 103

W

Walker 1847 Percussion Revolver, 296
Walther GSP Match Pistol, 143
Walther LP300 Match Pistol, 312
Walther P22 Pistol, 137
Walther P99 Auto Pistol, 137
Walther P990 Auto Pistol, 137
Walther PPK American Auto Pistol, 137
Walther PPK/S American Auto Pistol, 137
Weatherby Athena Grade III Classic Field O/U, 277
Weatherby Athena Grade V Classic Field O/U, 276
Weatherby Athena Side-By-Side, 283
Weatherby Custom Shop Bolt-Action Rifles, 102
Weatherby Mark V Accumark Rifle, 204
Weatherby Mark V Accumark Ultra Lightweight Rifles, 204
Weatherby Mark V Dangerous Game Rifle, 205
Weatherby Mark V Deluxe Bolt-Action Rifle, 203
Weatherby Mark V Euromark Rifle, 204
Weatherby Mark V Eurosport Rifle, 204
Weatherby Mark V Fibermark Rifles, 205
Weatherby Mark V Lazermark Rifle, 203
Weatherby Mark V Royal Custom Rifle, 205
Weatherby Mark V Special Varmint Rifle (SVR), 205
Weatherby Mark V Sporter Rifle, 203
Weatherby Mark V Stainless Rifle, 204
Weatherby Mark V Super Big Gamemaster Deer Rifle, 205

Weatherby Mark V SVM/SPM Rifles, 205
Weatherby Mark V Synthetic, 204
Weatherby Orion Grade II Classic Field O/U, 277
Weatherby Orion Grade III Field O/U Shotguns, 277
Weatherby Orion Side-By-Side, 283
Weatherby Orion SSC Over/Under Shotgun, 277
Weatherby Orion Upland O/U, 277
Weatherby SAS (Semi-Automatic Shotguns), 254
Weatherby SAS Auto Shotgun, 254
Weatherby Threat Response Rifles (TRR) Series, 205
Whiscombe JW Series Air Rifles, 315
White Model 97 Whitetail Hunter Rifle, 308
White Model 98 Elite Hunter Rifle, 308
White Model 2000 Blacktail Hunter Rifle, 308
White Model Thunderbolt Rifle, 308
White Tominator Shotgun, 309
Wilderness Explorer Multi-Caliber Carbine, 205
Wilkinson Linda Auto Pistol, 137
Wilkinson Linda Carbine, 172
Wilkinson Linda L2 Limited Edition, 172
Wilkinson Sherry Auto Pistol, 137
Wilkinson Terry Carbine, 172
Winchester Model 1300 Black Shadow Field Gun, 261
Winchester Model 1300 Camp Defender®, 291
Winchester Model 1300 Deer Black Shadow Gun, 261
Winchester Model 1300 Defender Pump Guns, 291
Winchester Model 1300 Ranger Pump Gun, 261
Winchester Model 1300 Stainless Marine Pump Gun, 291
Winchester Model 1300 Turkey and Universal Hunter Models, 261
Winchester Model 1300 Upland Pump Gun, 261
Winchester Model 1300 Walnut Field Pump, 260
Winchester Model 1885 Low Wall Rimfire, 236
Winchester Model 1886 Extra Light Lever-Action Rifle, 180
Winchester Model 1895 Lever-Action Rifle, 180
Winchester Model 52B Bolt-Action Rifle, 236
Winchester Model 70 Black Shadow, 206
Winchester Model 70 Classic Compact, 206
Winchester Model 70 Classic Custom Rifles, 102
Winchester Model 70 Classic Featherweight, 206
Winchester Model 70 Classic Safari Express, 207
Winchester Model 70 Classic Sporter LT, 206
Winchester Model 70 Classic Stainless Rifle, 206
Winchester Model 70 Classic Super Grade, 207
Winchester Model 70 Coyote, 207
Winchester Model 70 Stealth Rifle, 207
Winchester Model 70 WSM Rifles, 207
Winchester Model 94 Legacy, 180
Winchester Model 94 Ranger Compact, 180
Winchester Model 94 Ranger, 180
Winchester Model 94 Traditional Big Bore, 179
Winchester Model 94 Traditional-CW, 179
Winchester Model 94 Trails End, 180
Winchester Model 94 Trapper, 180
Winchester Model 9410 Lever-Action Shotgun, 261
Winchester Model 9422 Lever-Action Rifles, 228
Winchester Super X2 Auto Shotgun, 254
Winchester Super X2 Field 3" Auto Shotgun, 254
Winchester Super X2 Sporting Clays Auto Shotgun, 254
Winchester Supreme O/U Shotguns, 277
Winchester Timber Carbine, 179

Z

Zouave Percussion Rifle, 308

NUMBERS

1861 Navy Percussion Revolver, 296
1862 Pocket Navy Percussion Revolver, 296
1st U.S. Model Dragoon, 296
2nd U.S. Model Dragoon Revolver, 296
3rd U.S. Model Dragoon Revolver, 296

Browning Luxus Grade B2

Browning Luxus Renaissance Argent

Browning Luxus Renaissance OR

Ed Brown Classic Class A

Ed Brown Kobra Carry

Kimber Ultra CDP

Kimber Ultra Royal II

BRILEY 1911-STYLE AUTO PISTOLS

Caliber: 9mm Para., 38 Super, 40 S&W, 10-shot magazine; 45 ACP, 8-shot magazine. **Barrel:** 3.6" or 5". **Weight:** NA. **Length:** NA. **Grips:** Rosewood or rubber. **Sights:** Bo-Mar adjustable rear, Briley dovetail blade front. **Features:** Modular or Caspian alloy, carbon steel or stainless steel frame; match barrel and trigger group; lowered and flared ejection port; front and rear serrations on slide; beavertail grip safety; hot blue, hard chrome or stainless steel finish. Introduced 2000. Made in U.S. From Briley Manufacturing Inc.

Price: Fantom (3.6" bbl., fixed low-mount rear sight, armor coated lower receiver) . . . . from **$1,900.00**
Price: Fantom with two-port compensator . . . . from **$2,245.00**
Price: Advantage (5" bbl., adj. low-mount rear sight, checkered mainspring housing) . . . . from **$1,650.00**
Price: Versatility Plus (5" bbl., adj. low-mount rear sight, modular or Caspian frame) . . . . from **$1,850.00**
Price: Signature Series (5" bbl., adj. low-mount rear sight, 40 S&W only) . . . . from **$2,250.00**
Price: Plate Master (5" bbl. with compensator, lightened slide, Briley scope mount) . . . . from **$1,895.00**
Price: El Presidente (5" bbl. with Briley quad compensator, Briley scope mount) . . . . from **$2,550.00**

BROWNING HI-POWER LUXUS

The legendary Browning Hi-Power pistol still produced in Belgium is available in four grades in the Luxus series: Grade II, Renaissance Argent, Grade B2 and the gold-finished Renaissance OR. Other specifications NA.
Price: . . . . **NA**

ED BROWN CLASSIC CUSTOM AND CLASS A LIMITED 1911-STYLE AUTO PISTOLS

Caliber: 45 ACP; 7-shot magazine; 40 S&W, 400 Cor-Bon, 38 Super, 9x23, 9mm Para. **Barrel:** 4.25", 5", 6". **Weight:** NA. **Length:** NA. **Grips:** Hogue exotic checkered wood. **Sights:** Bo-Mar or Novak rear, blade front. **Features:** Blued or stainless steel frame; ambidextrous safety; beavertail grip safety; checkered forestrap and mainspring housing; match-grade barrel; slotted hammer; long lightweight or Videki short steel trigger. Many options offered. Made in U.S. by Ed Brown Products.
Price: Classic Custom (45 ACP, 5" barrel) . . . . from **$2,895.00**
Price: Class A Limited (all calibers; several bbl. lengths in competition and carry forms) . . . . from **$2,250.00**
Price: Commander Bobtail (most calibers, 4.25" bbl., has "bobtail" modification to reduce overall length) . . . . from **$2,300.00**

Price: Kobra (45 ACP only, 5" bbl., completely hand-fitted with heavy dehorning) . . . . from **$1,795.00**
Price: Kobra Carry (45 ACP only, 4.25" bbl., has exclusive snakeskin pattern on frame, top portion of mainspring housing and slide) . . . . from **$1,995.00**

KIMBER CUSTOM II 1911-STYLE AUTO PISTOLS

Caliber: 9mm Para., 38 Super, 9-shot magazines; 40 S&W, 8-shot magazine; 45 ACP, 7-shot magazine. **Barrel:** 5". **Weight:** 38 oz. **Length:** 8.7" overall. **Grips:** Black synthetic, smooth or double-diamond checkered rosewood, or double-diamond checkered walnut. **Sights:** McCormick low profile or Kimber adjustable rear, blade front. **Features:** Machined steel slide, frame and barrel; front and rear beveled slide serrations; cut and button-rifled, match-grade barrel; adjustable aluminum trigger; full-length guide rod; Commander-style hammer; high-ride beavertail safety; beveled magazine well. Other models available. Made in U.S. by Kimber Mfg. Inc.
Price: Custom II (black matte finish) **$730.00**
Price: Custom Royal II (polished blue finish, checkered rosewood grips) **$886.00**
Price: Custom Stainless II (satin-finished stainless steel frame and slide) **$832.00**
Price: Custom Target II (matte black or stainless finish, Kimber adj. sight) **$945.00**
Price: Custom Compact CDP II (4" bbl., alum. frame, tritium three-dot sights, 28 oz.) **$1,141.00**
Price: Custom Pro CDP II (4" bbl., alum. frame, tritium sights, full-length grip, 28 oz.) **$1,141.00**
Price: Ultra CDP II (3" bbl., aluminum frame, tritium sights, 25 oz.) **$1,141.00**
Price: Gold Match II (polished blue finish, hand-fitted barrel, ambid. safety) . . . . from **$1,168.00**
Price: Stainless Gold Match II (stainless steel frame and slide, hand-fitted bbl., amb. safety) . . . . **$1,315.00 to $1,345.00**

Les Baer Thunder Ranch Special

Rock River Arms Limited Match

Volquartsen Stingray

LES BAER CUSTOM 1911-STYLE AUTO PISTOLS

Caliber: 9mm Para., 38 Super, 40 S&W, 45 ACP, 400 Cor-Bon; 7- or 8-shot magazine. **Barrel:** 4-1/4", 5", 6". **Weight:** 28 to 40 oz. **Length:** NA. **Grips:** Checkered cocobolo. **Sights:** Low-mount combat fixed, combat fixed with tritium inserts or low-mount adjustable rear, dovetail front. **Features:** Forged steel or aluminum frame; slide serrated front and rear; lowered and flared ejection port; beveled magazine well; speed trigger with 4-pound pull; beavertail grip safety; ambidextrous safety. Other models available. Made in U.S. by Les Baer Custom.

Price: Baer 1911 Premier II 5" Model (5" bbl., optional stainless steel frame and slide) . . . . from **$1,498.00**
Price: Premier II 6" Model (6" barrel) . . . . from **$1,675.00**
Price: Premier II LW1 (forged aluminum frame, steel slide and barrel)
. . . . from **$1,835.00**
Price: Custom Carry (4" or 5" barrel, steel frame) . . . . . . from **$1,728.00**
Price: Custom Carry (4" barrel, aluminum frame) . . . . . . from **$2,039.00**
Price: Swift Response Pistol (fixed tritium sights, Bear Coat finish)
. . . . from **$2,339.00**
Price: Monolith (5" barrel and slide with extra-long dust cover)
. . . . from **$1,660.00**
Price: Stinger (4-1/4" barrel, steel or aluminum frame) . . . from **$1,552.00**
Price: Thunder Ranch Special (tritium fixed combat sight, Thunder Ranch logo) . . . . from **$1,685.00**
Price: National Match Hardball (low-mount adj. sight; meets DCM rules)
. . . . from **$1,425.00**
Price: Bullseye Wadcutter Pistol (Bo-Mar rib w/ adj. sight, guar. 2-1/2" groups) . . . . from **$1,560.00**
Price: Ultimate Master Combat (5" or 6" bbl., adj. sights, checkered front strap) . . . . from **$2,530.00**
Price: Ultimate Master Combat Compensated (four-port compensator, adj. sights) . . . . from **$2,558.00**

ROCK RIVER ARMS 1911-STYLE AUTO PISTOLS

Caliber: 9mm Para., 38 Super, 40 S&W, 45 ACP. **Barrel:** 4" or 5". **Weight:** NA. **Length:** NA. **Grips:** Double-diamond, checkered cocobolo or black synthetic. **Sights:** Bo-Mar low-mount adjustable, Novak fixed with tritium inserts, Heine fixed or Rock River scope mount; dovetail front blade. **Features:** Chrome-moly, machined steel frame and slide; slide serrated front and rear; aluminum speed trigger with 3.5-4 lb. pull; national match KART barrel; lowered and flared ejection port; tuned and polished extractor; beavertail grip safety; beveled mag. well. Other frames offered. Made in U.S. by Rock River Arms Inc.

Price: Elite Commando (4" barrel, Novak tritium sights) **$1,395.00**
Price: Standard Match (5" barrel, Heine fixed sights) **$1,150.00**
Price: National Match Hardball (5" barrel, Bo-Mar adj. sights)
. . . . from **$1,275.00**
Price: Bullseye Wadcutter (5" barrel, Rock River slide scope mount)
. . . . from **$1,380.00**
Price: Basic Limited Match (5" barrel, Bo-Mar adj. sights) from **$1,395.00**
Price: Limited Match (5" barrel, guaranteed 1-1/2" groups at 50 yards)
. . . . from **$1,795.00**
Price: Hi-Cap Basic Limited (5" barrel, four frame choices) from **$1,895.00**
Price: Ultimate Match Achiever (5" bbl. with compensator, mount and Aimpoint) . . . . from **$2,255.00**
Price: Match Master Steel (5" bbl. with compensator, mount and Aimpoint)
. . . . **$5,000.00**

STI COMPACT AUTO PISTOLS

Caliber: 9mm Para., 40 S&W. **Barrel:** 3.4". **Weight:** 28 oz. **Length:** 7" overall. **Grips:** Checkered double-diamond rosewood. **Sights:** Heine Low Mount fixed rear, slide integral front. **Features:** Similar to STI 2011 models except has compact frame, 7-shot magazine in 9mm (6-shot in 40 cal.), single-sided thumb safety, linkless barrel lockup system, matte blue finish. From STI International.

Price: (9mm Para. or 40 S&W) . . . . from **$746.50**

VOLQUARTSEN CUSTOM 22 CALIBER AUTO PISTOLS

Caliber: 22 LR; 10-shot magazine. **Barrel:** 3.5" to 10"; stainless steel air gauge. **Weight:** 2-1/2 to 3 lbs. 10 oz. **Length:** NA. **Grips:** Finger-grooved plastic or walnut. **Sights:** Adjustable rear and blade front or Weaver-style scope mount. **Features:** Conversions of Ruger Mk. II Auto pistol. Variety of configurations featuring compensators, underlug barrels, etc. Stainless steel finish; black Teflon finish available for additional $85; target hammer, trigger. Made in U.S. by Volquartsen Custom.

Price: 3.5 Compact (3.5" barrel, T/L adjustable rear sight, scope base optional) **$640.00**
Price: Deluxe (barrel to 10", T/L adjustable rear sight) **$675.00**
Price: Deluxe with compensator **$745.00**
Price: Masters (6.5" barrel, finned underlug, T/L adjustable rear sight, compensator) **$950.00**
Price: Olympic (7" barrel, recoil-reducing gas chamber, T/L adjustable rear sight) **$870.00**
Price: Stingray (7.5" ribbed, ported barrel; red-dot sight) **$995.00**
Price: Terminator (7.5" ported barrel, grooved receiver, scope rings)
. . . . **$730.00**
Price: Ultra-Light Match (6" tensioned barrel, Weaver mount, weighs 2-1/2 lbs.) **$885.00**
Price: V-6 (6", triangular, ventilated barrel with underlug, T/L adj. sight)
. . . . **$1,030.00**
Price: V-2000 (6" barrel with finned underlug, T/L adj. sight) . . **$1,095.00**
Price: V-Magic II (7.5" barrel, red-dot sight) **$1,055.00**

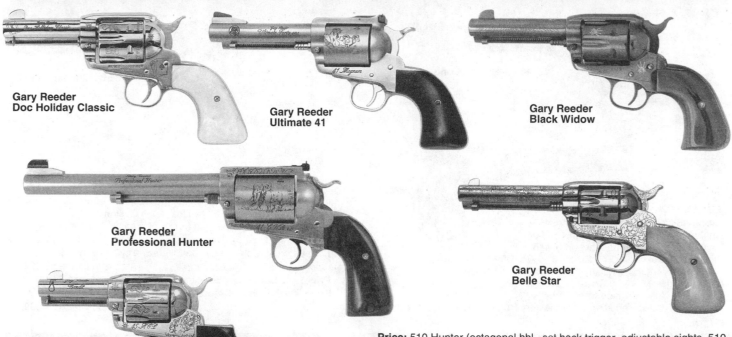

Gary Reeder
Doc Holliday Classic

Gary Reeder
Ultimate 41

Gary Reeder
Black Widow

Gary Reeder
Professional Hunter

Gary Reeder
Belle Star

Gary Reeder
Bandit

GARY REEDER CUSTOM GUNS REVOLVERS

Caliber: 22 WMR, 22 Hornet, 218 Bee, 356 GMR, 41 GNR, 410 GNR, 510 GNR, 357 Magnum, 45 Colt, 44-40, 41 Magnum, 44 Magnum, 454 Casull, 475 Linebaugh, 500 Linebaugh. **Barrel:** 2-1/2" to 12". **Weight:** Varies by model. **Length:** Varies by model. **Grips:** Black Cape buffalo horn, laminated walnut, simulated pearl, black and ivory micarta, others. **Sights:** Notch fixed or adjustable rear, blade or ramp front. **Features:** Custom conversions of Ruger Vaquero, Blackhawk Bisley and Super Blackhawk frames. Jeweled hammer and trigger, tuned action, model name engraved on barrel, additional engraving on frame and cylinder, integral muzzle brake, finish available in high-polish or satin stainless steel or black Chromex finish. Also available on customer's gun at reduced cost. Other models available. Made in U.S. by Gary Reeder Custom Guns.

Price: Gamblers Classic (2-1/2" bbl., engraved cards and dice, no ejector rod housing) . . . . from **$995.00**

Price: Tombstone Classic (3-1/2" bbl. with gold bands, notch sight, birdshead grips) . . . . from **$995.00**

Price: Doc Holliday Classic (3-1/2" bbl., engraved cards and dice, white pearl grips) . . . . from **$995.00**

Price: Ultimate Vaquero (engraved barrel, frame and cylinder, made to customer specs) . . . . from **$995.00**

Price: Black Widow (4-5/8" bbl., black Chromex finish, black widow spider engraving) . . . . from **$1,095.00**

Price: Cowboy Classic (stainless finish, cattle brand engraved, limited to 100 guns) . . . . from **$995.00**

Price: African Hunter (6" bbl., with or without muzzle brake, 475 or 500 Linebaugh) (on your gun from) **$1,295.00**

Price: Alaskan Survivalist (3" bbl., Redhawk frame, engraved bear, 45 Colt or 44 Magnum) . . . . from **$1,095.00**

Price: Ultimate Back-Up (3-1/2" bbl., fixed sights, choice of animal engraving, 475 Linebaugh, 500 Linebaugh) (on your gun from) **$1,295.00**

Price: Double Deuce (8" heavy bbl., adjustable sights, laminated grips, 22 WMR 8-shot) . . . . from **$1,195.00**

Price: Ultimate 41 (410 GNR 5-shot, built on customer furnished Ruger frame) . . . . from **$1,295.00**

Price: 510 Hunter (octagonal bbl., set back trigger, adjustable sights, 510 GNR 5-shot, built on customer furnished Ruger frame) . . from **$1,495.00**

Price: American Hunter (475 Linebaugh or 500 Linebaugh, built to customers specs on furnished Ruger frame) . . . . from **$1,295.00**

Price: Ultimate 44 ((ported, special recoil-taming grip frame, sling swivels, 44 Mag. 5-shot, built on customer furnished Ruger Hunter)
. . . . from **$1,295.00**

Price: Professional Hunter (stretch frame stainless 5-shot available in calibers including 475 Maximum and 500 Maximum) . . . . from **$2,395.00**

Price: Classic 45 (shoots 45 Colt, 45 ACP or 45 Schofield without moon clips, built to customer specs on customer furnished Ruger frame)
. . . . from **$1,295.00**

Price: Belle Starr Classic (engraved with gunfighter grip, 32 H&R)
. . . . from **$1,095.00**

Price: Bandit (3-1/2" bbl., special Lightning style grip frame built on a Ruger Vaquero frame, engraved, set back trigger, Colt-style hammer)
. . . . from **$1,095.00**

Price: Southern Comfort (5 shot cylinder, heavy duty base pin, tear drop hammer, special set back trigger, interchangeable blade system, special gripframe, satin Vapor Honed finish) . . . . from **$1,095.00**

Price: Ultimate 480 (choice of barrel lengths in any caliber, full vapor honed stainless steel, satin finish Black Chromex or two-toned finish, 5 shot cylinder, heavy barrel, Gunfighter grip, full action job, custom laminated grips, freewheeling cylinder, Belt Mountain base pin) . . . . from **$995.00**

Price: Coyote Classic (chambered in 22 Hornet, 22 K-Hornet, 218 Bee, 218 Mashburn Bee, 17 Ackley Bee, 17 Ackley Hornet, 256 Winchester, 25-20, 6-shot unfluted cylinder, heavy 8" barrel, Super Blackhawk gripframe, finish of satin stainless, satin Black Chromex or high polished, comes with laminated cherry grips and Gunfighter grip) . . . . from **$995.00**

Price: Ultimate 50 (choice of barrel lengths in any centerfire caliber, 5 shot stainless steel 50 Action Express, freewheeling cylinder) from **$1,195.00**

Price: Ultimate Black Widow (475 Linebaugh or 500 Linebaugh, heavy duty 5 shot cylinder, heavy high grade barrel, Gunfighter Grip with black Micarta grips, Belt Mountain base pin) . . . . from **$1,295.00**

Price: 45 Backpacker (weighs 28 oz., comes in 45 Long Colt, all stainless except for lightweight aircraft aluminum gripframe, black Micarta grips, not recommended for Plus P ammo) . . . . from **$995.00**

Price: Rio Grande Classic (built on any caliber Vaquero in barrel length of choice, Gunfighter grip, engraving is old southwest type with a few western features, specially designed base pin, long tapered hammer)
. . . . from **$995.00**

44 Linebaugh Long

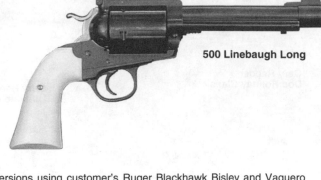

500 Linebaugh Long

500 Linebaugh

LINEBAUGH CUSTOM SIXGUNS REVOLVERS

Caliber: 45 Colt, 44 Linebaugh Long, 458 Linebaugh, 475 Linebaugh, 500 Linebaugh, 500 Linebaugh Long, 445 Super Mag. **Barrel:** 4-3/4", 5-1/2", 6", 7-1/2"; other lengths available. **Weight:** NA. **Length:** NA. **Grips:** Dustin Linebaugh Custom made to customer's specs. **Sights:** Bowen steel rear or factory Ruger; blade front. **Features:** Conversions using customer's Ruger Blackhawk Bisley and Vaquero Bisley frames. Made in U.S. by Linebaugh Custom Sixguns.
Price: Small 45 Colt conversion (rechambered cyl., new barrel) . . . . from **$1,200.00**
Price: Large 45 Colt conversion (oversized cyl., new barrel, 5- or 6-shot) . . . . from **$1,800.00**
Price: 475 Linebaugh, 500 Linebaugh conversions from **$1,800.00**
Price: Linebaugh and 445 Super Mag calibers on 357 Maximum frame . . . . from **$3,000.00**

Gary Reeder Ultimate Encore

Gary Reeder Kodiak Hunter Dall Sheep

SSK Industries Contender

GARY REEDER CUSTOM GUNS CONTENDER AND ENCORE PISTOLS

Caliber: 22 Cheetah, 218 Bee, 22 K-Hornet, 22 Hornet, 218 Mashburn Bee, 22-250 Improved, 6mm/284, 7mm STW, 7mm GNR, 30 GNR, 338 GNR, 300 Win. Magnum, 338 Win. Magnum, 350 Rem. Magnum, 358 STA, 375 H&H, 378 GNR, 416 Remington, 416 GNR, 450 GNR, 475 Linebaugh, 500 Linebaugh, 50 Alaskan, 50 AE, 454 Casull; others available. **Barrel:** 8" to 15" (others available). **Weight:** NA. **Length:** Varies with barrel length. **Grips:** Walnut fingergroove. **Sights:** Express-style adjustable rear and barrel band front (Kodiak Hunter); none furnished most models. **Features:** Offers complete guns and barrels in the T/C Contender and Encore. Integral muzzle brake, engraved animals and model name, tuned action, high-polish or satin stainless steel or black Chromex finish. Made in U.S. by Gary Reeder Custom Guns.
Price: Kodiak Hunter (50 AE, 475 Linebaugh, 500 Linebaugh, 510 GNR, or 454 Casull, Kodiak bear and Dall sheep engravings) from **$1,195.00**
Price: Ultimate Encore (15" bbl. with muzzle brake, custom engraving) . . . . from **$1,095.00**

SSK INDUSTRIES CONTENDER AND ENCORE PISTOLS

Caliber: More than 200, including most standard pistol and rifle calibers, as well as 226 JDJ, 6mm JDJ, 257 JDJ, 6.5mm JDJ, 7mm JDJ, 6.5mm Mini-Dreadnaught, 30-06 JDJ, 280 JDJ, 375 JDJ, 6mm Whisper, 300 Whisper and 338 Whisper. **Barrel:** 10" to 26"; blued or stainless; variety of configurations. **Weight:** Varies with barrel length and features. **Length:** Varies with barrel length. **Grips:** Pachmayr, wood models available. **Features:** Offers frames, barrels and complete guns in the T/C Contender and Encore. Fluted, diamond, octagon and round barrels; flatside Contender frames; chrome-plating; muzzle brakes; trigger jobs; variety of stocks and forends; sights and optics. Made in U.S. by SSK Industries.
Price: Blued Contender frame . . . . from **$390.00**
Price: Stainless Contender frame . . . . from **$390.00**
Price: Blued Encore frame . . . . from **$290.00**
Price: Stainless Encore frame . . . . from **$318.00**
Price: Contender barrels . . . . from **$315.00**
Price: Encore barrels . . . . from **$340.00**

SEMI-CUSTOM

Ed Brown 702 Varmint

Ed Brown 702 Bushveld

ED BROWN CUSTOM BOLT-ACTION RIFLES

Caliber: 222, 223, 22-250, 220 Swift, 243, 243 Ackley Imp., 25-06, 270 Win., 280 Rem., 280 Ackley Imp., 6mm, 6.5/284, 7mm/08, 7mm Rem. Mag., 7STW, 30/06, 308, 300 Win. Mag., 338 Win. Mag., 375 H&H, 404 Jeffery, 416 Rem. Mag., 416 Rigby, 458 Win. Mag. **Barrel:** 21", 24", 26". **Weight:** NA. **Length:** NA. **Stock:** Fiberglass synthetic; swivel studs; recoil pad. **Sights:** Optional; Talley scope rings and base furnished; scope mounting included in price (scope extra). **Features:** Machined receiver; hand-fitted bolt with welded handle; M16-type extractor; three-position safety; trigger adjustable for pull and overtravel; match-quality, hand-lapped barrel with deep countersunk crowning. Made in U.S. by Ed Brown Custom, Inc.

Price: Model 702 Savanna short- or long-action repeater (lightweight 24" or medium-weight 26"barrel) . . from **$2,800.00**
Price: Model 702 Tactical long-action repeater (heavy contour 26" barrel) . . . . from **$2,900.00**
Price: Model 702 Ozark short-action repeater (lightweight 21" barrel) . . . . from **$2,800.00**
Price: Model 702 Varmint short-action single shot (med. 26" or hvy. 24") . . . . from **$2,800.00**
Price: Model 702 Light Tactical short-action repeater (med. 21" barrel) . . . . from **$2,800.00**
Price: Model 702 Bushveld dangerous game rifle (24" med. or heavy barrel) from **$2,900.00**
Price: Model 702 Denali mountain hunting rifle (22" super light weight bbl. or 23" light weight bbl.) . . . . . . from **$2,800.00**
Price: Model 702 Tactical sniper rifle (26" heavy bbl.) . . . . from **$2,900.00**
Price: Model 702 Marine Sniper (24" heavy bbl.) . . . . from **$2,900.00**

Dakota 76 Classic

Dakota 97 Hunter

DAKOTA 76 RIFLE

Caliber: All calibers from 22-250 through 458 Win. Mag. **Barrel:** 23". **Weight:** 6-1/2 lbs. **Length:** NA. **Stock:** Choice of X-grade oil-finished English, Bastogne or Claro walnut. **Features:** Short, standard short magnum or long magnum actions, hand checkered stock with 1" black recoil pad, steel grip cap and single screw stud sling swivels. Many options and upgrades available.

Price: Dakota 76 Classic . . . . from **$3,795.00**
Price: Dakota 76 Safari (23" bbl., calibers from 257 Roberts through 458 Win. Mag.drop belly magazine
with straddle floorplate) . . . . from **$4,795.00**
Price: Dakota 76 African (24" bbl., 450 Dakota, 416 Dakota, 416 Rigby, 404 Jeffrey,
four-round magazine) . . . . from **$5,495.00**
Price: Dakota 97 Hunter (24" bbl., calibers from 25-06 to 375 Dakota, synthetic stock) . . . . from **$2,150.00**
Price: Longbow Tactical Engagement Rifle (28" bbl., 338 Lapua Mag., 330 Dakota, 300 Dakota,
McMillan fiberglass stock with full-length action bedding) . . . . from **$4,500.00**

SEMI-CUSTOM RIFLES — BOLT-ACTION

Legacy Sports Texas Safari

LEGACY SPORTS INTERNATIONAL TEXAS SAFARI RIFLES

Built by famed gunsmith Bill Wiseman, features include a variety of available calibers, fluted barrels, muzzle brake, customized mill cuts on receiver and bolt sleeve, three-position safety, receiver-mounted bolt release lever, Teflon finish on all metal parts, Leupold scope bases, detachable magazine, reinforced lug area, polymer stock with painted finish, glass bedding, free floating barrel, and sling swivel studs. Built to order.

    Price: Texas Safari Rifle . . . . **NA**

Remington Model ABG

REMINGTON MODEL 700 CUSTOM SHOP RIFLES

Caliber: 270 Win., 280 Rem., 30-06, 7mm Rem. Mag., 7mm STW, 300 Win. Mag., 300 Wea. Mag., 338 Win. Mag., 8mm Rem. Mag., 35 Whelen, 375 H&H Mag., 416 Rem. Mag., 458 Win. Mag., 7mm RUM, 300 RUM, 338 RUM, 375 RUM. **Barrel:** 22", 24", 26". **Weight:** 6 lbs. 6 oz. to 9 lbs. **Length:** 44-1/4" to 46-1/2" overall. **Stock:** Laminated hardwood, walnut or Kevlar-reinforced fiberglass. **Sights:** Adjustable rear (Safari models); all receivers drilled and tapped for scope mounts. **Features:** Black matte, satin blue or uncolored stainless steel finish; hand-fitted action is epoxy-bedded to stock; tuned trigger; bolt-supported extractor for sure extraction; fancy wood and other options available. Made in U.S. by Remington Arms Co.

    Price: Custom KS Mountain Rifle (24" barrel, synthetic stock, 6-3/4 lbs. in mag. cals.) . . . . from **$1,314.00**
    Price: Custom KS Safari Stainless (22" barrel, synthetic stock, 9 lbs.) . . . . from **$1,697.00**
    Price: Model ABG (African Big Game – 26" bbl., laminated stock, satin blue finish) . . . . from **$1,726.00**
    Price: APR (African Plains Rifle — 26" barrel, laminated stock, satin blue finish) . . . . from **$1,716.00**
    Price: AWR (Alaskan Wilderness Rifle — 24" barrel, syn. stock, black matte finish) . . . . from **$1,593.00**
    Price: Model 700 Custom C Grade – from $1,733.00; Custom High Grade . . . . from **$3,297.00**

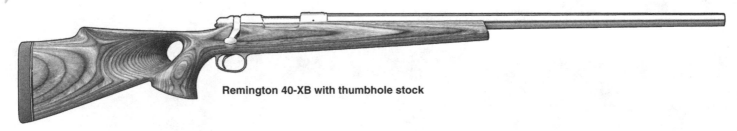

Remington 40-XB with thumbhole stock

REMINGTON MODEL 40-X CUSTOM SHOP TARGET RIFLES

Caliber: 22 LR, 22 WMR, 22 BR Rem., 222 Rem., 223 Rem., 22-250, 220 Swift, 6mm BR Rem., 6mm Rem., 243 Win., 25-06, 260 Rem., 7.62mm NATO, 7mm BR Rem., 7mm Rem. Mag., 7mm STW, 308 Win., 30-06, 300 Win. Mag. **Barrel:** 24", 27-1/4"; various twist rates offered. **Weight:** 9-3/4 to 11 lbs. **Length:** 40" to 47" overall. **Stock:** Walnut, laminated wood or Kevlar-reinforced fiberglass. **Sights:** None; receiver drilled and tapped for scope mounts. **Features:** Single shot or 5-shot repeater; carbon steel or stainless steel receiver; externally adjustable trigger (1-1/2 to 3-1/2 lbs.); rubber butt pad. From Remington Arms Co.

    Price: 40-XB Rangemaster (27-1/4" bbl., walnut stock, forend rail with hand stop) . . . . from **$1,636.00**
    Price: 40-XB (with thumbhole stock) . . . . from **$1,848.00**
    Price: 40-XB KS (27-1/4" bbl., black synthetic stock) . . . . from **$1,876.00**
    Price: 40-XRBR KS (24" bbl., Remington green synthetic stock with straight comb) . . . . from **$1,894.00**
    Price: 40-XC KS (24" bbl., gray synthetic stock with adj. comb) . . . . from **$1,821.00**
    Price: 40-XB Tactical (27-1/4" bbl., synthetic stock, matte finish) . . . . from **$2,108.00**

SEMI-CUSTOM

SEMI-CUSTOM RIFLES — BOLT-ACTION

Remington Model Seven Custom MS

REMINGTON MODEL SEVEN CUSTOM SHOP RIFLES

Caliber: 222 Rem., 223 Rem., 22-250 Rem., 243 Win., 6mm Rem., 250 Savage, 257 Roberts, 260 Rem., 308 Win., 7mm-08 Rem., 35 Rem., 350 Rem. Mag. **Barrel:** 20". **Weight:** 5-3/4 to 6-1/2 lbs. **Length:** 39-1/2" overall. **Stock:** Laminated hardwood or Kevlar-reinforced fiberglass. **Sights:** Adjustable ramp rear, hooded blade front. **Features:** Hand-fitted action; epoxy bedded; deep blue or non-reflective black matte finish; drilled and tapped for scope mounts. From Remington Arms Co.
    Price: Model Seven Custom MS (20" bbl., Mannlicher stock, deep blue finish) . . . . from **$1,332.00**
    Price: Model Seven Custom KS (20" bbl., synthetic stock, matte finish) . . . . from **$1,314.00**
    Price: Model Seven AWR Alaskan Wilderness Rifle (22" bbl., synthetic stock, 7mm Rem. SAUM, 300 Rem. SAUM) from **$1,546.00**

John Rigby African Express Rifle

JOHN RIGBY CUSTOM AFRICAN EXPRESS RIFLE

Caliber: 375 H&H Magnum, 416 Rigby, 450 Rigby, 458 Winchester, 505 Gibbs. **Barrel:** To customer specs. **Weight:** NA. **Length:** To customer specs. **Stock:** Customer's choice. **Sights:** Express- type rear, hooded ramp front; scope mounts offered. **Features:** Handcrafted bolt-action rifle built to customer specifications. Variety of engraving and stock wood options available. Imported from England by John Rigby & Co.
    Price: African Express Rifle
    . . . . from **$18,600.00**

John Rigby African Express Rifle engraving

JOHN RIGBY BOLT-ACTION RIFLES

Caliber: 300 H&H, 375 H&H, 416 Rigby, 458 Win., 500 Jeffrey (other calibers upon request) **Barrel:** NA. **Weight:** NA. **Length:** NA. **Stock:** Exhibition grade English walnut. **Sights:** Quarter rib with Express sights containing flip up night sight. **Features:** Stock custom-fitted to buyer specifications, detachable scope mounts included, Pac Nor Match grade barrel.
    Price: John Rigby Bolt Action Rifle . . . . from **$14,500.00**

TIME PRECISION BOLT-ACTION RIFLES

Caliber: 22 LR, 222, 223, 308, 378, 300 Win. Mag., 416 Rigby, others. **Barrel:** NA. **Weight:** 10 lbs. and up. **Length:** NA. **Stock:** Fiberglass. **Sights:** None; receiver drilled and tapped for scope mount. **Features:** Thirty different action types offered, including single shots and repeaters for bench rest, varmint and big-game hunting. Machined chrome-moly action; three-position safety; Shilen match trigger (other triggers available); twin cocking cams; dual firing pin. Built to customer specifications. From Time Precision.
    Price: 22 LR Bench Rest Rifle (Shilen match-grade stainless steel bbl., fiberglass stock) . . . . from **$2,202.00**
    Price: 22 LR Target Rifle . . . . from **$2,220.00**
    Price: 22 LR Sporter . . . . from **$1,980.00**
    Price: 22 LR Benchrest Rifle . . . . from **$2,202.00**
    Price: Hunting Rifle (calibers to 30-06) . . . . from **$2,202.00**
    Price: Benchrest Rifle (most calibers) . . . . from **$2,202.00**
    Price: Hunting Rifle (7mm Rem. Mag., 300 Win. Mag., 338 Win. Mag.) . . . . from **$2,322.00**

Weatherby Safari Grade

Weatherby Crown Custom

Weatherby Custom close-up

WEATHERBY CUSTOM SHOP BOLT-ACTION RIFLES

Caliber: 257 Wby. Mag., 270 Wby. Mag., 7mm Wby. Mag., 300 Wby. Mag., 340 Wby. Mag., 375 H&H Mag., 378 Wby. Mag., 416 Wby. Mag., 460 Wby. Mag. **Barrel:** 24", 26", 28". **Weight:** NA. **Length:** NA. **Stock:** Monte Carlo, modified Monte Carlo or Classic design in Exhibition- or Exhibition Special Select grades of claro or French walnut; injection-molded synthetic in Snow Camo, Alpine Camo or Dark Timber colors. **Sights:** Quarter-rib rear with one standing and one folding leaf, hooded ramp front (Safari Grade); drilled and tapped for scope mount. **Features:** Rosewood or ebony pistol-grip caps with inlaid diamonds in rosewood, walnut or maple; three grades of engraving patterns for receiver, bolt and handle; gold inlays; wooden inlaid buttstock, forearm and magazine box; three grades of engraved and gold inlaid rings and bases; canvas/leather, solid leather or leather with oak trim case. From the Weatherby Custom Shop.

Price: Safari Grade (engr. floorplate, oil-finished French wal. stock w/fleur-de-lis checkering.) **$5,654.00**
Price: Crown (engr., inlaid floorplate, engr. bbl. and receiver, hand-carved walnut stock) **$7,249.00**
Price: Crown Custom (engraved barrel, receiver and triggerguard, hand-carved walnut stock, damascened bolt and follower with checkered knob) . . . . from **$7,249.00**
Price: Outfitter Krieger (Krieger stainless steel bbl.) **$3,639.00**
Price: Outfitter Custom (standard barrel, Bell and Carlson syn. camo stock) . . . . from **$2,414.00**
Price: Dangerous Game Rifle (chrome moly Criterion barrel by Krieger Monte Carlo-style composite stock, Mark V action) . . . . from **$2,892.00**

Winchester African Express

WINCHESTER MODEL 70 CLASSIC CUSTOM RIFLES

Caliber: 375 H&H Mag., 416 Rem. Mag., 458 Win. Mag., 458 Lott, 470 Capstick, 257 Roberts, 260 Rem., 7mm-08 Rem., 300 WSM, 270 WSM, 7mm WSM, 308 Win., 358 Win., 450 Marlin, 270 Win., 7mm Win., 30-06 Spfld., 25-06 Rem., 6.5x55 Swe., 264 Win. Mag., 280 Rem., 35 Whelen, 7mm Rem. Mag., 7mm Ultra Mag., 7mm STW, 300 Win. Mag., 300 Wea. Mag., 300 Ultra. Mag., 338 Ultra Mag., 375 H&H (Lwt). **Barrel:** 22", 24", 26". **Weight:** 6.5 to 9.5 lbs. **Length:** NA. **Stock:** Various grades of walnut and synthetic stocks available. **Sights:** Three-leaf express rear, adjustable front, (Express models); none furnished on other models. **Features:** Match-grade cut rifled barrels with squared, hand-honed actions. Most are available in stainless or blued, and right- or left-handed, hand-fitted actions. All utilize the pre-'64 type action with controlled round feed, receiver-mounted blade ejector and specially-tuned trigger systems. All are shipped in a hard case. Made in U.S.A. by Winchester/U.S. Repeating Arms Co.

Price: Model 70 Classic Custom African Express (22" or 24" barrel, 9.25 to 9.5 lbs) . . . . from **$4,572.00**
Price: Safari Express (24" barrel, 9 to 9.25 lbs.) . . . . from **$3,043.00**
Price: Short Action (24" barrel, 7.5 to 8.25 lbs.) . . . . from **$2,708.00**
Price: Featherweight (22" barrel, 7.25 lbs., 270 Win., 7mm Win., 30-06 Spfld.) . . . . from **$2,708.00**
Price: Carbon (24" or 26" barrel, 6.5 to 7 lbs.) . . . . from **$3,233.00**
Price: Ultimate Classic (24" or 26" barrel, 7.5 to 7.75 lbs.) . . . . from **$2,941.00**
Price: Extreme Weather (22", 24" or 26" barrel, 7.25 to 7.5 lbs.) . . . . from **$2,525.00**

SEMI-CUSTOM

Bushmaster DCM Competition Rifle

Volquartsen Grey Ghost

BROWNING SEMI-AUTO 22 LUXE

Caliber: 22 LR. **Barrel:** 19-1/4". **Weight:** 5 lbs. 3 oz. **Length:** 37". **Stock:** Polished walnut. **Sights:** Adjustable folding leaf rear, gold bead front. **Features:** The traditional John Browning-designed .22 takedown autoloader with bottom eject. Grooved receiver will accept most groove or tip-off type mounts or receiver sights. Custom shop versions are available in two grades of: SA 22 Grade II, and SA 22 Grade III.

Price: . . . . **NA**

BROWNING BAR MARK I

The original Browning BAR Mark I from the Browning Custom Shop in Belgium available in two grades: Grade IV and Grade D.

Price: . . . . **NA**

BUSHMASTER SEMI-AUTO RIFLES

Caliber: 223. **Barrel:** 16" regular or fluted, 20" regular, heavy or fluted, 24" heavy or fluted. **Weight:** 6.9 to 8.37 lbs. **Length:** 34.5" to 38.25" overall. **Stock:** Polymer. **Sights:** Fully adjustable dual flip- up aperture rear, blade front or Picatinny rail for scope mount. **Features:** Versions of the AR-15 style rifle. Aircraft-quality aluminum receiver; chrome-lined barrel and chamber; chrome-moly-vanadium steel barrel with 1:9" twist; manganese phosphate matte finish; forged front sight; receiver takes down without tools; serrated, finger groove pistol grip. Made in U.S.A. by Bushmaster Firearms/Quality Parts Co.

Price: DCM Competition Rifle **$1,495.00**

LES BAER AR 223 AUTO RIFLES

Caliber: 223. **Barrel:** 16-1/4", 20", 22" or 24"; cryo-treated, stainless steel bench-rest grade. **Weight:** NA. **Length:** NA. **Stock:** Polymer. **Sights:** None; Picatinny rail for scope mount. **Features:** Forged and machined upper and lower receiver; single- or double-stage adjustable trigger; free-float handguard; Bear Coat protective finish. Made in U.S.A. by Les Baer Custom.

Price: Ultimate Super Varmint (Jewell two-stage trigger, guar. to shoot 1/2 MOA groups) . . . . from **$1,989.00**
Price: Ultimate M4 Flattop (16-1/4" bbl., Ultra single-stage trigger) . . . . from **$2,195.00**
Price: Ultimate IPSC Action (20" bbl., Jewell two-stage trigger) . . . . from **$2,230.00**

SSK INDUSTRIES AR-15 RIFLES

Caliber: 223, 6mm PPC, 6.5mm PPC, Whisper and other wildcats. **Barrel:** 16-1/2" and longer (to order). **Weight:** NA. **Length:** NA. **Stock:** Black plastic. **Sights:** Blade front, adjustable rear (scopes and red-dot sights available). **Features:** Variety of designs to full match-grade guns offered. Customer's gun can be rebarreled or accurized. From SSK Industries.

Price: Complete AR-15 . . . . from **$1,800.00**
Price: A2 upper unit (front sight, short handguard **$1,100.00**
Price: Match Grade upper unit (bull barrel, tubular handguard, scope mount) **$1,100.00**

VOLQUARTSEN CUSTOM 22 CALIBER AUTO RIFLES

Caliber: 22 LR, 22 Magnum. **Barrel:** 16-1/2" to 20"; stainless steel air gauge. **Weight:** 4-3/4 to 5-3/4 lbs. **Length:** NA. **Stock:** Synthetic or laminated. **Sights:** Not furnished; Weaver base provided. **Features:** Conversions of the Ruger 10/22 rifle. Tuned trigger with 2-1/2 to 3-1/2 lb. pull. Variety of configurations and features. From Volquartsen Custom.

Price: Ultra-Light (22 LR, 16-1/2" tensioned barrel, synthetic stock) . . . . from **$670.00**
Price: Grey Ghost (22 LR, 18-1/2" barrel, laminated wood stock) . . . . from **$690.00**
Price: Deluxe (22 LR, 20" barrel, laminated wood or fiberglass stock) . . . . from **$850.00**
Price: Mossad (22 LR, 20" fluted and ported barrel, fiberglass thumbhole stock) . . . . from **$970.00**
Price: VX-2500 (22 LR, 20" fluted and ported barrel, aluminum/fiberglass stock) . . . . from **$1,044.00**
Price: Volquartsen 22 LR (stainless steel receiver) . . . . from **$920.00**
Price: Volquartsen 22 Mag (22 WMR, stainless steel receiver) . . . . from **$950.00**

John Rigby Boxlock

John Rigby Sidelock close-up

BERETTA EXPRESS DOUBLE RIFLES

Caliber: 9.3x74R, 375 H&H Mag., 416 Rigby, 458 Win. Mag., 470 Nitro Express, 500 Nitro Express. **Barrel:** 23" to 25". **Weight:** 11 lbs. **Length:** NA. **Stock:** Hand-finished, hand-checkered walnut with cheek rest. **Sights:** Folding-leaf, Express-type rear, blade front. **Features:** High-strength steel action with reinforced receiver sides; top tang extends to stock comb for strength; double triggers (articulated front trigger and automatic blocking device eliminate chance of simultaneous discharge); hand-cut, stepped rib; engraved receiver; trapdoor compartment in stock for extra cartridges; spare front sights stored in pistol-grip cap. Imported from Italy by Beretta USA.

Price: SSO6 o/u (optional claw mounts for scope) . . . . from **$21,000.00**
Price: SSO6 EELL o/u (engraved game scenes or color case-hardened with gold inlays) . . . . from **$23,500.00**
Price: 455 s/s (color case-hardened action) . . . . from **$36,000.00**
Price: 455 EELL s/s (receiver engraved with big-game animals) . . . . from **$47,000.00**

BROWNING EXPRESS RIFLES

Still made in Belgium in the traditional manner, two models are available, Herstal and CCS 375. Produced in five different grades of embellishment. Other specifications NA.
Price: . . . . **NA**

JOHN RIGBY DOUBLE RIFLES

Caliber: 375 H&H, 500/416, 450 Nitro Express, 470 Nitro Express, 500 Nitro Express, 577 Nitro Express. **Barrel:** To customer specs. **Weight:** NA. **Length:** To customer specs. **Stock:** To customer specs. **Sights:** Dovetail, express-type sights; claw-foot scope mount available. **Features:** Handcrafted to customer specifications. Boxlock or sidelock action, hand-fitted; variety of engraving and other options offered. Imported from England by John Rigby & Co.
Price: Rigby Boxlock . . . . from **$23,500.00**
Price: Rigby Sidelock . . . . from **$41,700.00**

Ballard No. 1-3/4 Far West

BALLARD RIFLE, LLC

Caliber: 22 LR, 32-40, 38-55, 40-65 Win., 40-70 SS, 40-90, 45-70 Gov't., 45-90, 45-110, 50-70 Gov't., 50-90
Barrel: 24", 26", 30", 32", 34". **Weight:** 7-1/2 to 11-1/2 lbs.
Stock: American black walnut. **Sights:** Blade front, Rocky Mountain rear, others. **Features:** Authentic reproductions faithful to the original patent. Receivers and internal parts machined from solid 8620 steel stock, not castings. Hand finished. Many options.

Price: No. 1-1/2 Hunter's Rifle (30" round bbl., single trigger, S lever) . . . . from **$2,050.00**
Price: No. 1-3/4 Far West (30" round regular or heavyweight bbl., S lever) . . . . from **$2,250.00**
Price: No. 3 Gallery Rifle (24", 26" or 30" lightweight octagon bbl., rifle bottsrock with steel crescent buttplate, S lever) . . . . from **$2,050.00**
Price: No. 3F Fine Gallery Rifle (26", 28" or 30" octagon bbl., pistol grip, single or double set triggers) . . . . from **$2,500.00**
Price: No. 4 Perfection (30" or 32" octagon bbl.single or double set trigger) . . . . from **$2,250.00**
Price: No. 4-1/2 Mid Range (30" or 32" standard pr heavyweight half octagon bbl., single or double set triggers, pistol grip shotgun buttstock) . . . . . . from **$2,250.00**
Price: No. 5 Pacific (30" or 32" standard or heavyweight octagon bbl., standard stocks in rifle or shotgun configuration) . . . . from **$2,575.00**
Price: No. 5-1/2 Montana Model (30" or 32" heavyweight octagon bbl., under-barrel wiping rod, set triggers, ring lever) . . . . from **$2,725.00**
Price: No. 6 Off Hand Rifle (30", 32" or 34" half octagon bbl., blade front sight, pistol grip receiver, double set triggers) . . . . from **$2,550.00**
Price: No. 7 Long Range (32" or 34" standard or heavyweight half octagon bbl., pistol grip shotgun buttstock, single or double set trigger) . . . . . . from **$2,250.00**
Price: No. 8 Union Hill Model (30" half octagon standard or heavyweight bbl., double set triggers, pistol grip stock withcheekpiece, full loop lever) . . . . . from **$2,500.00**
Price: Standard Sporting Model 1885 High Wall (30" or 32" octragonal bbl.,single trigger, small S lever) . . . . from **$2,050.00**
Price: Special Sporting Model 1885 High Wall (32" bbl., shotgun buttstock with cheekpiece, shotgun buttplate, double set triggers) . . . . from **$2,200.00**

SEMI-CUSTOM

Ballard No. 3 Gallery

Ballard No. 6 Off Hand

Ballard No. 8 Union Hill

Ballard No. 5 Pacific

Ballard No. 5-1/2 Montana

Ballard Standard Sporting Model

Ballard No. 7 Long Range

Ballard Special Sporting Model

SEMI-CUSTOM

C. Sharps Model 1875 Sporting

C. Sharps Model 1875 Classic

C. Sharps Model 1877 Custom LR Target

C. Sharps Model 1885 Highwall Sporting

C. Sharps Model 1885 Highwall Classic Sporting

C. SHARPS ARMS RIFLES

Caliber: 22 RF to 50-140-3 1/4 Sharps. **Barrel:** Octagon 18" to 34". **Weight:** 9-18 lbs.. **Stock:** American English walnut (premium straight grain to presentation). **Sights:** Short range to long range target. **Features:** Authentic replicas of Sharps rifles. Models 1874, 1877 & 1885 Machined from solid steel. Made in U.S. by C. Sharps Arms Co. Inc.

Price: Model 1874 Hartford	from $1,775.00
Price: Model 1874 Bridgeport	from $1,495.00
Price: Model 1875 Sporting	from $1,095.00
Price: Model 1875 Classic	from $1,385.00
Price: Model 1875 Target	from $1,136.63
Price: Model 1877 Custom LR Target	from $5,500.00
Price: Model 1885 Highwall Sporting	from $1,350.00
Price: Model 1885 Highwall Classic Sporting	from $1,550.00

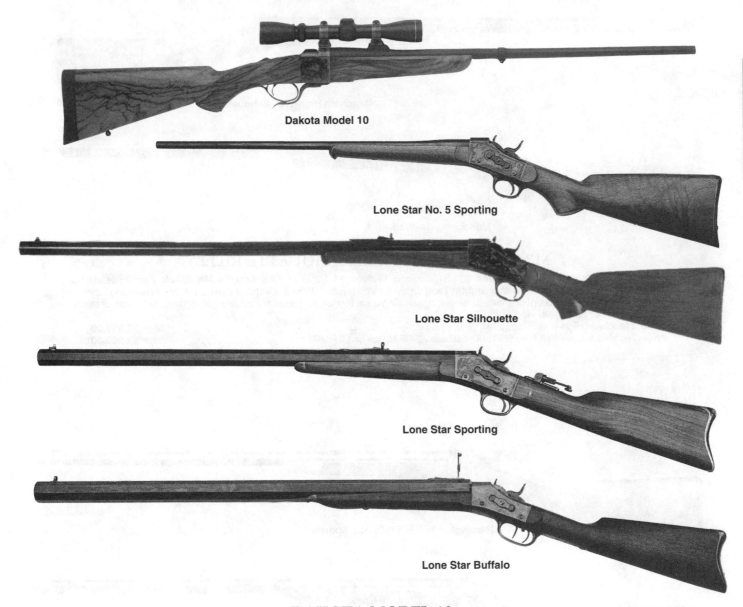

Dakota Model 10

Lone Star No. 5 Sporting

Lone Star Silhouette

Lone Star Sporting

Lone Star Buffalo

DAKOTA MODEL 10

Caliber: Most from 22 LR through 404 Dakota. **Barrel:** 23". **Length:** NA. **Weight:** 5-1/2 lbs. **Stock:** Walnut. **Sights:** NA. **Features:** Falling block action machined from prehardened 4140 bar stock. Many options.
    Price: Dakota Model 10 . . . . from **$3,795.00**

LONE STAR ROLLING BLOCK RIFLES

Caliber: 30-40 Krag, 30-30, 32-40, 38-55, 40-50 SS, 40-50 BN, 40-65, 40-70 SS, 40-70 BN, 40-82, 40-90 SBN, 40-90 SS, 44-90 Rem. Sp., 45 Colt, 45-110 (3-1/4"), 45-110 (2-7/8"), 45-100, 45-90, 45- 70, 50-70, 50-90. **Barrel:** 26" to 34". **Weight:** 6 to 11 lbs. **Length:** NA. **Stock:** American walnut. **Sights:** Buckhorn rear, blade or dovetail front. **Features:** Authentic replicas of Remington rolling block rifles. Round, tapered round, octagon, tapered octagon or half-octagon barrel; bone-pack, color case hardened action; drilled and tapped for vernier sight; single, single-set or double-set trigger; variety of sight, finish and engraving options. Fires blackpowder or factory ammo. Made in U.S. by Lone Star Rifle Co. Inc.
    Price: No. 5 Sporting Rifle (30-30 or 30-40 Krag, 26" barrel, buckhorn rear sight) **$1,595.00**
    Price: Cowboy Action Rifle (28" round barrel, buckhorn rear sight) **$1,595.00**
    Price: Silhouette Rifle (32" or 34" round barrel, drilled and tapped for vernier sight) **$1,595.00**
    Price: Sporting Rifle (straight grip, semi-crescent butt) . . . . from **$1,995.00**
    Price: Creedmoor (34" bbl identical to original rifle) **$2,195.00**
    Price: Buffalo Rifle (12 or 16 lbs) **$2,900.00**
    Price: Custer Commemorative (50-70 only) exact replica of General George Armstrong Custer's
Remington Sporting rifle **$2,900.00**

Meacham High-Wall Silhouette

Meacham Low-Wall

MEACHAM HIGH-WALL SILHOUETTE RIFLE

Caliber: 40-65 Match, 45-70 Match. **Barrel:** 30", 34" octagon. **Weight:** 11-1/2 to 11.9 lbs. **Length:** NA. **Stock:** Fancy eastern black walnut with cheekpiece and shadow line. **Sights:** Tang drilled for Win.base, 3/8" front dovetail. **Features:** Parts interchangeable copy of '85 Winchester. Numerous options include single trigger, single set trigger, or Schuetzen double set triggers, thick side or thin side bone charcoal color case-hardened action.
    Price: Meacham High-Wall Silhouette . . . . from **$2,999.00**
    Price: Meacham Low-Wall Rifle (28" bbl., calibers 22 RF Match or 17 HMR) . . . . from **$2,999.00**

Remington No. 1 Mid-Range Sporter

Remington No. 1 Silhouette

REMINGTON CUSTOM SHOP ROLLING BLOCK RIFLES

Caliber: 45-70. **Barrel:** 30". **Weight:** NA. **Length:** NA. **Stock:** American walnut. **Sights:** Buckhorn rear and blade front (optional tang-mounted vernier rear, globe with spirit level front). **Features:** Satin blue finish with case-colored receiver; single set trigger; steel Schnabel fore end tip; steel butt plate. From Remington Arms Co. Custom Gun Shop.
    Price: No. 1 Mid-Range Sporter (round or half-octagon barrel) **$1,450.00**
    Price: No. 1 Silhouette (heavy barrel with 1:18" twist; no sights) **$1,560.00**

SEMI-CUSTOM SHOTGUNS

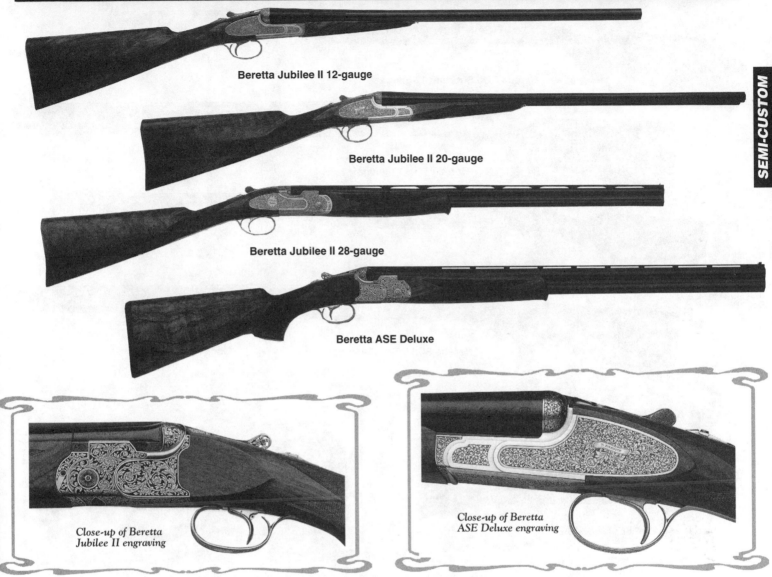

Beretta Jubilee II 12-gauge

Beretta Jubilee II 20-gauge

Beretta Jubilee II 28-gauge

Beretta ASE Deluxe

*Close-up of Beretta
Jubilee II engraving*

*Close-up of Beretta
ASE Deluxe engraving*

BERETTA PREMIUM GRADE SHOTGUNS

Gauge: 12, 20, 410, 3" chamber; 28, 2-3/4" chamber. **Barrel:** 26", 28", 30", 32". **Weight:** 5 to 7-1/2 lbs. **Length:** NA. **Stock:** Highly figured English or American walnut; straight or pistol grip; hand- checkered. **Features:** Machined nickel-chrome-moly action, hand-fitted; cross-bolt breech lock; Boehler Antinit steel barrels with fixed chokes or Mobilchoke tubes; single selective or non-selective or double trigger; numerous stock and engraving options. From Beretta USA.

Price: Giubileo (Jubilee) o/u (engraved sideplates, trigger guard, safety and top lever)	from **$12,900.00**
Price: Giubileo II (Jubilee II) s/s (English-style stock, engraved sideplates and fixtures)	from **$12,900.00**
Price: ASE Deluxe o/u (engraved receiver and forend cap)	from **$24,000.00**
Price: SO5 Trap (single, non-selective trigger, heavy beavertail fore end, fixed chokes)	from **$17,490.00**
Price: SO5 Skeet (26" or 28" bbl., heavy beavertail fore end, fixed chokes)	from **$17,490.00**
Price: SO5 Sporting (single, selective trigger, Mobilchoke tubes)	from **$17,490.00**
Price: SO6 EELL o/u (engraved receiver with gold inlays, custom-fit stock)	from **$34,900.00**
Price: SO6 EL o/u (light English scroll engravings on receiver)	from **$23,900.00**
Price: SO6 EESS o/u (enamel-colored receiver in green, red or blue, arabesque engravings)	from **$34,900.00**
Price: SO9 o/u (single, non-selective trigger, engraved receiver and fixtures)	from **$44,500.00**

Beretta SO5 Skeet 12-gauge

SEMI-CUSTOM SHOTGUNS

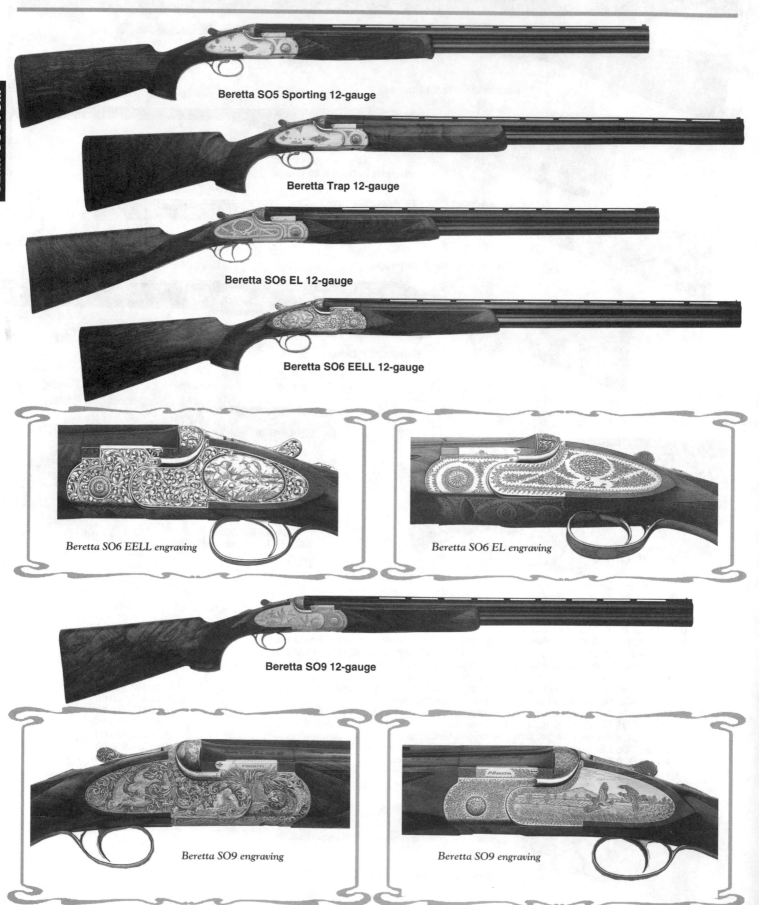

Beretta SO5 Sporting 12-gauge

Beretta Trap 12-gauge

Beretta SO6 EL 12-gauge

Beretta SO6 EELL 12-gauge

Beretta SO6 EELL engraving

Beretta SO6 EL engraving

Beretta SO9 12-gauge

Beretta SO9 engraving

Beretta SO9 engraving

SEMI-CUSTOM SHOTGUNS

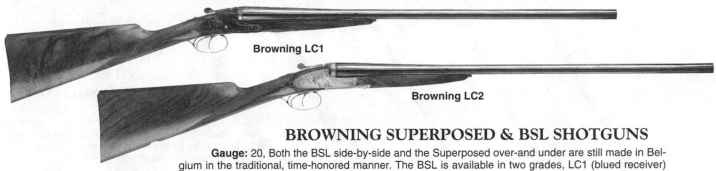

Browning LC1

Browning LC2

BROWNING SUPERPOSED & BSL SHOTGUNS

Gauge: 20, Both the BSL side-by-side and the Superposed over-and-under are still made in Belgium in the traditional, time-honored manner. The BSL is available in two grades, LC1 (blued receiver) and LC2 (silver-colored receiver). The Superposed is available in 18 grades. Custom options include: engraving of name or initials, second set of barrels, special finish or checkering, special stock dimensions, personalized engraving scenes and upgraded wood. Other specifications NA.
Price: . . . . **NA**

DAKOTA LEGEND/PREMIER SHOTGUNS

Available in all standard gauges, features include exhibition English walnut stock, French grey finish, 50% coverage engraving, straight grip, splinter forend, double trigger, 27" barrels, game rib with gold bead, selective ejectors, choice of chokes. Various options available.
Price: Dakota Premier Grade . . . . from **$13,950.00**
Price: Dakota Legend Shotgun (27" bbls., special selection English walnut stock, straight grip, splinter forend) . . . . from **$18,000**

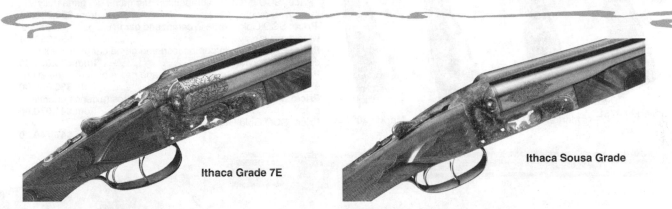

Ithaca Grade 7E

Ithaca Sousa Grade

ITHACA CLASSIC DOUBLES SIDE-BY-SIDE SHOTGUNS

Gauge: 20, 28, 2-3/4" chamber; 410, 3" chamber. **Barrel:** 26", 28", 30". **Weight:** 5 lbs. 5 oz. (410 bore) to 5 lbs. 14 oz. (20 ga.). **Length:** NA. **Stock:** Exhibition-grade American black walnut, hand-checkered with hand-rubbed oil finish. **Features:** Updated duplicates of original New Ithaca Double double-barrel shotguns. Hand-fitted boxlock action; splinter or beavertail forend; bone-charcoal color case-hardened receiver; chrome-moly steel rust-blued barrels; ejectors; gold double triggers; fixed chokes; hand-engraved game scenes. Made in U.S. by Ithaca Classic Doubles.
Price: Special Skeet Grade (plain color case-hardened receiver, feather crotch walnut stock) **$3,465.00**
Price: Grade 4E (gold-plated triggers, jeweled barrel flats, engraved game-bird scene) **$4,625.00**
Price: Grade 7E (gold-inlaid ducks, pheasants and bald eagle on scroll engraving) **$9,200.00**
Price: Sousa Grade (gold-inlaid setter, pointer, flying ducks and Sousa mermaid) **$11,550.00**

JOHN RIGBY SHOTGUNS

John Rigby Side-by-Side 12-gauge engraving

Gauge: 12, 16, 20, 28 and 410 bore. **Barrel:** To customer specs. **Weight:** NA. **Length:** To customer specs. **Stock:** Customer's choice. **Features:** True sidelock side-by-side and over-under shotguns made to customer's specifications. Hand-fitted actions and stocks; engraved receivers embellished with game scenes; over-under includes removable choke tubes. Imported from England by John Rigby & Co.
Price: Sidelock over-under (single selective, non-selective or double triggers) . . . . from **$36,500.00**
Price: Sidelock side-by-side (engraved receiver, choice of stock wood) . . . . from **$39,950.00**
Price: Hammer shotguns (manual-cocking hammers, rebounding firing pins and hammers; extractors only) . . . . from **$18,000.00**

SEMI-CUSTOM SHOTGUNS

MERKEL EXHIBITION, VINTAGERS EXPO AND CUSTOM ENGRAVED SHOTGUNS

Gauge: 12, 16, 20, 28, 410. **Barrel:** 26-3/4", 28"; others optional. **Weight:** NA. **Length:** NA. **Stock:** Highly figured walnut; English (straight) or pistol grip. **Features:** Highly engraved versions of Merkel over-under and side-by-side shotguns. Imported from Germany by GSI Inc.
Price: . . . . **NA**

PERAZZI SCO, SCO GOLD, EXTRA AND EXTRA GOLDSHOTGUNS

Gauge: 12, 20, 28, 410. **Barrel:** 23-5/8" to 34". **Weight:** 6 lbs. 3 oz. to 8 lb. 13 oz. **Length:** NA. **Stock:** To customer specs. **Features:** Enhanced, engraved models of game and competition over- under shotguns. Customer may choose from many engraved hunting and wildlife scenes. Imported from Italy by Perazzi USA Inc.
Price: SCO Grade in competition and game o/u guns (fully engraved receiver) . . . . from **$30,250.00**
Price: SCO Gold Grade in comp. and game o/u guns (engraved w/gold inlays) . . . . from **$30,250.00**
Price: Extra Grade in competition and game o/u guns (highly detailed engraving) . . . . from **$75,080.00**
Price: Extra Gold Grade in comp. and game o/u guns (detailed engraving w/ gold inlays) . . . . from **$80,850.00**
Price: SCO Grade with engraved sideplates (extends engraved area) . . . . from **$41,070.00**
Price: SCO Gold Grade with engraved sideplates . . . . from **$47,740.00**

Merkel 47E

Merkel 47SL

Merkel 280EL

Merkel 303EL

Merkel 2001EL

Perazzi MX-8

Perazzi MX-10

Perazzi SCO Grade engraving

Perazzi SCO Gold engraving

Perazzi Extra engraving

SEMI-CUSTOM

SEMI-CUSTOM SHOTGUNS

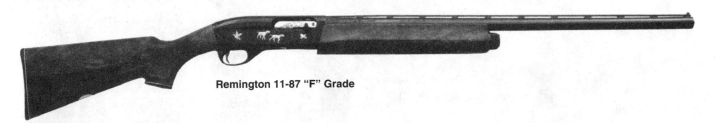

Remington 11-87 "F" Grade

REMINGTON CUSTOM SHOP AUTO SHOTGUNS

Gauge: 10, 12, 20, 28. **Barrel:** 21" to 30". **Weight:** NA. **Length:** NA. **Stock:** Two grades of American walnut. **Features:** Engraved versions of the Model 11-87 and Model 1100 shotgun. "D" or "F" grade fancy walnut, hand-checkered stock; choice of ebony, rosewood, skeleton steel or solid steel grip cap; choice of solid steel, standard, Old English or ventilated recoil pad; optional inletted gold oval with three initials on bottom of stock. From Remington Arms. Co. Custom Gun Shop.
    Price: 11-87 and 1100 "D" Grade (English scroll engraving on receiver, breech and trig. guard) **$3,723.00**
    Price: 11-87 and 1100 "F" Grade (engraved game scene, "F" Grade walnut stock) **$7,245.00**
    Price: 11-87 and 1100 "F" Grade with gold inlay (inlaid three-panel engraved game scene) **$10,663.00**

REMINGTON CUSTOM SHOP PUMP SHOTGUNS

Gauge: 10, 12, 20, 28, 410. **Barrel:** 20" to 30". **Weight:** NA. **Length:** NA. **Stock:** Two grades of American walnut. **Features:** Engraved versions of the Model 870 shotgun. "D" or "F" grade fancy walnut hand-checkered stock; choice of ebony, rosewood, skeleton steel or solid steel grip cap; choice of solid steel, standard, Old English or ventilated recoil pad; optional inletted gold oval with three initials on bottom of stock. From Remington Arms Co. Custom Gun Shop.
    Price: 870 "D" Grade (English scroll engraving on receiver, breech and trig. guard) **$3,723.00**
    Price: 870 "F" Grade (engraved game scene, "F" grade walnut stock) **$7,245.00**
    Price: 870 "F" Grade with gold inlay (inlaid three-panel engraved game scene) **$10,663.00**

REMINGTON CUSTOM SHOP OVER/UNDER SHOTGUNS

Gauge: 12. **Barrel:** 26", 28", 30". **Weight:** 7-1/2 to 8 lbs. **Length:** 42-1/2" to 47-1/4". **Stock:** American walnut. **Features:** Barrels made of chrome-moly steel with 3" chambers, finger grooved forend, fully brazed barrel side ribs, hardened trunions, automatic ejectors. Made in U.S. by Remington Arms Co. Custom Gun Shop.
    Price: Remington Model 332 D Grade . . . . from **$4,184.00**
    Price: Model 332 F Grade . . . . from **$7,706.00**
    Price: Model 332 F Grade w/gold inlay . . . . from **$11,122.00**

Tar-Hunt DSG

TAR-HUNT DSG (DESIGNATED SLUG GUN)

Gauge: 12, 16. **Barrel:** 23". **Weight:** NA. **Length:** NA. **Stock:** NA **Features:** Tar-Hunt converts the basic Remington 870 shotgun into a configuration for shooting slugs only by installation of a non-removable custom fit Shaw rifled slug barrel with muzzle brake. The 870 Wingmaster is fitted with a barrel with 2-3/4" chamber, the 870 Express Mag. and Wingmaster Mag. have a 3-inch chamber and the 870 Express Super Mag. will have a 3-1/2" chamber. Included are Leupold two-piece windage bases which will accept any standard type turn in rings.
    Price: Tar-Hunt DSG . . . . **$359.95** (with customer furnished Remington 870)
    Price: Tar-Hunt DSG . . . . **$635.00** (complete gun with black synthetic stock)

Includes models suitable for several forms of competition and other sporting purposes.

Accu-Tek HC-380

Accu-Tek XL-9

Auto-Ordnance 1911A1 Standard

Baer Custom Carry

Baer Premium II

Auto-Ordnance Deluxe

ACCU-TEK MODEL HC-380 AUTO PISTOL

Caliber: 380 ACP, 10-shot magazine. **Barrel:** 2.75". **Weight:** 26 oz. **Length:** 6" overall. **Grips:** Checkered black composition. **Sights:** Blade front, rear adjustable for windage. **Features:** External hammer; manual thumb safety with firing pin and trigger disconnect; bottom magazine release. Stainless steel construction. Introduced 1993. Price includes cleaning kit and gun lock. Made in U.S.A. by Accu-Tek.
Price: Satin stainless **$249.00**

ACCU-TEK XL-9 AUTO PISTOL

Caliber: 9mm Para., 5-shot magazine. **Barrel:** 3". **Weight:** 24 oz. **Length:** 5.6" overall. **Grips:** Black pebble composition. **Sights:** Three-dot system; rear adjustable for windage. **Features:** Stainless steel construction; double-action-only mechanism. Introduced 1999. Price includes cleaning kit and gun lock, two magazines. Made in U.S.A. by Accu-Tek.
Price: **$267.00**

AMERICAN DERRINGER LM-5 AUTOMATIC PISTOL

Caliber: 25 ACP, 5-shot magazine. **Barrel:** 2-1/4". **Weight:** 15 oz. **Length:** NA. **Grips:** Wood. **Sights:** Fixed. **Features:** Compact, stainless, semi-auto, single-action hammerless design. Hand assembled and fitted.
Price: **$425.00**

AUTO-ORDNANCE 1911A1 AUTOMATIC PISTOL

Caliber: 45 ACP, 7-shot magazine. **Barrel:** 5". **Weight:** 39 oz. **Length:** 8-1/2" overall. **Grips:** Checkered plastic with medallion. **Sights:** Blade front, rear adjustable for windage. **Features:** Same specs as 1911A1 military guns—parts interchangeable. Frame and slide blued; each radius has non-glare finish. Made in U.S.A. by Auto-Ordnance Corp.
Price: 45 ACP, blue **$511.00**
Price: 45 ACP, Parkerized **$515.00**
Price: 45 ACP Deluxe (three-dot sights, textured rubber
wraparound grips) **$525.00**

AUTAUGA 32 AUTO PISTOL

Caliber: 32 ACP, 6-shot magazine. **Barrel:** 2". **Weight:** 11.3 oz. **Length:** 4.3" overall. **Grips:** Black polymer. **Sights:** Fixed. **Features:** Double-action-only mechanism. Stainless steel construction. Uses Winchester Silver Tip ammunition.
Price: . . . . **NA**

BAER 1911 CUSTOM CARRY AUTO PISTOL

Caliber: 45 ACP, 7- or 10-shot magazine. **Barrel:** 5". **Weight:** 37 oz. **Length:** 8.5" overall. **Grips:** Checkered walnut. **Sights:** Baer improved ramp-style dovetailed front, Novak low-mount rear. **Features:** Baer forged NM frame, slide and barrel with stainless bushing; fitted slide to frame; double serrated slide (full-size only); Baer speed trigger with 4-lb. pull; Baer deluxe hammer and sear, tactical-style extended ambidextrous safety, beveled magazine well; polished feed ramp and throated barrel; tuned extractor; Baer extended ejector, checkered slide stop; lowered and flared ejection port, full-length recoil guide rod; recoil buff. Partial listing shown. Made in U.S.A. by Les Baer Custom, Inc.
Price: Standard size, blued **$1,640.00**
Price: Standard size, stainless **$1,690.00**
Price: Comanche size, blued **$1,640.00**
Price: Comanche size, stainless **$1,690.00**
Price: Comanche size, aluminum frame, blued slide **$1,923.00**
Price: Comanche size, aluminum frame, stainless slide **$1,995.00**

BAER 1911 PREMIER II AUTO PISTOL

Caliber: 9x23, 38 Super, 400 Cor-Bon, 45 ACP, 7- or 10-shot magazine. **Barrel:** 5". **Weight:** 37 oz. **Length:** 8.5" overall. **Grips:** Checkered rosewood, double diamond pattern. **Sights:** Baer dovetailed front, low-mount Bo-Mar rear with hidden leaf. **Features:** Baer NM forged steel frame and barrel with stainless bushing; slide fitted to frame; double serrated slide; lowered, flared ejection port; tuned, polished extractor; Baer extended ejector, checkered slide stop, aluminum speed trigger with 4-lb. pull, deluxe Commander hammer and sear, beavertail grip safety with pad, beveled magazine well, extended ambidextrous safety; flat mainspring housing; polished feed ramp and throated barrel; 30 lpi checkered front strap. Made in U.S.A. by Les Baer Custom, Inc.
Price: Blued **$1,428.00**
Price: Stainless **$1,558.00**
Price: 6" model, blued, from **$1,595.00**

BAER 1911 S.R.P. PISTOL

Caliber: 45 ACP. **Barrel:** 5". **Weight:** 37 oz. **Length:** 8.5" overall. **Grips:** Checkered walnut. **Sights:** Trijicon night sights. **Features:** Similar to the F.B.I. contract gun except uses Baer forged steel frame. Has Baer match barrel with supported chamber, Wolff springs, complete tactical action job. All parts Mag-na-fluxed; deburred for tactical carry. Has Baer Ultra Coat finish. Tuned for reliability. Contact Baer for complete details. Introduced 1996. Made in U.S.A. by Les Baer Custom, Inc.
Price: Government or Comanche length **$2,240.00**

Beretta 92 Billennium

Beretta 96

Beretta M8000/8040 Cougar

BERETTA MODEL 92 BILLENNIUM LIMITED EDITION
Caliber: 9mm. **Grips:** Carbon fiber. **Sights:** 3 dot. **Features:** Single action. Semiauto. Steel frame, frame mounted safety. Only 2000 made worldwide.
Price: **$1,429.00**

BERETTA MODEL 92FS PISTOL
Caliber: 9mm Para., 10-shot magazine. **Barrel:** 4.9". **Weight:** 34 oz. **Length:** 8.5" overall. **Grips:** Checkered black plastic. **Sights:** Blade front, rear adjustable for windage. Tritium night sights available. **Features:** Double action. Extractor acts as chamber loaded indicator, squared trigger guard, grooved front and backstraps, inertia firing pin. Matte or blued finish. Introduced 1977. Made in U.S.A. and imported from Italy by Beretta U.S.A.
Price: With plastic grips **$691.00**
Price: Vertec with access rail **$726.00**
Price: Vertec Inox **$776.00**

Beretta Model 92FS/96 Brigadier Pistols
Similar to the Model 92FS/96 except with a heavier slide to reduce felt recoil and allow mounting removable front sight. Wrap-around rubber grips. Three-dot sights dovetailed to the slide, adjustable for windage. Weighs 35.3 oz. Introduced 1999.
Price: 9mm or 40 S&W, 10-shot **$748.00**
Price: Inox models (stainless steel) **$798.00**

Beretta Model 92FS Compact and Compact Type M Pistol
Similar to the Model 92FS except more compact and lighter: overall length 7.8"; 4.3" barrel; weighs 30.9 oz. Has Bruniton finish, chrome-lined bore, combat trigger guard, ambidextrous safety/decock lever. Single column 8-shot magazine (Type M), or double column 10-shot (Compact), 9mm only. Introduced 1998. Imported from Italy by Beretta U.S.A.
Price: Compact (10-shot) **$691.00**
Price: Compact Type M (8-shot) **$691.00**
Price: Compact Inox (stainless) **$748.00**
Price: Compact Type M Inox (stainless) **$748.00**

Beretta Model 96 Pistol
Same as the Model 92FS except chambered for 40 S&W. Ambidextrous safety mechanism with passive firing pin catch, slide safety/decocking lever, trigger bar disconnect. Has 10-shot magazine. Available with three-dot sights. Introduced 1992.
Price: Model 96, plastic grips **$691.00**
Price: Stainless, rubber grips **$798.00**
Price: Vertec with access rail **$726.00**
Price: Vertec Inox **$776.00**

BERETTA MODEL 80 CHEETAH SERIES DA PISTOLS
Caliber: 380 ACP, 10-shot magazine (M84); 8-shot (M85); 22 LR, 7-shot (M87). **Barrel:** 3.82". **Weight:** About 23 oz. (M84/85); 20.8 oz. (M87). **Length:** 6.8" overall. **Grips:** Glossy black plastic (wood optional at extra cost). **Sights:** Fixed front, drift-adjustable rear. **Features:** Double action, quick takedown, convenient magazine release. Introduced 1977. Imported from Italy by Beretta U.S.A.
Price: Model 84 Cheetah, plastic grips **$599.00**
Price: Model 85 Cheetah, plastic grips, 8-shot **$563.00**

Price: Model 87 Cheetah, wood, 22 LR, 7-shot **$599.00**
Price: Model 87 Target, plastic grips **$682.00**

Beretta Model 86 Cheetah
Similar to the 380-caliber Model 85 except has tip-up barrel for first-round loading. Barrel length is 4.4", overall length of 7.33". Has 8-shot magazine, walnut grips. Introduced 1989.
Price: **$599.00**

Beretta Model 21 Bobcat Pistol
Similar to the Model 950 BS. Chambered for 22 LR or 25 ACP. Both double action. Has 2.4" barrel, 4.9" overall length; 7-round magazine on 22 cal.; 8 rounds in 25 ACP, 9.9 oz., available in nickel, matte, engraved or blue finish. Plastic grips. Introduced 1985.
Price: Bobcat, 22 or 25, blue **$292.00**
Price: Bobcat, 22, stainless **$315.00**
Price: Bobcat, 22 or 25, matte **$259.00**

BERETTA MODEL 3032 TOMCAT PISTOL
Caliber: 32 ACP, 7-shot magazine. **Barrel:** 2.45". **Weight:** 14.5 oz. **Length:** 5" overall. **Grips:** Checkered black plastic. **Sights:** Blade front, drift-adjustable rear. **Features:** Double action with exposed hammer; tip-up barrel for direct loading/unloading; thumb safety; polished or matte blue finish. Imported from Italy by Beretta U.S.A. Introduced 1996.
Price: Blue **$379.00**
Price: Matte **$349.00**
Price: Stainless **$428.00**
Price: Titanium **$589.00**
Price: With Tritium sights **$420.00**

BERETTA MODEL 8000/8040/8045 COUGAR PISTOL
Caliber: 9mm Para., 10-shot, 40 S&W, 10-shot magazine; 45 ACP, 8-shot. **Barrel:** 3.6". **Weight:** 33.5 oz. **Length:** 7" overall. **Grips:** Checkered plastic. **Sights:** Blade front, rear drift adjustable for windage. **Features:** Slide-mounted safety; rotating barrel; exposed hammer. Matte black Bruniton finish. Announced 1994. Imported from Italy by Beretta U.S.A.
Price: **$709.00**
Price: D model, 9mm, 40 S&W **$709.00**
Price: D model, 45 ACP **$764.00**

BERETTA MODEL 9000S COMPACT PISTOL
Caliber: 9mm Para., 40 S&W; 10-shot magazine. **Barrel:** 3.4". **Weight:** 26.8 oz. **Length:** 6.6". **Grips:** Soft polymer. **Sights:** Windage-adjustable white-dot rear, white-dot blade front. **Features:** Glass-reinforced polymer frame; patented tilt-barrel, open-slide locking system; chrome-lined barrel; external serrated hammer; automatic firing pin and manual safeties. Introduced 2000. Imported from Italy by Beretta USA.
Price: 9000S Type F (single and double action, external
hammer) **$558.00**
Price: 9000S Type D (double-action only, no external
hammer or safety) **$558.00**

Beretta Model 8000/8040/8045 Mini Cougar
Similar to the Model 8000/8040 Cougar except has shorter grip frame and weighs 27.6 oz. Introduced 1998. Imported from Italy by Beretta U.S.A.
Price: 9mm or 40 S&W **$709.00**
Price: 9mm or 40 S&W, DAO **$709.00**
Price: 45 ACP DAO **$764.00**

Beretta U22 Neos

Bersa Thunder 380

**Browning Micro
Buck Mark Standard**

**Browning Buck
Mark Challenge**

BERETTA MODEL U22 NEOS

Caliber: 22 LR, 10-shot magazine. **Barrel:** 4.2"; 6". **Weight:** 32 oz.; 36 oz. **Length:** 8.8"; 10.3". **Sights:** Target. **Features:** Integral rail for standard scope mounts, light, perfectly weighted, 100% American made by Beretta.

Price: **$265.00**
Price: Inox **$315.00**
Price: DLX **$336.00**
Price: Inox **$386.00**

BERSA THUNDER 380 AUTO PISTOLS

Caliber: 380 ACP, 7-shot (Thunder 380 Lite), 9-shot magazine (Thunder 380 DLX). **Barrel:** 3.5". **Weight:** 23 oz. **Length:** 6.6" overall. **Grips:** Black polymer. **Sights:** Blade front, notch rear adjustable for windage; three-dot system. **Features:** Double action; firing pin and magazine safeties. Available in blue, nickel, or duo tone. Introduced 1995. Distributed by Eagle Imports, Inc.

Price: Thunder 380, 7-shot, deep blue finish **$266.95**
Price: Thunder 380 Deluxe, 9-shot, satin nickel **$299.95**
Price: Thunder 380 Gold, 7-shot **$299.95**

NEW! Bersa Thunder 45 Ultra Compact Pistol

Similar to the Bersa Thunder 380 except in 45 ACP. Available in three finishes. Introduced 2003. Imported from Argentina by Eagle Imports, Inc.

Price: Thunder 45, matte blue **$400.95**
Price: Thunder 45, Duotone **$424.95**
Price: Thunder 45, Satin nickel **$441.95**

BLUE THUNDER/COMMODORE 1911-STYLE AUTO PISTOLS

Caliber: 45 ACP, 7-shot magazine. **Barrel:** 4-1/4", 5". **Weight:** NA. **Length:** NA. **Grips:** Checkered hardwood. **Sights:** Blade front, drift-adjustable rear. **Features:** Extended slide release and safety, spring guide rod, skeletonized hammer and trigger, magazine bumper, beavertail grip safety. Imported from the Philippines by Century International Arms Inc.

Price: . . . . **$464.80 to $484.80**

BROWNING HI-POWER 9mm AUTOMATIC PISTOL

Caliber: 9mm Para.,10-shot magazine. **Barrel:** 4-21/32". **Weight:** 32 oz. **Length:** 7-3/4" overall. **Grips:** Walnut, hand checkered, or black Polyamide. **Sights:** 1/8" blade front; rear screw-adjustable for windage and elevation. Also available with fixed rear (drift-adjustable for windage). **Features:** External hammer with half-cock and thumb safeties. A blow on the hammer cannot discharge a cartridge; cannot be fired with magazine removed. Fixed rear sight model available. Includes gun lock. Imported from Belgium by Browning.

Price: Fixed sight model, walnut grips **$680.00**
Price: Fully adjustable rear sight, walnut grips **$730.00**
Price: Mark III, standard matte black finish, fixed sight, moulded grips, ambidextrous safety **$662.00**

Browning Hi-Power Practical Pistol

Similar to the standard Hi-Power except has silver-chromed frame with blued slide, wrap-around Pachmayr rubber grips, round-style serrated hammer and removable front sight, fixed rear (drift-adjustable for windage). Available in 9mm Para. Includes gun lock. Introduced 1991.

Price: **$717.00**

BROWNING BUCK MARK STANDARD 22 PISTOL

Caliber: 22 LR, 10-shot magazine. **Barrel:** 5-1/2". **Weight:** 32 oz. **Length:** 9-1/2" overall. **Grips:** Black moulded composite with checkering. **Sights:** Ramp front, Browning Pro Target rear adjustable for windage and elevation. **Features:** All steel, matte blue finish or nickel, gold-colored trigger. Buck Mark Plus has laminated wood grips. Includes gun lock. Made in U.S.A. Introduced 1985. From Browning.

Price: Buck Mark Standard, blue **$286.00**
Price: Buck Mark Nickel, nickel finish with contoured rubber grips **$338.00**
Price: Buck Mark Plus, matte blue with laminated wood grips . . . **$350.00**
Price: Buck Mark Plus Nickel, nickel finish, laminated wood grips **$383.00**

Browning Buck Mark Camper

Similar to the Buck Mark except 5-1/2" bull barrel. Weight is 34 oz. Matte blue finish, molded composite grips. Introduced 1999. From Browning.

Price: **$258.00**
Price: Camper Nickel, nickel finish, molded composite grips **$287.00**

Browning Buck Mark Challenge

Similar to the Buck Mark except has a lightweight barrel and smaller grip diameter. Barrel length is 5-1/2", weight is 25 oz. Introduced 1999. From Browning.

Price: **$320.00**

Browning Buck Mark Micro

Same as the Buck Mark Standard and Buck Mark Plus except has 4" barrel. Available in blue or nickel. Has 16-click Pro Target rear sight. Introduced 1992.

Price: Micro Standard, matte blue finish **$286.00**
Price: Micro Nickel, nickel finish **$338.00**
Price: Buck Mark Micro Plus, matte blue, lam. wood grips **$350.00**
Price: Buck Mark Micro Plus Nickel **$383.00**

Charles Daly M-1911-A1P

Cobra FS380

Cobra Patriot

Cobra CA32

Colt 1991 Model O

Colt 1991 Model O Commander

Colt XSE Model O Commander

Browning Buck Mark Bullseye

Same as the Buck Mark Standard except has 7-1/4" fluted barrel, matte blue finish. Weighs 36 oz.
Price: Bullseye Standard, molded composite grips $420.00
Price: Bullseye Target, contoured rosewood grips $541.00

Browning Buck Mark 5.5

Same as the Buck Mark Standard except has a 5-1/2" bull barrel with integral scope mount, matte blue finish.
Price: 5.5 Field, Pro-Target adj. rear sight,
contoured walnut grips $459.00
Price: 5.5 Target, hooded adj. target sights, contoured walnut grips
. . . . $459.00

Buck Mark Commemorative

Same as the Buck Mark Standard except has a 6-3/4" Challenger-style barrel, matte blue finish and scrimshaw-style, bonded ivory grips. Includes pistol rug. Limited to 1,000 guns
Price: Commemorative $437.00

CHARLES DALY M-1911-A1P AUTOLOADING PISTOL

Caliber: 45 ACP, 7- or 10-shot magazine. **Barrel:** 5". **Weight:** 38 oz. **Length:** 8-3/4" overall. **Grips:** Checkered. **Sights:** Blade front, rear drift adjustable for windage; three-dot system. **Features:** Skeletonized combat hammer and trigger; beavertail grip safety; extended slide release; oversize thumb safety; Parkerized finish. Introduced 1996. Imported from the Philippines by K.B.I., Inc.
Price: $469.95

COBRA ENTERPRISES FS380 AUTO PISTOL

Caliber: 380 ACP, 7-shot magazine. **Barrel:** 3.5". **Weight:** 2.1 lbs. **Length:** 6-3/8" overall. **Grips:** Black composition. **Sights:** Fixed. **Features:** Choice of bright chrome, satin nickel or black finish. Introduced 2002. Made in U.S.A. by Cobra Enterprises.
Price: $98.00

COBRA ENTERPRISES FS32 AUTO PISTOL

Caliber: 32 ACP, 8-shot magazine. **Barrel:** 3.5". **Weight:** 2.1 lbs. **Length:** 6-3/8" overall. **Grips:** Black composition. **Sights:** Fixed. **Features:** Choice of black, satin nickel or bright chrome finish. Introduced 2002. Made in U.S.A. by Cobra Enterprises.
Price: $107.00

COBRA INDUSTRIES PATRIOT PISTOL

Caliber: 380ACP, 9mm Luger, 6-shot magazine. **Barrel:** 3.3". **Weight:** 20 oz. **Length:** 6" overall. **Grips:** Checkered polymer. **Sights:** Fixed. **Features:** Stainless steel slide with load indicator; double-action-only trigger system. Introduced 2002. Made in U.S.A. by Cobra Enterprises, Inc.
Price: . . . . About $325.00

COBRA INDUSTRIES CA32, CA380

Caliber: 32ACP, 380 ACP. **Barrel:** 2.8" **Weight:** 22 oz. **Length:** 5.4". **Grips:** Laminated wood (CA32); Black molded synthetic (CA380). **Sights:** Fixed. **Features:** True pocket pistol size and styling without bulk. Made in U.S.A. by Cobra Enterprises.
Price: . . . . NA

COLT MODEL 1991 MODEL O AUTO PISTOL

Caliber: 45 ACP, 7-shot magazine. **Barrel:** 5". **Weight:** 38 oz. **Length:** 8.5" overall. **Grips:** Checkered black composition. **Sights:** Ramped blade front, fixed square notch rear, high profile. **Features:** Matte finish. Continuation of serial number range used on original G.I. 1911 A1 guns. Comes with one magazine and moulded carrying case. Introduced 1991.
Price: $645.00
Price: Stainless $800.00

Colt Model 1991 Model O Commander Auto Pistol

Similar to the Model 1991 A1 except has 4-1/4" barrel. Overall length is 7-3/4". Comes with one 7-shot magazine, molded case.
Price: Blue $645.00
Price: Stainless steel $800.00

COLT XSE SERIES MODEL O AUTO PISTOLS

Caliber: 45 ACP, 8-shot magazine. **Barrel:** 4.25", 5". **Grips:** Checkered, double diamond rosewood. **Sights:** Drift-adjustable three-dot combat. **Features:** Brushed stainless finish; adjustable, two-cut aluminum trigger; extended ambidextrous thumb safety; upswept beavertail with palm swell; elongated slot hammer; beveled magazine well. Introduced 1999. From Colt's Manufacturing Co., Inc.
Price: XSE Government (5" barrel) $950.00
Price: XSE Commander (4.25" barrel) $950.00

Colt XSE Lightweight Commander

Colt Defender

Colt Series 70

Colt 38 Super

Colt Gunsite

CZ 75B 9mm

CZ 75B Decocker

COLT XSE LIGHTWEIGHT COMMANDER AUTO PISTOL

Caliber: 45 ACP, 8-shot. **Barrel:** 4-1/4". **Weight:** 26 oz. **Length:** 7-3/4" overall. **Grips:** Double diamond checkered rosewood. **Sights:** Fixed, glare-proofed blade front, square notch rear; three-dot system. **Features:** Brushed stainless slide, nickeled aluminum frame; McCormick elongated-slot enhanced hammer, McCormick two-cut adjustable aluminum hammer. Made in U.S.A. by Colt's Mfg. Co., Inc.
Price: 45, stainless **$950.00**

COLT DEFENDER

Caliber: 40 S&W, 45 ACP, 7-shot magazine. **Barrel:** 3". **Weight:** 22-1/2 oz. **Length:** 6-3/4" overall. **Grips:** Pebble-finish rubber wraparound with finger grooves. **Sights:** White dot front, snag-free Colt competition rear. **Features:** Stainless finish; aluminum frame; combat-style hammer; Hi Ride grip safety, extended manual safety, disconnect safety. Introduced 1998. Made in U.S.A. by Colt's Mfg. Co.
Price: **$773.00**
Price: 41 Magnum Model, from. **$825.00**

NEW! COLT SERIES 70

Caliber: 45 ACP. **Barrel:** 5". **Weight:** NA **Length:** NA **Grips:** Rosewood with double diamond checkering pattern. **Sights:** Fixed. **Features:** A custom replica of the Original Series 70 pistol with a Series 70 firing system, original rollmarks. Introduced 2002. Made in U.S.A. by Colt's Manufacturing.
Price: . . . . **NA**

NEW! COLT 38 SUPER

Caliber: 38 Super **Barrel:** 5" **Weight:** NA. **Length:** 8-1/2" **Grips:** Checkered rubber (Stainless and blue models); Wood with double diamond checkering pattern (Bright stainless model). **Sights:** 3-dot. **Features:** Beveled magazine well, standard thumb safety and service-style grip safety. Introduced 2003. Made in U.S.A. by Colt's Mfg. Co.
Price: . . . . (Blue) **$864.00** (Stainless steel) **$943.00**
Price: . . . . (Bright stainless steel) **$1,152.00**

NEW! COLT GUNSITE PISTOL

Caliber: 45 ACP **Barrel:** 5". **Weight:** NA. **Length:** NA. **Grips:** Rosewood. **Sights:** Heinie, front; Novak, rear. **Features:** Contains most all of the Gunsite school recommended features such as Series 70 firing system, Smith & Alexander metal grip safety w/palm swell, serrated flat mainspring housing, dehorned all around. Available in blue or stainless steel. Introduced 2003. Made in U.S.A. by Colt's Mfg. Co.
Price: . . . . **NA**

CZ 75B AUTO PISTOL

Caliber: 9mm Para., 40 S&W, 10-shot magazine. **Barrel:** 4.7". **Weight:** 34.3 oz. **Length:** 8.1" overall. **Grips:** High impact checkered plastic. **Sights:** Square post front, rear adjustable for windage; three-dot system. **Features:** Single action/double action design; firing pin block safety; choice of black polymer, matte or high-polish blue finishes. All-steel frame. Imported from the Czech Republic by CZ-USA.
Price: Black polymer. **$472.00**
Price: Glossy blue. **$486.00**
Price: Dual tone or satin nickel **$486.00**
Price: 22 LR conversion unit. **$279.00**

CZ 75B Decocker

Similar to the CZ 75B except has a decocking lever in place of the safety lever. All other specifications are the same. Introduced 1999. Imported from the Czech Republic by CZ-USA.
Price: 9mm, black polymer **$467.00**
Price: 40 S&W **$481.00**

CZ 75B Compact Auto Pistol

Similar to the CZ 75 except has 10-shot magazine, 3.9" barrel and weighs 32 oz. Has removable front sight, non-glare ribbed slide top. Trigger guard is squared and serrated; combat hammer. Introduced 1993. Imported from the Czech Republic by CZ-USA.
Price: 9mm, black polymer **$499.00**
Price: Dual tone or satin nickel **$513.00**
Price: D Compact, black polymer **$526.00**

CZ 85

CZ 97B

CZ 75/85 Kadet

CZ 100

**Dan Wesson Firearms
Pointman Major**

CZ 75M IPSC Auto Pistol

Similar to the CZ 75B except has a longer frame and slide, slightly larger grip to accommodate new heavy-duty magazine. Ambidextrous thumb safety, safety notch on hammer; two-port in-frame compensator; slide racker; frame-mounted Firepoint red dot sight. Introduced 2001. Imported from the Czech Republic by CZ USA.
Price: 40 S&W, 10-shot mag. **$1,551.00**
Price: CZ 75 Standard IPSC (40 S&W, adj. sights) **$1,038.00**

CZ 85B Auto Pistol

Same gun as the CZ 75 except has ambidextrous slide release and safety-levers; non-glare, ribbed slide top; squared, serrated trigger guard; trigger stop to prevent overtravel. Introduced 1986. Imported from the Czech Republic by CZ-USA.
Price: Black polymer. **$483.00**
Price: Combat, black polymer. **$540.00**
Price: Combat, dual tone **$487.00**
Price: Combat, glossy blue. **$499.00**

CZ 85 Combat

Similar to the CZ 85B (9mm only) except has an adjustable rear sight, adjustable trigger for overtravel, free-fall magazine, extended magazine catch. Does not have the firing pin block safety. Introduced 1999. Imported from the Czech Republic by CZ-USA.
Price: 9mm, black polymer **$540.00**
Price: 9mm, glossy blue **$566.00**
Price: 9mm, dual tone or satin nickel **$586.00**

CZ 83B DOUBLE-ACTION PISTOL

Caliber: 9mm Makarov, 32 ACP, 380 ACP, 10-shot magazine. **Barrel:** 3.8". **Weight:** 26.2 oz. **Length:** 6.8" overall. **Grips:** High impact checkered plastic. **Sights:** Removable square post front, rear adjustable for windage; three-dot system. **Features:** Single action/double action; ambidextrous magazine release and safety. Blue finish; non-glare ribbed slide top. Imported from the Czech Republic by CZ-USA.
Price: Blue **$378.00**
Price: Nickel **$397.00**

CZ 97B AUTO PISTOL

Caliber: 45 ACP, 10-shot magazine. **Barrel:** 4.85". **Weight:** 40 oz. **Length:** 8.34" overall. **Grips:** Checkered walnut. **Sights:** Fixed. **Features:** Single action/double action; full-length slide rails; screw-in barrel bushing; linkless barrel; all-steel construction; chamber loaded indicator; dual transfer bars. Introduced 1999. Imported from the Czech Republic by CZ-USA.
Price: Black polymer. **$625.00**
Price: Glossy blue. **$641.00**

CZ 75/85 KADET AUTO PISTOL

Caliber: 22 LR, 10-shot magazine. **Barrel:** 4.88". **Weight:** 36 oz. **Grips:** High impact checkered plastic. **Sights:** Blade front, fully adjustable rear. **Features:** Single action/double action mechanism; all-steel construction. Duplicates weight, balance and function of the CZ 75 pistol. Introduced 1999. Imported from the Czech Republic by CZ-USA.
Price: Black polymer................................... **$486.00**

CZ 100 AUTO PISTOL

Caliber: 9mm Para., 40 S&W, 10-shot magazine. **Barrel:** 3.7". **Weight:** 24 oz. **Length:** 6.9" overall. **Grips:** Grooved polymer. **Sights:** Blade front with dot, white outline rear drift adjustable for windage. **Features:** Double action only with firing pin block; polymer frame, steel slide; has laser sight mount. Introduced 1996. Imported from the Czech Republic by CZ-USA.
Price: 9mm Para..................................... **$405.00**
Price: 40 S&W **$424.00**

DAN WESSON FIREARMS POINTMAN MAJOR AUTO PISTOL

Caliber: 45 ACP. **Barrel:** 5". **Grips:** Rosewood checkered. **Sights: Features:** Blued or stainless steel frame and serrated slide; Chip McCormick match-grade trigger group, sear and disconnect; match-grade barrel; high-ride beavertail safety; checkered slide release; high rib; interchangeable sight system; laser engraved. Introduced 2000. Made in U.S.A. by Dan Wesson Firearms.
Price: Model PM1-B (blued) **$799.00**
Price: Model PM1-S (stainless) **$799.00**

Dan Wesson Firearms Pointman Seven Auto Pistols

Similar to Pointman Major, dovetail adjustable target rear sight and dovetail target front sight. Available in blued or stainless finish. Introduced 2000. Made in U.S.A. by Dan Wesson Firearms.
Price: PM7 (blued frame and slide) **$999.00**
Price: PM7S (stainless finish)......................... **$1,099.00**

Dan Wesson Firearms Pointman Guardian Auto Pistols

Similar to Pointman Major, more compact frame with 4.25" barrel. Available in blued or stainless finish with fixed or adjustable sights. Introduced 2000. Made in U.S.A. by Dan Wesson Firearms.
Price: PMG-FS, all new frame (fixed sights) **$769.00**
Price: PMG-AS (blued frame and slide, adjustable sights)...... **$799.00**
Price: PMGD-FS Guardian Duce, all new frame (stainless frame and blued slide, fixed sights) **$829.00**
Price: PMGD-AS Guardian Duce (stainless frame and blued slide, adj. sights)..................................... **$799.00**

Dan Wesson Firearms Major Aussie

Dan Wesson Firearms Patriot Marksman

Desert Baby Eagle

Desert Eagle Mark XIX

Dan Wesson Firearms Major Tri-Ops Packs

Similar to Pointman Major. Complete frame assembly fitted to 3 match grade complete slide assemblied (9mm, 10mm, 40 S&W). Includes recoil springs and magazines that come in hard cases fashioned after high-grade European rifle case. Constructed of navy blue cordura stretched over hardwood with black leather trim and comfortable black leather wrapped handle. Brass corner protectors, dual combination locks, engraved presentation plate on the lid. Inside, the Tri-Ops Pack components are nested in precision die-cut closed cell foam and held sercurely in place by convoluted foam in the inside of the lid. Introduced 2002. Made in U.S.A. by Dan Wesson Firearms.
Price: TOP1B (blued), TOP1-S (stainless) **$2.459.00**

Dan Wesson Firearms Major Aussie

Similar to Pointman Major. Available in 45 ACP. Features Bomar-style adjustable rear target sight, unique slide top configuration exclusive to this model (features radius from the flat side surfaces of the slide to a narrow flat on top and then a small radius and reveal ending in a flat, low (1/16" high) sight rib 3/8" wide with lengthwise serrations). Clearly identified by the Southern Cross flag emblem laser engraved on the sides of the slide (available in 45 ACP only). Introduced 2002. Made in U.S.A. by Dan Wesson Firearms.
Price: PMA-B (blued) **$999.00**
Price: PMA-S (stainless). **$1,099.00**

Dan Wesson Firearms Pointman Minor Auto Pistol

Similar to Pointman Major. Full size (5") entry level IDPA or action pistol model with blued carbon alloy frame and round top slide, bead blast matte finish on frame and slide top and radius, satin-brushed polished finish on sides of slide, chromed barrel, dovetail mount fixed rear target sight and tactical/target ramp front sight, match trigger, skeletonized target hammer, high ride beavertail, fitted extractor, serrations on thumb safety, slide release and mag release, lowered and relieved ejection port, beveled mag well, exotic hardwood grips, serrated mainspring housing, laser engraved. Introduced 2000. Made in U.S.A. by Dan Wesson Firearms.
Price: Model PM2-P **$599.00**

Dan Wesson Firearms Pointman Hi-Cap Auto Pistol

Similar to Pointman Minor, full-size high-capacity (10-shot) magazine with 5" chromed barrel, blued finish and dovetail fixed rear sight. Match adjustable trigger, ambidextrous extended thumb safety, beavertail safety. Introduced 2001. From Dan Wesson Firearms.
Price: PMHC (Pointman High-Cap) **$689.00**

Dan Wesson Firearms Pointman Dave Pruitt Signature Series

Similar to other full-sized Pointman models, customized by Master Pistol-smith and IDPA Grand Master Dave Pruitt. Alloy carbon-steel with black oxide bluing and bead-blast matte finish. Front and rear chevron cocking serrations, dovetail mount fixed rear target sight and tactical/target ramp front sight, ramped match barrel with fitted match bushing and link, Chip McCormick (or equivalent) match grade trigger group, serrated ambidextrous tactical/carry thumb safety, high ride beavertail, serrated slide release and checkered mag release, match grade sear and hammer, fitted extractor, lowered and relieved ejection port, beveled mag well, full length 2-piece recoil spring guide rod, cocobolo double diamond checkered grips, serrated steel mainspring housing, special laser engraving. Introduced 2001. From Dan Wesson Firearms.
Price: PMDP (Pointman Dave Pruitt) **$899.00**

DAN WESSON FIREARMS PATRIOT 1911 PISTOL

Caliber: 45 ACP. **Grips:** Exotic exhibition grade cocobolo, double diamond hand cut checkering. **Sights:** New innovative combat/carry rear sight that completely encloses the dovetail. **Features:** The new Patriot Expert and Patriot Marksman are full size match grade series 70 1911s machined from steel forgings. Available in blued chome moly steel or stainless steel. Beveled mag well, lowered and flared ejection port, high sweep beavertail safety. Delivery begins in June 2002.
Price: Model PTM-B (blued) **$797.00**
Price: Model PTM-S (stainless) **$898.00**
Price: Model PTE-B (blued) **$864.00**
Price: Model PTE-S (stainless). **$971.00**

DESERT EAGLE MARK XIX PISTOL

Caliber: 357 Mag., 9-shot; 44 Mag., 8-shot; 50 Magnum, 7-shot. **Barrel:** 6", 10", interchangeable. **Weight:** 357 Mag.—62 oz.; 44 Mag.—69 oz.; 50 Mag.— 72 oz. **Length:** 10-1/4" overall (6" bbl.). **Grips:** Polymer; rubber available. **Sights:** Blade on ramp front, combat-style rear. Adjustable available. **Features:** Interchangeable barrels; rotating three-lug bolt; ambidextrous safety; adjustable trigger. Military epoxy finish. Satin, bright nickel, hard chrome, polished and blued finishes available. 10" barrel extra. Imported from Israel by Magnum Research, Inc.
Price: 357, 6" bbl., standard pistol **$1,199.00**
Price: 44 Mag., 6", standard pistol **$1,199.00**
Price: 50 Magnum, 6" bbl., standard pistol **$1,199.00**

DESERT BABY EAGLE PISTOLS

Caliber: 9mm Para., 40 S&W, 45 ACP, 10-round magazine. **Barrel:** 3.5", 3.7", 4.72". **Weight:** NA. **Length:** 7.25" to 8.25" overall. **Grips:** Polymer. **Sights:** Drift-adjustable rear, blade front. **Features:** Steel frame and slide; polygonal rifling to reduce barrel wear; slide safety; decocker. Reintroduced in 1999. Imported from Israel by Magnum Research Inc.
Price: Standard (9mm or 40 cal.; 4.72" barrel, 8.25" overall) **$499.00**
Price: Semi-Compact (9mm, 40 or 45 cal.; 3.7" barrel,
7.75" overall) **$499.00**
Price: Compact (9mm or 40 cal.; 3.5" barrel, 7.25" overall) **$499.00**
Price: Polymer (9mm or 40 cal; polymer frame; 3.25" barrel,
7.25" overall) **$499.00**

HANDGUNS

EAA Witness

Ed Brown Commander Bobtail

Ed Brown Kobra Carry

Entréprise Elite P500

Entréprise Boxer P500

Entréprise Tactical 500

HANDGUNS

EAA WITNESS DA AUTO PISTOL

Caliber: 9mm Para., 10-shot magazine; 38 Super, 40 S&W, 10-shot magazine; 45 ACP, 10-shot magazine. **Barrel:** 4.50". **Weight:** 35.33 oz. **Length:** 8.10" overall. **Grips:** Checkered rubber. **Sights:** Undercut blade front, open rear adjustable for windage. **Features:** Double-action trigger system; round trigger guard; frame-mounted safety. Introduced 1991. Imported from Italy by European American Armory.

Price: 9mm, blue	$449.00
Price: 9mm, Wonder finish	$459.00
Price: 9mm Compact, blue, 10-shot	$449.00
Price: As above, Wonder finish	$459.60
Price: 40 S&W, blue	$449.60
Price: As above, Wonder finish	$459.60
Price: 40 S&W Compact, 9-shot, blue	$449.60
Price: As above, Wonder finish	$459.60
Price: 45 ACP, blue	$449.00
Price: As above, Wonder finish	$459.60
Price: 45 ACP Compact, 8-shot, blue	$449.00
Price: As above, Wonder finish	$459.60

EAA EUROPEAN MODEL AUTO PISTOLS

Caliber: 32 ACP or 380 ACP, 7-shot magazine. **Barrel:** 3.88". **Weight:** 26 oz. **Length:** 7-3/8" overall. **Grips:** European hardwood. **Sights:** Fixed blade front, rear drift-adjustable for windage. **Features:** Chrome or blue finish; magazine, thumb and firing pin safeties; external hammer; safety-lever takedown. Imported from Italy by European American Armory.

Price: Blue	$132.60
Price: Wonder finish	$163.80

EAA/BUL 1911 AUTO PISTOL

Caliber: 45 ACP. **Barrel:** 3", 4", 5". **Weight:** 24-30 oz. **Length:** 7-10". **Grips:** Full checkered. **Sights:** Tactical rear, dove tail front. **Features:** Lightweight polymer frame, extended beavertail, skeletonized trigger and hammer, beveled mag well.

Price: Blue	$559.00
Price: Chrome	$599.00

ED BROWN COMMANDER BOBTAIL

Caliber: 45 ACP, 400 Cor-Bon, 40 S&W, 357 SIG, 38 Super, 9mm Luger, 7-shot magazine. **Barrel:** 4.25". **Weight:** 34 oz. **Grips:** Hogue exotic wood. **Sights:** Customer preference front; fixed Novak low-mount, rear. Optional night inserts available. **Features:** Checkered forestrap and bobtailed mainspring housing. Other options available.

Price:	$2,300.00

ED BROWN KOBRA, KOBRA CARRY

Caliber: 45 ACP, 7-shot magazine. **Barrel:** 5" (Kobra); 4.25" (Kobra Carry). **Weight:** 39 oz. (Kobra); 34 oz. (Kobra Carry). **Grips:** Hogue exotic wood. **Sights:** Ramp, front; fixed Novak low-mount night sights, rear. **Features:** Has snakeskin pattern serrations on forestrap and mainspring housing, denorned edges, beavertail grip safety.

Price: .... **$1,795.00** (Kobra); **$1,995.00** (Kobra Carry)

ENTRÉPRISE ELITE P500 AUTO PISTOL

Caliber: 45 ACP, 10-shot magazine. **Barrel:** 5". **Weight:** 40 oz. **Length:** 8.5" overall. **Grips:** Black ultra-slim, double diamond, checkered synthetic. **Sights:** Dovetailed blade front, rear adjustable for windage; three-dot system. **Features:** Reinforced dust cover; lowered and flared ejection port; squared trigger guard; adjustable match trigger; bolstered front strap; high grip cut; high ride beavertail grip safety; steel flat mainspring housing; extended thumb lock; skeletonized hammer, match grade sear, disconnector; Wolff springs. Introduced 1998. Made in U.S.A. by Entréprise Arms.

Price: **$739.90**

Entréprise Boxer P500 Auto Pistol

Similar to the Medalist model except has adjustable Competizione "melded" rear sight with dovetailed Patridge front; high mass chiseled slide with sweep cut; machined slide parallel rails; polished breech face and barrel channel. Introduced 1998. Made in U.S.A. by Entréprise Arms.

Price: **$1,399.00**

Entréprise Medalist P500 Auto Pistol

Similar to the Elite model except has adjustable Competizione "melded" rear sight with dovetailed Patridge front; machined slide parallel rails with polished breech face and barrel channel; front and rear slide serrations; lowered and flared ejection port; full-length one-piece guide rod with plug; National Match barrel and bushing; stainless firing pin; tuned match extractor; oversize firing pin stop; throated barrel and polished ramp; slide lapped to frame. Introduced 1998. Made in U.S.A. by Entréprise Arms.

Price: 45 ACP	$979.00
Price: 40 S&W	$1,099.00

Entréprise Tactical P500 Auto Pistol

Similar to the Elite model except has Tactical2 Ghost Ring sight or Novak lo-mount sight; ambidextrous thumb safety; front and rear slide serrations; full-length guide rod; throated barrel, polished ramp; tuned match extractor; fitted barrel and bushing; stainless firing pin; slide lapped to frame; dehorned. Introduced 1998. Made in U.S.A. by Entréprise Arms.

Price:	$979.90
Price: Tactical Plus (full-size frame, Officer's slide)	$1,049.00

FEG PJK-9HP

Felk MTF 450

Firestorm Mini

Firestorm 45 Gov't

Glock 17C

Glock 22

ERMA KGP68 AUTO PISTOL

Caliber: 32 ACP, 6-shot, 380 ACP, 5-shot. **Barrel:** 4". **Weight:** 22-1/2 oz. **Length:** 7-3/8" overall. **Grips:** Checkered plastic. **Sights:** Fixed. **Features:** Toggle action similar to original "Luger" pistol. Action stays open after last shot. Has magazine and sear disconnect safety systems.
Price: **$499.95**

FEG PJK-9HP AUTO PISTOL

Caliber: 9mm Para., 10-shot magazine. **Barrel:** 4.75". **Weight:** 32 oz. **Length:** 8" overall. **Grips:** Hand-checkered walnut. **Sights:** Blade front, rear adjustable for windage; three dot system. **Features:** Single action; polished blue or hard chrome finish; rounded combat-style serrated hammer. Comes with two magazines and cleaning rod. Imported from Hungary by K.B.I., Inc.
Price: Blue **$259.95**
Price: Hard chrome. **$259.95**

FEG SMC-380 AUTO PISTOL

Caliber: 380 ACP, 6-shot magazine. **Barrel:** 3.5". **Weight:** 18.5 oz. **Length:** 6.1" overall. **Grips:** Checkered composition with thumbrest. **Sights:** Blade front, rear adjustable for windage. **Features:** Patterned after the PPK pistol. Alloy frame, steel slide; double action. Blue finish. Comes with two magazines, cleaning rod. Imported from Hungary by K.B.I., Inc.
Price: **$224.95**

FELK MTF 450 AUTO PISTOL

Caliber: 9mm Para. (10-shot); 40 S&W (8-shot); 45 ACP (9-shot magazine). **Barrel:** 3.5". **Weight:** 19.9 oz. **Length:** 6.4" overall. **Grips:** Checkered. **Sights:** Blade front; adjustable rear. **Features:** Double-action-only trigger, striker fired; polymer frame; trigger safety, firing pin safety, trigger bar safety; adjustable trigger weight; fully interchangeable slide/barrel to change calibers. Introduced 1998. Imported by Felk Inc.
Price: **$395.00**
Price: 45 ACP pistol with 9mm and 40 S&W slide/barrel
assemblies **$999.00**

FIRESTORM AUTO PISTOL

Features: 7 or 10 rd. double action pistols with matte, duotone or nickel finish. Distributed by SGS Importers International.
Price: 22 LR 10 rd, 380 7 rd. matte. **$264.95**
Price: Duotone **$274.95**
Price: Mini 9mm, 40 S&W, 10 rd. matte **$383.95**
Price: Duotone **$391.95**
Price: Nickel **$408.95**
Price: Mini 45, 7 rd. matte. **$383.95**

Price: Duotone 45. . . . . **$399.95**
Price: Nickel 45. . . . . **$416.95**
Price: 45 Government, Compact, 7 rd. matte **$324.95**
Price: Duotone **$333.95**
Price: Extra magazines. **$29.95-49.95**

GLOCK 17 AUTO PISTOL

Caliber: 9mm Para., 10-shot magazine. **Barrel:** 4.49". **Weight:** 22.04 oz. (without magazine). **Length:** 7.32" overall. **Grips:** Black polymer. **Sights:** Dot on front blade, white outline rear adjustable for windage. **Features:** Polymer frame, steel slide; double-action trigger with "Safe Action" system; mechanical firing pin safety, drop safety; simple takedown without tools; locked breech, recoil operated action. Adopted by Austrian armed forces 1983. NATO approved 1984. Imported from Austria by Glock, Inc.
Price: Fixed sight, with extra magazine, magazine loader, cleaning kit
. . . . **$641.00**
Price: Adjustable sight **$671.00**
Price: Model 17L (6" barrel) **$800.00**
Price: Model 17C, ported barrel (compensated) **$646.00**

Glock 19 Auto Pistol

Similar to the Glock 17 except has a 4" barrel, giving an overall length of 6.85" and weight of 20.99 oz. Magazine capacity is 10 rounds. Fixed or adjustable rear sight. Introduced 1988.
Price: Fixed sight **$641.00**
Price: Adjustable sight **$671.00**
Price: Model 19C, ported barrel **$646.00**

Glock 20 10mm Auto Pistol

Similar to the Glock Model 17 except chambered for 10mm Automatic cartridge. Barrel length is 4.60", overall length is 7.59", and weight is 26.3 oz. (without magazine). Magazine capacity is 10 rounds. Fixed or adjustable rear sight. Comes with an extra magazine, magazine loader, cleaning rod and brush. Introduced 1990. Imported from Austria by Glock, Inc.
Price: Fixed sight **$700.00**
Price: Adjustable sight **$730.00**

Glock 21 Auto Pistol

Similar to the Glock 17 except chambered for 45 ACP, 10-shot magazine. Overall length is 7.59", weight is 25.2 oz. (without magazine). Fixed or adjustable rear sight. Introduced 1991.
Price: Fixed sight **$700.00**
Price: Adjustable sight **$730.00**

Glock 26

Glock 30

Glock 31

Glock 35

Hammerli Trailside

Glock 22 Auto Pistol

Similar to the Glock 17 except chambered for 40 S&W, 10-shot magazine. Overall length is 7.28", weight is 22.3 oz. (without magazine). Fixed or adjustable rear sight. Introduced 1990.

Price: Fixed sight **$641.00**
Price: Adjustable sight **$671.00**
Price: Model 22C, ported barrel **$646.00**

Glock 23 Auto Pistol

Similar to the Glock 19 except chambered for 40 S&W, 10-shot magazine. Overall length is 6.85", weight is 20.6 oz. (without magazine). Fixed or adjustable rear sight. Introduced 1990.

Price: Fixed sight **$641.00**
Price: Model 23C, ported barrel **$646.00**
Price: Adjustable sight **$671.00**

GLOCK 26, 27 AUTO PISTOLS

Caliber: 9mm Para. (M26), 10-shot magazine; 40 S&W (M27), 9-shot magazine. **Barrel:** 3.46". **Weight:** 21.75 oz. **Length:** 6.29" overall. **Grips:** Integral. Stippled polymer. **Sights:** Dot on front blade, fixed or fully adjustable white outline rear. **Features:** Subcompact size. Polymer frame, steel slide; double-action trigger with "Safe Action" system, three safeties. Matte black Tenifer finish. Hammer-forged barrel. Imported from Austria by Glock, Inc. Introduced 1996.

Price: Fixed sight **$641.00**
Price: Adjustable sight **$671.00**

GLOCK 29, 30 AUTO PISTOLS

Caliber: 10mm (M29), 45 ACP (M30), 10-shot magazine. **Barrel:** 3.78". **Weight:** 24 oz. **Length:** 6.7" overall. **Grips:** Integral. Stippled polymer. **Sights:** Dot on front, fixed or fully adjustable white outline rear. **Features:** Compact size. Polymer frame steel slide; double-recoil spring reduces recoil; Safe Action system with three safeties; Tenifer finish. Two magazines supplied. Introduced 1997. Imported from Austria by Glock, Inc.

Price: Fixed sight **$700.00**
Price: Adjustable sight **$730.00**

Glock 31/31C Auto Pistols

Similar to the Glock 17 except chambered for 357 Auto cartridge; 10-shot magazine. Overall length is 7.32", weight is 23.28 oz. (without magazine). Fixed or adjustable sight. Imported from Austria by Glock, Inc.

Price: Fixed sight **$641.00**
Price: Adjustable sight **$671.00**
Price: Model 31C, ported barrel **$646.00**

Glock 32/32C Auto Pistols

Similar to the Glock 19 except chambered for the 357 Auto cartridge; 10-shot magazine. Overall length is 6.85", weight is 21.52 oz. (without magazine). Fixed or adjustable sight. Imported from Austria by Glock, Inc.

Price: Fixed sight **$616.00**
Price: Adjustable sight **$644.00**
Price: Model 32C, ported barrel **$646.00**

Glock 33 Auto Pistol

Similar to the Glock 26 except chambered for the 357 Auto cartridge; 9-shot magazine. Overall length is 6.29", weight is 19.75 oz. (without magazine). Fixed or adjustable sight. Imported from Austria by Glock, Inc.

Price: Fixed sight **$641.00**
Price: Adjustable sight **$671.00**

GLOCK 34, 35 AUTO PISTOLS

Caliber: 9mm Para. (M34), 40 S&W (M35), 10-shot magazine. **Barrel:** 5.32". **Weight:** 22.9 oz. **Length:** 8.15" overall. **Grips:** Integral. Stippled polymer. **Sights:** Dot on front, fully adjustable white outline rear. **Features:** Polymer frame, steel slide; double-action trigger with "Safe Action" system; three safeties; Tenifer finish. Imported from Austria by Glock, Inc.

Price: Model 34, 9mm. **$770.00**
Price: Model 35, 40 S&W **$770.00**

GLOCK 36 AUTO PISTOL

Caliber: 45 ACP, 6-shot magazine. **Barrel:** 3.78". **Weight:** 20.11 oz. **Length:** 6.77" overall. **Grips:** Integral. Stippled polymer. **Sights:** Dot on front, fully adjustable white outline rear. **Features:** Polymer frame, steel slide; double-action trigger with "Safe Action" system; three safeties; Tenifer finish. Imported from Austria by Glock, Inc.

Price: Fixed sight **$700.00**
Price: Adj. sight **$730.00**

HAMMERLI "TRAILSIDE" TARGET PISTOL

Caliber: 22 LR. **Barrel:** 4.5", 6". **Weight:** 28 oz. **Grips:** Synthetic. **Sights:** Fixed. **Features:** 10-shot magazine. Imported from Switzerland by Sigarms. Distributed by Hammerli U.S.A.

Price: **$579.00**

HECKLER & KOCH USP AUTO PISTOL

Caliber: 9mm Para., 10-shot magazine, 40 S&W, 10-shot magazine. **Barrel:** 4.25". **Weight:** 28 oz. (USP40). **Length:** 6.9" overall. **Grips:** Non-slip stippled black polymer. **Sights:** Blade front, rear adjustable for windage. **Features:** New HK design with polymer frame, modified Browning action with recoil reduction system, single control lever. Special "hostile environment" finish on all metal parts. Available in SA/DA, DAO, left- and right-hand versions. Introduced 1993. Imported from Germany by Heckler & Koch, Inc.

Price: Right-hand **$827.00**
Price: Left-hand **$852.00**
Price: Stainless steel, right-hand **$888.00**
Price: Stainless steel, left-hand **$913.00**

Heckler & Koch USP Compact

Heckler & Koch USP45

Heckler & Koch USP45 Compact

Heckler & Koch USP45 Tactical

Heckler & Koch Elite

Heckler & Koch Mark 23 Special Operations

Heckler & Koch P7M8

Heckler & Koch USP Compact Auto Pistol
Similar to the USP except has 3.58" barrel, measures 6.81" overall, and weighs 1.60 lbs. (9mm). Available in 9mm Para. 357 SIG or 40 S&W with 10-shot magazine. Introduced 1996. Imported from Germany by Heckler & Koch, Inc.

Price: Blue $786.00
Price: Blue with control lever on right $821.00
Price: Same as USP Compact DAO, enhanced trigger performance $821.00

Heckler & Koch USP45 Auto Pistol
Similar to the 9mm and 40 S&W USP except chambered for 45 ACP, 10-shot magazine. Has 4.13" barrel, overall length of 7.87" and weighs 30.4 oz. Has adjustable three-dot sight system. Available in SA/DA, DAO, left- and right-hand versions. Introduced 1995. Imported from Germany by Heckler & Koch, Inc.

Price: Right-hand $827.00
Price: Left-hand $862.00
Price: Stainless steel right-hand................... $888.00
Price: Stainless steel left-hand $923.00

Heckler & Koch USP45 Compact
Similar to the USP45 except has stainless slide; 8-shot magazine; modified and contoured slide and frame; extended slide release; 3.80" barrel, 7.09" overall length, weighs 1.75 lbs.; adjustable three-dot sights. Introduced 1998. Imported from Germany by Heckler & Koch, Inc.

Price: With control lever on left, stainless $909.00
Price: As above, blue $857.00
Price: With control lever on right, stainless............... $944.00
Price: As above, blue $892.00

HECKLER & KOCH USP45 TACTICAL PISTOL
Caliber: 45 ACP, 10-shot magazine. **Barrel:** 4.92". **Weight:** 2.24 lbs. **Length:** 8.64" overall. **Grips:** Non-slip stippled polymer. **Sights:** Blade front, fully adjustable target rear. **Features:** Has extended threaded barrel with rubber O-ring; adjustable trigger; extended magazine floorplate; adjustable trigger stop; polymer frame. Introduced 1998. Imported from Germany by Heckler & Koch, Inc.

Price: $1,124.00

HECKLER & KOCH MARK 23 SPECIAL OPERATIONS PISTOL
Caliber: 45 ACP, 10-shot magazine. **Barrel:** 5.87". **Weight:** 43 oz. **Length:** 9.65" overall. **Grips:** Integral with frame; black polymer. **Sights:** Blade front, rear drift adjustable for windage; three-dot. **Features:** Polymer frame; double action; exposed hammer; short recoil, modified Browning action. Civilian version of the SOCOM pistol. Introduced 1996. Imported from Germany by Heckler & Koch, Inc.

Price: $2,444.00

Heckler & Koch USP Expert Pistol
Combines features of the USP Tactical and HK Mark 23 pistols with a new slide design. Chambered for 45 ACP, 40 S&W & 9mm; 10-shot magazine. Has adjustable target sights, 5.20" barrel, 8.74" overall length, weighs 1.87 lbs. Match-grade single- and double-action trigger pull with adjustable stop; ambidextrous control levers; elongated target slide; barrel O-ring that seals and centers barrel. Suited to IPSC competition. Introduced 1999. Imported from Germany by Heckler & Koch, Inc.

Price: $1,533.00

Heckler & Koch Elite
A long slide version of the USP combining features found on standard-sized and specialized models of the USP. Most noteworthy is the 6.2-inch barrel, making it the most accurate of the USP series. In 9mm and 45 ACP. Imported from Germany by Heckler & Koch, Inc. Introduced 2003.

Price: $1,533.00

HECKLER & KOCH P7M8 AUTO PISTOL
Caliber: 9mm Para., 8-shot magazine. **Barrel:** 4.13". **Weight:** 29 oz. **Length:** 6.73" overall. **Grips:** Stippled black plastic. **Sights:** Blade front, adjustable rear; three dot system. **Features:** Unique "squeeze cocker" in frontstrap cocks the action. Gas-retarded action. Squared combat-type trigger guard. Blue finish. Compact size. Imported from Germany by Heckler & Koch, Inc.

Price: P7M8, blued $1,472.00

Hi-Point 9MM Comp

Kahr K9

Kahr MK40

Kel-Tec P-11

HECKLER & KOCH P2000 GPM PISTOL

Caliber: 9mmx19; 10-shot magazine, 13- or 16-round law enforcement/military magazines. **Barrel:** 3.62". **Weight:** 21.87 ozs. **Length:** 7". **Grips:** Interchangeable panels. **Sights:** Fixed partridge style, drift adjustable for windage, standard 3-dot. **Features:** German Pistol Model incorporating features of the HK USP Compact such as the pre-cocked hammer system which combines the advantages of a cocked striker with the double action hammer system. Introduced 2003. Imported from Germany by Heckler & Koch, Inc.

Price: .... **NA**

HI-POINT FIREARMS 9MM COMP PISTOL

Caliber: 9mm, Para., 10-shot magazine. **Barrel:** 4". **Weight:** 39 oz. **Length:** 7.72" overall. **Grips:** Textured acetal plastic. **Sights:** Adjustable; low profile. **Features:** Single-action design. Scratch-resistant, non-glare blue finish, alloy frame. Muzzle brake/compensator. Compensator is slotted for laser or flashlight mounting. Introduced 1998. From MKS Supply, Inc.

Price: Matte black **$159.00**

HI-POINT FIREARMS MODEL 9MM COMPACT PISTOL

Caliber: 9mm Para., 8-shot magazine. **Barrel:** 3.5". **Weight:** 29 oz. **Length:** 6.7" overall. **Grips:** Textured acetal plastic. **Sights:** Combat-style adjustable three-dot system; low profile. **Features:** Single-action design; frame-mounted magazine release; polymer or alloy frame. Scratch-resistant matte finish. Introduced 1993. Made in U.S.A. by MKS Supply, Inc.

Price: Black, alloy frame **$137.00**
Price: With polymer frame (29 oz.), non-slip grips **$137.00**
Price: Aluminum with polymer frame **$137.00**

Hi-Point Firearms Model 380 Polymer Pistol

Similar to the 9mm Compact model except chambered for 380 ACP, 8-shot magazine, adjustable three-dot sights. Weighs 29 oz. Polymer frame. Introduced 1998. Made in U.S.A. by MKS Supply.

Price: **$109.00**

Hi-Point Firearms 380 Comp Pistol

Similar to the 380 Polymer Pistol except has a 4" barrel with muzzle compensator; action locks open after last shot. Includes a 10-shot and an 8-shot magazine; trigger lock. Introduced 2001. Made in U.S.A. by MKS Supply Inc.

Price: **$125.00**
Price: With laser sight **$190.00**

HI-POINT FIREARMS 45 POLYMER FRAME

Caliber: 45 ACP, 9-shot. **Barrel:** 4.5". **Weight:** 35 oz. **Sights:** Adjustable 3-dot. **Features:** Last round lock-open, grip mounted magazine release, magazine disconnect safety, integrated accessory rail. Introduced 2002. Made in U.S.A. by MKS Supply Inc.

Price: **$169.00**

IAI M-2000 PISTOL

Caliber: 45 ACP, 8-shot. **Barrel:** 5", (Compact 4.25"). **Weight:** 36 oz. **Length:** 8.5", (6" Compact). **Grips:** Plastic or wood. **Sights:** Fixed. **Features:** 1911 Government U.S. Army-style. Steel frame and slide parkerized. GI grip safety. Beveled feed ramp barrel. By IAI, Inc.

Price: **$465.00**

KAHR K9, K40 DA AUTO PISTOLS

Caliber: 9mm Para., 7-shot, 40 S&W, 6-shot magazine. **Barrel:** 3.5". **Weight:** 25 oz. **Length:** 6" overall. **Grips:** Wrap-around textured soft polymer. **Sights:** Blade front, rear drift adjustable for windage; bar-dot combat style. **Features:** Trigger-cocking double-action mechanism with passive firing pin block. Made of 4140 ordnance steel with matte black finish. Contact maker for complete price list. Introduced 1994. Made in U.S.A. by Kahr Arms.

Price: E9, black matte finish **$425.00**
Price: Matte black, night sights 9mm **$668.00**
Price: Matte stainless steel, 9mm....................... **$638.00**
Price: 40 S&W, matte black **$580.00**
Price: 40 S&W, matte black, night sights **$668.00**
Price: 40 S&W, matte stainless **$638.00**
Price: K9 Elite 98 (high-polish stainless slide flats, Kahr combat trigger), from **$694.00**
Price: As above, MK9 Elite 98, from........................ **$694.00**
Price: As above, K40 Elite 98, from **$694.00**
Price: Covert, black, stainless slide, short grip........... **$599.00**
Price: Covert, black, tritium nite sights **$689.00**

Kahr K9 9mm Compact Polymer Pistol

Similar to K9 steel frame pistol except has polymer frame, matte stainless steel slide. Barrel length 3.5"; overall length 6"; weighs 17.9 oz. Includes two 7-shot magazines, hard polymer case, trigger lock. Introduced 2000. Made in U.S.A. by Kahr Arms.

Price: **$599.00**

Kahr MK9/MK40 Micro Pistol

Similar to the K9/K40 except is 5.5" overall, 4" high, has a 3" barrel. Weighs 22 oz. Has snag-free bar-dot sights, polished feed ramp, dual recoil spring system, DA-only trigger. Comes with 6- and 7-shot magazines. Introduced 1998. Made in U.S.A. by Kahr Arms.

Price: Matte stainless **$638.00**
Price: Elite 98, polished stainless, tritium night sights **$791.00**

KAHR PM9 PISTOL

Caliber: 9x19. **Barrel:** 3", 1:10 twist. **Weight:** 15.9 oz. **Length:** 5.3" overall. **Features:** Lightweight black polymer frame, polygonal rifling, stainless steel slide, DAO with passive striker block, trigger lock, hard case, 6 and 7 rd. mags.

Price: Matte stainless slide.......................... **$622.00**
Price: Tritium night sights **$719.00**

KEL-TEC P-11 AUTO PISTOL

Caliber: 9mm Para., 10-shot magazine. **Barrel:** 3.1". **Weight:** 14 oz. **Length:** 5.6" overall. **Grips:** Checkered black polymer. **Sights:** Blade front, rear adjustable for windage. **Features:** Ordnance steel slide, aluminum frame. Double-action-only trigger mechanism. Introduced 1995. Made in U.S.A. by Kel-Tec CNC Industries, Inc.

Price: Blue **$314.00**
Price: Hard chrome.......................... **$368.00**
Price: Parkerized **$355.00**

Kel-Tec P-32

Kimber Custom II

Kimber Pro Carry II

Kimber Ultra Carry II

Kimber Ten II High Capacity Polymer

Kimber Gold Match II

KEL-TEC P-32 AUTO PISTOL

Caliber: 32 ACP, 7-shot magazine. **Barrel:** 2.68". **Weight:** 6.6 oz. **Length:** 5.07" overall. **Grips:** Checkered composite. **Sights:** Fixed. **Features:** Double-action-only mechanism with 6-lb. pull; internal slide stop. Textured composite grip/frame. Now available in 380 ACP. Made in U.S.A. by Kel-Tec CNC Industries, Inc.

Price: Blue **$300.00**

Price: Hard chrome. **$340.00**

Price: Parkerized **$355.00**

KIMBER CUSTOM II AUTO PISTOL

Caliber: 45 ACP, 40 S&W, 38 Super. **Barrel:** 5", match grade, 40 S&W, 38 Super barrels ramped. **Weight:** 38 oz. **Length:** 8.7" overall. **Grips:** Checkered black rubber, walnut, rosewood. **Sights:** Dovetail front and rear, Kimber adjustable or fixed three dot (green) Meptrolight night sights. **Features:** Slide, frame and barrel machined from steel or stainless steel forgings. Match grade barrel, chamber and trigger group. Extended thumb safety, beveled magazine well, beveled front and rear slide serrations, high ride beavertail grip safety, checkered flat mainspring housing, kidney cut under trigger guard, high cut grip, match grade stainless steel berrel bushing, polished breech face, Commander-style hammer, lowered and flared ejection port, Wolff springs, bead blasted black oxide finish. Introduced in 1996. Made in U.S.A. by Kimber Mfg., Inc.

Price: Custom. **$730.00**

Price: Custom Walnut (double-diamond walnut grips) **$752.00**

Price: Custom Stainless **$832.00**

Price: Custom Stainless 40 S&W **$870.00**

Price: Custom Stainless Target 45 ACP (stainless, adj. sight) . . . **$945.00**

Price: Custom Stainless Target 38 Super **$974.00**

Kimber Custom II Auto Pistol

Similar to Compact II, 4" bull barrel fitted directly to the stainless steel slide without a bushing, grip is .400" shorter than standard, no front serrations. Weighs 34 oz. 45 ACP only. Introduced in 1998. Made in U.S.A. by Kimber Mfg., Inc.

Price: **$870.00**

Kimber Pro Carry II Auto Pistol

Similar to Custom II, has aluminum frame, 4" bull barrel fitted directly to the slide without bushing. HD with stainless steel frame. Introduced 1998. Made in U.S.A. by Kimber Mfg., Inc.

Price: 45 ACP **$773.00**

Price: HD II **$879.00**

Price: Pro Carry HD II Stainless 45 ACP **$845.00**

Price: Pro Carry HD II Stainless 38 Spec. **$917.00**

Kimber Ultra Carry II Auto Pistol

Similar to Compact Stainless II, lightweight aluminum frame, 3" match grade bull barrel fitted to slide without bushing. Grips .400" shorter. Special slide stop. Low effort recoil. Weighs 25 oz. Introduced in 1999. Made in U.S.A. by Kimber Mfg., Inc.

Price: **$767.00**

Price: Stainless. **$841.00**

Price: Stainless 40 S&W. **$884.00**

Kimber Ten II High Capacity Polymer Pistol

Similar to Custom II, Pro Carry II and Ultra Carry II depending on barrel length. Ten-round magazine capacity (double stack and flush fitting). Polymer grip frame molded over stainless steel or aluminum (Ultra Ten II only) frame insert. Checkered front strap and belly of trigger guard. All models have fixed sights except Gold Match Ten II, which has adjustable sight. Frame grip dimensions approximate that of the standard 1911 for natural aiming and better recoil control. Ultra Ten II weight is 24 oz. Others 32-34 oz. Additional 14-round magazines available where legal. Much-improved version of the Kimber Polymer series. Made in U.S.A. by Kimber Mfg., Inc.

Price: Ultra Ten II **$850.00**

Price: Pro Carry Ten II **$828.00**

Price: Stainless Ten II **$812.00**

Kimber Gold Match II Auto Pistol

Similar to Custom II models. Includes stainless steel barrel with match grade chamber and barrel bushing, ambidextrous thumb safety, adjustable sight, premium aluminum trigger, hand-checkered double diamond rosewood grips. Barrel hand-fitted to bushing and slide for target accuracy. Made in U.S.A. by Kimber Mfg., Inc.

Price: Gold Match II **$1,169.00**

Price: Gold Match Stainless II 45 ACP **$1,315.00**

Price: Gold Match Stainless II 40 S&W **$1,345.00**

Kimber Gold Match Ten II Polymer Auto Pistol

Similar to Stainless Gold Match II. High capacity polymer frame with ten-round magazine. No ambi thumb safety. Polished flats add elegant look. Introduced 1999. Made in U.S.A. by Kimber Mfg., Inc.

Price: **$1,118.00**

Kimber Gold Match II

Kimber Gold Combat II

Kimber CDP II

Kimber Eclipse II

Kimber Eclipse Pro II

Kimber LTP II

Llama Micromax 380

Kimber Gold Combat II Auto Pistol

Similar to Gold Match II except designed for concealed carry. Extended and beveled magazine well, Meprolight tritium night sights; premium aluminum trigger; 30 lpi front strap checkering; special Custom Shop markings; Kim Pro premium finish. Introduced 1999. Made in U.S.A. by Kimber Mfg., Inc.

Price: 45 ACP **$1,682.00**
Price: Gold Combat Stainless (satin-finished stainless frame and slide, special Custom Shop markings) **$1,623.00**

Kimber CDP II Series Auto Pistol

Similar to Custom II, but designed for concealed carry. Aluminum frame. Standard features include stainless steel slide, Meprolight tritium three dot (green) dovetail-mounted night sights, match grade barrel and chamber, 30 LPI front strap checkering, two tone finish, ambidextrous thumb safety, hand-checkered double diamond rosewood grips. Introduced in 2000. Made in U.S.A. by Kimber Mfg., Inc.

Price: Ultra CDP II 40 S&W **$1,120.00**
Price: Ultra CDP II (3 barrel, short grip) **$1,084.00**
Price: Compact CDP II (4 barrel, short grip) **$1,084.00**
Price: Pro CDP II (4 barrel, full length grip) **$1,084.00**
Price: Custom CDP II (5 barrel, full length grip) **$1,084.00**

Kimber Eclipse II Series Auto Pistol

Similar to Custom II and other stainless Kimber pistols. Stainless slide and frame, black anodized, two tone finish. Gray/black laminated grips. 30 LPI front strap checkering. All have night sights, with Target versions having Meprolight adjustable Bar/Dot version. Made in U.S.A. by Kimber Mfg., Inc.

Price: Eclipse Ultra II (3 barrel, short grip) **$1,052.00**
Price: Eclipse Pro II (4 barrel, full length grip) **$1,052.00**
Price: Eclipse Pro Target II (4 barrel, full length grip, adjustable sight) **$1,153.00**
Price: Eclipse Custom II (5 barrel, full length grip) **$1,071.00**
Price: Eclipse Target II (5 barrel, full length grip, adjustable sight) **$1,153.00**

Kimber LTP II Polymer Auto Pistol

Similar to Gold Match II. Built for Limited Ten competition. First Kimber pistol with new, innovative Kimber external extractor. KimPro premium finish. Stainless steel match grade barrel. Extended and beveled magazine well. Checkered front strap and trigger guard belly. Tungsten full length guide rod. Premium aluminum trigger. Ten-round single stack magazine. Wide ambidextrous thumb safety. Made in U.S.A. by Kimber Mfg., Inc.

Price: **$2,036.00**

Kimber Super Match II Auto Pistol

Similar to Gold Match II. Built for target and action shotting competition. Tested for accuracy. Target included. Stainless steel barrel and chamber. KimPro finish on stainless steel slide. Stainless steel frame. 30 LPI checkered front strap, premium aluminum trigger, Kimber adjustable sight. Introduced in 1999.

Price: **$1,926.00**

KORTH PISTOL

Caliber: 40 S&W, 357 SIG (9-shot); 9mm Para, 9x21 (10-shot). **Barrel:** 4" (standard), 5" (optional). Trigger **Weight:** 3.3 lbs. (single Action), 11 lbs. (double action). **Sights:** Fully adjustable. **Features:** All parts of surface-hardened steel; recoil-operated action, mechanically-locked via large pivoting bolt block maintaining parallel positioning of barrel during the complete cycle. Accessories include sound suppressor for qualified buyers. A masterpiece of German precision. Imported by Korth USA.

Price: **$5,413.00**

LLAMA MICROMAX 380 AUTO PISTOL

Caliber: 32 ACP, 8-shot, 380 ACP, 7-shot magazine. **Barrel:** 3-11/16". **Weight:** 23 oz. **Length:** 6-1/2" overall. **Grips:** Checkered high impact polymer. **Sights:** 3-dot combat. **Features:** Single-action design. Mini custom extended slide release; mini custom extended beavertail grip safety; combat-style hammer. Introduced 1997. Distributed by Import Sports, Inc.

Price: Matte blue. **$281.95**
Price: Satin chrome (380 only) **$298.95**

HANDGUNS

Llama Minimax

Llama Max-1
Government Deluxe

North American
Arms Guardian

Para-Ordnance P12.45

Para-Ordnance LDA

LLAMA MINIMAX SERIES
Caliber: 40 S&W, 7-shot; 45 ACP, 6-shot magazine. **Barrel:** 3-1/2".
Weight: 35 oz. **Length:** 7-1/3" overall. **Grips:** Checkered rubber. **Sights:**
Three-dot combat. **Features:** Single action, skeletonized combat-style
hammer, extended slide release, cone-style barrel, flared ejection port. In-
troduced 1996. Distributed by Import Sports, Inc.
Price: Blue **$333.95**
Price: Duo-Tone finish (45 only) **$342.95**
Price: Satin chrome **$349.95**

Llama Minimax Sub-Compact Auto Pistol
Similar to the Minimax except has 3.14" barrel, weighs 31 oz.; 6.8" overall
length; has 10-shot magazine with finger extension; beavertail grip safety.
Introduced 1999. Distributed by Import Sports, Inc.
Price: 45 ACP, matte blue **$349.95**
Price: As above, satin chrome **$367.95**
Price: Duo-Tone finish (45 only) **$358.95**

LLAMA MAX-I AUTO PISTOLS
Caliber: 45 ACP, 7-shot. **Barrel:** 5-1/8". **Weight:** 36 oz. **Length:** 8-1/2"
overall. **Grips:** Polymer. **Sights:** Blade front; three-dot system. **Features:**
Single-action trigger; skeletonized combat-style hammer; steel frame; extended manual and grip safeties, matte finish. Introduced 1995. Distributed by Import Sports, Inc.
Price: 45 ACP, 7-shot, Government model **$324.95**

NORTH AMERICAN ARMS GUARDIAN PISTOL
Caliber: 32 ACP, 380 ACP, 32NAA, 6-shot magazine. **Barrel:** 2.1".
Weight: 13.5 oz. **Length:** 4.36" overall. **Grips:** Black polymer. **Sights:**
Fixed. **Features:** Double-action-only mechanism. All stainless steel con-
struction; snag-free. Introduced 1998. Made in U.S.A. by North American
Arms.
Price: . . . . **$408.00 to $449.00**

OLYMPIC ARMS OA-96 AR PISTOL
Caliber: 223. **Barrel:** 6", 8", 4140 chrome-moly steel. **Weight:** 5 lbs.
Length: 15-3/4" overall. **Grips:** A2 stowaway pistol grip; no buttstock or
receiver tube. **Sights:** Flat-top upper receiver, cut-down front sight base.
Features: AR-15-type receivers with special bolt carrier; short aluminum
hand guard; Vortex flash hider. Introduced 1996. Made in U.S.A. by Olym-
pic Arms, Inc.
Price: **$858.00**

Olympic Arms OA-98 AR Pistol
Similar to the OA-93 except has removable 7-shot magazine, weighs 3
lbs. Introduced 1999. Made in U.S.A. by Olympic Arms, Inc.
Price: **$990.00**

PARA-ORDNANCE P-SERIES AUTO PISTOLS
Caliber: 9mm Para., 40 S&W, 45 ACP, 10-shot magazine. **Barrel:** 3", 3-
1/2", 4-1/4", 5". **Weight:** From 24 oz. (alloy frame). **Length:** 8.5" overall.
Grips: Textured composition. **Sights:** Blade front, rear adjustable for
windage. High visibility three-dot system. **Features:** Available with alloy,
steel or stainless steel frame with black finish (silver or stainless gun).
Steel and stainless steel frame guns weigh 40 oz. (P14.45), 36 oz.
(P13.45), 34 oz. (P12.45). Grooved match trigger, rounded combat-style
hammer. Beveled magazine well. Manual thumb, grip and firing pin lock
safeties. Solid barrel bushing. Contact maker for full details. Introduced
1990. Made in Canada by Para-Ordnance.
Price: Steel frame **$795.00**
Price: Alloy frame **$765.00**
Price: Stainless steel **$865.00**

Para-Ordnance Limited Pistols
Similar to the P-Series pistols except with full-length recoil guide system;
fully adjustable rear sight; tuned trigger with overtravel stop; beavertail
grip safety; competition hammer; front and rear slide serrations; ambidextrous safety; lowered ejection port; ramped match-grade barrel; dovetailed front sight. Introduced 1998. Made in Canada by Para-Ordnance.
Price: 9mm, 40 S&W, 45 ACP . . . . **$945.00 to $999.00**

Para-Ordnance LDA Auto Pistols
Similar to P-series except has double-action trigger mechanism. Steel
frame with matte black finish, checkered composition grips. Available in
9mm Para., 40 S&W, 45 ACP. Introduced 1999. Made in Canada by
Para-Ordnance.
Price: **$775.00**

Para-Ordnance LDA Limited Pistols
Similar to LDA, has ambidextrous safety, adjustable rear sight, front slide
serrations and full-length recoil guide system. Made in Canada by Para-
Ordnance.
Price: Black finish **$975.00**
Price: Stainless **$1,049.00**

PARA-ORDNANCE C5 45 LDA PARA CARRY
Caliber: 45 ACP. **Barrel:** 3", 6+1 shot. **Weight:** 30 oz. **Length:** 6.5". **Grips:**
Double diamond checkered Cocobolo. **Features:** Stainless finish and re-
ceiver, "world's smallest DAO 45 auto." Para LDA trigger system and safe-
ties.
Price: **$899.00**

Para-Ordnance C5
45 LDA Para Carry

Para-Ordnance C7
45 LDA Para Companion

Peters Stahl High Capacity

Peters Stahl Trophy Master

Peters Stahl Millenium

Phoenix
Arms HP22

Rock River Standard Match

Ruger P89

Ruger P90

HANDGUNS

PARA-ORDNANCE C7 45 LDA PARA COMPANION
Caliber: 45 ACP. **Barrel:** 3.5", 7+1 shot. **Weight:** 32 oz. **Length:** 7". **Grips:** Double diamond checkered Cocobolo. **Features:** Para LDA trigger system with Para LDA 3 safeties (slide lock, firing pin block and grip safety). Lightning speed, full size capacity.
Price: **$899.00**

PETERS STAHL AUTOLOADING PISTOLS
Caliber: 9mm Para., 45 ACP. **Barrel:** 5" or 6". **Grips:** Walnut or walnut with rubber wrap. **Sights:** Fully adjustable rear, blade front. **Features:** Stainless steel extended slide stop, safety and extended magazine release button; speed trigger with stop and approx. 3-lb. pull; polished ramp. Introduced 2000. Imported from Germany by Phillips & Rogers.
Price: High Capacity (accepts 15-shot magazines in 45 cal.; includes 10-shot magazine) **$1,695.00**
Price: Trophy Master (blued or stainless, 7-shot in 45, 8-shot in 9mm) **$1,995.00**
Price: Millenium Model (titanium coating on receiver and slide). **$2,195.00**

PHOENIX ARMS HP22, HP25 AUTO PISTOLS
Caliber: 22 LR, 10-shot (HP22), 25 ACP, 10-shot (HP25). **Barrel:** 3". **Weight:** 20 oz. **Length:** 5-1/2" overall. **Grips:** Checkered composition. **Sights:** Blade front, adjustable rear. **Features:** Single action, exposed hammer; manual hold-open; button magazine release. Available in satin nickel, polished blue finish. Introduced 1993. Made in U.S.A. by Phoenix Arms.
Price: With gun lock and cable lanyard. **$130.00**
Price: HP Rangemaster kit with 5" bbl., locking case and assessories **$171.00**
Price: HP Deluxe Rangemaster kit with 3" and 5" bbls., 2 mags., case **$210.00**

ROCK RIVER ARMS STANDARD MATCH AUTO PISTOL
Caliber: 45 ACP. **Barrel:** NA. **Weight:** NA. **Length:** NA. **Grips:** Cocobolo, checkered. **Sights:** Heine fixed rear, blade front. **Features:** Chrome-moly steel frame and slide; beavertail grip safety with raised pad; checkered slide stop; ambidextrous safety; polished feed ramp and extractor; aluminum speed trigger with 3.5 lb. pull. Made in U.S.A. From Rock River Arms.
Price: **$1,025.00**

ROCKY MOUNTAIN ARMS PATRIOT PISTOL
Caliber: 223, 10-shot magazine. **Barrel:** 7", with muzzle brake. **Weight:** 5 lbs. **Length:** 20.5" overall. **Grips:** Black composition. **Sights:** None furnished. **Features:** Milled upper receiver with enhanced Weaver base; milled lower receiver from billet plate; machined aluminum National Match handguard. Finished in DuPont Teflon-S matte black or NATO green. Comes with black nylon case, one magazine. Introduced 1993. From Rocky Mountain Arms, Inc.
Price: With A-2 handle top . . . . **$2,500.00 to $2,800.00**
Price: Flat top model. . . . . **$3,000.00 to $3,500.00**

RUGER P89 AUTOLOADING PISTOL
Caliber: 9mm Para., 10-shot magazine. **Barrel:** 4.50". **Weight:** 32 oz. **Length:** 7.84" overall. **Grips:** Grooved black synthetic composition. **Sights:** Square post front, square notch rear adjustable for windage, both with white dot inserts. **Features:** Double action, ambidextrous slide-mounted safety-levers. Slide 4140 chrome-moly steel or 400-series stainless steel, frame lightweight aluminum alloy. Ambidextrous magazine release. Blue, stainless steel. Introduced 1986; stainless 1990.
Price: P89, blue, extra mag and mag loader, plastic case locks . **$475.00**
Price: KP89, stainless, extra mag and mag loader, plastic case locks **$525.00**

Ruger P93D

Ruger KP94D

Ruger KP95DAO

Ruger KMK 4

Ruger P89D Decocker Autoloading Pistol

Similar to standard P89 except has ambidextrous decocking levers in place of regular slide-mounted safety. Decocking levers move firing pin inside slide where hammer can not reach, while simultaneously blocking firing pin from forward movement—allows shooter to decock cocked pistol without manipulating trigger. Conventional thumb decocking procedures are therefore unnecessary. Blue, stainless steel. Introduced 1990.
Price: P89D, blue, extra mag and mag loader, plastic case locks   **$475.00**
Price: KP89D, stainless, extra mag and mag loader,
plastic case locks **$525.00**

Ruger P89 Double-Action-Only Autoloading Pistol

Same as KP89 except operates only in double-action mode. Has spurless hammer, gripping grooves on each side of rear slide; no external safety or decocking lever. Internal safety prevents forward movement of firing pin unless trigger is pulled. Available 9mm Para., stainless steel only. Introduced 1991.
Price: Lockable case, extra mag and mag loader **$525.00**

RUGER P90 MANUAL SAFETY MODEL AUTOLOADING PISTOL

Caliber: 45 ACP, 8-shot magazine. **Barrel:** 4.50". **Weight:** 33.5 oz. **Length:** 7.75" overall. **Grips:** Grooved black synthetic composition. **Sights:** Square post front, square notch rear adjustable for windage, both with white dot. **Features:** Double action ambidextrous slide-mounted safety-levers move firing pin inside slide where hammer can not reach, simultaneously blocking firing pin from forward movement. Stainless steel only. Introduced 1991.
Price: KP90 with extra mag, loader, case and gunlock. **$565.00**
Price: P90 (blue). **$525.00**

Ruger KP90 Decocker Autoloading Pistol

Similar to the P90 except has a manual decocking system. The ambidextrous decocking levers move the firing pin inside the slide where the hammer can not reach it, while simultaneously blocking the firing pin from forward movement—allows shooter to decock a cocked pistol without manipulating the trigger. Available only in stainless steel. Overall length 7.75", weighs 33.5 oz. Introduced 1991.
Price: KP90D with case, extra mag and mag loading tool **$565.00**

RUGER P93 COMPACT AUTOLOADING PISTOL

Caliber: 9mm Para., 10-shot magazine. **Barrel:** 3.9". **Weight:** 31 oz. **Length:** 7.25" overall. **Grips:** Grooved black synthetic composition. **Sights:** Square post front, square notch rear adjustable for windage. **Features:** Front of slide crowned with convex curve; slide has seven finger grooves; trigger guard bow higher for better grip; 400-series stainless slide, lightweight alloy frame; also blue. Decocker-only or DAO-only. Includes hard case and lock. Introduced 1993. Made in U.S.A. by Sturm, Ruger & Co.
Price: KP93DAO, double-action-only **$575.00**
Price: KP93D ambidextrous decocker, stainless **$575.00**
Price: P93D, ambidextrous decocker, blue **$495.00**

Ruger KP94 Autoloading Pistol

Sized midway between full-size P-Series and compact P93. 4.25" barrel, 7.5" overall length, weighs about 33 oz. KP94 manual safety model; KP94DAO double-action-only (both 9mm Para., 10-shot magazine); KP94D is decocker-only in 40-caliber with 10-shot magazine. Slide gripping grooves roll over top of slide. KP94 has ambidextrous safety-levers; KP94DAO has no external safety, full-cock hammer position or decocking

lever; KP94D has ambidextrous decocking levers. Matte finish stainless slide, barrel, alloy frame. Also blue. Includes hard case and lock. Introduced 1994. Made in U.S.A. by Sturm, Ruger & Co.
Price: P94, P944, blue (manual safety) **$495.00**
Price: KP94 (9mm), KP944 (40-caliber) (manual
safety-stainless) **$575.00**
Price: KP94DAO (9mm), KP944DAO (40-caliber) **$575.00**
Price: KP94D (9mm), KP944D (40-caliber)-decock only **$575.00**

RUGER P95 AUTOLOADING PISTOL

Caliber: 9mm Para., 10-shot magazine. **Barrel:** 3.9". **Weight:** 27 oz. **Length:** 7.25" overall. **Grips:** Grooved; integral with frame. **Sights:** Blade front, rear drift adjustable for windage; three-dot system. **Features:** Moulded polymer grip frame, stainless steel or chrome-moly slide. Suitable for +P+ ammunition. Safety model, decocker or DAO. Introduced 1996. Made in U.S.A. by Sturm, Ruger & Co. Comes with lockable plastic case, spare magazine, loader and lock.
Price: P95 DAO double-action-only **$425.00**
Price: P95D decocker only **$425.00**
Price: KP95D stainless steel decocker only **$475.00**
Price: KP95DAO double-action only, stainless steel. **$475.00**
Price: KP95 safety model, stainless steel. **$475.00**
Price: P95 safety model, blued finish **$425.00**

RUGER P97 AUTOLOADING PISTOL

Caliber: 45ACP 8-shot magazine. **Barrel:** 4-1/8". **Weight:** 30-1/2 oz. **Length:** 7-1/4" overall. Grooved: Integral with frame. **Sights:** Blade front, rear drift adjustable for windage; three dot system. **Features:** Moulded polymer grip frame, stainless steel slide. Decocker or DAO. Introduced 1997. Made in U.S.A. by Sturm, Ruger & Co. Comes with lockable plastic case, spare magaline, loading tool.
Price: KP97D decocker only **$495.00**
Price: KP97DAO double-action only **$495.00**
Price: P97D decocker only, blued **$460.00**

RUGER MARK II STANDARD AUTOLOADING PISTOL

Caliber: 22 LR, 10-shot magazine. **Barrel:** 4-3/4" or 6". **Weight:** 35 oz. (4-3/4" bbl.). **Length:** 8-5/16" (4-3/4" bbl.). **Grips:** Checkered composition grip panels. **Sights:** Fixed, wide blade front, fixed rear. **Features:** Updated design of original Standard Auto. New bolt hold-open latch. 10-shot magazine, magazine catch, safety, trigger and new receiver contours. Introduced 1982.
Price: Blued (MK 4, MK 6) **$289.00**
Price: In stainless steel (KMK 4, KMK 6) **$379.00**

HANDGUNS

Ruger 22/45-P4

Ruger KP512

SIG Sauer P220

Ruger 22/45 Mark II Pistol

Similar to other 22 Mark II autos except has grip frame of Zytel that matches angle and magazine latch of Model 1911 45 ACP pistol. Available in 4" bull, 4-3/4" standard and 5-1/2" bull barrels. Comes with extra magazine, plastic case, lock. Introduced 1992.

Price: P4, 4" bull barrel, adjustable sights **$275.00**
Price: KP 4 (4-3/4" barrel), stainless steel, fixed sights **$305.00**
Price: KP512 (5-1/2" bull barrel), stainless steel, adj. sights **$359.00**
Price: P512 (5-1/2" bull barrel, all blue), adj. sights **$275.00**

SAFARI ARMS ENFORCER PISTOL

Caliber: 45 ACP, 6-shot magazine. **Barrel:** 3.8", stainless. **Weight:** 36 oz. **Length:** 7.3" overall. **Grips:** Smooth walnut with etched black widow spider logo. **Sights:** Ramped blade front, LPA adjustable rear. **Features:** Extended safety, extended slide release; Commander-style hammer; beavertail grip safety; throated, polished, tuned. Parkerized matte black or satin stainless steel finishes. Made in U.S.A. by Safari Arms.
Price: **$630.00**

SAFARI ARMS GI SAFARI PISTOL

Caliber: 45 ACP, 7-shot magazine. **Barrel:** 5", 416 stainless. **Weight:** 39.9 oz. **Length:** 8.5" overall. **Grips:** Checkered walnut. **Sights:** G.I.-style blade front, drift-adjustable rear. **Features:** Beavertail grip safety; extended thumb safety and slide release; Commander-style hammer. Parkerized finish. Reintroduced 1996.
Price: **$439.00**

SAFARI ARMS CARRIER PISTOL

Caliber: 45 ACP, 7-shot magazine. **Barrel:** 6", 416 stainless steel. **Weight:** 30 oz. **Length:** 9.5" overall. **Grips:** Wood. **Sights:** Ramped blade front, LPA adjustable rear. **Features:** Beavertail grip safety; extended controls; full-length recoil spring guide; Commander-style hammer. Throated, polished and tuned. Satin stainless steel finish. Introduced 1999. Made in U.S.A. by Safari Arms, Inc.
Price: **$714.00**

SAFARI ARMS COHORT PISTOL

Caliber: 45 ACP, 7-shot magazine. **Barrel:** 3.8", 416 stainless. **Weight:** 37 oz. **Length:** 8.5" overall. **Grips:** Smooth walnut with laser-etched black widow logo. **Sights:** Ramped blade front, LPA adjustable rear. **Features:** Combines the Enforcer model, slide and MatchMaster frame. Beavertail grip safety; extended thumb safety and slide release; Commander-style hammer. Throated, polished and tuned. Satin stainless finish. Introduced 1996. Made in U.S.A. by Safari Arms, Inc.
Price: **$654.00**

SAFARI ARMS MATCHMASTER PISTOL

Caliber: 45 ACP, 7-shot. **Barrel:** 5" or 6", 416 stainless steel. **Weight:** 38 oz. (5" barrel). **Length:** 8.5" overall. **Grips:** Smooth walnut. **Sights:** Ramped blade, LPA adjustable rear. **Features:** Beavertail grip safety; extended controls; Commander-style hammer; throated, polished, tuned.

Parkerized matte-black or satin stainless steel. Made in U.S.A. by Olympic Arms, Inc.
Price: 5" barrel **$594.00**
Price: 6" barrel **$654.00**

Safari Arms Carry Comp Pistol

Similar to the Matchmaster except has Wil Schueman-designed hybrid compensator system. Made in U.S.A. by Olympic Arms, Inc.
Price: **$1,067.00**

SEECAMP LWS 32 STAINLESS DA AUTO

Caliber: 32 ACP Win. Silvertip, 6-shot magazine. **Barrel:** 2", integral with frame. **Weight:** 10.5 oz. **Length:** 4-1/8" overall. **Grips:** Glass-filled nylon. **Sights:** Smooth, no-snag, contoured slide and barrel top. **Features:** Aircraft quality 17-4 PH stainless steel. Inertia-operated firing pin. Hammer fired double-action-only. Hammer automatically follows slide down to safety rest position after each shot—no manual safety needed. Magazine safety disconnector. Polished stainless. Introduced 1985. From L.W. Seecamp.
Price: **$425.00**

SEMMERLING LM-4 SLIDE-ACTION PISTOL

Caliber: 45 ACP, 4-shot magazine. **Barrel:** 2". **Weight:** 24 oz. **Length:** NA. **Grips:** NA. **Sights:** NA. **Features:** While outwardly appearing to be a semi-automatic, the Semmerling LM-4 is a unique and super compact pistol employing a thumb activated slide mechanism (the slide is manually retracted between shots). Hand-built and super reliable, it is intended for professionals in law enforcement and for concealed carry by licensed and firearms knowledgeable private citizens. From American Derringer Corp.
Price: **$2,635.00**

SIG SAUER P220 SERVICE AUTO PISTOL

Caliber: 45 ACP, (7- or 8-shot magazine). **Barrel:** 4-3/8". **Weight:** 27.8 oz. **Length:** 7.8" overall. **Grips:** Checkered black plastic. **Sights:** Blade front, drift adjustable rear for windage. Optional Siglite nightsights. **Features:** Double action. Decocking lever permits lowering hammer onto locked firing pin. Squared combat-type trigger guard. Slide stays open after last shot. Imported from Germany by SIGARMS, Inc.
Price: Blue SA/DA or DAO **$790.00**
Price: Blue, Siglite night sights **$880.00**
Price: K-Kote or nickel slide **$830.00**
Price: K-Kote or nickel slide with Siglite night sights. **$930.00**

SIG Sauer P220 Sport Auto Pistol

Similar to the P220 except has 4.9" barrel, ported compensator, all-stainless steel frame and slide, factory-tuned trigger, adjustable sights, extended competition controls. Overall length is 9.9", weighs 43.5 oz. Introduced 1999. From SIGARMS, Inc.
Price: **$1,320.00**

SIG Sauer P245 Compact

SIG Sauer Pro 2009

SIG Sauer P229 Sport

SIG Sauer P232

Smith & Wesson 457 TDA

SIG Sauer P245 Compact Auto Pistol

Similar to the P220 except has 3.9" barrel, shorter grip, 6-shot magazine, 7.28" overall length, and weighs 27.5 oz. Introduced 1999. From SIG-ARMS, Inc.

Price: Blue	**$780.00**
Price: Blue, with Siglite sights	**$850.00**
Price: Two-tone	**$830.00**
Price: Two-tone with Siglite sights	**$930.00**
Price: With K-Kote finish	**$830.00**
Price: K-Kote with Siglite sights	**$930.00**

SIG Sauer P229 DA Auto Pistol

Similar to the P228 except chambered for 9mm Para., 40 S&W, 357 SIG. Has 3.86" barrel, 7.08" overall length and 3.35" height. Weight is 30.5 oz. Introduced 1991. Frame made in Germany, stainless steel slide assembly made in U.S.; pistol assembled in U.S. From SIGARMS, Inc.

Price:	**$795.00**
Price: With nickel slide	**$890.00**
Price: Nickel slide Siglite night sights	**$935.00**

SIG PRO AUTO PISTOL

Caliber: 9mm Para., 40 S&W, 10-shot magazine. **Barrel:** 3.86". **Weight:** 27.2 oz. **Length:** 7.36" overall. **Grips:** Composite and rubberized one-piece. **Sights:** Blade front, rear adjustable for windage. Optional Siglite night sights. **Features:** Polymer frame, stainless steel slide; integral frame accessory rail; replaceable steel frame rails; left- or right-handed magazine release. Introduced 1999. From SIGARMS, Inc.

Price: SP2340 (40 S&W)	**$596.00**
Price: SP2009 (9mm Para.)	**$596.00**
Price: As above with Siglite night sights	**$655.00**

SIG Sauer P226 Service Pistol

Similar to the P220 pistol except has 4.4" barrel, and weighs 28.3 oz. 357 SIG or 40 S&W. Imported from Germany by SIGARMS, Inc.

Price: Blue SA/DA or DAO	**$830.00**
Price: With Siglite night sights	**$930.00**
Price: Blue, SA/DA or DAO 357 SIG	**$830.00**
Price: With Siglite night sights	**$930.00**
Price: K-Kote finish, 40 S&W only or nickel slide	**$830.00**
Price: K-Kote or nickel slide Siglite night sights	**$930.00**
Price: Nickel slide 357 SIG	**$875.00**
Price: Nickel slide, Siglite night sights	**$930.00**

SIG Sauer P229 Sport Auto Pistol

Similar to the P229 except available in 357 SIG only; 4.8" heavy barrel; 8.6" overall length; weighs 40.6 oz.; vented compensator; adjustable target sights; rubber grips; extended slide latch and magazine release. Made of stainless steel. Introduced 1998. From SIGARMS, Inc.

Price:	**$1,320.00**

SIG SAUER P232 PERSONAL SIZE PISTOL

Caliber: 380 ACP, 7-shot. **Barrel:** 3-3/4". **Weight:** 16 oz. **Length:** 6-1/2" overall. **Grips:** Checkered black composite. **Sights:** Blade front, rear adjustable for windage. **Features:** Double action/single action or DAO. Blowback operation, stationary barrel. Introduced 1997. Imported from Germany by SIGARMS, Inc.

Price: Blue SA/DA or DAO	**$505.00**
Price: In stainless steel	**$545.00**
Price: With stainless steel slide, blue frame	**$525.00**
Price: Stainless steel, Siglite night sights, Hogue grips	**$585.00**

SIG SAUER P239 PISTOL

Caliber: 9mm Para., 8-shot, 357 SIG 40 S&W, 7-shot magazine. **Barrel:** 3.6". **Weight:** 25.2 oz. **Length:** 6.6" overall. **Grips:** Checkered black composite. **Sights:** Blade front, rear adjustable for windage. Optional Siglite night sights. **Features:** SA/DA or DAO; blackened stainless steel slide, aluminum alloy frame. Introduced 1996. Made in U.S.A. by SIGARMS, Inc.

Price: SA/DA or DAO	**$620.00**
Price: SA/DA or DAO with Siglite night sights	**$720.00**
Price: Two-tone finish	**$665.00**
Price: Two-tone finish, Siglite sights	**$765.00**

SMITH & WESSON MODEL 22A SPORT PISTOL

Caliber: 22 LR, 10-shot magazine. **Barrel:** 4", 5-1/2", 7". **Weight:** 29 oz. **Length:** 8" overall. **Grips:** Two-piece polymer. **Sights:** Patridge front, fully adjustable rear. **Features:** Comes with a sight bridge with Weaver-style integral optics mount; alloy frame; .312" serrated trigger; stainless steel slide and barrel with matte blue finish. Introduced 1997. Made in U.S.A. by Smith & Wesson.

Price: 4"	**$264.00**
Price: 5-1/2"	**$292.00**
Price: 7"	**$331.00**

SMITH & WESSON MODEL 457 TDA AUTO PISTOL

Caliber: 45 ACP, 7-shot magazine. **Barrel:** 3-3/4". **Weight:** 29 oz. **Length:** 7-1/4" overall. **Grips:** One-piece Xenoy, wrap-around with straight backstrap. **Sights:** Post front, fixed rear, three-dot system. **Features:** Aluminum alloy frame, matte blue carbon steel slide; bobbed hammer; smooth trigger. Introduced 1996. Made in U.S.A. by Smith & Wesson.

Price:	**$591.00**

Smith & Wesson 908

Smith & Wesson 4013 TSW

Smith & Wesson 410 DA

Smith & Wesson 910 DA

Smith & Wesson 3913 LadySmith

Smith & Wesson 4006

SMITH & WESSON MODEL 908 AUTO PISTOL

Caliber: 9mm Para., 8-shot magazine. **Barrel:** 3-1/2". **Weight:** 26 oz. **Length:** 6-13/16". **Grips:** One-piece Xenoy, wrap-around with straight backstrap. **Sights:** Post front, fixed rear, three-dot system. **Features:** Aluminum alloy frame, matte blue carbon steel slide; bobbed hammer; smooth trigger. Introduced 1996. Made in U.S.A. by Smith & Wesson.
Price: $535.00

SMITH & WESSON MODEL 4013, 4053 TSW AUTOS

Caliber: 40 S&W, 9-shot magazine. **Barrel:** 3-1/2". **Weight:** 26.4 oz. **Length:** 6-7/8" overall. **Grips:** Xenoy one-piece wrap-around. **Sights:** Novak three-dot system. **Features:** Traditional double-action system; stainless slide, alloy frame; fixed barrel bushing; ambidextrous decocker; reversible magazine catch, equipment rail. Introduced 1997. Made in U.S.A. by Smith & Wesson.
Price: Model 4013 TSW $886.00
Price: Model 4053 TSW, double-action-only $886.00

Smith & Wesson Model 22S Sport Pistols

Similar to the Model 22A Sport except with stainless steel frame. Available only with 5-1/2" or 7" barrel. Introduced 1997. Made in U.S.A. by Smith & Wesson.
Price: 5-1/2" standard barrel. $358.00
Price: 5-1/2" bull barrel, wood target stocks with thumbrest $434.00
Price: 7" standard barrel. $395.00
Price: 5-1/2" bull barrel, two-piece target stocks with thumbrest . $353.00

SMITH & WESSON MODEL 410 DA AUTO PISTOL

Caliber: 40 S&W, 10-shot magazine. **Barrel:** 4". **Weight:** 28.5 oz. **Length:** 7.5 oz. **Grips:** One-piece Xenoy, wrap-around with straight backstrap. **Sights:** Post front, fixed rear; three-dot system. **Features:** Aluminum alloy frame; blued carbon steel slide; traditional double action with left-side slide-mounted decocking lever. Introduced 1996. Made in U.S.A. by Smith & Wesson.
Price: Model 410 . . . . $591.00
Price: Model 410, HiViz front sight $612.00

SMITH & WESSON MODEL 910 DA AUTO PISTOL

Caliber: 9mm Para., 10-shot magazine. **Barrel:** 4". **Weight:** 28 oz. **Length:** 7-3/8" overall. **Grips:** One-piece Xenoy, wrap-around with straight backstrap. **Sights:** Post front with white dot, fixed two-dot rear. **Features:** Alloy frame, blue carbon steel slide. Slide-mounted decocking lever. Introduced 1995.
Price: Model 910. . . . . $535.00
Price: Model 410, HiViz front sight $535.00

SMITH & WESSON MODEL 3913 TRADITIONAL DOUBLE ACTION

Caliber: 9mm Para., 8-shot magazine. **Barrel:** 3-1/2". **Weight:** 26 oz. **Length:** 6-13/16" overall. **Grips:** One-piece Delrin wrap-around, textured surface. **Sights:** Post front with white dot, Novak LoMount Carry with two dots. **Features:** Aluminum alloy frame, stainless slide (M3913) or blue steel slide (M3914). Bobbed hammer with no half-cock notch; smooth .304" trigger with rounded edges. Straight backstrap. Equipment rail. Extra magazine included. Introduced 1989.
Price: $760.00

Smith & Wesson Model 3913-LS LadySmith Auto

Similar to the standard Model 3913 except has frame that is upswept at the front, rounded trigger guard. Comes in frosted stainless steel with matching gray grips. Grips are ergonomically correct for a woman's hand. Novak LoMount Carry rear sight adjustable for windage, smooth edges for snag resistance. Extra magazine included. Introduced 1990.
Price: $782.00

Smith & Wesson Model 3953 DAO Pistol

Same as the Model 3913 except double-action-only. Model 3953 has stainless slide with alloy frame. Overall length 7"; weighs 25.5 oz. Extra magazine included. Equipment rail. Introduced 1990.
Price: $760.00

Smith & Wesson Model 3913TSW/3953TSW Auto Pistols

Similar to the Model 3913 and 3953 except TSW guns have tighter tolerances, ambidextrous manual safety/decocking lever, flush-fit magazine, delayed-unlock firing system; magazine disconnector. Compact alloy frame, stainless steel slide. Straight backstrap. Introduced 1998. Made in U.S.A. by Smith & Wesson.
Price: Single action/double action $760.00
Price: Double action only $760.00

SMITH & WESSON MODEL 4006 TDA AUTO

Caliber: 40 S&W, 10-shot magazine. **Barrel:** 4". **Weight:** 38.5 oz. **Length:** 7-7/8" overall. **Grips:** Xenoy wrap-around with checkered panels. **Sights:** Replaceable post front with white dot, Novak LoMount Carry fixed rear with two white dots, or micro. click adjustable rear with two white dots. **Features:** Stainless steel construction with non-reflective finish. Straight backstrap, quipment rail. Extra magazine included. Introduced 1990.
Price: With adjustable sights. $944.00
Price: With fixed sight. $907.00
Price: With fixed night sights. $1,040.00
Price: With Saf-T-Trigger, fixed sights $927.00

**Smith & Wesson
4566 TSW**

**Smith & Wesson
Sigma SW40V**

Smith & Wesson 99

SMITH & WESSON MODEL 4006 TSW

Caliber: 40, 10-shot. **Barrel:** 4". **Grips:** Straight back strap grip. **Sights:** Fixed Novak LoMount Carry. **Features:** Traditional double action, ambidextrous safety, Saf-T-Trigger, equipment rail, satin stainless.
Price: **$927.00**

Smith & Wesson Model 4043, 4046 DA Pistols

Similar to the Model 4006 except is double-action-only. Has a semi-bobbed hammer, smooth trigger, 4" barrel; Novak LoMount Carry rear sight, post front with white dot. Overall length is 7-1/2", weighs 28 oz. Model 4043 has alloy frame, equipment rail. Extra magazine included. Introduced 1991.
Price: Model 4043 (alloy frame) **$886.00**
Price: Model 4046 (stainless frame)...................... **$907.00**
Price: Model 4046 with fixed night sights **$1,040.00**

SMITH & WESSON MODEL 4500 SERIES AUTOS

Caliber: 45 ACP, 8-shot magazine. **Barrel:** 5" (M4506). **Weight:** 41 oz. (4506). **Length:** 8-1/2" overall. **Grips:** Xenoy one-piece wrap-around, arched or straight backstrap. **Sights:** Post front with white dot, adjustable or fixed Novak LoMount Carry on M4506. **Features:** M4506 has serrated hammer spur, equipment rail. All have two magazines. Contact Smith & Wesson for complete data. Introduced 1989.
Price: Model 4566 (stainless, 4-1/4", traditional DA, ambidextrous
safety, fixed sight) **$942.00**
Price: Model 4586 (stainless, 4-1/4", DA only) **$942.00**
Price: Model 4566 (stainless, 4-1/4" with Saf-T-Trigger,
fixed sight) **$961.00**

SMITH & WESSON MODEL 4513TSW/4553TSW PISTOLS

Caliber: 45 ACP, 7-shot magazine. **Barrel:** 3-3/4". **Weight:** 28 oz. (M4513TSW). **Length:** 6-7/8 overall. **Grips:** Checkered Xenoy; straight backstrap. **Sights:** White dot front, Novak LoMount Carry 2-Dot rear. **Features:** Model 4513TSW is traditional double action, Model 4553TSW is double action only. TSW series has tighter tolerances, ambidextrous manual safety/decocking lever, flush-fit magazine, delayed-unlock firing system; magazine disconnector. Compact alloy frame, stainless steel slide, equipment rail. Introduced 1998. Made in U.S.A. by Smith & Wesson.
Price: Model 4513TSW....................................... **$924.00**
Price: Model 4553TSW....................................... **$924.00**

SMITH & WESSON MODEL 4566 TSW

Caliber: 45 ACP. **Barrel:** 4-1/4", 8-shot. **Grips:** Straight back strap grip. **Sights:** Fixed Novak LoMount Carry. **Features:** Ambidextrous safety, equipment rail, Saf-T-Trigger, satin stainless finish. Traditional double action.
Price: **$961.00**

SMITH & WESSON MODEL 5900 SERIES AUTO PISTOLS

Caliber: 9mm Para., 10-shot magazine. **Barrel:** 4". **Weight:** 28-1/2 to 37-1/2 oz. (fixed sight); 38 oz. (adjustable sight). **Length:** 7-1/2" overall. **Grips:** Xenoy wrap-around with curved backstrap. **Sights:** Post front with white dot, fixed or fully adjustable with two white dots. **Features:** All stainless, stainless and alloy or carbon steel and alloy construction. Smooth .304" trigger, .260" serrated hammer. Equipment rail. Introduced 1989.
Price: Model 5906 (stainless, traditional DA, adjustable sight,
ambidextrous safety)................................... **$904.00**
Price: As above, fixed sight............................. **$841.00**

Price: With fixed night sights........................... **$995.00**
Price: With Saf-T-Trigger.............................. **$882.00**
Price: Model 5946 DAO (as above, stainless frame and slide)... **$863.00**

SMITH & WESSON ENHANCED SIGMA SERIES DAO PISTOLS

Caliber: 9mm Para., 40 S&W, 10-shot magazine. **Barrel:** 4". **Weight:** 26 oz. **Length:** 7.4" overall. **Grips:** Integral. **Sights:** White dot front, fixed rear; three-dot system. Tritium night sights available. **Features:** Ergonomic polymer frame; low barrel centerline; internal striker firing system; corrosion-resistant slide; Teflon-filled, electroless-nickel coated magazine, equipment rail. Introduced 1994. Made in U.S.A. by Smith & Wesson.
Price: SW9E, 9mm, 4" barrel, black finish, fixed sights **$447.00**
Price: SW9V, 9mm, 4" barrel, satin stainless, fixed night sights.. **$447.00**
Price: SW9VE, 4" barrel, satin stainless, Saf-T-Trigger,
fixed sights **$466.00**
Price: SW40E, 40 S&W, 4" barrel, black finish, fixed sights..... **$657.00**
Price: SW40V, 40 S&W, 4" barrel, black polymer, fixed sights ... **$447.00**
Price: SW40VE, 4" barrel, satin stainless, Saf-T-Trigger,
fixed sights **$466.00**

SMITH & WESSON MODEL CS9 CHIEF'S SPECIAL AUTO

Caliber: 9mm Para., 7-shot magazine. **Barrel:** 3". **Weight:** 20.8 oz. **Length:** 6-1/4" overall. **Grips:** Hogue wrap-around rubber. **Sights:** White dot front, fixed two-dot rear. **Features:** Traditional double-action trigger mechanism. Alloy frame, stainless or blued slide. Ambidextrous safety. Introduced 1999. Made in U.S.A. by Smith & Wesson.
Price: Blue or stainless................................. **$680.00**

Smith & Wesson Model CS40 Chief's Special Auto

Similar to CS9, chambered for 40 S&W (7-shot magazine), 3-1/4" barrel, weighs 24.2 oz., measures 6-1/2" overall. Introduced 1999. Made in U.S.A. by Smith & Wesson.
Price: Blue or stainless................................. **$717.00**

Smith & Wesson Model CS45 Chief's Special Auto

Similar to CS40, chambered for 45 ACP, 6-shot magazine, weighs 23.9 oz. Introduced 1999. Made in U.S.A. by Smith & Wesson.
Price: Blue or stainless................................. **$717.00**

SMITH & WESSON MODEL 99

Caliber: 9mm Para. 4" barrel; 40 S&W 4-1/8" barrel; 10-shot, adj. sights. **Features:** Traditional double action satin stainless, black polymer frame, equipment rail, Saf-T-Trigger.
Price: 4" barrel **$648.00**
Price: 4-1/8" barrel **$648.00**

SPRINGFIELD, INC. FULL-SIZE 1911A1 AUTO PISTOL

Caliber: 9mm Para., 9-shot; 38 Super, 9-shot; 40 S&W, 9-shot; 45 ACP, 7-shot. **Barrel:** 5". **Weight:** 35.6 oz. **Length:** 8-5/8" overall. **Grips:** Cocobolo. **Sights:** Fixed three-dot system. **Features:** Beveled magazine well; lowered and flared ejection port. All forged parts, including frame, barrel, slide. All new production. Introduced 1990. From Springfield, Inc.
Price: Mil-Spec 45 ACP, Parkerized **$559.00**
Price: Standard, 45 ACP, blued, Novak sights **$824.00**
Price: Standard, 45 ACP, stainless, Novak sights............ **$828.00**
Price: Lightweight 45 ACP (28.6 oz., matte finish, night sights).. **$877.00**
Price: 40 S&W, stainless **$860.00**
Price: 9mm, stainless **$837.00**

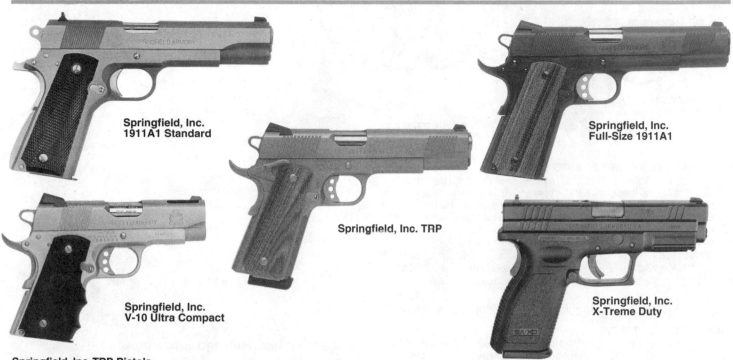

**Springfield, Inc.
1911A1 Standard**

**Springfield, Inc.
Full-Size 1911A1**

Springfield, Inc. TRP

**Springfield, Inc.
V-10 Ultra Compact**

**Springfield, Inc.
X-Treme Duty**

Springfield, Inc. TRP Pistols

Similar to 1911A1 except 45 ACP only, checkered front strap and mainspring housing, Novak Night Sight combat rear sight and matching dovetailed front sight, tuned, polished extractor, oversize barrel link; lightweight speed trigger and combat action job, match barrel and bushing, extended ambidextrous thumb safety and fitted beavertail grip safety. Carry bevel on entire pistol; checkered cocobolo wood grips, comes with two Wilson 7-shot magazines. Frame is engraved "Tactical," both sides of frame with "TRP." Introduced 1998. From Springfield, Inc.

Price: Standard with Armory Kote finish. **$1,395.00**
Price: Standard, stainless steel **$1,370.00**
Price: Standard with Operator Light Rail Armory Kote **$1,473.00**

Springfield, Inc. 1911A1 High Capacity Pistol

Similar to Standard 1911A1, available in 45 ACP with 10-shot magazine. Commander-style hammer, walnut grips, beveled magazine well, plastic carrying case. Can accept higher-capacity Para Ordnance magazines. Introduced 1993. From Springfield, Inc.

Price: Mil-Spec 45 ACP **$756.00**
Price: 45 ACP Ultra Compact (3-1/2" bbl.) **$909.00**

Springfield, Inc. 1911A1 V-Series Ported Pistols

Similar to standard 1911A1, scalloped slides with 10, 12 or 16 matching barrel ports to redirect powder gasses and reduce recoil and muzzle flip. Adjustable rear sight, ambi thumb safety, Videki speed trigger, and beveled magazine well. Checkered walnut grips standard. Available in 45 ACP, stainless or bi-tone. Introduced 1992.

Price: V-16 Long Slide, stainless **$1,121.00**
Price: Target V-12, stainless **$878.00**
Price: V-10 (Ultra-Compact, bi-tone) **$853.00**
Price: V-10 stainless **$863.00**

Springfield, Inc. 1911A1 Champion Pistol

Similar to standard 1911A1, slide is 4". Novak Night Sights. Delta hammer and cocobolo grips. Available in 45 ACP only; Parkerized or stainless. Introduced 1989.

Price: Stainless. **$849.00**

Springfield, Inc. Ultra Compact Pistol

Similar to 1911A1 Compact, shorter slide, 3.5" barrel, beavertail grip safety, beveled magazine well, Novak Low Mount or Novak Night Sights, Videki speed trigger, flared ejection port, stainless steel frame, blued slide, match grade barrel, rubber grips. Introduced 1996. From Springfield, Inc.

Price: Parkerized 45 ACP, Night Sights **$589.00**
Price: Stainless 45 ACP, Night Sights. **$849.00**
Price: Lightweight, 9mm, stainless **$837.00**

Springfield, Inc. Compact Lightweight

Mates a Springfield Inc. Champion length slide with the shorter Ultra-Compact forged alloy frame for concealability. In 45 ACP.

Price: **$733.00**

Springfield, Inc. Long Slide 1911 A1 Pistol

Similar to Full Size model, 6" barrel and slide for increased sight radius and higher velocity, fully adjustable sights, muzzle-forward weight distribution for reduced recoil and quicker shot-to-shot recovery. From Springfield Inc.

Price: Target, 45 ACP, stainless with Night Sights **$1,049.00**
Price: Trophy Match, stainless with adj. sights **$1,452.00**
Price: V-16 stainless steel **$1,121.00**

SPRINGFIELD, INC. MICRO-COMPACT 1911A1 PISTOL

Caliber: 45 ACP, 40 S&W 6+1 capacity. **Barrel:** 3" 1:16 LH. **Weight:** 24 oz. **Length:** 5.7". **Sights:** Novak LoMount tritium. Dovetail front. **Features:** Forged frame and slide, ambi thumb safety, extreme carry bevel treatment, lockable plastic case, 2 magazines.

Price: . . . . **$993.00 to $1,021.00**

SPRINGFIELD, INC. X-TREME DUTY

Caliber: 9mm, 40 S&W, 357 Sig. **Barrel:** 4.08". **Weight:** 22.88 oz. **Length:** 7.2". **Sights:** Dovetail front and rear. **Features:** Lightweight, ultra high-impact polymer frame. Trigger, firing pin and grip safety. Two 10-rod steel easy glide magazines. Imported from Croatia.

Price: . . . . **$489.00 to $1,099.00**

STEYR M & S SERIES AUTO PISTOLS

Caliber: 9mm Para., 40 S&W, 357 SIG; 10-shot magazine. **Barrel:** 4" (3.58" for Model S). **Weight:** 28 oz. (22.5 oz. for Model S). **Length:** 7.05" overall (6.53" for Model S). **Grips:** Ultra-rigid polymer. **Sights:** Drift-adjustable, white-outline rear; white-triangle blade front. **Features:** Polymer frame; trigger-drop firing pin, manual and key-lock safeties; loaded chamber indicator; 5.5-lb. trigger pull; 111-degree grip angle enhances natural pointing. Introduced 2000. Imported from Austria by GSI Inc.

Price: Model M (full-sized frame with 4" barrel) **$609.95**
Price: Model S (compact frame with 3.58" barrel) **$609.95**
Price: Extra 10-shot magazines (Model M or S) **$39.00**

HANDGUNS

Taurus PT 22

Taurus PT-911

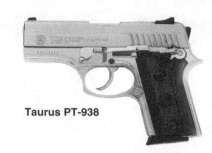

Taurus PT-938

Taurus PT-940

TAURUS MODEL PT 22/PT 25 AUTO PISTOLS

Caliber: 22 LR, 8-shot (PT 22); 25 ACP, 9-shot (PT 25). **Barrel:** 2.75". **Weight:** 12.3 oz. **Length:** 5.25" overall. **Grips:** Smooth rosewood or mother-of-pearl. **Sights:** Fixed. **Features:** Double action. Tip-up barrel for loading, cleaning. Blue, nickel, duotone or blue with gold accents. Introduced 1992. Made in U.S.A. by Taurus International.
Price: 22 LR, 25 ACP, blue, nickel or with duo-tone finish
with rosewood grips **$219.00**
Price: 22 LR, 25 ACP, blue with gold trim, rosewood grips **$234.00**
Price: 22 LR, 25 ACP, blue, nickel or duotone finish with checkered
wood grips. **$219.00**
Price: 22 LR, 25 ACP, blue with gold trim, mother of pearl grips . **$250.00**

TAURUS MODEL PT24/7

NEW!

Caliber: 9mm, 10+1 shot; 40 S&W, 10+1 shot. **Barrel:** 4". **Weight:** 27.2 oz. **Length:** 7-18". **Grips:** RIBBER rubber-finned overlay on polymer. **Sights:** Adjustable. **Features:** Accessory rail, four safeties, blue or stainless finish, consistent trigger pull weight and travel. Introduced 2003. Imported from Brazil by Taurus Int'l. Manufacturing.
Price: 9mm **$578.00**
Price: 40 Cal. **$594.00**

TAURUS MODEL PT92 AUTO PISTOL

Caliber: 9mm Para., 10-shot mag. **Barrel:** 5". **Weight:** 34 oz. **Length:** 8.5" overall. **Grips:** Checkered rubber, rosewood, mother-of-pearl. **Sights:** Fixed notch rear. Three-dot sight system. Also offered with micrometer-click adjustable night sights. **Features:** Double action, ambidextrous 3-way hammer drop safety, allows cocked & locked carry. Blue, stainless steel, blue with gold highlights, stainless steel with gold highlights, forged aluminum frame, integral key-lock. 22 LR conversion kit available. Imported from Brazil by Taurus International Manufacturing.
Price: Blue . . . . **$578.00 to $672.00**

Taurus Model PT99 Auto Pistol

Similar to PT92, fully adjustable rear sight.
Price: Blue . . . . **$575.00 to $670.00**
Price: 22 Conversion kit for PT 92 and PT99 (includes barrel and slide)
. . . . **$266.00**

TAURUS MODEL PT-100/101 AUTO PISTOL

Caliber: 40 S&W, 10-shot mag. **Barrel:** 5". **Weight:** 34 oz. **Length:** 8-1/2". **Grips:** Checkered rubber, rosewood, mother-of-pearl. **Sights:** 3-dot fixed or adjustable; night sights available. **Features:** Single/double action with three-position safety/decocker. Re-introduced in 2001. Imported by Taurus International.
Price: PT100. . . . . **$578.00 to $672.00**
Price: PT101. . . . . **$594.00 to $617.00**

TAURUS MODEL PT-111 MILLENNIUM PRO AUTO PISTOL

Caliber: 9mm Para., 10-shot mag. **Barrel:** 3.25". **Weight:** 18.7 oz. **Length:** 6-1/8" overall. **Grips:** Polymer. **Sights:** 3-dot fixed; night sights available. Low profile, three-dot combat. **Features:** Double action only, polymer frame, matte stainless or blue steel slide, manual safety, integral key-lock. Deluxe models with wood grip inserts. Now issued in a third generation series with many cosmetic and internal improvements.
Price: . . . . **$445.00 to $539.00**

Taurus Model PT-111 Millennium Titanium Pistol

Similar to PT-111, titanium slide, night sights.
Price: **$586.00**

TAURUS PT-132 MILLENIUM PRO AUTO PISTOL

Caliber: 32 ACP, 10-shot mag. **Barrel:** 3.25". **Weight:** 18.7 oz. **Grips:** Polymer. **Sights:** 3-dot fixed; night sights available. **Features:** Double action only, polymer frame, matte stainless or blue steel slide, manual safety, integral key-lock action. Introduced 2001.
Price: . . . . **$445.00 to $461.00**

TAURUS PT-138 MILLENIUM PRO SERIES

Caliber: 380 ACP, 10-shot mag. **Barrel:** 3.25". **Weight:** 18.7 oz. **Grips:** Polymer. **Sights:** Fixed 3-dot fixed. **Features:** Double action only, polymer frame, matte stainless or blue steel slide, manual safety, integral key-lock.
Price: . . . . **$445.00 to $461.00**

TAURUS PT-140 MILLENIUM PRO AUTO PISTOL

Caliber: 40 S&W, 10-shot mag. **Barrel:** 3.25". **Weight:** 18.7 oz. **Grips:** Checkered polymer. **Sights:** 3-dot fixed; night sights available. **Features:** Double-action only; matte stainless or blue steel slide, black polymer frame, manual safety, integral key-lock action. From Taurus International.
Price: . . . . **$484.00 to $578.00**

TAURUS PT-145 MILLENIUM AUTO PISTOL

Caliber: 45 ACP, 10-shot mag. **Barrel:** 3.27". **Weight:** 23 oz. **Stock:** Checkered polymer. **Sights:** 3-dot fixed; night sights available. **Features:** Double-action only, matte stainless or blue steel slide, black polymer frame, manual safety, integral key-lock. From Taurus International.
Price: . . . . **$484.00 to $578.00**

TAURUS MODEL PT-911 AUTO PISTOL

Caliber: 9mm Para., 10-shot mag. **Barrel:** 4". **Weight:** 28.2 oz. **Length:** 7" overall. **Grips:** Checkered rubber, rosewood, mother-of-pearl. **Sights:** Fixed, three-dot blue or stainless; night sights optional. **Features:** Double action, semi-auto ambidextrous 3-way hammer drop safety, allows cocked and locked carry. Blue, stainless steel, blue with gold highlights, or stainless steel with gold highlights, forged aluminum frame, integral key-lock.
Price: . . . . **$523.00 to $617.00**

TAURUS MODEL PT-938 AUTO PISTOL

Caliber: 380 ACP, 10-shot mag. **Barrel:** 3.72". **Weight:** 27 oz. **Length:** 6.5" overall. **Grips:** Checkered rubber. **Sights:** Fixed, three-dot. **Features:** Double action, ambidextrous 3-way hammer drop allows cocked & locked carry. Forged aluminum frame. Integral key-lock. Imported by Taurus International.
Price: Blue **$516.00**
Price: Stainless. **$531.00**

Taurus PT-945

Taurus PT-957

Walther PPK/S

Walther PPK

Walther P99

Walther P22

Wilkinson Sherry

TAURUS MODEL PT-940 AUTO PISTOL

Caliber: 40 S&W, 10-shot mag. **Barrel:** 3-5/8". **Weight:** 28.2 oz. **Length:** 7" overall. **Grips:** Checkered rubber, rosewood or mother-of-pearl. **Sights:** Fixed, three-dot blue or stainless; night sights optional. **Features:** Double action, semi-auto ambidextrous 3-way hammer drop safety, allows cocked & locked carry. Blue, stainless steel, blue with gold highlights, or stainless steel with gold hightlights, forged aluminum frame, integral key-lock.
Price: .... **$523.00 to $617.00**

TAURUS MODEL PT-945 SERIES

Caliber: 45 ACP, 8-shot mag. **Barrel:** 4.25". **Weight:** 28.2/29.5 oz. **Length:** 7.48" overall. **Grips:** Checkered rubber, rosewood or mother-of-pearl. **Sights:** Fixed, three-dot; night sights optional. **Features:** Double-action with ambidextrous 3-way hammer drop safety allows cocked & locked carry. Forged aluminum frame, PT-945C has poarted barrel/slide. Blue, stainless, blue with gold highlights, stainless with gold highlights, integral key-lock. Introduced 1995. Imported by Taurus International.
Price: .... **$563.00 to $641.00**

TAURUS MODEL PT-957 AUTO PISTOL

Caliber: 357 SIG, 10-shot mag. **Barrel:** 4". **Weight:** 28 oz. **Length:** 7" overall. **Grips:** Checkered rubber, rosewood or mother-of-pearl. **Sights:** Fixed, three-dot blue or stainless; night sights optional. **Features:** Double-action, blue, stainless steel, blue with gold accents or stainless with gold accents, ported barrel/slide, three-position safety with decocking lever and ambidextrous safety. Forged aluminum frame, integral key-lock. Introduced 1999. Imported by Taurus International.
Price: .... **$525.00 to $620.00**
Price: Non-ported .... **$525.00 to $535.00**

TAURUS MODEL 922 SPORT PISTOL

Caliber: 22 LR, 10-shot magazine. **Barrel:** 6". **Weight:** 24.8 oz. **Length:** 9-1/8". **Grips:** Polymer. **Sights:** Adjustable. **Features:** Matte blue steel finish, machined target crown, polymer frame, single and double action, easy disassembly for cleaning.
Price: .... (blue) **$310.00**
Price: .... (stainless) **$328.00**

WALTHER PPK/S AMERICAN AUTO PISTOL

Caliber: 380 ACP, 7-shot magazine. **Barrel:** 3.27". **Weight:** 23-1/2 oz. **Length:** 6.1" overall. **Stocks:** Checkered plastic. **Sights:** Fixed, white markings. **Features:** Double action; manual safety blocks firing pin and drops hammer; chamber loaded indicator on 32 and 380; extra finger rest magazine provided. Made entirely in the United States. Introduced 1980.
Price: 380 ACP only, blue **$540.00**
Price: As above, 32 ACP or 380 ACP, stainless **$540.00**

Walther PPK American Auto Pistol

Similar to Walther PPK/S except weighs 21 oz., has 6-shot capacity. Made in the U.S. Introduced 1986.
Price: Stainless, 32 ACP or 380 ACP **$540.00**
Price: Blue, 380 ACP only **$540.00**

WALTHER P99 AUTO PISTOL

Caliber: 9mm Para., 9x21, 40 S&W, 10-shot magazine. **Barrel:** 4". **Weight:** 25 oz. **Length:** 7" overall. **Grips:** Textured polymer. **Sights:** Blade front (comes with three interchangeable blades for elevation adjustment), micrometer rear adjustable for windage. **Features:** Double-action mechanism with trigger safety, decock safety, internal striker safety; chamber loaded indicator; ambidextrous magazine release levers; polymer frame with interchangeable backstrap inserts. Comes with two magazines. Introduced 1997. Imported from Germany by Carl Walther USA.
Price: **$799.00**

Walther P990 Auto Pistol

Similar to the P99 except is double action only. Available in blue or silver tenifer finish. Introduced 1999. Imported from Germany by Carl Walther USA.
Price: **$749.00**

WALTHER P22 PISTOL

Caliber: 22 LR. **Barrel:** 3.4", 5". **Weight:** 19.6 oz. (3.4"), 20.3 oz. (5"). **Length:** 6.26", 7.83". **Grips:** NA. **Sights:** Interchangeable white dot, front, 2-dot adjustable, rear. **Features:** A rimfire version of the Walther P99 pistol, available in nickel slide with black frame, or green frame with black slide versions. Made in Germany and distributed in the U.S. by Smith & Wesson.
Price: .... **NA**

WILKINSON SHERRY AUTO PISTOL

Caliber: 22 LR, 8-shot magazine. **Barrel:** 2-1/8". **Weight:** 9-1/4 oz. **Length:** 4-3/8" overall. **Grips:** Checkered black plastic. **Sights:** Fixed, groove. **Features:** Cross-bolt safety locks the sear into the hammer. Available in all blue finish or blue slide and trigger with gold frame. Introduced 1985.
Price: **$280.00**

WILKINSON LINDA AUTO PISTOL

Caliber: 9mm Para. **Barrel:** 8-5/16". **Weight:** 4 lbs., 13 oz. **Length:** 12-1/4" overall. **Grips:** Checkered black plastic pistol grip, walnut forend. **Sights:** Protected blade front, aperture rear. **Features:** Fires from closed bolt. Semi-auto only. Straight blowback action. Cross-bolt safety. Removable barrel. From Wilkinson Arms.
Price: **$675.00**

Includes models suitable for several forms of competition and other sporting purposes.

Baer 1911 Ultimate Master

Baer 1911 Bullseye Wadcutter

BF Ultimate

Browning Buck Mark Target 5.5

BAER 1911 ULTIMATE MASTER COMBAT PISTOL

Caliber: 9x23, 38 Super, 400 Cor-Bon 45 ACP (others available), 10-shot magazine. **Barrel:** 5", 6"; Baer NM. **Weight:** 37 oz. **Length:** 8.5" overall. **Grips:** Checkered rosewood. **Sights:** Baer dovetail front, low-mount Bo-Mar rear with hidden leaf. **Features:** Full-house competition gun. Baer forged NM blued steel frame and double serrated slide; Baer triple port, tapered cone compensator; fitted slide to frame; lowered, flared ejection port; Baer reverse recoil plug; full-length guide rod; recoil buff; beveled magazine well; Baer Commander hammer, sear; Baer extended ambidextrous safety, extended ejector, checkered slide stop, beavertail grip safety with pad, extended magazine release button; Baer speed trigger. Made in U.S.A. by Les Baer Custom, Inc.

Price: Compensated, open sights. **$2,476.00**
Price: 6" Model 400 Cor-Bon **$2,541.00**

BAER 1911 NATIONAL MATCH HARDBALL PISTOL

Caliber: 45 ACP, 7-shot magazine. **Barrel:** 5". **Weight:** 37 oz. **Length:** 8.5" overall. **Grips:** Checkered walnut. **Sights:** Baer dovetail front with undercut post, low-mount Bo-Mar rear with hidden leaf. **Features:** Baer NM forged steel frame, double serrated slide and barrel with stainless bushing; slide fitted to frame; Baer match trigger with 4-lb. pull; polished feed ramp, throated barrel; checkered front strap, arched mainspring housing; Baer beveled magazine well; lowered, flared ejection port; tuned extractor; Baer extended ejector, checkered slide stop; recoil buff. Made in U.S.A. by Les Baer Custom, Inc.

Price: **$1,335.00**

Baer 1911 Bullseye Wadcutter Pistol

Similar to National Match Hardball except designed for wadcutter loads only. Polished feed ramp and barrel throat; Bo-Mar rib on slide; full-length recoil rod; Baer speed trigger with 3-1/2-lb. pull; Baer deluxe hammer and sear; Baer beavertail grip safety with pad; flat mainspring housing checkered 20 lpi. Blue finish; checkered walnut grips. Made in U.S.A. by Les Baer Custom, Inc.

Price: From **$1,495.00**
Price: With 6" barrel, from **$1,690.00**

BF ULTIMATE SILHOUETTE HB SINGLE SHOT PISTOL

Caliber: 7mm U.S., 22 LR Match and 100 other chamberings. **Barrel:** 10.75" Heavy Match Grade with 11-degree target crown. **Weight:** 3 lbs.,

15 oz. **Length:** 16" overall. **Grips:** Thumbrest target style. **Sights:** Bo-Mar/Bond ScopeRib I Combo with hooded post front adjustable for height and width, rear notch available in .032", .062", .080" and .100" widths; 1/2-MOA clicks. **Features:** Designed to meet maximum rules for IHMSA Production Gun. Falling block action gives rigid barrel-receiver mating. Hand fitted and headspaced. Etched receiver; gold-colored trigger. Introduced 1988. Made in U.S.A. by E. Arthur Brown Co. Inc.

Price: **$669.00**

BF Classic Hunting Pistol

Similar to BF Ultimate Silhouette HB Single Shot Pistol, except no sights; drilled and tapped for scope mount. Barrels from 8" to 15". Variety of options offered. Made in U.S.A. by E. Arthur Brown Co. Inc.

Price: **$599.00**

BROWNING BUCK MARK SILHOUETTE

Caliber: 22 LR, 10-shot magazine. **Barrel:** 9-7/8". **Weight:** 53 oz. **Length:** 14" overall. **Grips:** Smooth walnut stocks and forend, or finger-groove walnut. **Sights:** Post-type hooded front adjustable for blade width and height; Pro Target rear fully adjustable for windage and elevation. **Features:** Heavy barrel with .900" diameter; 12-1/2" sight radius. Special sighting plane forms scope base. Introduced 1987. Made in U.S.A. From Browning.

Price: **$448.00**

Browning Buck Mark Target 5.5

Same as Buck Mark Silhouette, 5-1/2" barrel with .900" diameter. Hooded sights mounted on scope base that accepts optical or reflex sight. Rear sight is Browning fully adjustable Pro Target, front sight is adjustable post that customizes to different widths, can be adjusted for height. Contoured walnut grips with thumbrest, or finger-groove walnut. Matte blue finish. Overall length is 9-5/8", weighs 35-1/2 oz. Has 10-shot magazine. Introduced 1990. From Browning.

Price: **$425.00**
Price: Target 5.5 Gold (as above with gold anodized frame and top rib) **$477.00**
Price: Target 5.5 Nickel (as above with nickel frame and top rib) **$477.00**

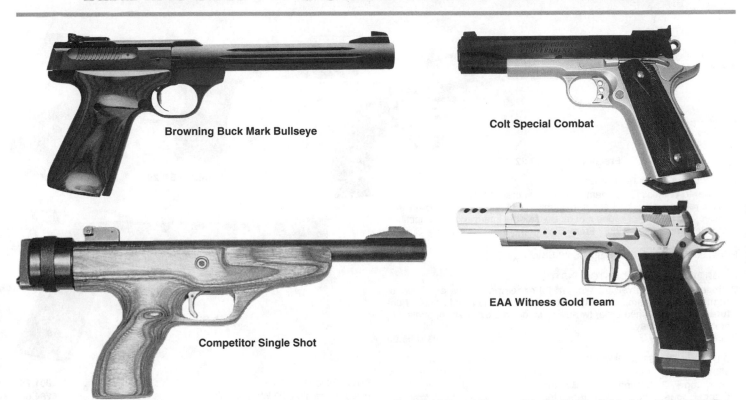

Browning Buck Mark Bullseye

Colt Special Combat

Competitor Single Shot

EAA Witness Gold Team

Browning Buck Mark Field 5.5

Same as Target 5.5, hoodless ramp-style front sight and low profile rear sight. Matte blue finish, contoured or finger-groove walnut stocks. Introduced 1991.

Price: **$425.00**

Browning Buck Mark Bullseye

Similar to Buck Mark Silhouette, 7-1/4" heavy barrel with three flutes per side; trigger adjusts from 2-1/2 to 5 lbs.; specially designed rosewood target or three-finger-groove stocks with competition-style heel rest, or with contoured rubber grip. Overall length 11-5/16", weighs 36 oz. Introduced 1996. Made in U.S.A. From Browning.

Price: With ambidextrous moulded composite stocks. **$389.00**
Price: With rosewood stocks, or wrap-around finger groove. **$500.00**

COLT GOLD CUP MODEL O PISTOL

Caliber: 45 ACP, 8-shot magazine. **Barrel:** 5", with new design bushing. **Weight:** 39 oz. **Length:** 8-1/2". **Grips:** Checkered rubber composite with silver-plated medallion. **Sights:** Patridge-style front, Bomar-style rear adjustable for windage and elevation, sight radius 6-3/4". **Features:** Arched or flat housing; wide, grooved trigger with adjustable stop; ribbed-top slide, hand fitted, with improved ejection port.

Price: Blue **$1,050.00**
Price: Stainless. **$1,116.00**

COLT SPECIAL COMBAT GOVERNMENT

Caliber: 45 ACP. **Barrel:** 5" **Weight:** NA. **Length:** 8-1/2" **Grips:** Rosewood w/double diamond checkering pattern. **Sights:** Clark dovetail, front; Bomar adjustable, rear. **Features:** A competition ready pistol with enhancements such as skeletonized trigger, upswept grip safety, custom tuned action, polished feed ramp. Blue or satin nickel finish. Introduced 2003. Made in U.S.A. by Colt's Mfg. Co.

Price: **$1,640.00**

COMPETITOR SINGLE SHOT PISTOL

Caliber: 22 LR through 50 Action Express, including belted magnums. **Barrel:** 14" standard; 10.5" silhouette; 16" optional. **Weight:** About 59 oz. (14" bbl.). **Length:** 15.12" overall. **Grips:** Ambidextrous; synthetic (standard) or laminated or natural wood. **Sights:** Ramp front, adjustable rear. **Features:** Rotary canon-type action cocks on opening; cammed ejector; interchangeable barrels, ejectors. Adjustable single stage trigger, sliding thumb safety and trigger safety. Matte blue finish. Introduced 1988. From Competitor Corp., Inc.

Price: 14", standard calibers, synthetic grip **$414.95**
Price: Extra barrels, from **$159.95**

CZ 75 CHAMPION COMPETITION PISTOL

Caliber: 9mm Para., 9x21, 40 S&W, 10-shot mag. **Barrel:** 4.49". **Weight:** 35 oz. **Length:** 9.44" overall. **Grips:** Black rubber. **Sights:** Blade front, fully adjustable rear. **Features:** Single-action trigger mechanism; three-port compensator (40 S&W, 9mm have two port) full-length guide rod; extended magazine release; ambidextrous safety; flared magazine well; fully adjustable match trigger. Introduced 1999. Imported from the Czech Republic by CZ USA.

Price: 9mm Para., 9x21, 40 S&W, dual-tone finish. **$1,551.00**

CZ 75 ST IPSC AUTO PISTOL

Caliber: 40 S&W, 10-shot magazine. **Barrel:** 5.12". **Weight:** 2.9 lbs. **Length:** 8.86" overall. **Grips:** Checkered walnut. **Sights:** Fully adjustable rear. **Features:** Single-action mechanism; extended slide release and ambidextrous safety; full-length slide rail; double slide serrations. Introduced 1999. Imported from the Czech Republic by CZ-USA.

Price: Dual-tone finish **$1,038.00**

EAA/BAIKAL IZH35 AUTO PISTOL

Caliber: 22 LR, 5-shot mag. **Barrel:** 6". **Grips:** Walnut; fully adjustable right-hand target-style. **Sights:** Fully adjustable rear, blade front; detachable scope mount. **Features:** Hammer-forged target barrel; machined steel receiver; adjustable trigger; manual slide hold back, grip and manual trigger-bar disconnect safeties; cocking indicator. Introduced 2000. Imported from Russia by European American Armory.

Price: Blued finish. **$539.00**

EAA WITNESS GOLD TEAM AUTO

Caliber: 9mm Para., 9x21, 38 Super, 40 S&W, 45 ACP. **Barrel:** 5.1". **Weight:** 41.6 oz. **Length:** 9.6" overall. **Grips:** Checkered walnut, competition style. **Sights:** Square post front, fully adjustable rear. **Features:** Triple-chamber cone compensator; competition SA trigger; extended safety and magazine release; competition hammer; beveled magazine well; beavertail grip. Hand-fitted major components. Hard chrome finish. Match-grade barrel. From E.A.A. Custom Shop. Introduced 1992. From European American Armory.

Price: **$2,150.00**

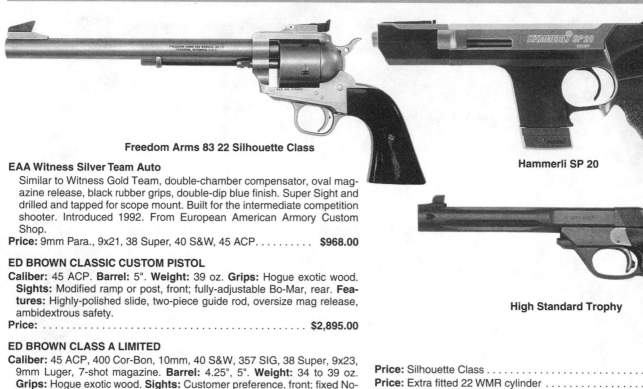

Freedom Arms 83 22 Silhouette Class

Hammerli SP 20

High Standard Trophy

EAA Witness Silver Team Auto

Similar to Witness Gold Team, double-chamber compensator, oval magazine release, black rubber grips, double-dip blue finish. Super Sight and drilled and tapped for scope mount. Built for the intermediate competition shooter. Introduced 1992. From European American Armory Custom Shop.
Price: 9mm Para., 9x21, 38 Super, 40 S&W, 45 ACP **$968.00**

ED BROWN CLASSIC CUSTOM PISTOL

Caliber: 45 ACP. **Barrel:** 5". **Weight:** 39 oz. **Grips:** Hogue exotic wood. **Sights:** Modified ramp or post, front; fully-adjustable Bo-Mar, rear. **Features:** Highly-polished slide, two-piece guide rod, oversize mag release, ambidextrous safety.
Price: **$2,895.00**

ED BROWN CLASS A LIMITED

Caliber: 45 ACP, 400 Cor-Bon, 10mm, 40 S&W, 357 SIG, 38 Super, 9x23, 9mm Luger, 7-shot magazine. **Barrel:** 4.25", 5". **Weight:** 34 to 39 oz. **Grips:** Hogue exotic wood. **Sights:** Customer preference, front; fixed Novak low-mount or fully-adjustable Bo-Mar, rear. **Features:** Checkered forestrap and mainspring housing, matte finished top sighting surface. Many options available.
Price: **$2,250.00**

ENTRÉPRISE TOURNAMENT SHOOTER MODEL I

Caliber: 45 ACP, 10-shot mag. **Barrel:** 6". **Weight:** 40 oz. **Length:** 8.5" overall. **Grips:** Black ultra-slim double diamond checkered synthetic. **Sights:** Dovetailed Patridge front, adjustable Competizione "melded" rear. **Features:** Oversized magazine release button; flared magazine well; fully machined parallel slide rails; front and rear slide serrations; serrated top of slide; stainless ramped bull barrel with fully supported chamber; full-length guide rod with plug; stainless firing pin; match extractor; polished ramp; tuned match extractor; black oxide. Introduced 1998. Made in U.S.A. by Entréprise Arms.
Price: **$2,300.00**
Price: TSMIII (Satin chrome finish, two-piece guide rod) **$2,700.00**

EXCEL INDUSTRIES CP-45, XP-45 AUTO PISTOL

Caliber: 45 ACP, 6-shot & 10-shot mags. **Barrel:** 3-1/4". **Weight:** 31 oz. & 25 oz. **Length:** 6-3/8" overall. **Grips:** Checkered black nylon. **Sights:** Fully adjustable rear. **Features:** Stainless steel frame and slide; single action with external hammer and firing pin block, manual thumb safety; last-shot hold open. Includes gun lock and cleaning kit. Introduced 2001. Made in U.S.A. by Excel Industries Inc.
Price: CP-45 . . . . **$425.00**
Price: XP-45 . . . . **$465.00**

FEINWERKEBAU AW93 TARGET PISTOL

Caliber: 22. **Barrel:** 6". **Grips:** Fully adjustable orthopaedic. **Sights:** Fully adjustable micrometer. **Features:** Advanced Russian design with German craftmanship. Imported from Germany by Nygord Precision Products.
Price: **$1,495.00**

FREEDOM ARMS MODEL 83 22 FIELD GRADE SILHOUETTE CLASS

Caliber: 22 LR, 5-shot cylinder. **Barrel:** 10". **Weight:** 63 oz. **Length:** 15.5" overall. **Grips:** Black Micarta. **Sights:** Removable patridge front blade; Iron Sight Gun Works silhouette rear, click adjustable for windage and elevation (optional adj. front sight and hood). **Features:** Stainless steel, matte finish, manual sliding-bar safety system; dual firing pins, lightened hammer for fast lock time, pre-set trigger stop. Introduced 1991. Made in U.S.A. by Freedom Arms.

Price: Silhouette Class **$1,901.75**
Price: Extra fitted 22 WMR cylinder **$264.00**

FREEDOM ARMS MODEL 83 CENTERFIRE SILHOUETTE MODELS

Caliber: 357 Mag., 41 Mag., 44 Mag.; 5-shot cylinder. **Barrel:** 10", 9" (357 Mag. only). **Weight:** 63 oz. (41 Mag.). **Length:** 15.5", 14-1/2" (357 only). **Grips:** Pachmayr Presentation. **Sights:** Iron Sight Gun Works silhouette rear sight, replaceable adjustable front sight blade with hood. **Features:** Stainless steel, matte finish, manual sliding-bar safety system. Made in U.S.A. by Freedom Arms.
Price: Silhouette Models. **$1,634.85**

GAUCHER GP SILHOUETTE PISTOL

Caliber: 22 LR, single shot. **Barrel:** 10". **Weight:** 42.3 oz. **Length:** 15.5" overall. **Grips:** Stained hardwood. **Sights:** Hooded post on ramp front, open rear adjustable for windage and elevation. **Features:** Matte chrome barrel, blued bolt and sights. Other barrel lengths available on special order. Introduced 1991. Imported by Mandall Shooting Supplies.
Price: **$425.00**

HAMMERLI SP 20 TARGET PISTOL

Caliber: 22 LR, 32 S&W. **Barrel:** 4.6". **Weight:** 34.6-41.8 oz. **Length:** 11.8" overall. **Grips:** Anatomically shaped synthetic Hi-Grip available in five sizes. **Sights:** Integral front in three widths, adjustable rear with changeable notch widths. **Features:** Extremely low-level sight line; anatomically shaped trigger; adjustable JPS buffer system for different recoil characteristics. Receiver available in red, blue, gold, violet or black. Introduced 1998. Imported from Switzerland by SIGARMS, Inc and Hammerli Pistols USA.
Price: Hammerli 22 LR **$1,668.00**
Price: Hammerli 32 S&W **$1,743.00**

HAMMERLI X-ESSE SPORT PISTOL

An all-steel 22 LR target pistol with a Hi-Grip in a new anatomical shape and an adjustable hand rest. Made in Switzerland. Introduced 2003.
Price: **$710.00**

HARRIS GUNWORKS SIGNATURE JR. LONG RANGE PISTOL

Caliber: Any suitable caliber. **Barrel:** To customer specs. **Weight:** 5 lbs. **Stock:** Gunworks fiberglass. **Sights:** None furnished; comes with scope rings. **Features:** Right- or left-hand benchrest action of titanium or stainless steel; single shot or repeater. Comes with bipod. Introduced 1992. Made in U.S.A. by Harris Gunworks, Inc.
Price: **$2,700.00**

High Standard Victor

Ruger Mark II Target

HIGH STANDARD TROPHY TARGET PISTOL

Caliber: 22 LR, 10-shot mag. **Barrel:** 5-1/2" bull or 7-1/4" fluted. **Weight:** 44 oz. **Length:** 9.5" overall. **Stock:** Checkered hardwood with thumbrest. **Sights:** Undercut ramp front, frame-mounted micro-click rear adjustable for windage and elevation; drilled and tapped for scope mounting. **Features:** Gold-plated trigger, slide lock, safety-lever and magazine release; stippled front grip and backstrap; adjustable trigger and sear. Barrel weights optional. From High Standard Manufacturing Co., Inc.
Price: 5-1/2", scope base **$540.00**
Price: 7.25" **$689.00**
Price: 7.25", scope base **$625.00**

HIGH STANDARD VICTOR TARGET PISTOL

Caliber: 22 LR, 10-shot magazine. **Barrel:** 4-1/2" or 5-1/2"; push-button takedown. **Weight:** 46 oz. **Length:** 9.5" overall. **Stock:** Checkered hardwood with thumbrest. **Sights:** Undercut ramp front, micro-click rear adjustable for windage and elevation. Also available with scope mount, rings, no sights. **Features:** Stainless steel construction. Full-length vent rib. Gold-plated trigger, slide lock, safety-lever and magazine release; stippled front grip and backstrap; polished slide; adjustable trigger and sear. Comes with barrel weight. From High Standard Manufacturing Co., Inc.
Price: 4-1/2" scope base **$564.00**
Price: 5-1/2", sights. **$625.00**
Price: 5-1/2" scope base. **$564.00**

KIMBER SUPER MATCH AUTO PISTOL

Caliber: 45 ACP, 7-shot magazine. **Barrel:** 5". **Weight:** 38 oz. **Length:** 18.7" overall. **Sights:** Blade front, Kimber fully adjustable rear. **Features:** Guaranteed to have shot 3" group at 50 yards. Stainless steel frame, black KimPro slide; two-piece magazine well; premium aluminum match-grade trigger; 30 lpi front strap checkering; stainless match-grade barrel; ambidextrous safety; special Custom Shop markings. Introduced 1999. Made in U.S.A. by Kimber Mfg., Inc.
Price: **$1,927.00**

KORTH MATCH REVOLVER

Caliber: 357 Mag., 38 Special, 32 S&W Long, 9mm Para., 22 WMR, 22 LR. **Barrel:** 5 π", 6". **Grips:** Adjustable match of oiled walnut with matte finish. **Sights:** Fully adjustable with rear sight leaves (wide th of sight notch: 3.4 mm, 3.5 mm, 3.6 mm), rear; undercut partridge, front. **Trigger:** Equipped with completely machined trigger shoe. Interchangeable caliber cylinders available as well as a variety of finishes. Made in Germany.
Price: . . . . From **$5,442.00**

MORINI MODEL 84E FREE PISTOL

Caliber: 22 LR, single shot. **Barrel:** 11.4". **Weight:** 43.7 oz. **Length:** 19.4" overall. **Grips:** Adjustable match type with stippled surfaces. **Sights:** Interchangeable blade front, match-type fully adjustable rear. **Features:** Fully adjustable electronic trigger. Introduced 1995. Imported from Switzerland by Nygord Precision Products.
Price: **$1,450.00**

PARDINI MODEL SP, HP TARGET PISTOLS

Caliber: 22 LR, 32 S&W, 5-shot magazine. **Barrel:** 4.7". **Weight:** 38.9 oz. **Length:** 11.6" overall. **Grips:** Adjustable; stippled walnut; match type. **Sights:** Interchangeable blade front, interchangeable, fully adjustable rear. **Features:** Fully adjustable match trigger. Introduced 1995. Imported from Italy by Nygord Precision Products.
Price: Model SP (22 LR) **$995.00**
Price: Model HP (32 S&W) **$1,095.00**

PARDINI GP RAPID FIRE MATCH PISTOL

Caliber: 22 Short, 5-shot magazine. **Barrel:** 4.6". **Weight:** 43.3 oz. **Length:** 11.6" overall. **Grips:** Wrap-around stippled walnut. **Sights:** Interchangeable post front, fully adjustable match rear. Introduced 1995. Imported from Italy by Nygord Precision Products.
Price: Model GP **$1,095.00**
Price: Model GP-E Electronic, has special parts **$1,595.00**

PARDINI K22 FREE PISTOL

Caliber: 22 LR, single shot. **Barrel:** 9.8". **Weight:** 34.6 oz. **Length:** 18.7" overall. **Grips:** Wrap-around walnut; adjustable match type. **Sights:** Interchangeable post front, fully adjustable match open rear. **Features:** Removable, adjustable match trigger. Toggle bolt pushes cartridge into chamber. Barrel weights mount above the barrel. New upgraded model introduced in 2002. Imported from Italy by Nygord Precision Products.
Price: **$1,295.00**

PARDINI GT45 TARGET PISTOL

Caliber: 45, 9mm, 40 S&W. **Barrel:** 5", 6". **Grips:** Checkered fore strap. **Sights:** Interchangeable post front, fully adjustable match open rear. **Features:** Ambi-safeties, trigger pull adjustable. Fits Helweg Glock holsters for defense shooters. Imported from Italy by Nygord Precision Products.
Price: 5" **$1,050.00**
Price: 6" **$1,125.00**
Price: Frame mount available . . . . **$75.00 extra**
Price: Slide mount available . . . . **$35.00 extra**

PARDINI/NYGORD "MASTER" TARGET PISTOL

Caliber: 22 cal. **Barrel:** 5-1/2". **Grips:** Semi-wrap-around. **Sights:** Micrometer rear and red dot. **Features:** Elegant NRA "Bullseye" pistol. Superior balance of Pardini pistols. Revolutionary recirpcating internal weight barrel shroud. Imported from Italy by Nygord Precision Products.
Price: **$1,145.00**

RUGER MARK II TARGET MODEL AUTOLOADING PISTOL

Caliber: 22 LR, 10-shot magazine. **Barrel:** 6-7/8". **Weight:** 42 oz. **Length:** 11-1/8" overall. **Grips:** Checkered composition grip panels. **Sights:** .125" blade front, micro-click rear, adjustable for windage and elevation. Sight radius 9-3/8". Plastic case with lock included.
Features: Introduced 1982.
Price: Blued (MK-678) **$349.00**
Price: Stainless (KMK-678) **$439.00**

Ruger Mark II Government Target Model

Same gun as Mark II Target Model except has 6-7/8" barrel, higher sights and is roll marked "Government Target Model" on right side of receiver below rear sight. Identical in all aspects to military model used for training U.S. Armed Forces except for markings. Comes with factory test target, also lockable plastic case. Introduced 1987.
Price: Blued (MK-678G) **$425.00**
Price: Stainless (KMK-678G) **$509.00**

Ruger Mark II Government Target

Ruger Mark II Bull Barrel - MK10

Safari Arms Big Deuce

Smith & Wesson Model 41

Springfield, Inc. 1911A1
Bullseye Wadcutter

Ruger Stainless Competition Model Pistol

Similar to Mark II Government Target Model stainless pistol, 6-7/8" slab-sided barrel; receiver top is fitted with Ruger scope base of blued, chrome moly steel; has Ruger 1" stainless scope rings for mounting variety of optical sights; checkered laminated grip panels with right-hand thumbrest. Blued open sights with 9-1/4" radius. Overall length 11-1/8", weight 45 oz. Case and lock included. Introduced 1991.
Price: KMK-678GC **$529.00**

Ruger Mark II Bull Barrel

Same gun as Target Model except has 5-1/2" or 10" heavy barrel (10" meets all IHMSA regulations). Weight with 5-1/2" barrel is 42 oz., with 10" barrel, 51 oz. Case with lock included.
Price: Blued (MK-512) **$349.00**
Price: Blued (MK-10) **$357.00**
Price: Stainless (KMK-10) **$445.00**
Price: Stainless (KMK-512) **$439.00**

SAFARI ARMS BIG DEUCE PISTOL

Caliber: 45 ACP, 7-shot magazine. **Barrel:** 6", 416 stainless steel. **Weight:** 40.3 oz. **Length:** 9.5" overall. **Grips:** Smooth walnut. **Sights:** Ramped blade front, LPA adjustable rear. **Features:** Beavertail grip safety; extended thumb safety and slide release; Commander-style hammer. Throated, polished and tuned. Parkerized matte black slide with satin stainless steel frame. Introduced 1995. Made in U.S.A. by Safari Arms, Inc.
Price: **$714.00**

SMITH & WESSON MODEL 41 TARGET

Caliber: 22 LR, 10-shot clip. **Barrel:** 5-1/2", 7". **Weight:** 44 oz. (5-1/2" barrel). **Length:** 9" overall (5-1/2" barrel). **Grips:** Checkered walnut with modified thumbrest, usable with either hand. **Sights:** 1/8" Patridge on ramp base; micro-click rear adjustable for windage and elevation. **Features:** 3/8" wide, grooved trigger; adjustable trigger stop drilled and tapped.
Price: S&W Bright Blue, either barrel **$958.00**

SMITH & WESSON MODEL 22A TARGET PISTOL

Caliber: 22 LR, 10-shot magazine. **Barrel:** 5-1/2" bull. **Weight:** 38.5 oz. **Length:** 9-1/2" overall. **Grips:** Dymondwood with ambidextrous thumbrests and flared bottom or rubber soft touch with thumbrest. **Sights:** Patridge front, fully adjustable rear. **Features:** Sight bridge with Weaver-style integral optics mount; alloy frame, stainless barrel and slide; blue finish. Introduced 1997. Made in U.S.A. by Smith & Wesson.
Price: **$367.00**
Price: HiViz front sight **$387.00**

Smith & Wesson Model 22S Target Pistol

Similar to the Model 22A except has stainless steel frame. Introduced 1997. Made in U.S.A. by Smith & Wesson.
Price: **$434.00**
Price: HiViz front sight **$453.00**

SPRINGFIELD, INC. 1911A1 BULLSEYE WADCUTTER PISTOL

Caliber: 38 Super, 45 ACP. **Barrel:** 5". **Weight:** 45 oz. **Length:** 8.59" overall (5" barrel). **Grips:** Checkered walnut. **Sights:** Bo-Mar rib with undercut blade front, fully adjustable rear. **Features:** Built for wadcutter loads only. Has full-length recoil spring guide rod, fitted Videki speed trigger with 3.5-lb. pull; match Commander hammer and sear; beavertail grip safety; lowered and flared ejection port; tuned extractor; fitted slide to frame; recoil buffer system; beveled and polished magazine well; checkered front strap and steel mainspring housing (flat housing standard); polished and throated National Match barrel and bushing. Comes with two magazines with slam pads, plastic carrying case, test target. Introduced 1992. From Springfield, Inc.
Price: **$1,499.00**

Springfield, Inc. Expert

Springfield, Inc. Distinguished

Springfield, Inc. N.M. Hardball

Springfield, Inc. 1911A1 Trophy Match

Springfield, Inc. Basic Competition Pistol

Has low-mounted Bo-Mar adjustable rear sight, undercut blade front; match throated barrel and bushing; polished feed ramp; lowered and flared ejection port; fitted Videki speed trigger with tuned 3.5-lb. pull; fitted slide to frame; recoil buffer system; checkered walnut grips; serrated, arched mainspring housing. Comes with two magazines with slam pads, plastic carrying case. Introduced 1992. From Springfield, Inc.

Price: 45 ACP, blue, 5" only **$1,295.00**

Springfield, Inc. Expert Pistol

Similar to the Competition Pistol except has triple-chamber tapered cone compensator on match barrel with dovetailed front sight; lowered and flared ejection port; fully tuned for reliability; fitted slide to frame; extended ambidextrous thumb safety, extended magazine release button; beavertail grip safety; Pachmayr wrap-around grips. Comes with two magazines, plastic carrying case. Introduced 1992. From Springfield, Inc.

Price: 45 ACP, Duotone finish. **$1,724.00**
Price: Expert Ltd. (non-compensated) **$1,624.00**

Springfield, Inc. Distinguished Pistol

Has all the features of the 1911A1 Expert except is full-house pistol with deluxe Bo-Mar low-mounted adjustable rear sight; full-length recoil spring guide rod and recoil spring retainer; checkered frontstrap; S&A magazine well; walnut grips. Hard chrome finish. Comes with two magazines with slam pads, plastic carrying case. From Springfield, Inc.

Price: 45 ACP. **$2,445.00**
Price: Distinguished Limited (non-compensated) **$2,345.00**

Springfield, Inc. 1911A1 N.M. Hardball Pistol

Has Bo-Mar adjustable rear sight with undercut front blade; fitted match Videki trigger with 4-lb. pull; fitted slide to frame; throated National Match barrel and bushing, polished feed ramp; recoil buffer system; tuned extractor; Herrett walnut grips. Comes with two magazines, plastic carrying case, test target. Introduced 1992. From Springfield, Inc.

Price: 45 ACP, blue. **$1,336.00**

Springfield, Inc. Leatham Legend TGO Series Pistols

Three models of 5" barrel, 45 ACP 1911 pistols built for serious competition. TGO 1 has deluxe low mount BoMar rear sight, Dawson fiber optics front sight, 3.5 lb. trigger pull. TGO 2 has BoMar low mount adjustable rear sight, Dawson fiber optic front sight, 4.5 to 5 lb. trigger pull. TGO 3 has Springfield Armory fully adjustable rear sight with low mount BoMar cut Dawson fiber optic front sight, 4.5 to 5 lb. trigger.

Price: TGO 1 . . . . **$2,999.00**
Price: TGO 2 . . . . **$1,899.00**
Price: TGO 3 . . . . **$1,295.00**

Springfield, Inc. Trophy Match Pistol

Similar to Springfield, Inc.'s Full Size model, but designed for bullseye and action shooting competition. Available with a Service Model 5" frame with matching slide and barrel in 5" and 6" lengths. Fully adjustable sights, checkered frame front strap, match barrel and bushing. In 45 ACP only. From Springfield Inc.

Price: **$1,248.00**

STI EAGLE 5.0, 6.0 PISTOL

Caliber: 0mm, 9x21, 38 & 40 Super, 40 S&W, 10mm, 45 ACP, 10-shot magazine. **Barrel:** 5", 6" bull. **Weight:** 34.5 oz. **Length:** 8.62" overall. **Grips:** Checkered polymer. **Sights:** STI front, Novak or Heine rear. **Features:** Standard frames plus 7 others; adjustable match trigger; skeletonized hammer; extended grip safety with locator pad; match-grade fit of all parts. Many options available. Introduced 1994. Made in U.S.A. by STI International.

Price: . . . . (5.0 Eagle) **$1,794.00**, (6.0 Eagle) **$1,894.00**

STI EXECUTIVE PISTOL

Caliber: 40 S&W. **Barrel:** 5" bull. **Weight:** 39 oz. **Length:** 8-5/8". **Grips:** Gray polymer. **Sights:** Dawson fiber optic, front; STI adjustable rear. **Features:** Stainless mag. well, front and rear serrations on slide. Made in U.S.A. by STI.

Price: **$2,389.00**

STI TROJAN

Caliber: 9mm, 38 Super, 40S&W, 45 ACP. **Barrel:** 5", 6". **Weight:** 36 oz. **Length:** 8.5". **Grips:** Rosewood. **Sights:** STI front with STI adjustable rear. **Features:** Stippled front strap, flat top slide, one-piece steel guide rod.

Price: (Trojan 5") **$1,024.00**
Price: (Trojan 6", not available in 38 Super) **$1,232.50**

WALTHER GSP MATCH PISTOL

Caliber: 22 LR, 32 S&W Long (GSP-C), 5-shot magazine. **Barrel:** 4.22". **Weight:** 44.8 oz. (22 LR), 49.4 oz. (32). **Length:** 11.8" overall. **Grips:** Walnut. **Sights:** Post front, match rear adjustable for windage and elevation. **Features:** Available with either 2.2-lb. (1000 gm) or 3-lb. (1360 gm) trigger. Spare magazine, barrel weight, tools supplied. Imported from Germany by Nygord Precision Products.

Price: GSP, with case **$1,495.00**
Price: GSP-C, with case **$1,595.00**

Includes models suitable for hunting and competitive courses of fire, both police and international.

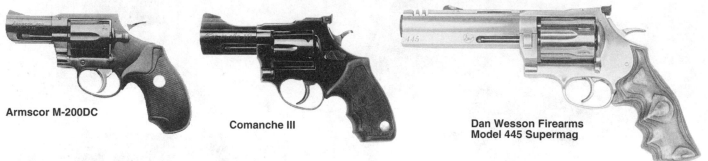

Armscor M-200DC

Comanche III

Dan Wesson Firearms Model 445 Supermag

ARMSCOR M-200DC REVOLVER
Caliber: 38 Spec., 6-shot cylinder. **Barrel:** 2-1/2", 4". **Weight:** 22 oz. (2-1/2" barrel). **Length:** 7-3/8" overall (2-1/2" barrel). **Grips:** Checkered rubber. **Sights:** Blade front, fixed notch rear. **Features:** All-steel construction; floating firing pin, transfer bar ignition; shrouded ejector rod; blue finish. Reintroduced 1996. Imported from the Philippines by K.B.I., Inc.
Price: 2-1/2" $199.99
Price: 4" $205.00

ARMSPORT MODEL 4540 REVOLVER
Caliber: 38 Special. **Barrel:** 4". **Weight:** 32 oz **Length:** 9" overall. **Sights:** Fixed rear, blade front. **Features:** Ventilated rib; blued finish. Imported from Argentina by Armsport Inc.
Price: $140.00

COMANCHE I, II, III DA REVOLVERS
Features: Adjustable sights. Blue or stainless finish. Distributed by SGS Importers.
Price: I 22 LR, 6" bbl, 9-shot, blue $236.95
Price: I 22LR, 6" bbl, 9-shot, stainless $258.95
Price: II 38 Special, 3", 4" bbl, 6-shot, blue. $219.95
Price: II 38 Special, 4" bbl, 6-shot, stainless. $236.95
Price: III 357 Mag, 3", 4", 6" bbl, 6-shot, blue $253.95
Price: III 357 Mag, 3", 4", 6" bbl, 6-shot, stainless $274.95
Price: II 38 Special, 3" bbl, 6-shot, stainless steel $236.95

DAN WESSON FIREARMS MODEL 722 SILHOUETTE REVOLVER
Caliber: 22 LR, 6-shot. **Barrel:** 10", vent heavy. **Weight:** 53 oz. **Grips:** Combat style. **Sights:** Patridge-style front, .080" narrow notch rear. **Features:** Single action only. Satin brushed stainless finish. Reintroduced 1997. Made in U.S.A. by Dan Wesson Firearms.
Price: 722 VH10 (vent heavy 10" bbl.) $888.00
Price: 722 VH10 SRS1 (Super Ram Silhouette, Bo-Mar sights, front hood, trigger job) $1,164.00

DAN WESSON FIREARMS MODEL 3220/73220 TARGET REVOLVER
Caliber: 32-20, 6-shot. **Barrel:** 2.5", 4", 6", 8", 10" standard vent, vent heavy. **Weight:** 47 oz. (6" VH). **Length:** 11.25" overall. **Grips:** Hogue Gripper rubber (walnut, exotic hardwoods optional). **Sights:** Red ramp interchangeable front, fully adjustable rear. **Features:** Bright blue (3220) or stainless (73220). Reintroduced 1997. Made in U.S.A. by Dan Wesson Firearms.
Price: 3220 VH2.5 (blued, 2.5" vent heavy bbl.) $643.00
Price: 73220 VH10 (stainless 10" vent heavy bbl.) $873.00

DAN WESSON FIREARMS MODEL 40/740 REVOLVERS
Caliber: 357 Maximum, 6-shot. **Barrel:** 4", 6", 8", 10". **Weight:** 72 oz. (8" bbl.). **Length:** 14.3" overall (8" bbl.). **Grips:** Hogue Gripper rubber (walnut or exotic hardwood optional). **Sights:** 1/8" serrated front, fully adjustable rear. **Features:** Blue or stainless steel. Made in U.S.A. by Dan Wesson Firearms.
Price: Blue, 4" $702.00
Price: Blue, 6" $749.00

Price: Blue, 8" $795.00
Price: Blue, 10" $858.00
Price: Stainless, 4" $834.00
Price: Stainless, 6" $892.00
Price: Stainless, 8" slotted $1,024.00
Price: Stainless, 10" $998.00
Price: 4", 6", 8" Compensated, blue .... $749.00 to $885.00
Price: As above, stainless. .... $893.00 to $1,061.00

Dan Wesson Firearms Model 414/7414 and 445/7445 SuperMag Revolvers
Similar size and weight as Model 40 revolvers. Chambered for 414 SuperMag or 445 SuperMag cartridge. Barrel lengths of 4", 6", 8", 10". Contact maker for complete price list. Reintroduced 1997. Made in the U.S. by Dan Wesson Firearms.
Price: 4", vent heavy, blue or stainless $904.00
Price: 8", vent heavy, blue or stainless $1,026.00
Price: 10", vent heavy, blue or stainless $1,103.00
Price: Compensated models .... $965.00 to $1,149.00

DAN WESSON FIREARMS MODEL 22/722 REVOLVERS
Caliber: 22 LR, 22 WMR, 6-shot. **Barrel:** 2-1/2", 4", 6", 8" or 10"; interchangeable. **Weight:** 36 oz. (2-1/2"), 44 oz. (6"). **Length:** 9-1/4" overall (4" barrel). **Grips:** Hogue Gripper rubber (walnut, exotic woods optional). **Sights:** 1/8" serrated, interchangeable front, white outline rear adjustable for windage and elevation. **Features:** Built on the same frame as the Wesson 357; smooth, wide trigger with over-travel adjustment, wide spur hammer, with short double-action travel. Available in blue or stainless steel. Reintroduced 1997. Contact Dan Wesson Firearms for complete price list.
Price: 22 VH2.5/722 VH2.5 (blued or stainless 2-1/2" bbl.) $551.00
Price: 22VH10/722 VH10 (blued or stainless 10" bbl.) $750.00

Dan Wesson 722M Small Frame Revolver
Similar to Model 22/722 except chambered for 22 WMR. Blued or stainless finish, 2-1/2", 4", 6", 8" or 10" barrels.
Price: Blued or stainless finish .... $643.00 to $873.00

DAN WESSON FIREARMS MODEL 15/715 and 32/732 REVOLVERS
Caliber: 32-20, 32 H&R Mag. (Model 32), 357 Mag. (Model 15). **Barrel:** 2-1/2", 4", 6", 8" (M32), 2-1/2", 4", 6", 8", 10" (M15); vent heavy. **Weight:** 36 oz. (2-1/2" barrel). **Length:** 9-1/4" overall (4" barrel). **Grips:** Checkered, interchangeable. **Sights:** 1/8" serrated front, fully adjustable rear. **Features:** New Generation Series. Interchangeable barrels; wide, smooth trigger, wide hammer spur; short double-action travel. Available in blue or stainless. Reintroduced 1997. Made in U.S.A. by Dan Wesson Firearms. Contact maker for full list of models.
Price: Model 15/715, 2-1/2" (blue or stainless) $551.00
Price: Model 15/715, 8" (blue or stainless) $612.00
Price: Model 15/715, compensated .... $704.00 to $827.00
Price: Model 32/732, 4" (blue or stainless) $674.00
Price: Model 32/732, 8" (blue or stainless) $766.00

Dan Wesson Firearms Model 744 VH8

**Dan Wesson Firearms
Super Ram Silhouette**

**Dan Wesson Firearms
Alaskan Guide Special**

DAN WESSON FIREARMS MODEL 41/741, 44/744 and 45/745 REVOLVERS

Caliber: 41 Mag., 44 Mag., 45 Colt, 6-shot. **Barrel:** 4", 6", 8", 10"; interchangeable; 4", 6", 8" Compensated. **Weight:** 48 oz. (4"). **Length:** 12" overall (6" bbl.) **Grips:** Smooth. **Sights:** 1/8" serrated front, white outline rear adjustable for windage and elevation. **Features:** Available in blue or stainless steel. Smooth, wide trigger with adjustable over-travel, wide hammer spur. Available in Pistol Pac set also. Reintroduced 1997. Contact Dan Wesson Firearms for complete price list.

Price: 41 Mag., 4", vent heavy (blue or stainless) **$643.00**
Price: 44 Mag., 6", vent heavy (blue or stainless) **$689.00**
Price: 45 Colt, 8", vent heavy (blue or stainless) **$766.00**
Price: Compensated models (all calibers) . . . . **$812.00 to $934.00**

DAN WESSON FIREARMS LARGE FRAME SERIES REVOLVERS

Caliber: 41, 741/41 Magnum; 44, 744/44 Magnum; 45, 745/45 Long Colt; 360, 7360/357; 460, 7460/45. **Barrel:** 2"-10". **Weight:** 49 oz.-69 oz. **Grips:** Standard, Hogue rubber Gripper Grips. **Sights:** Standard front, serrated ramp with color insert. Standard rear, adustable with color notch. Other sight options available. **Features:** Available in blue or stainless steel. Smooth, wide trigger with overtravel, wide hammer spur. Double and single action.

Price: . . . . **$769.00 to $889.00**

DAN WESSON FIREARMS MODEL 360/7360 REVOLVERS

Caliber: 357 Mag. **Barrel:** 4", 6", 8", 10"; vent heavy. **Weight:** 64 oz. (8" barrel). **Grips:** Hogue rubber finger groove. **Sights:** Interchangeable ramp or Patridge front, fully adjustable rear. **Features:** New Generation Large Frame Series. Interchangeable barrels and grips; smooth trigger, wide hammer spur. Blue (360) or stainless (7360). Introduced 1999. Made in U.S.A. by Dan Wesson Firearms.

Price: 4" bbl., blue or stainless **$735.00**
Price: 10" bbl., blue or stainless **$873.00**
Price: Compensated models . . . . **$858.00 to $980.00**

DAN WESSON FIREARMS MODEL 460/7460 REVOLVERS

Caliber: 45 ACP, 45 Auto Rim, 45 Super, 45 Winchester Magnum and 460 Rowland. **Barrel:** 4", 6", 8", 10"; vent heavy. **Weight:** 49 oz. (4" barrel). **Grips:** Hogue rubber finger groove; interchangeable. **Sights:** Interchangeable ramp or Patridge front, fully adjustable rear. **Features:** New Generation Large Frame Series. Shoots five cartridges (45 ACP, 45 Auto Rim, 45 Super, 45 Winchester Magnum and 460 Rowland; six half-moon

clips for auto cartridges included). Interchangeable barrels and grips. Available with non-fluted cylinder and Slotted Lightweight barrel shroud. Introduced 1999. Made in U.S.A. by Dan Wesson Firearms.

Price: 4" bbl., blue or stainless **$735.00**
Price: 10" bbl., blue or stainless **$888.00**
Price: Compensated models . . . . **$919.00 to $1,042.00**

DAN WESSON FIREARMS STANDARD SILHOUETTE REVOLVERS

Caliber: 357 SuperMag/Maxi, 41 Mag., 414 SuperMag, 445 SuperMag. **Barrel:** 8", 10". **Weight:** 64 oz. (8" barrel). **Length:** 14.3" overall (8" barrel). **Grips:** Hogue rubber finger groove; interchangeable. **Sights:** Patridge front, fully adjustable rear. **Features:** Interchangeable barrels and grips, fluted or non-fluted cylinder, satin brushed stainless finish. Introduced 1999. Made in U.S.A. by Dan Wesson Firearms.

Price: 357 SuperMag/Maxi, 8" **$1,057.00**
Price: 41 Mag., 10" **$888.00**
Price: 414 SuperMag., 8" **$1,057.00**
Price: 445 SuperMag., 8" **$1,057.00**

Dan Wesson Firearms Super Ram Silhouette Revolver

Similar to Standard Silhouette except has 10 land and groove Laser Coat barrel, Bo-Mar target sights with hooded front, special laser engraving. Fluted or non-fluted cylinder. Introduced 1999. Made in U.S.A. by Dan Wesson Firearms.

Price: 357 SuperMag/Maxi, 414 SuperMag., 445 SuperMag., 8", blue or stainless **$1,364.00**
Price: 41 Magnum, 44 Magnum, 8", blue or stainless **$1,241.00**
Price: 41 Magnum, 44 Magnum, 10", blue or stainless **$1,333.00**

DAN WESSON FIREARMS ALASKAN GUIDE SPECIAL

Caliber: 445 SuperMag, 44 Magnum. **Barrel:** Compensated 4" vent heavy barrel assembly. **Features:** Stainless steel with baked on, non-glare, matte black coating, special laser engraving.

Price: Model 7445 VH4C AGS **$995.00**
Price: Model 744 VH4C AGS **$855.00**

EAA STANDARD GRADE REVOLVERS

Caliber: 38 Spec., 6-shot; 357 magnum, 6-shot. **Barrel:** 2", 4". **Weight:** 38 oz. (22 rimfire, 4"). **Length:** 8.8" overall (4" bbl.). **Grips:** Rubber with finger grooves. **Sights:** Blade front, fixed or adjustable on rimfires; fixed only on 32, 38. **Features:** Swing-out cylinder; hammer block safety; blue finish. Introduced 1991. Imported from Germany by European American Armory.

Price: 38 Special 2" **$249.00**
Price: 38 Special, 4" **$259.00**
Price: 357 Magnum, 2" **$259.00**
Price: 357 Magnum, 4" **$279.00**

KORTH COMBAT REVOLVER

Caliber: 357 Mag., 32 S&W Long, 9mm Para., 22 WMR, 22 LR. **Barrel:** 3", 4", 5 π", 6", 8". **Sights:** Fully-adjustable, rear; Baughman ramp, front. **Grips:** Walnut (checkered or smooth). Also available as a Target model in 22 LR, 38 Spl., 32 S&W Long, 357 Mag. with undercut partridge front sight; fully-adjustable rear. Made in Germany. Imported by Korth USA.

Price: . . . . From **$5,442.00**

Medusa Model 47

Ruger GP-161

Ruger KGP-141

NEW!

KORTH TROJA REVOLVER

Caliber: 357 Mag. **Barrel:** 6". **Finish:** Matte blue. **Grips:** Smooth, oversized finger contoured walnut. **Features:** Maintaining all of the precision German craftsmanship that has made this line famous, the final surface finish is not as finely polished as the firm's other products – thus the lower price. Introduced 2003. Imported from Germany by Korth USA.

Price: . . . . From **$3,995.00**

MEDUSA MODEL 47 REVOLVER

Caliber: Most 9mm, 38 and 357 caliber cartridges; 6-shot cylinder. **Barrel:** 2-1/2", 3", 4", 5", 6"; fluted. **Weight:** 39 oz. **Length:** 10" overall (4" barrel). **Grips:** Gripper-style rubber. **Sights:** Changeable front blades, fully adjustable rear. **Features:** Patented extractor allows gun to chamber, fire and extract over 25 different cartridges in the 355 to 357 range, without half-moon clips. Steel frame and cylinder; match quality barrel. Matte blue finish. Introduced 1996. Made in U.S.A. by Phillips & Rogers, Inc.

Price: **$899.00**

ROSSI MODEL 351/352 REVOLVERS

Caliber: 38 Special +P, 5-shot. **Barrel:** 2". **Weight:** 24 oz. **Length:** 6-1/2" overall. **Grips:** Rubber. **Sights:** Blade front, fixed rear. **Features:** Patented key-lock Taurus Security System; forged steel frame handles +P ammunition. Introduced 2001. Imported by BrazTech/Taurus.

Price: Model 351 (blued finish) **$298.00**
Price: Model 352 (stainless finish) **$345.00**

ROSSI MODEL 461/462 REVOLVERS

Caliber: 357 Magnum +P, 6-shot. **Barrel:** 2". **Weight:** 26 oz. **Length:** 6-1/2" overall. **Grips:** Rubber. **Sights:** Fixed. **Features:** Single/double action. Patented key-lock Taurus Security System; forged steel frame handles +P ammunition. Introduced 2001. Imported by BrazTech/Taurus.

Price: Model 461 (blued finish) **$298.00**
Price: Model 462 (stainless finish) **$345.00**

ROSSI MODEL 971/972 REVOLVERS

Caliber: 357 Magnum +P, 6-shot. **Barrel:** 4", 6". **Weight:** 40-44 oz. **Length:** 8-1/2" or 10-1/2" overall. **Grips:** Rubber. **Sights:** Fully adjustable. **Features:** Single/double action. Patented key-lock Taurus Security System; forged steel frame handles +P ammunition. Introduced 2001. Imported by BrazTech/Taurus.

Price: Model 971 (blued finish, 4" barrel) **$345.00**
Price: Model 972 (stainless steel finish, 6" barrel) **$391.00**

Rossi Model 851

Similar to Model 971/972, chambered for 38 Special +P. Blued finish, 4" barrel. Introduced 2001. From BrazTech/Taurus.

Price: **$298.00**

RUGER GP-100 REVOLVERS

Caliber: 38 Spec., 357 Mag., 6-shot. **Barrel:** 3", 3" full shroud, 4", 4" full shroud, 6", 6" full shroud. **Weight:** 3" barrel—35 oz., 3" full shroud—36 oz., 4" barrel—37 oz., 4" full shroud—38 oz. **Sights:** Fixed; adjustable on 4" full shroud, all 6" barrels. **Grips:** Ruger Santoprene Cushioned Grip with Goncalo Alves inserts. **Features:** Uses action, frame incorporating improvements and features of both the Security-Six and Redhawk revolvers. Full length, short ejector shroud. Satin blue and stainless steel.

Price: GP-141 (357, 4" full shroud, adj. sights, blue) **$499.00**
Price: GP-160 (357, 6", adj. sights, blue) **$499.00**
Price: GP-161 (357, 6" full shroud, adj. sights, blue), 46 oz. **$499.00**
Price: GPF-331 (357, 3" full shroud) **$495.00**

Ruger KSP-331X

Price: GPF-340 (357, 4") **$495.00**
Price: GPF-341 (357, 4" full shroud) **$495.00**
Price: KGP-141 (357, 4" full shroud, adj. sights, stainless) **$555.00**
Price: KGP-160 (357, 6", adj. sights, stainless), 43 oz. **$555.00**
Price: KGP-161 (357, 6" full shroud, adj. sights, stainless) 46 oz. **$555.00**
Price: KGPF-330 (357, 3", stainless) **$555.00**
Price: KGPF-331 (357, 3" full shroud, stainless) **$555.00**
Price: KGPF-340 (357, 4", stainless), KGPF-840 (38 Special). . . **$555.00**
Price: KGPF-341 (357, 4" full shroud, stainless) **$555.00**
Price: KGPF-840 (38 Special, 4", stainless). **$555.00**

Ruger SP101 Double-Action-Only Revolver

Similar to standard SP101 except double-action-only with no single-action sear notch. Spurless hammer for snag-free handling, floating firing pin and Ruger's patented transfer bar safety system. Available with 2-1/4" barrel in 357 Magnum. Weighs 25 oz., overall length 7.06". Natural brushed satin, high-polish stainless steel. Introduced 1993.

Price: KSP321XL (357 Mag.) **$495.00**

RUGER SP101 REVOLVERS

Caliber: 22 LR, 32 H&R Mag., 6-shot; 38 Spec. +P, 357 Mag., 5-shot. **Barrel:** 2-1/4", 3-1/16", 4". **Weight:** (38 & 357 mag models) 2-1/4"—25 oz.; 3-1/16"—27 oz. **Sights:** Adjustable on 22, 32, fixed on others. **Grips:** Ruger Cushioned Grip with inserts. **Features:** Incorporates improvements and features found in the GP-100 revolvers into a compact, small frame, double-action revolver. Full-length ejector shroud. Stainless steel only. Introduced 1988.

Price: KSP-821X (2-1/4", 38 Spec.) **$495.00**
Price: KSP-831X (3-1/16", 38 Spec.) **$495.00**
Price: KSP-241X (4" heavy bbl., 22 LR), 34 oz. **$495.00**
Price: KSP-3231X (3-1/16", 32 H&R), 30 oz. **$495.00**
Price: KSP-321X (2-1/4", 357 Mag.) **$495.00**
Price: KSP-331X (3-1/16", 357 Mag.) **$495.00**
Price: KSP-3241X (32 Mag., 4" bbl) **$495.00**

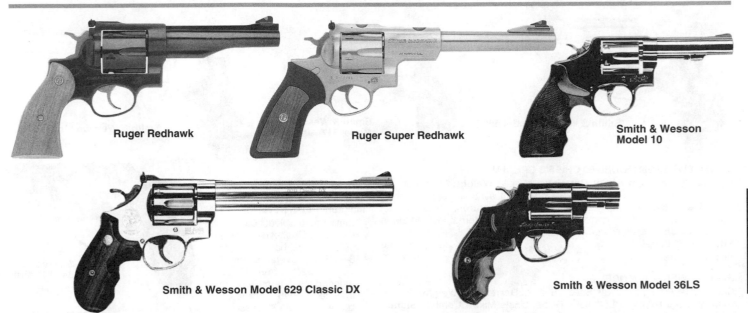

Ruger Redhawk

Ruger Super Redhawk

Smith & Wesson Model 10

Smith & Wesson Model 629 Classic DX

Smith & Wesson Model 36LS

RUGER REDHAWK

Caliber: 44 Rem. Mag., 45 Colt, 6-shot. **Barrel:** 5-1/2", 7-1/2". **Weight:** About 54 oz. (7-1/2" bbl.). **Length:** 13" overall (7-1/2" barrel). **Grips:** Square butt cushioned grip panels. **Sights:** Interchangeable Patridge-type front, rear adjustable for windage and elevation. **Features:** Stainless steel, brushed satin finish, blued ordnance steel. 9-1/2" sight radius. Introduced 1979.
Price: Blued, 44 Mag., 5-1/2" RH-445, 7-1/2" RH-44 . . . . **$585.00**
Price: Blued, 44 Mag., 7-1/2" RH44R, with scope mount, rings . . **$625.00**
Price: Stainless, 44 Mag., KRH445, 5-1/2", 7-1/2" KRH-44 . . . . . **$645.00**
Price: Stainless, 44 Mag., 7-1/2", with scope mount, rings KRH-44R. **$685.00**
Price: Stainless, 45 Colt, KRH455, 5-1/2", 7-1/2" KRH-45 . . . . . . **$645.00**
Price: Stainless, 45 Colt, 7-1/2", with scope mount and rings KRH-45R. **$685.00**

Ruger Super Redhawk Revolver

Similar to standard Redhawk except has heavy extended frame with Ruger Integral Scope Mounting System on wide topstrap. Also available 454 Casull and 480 Ruger. Wide hammer spur lowered for better scope clearance. Incorporates mechanical design features and improvements of GP-100. Choice of 7-1/2" or 9-1/2" barrel, both ramp front sight base with Redhawk-style Interchangeable Insert sight blades, adjustable rear sight. Comes with Ruger "Cushioned Grip" panels with wood panels. Target gray stainless steel. Introduced 1987.
Price: KSRH-7 (7-1/2"), KSRH-9 (9-1/2"), 44 Mag **$685.00**
Price: KSRH-7454 (7-1/2") 454 Casull, 9-1/2 KSRH-9454 . . . . . . **$775.00**
Price: KSRH-7480 (7-1/2") 480 Ruger **$775.00**
Price: KSRH-9480 (9-1/2") 480 Ruger **$775.00**

SMITH & WESSON MODEL 10 M&P HB REVOLVER

Caliber: 38 Spec., 6-shot. **Barrel:** 4". **Weight:** 33.5 oz. **Length:** 9-5/16" overall. **Grips:** Uncle Mike's Combat soft rubber; square butt. **Sights:** Fixed; ramp front, square notch rear.
Price: Blue **$496.00**

SMITH & WESSON COMMEMORATIVE MODEL 29

Features: Reflects original Model 29: 6-1/2" barrel, four-screw side plate, over-sized target grips, red vamp front and black blade rear sights, 150th Anniversary logo, engraved, gold-plated, blue, in wood presentation case. Limited.
Price: . . . . **NA**

SMITH & WESSON MODEL 629 REVOLVERS

Caliber: 44 Magnum, 44 S&W Special, 6-shot. **Barrel:** 5", 6", 8-3/8". **Weight:** 47 oz. (6" bbl.). **Length:** 11-3/8" overall (6" bbl.). **Grips:** Soft rubber; wood optional. **Sights:** 1/8" red ramp front, white outline rear, internal lock, adjustable for windage and elevation.
Price: Model 629, 4" **$717.00**
Price: Model 629, 6" **$739.00**
Price: Model 629, 8-3/8" barrel **$756.00**

Smith & Wesson Model 629 Classic Revolver

Similar to standard Model 629, full-lug 5", 6-1/2" or 8-3/8" barrel, chamfered front of cylinder, interchangeable red ramp front sight with adjustable white outline rear, Hogue grips with S&W monogram, frame is drilled and tapped for scope mounting. Factory accurizing and endurance packages. Overall length with 5" barrel is 10-1/2"; weighs 51 oz. Introduced 1990.
Price: Model 629 Classic (stainless), 5", 6-1/2" **$768.00**
Price: As above, 8-3/8" **$793.00**
Price: Model 629 with HiViz front sight **$814.00**

Smith & Wesson Model 629 Classic DX Revolver

Similar to Model 629 Classic, offered only with 6-1/2" or 8-3/8" full-lug barrel, five front sights: red ramp, black Patridge, black Patridge with gold bead, black ramp, black Patridge with white dot, white outline rear sight, adjustable sight, internal lock. Hogue combat-style and wood round butt grip. Introduced 1991.
Price: Model 629 Classic DX, 6-1/2" **$986.00**
Price: As above, 8-3/8" **$1,018.00**

SMITH & WESSON MODEL 37 CHIEF'S SPECIAL & AIRWEIGHT

Caliber: 38 Spec. +P, 5-shot. **Barrel:** 1-7/8". **Weight:** 19-1/2 oz. (2" bbl.); 13-1/2 oz. (Airweight). **Length:** 6-1/2" (round butt). **Grips:** Round butt soft rubber. **Sights:** Fixed, serrated ramp front, square notch rear. Glass beaded finish.
Price: Model 37. . . . . **$523.00**

Smith & Wesson Model 637 Airweight Revolver

Similar to the Model 37 Airweight except has alloy frame, stainless steel barrel, cylinder and yoke; rated for 38 Spec. +P; Uncle Mike's Boot Grip. Weighs 15 oz. Introduced 1996. Made in U.S.A. by Smith & Wesson.
Price: **$548.00**

SMITH & WESSON MODEL 36LS, 60LS LADYSMITH

Caliber: 38 S&W Special +P, 5-shot. **Barrel:** 1-7/8". **Weight:** 20 oz. **Length:** 6-5/16 overall (1-7/8" barrel). **Grips:** Combat Dymondwood® grips with S&W monogram. **Sights:** Serrated ramp front, fixed notch rear. **Features:** Speedloader cutout. Comes in a fitted carry/storage case. Introduced 1989.
Price: Model 36LS **$518.00**
Price: Model 60LS, 2-1/8" barrel stainless, 357 Magnum **$566.00**

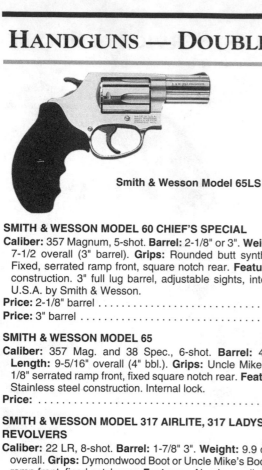

Smith & Wesson Model 65LS

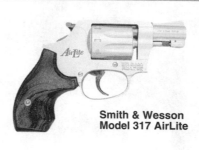

Smith & Wesson
Model 317 AirLite

Smith & Wesson Model 625

Smith & Wesson
Model 340 PD Airlite Sc

SMITH & WESSON MODEL 60 CHIEF'S SPECIAL
Caliber: 357 Magnum, 5-shot. **Barrel:** 2-1/8" or 3". **Weight:** 24 oz. **Length:** 7-1/2 overall (3" barrel). **Grips:** Rounded butt synthetic grips. **Sights:** Fixed, serrated ramp front, square notch rear. **Features:** Stainless steel construction. 3" full lug barrel, adjustable sights, internal lock. Made in U.S.A. by Smith & Wesson.
Price: 2-1/8" barrel **$541.00**
Price: 3" barrel **$574.00**

SMITH & WESSON MODEL 65
Caliber: 357 Mag. and 38 Spec., 6-shot. **Barrel:** 4". **Weight:** 34 oz. **Length:** 9-5/16" overall (4" bbl.). **Grips:** Uncle Mike's Combat. **Sights:** 1/8" serrated ramp front, fixed square notch rear. **Features:** Heavy barrel. Stainless steel construction. Internal lock.
Price: **$531.00**

SMITH & WESSON MODEL 317 AIRLITE, 317 LADYSMITH REVOLVERS
Caliber: 22 LR, 8-shot. **Barrel:** 1-7/8" 3". **Weight:** 9.9 oz. **Length:** 6-3/16" overall. **Grips:** Dymondwood Boot or Uncle Mike's Boot. **Sights:** Serrated ramp front, fixed notch rear. **Features:** Aluminum alloy, carbon and stainless steels, and titanium construction. Short spur hammer, smooth combat trigger. Clear Cote finish. Introduced 1997. Made in U.S.A. by Smith & Wesson.
Price: With Uncle Mike's Boot grip **$550.00**
Price: With DymondWood Boot grip, 3" barrel, HiViz front sight, internal lock. **$600.00**
Price: Model 317 LadySmith (DymondWood only, comes with display case) **$596.00**

SMITH & WESSON MODEL 64 STAINLESS M&P
Caliber: 38 Spec. +P, 6-shot. **Barrel:** 2", 3", 4". **Weight:** 34 oz. **Length:** 9-5/16" overall. **Grips:** Soft rubber. **Sights:** Fixed, 1/8" serrated ramp front, square notch rear. **Features:** Satin finished stainless steel, square butt.
Price: 2" **$522.00**
Price: 3", 4". **$532.00**

SMITH & WESSON MODEL 65LS LADYSMITH
Caliber: 357 Magnum, 38 Spec. +P, 6-shot. **Barrel:** 3". **Weight:** 31 oz. **Length:** 7.94" overall. **Grips:** Rosewood, round butt. **Sights:** Serrated ramp front, fixed notch rear. **Features:** Stainless steel with frosted finish. Smooth combat trigger, service hammer, shrouded ejector rod. Comes with case. Introduced 1992.
Price: **$584.00**

SMITH & WESSON MODEL 66 STAINLESS COMBAT MAGNUM
Caliber: 357 Mag. and 38 Spec. +P, 6-shot. **Barrel:** 2-1/2", 4", 6". **Weight:** 36 oz. (4" barrel). **Length:** 9-9/16" overall. **Grips:** Soft rubber. **Sights:** Red ramp front, micro-click rear adjustable for windage and elevation. **Features:** Satin finish stainless steel. Internal lock.
Price: 2-1/2" **$590.00**
Price: 4" **$579.00**
Price: 6" **$608.00**

SMITH & WESSON MODEL 67 COMBAT MASTERPIECE
Caliber: 38 Special, 6-shot. **Barrel:** 4". **Weight:** 32 oz. **Length:** 9-5/16" overall. **Grips:** Soft rubber. **Sights:** Red ramp front, micro-click rear adjustable for windage and elevation. **Features:** Stainless steel with satin finish. Smooth combat trigger, semi-target hammer. Introduced 1994.
Price: **$585.00**

Smith & Wesson Model 686 Magnum PLUS Revolver
Similar to the Model 686 except has 7-shot cylinder, 2-1/2", 4" or 6" barrel. Weighs 34-1/2 oz., overall length 7-1/2" (2-1/2" barrel). Hogue rubber grips. Internal lock. Introduced 1996. Made in U.S.A. by Smith & Wesson.
Price: 2-1/2" barrel **$631.00**
Price: 4" barrel **$653.00**
Price: 6" barrel **$663.00**

SMITH & WESSON MODEL 625 REVOLVER
Caliber: 45 ACP, 6-shot. **Barrel:** 5". **Weight:** 46 oz. **Length:** 11.375" overall. **Grips:** Soft rubber; wood optional. **Sights:** Patridge front on ramp, S&W micrometer click rear adjustable for windage and elevation. **Features:** Stainless steel construction with .400" semi-target hammer, .312" smooth combat trigger; full lug barrel. Glass beaded finish. Introduced 1989.
Price: 5" **$745.00**
Price: 4" with internal lock. **$745.00**

SMITH & WESSON MODEL 640 CENTENNIAL DA ONLY
Caliber: 357 Mag., 38 Spec. +P, 5-shot. **Barrel:** 2-1/8". **Weight:** 25 oz. **Length:** 6-3/4" overall. **Grips:** Uncle Mike's Boot Grip. **Sights:** Serrated ramp front, fixed notch rear. **Features:** Stainless steel. Fully concealed hammer, snag-proof smooth edges. Internal lock. Introduced 1995 in 357 Magnum.
Price: **$599.00**

SMITH & WESSON MODEL 617 K-22 MASTERPIECE
Caliber: 22 LR, 6- or 10-shot. **Barrel:** 4", 6", 8-3/8". **Weight:** 42 oz. (4" barrel). **Length:** NA. **Grips:** Soft rubber. **Sights:** Patridge front, adjustable rear. Drilled and tapped for scope mount. **Features:** Stainless steel with satin finish; 4" has .312" smooth trigger, .375" semi-target hammer; 6" has either .312" combat or .400" serrated trigger, .375" semi-target or .500" target hammer; 8-3/8" with .400" serrated trigger, .500" target hammer. Introduced 1990.
Price: 4" **$644.00**
Price: 6", target hammer, target trigger **$625.00**
Price: 6", 10-shot **$669.00**
Price: 8-3/8", 10 shot **$679.00**

SMITH & WESSON MODEL 610 CLASSIC HUNTER REVOLVER
Caliber: 10mm, 40 S&W, 6-shot cylinder. **Barrel:** 6-1/2" full lug. **Weight:** 52 oz. **Length:** 12" overall. **Grips:** Hogue rubber combat. **Sights:** Interchangeable blade front, micro-click rear adjustable for windage and elevation. **Features:** Stainless steel construction; target hammer, target trigger; unfluted cylinder; drilled and tapped for scope mounting. Introduced 1998.
Price: **$785.00**

SMITH & WESSON MODEL 340 PD AIRLITE Sc CENTENNIAL
Caliber: 357 Magnum, 38 Spec. +P, 5-shot. **Barrel:** 1-7/8". **Grips:** Rounded butt grip. **Sights:** HiViz front. **Features:** Synthetic grip, internal lock. Blue.
Price: **$799.00**

HANDGUNS

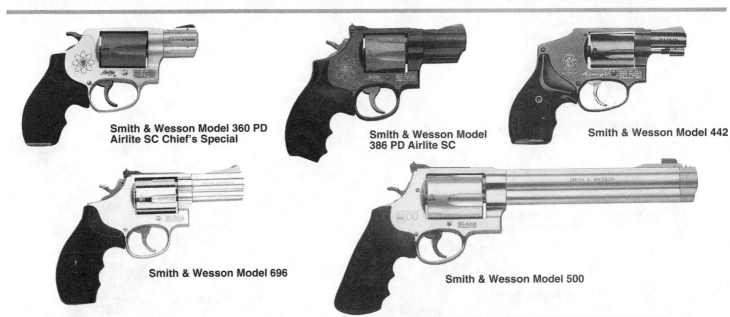

Smith & Wesson Model 360 PD Airlite SC Chief's Special

Smith & Wesson Model 386 PD Airlite SC

Smith & Wesson Model 442

Smith & Wesson Model 696

Smith & Wesson Model 500

SMITH & WESSON MODEL 360 PD AIRLITE Sc CHIEF'S SPECIAL

Caliber: 357 Magnum, 38 Spec. +P, 5-shot. **Barrel:** 1-7/8". **Grips:** Rounded butt grip. **Sights:** Fixed. **Features:** Synthetic grip, internal lock. Stainless.
Price: Red ramp front $767.00
Price: HiViz front $781.00

SMITH & WESSON MODEL 386 PD AIRLITE Sc

Caliber: 357 Magnum, 38 Spec. +P, 7-shot. **Barrel:** 2-1/2". **Grips:** Rounded butt grip. **Sights:** Adjustable, HiViz front. **Features:** Synthetic grip, internal lock.
Price: Blue $815.00

SMITH & WESSON MODEL 331, 332 AIRLITE Ti REVOLVERS

Caliber: 32 H&R Mag., 6-shot. **Barrel:** 1-7/8". **Weight:** 11.2 oz. (with wood grip). **Length:** 6-15/16" overall. **Grips:** Uncle Mike's Boot or Dymondwood Boot. **Sights:** Black serrated ramp front, fixed notch rear. **Features:** Aluminum alloy frame, barrel shroud and yoke; titanium cylinder; stainless steel barrel liner. Matte finish. Introduced 1999. Made in U.S.A. by Smith & Wesson.
Price: Model 331 Chiefs $716.00
Price: Model 332, internal lock $734.00

SMITH & WESSON MODEL 337 CHIEF'S SPECIAL AIRLITE Ti

Caliber: 38 Spec. +P, 5-shot. **Barrel:** 1-7/8". **Weight:** 11.2 oz. (Dymondwood grips). **Length:** 6-5/16" overall. **Grips:** Uncle Mike's Boot or Dymondwood Boot. **Sights:** Black serrated front, fixed notch rear. **Features:** Aluminum alloy frame, barrel shroud and yoke; titanium cylinder; stainless steel barrel liner. Matte finish. Introduced 1999. Made in U.S.A. by Smith & Wesson.
Price: $716.00

SMITH & WESSON MODEL 342 CENTENNIAL AIRLITE Ti

Caliber: 38 Spec. +P, 5-shot. **Barrel:** 1-7/8". **Weight:** 11.3 oz. (Dymondwood stocks). **Length:** 6-15/16" overall. **Grips:** Uncle Mike's Boot or Dymondwood Boot. **Sights:** Black serrated ramp front, fixed notch rear. **Features:** Aluminum alloy frame, barrel shroud and yoke; titanium cylinder; stainless steel barrel liner. Shrouded hammer. Matte finish. Internal lock. Introduced 1999. Made in U.S.A. by Smith & Wesson.
Price: $734.00

Smith & Wesson Model 442 Centennial Airweight

Similar to Model 640 Centennial, alloy frame giving weighs 15.8 oz. Chambered for 38 Special +P, 1-7/8" carbon steel barrel; carbon steel cylinder; concealed hammer; Uncle Mike's Boot grip. Fixed square notch rear sight, serrated ramp front. DA only, glass beaded finish. Introduced 1993.
Price: Blue $547.00

SMITH & WESSON MODEL 638 AIRWEIGHT BODYGUARD

Caliber: 38 Spec. +P, 5-shot. **Barrel:** 1-7/8". **Weight:** 15 oz. **Length:** 6-15/16" overall. **Grips:** Uncle Mike's Boot grip. **Sights:** Serrated ramp front, fixed notch rear. **Features:** Alloy frame, stainless cylinder and barrel; shrouded hammer. Glass beaded finish. Introduced 1997. Made in U.S.A. by Smith & Wesson.
Price: With Uncle Mike's Boot grip $564.00

Smith & Wesson Model 642 Airweight Revolver

Similar to Model 442 Centennial Airweight, stainless steel barrel, cylinder and yoke with matte finish; Uncle Mike's Boot Grip; DA only; weighs 15.8 oz. Introduced 1996. Made in U.S.A. by Smith & Wesson.
Price: $571.00

Smith & Wesson Model 642LS LadySmith Revolver

Same as Model 642 except has smooth combat wood grips, comes with deluxe soft case; Dymondwood grip; aluminum alloy frame, stainless cylinder, barrel and yoke; frosted matte finish. Weighs 15.8 oz. Introduced 1996. Made in U.S.A. by Smith & Wesson.
Price: 1-7/8" $597.00

SMITH & WESSON MODEL 649 BODYGUARD REVOLVER

Caliber: 357 Mag., 38 Spec. +P, 5-shot. **Barrel:** 2-1/8". **Weight:** 20 oz. **Length:** 6-5/16" overall. **Grips:** Uncle Mike's Combat. **Sights:** Black pinned ramp front, fixed notch rear. **Features:** Stainless steel construction; shrouded hammer; smooth combat trigger. Internal lock. Made in U.S.A. by Smith & Wesson.
Price: $594.00

SMITH & WESSON MODEL 657 REVOLVER

Caliber: 41 Mag., 6-shot. **Barrel:** 7-1/2" full lug. **Weight:** 48 oz. **Grips:** Soft rubber. **Sights:** Pinned 1/8" red ramp front, micro-click rear adjustable for windage and elevation. Target hammer, drilled and tapped, unfluted cylinder. **Features:** Stainless steel construction.
Price: $706.00

SMITH & WESSON MODEL 696 REVOLVER

Caliber: 44 Spec., 5-shot. **Barrel:** 3". **Weight:** 35.5 oz. **Length:** 8-1/4" overall. **Grips:** Uncle Mike's Combat. **Sights:** Red ramp front, click adjustable white outline rear. **Features:** Stainless steel construction; round butt frame; satin finish. Introduced 1997. Made in U.S.A. by Smith & Wesson.
Price: $620.00

SMITH & WESSON MODEL 500

Caliber: 50. **Barrel:** 8-3/8". **Weight:** 72.5 oz. **Length:** NA. **Grips:** Rubber. **Sights:** Interchangeable blade, front, adjustable rear. **Features:** Built on the massive, new X-Frame, recoil compensator, ball detent cylinder latch. Made in U.S.A. by Smith & Wesson.
Price: . . . . NA

Taurus Model 82

Taurus Model 85

Taurus Model 94 UL

Taurus Model 22H Raging Hornet

Taurus Model 44

TAURUS SILHOUETTE REVOLVERS

Available in calibers from 22 LR through 454 Casull, the common trait is a 12" vent rib barrel. An optional arm support that wraps around the forearm is available.
Price: . . . . **$414.00 to $859.00**

TAURUS MODEL 17 "TRACKER"

Caliber: 17 HMR, 7-shot. **Barrel:** 6-1/2". **Weight:** 45.8 oz. **Grips:** Rubber. **Sights:** Adjustable. **Features:** Double action, matte stainless, integral key-lock.
Price: . . . . **$430.00 to $438.00**

TAURUS MODEL 17-12 TARGET "SILHOUETTE"

Caliber: 17 HMR, 7-shot. **Barrel:** 12". **Weight:** 57.8 oz. **Grips:** Rubber. **Sights:** Adjustable. **Features:** Vent rib, double action, adjustable main spring and trigger stop. Matte stainless, integral key-lock.
Price: **$430.00**

Taurus Model 17-C Series

Similar to the Models 17 Tracker and Silhouette series but 8-shot cylinder, 2", 4" or 5" barrel, blue or stainless finish and regular (24 oz.) or UltraLite (18.5 oz.) versions available. All models have target crown for enhanced accuracy.
Price: . . . . **$359.00 to $391.00**

TAURUS MODEL 63

Caliber: 22 LR, 10 + 1 shot. **Barrel:** 23". **Weight:** 97.9 oz. **Grips:** Premium hardwood. **Sights:** Adjustable. **Features:** Auto loading action, round barrel, manual firing pin block, integral security system lock, trigger guard mounted safety, blue or stainless finish.
Price: . . . . **$295.00 to $310.00**

TAURUS MODEL 65 REVOLVER

Caliber: 357 Mag., 6-shot. **Barrel:** 4". **Weight:** 38 oz. **Length:** 10-1/2" overall. **Grips:** Soft rubber. **Sights:** Fixed. **Features:** Double action, integral key-lock. Imported by Taurus International.
Price: Blue or matte stainless . . . . **$375.00 to $422.00**

Taurus Model 66 Revolver

Similar to Model 65, 4" or 6" barrel, 7-shot cylinder, adjustable rear sight. Integral key-lock action. Imported by Taurus International.
Price: Blue or matte stainless . . . . **$422.00 to $469.00**

Taurus Model 66 Silhouette Revolver

Similar to Model 6, 12" barrel, 7-shot cylinder, adjustable sight. Integral key-lock action, blue or matte stainless steel finish, rubber grips. Introduced 2001. Imported by Taurus International.
Price: . . . . **$414.00 to $461.00**

TAURUS MODEL 82 HEAVY BARREL REVOLVER

Caliber: 38 Spec., 6-shot. **Barrel:** 4", heavy. **Weight:** 36.5 oz. **Length:** 9-1/4" overall (4" bbl.). **Grips:** Soft black rubber. **Sights:** Serrated ramp front, square notch rear. **Features:** Double action, solid rib, integral key-lock. Imported by Taurus International.
Price: Blue or matte stainless . . . . **$352.00 to $398.00**

TAURUS MODEL 85 REVOLVER

Caliber: 38 Spec., 5-shot. **Barrel:** 2". **Weight:** 17-24.5 oz., titanium 13.5-15.4 oz. **Grips:** Rubber, rosewood or mother-of-pearl. **Sights:** Ramp front, square notch rear. **Features:** Blue, matte stainless, blue with gold accents, stainless with gold accents; rated for +P ammo. Integral key-lock. Introduced 1980. Imported by Taurus International.
Price: . . . . **$375.00 to $547.00**
Price: Total Titanium **$531.00**

TAURUS MODEL 94 REVOLVER

Caliber: 22 LR, 9-shot cylinder. **Barrel:** 2", 4", 5". **Weight:** 18.5-27.5 oz. **Grips:** Soft black rubber. **Sights:** Serrated ramp front, click-adjustable rear. **Features:** Double action, integral key-lock. Introduced 1989. Imported by Taurus International.
Price: Blue **$325.00**
Price: Matte stainless **$375.00**
Price: Model 94 UL, forged aluminum alloy, 18-18.5 oz. **$365.00**
Price: As above, stainless. **$410.00**

TAURUS MODEL 22H RAGING HORNET REVOLVER

Caliber: 22 Hornet, 8-shot. **Barrel:** 10". **Weight:** 50 oz. **Length:** 6.5" overall. **Grips:** Soft black rubber. **Sights:** Fully adjustable, scope mount base included. **Features:** Ventilated rib, stainless steel construction with matte finish. Double action, integral key-lock. Introduced 1999. Imported by Taurus International.
Price: **$898.00**

TAURUS MODEL 30C RAGING THIRTY

Caliber: 30 carbine, 8-shot. **Barrel:** 10". **Weight:** 72.3 oz. **Grips:** Soft black rubber. **Sights:** Adjustable. **Features:** Double action, ventilated rib, matte stainless, comes with five "Stellar" full-moon clips, integral key-lock.
Price: **$898.00**

TAURUS MODEL 44 REVOLVER

Caliber: 44 Mag., 6-shot. **Barrel:** 4", 6-1/2", 8-3/8". **Weight:** 44-3/4 oz. **Grips:** Rubber. **Sights:** Adjustable. **Features:** Double action. Integral key-lock. Introduced 1994. New Model 44S12 has 12" vent rib barrel. Imported from Brazil by Taurus International Manufacturing, Inc.
Price: Blue or stainless steel . . . . **$445.00 to $602.00**

Taurus Model 415

Taurus Model 608

Taurus Model 450

HANDGUNS

TAURUS MODEL 217 TARGET "SILHOUETTE"

Caliber: 218 Bee, 8-shot. **Barrel:** 12". **Weight:** 52.3 oz. **Grips:** Rubber. **Sights:** Adjustable. **Features:** Double action, ventilated rib, adjustable mainspring and trigger stop, matte stainless, integral key-lock.
Price: **$461.00**

TAURUS MODEL 218 RAGING BEE

Caliber: 218 Bee, 7-shot. **Barrel:** 10". **Weight:** 74.9 oz. **Grips:** Rubber. **Sights:** Adjustable rear. **Features:** Ventilated rib, adjustable action, matte stainless, integral key-lock. Also Available as Model 218SS6 Tracker with 6-1/2" vent rib barrel.
Price: . . . . (Raging Bee) **$898.00**
Price: . . . . (Tracker) **$406.00**

TAURUS MODEL 415 REVOLVER

Caliber: 41 Mag., 5-shot. **Barrel:** 2-1/2". **Weight:** 30 oz. **Length:** 7-1/8" overall. **Grips:** Rubber. **Sights:** Fixed. **Features:** Stainless steel construction; matte finish; ported barrel. Double action. Integral key-lock. Introduced 1999. Imported by Taurus International.
Price: **$508.00**
Price: Total Titanium **$602.00**

TAURUS MODEL 425/627 TRACKER REVOLVERS

Caliber: 357 Mag., 7-shot; 41 Mag., 5-shot. **Barrel:** 4" and 6". **Weight:** 28.8-40 oz. (titanium) 24.3-28. (6"). **Grips:** Rubber. **Sights:** Fixed front, adjustable rear. **Features:** Double action stainless steel, Shadow Gray or Total Titanium; vent rib (steel models only); integral key-lock action. Imported by Taurus International.
Price: . . . . **$508.00 to $516.00**
Price: Total Titanium **$688.00**

TAURUS MODEL 445

Caliber: 44 Special, 5-shot. **Barrel:** 2". **Weight:** 20.3-28.25 oz. **Length:** 6-3/4" overall. **Grips:** Rubber. **Sights:** Ramp front, notch rear. **Features:** Blue or stainless steel. Standard or DAO concealed hammer, optional porting. Introduced 1997. Imported by Taurus International.
Price: . . . . **$345.00 to $500.00**
Price: Total Titanium 19.8 oz. **$600.00**

TAURUS MODEL 455 "STELLAR TRACKER"

Caliber: 45 ACP, 5-shot. **Barrel:** 2", 4", 6". **Weight:** 28/33/38.4 oz. **Grips:** Rubber. **Sights:** Adjustable. **Features:** Double action, matte stainless, includes five "Stellar" full-moon clips, integral key-lock.
Price: **$523.00**

TAURUS MODEL 460 "TRACKER"

Caliber: 45 Colt, 5-shot. **Barrel:** 4" or 6". **Weight:** 33/38.4 oz. **Grips:** Rubber. **Sights:** Adjustable. **Features:** Double action, ventilated rib, matte stainless steel, comes with five "Stellar" full-moon clips.
Price: **$516.00**
Price: . . . . (Shadow gray, Total Titanium) **$688.00**

TAURUS MODEL 605 REVOLVER

Caliber: 357 Mag., 5-shot. **Barrel:** 2". **Weight:** 24 oz. **Grips:** Rubber. **Sights:** Fixed. **Features:** Double action, blue or stainless, concealed hammer models DAO, porting optional, integral key-lock. Introduced 1995. Imported by Taurus International.
Price: . . . . **$375.00 to $438.00**

Taurus Model 731 Revolver

Similar to the Taurus Model 605, except in 32 Magnum.
Price: . . . . **$438.00 to $531.00**

Taurus Model 454 Raging Bull

TAURUS MODEL 608 REVOLVER

Caliber: 357 Mag. 38 Spec., 8-shot. **Barrel:** 4", 6-1/2", 8-3/8". **Weight:** 44-57 oz. **Length:** 9-3/8" overall. **Grips:** Soft black rubber. **Sights:** Adjustable. **Features:** Double action, integral key-lock action. Available in blue or stainless. Introduced 1995. Imported by Taurus International.
Price: . . . . **$469.00 to $547.00**

Taurus Model 44 Series Revolver

Similar to Taurus Model 60 series, but in 44 Rem. Mag. With six-shot cylinder, blue and matte stainless finishes.
Price: . . . . **$500.00 to $578.00**

TAURUS MODEL 650CIA REVOLVER

Caliber: 357 Magnum, 5-shot. **Barrel:** 2". **Weight:** 24.5 oz. **Grips:** Rubber. **Sights:** Ramp front, square notch rear. **Features:** Double-action only, blue or matte stainless steel, integral key-lock, internal hammer. Introduced 2001. From Taurus International.
Price: . . . . **$406.00 to $453.00**

TAURUS MODEL 651 CIA REVOLVER

Caliber: 357 Magnum, 5-shot. **Barrel:** 2". **Weight:** 17-24.5 oz. **Grips:** Rubber. **Sights:** Fixed. **Features:** Concealed single action/double action design. Shrouded cockable hammer, blue, matte stainless, Shadow Gray, Total Titanium, integral key-lock. Made in Brazil. Imported by Taurus International Manufacturing, Inc.
Price: . . . . **$406.00 to $578.00**

TAURUS MODEL 450 REVOLVER

Caliber: 45 Colt, 5-shot. **Barrel:** 2". **Weight:** 21.2-22.3 oz. **Length:** 6-5/8" overall. **Grips:** Rubber. **Sights:** Ramp front, notch rear. **Features:** Double action, blue or stainless, ported, integral key-lock. Introduced 1999. Imported from Brazil by Taurus International.
Price: **$492.00**
Price: Ultra-Lite (alloy frame) **$523.00**
Price: Total Titanium, 19.2 oz. **$600.00**

TAURUS MODEL 444/454/480 RAGING BULL REVOLVERS

Caliber: 44 Mag., 45 LC, 454 Casull, 480 Ruger, 5-shot. **Barrel:** 5", 6-1/2", 8-3/8". **Weight:** 53-63 oz. **Length:** 12" overall (6-1/2" barrel). **Grips:** Soft black rubber. **Sights:** Patridge front, adjustable rear. **Features:** Double action, ventilated rib, ported, integral key-lock. Introduced 1997. Imported by Taurus International.
Price: Blue . . . . **$578.00 to $797.00**
Price: Matte stainless . . . . **$641.00 to $859.00**

Taurus Raging Bull Model 416

Taurus Model 970 Tracker

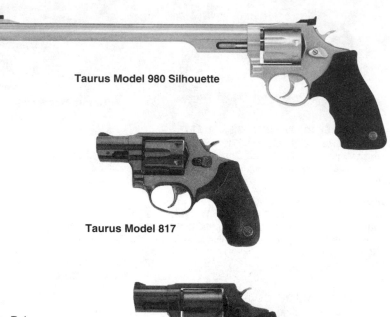

Taurus Model 980 Silhouette

Taurus Model 817

Taurus Model 905

TAURUS RAGING BULL MODEL 416

Caliber: 41 Magnum, 6-shot. **Barrel:** 6-1/2". **Weight:** 61.9 oz. **Grips:** Rubber. **Sights:** Adjustable. **Features:** Double action, ported, ventilated rib, matte stainless, integral key-lock.
Price: $641.00

TAURUS MODEL 617 REVOLVER

Caliber: 357 Magnum, 7-shot. **Barrel:** 2". **Weight:** 28.3 oz. **Length:** 6-3/4" overall. **Grips:** Soft black rubber. **Sights:** Fixed. **Features:** Double action, blue, shadow gray, bright spectrum blue or matte stainless steel, integral key-lock. Available with porting, concealed hammer. Introduced 1998. Imported by Taurus International.
Price: . . . . $391.00 to $453.00
Price: Total Titanium, 19.9 oz. $602.00

Taurus Model 445 Series Revolver

Similar to Taurus Model 617 series except in 44 Spl. with 5-shot cylinder.
Price: . . . . $389.00 to $422.00

Taurus Model 617ULT Revolver

Similar to Model 617 except aluminum alloy and titanium components, matte stainless finish, integral key-lock action. Weighs 18.5 oz. Available ported or non-ported. Introduced 2001. Imported by Taurus International.
Price: (5-shot cylinder) . . . . $530.00 to $545.00

TAURUS MODEL 817 ULTRA-LITE REVOLVER

Caliber: 38 Spec., 7-shot. **Barrel:** 2". **Weight:** 21 oz. **Length:** 6-1/2" overall. **Grips:** Soft rubber. **Sights:** Fixed. **Features:** Double action, integral key-lock. Rated for +P ammo. Introduced 1999. Imported from Brazil by Taurus International.
Price: Blue $375.00
Price: Blue, ported $395.00
Price: Matte, stainless. $420.00
Price: Matte, stainless, ported $440.00

TAURUS MODEL 850CIA REVOLVER

Caliber: 38 Special, 5-shot. **Barrel:** 2". **Weight:** 17-24.5 oz. **Grips:** Rubber. **Sights:** Ramp front, square notch rear. **Features:** Double action only, blue or matte stainless steel, rated for +P ammo, integral key-lock, internal hammer. Introduced 2001. From Taurus International.
Price: . . . . $406.00 to $453.00
Price: Total Titanium $578.00

TAURUS MODEL 851CIA REVOLVER

Caliber: 38 Spec., 5-shot. **Barrel:** 2". **Weight:** 17-24.5 oz. **Grips:** Rubber. **Sights:** Fixed-UL/ULT adjustable. **Features:** Concealed single action/double action design. Shrouded cockable hammer, blue, matte

stainless, Total Titanium, blue or stainless UL and ULT, integral key-lock. Rated for +P ammo.
Price: . . . . $406.00 to $578.00

TAURUS MODEL 94, 941 REVOLVER

Caliber: 22 LR (Mod. 94), 22 WMR (Mod. 941), 8-shot. **Barrel:** 2", 4", 5". **Weight:** 27.5 oz. (4" barrel). **Grips:** Soft black rubber. **Sights:** Serrated ramp front, rear adjustable. **Features:** Double action, integral key-lock. Introduced 1992. Imported by Taurus International.
Price: Blue . . . . $328.00 to $344.00
Price: Stainless (matte) . . . . $375.00 to $391.00
Price: Model 941 Ultra Lite,
forged aluminum alloy, 2" . . . . $359.00 to $375.00
Price: As above, stainless. . . . . $406.00 to $422.00

TAURUS MODEL 970/971 TRACKER REVOLVERS

Caliber: 22 LR (Model 970), 22 Magnum (Model 971); 7-shot. **Barrel:** 6". **Weight:** 53.6 oz. **Grips:** Rubber. **Sights:** Adjustable. **Features:** Double barrel, heavy barrel with ventilated rib; matte stainless finish, integral key-lock. Introduced 2001. From Taurus International.
Price: . . . . $391.00 to $406.00

TAURUS MODEL 980/981 SILHOUETTE REVOLVERS

Caliber: 22 LR (Model 980), 22 Magnum (Model 981); 7-shot. **Barrel:** 12". **Weight:** 68 oz. **Grips:** Rubber. **Sights:** Adjustable. **Features:** Double action, heavy barrel with ventilated rib and scope mount, matte stainless finish, integral key-lock. Introduced 2001. From Taurus International.
Price: (Model 980) $398.00
Price: (Model 981) $414.00

TAURUS MODEL 905, 405, 455 PISTOL CALIBER REVOLVERS

Caliber: 9mm, 40, 45 ACP, 5-shot. **Barrel:** 2", 4", 6-1/2". **Weight:** 21 oz. to 40.8 oz. **Grips:** Rubber. **Sights:** Fixed, adjustable on Model 455SS6 in 45 ACP. **Features:** Produced as a backup gun for law enforcement officers who desire to carry the same caliber ammunition in their back-up revolver as they do in their service sidearm. Introduced 2003. Imported from Brazil by Taurus International Manufacturing, Inc.
Price: . . . . $383.00 to $523.00

Both classic six-shooters and modern adaptations for hunting and sport.

Century Model 100

Cimarron Lightning

Cimarron Model P

Cimarron Model P
New Sheriff

Cimarron Bisley

Cimarron Roughrider

CABELA'S MILLENNIUM REVOLVER
Caliber: 45 Colt. **Barrel:** 4-3/4". **Weight:** NA. **Length:** 10" overall. **Grips:** Hardwood. **Sights:** Blade front, hammer notch rear. **Features:** Matte black finish; unpolished brass accents. Introduced 2001. From Cabela's.
Price: **$229.99**

CENTURY GUN DIST. MODEL 100 SINGLE-ACTION
Caliber: 30-30, 375 Win., 444 Marlin, 45-70, 50-70. **Barrel:** 6-1/2" (standard), 8", 10". **Weight:** 6 lbs. (loaded). **Length:** 15" overall (8" bbl.). **Grips:** Smooth walnut. **Sights:** Ramp front, Millett adjustable square notch rear. **Features:** Highly polished high tensile strength manganese bronze frame, blue cylinder and barrel; coil spring trigger mechanism. Contact maker for full price information. Introduced 1975. Made in U.S.A. From Century Gun Dist., Inc.
Price: 6-1/2" barrel, 45-70. . . . . **$2,000.00**

CIMARRON LIGHTNING SA
Caliber: 38 Colt, 38 Special. **Barrel:** 3-1/2", 4-3/4", 5-1/2". **Grips:** Smooth or checkered walnut. **Sights:** Blade front. **Features:** Replica of the Colt 1877 Lightning DA. Similar to Cimarron Thunderer™, except smaller grip frame to fit smaller hands. Standard blue, charcoal blue or nickel finish with forged, old model, or color case hardened frame. Introduced 2001. From Cimarron F.A. Co.
Price: . . . . **$489.00 to $554.00**

CIMARRON MODEL P
Caliber: 32 WCF, 38 WCF, 357 Mag., 44 WCF, 44 Spec., 45 Colt. **Barrel:** 4-3/4", 5-1/2", 7-1/2". **Weight:** 39 oz. **Length:** 10" overall (4" barrel). **Grips:** Walnut. **Sights:** Blade front, fixed or adjustable rear. **Features:** Uses "old model" blackpowder frame with "Bullseye" ejector or New Model frame. Imported by Cimarron F.A. Co.
Price: . . . . **$499.00 to $549.00**
Price: New Sheriff . . . . **$499.00 to $564.00**

Cimarron Bisley Model Single-Action Revolvers
Similar to 1873 Model P, special grip frame and trigger guard, knurled wide-spur hammer, curved trigger. Available in 357 Mag., 44 WCF, 44 Spl., 45 Colt. Introduced 1999. Imported by Cimarron F.A. Co.
Price: **$519.00**

Cimarron Flat Top Single-Action Revolvers
Similar to 1873 Model P, flat top strap with windage-adjustable rear sight, elevation-adjustable front sight. Available in 44 WCF, 45 Colt; 7-1/2" barrel. Introduced 1999. Imported by Cimarron F.A. Co.
Price: **$519.00**

CIMARRON MODEL "P" JR.
Caliber: 38 Special. **Barrel:** 3-1/2", 4-3/4", 5-1/2". **Grips:** Checkered walnut. **Sights:** Blade front. **Features:** Styled after 1873 Colt Peacemaker, except 20 percent smaller. Blue finish with color-case hardened frame; Cowboy Comp® action. Introduced 2001. From Cimarron F.A. Co.
Price: . . . . **$419.00 to $479.00**

CIMARRON ROUGHRIDER ARTILLERY MODEL SINGLE-ACTION
Caliber: 45 Colt. **Barrel:** 5-1/2". **Weight:** 39 oz. **Length:** 11-1/2" overall. **Grips:** Walnut. **Sights:** Fixed. **Features:** U.S. markings and cartouche, case-hardened frame and hammer; 45 Colt only. Imported by Cimarron F.A. Co.
Price: . . . . **$549.00 to $599.00**

HANDGUNS

Cimarron Thunderer

Colt Cowboy

Colt Single-Action Army

EMF Hartford

EAA Bounty Hunter

EMF 1894 Bisley

CIMARRON 1872 OPEN TOP REVOLVER
Caliber: 38, 44 Special, 45 S&W Schofield. **Barrel:** 5-1/2" and 7-1/2". **Grips:** Walnut. **Sights:** Blade front, fixed rear. **Features:** Replica of first cartridge-firing revolver. Blue, charcoal blue, nickel or Original® finish; Navy-style brass or steel Army-style frame. Introduced 2001 by Cimarron F.A. Co.
Price: .... **$529.00 to $599.00**

CIMARRON THUNDERER REVOLVER
Caliber: 357 Mag., 44 WCF, 44 Spl, 45 Colt, 6-shot. **Barrel:** 3-1/2", 4-3/4", 5-1/2", 7-1/2", with ejector. **Weight:** 38 oz. (3-1/2" barrel). **Grips:** Smooth walnut. **Sights:** Blade front, notch rear. **Features:** Thunderer grip; color case-hardened frame with balance blued. Introduced 1993. Imported by Cimarron F.A. Co.
Price: 3-1/2", 4-3/4", smooth grips .... **$519.00 to $549.00**
Price: As above, checkered grips .... **$564.00 to $584.00**
Price: 5-1/2", 7-1/2", smooth grips .... **$519.00 to $549.00**
Price: As above, checkered grips .... **$564.00 to $584.00**

COLT COWBOY SINGLE-ACTION REVOLVER
Caliber: 45 Colt, 6-shot. **Barrel:** 5-1/2". **Weight:** 42 oz. **Grips:** Black composition, first generation style. **Sights:** Blade front, notch rear. **Features:** Dimensional replica of Colt's original Peacemaker with medium-size color case-hardened frame; transfer bar safety system; half-cock loading. Introduced 1998. From Colt's Mfg. Co.
Price: About **$670.00**

COLT SINGLE-ACTION ARMY REVOLVER
Caliber: 44-40, 45 Colt, 6-shot. **Barrel:** 4-3/4", 5-1/2", 7-1/2". **Weight:** 40 oz. (4-3/4" barrel). **Length:** 10-1/4" overall (4-3/4" barrel). **Grips:** Black Eagle composite. **Sights:** Blade front, notch rear. **Features:** Available in full nickel finish with nickel grip medallions, or Royal Blue with color case-hardened frame, gold grip medallions. Reintroduced 1992.
Price: **$1,380.00**

EAA BOUNTY HUNTER SA REVOLVERS
Caliber: 22 LR/22 WMR, 357 Mag., 44 Mag., 45 Colt, 6-shot. **Barrel:** 4-1/2", 7-1/2". **Weight:** 2.5 lbs. **Length:** 11" overall (4-5/8" barrel). **Grips:** Smooth walnut. **Sights:** Blade front, grooved topstrap rear. **Features:** Transfer bar safety; three position hammer; hammer forged barrel. Introduced 1992. Imported by European American Armory.

Price: Blue or case-hardened **$369.00**
Price: Nickel **$399.00**
Price: 22LR/22WMR, blue **$269.00**
Price: As above, nickel **$299.00**

EMF HARTFORD SINGLE-ACTION REVOLVERS
Caliber: 357 Mag., 32-20, 38-40, 44-40, 44 Spec., 45 Colt. **Barrel:** 4-3/4", 5-1/2", 7-1/2". **Weight:** 45 oz. **Length:** 13" overall (7-1/2" barrel). **Grips:** Smooth walnut. **Sights:** Blade front, fixed rear. **Features:** Identical to the original Colts with inspector cartouche on left grip, original patent dates and U.S. markings. All major parts serial numbered using original Colt-style lettering, numbering. Bullseye ejector head and color case-hardening on frame and hammer. Introduced 1990. From E.M.F.
Price: **$500.00**
Price: Cavalry or Artillery **$390.00**
Price: Nickel plated, add **$125.00**
Price: Casehardened New Model frame **$365.00**

EMF 1894 Bisley Revolver
Similar to the Hartford single-action revolver except has special grip frame and trigger guard, wide spur hammer; available in 38-40 or 45 Colt, 4-3/4", 5-1/2" or 7-1/2" barrel. Introduced 1995. Imported by E.M.F.
Price: Casehardened/blue **$400.00**
Price: Nickel **$525.00**

EMF Hartford Pinkerton Single-Action Revolver
Same as the regular Hartford except has 4" barrel with ejector tube and birds head grip. Calibers: 357 Mag., 45 Colt. Introduced 1997. Imported by E.M.F.
Price: **$375.00**

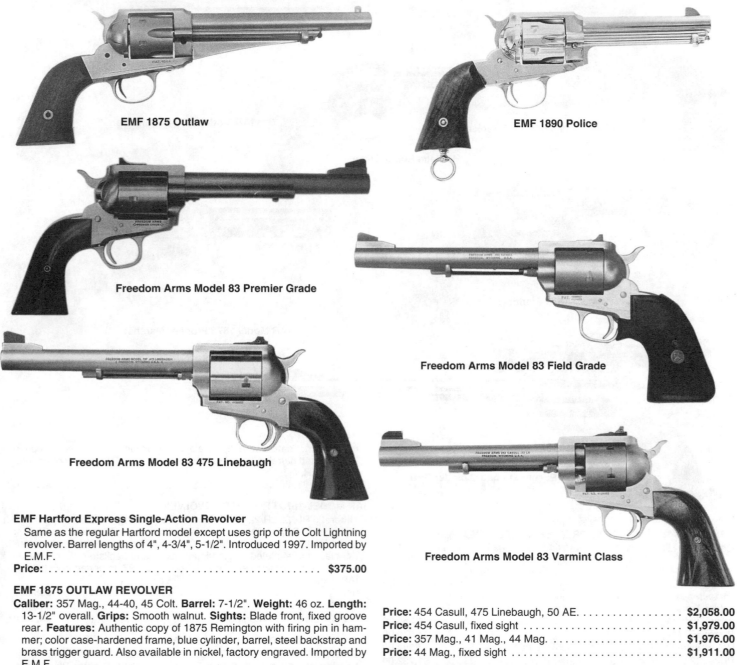

EMF 1875 Outlaw

EMF 1890 Police

Freedom Arms Model 83 Premier Grade

Freedom Arms Model 83 Field Grade

Freedom Arms Model 83 475 Linebaugh

Freedom Arms Model 83 Varmint Class

EMF Hartford Express Single-Action Revolver

Same as the regular Hartford model except uses grip of the Colt Lightning revolver. Barrel lengths of 4", 4-3/4", 5-1/2". Introduced 1997. Imported by E.M.F.

Price: **$375.00**

EMF 1875 OUTLAW REVOLVER

Caliber: 357 Mag., 44-40, 45 Colt. **Barrel:** 7-1/2". **Weight:** 46 oz. **Length:** 13-1/2" overall. **Grips:** Smooth walnut. **Sights:** Blade front, fixed groove rear. **Features:** Authentic copy of 1875 Remington with firing pin in hammer; color case-hardened frame, blue cylinder, barrel, steel backstrap and brass trigger guard. Also available in nickel, factory engraved. Imported by E.M.F.

Price: All calibers **$575.00**
Price: Nickel **$735.00**

EMF 1890 Police Revolver

Similar to the 1875 Outlaw except has 5-1/2" barrel, weighs 40 oz., with 12-1/2" overall length. Has lanyard ring in butt. No web under barrel. Calibers 357, 44-40, 45 Colt. Imported by E.M.F.

Price: All calibers **$590.00**
Price: Nickel **$750.00**

FREEDOM ARMS MODEL 83 PREMIER GRADE REVOLVER

Caliber: 357 Mag., 41 Mag., 44 Mag., 454 Casull, 475 Linebaugh, 50 AE, 5-shot. **Barrel:** 4-3/4", 6", 7-1/2", 9" (357 Mag. only), 10". **Weight:** 52.8 oz. **Length:** 13" (7-1/2" bbl.). **Grips:** Impregnated hardwood. **Sights:** Blade front, notch or adjustable rear. **Features:** All stainless steel construction; sliding bar safety system. Lifetime warranty. Made in U.S.A. by Freedom Arms, Inc.

Price: 454 Casull, 475 Linebaugh, 50 AE. **$2,058.00**
Price: 454 Casull, fixed sight **$1,979.00**
Price: 357 Mag., 41 Mag., 44 Mag. **$1,976.00**
Price: 44 Mag., fixed sight **$1,911.00**

Freedom Arms Model 83 Field Grade Revolver

Model 83 frame. Weighs 52-56 oz. Adjustable rear sight, replaceable front blade, matte finish, Pachmayr grips. All stainless steel. Introduced 1988. Made in U.S.A. by Freedom Arms Inc.

Price: 454 Casull, 475 Linebaugh, 50 AE, adj. sights. **$1,591.00**
Price: 454 Casull, fixed sights. **$1,553.00**
Price: 357 Mag., 41 Mag., 44 Mag. **$1,527.00**

FREEDOM ARMS MODEL 83 VARMINT CLASS REVOLVERS

Caliber: 22 LR, 5-shot. **Barrel:** 5-1/8, 7-1/2". **Weight:** 58 oz. (7-1/2" bbl.). **Length:** 11-1/2" (7-1/2" bbl.). **Grips:** Impregnated hardwood. **Sights:** Steel base adjustable "V" notch rear sight and replaceable brass bead front sight. **Features:** Stainless steel, matte finish, manual sliding-bar system, dual firing pins, pre-set trigger stop. One year limited warranty to original owner. Made in U.S.A. by Freedom Arms, Inc.

Price: Varmint Class **$1,828.00**
Price: Extra fitted 22 WMR cylinder **$264.00**

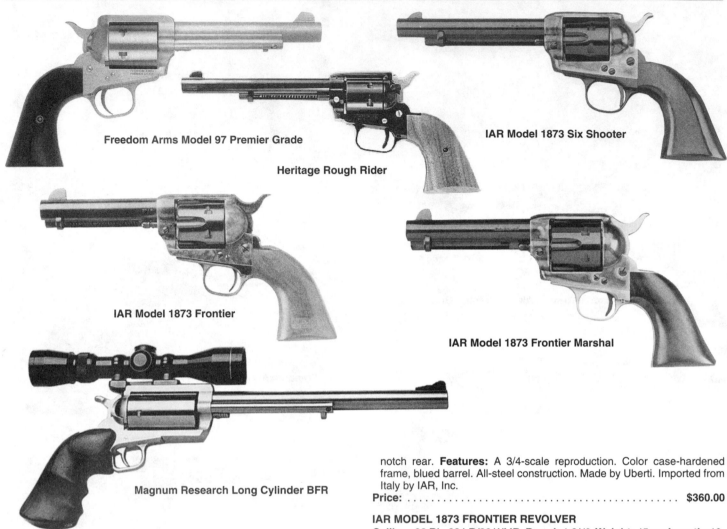

Freedom Arms Model 97 Premier Grade

Heritage Rough Rider

IAR Model 1873 Six Shooter

IAR Model 1873 Frontier

IAR Model 1873 Frontier Marshal

Magnum Research Long Cylinder BFR

FREEDOM ARMS MODEL 97 PREMIER GRADE REVOLVER
Caliber: 22 LR, 357 Mag., 41 Mag., 44 Special, 45 Colt, 5-shot. **Barrel:** 4-1/2", 5-1/2", 7-1/2", 10". **Weight:** 37 oz. (45 Colt 5-1/2"). **Length:** 10-3/4" (5-1/2" bbl.). **Grips:** Impregnated hardwood. **Sights:** Adjustable rear, replaceable blade front. **Features:** Stainless steel, brushed finish, automatic transfer bar safety system. Introduced in 1997. Made in U.S.A. by Freedom Arms.
Price: 357 Mag., 41 Mag., 45 Colt **$1,668.00**
Price: 357 Mag., 45 Colt, fixed sight **$1,576.00**
Price: Extra fitted cylinders 38 Special, 45 ACP **$264.00**
Price: 22 LR with sporting chambers **$1,732.00**
Price: Extra fitted 22 WMR cylinder **$264.00**
Price: Extra fitted 22 LR match grade cylinder **$476.00**
Price: 22 match grade chamber instead of 22 LR sport chamber
. . . . **$214.00**

HERITAGE ROUGH RIDER REVOLVER
Caliber: 22 LR, 22 LR/22 WMR combo, 6-shot. **Barrel:** 2-3/4", 3-1/2", 4-3/4", 6-1/2", 9". **Weight:** 31 to 38 oz. **Length:** NA. **Grips:** Exotic hardwood, laminated wood or mother of pearl; bird's head models offered. **Sights:** Blade front, fixed rear. Adjustable sight on 6-1/2" only. **Features:** Hammer block safety. High polish blue or nickel finish. Introduced 1993. Made in U.S.A. by Heritage Mfg., Inc.
Price: . . . . **$184.95 to $239.95**

IAR MODEL 1873 SIX SHOOTER
Caliber: 22 LR/22 WMR combo. **Barrel:** 5-1/2". **Weight:** 36-1/2" oz. **Length:** 11-3/8" overall. **Grips:** One-piece walnut. **Sights:** Blade front, notch rear. **Features:** A 3/4-scale reproduction. Color case-hardened frame, blued barrel. All-steel construction. Made by Uberti. Imported from Italy by IAR, Inc.
Price: **$360.00**

IAR MODEL 1873 FRONTIER REVOLVER
Caliber: 22 RL, 22 LR/22 WMR. **Barrel:** 4-3/4". **Weight:** 45 oz. **Length:** 10-1/2" overall. **Grips:** One-piece walnut with inspector's cartouche. **Sights:** Blade front, notch rear. **Features:** Color case-hardened frame, blued barrel, black nickel-plated brass trigger guard and backstrap. Bright nickel and engraved versions available. Introduced 1997. Imported from Italy by IAR, Inc.
Price: **$380.00**
Price: Nickel-plated. **$425.00**
Price: 22 LR/22WMR combo **$420.00**

IAR MODEL 1873 FRONTIER MARSHAL
Caliber: 357 Mag., 45 Colt. **Barrel:** 4-3/4", 5-1/2, 7-1/2". **Weight:** 39 oz. **Length:** 10-1/2" overall. **Grips:** One-piece walnut. **Sights:** Blade front, notch rear. **Features:** Bright brass trigger guard and backstrap, color case-hardened frame, blued barrel and cylinder. Introduced 1998. Imported from Italy by IAR, Inc.
Price: **$395.00**

MAGNUM RESEARCH BFR SINGLE-ACTION REVOLVER
(Long cylinder) Caliber: 45/70 Government, 444 Marlin, 45 LC/410, 450 Marlin, 500 S&W. **Barrel:** 7.5", 10". **Weight:** 4 lbs., 4.36 lbs. **Length:** 15", 17.5".
(Short cylinder) Caliber: 454 Casull, 22 Hornet, BFR 480/475. **Barrel:** 6.5", 7.5", 10". **Weight:** 3.2 lbs., 3.5 lbs., 4.36 lbs. (10"). **Length:** 12.75 (6"), 13.75", 16.25"
Sights: All have fully adjustable rear, black blade ramp front. **Features:** Stainless steel construction, rubber grips, all 5-shot capacity. Barrels are stress-relieved and cut rifled. Made in U.S.A. From Magnum Research, Inc.
Price: **$999.00**

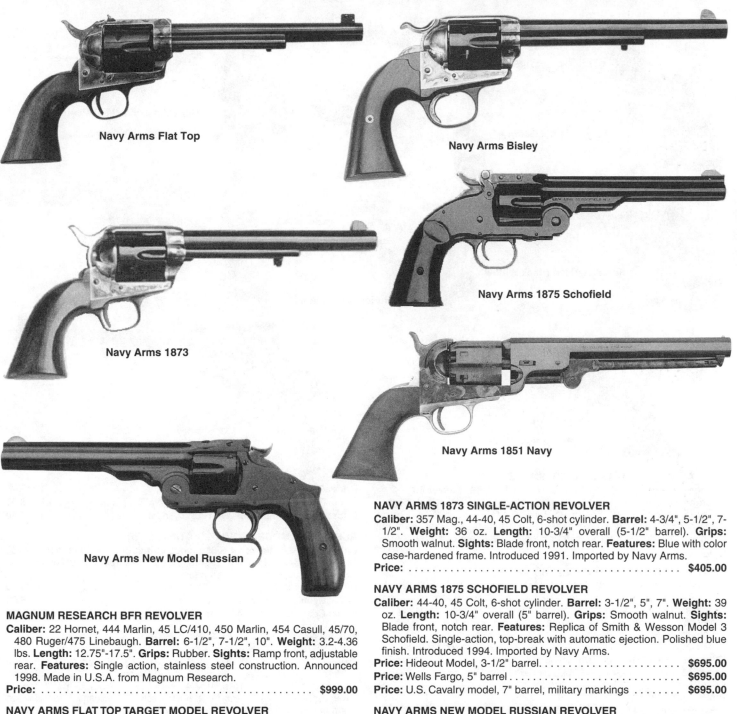

Navy Arms Flat Top

Navy Arms Bisley

Navy Arms 1875 Schofield

Navy Arms 1873

Navy Arms 1851 Navy

Navy Arms New Model Russian

MAGNUM RESEARCH BFR REVOLVER

Caliber: 22 Hornet, 444 Marlin, 45 LC/410, 450 Marlin, 454 Casull, 45/70, 480 Ruger/475 Linebaugh. **Barrel:** 6-1/2", 7-1/2", 10". **Weight:** 3.2-4.36 lbs. **Length:** 12.75"-17.5". **Grips:** Rubber. **Sights:** Ramp front, adjustable rear. **Features:** Single action, stainless steel construction. Announced 1998. Made in U.S.A. from Magnum Research.
Price: **$999.00**

NAVY ARMS FLAT TOP TARGET MODEL REVOLVER

Caliber: 45 Colt, 6-shot cylinder. **Barrel:** 7-1/2". **Weight:** 40 oz. **Length:** 13-1/4" overall. **Grips:** Smooth walnut. **Sights:** Spring-loaded German silver front, rear adjustable for windage. **Features:** Replica of Colt's Flat Top Frontier target revolver made from 1888 to 1896. Blue with color case-hardened frame. Introduced 1997. Imported by Navy Arms.
Price: **$450.00**

NAVY ARMS BISLEY MODEL SINGLE-ACTION REVOLVER

Caliber: 44-40 or 45 Colt, 6-shot cylinder. **Barrel:** 4-3/4", 5-1/2", 7-1/2". **Weight:** 40 oz. **Length:** 12-1/2" overall (7-1/2" barrel). **Grips:** Smooth walnut. **Sights:** Blade front, notch rear. **Features:** Replica of Colt's Bisley Model. Polished blue finish, color case-hardened frame. Introduced 1997. Imported by Navy Arms.
Price: . . . . **$425.00 to $460.00**

NAVY ARMS 1873 SINGLE-ACTION REVOLVER

Caliber: 357 Mag., 44-40, 45 Colt, 6-shot cylinder. **Barrel:** 4-3/4", 5-1/2", 7-1/2". **Weight:** 36 oz. **Length:** 10-3/4" overall (5-1/2" barrel). **Grips:** Smooth walnut. **Sights:** Blade front, notch rear. **Features:** Blue with color case-hardened frame. Introduced 1991. Imported by Navy Arms.
Price: **$405.00**

NAVY ARMS 1875 SCHOFIELD REVOLVER

Caliber: 44-40, 45 Colt, 6-shot cylinder. **Barrel:** 3-1/2", 5", 7". **Weight:** 39 oz. **Length:** 10-3/4" overall (5" barrel). **Grips:** Smooth walnut. **Sights:** Blade front, notch rear. **Features:** Replica of Smith & Wesson Model 3 Schofield. Single-action, top-break with automatic ejection. Polished blue finish. Introduced 1994. Imported by Navy Arms.
Price: Hideout Model, 3-1/2" barrel. **$695.00**
Price: Wells Fargo, 5" barrel **$695.00**
Price: U.S. Cavalry model, 7" barrel, military markings **$695.00**

NAVY ARMS NEW MODEL RUSSIAN REVOLVER

Caliber: 44 Russian, 6-shot cylinder. **Barrel:** 6-1/2". **Weight:** 40 oz. **Length:** 12" overall. **Grips:** Smooth walnut. **Sights:** Blade front, notch rear. **Features:** Replica of the S&W Model 3 Russian Third Model revolver. Spur trigger guard, polished blue finish. Introduced 1999. Imported by Navy Arms.
Price: **$769.00**

NAVY ARMS 1851 NAVY CONVERSION REVOLVER

Caliber: 38 Spec., 38 Long Colt. **Barrel:** 5-1/2", 7-1/2". **Weight:** 44 oz. **Length:** 14" overall (7-1/2" barrel). **Grips:** Smooth walnut. **Sights:** Bead front, notch rear. **Features:** Replica of Colt's cartridge conversion revolver. Polished blue finish with color case-hardened frame, silver plated trigger guard and backstrap. Introduced 1999. Imported by Navy Arms.
Price: **$165.00**

HANDGUNS

HANDGUNS — SINGLE ACTION REVOLVERS

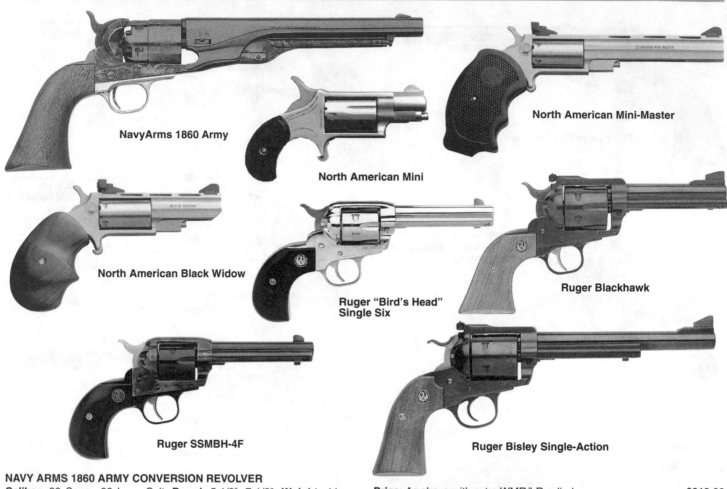

NavyArms 1860 Army

North American Mini

North American Mini-Master

North American Black Widow

Ruger "Bird's Head" Single Six

Ruger Blackhawk

Ruger SSMBH-4F

Ruger Bisley Single-Action

NAVY ARMS 1860 ARMY CONVERSION REVOLVER
Caliber: 38 Spec., 38 Long Colt. **Barrel:** 5-1/2", 7-1/2". **Weight:** 44 oz. **Length:** 13-1/2" overall (7-1/2" barrel). **Grips:** Smooth walnut. **Sights:** Blade front, notch rear. **Features:** Replica of Colt's conversion revolver. Polished blue finish with color case-hardened frame, full-size 1860 Army grip with blued steel backstrap. Introduced 1999. Imported by Navy Arms.
Price: **$190.00**

NORTH AMERICAN MINI REVOLVERS
Caliber: 22 Short, 22 LR, 22 WMR, 5-shot. **Barrel:** 1-1/8", 1-5/8". **Weight:** 4 to 6.6 oz. **Length:** 3-5/8" to 6-1/8" overall. **Grips:** Laminated wood. **Sights:** Blade front, notch fixed rear. **Features:** All stainless steel construction. Polished satin and matte finish. Engraved models available. From North American Arms.
Price: 22 Short, 22 LR . . . . **$186.00 to $221.00**
Price: 22 WMR, 1-1/8" or 1-5/8" bbl. **$205.00**
Price: 22 WMR, 1-1/8" or 1-5/8" bbl. with extra 22 LR cylinder. . . **$245.00**

NORTH AMERICAN MINI-MASTER
Caliber: 22 LR, 22 WMR, 17 HMR, 5-shot cylinder. **Barrel:** 4". **Weight:** 10.7 oz. **Length:** 7.75" overall. **Grips:** Checkered hard black rubber. **Sights:** Blade front, white outline rear adjustable for elevation, or fixed. **Features:** Heavy vent barrel; full-size grips. Non-fluted cylinder. Introduced 1989.
Price: Adjustable sight, 22 WMR, 17 HMR or 22 LR **$304.00**
Price: As above with extra WMR/LR cylinder **$343.00**
Price: Fixed sight, 22 WMR, 17 HMR or 22 LR **$286.00**
Price: As above with extra WMR/LR cylinder **$324.00**

North American Black Widow Revolver
Similar to Mini-Master, 2" heavy vent barrel. Built on 22 WMR frame. Non-fluted cylinder, black rubber grips. Available with Millett Low Profile fixed sights or Millett sight adjustable for elevation only. Overall length 5-7/8", weighs 8.8 oz. From North American Arms.
Price: Adjustable sight, 22 LR, 17 HMR or 22 WMR **$274.00**

Price: As above with extra WMR/LR cylinder **$312.00**
Price: Fixed sight, 22 LR, 17 HMR or 22 WMR **$256.00**
Price: As above with extra WMR/LR cylinder **$294.00**

RUGER NEW MODEL SINGLE SIX REVOLVER
Caliber: 32 H&R. **Barrel:** 4-5/8", 6-shot. **Grips:** Black Micarta "birds head", rosewood with color case. **Sights:** Fixed. **Features:** Instruction manual, high impact case, gun lock standard.
Price: Stainless, KSSMBH-4F, birds head **$576.00**
Price: Color case, SSMBH-4F, birds head **$576.00**
Price: Color case, SSM-4F-S, rosewood **$576.00**

RUGER NEW MODEL BLACKHAWK AND BLACKHAWK CONVERTIBLE
Caliber: 30 Carbine, 357 Mag./38 Spec., 41 Mag., 45 Colt, 6-shot. **Barrel:** 4-5/8" or 5-1/2", either caliber; 7-1/2" (30 Carbine and 45 Colt). **Weight:** 42 oz. (6-1/2" bbl.). **Length:** 12-1/4" overall (5-1/2" bbl.). **Grips:** American walnut. **Sights:** 1/8" ramp front, micro-click rear adjustable for windage and elevation. **Features:** Ruger transfer bar safety system, independent firing pin, hardened chrome-moly steel frame, music wire springs throughout. Case and lock included.
Price: Blue 30 Carbine, 7-1/2" (BN31) **$435.00**
Price: Blue, 357 Mag., 4-5/8", 6-1/2" (BN34, BN36) **$435.00**
Price: As above, stainless (KBN34, KBN36) **$530.00**
Price: Blue, 357 Mag./9mm Convertible, 4-5/8", 6-1/2" (BN34X, BN36X) includes extra cylinder **$489.00**
Price: Blue, 41 Mag., 4-5/8", 6-1/2" (BN41, BN42) **$435.00**
Price: Blue, 45 Colt, 4-5/8", 5-1/2", 7-1/2" (BN44, BN455, BN45) **$435.00**
Price: Stainless, 45 Colt, 4-5/8", 7-1/2" (KBN44, KBN45) **$530.00**
Price: Blue, 45 Colt/45 ACP Convertible, 4-5/8", 5-1/2" (BN44X, BN455X) includes extra cylinder **$489.00**

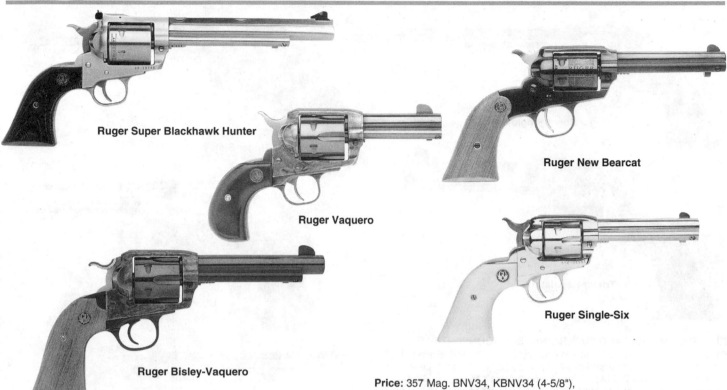

Ruger Super Blackhawk Hunter

Ruger Vaquero

Ruger New Bearcat

Ruger Single-Six

Ruger Bisley-Vaquero

Ruger Bisley Single-Action Revolver

Similar to standard Blackhawk, hammer is lower with smoothly curved, deeply checkered wide spur. The trigger is strongly curved with wide smooth surface. Longer grip frame has hand-filling shape. Adjustable rear sight, ramp-style front. Unfluted cylinder and roll engraving, adjustable sights. Chambered for 357, 44 Mags. and 45 Colt; 7-1/2" barrel; overall length of 13"; weighs 48 oz. Plastic lockable case. Introduced 1985.

Price: RB-35W, 357Mag, RBD-44W, 44Mag, RB-45W, 45 Colt . . **$535.00**

RUGER NEW MODEL SUPER BLACKHAWK

Caliber: 44 Mag., 6-shot. Also fires 44 Spec. **Barrel:** 4-5/8", 5-1/2", 7-1/2", 10-1/2" bull. **Weight:** 48 oz. (7-1/2" bbl.), 51 oz. (10-1/2" bbl.). **Length:** 13-3/8" overall (7-1/2" bbl.). **Grips:** American walnut. **Sights:** 1/8" ramp front, micro-click rear adjustable for windage and elevation. **Features:** Ruger transfer bar safety system, fluted or un-fluted cylinder, steel grip and cylinder frame, round or square back trigger guard, wide serrated trigger, wide spur hammer. With case and lock.

Price: Blue, 4-5/8", 5-1/2", 7-1/2" (S458N, S45N, S47N) **$519.00**
Price: Blue, 10-1/2" bull barrel (S411N) **$529.00**
Price: Stainless, 4-5/8", 5-1/2", 7-1/2" (KS458N, KS45N, KS47N) **$535.00**
Price: Stainless, 10-1/2" bull barrel (KS411N) **$545.00**

RUGER NEW MODEL SUPER BLACKHAWK HUNTER

Caliber: 44 Mag., 6-shot. **Barrel:** 7-1/2", full-length solid rib, unfluted cylinder. **Weight:** 52 oz. **Length:** 13-5/8". **Grips:** Black laminated wood. **Sights:** Adjustable rear, replaceable front blade. **Features:** Reintroduced Ultimate SA revolver. Includes instruction manual, high-impact case, set 1" medium scope rings, gun lock, ejector rod as standard.

Price: **$639.00**

RUGER VAQUERO SINGLE-ACTION REVOLVER

Caliber: 357 Mag., 44-40, 44 Mag., 45 LC, 6-shot. **Barrel:** 4-5/8", 5-1/2", 7-1/2". **Weight:** 38-41 oz. **Length:** 13-1/8" overall (7-1/2" barrel). **Grips:** Smooth rosewood with Ruger medallion. **Sights:** Blade front, fixed notch rear. **Features:** Uses Ruger's patented transfer bar safety system and loading gate interlock with classic styling. Blued model color case-hardened finish on frame, rest polished and blued. Stainless has high-gloss. Introduced 1993. From Sturm, Ruger & Co.

Price: 357 Mag. BNV34, KBNV34 (4-5/8"), BNV35, KBNV35 (5-1/2") **$535.00**
Price: 44-40 BNV40, KBNV40 (4-5/8"). BNV405, KBNV405 (5-1/2"). BNV407, KBNV407 (7-1/2") **$535.00**
Price: 44 Mag., BNV474, KBNV474 (4-5/8"). BNV475, KBNV475 (5-1/2"). BNV477, KBNV477 (7-1/2") **$535.00**
Price: 45 LC, BN444, KBNV44 (4-5/8"). BNV455, KBNV455 (5-1/2"). BNV45, KBNV45 (7-1/2") **$535.00**
Price: 45 LC, BNVBH453, KBNVBH453 3-3/4" with "birds head" grip **$576.00**
Price: 357 Mag., RBNV35 (5-1/2") **$535.00**; KRBNV35 (5-1/2") . **$555.00**
Price: 45 LC, RBNV44 (4-5/8"), RBNV455 (5-1/2") **$535.00**
Price: 45 LC, KRBNV44 (4-5/8"), KRBNV455 (5-1/2") **$555.00**

Ruger Bisley-Vaquero Single-Action Revolver

Similar to Vaquero, Bisley-style hammer, grip and trigger, available in 357 Magnum, 44 Magnum and 45 LC only, 4-5/8" or 5-1/2" barrel. Smooth rosewood grips with Ruger medallion. Roll-engraved, unfluted cylinder. Introduced 1997. From Sturm, Ruger & Co.

Price: Color case-hardened frame, blue grip frame, barrel and cylinder, RBNV-475, RBNV-474, 44 Mag. **$535.00**
Price: High-gloss stainless steel, KRBNV-475, KRBNV-474 . . . . **$555.00**
Price: For simulated ivory grips add . . . . **$41.00 to $44.00**

RUGER NEW BEARCAT SINGLE-ACTION

Caliber: 22 LR, 6-shot. **Barrel:** 4". **Weight:** 24 oz. **Length:** 8-7/8" overall. **Grips:** Smooth rosewood with Ruger medallion. **Sights:** Blade front, fixed notch rear. **Features:** Reintroduction of the Ruger Bearcat with slightly lengthened frame, Ruger patented transfer bar safety system. Available in blue only. Introduced 1993. With case and lock. From Sturm, Ruger & Co.

Price: SBC4, blue **$379.00**
Price: KSBC-4, ss **$429.00**

RUGER MODEL SINGLE-SIX REVOLVER

Caliber: 32 H&R Magnum. **Barrel:** 4-5/8", 6-shot. **Weight:** 33 oz. **Length:** 10-1/8". **Grips:** Blue, rosewood, stainless, simulated ivory. **Sights:** Blade front, notch rear fixed. **Features:** Transfer bar and loading gate interlock safety, instruction manual, high impact case and gun lock.

Price: **$576.00**
Price: Blue, SSM4FS **$576.00**
Price: SS, KSSM4FSI. **$576.00**

HANDGUNS

Ruger Super Single-Six

Tristar Regulator

Ruger Bisley

Uberti 1873 Cattleman

Uberti 1875 Army Outlaw

RUGER SINGLE-SIX AND SUPER SINGLE-SIX CONVERTIBLE
Caliber: 22 LR, 6-shot; 22 WMR in extra cylinder; 17 HMR. **Barrel:** 4-5/8", 5-1/2", 6-1/2", 9-1/2" (6-groove). **Weight:** 35 oz. (6-1/2" bbl.). **Length:** 11-13/16" overall (6-1/2" bbl.). **Grips:** Smooth American walnut. **Sights:** Improved Patridge front on ramp, fully adjustable rear protected by integral frame ribs (super single-six); or fixed sight (single six). **Features:** Ruger transfer bar safety system, loading gate interlock, hardened chrome-moly steel frame, wide trigger, music wire springs throughout, independent firing pin.
Price: 4-5/8", 5-1/2", 6-1/2", 9-1/2" barrel, blue, adjustable sight NR4, NR5, NR6, NR9 . . . . **$389.00**
Price: 5-1/2", 6-1/2" bbl. only, stainless steel, adjustable sight KNR5, KNR6 . . . . **$469.00**
Price: 5-1/2", 6-1/2" barrel, blue fixed sights **$379.00**
Price: 6-1/2" barrel, NR 617, 17 HMR **$389.00**
Price: Ruger 50th Anniversary Single Six with 4-5/8" barrel and a gold-colored rollmark "50 years of Single Six 1953 to 2003," blued steel finish, Cocobolo wood grips with red Ruger medallions and both 22 LR and 22 WMR cylinders **$425.00**

Ruger Bisley Small Frame Revolver
Similar to Single-Six, frame is styled after classic Bisley "flat-top." Most mechanical parts are unchanged. Hammer is lower and smoothly curved with deeply checkered spur. Trigger is strongly curved with wide smooth surface. Longer grip frame designed with hand-filling shape, and trigger guard is a large oval. Adjustable dovetail rear sight; front sight base accepts interchangeable square blades of various heights and styles. Unfluted cylinder and roll engraving. Weighs 41 oz. Chambered for 22 LR, 6-1/2" barrel only. Plastic lockable case. Introduced 1985.
Price: RB-22AW **$422.00**

SMITH & WESSON COMMEMORATIVE MODEL 2000
Caliber: 45 S&W Schofield. **Barrel:** 7". **Features:** 150th Anniversary logo, engraved, gold-plated, walnut grips, blue, original style hammer, trigger, and barrel latch. Wood presentation case. Limited.
Price: . . . . **NA**

TRISTAR/UBERTI REGULATOR REVOLVER
Caliber: 45 Colt. **Barrel:** 4-3/4", 5-1/2". **Weight:** 32-38 oz. **Length:** 8-1/4" overall (4-3/4" bbl.) **Grips:** One-piece walnut. **Sights:** Blade front, notch rear. **Features:** Uberti replica of 1873 Colt Model "P" revolver. Color-case hardened steel frame, brass backstrap and trigger guard, hammer-block safety. Imported from Italy by Tristar Sporting Arms.
Price: Regulator **$335.00**
Price: Regulator Deluxe (blued backstrap, trigger guard) **$367.00**

UBERTI 1873 CATTLEMAN SINGLE-ACTION
Caliber: 22 LR/22 WMR, 38 Spec., 357 Mag., 44 Spec., 44-40, 45 Colt/45 ACP, 6-shot. **Barrel:** 4-3/4", 5-1/2", 7-1/2"; 44-40, 45 Colt also with 3", 3-1/2", 4". **Weight:** 38 oz. (5-1/2" bbl.). **Length:** 10-3/4" overall (5-1/2" bbl.). **Grips:** One-piece smooth walnut. **Sights:** Blade front, groove rear; fully adjustable rear available. **Features:** Steel or brass backstrap, trigger guard; color case-hardened frame, blued barrel, cylinder. Imported from Italy by Uberti U.S.A.
Price: Steel backstrap, trigger guard, fixed sights **$410.00**
Price: Brass backstrap, trigger guard, fixed sights **$359.00**
Price: Bisley model **$435.00**

Uberti 1873 Buckhorn Single-Action
A slightly larger version of the Cattleman revolver. Available in 44 Magnum or 44 Magnum/44-40 convertible, otherwise has same specs.
Price: Steel backstrap, trigger guard, fixed sights **$410.00**

UBERTI 1875 SA ARMY OUTLAW REVOLVER
Caliber: 357 Mag., 44-40, 45 Colt, 45 Colt/45 ACP convertible, 6-shot. **Barrel:** 5-1/2", 7-1/2". **Weight:** 44 oz. **Length:** 13-3/4" overall. **Grips:** Smooth walnut. **Sights:** Blade front, notch rear. **Features:** Replica of the 1875 Remington S.A. Army revolver. Brass trigger guard, color case-hardened frame, rest blued. Imported by Uberti U.S.A.
Price: **$483.00**
Price: 45 Colt/45 ACP convertible **$525.00**

UBERTI 1890 ARMY OUTLAW REVOLVER
Caliber: 357 Mag., 44-40, 45 Colt, 45 Colt/45 ACP convertible, 6-shot. **Barrel:** 5-1/2", 7-1/2". **Weight:** 37 oz. **Length:** 12-1/2" overall. **Grips:** American walnut. **Sights:** Blade front, groove rear. **Features:** Replica of the 1890 Remington single-action. Brass trigger guard, rest is blued. Imported by Uberti U.S.A.
Price: **$483.00**

Uberti 1890 Army Outlaw

Uberti Russian

Uberti 1875 Schofield

Uberti Bisley

Uberti Bisley Flat Top

UBERTI NEW MODEL RUSSIAN REVOLVER

Caliber: 44 Russian, 6-shot cylinder. **Barrel:** 6-1/2". **Weight:** 40 oz. **Length:** 12" overall. **Grips:** Smooth walnut. **Sights:** Blade front, notch rear. **Features:** Repica of the S&W Model 3 Russian Third Model revolver. Spur trigger guard, polished blue finish. Introduced 1999. Imported by Uberti USA.
Price: **$800.00**

UBERTI 1875 SCHOFIELD-STYLE BREAK-TOP REVOLVER

Caliber: 44-40, 45 Colt, 6-shot cylinder. **Barrel:** 5", 7". **Weight:** 39 oz. **Length:** 10-3/4" overall (5" barrel). **Grips:** Smooth walnut. **Sights:** Blade front, notch rear. **Features:** Replica of Smith & Wesson Model 3 Schofield. Single-action, top-break with automatic ejection. Polished blue finish. Introduced 1994. Imported by Uberti USA.
Price: **$750.00**

UBERTI BISLEY MODEL SINGLE-ACTION REVOLVER

Caliber: 38-40, 357 Mag., 44 Spec., 44-40 or 45 Colt, 6-shot cylinder. **Barrel:** 4-3/4", 5-1/2", 7-1/2". **Weight:** 40 oz. **Length:** 12-1/2" overall (7-1/2" barrel). **Grips:** Smooth walnut. **Sights:** Blade front, notch rear. **Features:** Replica of Colt's Bisley Model. Polished blue finish, color case-hardened frame. Introduced 1997. Imported by Uberti USA.
Price: **$435.00**

Uberti Bisley Model Flat Top Target Revolver

Similar to standard Bisley model, flat top strap, 7-1/2" barrel only, spring-loaded German silver front sight blade, standing leaf rear sight adjustable for windage. Polished blue finish, color case-hardened frame. Introduced 1998. Imported by Uberti USA.
Price: **$435.00**

Uberti Bisley Flat Top

U.S. FIRE-ARMS SINGLE ACTION ARMY REVOLVER

Caliber: 45 Colt (standard); 32 WCF, 38 WCF, 38 S&W, 41 Colt, 44WCF, 44 S&W (optional, additional charge), 6-shot cylinder. **Barrel:** 4-3/4", 5-1/2", 7-1/2". **Weight:** 37 oz. **Length:** NA. **Grips:** Hard rubber. **Sights:** Blade front, notch rear. **Features:** Recreation of original guns; 3" and 4" have no ejector. Available with all-blue, blue with color case-hardening, or full nickel-plate finish. Made in U.S.A. by United States Fire-Arms Mfg. Co.
Price: Blue/cased-colors **$1,250.00**
Price: Carbonal blue/case-colors **$1,400.00**
Price: Nickel **$1,450.00**

U.S. Fire-Arms "China Camp" Cowboy Action Revolver

Similar to Single Action Army revolver, available in Silver Steel finish only. Offered in 4-3/4", 5-1/2", 7-1/2" barrels. Made in U.S.A. by United States Fire-Arms Mfg. Co.
Price: **$1,200.00**

U.S. FIRE-ARMS RODEO COWBOY ACTION REVOLVER

Caliber: 45 Colt. **Barrel:** 4-3/4", 5-1/2". **Grips:** Rubber. **Features:** Historically correct armory bone case hammer, blue satin finish, transfer bar safety system, correct solid firing pin. Entry level basic cowboy SASS gun for beginner or expert.
Price: **$550.00**

U.S. FIRE-ARMS UNITED STATES PRE-WAR

Caliber: 45 Colt, other caliber available. **Barrel:** 4-3/4", 5-1/2", 7-1/2". **Grips:** Hard rubber. **Features:** Armory bone case/Armory blue finish standard, cross-pin or black powder frame. Introduced 2002. Made in U.S.A. by United States Firearms Manufacturing Co.
Price: **$1,525.00**

Specially adapted single-shot and multi-barrel arms.

American Derringer Model 1

American Derringer Model 4

American Derringer Model 6

American Derringer Model 7

American Derringer Lady Derringer

American Derringer DA 38

AMERICAN DERRINGER MODEL 1

Caliber: 22 LR, 22 WMR, 30 Carbine, 30 Luger, 30-30 Win., 32 H&R Mag., 32-20, 380 ACP, 38 Super, 38 Spec., 38 Spec. shotshell, 38 Spec. +P, 9mm Para., 357 Mag., 357 Mag./45/410, 357 Maximum, 10mm, 40 S&W, 41 Mag., 38-40, 44-40 Win., 44 Spec., 44 Mag., 45 Colt, 45 Win. Mag., 45 ACP, 45 Colt/410, 45-70 single shot. **Barrel:** 3". **Weight:** 15-1/2 oz. (38 Spec.). **Length:** 4.82" overall. **Grips:** Rosewood, Zebra wood. **Sights:** Blade front. **Features:** Made of stainless steel with high-polish or satin finish. Two-shot capacity. Manual hammer block safety. Introduced 1980. Available in almost any pistol caliber. Contact the factory for complete list of available calibers and prices. From American Derringer Corp.

Price: 22 LR	$320.00
Price: 38 Spec.	$320.00
Price: 357 Maximum	$345.00
Price: 357 Mag.	$335.00
Price: 9mm, 380	$320.00
Price: 40 S&W	$335.00
Price: 44 Spec.	$398.00
Price: 44-40 Win.	$398.00
Price: 45 Colt	$385.00
Price: 30-30, 45 Win. Mag.	$460.00
Price: 41, 44 Mags.	$470.00
Price: 45-70, single shot	$387.00
Price: 45 Colt, 410, 2-1/2"	$385.00
Price: 45 ACP, 10mm Auto	$340.00

American Derringer Model 4

Similar to the Model 1 except has 4.1" barrel, overall length of 6", and weighs 16-1/2 oz.; chambered for 357 Mag., 357 Maximum, 45-70, 3" 410-bore shotshells or 45 Colt or 44 Mag. Made of stainless steel. Manual hammer block safety. Introduced 1980.

Price: 3" 410/45 Colt	$425.00
Price: 45-70	$560.00
Price: 44 Mag. with oversize grips	$515.00
Price: Alaskan Survival model (45-70 upper barrel, 410 or 45 Colt lower)	$475.00

American Derringer Model 6

Similar to the Model 1 except has 6" barrel chambered for 3" 410 shotshells or 22 WMR, 357 Mag., 45 ACP, 45 Colt; rosewood stocks; 8.2" o.a.l. and weighs 21 oz. Shoots either round for each barrel. Manual hammer block safety. Introduced 1980.

Price: 22 WMR	$440.00
Price: 357 Mag.	$440.00
Price: 45 Colt/410	$450.00
Price: 45 ACP	$440.00

American Derringer Model 7 Ultra Lightweight

Similar to Model 1 except made of high strength aircraft aluminum. Weighs 7-1/2 oz., 4.82" o.a.l., rosewood stocks. Available in 22 LR, 22 WMR, 32 H&R Mag., 380 ACP, 38 Spec., 44 Spec. Introduced 1980.

Price: 22 LR, WMR	$325.00
Price: 38 Spec.	$325.00
Price: 380 ACP	$325.00
Price: 32 H&R Mag/32 S&W Long	$325.00
Price: 44 Spec.	$565.00

American Derringer Model 10 Ultra Lightweight

Similar to the Model 1 except frame is of aluminum, giving weight of 10 oz. Stainless barrels. Available in 38 Spec., 45 Colt or 45 ACP only. Matte gray finish. Introduced 1980.

Price: 45 Colt	$385.00
Price: 45 ACP	$330.00
Price: 38 Spec.	$305.00

American Derringer Lady Derringer

Same as the Model 1 except has tuned action, is fitted with scrimshawed synthetic ivory grips; chambered for 32 H&R Mag. and 38 Spec.; 357 Mag., 45 Colt, 45/410. Deluxe Grade is highly polished; Deluxe Engraved is engraved in a pattern similar to that used on 1880s derringers. All come in a French fitted jewelry box. Introduced 1989.

Price: 32 H&R Mag.	$375.00
Price: 357 Mag.	$405.00
Price: 38 Spec.	$360.00
Price: 45 Colt, 45/410	$435.00

American Derringer Texas Commemorative

A Model 1 Derringer with solid brass frame, stainless steel barrel and rosewood grips. Available in 38 Spec., 44-40 Win., or 45 Colt. Introduced 1980.

Price: 38 Spec.	$365.00
Price: 44-40	$420.00
Price: Brass frame, 45 Colt	$450.00

AMERICAN DERRINGER DA 38 MODEL

Caliber: 22 LR, 9mm Para., 38 Spec., 357 Mag., 40 S&W. **Barrel:** 3". **Weight:** 14.5 oz. **Length:** 4.8" overall. **Grips:** Rosewood, walnut or other hardwoods. **Sights:** Fixed. **Features:** Double-action only; two-shots. Manual safety. Made of satin-finished stainless steel and aluminum. Introduced 1989. From American Derringer Corp.

Price: 22 LR	$435.00
Price: 38 Spec.	$460.00
Price: 9mm Para.	$445.00
Price: 357 Mag.	$450.00
Price: 40 S&W	$475.00

ANSCHUTZ MODEL 64P SPORT/TARGET PISTOL

Caliber: 22 LR, 22 WMR, 5-shot magazine. **Barrel:** 10". **Weight:** 3 lbs., 8 oz. **Length:** 18-1/2" overall. **Stock:** Choate Rynite. **Sights:** None furnished; grooved for scope mounting. **Features:** Right-hand bolt; polished blue finish. Introduced 1998. Imported from Germany by AcuSport.

Price: 22 LR	$455.95
Price: 22 WMR	$479.95

Bond Arms Texas Defender

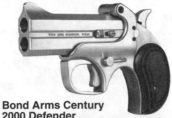

Bond Arms Century 2000 Defender

Cobra Big Bore

Cobra D-Series

Comanche Super Single Shot

Downsizer WSP Single Shot

IAR Model 1872 Derringer

Gaucher GN1 Silhouette

BOND ARMS DEFENDER DERRINGER

Caliber: 410 Buckshot or slug, 45 Colt/45 Schofield (2.5" chamber), 45 Colt (only), 450 Bond Super/45 ACP/45 Super, 44 Mag./44 Special/44 Russian, 10mm, 40 S&W, 357 SIG, 357 Maximum/357 Mag./38 Special, 357 Mag/38 Special & 38 Long Colt, 38 Short Colt, 9mm Luger (9x19), 32 H&R Mag./38 S&W Long/32 Colt New Police, 22 Mag., 22 LR., 38-40, 44-40. **Barrel:** 3", 3-1/2". **Weight:** 20-21 oz. **Length:** 5"-5-1/2". **Grips:** Exotic woods or animal horn. **Sights:** Blade front, fixed rear. **Features:** Interchangeable barrels, retracting and rebounding firing pins, cross-bolt safety, automatic extractor for rimmed calibers. Stainless steel construction. Right or left hand.
Price: Texas (with TG) 3" bbl. **$359.00**
Price: Super (with TG) 3" bbl., 450 Bond Super and 45 ACP ... **$359.00**
Price: Cowboy (no TG) **$359.00**
Price: Century 2000 (with TG), Cowboy Century 2000 (no TG), 3-1/2" bbls., 410/45 Colt **$379.00**
Price: additional calibers available separately

BROWN CLASSIC SINGLE SHOT PISTOL

Caliber: 17 Ackley Hornet through 45-70 Govt. **Barrel:** 15" airgauged match grade. **Weight:** About 3 lbs., 7 oz. **Grips:** Walnut; thumbrest target style. **Sights:** None furnished; drilled and tapped for scope mounting. **Features:** Falling block action gives rigid barrel-receiver mating; hand-fitted and headspaced. Introduced 1998. Made in U.S.A. by E.A. Brown Mfg.
Price: **$499.00**

COBRA BIG BORE DERRINGERS

Caliber: 22 WMR, 38 Spec., 9mm Para. **Barrel:** 2.75". **Weight:** 11.5 oz. **Length:** 4.65" overall. **Grips:** Textured black synthetic. **Sights:** Blade front, fixed notch rear. **Features:** Alloy frame, steel-lined barrels, steel breech block. Plunger-type safety with integral hammer block. Chrome or black Teflon finish. Introduced 2002. Made in U.S.A. by Cobra Enterprises.
Price: **$98.00**
Price: 9mm Para. **$104.00**

COBRA LONG-BORE DERRINGERS

Caliber: 22 WMR, 38 Spec., 9mm Para. **Barrel:** 3.5". **Weight:** 13 oz. **Length:** 5.65" overall. **Grips:** Textured black synthetic. **Sights:** Fixed. **Features:** Chrome or black Teflon finish. Larger than Davis D-Series models. Introduced 2002. Made in U.S.A. by Cobra Enterprises.
Price: **$104.00**
Price: 9mm Para. **$110.00**
Price: Big-Bore models (same calibers, 3/4" shorter barrels)..... **$98.00**

COBRA D-SERIES DERRINGERS

Caliber: 22 LR, 22 WMR, 25 ACP, 32 ACP. **Barrel:** 2.4". **Weight:** 9.5 oz. **Length:** 4" overall. **Grips:** Laminated wood or pearl. **Sights:** Blade front, fixed notch rear. **Features:** Choice of black Teflon or chrome finish; spur trigger. Introduced 2002. Made in U.S.A. by Cobra Enterprises.
Price: **$99.50**

COMANCHE SUPER SINGLE SHOT PISTOL

Caliber: 45 LC, 410 ga. **Barrel:** 10". **Sights:** Adjustable. **Features:** Blue finish, not available for sale in CA, MA. Distributed by SGS Importers International, Inc.
Price: **$174.95**
Price: Satin nickel **$191.95**
Price: Duo tone **$185.95**

DOWNSIZER WSP SINGLE SHOT PISTOL

Caliber: 357 Magnum, 45 ACP. **Barrel:** 2.10". **Weight:** 11 oz. **Length:** 3.25" overall. **Grips:** Black polymer. **Sights:** None. **Features:** Single shot, tip-up barrel. Double action only. Stainless steel construction. Measures .900" thick. Introduced 1997. From Downsizer Corp.
Price: **$499.00**

GAUCHER GN1 SILHOUETTE PISTOL

Caliber: 22 LR, single shot. **Barrel:** 10". **Weight:** 2.4 lbs. **Length:** 15.5" overall. **Grips:** European hardwood. **Sights:** Blade front, open adjustable rear. **Features:** Bolt action, adjustable trigger. Introduced 1990. Imported from France by Mandall Shooting Supplies.
Price: About **$525.00**
Price: Model GP Silhouette **$425.00**

IAR MODEL 1872 DERRINGER

Caliber: 22 Short. **Barrel:** 2-3/8". **Weight:** 7 oz. **Length:** 5-1/8" overall. **Grips:** Smooth walnut. **Sights:** Blade front, notch rear. **Features:** Gold or nickel frame with blue barrel. Reintroduced 1996 using original Colt designs and tooling for the Colt Model 4 Derringer. Made in U.S.A. by IAR, Inc.
Price: **$109.00**
Price: Single cased gun **$125.00**
Price: Double cased set **$215.00**

IAR MODEL 1866 DOUBLE DERRINGER

Caliber: 38 Special. **Barrel:** 2-3/4". **Weight:** 16 oz. **Grips:** Smooth walnut. **Sights:** Blade front, notch rear. **Features:** All steel construction. Blue barrel, color case-hardened frame. Uses original designs and tooling for the Uberti New Maverick Derringer. Introduced 1999. Made in U.S.A. by IAR, Inc.
Price: **$395.00**

Maximum Single Shot

RPM XL Pistol

Thompson/Center C2 Contender

MAXIMUM SINGLE SHOT PISTOL

Caliber: 22 LR, 22 Hornet, 22 BR, 22 PPC, 223 Rem., 22-250, 6mm BR, 6mm PPC, 243, 250 Savage, 6.5mm-35M, 270 MAX, 270 Win., 7mm TCU, 7mm BR, 7mm-35, 7mm INT-R, 7mm-08, 7mm Rocket, 7mm Super-Mag., 30 Herrett, 30 Carbine, 30-30, 308 Win., 30x39, 32-20, 350 Rem. Mag., 357 Mag., 357 Maximum, 358 Win., 375 H&H, 44 Mag., 454 Casull. **Barrel:** 8-3/4", 10-1/2", 14". **Weight:** 61 oz. (10-1/2" bbl.); 78 oz. (14" bbl.). **Length:** 15", 18-1/2" overall (with 10-1/2" and 14" bbl., respectively). **Grips:** Smooth walnut stocks and forend. Also available with 17" finger groove grip. **Sights:** Ramp front, fully adjustable open rear. **Features:** Falling block action; drilled and tapped for M.O.A. scope mounts; integral grip frame/receiver; adjustable trigger; Douglas barrel (interchangeable). Introduced 1983. Made in U.S.A. by M.O.A. Corp.

Price: Stainless receiver, blue barrel	**$799.00**
Price: Stainless receiver, stainless barrel	**$883.00**
Price: Extra blued barrel	**$254.00**
Price: Extra stainless barrel	**$317.00**
Price: Scope mount	**$60.00**

RPM XL SINGLE SHOT PISTOL

Caliber: 22 LR through 45-70. **Barrel:** 8", 10-3/4", 12", 14". **Weight:** About 60 oz. **Grips:** Smooth Goncalo Alves with thumb and heel rests. **Sights:** Hooded front with interchangeable post, or Patridge; ISGW rear adjustable for windage and elevation. **Features:** Barrel drilled and tapped for scope mount. Visible cocking indicator. Spring-loaded barrel lock, positive hammer-block safety. Trigger adjustable for weight of pull and over-travel. Contact maker for complete price list. Made in U.S.A. by RPM.

Price: XL Hunter model (action only)	**$1,045.00**
Price: Extra barrel, 8" through 10-3/4"	**$407.50**
Price: Extra barrel, 12" through 14"	**$547.50**
Price: Muzzle brake	**$160.00**
Price: Left hand action, add	**$50.00**

SAVAGE STRIKER BOLT-ACTION HUNTING HANDGUN

Caliber: 223, 243, 7mm-08, 308, 300 WSM 2-shot mag. **Barrel:** 14". **Weight:** About 5 lbs. **Length:** 22-1/2" overall. **Stock:** Black composite ambidextrous mid-grip; grooved forend; "Dual Pillar" bedding. **Sights:** None furnished; drilled and tapped for scope mounting. **Features:** Short left-hand bolt with right-hand ejection; free-floated barrel; uses Savage Model 110 rifle scope rings/bases. Introduced 1998. Made in U.S.A. by Savage Arms, Inc.

Price: Model 510F (blued barrel and action)	**$425.00**
Price: Model 516FSS (stainless barrel and action)	**$462.00**
Price: Model 516FSAK (stainless, adjustable muzzle brake)	**$512.00**
Price: Model 516FSAK black stock (ss, aMB, 300WSM)	**$588.00**

Savage Sport Striker Bolt-Action Hunting Handgun

Similar to Striker, but chambered in 22 LR and 22 WMR. Detachable, 10-shot magazine (5-shot magazine for 22 WMR). Overall length 19", weighs 4 lbs. Ambidextrous fiberglass/graphite composite rear grip. Drilled and tapped, scope mount installed. Introduced 2000. Made in U.S.A. by Savage Arms Inc.

Price: Model 501F (blue finish, 22LR)	**$216.00**
Price: Model 501FXP with soft case, 1.25-4x28 scope	**$258.00**
Price: Model 502F (blue finish, 22 WMR)	**$238.00**

SPRINGFIELD M6 SCOUT PISTOL

Caliber: 22 LR/45 LC/.410, 22 Hornet, 45 LC/.410. **Barrel:** 10". **Weight:** NA. **Length:** NA. **Grip:** NA. **Sights:** NA. **Features:** Adapted from the U.S. Air Force M6 Survival Rifle, it is also available as a carbine with 16" barrel.

Price:	**$169.00 to $197.00**
Price: Pistol/Carbine	**$183.00 to $209.00**

THOMPSON/CENTER ENCORE PISTOL

Caliber: 22-250, 223, 260 Rem., 7mm-08, 243, 308, 270, 30-06, 44 Mag., 454 Casull, 480 Ruger, 444 Marlin single shot, 450 Marlin with muzzle tamer, no sights. **Barrel:** 12", 15", tapered round. **Weight:** NA. **Length:** 21" overall with 12" barrel. **Grips:** American walnut with finger grooves, walnut forend. **Sights:** Blade on ramp front, adjustable rear, or none. **Features:** Interchangeable barrels; action opens by squeezing the trigger guard; drilled and tapped for scope mounting; blue finish. Announced 1996. Made in U.S.A. by Thompson/Center Arms.

Price:	**$582.00 to $588.00**
Price: Extra 12" barrels	**$258.00**
Price: Extra 15" barrels	**$263.00**
Price: 45 Colt/410 barrel, 12"	**$282.00**
Price: 45 Colt/410 barrel, 15"	**$297.00**

Thompson/Center Stainless Encore Pistol

Similar to blued Encore, made of stainless steel, available with 15" barrel in 223, 22-250, 243 Win., 7mm-08, 308, 30/06 Sprgfld., 45/70 Gov't., 45/410 VR. With black rubber grip and forend. Made in U.S.A. by Thompson/Center Arms.

Price:	**$622.00 to $644.00**

Thompson/Center G2 Contender Pistol

A second generation Contender pistol maintaining the same barrel interchangeability with older Contender barrels and their corresponding forends (except Herrett forend). The G2 frame will not accept old-style grips due to the change in grip angle. Incorporates an automatic hammer block safety with built-in interlock. Features include trigger adjustable for overtravel, adjustable rear sight; ramp front sight blade, blued steel finish.

Price:	**$566.75**

UBERTI ROLLING BLOCK TARGET PISTOL

Caliber: 22 LR, 22 WMR, 22 Hornet, 357 Mag., 45 Colt, single shot. **Barrel:** 9-7/8", half-round, half-octagon. **Weight:** 44 oz. **Length:** 14" overall. **Stock:** Walnut grip and forend. **Sights:** Blade front, fully adjustable rear. **Features:** Replica of the 1871 rolling block target pistol. Brass trigger guard, color case-hardened frame, blue barrel. Imported by Uberti U.S.A.

Price:	**$410.00**

Both classic arms and recent designs in American-style repeaters for sport and field shooting.

Armalite M15A2

Armalite AR-10A4

Armalite AR-180B

Auto-Ordnance 1927 A-1 Thompson

ARMALITE M15A2 CARBINE
Caliber: 223, 7-shot magazine. **Barrel:** 16" heavy chrome lined; 1:9" twist. **Weight:** 7 lbs. **Length:** 35-11/16" overall. **Stock:** Green or black composition. **Sights:** Standard A2. **Features:** Upper and lower receivers have push-type pivot pin; hard coat anodized; A2-style forward assist; M16A2-type raised fence around magazine release button. Made in U.S.A. by ArmaLite, Inc.
Price: Green **$930.00**
Price: Black **$945.00**

ARMALITE AR-10A4 SPECIAL PURPOSE RIFLE
Caliber: 308 Win., 10-shot magazine. **Barrel:** 20" chrome-lined, 1:12" twist. **Weight:** 9.6 lbs. **Length:** 41" overall **Stock:** Green or black composition. **Sights:** Detachable handle, front sight, or scope mount available; comes with international style flattop receiver with Picatinny rail. **Features:** Proprietary recoil check. Forged upper receiver with case deflector. Receivers are hard-coat anodized. Introduced 1995. Made in U.S.A. by ArmaLite, Inc.
Price: Green **$1,383.00**
Price: Black **$1,383.00**
Price: Green or black with match trigger **$1,483.00**
Price: Green or Black with match trigger and stainless barrel . . **$1,583.00**

Armalite AR-10(T)
Similar to the Armalite AR-10A4 but with stainless steel, barrel, machined tool steel, two-stage National Match trigger group and other features.
Price: AR-10(T) Rifle **$2,080.00**
Price: AR-10(T) Carbine **$2,080.00**

Armalite AR-10A2
Utilizing the same 20" double-lapped, heavy barrel as the Armalite AR-10A4 Special Purpose Rifle, the AR-10A2 has a clamping front sight base allowing the removeable front sight to be rotated to zero the front sight. This assures the rear sight is centered and full left and right windage movement is available when shooting in strong winds. Offered in 308 caliber only. Made in U.S.A. by Armalite, Inc.
Price: AR-10A2 Rifle or Carbine. **$1,435.00**
Price: AR-10A2 Rifle or Carbine with match trigger **$1,535.00**
Price: AR-10A2 Rifle with stainless steel barrel **$1,535.00**

ARMALITE AR-180B RIFLE
Caliber: 223, 10-shot magazine. **Barrel:** 19.8" **Weight:** 6 lbs. **Length:** 38". **Stock:** Synthetic. **Sights:** Rear sight adjustable for windage, small and large apertures. **Features:** Lower receiver made of polymer, upper formed of sheet metal. Uses standard AR-15 magazines. Made in U.S.A. by Armalite. **Price:** **$650.00**
Price: With match trigger **$750.00**

ARSENAL USA SSR-56
Caliber: 7.62x39mm **Barrel:** 16.25" **Weight:** 7.4 lbs. **Length:** 35.5" **Stock:** Black polymer. **Sights:** Adjustable rear. **Features:** An AK-47 style rifle built on a hardened Hungarian FEG receiver with the required six U.S. made parts to make it legal for use with all extra-capacity magazines. From Arsenal I, LLC.
Price: **$565.00**

Barrett Model 82A-1

Browning Mark II Safari

ARSENAL USA SSR-74-2

Caliber: 5.45x39mm **Barrel:** 16.25" **Weight:** 7 lbs. **Length:** 36.75" **Stock:** Polymer or wood. **Sights:** Adjustable. **Features:** Built with parts from an unissued Bulgarian AK-74 rifle, it has a Buffer Technologies recoil buffer, and enough U.S.-made parts to allow pistol grip stock, and use with all extra-capacity magazines. Assembled in U.S.A. From Arsenal I, LLC.
Price: **$499.00**

ARSENAL USA SSR-85C-2

Caliber: 7.62x39mm **Barrel:** 16.25" **Weight:** 7.1 lbs. **Length:** 35.5" **Stock:** Polymer or wood. **Sights:** Adjustable rear calibrated to 800 meters. **Features:** Built from parts obtained from unissued Polish AK-47 rifles, the gas tube is vented and the receiver cover is plain. Rifle contains enough U.S.-sourced parts to allow pistol grip stock and use with all extra-capacity magazines. Assembled in U.S.A. by Arsenal USA I, LLC.
Price: **$499.00**

AUTO-ORDNANCE 1927 A-1 THOMPSON

Caliber: 45 ACP. **Barrel:** 16-1/2". **Weight:** 13 lbs. **Length:** About 41" overall (Deluxe). **Stock:** Walnut stock and vertical forend. **Sights:** Blade front, open rear adjustable for windage. **Features:** Recreation of Thompson Model 1927. Semi-auto only. Deluxe model has finned barrel, adjustable rear sight and compensator; Standard model has plain barrel and military sight. From Auto-Ordnance Corp.
Price: Deluxe **$950.00**
Price: 1927A1C Lightweight model (9-1/2 lbs.) **$950.00**

Auto-Ordnance Thompson M1/M1-C

Similar to the 1927 A-1 except is in the M-1 configuration with side cocking knob, horizontal forend, smooth unfinned barrel, sling swivels on butt and forend. Matte black finish. Introduced 1985.
Price: M1 semi-auto carbine. **$950.00**
Price: M1-C lightweight semi-auto **$925.00**

Auto-Ordnance 1927A1 Commando

Similar to the 1927A1 except has Parkerized finish, black-finish wood butt, pistol grip, horizontal forend. Comes with black nylon sling. Introduced 1998. Made in U.S.A. by Auto-Ordnance Corp.
Price: **$950.00**

BARRETT MODEL 82A-1 SEMI-AUTOMATIC RIFLE

Caliber: 50 BMG, 10-shot detachable box magazine. **Barrel:** 29". **Weight:** 28.5 lbs. **Length:** 57" overall. **Stock:** Composition with energy-absorbing recoil pad. **Sights:** Scope optional. **Features:** Semi-automatic, recoil operated with recoiling barrel. Three-lug locking bolt; muzzle brake. Adjustable bipod. Introduced 1985. Made in U.S.A. by Barrett Firearms.
Price: From **$7,200.00**

BENELLI RI RIFLE

Caliber: 300 Win. Mag., 30-06 Springfield. **Barrel:** 20", 22", 24". **Weight:** 7.1 lbs. **Length:** 43.75" **Stock:** Select satin walnut. **Sights:** None. **Features:** Auto-regulating gas-operated system, three-lugged rotary bolt, interchangeable barrels. Introduced 2003. Imported from Italy by Benelli USA.
Price: . . . . **$1065.00 to $1,080.00**

BROWNING BAR MARK II SAFARI SEMI-AUTO RIFLE

Caliber: 243, 25-06, 270, 30-06, 308, 270 WSM, 7mm WSM. **Barrel:** 22" round tapered. **Weight:** 7-3/8 lbs. **Length:** 43" overall. **Stock:** French walnut pistol grip stock and forend, hand checkered. **Sights:** Gold bead on hooded ramp front, click adjustable rear, or no sights. **Features:** Has new bolt release lever; removable trigger assembly with larger trigger guard; redesigned gas and buffer systems. Detachable 4-round box magazine. Scroll-engraved receiver is tapped for scope mounting. BOSS barrel vibration modulator and muzzle brake system available only on models without sights. Mark II Safari introduced 1993. Imported from Belgium by Browning.
Price: Safari, with sights **$833.00**
Price: Safari, no sights **$815.00**
Price: Safari, 270 and 30-06, no sights, BOSS **$891.00**

Browning BAR Mark II Lightweight Semi-Auto

Similar to the Mark II Safari except has lighter alloy receiver and 20" barrel. Available in 243, 308, 270, 30-06, 7mm Rem. Mag., 300 Win. Mag., 338 Win. Mag. Weighs 7 lbs., 2 oz.; overall length 41". Has dovetailed, gold bead front sight on hooded ramp, open rear click adjustable for windage and elevation. Introduced 1997. Imported from Belgium by Browning.
Price: 243, 308, 270, 30-06 . . . . **$833.00**
Price: 7mm Rem. Mag., 300 Win. Mag., 338 Win. Mag **$909.00**

Browning BAR Mark II Safari Rifle in magnum calibers

Same as the standard caliber model, except weighs 8-3/8 lbs., 45" overall, 24" bbl., 3-round mag. Cals. 7mm Mag., 300 Win. Mag., 338 Win. Mag. BOSS barrel vibration modulator and muzzle brake system available only on models without sights. Introduced 1993.
Price: Safari, with sights **$909.00**
Price: Safari, no sights **$890.00**
Price: Safari, no sights, BOSS **$967.00**

CENTERFIRE RIFLES — AUTOLOADERS

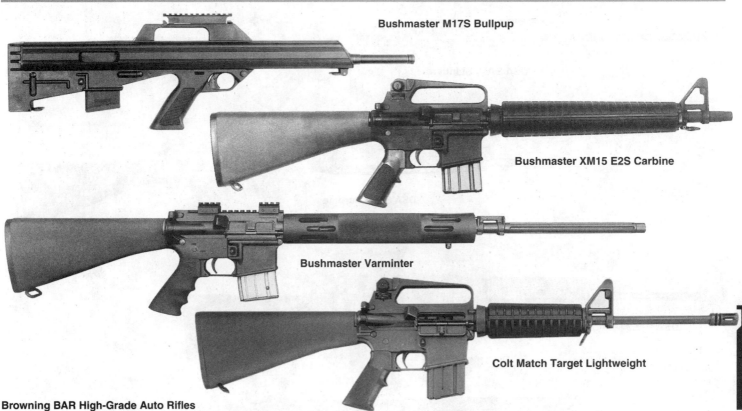

Bushmaster M17S Bullpup

Bushmaster XM15 E2S Carbine

Bushmaster Varminter

Colt Match Target Lightweight

Browning BAR High-Grade Auto Rifles

Similar to BAR Mark II Safari model except has grayed receiver with big-game scenes framed in gold with select walnut stock and forearm. Furnished with no sights. Introduced 2001.
Price: 270, 30-06 (whitetail and mule deer scenes) **$1,820.00**
Price: 7mm Rem. Mag., 300 Win. Mag. (moose and elk scenes)
. . . . **$1,876.00**

BROWNING BAR STALKER AUTO RIFLES

Caliber: 243, 308, 270, 30-06, 7mm Rem. Mag., 300 Win. Mag., 338 Win. Mag., 270 WSM< 7mm WSM. **Barrel:** 20", 22" and 24". **Weight:** 6 lbs., 12 oz. (243) to 8 lbs., 2 oz. (magnum cals.) **Length:** 41" to 45" overall. **Stock:** Black composite stock and forearm. **Sights:** Hooded front and adjustable rear or none. **Features:** Optional BOSS (no sights); gas-operated action with seven-lug rotary bolt; dual action bars; 3- or 4-shot magazine (depending on caliber). Introduced 2001. Imported by Browning.
Price: BAR Stalker, open sights (243, 308, 270, 30-06) **$809.00**
Price: BAR Stalker, open sights (7mm, 300 Win. Mag.,
338 Win. Mag.) **$883.00**
Price: BAR Stalker, BOSS (7mm, 300 Win. Mag., 338 Win. Mag.) **$941.00**

BUSHMASTER M17S BULLPUP RIFLE

Caliber: 223, 10-shot magazine. **Barrel:** 21.5", chrome lined;1:9" twist. **Weight:** 8.2 lbs. **Length:** 30" overall. **Stock:** Fiberglass-filled nylon. **Sights:** Designed for optics—carrying handle incorporates scope mount rail for Weaver-type rings; also includes 25-meter open iron sights. **Features:** Gas-operated, short-stroke piston system; ambidextrous magazine release. Introduced 1993. Made in U.S.A. by Bushmaster Firearms, Inc./Quality Parts Co.
Price: **$765.00**

BUSHMASTER SHORTY XM15 E2S CARBINE

Caliber: 223,10-shot magazine. **Barrel:** 16", heavy; 1:9" twist. **Weight:** 7.2 lbs. **Length:** 34.75" overall. **Stock:** A2 type; fixed black composition. **Sights:** Fully adjustable M16A2 sight system. **Features:** Patterned after Colt M-16A2. Chrome-lined barrel with manganese phosphate finish. "Shorty" handguards. Has forged aluminum receivers with push-pin. Made in U.S.A. by Bushmaster Firearms Inc.
Price: . . . . (A2) **$985.00**
Price: (A3) **$1,085.00**

Bushmaster XM15 E2S Dissipator Carbine

Similar to the XM15 E2S Shorty carbine except has full-length "Dissipator" handguards. Weighs 7.6 lbs.; 34.75" overall; forged aluminum receivers with push-pin style takedown. Made in U.S.A. by Bushmaster Firearms, Inc.
Price: . . . . (A2 type) **$995.00**
Price: (A3 type) **$1,095.00**

Bushmaster XM15 E25 AK Shorty Carbine

Similar to the XM15 E2S Shorty except has 14.5" barrel with an AK muzzle brake permanently attached giving 16" barrel length. Weighs 7.3 lbs. Introduced 1999. Made in U.S.A. by Bushmaster Firearms, Inc.
Price: . . . . (A2 type) **$1,005.00**
Price: (A3 type) **$1,105.00**

Bushmaster M4/M4A3 Post-Ban Carbine

Similar to the XM15 E2S except has 14.5" barrel with Mini Y compensator, and fixed tele-stock. MR configuration has fixed carry handle; M4A3 has removeable carry handle.
Price: (M4) **$1,065.00**
Price: (M4A3) **$1,165.00**

BUSHMASTER VARMINTER RIFLE

Caliber: 223 Rem., 5-shot. **Barrel:** 24", 1:9" twist, fluted, heavy, stainless. **Weight:** 8/3/4 lbs. **Length:** 42-1/4". **Stock:** Rubberized pistol grip. **Sights:** 1/2" scope risers. **Features:** Gas-operated, semi-auto, 2 stage trigger, slotted free floater forend, lockable hard case.
Price: **$1,245.00**

COLT MATCH TARGET RIFLE

Caliber: 223 Rem., 5-shot magazine. **Barrel:** 16.1" or 20". **Weight:** 7.1 to 8-1/2 lbs. **Length:** 34-1/2" to 39". **Stock:** Composition stock, grip, forend. **Sights:** Post front, rear adjustable for windage and elevation. **Features:** 5-round detachable box magazine, flash suppressor, sling swivels. Forward bolt assist included. Introduced 1991. Made in U.S.A. by Colt's Manufacturing Co. Inc.
Price: Colt Light Rifle **$779.00**
Price: Match Target HBAR, from **$1,194.00**

CENTERFIRE RIFLES — AUTOLOADERS

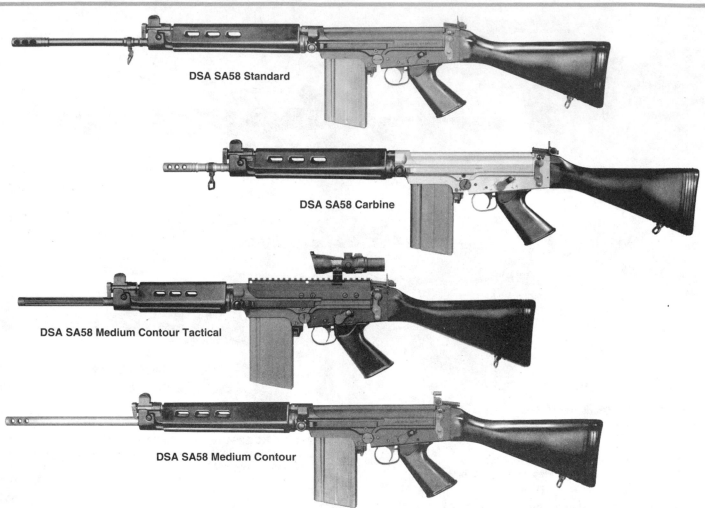

DSA SA58 Standard

DSA SA58 Carbine

DSA SA58 Medium Contour Tactical

DSA SA58 Medium Contour

DPMS PANTHER ARMS A-15 RIFLES

Caliber: 223 Rem., 7.62x39. **Barrel:** 16" to 24". **Weight:** 7-3/4 to 11-3/4 lbs. **Length:** 34-1/2 to 42-1/4" overall. **Stock:** Black Zytel® composite. **Sights:** Square front post, adjustable A2 rear. **Features:** Steel or stainless steel heavy or bull barrel; hard-coat anodized receiver; aluminum free-float tube handguard; many options. From DPMS Panther Arms.

Price: Panther Bull A-15 (20" stainless bull barrel) **$915.00**
Price: Panther Bull Twenty-Four (24" stainless bull barrel) **$945.00**
Price: Bulldog (20" stainless fluted barrel, flat top receiver) **$1,219.00**
Price: Panther Bull Sweet Sixteen (16" stainless bull barrel) **$885.00**
Price: DCM Panther (20" stainless heavy bbl., n.m. sights) **$1,099.00**
Price: Panther 7.62x39 (20" steel heavy barrel) **$849.00**

DSA SA58 CONGO, PARA CONGO

Caliber: 308 Win. **Barrel:** 18" w/short muzzle brake. **Weight:** 8.6 lbs. (Congo); 9.85 lbs. (Para Congo). **Length:** 39.75" **Stock:** Synthetic w/military grade furniture (Congo); Synthetic with non-folding steel para stock (Para Congo). **Sights:** Post, front, windage adjustable peep, rear (Congo); Belgian style para flip peep, rear (Para Congo). **Features:** Fully-adjustable gas system, high-grade steel upper receiver with carry handle. Made in U.S.A. by DSA, Inc.

Price: . . . . $1,695.00 (Congo); $1,995.00 (Para Congo)

DSA SA58 GRAY WOLF

Caliber: 308 Win., 300 WSM. **Barrel:** 21" match-grade bull w/target crown. **Weight:** 13 lbs. **Length:** 41.75" **Stock:** Synthetic. **Sights:** Elevation adjustable post, front; windage adjustable match peep, rear. **Features:** Fully-adjustable gas system, high-grade steel upper receiver, Picatinny scope mount, DuraCoat finish. Made in U.S.A. by DSA, Inc.

Price: **$2,120.00**

DSA SA58 PREDATOR

Caliber: 260 Rem., 243 Win., 308 Win. **Barrel:** 16" and 19" w/target crown. **Weight:** 9 to 9.3 lbs. **Length:** 36.25" to 39.25". **Stock:** Synthetic. **Sights:** Elevation adjustable post, front; windage adjustable match peep, rear. **Features:** Fully-adjustable gas system, high-grade steel upper receiver, Picatinny scope mount, DuraCoat solid and camo finishes.

Price: . . . . **$1,595.00** (308 win.); **$1,695.00** (243 Win., 260 Rem.)

DSA SA58 T48

Caliber: 308 Win. **Barrel:** 16.25" with Browning replica flash hider. **Weight:** 9.3 lbs. **Length:** 44.5". **Stock:** European walnut. **Sights:** Adjustable post front, adjustable rear peep. **Features:** Gas-operated semi-auto with fully adjustable gas system, high grade steel upper receiver. DuraCoat finishes. Made in U.S.A. by DSA, Inc.

Price: **$1,795.00**

DSA SA58 GI

Similar to the SA58 T48, except has steel bipod cut handguard with haardwood stock and synthetic pistol grip, original GI steel lower receiver with GI bipod. Made in U.S.A. by DSA, Inc.

Price: **$1,695.00**

DSA SA58 TACTICAL CARBINE, CARBINE

Caliber: 308 Win., limited 243 and 260. **Barrel:** 16.25" with integrally machined muzzle brake. **Weight:** 8.75 lbs. **Length:** 38.25". **Stock:** Fiberglass reinforced synthetic handguard. **Sights:** Adjustable post front, adjustable rear peep. **Features:** Gas-operated semi-auto with fully adjustable gas system, high grade steel or 416 stainless upper receiver. In variety of camo finishes. Made in U.S.A. by DSA, Inc.

Price: Tactical Fluted bbl. **$1,475.00**
Price: Carbine stainless steel bbl. **$1,645.00**
Price: Carbine high-grade steel bbl. **$1,395.00**

DSA SA58 Bull

DSA SA58 T48 Replica

DSA SA58 OSW

EAA/Saiga 380

RIFLES

DSA SA58 MEDIUM CONTOUR

Caliber: 308 Win., limited 243 and 260. **Barrel:** 21" with integrally machined muzzle brake. **Weight:** 9.75 lbs. **Length:** 43". **Stock:** Fiberglass reinforced synthetic handguard. **Sights:** Adjustable post front with match rear peep. **Features:** Gas-operated semi-auto with fully adjustable gas system, high grade steel or 416 stainless upper receiver. In variety of camo finishes. Made in U.S.A. by DSA, Inc.
Price: chrome moly **$1,475.00**
Price: stainless steel **$1,725.00**

DSA SA58 21" OR 24" BULL BARREL RIFLE

Caliber: 308 Win., 300 WSM. **Barrel:** 21" or 24". **Weight:** 11.1 and 11.5 lbs. **Length:** 41.5" and 44.5". **Stock:** Synthetic, free floating handguard. **Sights:** Elevation adjustable protected post front, match rear peep. **Features:** Gas-operated semi-auto with fully adjustable gas system, high grade steel or stainless upper receiver. Made in U.S.A. by DSA, Inc.
Price: 21", 24" **$1,745.00**
Price: 24" fluted bbl. **$1,795.00**

DSA SA58 MINI OSW

Caliber: 7.62 NATO. **Barrel:** 11" or 13" with muzzle brake. **Weight:** 9 to 9.35 lbs. **Length:** 33". **Stock:** Synthetic. **Features:** Gas-operated semi-auto or select fire with fully adjustable short gas system, optional FAL Rail Interface Handguard, SureFire Vertical Foregrip System, EOTech HOLOgraphic Sight and ITC Cheekrest. Made in U.S.A. by DSA, Inc.
Price: **$1,525.00**

EAA/SAIGA SEMI-AUTO RIFLE

Caliber: 7.62x39, 308, 223. **Barrel:** 20.5", 22", 16.3". **Weight:** 7 to 8-1/2 lbs. **Length:** 43". **Stock:** Synthetic or wood. **Sights:** Adjustable, sight base. **Features:** Based on AK Combat rifle by Kalashnikov. Imported from Russia by EAA Corp.
Price: 7.62x39 (syn.) **$239.00**
Price: 308 (syn. or wood) **$429.00**
Price: 223 (syn.) **$389.00**

EAGLE ARMS AR-10 RIFLE

Caliber: 308. **Barrel:** 20", 24". **Weight:** NA **Length:** NA **Stock:** Synthetic. **Sights:** Adjustable A2, front, Std. A2, rear; Flat top and Match Rifle have no sights but adjustable Picatinny rail furnished. **Features:** A product of the latest in manufacturing technology to provide a quality rifle at a reasonable price. Introduced 2003. Made in U.S.A. by Eagle Arms.
Price: AR-10 Service Rifle **$1,055.00**
Price: AR-10 Flat Top Rifle **$999.95**
Price: AR-10 Match Rifle **$1,480.00**

EAGLE ARMS M15 RIFLE

Caliber: 223. **Barrel:** 16", 20". **Weight:** NA **Length:** NA **Stock:** Synthetic. **Sights:** Adjustable A2, front; Std. A2, rear; Flat Top Rifle & Carbine versions, no sights furnished. **Features:** Available in 4 different configurations, the latest manufacturing technology has been employed to keep the price reasonable. Introduced 2003. Made in U.S.A. by Eagle Arms.
Price: A2 Rifle **$795.00**
Price: A2 Carbine **$795.00**
Price: Flat Top Rifle **$835.00**
Price: Flat Top Carbine **$835.00**

Heckler & Koch SLB 2000

Heckler & Koch SL8-1

Heckler & Koch USC

Hi-Point Carbine

HECKLER & KOCH SLB 2000 RIFLE

Caliber: 30-06; 2-, 5- and 10-shot magazines. **Barrel:** 19.7". **Weight:** 8 lb. **Length:** 41.3". **Stock:** Oil-finished, checkered walnut. **Sights:** Ramp front, patridge rear. **Features:** Short-stroke, piston-actuated gas operation; modular steel and polymer construction; free-floating barrel; pistol grip angled for natural feel. Introduced 2001. From H&K.
Price: **$1,299.00**

HECKLER & KOCH SL8-1 RIFLE

Caliber: 223; 10-shot magazine. **Barrel:** 17.7". **Weight:** 8.6 lbs. **Length:** 38.6" overall. **Stock:** Polymer thumbhole. **Sights:** Blade front with integral hood; fully adjustable rear diopter. Picatinny rail. **Features:** Based on German military G36 rifle. Uses short-stroke piston-actuated gas operation; almost entirely constructed of carbon fiber-reinforced polymer. Free-floating heavy target barrel. Introduced 2000. From H&K.
Price: **$1,249.00**

HECKLER & KOCH USC CARBINE

Caliber: 45 ACP, 10-shot magazine. **Barrel:** 16". **Weight:** 8.6 lb. **Length:** 35.4" overall. **Stock:** Skeletonized polymer thumbhole. **Sights:** Blade front with integral hood, fully adjustable diopter. **Features:** Based on German UMP submachine gun. Blowback operation; almost entirely constructed of carbon fiber-reinforced polymer. Free-floating heavy target barrel. Introduced 2000. From H&K.
Price: **$1,249.00**

HI-POINT 9MM CARBINE

Caliber: 9mm Para., 40 S&W, 10-shot magazine. **Barrel:** 16-1/2" (17-1/2" for 40 S&W). **Weight:** 4-1/2 lbs. **Length:** 31-1/2" overall. **Stock:** Black polymer, camouflage. **Sights:** Protected post front, aperture rear. Integral scope mount. **Features:** Grip-mounted magazine release. Black or

chrome finish. Sling swivels. Available with laser or red dot sights. Introduced 1996. Made in U.S.A. by MKS Supply, Inc.
Price: Black or chrome, 9mm **$199.00**
Price: 40 S&W **$225.00**
Price: Camo stock **$210.00**

IAI M-333 M1 GARAND

Caliber: 30-06, 8-shot clip. **Barrel:** 24". **Weight:** 9-1/2 lbs. **Length:** 43.6" overall. **Stock:** Hardwood. **Sights:** Blade front, aperture adjustable rear. **Features:** Parkerized finish; gas-operated semi-automatic; remanufactured to military specifications. From IAI.
Price: **$971.75**

IAI M-888 M1 CARBINE SEMI-AUTOMATIC RIFLE

Caliber: 22, 30 Carbine. **Barrel:** 18"-20". **Weight:** 5-1/2 lbs. **Length:** 35"-37" overall. **Stock:** Laminate, walnut or birch. **Sights:** Blade front, adjustable rear. **Features:** Gas-operated, air cooled, manufactured to military specifications. 10/15/30 rnd. mag. scope available. From IAI.
Price: 30 cal. .... **$556.00 to $604.00**
Price: 22 cal. .... **$567.00 to $654.00**

Intrac Arms IAI-65 Rifle

A civilian-legal version of the original HKM rifle manufactured in Hungary. Manufactured by Gordon Technologies using an original AMD-65 matching parts kit built on an AKM receiver. The original wire stock is present, but it is welded in the open position as per BATF regulations. Furnished with a 12.6" barrel with large weld-in-place muzzle brake to bring its length over the 16" federal minimum. This rifle accepts all 7.62x39mm magazines and drums. Introduced 2002. From Intrac Arms International, Inc.
Price: **$799.00**

Remington Model 7400

Ruger Deerfield 99/44 Carbine

Ruger PC4 Carbine

Ruger Ranch Mini 14/5R

LES BAER CUSTOM ULTIMATE AR 223 RIFLES

Caliber: 223. **Barrel:** 18", 20", 22", 24". **Weight:** 7-3/4 to 9-3/4 lb. **Length:** NA. **Stock:** Black synthetic. **Sights:** None furnished; Picatinny-style flat top rail for scope mounting. **Features:** Forged receiver; Ultra single-stage trigger (Jewell two-stage trigger optional); titanium firing pin; Versa-Pod bi-pod; chromed National Match carrier; stainless steel, hand-lapped and cryo-treated barrel; guaranteed to shoot 1/2 or 3/4 MOA, depending on model. Made in U.S.A. by Les Bear Custom Inc.

Price: Super Varmint Model **$1,989.00**
Price: M4 Flattop Model **$2,195.00**
Price: IPSC Action Model **$2,195.00**

LR 300 SR LIGHT SPORT RIFLE

Caliber: 223. **Barrel:** 16-1/4"; 1:9" twist. **Weight:** 7.2 lbs. **Length:** 36" overall (extended stock), 26-1/4" (stock folded). **Stock:** Folding, tubular steel, with thumbhold-type grip. **Sights:** Trijicon post front, Trijicon rear. **Features:** Uses AR-15 type upper and lower receivers; flattop receiver with weaver base. Accepts all AR-15/M-16 magazines. Introduced 1996. Made in U.S.A. from Z-M Weapons.

Price: **$2,550.00**

OLYMPIC ARMS CAR-97 RIFLES

Caliber: 223, 7-shot; 9mm Para., 45 ACP, 40 S&W, 10mm, 10-shot. **Barrel:** 16". **Weight:** 7 lbs. **Length:** 34.75" overall. **Stock:** A2 stowaway grip, telescoping-look butt. **Sights:** Post front, fully adjustable aperature rear. **Features:** Based on AR-15 rifle. Post-ban version of the CAR-15. Made in U.S.A. by Olympic Arms, Inc.

Price: 223 . . . . **$780.00**
Price: 9mm Para., 45 ACP, 40 S&W, 10mm **$840.00**
Price: PCR Eliminator (223, full-length handguards) **$803.00**

OLYMPIC ARMS PCR-4 RIFLE

Caliber: 223, 10-shot magazine. **Barrel:** 20". **Weight:** 8 lbs., 5 oz. **Length:** 38.25" overall. **Stock:** A2 stowaway grip, trapdoor buttstock. **Sights:** Post front, A1 rear adjustable for windage. **Features:** Based on the AR-15 rifle. Barrel is button rifled with 1:9" twist. No bayonet lug. Introduced 1994. Made in U.S.A. by Olympic Arms, Inc.

Price: **$792.00**

OLYMPIC ARMS PCR-6 RIFLE

Caliber: 7.62x39mm (PCR-6), 10-shot magazine. **Barrel:** 16". **Weight:** 7 lbs. **Length:** 34" overall. **Stock:** A2 stowaway grip, trapdoor buttstock.

Sights: Post front, A1 rear adjustable for windage. **Features:** Based on the CAR-15. No bayonet lug. Button-cut rifling. Introduced 1994. Made in U.S.A. by Olympic Arms, Inc.

Price: **$845.00**

REMINGTON MODEL 7400 AUTO RIFLE

Caliber: 243 Win., 270 Win., 308 Win., 30-06, 4-shot magazine. **Barrel:** 22" round tapered. **Weight:** 7-1/2 lbs. **Length:** 42-5/8" overall. **Stock:** Walnut, deluxe cut checkered pistol grip and forend. Satin or high-gloss finish. **Sights:** Gold bead front sight on ramp; step rear sight with windage adjustable. **Features:** Redesigned and improved version of the Model 742. Positive cross-bolt safety. Receiver tapped for scope mount. Introduced 1981.

Price: **$624.00**
Price: Carbine (18-1/2" bbl., 30-06 only) **$624.00**
Price: With black synthetic stock, matte black metal,
rifle or carbine **$520.00**
Price: Weathermaster, nickel-plated w/synthetic stock and forend,
270, 30-06 . . . . **$624.00**

ROCK RIVER ARMS STANDARD A2 RIFLE

Caliber: 45 ACP. **Barrel:** NA. **Weight:** 8.2 lbs. **Length:** NA. **Stock:** Thermoplastic. **Sights:** Standard AR-15 style sights. **Features:** Two-stage, national match trigger; optional muzzle brake. Made in U.S.A. From River Rock Arms.

Price: **$925.00**

RUGER DEERFIELD 99/44 CARBINE

Caliber: 44 Mag., 4-shot rotary magazine. **Barrel:** 18-1/2". **Weight:** 6-1/4 lbs. **Length:** 36-7/8" overall. **Stock:** Hardwood. **Sights:** Gold bead front, folding adjustable aperture rear. **Features:** Semi-automatic action; dual front-locking lugs lock directly into receiver; integral scope mount; push-button safety; includes 1" rings and gun lock. Introduced 2000. Made in U.S.A. by Sturm, Ruger & Co.

Price: **$675.00**

RUGER PC4, PC9 CARBINES

Caliber: 9mm Para., 40 cal., 10-shot magazine. **Barrel:** 16.25". **Weight:** 6 lbs., 4 oz. **Length:** 34.75" overall. **Stock:** Black high impact synthetic checkered grip and forend. **Sights:** Blade front, open adjustable rear; integral Ruger scope mounts. **Features:** Delayed blowback action; manual push-button cross bolt safety and internal firing pin block safety automatic slide lock. Introduced 1997. Made in U.S.A. by Sturm, Ruger & Co.

Price: PC9, PC4, (9mm, 40 cal.) **$605.00**
Price: PC4GR, PC9GR, (40 auto, 9mm, post sights, ghost ring) **$628.00**

CENTERFIRE RIFLES — AUTOLOADERS

Springfield M1A

Springfield National Match M1A

Springfield Super Match with Camo M1A

RUGER MINI-14/5 AUTOLOADING RIFLE

Caliber: 223 Rem., 5-shot detachable box magazine. **Barrel:** 18-1/2". Rifling twist 1:9". **Weight:** 6.4 lbs. **Length:** 37-1/4" overall. **Stock:** American hardwood, steel reinforced. **Sights:** Ramp front, fully adjustable rear. **Features:** Fixed piston gas-operated, positive primary extraction. New buffer system, redesigned ejector system. Ruger S100RM scope rings included on Ranch Rifle.
Price: Mini-14/5R, Ranch Rifle, blued, scope rings **$695.00**
Price: K-Mini-14/5R, Ranch Rifle, stainless, scope rings. **$770.00**
Price: Mini-14/5, blued. **$655.00**
Price: K-Mini-14/5, stainless. **$715.00**
Price: K-Mini-14/5P, stainless, synthetic stock. **$715.00**
Price: K-Mini-14/5RP, Ranch Rifle, stainless, synthetic stock. . . . **$770.00**

Ruger Mini Thirty Rifle

Similar to the Mini-14 Ranch Rifle except modified to chamber the 7.62x39 Russian service round. Weight is about 6-7/8 lbs. Has 6-groove barrel with 1:10" twist, Ruger Integral Scope Mount bases and folding peep rear sight. Detachable 5-shot staggered box magazine. Blued finish. Introduced 1987.
Price: Blue, scope rings **$695.00**
Price: Stainless, scope rings **$770.00**

SPRINGFIELD, INC. M1A RIFLE

Caliber: 7.62mm NATO (308), 5- or 10-shot box magazine. **Barrel:** 25-1/16" with flash suppressor, 22" without suppressor. **Weight:** 9-3/4 lbs. **Length:** 44-1/4" overall. **Stock:** American walnut with walnut-colored heat-resistant fiberglass handguard. Matching walnut handguard available. Also available with fiberglass stock. **Sights:** Military, square blade front, full click-adjustable aperture rear. **Features:** Commercial equivalent of the U.S. M-14 service rifle with no provision for automatic firing. From Springfield, Inc.
Price: Standard M1A, black fiberglass stock **$1,319.00**
Price: Standard M1A, black fiberglass stock, stainless **$1,629.00**
Price: Standard M1A, black stock, carbon barrel **$1,379.00**
Price: Standard M1A, Mossy Oak stock, carbon barrel **$1,443.00**
Price: Scout Squad M1A . . . . **$1,529 to $1,639.00**
Price: National Match . . . . **$1,995.00 to $2,040.00**
Price: Super Match (heavy premium barrel), about **$2,449.00**

Price: M21 Tactical Rifle (adj. cheekpiece), about **$2,975.00**
Price: M25 White Feather Tactical Rifle **$4,195.00**

SPRINGFIELD M1 GARAND RIFLE

Caliber: 308, 30-06. **Barrel:** 24". **Weight:** 9.5 lbs. **Length:** 43-3/5". **Stock:** Walnut. **Sights:** Military aperture with MOA adjustments for both windage and elevation, rear; military square post, front. **Features:** Original U.S. government-issue parts on a new walnut stock.
Price: . . . . **$1,099 to $1,129.00**

STONER SR-15 M-5 RIFLE

Caliber: 223. **Barrel:** 20". **Weight:** 7.6 lbs. **Length:** 38" overall. **Stock:** Black synthetic. **Sights:** Post front, fully adjustable rear (300-meter sight). **Features:** Modular weapon system; two-stage trigger. Black finish. Introduced 1998. Made in U.S.A. by Knight's Mfg.
Price: **$1,650.00**
Price: M-4 Carbine (16" barrel, 6.8 lbs) **$1,555.00**

STONER SR-25 CARBINE

Caliber: 7.62 NATO, 10-shot steel magazine. **Barrel:** 16" free-floating **Weight:** 7-3/4 lbs. **Length:** 35.75" overall. **Stock:** Black synthetic. **Sights:** Integral Weaver-style rail. Scope rings, iron sights optional. **Features:** Shortened, non-slip handguard; removable carrying handle. Matte black finish. Introduced 1995. Made in U.S.A. by Knight's Mfg. Co.
Price: **$3,345.00**

WILKINSON LINDA CARBINE

Caliber: 9mm Para. **Barrel:** 16-3/16". **Weight:** 7 lbs. **Stocks:** Fixed tubular with wood pad. **Sights:** Aperture rear sight. **Features:** Aluminum receiver, pre-ban configuration (limited supplies), vent. barrel shroud, small wooden forearm, 18 or 31 shot mag. Many accessories.
Price: **$1,800.00**

Wilkinson Linda L2 Limited Edition

Manufactured from the last 600 of the original 2,200 pre-ban Linda Carbines, includes many upgrades and accessories. New 2002.
Price: **$4,800.00**

WILKINSON TERRY CARBINE

Caliber: 9mm Para. **Barrel:** 16-3/16". **Weight:** 7 lbs. **Stocks:** Black or maple. **Sights:** Adjustable. **Features:** Blowback semi-auto action, 31 shot mag., closed breech.
Price: . . . . **NA**

RIFLES

Both classic arms and recent designs in American-style repeaters for sport and field shooting.

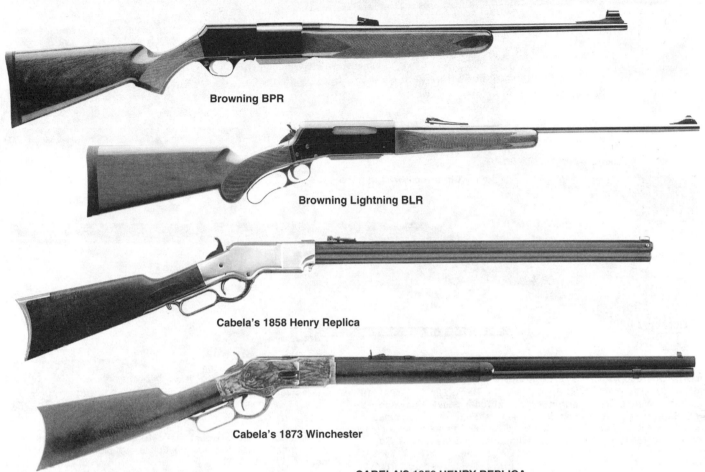

Browning BPR

Browning Lightning BLR

Cabela's 1858 Henry Replica

Cabela's 1873 Winchester

BROWNING BPR PUMP RIFLE

Caliber: 243, 308 (short action); 270, 30-06, 7mm Rem. Mag., 300 Win. Mag., 4-shot magazine (3 for magnums). **Barrel:** 22"; 24" for magnum calibers. **Weight:** 7 lbs., 3 oz. **Length:** 43" overall (22" barrel). **Stock:** Select walnut with full pistol grip, high gloss finish. **Sights:** Gold bead on hooded ramp front, open click adjustable rear. **Features:** Slide-action mechanism cams forend down away from the barrel. Seven-lug rotary bolt; cross-bolt safety behind trigger; removable magazine; alloy receiver. Introduced 1997. Imported from Belgium by Browning.
Price: Standard calibers $718.00
Price: Magnum calibers $772.00

BROWNING LIGHTNING BLR LEVER-ACTION RIFLE

Caliber: 22-250, 243, 7mm-08, 308 Win., 270 WSM, 7mm WSM, 300 WSM, 358, 450 Marlin, 270 Win., 30-06 Sprg., 7mm Rem. Mag., 300 Win. Mag. 4-shot detachable magazine. **Barrel:** 20" round tapered. **Weight:** 6 lbs., 8 oz. **Length:** 39-1/2" overall. **Stock:** Walnut. Checkered grip and forend, high-gloss finish. **Sights:** Gold bead on ramp front; low profile square notch adjustable rear. **Features:** Wide, grooved trigger; half-cock hammer safety; fold-down hammer. Receiver tapped for scope mount. Recoil pad installed. Introduced 1996. Imported from Japan by Browning.
Price: $649.00

Browning Lightning BLR Long Action

Similar to the standard Lightning BLR except has long action to accept 30-06, 270, 7mm Rem. Mag. and 300 Win. Mag. Barrel lengths are 22" for 30-06 and 270, 24" for 7mm Rem. Mag. and 300 Win. Mag. Has six-lug rotary bolt; bolt and receiver are full-length fluted. Fold-down hammer at half-cock. Weighs about 7 lbs., overall length 42-7/8" (22" barrel). Introduced 1996.
Price: $686.00

CABELA'S 1858 HENRY REPLICA

Caliber: 44-40, 45 Colt. **Barrel:** 24-1/4". **Weight:** 9.3 lbs. **Length:** 43.75" overall. **Stock:** American walnut. **Sights:** Bead front, open adjustable rear. **Features:** Brass receiver and buttplate. Uses original Henry loading system. Faithful to the original rifle. Introduced 1994. Imported by Cabela's.
Price: $999.99

CABELA'S 1866 WINCHESTER REPLICA

Caliber: 44-40, 45 Colt. **Barrel:** 24-1/4". **Weight:** 9 lbs. **Length:** 43" overall. **Stock:** European walnut. **Sights:** Bead front, open adjustable rear. **Features:** Solid brass receiver, buttplate, forend cap. Octagonal barrel. Faithful to the original Winchester '66 rifle. Introduced 1994. Imported by Cabela's.
Price: $799.99

CABELA'S 1873 WINCHESTER REPLICA

Caliber: 44-40, 45 Colt. **Barrel:** 24-1/4", 30". **Weight:** 8.5 lbs. **Length:** 43-1/4", 50" overall. **Stock:** European walnut. **Sights:** Bead front, open adjustable rear; globe front, tang rear. **Features:** Color case-hardened steel receiver. Faithful to the original Model 1873 rifle. Introduced 1994. Imported by Cabela's.
Price: Sporting model, 30" barrel, 44-40, 45 Colt $999.99
Price: Sporting model, 24" or 25" barrel $899.99

CIMARRON 1860 HENRY REPLICA

Caliber: 44 WCF, 13-shot magazine. **Barrel:** 24-1/4" (rifle), 22" (carbine). **Weight:** 9-1/2 lbs. **Length:** 43" overall (rifle). **Stock:** European walnut. **Sights:** Bead front, open adjustable rear. **Features:** Brass receiver and buttplate. Uses original Henry loading system. Faithful to the original rifle. Introduced 1991. Imported by Cimarron F.A. Co.
Price: $1,029.00

Cimarron 1866 Winchester Replica

Cimarron 1873 Long Range

Dixie 1873

IAR 1873
Revolver Carbine

CIMARRON 1866 WINCHESTER REPLICAS

Caliber: 22 LR, 22 WMR, 38 Spec., 44 WCF. **Barrel:** 24-1/4" (rifle), 19" (carbine). **Weight:** 9 lbs. **Length:** 43" overall (rifle). **Stock:** European walnut. **Sights:** Bead front, open adjustable rear. **Features:** Solid brass receiver, buttplate, forend cap. Octagonal barrel. Faithful to the original Winchester '66 rifle. Introduced 1991. Imported by Cimarron F.A. Co.
Price: Rifle **$839.00**
Price: Carbine **$829.00**

CIMARRON 1873 SHORT RIFLE

Caliber: 357 Mag., 38 Spec., 32 WCF, 38 WCF, 44 Spec., 44 WCF, 45 Colt. **Barrel:** 20" tapered octagon. **Weight:** 7.5 lbs. **Length:** 39" overall. **Stock:** Walnut. **Sights:** Bead front, adjustable semi-buckhorn rear. **Features:** Has half "button" magazine. Original-type markings, including caliber, on barrel and elevator and "Kings" patent. From Cimarron F.A. Co.
Price: . . . . **$949.00 to $999.00**

CIMARRON 1873 LONG RANGE RIFLE

Caliber: 44 WCF, 45 Colt. **Barrel:** 30", octagonal. **Weight:** 8-1/2 lbs. **Length:** 48" overall. **Stock:** Walnut. **Sights:** Blade front, semi-buckhorn ramp rear. Tang sight optional. **Features:** Color case-hardened frame; choice of modern blue-black or charcoal blue for other parts. Barrel marked "Kings Improvement." From Cimarron F.A. Co.
Price: . . . . **$999.00 to $1,199.00**

Cimarron 1873 Sporting Rifle

Similar to the 1873 Short Rifle except has 24" barrel with half-magazine.
Price: . . . . **$949.00 to $999.00**

DIXIE ENGRAVED 1873 RIFLE

Caliber: 44-40, 11-shot magazine. **Barrel:** 20", round. **Weight:** 7-3/4 lbs. **Length:** 39" overall. **Stock:** Walnut. **Sights:** Blade front, adjustable rear. **Features:** Engraved and case-hardened frame. Duplicate of Winchester 1873. Made in Italy. From 21 Gun Works.
Price: **$1,350.00**
Price: Plain, blued carbine **$850.00**

E.M.F. 1860 HENRY RIFLE

Caliber: 44-40 or 45 Colt. **Barrel:** 24.25". **Weight:** About 9 lbs. **Length:** About 43.75" overall. **Stock:** Oil-stained American walnut. **Sights:** Blade front, rear adjustable for elevation. **Features:** Reproduction of the original Henry rifle with brass frame and buttplate, rest blued. From E.M.F.
Price: Brass frame **$850.00**
Price: Steel frame **$950.00**

E.M.F. 1866 YELLOWBOY LEVER ACTIONS

Caliber: 38 Spec., 44-40. **Barrel:** 19" (carbine), 24" (rifle). **Weight:** 9 lbs. **Length:** 43" (rifle). **Stock:** European walnut. **Sights:** Bead front, open adjustable rear. **Features:** Solid brass frame, blued barrel, lever, hammer, buttplate. Imported from Italy by E.M.F.
Price: Rifle **$690.00**
Price: Carbine. **$675.00**

E.M.F. HARTFORD MODEL 1892 LEVER-ACTION RIFLE

Caliber: 45 Colt. **Barrel:** 24", octagonal. **Weight:** 7-1/2 lbs. **Length:** 43" overall. **Stock:** European walnut. **Sights:** Blade front, open adjustable rear. **Features:** Color case-hardened frame, lever, trigger and hammer with blued barrel, or overall blue finish. Introduced 1998. Imported by E.M.F.
Price: Standard. **$590.00**

E.M.F. MODEL 1873 LEVER-ACTION RIFLE

Caliber: 32/20, 357 Mag., 38/40, 44-40, 44 Spec., 45 Colt. **Barrel:** 24". **Weight:** 8 lbs. **Length:** 43-1/4" overall. **Stock:** European walnut. **Sights:** Bead front, rear adjustable for windage and elevation. **Features:** Color case-hardened frame (blue on carbine). Imported by E.M.F.
Price: Rifle **$865.00**
Price: Carbine, 19" barrel **$865.00**

IAR MODEL 1873 REVOLVER CARBINE

Caliber: 357 Mag., 45 Colt. **Barrel:** 18". **Weight:** 4 lbs., 8 oz. **Length:** 34" overall. **Stock:** One-piece walnut. **Sights:** Blade front, notch rear. **Features:** Color case-hardened frame, blue barrel, backstrap and triggerguard. Introduced 1998. Imported from Italy by IAR, Inc.
Price: Standard. **$490.00**

Marlin 336C

Marlin 336 Cowboy

Marlin 336Y Spikehorn

Marlin 444P Outfitter

MARLIN MODEL 336C LEVER-ACTION CARBINE

Caliber: 30-30 or 35 Rem., 6-shot tubular magazine. **Barrel:** 20" Micro-Groove®. **Weight:** 7 lbs. **Length:** 38-1/2" overall. **Stock:** Checkered American black walnut, capped pistol grip. Mar-Shield® finish; rubber butt pad; swivel studs. **Sights:** Ramp front with Wide-Scan hood, semi-buck-horn folding rear adjustable for windage and elevation. **Features:** Hammer-block safety. Receiver tapped for scope mount, offset hammer spur; top of receiver sandblasted to prevent glare. Includes safety lock.
Price: **$529.00**

Marlin Model 336 Cowboy

Similar to the Model 336C except chambered for 38-55 Win., 24" tapered octagon barrel with deep-cut Ballard-type rifling; straight-grip walnut stock with hard rubber buttplate; blued steel forend cap; weighs 7-1/2 lbs.; 42-1/2" overall. Introduced 1999. Includes safety lock. Made in U.S.A. by Marlin.
Price: **$735.00**

Marlin Model 336A Lever-Action Carbine

Same as the Marlin 336C except has cut-checkered, walnut-finished hardwood pistol grip stock with swivel studs, 30-30 only, 6-shot. Hammer-block safety. Adjustable rear sight, brass bead front. Includes safety lock.
Price: **$451.00**
Price: With 4x scope and mount. **$501.00**

Marlin Model 336CC Lever-Action Carbine

Same as the Marlin 336A except has Mossy Oak® Break-Up camouflage stock and forearm. 30-30 only, 6-shot; receiver tapped for scope mount or receiver sight. Introduced 2001. Includes safety lock. Made in U.S.A. by Marlin.
Price: **$503.00**

Marlin Model 336SS Lever-Action Carbine

Same as the 336C except receiver, barrel and other major parts are machined from stainless steel. 30-30 only, 6-shot; receiver tapped for scope. Includes safety lock.
Price: **$640.00**

Marlin Model 336W Lever-Action Rifle

Similar to the Model 336CS except has walnut-finished, cut-checkered Maine birch stock; blued steel barrel band has integral sling swivel; no front sight hood; comes with padded nylon sling; hard rubber butt plate. Introduced 1998. Includes safety lock. Made in U.S.A. by Marlin.
Price: **$457.00**
Price: With 4x scope and mount. **$506.00**

Marlin Model 336 Y "Spikehorn"

Similar to the Models in the 336 series except in a compact format with 16-1/2" barrel measuring only 34" in overall length. Weight is 6-1/2 lbs., length of pull 12-1/2". Blued steel barrel and receiver. Chambered for 30/30 cartridge. Introduced 2003.
Price: **$536.00**

MARLIN MODEL 444 LEVER-ACTION SPORTER

Caliber: 444 Marlin, 5-shot tubular magazine. **Barrel:** 22" deep cut Ballard rifling. **Weight:** 7-1/2 lbs. **Length:** 40-1/2" overall. **Stock:** Checkered American black walnut, capped pistol grip, rubber rifle butt pad. Mar-Shield® finish; swivel studs. **Sights:** Hooded ramp front, folding semi-buckhorn rear adjustable for windage and elevation. **Features:** Hammer-block safety. Receiver tapped for scope mount; offset hammer spur. Includes safety lock.
Price: **$618.00**

Marlin Model 444P Outfitter Lever-Action

Similar to the 444SS with deep-cut Ballard-type rifling; weighs 6-3/4 lbs.; overall length 37". Available only in 444 Marlin. Introduced 1999. Includes safety lock. Made in U.S.A. by Marlin.
Price: **$631.00**

MARLIN MODEL 1894 LEVER-ACTION CARBINE

Caliber: 44 Spec./44 Mag., 10-shot tubular magazine. **Barrel:** 20" Ballard-type rifling. **Weight:** 6 lbs. **Length:** 37-1/2" overall. **Stock:** Checkered American black walnut, straight grip and forend. Mar-Shield® finish. Rubber rifle butt pad; swivel studs. **Sights:** Wide-Scan hooded ramp front, semi-buckhorn folding rear adjustable for windage and elevation. **Features:** Hammer-block safety. Receiver tapped for scope mount, offset hammer spur, solid top receiver sand blasted to prevent glare. Includes safety lock.
Price: **$544.00**

RIFLES

NEW!

CENTERFIRE RIFLES — LEVER AND SLIDE

Marlin 1894PG

Marlin 1894 Cowboy

Marlin 1894SS

Marlin 1895

Marlin 1895GS

Marlin Model 1894PG/1894FG
Pistol-gripped versions of the Model 1894. Model 1894PG is chambered for .44 Magnum; Model 1894FG is chambered for .41 Magnum.
Price: (Model 1894PG) $610.00
Price: (Model 1894FG) $610.00

Marlin Model 1894C Carbine
Similar to the standard Model 1894S except chambered for 38 Spec./357 Mag. with full-length 9-shot magazine, 18-1/2" barrel, hammer-block safety, hooded front sight. Introduced 1983. Includes safety lock.
Price: $556.00

MARLIN MODEL 1894 COWBOY
Caliber: 357 Mag., 44 Mag., 45 Colt, 10-shot magazine. Barrel: 20" except .45 Colt which has a 24" tapered octagon, deep cut rifling. Weight: 7-1/2 lbs. Length: 41-1/2" overall. Stock: Straight grip American black walnut, hard rubber buttplate, Mar-Shield® finish. Sights: Marble carbine front, adjustable Marble semi-buckhorn rear. Features: Squared finger lever; straight grip stock; blued steel forend tip. Designed for Cowboy Shooting events. Introduced 1996. Includes safety lock. Made in U.S.A. by Marlin.
Price: $820.00

Marlin Model 1894 Cowboy Competition Rifle
Similar to Model 1894 except 20" barrel, 37-1/2" long, weighs only 6 lbs., antique finish on receiver, lever and bolt. Factory-tuned for competitive cowboy action shooting.Available in .38 Spl. And .45 Colt.
Price: $986.00

Marlin Model 1894SS
Similar to Model 1894 except has stainless steel barrel, receiver, lever, guard plate, magazine tube and loading plate. Nickel-plated swivel studs.
Price: $680.00

MARLIN MODEL 1895 LEVER-ACTION RIFLE
Caliber: 45-70, 4-shot tubular magazine. Barrel: 22" round. Weight: 7-1/2 lbs. Length: 40-1/2" overall. Stock: Checkered American black walnut, full pistol grip. Mar-Shield® finish; rubber butt pad; quick detachable swivel studs. Sights: Bead front with Wide-Scan hood, semi-buckhorn folding rear adjustable for windage and elevation. Features: Hammer-block safety. Solid receiver tapped for scope mounts or receiver sights; offset hammer spur. Includes safety lock.
Price: $631.00

Marlin Model 1895G Guide Gun Lever-Action Rifle
Similar to Model 1895 with deep-cut Ballard-type rifling; straight-grip walnut stock. Overall length is 37", weighs 7 lbs. Introduced 1998. Includes safety lock. Made in U.S.A. by Marlin.
Price: $646.00

Marlin Model 1895GS Guide Gun
Similar to Model 1895G except receiver, barrel and most metal parts are machined from stainless steel. Chambered for 45-70, 4-shot, 18-1/2" barrel. Overall length is 37", weighs 7 lbs. Introduced 2001. Includes safety lock. Made in U.S.A. by Marlin.
Price: $760.00

Marlin Model 1895 Cowboy Lever-Action Rifle
Similar to Model 1895 except has 26" tapered octagon barrel with Ballard-type rifling, Marble carbine front sight and Marble adjustable semi-buckhorn rear sight. Receiver tapped for scope or receiver sight. Overall length is 44-1/2", weighs about 8 lbs. Introduced 2001. Includes safety lock. Made in U.S.A. by Marlin.
Price: $802.00

Marlin Model 1895M Lever-Action Rifle
Similar to Model 1895 except has an 18-1/2" barrel with Ballard-type cut rifling. New Model 1895MR variant has 22" barrel, pistol grip. Chambered for 450 Marlin. Includes safety lock.
Price: (Model 1895M). $695.00
Price: (Model 1895MR) $761.00

RIFLES

NEW!

CENTERFIRE RIFLES — LEVER AND SLIDE

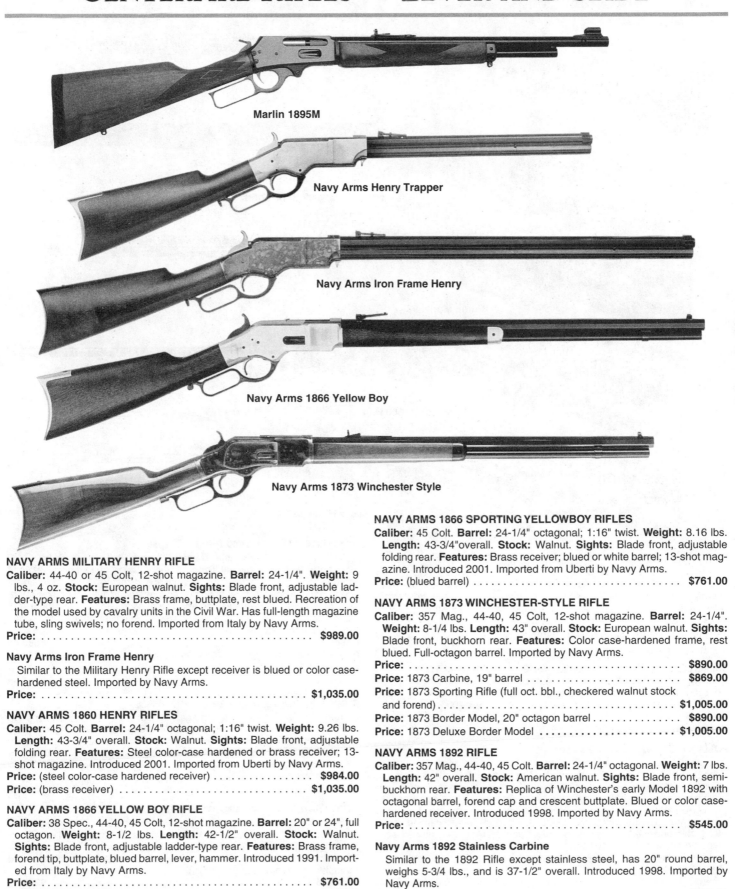

Marlin 1895M

Navy Arms Henry Trapper

Navy Arms Iron Frame Henry

Navy Arms 1866 Yellow Boy

Navy Arms 1873 Winchester Style

NAVY ARMS MILITARY HENRY RIFLE

Caliber: 44-40 or 45 Colt, 12-shot magazine. **Barrel:** 24-1/4". **Weight:** 9 lbs., 4 oz. **Stock:** European walnut. **Sights:** Blade front, adjustable ladder-type rear. **Features:** Brass frame, buttplate, rest blued. Recreation of the model used by cavalry units in the Civil War. Has full-length magazine tube, sling swivels; no forend. Imported from Italy by Navy Arms.
Price: **$989.00**

Navy Arms Iron Frame Henry

Similar to the Military Henry Rifle except receiver is blued or color case-hardened steel. Imported by Navy Arms.
Price: **$1,035.00**

NAVY ARMS 1860 HENRY RIFLES

Caliber: 45 Colt. **Barrel:** 24-1/4" octagonal; 1:16" twist. **Weight:** 9.26 lbs. **Length:** 43-3/4" overall. **Stock:** Walnut. **Sights:** Blade front, adjustable folding rear. **Features:** Steel color case hardened or brass receiver; 13-shot magazine. Introduced 2001. Imported from Uberti by Navy Arms.
Price: (steel color-case hardened receiver) **$984.00**
Price: (brass receiver) **$1,035.00**

NAVY ARMS 1866 YELLOW BOY RIFLE

Caliber: 38 Spec., 44-40, 45 Colt, 12-shot magazine. **Barrel:** 20" or 24", full octagon. **Weight:** 8-1/2 lbs. **Length:** 42-1/2" overall. **Stock:** Walnut. **Sights:** Blade front, adjustable ladder-type rear. **Features:** Brass frame, forend tip, buttplate, blued barrel, lever, hammer. Introduced 1991. Imported from Italy by Navy Arms.
Price: **$761.00**
Price: Carbine, 19" barrel **$746.00**

NAVY ARMS 1866 SPORTING YELLOWBOY RIFLES

Caliber: 45 Colt. **Barrel:** 24-1/4" octagonal; 1:16" twist. **Weight:** 8.16 lbs. **Length:** 43-3/4" overall. **Stock:** Walnut. **Sights:** Blade front, adjustable folding rear. **Features:** Brass receiver; blued or white barrel; 13-shot magazine. Introduced 2001. Imported from Uberti by Navy Arms.
Price: (blued barrel) **$761.00**

NAVY ARMS 1873 WINCHESTER-STYLE RIFLE

Caliber: 357 Mag., 44-40, 45 Colt, 12-shot magazine. **Barrel:** 24-1/4". **Weight:** 8-1/4 lbs. **Length:** 43" overall. **Stock:** European walnut. **Sights:** Blade front, buckhorn rear. **Features:** Color case-hardened frame, rest blued. Full-octagon barrel. Imported by Navy Arms.
Price: **$890.00**
Price: 1873 Carbine, 19" barrel **$869.00**
Price: 1873 Sporting Rifle (full oct. bbl., checkered walnut stock and forend) **$1,005.00**
Price: 1873 Border Model, 20" octagon barrel **$890.00**
Price: 1873 Deluxe Border Model **$1,005.00**

NAVY ARMS 1892 RIFLE

Caliber: 357 Mag., 44-40, 45 Colt. **Barrel:** 24-1/4" octagonal. **Weight:** 7 lbs. **Length:** 42" overall. **Stock:** American walnut. **Sights:** Blade front, semi-buckhorn rear. **Features:** Replica of Winchester's early Model 1892 with octagonal barrel, forend cap and crescent buttplate. Blued or color case-hardened receiver. Introduced 1998. Imported by Navy Arms.
Price: **$545.00**

Navy Arms 1892 Stainless Carbine

Similar to the 1892 Rifle except stainless steel, has 20" round barrel, weighs 5-3/4 lbs., and is 37-1/2" overall. Introduced 1998. Imported by Navy Arms.
Price: **$585.00**

RIFLES

CENTERFIRE RIFLES — LEVER AND SLIDE

Navy Arms 1892 Rifle

Navy Arms 1892 Short Rifle

Puma Model 92

Remington 7600 Rifle

Ruger Model 96/44

Navy Arms 1892 Short Rifle

Similar to the 1892 Rifle except has 20" octagonal barrel, weighs 6-1/4 lbs., and is 37-3/4" overall. Replica of the rare, special order 1892 Winchester nicknamed the "Texas Special." Blued or color case-hardened receiver and furniture. Introduced 1998. Imported by Navy Arms.

Price: **$545.00**
Price: (stainless steel, 20" octagon barrel) **$585.00**

NAVY ARMS 1892 STAINLESS RIFLE

Caliber: 357 Mag., 44-40, 45 Colt. **Barrel:** 24-1/4" octagonal. **Weight:** 7 lbs. **Length:** 42". **Stock:** American walnut. **Sights:** Brass bead front, semi-buckhorn rear. **Features:** Designed for the Cowboy Action Shooter. Stainless steel barrel, receiver and furniture. Introduced 2000. Imported by Navy Arms.

Price: **$585.00**

PUMA MODEL 92 RIFLES & CARBINES

Caliber: 38 Spec./357 Mag., 44 Mag., 45 Colt, 454 Casull (20" carbine only), 480 Ruger. **Barrel:** 20" round, 24"octagonal. **Weight:** 6.1-7.7 lbs. **Stock:** Walnut-stained hardwood. **Sights:** Open, buckhorn front & rear available. **Features:** Blue, case-hardened, stainless steel and brass receivers, matching buttplates. Blued, stainless steel barrels, full-length magazines. Thumb safety on top of both. 454 Casull carbine loads through magazine tube, has rubber recoil pad. 45 Colt brass-framed, saddle-ring rifle and 454 Casull carbine introduced 2002. The 480 Ruger version was introduced in 2003. Imported from Brazil by Legacy Sports International.

Price: Octagonal barrel. . . . . **$500.00 to $561.00**
Price: Round barrel. . . . . **$407.00 to $549.00**

REMINGTON MODEL 7600 PUMP ACTION

Caliber: 243, 270, 30-06, 308. **Barrel:** 22" round tapered. **Weight:** 7--1/2 lbs. **Length:** 42-5/8" overall. **Stock:** Cut-checkered walnut pistol grip and forend, Monte Carlo with full cheekpiece. Satin or high-gloss finish. **Sights:** Gold bead front sight on matted ramp, open step adjustable sporting rear. **Features:** Redesigned and improved version of the Model 760. Detachable 4-shot clip. Cross-bolt safety. Receiver tapped for scope mount. Introduced 1981.

Price: **$588.00**
Price: Carbine (18-1/2" bbl., 30-06 only) **$588.00**
Price: With black synthetic stock, matte black metal, rifle or carbine **$484.00**

RUGER MODEL 96/44 LEVER-ACTION RIFLE

Caliber: 44 Mag., 4-shot rotary magazine. **Barrel:** 18-1/2". **Weight:** 5-7/8 lbs. **Length:** 37-5/16" overall. **Stock:** American hardwood. **Sights:** Gold bead front, folding leaf rear. **Features:** Solid chrome-moly steel receiver. Manual cross-bolt safety, visible cocking indicator; short-throw lever action; integral scope mount; blued finish; color case-hardened lever. Introduced 1996. Made In U.S. by Sturm, Ruger & Co.

Price: 96/44M, 44 Mag **$525.00**

TRISTAR/UBERTI 1873 SPORTING RIFLE

Caliber: 44-40, 45 Colt. **Barrel:** 24-1/4", 30", octagonal. **Weight:** 8.1 lbs. **Length:** 43-1/4" overall. **Stock:** Walnut. **Sights:** Blade front adjustable for windage, open rear adjustable for elevation. **Features:** Color case-hardened frame, blued barrel, hammer, lever, buttplate, brass elevator. Imported from Italy by Tristar Sporting Arms Ltd.

Price: 24-1/4" barrel **$925.00**
Price: 30" barrel **$969.00**

RIFLES

Tristar 1873 Sporting Rifle

Tristar 1866 Yellowboy Carbine

Tristar 1860 Henry

Winchester Model 94 Big Bore

Winchester 94 Traditional

TRISTAR/UBERTI 1866 SPORTING RIFLE, CARBINE

Caliber: 22 LR, 22 WMR, 38 Spec., 44-40, 45 Colt. **Barrel:** 24-1/4", octagonal. **Weight:** 8.1 lbs. **Length:** 43-1/4" overall. **Stock:** Walnut. **Sights:** Blade front adjustable for windage, rear adjustable for elevation. **Features:** Frame, buttplate, forend cap of polished brass, balance charcoal blued. Imported by Tristar Sporting Arms Ltd.
Price: **$779.00**
Price: Yellowboy Carbine (19" round bbl.) **$739.00**

TRISTAR/UBERTI 1860 HENRY RIFLE

Caliber: 44-40, 45 Colt. **Barrel:** 24-1/4", half-octagon. **Weight:** 9.2 lbs. **Length:** 43-3/4" overall. **Stock:** American walnut. **Sights:** Blade front, rear adjustable for elevation. **Features:** Frame, elevator, magazine follower, buttplate are brass, balance blue. Imported by Tristar Sporting Arms Ltd. Arms, Inc.
Price: **$989.00**

Tristar/Uberti 1860 Henry Trapper Carbine

Similar to the 1860 Henry Rifle except has 18-1/2" barrel, measures 37-3/4" overall, and weighs 8 lbs. Introduced 1999. Imported from Italy by Tristar Sporting Arms Ltd.
Price: Brass frame, blued barrel **$989.00**

U.S. FIRE-ARMS LIGHTNING MAGAZINE RIFLE

Caliber: .45 Colt, .44 WCF, .44 Spl., .38 WCF, .32 WCF, 15-shot. **Barrel:** 26" (rifle); 20" carbine, round or octagonal. **Stock:** Oiled walnut. **Finish:** Dome blue. Introduced 2002. Made in U.S.A. by United States Fire Arms Manufacturing Co.
Price: **$995.00**

VEKTOR H5 SLIDE-ACTION RIFLE

Caliber: 223 Rem., 5-shot magazine. **Barrel:** 18", 22". **Weight:** 9 lbs., 15 oz. **Length:** 42-1/2" overall (22" barrel). **Stock:** Walnut thumbhole. **Sights:** Comes with 1" 4x32 scope with low-light reticle. **Features:** Rotating bolt mechanism. Matte black finish. Introduced 1999. Imported from South Africa by Vektor USA.
Price: **$849.95**

WINCHESTER MODEL 94 TRADITIONAL BIG BORE

Caliber: 444 Marlin, 6-shot magazine. **Barrel:** 20". **Weight:** 6-1/2 lbs. **Length:** 38-5/8" overall. **Stock:** American walnut. Satin finish. **Sights:** Hooded ramp front, semi-buckhorn rear adjustable for windage and elevation. **Features:** All external metal parts have Winchester's deep blue finish. Rifling twist 1:12". Rubber recoil pad fitted to buttstock. Introduced 1983. From U.S. Repeating Arms Co., Inc.
Price: **$465.00**

Winchester Timber Carbine

Similar to the Model 94 Big Bore. Chambered for 444 Marlin; 18" barrel is ported; half-pistol grip stock with butt pad; checkered grip and forend. Introduced 1999. Made in U.S.A. by U.S. Repeating Arms Co., Inc.
Price: **$573.00**

WINCHESTER MODEL 94 TRADITIONAL-CW

Caliber: 30-30 Win., 6-shot; 44 Mag., 11-shot tubular magazine. **Barrel:** 20". **Weight:** 6-1/2 lbs. **Length:** 37-3/4" overall. **Stock:** Straight grip checkered walnut stock and forend. **Sights:** Hooded blade front, semi-buckhorn rear. Drilled and tapped for scope mount. Post front sight on Trapper model. **Features:** Solid frame, forged steel receiver; side ejection, exposed rebounding hammer with automatic trigger-activated transfer bar. Introduced 1984.
Price: 30-30 . . . . **$440.00**
Price: 44 Mag. **$463.00**
Price: Traditional (no checkering, 30-30 only) **$407.00**

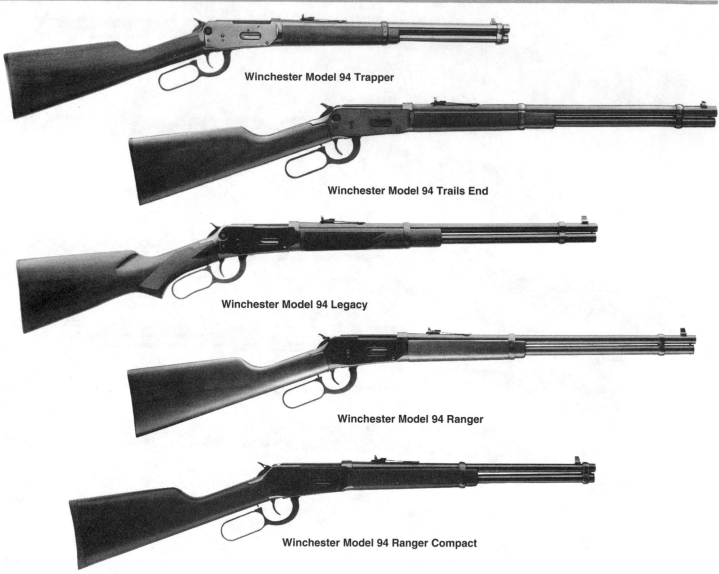

Winchester Model 94 Trapper

Winchester Model 94 Trails End

Winchester Model 94 Legacy

Winchester Model 94 Ranger

Winchester Model 94 Ranger Compact

Winchester Model 94 Trapper
Similar to Model 94 Traditional except has 16" barrel, 5-shot magazine in 30-30, 9-shot in 357 Mag., 44 Magnum/44 Special, 45 Colt. Has stainless steel claw extractor, saddle ring, hammer spur extension, smooth walnut wood.
Price: 30-30 . . . . **$407.00**
Price: 44 Mag., 357 Mag., 45 Colt **$431.00**

Winchester Model 94 Trails End
Similar to the Model 94 Walnut except chambered only for 357 Mag., 44-40, 44 Mag., 45 Colt; 11-shot magazine. Available with standard lever loop. Introduced 1997. From U.S. Repeating Arms Co., Inc.
Price: With standard lever loop. **$445.00**

Winchester Model 94 Legacy
Similar to the Model 94 Traditional-CW except has half-pistol grip walnut stock, checkered grip and forend. Chambered for 30-30, 357 Mag., 44 Mag., 45 Colt; 24" barrel. Introduced 1995. Made in U.S.A. by U.S. Repeating Arms Co., Inc.
Price: With 24" barrel **$457.00**

Winchester Model 94 Ranger
Similar to the Model 94 Traditional except has a hardwood stock, post-style front sight and hammer-spur extension.
Price: (20" barrel) **$355.00**

Winchester Model 94 Ranger Compact
Similar to the Model 94 Ranger except has 16" barrel and 12-1/2" length of pull, rubber recoil pad, post front sight. Introduced 1998. Made in U.S.A. by U.S. Repeating Arms Co., Inc.
Price: 357 Mag. **$378.00**
Price: 30-30 . . . . **$355.00**

WINCHESTER MODEL 1895 LEVER-ACTION RIFLE
Caliber: 405 Win, 4-shot magazine. **Barrel:** 24", round. **Weight:** 8 lbs. **Length:** 42" overall. **Stock:** American walnut. **Sights:** Gold bead front, buckhorn rear adjustable for elevation. **Features:** Recreation of the original Model 1895. Polished blue finish with Nimschke-style scroll engraving on receiver. Scalloped receiver, two-piece cocking lever, Schnabel forend, straight-grip stock. Introduced 1995. From U.S. Repeating Arms Co., Inc.
Price: Grade I **$1,045.00**
Price: High Grade **$1,532.00**

WINCHESTER MODEL 1886 EXTRA LIGHT LEVER-ACTION RIFLE
Caliber: 45-70, 4-shot magazine. **Barrel:** 22", round tapered. **Weight:** 7-1/4 lbs. **Length:** 40-1/2" overall. **Stock:** Smooth walnut. **Sights:** Bead front, ramp-adjustable buckhorn-style rear. **Features:** Recreation of the Model 1886. Polished blue finish; crescent metal butt plate; metal forend cap; pistol grip stock. Reintroduced 1998. From U.S. Repeating Arms Co., Inc.
Price: Grade I **$1,152.00**
Price: High Grade **$1,440.00**

Includes models for a wide variety of sporting and competitive purposes and uses.

Anschutz 1733D

Barrett Model 95

Blaser R93 Classic

ANSCHUTZ 1743D BOLT-ACTION RIFLE

Caliber: 222 Rem., 3-shot magazine. **Barrel:** 19.7". **Weight:** 6.4 lbs. **Length:** 39" overall. **Stock:** European walnut. **Sights:** Hooded blade front, folding leaf rear. **Features:** Receiver grooved for scope mounting; single stage trigger; claw extractor; sling safety; sling swivels. Imported from Germany by AcuSport Corp.

Price: **$1,588.95**

ANSCHUTZ 1740 MONTE CARLO RIFLE

Caliber: 22 Hornet, 5-shot clip; 222 Rem., 3-shot clip. **Barrel:** 24". **Weight:** 6-1/2 lbs. **Length:** 43.25" overall. **Stock:** Select European walnut. **Sights:** Hooded ramp front, folding leaf rear; drilled and tapped for scope mounting. **Features:** Uses match 54 action. Adjustable single stage trigger. Stock has roll-over Monte Carlo cheekpiece, slim forend with Schnabel tip, Wundhammer palm swell on grip, rosewood gripcap with white diamond insert. Skip-line checkering on grip and forend. Introduced 1997. Imported from Germany by AcuSport Corp.

Price: From. **$1,439.00**
Price: Model 1730 Monte Carlo, as above except in
22 Hornet **$1,439.00**

Anschutz 1733D Rifle

Similar to the 1740 Monte Carlo except has full-length, walnut, Mannlicher-style stock with skip-line checkering, rosewood Schnabel tip, and is chambered for 22 Hornet. Weighs 6.4 lbs., overall length 39", barrel length 19.7". Imported from Germany by AcuSport Corp.

Price: **$1,588.95**

BARRETT MODEL 95 BOLT-ACTION RIFLE

Caliber: 50 BMG, 5-shot magazine. **Barrel:** 29". **Weight:** 22 lbs. **Length:** 45" overall. **Stock:** Energy-absorbing recoil pad. **Sights:** Scope optional. **Features:** Bolt-action, bullpup design. Disassembles without tools; extendable bipod legs; match-grade barrel; high efficiency muzzle brake. Introduced 1995. Made in U.S.A. by Barrett Firearms Mfg., Inc.

Price: From. **$4,950.00**

BLASER R93 BOLT-ACTION RIFLE

Caliber: 22-250, 243, 6.5x55, 270, 7x57, 7mm-08, 308, 30-06, 257 Wea. Mag., 7mm Rem. Mag., 300 Win. Mag., 300 Wea. Mag., 338 Win Mag.,

375 H&H, 416 Rem. Mag. **Barrel:** 22" (standard calibers), 26" (magnum). **Weight:** 7 lbs. **Length:** 40" overall (22" barrel). **Stock:** Two-piece European walnut. **Sights:** None furnished; drilled and tapped for scope mounting. **Features:** Straight pull-back bolt action with thumb-activated safety slide/cocking mechanism; interchangeable barrels and bolt heads. Introduced 1994. Imported from Germany by SIGARMS.

Price: R93 Classic **$3,680.00**
Price: R93 LX **$1,895.00**
Price: R93 Synthetic (black synthetic stock) **$1,595.00**
Price: R93 Safari Synthetic (416 Rem. Mag. only) **$1,855.00**
Price: R93 Grand Lux **$4,915.00**
Price: R93 Attaché **$5,390.00**

BRNO 98 BOLT-ACTION RIFLE

Caliber: 7x64, 243, 270, 308, 30-06, 300 Win. Mag., 9.3x62. **Barrrel:** 23.6". **Weight:** 7.2 lbs. **Length:** 40.9" overall. **Stock:** European walnut. **Sights:** Blade on ramp front, open adjustable rear. **Features:** Uses Mauser 98-type action; polished blue. Announced 1998. Imported from the Czech Republic by Euro-Imports.

Price: Standard calibers **$507.00**
Price: Magnum calibers **$547.00**
Price: With set trigger, standard calibers **$615.00**
Price: As above, magnum calibers **$655.00**
Price: With full stock, set trigger, standard calibers **$703.00**
Price: As above, magnum calibers **$743.00**
Price: 300 Win. Mag., with BOSS. **$933.00**

BROWNING A-BOLT RIFLES

Caliber: 223, 22-250, 243, 7mm-08, 308, 25-06, 260, 270, 30-06, 260 Rem., 7mm Rem. Mag., 300 Win. Short Mag., 300 Win. Mag., 338 Win. Mag., 375 H&H Mag, 223 WSSM, 243 WSSM, 270 WSM, 7mm WSM, 300 WSM. **Barrel:** 22" medium sporter weight with recessed muzzle; 26" on mag. cals. **Weight:** 6-1/2 to 7-1/2 lbs. **Length:** 44-3/4" overall (magnum and standard); 41-3/4" (short action). **Stock:** Classic style American walnut; recoil pad standard on magnum calibers. **Features:** Short-throw (60") fluted bolt, three locking lugs, plunger-type ejector; adjustable trigger is grooved and gold-plated. Hinged floorplate, detachable box magazine (4 rounds std. cals., 3 for magnums). Slide tang safety. BOSS barrel vibration modulator and muzzle brake system not available in 375 H&H. Introduced 1985. Imported from Japan by Browning.

Price: Hunter, no sights **$620.00**
Price: Hunter, no sights, magnum calibers. **$646.00**
Price: For BOSS add **$80.00**

Browning A-Bolt Hunter

Browning A-Bolt Medallion

Browning A-Bolt White Gold Medallion

Browning A-Bolt Eclipse M-1000

Browning A-Bolt Medallion

Similar to standard A-Bolt except has glossy stock finish, rosewood grip and forend caps, engraved receiver, high-polish blue, no sights. New calibers include 223 WSSM, 243 WSSM< 270 WSM, 7mm WSM.

Price: Short-action calibers. $730.00
Price: Long-action calibers $756.00
Price: Medallion, 375 H&H Mag., open sights $767.00
New! **Price:** 300 Win. Short Magnum $756.00
New! **Price:** 300 Rem. Ultra Mag., 338 Rem. Ultra Mag. $756.00
Price: For BOSS, add. $80.00

Browning A-Bolt Medallion Left-Hand

Same as the Medallion model A-Bolt except has left-hand action and is available in 270, 30-06, 7mm Rem. Mag., 300 Win. Mag. Introduced 1987.

Price: 270, 30-06 (no sights) $758.00
Price: 7mm Mag., 300 Win. Mag. (no sights) $784.00
Price: For BOSS, add. $80.00

Browning A-Bolt White Gold Medallion

Similar to the standard A-Bolt except has select walnut stock with brass spacers between rubber recoil pad and between the rosewood gripcap and forend tip; gold-filled barrel inscription; palm-swell pistol grip, Monte Carlo comb, 22 lpi checkering with double borders; engraved receiver flats. In 270, 30-06, 7mm Rem. Mag. and 300 Win. Mag. Introduced 1988.

Price: 270, 30-06 . . . . $1,046.00
Price: 7mm Rem. Mag, 300 Win. Mag.. . . . . $1,072.00
Price: For BOSS, add. $76.00

Browning A-Bolt Custom Trophy Rifle

Similar to the A-Bolt Medallion except has select American walnut stock with recessed swivel studs, octagon barrel, skeleton pistol gripcap, gold

highlights, shadowline cheekpiece. Calibers 270, 30-06, 7mm Rem. Mag., 300 Win. Mag. Introduced 1998. Imported from Japan by Browning.
Price: $1,360.00

Browning A-Bolt Eclipse Hunter

Similar to the A-Bolt II except has gray/black laminated, thumbhole stock, BOSS barrel vibration modulator and muzzle brake. Available in long and short action with heavy barrel. In 270 Win., 30-06, 7mm Rem. Mag. Introduced 1996. Imported from Japan by Browning.
Price: 270, 30-06, with BOSS. $1,017.00
Price: 7mm Rem. Mag, with BOSS $1,043.00

Browning A-Bolt Eclipse M-1000

Similar to the A-Bolt II Eclipse except has long action and heavy target barrel. Chambered only for 300 Win. Mag. Adjustable trigger, bench-style forend, 3-shot magazine; laminated thumbhold stock; BOSS system standard. Introduced 1997. Imported for Japan by Browning.
Price: $1,048.00

Browning A-Bolt Micro Hunter

Similar to the A-Bolt II Hunter except has 13-5/16" length of pull, 20" barrel, and comes in 260 Rem., 243, 308, 7mm-08, 223, 22-250, 22 Hornet, 270 WSM, 7mm WSM, 300 WSM. Weighs 6 lbs., 1 oz. Introduced 1999. Imported by Browning.
Price: (no sights) $614.00

Browning A-Bolt Classic Hunter

Similar to the A-Bolt unter except has low-luster bluing and walnut stock with Monte Carlo comb, pistol grip palm swell, double-border checkering. Available in 270, 30-06, 7mm Rem. Mag., 300 Win. Mag, 223 WSSM, 243 WSSM. Introduced 1999. Imported by Browning.
Price: 270, 30-06 . . . . $698.00
Price: 7mm Mag., 300 Mag.. . . . . $724.00

Browning A-Bolt Stalker

Charles Daly Superior

CZ 527 Lux

CZ 550 Lux

Browning A-Bolt Stainless Stalker

Similar to the Hunter model A-Bolt except receiver and barrel are made of stainless steel; the rest of the exposed metal surfaces are finished with a durable matte silver-gray. Graphite-fiberglass composite textured stock. No sights are furnished. Available in 260, 243, 308, 7mm-08, 270, 280,30-06, 7mm Rem. Mag., 300 WSM, 300 Rem. Ultra Mag., 338 Win. Mag., 338 Rem. Ultra Mag., 375 H&H, 223 WSSM, 243 WSSM, 270 WSM, 7mm WSM. Introduced 1987.

Price: Short-action calibers...........................	$813.00
Price: Magnum calibers	$839.00
New! **Price:** 300 Win. Short Magnum......................	$839.00
New! **Price:** 300 Rem. Ultra Mag., 338 Rem. Ultra Mag.	$839.00
Price: For BOSS, add................................	$80.00
Price: Left-hand, 270, 30-06.........................	$838.00
Price: Left-hand, 7mm, 300 Win. Mag., 338 Win. Mag.	$864.00
Price: Left-hand, 375 H&H, with sights....................	$864.00
Price: Left-hand, for BOSS, add..........................	$80.00
Price: Carbon-fiber barrel, 22-250......................	$1,750.00
Price: Carbon-fiber barrel, 300 Win. Mag.	$1,776.00

Browning A-Bolt Composite Stalker

Similar to the A-Bolt Hunter except has black graphite-fiberglass stock with textured finish. Matte blue finish on all exposed metal surfaces. Available in 223, 22-250, 243, 7mm-08, 308, 30-06, 270, 280, 25-06, 7mm Rem. Mag., 300 WSM, 300 Win. Mag., 338 Win. Mag, 223 WSSM, 243 WSSM, 270 WSM, 7mm WSM. BOSS barrel vibration modulator and muzzle brake system offered in all calibers. Introduced 1994.

Price: Standard calibers, no sights......................	$639.00
Price: Magnum calibers, no sights	$665.00
Price: For BOSS, add................................	$77.00

CARBON ONE BOLT-ACTION RIFLE

Caliber: 22-250 to 375 H&H. **Barrel:** Up to 28". **Weight:** 5-1/2 to 7-1/4 lbs. **Length:** Varies. **Stock:** Synthetic or wood. **Sights:** None furnished. **Features:** Choice of Remington, Browning or Winchester action with free-floated Christensen graphite/epoxy/steel barrel, trigger pull tuned to 3 to 3-1/2 lbs. Made in U.S.A. by Christensen Arms.

Price: Carbon One Hunter Rifle, 6-1/2 to 7 lbs.	$1,499.00
Price: Carbon One Custom, 5-1/2 to 6-1/2 lbs., Shilen trigger ..	$2,750.00
Price: Carbon Ranger, 50 BMG, 5-shot repeater...........	$4,750.00
Price: Carbon Ranger, 50 BMG, single shot	$3,950.00

CHARLES DALY SUPERIOR BOLT-ACTION RIFLE

Caliber: 22 Hornet, 5-shot magazine. **Barrel:** 22.6". **Weight:** 6.6 lbs. **Length:** 41.25" overall. **Stock:** Walnut-finished hardwood with Monte Carlo comb and cheekpiece. **Sights:** Ramped blade front, fully adjustable open rear. **Features:** Receiver dovetailed for tip-off scope mount. Introduced 1996. Imported by K.B.I., Inc.

Price:	$364.95

Charles Daly Empire Grade Rifle

Similar to the Superior except has oil-finished American walnut stock with 18 lpi hand checkering; black hardwood gripcap and forend tip; highly polished barreled action; jewelled bolt; recoil pad; swivel studs. Imported by K.B.I., Inc.

Price:	$469.95

CZ 527 LUX BOLT-ACTION RIFLE

Caliber: 22 Hornet, 222 Rem., 223 Rem., detachable 5-shot magazine. **Barrel:** 23-1/2"; standard or heavy barrel. **Weight:** 6 lbs., 1 oz. **Length:** 42-1/2" overall. **Stock:** European walnut with Monte Carlo. **Sights:** Hooded front, open adjustable rear. **Features:** Improved mini-Mauser action with non-rotating claw extractor; single set trigger; grooved receiver. Imported from the Czech Republic by CZ-USA.

Price:	$566.00
Price: Model FS, full-length stock, cheekpiece..............	$658.00

CZ 527 American Classic Bolt-Action Rifle

Similar to the CZ 527 Lux except has classic-style stock with 18 l.p.i. checkering; free-floating barrel; recessed target crown on barrel. No sights furnished. Introduced 1999. Imported from the Czech Republic by CZ-USA.

Price: 22 Hornet, 222 Rem., 223 Rem.	$586.00 to $609.00

CZ 550 LUX BOLT-ACTION RIFLE

Caliber: 22-250, 243, 6.5x55, 7x57, 7x64, 308 Win., 9.3x62, 270 Win., 30-06. **Barrel:** 20.47". **Weight:** 7.5 lbs. **Length:** 44.68" overall. **Stock:** Turkish walnut in Bavarian style or FS (Mannlicher). **Sights:** Hooded front, adjustable rear. **Features:** Improved Mauser-style action with claw extractor, fixed ejector, square bridge dovetailed receiver; single set trigger. Imported from the Czech Republic by CZ-USA.

Price: Lux	$566.00 to $609.00
Price: FS (full stock)	$706.00

CENTERFIRE RIFLES — BOLT ACTION

CZ 550 American Classic

CZ 550 Magnum

Dakota 76 Classic

Dakota 76 Safari

CZ 550 American Classic Bolt-Action Rifle

Similar to CZ 550 Lux except has American classic-style stock with 18 l.p.i. checkering; free-floating barrel; recessed target crown. Has 25.6" barrel; weighs 7.48 lbs. No sights furnished. Introduced 1999. Imported from the Czech Republic by CZ-USA.
Price: ....$586.00 to $609.00

CZ 550 Medium Magnum Bolt-Action Rifle

Similar to the CZ 550 Lux except chambered for the 300 Win. Mag. and 7mm Rem. Mag.; 5-shot magazine. Adjustable iron sights, hammer-forged barrel, single-set trigger, Turkish walnut stock. Weighs 7.5 lbs. Introduced 2001. Imported from the Czech Republic by CZ USA.
Price: $621.00

CZ 550 Magnum Bolt-Action Rifle

Similar to CZ 550 Lux except has long action for 300 Win. Mag., 375 H&H, 416 Rigby, 458 Win. Mag. Overall length is 46.45"; barrel length 25"; weighs 9.24 lbs. Hooded front sight, express rear with one standing, two folding leaves. Imported from the Czech Republic by CZ-USA.
Price: 300 Win. Mag. $717.00
Price: 375 H&H...$756.00
Price: 416 Rigby $809.00
Price: 458 Win. Mag. $744.00

CZ 700 M1 SNIPER RIFLE

Caliber: 308 Winchester, 10-shot magazine. **Barrel:** 25.6". **Weight:** 11.9 lbs. **Length:** 45" overall. **Stock:** Laminated wood thumbhole with adjustable buttplate and cheekpiece. **Sights:** None furnished; permanently attached Weaver rail for scope mounting. **Features:** 60-degree bolt throw; oversized trigger guard and bolt handle for use with gloves; full-length equipment rail on forend; fully adjustable trigger. Introduced 2001. Imported from the Czech Republic by CZ USA.
Price: $2,097.00

DAKOTA 76 TRAVELER TAKEDOWN RIFLE

Caliber: 257 Roberts, 25-06, 7x57, 270, 280, 30-06, 338-06, 35 Whelen (standard length); 7mm Rem. Mag., 300 Win. Mag., 338 Win. Mag., 416 Taylor, 458 Win. Mag. (short magnums); 7mm, 300, 330, 375 Dakota Magnums. **Barrel:** 23". **Weight:** 7-1/2 lbs. **Length:** 43-1/2" overall. **Stock:** Medium fancy-grade walnut in classic style. Checkered grip and forend; solid butt pad. **Sights:** None furnished; drilled and tapped for scope mounts. **Features:** Threadless disassembly—no threads to wear or stretch, no interrupted cuts, and headspace remains constant. Uses modified Model 76 design with many features of the Model 70 Winchester. Left-hand model also available. Introduced 1989. Made in U.S.A. by Dakota Arms, Inc.
Price: Classic $4,495.00
Price: Safari $5,495.00
Price: Extra barrels......................$1,650.00 to $1,950.00

DAKOTA 76 CLASSIC BOLT-ACTION RIFLE

Caliber: 257 Roberts, 270, 280, 30-06, 7mm Rem. Mag., 338 Win. Mag., 300 Win. Mag., 375 H&H, 458 Win. Mag. **Barrel:** 23". **Weight:** 7-1/2 lbs. **Length:** 43-1/2" overall. **Stock:** Medium fancy grade walnut in classic style. Checkered pistol grip and forend; solid butt pad. **Sights:** None furnished; drilled and tapped for scope mounts. **Features:** Has many features of the original Model 70 Winchester. One-piece rail trigger guard assembly; steel gripcap. Model 70-style trigger. Many options available. Left-hand rifle available at same price. Introduced 1988. From Dakota Arms, Inc.
Price: $3,595.00

DAKOTA 76 SAFARI BOLT-ACTION RIFLE

Caliber: 270 Win., 7x57, 280, 30-06, 7mm Dakota, 7mm Rem. Mag., 300 Dakota, 300 Win. Mag., 330 Dakota, 338 Win. Mag., 375 Dakota, 458 Win. Mag., 300 H&H, 375 H&H, 416 Rem. **Barrel:** 23". **Weight:** 8-1/2 lbs. **Length:** 43-1/2" overall. **Stock:** XXX fancy walnut with ebony forend tip; point-pattern with wrap-around forend checkering. **Sights:** Ramp front, standing leaf rear. **Features:** Has many features of the original Model 70 Winchester. Barrel band front swivel, inletted rear. Cheekpiece with shadow line. Steel gripcap. Introduced 1988. From Dakota Arms, Inc.
Price: Wood stock $4,595.00

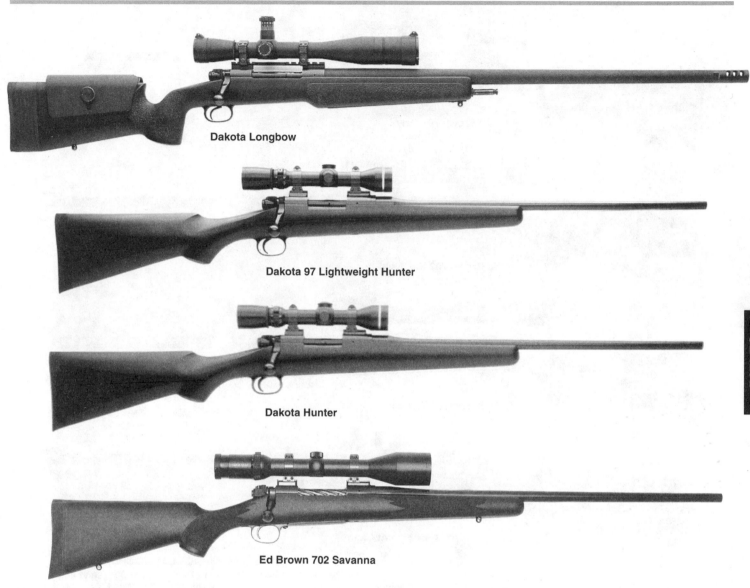

Dakota Longbow

Dakota 97 Lightweight Hunter

Dakota Hunter

Ed Brown 702 Savanna

Dakota African Grade

Similar to 76 Safari except chambered for 338 Lapua Mag., 404 Jeffery, 416 Rigby, 416 Dakota, 450 Dakota, 4-round magazine, select wood, two stock cross-bolts. 24" barrel, weighs 9-10 lbs. Ramp front sight, standing leaf rear. Introduced 1989.

Price: $4,995.00

DAKOTA LONGBOW TACTICAL E.R. RIFLE

Caliber: 300 Dakota Magnum, 330 Dakota Magnum, 338 Lapua Magnum. **Barrel:** 28", .950" at muzzle **Weight:** 13.7 lbs. **Length:** 50" to 52" overall. **Stock:** Ambidextrous McMillan A-2 fiberglass, black or olive green color; adjustable cheekpiece and buttplate. **Sights:** None furnished. Comes with Picatinny one-piece optical rail. **Features:** Uses the Dakota 76 action with controlled-round feed; three-position firing pin block safety, claw extractor; Model 70-style trigger. Comes with bipod, case tool kit. Introduced 1997. Made in U.S.A. by Dakota Arms, Inc.

Price: $4,250.00

DAKOTA 97 LIGHTWEIGHT HUNTER

Caliber: 22-250 to 330. **Barrel:** 22"-24". **Weight:** 6.1-6.5 lbs. **Length:** 43" overall. **Stock:** Fiberglass. **Sights:** Optional. **Features:** Matte blue finish, black stock. Right-hand action only. Introduced 1998. Made in U.S.A. by Dakota Arms, Inc.

Price: $1,995.00

DAKOTA LONG RANGE HUNTER RIFLE

Caliber: 25-06, 257 Roberts, 270 Win., 280 Rem., 7mm Rem. Mag., 7mm Dakota Mag., 30-06, 300 Win. Mag., 300 Dakota Mag., 338 Win. Mag., 330 Dakota Mag., 375 H&H Mag., 375 Dakota Mag. **Barrel:** 24", 26", match-quality; free-floating. **Weight:** 7.7 lbs. **Length:** 45" to 47" overall. **Stock:** H-S Precision black synthetic, with one-piece bedding block system. **Sights:** None furnished. Drilled and tapped for scope mounting. **Features:** Cylindrical machined receiver controlled round feed; Mauser-style extractor; three-position striker blocking safety; fully adjustable match trigger. Right-hand action only. Introduced 1997. Made in U.S.A. by Dakota Arms, Inc.

Price: $1,995.00

ED BROWN MODEL 702, SAVANNA

Caliber: (long action) 25-06, 270 Win., 280 Rem., 7mm Rem. Mag., 7STW, 30-06, 300 Win. Mag., 300 Weatherby, 338 Win. Mag. (Short action) 223, 22-250, 243, 6mm, 260 Rem. 7mm-08, 308, 300 WSM, 270 WSM, 7mm WSM. **Barrel:** 23" (standard calibers) light weight #3 contour; medium weight 24", 26" with #4 contour on medium calibers. **Weight:** 8 to 8.5-lbs. **Stock:** Fully glass-bedded McMillan fiberglass sporter. **Sights:** None furnished. Talley scope mounts utilzing heavy duty 8-40 screws. **Features:** Custom action with machined steel trigger guard and hinged floor plate. Available in left-hand version.

Price: From $2,800.00

Ed Brown 702 Ozark

Ed Brown 702 Bushveld

Ed Brown 702 Varmint

Harris Gunworks Alaskan

Ed Brown Model 702 Denali, Ozark

Similar to the Ed Brown Model 702 Savanna but the Denali is a lighter weight rifle designed specifically for mountain hunting, especially suited to the 270 and 280 calibers. Right hand only. Weighs about 7.75 lbs. The Model 702 Ozark is another lighter weight rifle made on a short action with a very light weight stock. Ozark calibers are 223, 243, 6mm, 260 Rem., 7mm-08, 308. Weight 6.5 lbs.
Price: From (either model) **$2,800.00**

ED BROWN MODEL 702 BUSHVELD

Caliber: 338 Win. Mag., 375 H&H, 416 Rem. Mag., 458 Win. Mag. And all Ed Brown Savanna long action calibers. **Barrel:** 24" medium or heavy weight. **Weight:** 8.25 lbs. **Stock:** Fully bedded McMillan fiberglass with Monte Carlo style cheekpiece, Pachmayr Decelerator recoil pad. **Sights:** None furnish. Talley scope mounts utilizing heavy duty 8-40 screws. **Features:** A dangerous game rifle with options including left-hand action, stainless steel barrel, additional calibers, iron sights.
Price: From **$2,900.00**

ED BROWN MODEL 702 VARMINT

Caliber: 223, 22-250, 220 Swift, 243, 6mm, 308. **Barrel:** Medium weight #5 contour 24"; heavy weight #17 contour 24"; 26" optional. **Weight:** 9 lbs. **Stock:** Fully glass-bedded McMillan fiberglass with recoil pad. **Sights:** None furnished. Talley scope mounts with heavy duty 8-40 screws. **Features:** Fully-adjustable trigger, steel trigger guard and floor plate, many options available.
Price: From **$2,500.00**

HARRIS GUNWORKS SIGNATURE CLASSIC SPORTER

Caliber: 22-250, 243, 6mm Rem., 7mm-08, 284, 308 (short action); 25-06, 270, 280 Rem., 30-06, 7mm Rem. Mag., 300 Win. Mag., 300 Wea. (long action); 338 Win. Mag., 340 Wea., 375 H&H (magnum action). **Barrel:** 22", 24", 26". **Weight:** 7 lbs. (short action). **Stock:** Fiberglass in green, beige, brown or black. Recoil pad and 1" swivels installed. Length of pull up to 14-1/4". **Sights:** None furnished. Comes with 1" rings and bases. **Features:** Uses right- or left-hand action with matte black finish. Trigger pull set at 3 lbs. Four-round magazine for standard calibers; three for magnums. Aluminum floorplate. Wood stock optional. Introduced 1987. From Harris Gunworks, Inc.
Price: **$2,700.00**

Harris Gunworks Signature Classic Stainless Sporter

Similar to Signature Classic Sporter except action is made of stainless steel. Same calibers, in addition to 416 Rem. Mag. Fiberglass stock, right- or left-hand action in natural stainless, glass bead or black chrome sulfide finishes. Introduced 1990. From Harris Gunworks, Inc.
Price: **$2,900.00**

Harris Gunworks Signature Alaskan

Similar to Classic Sporter except match-grade barrel with single leaf rear sight, barrel band front, 1" detachable rings and mounts, steel floorplate, electroless nickel finish. Wood Monte Carlo stock with cheekpiece, palm-swell grip, solid butt pad. Chambered for 270, 280 Rem., 30-06, 7mm Rem. Mag., 300 Win. Mag., 300 Wea., 358 Win., 340 Wea., 375 H&H. Introduced 1989.
Price: **$3,800.00**

Harris Gunworks Signature Titanium Mountain

Harris Gunworks Signature Super Varminter

Harris Gunworks Talon Safari

Howa Lightning

Harris Gunworks Signature Titanium Mountain Rifle

Similar to Classic Sporter except action made of titanium alloy, barrel of chrome-moly steel. Stock is graphite reinforced fiberglass. Weight is 5-1/2 lbs. Chambered for 270, 280 Rem., 30-06, 7mm Rem. Mag., 300 Win. Mag. Fiberglass stock optional. Introduced 1989.

Price: **$3,300.00**
Price: With graphite-steel composite light weight barrel **$3,700.00**

Harris Gunworks Signature Varminter

Similar to Signature Classic Sporter except has heavy contoured barrel, adjustable trigger, field bipod and special hand-bedded fiberglass stock. Chambered for 223, 22-250, 220 Swift, 243, 6mm Rem., 25-06, 7mm-08, 7mm BR, 308, 350 Rem. Mag. Comes with 1" rings and bases. Introduced 1989.

Price: **$2,700.00**

HARRIS GUNWORKS TALON SAFARI RIFLE

Caliber: 300 Win. Mag., 300 Wea. Mag., 300 Phoenix, 338 Win. Mag., 30/378, 338 Lapua, 300 H&H, 340 Wea. Mag., 375 H&H, 404 Jeffery, 416 Rem. Mag., 458 Win. Mag. (Safari Magnum); 378 Wea. Mag., 416 Rigby, 416 Wea. Mag., 460 Wea. Mag. (Safari Super Magnum). **Barrel:** 24". **Weight:** About 9-10 lbs. **Length:** 43" overall. **Stock:** Gunworks fiberglass Safari. **Sights:** Barrel band front ramp, multi-leaf express rear. **Features:** Uses Harris Gunworks Safari action. Has quick detachable 1" scope mounts, positive locking steel floorplate, barrel band sling swivel. Match-grade barrel. Matte black finish standard. Introduced 1989. From Harris Gunworks, Inc.

Price: Talon Safari Magnum **$3,900.00**
Price: Talon Safari Super Magnum **$4,200.00**

HARRIS GUNWORKS TALON SPORTER RIFLE

Caliber: 22-250, 243, 6mm Rem., 6mm BR, 7mm BR, 7mm-08, 25-06, 270, 280 Rem., 284, 308, 30-06, 350 Rem. Mag. (long action); 7mm Rem. Mag., 7mm STW, 300 Win. Mag., 300 Wea. Mag., 300 H&H, 338 Win. Mag., 340 Wea. Mag., 375 H&H, 416 Rem. Mag. **Barrel:** 24" (standard). **Weight:** About 7-1/2 lbs. **Length:** NA. **Stock:** Choice of walnut or fiberglass. **Sights:** None furnished; comes with rings and bases. Open sights optional. **Features:** Uses pre-'64 Model 70-type action with cone breech, controlled feed, claw extractor and three-position safety. Barrel and action are of stainless steel; chrome-moly optional. Introduced 1991. From Harris Gunworks, Inc.

Price: **$2,900.00**

HOWA LIGHTNING BOLT-ACTION RIFLE

Caliber: 223, 22-250, 243, 6.5x55, 270, 308, 30-06, 7mm Rem. Mag., 300 Win. Mag., 338 Win. Mag, 300 WSM, 7mm WSM, 270 WSM. **Barrel:** 22", 24" magnum calibers. **Weight:** 7-1/2 lbs. **Length:** 42" overall (22" barrel). **Stock:** Black Bell & Carlson Carbelite composite with Monte Carlo comb; checkered grip and forend. **Sights:** None furnished. Drilled and tapped for scope mounting. **Features:** Sliding thumb safety; hinged floorplate; polished blue/black finish. Introduced 1993. From Legacy Sports International.

Price: Blue, standard calibers. **$479.00**
Price: Blue, magnum calibers. **$502.00**
Price: Stainless, standard calibers **$585.00**
Price: Stainless, magnum calibers **$612.00**

Howa M-1500 Hunter Bolt-Action Rifle

Similar to Lightning Model except has walnut-finished hardwood stock. Polished blue finish or stainless steel. Introduced 1999. From Legacy Sports International.

Price: Blue, standard calibers. **$539.00**
Price: Stainless, standard calibers **$638.00**
Price: Blue, magnum calibers. **$560.00**
Price: Stainless, magnum calibers **$662.00**

RIFLES

Howa M-1500 Hunter

Howa M-1500 Ultralight

Howa M-1500 Varmint Supreme

Kimber 84M Classic

Kimber 84M Varmint

Howa M-1500 Supreme Rifles

Similar to Howa M-1500 Lightning except stocked with JRS Classic or Thumbhole Sporter laminated wood stocks in Nutmeg (brown/black) or Pepper (gray/black) colors. Barrel 22"; 24" magnum calibers. Weights are JRS stock 8 lbs., THS stock 8.3 lbs. Introduced 2001. Imported from Japan by Legacy Sports International.

Price: Blue, standard calibers, JRS stock. **$616.00**
Price: Blue, standard calibers, THS stock **$668.00**
Price: Blue, magnum calibers, JRS stock. **$638.00**
Price: Blue, magnum calibers, THS stock **$638.00**
Price: Stainless, standard calibers, JRS stock **$720.00**
Price: Stainless, standard calibers, THS stock **$771.00**
Price: Stainless, magnum calibers, JRS stock **$720.00**
Price: Stainless, magnum calibers, THS stock. **$742.00**

Howa M-1500 Ultralight

Similar to Howa M-1500 Lightning except receiver milled to reduce weight, tapered 22" barrel; 1-10" twist. Chambered for 243 Win. Stocks are black texture-finished hardwood. Weighs 6.4 lbs. Length 40"overall.
Price: Blued **$511.00**

Howa M-1500 Varmint and Varmint Supreme Rifles

Similar to M-1500 Lightning except has heavy 24" hammer-forged barrel. Chambered for 223, 22-250, 308. Weighs 9.3 lbs.; overall length 44.5". Introduced 1999. Imported from Japan by Interarms/Howa.

Varminter Supreme has heavy barrel, target crown muzzle. Heavy 24" barrel, laminated wood with raised comb stocks, rollover cheekpiece, vented beavertail forearm; available in 223 Rem., 22-250 Rem., 308 Win. Weighs 9.9 lbs. Introduced 2001. Imported from Japan by Legacy Sports International.

Price: Varminter, blue, polymer stock. **$517.00**
Price: Varminter, stainless, polymer stock **$626.00**
Price: Varminter, blue, wood stock. **$575.00**
Price: Varminter, stainless, wood stock **$677.00**
Price: Varminter Supreme, blued . . . . **$612.00 to $641.00**
Price: Varminter Supreme, stainless . . . . **$714.00 to $743.00**

KIMBER MODEL 84M BOLT-ACTION RIFLE

Caliber: 22-250, 243, 260 Rem., 7mm-08, 308, 5-shot. **Barrel:** 22", 24", 26". **Weight:** 5 lbs., 10 oz. to 10 lbs. **Length:** 41"-45". **Stock:** Claro walnut, checkered with steel grip cap or gray laminate. **Sights:** None; drilled and tapped for bases. **Features:** Mauser claw extractor, two-position wing safety, action bedded on aluminum pillars, free-floated barrel, match-grade trigger set at 4 lbs., matte blue finish. Includes cable lock. Introduced 2001. Made in U.S.A. by Kimber Mfg. Inc.
Price: Classic (243, 260, 7mm-08, 308) **$917.00**
Price: Varmint (22-250) **$1,001.00**

RIFLES

L.A.R. Grizzly

Legacy Sports International M-1500

Legacy Sports International Texas Safari

Legacy Sports International Mauser 98

L.A.R. GRIZZLY 50 BIG BOAR RIFLE
Caliber: 50 BMG, single shot. **Barrel:** 36". **Weight:** 30.4 lbs. **Length:** 45.5" overall. **Stock:** Integral. Ventilated rubber recoil pad. **Sights:** None furnished; scope mount. **Features:** Bolt-action bullpup design, thumb and bolt stop safety. All-steel construction. Unsurpassed accuracy and impact. Introduced 1994. Made in U.S.A. by L.A.R. Mfg., Inc.
Price: **$2,195.00**

LEGACY SPORTS INTERNATIONAL M-1500 CUSTOM RIFLES
Caliber: 300 WSM, 300 Win. Mag.; 3 plus 1 in chamber. **Weight:** 7.6-8.3 lbs. **Length:** 42.5" overall. **Stock:** Black polymer, laminated wood. **Features:** Built on Howa M-1500 stainless steel short-action, 3-position thumb safety, hinged floorplate, drilled and tapped for standard scope mounts. 300 WSM has stainless steel short action, 22 bbl. 300 Win. Mag. has blued long action, 24" bbl. with integral ported muzzle brake by Bill Wiseman. Introduced 2001 by Legacy Sports International.
Price: JRS Classic Pepper stock **$995.00**
Price: Thumbhole Pepper stock **$1,035.00**
Price: 300 WSM, polymer stock **$895.00**
Price: 300 Win. Mag., JRS Nutmeg stock **$855.00**

LEGACY SPORTS INTERNATIONAL TEXAS SAFARI RIFLES
Caliber: 270 Win., 300 Win. Mag. 270 Win.: 5 plus 1 in chamber; 300 Mag., 3 plus 1 in chamber. **Weight:** 7.8 lbs. **Length:** 42.5" overall; 44.5" in 300 Win. Mag. **Stock:** Brown/black laminated wood. **Features:** Built on Howa M-1500 action customized by Bill Wiseman, College Station, TX; Wiseman-designed 3-position thumb safety and bolt-release, hinged floorplate, drilled and tapped for standard scope mounts. Action glass-bedded, farrel free floated. 300 Win. Mag. has integral muzzle brake. Introduced 2001 by Legacy Sports International.
Price: 270 Win. **$1,522.00**
Price: 300 Win. Mag. **$1,753.00**

LEGACY SPORTS INTERNATIONAL MAUSER 98 RIFLE
Caliber: 300 Win. Mag. **Barrel:** 24", 1-10" twist. **Weight:** 8.4 lbs. **Length:** 45" overall. **Stock:** Premium American walnut. **Sights:** None. **Features:** Square-bridge Mauser 98 action dovetailed for ring mounts (scope and rings not included). 3-position thumb safety, hinged floorplate, adjustable trigger. Introduced 2001. Imported from Italy by Legacy Sports International.
Price: **$955.00**

MAGNUM RESEARCH MAGNUM LITE TACTICAL RIFLE
Caliber: 223 Rem., 22-250, 308 Win., 300 Win. Mag., 300 WSM. **Barrel:** 26" Magnum Lite™ graphite. **Weight:** 8.3 lbs. **Length:** NA. **Stock:** H-S Precision™ tactical black synthetic. **Sights:** None furnished; drilled and tapped for scope mount. **Features:** Accurized Remington 700 action; adjustable trigger; adjustable comb height. Tuned to shoot 1/2" MOA or better. Introduced 2001. From Magnum Research Inc.
Price: **$2,400.00**

CENTERFIRE RIFLES — BOLT ACTION

Magnum Research Tactical

Raptor Bolt-Action

Remington 673 Guide

Remington 700 Classic

Remington 700 ADL Synthetic

MOUNTAIN EAGLE MAGNUM LITE RIFLE
Caliber: 22-250, 223 Rem. (Varmint); 280, 30-06 (long action); 7mm Rem. Mag., 300 Win. Mag., (magnum action). **Barrel:** 24", 26", free floating. **Weight:** 7 lbs., 13 oz. **Length:** 44" overall (24" barrel). **Stock:** Kevlar-graphite with aluminum bedding block, high comb, recoil pad, swivel studs; made by H-S Precision. **Sights:** None furnished; accepts any Remington 700-type base. **Features:** Special Sako action with one-piece forged bolt, hinged steel floorplate, lengthened receiver ring; adjustable trigger. Krieger cut-rifled benchrest barrel. Introduced 1996. From Magnum Research, Inc.
Price: Magnum Lite (graphite barrel) **$2,295.00**

NEW ULTRA LIGHT ARMS BOLT-ACTION RIFLES
Caliber: 17 Rem. to 416 Rigby (numerous calibers available). **Barrel:** Douglas, length to order. **Weight:** 4-3/4 to 7-1/2 lbs. **Length:** Varies. **Stock:** Kevlar®/ graphite composite, variety of finishes. **Sights:** None furnished; drilled and tapped for scope mount. **Features:** Timney trigger, hand-lapped action, button-rifled barrel, hand-bedded action, recoil pad, sling-swivel studs, optional Jewell Trigger. Made in U.S.A. by New Ultra Light Arms.
Price: Model 20 (short action). **$2,500.00**
Price: Model 24 (long action) **$2,600.00**
Price: Model 28 (magnum action). **$2,900.00**

Price: Model 40 (300 Wea. Mag., 416 Rigby) **$2,900.00**
Price: Left-hand models, add **$100.00**

RAPTOR BOLT-ACTION RIFLE
Caliber: 270, 30-06, 243, 25-06, 308; 4-shot magazine. **Barrel:** 22". **Weight:** 7 lbs., 6 oz. **Length:** 42.5" overall. **Stock:** Black synthetic, fiberglass reinforced; checkered grip and forend; vented recoil pad; Monte Carlo cheekpiece. **Sights:** None furnished; drilled and tapped for scope mounts. **Features:** Rust-resistant "Taloncote" treated barreled action; pillar bedded; stainless bolt with three locking lugs; adjustable trigger. Announced 1997. Made in U.S.A. by Raptor Arms Co., Inc.
Price: **$249.00**

Remington Model 673 Guide Rifle
Available in 350 Rem. Mag., 300 Rem. SAUM with 22" magnum contour barrel with machined steel ventilated rib, iron sights, wide laminate stock.
Price: **$825.00**

REMINGTON MODEL 700 CLASSIC RIFLE
Caliber: 300 Savage. **Barrel:** 24". **Weight:** About 7-1/4 lbs. **Length:** 44-1/2" overall. **Stock:** American walnut, 20 lpi checkering on pistol grip and forend. Classic styling. Satin finish. **Sights:** None furnished. Receiver drilled and tapped for scope mounting. **Features:** A "classic" version of the BDL with straight comb stock. Fitted with rubber recoil pad. Sling swivel studs installed. Hinged floorplate. Limited production in 2003 only.
Price: **$683.00**

Remington 700 BDL

Remington 700 BDL Left Hand

Remington 700 BDL SS

Remington 700 BDL SS DM

REMINGTON MODEL 700 ADL DELUXE RIFLE
Caliber: 270, 30-06. **Barrel:** 22" round tapered. **Weight:** 7-1/4 lbs. **Length:** 41-5/8" overall. **Stock:** Walnut. Satin-finished pistol grip stock with fine-line cut checkering, Monte Carlo. **Sights:** Gold bead ramp front; removable, step-adjustable rear with windage screw. **Features:** Side safety, receiver tapped for scope mounts.
Price: **$580.00**

Remington Model 700 ADL Synthetic
Similar to the 700 ADL except has a fiberglass-reinforced synthetic stock with straight comb, raised cheekpiece, positive checkering, and black rubber butt pad. Metal has matte finish. Available in 22-250, 223, 243, 270, 308, 30-06 with 22" barrel, 300 Win. Mag., 7mm Rem. Mag. with 24" barrel. Introduced 1996.
Price: From .... **$500.00 to $527.00**

Remington Model 700 ADL Synthetic Youth
Similar to the Model 700 ADL Synthetic except has 1" shorter stock, 20" barrel. Chambered for 243, 308. Introduced 1998.
Price: **$500.00**

Remington Model 700 BDL Custom Deluxe Rifle
Same as 700 ADL except chambered for 222, 223 (short action, 24" barrel), 7mm-08, 280, 22-250, 25-06. (short action, 22" barrel), 243, 270, 30-06, skip-line checkering, black forend tip and gripcap with white line spacers. Matted receiver top, quick-release floorplate. Hooded ramp front sight, quick detachable swivels.
Price: **$683.00**

Also available in 17 Rem., 7mm Rem. Mag., 7mm Rem. Ultra Mag., 300 Win. Mag. (long action, 24" barrel); 300 Rem. Ultra Mag. (26" barrel). Overall length 44-1/2", weight about 7-1/2 lbs.
Price: .... **$709.00 to $723.00**

Remington Model 700 BDL Left Hand Custom Deluxe
Same as 700 BDL except mirror-image left-hand action, stock. Available in 270, 30-06, 7mm Rem. Mag., 300 Rem. Ultra Mag, 338 Rem. Ultra Mag., 7mm Rem. Ultra Mag.
Price: .... **$709.00 to $749.00**

Remington Model 700 BDL DM Rifle
Same as 700 BDL except detachable box magazine (4-shot, standard calibers, 3-shot for magnums). Glossy stock finish, open sights, recoil pad, sling swivels. Available in 270, 30-06, 7mm Rem. Mag., 300 Win. Mag. Introduced 1995.
Price: From................................. **$749.00 to $776.00**

Remington Model 700 BDL SS Rifle
Similar to 700 BDL rifle except hinged floorplate, 24" standard weight barrel in all calibers; magnum calibers have magnum-contour barrel. No sights supplied, but comes drilled and tapped. Corrosion-resistant follower and fire control, stainless BDL-style barreled action with fine matte finish. Synthetic stock has straight comb and cheekpiece, textured finish, positive checkering, plated swivel studs. Calibers—270, 30-06; magnums—7mm Rem. Mag., 7mm Rem. UltraMag., 300 Rem. Ultra Mag. (26" barrel) 300 Win. Mag., 338 Rem. Ultra Mag., 7mm Rem. SAUM, 300 Rem. SAUM. Weighs 7-3/8 to 7-1/2 lbs. Introduced 1993.
Price: From................................. **$735.00 to $775.00**

Remington Model 700 BDL SS DM Rifle
Same as 700 BDL SS except detachable box magazine. Barrel, receiver and bolt made of #416 stainless steel; black synthetic stock, fine-line engraving. Available in 270, 30-06, 7mm Rem. Mag., 300 Win. Mag. Introduced 1995.
Price: From................................. **$801.00 to $828.00**

Remington 700 LSS Mountain

Remington 700 Safari KS

Remington 700 APR African Plains

Remington 700 Titanium

Remington Model 700 Custom KS Mountain Rifle

Similar to 700 BDL except custom finished with aramid fiber reinforced resin synthetic stock. Available in left- and right-hand versions. Chambered 270 Win., 280 Rem., 30-06, 7mm Rem. Mag., 7mm STW, 300 Rem. Ultra Mag., 338 Rem. Ultra Mag., 300 Win. Mag., 300 Wea. Mag., 35 Whelen, 338 Win. Mag., 8mm Rem. Mag., 375 H&H, with 24" barrel (except 300 Rem. Ultra Mag., 26"), 7mm RUM, 375 RUM. Weighs 6 lbs., 6 oz. Introduced 1986.

Price: Right-hand **$1,314.00**
Price: Left-hand **$1,393.00**
Price: Stainless. . . . . **$1,500 to $1,580.00**

Remington Model 700 LSS Mountain Rifle

Similar to Model 700 Custom KS Mountain Rifle except stainless steel 22" barrel and two-tone laminated stock. Chambered in 260 Rem., 7mm-08, 270 Winchester and 30-06. Overall length 42-1/2", weighs 6-5/8 oz. Introduced 1999.

Price: **$800.00**

Remington Model 700 Safari Grade

Similar to 700 BDL aramid fiber reinforced fiberglass stock, blued carbon steel bbl. and action, or stainless, w/cheekpiece, custom finished and tuned. In 8mm Rem. Mag., 375 H&H, 416 Rem. Mag. or 458 Win. Mag. calibers only with heavy barrel. Right- and left-hand versions.

Price: Safari KS . . . . **$1,520.00 to $1,601.00**
Price: Safari KS (stainless right-hand only) **$1,697.00**

Remington Model 700 AWR Alaskan Wilderness Rifle

Similar to the 700 BDL except has stainless barreled action finishBlack Teflon 24" bbl. 26" Ultra Mag raised cheekpiece, magnum-grade black rubber recoil pad. Chambered for 7mm RUM., 375 RUM, 7mm STW, 300 Rem. Ultra Mag., 300 Win. Mag., 300 Wea. Mag., 338 Rem. Ultra Mag., 338 Win. Mag., 375 H&H. Aramid fiber reinforced fiberglass stock. Introduced 1994.

Price: . . . . **$1,593.00** (right-hand); **$1,673.00** (left-hand)

Remington Model 700 APR African Plains Rifle

Similar to Model 700 BDL except magnum receiver and specially contoured 26" Custom Shop barrel with satin blued finish, laminated wood stock with raised cheekpiece, satin finish, black butt pad, 20 lpi cut checkering. Chambered for 7mm Rem. Mag., 7mm RUM, 375 RUM, 300 Rem. Ultra Mag., 300 Win. Mag., 300 Wea. Mag., 338 Win. Mag., 338 Rem. Ultra Mag., 375 H&H. Introduced 1994.

Price: **$1,716.00**

Remington Model 700 LSS Rifle

Similar to 700 BDL except stainless steel barreled action, gray laminated wood stock with Monte Carlo comb and cheekpiece. No sights furnished. Available in (RH) 7mm Rem. Mag., 300 Win. Mag., 300 RUM, 338 RUM, 7mm Rem. Ultra Mag., 375 Rem. Ultra Mag., (LH) 7mm Rem. Ultra Mag., 300 Rem. Ultra Mag., and 338 Rem. RUM. Introduced 1996.

Price: From . . . . (Right-hand) **$820.00 to $840.00**; (LH) **$867.00**

Remington Model 700 MTN DM Rifle

Similar to 700 BDL except weighs 6-1/2 to 6-5/8 lbs., 22" tapered barrel. Redesigned pistol grip, straight comb, contoured cheekpiece, hand-rubbed oil stock finish, deep cut checkering, hinged floorplate and magazine follower, two-position thumb safety. Chambered for 260 Rem., 270 Win., 7mm-08, 25-06, 280 Rem., 30-06, 4-shot detachable box magazine. Overall length is 41-5/8"-42-1/2". Introduced 1995.

Price: **$728.00**

Remington Model 700 Titanium

Similar to 700 BDL except has titanium receiver, spiral-cut fluted bolt, skeletonized bolt handle and carbon-fiber and aramid fiber reinforced stock with sling swivel studs. Barrel 22"; weighs 5-1/4 lbs. (short action) or 5-1/2 lbs. (long action). Satin stainless finish. 260 Rem., 270 Win., 7mm-08, 30-06, 308 Win. Introduced 2001.

Price: **$1,239.00**

Remington Model 700 VLS Varmint Laminated Stock

Similar to 700 BDL except 26" heavy barrel without sights, brown laminated stock with beavertail forend, gripcap, rubber butt pad. Available in 223 Rem., 22-250, 6mm, 243, 308. Polished blue finish. Introduced 1995.

Price: From **$705.00**

Remington 700 VLS

Remington 700 VS

Remington 700 VS SF

Remington 700 Sendero SF

Remington Seven LS

Remington Model 700 VS Varmint Synthetic Rifles

Similar to 700 BDL Varmint Laminated except composite stock reinforced with aramid fiber reinforced, fiberglass and graphite. Aluminum bedding block that runs full length of receiver. Free-floating 26" barrel. Metal has black matte finish; stock has textured black and gray finish and swivel studs. Available in 223, 22-250, 308. Right- and left-hand. Introduced 1992.
Price: .... **$811.00 to $837.00**

Remington Model 700 VS SF Rifle

Similar to Model 700 Varmint Synthetic except satin-finish stainless barreled action with 26" fluted barrel, spherical concave muzzle crown. Chambered for 223, 220 Swift, 22-250. Introduced 1994.
Price: **$976.00**

Remington Model 700 EtronX VSSF Rifle

Similar to Model 700 VS SF except features battery-powered ignition system for near-zero lock time and electronic trigger mechanism. Requires ammunition with EtronX electrically fired primers. Aluminum-bedded 26" heavy, stainless steel, fluted barrel; overall length 45-7/8"; weight 8 lbs., 14 oz. Black, Kevlar-reinforced composite stock. Light-emitting diode display on grip top indicates fire or safe mode, loaded or unloaded chamber, battery condition. Introduced 2000.
Price: 220 Swift, 22-250 or 243 Win. **$1,332.00**

Remington Model 700 Sendero SF Rifle

Similar to 700 Sendero except stainless steel action and 26" fluted stainless barrel. Weighs 8-1/2 lbs. Chambered for 7mm Rem. SAUM, 300 Rem. SAUM, 7mm Rem. Mag., 7mm STW, 300 Rem. Ultra Mag., 338 Rem. Ultra Mag., 300 Win. Mag., 7mm Rem. Ultra Mag. Introduced 1996.
Price: .... **$1,003.00 to $1,016.00**

REMINGTON MODEL 700 RMEF

Caliber: 300 Rem. SAUM. **Barrel:** 26". **Weight:** 7-5/8 lbs. **Length:** 46.5". **Stock:** Synthetic, Realtree Hardwoods HD finish. **Sights:** None; drilled and tapped. **Features:** Special Edition (sold one year only), Rocky Mountain Elk Foundation rifle, 416 stainless bolt, varrel, receiver. Portion of proceeds to RMEF.
Price: **$835.00**

REMINGTON MODEL 710 BOLT-ACTION RIFLE

Caliber: 270 Win., 30-06. **Barrel:** 22". **Weight:** 7-1/8 lbs. **Length:** 42-1/2" overall. **Stock:** Gray synthetic. **Sights:** Bushnell Sharpshooter 3-9x scope mounted and bore-sighted. **Features:** Unique action locks bolt directly into barrel; 60-degree bolt throw; 4-shot dual-stack magazine; key-operated Integrated Security System locks bolt open. Introduced 2001. Made in U.S.A. by Remington Arms Co.
Price: **$425.00**

REMINGTON MODEL SEVEN LS

Caliber: 223 Rem., 243 Win., 7mm-08 Rem., 308 Win. **Barrel:** 20". **Weight:** 6-1/2 lbs. **Length:** 39-1/4" overall. **Stock:** Brown laminated, satin finished. **Features:** Satin finished carbone steel barrel and action, 4-round magazine, hinged magazine floorplate. Furnished with iron sights and sling swivel studs, drilled and tapped for scope mounts.
Price: **$701.00**
Price: 7mmRSAUM, 300RSAUM, LS Magnum, 22" bbl. **$741.00**

Remington Model Seven SS

Similar to Model Seven LS except stainless steel barreled action and black synthetic stock, 20" barrel. Chambered for 243, 260 Rem., 7mm-08, 308. Introduced 1994.
Price: **$729.00**
Price: 7mmRSAUM, 300RSAUM, Model Seven SS Magnum, 22" bbl. **$769.00**

Remington Model Seven LS Mag

Remington Model Seven SS Mag

Remington Model Seven Custom MS

Remington Seven Custom KS

Ruger Magnum

Ruger 77/22 Hornet Varmint

Remington Model Seven Custom MS Rifle

Similar to Model Seven LS except full-length Mannlicher-style stock of laminated wood with straight comb, solid black recoil pad, black steel forend tip, cut checkering, gloss finish. Barrel length 20", weighs 6-3/4 lbs. Available in 222 Rem., 223, 22-250, 243, 6mm Rem., 260 Rem., 7mm-08 Rem., 308, 350 Rem. Mag. Calibers 250 Savage, 257 Roberts, 35 Rem. Polished blue finish. Introduced 1993. From Remington Custom Shop.

Price: From **$1,332.00**

Remington Model Seven Youth Rifle

Similar to Model Seven LS except hardwood stock, 1" shorter length of pull, chambered for 223, 243, 260 Rem., 7mm-08. Introduced 1993.

Price: **$547.00**

Remington Model Seven Custom KS

Similar to Model Seven LS except gray aramid fiber reinforced stock with 1" black rubber recoil pad and swivel studs. Blued satin carbon steel barreled action. No sights on 223, 260 Rem., 7mm-08, 308; 35 Rem. and 350 Rem. have iron sights.

Price: **$1,314.00**

RUGER MAGNUM RIFLE

Caliber: 375 H&H, 416 Rigby, 458 Lott. **Barrel:** 23". **Weight:** 9-1/2 to 10-1/4 lbs. **Length:** 44". **Stock:** AAA Premium Grade Circassian walnut with live-rubber recoil pad, metal grip cap, and studs for mounting sling swivels. **Sights:** Blade, front; V-notch rear express sights (one stationary, two folding) drift-adjustable for windage. **Features:** Patented floorplate latch secures the hinged floorplate against accidental dumping of cartridges; one-piece bolt has a non-rotating Mauser-type controlled-feed extractor; fixed-blade ejector.

Price: M77RSMMKII **$1,695.00**

RUGER 77/22 HORNET BOLT-ACTION RIFLE

Caliber: 22 Hornet, 6-shot rotary magazine. **Barrel:** 20". **Weight:** About 6 lbs. **Length:** 39-3/4" overall. **Stock:** Checkered American walnut, black rubber butt pad. **Sights:** Brass bead front, open adjustable rear; also available without sights. **Features:** Same basic features as rimfire model except slightly lengthened receiver. Uses Ruger rotary magazine. Three-position safety. Comes with 1" Ruger scope rings. Introduced 1994.

Price: 77/22RH (rings only) **$589.00**
Price: 77/22RSH (with sights) **$609.00**
Price: K77/22VHZ Varmint, laminated stock, no sights **$625.00**

Ruger M77 Mark II

Ruger KM77RLFP MKII

Ruger KM77RSFP MKII

Ruger KM77RFP MKII

Ruger 77/44

RUGER M77 MARK II RIFLE

Caliber: 223, 220 Swift, 22-250, 243, 6mm Rem., 257 Roberts, 25-06, 6.5x55 Swedish, 270, 7x57mm, 260 Rem., 280 Rem., 308, 30-06, 7mm Rem. Mag., 7mm Rem. Short Ultra Mag., 300 Rem. Short Ultra Mag., 300 WSM, 300 Win. Mag., 338 Win. Mag., 4-shot magazine. **Barrel:** 20", 22"; 24" (magnums). **Weight:** About 7 lbs. **Length:** 39-3/4" overall. **Stock:** Synthetic American walnut; swivel studs, rubber butt pad. **Sights:** None furnished. Receiver has Ruger integral scope mount base, Ruger 1" rings. Some with iron sights. **Features:** Short action with new trigger, 3-position safety. Steel trigger guard. Left-hand available. Introduced 1989.

Price: M77RMKII (no sights)............................. **$675.00**
Price: M77RSMKII (open sights) **$759.00**
Price: M77LRMKII (left-hand, 270, 30-06, 7mm Rem. Mag.,300 Win. Mag.) **$675.00**
Price: KM77REPMKII (Shorts) **$675.00**

Ruger M77RSI International Carbine

Same as standard Model 77 except 18" barrel, full-length International-style stock, steel forend cap, loop-type steel sling swivels. Integral-base receiver, open sights, Ruger 1" steel rings. Improved front sight. Available in 243, 270, 308, 30-06. Weighs 7 lbs. Length overall is 38-3/8".
Price: M77RSIMKII.................................... **$769.00**

Ruger M77 Mark II All-Weather and Sporter Model Stainless Rifle

Similar to wood-stock M77 Mark II except all metal parts are stainless steel, has an injection-moulded, glass-fiber-reinforced polymer stock. Laminated wood stock. Chambered for 223, 243, 270, 308, 30-06, 7mm Rem. Mag., 300 Win. Mag., 338 Win. Mag. Fixed-blade-type ejector, 3-position safety, new trigger guard with patented floorplate latch. Integral Scope Base Receiver, 1" Ruger scope rings, built-in sling swivel loops. Introduced 1990.

Price: K77RFPMKII **$675.00**
Price: K77RLFPMKII Ultra-Light, synthetic stock, rings, no sights **$675.00**
Price: K77LRBBZMKII, left-hand bolt, rings, no sights, laminated stock.. **$729.00**
Price: K77RSFPMKII, synthetic stock, open sights **$759.00**
Price: K77RBZMKII, no sights, laminated wood stock, 223, 22/250, 243, 270, 280 Rem., 7mm Rem. Mag., 30-06, 308, 300 Win. Mag., 338 Win. Mag....................... **$729.00**
Price: K77RSBZMKII, open sights, laminated wood stock, 243, 270, 7mm Rem. Mag., 30-06, 300 Win. Mag., 338 Win. Mag... **$799.00**
Price: KM77RFPMKII (Shorts), M77RMKII **$675.00**

Ruger M77RL Ultra Light

Similar to standard M77 except weighs 6 lbs., chambered for 223, 243, 308, 270, 30-06, 257 Roberts, barrel tapped for target scope blocks, 20" Ultra Light barrel. Overall length 40". Ruger's steel 1" scope rings supplied. Introduced 1983.
Price: M77RLMKII **$729.00**

Ruger M77 Mark II Compact Rifles

Similar to standard M77 except reduced 16-1/2" barrel, weighs 5-3/4 lbs. Chambered for 223, 243, 260 Rem., 308, and 7mm-08.
Price: M77CR MKII (blued finish, walnut stock) **$675.00**
Price: KM77CRBBZ MkII (stainless finish, black laminated stock) **$729.00**

RUGER 77/44 BOLT-ACTION RIFLE

Caliber: 44 Magnum, 4-shot magazine. **Barrel:** 18-1/2". **Weight:** 6 lbs. **Length:** 38-1/4" overall. **Stock:** American walnut with rubber butt pad and swivel studs or black polymer (stainless only). **Sights:** Gold bead front, folding leaf rear. Comes with Ruger 1" scope rings. **Features:** Uses same action as the Ruger 77/22. Short bolt stroke; rotary magazine; three-position safety. Introduced 1997. Made in U.S.A. by Sturm, Ruger & Co.
Price: Blue, walnut, 77/44RS **$605.00**
Price: Stainless, polymer, stock, K77/44RS **$605.00**

RIFLES

Ruger M77VT Target

Sako TRG-S

Sako 75 Hunter

Sako 75 Stainless Hunter

Sako 75 Deluxe

RUGER M77VT TARGET RIFLE
Caliber: 22-250, 220 Swift, 223, 243, 25-06, 308. **Barrel:** 26" heavy stainless steel with target gray finish. **Weight:** 9-3/4 lbs. **Length:** Approx. 44" overall. **Stock:** Laminated American hardwood with beavertail forend, steel swivel studs; no checkering or gripcap. **Sights:** Integral scope mount bases in receiver. **Features:** Ruger diagonal bedding system. Ruger steel 1" scope rings supplied. Fully adjustable trigger. Steel floorplate and trigger guard. New version introduced 1992.
Price: K77VTMKII **$819.00**

SAKO TRG-S BOLT-ACTION RIFLE
Caliber: 338 Lapua Mag., 30-378 Weatherby, 3-shot magazine. **Barrel:** 26". **Weight:** 7.75 lbs. **Length:** 45.5" overall. **Stock:** Reinforced polyurethane with Monte Carlo comb. **Sights:** None furnished. **Features:** Resistance-free bolt with 60-degree lift. Recoil pad adjustable for length. Free-floating barrel, detachable magazine, fully adjustable trigger. Matte blue metal. Introduced 1993. Imported from Finland by Beretta USA.
Price: **$896.00**

Sako TRG-42 Bolt-Action Rifle
Similar to TRG-S except 5-shot magazine, fully adjustable stock and competition trigger. Offered in 338 Lapua Mag. and 300 Win. Mag. Imported from Finland by Beretta USA.
Price: **$2,829.00**

SAKO 75 HUNTER BOLT-ACTION RIFLE
Caliber: 17 Rem., 222, 223, 22-250, 243, 7mm-08, 308 Win., 25-06, 270, 280, 30-06; 270 Wea. Mag., 7mm Rem. Mag., 7mm STW, 7mm Wea. Mag., 300 Win. Mag., 300 Wea. Mag., 338 Win. Mag., 340 Wea. Mag., 375 H&H, 416 Rem. Mag. **Barrel:** 22", standard calibers; 24", 26" magnum calibers. **Weight:** About 6 lbs. **Length:** NA. **Stock:** European walnut with matte lacquer finish. **Sights:** None furnished; dovetail scope mount rails.

Features: New design with three locking lugs and a mechanical ejector, key locks firing pin and bolt, cold hammer-forged barrel is free-floating, 2-position safety, hinged floorplate or detachable magazine that can be loaded from the top, short 70 degree bolt lift. Five action lengths. Introduced 1997. Imported from Finland by Beretta USA.
Price: Standard calibers **$1,129.00**
Price: Magnum Calibers **$1,163.00**

Sako 75 Stainless Synthetic Rifle
Similar to 75 Hunter except all metal is stainless steel, synthetic stock has soft composite panels moulded into forend and pistol grip. Available in 22-250, 243, 308 Win., 25-06, 270, 30-06 with 22" barrel, 7mm Rem. Mag., 7mm STW, 300 Win. Mag., 338 Win. Mag. and 375 H&H Mag. with 24" barrel and 300 Wea. Mag., 300 Rem.Ultra Mag. with 26" barrel. Introduced 1997. Imported from Finland by Beretta USA.
Price: Standard calibers **$1,212.00**
Price: Magnum calibers **$1,246.00**

Sako 75 Deluxe Rifle
Similar to 75 Hunter except select wood rosewood gripcap and forend tip. Available in 17 Rem., 222, 223, 25-06, 243, 7mm-08, 308, 25-06, 270, 280, 30-06; 270 Wea. Mag., 7mm Rem. Mag., 7mm STW, 7mm Wea. Mag., 300 Win. Mag., 300 Wea. Mag., 338 Win. Mag., 340 Wea. Mag., 375 H&H, 416 Rem. Mag. Introduced 1997. Imported from Finland by Beretta USA.
Price: Standard calibers **$1,653.00**
Price: Magnum calibers **$1,688.00**

Sako 75 Varmint Stainless Laminated Rifle
Similar to Sako 75 Hunter except chambered only for 222, 223, 22-250, 22 PPC USA, 6mm PPC, heavy 24" barrel with recessed crown, all metal is stainless steel, laminated wood stock with beavertail forend. Introduced 1999. Imported from Finland by Beretta USA.
Price: **$1,448.00**

Sako 75 Varmint

Savage 110GXP3

Savage 111FXP3

Savage 111FCXP3

Sako 75 Varmint Rifle

Similar to Model 75 Hunter except chambered only for 17 Rem., 222 Rem., 223 Rem., 22-250 Rem., 22 PPC and 6mm PPC, 24" heavy barrel with recessed crown, beavertail forend. Introduced 1998. Imported from Finland by Beretta USA.

Price: **$1,337.00**

SAUER 202 BOLT-ACTION RIFLE

Caliber: Standard—243, 6.5x55, 270 Win., 308 Win., 30-06; magnum—7mm Rem. Mag., 300 Win. Mag., 300 Wea. Mag., 375 H&H. **Barrel:** 23.6" (standard), 26" (magnum). **Weight:** 7.7 lbs. (standard). **Length:** 44.3" overall (23.6" barrel). **Stock:** Select American Claro walnut with high-gloss epoxy finish, rosewood grip and forend caps; 22 lpi checkering. Synthetic also available. **Sights:** None furnished; drilled and tapped for scope mounting. **Features:** Short 60" bolt throw; detachable box magazine; six-lug bolt; quick-change barrel; tapered bore; adjustable two-stage trigger; firing pin cocking indicator. Introduced 1994. Imported from Germany by Sigarms, Inc.

Price: Standard calibers, right-hand. **$1,035.00**
Price: Magnum calibers, right-hand **$1,106.00**
Price: Standard calibers, synthetic stock **$985.00**
Price: Magnum calibers, synthetic stock **$1,056.00**

SAVAGE MODEL 10GXP3, 110GXP3 PACKAGE GUNS

Caliber: 223 Rem., 22-250 Rem., 243 Win., 7mm-08 Rem., 308 Win., 300 WSM (10GXP3). 25-06 Rem., 270 Win., 30-06 Spfld., 7mm Rem. Mag., 300 Win. Mag., 300 Rem. Ultra Mag. (110GXP3). **Barrel:** 22" 24", 26". **Weight:** 7.5 lbs. average. **Length:** 43"-47". **Stock:** Walnut Monte Carlo with checkering. **Sights:** 3-9X40mm scope, mounted & bore sighted. **Features:** Blued, free floating and button rifled, internal box magazines, swivel studs, leather sling. Left-hand available.

Price: **$495.00**

SAVAGE MODEL 11FXP3, 111FXP3, 111FCXP3, 11FYXP3 (Youth) PACKAGE GUNS

Caliber: 223 Rem., 22-250 Rem., 243 Win., 308 Win., 300 WSM (11FXP3). 270 Win., 30-06 Spfld., 25-06 Rem., 7mm Rem. Mag., 300 Win. Mag., 338 Win. Mag., 300 Rem. Ultra Mag. (11FCXPE & 111FXP3). **Barrel:** 22"-26". **Weight:** 6.5 lbs. **Length:** 41"-47". **Stock:** Synthetic checkering, dual pillar bed. **Sights:** 3-9X40mm scope, mounted & bore sighted. **Features:** Blued, free floating and button rifled, Top loading internal box mag (except 111FXCP3 has detachable box mag.). Nylon sling and swivel studs. Some left-hand available.

Price: Model 11FXP3 . . . . **$505.00**
Price: Model 111FCXP3 . . . . **$425.00**
Price: Model 11FYXP3, 243 Win., 12.5" pull (youth) **$471.00**

RIFLES

Savage 11FYXP3

Savage 16FXP3

Savage 10FM Sierra Ultra Light

Savage 10FCM Scout Ultra Light

Savage Model 10FP

SAVAGE MODEL 16FXP3, 116FXP3 SS ACTION PACKAGE GUNS

Caliber: 223 Rem., 243 Win., 308 Win., 300 WSM, 270 Win., 30-06 Spfld., 7mm Rem. Mag., 300 Win. Mag., 338 Win. Mag., 375 H&H, 7mm S&W, 7mm Rem. Ultra Mag., 300 Rem. Ultra Mag. **Barrel:** 22", 24", 26". **Weight:** 6.75 lbs. average. **Length:** 41"-46". **Stock:** Synthetic checkering, dual pillar bed. **Sights:** 3-9X40mm scope, mounted & bore sighted. **Features:** Free floating and button rifled. Internal box mag., nylon sling and swivel studs.
Price: **$556.00**

SAVAGE MODEL 10FM SIERRA ULTRA LIGHT RIFLE

Caliber: 223, 243, 308. **Barrel:** 20". **Weight:** 6 lbs. **Length:** 41-1/2". **Stock:** "Dual Pillar" bedding in black synthetic stock with silver medallion in gripcap. **Sights:** None furnished; drilled and tapped for scope mounting. **Features:** True short action. Comes with sling and quick-detachable swivels. Introduced 1998. Made in U.S.A. by Savage Arms, Inc.
Price: **$495.00**

SAVAGE MODEL 10FCM SCOUT ULTRA LIGHT RIFLE

Caliber: 7mm-08 Rem., 308 Win. **Barrel:** 20", 4-shot. **Weight:** 6.25 lbs. **Length:** 39.75" overall. **Stock:** Synthetic checkering, dual pillar bed. **Sights:** Ghost ring rear, gold bead front. **Features:** Blued, detachable box magazine, Savage shooting sling/carry strap. Quick detach swivels.
Price: **$581.00**

SAVAGE MODEL 10/110FP LONG RANGE RIFLE

Caliber: 223, 25-06, 308, 30-06, 300 Win. Mag., 7mm Rem. Mag., 4-shot magazine. **Barrel:** 24", heavy; recessed target muzzle. **Weight:** 8-1/2 lbs. **Length:** 45.5" overall. **Stock:** Black graphite/fiberglass composition; positive checkering. **Sights:** None furnished. Receiver drilled and tapped for scope mounting. **Features:** Pillar-bedded stock. Black matte finish on all metal parts. Double swivel studs on the forend for sling and/or bipod mount. Right or left-hand. Introduced 1990. From Savage Arms, Inc.
Price: Right- or left-hand **$558**

Savage Model 10FP Tactical Rifle

Similar to the Model 110FP except has true short action, chambered for 223, 308; black synthetic stock with "Dual Pillar" bedding. Introduced 1998. Made in U.S.A. by Savage Arms, Inc.
Price: **$558.00**
Price: Model 10FLP (left-hand) **$558.00**
Price: Model 10FP-LE1 (20"), 10FPLE2 (26") **$566.00**
Price: Model 10FPXP-LE w/Burris 3.5-10X50 scope,
Harris bipod package **$1,632.00**

Savage Model 10FP-LE1A Tactical Rifle

Similar to the Model 110FP except weighs 10.75 lbs. and has overall length of 39.75". Chambered for 223 Rem., 308 Win. Black synthetic Choate™ adjustable stock with accessory rail and swivel studs.
Price: **$684.00**

RIFLES

Savage Model 10FPLE1

Savage Model 10FPXP-LE

Savage Model 111F

Savage Hunter 111G

Savage Model 11F

Savage Hunter 11G

SAVAGE MODEL 111 CLASSIC HUNTER RIFLES

Caliber: 25-06 Rem., 270 Win., 30-06 Spfld., 7mm Rem. Mag., 300 Win. Mag., 7mm RUM, 300 RUM. **Barrel:** 22", 24", 26" (magnum calibers). **Weight:** 6.5 to 7.5 lbs. **Length:** 42.75" to 47.25". **Stock:** Walnut-finished hardwood (M111G, GC); graphite/fiberglass filled composite. **Sights:** Ramp front, open fully adjustable rear; drilled and tapped for scope mounting. **Features:** Three-position top tang safety, double front locking lugs, free-floated button-rifled barrel. Comes with trigger lock, target, ear puffs. Introduced 1994. Made in U.S.A. by Savage Arms, Inc.

Price: Model 111F (270 Win., 30-06 Spfld., 7mm Rem. Mag., 300 win. Mag.) **$411.00**

Price: Model 111F (25-06 Rem., 338 Win. Mag., 7mm Rem. Ultra Mag, 300 Rem. Ultra Mag.) **$461.00**

Price: Model 111G (wood stock, top-loading magazine, right- or left-hand) **$436.00**

Price: Model 111GNS (wood stock, top-loading magazine, no sights, right-hand only) **$428.00**

Savage Model 11 Classic Hunter Rifles, Short Action

Similar to the Model 111F except has true short action, chambered for 22-250, Rem., 243 Win., 7mm-08 Rem., 308 Win.; black synthetic stock with "Dual Pillar" bedding, positive checkering. Introduced 1998. Made in U.S.A. by Savage Arms, Inc.

Price: Model 11F **$461.00**

Price: Model 11FL (left-hand) **$461.00**

Price: Model 11FNS (right-hand, no sights) **$453.00**

Price: Model 11G (wood stock) **$436.00**

Price: Model 11GL (as above, left-hand) **$436.00**

Price: Model 11FC (right hand, open sights) **$487.00**

RIFLES

Savage Model 10GY

Savage Model 114U

Savage Model 12FV

Savage Model 12VSS Varminter

Savage Model 10GY

Similar to the Model 111G except weighs 6.3 lbs., is 42-1/2" overall, and the stock is scaled for ladies, small-framed adults and youths. Chambered for 223, 243, 308. Ramp front sight, open adjustable rear; drilled and tapped for scope mounts. Made in U.S.A. by Savage Arms, Inc.

Price: Model 10GY (short action, calibers 223, 243, 308) **$436.00**

SAVAGE MODEL 114U ULTRA RIFLE

Caliber: 270 Win., 30-06 Spfld., 7mm Rem. Mag., 7mm STW, 300 Win. Mag. **Barrel:** 22"-24". **Weight:** 7-7.5 lbs. **Length:** 43.25"-45.25" overall. **Stock:** Ultra high gloss American walnut with black tip and custom cut checkering. **Sights:** None furnished; drilled and tapped for scope mounting. **Features:** High-luster blued barrel action, internal box magazine.

Price: **$552.00**

SAVAGE MODEL 112 LONG RANGE RIFLES

Caliber: 22-250, 223, 5-shot magazine. **Barrel:** 26" heavy. **Weight:** 8.8 lbs. **Length:** 47.5" overall. **Stock:** Black graphite/fiberglass filled composite with positive checkering. **Sights:** None furnished; drilled and tapped for scope mounting. **Features:** Pillar-bedded stock. Blued barrel with recessed target-style muzzle. Double front swivel studs for attaching bipod. Introduced 1991. Made in U.S.A. by Savage Arms, Inc.

Price: Model 112FVSS (cals. 223, 22-250, 25-06, 7mm Rem. Mag., 300 Win. Mag., stainless barrel, bolt handle, trigger guard),
right- or left-hand **$626.00**
Price: Model 112FVSS-S (as above, single shot) **$675.00**
Price: Model 112BVSS (heavy-prone laminated stock with high comb, Wundhammer swell, fluted stainless barrel, bolt handle,
trigger guard) **$675.00**
Price: Model 112BVSS-S (as above, single shot) **$675.00**

Savage Model 12 Long Range Rifles

Similar to the Model 112 Long Range except with true short action, chambered for 223, 22-250, 308. Models 12FV, 12FVSS have black synthetic stocks with "Dual Pillar" bedding, positive checkering, swivel studs; model 12BVSS has brown laminated stock with beavertail forend, fluted stainless barrel. Introduced 1998. Made in U.S.A. by Savage Arms, Inc.

Price: Model 12FV (223, 22-250, 243 Win., 308 Win., blue) **$515.00**
Price: Model 12FVSS (blue action, fluted stainless barrel) **$626.00**
Price: Model 12FLVSS (as above, left-hand) **$626.00**
Price: Model 12FVSS-S
(blue action, fluted stainless barrel, single shot) **$934.00**
Price: Model 12BVSS (laminated stock) **$675.00**
Price: Model 12BVSS-S (as above, single shot) **$675.00**
Price: Model 12BVSS-XP (hard case, Burris 6-18X37) **$1,100.00**

Savage Model 12VSS Varminter Rifle

Similar to other Model 12s except blue/stainless steel action, fluted stainless barrel, Choate full pistol-grip, adjustable synthetic stock, Sharp Shooter trigger. Overall length 47-1/2 inches, weighs appx. 15 lbs. No sights; drilled and tapped for scope mounts. Chambered in 223, 22-250, 308 Win. Made in U.S.A. by Savage Arms Inc.

Price: **$934.00**

SAVAGE MODEL 116SE SAFARI EXPRESS RIFLE

Caliber: 458 Win. Mag. **Barrel:** 24". **Weight:** 8.5 lbs. **Length:** 45.5" overall. **Stock:** Classic-style select walnut with ebony forend tip, deluxe cut checkering. Two cross bolts; internally vented recoil pad. **Sights:** Bead on ramp front, three-leaf express rear. **Features:** Controlled-round feed design; adjustable muzzle brake; one-piece barrel band stud. Satin-finished stainless steel barreled action. Introduced 1994. Made in U.S.A. by Savage Arms, Inc.

Price: **$1,013.00**

RIFLES

Savage Model 116SE Safari Express

Savage Model 116SE Safari Express

Savage Model 16FSS

Savage Model 116FSAK

Sigarms SHR 970

Steyr Mannlicher SBS

SAVAGE MODEL 116 WEATHER WARRIORS

Caliber: 375 H&H, 300 Rem. Ultra Mag., 308 Win., 300 Rem. Ultra Mag., 300 WSM, 7mm Rem. Ultra Mag., 7mm Rem. Short Ultra Mag., 7mm S&W, 7mm-08 Rem. **Barrel:** 22", 24" for 7mm Rem. Mag., 300 Win. Mag., 338 Win. Mag. (M116FSS only). **Weight:** 6.25 to 6.5 lbs. **Length:** 41"-47". **Stock:** Graphite/fiberglass filled composite. **Sights:** None furnished; drilled and tapped for scope mounting. **Features:** Stainless steel with matte finish; free-floated barrel; quick-detachable swivel studs; laser-etched bolt; scope bases and rings. Left-hand models available in all models, calibers at same price. Model 116FSS introduced 1991; 116FSAK introduced 1994. Made in U.S.A. by Savage Arms, Inc.
Price: Model 116FSS (top-loading magazine) **$520.00**
Price: Model 116FSAK (top-loading magazine, Savage Adjustable Muzzle Brake system). **$601.00**
Price: Model 16BSS (brown laminate, 24") **$668.00**
Price: Model 116BSS (brown laminate, 26") **$668.00**

Savage Model 16FSS Rifle

Similar to Model 116FSS except true short action, chambered for 223, 243, 22" free-floated barrel; black graphite/fiberglass stock with "Dual Pillar" bedding. Also left-hand. Introduced 1998. Made in U.S.A. by Savage Arms, Inc.
Price: **$520.00**

SIGARMS SHR 970 SYNTHETIC RIFLE

Caliber: 270, 30-06. **Barrel:** 22". **Weight:** 7.2 lbs. **Length:** 41.9" overall. **Stock:** Textured black fiberglass or walnut. **Sights:** None furnished; drilled and tapped for scope mounting. **Features:** Quick takedown; interchangeable barrels; removable box magazine; cocking indicator; three-position safety. Introduced 1998. Imported by Sigarms, Inc.
Price: Synthetic stock **$499.00**
Price: Walnut stock **$550.00**

STEYR CLASSIC MANNLICHER SBS RIFLE

Caliber: 243, 25-06, 308, 6.5x55, 6.5x57, 270, 7x64 Brenneke, 7mm-08, 7.5x55, 30-06, 9.3x62, 6.5x68, 7mm Rem. Mag., 300 Win. Mag., 8x685, 4-shot magazine. **Barrel:** 23.6" standard; 26" magnum; 20" full stock standard calibers. **Weight:** 7 lbs. **Length:** 40.1" overall. **Stock:** Hand-checkered fancy European oiled walnut with standard forend. **Sights:** Ramp front adjustable for elevation, V-notch rear adjustable for windage. **Features:** Single adjustable trigger; 3-position roller safety with "safe-bolt" setting; drilled and tapped for Steyr factory scope mounts. Introduced 1997. Imported from Austria by GSI, Inc.
Price: Full-stock, standard calibers **$1,749.00**

Steyr SBS Forester

Steyr SBS Prohunter

Steyr Scout Rifle

Tikka Whitetail Hunter

STEYR SBS FORESTER RIFLE

Caliber: 243, 25-06, 270, 7mm-08, 308 Win., 30-06, 7mm Rem. Mag., 300 Win. Mag. Detachable 4-shot magazine. **Barrel:** 23.6", standard calibers; 25.6", magnum calibers. **Weight:** 7.5 lbs. **Length:** 44.5" overall (23.6" barrel). **Stock:** Oil-finished American walnut with Monte Carlo cheekpiece. Pachmayr 1" swivels. **Sights:** None furnished. Drilled and tapped for Browning A-Bolt mounts. **Features:** Steyr Safe Bolt systems, three-position ambidextrous roller tang safety, for Safe, Loading Fire. Matte finish on barrel and receiver; adjustable trigger. Rotary cold-hammer forged barrel. Introduced 1997. Imported by GSI, Inc.

Price: Standard calibers $799.00
Price: Magnum calibers $829.00

Steyr SBS Prohunter Rifle

Similar to the SBS Forester except has ABS synthetic stock with adjustable butt spacers, straight comb without cheekpiece, palm swell, Pachmayr 1" swivels. Special 10-round magazine conversion kit available. Introduced 1997. Imported by GSI.

Price Standard calibers $769.00
Price Magnum calibers $799.00

STEYR SCOUT BOLT-ACTION RIFLE

Caliber: 308 Win., 5-shot magazine. **Barrel:** 19", fluted. **Weight:** NA. **Length:** NA. **Stock:** Gray Zytel. **Sights:** Pop-up front & rear, Leupold M8 2.5x28 IER scope on Picatinny optic rail with Steyr mounts. **Features:** luggage case, scout sling, two stock spacers, two magazines. Introduced 1998. From GSI.

Price: From $1,969.00

STEYR SSG BOLT-ACTION RIFLE

Caliber: 308 Win., detachable 5-shot rotary magazine. **Barrel:** 26" **Weight:** 8.5 lbs. **Length:** 44.5" overall. **Stock:** Black ABS Cycolac with spacers for length of pull adjustment. **Sights:** Hooded ramp front adjustable for elevation, V-notch rear adjustable for windage. **Features:** Sliding safety; NATO rail for bipod; 1" swivels; Parkerized finish; single or double-set triggers. Imported from Austria by GSI, Inc.

Price: SSG-PI, iron sights. $1,699.00
Price: SSG-PII, heavy barrel, no sights $1,699.00
Price: SSG-PIIK, 20" heavy barrel, no sights $1,699.00
Price: SSG-PIV, 16.75" threaded heavy barrel with flash hider . $2,659.00

TIKKA WHITETAIL HUNTER LEFT-HAND BOLT-ACTION RIFLE

Caliber: 22-250, 223, 243, 7mm-08, 25-06, 270, 308, 30-06, 7mm Rem. Mag., 300 Win. Mag., 338 Win. Mag. **Barrel:** 22-1/2" (std. cals.), 24-1/2" (magnum cals.). **Weight:** 7-1/8 lbs. **Length:** 43" overall (std. cals.). **Stock:** European walnut with Monte Carlo comb, rubber butt pad, checkered grip and forend. **Sights:** None furnished. **Features:** Detachable four-shot magazine (standard calibers), three-shot in magnums. Receiver dovetailed for scope mounting. Reintroduced 1996. Imported from Finland by Beretta USA.

Price: Left-hand $710.00

Tikka Continental Varmint

Tikka Whitetail Hunter Stainless Synthetic

Weatherby Mark V Lazermark

Weatherby Mark V Sporter

Tikka Continental Varmint Rifle
Similar to the standard Tikka rifle except has 26" heavy barrel, extra-wide forend. Chambered for 17 Rem., 22-250, 223, 308. Reintroduced 1996. Made in Finland by Sako. Imported by Beretta USA.
Price: **$720.00**

Tikka Continental Long Range Hunting Rifle
Similar to the Whitetail Hunter except has 26" heavy barrel. Available in 25-06, 270 Win., 7mm Rem. Mag., 300 Win. Mag. Introduced 1996. Imported from Finland by Beretta USA.
Price: 25-06, 270 Win. **$720.00**
Price: 7mm Rem. Mag., 300 Win. Mag. **$750.00**

Tikka Whitetail Hunter Stainless Synthetic
Similar to the Whitetail Hunter except all metal is of stainless steel, and it has a black synthetic stock. Available in 22-250, 223, 243, 7mm-08, 25-06, 270, 308, 30-06, 7mm Rem. Mag., 300 Win. Mag., 338 Win. Mag. Introduced 1997. Imported from Finland by Beretta USA.
Price: Standard calibers **$775.00**
Price: Magnum calibers **$745.00**

VEKTOR BUSHVELD BOLT-ACTION RIFLE
Caliber: 243, 308, 7x57, 7x64 Brenneke, 270 Win., 30-06, 300 Win. Mag., 300 H&H, 9.3x62. **Barrel:** 22"-26". **Weight:** NA. **Length:** NA. **Stock:** Turkish walnut with wrap-around hand checkering. **Sights:** Blade on ramp front, fixed standing leaf rear. **Features:** Combines the best features of the Mauser 98 and Winchester 70 actions. Controlled-round feed; Mauser-type extractor; no cut-away through the bolt locking lug; M70-type three-position safety; Timney-type adjustable trigger. Introduced 1999. Imported from South Africa by Vektor USA.
Price: .... **$1,595.00 to $1,695.00**

VEKTOR MODEL 98 BOLT-ACTION RIFLE
Caliber: 243, 308, 7x57, 7x64 Brenneke, 270 Win., 30-06, 300 Win. Mag., 300 H&H, 375 H&H, 9.3x62. **Barrel:** 22"-26". **Weight:** NA. **Length:** NA.

Stock: Turkish walnut with hand-checkered grip and forend. **Sights:** None furnished; drilled and tapped for scope mounting. **Features:** Bolt has guide rib; non-rotating, long extractor enhances positive feeding; polished blue finish. Updated Mauser 98 action. Introduced 1999. Imported from South Africa by Vektor USA.
Price: .... **$1,149.00 to $1,249.00**

WEATHERBY MARK V DELUXE BOLT-ACTION RIFLE
Caliber: All Weatherby calibers plus 22-250, 243, 25-06, 270 Win., 280 Rem., 7mm-08, 30-06, 308 Win. **Barrel:** 24" barrel on standard calibers. **Weight:** 8-1/2 to 10-1/2 lbs. **Length:** 46-5/8" to 46-3/4" overall. **Stock:** Walnut, Monte Carlo with cheekpiece; high luster finish; checkered pistol grip and forend; recoil pad. **Sights:** None furnished. **Features:** Cocking indicator; adjustable trigger; hinged floorplate, thumb safety; quick detachable sling swivels. Made in U.S.A. From Weatherby.
Price: 257, 270, 7mm. 300, 340 Wea. Mags., 26" barrel **$1,767.00**
Price: 416 Wea. Mag. with Accubrake, 28" barrel **$2,079.00**
Price: 460 Wea. Mag. with Accubrake, 28" barrel **$2,443.00**
Price: 24" barrel **$1,715.00**

Weatherby Mark V Lazermark Rifle
Same as Mark V Deluxe except stock has extensive oak leaf pattern laser carving on pistol grip and forend. Introduced 1981.
Price: 257, 270, 7mm Wea. Mag., 300, 340, 26" **$1,923.00**
Price: 378 Wea. Mag., 28" **$2,266.00**
Price: 416 Wea. Mag., 28", Accubrake **$2,266.00**
Price: 460 Wea. Mag., 28", Accubrake **$2,661.00**

Weatherby Mark V Sporter Rifle
Same as the Mark V Deluxe without the embellishments. Metal has low-luster blue, stock is Claro walnut with matte finish, Monte Carlo comb, recoil pad. Introduced 1993. From Weatherby.
Price: 22-250, 243, 240 Wea. Mag., 25-06, 7mm-08, 270 WCF, 280, 30-06, 308; 24" **$1,091.00**
Price: 257 Wea., 270, 7 mm Wea., 7mm Rem., 300 Wea., 300 Win., 340 Wea., 338 Win. Mag., 26" barrel for Wea. Calibers; 24" for non-Wea. Calibers. **$1,143.00**

CENTERFIRE RIFLES — BOLT ACTION

Weatherby Mark V Euromark

Weatherby Mark V Stainless

Weatherby Mark V Synthetic

Weatherby Mark V Accumark

RIFLES

Weatherby Mark V Euromark Rifle

Similar to the Mark V Deluxe except has raised-comb Monte Carlo stock with hand-rubbed oil finish, fine-line hand-cut checkering, ebony grip and forend tips. All metal has low-luster blue. Right-hand only. Uses Mark V action. Introduced 1995. Made in U.S.A. From Weatherby.
Price: 257, 270, 7mm, 300, 340 Wea. Mags., 26" barrel **$1,819.00**
Price: 7mm Rem. Mag., 300 Win. Mag., 338 Win. Mag.,
375 H&H, 24" barrel **$1,819.00**
Price: 378 Wea. Mag., 416 Wea. Mag., 28" barrel **$2,131.00**

Weatherby Mark V Stainless Rifle

Similar to the Mark V Deluxe except made of 410-series stainless steel. Also available in 30-378 Wea. Mag. Has lightweight injection-moulded synthetic stock with raised Monte Carlo comb, checkered grip and forend, custom floorplate release. Right-hand only. Introduced 1995. Made in U.S.A. From Weatherby.
Price: 22-250 Rem., 243 Win., 240 Wby. Mag., 25-06 Rem., 270 Win.,
280 Rem., 7mm-08 Rem., 30-06 Spfld., 308 Win., 24" barrel . **$1,018.00**
Price: 257, 270, 7mm, 300, 340 Wby. Mag., 26" barrel **$1,070.00**
Price: 7mm Rem. Mag., 300 Win. Mag., 338 Win. Mag.,
375 H&H Mag., 24" barrel. **$1,070.00**

Weatherby Mark V Eurosport Rifle

Similar to the Mark V Deluxe except has raised-comb Monte Carlo stock with hand-rubbed satin oil finish, low-luster blue metal. No gripcap or forend tip. Right-hand only. Introduced 1995. Made in U.S.A. From Weatherby.
Price: 257, 270, 7mm, 300, 340 Wea. Mags., 26" barrel **$1,143.00**
Price: 7mm Rem. Mag., 300, 338 Win. Mags., 24" barrel **$1,143.00**
Price: 375 H&H, 24" barrel **$1,143.00**

Weatherby Mark V Synthetic

Similar to the Mark V Stainless except made of matte finished blued steel. Injection moulded synthetic stock. Weighs 6-1/2 lbs., 24" barrel. Available in 22-250, 240 Wea. Mag., 243, 25-06, 270, 7mm-08, 280, 30-06, 308. Introduced 1997. Made in U.S.A. From Weatherby.
Price: **$923.00**
Price: 257, 270, 7mm, 300, 340 Wea. Mags., 26" barrel **$975.00**
Price: 7mm STW, 7mm Rem. Mag., 300, 338 Win. Mags **$975.00**
Price: 375 H&H, 24" barrel **$975.00**
Price: 30-378 Wea. Mag., 338-378 Wea 28" barrel.......... **$1,151.00**

WEATHERBY MARK V ACCUMARK RIFLE

Caliber: 257, 270, 7mm, 300, 340 Wea. Mags., 338-378 Wea. Mag., 30-378 Wea. Mag., 7mm STW, 7mm Rem. Mag., 300 Win. Mag. **Barrel:** 26", 28". **Weight:** 8-1/2 lbs. **Length:** 46-5/8" overall. **Stock:** Bell & Carlson with full length aluminum bedding block. **Sights:** None furnished. Drilled and tapped for scope mounting. **Features:** Uses Mark V action with heavy-contour stainless barrel with black oxidized flutes, muzzle diameter of .705". Introduced 1996. Made in U.S.A. From Weatherby.
Price: 26" **$1,507.00**
Price: 30-378 Wea. Mag., 338-378 Wea. Mag., 28",
Accubrake....................................... **$1,724.00**
Price: 223, 22-250, 243, 240 Wea. Mag., 25-06, 270,
280 Rem., 7mm-08, 30-06, 308; 24" **$1,455.00**
Price: Accumark Left-Hand 257, 270, 7mm, 300, 340 Wea.
Mag., 7mm Rem. Mag., 7mm STW, 300 Win. Mag......... **$1,559.00**
Price: Accumark Left-Hand 30-378, 333-378 Wea. Mags...... **$1,788.00**

Weatherby Mark V Accumark Ultra Lightweight Rifles

Similar to the Mark V Accumark except weighs 5-3/4 lbs, 6-3/4 lbs. in Mag. calibers.; 24", 26" fluted barrel with recessed target crown; hand-laminated stock with CNC-machined aluminum bedding plate and faint gray "spider web" finish. Available in 257, 270, 7mm, 300 Wea. Mags., (26"); 243, 240 Wea. Mag., 25-06, 270 Win., 280 Rem., 7mm-08, 7mm Rem. Mag., 30-06, 338-06 A-Square, 308, 300 Win. Mag. (24"). Introduced 1998. Made in U.S.A. by Weatherby.
Price: .... **$1,459.00 to $1,517.00**
Price: Left-hand models **$1,559.00**

Weatherby Mark V SVR

Weatherby Mark V Fibermark

Weatherby Mark V Dangerous Game Rifle

Wilderness Explorer

Weatherby Mark V Special Varmint Rifle (SVR)

A new entrant in the Mark V series similar to the Super VarmintMaster and Accumark with 22", #3 contour chrome moly 4140 steel Krieger Criterion botton-rifled barrel with 1-degree target crown and hand-laminated composite stock. Available in .223 Rem. (5+1 magazine capacity) and .22-250 Rem. (4+1 magazine capacity) in right-hand models only.
Price: **$999.00**

Weatherby Mark V SVM/SPM Rifles

Similar to the Mark V Accumark except has 26" fluted (SVM) or 24" fluted Krieger barrel, spiderweb-pattern tan laminated synthetic stock. SVM has a fully adjustable trigger. Chambered for 223, 22-250, 220 Swift (SVM only), 243, 7mm-08 and 308. Made in U.S.A. by Weatherby.
Price: SVM (Super VarmintMaster), repeater or single-shot ... **$1,517.00**
New! **Price:** SPM (Super PredatorMaster) **$1,459.00**

Weatherby Mark V Fibermark Rifles

Similar to other Mark V models except has black Kevlar® and fiberglass composite stock and bead-blast blue or stainless finish. Chambered for 19 standard and magnum calibers. Introduced 1983; reintroduced 2001. Made in U.S.A. by Weatherby.
Price: Fibermark .... **$1,070.00 to $1,347.00**
Price: Fibermark Stainless .... **$1,165.00 to $1,390.00**

WEATHERBY MARK V DANGEROUS GAME RIFLE

Caliber: 375 H&H, 375 Wea. Mag., 378 Wea. Mag., 416 Rem. Mag., 416 Wea. Mag., 458 Win. Mag., .458 Lott, 460 Wea. Mag. 300 Win. Mag., 300 Wby., Mag., 338 Win. Mag., 340 Wby. Mag., 24" only **Barrel:** 24" or 26". **Weight:** 8-3/4 to 9-1/2 lbs. **Length:** 44-5/8" to 46-5/8" overall. **Stock:** Kevlar® and fiberglass composite. **Sights:** Barrel-band hooded front with large gold bead, adjustable ramp/shallow "V" rear. **Features:** Designed for dangerous-game hunting. Black oxide matte finish on all metalwork; Pachmayr Decelerator™ recoil pad, short-throw Mark V action. Introduced 2001. Made in U.S.A. by Weatherby.
Price: .... **$2,703.00 to $2,935.00**

WEATHERBY MARK V SUPER BIG GAMEMASTER DEER RIFLE

Caliber: 240 Wby. Mag., 25-06 Rem., 270 Win., 280 Rem., 30-06 Spfld., 257 Wby. Mag., 270 Wby. Mag., 7mm Rem., Mag., 7mm Wby. Mag., 338-06 A-Square, 300 Win. Mag., 300 Wby. Mag. **Barrel:** 26", target crown. **Weight:** 5-3/4 lbs., (6-3/4 lbs. Magnum). **Stock:** Raised comb Monte Carlo composite. **Features:** Fluted barrel, aluminum bedding block, Pachmayr decelerator, 54-degree bolt lift, adj. trigger.
Price: **$1,459.00**
Price: Magnum **$1,517.00**

WEATHERBY MARK V ROYAL CUSTOM RIFLE

Caliber: 257, 270, 7mm, 300, 340 all Wby. Mags. Other calibers available upon request. **Barrel:** 26". **Stock:** Monte Carlo hand-checkered claro walnut with high gloss finish. **Features:** Bolt and follower are damascened with checkered knob. Engraved receiver, bolt sleeve and floorplate sport scroll pattern. Animal images on floorplate optional. High gloss blue, 24-karat gold and nickel-plating. Made in U.S.A. From Weatherby.
Price: **$5,831.00**

WEATHERBY THREAT RESPONSE RIFLES (TRR) SERIES

Caliber: TRR 223 Rem., 300 Win. TRR Magnum and Magnum Custom 300 Win. Mag., 300 Wby. Mag., 30-378 Wby. Mag., 328-378 Wby. Mag. **Barrel:** 22", 26", target crown. **Stock:** Hand-laminated composite. TTR & TRR Magnum have raised comb Monte Carlo style. TRR Magnum Custom adjustable ergonomic stock. **Features:** Adjustable trigger, aluminum bedding block, beavertail forearms dual tapered, flat-bottomed. "Rocker Arm" lockdown scope mounting. 54 degree bolt. Pachmayr decelerator pad. Made in U.S.A.
Price: TRR Magnum Custom 300 .... **$2,699.00**
Price: 30-378, 338-378 with accubrake **$2,861.00**

WILDERNESS EXPLORER MULTI-CALIBER CARBINE

Caliber: 22 Hornet, 218 Bee, 44 Magnum, 50 A.E. (interchangeable). **Barrel:** 18", match grade. **Weight:** 5.5 lbs **Length:** 38-1/2" overall. **Stock:** Synthetic or wood. **Sights:** None furnished; comes with Weaver-style mount on barrel. **Features:** Quick-change barrel and bolt face for caliber switch. Removable box magazine; adjustable trigger with side safety; detachable swivel studs. Introduced 1997. Made in U.S.A. by Phillips & Rogers, Inc.
Price: **$995.00**

Winchester Model 70 Classic

Winchester Model 70 Classic Stainless

Winchester Model 70 Classic Compact

Winchester Model 70 Classic Featherweight

Winchester Model 70 Black Shadow

WINCHESTER MODEL 70 CLASSIC SPORTER LT

Caliber: 25-06, 270 Win., 30-06, 7mm STW, 7mm Rem. Mag., 300 Win. Mag., 338 Win. Mag., 3-shot magazine; 5-shot for 25-06, 270 Win., 30-06. **Barrel:** 24", 26" for magnums. **Weight:** 7-3/4 to 8 lbs. **Length:** 46-3/4" overall (26" bbl.). **Stock:** American walnut with cut checkering and satin finish. Classic style with straight comb. **Sights:** None furnished. Drilled and tapped for scope mounting. **Features:** Uses pre-64-type action with controlled round feeding. Three-position safety, stainless steel magazine follower; rubber butt pad; epoxy bedded receiver recoil lug. From U.S. Repeating Arms Co.

Price: 25-06, 270, 30-06 . . . . **$727.00**
Price: Other calibers **$756.00**
Price: Left-hand, 270 or 30-06 . . . . **$762.00**
Price: Left-hand, 7mm Rem. Mag or 300 Win. Mag. **$793.00**

Winchester Model 70 Classic Stainless Rifle

Same as Model 70 Classic Sporter except stainless steel barrel and pre-64-style action with controlled round feeding and matte gray finish, black composite stock impregnated with fiberglass and graphite, contoured rubber recoil pad. No sights (except 375 H&H). Available in 270 Win., 30-06, 7mm STW, 7mm Rem. Mag., 300 Win. Mag., 300 Ultra Mag., 338 Win. Mag., 375 H&H Mag. (24" barrel), 3- or 5-shot magazine. Weighs 7-1/2 lbs. Introduced 1994.

Price: 270, 30-06 . . . . **$800.00**
Price: 375 H&H Mag., with sights **$924.00**
Price: Other calibers **$829.00**

Winchester Model 70 Classic Featherweight

Same as Model 70 Classic except action bedded in standard-grade walnut stock. Available in 22-250, 243, 6.5x55, 308, 7mm-08, 270 Win., 30-06. Drilled and tapped for scope mounts. Weighs 7 lbs. Introduced 1992.
Price: **$726.00**

Winchester Model 70 Classic Compact

Similar to Classic Featherweight except scaled down for smaller shooters. 20" barrel, 12-1/2" length of pull. Pre-'64-type action. Available in 243, 308 or 7mm-08. Introduced 1998. Made in U.S.A. by U. S. Repeating Arms Co.
Price: **$740.00**

Winchester Model 70 Black Shadow

Similar to Model 94 Ranger except black composite stock, matte blue barrel and action. Push-feed bolt design; hinged floorplate. Available in 270, 30-06, 7mm Rem. Mag., 300 Win. Mag. Made in U.S.A. by U.S. Repeating Arms Co.
Price: 270, 30-06 . . . . **$523.00**
Price: 7mm Rem. Mag., 300 Win. Mag. **$553.00**

Winchester Model 70 Coyote

Winchester Model 70 Stealth

Winchester Model 70 Classic Super Grade

Winchester Model 70 Safari Express

Winchester Model 70 WSM

Winchester Model 70 Coyote

Similar to Model 70 Black Shadow except laminated wood stock, 24" medium-heavy stainless steel barrel Available in 223 Rem., 22-250 Rem., 243 Win., or 308 Win.

Price: **$705.00**

WINCHESTER MODEL 70 STEALTH RIFLE

Caliber: 223, 22-250, 308 Win. **Barrel:** 26". **Weight:** 10-3/4 lbs. **Length:** 46" overall. **Stock:** Kevlar/fiberglass/graphite Pillar Plus Accu-Block with full-length aluminum bedding block. **Sights:** None furnished. **Features:** Push-feed bolt design; matte finish. Introduced 1999. Made in U.S.A. by U.S. Repeating Arms Co.

Price: **$785.00**

WINCHESTER MODEL 70 CLASSIC SUPER GRADE

Caliber: 25-06, 270, 30-06, 5-shot magazine; 7mm Rem. Mag., 300 Win. Mag., 338 Win. Mag., 3-shot magazine. **Barrel:** 24", 26" for magnums. **Weight:** 7-3/4 lbs. to 8 lbs. **Length:** 44-1/2" overall (24" bbl.) **Stock:** Walnut with straight comb, sculptured cheekpiece, wrap-around cut checkering, tapered forend, solid rubber butt pad. **Sights:** None furnished; comes with scope bases and rings. **Features:** Controlled round feeding with stainless steel claw extractor, bolt guide rail, three-position safety; all steel bottom metal, hinged floorplate, stainless magazine follower. Introduced 1994. From U.S. Repeating Arms Co.

Price: 25-06, 270, 30-06 . . . . **$995.00**
Price: Other calibers **$1,024.00**

WINCHESTER MODEL 70 CLASSIC SAFARI EXPRESS

Caliber: 375 H&H Mag., 416 Rem. Mag., 458 Win. Mag., 3-shot magazine. **Barrel:** 24". **Weight:** 8-1/4 to 8-1/2 lbs. **Stock:** American walnut with Monte Carlo cheekpiece. Wrap-around checkering and finish. **Sights:** Hooded ramp front, open rear. **Features:** Controlled round feeding. Two steel cross bolts in stock for added strength. Front sling swivel stud mounted on barrel. Contoured rubber butt pad. From U.S. Repeating Arms Co.

Price: **$1,124.00**
Price: Left-hand, 375 H&H only **$1,163.00**

WINCHESTER MODEL 70 WSM RIFLES

Caliber: 300 WSM, 3-shot magazine. **Barrel:** 24". **Weight:** 7-1/4 to 7-3/4 lbs. **Length:** 44" overall. **Stock:** Checkered walnut, black synthetic or laminated wood. **Sights:** None. **Features:** Model 70 designed for the new 300 Winchester Short Magnum cartridge. Short-action receiver, three-position safety, knurled bolt handle. Introduced 2001. From U.S. Repeating Arms Co.

Price: Classic Featherweight WSM (checkered walnut stock
and forearm) **$769.00**
Price: Classic Stainless WSM (black syn. stock,
stainless steel bbl.) **$829.00**
Price: Classic Laminated WSM (laminated wood stock) **$793.00**

RIFLES

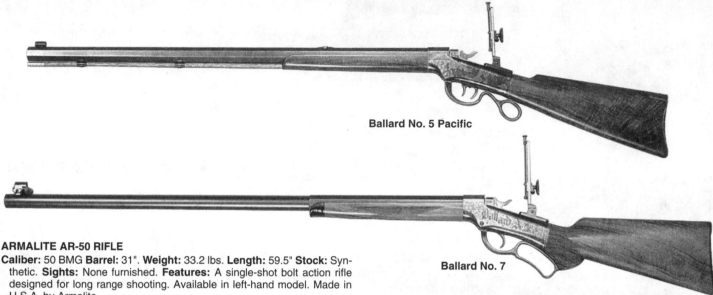

Ballard No. 5 Pacific

Ballard No. 7

ARMALITE AR-50 RIFLE
Caliber: 50 BMG **Barrel:** 31". **Weight:** 33.2 lbs. **Length:** 59.5" **Stock:** Synthetic. **Sights:** None furnished. **Features:** A single-shot bolt action rifle designed for long range shooting. Available in left-hand model. Made in U.S.A. by Armalite.
Price: **$2,745.00**

ARMSPORT 1866 SHARPS RIFLE, CARBINE
Caliber: 45-70. **Barrel:** 28", round or octagonal. **Weight:** 8.10 lbs. **Length:** 46" overall. **Stock:** Walnut. **Sights:** Blade front, folding adjustable rear. Tang sight set optionally available. **Features:** Replica of the 1866 Sharps. Color case-hardened frame, rest blued. Imported by Armsport.
Price: **$865.00**
Price: With octagonal barrel **$900.00**
Price: Carbine, 22" round barrel **$850.00**

BALLARD NO. 1 3/4 FAR WEST RIFLE
Caliber: 22 LR, 32-40, 38-55, 40-65, 40-70, 45-70, 45-110, 50-70, 50-90. **Barrel:** 30" std. or heavyweight. **Weight:** 10-1/2 lbs. (std.) or 11-3/4 lbs. (heavyweight bbl.) **Length:** NA. **Stock:** Walnut. **Sights:** Blade front, Rocky Mountain rear. **Features:** Single or double-set triggers, S-lever or ring-style lever; color case-hardened finish; hand polished and lapped Badger barrel. Made in U.S.A. by Ballard Rifle & Cartridge Co.
Price: **$2,250.00**

BALLARD NO. 4 PERFECTION RIFLE
Caliber: 22 LR, 32-40, 38-55, 40-65, 40-70, 45-70, 45-90, 45-110, 50-70, 50-90. **Barrel:** 30" or 32" octagon, standard or heavyweight. **Weight:** 10-1/2 lbs. (standard) or 11-3/4 lbs. (heavyweight bbl.). **Length:** NA. **Stock:** Smooth walnut. **Sights:** Blade front, Rocky Mountain rear. **Features:** Rifle or shotgun-style buttstock, straight grip action, single or double-set trigger, "S" or right lever, hand polished and lapped Badger barrel. Made in U.S.A. by Ballard Rifle & Cartridge Co.
Price: **$2,250.00**

BALLARD NO. 5 PACIFIC SINGLE-SHOT RIFLE
Caliber: 32-40, 38-55, 40-65, 40-90, 40-70 SS, 45-70 Govt., 45-110 SS, 50-70 Govt., 50-90 SS. **Barrel:** 30", or 32" octagonal. **Weight:** 10-1/2 lbs. **Length:** NA. **Stock:** High-grade walnut; rifle or shotgun style. **Sights:** Blade front, Rocky Mountain rear. **Features:** Standard or heavy barrel; double-set triggers; under-barrel wiping rod; ring lever. Introduced 1999. Made in U.S.A. by Ballard Rifle & Cartridge Co.
Price: **$2,575.00**

BALLARD NO. 7 LONG RANGE RIFLE
Caliber: 32-40, 38-55, 40-65, 40-70 SS, 45-70 Govt., 45-90, 45-110. **Barrel:** 32", 34" half-octagon. **Weight:** 11-3/4 lbs. **Length:** NA. **Stock:** Walnut; checkered pistol grip shotgun butt, ebony forend cap. **Sights:** Globe front. **Features:** Designed for shooting up to 1000 yards. Standard or heavy barrel; single or double-set trigger; hard rubber or steel buttplate. Introduced 1999. Made in U.S.A. by Ballard Rifle & Cartridge Co.
Price: From **$2,475.00**

BALLARD NO. 8 UNION HILL RIFLE
Caliber: 22 LR, 32-40, 38-55, 40-65 Win., 40-70 SS. **Barrel:** 30" half-octagon. **Weight:** About 10-1/2 lbs. **Length:** NA. **Stock:** Walnut; pistol grip butt with cheekpiece. **Sights:** Globe front. **Features:** Designed for 200-yard offhand shooting. Standard or heavy barrel; double-set triggers; full loop lever; hook Schuetzen buttplate. Introduced 1999. Made in U.S.A. by Ballard Rifle & Cartridge Co.
Price: From **$2,500.00**

BALLARD MODEL 1885 HIGH WALL SINGLE SHOT RIFLE
Caliber: 17 Bee, 22 Hornet, 218 Bee, 219 Don Wasp, 219 Zipper, 22 Hi-Power, 225 Win., 25-20 WCF, 25-35 WCF, 25 Krag, 7mmx57R, 30-30, 30-40 Krag, 303 British, 33 WCF, 348 WCF, 35 WCF, 35-30/30, 9.3x74R, 405 WCF, 50-110 WCF, 500 Express, 577 Express. **Barrel:** Lengths to 34". **Weight:** NA. **Length:** NA. **Stock:** Straight-grain American walnut. **Sights:** buckhorn or flat top rear, blade front. **Features:** Faithful copy of original Model 1885 High Wall; parts interchange with original rifles; variety of options available. Introduced 2000. Made in U.S.A. by Ballard Rifle & Cartridge LLC.
Price: From **$2,255.00**
Price: With single set trigger from **$2,355.00**

BARRETT MODEL 99 SINGLE SHOT RIFLE
Caliber: 50 BMG. **Barrel:** 33". **Weight:** 25 lbs. **Length:** 50.4" overall. **Stock:** Anodized aluminum with energy-absorbing recoil pad. **Sights:** None furnished; integral M1913 scope rail. **Features:** Bolt action; detachable bipod; match-grade barrel with high-efficiency muzzle brake. Introduced 1999. Made in U.S.A. by Barrett Firearms.
Price: From **$3,000.00**

BROWN MODEL 97D SINGLE SHOT RIFLE
Caliber: 17 Ackley Hornet through 45-70 Govt. **Barrel:** Up to 26", air gauged match grade. **Weight:** About 5 lbs., 11 oz. **Stock:** Sporter style with pistol grip, cheekpiece and Schnabel forend. **Sights:** None furnished; drilled and tapped for scope mounting. **Features:** Falling block action gives rigid barrel-receiver matting; polished blue/black finish. Hand-fitted action. Many options. Made in U.S.A. by E. Arthur Brown Co. Inc.
Price: From **$699.00**

BROWNING MODEL 1885 HIGH WALL SINGLE SHOT RIFLE
Caliber: 22-250, 30-06, 270, 7mm Rem. Mag., 454 Casull, 45-70. **Barrel:** 28". **Weight:** 8 lbs., 12 oz. **Length:** 43-1/2" overall. **Stock:** Walnut with straight grip, Schnabel forend. **Sights:** None furnished; drilled and tapped for scope mounting. **Features:** Replica of J.M. Browning's high-wall falling block rifle. Octagon barrel with recessed muzzle. Imported from Japan by Browning. Introduced 1985.
Price: **$1,027.00**

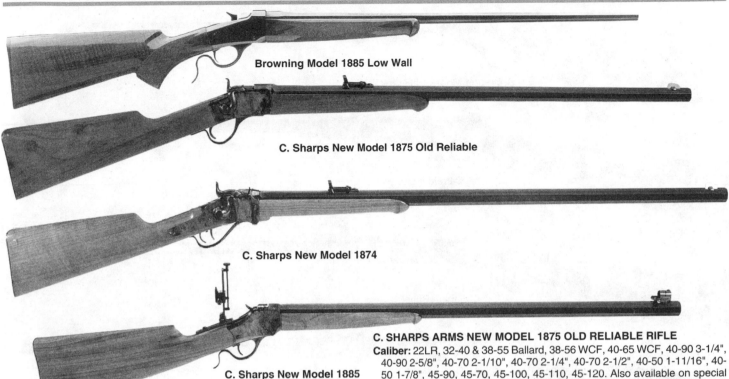

Browning Model 1885 Low Wall

C. Sharps New Model 1875 Old Reliable

C. Sharps New Model 1874

C. Sharps New Model 1885

Browning Model 1885 BPCR Rifle

Similar to the 1885 High Wall rifle except the ejector system and shell deflector have been removed; chambered only for 40-65 and 45-70; color case-hardened full-tang receiver, lever, buttplate and gripcap; matte blue 30" part octagon, part round barrel. The Vernier tang sight has indexed elevation, is screw adjustable windage, and has three peep diameters. The hooded front sight has a built-in spirit level and comes with sight interchangeable inserts. Adjustable trigger. Overall length 46-1/8", weighs about 11 lbs. Introduced 1996. Imported from Japan by Browning.

Price: **$1,766.00**

Browning Model 1885 Low Wall Traditional Hunter

Similar to the Model 1885 Low Wall except chambered for 357 Mag., 44 Mag. and 45 Colt; steel crescent buttplate; 1/16" gold bead front sight, adjustable buckhorn rear, and tang-mounted peep sight with barrel-type elevation adjuster and knob-type windage adjustments. Barrel is drilled and tapped for a Browning scope base. Oil-finished select walnut stock with swivel studs. Introduced 1997. Imported for Japan by Browning.

Price: **$1,289.00**

Browning Model 1885 Low Wall Rifle

Similar to the Model 1885 High Wall except has trimmer receiver, thinner 24" octagonal barrel. Forend is mounted to the receiver. Adjustable trigger. Walnut pistol grip stock, trim Schnabel forend with high-gloss finish. Available in 22 Hornet and 260 Rem. Overall length 39-1/2", weighs 6 lbs., 11 oz. Rifling twist rates: 1:16" (22 Hornet); 1:9" (260). Polished blue finish. Introduced 1995. Imported from Japan by Browning.

Price: **$997.00**

BRNO ZBK 110 SINGLE SHOT RIFLE

Caliber: 222 Rem., 5.6x52R, 22 Hornet, 5.6x50 Mag., 6.5x57R, 7x57R, 8x57JRS. **Barrel:** 23.6". **Weight:** 5.9 lbs. **Length:** 40.1" overall. **Stock:** European walnut. **Sights:** None furnished; drilled and tapped for scope mounting. **Features:** Top tang opening lever; cross-bolt safety; polished blue finish. Announced 1998. Imported from The Czech Republic by Euro-Imports.

Price: Standard calibers **$223.00**
Price: 7x57R, 8x57JRS **$245.00**
Price: Lux model, standard calibers **$311.00**
Price: Lux model, 7x57R, 8x57JRS **$333.00**

C. SHARPS ARMS NEW MODEL 1875 OLD RELIABLE RIFLE

Caliber: 22LR, 32-40 & 38-55 Ballard, 38-56 WCF, 40-65 WCF, 40-90 3-1/4", 40-90 2-5/8", 40-70 2-1/10", 40-70 2-1/4", 40-70 2-1/2", 40-50 1-11/16", 40-50 1-7/8", 45-90, 45-70, 45-100, 45-110, 45-120. Also available on special order only in 50-70, 50-90, 50-140. **Barrel:** 24", 26", 30" (standard), 32", 34" optional. **Weight:** 8-12 lbs. **Stock:** Walnut, straight grip, shotgun butt with checkered steel buttplate. **Sights:** Silver blade front, Rocky Mountain buckhorn rear. **Features:** Recreation of the 1875 Sharps rifle. Production guns will have case colored receiver. Available in Custom Sporting and Target versions upon request. Announced 1986. From C. Sharps Arms Co.

Price: 1875 Sporting Rifle (30" tapered oct. bbl.) **$1,185.00**

C. Sharps Arms 1875 Classic Sharps

Similar to New Model 1875 Sporting Rifle except 26", 28" or 30" full octagon barrel, crescent buttplate with toe plate, Hartford-style forend with cast German silver nose cap. Blade front sight, Rocky Mountain buckhorn rear. Weighs 10 lbs. Introduced 1987. From C. Sharps Arms Co.

Price: **$1,470.00**

C. Sharps Arms New Model 1875 Target & Long Range

Similar to New Model 1875 in all listed calibers except 22 LR; 34" tapered octagon barrel; globe with post front sight, Long Range Vernier tang sight with windage adjustments. Pistol grip stock with cheek rest; checkered steel buttplate. Introduced 1991. From C. Sharps Arms Co.

Price: **$1,549.50**

C. SHARPS ARMS NEW MODEL 1874 OLD RELIABLE

Caliber: 40-50, 40-70, 40-90, 45-70, 45-90, 45-100, 45-110, 45-120, 50-70, 50-90, 50-140. **Barrel:** 26", 28", 30" tapered octagon. **Weight:** About 10 lbs. **Length:** NA. **Stock:** American black walnut; shotgun butt with checkered steel buttplate; straight grip, heavy forend with Schnabel tip. **Sights:** Blade front, buckhorn rear. Drilled and tapped for tang sight. **Features:** Recreation of the Model 1874 Old Reliable Sharps Sporting Rifle. Double set triggers. Reintroduced 1991. Made in U.S.A. by C. Sharps Arms.

Price: **$1,584.00**

C. SHARPS ARMS NEW MODEL 1885 HIGHWALL RIFLE

Caliber: 22 LR, 22 Hornet, 219 Zipper, 25-35 WCF, 32-40 WCF, 38-55 WCF, 40-65, 30-40-Krag, 40-50 ST or BN, 40-70 ST or BN, 40-90 ST or BN, 45-70 2-1/10" ST, 45-90 2-4/10" ST, 45-100 2-6/10" ST, 45-110 2-7/8" ST, 45-120 3-1/4" ST. **Barrel:** 26", 28", 30", tapered full octagon. **Weight:** About 9 lbs., 4 oz. **Length:** 47" overall. **Stock:** Oil-finished American walnut; Schnabel-style forend. **Sights:** Blade front, buckhorn rear. Drilled and tapped for optional tang sight. **Features:** Single trigger; octagonal receiver top; checkered steel buttplate; color case-hardened receiver and buttplate, blued barrel. Many options available. Made in U.S.A. by C. Sharps Arms Co.

Price: From **$1,439.00**

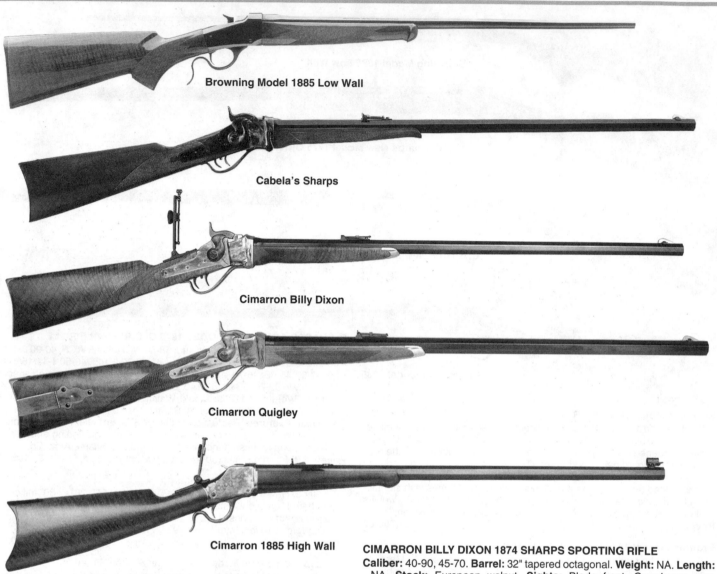

Browning Model 1885 Low Wall

Cabela's Sharps

Cimarron Billy Dixon

Cimarron Quigley

Cimarron 1885 High Wall

RIFLES

C. SHARPS ARMS CUSTOM NEW MODEL 1877 LONG RANGE TARGET RIFLE

Caliber: 44-90 Sharps/Rem., 45-70, 45-90, 45-100 Sharps. **Barrel:** 32", 34" tapered round with Rigby flat. **Weight:** Appx. 10 lbs. **Stock:** Walnut checkered. Pistol grip/forend. **Sights:** Classic long range with windage. **Features:** Elegant single shot, limited to custom production only.
Price: . . . . **$5,550.00 and up**

CABELA'S SHARPS BASIC RIFLE

Caliber: .45-70. **Barrel:** 28" tapered round. **Weight:** 8.7 lbs. **Length:** 44" overall. **Stock:** European walnut. **Sights:** Buckhorn rear, blade front. **Features:** Utilitarian look of the original with single trigger and 1-in-18 twist rate. Imported by Cabela's.
Price: **$799.99**

CABELA'S SHARPS SPORTING RIFLE

Caliber: 45-70, 45-120, .45-110, .50-70. **Barrel:** 32", tapered octagon. **Weight:** 9 lbs. **Length:** 47-1/4" overall. **Stock:** Checkered walnut. **Sights:** Blade front, open adjustable rear. **Features:** Color case-hardened receiver and hammer, rest blued. Introduced 1995. Imported by Cabela's.
Price: **$949.99**
Price: (Deluxe engraved Sharps, .45-70) **$1,599.99**
Price: (Heavy target Sharps, 45-70, 45-120, .50-70) **$1,099.99**
Price: (Quigley Sharps, 45-70, 45-120, 45-110) **$1,399.99**

CIMARRON BILLY DIXON 1874 SHARPS SPORTING RIFLE

Caliber: 40-90, 45-70. **Barrel:** 32" tapered octagonal. **Weight:** NA. **Length:** NA. **Stock:** European walnut. **Sights:** Blade front, Creedmoor rear. **Features:** Color case-hardened frame, blued barrel. Hand-checkered grip and forend; hand-rubbed oil finish. Introduced 1999. Imported by Cimarron F.A. Co.
Price: **$1,525.00**

CIMARRON QUIGLEY MODEL 1874 SHARPS SPORTING RIFLE

Caliber: 45-70, 45-90, 45-120. **Barrel:** 34" octagonal. **Weight:** NA. **Length:** NA. **Stock:** Checkered walnut. **Sights:** Blade front, adjustable rear. **Features:** Blued finish; double set triggers. From Cimarron F.A. Co.
Price: **$1,625.00**

CIMARRON SILHOUETTE MODEL 1874 SHARPS SPORTING RIFLE

Caliber: 45-70. **Barrel:** 32" octagonal. **Weight:** NA. **Length:** NA. **Stock:** Walnut. **Sights:** Blade front, adjustable rear. **Features:** Pistol-grip stock with shotgun-style butt plate; cut-rifled barrel. From Cimarron F.A. Co.
Price: **$1,299.00**

CIMARRON MODEL 1885 HIGH WALL RIFLE

Caliber: 38-55, 40-65, 45-70, 45-90, 45-120. **Barrel:** 30" octagonal. **Weight:** NA. **Length:** NA. **Stock:** European walnut. **Sights:** Bead front, semi-buckhorn rear. **Features:** Replica of the Winchester 1885 High Wall rifle. Color case-hardened receiver and lever, blued barrel. Curved buttplate. Optional double set triggers. Introduced 1999. Imported by Cimarron F.A. Co.
Price: **$995.00**
Price: With pistol grip **$1,175.00**

Cumberland Mountain Plateau

Dakota Single Shot

Dixie 1874 Sharps Silhouette

H&R Ultra Hunter

CUMBERLAND MOUNTAIN PLATEAU RIFLE

Caliber: 40-65, 45-70. **Barrel:** Up to 32"; round. **Weight:** About 10-1/2 lbs. (32" barrel). **Length:** 48" overall (32" barrel). **Stock:** American walnut. **Sights:** Marble's bead front, Marble's open rear. **Features:** Falling block action with underlever. Blued barrel and receiver. Stock has lacquer finish, crescent buttplate. Introduced 1995. Made in U.S.A. by Cumberland Mountain Arms, Inc.

Price: **$1,085.00**

DAKOTA MODEL 10 SINGLE SHOT RIFLE

Caliber: Most rimmed and rimless commercial calibers. **Barrel:** 23". **Weight:** 6 lbs. **Length:** 39-1/2" overall. **Stock:** Medium fancy grade walnut in classic style. Checkered grip and forend. **Sights:** None furnished. Drilled and tapped for scope mounting. **Features:** Falling block action with under-lever. Top tang safety. Removable trigger plate for conversion to single set trigger. Introduced 1990. Made in U.S.A. by Dakota Arms.

Price: **$3,595.00**
Price: Barreled action **$2,095.00**
Price: Action only **$1,850.00**
Price: Magnum calibers **$3,595.00**
Price: Magnum barreled action. **$2,050.00**
Price: Magnum action only **$1,675.00**

DIXIE 1874 SHARPS BLACKPOWDER SILHOUETTE RIFLE

Caliber: 45-70. **Barrel:** 30"; tapered octagon; blued; 1:18" twist. **Weight:** 10 lbs., 3 oz. **Length:** 47-1/2" overall. **Stock:** Oiled walnut. **Sights:** Blade front, ladder-type hunting rear. **Features:** Replica of the Sharps #1 Sporter. Shotgun-style butt with checkered metal buttplate; color case-hardened receiver, hammer, lever and buttplate. Tang is drilled and tapped for tang sight. Double-set triggers. Meets standards for NRA blackpowder cartridge matches. Introduced 1995. Imported from Italy by Dixie Gun Works.

Price: **$1,025.00**

Dixie 1874 Sharps Lightweight Hunter/Target Rifle

Same as the Dixie 1874 Sharps Blackpowder Silhouette model except has a straight-grip buttstock with military-style buttplate. Based on the 1874 military model. Introduced 1995. Imported from Italy by Dixie Gun Works.

Price: **$995.00**

E.M.F. 1874 METALLIC CARTRIDGE SHARPS RIFLE

Caliber: 45-70, 45/120. **Barrel:** 28", octagon. **Weight:** 10-3/4 lbs. **Length:** NA. **Stock:** Oiled walnut. **Sights:** Blade front, flip-up open rear. **Features:** Replica of the 1874 Sharps Sporting rifle. Color case-hardened lock; double-set trigger; blue finish. Imported by E.M.F.

Price: From **$700.00**
Price: With browned finish **$1,000.00**
Price: Military Carbine **$650.00**

HARRINGTON & RICHARDSON ULTRA VARMINT RIFLE

Caliber: 223, 243. **Barrel:** 24", heavy. **Weight:** About 7.5 lbs. **Stock:** Hand-checkered laminated birch with Monte Carlo comb. **Sights:** None furnished. Drilled and tapped for scope mounting. **Features:** Break-open action with side-lever release, positive ejection. Scope mount. Blued receiver and barrel. Swivel studs. Introduced 1993. From H&R 1871, Inc.

Price: **$332.00**

Harrington & Richardson Ultra Hunter Rifle

Similar to Ultra Varmint rifle except chambered for 25-06 with 26" barrel, or 308 Win., 450 Marlin with 22" barrel. Stock and forend are of cinnamon-colored laminate; hand-checkered grip and forend. Introduced 1995. Made in U.S.A. by H&R 1871, LLC.

Price: **$332.00**

Harrington & Richardson Ultra Comp Rifle

Similar to Ultra Varmint except chambered for 270 or 30-06; compensator to reduce recoil; camo-laminate stock and forend; blued, highly polished frame; scope mount. Made in U.S.A. by H&R 1871, LLC.

Price: **$376.00**

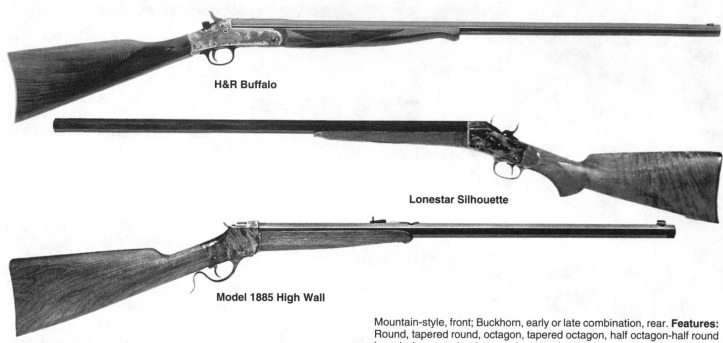

H&R Buffalo

Lonestar Silhouette

Model 1885 High Wall

HARRINGTON & RICHARDSON BUFFALO CLASSIC RIFLE

Caliber: 45-70. **Barrel:** 32" heavy. **Weight:** 8 lbs. **Length:** 52" overall. **Stock:** American black walnut. **Sights:** Williams receiver sight; Lyman target front sight with 8 aperture inserts. **Features:** Color case-hardened Handi-Rifle action with exposed hammer; color case-hardened crescent buttplate; 19th century checkering pattern. Introduced 1995. Made in U.S.A. by H&R 1871, LLC.
Price: About $418.00

Harrington & Richardson 38-55 Target Rifle

Similar to the Buffalo Classic rifle except chambered for 38-55 Win., has 28" barrel. The barrel, steel trigger guard and forend spacer, are highly polished and blued. Color case-hardened receiver and buttplate. Williams receiver sight; Lyman target front sight with 8 aperture inserts. Introduced 1998. Made in U.S.A. by H&R 1871, LLC.
Price: $418.00

HARRIS GUNWORKS ANTIETAM SHARPS RIFLE

Caliber: 40-65, 45-75. **Barrel:** 30", 32", octagon or round, hand-lapped stainless or chrome-moly. **Weight:** 11.25 lbs. **Length:** 47" overall. **Stock:** Choice of straight grip, pistol grip or Creedmoor with Schnabel forend; pewter tip optional. Standard wood is A Fancy; higher grades available. **Sights:** Montana Vintage Arms #111 Low Profile Spirit Level front, #108 mid-range tang rear with windage adjustments. **Features:** Recreation of the 1874 Sharps sidehammer. Action is color case-hardened, barrel satin black. Chrome-moly barrel optionally blued. Optional sights include #112 Spirit Level Globe front with windage, #107 Long Range rear with windage. Introduced 1994. Made in U.S.A. by Harris Gunworks.
Price: $2,400.00

KRIEGHOFF HUBERTUS SINGLE-SHOT RIFLE

Caliber: 222, 243, 270, 308, 30-06, 5.6x50R Mag., 5.6x52R, 6x62R Freres, 6.5x57R, 6.5x65R, 7x57R, 7x65R, 8x57JRS, 8x75RS, 7mm Rem. Mag., 300 Win. Mag. **Barrel:** 23-1/2". **Weight:** 6-1/2 lbs. **Length:** NA. **Stock:** High-grade walnut. **Sights:** Blade front, open rear. **Features:** Break-loading with manual cocking lever on top tang; take-down; extractor; Schnabel forearm; many options. Imported from Germany by Krieghoff International Inc.
Price: Hubertus single shot, from $5,850.00
Price: Hubertus, magnum calibers $6,850.00

LONE STAR NO. 5 REMINGTON PATTERN ROLLING BLOCK RIFLE

Caliber: 25-35, 30-30, 30-40 Krag. **Barrel:** 26" to 34". **Weight:** NA. **Length:** NA **Stock:** American walnut. **Sights:** Beech style, Marble bead, Rocky Mountain-style, front; Buckhorn, early or late combination, rear. **Features:** Round, tapered round, octagon, tapered octagon, half octagon-half round barrels; bone-pack color case-hardened actions; single, single set, or double set triggers. Made in U.S.A. by Lone Star Rifle Co., Inc.
Price: $1,595.00

Lone Star Cowboy Action Rifle

Similar to the Lone Star No. 5 rifle, but designed for Cowboy Action Shooting with 28-33" barrel, buckhorn rear sight.
Price: $1,595.00

Lone Star Standard Silhouette Rifle

Similar to the Lone Star No. 5 rifle but designed for silhouette shooting with 30-34" barrel.
Price: $1,595.00

MEACHAM HIGHWALL SILHOUETTE RIFLE

Caliber: 40-65 Match, 45-70 Match. **Barrel:** 30", 34" octagon. **Stock:** Black walnut with cheekpiece. **Weight:** 11.5 to 11.9 lbs. **Sights:** None. Tang drilled for Win. base, 3/8" dovetail notch, front. **Length of pull:** 13-5/8". **Features:** Parts interchangeable copy of '85 Winchester. Available with single trigger, single set trigger, or Schuetzen-style double set triggers. Color case-hardened action. Introduced 2002. From Meacham T&H, Inc.
Price: $2,999.00

MERKEL K-1 MODEL LIGHTWEIGHT STALKING RIFLE

Caliber: 243 Win., 270 Win., 7x57R, 308 Win., 30-06, 7mm Rem. Mag., 300 Win. Mag., 9.3x74R. **Barrel:** 23.6". **Weight:** 5.6 lbs. unscoped. **Stock:** Satin-finished walnut, fluted and checkered; sling-swivel studs. **Sights:** None (scope base furnished). **Features:** Franz Jager single-shot break-open action, cocking/uncocking slide-type safety, matte silver receiver, selectable trigger pull weights, integrated, quick detach 1" or 30mm optic mounts (optic not included). Imported from Germany by GSI.
Price: Standard, simple border engraving $3,795.00
Price: Premium, light arabesque scroll. $3,795.00
Price: Jagd, fine engraved hunting scenes $4,395.00

MODEL 1885 HIGH WALL RIFLE

Caliber: 30-40 Krag, 32-40, 38-55, 40-65 WCF, 45-70. **Barrel:** 26" (30-40), 28"-30" all others. Douglas Premium #3 tapered octagon. **Weight:** 9 lbs, 4 oz. **Length:** 47" overall. **Stock:** Premium American black walnut. **Sights:** Marble's standard ivory bead front, #66 long blade top rear with reversible notch and elevator. **Features:** Receiver with octagon top, thick-wall High Wall with coil spring action. Tang drilled, tapped for High Wall tang sight. Receiver, lever, hammer and breechblock color case-hardened. Available from Montana Armory, Inc.
Price: $1,350.00

CENTERFIRE RIFLES — SINGLE SHOT

Mossberg SSi-One Sporter

Mossberg SSi-One Varminter

Navy Arms 1874 Sharps Cavalry Carbine

Navy Arms 1874 Sharps Plains

Navy Arms 1874 Sharps Sporting

MOSSBERG SSi-ONE SINGLE SHOT RIFLE
Caliber: 223 Rem., 22-250 Rem., 243 Win., 270 Win., 308 Rem., 30-06. **Barrel:** 24". **Weight:** 8 lbs. **Length:** 40". **Stock:** Satin-finished walnut, fluted and checkered; sling-swivel studs. **Sights:** None (scope base furnished). **Features:** Frame accepts interchangeable barrels, including 12-gauge, fully rifled slug barrel and 12 ga., 3-1/2" chambered barrel with Ulti-Full Turkey choke tube. Lever-opening, break-action design; single-stage trigger; ambidextrous, top-tang safety; internal eject/extract selector. Introduced 2000. From Mossberg.
Price: SSi-One Sporter (standard barrel) or 12 ga.,
3-1/2" chamber **$459.00**
Price: SSi-One Varmint (bull barrel, 22-250 Rem. only;
weighs 10 lbs.) **$480.00**
Price: SSi-One 12-gauge Slug (fully rifled barrel, no sights,
scope base) **$480.00**

NAVY ARMS 1873 SHARPS "QUIGLEY"
Caliber: 45/70. **Barrel:** 34" heavy octagonal. **Stock:** Walnut. **Features:** Case-hardened receiver and military patchbox. Exact reproduction from "Quigley Down Under."
Price: **$1,390.00**

NAVY ARMS 1873 SHARPS NO. 2 CREEDMOOR RIFLE
Caliber: 45/70. **Barrel:** 30" tapered round. **Stock:** Walnut. **Sights:** Front globe, "soule" tang rear. **Features:** Nickel receiver and action. Lightweight sporting rifle.
Price: **$1,300.00**

NAVY ARMS 1874 SHARPS CAVALRY CARBINE
Caliber: 45-70. **Barrel:** 22". **Weight:** 7 lbs., 12 oz. **Length:** 39" overall. **Stock:** Walnut. **Sights:** Blade front, military ladder-type rear. **Features:** Replica of the 1874 Sharps miltary carbine. Color case-hardened receiver and furniture. Imported by Navy Arms.
Price: **$1,000.00**

NAVY ARMS 1874 SHARPS BUFFALO RIFLE
Caliber: 45-70, 45-90. **Barrel:** 28" heavy octagon. **Weight:** 10 lbs., 10 oz. **Length:** 46" overall. **Stock:** Walnut; checkered grip and forend. **Sights:** Blade front, ladder rear; tang sight optional. **Features:** Color case-hardened receiver, blued barrel; double-set triggers. Imported by Navy Arms.
Price: **$1,160.00**

Navy Arms Sharps Plains Rifle
Similar to Sharps Buffalo rifle except 45-70 only, 32" medium-weight barrel, weighs 9 lbs., 8 oz., and is 49" overall. Imported by Navy Arms.
Price: **$1,125.00**

Navy Arms Sharps Sporting Rifle
Same as the Navy Arms Sharps Plains Rifle except has pistol grip stock. Introduced 1997. Imported by Navy Arms.
Price: 45-70 only **$1,160.00**

NAVY ARMS 1885 HIGH WALL RIFLE
Caliber: 45-70; others available on special order. **Barrel:** 28" round, 30" octagonal. **Weight:** 9.5 lbs. **Length:** 45-1/2" overall (30" barrel). **Stock:** Walnut. **Sights:** Blade front, vernier tang-mounted peep rear. **Features:** Replica of Winchester's High Wall designed by Browning. Color case-hardened receiver, blued barrel. Introduced 1998. Imported by Navy Arms.
Price: 28", round barrel, target sights **$920.00**
Price: 30" octagonal barrel, target sights **$995.00**

RIFLES

CENTERFIRE RIFLES — SINGLE SHOT

Navy Arms 1873 Springfield

Navy Arms Rolling Block buffalo

Navy Arms #2 Creedmoor

Navy Arms John Bodine

Navy Arms No. 3 Long Range

NAVY ARMS 1873 SPRINGFIELD CAVALRY CARBINE
Caliber: 45-70. **Barrel:** 22". **Weight:** 7 lbs. **Length:** 40-1/2" overall. **Stock:** Walnut. **Sights:** Blade front, military ladder rear. **Features:** Blued lockplate and barrel; color case-hardened breechblock; saddle ring with bar. Replica of 7th Cavalry gun. Imported by Navy Arms.
Price: $930.00

NAVY ARMS ROLLING BLOCK RIFLE
Caliber: 45-70. **Barrel:** 26", 30". **Stock:** Walnut. **Sights:** Blade front, adjustable rear. **Features:** Reproduction of classic rolling block action. Available with full-octagon or half-octagon-half-round barrel. Color case-hardened action, steel fittings. From Navy Arms.

Price: Buffalo $825.00
Price: Special Sporting, 26" half round bbl. $730.00

NAVY ARMS "JOHN BODINE" ROLLING BLOCK RIFLE
Caliber: 45-70. **Barrel:** 30" heavy octagonal. **Stock:** Walnut. **Sights:** Globe front, "soule" tang rear. **Features:** Double set triggers.
Price: $1,385.00

NAVY ARMS SHARPS NO. 3 LONG RANGE RIFLE
Caliber: 45-70, 45-90. **Barrel:** 34" octagon. **Weight:** 10 lbs., 12 oz. **Length:** 51-1/2". **Stock:** Deluxe walnut. **Sights:** Globe target front and match grade rear tang. **Features:** Shotgun buttplate, German silver forend cap, color case hardenend receiver. Imported by Navy Arms.
Price: $1,885.00

New England
Firearms Handi-Rifle

New England Firearms Super Light

New England Firearms Survivor

Remington No. 1 Mid-Range

NEW ENGLAND FIREARMS HANDI-RIFLE

Caliber: 22 Hornet, 223, 243, 30-30, 270, 280 Rem., 308, 30-06, 357 Mag., 44 Mag., 45-70. **Barrel:** 22", 24"; 26" for 280 Rem. **Weight:** 7 lbs. **Stock:** Walnut-finished hardwood; black rubber recoil pad. **Sights:** Ramp front, folding rear (22 Hornet, 30-30, 45-70). Drilled and tapped for scope mount; 223, 243, 270, 280, 30-06 have no open sights, come with scope mounts. **Features:** Break-open action with side-lever release. The 223, 243, 270 and 30-06 have recoil pad and Monte Carlo stock for shooting with scope. Swivel studs on all models. Blue finish. Introduced 1989. From New England Firearms.

Price:	**$270.00**
Price: 280 Rem., 26" barrel	**$270.00**
Price: Synthetic Handi-Rifle (black polymer stock and forend, swivels, recoil pad)	**$281.00**
Price: Handi-Rifle Youth (223, 243)	**$270.00**
Price: Stainless Handi-Rifle (223 Rem., 243 Rem.)	**$337.00**

New England Firearms Super Light Rifle

Similar to Handi-Rifle except new barrel taper, shorter 20" barrel with recessed muzzle, special lightweight synthetic stock and forend. No sights furnished on 223 and 243 versions, but have factory-mounted scope base and offset hammer spur; Monte Carlo stock; 22 Hornet has ramp front, fully adjustable open rear. Overall length 36", weight is 5.5 lbs. Introduced 1997. Made in U.S.A. by New England Firearms.

Price: 22 Hornet, 223 Rem. or 243 Win. **$281.00**

NEW ENGLAND FIREARMS SURVIVOR RIFLE

Caliber: 223, 308 Win., single shot. **Barrel:** 22". **Weight:** 6 lbs. **Length:** 36" overall. **Stock:** Black polymer, thumbhole design. **Sights:** None furnished; scope mount provided. **Features:** Receiver drilled and tapped for scope mounting. Stock and forend have storage compartments for ammo, etc.; comes with integral swivels and black nylon sling. Introduced 1996. Made in U.S.A. by New England Firearms.

Price: Blue finish. **$284.00**

REMINGTON NO. 1 ROLLING BLOCK MID-RANGE SPORTER

Caliber: 45-70. **Barrel:** 30" round. **Weight:** 8-3/4 lbs. **Length:** 46-1/2" overall. **Stock:** American walnut with checkered pistol grip and forend. **Sights:** Beaded blade front, adjustable center-notch buckhorn rear. **Features:** Recreation of the original. Polished blue metal finish. Many options available. Introduced 1998. Made in U.S.A. by Remington.

Price: **$1,450.00**
Price: Silhouette model with single-set trigger, heavy barrel . . . **$1,560.00**

RIFLES

Ruger No. 1B

Ruger K1-B-BBZ

Ruger No. 1A Light Sporter

Ruger No. 1V Varminter

Ruger No. 1 RSI

ROSSI SINGLE SHOT CENTERFIRE RIFLE

Caliber: 308 Win., 270 Win., 30-06 Spfld., 223 Rem., 243 Win. **Barrel:** 23". **Weight:** 6-6.5 lbs. **Stock:** Monte carlo, exotic woods, walnut finish & swivels with white line space and recoil pad. **Sights:** None, scope rails and hammer extension included. **Features:** Break Open, positive ejection, internal transfer bar mechanism and manual external safety. Trigger block system included.
Price: $179.95

ROSSI CENTERFIRE/SHOTGUN "MATCHED PAIRS"

Caliber: 12 ga./223 Rem., full size, 20 ga./223 Rem. full & youth, 12 ga./342 Win. full, 20 ga./243 Win., full & youth, 12 ga./308 Win. full, 20 ga./308 Win. full & youth, 12 ga./30-06 Spfld. full, 20 ga./30-06 Spfld. full, 12 ga./270 Win. full, 20 ga./270 Win. full. **Barrel:** 28"/23" full, 22"/22" youth. **Weight:** 5-7 lbs. **Stock:** Straight, exotic woods, walnut finish and swivels wtih white line space and recoil pad. **Sights:** Bead front shotgun, fully adjustable rifle, drilled and tapped. **Features:** Break Open, positive ejection, internal transfer bar mechanism and manual external safety. Trigger block system included.
Price: 350.00

RUGER NO. 1B SINGLE SHOT

Caliber: 218 Bee, 22 Hornet, 220 Swift, 22-250, 223, 243, 6mm Rem., 25-06, 257 Roberts, 270, 280, 30-06, 7mm Rem. Mag., 300 Win. Mag., 308 Win., 338 Win. Mag., 270 Wea., 300 Wea. **Barrel:** 26" round tapered with quarter-rib; with Ruger 1" rings. **Weight:** 8 lbs. **Length:** 42-1/4" overall. **Stock:** Walnut, two-piece, checkered pistol grip and semi-beavertail

forend. **Sights:** None, 1" scope rings supplied for integral mounts. **Features:** Under-lever, hammerless falling block design has auto ejector, top tang safety.
Price: 1B. $875.00
Price: Barreled action $600.00
Price: K1-B-BBZ Stainless steel, laminated stock 25-06, 7MM mag, 7MM STW, 300 Win Mag., 243 Win., 30-06, 308 Win. $910.00

Ruger No. 1A Light Sporter

Similar to the No. 1B Standard Rifle except has lightweight 22" barrel, Alexander Henry-style forend, adjustable folding leaf rear sight on quarter-rib, dovetailed ramp front with gold bead. Calibers 243, 30-06, 270 and 7x57. Weighs about 7-1/4 lbs.
Price: No. 1A $875.00
Price: Barreled action $600.00

Ruger No. 1V Varminter

Similar to the No. 1B Standard Rifle except has 24" heavy barrel. Semi-beavertail forend, barrel ribbed for target scope block, with 1" Ruger scope rings. Calibers 22-250, 220 Swift, 223, 25-06, 6mm Rem. Weight about 9 lbs.
Price: No. 1V $875.00
Price: Barreled action $600.00
Price: K1-V-BBZ stainless steel, laminated stock 22-250 . . . . . . $910.00

Ruger No. 1 RSI International

Similar to the No. 1B Standard Rifle except has lightweight 20" barrel, full-length International-style forend with loop sling swivel, adjustable folding leaf rear sight on quarter-rib, ramp front with gold bead. Calibers 243, 30-06, 270 and 7x57. Weight is about 7-1/4 lbs.
Price: No. 1 RSI $890.00
Price: Barreled action $600.00

Ruger No. 1H Tropical

Ruger No. 1S Medium Sporter

Shiloh 1874 Long Range Express

Shiloh 1874 Quigley

Shiloh 1874 Saddle

Ruger No. 1H Tropical Rifle

Similar to the No. 1B Standard Rifle except has Alexander Henry forend, adjustable folding leaf rear sight on quarter-rib, ramp front with dovetail gold bead, 24" heavy barrel. Calibers 375 H&H, 416 Rem. Mag., 416 Rigby, and 458 Win. Mag. (weighs about 9 lbs.).

Price: No. 1H **$875.00**
Price: Barreled action **$600.00**
Price: K1-H-BBZ, S/S, 375 H&H, 416 Rigby **$910.00**

Ruger No. 1S Medium Sporter

Similar to the No. 1B Standard Rifle except has Alexander Henry-style forend, adjustable folding leaf rear sight on quarter-rib, ramp front sight base and dovetail-type gold bead front sight. Calibers 218 Bee, 7mm Rem. Mag., 338 Win. Mag., 300 Win. Mag. with 26" barrel, 45-70 with 22" barrel. Weighs about 7-1/2 lbs. In 45-70.

Price: No. 1S **$875.00**
Price: Barreled action **$600.00**
Price: K1-S-BBZ, S/S, 45-70 . . . . **$910.00**

SHILOH RIFLE CO. SHARPS 1874 LONG RANGE EXPRESS

Caliber: 40-50 BN, 40-70 BN, 40-90 BN, 45-70 ST, 45-90 ST, 45-110 ST, 50-70 ST, 50-90 ST, 38-55, 40-70 ST, 40-90 ST. **Barrel:** 34" tapered octagon. **Weight:** 10-1/2 lbs. **Length:** 51" overall. **Stock:** Oil-finished semi-fancy walnut with pistol grip, shotgun-style butt, traditional cheek rest,

Schnabel forend. **Sights:** Globe front, sporting tang rear. **Features:** Recreation of the Model 1874 Sharps rifle. Double set triggers. Made in U.S.A. by Shiloh Rifle Mfg. Co.

Price: **$1,796.00**
Price: Sporting Rifle No. 1 (similar to above except with 30" bbl., blade front, buckhorn rear sight). **$1,706.00**
Price: Sporting Rifle No. 3 (similar to No. 1 except straight-grip stock, standard wood) **$1,504.00**
Price: 1874 Hartford (Hartford collar, pewter tip) **$1,702.00**
Price: 1874 Sporter #1 (30" bbl, blade, buckhorn sights) **$1,706.00**
Price: 1874 Sporter #3 (walnut, shotgun or military stock) **$1,504.00**

SHILOH RIFLE CO. SHARPS 1874 QUIGLEY

Caliber: 45-70, 45-110. **Barrel:** 34" heavy octagon. **Stock:** Military-style with patch box, standard grade American walnut. **Sights:** Semi buckhorn, interchangeable front and midrange vernier tang wight with windage. **Features:** Gold inlay initials, pewter tip, hartford collar, case color or antique finish. Double set triggers.

Price: **$2,860.00**

SHILOH RIFLE CO. SHARPS 1874 SADDLE RIFLE

Caliber: 38-55, 40-50 BN, 40-65 Win., 40-70 BN, 40-70 ST, 40-90 BN, 40-90 ST, 44-77 BN, 44-90 BN, 45-70 ST, 45-90 ST, 45-100 ST, 45-110 ST, 45-120 ST, 50-70 ST, 50-90 ST. **Barrel:** 26" full or h alf octagon. **Stock:** Semi fancy American walnut. Shotgun style with cheekrest. **Sights:** Buckhorn and blade. **Features:** Double set trigger, numerous custom features can be added.

Price: **$1,504.00**

RIFLES

CENTERFIRE RIFLES — SINGLE SHOT

Shiloh 1874 Montana Roughrider

Shiloh 1874 Creedmoor

Thompson/Center Encore

Thompson/Center Encore "Katahdin"

Thompson/Center Encore

SHILOH RIFLE CO. SHARPS 1874 MONTANA ROUGHRIDER
Caliber: 38-55, 40-50 BN, 40-65 Win., 40-70 BN, 40-70 ST, 40-90 BN, 40-90 ST, 44-77 BN, 44-90 BN, 45-70 ST, 45-90 ST, 45-100 ST, 45-110 ST, 45-120 ST, 50-70 ST, 50-90 ST. **Barrel:** 30" full or half octagon. **Stock:** American walnut in shotgun or military style. **Sights:** Buckhorn and blade. **Features:** Double set triggers, numerous custom features can be added.
Price: **$1,504.00**

SHILOH RIFLE CO. SHARPS CREEDMOOR TARGET
Caliber: 38-55, 40-50 BN, 40-65 Win., 40-70 BN, 40-70 ST, 40-90 BN, 40-90 ST, 44-77 BN, 44-90 BN, 45-70 ST, 45-90 ST, 45-100 ST, 45-110 ST, 45-120 ST, 50-70 ST, 50-90 ST. **Barrel:** 32", half round-half octagon. **Stock:** Extra fancy American walnut. Shotgun style with pistol grip. **Sights:** Customer's choice. **Features:** Single trigger, AA finish on stock, polished barrel and screws, pewter tip.
Price: **$2,442.00**

THOMPSON/CENTER ENCORE RIFLE
Caliber: 22-250, 223, 243, 25-06, 270, 7mm-08, 308, 30-06, 7mm Rem. Mag., 300 Win. Mag. **Barrel:** 24", 26". **Weight:** 6 lbs., 12 oz. (24" barrel). **Length:** 38-1/2" (24" barrel). **Stock:** American walnut. Monte Carlo style; Schnabel forend or black composite. **Sights:** Ramp-style white bead front, fully adjustable leaf-type rear. **Features:** Interchangeable barrels; action opens by squeezing trigger guard; drilled and tapped for T/C scope mounts; polished blue finish. Introduced 1996. Made in U.S.A. by Thompson/Center Arms.
Price: . . . . **$599 to $632.00**
Price: Extra barrels **$270.00**

Thompson/Center Stainless Encore Rifle
Similar to blued Encore except stainless steel with blued sights, black composite stock and forend. Available in 22-250, 223, 7mm-08, 30-06, 308. Introduced 1999. Made in U.S.A. by Thompson/Center Arms.
Price: . . . . **$670.00 to $676.00**

THOMPSON/CENTER ENCORE "KATAHDIN" CARBINE
Caliber: 45-70 Gov't., 444 Marlin, 450 Marlin. **Barrel:** 18" with muzzle tamer. **Stock:** Composite.
Price: **$619.00**

Thompson/Center G2 Contender Rifle
Similar to the G2 Contender pistol, but in a compact rifle format. **Features:** Interchangeable 23" barrels, chambered for .17 HMR, .22LR, .223 Rem., 30/30 Win. and .45/70 Gov't; plus a .45 Cal. Muzzleloading barrel. All of the 16-1/4" and 21" barrels made for the old style Contender will fit. **Weight:** 5-1/2 lbs. Introduced 2003. Made in U.S.A. by Thompson/Center Arms.
Price: . . . . **$592.40 to $607.00**

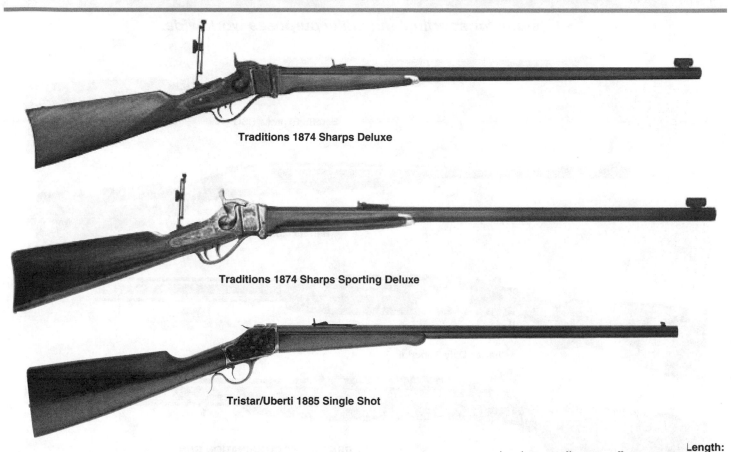

Traditions 1874 Sharps Deluxe

Traditions 1874 Sharps Sporting Deluxe

Tristar/Uberti 1885 Single Shot

TRADITIONS 1874 SHARPS DELUXE RIFLE

Caliber: 45-70. **Barrel:** 32" octagonal; 1:18" twist. **Weight:** 11.67 lbs. **Length:** 48.8" overall. **Stock:** Checkered walnut with German silver nose cap and steel butt plate. **Sights:** Globe front, adjustable creedmore rear with 12 inserts. **Features:** Color-case hardened receiver; double-set triggers. Introduced 2001. Imported from Pedersoli by Traditions.
Price: **$999.00**

Traditions 1874 Sharps Sporting Deluxe Rifle

Similar to Sharps Deluxe but custom silver engraved receiver, European walnut stock and forend, satin finish, set trigger, fully adjustable.
Price: **$1,999.00**

Traditions 1874 Sharps Standard Rifle

Similar to 1874 Sharps Deluxe Rifle, except has blade front and adjustable buckhorn-style rear sight. Weighs 10.67 pounds. Introduced 2001. Imported from Pedersoli by Traditions.
Price: **$769.00**

TRADITIONS ROLLING BLOCK SPORTING RIFLE

Caliber: 45-70. **Barrel:** 30" octagonal; 1:18" twist. **Weight:** 11.67 lbs. **Length:** 46.7" overall. **Stock:** Walnut. **Sights:** Blade front, adjustable rear. **Features:** Antique silver, color-case hardened receiver, drilled and tapped for tang/globe sights; brass butt plate and trigger guard. Introduced 2001. Imported from Pedersoli by Traditions.
Price: **$769.00**

TRADITIONS ROLLING BLOCK SPORTING RIFLE IN 30-30 WINCHESTER

Caliber: 45-70. **Barrel:** 28" round, blued. **Weight:** 8.25 lbs. **Stock:** Walnut. **Sights:** Fixed front, adjustable rear. **Features:** For hunting like in the Old West. Steel butt plate, trigger guard, barrel band. Classic reproduction.
Price: **$769.00**

Length: 44.5" overall. **Stock:** Walnut. **Sights:** Dovetail front, adjustable rear. **Features:** Cut checkering, case colored frame finish.
Price: **$795.00**

TRISTAR/UBERTI 1885 SINGLE SHOT

Caliber: 45-70. **Barrel:** 28". **Weight:** 8.75 lbs. **Length:** 44.5" overall. **Stock:** European walnut. **Sights:** Bead on blade front, open step-adjustable rear. **Features:** Recreation of the 1885 Winchester. Color case-hardened receiver and lever, blued barrel. Introduced 1998. Imported from Italy by Tristar Sporting Arms Ltd.
Price: **$765.00**

UBERTI BABY ROLLING BLOCK CARBINE

Caliber: 22 LR, 22 WMR, 22 Hornet, 357 Mag., single shot. **Barrel:** 22". **Weight:** 4.8 lbs. **Length:** 35-1/2" overall. **Stock:** Walnut stock and forend. **Sights:** Blade front, fully adjustable open rear. **Features:** Resembles Remington New Model No. 4 carbine. Brass trigger guard and buttplate; color case-hardened frame, blued barrel. Imported by Uberti USA Inc.
Price: **$490.00**
Price: Baby Rolling Block Rifle, 26" bbl. **$590.00**

DRILLINGS, COMBINATION GUNS, DOUBLE GUNS

Designs for sporting and utility purposes worldwide.

Beretta Express SSO

Beretta Model 455 SxS

Charles Daly Superior

Charles Daly Empire Combo

BERETTA EXPRESS SSO O/U DOUBLE RIFLES
Caliber: 375 H&H, 458 Win. Mag., 9.3x74R. **Barrel:** 25.5". **Weight:** 11 lbs. **Stock:** European walnut with hand-checkered grip and forend. **Sights:** Blade front on ramp, open V-notch rear. **Features:** Sidelock action with color case-hardened receiver (gold inlays on SSO6 Gold). Ejectors, double triggers, recoil pad. Introduced 1990. Imported from Italy by Beretta U.S.A.
Price: SSO6 . . . . **$21,000.00**
Price: SSO6 Gold **$23,500.00**

BERETTA MODEL 455 SxS EXPRESS RIFLE
Caliber: 375 H&H, 458 Win. Mag., 470 NE, 500 NE 3", 416 Rigby. **Barrel:** 23-1/2" or 25-1/2". **Weight:** 11 lbs. **Stock:** European walnut with hand-checkered grip and forend. **Sights:** Blade front, folding leaf V-notch rear. **Features:** Sidelock action with easily removable sideplates; color case-hardened finish (455), custom big game or floral motif engraving (455EELL). Double triggers, recoil pad. Introduced 1990. Imported from Italy by Beretta U.S.A.
Price: Model 455. . . . . **$36,000.00**
Price: Model 455EELL **$47,000.00**

BRNO 500 COMBINATION GUNS
Caliber/Gauge: 12 (2-3/4" chamber) over 5.6x52R, 5.6x50R, 222 Rem., 243, 6.x55, 308, 7x57R, 7x65R, 30-06. **Barrel:** 23.6". **Weight:** 7.6 lbs. **Length:** 40.5" overall. **Stock:** European walnut. **Sights:** Bead front, V-notch rear; grooved for scope mounting. **Features:** Boxlock action; double set trigger; blue finish with etched engraving. Announced 1998. Imported from The Czech Republic by Euro-Imports.
Price: **$1,023.00**
Price: O/U double rifle, 7x57R, 7x65R, 8x57JRS. **$1,125.00**

BRNO ZH 300 COMBINATION GUN
Caliber/Gauge: 22 Hornet, 5.6x50R Mag., 5.6x52R, 7x57R, 7x65R, 8x57JRS over 12, 16 (2-3/4" chamber). **Barrel:** 23.6". **Weight:** 7.9 lbs. **Length:** 40.5" overall. **Stock:** European walnut. **Sights:** Blade front, open adjustable rear. **Features:** Boxlock action; double triggers; automatic safety. Announced 1998. Imported from The Czech Republic by Euro-Imports.
Price: **$724.00**

BRNO ZH Double Rifles
Similar to ZH 300 combination guns except double rifle barrels. Available in 7x65R, 7x57R and 8x57JRS. Announced 1998. Imported from The Czech Republic by Euro-Imports.
Price: **$1,125.00**

CHARLES DALY SUPERIOR COMBINATION GUN
Caliber/Gauge: 12 ga. over 22 Hornet, 223 Rem., 22-250, 243 Win., 270 Win., 308 Win., 30-06. **Barrel:** 23.5", shotgun choked Imp. Cyl. **Weight:** About 7.5 lbs. **Stock:** Checkered walnut pistol grip and semi-beavertail forend. **Features:** Silvered, engraved receiver; chrome-moly steel barrels; double triggers; extractors; sling swivels; gold bead front sight. Introduced 1997. Imported from Italy by K.B.I. Inc.
Price: **$1,249.95**

Charles Daly Empire Combination Gun
Same as the Superior grade except has deluxe wood with European-style comb and cheekpiece; slim forend. Introduced 1997. Imported from Italy by K.B.I., Inc.
Price: **$1,789.95**

CZ 584 SOLO COMBINATION GUN
Caliber/Gauge: 7x57R; 12, 2-3/4" chamber. **Barrel:** 24.4". **Weight:** 7.37 lbs. **Length:** 45.25" overall. **Stock:** Circassian walnut. **Sights:** Blade front, open rear adjustable for windage. **Features:** Kersten-style double lump locking system; double-trigger Blitz-type mechanism with drop safety and adjustable set trigger for the rifle barrel; auto safety, dual extractors; receiver dovetailed for scope mounting. Imported from the Czech Republic by CZ-USA.
Price: **$851.00**

RIFLES

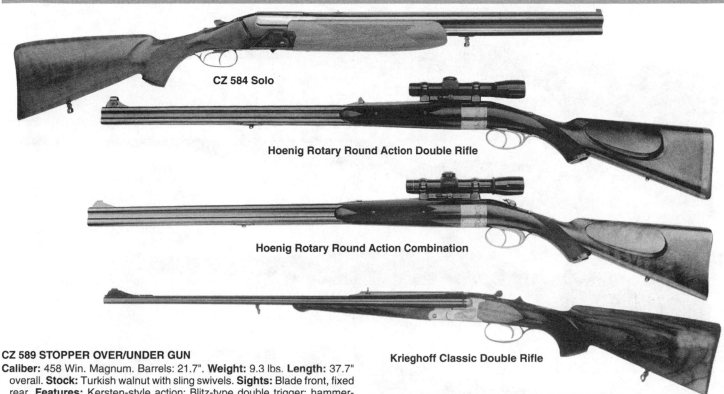

CZ 584 Solo

Hoenig Rotary Round Action Double Rifle

Hoenig Rotary Round Action Combination

Krieghoff Classic Double Rifle

CZ 589 STOPPER OVER/UNDER GUN

Caliber: 458 Win. Magnum. **Barrels:** 21.7". **Weight:** 9.3 lbs. **Length:** 37.7" overall. **Stock:** Turkish walnut with sling swivels. **Sights:** Blade front, fixed rear. **Features:** Kersten-style action; Blitz-type double trigger; hammer-forged, blued barrels; satin-nickel, engraved receiver. Introduced 2001. Imported from the Czech Republic by CZ USA.
Price: **$2,999.00**
Price: Fully engraved model **$3,999.00**

DAKOTA DOUBLE RIFLE

Caliber: 470 Nitro Express, 500 Nitro Express. **Barrel:** 25". **Stock:** Exhibition-grade walnut. **Sights:** Express. **Features:** Round action; selective ejectors; recoil pad; Americase. From Dakota Arms Inc.
Price: **$25,000.00**

EAA/BAIKAL IZH-94 COMBINATION GUN

Caliber/Gauge: 12, 3" chamber; 222 Rem., 223, 5.6x50R, 5.6x55E, 7x57R, 7x65R, 7.62x39, 7.62x51, 308, 7.62x53R, 7.62x54R, 30-06. **Barrel:** 24", 26"; imp., mod. and full choke tubes. **Weight:** 7.28 lbs. **Stock:** Walnut; rubber butt pad. **Sights:** Express style. **Features:** Hammer-forged barrels with chrome-lined bores; machined receiver; single-selective or double triggers. Imported by European American Armory.
Price: Blued finish. **$549.00**
Price: 20 ga./22 LR, 20/22 Mag, 3" **$629.00**

GARBI EXPRESS DOUBLE RIFLE

Caliber: 7x65R, 9.3x74R, 375 H&H. **Barrel:** 24-3/4". **Weight:** 7-3/4 to 8-1/2 lbs. **Length:** 41-1/2" overall. **Stock:** Turkish walnut. **Sights:** Quarter-rib with express sight. **Features:** Side-by-side double; H&H-pattern sidelock ejector with reinforced action, chopper lump barrels of Boehler steel; double triggers; fine scroll and rosette engraving, or full coverage ornamental; coin-finished action. Introduced 1997. Imported from Spain by Wm. Larkin Moore.
Price: **$19,900.00**

HOENIG ROTARY ROUND ACTION DOUBLE RIFLE

Caliber: Most popular calibers from 225 Win. to 9.3x74R. **Barrel:** 22"-26". **Stock:** English Walnut; to customer specs. **Sights:** Swivel hood front with button release (extra bead stored in trap door gripcap), express-style rear on quarter-rib adjustable for windage and elevation; scope mount. **Features:** Round action opens by rotating barrels, pulling forward. Inertia extractor system, rotary safety blocks strikers. single lever quick-detachable scope mount. Simple takedown without removing forend. Introduced 1997. Made in U.S.A. by George Hoenig.
Price: **$24,975.00**

HOENIG ROTARY ROUND ACTION COMBINATION

Caliber: 28 ga. **Barrel:** 26". **Weight:** 7 lbs. **Stock:** English Walnut to customer specs. **Sights:** Front ramp with button release blades. Foldable aperture tang sight windage and elevation adjustable. Quarter rib with scope mount. **Features:** Round action opens by rotating barrels, pulling forward. Inertia extractor; rotary safety blocks strikers. Simple takedown without removing forend. Made in U.S.A. by George Hoenig.
Price: **$24,975.00**

KRIEGHOFF CLASSIC DOUBLE RIFLE

Caliber: 7x65R, 308 Win., 30-06, 8x57 JRS, 8x75RS, 9.3x74R. **Barrel:** 23.5". **Weight:** 7.3 to 8 lbs. **Stock:** High grade European walnut. Standard has conventional rounded cheekpiece, Bavaria has Bavarian-style cheekpiece. **Sights:** Bead front with removable, adjustable wedge (375 H&H and below), standing leaf rear on quarter-rib. **Features:** Boxlock action; double triggers; short opening angle for fast loading; quiet extractors; sliding, self-adjusting wedge for secure bolting; Purdey-style barrel extension; horizontal firing pin placement. Many options available. Introduced 1997. Imported from Germany by Krieghoff International.
Price: With small Arabesque engraving **$7,850.00**
Price: With engraved sideplates **$9,800.00**
Price: For extra barrels **$4,500.00**
Price: Extra 20-ga., 28" shotshell barrels **$3,200.00**

Krieghoff Classic Big Five Double Rifle

Similar to the standard Classic excpet available in 375 Flanged Mag. N.E., 500/416 N.E., 470 N.E., 500 N.E. 3". Has hinged front trigger, non-removable muzzle wedge (larger than 375-caliber), Universal Trigger System, Combi Cocking Device, steel trigger guard, specially weighted stock bolt for weight and balance. Many options available. Introduced 1997. Imported from Germany by Krieghoff International.
Price: **$9,450.00**
Price: With engraved sideplates. **$11,400.00**

LEBEAU - COURALLY EXPRESS RIFLE SxS

Caliber: 7x65R, 8x57JRS, 9.3x74R, 375 H&H, 470 N.E. **Barrel:** 24" to 26". **Weight:** 7-3/4 to 10-1/2 lbs. **Stock:** Fancy French walnut with cheekpiece. **Sights:** Bead on ramp front, standing left express rear on quarter-rib. **Features:** Holland & Holland-type sidelock with automatic ejectors; double triggers. Built to order only. Imported from Belgium by Wm. Larkin Moore.
Price: **$41,000.00**

Merkel 96K Engraved

Merkel 140-1

Rizzini Express

Savage 24F Combination

Springfield M6 Scout

MERKEL DRILLINGS

Caliber/Gauge: 12, 20, 3" chambers, 16, 2-3/4" chambers; 22 Hornet, 5.6x50R Mag., 5.6x52R, 222 Rem., 243 Win., 6.5x55, 6.5x57R, 7x57R, 7x65R, 308, 30-06, 8x57JRS, 9.3x74R, 375 H&H. **Barrel:** 25.6". **Weight:** 7.9 to 8.4 lbs. depending upon caliber. **Stock:** Oil-finished walnut with pistol grip; cheekpiece on 12-, 16-gauge. **Sights:** Blade front, fixed rear. **Features:** Double barrel locking lug with Greener cross-bolt; scroll-engraved, case-hardened receiver; automatic trigger safety; Blitz action; double triggers. Imported from Germany by GSI.
Price: Model 96K (manually cocked rifle system), from **$7,495.00**
Price: Model 96K Engraved (hunting series on receiver) **$8,595.00**

Merkel Boxlock Double Rifles

Similar to the Model 160 double rifle except with Anson & Deely boxlock action with cocking indicators, double triggers, engraved color case-hardened receiver. Introduced 1995. Imported from Germany by GSI.
Price: Model 140-1, from **$6,695.00**
Price: Model 140-1.1 (engraved silver-gray receiver), from **$7,795.00**

RIZZINI EXPRESS 90L DOUBLE RIFLE

Caliber: 30-06, 7x65R, 9.3x74R. **Barrel:** 24". **Weight:** 7-1/2 lbs. **Length:** 40" overall. **Stock:** Select European walnut with satin oil finish; English-style cheekpiece. **Sights:** Ramp front, quarter-rib with express sight. **Features:** Color case-hardened boxlock action; automatic ejectors; single selective trigger; polished blue barrels. Extra 20-gauge shotshell barrels available. Imported for Italy by Wm. Larkin Moore.
Price: With case **$3,850.00**

SAVAGE 24F PREDATOR O/U COMBINATION GUN

Caliber/Gauge: 22 Hornet, 223, 30-30 over 12 (24F-12) or 22 LR, 22 Hornet, 223, 30-30 over 20-ga. (24F-20); 3" chambers. Action: Takedown, low rebounding visible hammer. Single trigger, barrel selector spur on hammer. **Barrel:** 24" separated barrels; 12-ga. has mod. choke tubes, 20-ga. has fixed Mod. choke. **Weight:** 8 lbs. **Length:** 40-1/2" overall. **Stock:** Black Rynite composition. **Sights:** Blade front, rear open adjustable for elevation. **Features:** Introduced 1989.
Price: 24F-12 . . . . **$586.00**
Price: 24F-20 . . . . **$556.00**

SPRINGFIELD, INC. M6 SCOUT RIFLE/SHOTGUN

Caliber/Gauge: 22 LR or 22 Hornet over 410-bore. **Barrel:** 18.25". **Weight:** 4 lbs. **Length:** 32" overall. **Stock:** Folding detachable with storage for 15 22 LR, four 410 shells. **Sights:** Blade front, military aperture for 22; V-notch for 410. **Features:** All-metal construction. Designed for quick disassembly and minimum maintenance. Folds for compact storage. Introduced 1982; reintroduced 1996. Imported from the Czech Republic by Springfield, Inc.
Price: Parkerized **$185.00**
Price: Stainless steel **$219.00**

RIMFIRE RIFLES — AUTOLOADERS

Designs for hunting, utility and sporting purposes, including training for competition

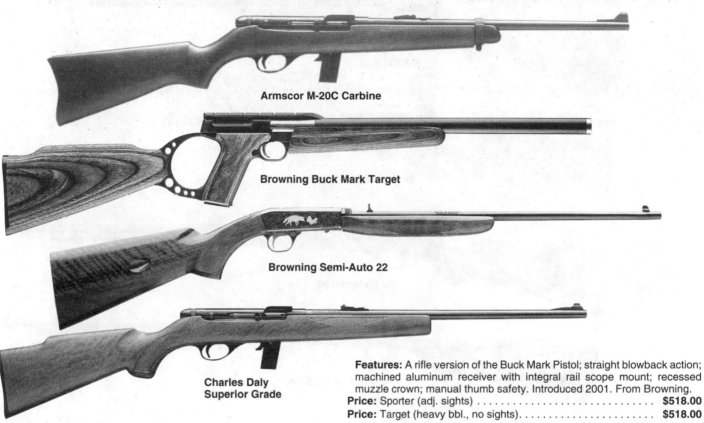

Armscor M-20C Carbine

Browning Buck Mark Target

Browning Semi-Auto 22

Charles Daly Superior Grade

AR-7 EXPLORER CARBINE

Caliber: 22 LR, 8-shot magazine. **Barrel:** 16". **Weight:** 2-1/2 lbs. **Length:** 34-1/2" / 16-1/2" stowed. **Stock:** Moulded Cycolac; snap-on rubber butt pad. **Sights:** Square blade front, aperture rear. **Features:** Takedown design stores barrel and action in hollow stock. Light enough to float. Reintroduced 1999. From AR-7 Industries, LLC.
Price: Black matte finish **$150.00**
Price: AR-20 Sporter (tubular stock, barrel shroud) **$200.00**
New! **Price:** AR-7 camo- or walnut-finish stock **$164.95**

ARMSCOR MODEL AK22 AUTO RIFLE

Caliber: 22 LR, 10-shot magazine. **Barrel:** 18.5". **Weight:** 7.5 lbs. **Length:** 38" overall. **Stock:** Plain mahogany. **Sights:** Adjustable post front, leaf rear adjustable for elevation. **Features:** Resembles the AK-47. Matte black finish. Introduced 1987. Imported from the Philippines by K.B.I., Inc.
Price: About **$219.95**

ARMSCOR M-1600 AUTO RIFLE

Caliber: 22 LR, 10-shot magazine. **Barrel:** 18.25". **Weight:** 6.2 lbs. **Length:** 38.5" overall. **Stock:** Black finished mahogany. **Sights:** Post front, aperture rear. **Features:** Resembles Colt AR-15. Matte black finish. Introduced 1987. Imported from the Philippines by K.B.I., Inc.
Price: About **$199.95**

ARMSCOR M-20C AUTO CARBINE

Caliber: 22 LR, 10-shot magazine. **Barrel:** 18.25". **Weight:** 6.5 lbs. **Length:** 38" overall. **Stock:** Walnut-finished mahogany. **Sights:** Hooded front, rear adjustable for elevation. **Features:** Receiver grooved for scope mounting. Blued finish. Introduced 1990. Imported from the Philippines by K.B.I., Inc.
Price: **$154.95**

BROWNING BUCK MARK SEMI-AUTO RIFLES

Caliber: 22 LR, 10-shot magazine. **Barrel:** 18" tapered (Sporter), heavy bull (Target), or carbon composite barrel (Classic Carbon). **Weight:** 4 lbs., 2 oz. (Sporter) or 5 lbs., 4 oz. (Target). **Length:** 34" overall. **Stock:** Walnut stock and forearm with full pistol grip. **Sights:** Hi-Viz adjustable (Sporter).

Features: A rifle version of the Buck Mark Pistol; straight blowback action; machined aluminum receiver with integral rail scope mount; recessed muzzle crown; manual thumb safety. Introduced 2001. From Browning.
Price: Sporter (adj. sights) **$518.00**
Price: Target (heavy bbl., no sights). **$518.00**

BROWNING SEMI-AUTO 22 RIFLE

Caliber: 22 LR, 11-shot. **Barrel:** 19-1/4". **Weight:** 5 lbs., 3 oz. **Length:** 37" overall. **Stock:** Checkered select walnut with pistol grip and semi-beavertail forend. **Sights:** Gold bead front, folding leaf rear. **Features:** Engraved receiver with polished blue finish; cross-bolt safety; tubular magazine in buttstock; easy takedown for carrying or storage. Imported from Japan by Browning.
Price: Grade I **$479.00**

Browning Semi-Auto 22, Grade VI

Same as the Grade I Auto-22 except available with either grayed or blued receiver with extensive engraving with gold-plated animals: right side pictures a fox and squirrel in a woodland scene; left side shows a beagle chasing a rabbit. On top is a portrait of the beagle. Stock and forend are of high-grade walnut with a double-bordered cut checkering design. Introduced 1987.
Price: Grade VI, blue or gray receiver **$1,028.00**

BRNO ZKM 611 AUTO RIFLE

Caliber: 22 WMR, 6- or 10-shot magazine. **Barrel:** 20.4". **Weight:** 5.9 lbs. **Length:** 38.9" overall. **Stock:** European walnut. **Sights:** Hooded blade front, open adjustable rear. **Features:** Removable box magazine; polished blue finish; cross-bolt safety; grooved receiver for scope mounting; easy takedown for storage. Imported from The Czech Republic by Euro-Imports.
Price: **$475.00**

CHARLES DALY FIELD GRADE AUTO RIFLE

Caliber: 22 LR, 10-shot magazine. **Barrel:** 20-3/4". **Weight:** 6.5 lbs. **Length:** 40-1/2" overall. **Stock:** Walnut-finished hardwood with Monte Carlo. **Sights:** Hooded front, adjustable open rear. **Features:** Receiver grooved for scope mounting; blue finish; shell deflector. Introduced 1998. Imported by K.B.I.
Price: **$124.00**
Price: Superior Grade (cut checkered stock, fully adjustable sight). **$199.00**

RIFLES

CZ 511 Auto

Henry U.S. Survival

Marlin Model 60

Marlin Model 60SSK

Marlin Model 70PSS

Charles Daly Empire Grade Auto Rifle

Similar to the Field Grade except has select California walnut stock with 24 l.p.i. hand checkering, contrasting forend and gripcaps, damascened bolt, high-polish blue. Introduced 1998. Imported by K.B.I.
Price: **$369.00**

CZ 511 AUTO RIFLE

Caliber: 22 LR, 8-shot magazine. **Barrel:** 22.2". **Weight:** 5.39 lbs. **Length:** 38.6" overall. **Stock:** Walnut with checkered pistol grip. **Sights:** Hooded front, adjustable rear. **Features:** Polished blue finish; detachable magazine; sling swivel studs. Imported from the Czech Republic by CZ-USA.
Price: **$351.00**

HENRY U.S. SURVIVAL RIFLE .22

Caliber: 22 LR, 8-shot magazine. **Barrel:** 16" steel lined. **Weight:** 2.5 lbs. **Stock:** ABS plastic. **Sights:** Blade front on ramp, aperture rear. **Features:** Takedown design stores barrel and action in hollow stock. Light enough to float. Silver, black or camo finish. Comes with two magazines. Introduced 1998. From Henry Repeating Arms Co.
Price: **$165.00**

MAGTECH MT 7022 AUTO RIFLE

Caliber: 22 LR, 10-shot magazine. **Barrel:** 18". **Weight:** 4.8 lbs. **Length:** 37" overall. **Stock:** Brazilian hardwood. **Sights:** Hooded blade front, fully adjustable open rear. **Features:** Cross-bolt safety; last-shot bolt hold-open; alloy receiver is drilled and tapped for scope mounting. Introduced 1998. Imported from Brazil by Magtech Ammunition Co.
Price: **$100.00**

MARLIN MODEL 60 AUTO RIFLE

Caliber: 22 LR, 14-shot tubular magazine. **Barrel:** 19" round tapered. **Weight:** About 5-1/2 lbs. **Length:** 37-1/2" overall. **Stock:** Press-checkered, walnut-finished Maine birch with Monte Carlo, full pistol grip; Mar-Shield® finish. **Sights:** Ramp front, open adjustable rear. **Features:** Matted receiver is grooved for scope mount. Manual bolt hold-open; automatic last-shot bolt hold-open. Model 60C is similar except has hardwood Monte Carlo stock with Mossy Oak Break-Up camouflage pattern. From Marlin.
Price: **$185.00**
Price: With 4x scope. **$193.00**
Price: (Model 60C) $220.00

Marlin Model 60SS Self-Loading Rifle

Same as the Model 60 except breech bolt, barrel and outer magazine tube are made of stainless steel; most other parts are either nickel-plated or coated to match the stainless finish. Monte Carlo stock is of black/gray Maine birch laminate, and has nickel-plated swivel studs, rubber butt pad. Introduced 1993. From Marlin.
Price: **$297.00**
Price: Model 60SSK (black fiberglass-filled stock) **$257.00**
Price: Model 60SB (walnut-finished birch stock) **$235.00**
Price: Model 60SB with 4x scope. **$251.00**

MARLIN 70PSS PAPOOSE STAINLESS RIFLE

Caliber: 22 LR, 7-shot magazine. **Barrel:** 16-1/4" stainless steel, Micro-Groove® rifling. **Weight:** 3-1/4 lbs. **Length:** 35-1/4" overall. **Stock:** Black fiberglass-filled synthetic with abbreviated forend, nickel-plated swivel studs, moulded-in checkering. **Sights:** Ramp front with orange post, cut-away Wide Scan® hood; adjustable open rear. Receiver grooved for scope mounting. **Features:** Takedown barrel; cross-bolt safety; manual bolt hold-open; last shot bolt hold-open; comes with padded carrying case. Introduced 1986. Made in U.S.A. by Marlin.
Price: **$304.00**

RIFLES

RIMFIRE RIFLES — AUTOLOADERS

Marlin 7000

Marlin 795

Marlin 552 BDL Speedmaster

Remington 597

Ruger 10/22 International

MARLIN MODEL 7000 AUTO RIFLE

Caliber: 22 LR, 10-shot magazine **Barrel:** 18" heavy target with 12-groove Micro-Groove® rifling, recessed muzzle. **Weight:** 5-1/2 lbs. **Length:** 37" overall. **Stock:** Black fiberglass-filled synthetic with Monte Carlo combo, swivel studs, moulded-in checkering. **Sights:** None furnished; comes with ring mounts. **Features:** Automatic last-shot bolt hold-open, manual bolt hold-open; cross-bolt safety; steel charging handle; blue finish, nickel-plated magazine. Introduced 1997. Made in U.S.A. by Marlin Firearms Co.
Price: **$249.00**

Marlin Model 795 Auto Rifle

Similar to Model 7000 except standard-weight 18" barrel with 16-groove Micro-Groove rifling. Ramp front sight with brass bead, screw adjustable open rear. Receiver grooved for scope mount. Introduced 1997. Made in U.S.A. by Marlin Firearms Co.
Price: **$176.00**

Marlin Model 795SS Auto Rifle

Similar to Model 795 excapt stainless steel barrel. Most other parts nickel-plated. Adjustable folding semi-buckhorn rear sights, ramp front high-visibility post and removeable cutaway wide scan hood.
Price: **$235.00**

REMINGTON MODEL 552 BDL DELUXE SPEEDMASTER RIFLE

Caliber: 22 S (20), L (17) or LR (15) tubular mag. **Barrel:** 21" round tapered. **Weight:** 5-3/4 lbs. **Length:** 40" overall. **Stock:** Walnut. Checkered grip and forend. **Sights:** Big game. **Features:** Positive cross-bolt safety, receiver grooved for tip-off mount.
Price: **$393.00**

REMINGTON 597 AUTO RIFLE

Caliber: 22 LR, 10-shot clip. **Barrel:** 20". **Weight:** 5-1/2 lbs. **Length:** 40" overall. **Stock:** Black synthetic. **Sights:** Big game. **Features:** Matte black finish, nickel-plated bolt. Receiver is grooved and drilled and tapped for scope mounts. Introduced 1997. Made in U.S.A. by Remington.
Price: **$169.00**
Price: Model 597 Magnum, 22 WMR, 8-shot clip **$335.00**
Price: Model 597 LSS (laminated stock, stainless) **$279.00**
Price: Model 597 SS
(22 LR, stainless steel, black synthetic stock) **$224.00**
Price: Model 597 LS Heavy Barrel (22 LR, laminated stock) **$265.00**
Price: Model 597 Magnum LS Heavy Barrel
(22 WMR, lam. stock) **$399.00**
Price: Model 597 Magnum 17 HMR, 8-shot clip **$361.00**

RUGER 10/22 AUTOLOADING CARBINE

Caliber: 22 LR, 10-shot rotary magazine. **Barrel:** 18-1/2" round tapered. **Weight:** 5 lbs. **Length:** 37-1/4" overall. **Stock:** American hardwood with pistol grip and barrel band or synthetic. **Sights:** Brass bead front, folding leaf rear adjustable for elevation. **Features:** Detachable rotary magazine fits flush into stock, cross-bolt safety, receiver tapped and grooved for scope blocks or tip-off mount. Scope base adaptor furnished with each rifle.
Price: Model 10/22 RB (blue) **$239.00**
Price: Model K10/22RB (bright finish stainless barrel) **$279.00**
Price: Model 10/22RPF (blue, synthetic stock) **$239.00**

Ruger 10/22 International Carbine

Similar to the Ruger 10/22 Carbine except has full-length International stock of American hardwood, checkered grip and forend; comes with rubber butt pad, sling swivels. Reintroduced 1994.
Price: Blue (10/22RBI) **$279.00**
Price: Stainless (K10/22RBI) **$299.00**

RIFLES

Ruger 10/22 Deluxe Sporter

Ruger 10/22 Target

Ruger 10/22 International

Savage Model 64FV

Ruger 10/22 Deluxe Sporter

Same as 10/22 Carbine except walnut stock with hand checkered pistol grip and forend; straight buttplate, no barrel band, has sling swivels.
Price: Model 10/22 DSP **$299.00**

Ruger 10/22T Target Rifle

Similar to the 10/22 except has 20" heavy, hammer-forged barrel with tight chamber dimensions, improved trigger pull, laminated hardwood stock dimensioned for optical sights. No iron sights supplied. Introduced 1996. Made in U.S.A. by Sturm, Ruger & Co.
Price: 10/22T **$425.00**
Price: K10/22T, stainless steel **$485.00**

Ruger K10/22RPF All-Weather Rifle

Similar to the stainless K10/22/RB except has black composite stock of thermoplastic polyester resin reinforced with fiberglass; checkered grip and forend. Brushed satin, natural metal finish with clear hardcoat finish. Weighs 5 lbs., measures 36-3/4" overall. Introduced 1997. From Sturm, Ruger & Co.
Price: **$279.00**

RUGER 10/22 MAGNUM AUTOLOADING CARBINE

Caliber: 22 WMR, 9-shot rotary magazine. **Barrel:** 18-1/2". **Weight:** 6 lbs. **Length:** 37-1/4" overall. **Stock:** Birch. **Sights:** Gold bead front, folding rear. **Features:** All-steel receiver has integral Ruger scope bases for the included 1" rings. Introduced 1999. Made in U.S.A. by Sturm, Ruger & Co.
Price: 10/22RBM **$499.00**

SAVAGE MODEL 64G AUTO RIFLE

Caliber: 22 LR, 10-shot magazine. **Barrel:** 20", 21". **Weight:** 5-1/2 lbs. **Length:** 40", 41". **Stock:** Walnut-finished hardwood with Monte Carlo-type comb, checkered grip and forend. **Sights:** Bead front, open adjustable rear. Receiver grooved for scope mounting. **Features:** Thumb-operated rotating safety. Blue finish. Side ejection, bolt hold-open device. Introduced 1990. Made in Canada, from Savage Arms.

Price: **$151.00**
Price: Model 64FSS, stainless **$196.00**
Price: Model 64F, black synthetic stock **$135.00**
Price: Model 64GXP Package Gun includes
4x15 scope and mounts **$156.00**
Price: Model 64FXP (black stock, 4x15 scope) **$144.00**
Price: Model 64F Camo **$166.00**

Savage Model 64FV Auto Rifle

Similar to the Model 64F except has heavy 21" barrel with recessed crown; no sights provided—comes with Weaver-style bases. Introduced 1998. Imported from Canada by Savage Arms, Inc.
Price: **$182.00**
Price: Model 64FVSS, stainless **$235.00**

THOMPSON/CENTER 22 LR CLASSIC RIFLE

Caliber: 22 LR, 8-shot magazine. **Barrel:** 22" match-grade. **Weight:** 5-1/2 pounds. **Length:** 39-1/2" overall. **Stock:** Satin-finished American walnut with Monte Carlo-type comb and pistol grip cap, swivel studs. **Sights:** Ramp-style front and fully adjustable rear, both with fiber optics. **Features:** All-steel receiver drilled and tapped for scope mounting; barrel threaded to receiver; thumb-operated safety; trigger-guard safety lock included. New .22 Classic Benchmark TGT target rifle variant has 18" heavy barrel, brown laminated target stock, blued with matte finish, 10-shot magazine and no sights; drilled and tapped.
Price: T/C 22 LR Classic (blue) **$370.00**
Price: T/C 22 LR Classic Benchmark **$472.00**

TAURUS MODEL 63 RIFLE

Caliber: .22 LR, 10-shot tube-fed magazine. **Barrel:** 23". **Weight:** 72 oz. **Length:** 32-1/2". **Stock:** Hand-fitted walnut-finished hardwood. **Sights:** Adjustable rear, fixed front. **Features:** Manual safety, metal buttplate, can accept Taurus tang sight. Charged and cocked with operating plunger at front of forend. Available in blue or polished stainless steel.
Price: 63 . . . . **$295.00**
Price: 63SS **$311.00**

Classic and modern models for sport and utility, including training.

Browning BL-22

Henry Lever-Action 22

Henry Golden Boy 22

Henry Pump-Action 22

Marlin Model 39AS

Marlin Model 1897T

BROWNING BL-22 LEVER-ACTION RIFLE

Caliber: 22 S (22), L (17) or LR (15), tubular magazine. **Barrel:** 20" round tapered. **Weight:** 5 lbs. **Length:** 36-3/4" overall. **Stock:** Walnut, two-piece straight grip Western style. **Sights:** Bead post front, folding-leaf rear. **Features:** Short throw lever, half-cock safety, receiver grooved for tip-off scope mounts, gold-colored trigger. Imported from Japan by Browning.

Price: Grade I $415.00
Price: Grade II (engraved receiver, checkered grip and forend) . $471.00
Price: Classic, Grade I (blued trigger, no checkering) $415.00
Price: Classic, Grade II (cut checkering, satin wood finish, polished blueing) $471.00

HENRY LEVER-ACTION 22

Caliber: 22 Long Rifle (15-shot). **Barrel:** 18-1/4" round. **Weight:** 5-1/2 lbs. **Length:** 34" overall. **Stock:** Walnut. **Sights:** Hooded blade front, open adjustable rear. **Features:** Polished blue finish; full-length tubular magazine; side ejection; receiver grooved for scope mounting. Introduced 1997. Made in U.S.A. by Henry Repeating Arms Co.

Price: $239.95
Price: Youth model (33" overall, 11-rounds 22 LR) $229.95

HENRY GOLDEN BOY 22 LEVER-ACTION RIFLE

Caliber: 22 LR, 22 Magnum, 16-shot. **Barrel:** 20" octagonal. **Weight:** 6.25 lbs. **Length:** 38" overall. **Stock:** American walnut. **Sights:** Blade front,

open rear. **Features:** Brasslite receiver, brass buttplate, blued barrel and lever. Introduced 1998. Made in U.S.A. from Henry Repeating Arms Co.

Price: $379.95
Price: Magnum $449.95

HENRY PUMP-ACTION 22 PUMP RIFLE

Caliber: 22 LR, 15-shot. **Barrel:** 18.25". **Weight:** 5.5 lbs. **Length:** NA. **Stock:** American walnut. **Sights:** Bead on ramp front, open adjustable rear. **Features:** Polished blue finish; receiver groved for scope mount; grooved slide handle; two barrel bands. Introduced 1998. Made in U.S.A. from Henry Repeating Arms Co.

Price: $249.95

MARLIN MODEL 39A GOLDEN LEVER-ACTION RIFLE

Caliber: 22, S (26), L (21), LR (19), tubular mag. **Barrel:** 24" Micro-Groove®. **Weight:** 6-1/2 lbs. **Length:** 40" overall. **Stock:** Checkered American black walnut; Mar-Shield® finish. Swivel studs; rubber butt pad. **Sights:** Bead ramp front with detachable Wide-Scan™ hood, folding rear semi-buckhorn adjustable for windage and elevation. **Features:** Hammer block safety; rebounding hammer. Takedown action, receiver tapped for scope mount (supplied), offset hammer spur, gold-plated steel trigger. From Marlin Firearms.

Price: $552.00

MARLIN MODEL 1897T RIFLE

Caliber: 22, S (21), L (16), LR (14), tubular mag. **Barrel:** 20" tapered octagon. **Weight:** Marble semi-buckhorn rear, Marble front brass beaded. **Features:** Hammer block safety solid top receiver tapped, 2-level base for 3/4", 7/8" scope ring and " detached, blued, safety lock. From Marlin Firearms.

Price: $748.00

Remington Model 572 BDL Deluxe Fieldmaster

Ruger Model 96/22

Taurus 62R

Taurus 72C-SS

Winchester 9422 Legacy

REMINGTON 572 BDL DELUXE FIELDMASTER PUMP RIFLE

Caliber: 22 S (20), L (17) or LR (15), tubular mag. **Barrel:** 21" round tapered. **Weight:** 5-1/2 lbs. **Length:** 40" overall. **Stock:** Walnut with checkered pistol grip and slide handle. **Sights:** Big game. **Features:** Cross-bolt safety; removing inner magazine tube converts rifle to single shot; receiver grooved for tip-off scope mount.

Price: **$407.00**

RUGER MODEL 96 LEVER-ACTION RIFLE

Caliber: 22 LR, 10 rounds; 22 WMR, 9 rounds; 44 Magnum, 4 rounds; 17 HMR 9 rounds. **Barrel:** 18-1/2". **Weight:** 5-1/4 lbs. **Length:** 37-1/4" overall. **Stock:** Hardwood. **Sights:** Gold bead front, folding leaf rear. **Features:** Sliding cross button safety, visible cocking indicator; short-throw lever action. Introduced 1996. Made in U.S.A. by Sturm, Ruger & Co.

Price: 96/22 (22 LR) **$349.00**
Price: 96/22M (22 WMR) **$375.00**
Price: 96/22M (44 Mag.) **$525.00**
New! **Price:** 96/17M (17 HMR) **$375.00**

TAURUS MODEL 62 PUMP RIFLE

Caliber: 22 LR, 12- or 13-shot. **Barrel:** 16-1/2" or 23" round. **Weight:** 72 oz-80 oz. **Length:** 39" overall. **Stock:** Premium hardwood. **Sights:** Adjustable rear, bead blade front, optional tang. **Features:** Blue, case hardened or stainless, bolt-mounted safety, pump action, manual firing pin block, integral security lock system. Imported from Brazil by Taurus International.

Price: M62C (blue) **$280.00**
Price: M62C-CH (case hardened-blue) **$280.00**
Price: M62CCH-T (case hardened-blue) **$358.00**
Price: M62C-SS (stainless steel) **$295.00**
Price: M62CSS-T (stainless steel) **$373.00**
Price: M62C-SS-Y (stainless steel) **$327.00**

Price: M62C-T (blue) **$358.00**
Price: M62C-Y (blue) **$311.00**
Price: M62R (blue) **$280.00**
Price: M62R-CH (case hardened-blue) **$280.00**
Price: M62RCH-T (case hardened-blue) **$358.00**
Price: M62R-SS (stainless steel) **$295.00**
Price: M62RSS-T (stainless steel) **$373.00**
Price: M62R-T (blue) **$358.00**

Taurus Model 72 Pump Rifle

Same as Model 62 except chambered in 22 Magnum or .17 HMR; 16-1/2" bbl. holds 10-12 shots, 23" bbl. holds 11-13 shots. Weighs 72 oz.-80 oz. Introduced 2001. Imported from Brazil by Taurus International.

Price: M72C (blue) **$295.00**
Price: M72C-CH (case hardened-blue) **$295.00**
Price: M72CCH-T (case hardened-blue) **$373.00**
Price: M72C-SS (stainless steel) **$311.00**
Price: M72CSS-T (stainless steel) **$389.00**
Price: M72C-T (blue) **$373.00**
Price: M72R (blue) **$295.00**
Price: M72R-CH (case hardened-blue) **$295.00**
Price: M72RCH-T (case hardened-blue) **$373.00**
Price: M72R-SS (stainless steel) **$311.00**
Price: M72RSS-T (stainless steel) **$389.00**
Price: M72R-T (blue) **$373.00**

WINCHESTER MODEL 9422 LEVER-ACTION RIFLES

Caliber: 22 LR, 22 WMR, tubular magazine. **Barrel:** 20-1/2". **Weight:** 6-1/4 lbs. **Length:** 37-1/8" overall. **Stock:** American walnut, two-piece, straight grip (Traditional) or semi-pistol grip (Legacy). **Sights:** Hooded ramp front, adjustable semi-buckhorn rear. **Features:** Side ejection, receiver grooved for scope mounting, takedown action. From U.S. Repeating Arms Co.

Price: Traditional, 22 LR 15-shot **$465.00**
Price: Traditional, 22WMR, 11-shot **$487.00**
Price: Legacy, 22 LR 15-shot **$498.00**
Price: Legacy 22 WMR, 11-shot **$521.00**

RIFLES

Includes models for a variety of sports, utility and competitive shooting.

Anschutz 1518D Luxus

Anschutz 1710D

Charles Daly Field Grade

ANSCHUTZ 1416D/1516D CLASSIC RIFLES

Caliber: 22 LR (1416D), 5-shot clip; 22 WMR (1516D), 4-shot clip. **Barrel:** 22-1/2". **Weight:** 6 lbs. **Length:** 41" overall. **Stock:** European hardwood with walnut finish; classic style with straight comb, checkered pistol grip and forend. **Sights:** Hooded ramp front, folding leaf rear. **Features:** Uses Match 64 action. Adjustable single stage trigger. Receiver grooved for scope mounting. Imported from Germany by AcuSport Corp.

Price: 1416D, 22 LR **$755.95**
Price: 1516D, 22 WMR **$779.95**
Price: 1416D Classic left-hand **$679.95**

Anschutz 1416D/1516D Walnut Luxus Rifles

Similar to the Classic models except have European walnut stocks with Monte Carlo cheekpiece, slim forend with Schnabel tip, cut checkering on grip and forend. Introduced 1997. Imported from Germany by AcuSport Corp.

Price: 1416D (22 LR) **$755.95**
Price: 1516D (22 WMR) **$779.95**

ANSCHUTZ 1518D LUXUS BOLT-ACTION RIFLE

Caliber: 22 WMR, 4-shot magazine. **Barrel:** 19-3/4". **Weight:** 5-1/2 lbs. **Length:** 37-1/2" overall. **Stock:** European walnut. **Sights:** Blade on ramp front, folding leaf rear. **Features:** Receiver grooved for scope mounting; single stage trigger; skip-line checkering; rosewood forend tip; sling swivels. Imported from Germany by AcuSport Corp.

Price: **$1,186.95**

ANSCHUTZ 1710D CUSTOM RIFLE

Caliber: 22 LR, 5-shot clip. **Barrel:** 24-1/4". **Weight:** 7-3/8 lbs. **Length:** 42-1/2" overall. **Stock:** Select European walnut. **Sights:** Hooded ramp front, folding leaf rear; drilled and tapped for scope mounting. **Features:** Match 54 action with adjustable single-stage trigger; roll-over Monte Carlo cheekpiece, slim forend with Schnabel tip, Wundhammer palm swell on pistol grip, rosewood gripcap with white diamond insert; skip-line checkering on grip and forend. Introduced 1988. Imported from Germany by AcuSport Corp.

Price: **$1,289.95**

CABANAS MASTER BOLT-ACTION RIFLE

Caliber: 177, round ball or pellet; single shot. **Barrel:** 19-1/2". **Weight:** 8 lbs. **Length:** 45-1/2" overall. **Stocks:** Walnut target-type with Monte Carlo. **Sights:** Blade front, fully adjustable rear. **Features:** Fires round ball or pellet with 22-cal. blank cartridge. Bolt action. Imported from Mexico by Mandall Shooting Supplies. Introduced 1984.

Price: **$189.95**
Price: Varmint model (has 21-1/2" barrel, 4-1/2 lbs., 41" overall length, varmint-type stock) **$119.95**

Cabanas Leyre Bolt-Action Rifle

Similar to Master model except 44" overall, has sport/target stock.

Price: **$149.95**
Price: Model R83 (17" barrel, hardwood stock, 40" o.a.l.) **$79.95**
Price: Mini 82 Youth (16-1/2" barrel, 33" overall length, 3-1/2 lbs.) **$69.95**
Price: Pony Youth (16" barrel, 34" overall length, 3.2 lbs.) **$69.95**

Cabanas Espronceda IV Bolt-Action Rifle

Similar to the Leyre model except has full sporter stock, 18-3/4" barrel, 40" overall length, weighs 5-1/2 lbs.

Price: **$134.95**

CABANAS LASER RIFLE

Caliber: 177. **Barrel:** 19". **Weight:** 6 lbs., 12 oz. **Length:** 42" overall. **Stock:** Target-type thumbhole. **Sights:** Blade front, open fully adjustable rear. **Features:** Fires round ball or pellets with 22 blank cartridge. Imported from Mexico by Mandall Shooting Supplies.

Price: **$159.95**

CHARLES DALY SUPERIOR BOLT-ACTION RIFLE

Caliber: 22 LR, 10-shot magazine. **Barrel:** 22-5/8". **Weight:** 6.7 lbs. **Length:** 41.25" overall. **Stock:** Walnut-finished mahogany. **Sights:** Bead front, rear adjustable for elevation. **Features:** Receiver grooved for scope mounting. Blued finish. Introduced 1998. Imported by K.B.I., Inc.

Price: **$189.95**

Charles Daly Field Grade Rifle

Similar to the Superior except has short walnut-finished hardwood stock for small shooters. Introduced 1998. Imported by K.B.I., Inc.

Price: **$134.95**
Price: Field Youth (17.5" barrel) **$144.95**

Charles Daly Superior Magnum Grade Rifle

Similar to the Superior except chambered for 22 WMR. Has 22.6" barrel, double lug bolt, checkered stock, weighs 6.5 lbs. Introduced 1987.

Price: About **$204.95**

Charles Daly Empire Magnum Grade Rifle

Similar to the Superior Magnum except has oil-finished American walnut stock with 18 lpi hand checkering; black hardwood gripcap and forend tip; highly polished barreled action; jewelled bolt; recoil pad; swivel studs. Imported from the Philippines by K.B.I., Inc.

Price: **$364.95**

Chipmunk Deluxe

CZ 452 Lux

CZ 452 Varmint

CZ 452 American Classic

Charles Daly Empire Grade Rifle

Similar to the Superior except has oil-finished American walnut stock with 18 lpi hand checkering; black hardwood gripcap and forend tip; highly polished barreled action; jewelled bolt; recoil pad; swivel studs. Imported by K.B.I., Inc.

Price: **$329.00**

CHARLES DALY TRUE YOUTH BOLT-ACTION RIFLE

Caliber: 22 LR, single shot. **Barrel:** 16-1/4". **Weight:** About 3 lbs. **Length:** 32" overall. **Stock:** Walnut-finished hardwood. **Sights:** Blade front, adjustable rear. **Features:** Scaled-down stock for small shooters. Blue finish. Introduced 1998. Imported by K.B.I., Inc.

Price: **$154.95**

CHIPMUNK SINGLE SHOT RIFLE

Caliber: 22 LR, 22 WMR, single shot. **Barrel:** 16-1/8". **Weight:** About 2-1/2 lbs. **Length:** 30" overall. **Stocks:** American walnut. **Sights:** Post on ramp front, peep rear adjustable for windage and elevation. **Features:** Drilled and tapped for scope mounting using special Chipmunk base ($13.95). Engraved model also available. Made in U.S.A. Introduced 1982. From Rogue Rifle Co., Inc.

Price: Standard. **$194.25**
Price: Standard 22 WMR **$209.95**
Price: Deluxe (better wood, checkering). **$246.95**
Price: Deluxe 22 WMR **$262.95**
Price: Laminated stock **$209.95**
Price: Laminated stock, 22 WMR **$225.95**
Price: Bull barrel models of above, add **$16.00**

CHIPMUNK TM (TARGET MODEL)

Caliber: 22 S, L, or LR. **Barrel:** 18" blue. **Weight:** 5 lbs. **Length:** 33". Stocks: Walnut with accessory rail. **Sights:** 1/4 minute micrometer adjustable. **Features:** Manually cocking single shot bolt action, blue receiver, adjustable butt plate and butt pad.

Price: **$329.95**

COOPER MODEL 57-M BOLT-ACTION RIFLE

Caliber: 22 LR, 22 WMR, 17 HMR. **Barrel:** 23-3/4" stainless steel or 41-40 match grade. **Weight:** 6.6 lbs. **Stock:** Claro walnut, 22 lpi hand checkering. **Sights:** None furnished. **Features:** Three rear locking lug, repeating bolt-action with 5-shot mag. Fully adjustable trigger. Many options. Made 100% in the U.S.A. by Cooper Firearms of Montana, Inc.

Price: Classic **$1,100.00**
Price: LVT. **$1,295.00**
Price: Custom Classic **$1,895.00**
Price: Western Classic **$2,495.00**

CZ 452 M 2E LUX BOLT-ACTION RIFLE

Caliber: 22 LR, 22 WMR, 5-shot detachable magazine. **Barrel:** 24.8". **Weight:** 6.6 lbs. **Length:** 42.63" overall. **Stock:** Walnut with checkered pistol grip. **Sights:** Hooded front, fully adjustable tangent rear. **Features:** All-steel construction, adjustable trigger, polished blue finish. Imported from the Czech Republic by CZ-USA.

Price: 22 LR **$351.00**
Price: 22 WMR **$378.00**
Price: Synthetic stock, nickel finish, 22 LR. **$344.00**

CZ 452 M 2E Varmint Rifle

Similar to the Lux model except has heavy 20.8" barrel; stock has beavertail forend; weighs 7 lbs.; no sights furnished. Available only in 22 LR. Imported from the Czech Republic by CZ-USA.

Price: **$378.00**

CZ 452 American Classic Bolt-Action Rifle

Similar to the CZ 452 M 2E Lux except has classic-style stock of Circassian walnut; 22.5" free-floating barrel with recessed target crown; receiver dovetail for scope mounting. No open sights furnished. Introduced 1999. Imported from the Czech Republic by CZ-USA.

Price: 22 LR **$351.00**
Price: 22 WMR **$378.00**

HARRINGTON & RICHARDSON ULTRA HEAVY BARREL 22 MAG RIFLE

Caliber: 22 WMR, single shot. **Barrel:** 22" bull. **Stock:** Cinnamon laminated wood with Monte Carlo cheekpiece. **Sights:** None furnished; scope mount rail included. **Features:** Hand-checkered stock and forend; deep-crown rifling; tuned trigger; trigger locking system; hammer extension. Introduced 2001. From H&R 1871 LLC.

Price: **$193.00**

Henry "Mini" Bolt 22

Kimber 22 Classic

Kimber 22 SuperAmerica

Kimber 22 SVT

Kimber 22 HS

HENRY "MINI" BOLT 22 RIFLE
Caliber: 22 LR, single shot. **Barrel:** 16" stainless, 8-groove rifling. **Weight:** 3.25 lbs. **Length:** 30", LOP 11-1/2". **Stock:** Synthetic, pistol grip, wraparound checkering and beavertail forearm. **Sights:** William Fire sights. **Features:** One piece bolt configuration manually operated safety. Ideal for beginners or ladies.
Price: **$169.95**

KIMBER 22 CLASSIC BOLT-ACTION RIFLE
Caliber: 22 LR, 5-shot magazine. **Barrel:** 18", 22", 24" match grade; 11-degree target crown. **Weight:** 5-8 lbs. **Length:** 35"-43". **Stock:** Classic Claro walnut, hand-cut checkering, steel gripcap, swivel studs. **Sights:** None, drilled and tapped. **Features:** All-new action with Mauser-style full-length claw extractor, two-position wing safety, match trigger, pillar-bedded action with recoil lug. Introduced 1999. Made in U.S.A. by Kimber Mfg., Inc.
Price: New Classic **$1,085.00**
Price: Classic **$949.00**
Price: Hunter **$678.00**
Price: Youth **$746.00**

Kimber 22 SuperAmerica Bolt-Action Rifle
Similar to 22 Classic except has AAA Claro walnut stock with wraparound 22 l.p.i. hand-cut checkering, ebony forened tip, beaded cheekpiece. Introduced 1999. Made in U.S.A. by Kimber Mfg., Inc.
Price: **$1,764.00**

Kimber 22 SVT Bolt-Action Rilfe
Similar to 22 Classic except has 18" stainless steel, fluted bull barrel, gray laminated, high-comb target-style stock with deep pistol grip, high comb, beavertail forend with bipod stud. Weighs 7.5 lbs., overall length 36.5". Matte finish on action. Introduced 1999. Made in U.S.A. by Kimber Mfg., Inc.
Price: **$949.00**

Kimber 22 HS (Hunter Silhouette) Bolt-Action Rifle
Similar to 22 Classic except 24" medium sporter match-grade barrel with half-fluting; high comb, walnut, Monte Carlo target stock with 18 l.p.i. checkering; matte blue metal finish. Introduced 1999. Made in U.S.A. by Kimber Mfg., Inc.
Price: **$814.00**

Marlin 17V

Marlin Model 15YN "Little Buckaroo"

Marlin Model 880SS

Marlin 880SQ Squirrel

Marlin 25N

Marlin 25MNC

MARLIN MODEL 17V HORNADY MAGNUM
Caliber: 17 Magnum, 7-shot. **Barrel:** 22. **Weight:** 6 lbs., stainless 7 lbs. **Length:** 41". **Stock:** Checkered walnut Monte Carlo SS, laminated black/grey. **Sights:** No sights but receiver grooved. **Features:** Swivel studs, positive thumb safety, red cocking indicator, safety lock, SS 1" brushed aluminum scope rings.
Price: **$269.00**
Price: Bead blasted SS barrel & receiver **$402.00**

MARLIN MODEL 15YN "LITTLE BUCKAROO"
Caliber: 22 S, L, LR, single shot. **Barrel:** 16-1/4" Micro-Groove®. **Weight:** 4-1/4 lbs. **Length:** 33-1/4" overall. **Stock:** One-piece walnut-finished, press-checkered Maine birch with Monte Carlo; Mar-Shield® finish. **Sights:** Ramp front, adjustable open rear. **Features:** Beginner's rifle with thumb safety, easy-load feed throat, red cocking indicator. Receiver grooved for scope mounting. Introduced 1989.
Price: **$209.00**
Price: Stainless steel with fire sights **$233.00**

MARLIN MODEL 880SS BOLT-ACTION RIFLE
Caliber: 22 LR, 7-shot clip magazine. **Barrel:** 22" Micro-Groove®. **Weight:** 6 lbs. **Length:** 41" overall. **Stock:** Black fiberglass-filled synthetic with nickel-plated swivel studs and moulded-in checkering. **Sights:** Ramp front with orange post and cutaway Wide-Scan™ hood, adjustable semi-

buckhorn folding rear. **Features:** Stainless steel barrel, receiver, front breech bolt and striker; receiver grooved for scope mounting. Introduced 1994. Model 880SQ (Squirrel Rifle) is similar but has heavy 22" barrel. Made in U.S.A. by Marlin.
Price: (Model 880SS) **$316.00**
Price: (Model 880SQ) $330.00

Marlin Model 81TS Bolt-Action Rifle
Same as Marlin 880SS except blued steel, tubular magazine, holds 17 Long Rifle cartridges. Weighs 6 lbs.
Price: **$213.00**

Marlin Model 880SQ Squirrel Rifle
Similar to Model 880SS except uses heavy target barrel. Black synthetic stock with moulded-in checkering, double bedding screws, matte blue finish. Without sights, no dovetail or filler screws; receiver grooved for scope mount. Weighs 7 lbs. Introduced 1996. Made in U.S.A. by Marlin.
Price: **$322.00**

Marlin Model 25N Bolt-Action Repeater
Similar to Marlin 880, except walnut-finished hardwood stock, adjustable open rear sight, ramp front.
Price: **$212.00**
Price: With 4x scope and mount. **$220.00**

Marlin Model 25NC Bolt-Action Repeater
Same as Model 25N except Mossy Oak® Break-Up camouflage stock. Made in U.S.A. by Marlin.
Price: **$248.00**

RIFLES

Marlin 883SS

Marlin 83TS

Ruger K77/22 Varmint

Marlin Model 25MN/25MNC Bolt-Action Rifles

Similar to the Model 25N except chambered for 22 WMR. Has 7-shot clip magazine, 22" Micro-Groove® barrel, checkered walnut-finished Maine birch stock. Introduced 1989.
Price: 25MN **$241.00**
New! **Price:** 25MNC (Mossy Oak® Break-Up camouflage stock). **$278.00**

Marlin Model 882 Bolt-Action Rifle

Same as the Marlin 880 except 22 WMR cal. only with 7-shot clip magazine; weight about 6 lbs. Comes with swivel studs.
Price: **$324.00**
Price: Model 882L (laminated hardwood stock; weighs 6-1/4 lbs.) **$342.00**

Marlin Model 882SS Bolt-Action Rifle

Same as the Marlin Model 882 except has stainless steel front breech bolt, barrel, receiver and bolt knob. All other parts are either stainless steel or nickel-plated. Has black Monte Carlo stock of fiberglass-filled polycarbonate with moulded-in checkering, nickel-plated swivel studs. Introduced 1995. Made in U.S.A. by Marlin Firearms Co.
Price: **$345.00**

Marlin Model 882SSV Bolt-Action Rifle

Similar to the Model 882SS except has selected heavy 22" stainless steel barrel with recessed muzzle, and comes without sights; receiver is grooved for scope mount and 1" ring mounts are included. Weighs 7 lbs. Introduced 1997. Made in U.S.A. by Marlin Firearms Co.
Price: **$338.00**

MARLIN MODEL 883 BOLT-ACTION RIFLE

Caliber: 22 WMR. **Barrel:** 22"; 1:16" twist. **Weight:** 6 lbs. **Length:** 41" overall. **Stock:** Walnut Monte Carlo with sling swivel studs, rubber butt pad. **Sights:** Ramp front with brass bead, removable hood; adjustable semi-buckhorn folding rear. **Features:** Thumb safety, red cocking indicator, receiver grooved for scope mount. Made in U.S.A. by Marlin Firearms Co.
Price: **$337.00**

Marlin Model 883SS Bolt-Action Rifle

Same as the Model 883 except front breech bolt, striker knob, trigger stud, cartridge lifter stud and outer magazine tube are of stainless steel; other parts are nickel-plated. Has two-tone brown laminated Monte Carlo stock with swivel studs, rubber butt pad. Introduced 1993.
Price: **$358.00**

Marlin Model 83TS Bolt-Action Rifle

Same as the Model 883 except has a black Monte Carlo fiberglass-filled synthetic stock with sling swivel studs. Weighs 6 lbs., length 41" overall. Introduced 2001. Made in U.S.A. by Marlin Firearms Co.
Price: **$259.00**

MEACHAM LOW WALL RIFLE

Caliber: 22 RF Match, .17 HMR. **Barrel:** 28". **Weight:** 10 lbs. **Sights:** None. Tang drilled for Win. base, 3/8" dovetail slot, front. **Stock:** Fancy eastern black walnut with cheekpiece; ebony insert in forend. **Features:** Available with single trigger, single set trigger, or Schuetzen-style double set triggers. Introduced 2002. From Meacham T&H, Inc.
Price: **$2,999.00**

NEW ENGLAND FIREARMS SPORTSTER™ SINGLE-SHOT RIFLES

Caliber: 22 LR, 22 WMR, 17 HMR, single-shot. **Barrel:** 20". **Weight:** 5-1/2 lbs. **Length:** 36-1/4" overall. **Stock:** Black polymer. **Sights:** None furnished; scope mount included. **Features:** Break open, side-lever release; automatic ejection; recoil pad; sling swivel studs; trigger locking system. Introduced 2001. Made in U.S.A. by New England Firearms.
Price: **$149.00**
Price: Youth model (20" bbl., 33" overall, weighs 5-1/3 lbs.) **$149.00**
Price: Sportster 17 HMR **$180.00**

NEW ULTRA LIGHT ARMS 20RF BOLT-ACTION RIFLE

Caliber: 22 LR, single shot or repeater. **Barrel:** Douglas, length to order. **Weight:** 5-1/4 lbs. **Length:** Varies. **Stock:** Kevlar®/graphite composite, variety of finishes. **Sights:** None furnished; drilled and tapped for scope mount. **Features:** Timney trigger, hand-lapped action, button-rifled barrel, hand-bedded action, recoil pad, sling-swivel studs, optional Jewell Trigger. Made in U.S.A. by New Ultra Light Arms.
Price: 20 RF single shot **$800.00**
Price: 20 RF repeater **$850.00**

ROSSI MATCHED PAIR SINGLE-SHOT RIFLE/SHOTGUN

Caliber: 22 LR or 22 Mag. **Barrel:** 18-1/2" or 23". **Weight:** 6 lbs. **Stock:** Hardwood (brown or black finish). **Sights:** Fully adjustable front and rear. **Features:** Break-open breech, transfer-bar manual safety, includes matched 410-, 20- or 12-gauge shotgun barrel with bead front sight. Introduced 2001. Imported by BrazTech/Taurus.
Price: blue **$139.95**
Price: stainless steel **$169.95**

RUGER K77/22 VARMINT RIFLE

Caliber: 22 LR, 10-shot, 22 WMR, 9-shot detachable rotary magazine. **Barrel:** 24", heavy. **Weight:** 6-7/8 lbs. **Length:** 43.25" overall. **Stock:** Laminated hardwood with rubber butt pad, quick-detachable swivel studs. **Sights:** None furnished. Comes with Ruger 1" scope rings. **Features:** Stainless steel or blued finish. Three-position safety, dual extractors. Stock has wide, flat forend. Introduced 1993.
Price: K77/22VBZ, 22 LR **$645.00**
Price: K77/22VMBZ, 22 WMR **$645.00**

Ruger 77/22R

Sako Finnfire

Savage Mark I-G

Savage Mark I-Y

RUGER 77/22 RIMFIRE BOLT-ACTION RIFLE

Caliber: 22 LR, 10-shot rotary magazine; 22 WMR, 9-shot rotary magazine. **Barrel:** 20". **Weight:** About 5-3/4 lbs. **Length:** 39-3/4" overall. **Stock:** Checkered American walnut, laminated hardwood, or synthetic stocks, stainless sling swivels. **Sights:** Brass bead front, adjustable folding leaf rear or plain barrel with 1" Ruger rings. **Features:** Mauser-type action uses Ruger's rotary magazine. Three-position safety, simplified bolt stop, patented bolt locking system. Uses the dual-screw barrel attachment system of the 10/22 rifle. Integral scope mounting system with 1" Ruger rings. Blued model introduced 1983. Stainless steel and blued with synthetic stock introduced 1989.

Price: 77/22R (no sights, rings, walnut stock) **$580.00**
Price: 77/22RS (open sights, rings, walnut stock) **$605.00**
Price: K77/22RP (stainless, no sights, rings, synthetic stock) . . . **$580.00**
Price: K77/22RSP (stainless, open sights, rings, synthetic stock) **$605.00**
Price: 77/22RM (22 WMR, blue, walnut stock) **$580.00**
Price: K77/22RSMP (22 WMR, stainless, open sights, rings, synthetic
stock) **$605.00**
Price: K77/22RMP (22 WMR, stainless, synthetic stock) **$580.00**
Price: 77/22RSM
(22 WMR, blue, open sights, rings, walnut stock) **$585.00**
New!! **Price:** K77/17RM, 17RMP, 17VMBBZ (17 HMR, walnut, synthetic or laminate stocks, no sights, rings, blued or stainless) **$580.00 to $645.00**

SAKO FINNFIRE HUNTER BOLT-ACTION RIFLE

Caliber: 22 LR, 5-shot magazine. **Barrel:** 22". **Weight:** 5.75 lbs. **Length:** 39-1/2" overall. **Stock:** European walnut with checkered grip and forend. **Sights:** Hooded blade front, open adjustable rear. **Features:** Adjustable single-stage trigger; has 50-degree bolt lift. Introduced 1994. Imported from Finland by Beretta USA.

Price: **$854.00**
Price: Varmint (heavy barrel) **$896.00**

SAKO FINNFIRE TARGET RIFLE

Caliber: 22 LR. **Barrel:** 22"; heavy, free-floating. **Stock:** Match style of European walnut; adjustable cheekpiece and buttplate; stippled pistol grip and forend. **Sights:** None furnished; has 11mm integral dovetail scope mount. **Features:** Based on the Sako P94S action with two bolt locking lugs, 50-degree bolt lift and 30mm throw; adjustable trigger. Introduced 1999. Imported from Finland by Beretta USA.

Price: **$951.00**

SAKO 75 FINNLIGHT

Caliber: 243 Rem., 7mm-08 Rem., 308 Win., 25-06 Rem., 270 Win., 280 Rem, 30-06 Spfld, 6.5x55, 7mm Rem. Mag., 300 Win. Mag. **Barrel:** 20", 22". **Weight:** 6-1/2 lbs. **Stock:** Synthetic. **Sights:** None. **Features:** Bolt-action with 3 locking lugs, mechanical ejector, 2 position safety with bolt handle release, single-stage adjustable trigger, detachable magazine with hinged floor plate, stainless steel action and internal parts. Imported from Finland bu Beretta USA.

Price: From . . . . **$1,267.00 to $1,301.00**

SAVAGE MARK I-G BOLT-ACTION RIFLE

Caliber: 22 LR, single shot. **Barrel:** 20-3/4". **Weight:** 5-1/2 lbs. **Length:** 39-1/2" overall. **Stock:** Walnut-finished hardwood with Monte Carlo-type comb, checkered grip and forend. **Sights:** Bead front, open adjustable rear. **Features:** Thumb-operated rotating safety. Blue finish. Rifled or smooth bore. Introduced 1990. Made in Canada, from Savage Arms Inc.

Price: Mark IG, rifled or smooth bore, right- or left-handed **$144.00**
Price: Mark I-GY (Youth), 19" bbl., 37" overall, 5 lbs.. . . . . . **$144.00**
Price: Mark I-LY (Youth), 19" bbl., color laminate **$175.00**
Price: Mark I-Y (Youth), 19" bbl., camo **$174.00**
Price: Mark I-GYXP (Youth), with scope **$162.00**
Price: Mark I-GSB (22 LR shot cartridge). **$144.00**

Savage Mark II-BV

Savage Mark II-FXP

Savage Mark II-FSS

Savage Model 93G

Savage Model 93FSS

SAVAGE MARK II BOLT-ACTION RIFLE

Caliber: 22 LR, 10-shot magazine. **Barrel:** 20-1/2". **Weight:** 5-1/2 lbs. **Length:** 39-1/2" overall. **Stock:** Walnut-finished hardwood with Monte Carlo-type comb, checkered grip and forend. **Sights:** Bead front, open adjustable rear. Receiver grooved for scope mounting. **Features:** Thumb-operated rotating safety. Blue finish. Introduced 1990. Made in Canada, from Savage Arms, Inc.

Price: Mark II-BV **$248.00**
Price: Mark II Camo **$174.00**
Price: Mark II-GY (youth), 19" barrel, 37" overall, 5 lbs. **$156.00**
Price: Mark II-GL, left-hand **$156.00**
Price: Mark II-GLY (youth) left-hand $156.00
Price: Mark II-GXP Package Gun (comes with 4x15 scope),
right- or left-handed **$164.00**
Price: Mark II-FXP (as above with black synthetic stock) **$151.00**
Price: Mark II-F (as above, no scope) **$144.00**
Price: Mark II-FVXP (as above, with scope and rings) **$252.00**

Savage Mark II-LV Heavy Barrel Rifle

Similar to Mark II-G except heavy 21" barrel with recessed target-style crown, gray, laminated hardwood stock with cut checkering. No sights furnished, has dovetailed receiver for scope mounting. Overall length is 39-3/4", weight is 6-1/2 lbs. Comes with 10-shot clip magazine. Introduced 1997. Imported from Canada by Savage Arms, Inc.

Price: **$235.00**
Price: Mark II-FV, with black graphite/polymer stock **$205.00**

Savage Mark II-FSS Stainless Rifle

Similar to the Mark II-G except has stainless steel barreled action and graphite/polymer filled stock; free-floated barrel. Weighs 5 lbs. Introduced 1997. Imported from Canada by Savage Arms, Inc.

Price: **$205.00**

SAVAGE MODEL 93G MAGNUM BOLT-ACTION RIFLE

Caliber: 22 WMR, 5-shot magazine. **Barrel:** 20-3/4". **Weight:** 5-3/4 lbs. **Length:** 39-1/2" overall. **Stock:** Walnut-finished hardwood with Monte Carlo-type comb, checkered grip and forend. **Sights:** Bead front, adjustable open rear. Receiver grooved for scope mount. **Features:** Thumb-operated rotary safety. Blue finish. Introduced 1994. Made in Canada, from Savage Arms.

Price: **$182.00**
Price: Model 93F (as above with black graphite/fiberglass stock) **$175.00**

Savage Model 93FSS Magnum Rifle

Similar to Model 93G except stainless steel barreled action and black synthetic stock with positive checkering. Weighs 5-1/2 lbs. Introduced 1997. Imported from Canada by Savage Arms, Inc.

Price: **$236.00**

Savage Model 93FVSS Magnum Rifle

Similar to Model 93FSS Magnum except 21" heavy barrel with recessed target-style crown, satin-finished stainless barreled action, black graphite/fiberglass stock. Drilled and tapped for scope mounting; comes with Weaver-style bases. Introduced 1998. Imported from Canada by Savage Arms, Inc.

Price: . . . . **$252.00**, With scope **$287.00**

Savage Model 93FVSS

Savage Model 30G Stevens "Favorite"

Savage Cub G Youth

Winchester Model 52B

Winchester Model 1885 Low Wall

SAVAGE MARK 30G STEVENS "FAVORITE"

Caliber: 22 LR, 22WMR - Model 30GM, 17 HMR - Model 30R17. **Barrel:** 21". **Weight:** 4.25 lbs. **Length:** 36.75". **Stock:** Walnut, straight grip, Schnabel forend. **Sights:** Adjustable rear, bead post front. **Features:** Lever action falling block, inertia firing pin system, Model 30G half octagonal bbl. Model 30GM full octagonal bbl.

Price: Model 30G $221.00
Price: Model 30GM $258.00
Price: Model 30R17 .... $284.00

NEW!

Savage Cub G Youth

Caliber: 22 S, L, LR. **Barrel:** 16.125" **Weight:** 3.3 lbs. **Length:** 33" **Stock:** Walnut finished hardwood. **Sights:** Bead post, front; peep, rear. **Features:** Mini single shot bolt action, free-floating button-rifled barrel, blued finish. From Savage Arms.

Price: $149.00

WINCHESTER MODEL 52B BOLT-ACTION RIFLE

Caliber: 22 Long Rifle, 5-shot magazine. **Barrel:** 24". **Weight:** 7 lbs. **Length:** 41-3/4" overall. **Stock:** Walnut with checkered grip and forend. **Sights:** None furnished; grooved receiver and drilled and tapped for scope mounting. **Features:** Has Micro Motion trigger adjustable for pull and over-travel; match chamber; detachable magazine. Reintroduced 1997. From U.S. Repeating Arms Co.

Price: $662.00

WINCHESTER MODEL 1885 LOW WALL RIMFIRE

Caliber: 22 LR, single-shot. **Barrel:** 24-1/2"; half-octagon. **Weight:** 8 lbs. **Length:** 41" overall. **Stock:** Walnut. **Sights:** Blade front, semi-buckhorn rear. **Features:** Drilled and tapped for scope mount or tang sight; target chamber. Limited production. From U.S. Repeating Arms Co.

Price: Grade I (2,400 made) $936.00

Includes models for classic American and ISU target competition and other sporting and competitive shooting.

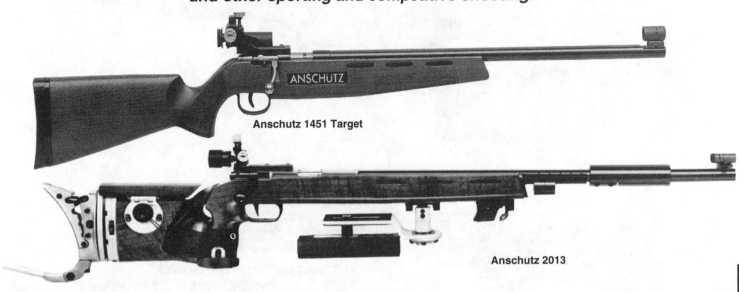

Anschutz 1451 Target

Anschutz 2013

ANSCHUTZ 1451R SPORTER TARGET RIFLE

Caliber: 22 LR, 5-shot magazine. **Barrel:** 22" heavy match. **Weight:** 6.4 lbs. **Length:** 39.75" overall. **Stock:** European hardwood with walnut finish. **Sights:** None furnished. Grooved receiver for scope mounting or Anschutz micrometer rear sight. **Features:** Sliding safety, two-stage trigger. Adjustable buttplate; forend slide rail to accept Anschutz accessories. Imported from Germany by AcuSport Corp.
Price: **$549.00**

ANSCHUTZ 1451 TARGET RIFLE

Caliber: 22 LR. **Barrel:** 22". **Weight:** About 6.5 lbs. **Length:** 40". **Sights:** Optional. Receiver grooved for scope mounting. **Features:** Designed for the beginning junior shooter with adjustable length of pull from 13.25" to 14.25" via removable butt spacers. Two-stage trigger factory set at 2.6 lbs. Introduced 1999. Imported from Germany by Gunsmithing, Inc.
Price: **$347.00**
Price: #6834 Match Sight Set........................ **$227.10**

ANSCHUTZ 1808D-RT SUPER RUNNING TARGET RIFLE

Caliber: 22 LR, single shot. **Barrel:** 32-1/2". **Weight:** 9 lbs. **Length:** 50" overall. **Stock:** European walnut. Heavy beavertail forend; adjustable cheekpiece and buttplate. Stippled grip and forend. **Sights:** None furnished. Grooved for scope mounting. **Features:** Designed for Running Target competition. Nine-way adjustable single-stage trigger, slide safety. Introduced 1991. Imported from Germany by Accuracy International, Gunsmithing, Inc.
Price: Right-hand **$1,364.10**

ANSCHUTZ 1903 MATCH RIFLE

Caliber: 22 LR, single shot. **Barrel:** 25.5", .75" diameter. **Weight:** 10.1 lbs. **Length:** 43.75" overall. **Stock:** Walnut-finished hardwood with adjustable cheekpiece; stippled grip and forend. **Sights:** None furnished. **Features:** Uses Anschutz Match 64 action and #5098 two-stage trigger. A medium weight rifle for intermediate and advanced Junior Match competition. Introduced 1987. Imported from Germany by Accuracy International, Gunsmithing, Inc.
Price: Right-hand **$720.40**
Price: Left-hand **$757.90**

ANSCHUTZ 64-MS R SILHOUETTE RIFLE

Caliber: 22 LR, 5-shot magazine. **Barrel:** 21-1/2", medium heavy; 7/8" diameter. **Weight:** 8 lbs. **Length:** 39.5" overall. **Stock:** Walnut-finished hardwood, silhouette-type. **Sights:** None furnished. **Features:** Uses Match 64 action. Designed for metallic silhouette competition. Stock has stippled checkering, contoured thumb groove with Wundhammer swell.

Two-stage #5098 trigger. Slide safety locks sear and bolt. Introduced 1980. Imported from Germany by AcuSport Corp., Accuracy International, Gunsmithing, Inc.
Price: 64-MS R **$704.30**

ANSCHUTZ 2013 BENCHREST RIFLE

Caliber: 22 LR, single shot. **Barrel:** 19.6". **Weight:** About 10.3 lbs. **Length:** 37.75" to 42.5" overall. **Stock:** Benchrest style of European hardwood. Stock length adjustable via spacers and buttplate. **Sights:** None furnished. Receiver grooved for mounts. **Features:** Uses the Anschutz 2013 target action, #5018 two-stage adjustable target trigger factory set at 3.9 oz. Introduced 1994. Imported from Germany by Accuracy International, Gunsmithing, Inc.
Price: **$1,757.20**

Anschutz 2007 Match Rifle

Uses same action as the Model 2013, but has a lighter barrel. European walnut stock in right-hand, true left-hand or extra-short models. Sights optional. Available with 19.6" barrel with extension tube, or 26", both in stainless or blue. Introduced 1998. Imported from Germany by Gunsmithing, Inc., Accuracy International.
Price: Right-hand, blue, no sights **$1,766.60**
Price: Right-hand, blue, no sights, extra-short stock **$1,756.60**
Price: Left-hand, blue, no sights................... **$1,856.80**

ANSCHUTZ 1827 BIATHLON RIFLE

Caliber: 22 LR, 5-shot magazine. **Barrel:** 21-1/2". **Weight:** 8-1/2 lbs. with sights. **Length:** 42-1/2" overall. **Stock:** European walnut with cheekpiece, stippled pistol grip and forend. **Sights:** Optional globe front specially designed for Biathlon shooting, micrometer rear with hinged snow cap. **Features:** Uses Super Match 54 action and nine-way adjustable trigger; adjustable wooden buttplate, Biathlon butthook, adjustable hand-stop rail. Introduced 1982. Imported from Germany by Accuracy International, Gunsmithing, Inc.
Price: Right-hand, with sights, about .... **$1,500.50 to $1,555.00**

Anschutz 1827BT Fortner Biathlon Rifle

Similar to the Anschutz 1827 Biathlon rifle except uses Anschutz/Fortner system straight-pull bolt action, blued or stainless steel barrel. Introduced 1982. Imported from Germany by Accuracy International, Gunsmithing, Inc.
Price: Right-hand, with sights............... **$1,908.00 to $2,210.00**
Price: Left-hand, with sights .... **$2,099.20 to $2,395.00**
Price: Right-hand, sights, stainless barrel (Gunsmithing, Inc.).. **$2,045.20**

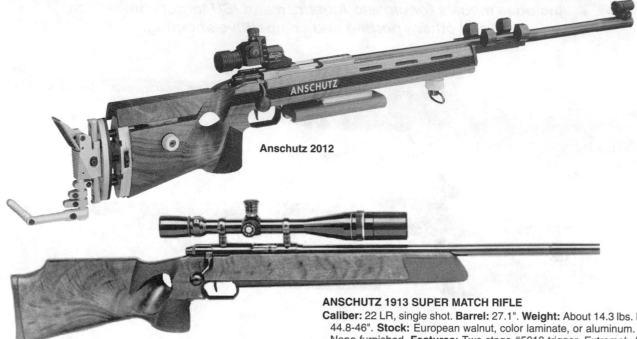

Anschutz 2012

Anschutz 54.18MS REP

ANSCHUTZ SUPER MATCH SPECIAL MODEL 2013 RIFLE

Caliber: 22 LR, single shot. **Barrel:** 25.9". **Weight:** 13 lbs. **Length:** 41.7-42.9". **Stock:** A thumbhole version made of European walnut, both the cheekpiece and buttplate are highly adjustable. **Sights:** None furnished. **Features:** Developed by Anschütz for women to shoot in the sport rifle category. Stainless or blue. This top of the line rifle was introduced in 1997.
Price: Right-hand, blue, no sights, walnut **$2,219.30**
Price: Right-hand, stainless, no sights, walnut **$2,345.30**
Price: Left-hand, blue, no sights, walnut **$2,319.50**

ANSCHUTZ 2012 SPORT RIFLE

Caliber: 22 LR, 5-shot magazine. **Barrel:** 22.4" match; detachable muzzle tube. **Weight:** 7.9 lbs. **Length:** 40.9" overall. **Stock:** European walnut, thumbhole design. **Sights:** None furnished. **Features:** Uses Anschutz 54.18 barreled action with two-stage match trigger. Introduced 1997. Imported from Germany by Accuracy International, AcuSport Corp.
Price: . . . . **$1,425.00 to $2,219.95**

ANSCHUTZ 1911 PRONE MATCH RIFLE

Caliber: 22 LR, single shot. **Barrel:** 27-1/4". **Weight:** 11 lbs. **Length:** 46" overall. **Stock:** Walnut-finished European hardwood; American prone-style with adjustable cheekpiece, textured pistol grip, forend with swivel rail and adjustable rubber buttplate. **Sights:** None furnished. Receiver grooved for Anschutz sights (extra). **Features:** Two-stage #5018 trigger adjustable from 2.1 to 8.6 oz. Extremely fast lock time. Stainless or blue barrel. Imported from Germany by Accuracy International, Gunsmithing, Inc.
Price: Right-hand, no sights **$1,714.20**

ANSCHUTZ 1912 SPORT RIFLE

Caliber: 22 LR, single shot. **Barrel:** 25.9". **Weight:** About 11.4 lbs. **Length:** 41.7-42.9". **Stock:** European walnut or aluminum. **Sights:** None furnished. **Features:** Light weight sport rifle version. Still uses the 54 match action like the 1913 but weighs 1.5 pounds less. Stainless or blue barrel. Introduced 1997.
Price: Right-hand, blue, no sights, walnut **$1,789.50**
Price: Right-hand, blue, no sights, aluminum **$2,129.80**
Price: Right-hand, stainless, no sights, walnut **$1,910.30**
Price: Left-hand, blue, no sights, walnut **$1,879.00**

ANSCHUTZ 1913 SUPER MATCH RIFLE

Caliber: 22 LR, single shot. **Barrel:** 27.1". **Weight:** About 14.3 lbs. **Length:** 44.8-46". **Stock:** European walnut, color laminate, or aluminum. **Sights:** None furnished. **Features:** Two-stage #5018 trigger. Extremely fast lock time. Stainless or blue barrel.
Price: Right-hand, blue, no sights, walnut stock **$2,262.90**
Price: Right-hand, blue, no sights, color laminate stock **$2,275.10**
Price: Right-hand, blue, no sights, aluminum stock **$2,262.90**
Price: Left-hand, blue, no sights, walnut stock **$2,382.20**

Anschutz 1913 Super Match Rifle

Same as the Model 1911 except European walnut International-type stock with adjustable cheekpiece, or color laminate, both available with straight or lowered forend, adjustable aluminum hook buttplate, adjustable hand stop, weighs 15.5 lbs., 46" overall. Stainless or blue barrel. Imported from Germany by Accuracy International, Gunsmithing, Inc.
Price: Right-hand, blue, no sights, walnut stock. . **$2,139.00 to $2,175.00**
Price: Right-hand, blue, no sights, color laminate stock **$2,199.40**
Price: Right-hand, blue, no sights, walnut, lowered forend **$2,181.80**
Price: Right-hand, blue, no sights, color laminate,
lowered forend **$2,242.20**
Price: Left-hand, blue, no sights, walnut stock. . . **$2,233.10 to $2,275.00**

Anschutz 54.18MS REP Deluxe Silhouette Rifle

Same basic action and trigger specifications as the Anschutz 1913 Super Match but with removable 5-shot clip magazine, 22.4" barrel extendable to 30" using optional extension and weight set. Weight is 8.1 lbs. Receiver drilled and tapped for scope mounting. Stock is thumbhole silhouette version or standard silhouette version, both are European walnut. Introduced 1990. Imported from Germany by Accuracy International, Gunsmithing, Inc.
Price: Thumbhole stock **$1,461.40**
Price: Standard stock **$1,212.10**

Anschutz 1907 Standard Match Rifle

Same action as Model 1913 but with 7/8" diameter 26" barrel (stainless or blue). Length is 44.5" overall, weighs 10.5 lbs. Choice of stock configurations. Vented forend. Designed for prone and position shooting ISU requirements; suitable for NRA matches. Also available with walnut flat-forend stock for benchrest shooting. Imported from Germany by Accuracy International, Gunsmithing, Inc.
Price: Right-hand, blue, no sights,
hardwood stock . . . . **$1,253.40 to $1,299.00**
Price: Right-hand, blue, no sights, colored laminated
stock . . . . **$1,316.10 to $1,375.00**
Price: Right-hand, blue, no sights, walnut stock. **$1,521.10**
Price: Left-hand, blue barrel, no sights, walnut stock. **$1,584.60**

RIFLES

Anschutz 1907

Armalite AR-10 (T)

Bushmaster XM15

ARMALITE AR-10 (T) RIFLE

Caliber: 308, 10-shot magazine. **Barrel:** 24" target-weight Rock 5R custom. **Weight:** 10.4 lbs. **Length:** 43.5" overall. **Stock:** Green or black compostion; N.M. fiberglass handguard tube. **Sights:** Detachable handle, front sight, or scope mount available. Comes with international-style flattop receiver with Picatinny rail. **Features:** National Match two-stage trigger. Forged upper receiver. Receivers hard-coat anodized. Introduced 1995. Made in U.S.A. by ArmaLite, Inc.

Price: Green $2,075.00
Price: Black $2,090.00
Price: AR-10 (T) Carbine, lighter 16" barrel, single stage trigger,
   weighs 8.8 lbs. Green $1,970.00
Price: Black $1,985.00

ARMALITE M15A4 (T) EAGLE EYE RIFLE

Caliber: 223, 7-shot magazine. **Barrel:** 24" heavy stainless; 1:8" twist. **Weight:** 9.2 lbs. **Length:** 42-3/8" overall. **Stock:** Green or black butt, N.M. fiberglass handguard tube. **Sights:** One-piece international-style flattop receiver with Weaver-type rail, including case deflector. **Features:** Detachable carry handle, front sight and scope mount (30mm or 1") available. Upper and lower receivers have push-type pivot pin, hard coat anodized. Made in U.S.A. by ArmaLite, Inc.

Price: Green $1,378.00
Price: Black $1,393.00

ARMALITE M15A4 ACTION MASTER RIFLE

Caliber: 223, 7-shot magazine. **Barrel:** 20" heavy stainless; 1:9" twist. **Weight:** 9 lbs. **Length:** 40-1/2" overall. **Stock:** Green or black plastic; N.M. fiberglass handguard tube. **Sights:** One-piece international-style flattop receiver with Weaver-type rail. **Features:** Detachable carry handle, front sight and scope mount available. National Match two-stage trigger group; Picatinny rail; upper and lower receivers have push-type pivot pin; hard coat anodized finish. Made in U.S.A. by ArmaLite, Inc.

Price: $1,175.00

BLASER R93 LONG RANGE RIFLE

Caliber: 308 Win., 10-shot detachable box magazine. **Barrel:** 24". **Weight:** 10.4 lbs. **Length:** 44" overall. **Stock:** Aluminum with synthetic lining. **Sights:** None furnished; accepts detachable scope mount. **Features:** Straight-pull bolt action with adjustable trigger; fully adjustable stock; quick takedown; corrosion resistant finish. Introduced 1998. Imported from Germany by Sigarms.

Price: $2,360.00

BUSHMASTER XM15 E2S TARGET MODEL RIFLE

Caliber: 223. **Barrel:** 20", 24"; 1:9" twist; heavy. **Weight:** 8.3 lbs. **Length:** 38.25" overall (20" barrel). **Stock:** Black composition; A2 type. **Sights:** Adjustable post front, adjustable aperture rear. **Features:** Patterned after Colt M-16A2. Chrome-lined barrel with manganese phosphate exterior. Forged aluminum receivers with push-pin takedown. Available in stainless barrel and camo stock versions. Made in U.S.A. by Bushmaster Firearms Co.

Price: 20" match heavy barrel (A2 type) $965.00
Price: (A3 type) $1,095.00

BUSHMASTER DCM COMPETITION RIFLE

Similar to the XM15 E2S Target Model except has 20" extra-heavy (1" diameter) barrel with 1.8" twist for heavier competition bullets. Weighs about 12 lbs. with balance weights. Has special competition rear sight with interchangeable apertures, extra-fine 1/2- or 1/4-MOA windage and elevation adjustments; specially ground front sight post in choice of three widths. Full-length handguards over free-floater barrel tube. Introduced 1998. Made in U.S.A. by Bushmaster Firearms, Inc.

Price: $1,495.00

Bushmaster DCM

Bushmaster XM15 E2S V-Match Carbine

Colt Accurized

Colt Match Target HBAR

Colt Match Target HBAR II

BUSHMASTER XM15 E2S V-MATCH RIFLE
Caliber: 223. **Barrel:** 20", 24""; 1:9" twist; heavy. **Weight:** 8.1 lbs. **Length:** 38.25" overall (20" barrel). **Stock:** Black composition. A2 type. **Sights:** None furnished; upper receiver has integral scope mount base. **Features:** Chrome-lined .950" heavy barrel with counter-bored crown, manganese phosphate finish, free-floating aluminum handguard, forged aluminum receivers with push-pin takedown, hard anodized mil-spec finish. Competition trigger optional. Made in U.S.A. by Bushmaster Firearms, Inc.
Price: 20" Match heavy barrel **$1,055.00**
Price: 24" Match heavy barrel **$1,065.00**
Price: V-Match Carbine (16" barrel) **$1,045.00**

COLT MATCH TARGET MODEL RIFLE
Caliber: 223 Rem., 8-shot magazine. **Barrel:** 20". **Weight:** 7.5 lbs. **Length:** 39" overall. **Stock:** Composition stock, grip, forend. **Sights:** Post front, aperture rear adjustable for windage and elevation. **Features:** Five-round detachable box magazine, standard-weight barrel, sling swivels. Has forward bolt assist. Military matte black finish. Model introduced 1991.
Price: **$1,144.00**
Price: With compensator **$1,150.00**

Colt Accurized Rifle
Similar to the Colt Match Target Model except has 24" stainless steel heavy barrel with 1.9" rifling, flattop receiver with scope mount and 1" rings, weighs 9.25 lbs. Introduced 1998. Made in U.S.A. by Colt's Mfg. Co., Inc.
Price: **$1,424.00**

Colt Match Target HBAR Rifle
Similar to the Target Model except has heavy barrel, 800-meter rear sight adjustable for windage and elevation. Introduced 1991.
Price: **$1,194.00**

Colt Match Target Competition HBAR Rifle
Similar to the Sporter Target except has flat-top receiver with integral Weaver-type base for scope mounting. Counter-bored muzzle, 1:9" rifling twist. Introduced 1991.
Price: Model R6700 . . . . **$1,199.00**

Colt Match Target Competition HBAR II Rifle
Similar to the Match Target Competition HBAR except has 16:1" barrel, weighs 7.1 lbs., overall length 34.5"; 1:9" twist barrel. Introduced 1995.
Price: **$1,172.00**

EAA/IZHMASH URAL 5.1

EAA/IZHMASH Biathlon

EAA/IZHMASH Biathlon Target

Ed Brown Model 702 Light Tactical

Ed Brown Model 702 Tactical

EAA/HW 660 MATCH RIFLE
Caliber: 22 LR. **Barrel:** 26". **Weight:** 10.7 lbs. **Length:** 45.3" overall. **Stock:** Match-type walnut with adjustable cheekpiece and buttplate. **Sights:** Globe front, match aperture rear. **Features:** Adjustable match trigger; stippled pistol grip and forend; forend accessory rail. Introduced 1991. Imported from Germany by European American Armory.
Price: About **$999.00**
Price: With laminate stock **$1,159.00**

EAA/IZHMASH URAL 5.1 TARGET RIFLE
Caliber: 22 LR. **Barrel:** 26.5". **Weight:** 11.3 lbs. **Length:** 44.5". **Stock:** Wood, international style. **Sights:** Adjustable click rear, hooded front with inserts. **Features:** Forged barrel with rifling, adjustable trigger, aluminum rail for accessories, hooked adjustable butt plate. Adjustable comb, adjustable large palm rest. Hand stippling on grip area.
Price: . . . . **NA**

EAA/Izhmash Biathlon Target Rifle
Similar to URAL with addition of snow covers for barrel and sights, stock holding extra mags, round trigger block. Unique bolt utilizes toggle action.

Designed to compete in 40 meter biathlon event. 22 LR, 19.5" bbl.
Price: **$979.00**

EAA/Izhmash Biathalon Basic Target Rifle
Same action as Biathlon but designed for plinking or fun. Beech stock, heavy barrel with Weaver rail for scope mount. 22 LR, 19.5" bbl.
Price: **$339.00**

ED BROWN MODEL 702 LIGHT TACTICAL
Caliber: 223, 308. **Barrel:** 21". **Weight:** 8.75 lbs. **Stock:** Fully glass-bedded fiberglass with recoil pad. Wide varmint-style forend. **Sights:** None furnished. Talley scope mounts utilizing heavy duty 8-40 screws. **Features:** Compact and super accurate, it is ideal for police, military and varmint hunters.
Price: From **$2,800.00**

ED BROWN MODEL 702 TACTICAL
Caliber: 308, 300 Win. Mag. **Barrel:** 26". **Weight:** 11.25 lbs. **Stock:** Hand bedded McMillan A-3 fiberglass tactical stock with recoil pad. **Sights:** None furnished. Leupold Mark 4 30mm scope mounts utilizing heavy-duty 8-40 screws. **Features:** Custom short or long action, steel trigger guard, hinged floor plate, additional caliber available.
Price: From **$2,900.00**

Ed Brown 702

Harris Gunworks Long Range

Harris Gunworks M-86

ED BROWN MODEL 702, M40A2 MARINE SNIPER

Caliber: 308 Win., 30-06 Springfield. **Barrel:** Match-grade 24". **Weight:** 9.25 lbs. **Stock:** Hand bedded McMillan GP fiberglass tactical stock with recoil pad in special Woodland Camo molded-in colors. **Sights:** None furnished. Leupold Mark 4 30mm scope mounts with heavy-duty 8-40 screws. **Features:** Steel trigger guard, hinged floor plate, three position safety. Left-hand model available.
Price: From **$2,900.00**

HARRIS GUNWORKS NATIONAL MATCH RIFLE

Caliber: 7mm-08, 308, 5-shot magazine. **Barrel:** 24", stainless steel. **Weight:** About 11 lbs. (std. bbl.). **Length:** 43" overall. **Stock:** Fiberglass with adjustable buttplate. **Sights:** Barrel band and Tompkins front; no rear sight furnished. **Features:** Gunworks repeating action with clip slot, Canjar trigger. Match-grade barrel. Available in right-hand only. Fiberglass stock, sight installation, special machining and triggers optional. Introduced 1989. From Harris Gunworks, Inc.
Price: **$3,500.00**

HARRIS GUNWORKS LONG RANGE RIFLE

Caliber: 300 Win. Mag., 7mm Rem. Mag., 300 Phoenix, 338 Lapua, single shot. **Barrel:** 26", stainless steel, match-grade. **Weight:** 14 lbs. **Length:** 46-1/2" overall. **Stock:** Fiberglass with adjustable buttplate and cheekpiece. Adjustable for length of pull, drop, cant and cast-off. **Sights:** Barrel band and Tompkins front; no rear sight furnished. **Features:** Uses Gunworks solid bottom single shot action and Canjar trigger. Barrel twist 1:12". Introduced 1989. From Harris Gunworks, Inc.
Price: **$3,620.00**

HARRIS GUNWORKS M-86 SNIPER RIFLE

Caliber: 308, 30-06, 4-shot magazine; 300 Win. Mag., 3-shot magazine. **Barrel:** 24", Gunworks match-grade in heavy contour. **Weight:** 11-1/4 lbs. (308), 11-1/2 lbs. (30-06, 300). **Length:** 43-1/2" overall. **Stock:** Specially designed McHale fiberglass stock with textured grip and forend, recoil pad. **Sights:** None furnished. **Features:** Uses Gunworks repeating action. Comes with bipod. Matte black finish. Sling swivels. Introduced 1989. From Harris Gunworks, Inc.
Price: **$2,700.00**

HARRIS GUNWORKS M-89 SNIPER RIFLE

Caliber: 308 Win., 5-shot magazine. **Barrel:** 28" (with suppressor). **Weight:** 15 lbs., 4 oz. **Stock:** Fiberglass; adjustable for length; recoil pad. **Sights:** None furnished. Drilled and tapped for scope mounting. **Features:** Uses Gunworks repeating action. Comes with bipod. Introduced 1990. From Harris Gunworks, Inc.
Price: Standard (non-suppressed) **$3,200.00**

HARRIS GUNWORKS
COMBO M-87 SERIES 50-CALIBER RIFLES

Caliber: 50 BMG, single shot. **Barrel:** 29, with muzzle brake. **Weight:** About 21-1/2 lbs. **Length:** 53" overall. **Stock:** Gunworks fiberglass. **Sights:** None furnished. **Features:** Right-handed Gunworks stainless steel receiver, chrome-moly barrel with 1:15" twist. Introduced 1987. From Harris Gunworks, Inc.
Price: **$3,885.00**
Price: M87R 5-shot repeater **$4,000.00**
Price: M-87 (5-shot repeater) "Combo" **$4,300.00**
Price: M-92 Bullpup (shortened M-87 single shot with bullpup stock) **$4,770.00**
Price: M-93 (10-shot repeater with folding stock, detachable magazine) **$4,150.00**

OLYMPIC ARMS PCR-SERVICEMATCH RIFLE

Caliber: 223, 10-shot magazine. **Barrel:** 20", broach-cut 416 stainless steel. **Weight:** About 10 lbs. **Length:** 39.5" overall. **Stock:** A2 stowaway grip and trapdoor buttstock. **Sights:** Post front, E2-NM fully adjustable aperture rear. **Features:** Based on the AR-15. Conforms to all DCM standards. Free-floating 1:8.5" or 1:10" barrel; crowned barrel; no bayonet lug. Introduced 1996. Made in U.S.A. by Olympic Arms, Inc.
Price: $1,062.00

OLYMPIC ARMS PCR-1 RIFLE

Caliber: 223, 10-shot magazine. **Barrel:** 20", 24"; 416 stainless steel. **Weight:** 10 lbs., 3 oz. **Length:** 38.25" overall with 20" barrel. **Stock:** A2 stowaway grip and trapdoor butt. **Sights:** None supplied; flattop upper receiver, cut-down front sight base. **Features:** Based on the AR-15 rifle. Broach-cut, free-floating barrel with 1:8.5" or 1:10" twist. No bayonet lug. Crowned barrel; fluting available. Introduced 1994. Made in U.S.A. by Olympic Arms, Inc.
Price: $1,038.00

RIFLES

Remington 40-XB Rangemaster

Remington 40-XC KS

Springfield, Inc. M1A Super Match

Springfield, Inc. M1A/M-21

RIFLES

Olympic Arms PCR-2, PCR-3 Rifles

Similar to the PCR-1 except has 16" barrel, weighs 8 lbs., 2 oz.; has post front sight, fully adjustable aperture rear. Model PCR-3 has flattop upper receiver, cut-down front sight base. Introduced 1994. Made in U.S.A. by Olympic Arms, Inc.

Price: **$958.00**

REMINGTON 40-XB RANGEMASTER TARGET CENTERFIRE

Caliber: 15 calibers from 220 Swift to 300 Win. Mag. **Barrel:** 27-1/4". **Weight:** 11-1/4 lbs. **Length:** 47" overall. **Stock:** American walnut, laminated thumbhole or Kevlar with high comb and beavertail forend stop. Rubber non-slip buttplate. **Sights:** None. Scope blocks installed. **Features:** Adjustable trigger. Stainless barrel and action. Receiver drilled and tapped for sights.

Price: Standard single shot. . $1,636.00 (right-hand), $1,761.00 (left-hand)
Price: Repeater. **$1,734.00**

REMINGTON 40-XBBR KS

Caliber: Five calibers from 22 BR to 308 Win. **Barrel:** 20" (light varmint class), 24" (heavy varmint class). **Weight:** 7-1/4 lbs. (light varmint class); 12 lbs. (heavy varmint class). **Length:** 38" (20" bbl.), 42" (24" bbl.). **Stock:** Aramid fiber. **Sights:** None. Supplied with scope blocks. **Features:** Unblued benchmaster with stainless steel barrel, trigger adjustable from 1-1/2 lbs. to 3-1/2 lbs. Special 2-oz. trigger extra cost. Scope and mounts extra.

Price: Single shot **$1,876.00**

REMINGTON 40-XC KS TARGET RIFLE

Caliber: 7.62 NATO, 5-shot. **Barrel:** 24", stainless steel. **Weight:** 11 lbs. without sights. **Length:** 43-1/2" overall. **Stock:** Aramid fiber. **Sights:** None furnished. **Features:** Designed to meet the needs of competitive shooters. Stainless steel barrel and action.

Price: **$1,821.00**

REMINGTON 40-XR CUSTOM SPORTER

Caliber: 22 LR, 22 WM. **Features:** Model XR-40 Target rifle action with craftsmanship of Model 700 Custom. Many options available.
Price: Single shot **$3,383.00**

SAKO TRG-22 BOLT-ACTION RIFLE

Caliber: 308 Win., 10-shot magazine. **Barrel:** 26". **Weight:** 10-1/4 lbs. **Length:** 45-1/4" overall. **Stock:** Reinforced polyurethane with fully adjustable cheekpiece and buttplate. **Sights:** None furnished. Optional quick-detachable, one-piece scope mount base, 1" or 30mm rings. **Features:** Resistance-free bolt, free-floating heavy stainless barrel, 60-degree bolt lift. Two-stage trigger is adjustable for length, pull, horizontal or vertical pitch. Introduced 2000. Imported from Finland by Beretta USA.

Price: Green **$2,898.00**
Price: Model TRG-42, as above except in 338 Lapua Mag or 300 Win. Mag. **$2,829.00**
Price: Green (new) **$3,243.00**

SPRINGFIELD, INC. M1A SUPER MATCH

Caliber: 308 Win. **Barrel:** 22", heavy Douglas Premium. **Weight:** About 11 lbs. **Length:** 44.31" overall. **Stock:** Heavy walnut competition stock with longer pistol grip, contoured area behind the rear sight, thicker butt and forend, glass bedded. **Sights:** National Match front and rear. **Features:** Has figure-eight-style operating rod guide. Introduced 1987. From Springfield, Inc.

Price: About **$2,479.00**

Springfield, Inc. M1A/M-21 Tactical Model Rifle

Similar to M1A Super Match except special sniper stock with adjustable cheekpiece and rubber recoil pad. Weighs 11.6 lbs. From Springfield, Inc.
Price: **$2,975.00**

SPRINGFIELD, INC. M-1 GARAND AMERICAN COMBAT RIFLES

Caliber: 30-06, 308 Win., 8-shot. **Barrel:** 24". **Weight:** 9.5 lbs. **Length:** 43.6". **Stock:** American walnut. **Sights:** Military square post front, military aperture, MOA adjustable rear. **Features:** Limited production, certificate of authenticity, all new receiver, barrel and stock wtih remaining parts USGI mil-spec. 2-stage military trigger.

Price: About **$2,479.00**

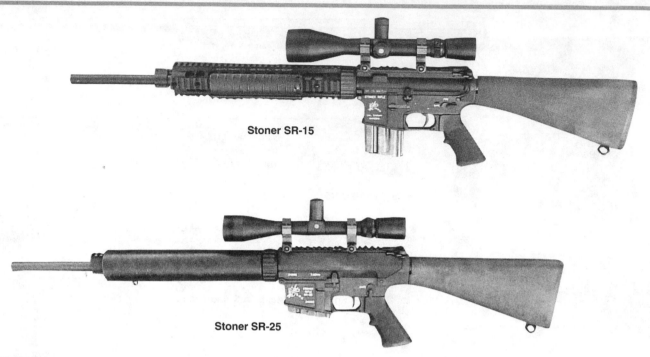

Stoner SR-15

Stoner SR-25

STONER SR-15 MATCH RIFLE

Caliber: 223. **Barrel:** 20". **Weight:** 7.9 lbs. **Length:** 38" overall. **Stock:** Black synthetic. **Sights:** None furnished; flat-top upper receiver for scope mounting. **Features:** Short Picatinny rail, two-stage match trigger. Introduced 1998. Made in U.S.A. by Knight's Mfg.Co.
Price: **$1,650.00**

STONER SR-25 MATCH RIFLE

Caliber: 7.62 NATO, 10-shot steel magazine, 5-shot optional. **Barrel:** 24" heavy match; 1:11.25" twist. **Weight:** 10.75 lbs. **Length:** 44" overall. **Stock:** Black synthetic AR-15A2 design. Full floating forend of Mil-spec synthetic attaches to upper receiver at a single point. **Sights:** None furnished. Has integral Weaver-style rail. Rings and iron sights optional. **Features:** Improved AR-15 trigger, AR-15-style seven-lug rotating bolt. Gas block rail mounts detachable front sight. Introduced 1993. Made in U.S.A. by Knight's Mfg. Co.
Price: **$3,345.00**
Price: SR-25 Lightweight Match (20" medium match target contour barrel, 9.5 lbs., 40" overall) **$3,345.00**

TANNER 50 METER FREE RIFLE

Caliber: 22 LR, single shot. **Barrel:** 27.7". **Weight:** 13.9 lbs. **Length:** 44.4" overall. **Stock:** Seasoned walnut with palm rest, accessory rail, adjustable hook buttplate. **Sights:** Globe front with interchangeable inserts, Tanner micrometer-diopter rear with adjustable aperture. **Features:** Bolt action with externally adjustable set trigger. Supplied with 50-meter test target. Imported from Switzerland by Mandall Shooting Supplies. Introduced 1984.
Price: About **$3,900.00**

TANNER STANDARD UIT RIFLE

Caliber: 308, 7.5mm Swiss, 10-shot. **Barrel:** 25.9". **Weight:** 10.5 lbs. **Length:** 40.6" overall. **Stock:** Match style of seasoned nutwood with accessory rail; coarsely stippled pistol grip; high cheekpiece; vented forend. **Sights:** Globe front with interchangeable inserts, Tanner micrometer-diopter rear with adjustable aperture. **Features:** Two locking lug revolving bolt encloses case head. Trigger adjustable from 1/2 to 6-1/2 lbs., match trigger optional. Comes with 300-meter test target. Imported from Switzerland by Mandall Shooting Supplies. Introduced 1984.
Price: About **$4,700.00**

TANNER 300 METER FREE RIFLE

Caliber: 308 Win., 7.5 Swiss, single shot. **Barrel:** 27.58". **Weight:** 15 lbs. **Length:** 45.3" overall. **Stock:** Seasoned walnut, thumbhole style, with accessory rail, palm rest, adjustable hook butt. **Sights:** Globe front with interchangeable inserts, Tanner-design micrometer-diopter rear with adjustable aperture. **Features:** Three-lug revolving-lock bolt design, adjustable set trigger; short firing pin travel, supplied with 300-meter test target. Imported from Switzerland by Mandall Shooting Supplies. Introduced 1984.
Price: About **$4,900.00**

TIKKA TARGET RIFLE

Caliber: 223, 22-250, 308, detachable 5-shot magazine. **Barrel:** 23-1/2" heavy. **Weight:** 9 lbs. **Length:** 43-5/8" overall. **Stock:** European walnut with adjustable comb, adjustable buttplate; stippled grip and forend. **Sights:** None furnished; drilled and tapped for scope mounting. **Features:** Buttplate adjustable for distance, angle, height and pitch, adjustable trigger, free-floating barrel. Introduced 1998. Imported from Finland by Beretta USA.
Price: **$950.00**

RIFLES

SHOTGUNS — AUTOLOADERS

Includes a wide variety of sporting guns and guns suitable for various competitions.

Benelli Legacy

Benelli M1 Field Camouflage

Benelli Super Black Eagle

BENELLI LEGACY SHOTGUN
Gauge: 12, 20, 2-3/4" and 3" chamber. **Barrel:** 24", 26", 28" (Full, Mod., Imp. Cyl., Imp. Mod., cylinder choke tubes). Mid-bead sight. **Weight:** 5.8 to 7.6 lbs. **Length:** 49-5/8" overall (28" barrel). **Stock:** Select European walnut with satin finish. **Features:** Uses the rotating bolt inertia recoil operating system with a two-piece steel/aluminum etched receiver (bright on lower, blue upper). Drop adjustment kit allows the stock to be custom fitted without modifying the stock. Introduced 1998. Imported from Italy by Benelli USA, Corp.
Price: **$1,400.00**

Benelli Sport II Shotgun
Similar to the Legacy model except has dual tone blue/silver receiver, two carbon fiber interchangeable ventilated ribs, adjustable butt pad, adjustable buttstock, and functions with ultra-light target loads. Walnut stock with satin finish. Introduced 1997. Imported from Italy by Benelli U.S.A.
Price: **$1,400.00**

BENELLI M1 FIELD SHOTGUN
Gauge: 12, 20 ga. **Barrel:** 21", 24", 26", 28". **Weight:** 7 lbs., 4 oz. **Stock:** High impact polymer; wood on 26", 28". **Sights:** Red bar. **Features:** Sporting version of the military & police gun. Uses the rotating Montefeltro bolt system. Ventilated rib; blue finish. Comes with set of five choke tubes. Imported from Italy by Benelli U.S.A.
Price: . . . (Synthetic) **$985.00**; (Wood) **$1,000.00**; (Timber HD) **$1,085.00**
Price: 24" rifled barrel . . . . . (Synthetic) **$1,060.00**; Timber HD **$1,165.00**
Price: Synthetic stock, left-hand version (24", 26", 28" brls.) . . **$1,005.00**
Price: Timber HD camo left-hand, 21", 24" barrel **$1,105.00**
Price: MI Field Steadygrip **$1,175.00**

Benelli Montefeltro Shotgun
Similar to the M1 Super except has checkered walnut stock with satin finish. Uses the Montefeltro rotating bolt system with a simple inertia recoil design. Full, Imp. Mod., Mod., Imp. Cyl. choke tubes, 12 and 20 ga. Weighs 6.8-7.1 lbs. Finish is blue. Introduced 1987.
Price: 24", 26", 28" **$1,005.00**
Price: Left-hand, 26", 28" **$1,020.00**

BENELLI SUPER BLACK EAGLE SHOTGUN
Gauge: 12, 3-1/2" chamber. **Barrel:** 24", 26", 28" (Cyl. Imp. Cyl., Mod., Imp. Mod., Full choke tubes). **Weight:** 7 lbs., 5 oz. **Length:** 49-5/8" overall (28"

barrel). **Stock:** European walnut with satin finish, or polymer. Adjustable for drop. **Sights:** Red bar front. **Features:** Uses Montefeltro inertia recoil bolt system. Fires all 12 gauge shells from 2-3/4" to 3-1/2" magnums, vent rib. Introduced 1991. Imported from Italy by Benelli U.S.A.
Price: With 26" and 28" barrel, wood stock **$1,300.00**
Price: Timber HD Camo 24", 26", 28" barrel **$1,385.00**
Price: With 24", 26" and 28" barrel, polymer stock. **$1,290.00**
Price: Left-hand, 24", 26", 28", polymer stock **$1,345.00**
Price: Left-hand, 24", 26", 28", camo stock **$1,435.00**
Price: Steadygrip Turkey Gun **$1,465.00**

Benelli Super Black Eagle Slug Gun
Similar to the Benelli Super Black Eagle except has 24" rifled barrel with 2-3/4" and 3" chamber, drilled and tapped for scope. Uses the inertia recoil bolt system. Matte-finish receiver. Weight is 7.5 lbs., overall length 45.5". Wood or polymer stocks available. Introduced 1992. Imported from Italy by Benelli U.S.A.
Price: With wood stock. **$1,345.00**
Price: With polymer stock. **$1,335.00**
Price: 24" barrel, Timber HD Camo **$1,460.00**

Benelli Executive Series Shotguns
Similar to the Legacy except has grayed steel lower receiver, hand-engraved and gold inlaid (Grade III), and has highest grade of walnut stock with drop adjustment kit. Barrel lengths 26" or 28"; 2-3/4" and 3" chamber. Special order only. Introduced 1995. Imported from Italy by Benelli U.S.A.
Price: Grade I (engraved game scenes) **$5,465.00**
Price: Grade II (game scenes with scroll engraving) **$6,135.00**
Price: Grade III (full coverage, gold inlays) **$7,065.00**

BERETTA AL391 URIKA AUTO SHOTGUNS
Gauge: 12, 20 gauge; 3" chamber. **Barrel:** 22", 24", 26", 28", 30"; five Mobilchoke choke tubes. **Weight:** 5.95 to 7.28 lbs. **Length:** Varies by model. **Stock:** Walnut, black or camo synthetic; shims, spacers and interchangeable recoil pads allow custom fit. **Features:** Self-compensating gas operation handles full range of loads; recoil reducer in receiver; enlarged trigger guard; reduced-weight receiver, barrel and forend; hard-chromed bore. Introduced 2000. Imported from Italy by Beretta USA.
Price: AL391 Urika (12 ga., 26", 28", 30" barrels) **$1,017.00**
Price: AL391 Urika (20 ga., 24", 26", 28" barrels) **$1,017.00**
Price: AL391 Urika Synthetic (12 ga., 24", 26", 28", 30" barrels) **$991.00**
Price: AL391 Urika Camo. (12 ga., Realtree Hardwoods
or Advantage Wetlands) **$1,108.00**

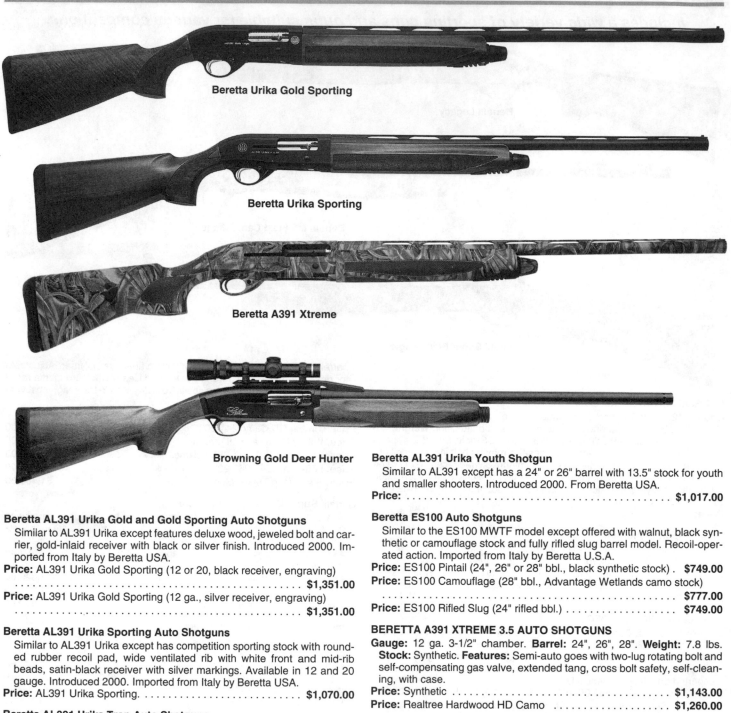

Beretta Urika Gold Sporting

Beretta Urika Sporting

Beretta A391 Xtreme

Browning Gold Deer Hunter

Beretta AL391 Urika Gold and Gold Sporting Auto Shotguns

Similar to AL391 Urika except features deluxe wood, jeweled bolt and carrier, gold-inlaid receiver with black or silver finish. Introduced 2000. Imported from Italy by Beretta USA.
Price: AL391 Urika Gold Sporting (12 or 20, black receiver, engraving)
.... **$1,351.00**
Price: AL391 Urika Gold Sporting (12 ga., silver receiver, engraving)
.... **$1,351.00**

Beretta AL391 Urika Sporting Auto Shotguns

Similar to AL391 Urika except has competition sporting stock with rounded rubber recoil pad, wide ventilated rib with white front and mid-rib beads, satin-black receiver with silver markings. Available in 12 and 20 gauge. Introduced 2000. Imported from Italy by Beretta USA.
Price: AL391 Urika Sporting. **$1,070.00**

Beretta AL391 Urika Trap Auto Shotguns

Similar to AL391 Urika except in 12 ga. only, has wide ventilated rib with white front and mid-rib beads, Monte Carlo stock and special trap recoil pad. Gold Trap features highly figured walnut stock and forend, gold-filled Beretta logo and signature on receiver. Optima bore and Optima choke tubes. Introduced 2000. Imported from Italy by Beretta USA.
Price: AL391 Urika Trap **$1,070.00**

Beretta AL391 Urika Parallel Target RL and SL Auto Shotguns

Similar to AL391 Urika except has parallel-comb, Monte Carlo stock with tighter grip radius to reduce trigger reach and stepped ventilated rib. SL model has same features but with 13.5" length of pull stock. Introduced 2000. Imported from Italy by Beretta USA.
Price: AL391 Urika Parallel Target RL **$1,070.00**
Price: AL391 Urika Parallel Target SL **$1,070.00**

Beretta AL391 Urika Youth Shotgun

Similar to AL391 except has a 24" or 26" barrel with 13.5" stock for youth and smaller shooters. Introduced 2000. From Beretta USA.
Price: **$1,017.00**

Beretta ES100 Auto Shotguns

Similar to the ES100 MWTF model except offered with walnut, black synthetic or camouflage stock and fully rifled slug barrel model. Recoil-operated action. Imported from Italy by Beretta U.S.A.
Price: ES100 Pintail (24", 26" or 28" bbl., black synthetic stock) . **$749.00**
Price: ES100 Camouflage (28" bbl., Advantage Wetlands camo stock)
.... **$777.00**
Price: ES100 Rifled Slug (24" rifled bbl.) **$749.00**

BERETTA A391 XTREME 3.5 AUTO SHOTGUNS

Gauge: 12 ga. 3-1/2" chamber. **Barrel:** 24", 26", 28". **Weight:** 7.8 lbs. **Stock:** Synthetic. **Features:** Semi-auto goes with two-lug rotating bolt and self-compensating gas valve, extended tang, cross bolt safety, self-cleaning, with case.
Price: Synthetic **$1,143.00**
Price: Realtree Hardwood HD Camo **$1,260.00**

BROWNING GOLD HUNTER AUTO SHOTGUN

Gauge: 12, 3" or 3-1/2" chamber; 20, 3" chamber. **Barrel:** 12 ga.—26", 28", 30", Invector Plus choke tubes; 20 ga.—26", 30", Invector choke tubes. **Weight:** 7 lbs., 9 oz. (12 ga.), 6 lbs., 12 oz. (20 ga.). **Length:** 46-1/4" overall (20 ga., 26" barrel). **Stock:** 14"x1-1/2"x2-1/3"; select walnut with gloss finish; palm swell grip. **Features:** Self-regulating, self-cleaning gas system shoots all loads; lightweight receiver with special non-glare deep black finish; large reversible safety button; large rounded trigger guard, gold trigger. The 20 gauge has slightly smaller dimensions; 12 gauge have back-bored barrels, Invector Plus tube system. Introduced 1994. Imported by Browning.
Price: 12 or 20 gauge, 3" chamber. **$894.00**
Price: 12 ga., 3-1/2" chamber. **$1,038.00**
Price: Extra barrels. .... **$336.00 to $415.00**

Browning Gold Sporting Golden Clays

Browning NWTF Mossy Oak Break-Up

Browning Gold Classic Stalker

Browning Gold Fusion

Browning Gold Rifled Deer Hunter Auto Shotgun

Similar to the Gold Hunter except 12 or 20 gauge, 22" rifled barrel with cantilever scope mount, walnut stock with extra-thick recoil pad. Weighs 7 lbs., 12 oz., overall length 42-1/2". Sling swivel studs fitted on the magazine cap and butt. Introduced 1997. Imported by Browning.

Price: 12 gauge **$887.00**
Price: With Mossy Oak Break-up camouflage **$1,046.00**
Price: 20 ga. (satin-finish walnut stock, 3" chamber) **$987.00**

Browning Gold Deer Stalker

Similar to the Gold Deer Hunter except has black composite stock and forend, fully rifled barrel, cantilever scope mount. Introduced 1999. Imported by Browning.

Price: 12 gauge **$967.00**

Browning Gold Sporting Clays Auto

Similar to the Gold Hunter except 12 gauge only with 28" or 30" barrel; front Hi-Viz Pro-Comp and center bead on tapered ventilated rib; ported and back-bored Invector Plus barrel; 2-3/4" chamber; satin-finished stock with solid, radiused recoil pad with hard heel insert; non-glare black alloy receiver has "Sporting Clays" inscribed in gold. Introduced 1996. Imported from Japan by Browning.

Price: **$984.00**

Browning Gold Sporting Golden Clays

Similar to the Sporting Clays except has silvered receiver with gold engraving, high grade wood. Introduced 1999. Imported by Browning.

Price: **$1,457.00**

Browning Gold Ladies/Youth Sporting Clays Auto

Similar to the Gold Sporting Clays except has stock dimensions of 14-1/4"x1-3/4"x2" for women and younger shooters. Introduced 1999. Imported by Browning.

Price: **$920.00**

Browning Gold Micro Auto Shotgun

Similar to the Gold Hunter except has a 26" barrel, 13-7/8" pull length and smaller pistol grip for youths and other small shooters. Weighs 6 lbs., 10 oz. Introduced 2001. From Browning.

Price: **$894.00**

Browning Gold Stalker Auto Shotguns

Similar to the Gold Hunter except has black composite stock and forend. Choice of 3" or 3-1/2" chamber.

Price: 12 ga. with 3" chamber. **$856.00**
Price: With 3-1/2" chamber. **$1,002.00**

Browning Gold Mossy Oak® Shadow Grass Shotguns

Similar to the Gold Hunter except 12 gauge only, completely covered with Mossy Oak® Shadow Grass camouflage. Choice of 3" or 3-1/2" chamber and 26" or 28" barrel. Introduced 1999. Imported by Browning.

Price: 12 ga. 3" chamber **$967.00**
Price: 12 ga., 3-1/2" chamber. **$1,146.00**

Browning Gold Mossy Oak® Break-Up Shotguns

Similar to the Gold Hunter except 12 gauge only, completely covered with Mossy Oak® Break-Up camouflage. Imported by Browning.

Price: 3" chamber. **$1,069.00**
Price: 3-1/2" chamber. **$1,282.00**
Price: NWTF model, 3" chamber, 24" bbl. with Hi-Viz sight **$998.00**
Price: NWTF model, 3-1/2" chamber, 24" bbl. with Hi-Viz sight . **$1,177.00**
Price: Gold Rifled Deer (22" rifled bbl., Cantilever scope mount) **$1,046.00**

Browning Gold Classic Hunter Auto Shotgun

Similar to the Gold Hunter 3" except has semi-hump back receiver, magazine cut-off, adjustable comb, and satin-finish wood. Introduced 1999. Imported by Browning.

Price: 12 or 20 gauge. **$912.00**
Price: Classic High Grade (silvered, gold engraved receiver, high-grade wood) **$1,750.00**

Browning Gold Classic Stalker

Similar to the Gold Classic Hunter except has adjustable composite stock and forend. Introduced 1999. Imported by Browning.

Price: **$856.00**

SHOTGUNS — AUTOLOADERS

Browning Gold Waterfowl

Browning Gold Light 10 Gauge

EAA/Baikal MP-153

Browning Gold Fusion™ Auto Shotgun

Similar to the Gold Hunter except is 1/2 lb. lighter, has a new-style vent rib, adjustable comb system, Hi-Viz Pro-Comp front sight and five choke tubes. Offered with 26", 28" or 30" barrel, 12 gauge, 3" chamber only. Includes hard case. Introduced 2001. Imported by Browning.
Price: **$1,005.00**

Browning NWTF Gold Turkey Stalker

Similar to the Gold Hunter except 12 ga., 3" chamber only, has 24" barrel with Hi-Viz front sight and National Wild Turkey Federation logo on stock. Imported by Browning.
Price: **$876.00**

Browning Gold Turkey/Waterfowl Camo Shotgun

Similar to the Gold Turkey/Waterfowl Hunter except 12 gauge only, 3" or 3-1/2" chamber, 24" barrel with extra-full turkey choke tube, Hi-Viz front sight. Completely covered with Mossy Oak Break-Up camouflage. Introduced 1999. Imported by Browning.
Price: **$929.00**
Price: Turkey/Waterfowl Stalker (black stock and metal) **$949.00**

Browning Gold NWTF Turkey Series Camo Shotgun

Similar to the Gold Turkey/Waterfowl model except 10- or 12-gauge (3" or 3-1/2" chamber), 24" barrel with extra-full choke tube, Hi-Viz fiber-optic sights and complete gun coverage in Mossy Oak Break-Up camouflage with National Wild Turkey Federation logo on stock. Introduced 2001. From Browning.
Price: 10 gauge **$1,249.00**
Price: 12 gauge, 3-1/2" chamber **$1,177.00**
Price: 12 gauge, 3" chamber **$998.00**

Browning Gold Upland Special Auto Shotgun

Similar to the Gold Classic Hunter except has straight-grip walnut stock, 12 or 20 gauge, 3" chamber. Introduced 2001. From Browning
Price: 12-gauge model (24" bbl., weighs 7 lbs.) **$912.00**
Price: 20-gauge model (26" bbl., weighs 6 lbs., 12 oz.) **$912.00**

BROWNING GOLD 10 AUTO SHOTGUN

Gauge: 10, 3-1/2" chamber, 5-shot magazine. **Barrel:** 26", 28", 30" (Imp. Cyl., Mod., Full standard Invector). **Weight:** 10 lbs. 7 oz. (28" barrel). **Stock:** 14-3/8"x1-1/2"x2-3/8". Select walnut with gloss finish, cut checkering, recoil pad. **Features:** Short-stroke, gas-operated action, cross-bolt safety. Forged steel receiver with polished blue finish. Introduced 1993. Imported by Browning.
Price: **$1,007.95**
Price: Extra barrel. **$293.00**

Browning Gold 10 Gauge Auto Combo

Similar to the Gold 10 except comes with 24" and 26" barrels with Imp. Cyl., Mod., Full Invector choke tubes. Introduced 1999. Imported by Browning.
Price: **$1,059.00**

Browning Gold Light 10 Gauge Auto Shotgun

Similar to the Browning Gold 10, except has an alloy receiver that is 1 lb. lighter than standard model. Offered in 26" or 28" bbls. With Mossy Oak Break-Up or Shadow Grass coverage; 5-shot magazine. Weighs 9 lbs., 10 oz. (28" bbl.). Introduced 2001. Imported by Browning.
Price: **$1,224.00**
Price: Gold Light 10 Stalker (black composite stock and forearm)
. . . . **$1,155.00**

DIAMOND SEMI-AUTO SHOTGUNS

Gauge: 12 ga., 2-3/4" and 3" chambers. **Barrel:** 20"-30". **Stock:** Walnut, synthetic. **Features:** One-piece receiver, rotary butt, gas ejection, high strength steel. Gold, Silver Marine, Elite and Panther series with vented barrels and all but Silver have 3 chokes. Slug guns available, all but Panther with sights. Imported from Istanbul by Adco Sales, Inc.
Price: Gold, 28", walnut **$549.00**
Price: Gold, 28", synthetic **$499.00**
Price: Gold Slug, 24", w/sights, walnut **$549.00**
Price: Gold Slug, 24", w/sights, synthetic **$499.00**
Price: Silver Mariner, 22", synthetic **$499.00**
Price: Silver Mariner, 20" slug w/sights, synthetic **$479.00**
Price: Elite, 22" Slug, 24"-28", walnut. . . . . **$429.00 to $449.00**
Price: Panther, 22" slug; 26", 28", vent rin w/3 chokes,
synthetic . . . . **$379.00 to $399.00**
Price: Imperial12, 20 ga., 24" slug w/sights, 26",
28" vent rib w/3 chokes, walnut . . . . **$479.00 to $499.00**
Price: Imperial, 12 ga., 28" vent rib w/3 chokes,
3.5" chamber, walnut **$499.00**

EAA/BAIKAL MP-153 AUTO SHOTGUN

Gauge: 12, 3-1/2" chamber. **Barrel:** 18-1/2", 20", 24", 26", 28"; imp., mod. and full choke tubes. **Weight:** 7.8 lbs. **Stock:** Walnut. **Features:** Gas-operated action with automatic gas-adjustment valve allows use of light and heavy loads interchangeably; 4-round magazine; rubber recoil pad. Introduced 2000. Imported by European American Armory.
Price: MP-153 (blued finish, walnut stock and forend) **$509.00**
Price: MP-153 (field grade, synthetic stock) **$419.00**

EAA/SAIGA AUTO SHOTGUN

Gauge: 12, 20, 410, 3" chamber. **Barrel:** 19", 21", 22". **Weight:** 6.6-7.6 lbs. **Length:** 40"-45". **Stock:** Synthetic. **Features:** Retains best features of the AK Rifle by Kalashnikov as the semi-auto shotgun. Magazine fed. Imported from Russia by EAA Corp.
Price: 410 ga. **$239.00**
Price: 20 ga. **$389.00**
Price: 12 ga. . . . . **$429.00 to $469.00**

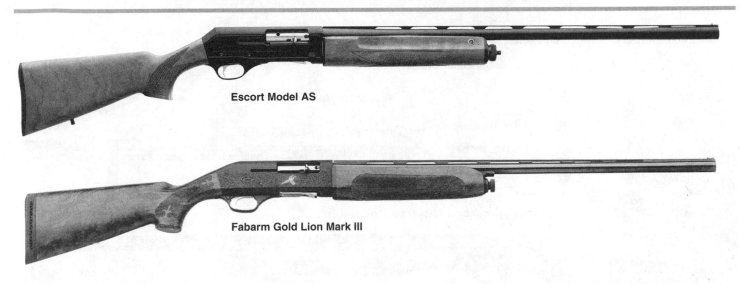

Escort Model AS

Fabarm Gold Lion Mark III

ESCORT AUTO SHOTGUN

Gauge: 12. **Barrel:** 28" (choke tubes, M, IM, F); 3" chambers. **Weight:** 7 lbs. **Stock:** Turkish walnut, checkered pistol grip and forend. **Features:** Aluminum-alloy receiver, blued finish, chrome-plated bolt, adjustment for normal and magnum loads. Gold-plated trigger, trigger-guard safety, magazine cut-off. Tree choke tubes and wrench, two stock-adjustment shims, waterfowl plug, 7-shot magazine extender. Introduced 2002. Camo model introduced 2003. Imported from Turkey by Legacy Sports International.

Price: **$386.00**
Price: Model PS, black polymer stock **$364.00**
Price: Camo with HiViz sights. **$479.00**

FABARM GOLD LION MARK III AUTO SHOTGUN

Gauge: 12, 3" chamber. **Barrel:** 24", 26", 28", choke tubes. **Weight:** 7 lbs. **Length:** 45.5" overall. **Stock:** European walnut with gloss finish; olive wood grip cap. **Features:** TriBore barrel, reversible safety; gold-plated trigger and carrier release button; leather-covered rubber recoil pad. Introduced 1998. Imported from Italy by Heckler & Koch, Inc.

Price: **$939.00**

Fabarm Sporting Clays Extra Auto Shotgun

Similar to Gold Lion except 28" TriBore ported barrel with interchangeable colored front-sight beads, mid-rib bead, 10mm channeled vent rib, carbon-fiber finish, oil-finished walnut stock and forend with olive wood grip-cap. Stock dimensions are 14.58"x1.58"x2.44". Distinctive gold-colored receiver logo. Available in 12 gauge only, 3" chamber. Introduced 1999. Imported from Italy by Heckler & Koch, Inc.

Price: **$1,249.00**

FRANCHI 48AL SHOTGUN

Gauge: 20 or 28, 2-3/4" chamber. **Barrel:** 24", 26", 28" (Full, cyl., mod., choke tubes). **Weight:** 5.5 lbs. (20 gauge). **Length:** 44"-48.". **Stock:** 14-1/4"x1-5/ 8"x2-1/2". Walnut with checkered grip and forend. **Features:** Long recoil-operated action. Chrome-lined bore; cross-bolt safety. Imported from Italy by Benelli U.S.A.

Price: 20 ga. **$715.00**
Price: 28 ga. **$825.00**

Franchi 48AL Deluxe Shotgun

Similar to 48AL but with select walnut stock and forend and high-polish blue finish with gold trigger. Introduced 2000.

Price: (20 gauge, 26" barrel) **$940.00**
Price: (28 gauge, 26" barrel) **$990.00**

Franchi 48AL English

Similar to 48AL Deluxe but with straight grip "English style" stock. 20 ga., 28 ga., 26" bbl, ICMF tubes.

Price: 20 gauge **$940.00**
Price: 28 gauge **$990.00**

Franchi 48AL Short Stock Shotgun

Similar to 48AL but with stock shortened to 12-1/2" length of pull.

Price: (20 gauge, 26" barrel) **$715.00**

FRANCHI 612 AND 620 SHOTGUNS

Gauge: 12, 20, 3" chamber. **Barrel:** 24", 26", 28", IC, MF tubes. **Weight:** 7 lbs. **Stock:** European walnut, synthetic and Timber HD. **Features:** Alloy frame with matte black finish; gas-operated with Vario System, four-lug rotating bolt. Introduced 1996. Imported from Italy by Benelli U.S.A.

Price: Walnut wood **$750.00**
Price: Camo, Timber HD **$875.00**
Price: Synthetic (black synthetic stock, forend) **$710.00**
Price: 20 ga., 24", 26", 28", walnut. **$750.00**
Price: Variopress 620 (Timber HD Camo) **$875.00**

Franchi 612 Defense Shotgun

Similar to 612 except has 18-1/2", cylinder-bore barrel with black, synthetic stock. Available in 12 gauge, 3" chamber only. Weighs 6-1/2 lbs. 2-shot magazine extension available. Introduced 2000.

Price: **$635.00**

Franchi 612 Sporting Shotgun

Similar to 612 except has 30" ported barrel to reduce muzzle jump. Available in 12 gauge, 3" chamber only. Introduced 2000.

Price: **$1,275.00**

Franchi 620 Short Stock Shotgun

Similar to 620 but with stock shortened to 12-1/2" length of pull for smaller shooters. Introduced 2000.

Price: (20 gauge, 26" barrel) **$730.00**

FRANCHI MODEL 912

Gauge: 12. **Barrel:** 24", 26", 28", 30". **Weight:** 7.5 to 7.8lbs. **Length:** 46" to 52". **Stock:** Satin walnut; synthetic. **Sights:** White bead, front. **Features:** Chambered for 3-1/2" magnum shells with Dual-Recoil-Reduction-System, multi-lugged rotary bolt. Made in Italy and imported by Benelli USA.

Price: (Walnut) .... **$1,000.00**; (Synthetic) **$940.00**
Price: Timber HD Camo **$1,050.00**

Remington Model 11-87 Premier

Remington Model 11-87 Dale Earnhardt Tribute

Remington Model 11-87 Special Purpose Magnum

Remington Model 11-87 SPS Camo

Remington Model 11-87 SPS-T Turkey Camo

REMINGTON MODEL 11-87 PREMIER SHOTGUN

Gauge: 12, 20, 3" chamber. **Barrel:** 26", 28", 30" Rem Choke tubes. Light Contour barrel. **Weight:** About 7-3/4 lbs. **Length:** 46" overall (26" bbl.). **Stock:** Walnut with satin or high-gloss finish; cut checkering; solid brown buttpad; no white spacers. **Sights:** Bradley-type white-faced front, metal bead middle. **Features:** Pressure compensating gas system allows shooting 2-3/4" or 3" loads interchangeably with no adjustments. Stainless magazine tube; redesigned feed latch, barrel support ring on operating bars; pinned forend. Introduced 1987.

Price: Light contour barrel **$777.00**
Price: Left-hand, 28" barrel **$831.00**
Price: Premier cantilever deer barrel, fully-rifled, 21" sling, swivels, Monte Carlo stock **$859.00**
Price: 3-1/2" Super Magnum, 28" barrel **$865.00**
Price: Dale Earnhardt Tribute, 12 ga., 28" barrel **$972.00**

Remington Model 11-87 Special Purpose Magnum

Similar to the 11-87 Premier except has dull stock finish, Parkerized exposed metal surfaces. Bolt and carrier have dull blackened coloring. Comes with 26" or 28" barrel with Rem Chokes, padded Cordura nylon sling and quick detachable swivels. Introduced 1987.

Price: With synthetic stock and forend (SPS) **$791.00**

Remington Model 11-87 SPS Special Purpose Synthetic Camo

Similar to the 11-87 Special Purpose Magnum except has synthetic stock and all metal (except bolt and trigger guard) and stock covered with

Mossy Oak Break-Up camo finish. In 12 gauge only, 26", Rem Choke. Comes with camo sling, swivels. Introduced 1992.

Price: **$905.00**

Remington Model 11-87 SPS-T Turkey Camo

Similar to the 11-87 Special Purpose Magnum except with synthetic stock, 21" vent. rib barrel with Rem Choke tube. Completely covered with Mossy Oak Break-Up Brown camouflage. Bolt body, trigger guard and recoil pad are non-reflective black.

Price: **$905.00**
Price: Model 11-87 SPS-T Camo CL cantilever **$907.00**

Remington Model 11-87 SPS-T Super Magnum Synthetic Camo

Similar to the 11-87 SPS-T Turkey Camo except has 23" vent rib barrel with Turkey Super full choke tube, chambered for 12 ga., 3-1/2", TruGlo rifle sights. Version available without TruGlo sights. Introduced 2001.

Price: **$963.00**

Remington Model 11-87 SPS-Deer Shotgun

Similar to the 11-87 Special Purpose Camo except has fully-rifled 21" barrel with rifle sights, black non-reflective, synthetic stock and forend, black carrying sling. Introduced 1993.

Price: **$824.00**
Price: With wood stock (Model 11-87 SP Deer Gun) Rem choke, 21" barrel w/rifle sights **$756.00**

Remington Model 11-87 SPS-T Synthetic Camo

Remington Model 11-87 SPS-Deer

Remington Model 11-87 SPS Cantilever

Remington Model 11-87 SP

Remington Model 1100 Youth Turkey Camo

Remington Model 11-87 SPS Cantilever Shotgun

Similar to the 11-87 SPS except has fully rifled barrel; synthetic stock with Monte Carlo comb; cantilever scope mount deer barrel. Comes with sling and swivels. Introduced 1994.

Price: **$872.00**

Remington Model 11-87 SP and SPS Super Magnum Shotguns

Similar to Model 11-87 Special Purpose Magnum except has 3-1/2" chamber. Available in flat-finish American walnut or black synthetic stock, 26" or 28" black-matte finished barrel and receiver; imp. cyl., modified and full Rem Choke tubes. Overall length 45-3/4", weighs 8 lbs., 2 oz. Introduced 2000. From Remington Arms Co.

Price: 11-87 SP Super Magnum (walnut stock) **$865.00**
Price: 11-87 SPS Super Magnum (synthetic stock) **$879.00**
Price: 11-87 SPS Super Magnum, 28" (camo) **$963.00**

Remington Model 11-87 Upland Special Shotgun

Similar to 11-87 Premier except has 23" ventilated rib barrel with straight-grip, English-style walnut stock. Available in 12 or 20 gauge. Overall length 43-1/2", weighs 7-1/4 lbs. (6-1/2 lbs. in 20 ga.). Comes with imp. cyl., modified and full choke tubes. Introduced 2000.

Price: 12 or 20 gauge **$777.00**

REMINGTON MODEL 1100 SYNTHETIC LT-20 SHOTGUN

Gauge: 20. **Barrel:** 26" Rem Chokes. **Weight:** 6-3/4 lbs. **Stock:** 14"x1-1/2"x2-1/2". Black synthetic, checkered pistol grip and forend. **Features:** Matted receiver top with scroll work on both sides of receiver.

Price: **$549.00**
Price: Youth Gun LT-20 (21" Rem Choke) **$549.00**
Price: Remington Model 1100 Synthetic, 12 gauge, black synthetic stock; vent. rib 28" barrel, Mod. Rem Choke tube. Weighs about 7-1/2 lbs. Introduced 1996.. .... **$549.00**

Remington Model 1100 Youth Synthetic Turkey Camo

Similar to the Model 1100 LT-20 except has 1" shorter stock, 21" vent rib barrel with Full Rem Choke tube; 3" chamber; synthetic stock and forend are covered with Skyline Excel camo, and barrel and receiver have non-reflective, black matte finish. Introduced 2003.

Price: **$612.00**

Remington Model 1100 LT-20 Synthetic Deer Shotgun

Similar to the Model 1100 LT-20 except has 21" fully rifled barrel with rifle sights, 2-3/4" chamber, and fiberglass-reinforced synthetic stock. Introduced 1997. Made in U.S. by Remington.

Price: **$583.00**

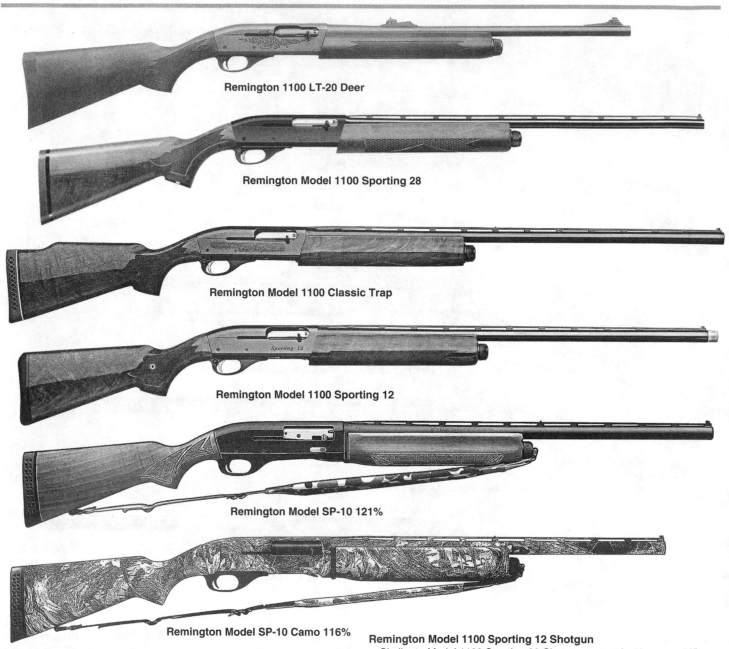

Remington 1100 LT-20 Deer

Remington Model 1100 Sporting 28

Remington Model 1100 Classic Trap

Remington Model 1100 Sporting 12

Remington Model SP-10 121%

Remington Model SP-10 Camo 116%

Remington Model 1100 Sporting 28

Similar to the 1100 LT-20 except in 28 gauge with 25" barrel; comes with Skeet, Imp. Cyl., Light Mod., Mod. Rem Choke tube. Semi-Fancy walnut with gloss finish, Sporting rubber butt pad. Made in U.S. by Remington. Introduced 1996.
Price: **$868.00**

Remington Model 1100 Sporting 20 Shotgun

Similar to Model 1100 LT-20 except tournament-grade American walnut stock with gloss finish and sporting-style recoil pad, 28" Rem choke barrel for Skeet, Imp. Cyl., Light Modified and Modified. Introduced 1998.
Price: **$868.00**

Remington Model 1100 Classic Trap Shotgun

Similar to Standard Model 1100 except 12 gauge with 30", low-profile barrel, semi-fancy American walnut stock, high-polish blued receiver with engraving and gold eagle inlay. Singles, mid handicap and long handicap choke tubes. Overall length 50-1/2", weighs 8 lbs., 4 oz. Introduced 2000. From Remington Arms Co.
Price: **$895.00**

Remington Model 1100 Sporting 12 Shotgun

Similar to Model 1100 Sporting 20 Shotgun except in 12 gauge, 28" ventilated barrel with semi-fancy American walnut stock, gold-plated trigger. Overall length 49", weighs 8 lbs. Introduced 2000. From Remington Arms Co.
Price: **$868.00**

Remington Model 1100 Synthetic Deer Shotgun

Similar to Model 1100 LT-20 except 12 gauge, 21" fully rifled barrel with cantilever scope mount and fiberglass-reinforced synthetic stock with Monte Carlo comb. Introduced 1997. Made in U.S. by Remington.
Price: **$629.00**

REMINGTON MODEL SP-10 MAGNUM SHOTGUN

Gauge: 10, 3-1/2" chamber, 2-shot magazine. **Barrel:** 26", 30" (full and mod. Rem chokes). **Weight:** 10-3/4 to 11 lbs. **Length:** 47-1/2" overall (26" barrel). **Stock:** Walnut with satin finish or black synthetic with 26" barrel. Checkered grip and forend. **Sights:** Twin bead. **Features:** Stainless steel gas system with moving cylinder; 3/8" ventilated rib. Receiver and barrel have matte finish. Brown recoil pad. Comes with padded Cordura nylon sling. Introduced 1989.
Price: **$1,317.00**

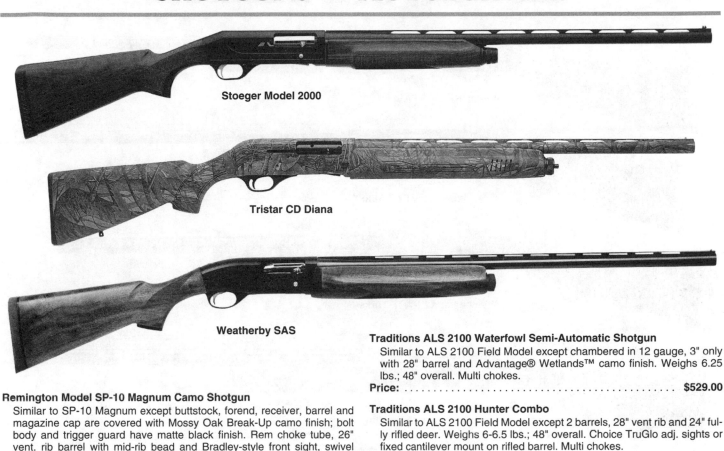

Stoeger Model 2000

Tristar CD Diana

Weatherby SAS

Remington Model SP-10 Magnum Camo Shotgun

Similar to SP-10 Magnum except buttstock, forend, receiver, barrel and magazine cap are covered with Mossy Oak Break-Up camo finish; bolt body and trigger guard have matte black finish. Rem choke tube, 26" vent. rib barrel with mid-rib bead and Bradley-style front sight, swivel studs and quick-detachable swivels, non-slip Cordura carrying sling in same camo pattern. Introduced 1993.

Price: **$1,453.00**

SARSILMAZ SEMI-AUTOMATIC SHOTGUN

Gauge: 12, 3" chamber. **Barrel:** 26" or 28"; fixed chokes. **Stock:** Walnut or synthetic. **Features:** Handles 2-3/4" or 3" magnum loads. Introduced 2000. Imported from Turkey by Armsport Inc.

Price: With walnut stock **$969.95**
Price: With synthetic stock **$919.95**

STOEGER MODEL 2000

Gauge: 12, 3" chamber, set of 5 choke tubes. **Barrel:** 24", 26", 28", 30". **Stock:** Walnut, deluxe, synthetic, and Timber HD. **Sights:** White bar. **Features:** Inertia-recoil for light target to turkey leads. Single trigger combo 26"/24" pack with optional 24" slug barrel.

Price: Walnut, 26", 28", 30" bbl. **$499.00**
Price: Synthetic, 24", 26", 28" bbl. **$480.00**
Price: Synthetic combo, 26"/24" bbl. **$560.00**
Price: Optional slug bbl., 26" **$105.00**
Price: Timber HD, 24", 26", 28" bbl. **$550.00**

TRADITIONS ALS 2100 SERIES SEMI-AUTOMATIC SHOTGUNS

Gauge: 12, 3" chamber; 20, 3" chamber. **Barrel:** 24", 26", 28" (imp. cyl., mod. and full choke tubes). **Weight:** 5 lbs., 10 oz. to 6 lbs., 5 oz. **Length:** 44" to 48" overall. **Stock:** Walnut or black composite. **Features:** Gas-operated; vent-rib barrelwith Beretta-style threaded muzzle. Introduced 2001 by Traditions.

Price: (12 or 20 ga., 26" or 28" barrel, walnut stock) **$479.00**
Price: (12 or 20 ga., 24" barrel Youth Model, walnut stock) **$479.00**
Price: (12 or 20 ga., 26" or 28" barrel, composite stock) **$459.00**

Traditions ALS 2100 Turkey Semi-Automatic Shotgun

Similar to ALS 2100 Field Model except chambered in 12 gauge, 3" only with 26" barrel and Mossy Oak® Break Up™ camo finish. Weighs 6 lbs., 46" overall.

Price: **$519.00**

Traditions ALS 2100 Waterfowl Semi-Automatic Shotgun

Similar to ALS 2100 Field Model except chambered in 12 gauge, 3" only with 28" barrel and Advantage® Wetlands™ camo finish. Weighs 6.25 lbs.; 48" overall. Multi chokes.

Price: **$529.00**

Traditions ALS 2100 Hunter Combo

Similar to ALS 2100 Field Model except 2 barrels, 28" vent rib and 24" fully rifled deer. Weighs 6-6.5 lbs.; 48" overall. Choice TruGlo adj. sights or fixed cantilever mount on rifled barrel. Multi chokes.

Price: Walnut, rifle barrel **$609.00**
Price: Walnut, cantilever **$629.00**
Price: Synthetic **$579.00**

Traditions ALS 2100 Slug Hunter

Similar to ALS 2100 Field Model, 12 ga., 24" barrel, overall length 44", weighs 6.25 lbs. Designed specifically for the deer hunter. Rifled barrel has 1 in 36" twist. Fully adjustable sights are fiber optic.

Price: Walnut, rifle barrel **$529.00**
Price: Synthetic, rifle barrel **$499.00**
Price: Walnut, cantilever. **$549.00**
Price: Synthetic, cantilever **$529.00**

Traditions ALS 2100 Home Security

Similar to ALS 2100 Field Model, 12 ga., 20" barrel, overall length 40", weighs 6 lbs. Can be reloaded with one hand while shouldered and on-target. Swivel studs installed in stock.

Price: **$399.00**

TRISTAR CD DIANA AUTO SHOTGUNS

Gauge: 12, shoots 2-3/4" or 3" interchangeably. **Barrel:** 24", 26", 28" (Imp. Cyl., Mod., Full choke tubes). **Stock:** European walnut or black synthetic. **Features:** Gas-operated action; blued barrel; checkered pistol grip and forend; vent rib barrel. Available with synthetic and camo stock and in slug model. First introduced 1999 under the name "Tristar Phantom." Imported by Tristar Sporting Arms Ltd.

Price: . . . . **$399.00 to $576.00**

VERONA MODEL SX400 SEMI AUTO SHOTGUN

Gauge: 12. **Barrel:** 26", 30". **Weight:** 6-1/2 lbs. **Stock:** Walnut, black composite. **Sights:** Red dot. **Features:** Aluminum receivers, gas-operated, 2-3/4" or 3" Magnum shells without adj. or mod., 4 screw-in chokes and wrench included. Sling swivels, gold trigger. Blued barrel. Imported from Italy by B.C. Outdoors.

Price: 401S, 12 ga. **$398.40**
Price: 405SDS, 12 ga. **$610.00**
Price: 405L, 12 ga. **$331.20**

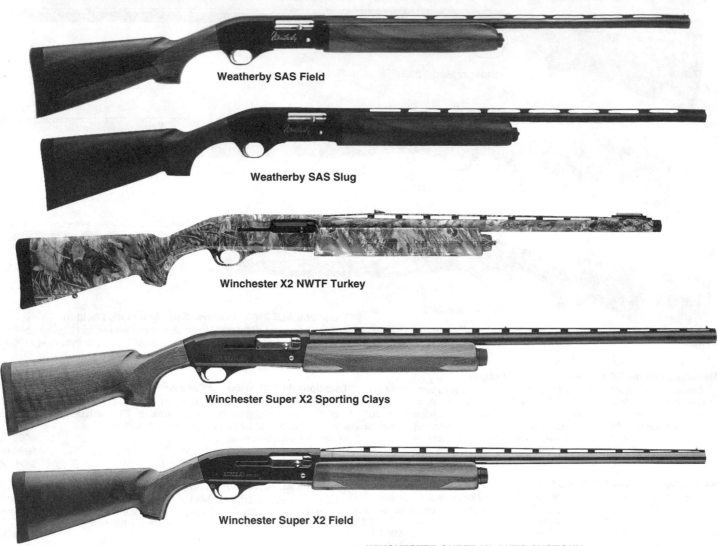

Weatherby SAS Field

Weatherby SAS Slug

Winchester X2 NWTF Turkey

Winchester Super X2 Sporting Clays

Winchester Super X2 Field

WEATHERBY SAS AUTO SHOTGUN

Gauge: 12, 2-3/4" or 3" chamber. **Barrel:** 26", 28" (20 ga.); 26", 28", 30" (12 ga.); Briley Multi-Choke tubes. **Weight:** 6-3/4 to 7-3/4 lbs. **Stock:** 14-1/4"x2-1/ 4"x1-1/2". Claro walnut; black, Shadow Grass or Mossy Oak Break-Up camo synthetic. **Features:** Alloy receiver with matte finish; gold-plated trigger; magazine cut-off. Introduced 1999. Imported by Weatherby.

Price: 12 or 20 ga. (walnut stock) **$945.00**
Price: 12 or 20 ga. (black synthetic stock) **$979.00**
Price: 12 ga. (camo stock) **$1,115.00**

WEATHERBY SAS (SEMI-AUTOMATIC SHOTGUNS)

6 Models: SAS Field, SAS Sporting Clays, SAS Shadow Grass, SAS Break-Up, SAS Synthetic and a Slug Gun.
Gauge: 12 ga. **Barrel:** Vent ribbed, 24"-30". **Stock:** SAS Field and Sporting Clays, walnut. SAS Shadow Grass, Break-Up, Synthetic, composite. **Sights:** SAS Sporting Clays, frass front and mid-point back. SAS Shadow Grass and Break-Up, HiViz front and brass mid. Synthetic has brass front. **Features:** Easy to shoot, load, clean, lightweight, lessened recoil, IMC system includes 3 chrome moly screw-in choke tubes. Slug gun has 22" rifled barrel with matte blue finish and cantilever base for scope mounting.
Price: . . . .**$649.00 to 749.00**

WINCHESTER SUPER X2 AUTO SHOTGUN

Gauge: 12, 3", 3-1/2" chamber. **Barrel:** 24", 26", 28"; Invector Plus choke tubes. **Weight:** 7-1/4 to 7-1/2 lbs. **Stock:** 14-1/4"x1-3/4"x2". Walnut or black synthetic. **Features:** Gas-operated action shoots all loads without adjustment; vent. rib barrels; 4-shot magazine. Introduced 1999. Made in U.S. by U.S. Repeating Arms Co.

Price: Field, walnut or synthetic stock, 3" **$819.00**
Price: Magnum, 3-1/2", synthetic stock, 26" or 28" bbl. **$936.00**
Price: Camo Waterfowl, 3-1/2", Mossy Oak Shadow Grass. . . . **$1,080.00**
Price: NWTF Turkey, 3-1/2", black synthetic stock, 24" bbl. **$997.00**
Price: NWTF Turkey, 3-1/2", Mossy Oak Break-Up camo **$1,080.00**

Winchester Super X2 Sporting Clays Auto Shotgun

Similar to the Super X2 except has two gas pistons (one for target loads, one for heavy 3" loads), adjustable comb system and high-post rib. Back-bored barrel with Invector Plus choke tubes. Offered in 28" and 30" barrels. Introduced 2001. From U.S. Repeating Arms Co.
Price: Super X2 Sporting Clays **$1,206.00**

Winchester Super X2 Field 3" Auto Shotgun

Similar to the Super X2 except has a 3" chamber, walnut stock and fore-arm and high-profile rib. Back-bored barrel and Invector Plus choke tubes. Introduced 2001. From U.S. Repeating Arms Co.
Price: Super X2 Field 3", 26" or 28" bbl.. . . . . **$819.00**

Includes a wide variety of sporting guns and guns suitable for competitive shooting.

Armscor M-30F Field

Benelli Nova Pump

Benelli Nova Pump Slug

Browning BPS 10 gauge

Browning BPS 10 gauge Mossy Oak® Shadow Grass

SHOTGUNS

ARMSCOR M-30F FIELD PUMP SHOTGUN
Gauge: 12, 3" chamber. **Barrel:** 28" fixed Mod., or with Mod. and Full choke tubes. **Weight:** 7.6 lbs. **Stock:** Walnut-finished hardwood. **Features:** Double action slide bars; blued steel receiver; damascened bolt. Introduced 1996. Imported from the Philippines by K.B.I., Inc.
Price: With fixed choke **$239.00**
Price: With choke tubes **$269.00**

BENELLI NOVA PUMP SHOTGUN
Gauge: 12, 20. **Barrel:** 24", 26", 28". **Stock:** Synthetic, X-tra Brown 12 ga., Timber HD 20 ga. **Sights:** Red bar. **Features:** 2-3/4", 3" chamber (3-2/1" 12 ga. only). Montefeltro rotating bolt design with dual action bars, magazine cut-off, synthetic trigger assembly, 4-shot magazine. Introduced 1999. Imported from Italy by Benelli USA.
Price: Synthetic **$335.00**
Price: Timber HD **$400.00**

Benelli Nova Pump Slug Gun
Similar to the Nova except has 18.5" barrel with adjustable rifle-type or ghost ring sights; weighs 7.2 lbs.; black synthetic stock. Introduced 1999. Imported from Italy by Benelli USA.
Price: With rifle sights **$355.00**
Price: With ghost-ring sights **$395.00**

Benelli Nova Pump Rifled Slug Gun
Similar to Nova Pump Slug Gun except has 24" barrel and rifled bore; open rifle sights; synthetic stock; weighs 8.1 pounds.
Price: . . . . (Synthetic) **$500.00**; Timber HD **$575.00**

BROWNING BPS PUMP SHOTGUN
Gauge: 10, 12, 3-1/2" chamber; 12 or 20, 3" chamber (2-3/4" in target guns), 28, 2-3/4" chamber, 5-shot magazine, 410 ga., 3" chamber. **Barrel:**

10 ga.— 24" Buck Special, 28", 30", 32" Invector; 12, 20 ga.—22", 24", 26", 28", 30", 32" (Imp. Cyl., mod. or full). 410 ga.—26" barrel. (Imp. Cyl., mod. and full choke tubes.) Also available with Invector choke tubes, 12 or 20 ga.; Upland Special has 22" barrel with Invector tubes. BPS 3" and 3-1/2" have back-bored barrel. **Weight:** 7 lbs., 8 oz. (28" barrel). **Length:** 48-3/4" overall (28" barrel). **Stock:** 14-1/4"x1-1/2"x2-1/2". Select walnut, semi-beavertail forend, full pistol grip stock. **Features:** All 12 gauge 3" guns except Buck Special and game guns have back-bored barrels with Invector Plus choke tubes. Bottom feeding and ejection, receiver top safety, high post vent. rib. Double action bars eliminate binding. Vent. rib barrels only. All 12 and 20 gauge guns with 3" chamber available with fully engraved receiver flats at no extra cost. Each gauge has its own unique game scene. Introduced 1977. Imported from Japan by Browning.
Price: 12 ga., 3-1/2" Magnum Hunter, Invector Plus **$548.00**
Price: 12 ga., 3-1/2" Magnum Stalker (black syn. stock) **$548.00**
Price: 12, 20 ga., Hunter, Invector Plus **$464.00**
Price: 12 ga. Deer Hunter (22" rifled bbl., cantilever mount) **$568.00**
Price: 28 ga., Hunter, Invector **$495.00**
Price: 410 ga., Hunter, Invector **$495.00**

Browning BPS 10 Gauge Shotguns
Chambered for the 10 gauge, 3-1/2" load. Offered in 24", 26" and 28" barrels. Offered with walnut, black composite (Stalker models) or camouflage stock and forend. Introduced 1999. Imported by Browning.
Price: Hunter (walnut). **$548.00**
Price: Stalker (composite) **$548.00**
Price: Mossy Oak® Shadow Grass or Break-Up Camo. **$652.00**

Browning BPS 10 gauge Camo Pump
Similar to the BPS 10 gauge Hunter except completely covered with Mossy Oak Shadow Grass camouflage. Available with 24", 26", 28" barrel. Introduced 1999. Imported by Browning.
Price: **$652.00**

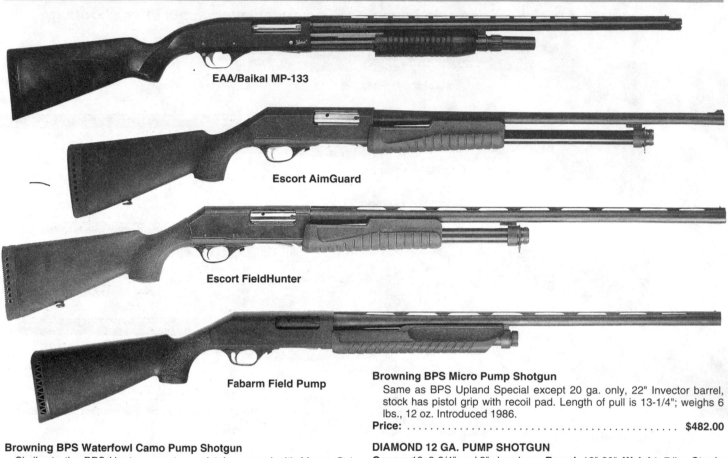

EAA/Baikal MP-133

Escort AimGuard

Escort FieldHunter

Fabarm Field Pump

Browning BPS Waterfowl Camo Pump Shotgun
Similar to the BPS Hunter except completely covered with Mossy Oak Shadow Grass camouflage. Available in 12 gauge, with 24", 26" or 28" barrel, 3" chamber. Introduced 1999. Imported by Browning.
Price: $652.00

Browning BPS Game Gun Deer Hunter
Similar to the standard BPS except has newly designed receiver/magazine tube/barrel mounting system to eliminate play, heavy 20.5" barrel with rifle-type sights with adjustable rear, solid receiver scope mount, "rifle" stock dimensions for scope or open sights, sling swivel studs. Gloss or matte finished wood with checkering, polished blue metal. Introduced 1992.
Price: $568.00

Browning BPS Game Gun Turkey Special
Similar to the standard BPS except has satin-finished walnut stock and dull-finished barrel and receiver. Receiver is drilled and tapped for scope mounting. Rifle-style stock dimensions and swivel studs. Has Extra-Full Turkey choke tube. Introduced 1992.
Price: $500.00

Browning BPS Stalker Pump Shotgun
Same gun as the standard BPS except all exposed metal parts have a matte blued finish and the stock has a durable black finish with a black recoil pad. Available in 10 ga. (3-1/2") and 12 ga. with 3" or 3-1/2" chamber, 22", 28", 30" barrel with Invector choke system. Introduced 1987.
Price: 12 ga., 3" chamber, Invector Plus $448.00
Price: 10, 12 ga., 3-1/2" chamber. $537.00

Browning BPS NWTF Turkey Series Pump Shotgun
Similar to the BPS Stalker except has full coverage Mossy Oak® Break-Up camo finish on synthetic stock, forearm and exposed metal parts. Offered in 10 and 12 gauge, 3" or 3-1/2" chamber; 24" bbl. has extra-full choke tube and Hi-Viz fiber optic sights. Introduced 2001. From Browning.
Price: 10 ga., 3-1/2" chamber. $637.00
Price: 12 ga., 3-1/2" chamber. $637.00
Price: 12 ga., 3" chamber $549.00

Browning BPS Micro Pump Shotgun
Same as BPS Upland Special except 20 ga. only, 22" Invector barrel, stock has pistol grip with recoil pad. Length of pull is 13-1/4"; weighs 6 lbs., 12 oz. Introduced 1986.
Price: $482.00

DIAMOND 12 GA. PUMP SHOTGUN
Gauge: 12, 2-3/4" and 3" chambers. **Barrel:** 18"-30". **Weight:** 7 lbs. **Stock:** Walnut, synthetic. **Features:** Aluminum one-piece receiver sculpted for lighter weight. Double locking on fixed bolt. Gold, Elite and Panther series with vented barrels and 3 chokes. All series slug guns available (Gold and Elite with sights). Imported from Istanbul by ADCO Sales.
Price: Gold, 28" vent rib w/3 chokes, walnut $359.00
Price: Gold, 28", synthetic $329.00
Price: Gold Slug, 24" w/sights, walnut or synthetic . . $329.00 to $359.00
Price: Silver Mariner 18.5" Slug, synthetic $399.00
Price: Silver Mariner 22" vent rib w/3 chokes $419.00
Price: Elite, 22" slug w/sights; 24", 28" ventib w/3 chokes,
walnut. . . . . $329.00 to $349.00
Price: Panther, 28", 30" ventib w/3 chokes, synthetic $279.00
Price: Panther,18.5", 22" Slug, synthetic . . . . $209.00 to $265.00
Price: Imperial 12 ga., 28" vent rib w/3 chokes, 3.5" chamber,
walnut $399.00

EAA/BAIKAL MP-133 PUMP SHOTGUN
Gauge: 12, 3-1/2" chamber. **Barrel:** 18-1/2", 20", 24", 26", 28"; imp., mod. and full choke tubes. **Weight:** NA. **Stock:** Walnut; checkered grip and grooved forearm. **Features:** Hammer-forged, chrome-lined barrel with ventilated rib; machined steel parts; dual action bars; trigger-block safety; 4-shot magazine tube; handles 2-3/4" through 3-1/2" shells. Introduced 2000. Imported by European American Armory.
Price: MP-133 (blued finish, walnut stock and forend) $329.00

ESCORT PUMP SHOTGUN
Gauge: 12, 3" chamber. **Barrel:** 20", fixed (AimGuard model); Multi (M, IC, F) (FieldHunter model). **Weight:** 6.4 to 7 lbs. **Stock:** Polymer. **Features:** AimGuard model has an included pistol grip accessory. FieldHunter has migratory bird magazine plug. Stock drop adjusting spacers included with both models. Mossy Oak camo stock available in FieldHunter. Introduced 2003. From Legacy Sports International.
Price: AimGuard $189.95
Price: FieldHunter . . . . $199.95 to $219.95

Ithaca Model 37 Waterfowl

Ithaca Model 37 Deerslayer II

Mossberg Model 835 Mossy Oak Camo

FABARM FIELD PUMP SHOTGUN

Gauge: 12, 3" chamber. **Barrel:** 28" (24" rifled slug barrel available). **Weight:** 76.6 lbs. **Length:** 48.25" overall. **Stock:** Polymer. **Features:** Similar to Fabarm FP6 Pump Shotgun. Alloy receiver; twin action bars; available in black or Mossy Oak Break-Up™ camo finish. Includes cyl., mod. and full choke tubes. Introduced 2001. Imported from Italy by Heckler & Koch Inc.

Price: Matte black finish $399.00
Price: Mossy Oak Break-Up™ finish $469.00

ITHACA MODEL 37 DELUXE PUMP SHOTGUN

Gauge: 12, 16, 20, 3" chamber. **Barrel:** 26", 28", 30" (12 gauge), 26", 28" (16 and 20 gauge), choke tubes. **Weight:** 7 lbs. **Stock:** Walnut with cut-checkered grip and forend. **Features:** Steel receiver; bottom ejection; brushed blue finish, vent rib barrels. Reintroduced 1996. Made in U.S. by Ithaca Gun Co.

Price: $633.00
Price: With straight English-style stock. $803.00
Price: Model 37 New Classic (ringtail forend, sunburst recoil pad, hand-finished walnut stock, 26" or 28" barrel) $803.00

ITHACA MODEL 37 WATERFOWL

Similar to Model 37 Deluxe except in 12 gauge only with 24", 26", or 30" barrel, special extended steel shot choke tube system. Complete coverage of Advantage Wetlands or Hardwoods camouflage. Introduced 1999. Made in U.S. by Ithaca Gun Co. Storm models have synthetic stock.

Price: . . . . $499.00 to $549.00

ITHACA MODEL 37 DEERSLAYER II PUMP SHOTGUN

Gauge: 12, 16, 20; 3" chamber. **Barrel:** 24", 26", fully rifled. **Weight:** 11 lbs. **Stock:** Cut-checkered American walnut with Monte Carlo comb. **Sights:** Rifle-type. **Features:** Integral barrel and receiver. Bottom ejection. Brushed blue finish. Reintroduced 1997. Made in U.S. by Ithaca Gun Co. Storm models have synthetic stock.

Price: $633.00
Price: Smooth Bore Deluxe $582.00
Price: Rifled Deluxe $582.00
Price: Storm $399.00

ITHACA MODEL 37 DEERSLAYER III PUMP SHOTGUN

Gauge: 12, 20, 2-3/4" and 3" chambers. **Barrel:** 26" free floated. **Weight:** 9 lbs. **Stock:** Monte Carlo laminate. **Sights:** Rifled. **Features:** Barrel length gives increased velocity. Trigger and sear set hand filed and stoned for creep free operation. Weaver-style scope base. Swivel studs. Matte blue.

Price: $900.00

ITHACA MODEL 37 RUFFED GROUSE SPECIAL EDITION

Gauge: 20 ga. **Barrel:** 22", 24", interchangeable choke tubes. **Weight:** 5.25 lbs. **Stock:** American black walnut. **Features:** Laser engraved stock with line art drawing. Bottom eject. Vent rib and English style. Right- or left-hand thru simple safety change. Aluminum receiver. Made in U.S.A. by Ithaca Gun Co.

Price: $840.00

ITHACA ELLETT SPECIAL MODEL 37 TURKEYSLAYER

Gauge: 12 ga., 3" chamber. **Barrel:** 22" ported. **Stock:** Composite. **Sights:** Fully adjustable, TruGlo front and rear. **Features:** Recreated from "Golden Age." Complete camo covering. Drilled and tapped. Extended turkey chokes. Matte metal, Realtree Hardwoods 20/200 or Advantage Timber patterns. Storm models are available in 12 or 20 gauge.

Price: $654.00
Price: Storm $459.00

ITHACA QUAD BORE MODEL 37 TURKEYSLAYER

Gauge: 20 ga. **Barrel:** 22" ported. **Weight:** 6.25 lbs. **Stock:** Black walnut stock and forend. **Sights:** Fully adjustable, TruGlo. **Features:** Sling swivel studs, matte blue, turkey full choke tube, 100% American made.

Price: $680.00

ITHACA MODEL 37 ULTRALIGHT DELUXE

Gauge: 16 ga. 2-3/4" chamber. **Barrel:** 24", 26", 28". **Weight:** 5.25 lbs. **Stock:** Standard deluxe. **Sights:** Raybar. **Features:** Vent rib, drilled and tapped, interchangeable barrel. F, M, IC choke tubes.

Price: Deluxe $649.00
Price: Classic/English $824.00
Price: Classic/Pistol $824.00

MOSSBERG MODEL 835 ULTI-MAG PUMP

Gauge: 12, 3-1/2" chamber. **Barrel:** Ported 24" rifled bore, 24", 28", Accu-Mag choke tubes for steel or lead shot. **Weight:** 7-3/4 lbs. **Length:** 48-1/2" overall. **Stock:** 14"x1-1/2"x2-1/2". Dual Comb. Cut-checkered hardwood or camo synthetic; both have recoil pad. **Sights:** White bead front, brass mid-bead; Fiber Optic. **Features:** Shoots 2-3/4", 3" or 3-1/2" shells. Back-bored and ported barrel to reduce recoil, improve patterns. Ambidextrous thumb safety, twin extractors, dual slide bars. Mossberg Cablelock included. Introduced 1988.

Price: 28" vent. rib, hardwood stock $370.00
Price: Combo, 24" rifled bore, rifle sights, 24" vent. rib, Accu-Mag Ulti-Full choke tube, Woodlands camo finish $572.00
Price: RealTree Camo Turkey, 24" vent. rib, Accu-Mag Extra-Full tube, synthetic stock. $525.00
Price: Mossy Oak Camo, 28" vent. rib, Accu-Mag tubes, synthetic stock $583.00
Price: OFM Camo, 28" vent. rib, Accu-Mag Mod. tube, synthetic stock $407.00

SHOTGUNS

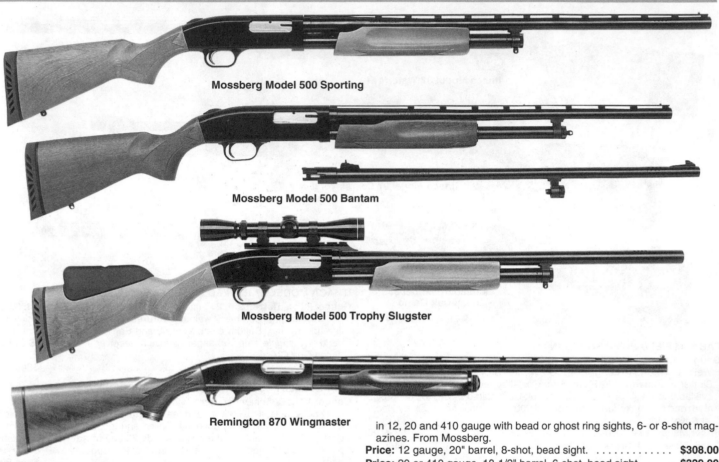

Mossberg Model 500 Sporting

Mossberg Model 500 Bantam

Mossberg Model 500 Trophy Slugster

Remington 870 Wingmaster

Mossberg Model 835 Synthetic Stock

Similar to the Model 835, except with 28" ported barrel with Accu-Mag Mod. choke tube, Parkerized finish, black synthetic stock and forend. Introduced 1998. Made in U.S. by Mossberg.

Price: **$370.00**

MOSSBERG MODEL 500 SPORTING PUMP

Gauge: 12, 20, 410, 3" chamber. **Barrel:** 18-1/2" to 28" with fixed or Accu-Choke, plain or vent. rib. **Weight:** 6-1/4 lbs. (410), 7-1/4 lbs. (12). **Length:** 48" overall (28" barrel). **Stock:** 14"x1-1/2"x2-1/2". Walnut-stained hardwood. Cut-checkered grip and forend. **Sights:** White bead front, brass mid-bead; Fiber Optic. **Features:** Ambidextrous thumb safety, twin extractors, disconnecting safety, dual action bars. Quiet Carry forend. Many barrels are ported. Mossberg Cablelock included. From Mossberg.

Price: From about............................... **$301.00**
Price: Sporting Combos (field barrel and Slugster barrel), from . . **$403.00**

Mossberg Model 500 Bantam Pump

Same as the Model 500 Sporting Pump except 12 (new for 2001) or 20 gauge, 22" vent. rib Accu-Choke barrel with choke tube set; has 1" shorter stock, reduced length from pistol grip to trigger, reduced forend reach. Introduced 1992.

Price: **$301.00**
Price: With full Woodlands camouflage finish (20 ga. only) **$384.00**

Mossberg Model 500 Camo Pump

Same as the Model 500 Sporting Pump except 12 gauge only and entire gun is covered with special camouflage finish. Receiver drilled and tapped for scope mounting. Comes with quick detachable swivel studs, swivels, camouflage sling, Mossberg Cablelock.

Price: From about................................ **$370.00**

Mossberg Model 500 Persuader/Cruiser Shotguns

Similar to Mossberg Model 500 except has 18-1/2" or 20" barrel with cylinder bore choke, synthetic stock and blue or parkerized finish. Available in 12, 20 and 410 gauge with bead or ghost ring sights, 6- or 8-shot magazines. From Mossberg.

Price: 12 gauge, 20" barrel, 8-shot, bead sight. **$308.00**
Price: 20 or 410 gauge, 18-1/2" barrel, 6-shot, bead sight **$329.00**
Price: 12 gauge, parkerized finish, 6-shot, 18-1/2" barrel, ghost ring sights **$437.00**
Price: Home Security 410 (410 gauge, 18-1/2" barrel with spreader choke) **$335.00**

Mossberg Model 590 Special Purpose Shotguns

Similar to Model 500 except has parkerized or Marinecote finish, 9-shot magazine and black synthetic stock (some models feature Speed Feed. Available in 12 gauge only with 20", cylinder bore barrel. Weighs 7-1/4 lbs. From Mossberg.

Price: Bead sight, heat shield over barrel **$389.00**
Price: Ghost ring sight, Speed Feed stock. **$546.00**

MOSSBERG MODEL 500 SLUGSTER

Gauge: 12, 20, 3" chamber. **Barrel:** 24", ported rifled bore. Integral scope mount. **Weight:** 7-1/4 lbs. **Length:** 44" overall. **Stock:** 14" pull, 1-3/8" drop at heel. Walnut; Dual Comb design for proper eye positioning with or without scoped barrels. Recoil pad and swivel studs. **Features:** Ambidextrous thumb safety, twin extractors, dual slide bars. Comes with scope mount. Mossberg Cablelock included. Introduced 1988.

Price: Rifled bore, with integral scope mount, Dual-Comb stock, 12 or 20 .... **$398.00**
Price: Fiber Optic, rifle sights **$398.00**
Price: Rifled bore, rifle sights **$367.00**
Price: 20 ga., Standard or Bantam, from **$367.00**

REMINGTON MODEL 870 WINGMASTER

Gauge: 12ga., 16 ga., 3" chamber. **Barrel:** 26", 28", 30" (Rem chokes). **Weight:** 7-1/4 lbs.. **Length:** 46", 48". **Stock:** Walnut, hardwood, synthetic. **Sights:** Single bead (Twin bead Wingmaster). **Features:** Balistically balanced performance, milder recoil. Light contour barrel. Double action bars, cross-bolt safety, blue finish.

Price: Wingmaster, walnut, blued, 26", 28", 30" **$584.00**
Price: 870 Wingmaster Super Magnum, 3-1/2" chamber, 28" ... **$665.00**

SHOTGUNS — SLIDE & LEVER ACTIONS

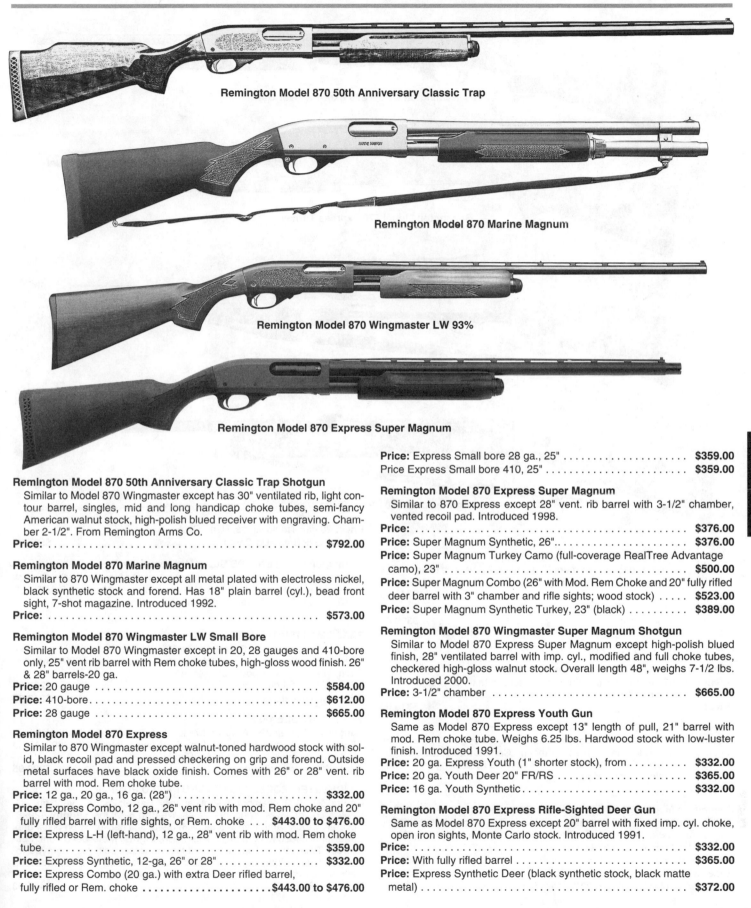

Remington Model 870 50th Anniversary Classic Trap

Remington Model 870 Marine Magnum

Remington Model 870 Wingmaster LW 93%

Remington Model 870 Express Super Magnum

Remington Model 870 50th Anniversary Classic Trap Shotgun
Similar to Model 870 Wingmaster except has 30" ventilated rib, light contour barrel, singles, mid and long handicap choke tubes, semi-fancy American walnut stock, high-polish blued receiver with engraving. Chamber 2-1/2". From Remington Arms Co.
Price: **$792.00**

Remington Model 870 Marine Magnum
Similar to 870 Wingmaster except all metal plated with electroless nickel, black synthetic stock and forend. Has 18" plain barrel (cyl.), bead front sight, 7-shot magazine. Introduced 1992.
Price: **$573.00**

Remington Model 870 Wingmaster LW Small Bore
Similar to Model 870 Wingmaster except in 20, 28 gauges and 410-bore only, 25" vent rib barrel with Rem choke tubes, high-gloss wood finish. 26" & 28" barrels-20 ga.
Price: 20 gauge **$584.00**
Price: 410-bore. **$612.00**
Price: 28 gauge **$665.00**

Remington Model 870 Express
Similar to 870 Wingmaster except walnut-toned hardwood stock with solid, black recoil pad and pressed checkering on grip and forend. Outside metal surfaces have black oxide finish. Comes with 26" or 28" vent. rib barrel with mod. Rem choke tube.
Price: 12 ga., 20 ga., 16 ga. (28") **$332.00**
Price: Express Combo, 12 ga., 26" vent rib with mod. Rem choke and 20" fully rifled barrel with rifle sights, or Rem. choke . . . **$443.00 to $476.00**
Price: Express L-H (left-hand), 12 ga., 28" vent rib with mod. Rem choke tube. **$359.00**
Price: Express Synthetic, 12-ga, 26" or 28" **$332.00**
Price: Express Combo (20 ga.) with extra Deer rifled barrel, fully rifled or Rem. choke . . . . **$443.00 to $476.00**

Price: Express Small bore 28 ga., 25" **$359.00**
Price Express Small bore 410, 25" **$359.00**

Remington Model 870 Express Super Magnum
Similar to 870 Express except 28" vent. rib barrel with 3-1/2" chamber, vented recoil pad. Introduced 1998.
Price: **$376.00**
Price: Super Magnum Synthetic, 26".. . . . . **$376.00**
Price: Super Magnum Turkey Camo (full-coverage RealTree Advantage camo), 23" **$500.00**
Price: Super Magnum Combo (26" with Mod. Rem Choke and 20" fully rifled deer barrel with 3" chamber and rifle sights; wood stock) **$523.00**
Price: Super Magnum Synthetic Turkey, 23" (black) **$389.00**

Remington Model 870 Wingmaster Super Magnum Shotgun
Similar to Model 870 Express Super Magnum except high-polish blued finish, 28" ventilated barrel with imp. cyl., modified and full choke tubes, checkered high-gloss walnut stock. Overall length 48", weighs 7-1/2 lbs. Introduced 2000.
Price: 3-1/2" chamber **$665.00**

Remington Model 870 Express Youth Gun
Same as Model 870 Express except 13" length of pull, 21" barrel with mod. Rem choke tube. Weighs 6.25 lbs. Hardwood stock with low-luster finish. Introduced 1991.
Price: 20 ga. Express Youth (1" shorter stock), from **$332.00**
Price: 20 ga. Youth Deer 20" FR/RS **$365.00**
Price: 16 ga. Youth Synthetic. **$332.00**

Remington Model 870 Express Rifle-Sighted Deer Gun
Same as Model 870 Express except 20" barrel with fixed imp. cyl. choke, open iron sights, Monte Carlo stock. Introduced 1991.
Price: **$332.00**
Price: With fully rifled barrel **$365.00**
Price: Express Synthetic Deer (black synthetic stock, black matte metal) **$372.00**

SHOTGUNS

Remington Model 870 Express Deer Gun

Remington Model 870 Express Turkey

Remington Model 870 SPS Super Slug Deer Gun

Remington Model 870 SPS-T Camo

Remington Model 870 Express Turkey

Same as Model 870 Express except 3" chamber, 21" vent rib turkey barrel and extra-full Rem. choke turkey tube; 12 ga. only. Introduced 1991.
Price: $345.00
Price: Express Turkey Camo stock has Skyline Excel
camo, matte black metal. $399.00
Price: Express Youth Turkey camo (as above with 1" shorter
length of pull), 20 ga., Skyline Excel camo. $399.00

Remington Model 870 Express Synthetic 18"

Similar to 870 Express with 18" barrel except synthetic stock and forend; 7-shot. Introduced 1994.
Price: $319.00

Remington Model 870 SPS Super Slug Deer Gun

Similar to the Model 870 Express Synthetic except has 23" rifled, modified contour barrel with cantilever scope mount. Comes with black synthetic stock and forend with swivel studs, black Cordura nylon sling. Introduced 1999. Fully rifled centilever barrel.
Price: $580.00

Remington Model 870 SPS-T Synthetic Camo Shotgun

Chambered for 12 ga., 3" shells, has Mossy Oak Break-Up® synthetic stock and metal treatment, TruGlo fiber optic sights. Introduced 2001.
Price: 20" RS, Rem. choke. $595.00
Price: Youth version $595.00
Price: Super Magnum Camo, 23", CL Rem. Choke $609.00
Price: Super Magnum Camo 23", VT Rem. Choke $591.00

Price: 20 ga., Truglo sights, Rem. Choke,
Mossy Oak Break-Up Camo $595.00

Remington Model 870 SPS Super Magnum Camo

Has synthetic stock and all metal (except bolt and trigger guard) and stock covered with Mossy Oak Break-Up camo finish. In 12 gauge 3-1/2", 26", 28" vent rib, Rem choke. Comes with camo sling, swivels.
Price: $591.00

SARSILMAZ PUMP SHOTGUN

Gauge: 12, 3" chamber. **Barrel:** 26" or 28". Stocks: Oil-finished hardwood. **Features:** Includes extra pistol-grip stock. Introduced 2000. Imported from Turkey by Armsport Inc.
Price: With pistol-grip stock $299.95
Price: With metal stock. $349.95

TRISTAR MODEL 1887

Gauge: 12. **Barrel:** 22". **Weight:** 8.75 lbs. **Length:** 40-1/2". Stocks: Walnut. **Features:** Imp. cylinder choke, 5 shell, oil finish. Introduced 2002. Made in Australia. Available through AcuSport Corp.
Price: With pistol-grip stock $299.95

WINCHESTER MODEL 1300 WALNUT FIELD PUMP

Gauge: 12, 20, 3" chamber, 5-shot capacity. **Barrel:** 26", 28", vent rib, with Full, Mod., Imp. Cyl. Winchoke tubes. **Weight:** 6-3/8 lbs. **Length:** 42-5/8" overall. **Stock:** American walnut, with deep cut checkering on pistol grip, traditional ribbed forend; high luster finish. **Sights:** Metal bead front. **Features:** Twin action slide bars; front-locking rotary bolt; roll-engraved receiver; blued, highly polished metal; cross-bolt safety with red indicator. Introduced 1984. From U.S. Repeating Arms Co., Inc.
Price: $405.00

Winchester 1300 Walnut Field Pump

Winchester 1300 Black Shadow Field Gun

Winchester 1300 Deer Black Shadow Gun

Winchester 1300 Ranger Compact

Winchester 9410

SHOTGUNS *(side tab)*

Winchester Model 1300 Upland Pump Gun

Similar to Model 1300 Walnut except straight-grip stock, 24" barrel. Introduced 1999. Made in U.S. by U.S. Repeating Arms Co.

Price: **$405.00**

Winchester Model 1300 Black Shadow Field Gun

Similar to Model 1300 Walnut except black composite stock and forend, matte black finish. Has vent rib 26" or 28" barrel, 3" chamber, mod. WinChoke tube. Introduced 1995. From U.S. Repeating Arms Co., Inc.

Price: 12 or 20 gauge................................. **$343.00**

Winchester Model 1300 Deer Black Shadow Gun

Similar to Model 1300 Black Shadow Turkey Gun except ramp-type front sight, fully adjustable rear, drilled and tapped for scope mounting. Black composite stock and forend, matte black metal. Smoothbore 22" barrel with one imp. cyl. WinChoke tube; 12 gauge only, 3" chamber. Weighs 6-3/4 lbs. Introduced 1994. From U.S. Repeating Arms Co., Inc.

Price: **$341.00**
Price: With rifled barrel................................ **$366.00**
Price: With cantilever scope mount **$409.00**
Price: Combo (22" rifled and 28" smoothbore bbls.) **$442.00**
Price: Compact (20 ga., 22" rifled barrel, shorter stock)........ **$409.00**

WINCHESTER MODEL 1300 RANGER PUMP GUN

Gauge: 12, 20, 3" chamber, 5-shot magazine. **Barrel:** 28" vent. rib with Full, Mod., Imp. Cyl. Winchoke tubes. **Weight:** 7 to 7-1/4 lbs. **Length:** 48-5/8" to 50-5/8" overall. **Stock:** Walnut-finished hardwood with ribbed forend. **Sights:** Metal bead front. **Features:** Cross-bolt safety, black rubber recoil pad, twin action slide bars, front-locking rotating bolt. From U.S. Repeating Arms Co., Inc.

Price: Vent. rib barrel, Winchoke **$357.00**
Price: Model 1300 Compact, 24" vent. rib **$356.00**

Winchester Model 1300 Turkey and Universal Hunter Models

Rotary bolt action. Durable Mossy oak break-up finish on 26" VR barrel extra full turkey improved cylinder, modified and full WinChoke tubes included. 3", 12 gauge chamber.

Price: Universal Hunter **$550.00**
Price: Buck and Tom **$525.00**
Price: Short Turkey **$439.00**

WINCHESTER MODEL 9410 LEVER-ACTION SHOTGUN

Gauge: 410, 2-1/2" chamber. **Barrel:** 24" (Cyl. bore). **Weight:** 6-3/4 lbs. **Length:** 42-1/8" overall. **Stock:** Checkered walnut straight-grip; checkered walnut forearm. **Sights:** Adjustable "V" rear, TruGlo® front. **Features:** Model 94 rifle action (smoothbore) chambered for 410 shotgun. Angle Controlled Eject extractor/ejector; choke tubes; 9-shot tubular magazine; 13-1/2" length of pull. Introduced 2001. From U.S. Repeating Arms Co.

Price: 9410 Lever-Action Shotgun **$553.00**
Price: 9410 Packer Shotgun............................. **$574.00**

Includes a variety of game guns and guns for competitive shooting.

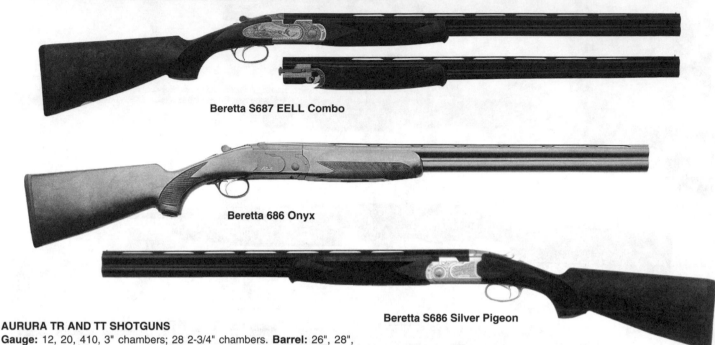

Beretta S687 EELL Combo

Beretta 686 Onyx

Beretta S686 Silver Pigeon

AURURA TR AND TT SHOTGUNS
Gauge: 12, 20, 410, 3" chambers; 28 2-3/4" chambers. **Barrel:** 26", 28", 30", 32". **Weight:** 5.95 to 7.25 lbs. **Stock:** Oil-finished European walnut. **Features:** Boxlock action, hard-chromed bores, automatic ejectors, single selective trigger, choke tubes (12 and 20 ga. only). From Sigarms.
Price: Aurura TR 20 Field $1,935.00
Price: Aurura TR 30 Field $2,301.00
Price: Aurura TR 40 Silver $2,704.00
Price: Aurura TR 40 Gold $2,767.00
Price: Aurura TT 25 Competition $2,073.00
Price: Aurura TT 45 Competition $2,905.00

BERETTA DT10 TRIDENT SHOTGUNS
Gauge: 12, 2-3/4", 3" chambers. **Barrel:** 28", 30", 32", 34"; competition-style vent rib; fixed or Optima Choke tubes. **Weight:** 7.9 to 9 lbs. **Stock:** High-grade walnut stock with oil finish; hand-checkered grip and forend, adjustable stocks available. **Features:** Detachable, adjustable trigger group, raised and thickened receiver, forend iron has replaceable nut to guarantee wood-to-metal fit, Optima Bore to improve shot pattern and reduce felt recoil. Introduced 2000. Imported from Italy by Beretta USA.
Price: DT10 Trident Trap (selective, lockable single trigger, adjustable stock). $8,500.00
Price: DT10 Trident Double Trap . . . . NA
Price: DT10 Trident X Trap . . . . NA
Price: DT10 Trident X Trap Combo (single and o/u barrels) . . $10,790.00
Price: DT10 Trident Skeet (skeet stock with rounded recoil pad, tapered rib) $8,030.00
Price: DT10 Trident Sporting (sporting clays stock with rounded recoil pad) $7,850.00

BERETTA SERIES 682 GOLD E SKEET, TRAP, SPORTING OVER/UNDERS
Gauge: 12, 2-3/4" chambers. **Barrel:** Skeet—28"; trap—30" and 32", imp. mod. & full and Mobilchoke; trap mono shotguns—32" and 34" Mobilchoke; trap top single guns—32" and 34" full and Mobilchoke; trap combo sets—from 30" O/U to 32" O/U, 34" top single. **Stock:** Close-grained walnut, hand checkered. **Sights:** White Bradley bead front sight and center bead. **Features:** Receiver has Greystone gunmetal gray finish with gold accents. Trap Monte Carlo stock has deluxe trap recoil pad. Various grades available; contact Beretta USA for details. Imported from Italy by Beretta USA.
Price: 682 Gold E Trap with adjustable stock. $3,905.00
Price: 682 Gold E X Trap . . . . NA

Price: 682 Gold E X Trap Top Combo . . . . NA
Price: 682 Gold E Sporting $3,436.00
Price: 682 Gold E Skeet, adjustable stock $3,905.00
Price: 682 Gold E Double Trap . . . . NA
Price: 687 EELL Diamond Pigeon Skeet, adjustable stock $6,050.00
Price: 687 EELL Diamond Pigeon Sporting $6,071.00

BERETTA MODEL 686 WHITEWING O/U
Gauge: 12, 20. **Barrel:** 26", 28", Mobilchoke tubes (Imp. Cyl., Mod., Full). **Weight:** 6.7 lbs. **Length:** 45.7" overall (28" barrels). **Stock:** 14.5"x2.2"x1.4". American walnut, radiused black buttplate. **Features:** Matte chrome finish on receiver, matte blue barrels, hard-chrome bores; low-profile receiver with dual conical locking lugs, single selective trigger, ejectors. Imported from Italy by Beretta U.S.A.
Price: Whitewing $1,295.00

BERETTA 686 ONYX O/U SHOTGUN
Gauge: 12, 3" chambers. **Barrel:** 28", 30" (Mobilchoke tubes). **Weight:** 7.7 lbs. **Stock:** Checkered American walnut. **Features:** Intended for the beginning Sporting Clays shooter. Has wide, vented 12.5mm target rib, radiused recoil pad. Polished black finish on receiver and barrels. Introduced 1993. Imported from Italy by Beretta U.S.A.
Price: $1,583.00

BERETTA 686 SILVER PIGEON O/U SHOTGUN
Gauge: 12, 20, 28, 3" chambers (2-3/4" 28 ga.). **Barrel:** 26", 28". **Weight:** 6.8 lbs. **Stock:** Checkered walnut. **Features:** Interchangeable barrels (20 and 28 ga.), single selective gold-plated trigger, boxlock action, auto safety, schnabel forend.
Price: $1,931.00
Price: 20 ga. and 28 ga. $2,676.00

BERETTA ULTRALIGHT OVER/UNDER
Gauge: 12, 2-3/4" chambers. **Barrel:** 26", 28", Mobilchoke choke tubes. **Weight:** About 5 lbs., 13 oz. **Stock:** Select American walnut with checkered grip and forend. **Features:** Low-profile aluminum alloy receiver with titanium breech face insert. Electroless nickel receiver with game scene engraving. Single selective trigger; automatic safety. Introduced 1992. Imported from Italy by Beretta U.S.A.
Price: $1,931.00

SHOTGUNS

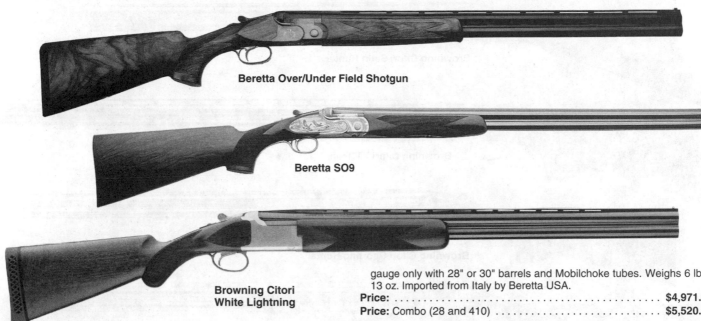

Beretta Over/Under Field Shotgun

Beretta SO9

**Browning Citori
White Lightning**

Beretta Ultralight Deluxe Over/Under Shotgun

Similar to the Ultralight except has matte electroless nickel finish receiver with gold game scene engraving; matte oil-finished, select walnut stock and forend. Imported from Italy by Beretta U.S.A.
Price: **$2,323.00**

BERETTA OVER/UNDER FIELD SHOTGUNS

Gauge: 12, 20, 28, and 410 bore, 2-3/4", 3" and 3-1/2" chambers. **Barrel:** 26" and 28" (Mobilchoke tubes). **Stock:** Close-grained walnut. **Features:** Highly-figured, American walnut stocks and forends, and a unique, weather-resistant finish on barrels. Silver designates standard 686, 687 models with silver receivers; 686 Silver Pigeon has enhanced engraving pattern, Schnabel forend; 686 Silver Essential has matte chrome finish; Gold indicates higher grade 686EL, 687EL models with full sideplates; Diamond is for 687EELL models with highest grade wood, engraving. Case provided with Gold and Diamond grades. Imported from Italy by Beretta U.S.A.
Price: S686 Silver Pigeon two-bbl. set **$2,587.00**
Price: S686 Silver Pigeon. **$1,817.00**
Price: S687 Silver Pigeon II Sporting **$2,196.00**
Price: Combo 29" and 30" **$3,151.00**
Price: S687EL Gold Pigeon (gold inlays, sideplates) **$4,099.00**
Price: S687EL Gold Pigeon, 410, 26"; 28 ga., 28" **$4,273.00**
Price: S687 EL Gold Pigeon II (deep relief engraving) **$4,513.00**
Price: S687 EL Gold Pigeon II Sporting (d.r. engraving) **$4,554.00**

BERETTA MODEL SO5, SO6, SO9 SHOTGUNS

Gauge: 12, 2-3/4" chambers. **Barrel:** To customer specs. **Stock:** To customer specs. **Features:** SO5—Trap, Skeet and Sporting Clays models SO5; SO6— SO6 and SO6 EELL are field models. SO6 has a case-hardened or silver receiver with contour hand engraving. SO6 EELL has hand-engraved receiver in a fine floral or "fine English" pattern or game scene, with bas-relief chisel work and gold inlays. SO6 and SO6 EELL are available with sidelocks removable by hand. Imported from Italy by Beretta U.S.A.
Price: SO5 Trap, Skeet, Sporting. **$13,000.00**
Price: SO6 Trap, Skeet, Sporting. **$17,500.00**
Price: SO6 EELL Field, custom specs **$28,000.00**
Price: SO9 (12, 20, 28, 410, 26", 28", 30", any choke) **$31,000.00**

Beretta S687EL Gold Pigeon Sporting O/U

Similar to S687 Silver Pigeon Sporting except sideplates with gold inlay game scene, vent side and top ribs, bright orange front sight. Stock and forend are high grade walnut with fine-line checkering. Available in 12

gauge only with 28" or 30" barrels and Mobilchoke tubes. Weighs 6 lbs., 13 oz. Imported from Italy by Beretta USA.
Price: **$4,971.00**
Price: Combo (28 and 410) **$5,520.00**

BRNO ZH 300 OVER/UNDER SHOTGUN

Gauge: 12, 2-3/4" chambers. **Barrel:** 26", 27-1/2", 29" (Skeet, Imp. Cyl., Mod., Full). **Weight:** 7 lbs. **Length:** 44.4" overall. **Stock:** European walnut. **Features:** Double triggers; automatic safety; polished blue finish engraved receiver. Announced 1998. Imported from the Czech Republic by Euro-Imports.
Price: ZH 301, field. **$594.00**
Price: ZH 302, Skeet **$608.00**
Price: ZH 303, 12 ga. trap **$608.00**
Price: ZH 321, 16 ga. **$595.00**

BRNO 501.2 OVER/UNDER SHOTGUN

Gauge: 12, 2-3/4" chambers. **Barrel:** 27.5" (Full & Mod.). **Weight:** 7 lbs. **Length:** 44" overall. **Stock:** European walnut. **Features:** Boxlock action with double triggers, ejectors; automatic safety; hand-cut checkering. Announced 1998. Imported from The Czech Republic by Euro-Imports.
Price: **$850.00**

BROWNING CITORI O/U SHOTGUNS

Gauge: 12, 20, 28 and 410. **Barrel:** 26", 28" in 28 and 410. Offered with Invector choke tubes. All 12 and 20 gauge models have back-bored barrels and Invector Plus choke system. **Weight:** 6 lbs., 8 oz. (26" 410) to 7 lbs., 13 oz. (30" 12 ga.). **Length:** 43" overall (26" bbl.). **Stock:** Dense walnut, hand checkered, full pistol grip, beavertail forend. Field-type recoil pad on 12 ga. field guns and trap and Skeet models. **Sights:** Medium raised beads, German nickel silver. **Features:** Barrel selector integral with safety, automatic ejectors, three-piece takedown. Imported from Japan by Browning. Contact Browning for complete list of models and prices.
Price: Grade I, Hunter, Invector, 12 and 20 . . . . **$1,486.00**
Price: Grade I, Lightning, 28 and 410, Invector **$1,594.00**
Price: Grade III, Lightning, 28 and 410, Invector **$2,570.00**
Price: Grade VI, 28 and 410 Lightning, Invector **$3,780.00**
Price: Grade I, Lightning, Invector Plus, 12, 20 . . . . **$1,534.00**
Price: Grade I, Hunting, 28", 30" only, 3-1/2", Invector Plus . . . **$1,489.00**
Price: Grade III, Lightning, Invector, 12, 20 . . . . **$2,300.00**
Price: Grade VI, Lightning, Invector, 12, 20 . . . . **$3,510.00**
Price: Gran Lightning, 26", 28", Invector, 12, 20 . . . . **$2,184.00**
Price: Gran Lightning, 28, 410 . . . . **$2,302.00**
Price: Micro Lightning, 20 ga., 24" bbl., 6 lbs., 4 oz. **$1,591.00**
Price: White Lightning (silver nitride receiver w/engraving, 12 or 20 ga., 26", 28") **$1,583.00**
Price: White Lightning, 28 or 410 gauge **$1,654.00**
Price: Citori Satin Hunter (12 ga., satin-finished wood, matte-finished barrels and receiver) 3-1/2" chambers **$1,535.00**

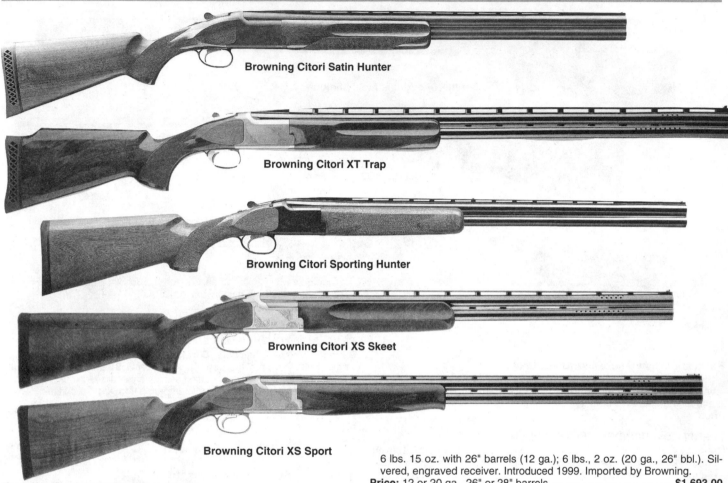

Browning Citori Satin Hunter

Browning Citori XT Trap

Browning Citori Sporting Hunter

Browning Citori XS Skeet

Browning Citori XS Sport

Browning Superlight Citori Over/Under

Similar to the standard Citori except available in 12, 20 with 24", 26" or 28" Invector barrels, 28 or 410 with 26" barrels choked Imp. Cyl. & Mod. or 28" choked Mod. & Full. Has straight grip stock, Schnabel forend tip. Superlight 12 weighs 6 lbs., 9 oz. (26" barrels); Superlight 20, 5 lbs., 12 oz. (26" barrels). Introduced 1982.

Price: Grade I, 28 or 410, Invector **$1,666.00**
Price: Grade III, Invector, 12. . . . . **$2,300.00**
Price: Grade VI, Invector, 12 or 20, gray or blue **$3,510.00**
Price: Grade VI, Invector, 28 or 410, Invector, gray or blue **$3,780.00**
Price: Grade I Invector, 12 or 20 . . . . **$1,580.00**
Price: Grade I Invector, White Upland Special (24" bbls.),
12 or 20 . . . . **$1,583.00**
Price: Citori Superlight Feather (12 ga., alloy receiver,
6 lbs. 4 oz.) **$1,756.00**

Browning Citori XT Trap Over/Under

Similar to the Citori Special Trap except has engraved silver nitride receiver with gold highlights, vented side barrel rib. Available in 12 gauge with 30" or 32" barrels, Invector-Plus choke tubes. Introduced 1999. Imported by Browning.

Price: **$1,834.00**
Price: With adjustable-comb stock **$2,054.00**

Browning Micro Citori Lightning

Similar to the standard Citori 20 ga. Lightning except scaled down for smaller shooter. Comes with 24" Invector Plus back-bored barrels, 13-3/4" length of pull. Weighs about 6 lbs., 3 oz. Introduced 1991.

Price: Grade I **$1,486.00**

Browning Citori Lightning Feather O/U

Similar to the 12 gauge Citori Grade I except has 2-3/4" chambers, rounded pistol grip, Lightning-style forend, and lighweight alloy receiver. Weighs

6 lbs. 15 oz. with 26" barrels (12 ga.); 6 lbs., 2 oz. (20 ga., 26" bbl.). Silvered, engraved receiver. Introduced 1999. Imported by Browning.

Price: 12 or 20 ga., 26" or 28" barrels **$1,693.00**
Price: Lightning Feather Combo (20 and 28 ga. bbls., 27" each) **$2,751.00**

Browning Citori Sporting Hunter

Similar to the Citori Hunting I except has Sporting Clays stock dimensions, a Superposed-style forend, and Sporting Clays butt pad. Available in 12 gauge with 3" chambers, back-bored 26", 28" and 30", all with Invector Plus choke tube system. Introduced 1998. Imported from Japan by Browning.

Price: 12 gauge, 3-1/2" **$1,709.00**
Price: 12, 20 gauge, 3" **$1,607.00**

Browning Citori Ultra XS Skeet

Similar to other Citori Ultra models except features a semi-beavertail forearm with deep finger grooves, ported barrels and triple system. Adjustable comb is optional. Introduced 2000.

Price: 12 ga., 28" or 30" barrel **$2,162.00**
Price: 20 ga., 28" or 30" barrel **$2,162.00**
Price: Adjustable comb model, 12 or 20 ga. **$2,380.00**

Browning Citori Ultra XS Trap

Similar to other Citori Ultra models except offered in 12 ga. only with 30" or 32" ported barrel, high-post rib, ventilated side ribs, Triple Trigger System™ and silver nitride receiver. Includes full, modified and imp. cyl. choke tubes. From Browning.

Price: 30" or 32" barrel **$2,022.00**
Price: Adjustable-comb model **$2,265.00**

Browning Citori Ultra XS Sporting

Similar to other Citori Ultra XS models except offered in 12, 20, 28 and 410 gauge. Silver nitride receiver, Schnabel forearm, ventilated side rib. Imported by Browning.

Price: 410 or 28 ga. **$2,268.00**
Price: 12 or 20 ga. **$2,196.00**

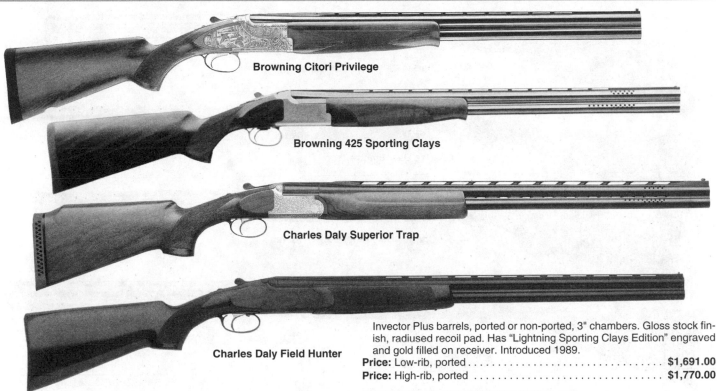

Browning Citori Privilege

Browning 425 Sporting Clays

Charles Daly Superior Trap

Charles Daly Field Hunter

Browning Citori Feather XS Shotguns

Similar to the standard Citori except has lightweight alloy receiver, silver nitrade Nitex receiver, Schnabel forearm, ventilated side rib and Hi-Viz Comp fiber optics sight. Available in 12, 20, 28 and 410 gauges. Introduced 2000.
Price: 28" or 30" barrel . . . . **$2,266.00 to $2,338.00**

Browning Citori High Grade Shotguns

Similar to standard Citori except has full sideplates with engraved hunting scenes and gold inlays, high-grade, hand-oiled walnut stock and forearm. Introduced 2000. From Browning.
Price: Citori Privilege (fully embellished sideplates), 12 or 20 ga.
. . . . **$5,376.00**
Price: Citori BG VI Lightning (gold inlays of ducks and pheasants)
From **$3,340.00**
Price: Citori BG III Superlight (scroll engraving on grayed receiver, gold inlays) **$2,190.00**
Price: Citori 425 Golden Clays (engraving of game bird-clay bird transition, gold accents), 12 or 20 ga. **$3,977.00**

Browning Nitra Citori XS Sporting Clays

Similar to the Citori Grade I except has silver nitride receiver with gold accents, stock dimensions of 14-3/4"x1-1/2"x2-1/4" with satin finish, right-hand palm swell, Schnabel forend. Comes with Modified, Imp. Cyl. and Skeet Invector-Plus choke tubes. Back-bored barrels; vented side ribs. Introduced 1999. Imported by Browning.
Price: 12, 20 ga. **$2,011.00**
Price: 28 ga., 410-bore **$2,077.00**

Browning Special Sporting Clays

Similar to the Citori Ultra Sporter except has full pistol grip stock with palm swell, gloss finish, 28", 30" or 32" barrels with back-bored Invector Plus chokes (ported or non-ported); high post tapered rib. Also available as 28" and 30" two-barrel set. Introduced 1989.
Price: With ported barrels **$1,636.00**
Price: As above, adjustable comb **$1,856.00**

Browning Lightning Sporting Clays

Similar to the Citori Lightning with rounded pistol grip and classic forend. Has high post tapered rib or lower hunting-style rib with 30" back-bored Invector Plus barrels, ported or non-ported, 3" chambers. Gloss stock finish, radiused recoil pad. Has "Lightning Sporting Clays Edition" engraved and gold filled on receiver. Introduced 1989.
Price: Low-rib, ported **$1,691.00**
Price: High-rib, ported **$1,770.00**

BROWNING LIGHT SPORTING 802 ES O/U

Gauge: 12, 2-3/4" chambers. **Barrel:** 28", back-bored Invector Plus. Comes with flush-mounted Imp. Cyl. and Skeet; 2" extended Imp. Cyl. and Mod.; and 4" extended Imp. Cyl. and Mod. tubes. **Weight:** 7 lbs., 5 oz. **Length:** 45" overall. **Stock:** 14-3/8" x 1/8" x 1-9/16" x 1-3/4". Select walnut with radiused solid recoil pad, Schnabel-type forend. **Features:** Trigger adjustable for length of pull; narrow 6.2mm ventilated rib; ventilated barrel side rib; blued receiver. Introduced 1996. Imported from Japan from Browning.
Price: **$2,063.00**

BROWNING 425 SPORTING CLAYS

Gauge: 12, 20, 2-3/4" chambers. **Barrel:** 12 ga.—28", 30", 32" (Invector Plus tubes), back-bored; 20 ga.—28", 30" (Invector Plus tubes). **Weight:** 7 lbs., 13 oz. (12 ga., 28"). **Stock:** 14-13/16" (1/8")x1-7/16"x2-3/16" (12 ga.). Select walnut with gloss finish, cut checkering, Schnabel forend. **Features:** Grayed receiver with engraving, blued barrels. Barrels are ported on 12 gauge guns. Has low 10mm wide vent rib. Comes with three interchangeable trigger shoes to adjust length of pull. Introduced in U.S. 1993. Imported by Browning.
Price: Grade I, 12, 20 ga., Invector Plus **$2,006.00**
Price: Golden Clays, 12, 20 ga., Invector Plus. **$3,977.00**

CHARLES DALY SUPERIOR TRAP AE MC

Gauge: 12, 2-3/4" chambers. **Barrel:** 30" choke tubes. **Weight:** About 7 lbs. **Stock:** Checkered walnut; pistol grip, semi-beavertail forend. **Features:** Silver engraved receiver, chrome moly steel barrels; gold single selective trigger; automatic safety; automatic ejectors; red bead front sight, metal bead center; recoil pad. Introduced 1997. Imported from Italy by K.B.I., Inc.
Price: **$1,339.00**

CHARLES DALY FIELD HUNTER OVER/UNDER SHOTGUN

Gauge: 12, 20, 28 and 410 bore (3" chambers, 28 ga. has 2-3/4"). **Barrel:** 28" Mod & Full, 26" Imp. Cyl. & Mod (410 is Full & Full). **Weight:** About 7 lbs. **Length:** NA. **Stock:** Checkered walnut pistol grip and forend. **Features:** Blued engraved receiver, chrome moly steel barrels; gold single selective trigger; automatic safety; extractors; gold bead front sight. Introduced 1997. Imported from Italy by K.B.I., Inc.
Price: 12 or 20 ga. **$799.00**
Price: 28 ga. **$879.00**
Price: 410 bore **$919.00**

SHOTGUNS

Charles Daly Superior Hunter

Charles Daly Empire Trap

Charles Daly Empire EDL Hunter

Charles Daly Empire Sporting O/U

Charles Daly Field Hunter AE Shotgun

Similar to the Field Hunter except 28 gauge only; 26" (Imp. Cyl. & Mod., 28 gauge), 26" (Full & Full, 410); automatic; ejectors. Introduced 1997. Imported from Italy by K.B.I., Inc.

Price: 28 .... **$999.00**

Charles Daly Superior Hunter AE Shotgun

Similar to the Field Hunter AE except has silvered, engraved receiver. Introduced 1997. Imported from Italy by F.B.I., Inc.

Price: 28 ga. **$1,129.00**
Price: 410 bore **$1,129.00**

Charles Daly Field Hunter AE-MC

Similar to the Field Hunter except in 12 or 20 only, 26" or 28" barrels with five multichoke tubes; automatic ejectors. Introduced 1997. Imported from Italy by K.B.I., Inc.

Price: 12 or 20 .... **$979.95**

Charles Daly Superior Sporting O/U

Similar to the Field Hunter AE-MC except 28" or 30" barrels; silvered, engraved receiver; five choke tubes; ported barrels; red bead front sight. Introduced 1997. Imported from Italy by K.B.I., Inc.

Price: **$1,259.95**

CHARLES DALY EMPIRE TRAP AE MC

Gauge: 12, 2-3/4" chambers. **Barrel:** 30" choke tubes. **Weight:** About 7 lbs. **Stock:** Checkered walnut; pistol grip, semi-beavertail forend. **Features:** Silvered, engraved, reinforced receiver; chrome moly steel barrels; gold single selective trigger; automatic safety, automatic ejector; red bead front sight, metal bead center; recoil pad. Imported from Italy by K.B.I., Inc.

Price: **$1,539.95**

CHARLES DALY DIAMOND REGENT GTX DL HUNTER O/U

Gauge: 12, 20, 410, 3" chambers, 28, 2-3/4" chambers. **Barrel:** 26", 28", 30" (choke tubes), 26" (Imp. Cyl. & Mod. in 28, 26" (Full & Full). **Weight:** About 7 lbs. **Stock:** Extra select fancy European walnut with 24" hand checkering, hand rubbed oil finish. **Features:** Boss-type action with internal side lumps. Deep cut hand-engraved scrollwork and game scene set in full sideplates. GTX detachable single selective trigger system with coil springs; chrome moly steel barrels; automatic safety; automatic ejectors, white bead front sight, metal bead center sight. Introduced 1997. Imported from Italy by K.B.I., Inc.

Price: 12 or 20 .... **$22,299.00**
Price: 28 .... **$22,369.00**
Price: 410 .... **$22,419.00**
Price: Diamond Regent GTX EDL Hunter (as above with engraved scroll and birds, 10 gold inlays), 12 or 20 .... **$26,249.00**
Price: As above, 28 .... **$26,499.00**
Price: As above, 410 .... **$26,549.00**

CHARLES DALY EMPIRE EDL HUNTER O/U

Gauge: 12, 20, 410, 3" chambers, 28 ga., 2-3/4". **Barrel:** 26", 28" (12, 20, choke tubes), 26" (Imp. Cyl. & Mod., 28 ga.), 26" (Full & Full, 410). **Weight:** About 7 lbs. Stocks: Checkered walnut pistol grip buttstock, semi-beavertail forend; recoil pad. **Features:** Silvered, engraved receiver; chrome moly barrels; gold single selective trigger; automatic safety; automatic ejectors; red bead front sight, metal bead middle sight. Introduced 1997. Imported from Italy by K.B.I., Inc.

Price: Empire EDL (dummy sideplates) 12 or 20 .... **$1,559.95**
Price: Empire EDL, 28 .... **$1,559.95**
Price: Empire EDL, 410 .... **$1,599.95**

Charles Daly Empire Sporting O/U

Similar to the Empire EDL Hunter except 12 or 20 gauge only, 28", 30" barrels with choke tubes; ported barrels; special stock dimensions. Introduced 1997. Imported from Italy by K.B.I., Inc.

Price: **$1,499.95**

CHARLES DALY DIAMOND GTX SPORTING O/U SHOTGUN

Gauge: 12, 20, 3" chambers. **Barrel:** 28", 30" with choke tubes. **Weight:** About 8.5 lbs. **Stock:** Checkered deluxe walnut; Sporting clays dimensions. Pistol grip; semi-beavertail forend; hand rubbed oil finish. **Features:** Chromed, hand-engraved receiver; chrome moly steel barrels; GTX detachable single selective trigger system with coil springs, automatic safety; automatic ejectors; red bead front sight; ported barrels. Introduced 1997. Imported from Italy by K.B.I., Inc.

Price: **$5,804.95**

CHARLES DALY DIAMOND GTX TRAP AE-MC O/U SHOTGUN

Gauge: 12, 2-3/4" chambers. **Barrel:** 30" (Full & Full). **Weight:** About 8.5 lbs. **Stock:** Checkered deluxe walnut; pistol grip; trap dimensions; semi-beavertail forend; hand-rubbed oil finish. **Features:** Silvered, hand-engraved receiver; chrome moly steel barrels; GTX detachable single selective trigger system with coil springs, automatic safety, automatic-ejectors, red bead front sight, metal bead middle; recoil pad. Imported from Italy by K.B.I., Inc.

Price: **$5,804.95**

SHOTGUNS

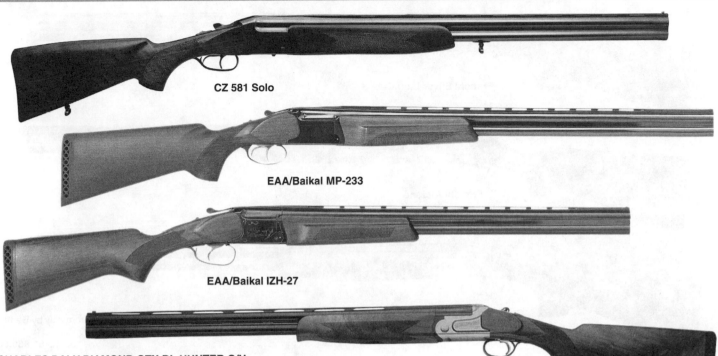

CZ 581 Solo

EAA/Baikal MP-233

EAA/Baikal IZH-27

Fabarm Max Lion

CHARLES DALY DIAMOND GTX DL HUNTER O/U

Gauge: 12, 20, 410, 3" chambers, 28, 2-3/4" chambers. **Barrel:** 26, 28", choke tubes in 12 and 20 ga., 26" (Imp. Cyl. & Mod.), 26" (Full & Full) in 410-bore. **Weight:** About 8.5 lbs. **Stock:** Select fancy European walnut stock, with 24 lpi hand checkering; hand-rubbed oil finish. **Features:** Boss-type action with internal side lugs, hand-engraved scrollwork and game scene. GTX detachable single selective trigger system with coil springs; chrome moly steel barrels, automatic safety, automatic ejectors, red bead front sight, recoil pad. Introduced 1997. Imported from Italy by K.B.I., Inc.

Price: 12 or 20 . . . . **$12,399.00**
Price: 28 . . . . **$12,489.00**
Price: 410 . . . . **$12,529.00**
Price: GTX EDL Hunter (with gold inlays), 12, 20 . . . . **$15,999.00**
Price: As above, 28 . . . . **$16,179.00**
Price: As above, 410 . . . . **$16,219.00**

CZ 581 SOLO OVER/UNDER SHOTGUN

Gauge: 12, 2-3/4" chambers. **Barrel:** 27.6" (Mod. & Full). **Weight:** 7.37 lbs. **Length:** 44.5" overall. **Stock:** Circassian walnut. **Features:** Automatic ejectors; double triggers; Kersten-style double lump locking system. Imported from the Czech Republic by CZ-USA.

Price: **$799.00**

EAA/BAIKAL MP-233 OVER/UNDER SHOTGUN

Gauge: 12, 3" chambers. **Barrel:** 26", 28", 30"; imp., mod. and full choke tubes. **Weight:** 7.28 lbs. **Stock:** Walnut; checkered forearm and grip. **Features:** Hammer-forged barrels; chrome-lined bores; removable trigger assembly (optional single selective trigger or double trigger); ejectors. Introduced 2000. Imported by European American Armory.

Price: MP-233. . . . . **$939.00**

EAA/BAIKAL IZH-27 OVER/UNDER SHOTGUN

Gauge: 12 (3" chambers), 16 (2-3/4" chambers), 20 (3" chambers), 28 (2-3/4" chambers), 410 (3"). **Barrel:** 26-1/2", 28-1/2" (imp., mod. and full choke tubes for 12 and 20 gauges; improved cylinder and modified for 16 and 28 gauges; improved modified and full for 410; 16 also offered in mod. and full). **Weight:** NA. **Stock:** Walnut, checkered forearm and grip. Imported by European American Armory.

Price: IZH-27 (12, 16 and 20 gauge) **$509.00**
Price: IZH-27 (28 and 410 gauge) **$569.00**

EAA IZH-27 Sporting O/U

Basic IZH-27 with barrel porting, wide vent rib with double sight beads, engraved nickel receiver, checkered walnut stock and forend with palm

swell and semi beavertail, 3 screw chokes, SS trigger, selectable ejectors, auto tang safety

Price: 12 ga., 29" bbl. **$589.00**

FABARM MAX LION OVER/UNDER SHOTGUNS

Gauge: 12, 3" chambers, 20, 3" chambers. **Barrel:** 26", 28", 30" (12 ga.); 26", 28" (20 ga.), choke tubes. **Weight:** 7.4 lbs. **Length:** 47.5" overall (26" barrel). **Stock:** European walnut; leather-covered recoil pad. **Features:** TriBore barrel, boxlock action with single selective trigger, manual safety, automatic ejectors; chrome-lined barrels; adjustable trigger. Silvered, engraved receiver. Comes with locking, fitted luggage case. Introduced 1998. Imported from Italy by Heckler & Koch, Inc.

Price: 12 or 20 . . . . **$1,799.00**

FABARM ULTRA CAMO MAG LION O/U SHOTGUN

Gauge: 12, 3-1/2" chambers. **Barrel:** 28" (cyl., imp. cyl., mod., imp. mod., full, SS-mod., SS-full choke tubes). **Weight:** 7.9 lbs. **Length:** 50" overall. **Stock:** Camo-colored walnut. **Features:** TriBore barrel, Wetlands Camo finished metal surfaces, single selective trigger, non-auto ejectors, leather-covered recoil pad. Locking hard plastic case. Introduced 1998. Imported from Italy by Heckler & Koch, Inc.

Price: **$1,229.00**

FABARM MAX LION PARADOX

Gauge: 12, 20, 3" chambers. **Barrel:** 24". **Weight:** 7.6 lbs. **Length:** 44.5" overall. **Stock:** Walnut with special enhancing finish. **Features:** TriBore upper barrel, both wood and receiver are enhanced with special finishes, color-case hardened type finish.

Price: 12 or 20 . . . . **$1,129.00**

FABARM SILVER LION OVER/UNDER SHOTGUNS

Gauge: 12, 3" chambers, 20, 3" chambers. **Barrel:** 26", 28", 30" (12 ga.); 26", 28" (20 ga.), choke tubes. **Weight:** 7.2 lbs. **Length:** 47.5" overall (26" barrels). **Stock:** Walnut; leather-covered recoil pad. **Features:** TriBore barrel, boxlock action with single selective trigger; silvered receiver with engraving; automatic ejectors. Comes with locking hard plastic case. Introduced 1998. Imported from Italy by Heckler & Koch, Inc.

Price: 12 or 20 . . . . **$1,229.00**

SHOTGUNS

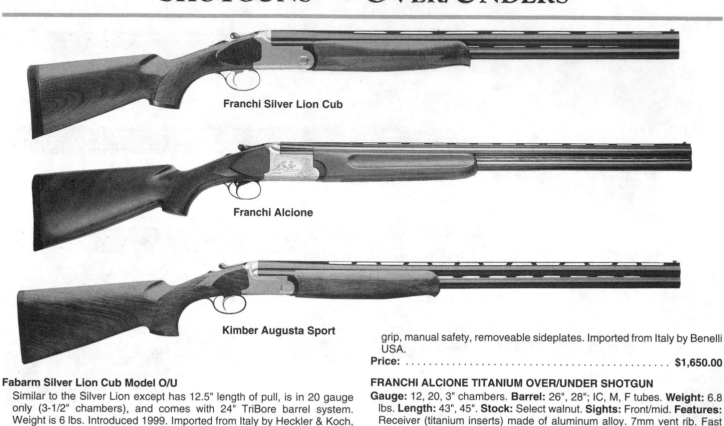

Franchi Silver Lion Cub

Franchi Alcione

Kimber Augusta Sport

Fabarm Silver Lion Cub Model O/U

Similar to the Silver Lion except has 12.5" length of pull, is in 20 gauge only (3-1/2" chambers), and comes with 24" TriBore barrel system. Weight is 6 lbs. Introduced 1999. Imported from Italy by Heckler & Koch, Inc.

Price: **$1,229.00**

FABARM CAMO TURKEY MAG O/U SHOTGUN

Gauge: 12, 3-1/2" chambers. **Barrel:** 20" TriBore (Ultra-Full ported tubes). **Weight:** 7.5 lbs. **Length:** 46" overall. **Stock:** 14.5"x1.5"x2.29". Walnut. **Sights:** Front bar, Picatinny rail scope base. **Features:** Completely covered with Xtra Brown camouflage finish. Unported barrels. Introduced 1999. Imported from Italy by Heckler & Koch, Inc.

Price: **$1,199.00**

FABARM SPORTING CLAYS COMPETITION EXTRA O/U

Gauge: 12, 20, 3" chambers. **Barrel:** 12 ga. has 30", 20 ga. has 28"; ported TriBore barrel system with five tubes. **Weight:** 7 to 7.8 lbs. **Length:** 49.6" overall (20 ga.). **Stock:** 14.50"x1.38"x2.17" (20 ga.); deluxe walnut; leather-covered recoil pad. **Features:** Single selective trigger, auto ejectors; 10mm channeled rib; carbon fiber finish. Introduced 1999. Imported from Italy by Heckler & Koch, Inc.

Price: **$1,749.00**

FRANCHI ALCIONE FIELD OVER/UNDER SHOTGUN

Gauge: 12, 20, 3" chambers. **Barrel:** 26", 28"; IC, M, F tubes. **Weight:** 7.5 lbs. **Length:** 43" overall with 26" barrels. **Stock:** European walnut. **Features:** Boxlock action with ejectors, barrel selector mounted on trigger; silvered, engraved receiver, vent center rib, automatic safety, interchangeable 20 ga. bbls., left-hand available. Imported from Italy by Benelli USA. Hard case included.

Price: **$1,275.00**
Price: (20 gauge barrel set) **$460.00**

Franchi Alcione SX O/U Shotgun

Similar to Alcione Field model with high grade walnut stock and forend. Gold engraved removeable sideplates, interchangeable barrels.

Price: **$1,800.00**
Price: (12 gauge barrel set) .... **$450.00 to $500.00**
Price: (20 gauge barrel set) **$450.00**

Franchi Alcione Sport SL O/U Shotgun

Similar to Alcione except 2-3/4" chambers, elongated forcing cones and porting for Sporting Clays shooting. 10mm vent rib, tightly curved pistol grip, manual safety, removeable sideplates. Imported from Italy by Benelli USA.

Price: **$1,650.00**

FRANCHI ALCIONE TITANIUM OVER/UNDER SHOTGUN

Gauge: 12, 20, 3" chambers. **Barrel:** 26", 28"; IC, M, F tubes. **Weight:** 6.8 lbs. **Length:** 43", 45". **Stock:** Select walnut. **Sights:** Front/mid. **Features:** Receiver (titanium inserts) made of aluminum alloy. 7mm vent rib. Fast locking triggers. Left-hand available.

Price: **$1,425.00**

FRANCHI 912 SHOTGUN

Gauge: 12 ga., 2-3/4", 3", 3-1/2"" chambers. **Barrel:** 24"-30". **Weight:** Appx. 7.6 lbs. **Length:** 46"-52". **Stock:** Walnut, synthetic, Timber HD. **Sights:** White bead front. **Features:** Based on 612 design, magazine cut-off, stepped vent rib, dual-recoil-reduction system.

Price: Satin walnut **$1,000.00**
Price: Synthetic **$940.00**
Price: Timber HD Camo **$1,050.00**

FRANCHI VELOCE OVER/UNDER SHOTGUN

Gauge: 20, 28. **Barrel:** 26", 28"; IC, M, F tubes. **Weight:** 5.5-5.8 lbs. **Length:** 43"-45". **Stock:** High grade walnut. **Features:** Aluminum receiver with steel reinforcement scaled to 20 gauge for light weight. Pistol grip stock with slip recoil pad. Imported by Benelli USA. Hard case included.

Price: **$1,425.00**
Price: 28 ga. **$1,500.00**

Franchi Veloce English Over/Under Shotgun

Similar to Veloce standard model with straight grip "English" style stock. Available with 26" barrels in 20 and 28 gauge. Hard case included.

Price: **$1,425.00**
Price: 28 ga. **$1,500.00**

HOENIG ROTARY ROUND ACTION GAME GUN

Gauge: 28. **Barrel:** 26", 28", solid tapered rib. **Weight:** 6 lbs. **Stock:** English walnut. **Features:** Round action opens by rotating barrels, pulling forward. Inertia extractor, rotary safety blocks strikers. Simple takedown without removing forend. Elegance and class of guns of yesteryear. Made in U.S.A. by George Hoenig.

Price: **$19,980.00**

KIMBER AUGUSTA SHOTGUN

Premium over/under, Boss type action. 12 ga. only. Tri-alloy barrel with choke tubes. Backbored 736. Long forcing cones. HiViz sight with center bead on vent ribl. Available with many features. Custom dimensions available. Imported from Italy by Kimber Mfg., Inc.

Price: **$5,000.00**

SHOTGUNS

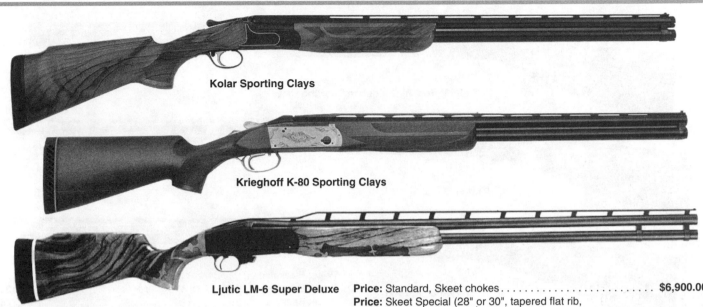

Kolar Sporting Clays

Krieghoff K-80 Sporting Clays

Ljutic LM-6 Super Deluxe

KOLAR SPORTING CLAYS O/U SHOTGUN

Gauge: 12, 2-3/4" chambers. **Barrel:** 30", 32"; extended choke tubes. **Stock:** 14-5/8"x2-1/2"x1-7/8"x1-3/8". French walnut. **Features:** Single selective trigger, detachable, adjustable for length; overbored barrels with long forcing cones; flat tramline rib; matte blue finish. Made in U.S. by Kolar.

Price: Standard **$7,250.00**
Price: Elite **$10,245.00**
Price: Elite Gold **$12,245.00**
Price: Legend **$13,245.00**
Price: Custom Gold **$24,750.00**

Kolar AAA Competition Trap Over/Under Shotgun

Similar to the Sporting Clays gun except has 32" O/U /34" Unsingle or 30" O/U /34" Unsingle barrels as an over/under, unsingle, or combination set. Stock dimensions are 14-1/2"x2-1/2"x1-1/2"; American or French walnut; step parallel rib standard. Contact maker for full listings. Made in U.S. by Kolar.

Price: Over/under, choke tubes, Standard **$7,025.00**
Price: Unsingle, choke tubes, Standard **$7,775.00**
Price: Combo (30"/34", 32"/34"), Standard. **$10,170.00**

Kolar AAA Competition Skeet Over/Under Shotgun

Similar to the Sporting Clays gun except has 28" or 30" barrels with Kolarite AAA sub gauge tubes; stock of American or French walnut with matte finish; flat tramline rib; under barrel adjustable for point of impact. Many options available. Contact maker for complete listing. Made in U.S. by Kolar.

Price: Standard, choke tubes **$8,645.00**
Price: Standard, choke tubes, two-barrel set **$10,710.00**

KRIEGHOFF K-80 SPORTING CLAYS O/U

Gauge: 12. **Barrel:** 28", 30" or 32" with choke tubes. **Weight:** About 8 lbs. **Stock:** #3 Sporting stock designed for gun-down shooting. **Features:** Standard receiver with satin nickel finish and classic scroll engraving. Selective mechanical trigger adjustable for position. Choice of tapered flat or 8mm parallel flat barrel rib. Free-floating barrels. Aluminum case. Imported from Germany by Krieghoff International, Inc.

Price: Standard grade with five choke tubes, from. **$8,150.00**

KRIEGHOFF K-80 SKEET SHOTGUN

Gauge: 12, 2-3/4" chambers. **Barrel:** 28", 30", (Skeet & Skeet), optional choke tubes). **Weight:** About 7-3/4 lbs. **Stock:** American Skeet or straight Skeet stocks, with palm-swell grips. Walnut. **Features:** Satin gray receiver finish. Selective mechanical trigger adjustable for position. Choice of ventilated 8mm parallel flat rib or ventilated 8-12mm tapered flat rib. Introduced 1980. Imported from Germany by Krieghoff International, Inc.

Price: Standard, Skeet chokes **$6,900.00**
Price: Skeet Special (28" or 30", tapered flat rib,
Skeet & Skeet choke tubes) **$7,575.00**

KRIEGHOFF K-80 O/U TRAP SHOTGUN

Gauge: 12, 2-3/4" chambers. **Barrel:** 30", 32" (Imp. Mod. & Full or choke tubes). **Weight:** About 8-1/2 lbs. **Stock:** Four stock dimensions or adjustable stock available; all have palm swell grips. Checkered European walnut. **Features:** Satin nickel receiver. Selective mechanical trigger, adjustable for position. Ventilated step rib. Introduced 1980. Imported from Germany by Krieghoff International, Inc.

Price: K-80 O/U (30", 32", Imp. Mod. & Full), from. **$7,375.00**
Price: K-80 Unsingle (32", 34", Full), Standard, from **$7,950.00**
Price: K-80 Combo (two-barrel set), Standard, from **$10,475.00**

Krieghoff K-20 O/U Shotguns

Similar to the K-80 except built on a 20-gauge frame. Designed for skeet, sporting clays and field use. Offered in 20, 28 and 410 gauge, 28" and 30" barrels. Imported from Germany by Krieghoff International Inc.

Price: K-20, 20 gauge, from **$8,150.00**
Price: K-20, 28 gauge, from **$8,425.00**
Price: K-20, 410 gauge, from **$8,425.00**

LEBEAU - COURALLY BOSS-VEREES O/U

Gauge: 12, 20, 2-3/4" chambers. **Barrel:** 25" to 32". **Weight:** To customer specifications. **Stock:** Exhibition-quality French walnut. **Features:** Boss-type sidelock with automatic ejectors; single or double triggers; chopper lump barrels. A custom gun built to customer specifications. Imported from Belgium by Wm. Larkin Moore.

Price: From **$70,000.00**

LJUTIC LM-6 SUPER DELUXE O/U SHOTGUN

Gauge: 12. **Barrel:** 28" to 34", choked to customer specs for live birds, trap, International Trap. **Weight:** To customer specs. **Stock:** To customer specs. Oil finish, hand checkered. **Features:** Custom-made gun. Hollow-milled rib, pull or release trigger, pushbutton opener in front of trigger guard. From Ljutic Industries.

Price: Super Deluxe LM-6 O/U. **$17,995.00**
Price: Over/Under Combo (interchangeable single barrel, two trigger guards, one for single trigger, one for doubles) **$24,995.00**
Price: Extra over/under barrel sets, 29"-32" **$5,995.00**

LUGER CLASSIC O/U SHOTGUNS

Gauge: 12, 3" and 3-1/2" chambers. **Barrel:** 26", 28", 30"; imp. cyl. mod. and full choke tubes. **Weight:** 7-1/2 lbs. **Length:** 45" overall (28" barrel) **Stock:** Select-grade European walnut, hand-checkered grip and forend. **Features:** Gold, single selective trigger; automatic ejectors. Introduced 2000.

Price: Classic (26", 28" or 30" barrel; 3-1/2" chambers) **$919.00**
Price: Classic Sporting (30" barrel; 3" chambers) **$964.00**

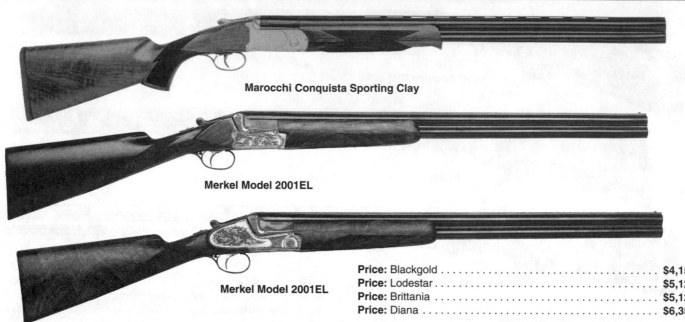

Marocchi Conquista Sporting Clay

Merkel Model 2001EL

Merkel Model 2001EL

MAROCCHI CONQUISTA SPORTING CLAYS O/U SHOTGUNS
Gauge: 12, 2-3/4" chambers. **Barrel:** 28", 30", 32" (ContreChoke tubes); 10mm concave vent rib. **Weight:** About 8 lbs. **Stock:** 14-1/2"-14-7/8"x2-3/16"x1-7/16"; American walnut with checkered grip and forend; Sporting Clays butt pad. **Sights:** 16mm luminescent front. **Features:** Lower monoblock and frame profile. Fast lock time. Ergonomically-shaped trigger adjustable for pull length. Automatic selective ejectors. Coin-finished receiver, blued barrels. Five choke tubes, hard case. Available as true left-hand model—opening lever operates from left to right; stock has left-hand cast. Introduced 1994. Imported from Italy by Precision Sales International.
Price: Grade I, right-hand $1,490.00
Price: Grade I, left-hand $1,615.00
Price: Grade II, right-hand $1,828.00
Price: Grade II, left-hand $2,180.00
Price: Grade III, right-hand, from $3,093.00
Price: Grade III, left-hand, from $3,093.00

Marocchi Conquista Trap Over/Under Shotgun
Similar to Conquista Sporting Clays model except 30" or 32" barrels choked Full & Full, stock dimensions of 14-1/2"-14-7/8"x1-11/16"x1-9/32"; weighs about 8-1/4 lbs. Introduced 1994. Imported from Italy by Precision Sales International.
Price: Grade I, right-hand $1,490.00
Price: Grade II, right-hand $1,828.00
Price: Grade III, right-hand, from $3,093.00

Marocchi Conquista Skeet Over/Under Shotgun
Similar to Conquista Sporting Clays except 28" (Skeet & Skeet) barrels, stock dimensions of 14-3/8"-14-3/4"x2-3/16"x1-1/2". Weighs about 7-3/4 lbs. Introduced 1994. Imported from Italy by Precision Sales International.
Price: Grade I, right-hand $1,490.00
Price: Grade II, right-hand $1,828.00
Price: Grade III, right-hand, from $3,093.00

MAROCCHI MODEL 99 SPORTING TRAP AND SKEET
Gauge: 12, 2-3/4", 3" chambers. **Barrel:** 28", 30", 32". **Stock:** French walnut. **Features:** Boss Locking system, screw-in chokes, low recoil, lightweight monoblock barrels and ribs. Imported from Italy by Precision Sales International.
Price: Grade I $2,350.00
Price: Grade II $2,870.00
Price: Grade II Gold $3,025.00
Price: Grade III $3,275.00
Price: Grade III Gold $3,450.00

Price: Blackgold $4,150.00
Price: Lodestar $5,125.00
Price: Brittania $5,125.00
Price: Diana $6,350.00

MAROCCHI CONQUISTA USA
MODEL 92 SPORTING CLAYS O/U SHOTGUN
Gauge: 12, 3" chambers. **Barrel:** 30"; back-bored, ported (ContreChoke Plus tubes); 10 mm concave ventilated top rib, ventilated middle rib. **Weight:** 8 lbs. 2 oz. **Stock:** 14-1/4"-14-5/8"x 2-1/8"x1-3/8"; American walnut with checkered grip and forend; Sporting Clays butt pad. **Features:** Low profile frame; fast lock time; automatic selective ejectors; blued receiver and barrels. Comes with three choke tubes. Ergonomically shaped trigger adjustable for pull length without tools. Barrels are back-bored and ported. Introduced 1996. Imported from Italy by Precision Sales International.
Price: $1,490.00

MERKEL MODEL 2001EL O/U SHOTGUN
Gauge: 12, 20, 3" chambers, 28, 2-3/4" chambers. **Barrel:** 12—28"; 20, 28 ga.—26-3/4". **Weight:** About 7 lbs. (12 ga.). **Stock:** Oil-finished walnut; English or pistol grip. **Features:** Self-cocking Blitz boxlock action with cocking indicators; Kersten double cross-bolt lock; silver-grayed receiver with engraved hunting scenes; coil spring ejectors; single selective or double triggers. Imported from Germany by GSI, Inc.
Price: 12, 20 . . . . $7,295.00
Price: 28 ga. $7,295.00
Price: Model 2000EL (scroll engraving, 12, 20 or 28) $5,795.00

Merkel Model 303EL O/U Shotgun
Similar to Model 2001 EL except Holland & Holland-style sidelock action with cocking indicators; English-style Arabesque engraving. Available in 12, 20, 28 gauge. Imported from Germany by GSI, Inc.
Price: $19,995.00

Merkel Model 2002 EL O/U Shotgun
Similar to Model 2001 EL except dummy sideplates, Arabesque engraving with hunting scenes; 12, 20, 28 gauge. Imported from Germany by GSI, Inc.
Price: $10,995.00

PERAZZI MX8 OVER/UNDER SHOTGUNS
Gauge: 12, 2-3/4" chambers. **Barrel:** 28-3/8" (Imp. Mod. & Extra Full), 29-1/2" (choke tubes). **Weight:** 7 lbs., 12 oz. **Stock:** Special specifications. **Features:** Has single selective trigger; flat 7/16"x5/16" vent. rib. Many options available. Imported from Italy by Perazzi U.S.A., Inc.
Price: Sporting $10,800.00
Price: Trap Double Trap (removable trigger group) $9,560.00
Price: Skeet $9,560.00
Price: SC3 grade (variety of engraving patterns) . . . . **Starting at $16,200**
Price: SCO grade (more intricate engraving, gold inlays)
. . . . **Starting at $26,000**

SHOTGUNS

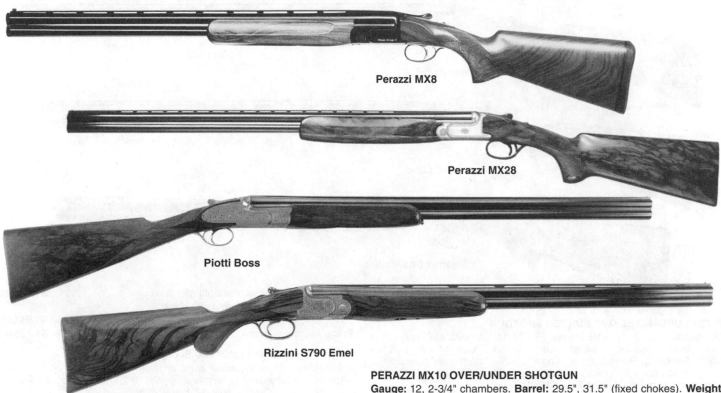

Perazzi MX8

Perazzi MX28

Piotti Boss

Rizzini S790 Emel

PERAZZI MX12 HUNTING OVER/UNDER

Gauge: 12, 2-3/4" chambers. **Barrel:** 26-3/4", 27-1/2", 28-3/8", 29-1/2" (Mod. & Full); choke tubes available in 27-5/8", 29-1/2" only (MX12C). **Weight:** 7 lbs., 4 oz. **Stock:** To customer specs; Interchangeable. **Features:** Single selective trigger; coil springs used in action; Schnabel forend tip. Imported from Italy by Perazzi U.S.A., Inc.
Price: From..................................... $9,560.00
Price: MX12C (with choke tubes), from $10,240.00

Perazzi MX20 Hunting Over/Under

Similar to the MX12 except 20 ga. frame size. Non-removable trigger group. Available in 20, 28, 410 with 2-3/4" or 3" chambers. 26" standard, and choked Mod. & Full. Weight is 6 lbs., 6 oz. Imported from Italy by Perazzi U.S.A., Inc.
Price: From..................................... $9,560.00
Price: MX20C (as above, 20 ga. only, choke tubes), from $10,120.00

PERAZZI MX8/MX8 SPECIAL TRAP, SKEET

Gauge: 12, 2-3/4" chambers. **Barrel:** Trap—29-1/2" (Imp. Mod. & Extra Full), 31-1/2" (Full & Extra Full). Choke tubes optional. Skeet—27-5/8" (Skeet & Skeet). **Weight:** About 8-1/2 lbs. (Trap); 7 lbs., 15 oz. (Skeet). **Stock:** Interchangeable and custom made to customer specs. **Features:** Has detachable and interchangeable trigger group with flat V springs. Flat 7/16" ventilated rib. Many options available. Imported from Italy by Perazzi U.S.A., Inc.
Price: From..................................... $9,560.00
Price: MX8 Special (adj. four-position trigger), from $10,120.00
Price: MX8 Special Combo (o/u and single barrel sets), from . $13,340.00

Perazzi MX8 Special Skeet Over/Under

Similar to the MX8 Skeet except has adjustable four-position trigger, Skeet stock dimensions. Imported from Italy by Perazzi U.S.A., Inc.
Price: From..................................... $9,560.00

Perazzi MX8/20 Over/Under Shotgun

Similar to the MX8 except has smaller frame and has a removable trigger mechanism. Available in trap, Skeet, sporting or game models with fixed chokes or choke tubes. Stock is made to customer specifications. Introduced 1993. Imported from Italy by Perazzi U.S.A., Inc.
Price: From..................................... $9,560.00

PERAZZI MX10 OVER/UNDER SHOTGUN

Gauge: 12, 2-3/4" chambers. **Barrel:** 29.5", 31.5" (fixed chokes). **Weight:** NA. **Stock:** Walnut; cheekpiece adjustable for elevation and cast. **Features:** Adjustable rib; vent. side rib. Externally selective trigger. Available in single barrel, combo, over/under trap, Skeet, pigeon and sporting models. Introduced 1993. Imported from Italy by Perazzi U.S.A., Inc.
Price: From..................................... $11,500.00

PERAZZI MX28, MX410 GAME O/U SHOTGUNS

Gauge: 28, 2-3/4" chambers, 410, 3" chambers. **Barrel:** 26" (Imp. Cyl. & Full). **Weight:** NA. **Stock:** To customer specifications. **Features:** Made on scaled-down frames proportioned to the gauge. Introduced 1993. Imported from Italy by Perazzi U.S.A., Inc.
Price: From..................................... $19,120.00

PIOTTI BOSS OVER/UNDER SHOTGUN

Gauge: 12, 20. **Barrel:** 26" to 32", chokes as specified. **Weight:** 6.5 to 8 lbs. **Stock:** Dimensions to customer specs. Best quality figured walnut. **Features:** Essentially a custom-made gun with many options. Introduced 1993. Imported from Italy by Wm. Larkin Moore.
Price: From..................................... $35,780.00

REMINGTON MODEL 332 O/U SHOTGUN

Gauge: 12, 3" chambers. **Barrel:** 26", 28", 30". **Weight:** 7.75 lbs. **Length:** 42"-47" **Stock:** Satin-finished American walnut. **Sights:** Twin bead. **Features:** Light-contour, vent rib, Rem chock barrel, blued, traditional M-32 experience with M-300 Ideal performance, standard auto ejectors, set trigger. Proven boxlock action.
Price: $1,624.00

RIZZINI S790 EMEL OVER/UNDER SHOTGUN

Gauge: 20, 28, 410. **Barrel:** 26", 27.5" (Imp. Cyl. & Imp. Mod.). **Weight:** About 6 lbs. **Stock:** 14"x1-1/2"x2-1/8". Extra-fancy select walnut. **Features:** Boxlock action with profuse engraving; automatic ejectors; single selective trigger; silvered receiver. Comes with Nizzoli leather case. Introduced 1996. Imported from Italy by Wm. Larkin Moore & Co.
Price: From..................................... $8,200.00

Rizzini S792 EMEL Over/Under Shotgun

Similar to S790 EMEL except dummy sideplates with extensive engraving coverage. Nizzoli leather case. Introduced 1996. Imported from Italy by Wm. Larkin Moore & Co.
Price: From..................................... $7,900.00

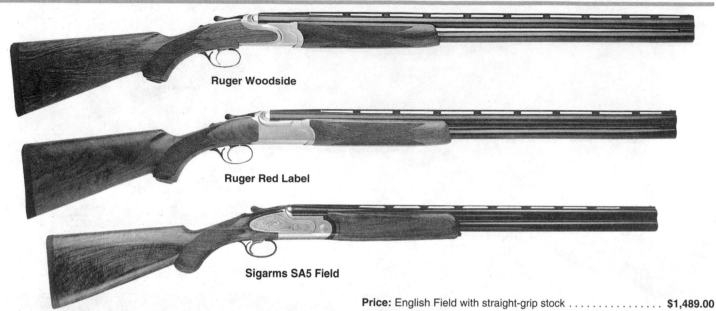

Ruger Woodside

Ruger Red Label

Sigarms SA5 Field

RIZZINI UPLAND EL OVER/UNDER SHOTGUN

Gauge: 12, 16, 20, 28, 410. **Barrel:** 26", 27-1/2", Mod. & Full, Imp. Cyl. & Imp. Mod. choke tubes. **Weight:** About 6.6 lbs. **Stock:** 14-1/2"x1-1/2"x2-1/4". **Features:** Boxlock action; single selective trigger; ejectors; profuse engraving on silvered receiver. Comes with fitted case. Introduced 1996. Imported from Italy by Wm. Larkin Moore & Co.
Price: From **$2,750.00**

Rizzini Artemis Over/Under Shotgun

Same as Upland EL model except dummy sideplates with extensive game scene engraving. Fancy European walnut stock. Fitted case. Introduced 1996. Imported from Italy by Wm. Larkin Moore & Co.
Price: From **$1,800.00**

RIZZINI S782 EMEL OVER/UNDER SHOTGUN

Gauge: 12, 2-3/4" chambers. **Barrel:** 26", 27.5" (Imp. Cyl. & Imp. Mod.). **Weight:** About 6.75 lbs. **Stock:** 14-1/2"x1-1/2"x2-1/4". Extra fancy select walnut. **Features:** Boxlock action with dummy sideplates, extensive engraving with gold inlaid game birds, silvered receiver, automatic ejectors, single selective trigger. Nizzoli leather case. Introduced 1996. Imported from Italy by Wm. Larkin Moore & Co.
Price: From **$9,900.00**

RUGER WOODSIDE OVER/UNDER SHOTGUN

Gauge: 12, 3" chambers. **Barrel:** 26", 28", 30" (Full, Mod., Imp. Cyl. and two Skeet tubes). **Weight:** 7-1/2 to 8 lbs. **Stock:** 14-1/8"x1-1/2"x2-1/2". Select Circassian walnut; pistol grip or straight English grip. **Features:** Newly patented Ruger cocking mechanism for easier, smoother opening. Buttstock extends forward into action as two side panels. Single selective mechanical trigger, selective automatic ejectors; serrated free-floating rib; back-bored barrels with stainless steel choke tubes. Blued barrels, stainless steel receiver. Engraved action available. Introduced 1995. Made in U.S. by Sturm, Ruger & Co.
Price: **$1,889.00**
Price: Woodside Sporting Clays (30" barrels) **$1,889.00**

RUGER RED LABEL O/U SHOTGUN

Gauge: 12, 20, 3" chambers; 28 2-3/4" chambers. **Barrel:** 26", 28" (Skeet [two], Imp. Cyl., Full, Mod. screw-in choke tubes). Proved for steel shot. **Weight:** About 7 lbs. (20 ga.); 7-1/2 lbs. (12 ga.). **Length:** 43" overall (26" barrels). **Stock:** 14"x1-1/2"x2-1/2". Straight grain American walnut or black synthetic. Checkered pistol grip and forend, rubber butt pad. **Features:** Stainless steel receiver. Single selective mechanical trigger, selective automatic ejectors; serrated free-floating vent. rib. Comes with two Skeet, one Imp. Cyl., one Mod., one Full choke tube and wrench. Made in U.S. by Sturm, Ruger & Co.
Price: Red Label with pistol grip stock **$1,489.00**

Price: English Field with straight-grip stock **$1,489.00**
Price: All-Weather Red Label with black
synthetic stock . . . . **$1,489.00 to $1,545.00**
Price: Factory engraved All-Weather models . . . . **$1,650.00 to $1,725.00**

Ruger Engraved Red Label O/U Shotguns

Similar to Red Label except scroll engraved receiver with 24-carat gold game bird (pheasant in 12 gauge, grouse in 20 gauge, woodcock in 28 gauge, duck on All-Weather 12 gauge). Introduced 2000.
Price: Engraved Red Label (12 gauge, 30" barrel) **$1,725.00**
Price: Engraved Red Label (12, 20 and 28 gauge in 26"
and 28" barrels) **$1,650.00**
Price: Engraved Red Label, All-Weather (synthetic stock, 12 gauge only;
26" and 28" brls.) **$1,650.00**
Price: Engraved Red Label, All-Weather (synthetic stock, 12 gauge only,
30" barrel) **$1,650.00**

Ruger Sporting Clays O/U Shotgun

Similar to Red Label except 30" back-bored barrels, stainless steel choke tubes. Weighs 7.75 lbs., overall length 47". Stock dimensions of 14-1/8"x1-1/ 2"x2-1/2". Free-floating serrated vent rib with brass front and mid-rib beads. No barrel side spacers. Comes with two Skeet, one imp. cyl., one mod. + full choke tubes. 12 ga. introduced 1992, 20 ga. introduced 1994.
Price: 12 or 20 . . . . **$1,545.00**
Price: All-Weather with black synthetic stock **$1,545.00**

SARSILMAZ OVER/UNDER SHOTGUN

Gauge: 12, 3" chambers. **Barrel:** 26", 28"; fixed chokes or choke tubes. **Weight:** NA. **Length:** NA. **Stock:** Oil-finished hardwood. **Features:** Double or single selective trigger, wide ventilated rib, chrome-plated parts, blued finish. Introduced 2000. Imported from Turkey by Armsport Inc.
Price: Double triggers; mod. and full or imp. cyl. and mod. fixed
chokes **$499.95**
Price: Single selective trigger; imp. cyl. and mod. or mod.
and full fixed chokes **$575.00**
Price: Single selective trigger; five choke tubes and wrench **$695.00**

SIGARMS SA5 OVER/UNDER SHOTGUN

Gauge: 12, 20, 3" chamber. **Barrel:** 26-1/2", 27" (Full, Imp. Mod., Mod., Imp. Cyl., Cyl. choke tubes). **Weight:** 6.9 lbs. (12 gauge), 5.9 lbs. (20 gauge). **Stock:** 14-1/2" x 1-1/2" x 2-1/2". Select grade walnut; checkered 20 l.p.i. at grip and forend. **Features:** Single selective trigger, automatic ejectors; hand-engraved detachable sideplated; matte nickel receiver, rest blued; tapered bolt lock-up. Introduced 1997. Imported by Sigarms, Inc.
Price: Field, 12 gauge **$2,670.00**
Price: Sporting Clays **$2,800.00**
Price: Field 20 gauge **$2,670.00**

SHOTGUNS

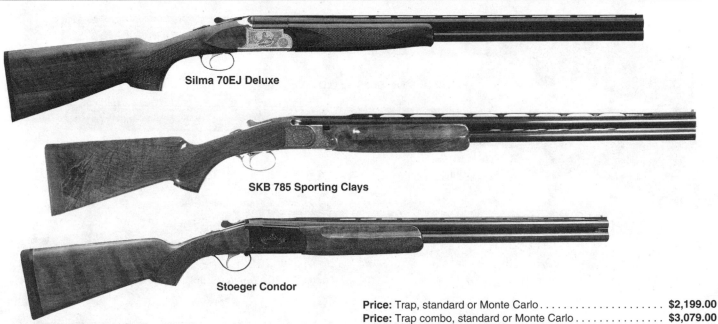

Silma 70EJ Deluxe

SKB 785 Sporting Clays

Stoeger Condor

SILMA MODEL 70EJ DELUXE

Gauge: 12 (3-1/2" chambers), 20, 410 (3" chambers), 28 (2-3/4" chambers). **Barrel:** 28" (12 and 20 gauge, fixed and tubed, 28 and 410 fixed), 26" (12 and 20 fixed). **Weight:** 7.6 lbs 12 gauge, 6.9 lbs, 20, 28 and 410. **Stock:** Checkered select European walnut, pistol grip, solid rubber recoil pad. **Features:** Monobloc construction, chrome-moly blued steel barrels, raised vent rib, automatic safety and ejectors, single mechanical gold-plated trigger, bead front sight. Brushed, engraved receiver. Introduced 2002. Clays models introduced 2003. Imported from Italy by Legacy sports International.

Price: 12, 20 multichokes (IC, M, F) **$823.00**
Price: 28, 410 multichokes (IC, M, F), fixed (M&F) **$961.00**
Price: Clays model, 12, multichokes (IC,M,F) **$1,237.00**

Silma Model 70 EJ Superlight

Similar to Silma 70EJ Deluxe except 12 gauge, 3" chambers, alloy receiver, weighs 5.6 lbs.

Price: 12, 20 multichokes (IC, M, F) **$1,004.00**

Silma Model 70 EJ Standard

Similar to Silma 70EJ Deluxe except 12 and 20 gauge only, standard walnut stock, light engraving, silver-plated trigger.

Price: 12 multichokes (IC, M, F) **$765.00**

SKB MODEL 785 OVER/UNDER SHOTGUN

Gauge: 12, 20, 3"; 28, 2-3/4"; 410, 3". **Barrel:** 26", 28", 30", 32" (Inter-Choke tubes). **Weight:** 6 lbs., 10 oz. to 8 lbs. **Stock:** 14-1/8"x1-1/2"x2-3/16" (Field). Hand-checkered American black walnut with high-gloss finish; semi-beavertail forend. Target stocks available in standard or Monte Carlo styles. **Sights:** Metal bead front (Field), target style on Skeet, trap, Sporting Clays models. **Features:** Boxlock action with Greener-style cross bolt; single selective chrome-plated trigger, chrome-plated selective ejectors; manual safety. Chrome-plated, over-size, back-bored barrels with lengthened forcing cones. Introduced 1995. Imported from Japan by G.U. Inc.

Price: Field, 12 or 20 . . . . **$2,119.00**
Price: Field, 28 or 410 . . . . **$2,199.00**
Price: Field set, 12 and 20 . . . . **$3,079.00**
Price: Field set, 20 and 28 or 28 and 410 . . . . **$3,179.00**
Price: Sporting Clays, 12 or 20 . . . . **$2,269.00**
Price: Sporting Clays, 28 . . . . **$2,349.00**
Price: Sporting Clays set, 12 and 20 . . . . **$3,249.00**
Price: Skeet, 12 or 20 . . . . **$2,199.00**
Price: Skeet, 28 or 410 . . . . **$2,239.00**
Price: Skeet, three-barrel set, 20, 28, 410 . . . . **$4,439.00**

Price: Trap, standard or Monte Carlo **$2,199.00**
Price: Trap combo, standard or Monte Carlo **$3,079.00**

SKB MODEL 585 OVER/UNDER SHOTGUN

Gauge: 12 or 20, 3"; 28, 2-3/4"; 410, 3". **Barrel:** 12 ga.—26", 28", 30", 32", 34" (Inter-Choke tubes); 20 ga.—26", 28" (Inter-Choke tube); 28—26", 28" (Inter-Choke tubes); 410—26", 28" (Inter-Choke tubes). Ventilated side ribs. **Weight:** 6.6 to 8.5 lbs. **Length:** 43" to 51-3/8" overall. **Stock:** 14-1/8"x1-1/ 2"x2-3/16". Hand checkered walnut with high-gloss finish. Target stocks available in standard and Monte Carlo. **Sights:** Metal bead front (field), target style on Skeet, trap, Sporting Clays. **Features:** Boxlock action; silver nitride finish with Field or Target pattern engraving; manual safety, automatic ejectors, single selective trigger. All 12 gauge barrels are back-bored, have lengthened forcing cones and longer choke tube system. Sporting Clays models in 12 gauge with 28" or 30" barrels available with optional 3/8" step-up target-style rib, matte finish, nickel center bead, white front bead. Introduced 1992. Imported from Japan by G.U., Inc.

Price: Field **$1,499.00**
Price: Two-barrel Field Set, 12 & 20 . . . . **$2,399.00**
Price: Two-barrel Field Set, 20 & 28 or 28 & 410 . . . . **$2,469.00**
Price: Trap, Skeet **$1,619.00**
Price: Two-barrel trap combo **$2,419.00**
Price: Sporting Clays model . . . . **$1,679.00 to $1,729.00**
Price: Skeet Set (20, 28, 410) **$3,779.00**

SKB Model 585 Gold Package

Similar to Model 585 Field except gold-plated trigger, two gold-plated game inlays, Schnabel forend. Silver or blue receiver. Introduced 1998. Imported from Japan by G.U. Inc.

Price: 12, 20 ga. **$1,689.00**
Price: 28, 410 . . . . **$1,749.00**

SKB Model 505 Shotguns

Similar to Model 585 except blued receiver, standard bore diameter, standard Inter-Choke system on 12, 20, 28, different receiver engraving. Imported from Japan by G.U. Inc.

Price: Field, 12 (26", 28"), 20 (26", 28") **$1,189.00**
Price: Sporting Clays, 12 (28", 30") **$1,299.00**

STOEGER CONDOR SPECIAL

Gauge: 12, 20, 2-3/4" 3" chambers. **Barrel:** 26", 28". **Weight:** 7.7 lbs. **Sights:** Brass bead. **Features:** IC and M screw-in choke trubes with each gun. Oil finished hardwood with pistol grip and forend. Auto safety, single trigger, automatic extractors.

Price: **$390.00**
Price: Condor Special **$440.00**
Price: Supreme Deluxe w/SS and red bar sights **$500.00**

SHOTGUNS

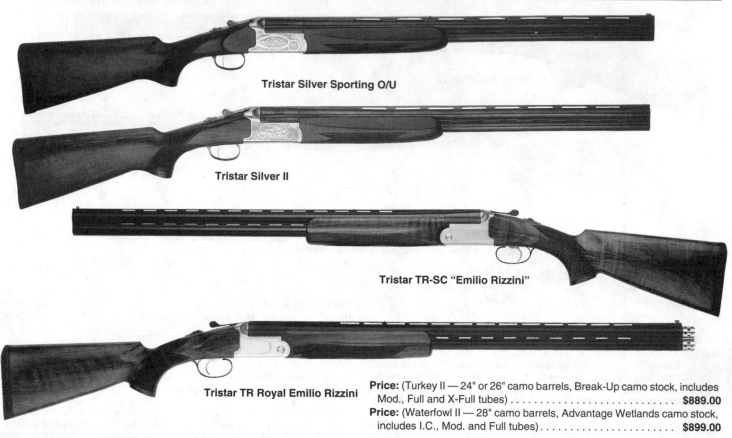

Tristar Silver Sporting O/U

Tristar Silver II

Tristar TR-SC "Emilio Rizzini"

Tristar TR Royal Emilio Rizzini

Price: (Turkey II — 24" or 26" camo barrels, Break-Up camo stock, includes Mod., Full and X-Full tubes) **$889.00**
Price: (Waterfowl II — 28" camo barrels, Advantage Wetlands camo stock, includes I.C., Mod. and Full tubes) **$899.00**

TRISTAR SILVER SPORTING O/U

Gauge: 12, 2-3/4" chambers, 20 3" chambers. **Barrel:** 28", 30" (Skeet, Imp. Cyl., Mod., Full choke tubes). **Weight:** 7-3/8 lbs. **Length:** 45-1/2" overall. **Stock:** 14-3/8"x1-1/2"x2-3/8". Figured walnut, cut checkering; Sporting Clays quick-mount buttpad. **Sights:** Target bead front. **Features:** Boxlock action with single selective trigger, automatic selective ejectors; special broadway channeled rib; vented barrel rib; chrome bores. Chrome-nickel finish on frame, with engraving. Introduced 1990. Imported from Italy by Tristar Sporting Arms Ltd.
Price: **$799.00**

Tristar Silver II Shotgun

Similar to the Silver I except 26" barrel (Imp. Cyl., Mod., Full choke tubes, 12 and 20 ga.), 28" (Imp. Cyl., Mod., Full choke tubes, 12 ga. only), 26" (Imp. Cyl. & Mod. fixed chokes, 28 and 410), automatic selective ejectors. Weight is about 6 lbs., 15 oz. (12 ga., 26").
Price: **$669.00**

TRISTAR TR-SC "EMILIO RIZZINI" OVER/UNDER

Gauge: 12, 20, 3" chambers. **Barrel:** 28", 30" (Imp. Cyl., Mod., Full choke tubes). **Weight:** 7-1/2 lbs. **Length:** 46" overall (28" barrel). **Stock:** 1-1/2"x2-3/ 8"x14-3/8". Semi-fancy walnut; pistol grip with palm swell; semi-beavertail forend; black Sporting Clays recoil pad. **Features:** Silvered boxlock action with Four Locks locking system, auto ejectors, single selective (inertia) trigger, auto safety. Hard chrome bores. Vent. 10mm rib with target-style front and mid-rib beads. Introduced 1998. Imported from Italy by Tristar Sporting Arms, Ltd.
Price: Sporting Clay model. **$1,047.00**
Price: 20 ga. **$1,127.00**

Tristar TR-Royal "Emilio Rizzini" Over/Under

Similar to the TR-SC except has special parallel stock dimensions (1-1/2"x1-5/8"x14-3/8") to give low felt recoil; Rhino ported, extended choke tubes; solid barrel spacer; has "TR-Royal" gold engraved on the silvered receiver. Available in 12 gauge (28", 30") 20 and 28 gauge (28" only). Introduced 1999. Imported from Italy by Tristar Sporting Arms, Ltd.
Price: 12, 20, 28 ga. **$1,319.00**

TRADITIONS CLASSIC SERIES O/U SHOTGUNS

Gauge: 12, 3"; 20, 3"; 16, 2-3/4"; 28, 2-3/4"; 410, 3". **Barrel:** 26" and 28". **Weight:** 6 lbs., 5 oz. to 7 lbs., 6 oz. **Length:** 43" to 45" overall. **Stock:** Walnut. **Features:** Single-selective trigger; chrome-lined barrels with screw-in choke tubes; extractors (Field Hunter and Field I models) or automatic ejectors (Field II and Field III models); rubber butt pad; top tang safety. Imported from Fausti of Italy by Traditions.
Price: (Field Hunter — blued receiver; 12 or 20 ga.; 26" bbl. has I.C. and mod. tubes, 28" has mod. and full tubes) **$669.00**
Price: (Field I — blued receiver; 12, 20, 28 or 410 ga.; fixed chokes [26" has I.C. and mod., 28" has mod. and full]) **$619.00**
Price: (Field II — coin-finish receiver; 12, 16, 20, 28 or 410 ga.; gold trigger; choke tubes) **$789.00**
Price: (Field III — coin-finish receiver; gold engraving and trigger; 12 ga.; 26" or 28" bbl.; choke tubes) **$999.00**
Price: (Upland II — blued receiver; 12 or 20 ga.; English-style straight walnut stock; choke tubes) **$839.00**
Price: (Upland III — blued receiver, gold engraving; 20 ga.; high-grade pistol grip walnut stock; choke tubes) **$1,059.00**
Price: (Upland III — blued, gold engraved receiver, 12 ga. Round pistol grip stock, choke tubes) **$1,059.00**
Price: (Sporting Clay II — silver receiver; 12 ga.; ported barrels with skeet, i.c., mod. and full extended tubes) **$959.00**
Price: (Sporting Clay III — engraved receivers, 12 and 20 ga., walnut stock, vent rib, extended choke tubes) **$1,189.00**

TRADITIONS MAG 350 SERIES O/U SHOTGUNS

Gauge: 12, 3-1/2". **Barrels:** 24", 26" and 28". **Weight:** 7 lbs. to 7 lbs., 4 oz. **Length:** 41" to 45" overall. **Stock:** Walnut or composite with Mossy Oak® Break-Up™ or Advantage® Wetlands ™ camouflage. **Features:** Black matte, engraved receiver; vent rib; automatic ejectors; single-selective trigger; three screw-in choke tubes; rubber recoil pad; top tang safety. Imported from Fausti of Italy by Traditions.
Price: (Mag Hunter II — 28" black matte barrels, walnut stock, includes I.C., Mod. and Full tubes) **$799.00**

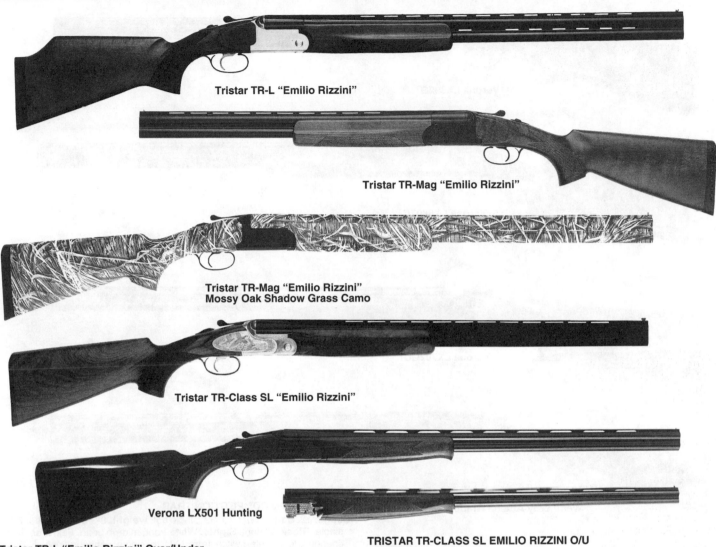

Tristar TR-L "Emilio Rizzini"

Tristar TR-Mag "Emilio Rizzini"

Tristar TR-Mag "Emilio Rizzini"
Mossy Oak Shadow Grass Camo

Tristar TR-Class SL "Emilio Rizzini"

Verona LX501 Hunting

Tristar TR-L "Emilio Rizzini" Over/Under

Similar to the TR-SC except has stock dimensions designed for female shooters (1-1/2" x 3" x 13-1/2"). Standard grade walnut. Introduced 1998. Imported from Italy by Tristar Sporting Arms, Ltd.
Price: **$1,063.00**

TRISTAR TR-I, II "EMILIO RIZZINI" OVER/UNDERS

Gauge: 12, 20, 3" chambers (TR-I); 12, 16, 20, 28, 410 3" chambers. **Barrel:** 12 ga., 26" (Imp. Cyl. & Mod.), 28" (Mod. & Full); 20 ga., 26" (Imp. Cyl. & Mod.), fixed chokes. **Weight:** 7-1/2 lbs. **Stock:** 1-1/2"x2-3/8"x14-3/8". Walnut with palm swell pistol grip, hand checkering, semi-beavertail forend, black recoil pad. **Features:** Boxlock action with blued finish, Four Locks locking system, gold single selective (inertia) trigger system, automatic safety, extractors. Introduced 1998. Imported from Italy by Tristar Sporting Arms, Ltd.

Price: TR-I **$779.00**
Price: TR-II (automatic ejectors, choke tubes) 12, 16 ga. **$919.00**
Price: 20, 28 ga., 410 . . . . **$969.00**

Tristar TR-Mag "Emilio Rizzini" Over/Under

Similar to TR-I, 3-1/2" chambers; choke tubes; 24" or 28" barrels with three choke tubes; extractors; auto safety. Matte blue finish on all metal, non-reflective wood finish. Introduced 1998. Imported from Italy by Tristar Sporting Arms, Ltd.

Price: **$799.00**
Price: Mossy Oak® Break-Up camo. **$969.00**
Price: Mossy Oak® Shadow Grass camo **$969.00**
Price: 10 ga., Mossy Oak® camo patterns. **$1,132.10**

TRISTAR TR-CLASS SL EMILIO RIZZINI O/U

Gauge: 12, 2-3/4" chambers. **Barrel:** 28", 30". **Weight:** 7-3/4 lbs. **Stock:** Fancy walnut, hand checkering, semi-beavertail forend, black recoil pad, gloss finish. **Features:** Boxlock action with silvered, engraved sideplates; Four Lock locking system; automatic ejectors; hard chrome bores; vent tapered 7mm rib with target-style front bead. hand-fitted gun. Introduced 1999. Imported from Italy by Tristar Sporting Arms, Ltd.
Price: **$1,775.00**

TRISTAR WS/OU 12 SHOTGUN

Gauge: 12, 3-1/2" chambers. **Barrel:** 28" or 30" (imp. cyl., mod., full choke tubes). **Weight:** 6 lbs., 15 oz. **Length:** 46" overall. **Stock:** 14-1/8"x1-1/8"x2-3/8". European walnut with cut checkering, black vented recoil pad, matte finish. **Features:** Boxlock action with single selective trigger, automatic selective ejectors; chrome bores. Matte metal finish. Imported by Tristar Sporting Arms Ltd.
Price: **$645.00**

VERONA LX501 HUNTING O/U SHOTGUNS

Gauge: 12, 20, 28, 410 (2-3/4", 3" chambers). **Barrel:** 28"; 12, 20 ga. have Interchoke tubes, 28 ga. and 410 have fixed Full & Mod. **Weight:** 6-7 lbs. **Stock:** Matte-finished walnut with machine-cut checkering. **Features:** Gold-plated single-selective trigger; ejectors; engraved, blued receiver, non-automatic safety; coil spring-operated firing pins. Introduced 1999. Imported from Italy by B.C. Outdoors.

Price: 12 and 20 ga. **$878.08**
Price: 28 ga. and 410 . . . . **$926.72**
Price: 410 . . . . **$907.01**
Price: Combos 20/28, 28/410. . . . . **$1,459.20**

SHOTGUNS — OVER/UNDERS

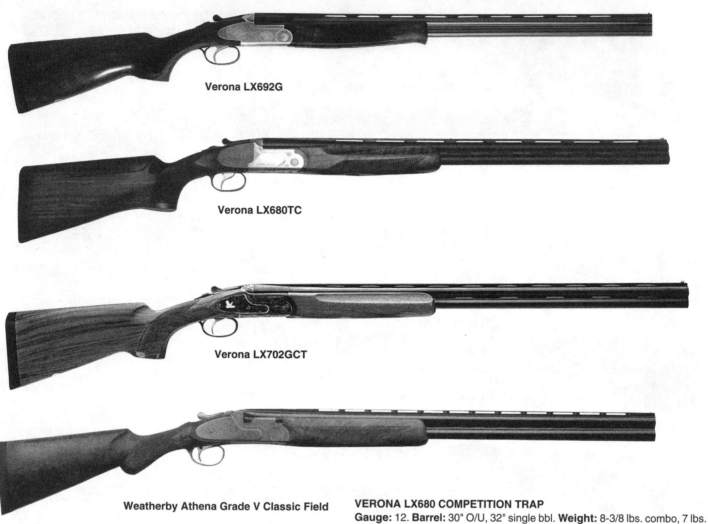

Verona LX692G

Verona LX680TC

Verona LX702GCT

Weatherby Athena Grade V Classic Field

Verona LX692 Gold Hunting Over/Under Shotguns

Similar to Verona LX501 except engraved, silvered receiver with false sideplates showing gold-inlaid bird hunting scenes on three sides; Schnabel forend tip; hand-cut checkering; black rubber butt pad. Available in 12 and 20 gauge only, five InterChoke tubes. Introduced 1999. Imported from Italy by B.C. Outdoors.

Price: **$1,295.00**
Price: LX692G Combo 28/410 . . . . **$2,192.40**

Verona LX680 Sporting Over/Under Shotguns

Similar to Verona LX501 except engraved, silvered receiver; ventilated middle rib; beavertail forend; hand-cut checkering; available in 12 or 20 gauge only with 2-3/4" chambers. Introduced 1999. Imported from Italy by B.C. Outdoors.

Price: **$1,159.68**

Verona LX680 Skeet/Sporting, Trap O/U Shotguns

Similar to Verona LX501 except skeet or trap stock dimensions; beavertail forend, palm swell on pistol grip; ventilated center barrel rib. Introduced 1999. Imported from Italy by B.C. Outdoors.

Price: **$1,736.96**

Verona LX692 Gold Sporting Over/Under Shotguns

Similar to Verona LX680 except false sideplates have gold-inlaid bird hunting scenes on three sides; red high-visibility front sight. Introduced 1999. Imported from Italy by B.C. Outdoors.

Price: Skeet/Sporting **$1,765.12**
Price: trap (32" barrel, 7-7/8 lbs.) **$1,594.80**

VERONA LX680 COMPETITION TRAP

Gauge: 12. **Barrel:** 30" O/U, 32" single bbl. **Weight:** 8-3/8 lbs. combo, 7 lbs. single. **Stock:** Walnut. **Sights:** White front, mid-rib bead. **Features:** Interchangeable barrels switch from O/U to single configurations. 5 Briley chokes in combo, 4 in single bbl. extended forcing cones, parted barrels 32" with raised rib. By B.C. Outdoors.

Price: Trap Single (LX680TGTSB) **$1,736.96**
Price: Trap Combo (LX680TC) **$2,553.60**

VERONA LX702 GOLD TRAP COMBO

Gauge: 20/28, 2-3/4"chamber. **Barrel:** 30". **Weight:** 7 lbs. **Stock:** Turkish walnut with beavertail forearm. **Sights:** White front bead. **Features:** 2-barrel competition gun. Color case-hardened side plates and receiver with gold inlaid pheasant. Ventilated rib between barrels. 5 interchokes. Imported from Italy by B.C. Outdoors.

Price: Combo **$2,467.84**
Price: 20 ga. **$1,829.12**

Verona LX702 Skeet/Trap O/U Shotguns

Similar to Verona LX702. Both are 12 gauge and 2-3/4" chamber. Skeet has 28" barrel and weighs 7-3/4 lbs. Trap has 32" barrel and weighs 7-7/8 lbs. By B.C. Outdoors.

Price: Skeet **$1,829.12**
Price: Trap **$1,829.12**

WEATHERBY ATHENA GRADE V CLASSIC FIELD O/U

Gauge: 12, 20, 3" chambers. **Barrel:** 26", 28", IMC Multi-Choke tubes. **Weight:** 12 ga., 7-1/4-8 lbs.; 20 ga. 6-1/2-7-1/4 lbs. **Stock:** Oil-finished American Claro walnut with fine-line checkering, rounded pistol grip and slender forend. **Features:** Old English recoil pad. Sideplate receiver has rose and scroll engraving.

Price: **$3,037.00**

Weatherby Orion Grade III Field

Weatherby Orion Grade II Classic Field

Weatherby Orion Upland

Winchester Supreme Field

Winchester Supreme Sporting

Weatherby Athena Grade III Classic Field O/U

Similar to Athena Grade V, has Grade III Claro walnut with oil finish, rounded pistol grip, slender forend; silver nitride/gray receiver has rose and scroll engraving with gold-overlay upland game scenes. Introduced 1999. Imported from Japan by Weatherby.
Price: 12, 20, 28 ga. **$2,173.00**

WEATHERBY ORION GRADE III FIELD O/U SHOTGUNS

Gauge: 12, 20, 3" chambers. **Barrel:** 26", 28", IMC Multi-Choke tubes. **Weight:** 6-1/2 to 8 lbs. **Stock:** 14-1/4"x1-1/2"x2-1/2". American walnut, checkered grip and forend. Rubber recoil pad. **Features:** Selective automatic ejectors, single selective inertia trigger. Top tang safety, Greener cross bolt. Has silver-gray receiver with engraving and gold duck/pheasant. Imported from Japan by Weatherby.
Price: Orion III, Field, 12, IMC, 26", 28" **$1,955.00**
Price: Orion III, Field, 20, IMC, 26", 28" **$1,955.00**

Weatherby Orion Grade II Classic Field O/U

Similar to Orion III Classic Field except stock has high-gloss finish, and bird on receiver is not gold. Available in 12 gauge, 26", 28", 30" barrels, 20 gauge, 26" 28", both with 3" chambers, 28 gauge, 26", 2-3/4" chambers. All have IMC choke tubes. Imported from Japan by Weatherby.
Price: **$1,622.00**

Weatherby Orion Upland O/U

Similar to Orion Grade I. Plain blued receiver, gold W on trigger guard; rounded pistol grip, slender forend of Claro walnut with high-gloss finish; black butt pad. Available in 12 and 20 gauge with 26" and 28" barrels. Introduced 1999. Imported from Japan by Weatherby.
Price: **$1,299.00**

WEATHERBY ORION SSC OVER/UNDER SHOTGUN

Gauge: 12, 3" chambers. **Barrel:** 28", 30", 32" (Skeet, SC1, Imp. Cyl., SC2, Mod. IMC choke tubes). **Weight:** About 8 lbs. **Stock:** 14-3/4"x2-1/4"x1-1/2". Claro walnut with satin oil finish; Schnabel forend tip; Sporter-style pistol grip; Pachmayr Decelerator recoil pad. **Features:** Designed for Sporting Clays competition. Has lengthened forcing cones and back-boring; ported barrels with 12mm grooved rib with mid-bead sight; mechanical trigger is adjustable for length of pull. Introduced 1998. Imported from Japan by Weatherby.
Price: SSC (Super Sporting Clays) **$2,059.00**

WINCHESTER SUPREME O/U SHOTGUNS

Gauge: 12, 2-3/4", 3" chambers. **Barrel:** 28", 30", Invector Plus choke tubes. **Weight:** 7 lbs. 6 oz. to 7 lbs. 12. oz. **Length:** 45" overall (28" barrel). **Stock:** Checkered walnut stock. **Features:** Chrome-plated chambers; back-bored barrels; tang barrel selector/safety; deep-blued finish. Introduced 2000. From U.S. Repeating Arms. Co.
Price: Supreme Field (26" or 28" barrel, 6mm ventilated rib) . . **$1,383.00**
Price: Supreme Sporting (28" or 30" barrel, 10mm rib,
adj. trigger) **$1,551.00**

Variety of models for utility and sporting use, including some competitive shooting.

Charles Daly Superior Hunter

Charles Daly Empire Hunter AE-MC

Charles Daly Diamond DL

Charles Daly Diamond Regent DL

ARRIETA SIDELOCK DOUBLE SHOTGUNS
Gauge: 12, 16, 20, 28, 410. **Barrel:** Length and chokes to customer specs. **Weight:** To customer specs. **Stock:** To customer specs. Straight English with checkered butt (standard), or pistol grip. Select European walnut with oil finish. **Features:** Essentially custom gun with myriad options. H&H pattern hand-detachable sidelocks, selective automatic ejectors, double triggers (hinged front) standard. Some have self-opening action. Finish and engraving to customer specs. Imported from Spain by Wingshooting Adventures.

Price: Model 557, auto ejectors, from **$3,250.00**
Price: Model 570, auto ejectors, from **$3,950.00**
Price: Model 578, auto ejectors, from **$4,350.00**
Price: Model 600 Imperial, self-opening, from **$6,050.00**
Price: Model 601 Imperial Tiro, self-opening, from **$6,950.00**
Price: Model 801, from **$9,135.00**
Price: Model 802, from **$9,135.00**
Price: Model 803, from **$6,930.00**
Price: Model 871, auto ejectors, from **$5,060.00**
Price: Model 872, self-opening, from **$12,375.00**
Price: Model 873, self-opening, from **$8,200.00**
Price: Model 874, self-opening, from **$9,250.00**
Price: Model 875, self-opening, from **$14,900.00**

CHARLES DALY SUPERIOR HUNTER AND SUPERIOR MC DOUBLE SHOTGUN
Gauge: 12, 20, 3" chambers, 28, 2-3/4" chambers. **Barrel:** 28" (Mod. & Full) 26" (Imp. Cyl. & Mod.). **Weight:** About 7 lbs. **Stock:** Checkered walnut pistol grip buttstock, splinter forend. **Features:** Silvered, engraved receiver; chrome-lined barrels; gold single trigger; automatic safety; extractors; gold bead front sight. Introduced 1997. Imported from Italy by K.B.I., Inc.
Price: Superior Hunter, 28 and 410 gauge **$1,029.00**
Price: Superior Hunter MC 26"-28" **$1,059.00**

Charles Daly Empire Hunter AE-MC Double Shotgun
Similar to Superior Hunter except deluxe wood English-style stock, game scene engraving, automatic ejectors. Introduced 1997. Imported from Italy by K.B.I., Inc.
Price: 12 or 20 . . . . **$1,349.00**

CHARLES DALY DIAMOND DL DOUBLE SHOTGUN
Gauge: 12, 20, 410, 3" chambers, 28, 2-3/4" chambers. **Barrel:** 28" (Mod. & Full), 26" (Imp. Cyl. & Mod.), 26" (Full & Full, 410). **Weight:** About 5-7 lbs. **Stock:** Select fancy European walnut, English-style butt, beavertail forend; hand-checkered, hand-rubbed oil finish. **Features:** Drop-forged action with gas escape valves; demiblock barrels with concave rib; selective automatic ejectors; hand-detachable double safety sidelocks with hand-engraved rose and scrollwork. Hinged front trigger. Color case-hardened receiver. Introduced 1997. Imported from Spain by K.B.I., Inc.
Price: **$6,999.00**

CHARLES DALY DIAMOND REGENT DL DOUBLE SHOTGUN
Gauge: 12, 20, 410, 3" chambers, 28, 2-3/4" chambers. **Barrel:** 28" (Mod. & Full), 26" (Imp. Cyl. & Mod.), 26" (Full & Full, 410). **Weight:** About 5-7 lbs. **Stock:** Special select fancy European walnut, English-style butt, splinter forend; hand-checkered; hand-rubbed oil finish. **Features:** Drop-forged action with gas escape valves; demiblock barrels of chrome-nickel steel with concave rib; selective automatic-ejectors; hand-detachable, double-safety H&H sidelocks with demi-relief hand engraving; H&H pattern easy-opening feature; hinged trigger; coin finished action. Introduced 1997. Imported from Spain by K.B.I., Inc.
Price: Special Custom Order . . . . **NA**

CHARLES DALY FIELD II, AE-MC HUNTER DOUBLE SHOTGUN
Gauge: 12, 20, 28, 410 (3" chambers; 28 has 2-3/4"). **Barrel:** 32" (Mod. & Mod.), 28, 30" (Mod. & Full), 26" (Imp. Cyl. & Mod.) 410 (Full & Full). **Weight:** 6 lbs. to 11.4 lbs. **Stock:** Checkered walnut pistol grip and forend. **Features:** Silvered, engraved receiver; gold single selective trigger in 10-, 12, and 20 ga.; double triggers in 28 and 410; automatic safety; extractors; gold bead front sight. Introduced 1997. Imported from Spain by K.B.I., Inc.
Price: 28 ga., 410-bore **$729.00**
Price: 12 or 20 AE-MC **$799.00**

SHOTGUNS

SHOTGUNS — SIDE-BY-SIDES

Charles Daly Field Hunter

EAA/Baikal Bounty Hunter IZH-43K

EAA/Baikal IZH-43 Bounty Hunter

EAA/Baikal MP-213

EAA/Baikal Bounty Hunter MP-213 Coach

DAKOTA PREMIER GRADE SHOTGUNS
Gauge: 12, 16, 20, 28, 410. **Barrel:** 27". **Weight:** NA. **Length:** NA. **Stock:** Exhibition-grade English walnut, hand-rubbed oil finish with straight grip and splinter forend. **Features:** French grey finish; 50 percent coverage engraving; double triggers; selective ejectors. Finished to customer specifications. Made in U.S. by Dakota Arms.
Price: 12, 16, 20 gauge **$13,950.00**
Price: 28 and 410 gauge **$15,345.00**

Dakota The Dakota Legend Shotguns
Similar to Premier Grade except has special selection English walnut, full-coverage scroll engraving, oak and leather case. Made in U.S. by Dakota Arms.
Price: 12, 16, 20 gauge **$18,000.00**
Price: 28 and 410 gauge **$19,800.00**

EAA/BAIKAL BOUNTY HUNTER IZH-43K SHOTGUN
Gauge: 12 (2-3/4", 3" chambers), 20 (3" chambers), 28 (2-3/4" chambers), 410 (3" chambers). **Barrel:** 18-1/2", 20", 24", 26", 28", three choke tubes. **Weight:** 7.28 lbs. Overall length: NA. **Stock:** Walnut, checkered forearm and grip. **Features:** Machined receiver; hammer-forged barrels with chrome-line bores; external hammers; double triggers (single, selective trigger available); rifle barrel inserts optional. Imported by European American Armory.
Price: . . . . **$379.00 to $429.00**

EAA/BAIKAL IZH-43 BOUNTY HUNTER SHOTGUNS
Gauge: 12 (2-3/4", 3" chambers), 16 (2-3/4" chambers), 20 (2-3/4" and 3" chambers). **Barrel:** 20", 24", 26", 28"; imp., mod. and full choke tubes.

Stock: Hardwood or walnut; checkered forend and grip. **Features:** Hammer forged barrel; internal hammers; extractors; engraved receiver; automatic tang safety; non-glare rib. Imported by European American Armory.
Price: IZH-43 Bounty Hunter (12 gauge, 2-3/4" chambers, 20" brl., dbl. triggers, hardwood stock) **$299.00**
Price: IZH-43 Bounty Hunter (12 or 20 gauge, 2-3/4" chambers, 20" brl., dbl. triggers, walnut stock) **$359.00**

EAA/BAIKAL MP-213 SHOTGUN
Gauge: 12, 3" chambers. **Barrel:** 24", 26", 28"; imp., mod. and full choke tubes. **Weight:** 7.28 lbs. **Stock:** Walnut, checkered forearm and grip; rubber butt pad. **Features:** Hammer-forged barrels; chrome-lined bores; machined receiver; double trigger (each trigger fires both barrels independently); ejectors. Introduced 2000. Imported by European American Armory.
Price: IZH-213 . . . . **$939.00**

EAA/BAIKAL BOUNTY HUNTER MP-213 COACH GUN
Gauge: 12, 2-3/4" chambers. **Barrel:** 20", imp., mod. and full choke tubes. **Weight:** 7 lbs. **Stock:** Walnut, checkered forend and grip. **Features:** Selective double trigger with removable assembly (single trigger and varied pull weights available); ejectors; engraved receiver. Imported by European American Armory.
Price: MP-213. . . . . **$939.00**

E.M.F. HARTFORD MODEL COWBOY SHOTGUN
Gauge: 12. **Barrel:** 20". **Weight:** NA. **Length:** NA. **Stock:** Checkered walnut. **Sights:** Center bead. **Features:** Exposed hammers; color-case hardened receiver; blued barrel. Introduced 2001. Imported from Spain by E.M.F. Co. Inc.
Price: **$625.00**

SHOTGUNS

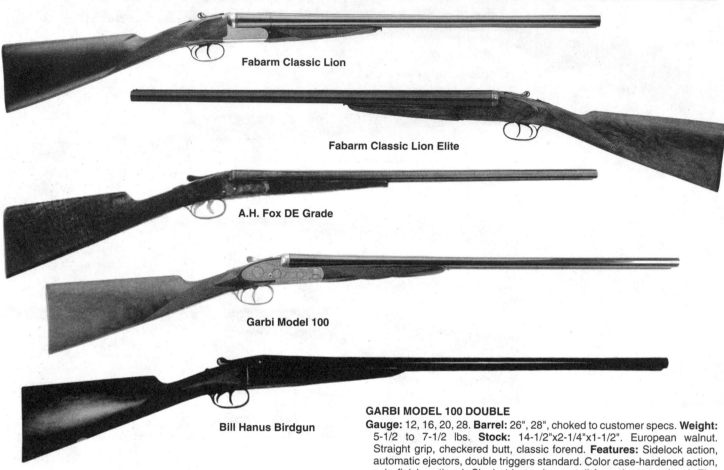

Fabarm Classic Lion

Fabarm Classic Lion Elite

A.H. Fox DE Grade

Garbi Model 100

Bill Hanus Birdgun

FABARM CLASSIC LION DOUBLE SHOTGUN

Gauge: 12, 3" chambers. **Barrel:** 26", 28", 30" (Cyl., Imp. Cyl., Mod., Imp. Mod., Full choke tubes). **Weight:** 7.2 lbs. **Length:** 44.5"-48.5. **Stock:** English-style or pistol grip oil-finished European walnut. **Features:** Boxlock action with double triggers, automatic ejectors, automatic safety. Introduced 1998. Imported from Italy by Heckler & Koch, Inc.
Price: Grade I $1,499.00
Price: Grade II $2,099.00
Price: Elite (color-case hardened type finish, 44.5") $1,689.00

FOX, A.H., SIDE-BY-SIDE SHOTGUNS

Gauge: 16, 20, 28, 410. **Barrel:** Length and chokes to customer specifications. Rust-blued Chromox or Krupp steel. **Weight:** 5-1/2 to 6-3/4 lbs. **Stock:** Dimensions to customer specifications. Hand-checkered Turkish Circassian walnut with hand-rubbed oil finish. Straight, semi or full pistol grip; splinter, Schnabel or beavertail forend; traditional pad, hard rubber buttplate or skeleton butt. **Features:** Boxlock action with automatic ejectors; double or Fox single selective trigger. Scalloped, rebated and color case-hardened receiver; hand finished and hand-engraved. Grades differ in engraving, inlays, grade of wood, amount of hand finishing. Add $1,500 for 28 or 410-bore. Introduced 1993. Made in U.S. by Connecticut Shotgun Mfg.
Price: CE Grade $11,000.00
Price: XE Grade $12,500.00
Price: DE Grade $15,000.00
Price: FE Grade $20,000.00
Price: Exhibition Grade $30,000.00
Price: 28/410 CE Grade $12,500.00
Price: 28/410 XE Grade $14,000.00
Price: 28/410 DE Grade $16,500.00
Price: 28/410 FE Grade $21,500.00
Price: 28/410 Exhibition Grade $30,000.00

GARBI MODEL 100 DOUBLE

Gauge: 12, 16, 20, 28. **Barrel:** 26", 28", choked to customer specs. **Weight:** 5-1/2 to 7-1/2 lbs. **Stock:** 14-1/2"x2-1/4"x1-1/2". European walnut. Straight grip, checkered butt, classic forend. **Features:** Sidelock action, automatic ejectors, double triggers standard. Color case-hardened action, coin finish optional. Single trigger; beavertail forend, etc. optional. Five other models are available. Imported from Spain by Wm. Larkin Moore.
Price: From $4,000.00

Garbi Model 200 Side-by-Side

Similar to the Garbi Model 100 except has heavy-duty locks, magnum proofed. Very fine Continental-style floral and scroll engraving, well figured walnut stock. Other mechanical features remain the same. Imported from Spain by Wm. Larkin Moore.
Price: $8,700.00

Garbi Model 101 Side-by-Side

Similar to the Garbi Model 100 except is hand engraved with scroll engraving, select walnut stock. Better overall quality than the Model 100. Imported from Spain by Wm. Larkin Moore.
Price: From $5,150.00

Garbi Model 103A, B Side-by-Side

Similar to the Garbi Model 100 except has Purdey-type fine scroll and rosette engraving. Better overall quality than the Model 101. Model 103B has nickel-chrome steel barrels, H&H-type easy opening mechanism; other mechanical details remain the same. Imported from Spain by Wm. Larkin Moore.
Price: Model 103A, from $6,600.00
Price: Model 103B, from $9,100.00

HANUS, BILL, BIRDGUN

Gauge: 16, 20, 28. **Barrel:** 27", 20 and 28 ga.; 28", 16 ga. (Skeet 1 & Skeet 2). **Weight:** 5 lbs., 4 oz. to 6 lbs., 4 oz. **Stock:** 14-3/8"x1-1/2"x2-3/8", with 1/4" cast-off. Select walnut. **Features:** Boxlock action with ejectors; splinter forend, straight English grip; checkered butt; English leather-covered handguard and Aya snap caps included. Made by AYA. Introduced 1998. Imported from Spain by Bill Hanus Birdguns.
Price: $2,295.00
Price: Single-selective trigger, add $350.00

SHOTGUNS

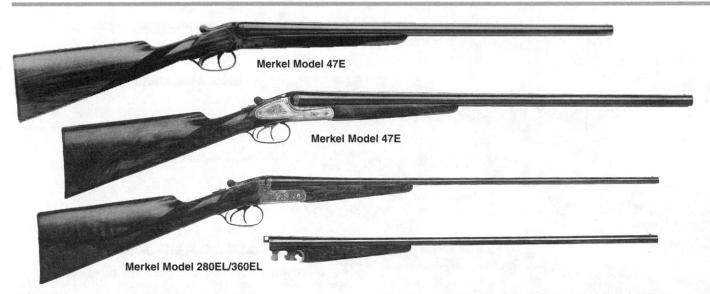

Merkel Model 47E

Merkel Model 47E

Merkel Model 280EL/360EL

ITHACA CLASSIC DOUBLES SKEET GRADE SxS

Gauge: 20, 28, 2-3/4" chambers, 410, 3". **Barrel:** 26", 28", 30", fixed chokes. **Weight:** 5 lbs., 14 oz. (20 gauge). **Stock:** 14-1/2"x2-1/4"x1-3/8". High-grade American black walnut, hand-rubbed oil finish; splinter or beavertail forend, straight or pistol grip. **Features:** Double triggers, ejectors; color case-hardened, engraved action body with matted top surfaces. Introduced 1999. Made in U.S. by Ithaca Classic Doubles.
Price: From **$5,999.00**

Ithaca Classic Doubles Grade 4E Classic SxS Shotgun

Gold-plated triggers, jeweled barrel flats and hand-turned locks. Feather crotch and flame-grained black walnut hand-checkered 28 lpi with fleur de lis pattern. Action body engraved with three game scenes and bank note scroll, color case-hardened. Introduced 1999. Made in U.S. by Ithaca Classic Doubles.
Price: From **$7,500.00**

ITHACA CLASSIC DOUBLES GRADE 7E CLASSIC SxS SHOTGUN

Engraved with bank note scroll and flat 24k gold game scenes: gold setter and gold pointer on opposite action sides, American bald eagle inlaid on bottom plate. Hand-timed, polished, jeweled ejectors and locks. Exhibition grade American black walnut stock and forend with eight-panel fleur de lis borders. Introduced 1999. Made in U.S. by Ithaca Classic Doubles.
Price: From **$11,000.00**

ITHACA CLASSIC DOUBLES GRADE 5E SxS SHOTGUN

Completely hand-made, it is based on the early Ithaca engraving patterns of master engraver William McGraw. The hand engraving is at 90% coverage in deep chiseled floral scroll with game scenes in 24kt gold inlays. Stocks are of high-grade Turkish and American walnut and are hand-checkered. Available in 12, 16, 20, 28 gauges and .410 bore including two barrel combination sets in 16/20 ga. and 28/410 bore. Introduced 2003. Made in U.S.A. by Ithaca Classic Doubles.
Price: From **$8,500.00**

ITHACA CLASSIC DOUBLES GRADE 6E SxS SHOTGUN

Features hand engraving of fine English scroll coupled with game scenes and 24kt gold inlays. Stockare hand-made of best quality American, Turkish or English walnut with hand checkering. All metal work is finished in traditional bone and charcoal color case hardening and deep rust blue. Available in 12, 16, 20, 28 gauges and .410 bore. Introduced 2003. Made in U.S.A. by Ithaca Classic Doubles.
Price: From **$9,999.00**

ITHACA CLASSIC DOUBLES SOUSA SPECIAL GRADE SxS SHOTGUN

Presentation grade American black walnut, hand-carved and checkered; hand-engraving with 24-karat gold inlays; tuned action and hand-applied finishes. Made in U.S. by Ithaca Classic Doubles.
Price: From **$18,000.00**

LEBEAU - COURALLY BOXLOCK SxS SHOTGUN

Gauge: 12, 16, 20, 28, 410-bore. **Barrel:** 25" to 32". **Weight:** To customer specifications. **Stock:** French walnut. **Features:** Anson & Deely-type action with automatic ejectors; single or double triggers. Essentially a custom gun built to customer specifications. Imported from Belgium by Wm. Larkin Moore.
Price: From **$21,000.00**

LEBEAU - COURALLY SIDELOCK SxS SHOTGUN

Gauge: 12, 16, 20, 28, 410-bore. **Barrel:** 25" to 32". **Weight:** To customer specifications. **Stock:** Fancy French walnut. **Features:** Holland & Holland-type action with automatic ejectors; single or double triggers. Essentially a custom gun built to customer specifications. Imported from Belgium by Wm. Larkin Moore.
Price: From **$43,000.00**

MERKEL MODEL 47E, 147E SIDE-BY-SIDE SHOTGUNS

Gauge: 12, 3" chambers, 16, 2-3/4" chambers, 20, 3" chambers. **Barrel:** 12, 16 ga.—28"; 20 ga.—26-3/4" (Imp. Cyl. & Mod., Mod. & Full). **Weight:** About 6-3/4 lbs. (12 ga.). **Stock:** Oil-finished walnut; straight English or pistol grip. **Features:** Anson & Deeley-type boxlock action with single selective or double triggers, automatic safety, cocking indicators. Color case-hardened receiver with standard Arabesque engraving. Imported from Germany by GSI.
Price: Model 47E (H&H ejectors) **$3,295.00**
Price: Model 147E (as above with ejectors) **$3,995.00**

Merkel Model 47SL, 147SL Side-by-Sides

Similar to Model 122 except H&H style sidelock action with cocking indicators, ejectors. Silver-grayed receiver and sideplates have Arabesque engraving, engraved border and screws (Model 47S), or fine hunting scene engraving (Model 147S). Imported from Germany by GSI.
Price: Model 47SL **$5,995.00**
Price: Model 147SL **$7,995.00**
Price: Model 247SL (English-style engraving, large scrolls) . . . **$7,995.00**
Price: Model 447SL (English-style engraving, small scrolls) . . . **$9,995.00**

Merkel Model 280EL and 360EL Shotguns

Similar to Model 47E except smaller frame. Greener cross bolt with double under-barrel locking lugs, fine engraved hunting scenes on silver-grayed receiver, luxury-grade wood, Anson and Deely box-lock action. H&H ejectors, single-selective or double triggers. Introduced 2000. From Merkel.
Price: Model 280EL (28 gauge, 28" barrel, imp. cyl. and
mod. chokes) 4 mod. chokes) **$5,795.00**
Price: Model 360EL (410 gauge, 28" barrel, mod. and
full chokes) **$5,795.00**
Price: Model 280/360EL two-barrel set (28 and 410 gauge
as above) **$8,295.00**

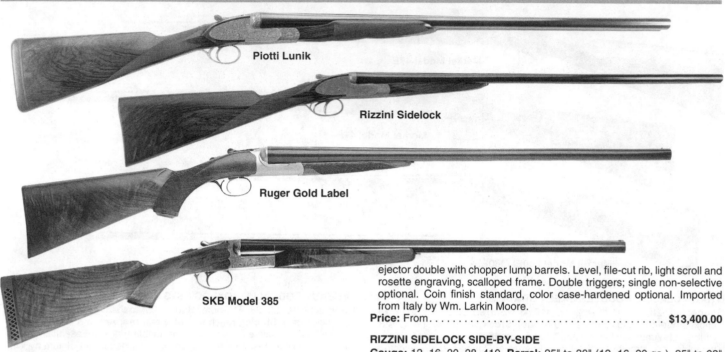

Piotti Lunik

Rizzini Sidelock

Ruger Gold Label

SKB Model 385

Merkel Model 280SL and 360SL Shotguns

Similar to Model 280EL and 360EL except has sidelock action, double triggers, English-style Arabesque engraving. Introduced 2000. From Merkel.

Price: Model 280SL (28 gauge, 28" barrel, imp. cyl. and
mod. chokes) **$8,495.00**
Price: Model 360SL (410 gauge, 28" barrel, mod. and
full chokes) **$8,495.00**
Price: Model 280/360SL two-barrel set **$11,995.00**

PIOTTI KING NO. 1 SIDE-BY-SIDE

Gauge: 12, 16, 20, 28, 410. **Barrel:** 25" to 30" (12 ga.), 25" to 28" (16, 20, 28, 410). To customer specs. Chokes as specified. **Weight:** 6-1/2 lbs. to 8 lbs. (12 ga. to customer specs.). **Stock:** Dimensions to customer specs. Finely figured walnut; straight grip with checkered butt with classic splinter forend and hand-rubbed oil finish standard. Pistol grip, beavertail forend. **Features:** Holland & Holland pattern sidelock action, automatic ejectors. Double trigger; non-selective single trigger optional. Coin finish standard; color case-hardened optional. Top rib; level, file-cut; concave, ventilated optional. Very fine, full coverage scroll engraving with small floral bouquets. Imported from Italy by Wm. Larkin Moore.

Price: From. **$20,900.00**

Piotti King Extra Side-by-Side

Similar to the Piotti King No. 1 except with upgraded engraving. Choice of any type of engraving, including bulino game scene engraving and game scene engraving with gold inlays. Engraved and signed by a master engraver. Other mechanical specifications remain the same. Imported from Italy by Wm. Larkin Moore.

Price: From. **$25,900.00**

Piotti Lunik Side-by-Side

Similar to the Piotti King No. 1 in overall quality. Has Renaissance-style large scroll engraving in relief. Best quality Holland & Holland-pattern sidelock ejector double with chopper lump (demi-bloc) barrels. Other mechanical specifications remain the same. Imported from Italy by Wm. Larkin Moore.

Price: From. **$21,900.00**

PIOTTI PIUMA SIDE-BY-SIDE

Gauge: 12, 16, 20, 28, 410. **Barrel:** 25" to 30" (12 ga.), 25" to 28" (16, 20, 28, 410). **Weight:** 5-1/2 to 6-1/4 lbs. (20 ga.). **Stock:** Dimensions to customer specs. Straight grip stock with walnut checkered butt, classic splinter forend, hand-rubbed oil finish are standard; pistol grip, beavertail forend, satin luster finish optional. **Features:** Anson & Deeley boxlock

ejector double with chopper lump barrels. Level, file-cut rib, light scroll and rosette engraving, scalloped frame. Double triggers; single non-selective optional. Coin finish standard, color case-hardened optional. Imported from Italy by Wm. Larkin Moore.

Price: From. **$13,400.00**

RIZZINI SIDELOCK SIDE-BY-SIDE

Gauge: 12, 16, 20, 28, 410. **Barrel:** 25" to 30" (12, 16, 20 ga.), 25" to 28" (28, 410). To customer specs. Chokes as specified. **Weight:** 6-1/2 lbs. to 8 lbs. (12 ga. to customer specs). **Stock:** Dimensions to customer specs. Finely figured walnut; straight grip with checkered butt with classic splinter forend and hand-rubbed oil finish standard. Pistol grip, beavertail forend. **Features:** Sidelock action, auto ejectors. Double triggers or non-selective single trigger standard. Coin finish standard. Imported from Italy by Wm. Larkin Moore.

Price: 12, 20 ga., from **$52,000.00**
Price: 28, 410 bore, from **$60,000.00**

RUGER GOLD LABEL SIDE-BY-SIDE SHOTGUN

Gauge: 12, 3" chambers. **Barrel:** 28" with skeet tubes. **Weight:** 6-1/2 lbs. **Length:** 45". **Stock:** American walnut straight or pistol grip. **Sights:** Gold bead front, full length rib, serrated top. **Features:** Spring-assisted break-open, SS trigger, auto eject. 5 interchangeable screw-in choke tubes, combination safety/barrel selector with auto safety reset.

Price: **$1,950.00**

SKB MODEL 385 SIDE-BY-SIDE

Gauge: 12, 20, 3" chambers; 28, 2-3/4" chambers. **Barrel:** 26" (Imp. Cyl., Mod., Skeet choke tubes). **Weight:** 6-3/4 lbs. **Length:** 42-1/2" overall. **Stock:** 14-1/8"x1-1/2"x2-1/2" American walnut with straight or pistol grip stock, semi-beavertail forend. **Features:** Boxlock action. Silver nitrided receiver with engraving; solid barrel rib; single selective trigger, selective automatic ejectors, automatic safety. Introduced 1996. Imported from Japan by G.U. Inc.

Price: **$2,049.00**
Price: Field Set, 20, 28 ga., 26" or 28", English or pistol grip. . . **$2,929.00**

SKB Model 385 Sporting Clays

Similar to the Field Model 385 except 12 gauge only; 28" barrel with choke tubes; raised ventilated rib with metal middle bead and white front. Stock dimensions 14-1/4"x1-7/16"x1-7/8". Introduced 1998. Imported from Japan by G.U. Inc.

Price: **$2,159.00**
Price: Sporting Clays set, 20, 28 ga. **$3,059.00**

SKB Model 485 Side-by-Side

Similar to the Model 385 except has dummy sideplates, raised ventilated rib with metal middle bead and white front, extensive upland game scene engraving, semi-fancy American walnut English or pistol grip stock. Imported from Japan by G.U. Inc.

Price: **$2,769.00**
Price: Field set, 20, 28 ga., 26" **$2,769.00**

SHOTGUNS

Stoeger Uplander

Stoeger Silverado Coach

Traditions Uplander V

Tristar Rota
Model 411

STOEGER UPLANDER SIDE-BY-SIDE SHOTGUN

Gauge: 16, 28, 2-3/4 chambers. 12, 20, 410, 3" chambers. **Barrel:** 26", 28". **Weight:** 7.3 lbs. **Sights:** Brass bead. **Features:** Double trigger, IC, M fixed choke tubes with gun.
Price: .... (With fixed chokes) **$335.00**; (With screw-in chokes) **$350.00**
Price: With English stock .... **$335.00 to $350.00**
Price: Upland Special **$375.00**
Price: Upland Supreme with SST, red bar sights **$445.00**
Price: Upland Short Stock (Youth) **$335.00**

STOEGER COACH GUN SIDE-BY-SIDE SHOTGUN

Gauge: 12, 20, 410, 2-3/4", 3" chambers. **Barrel:** 20". **Weight:** 6-1/2 lbs. **Stock:** Brown hardwood, classic beavertail forend. **Sights:** Brass bead. **Features:** IC & M fixed chokes, tang auto safety, auto extractors, black plastic butt plate. 12 ga. and 20 ga. also with English style stock.
Price: .... **$320.00**; (Nickel) **$375.00**
Price: Silverado .... **$375.00**; (With English stock) **$375.00**

TRADITIONS ELITE SERIES SIDE-BY-SIDE SHOTGUNS

Gauge: 12, 3"; 20, 3"; 28, 2-3/4"; 410, 3". **Barrel:** 26". **Weight:** 5 lbs., 12 oz. to 6-1/2 lbs. **Length:** 43" overall. **Stock:** Walnut. **Features:** Chrome-lined barrels; fixed chokes (Elite Field III ST, Field I DT and Field I ST) or choke tubes (Elite Hunter ST); extractors (Hunter ST and Field I models) or automatic ejectors (Field III ST); top tang safety. Imported from Fausti of Italy by Traditions.
Price: (Elite Field I DT — 12, 20, 28 or 410 ga.; I.C. and Mod. fixed chokes [F and F on 410]; double triggers) .... **$789.00 to $969.00**
Price: (Elite Field I ST — 12, 20, 28 or 410 ga.; same as DT but with single trigger) .... **$969.00 to $1,169.00**
Price: (Elite Field III ST — 28 or 410 ga.; gold-engraved receiver; high-grade walnut stock) **$2,099.00**
Price: (Elite Hunter ST — 12 or 20 ga.; blued receiver; I.C. and Mod. choke tubes) **$999.00**

TRADITIONS UPLANDER SERIES SIDE-BY-SIDE SHOTGUNS

Gauge: 12, 3"; 20, 3". **Barrel:** 26", 28". **Weight:** 6-1/4 lbs. to 6-1/2 lbs. **Length:** 43"-45" overall. **Stock:** Walnut. **Features:** Barrels threaded for choke tubes (Improved Cylinder, Modified and Full); top tang safety, extended trigger guard. Engraved silver receiver with side plates and lavish gold inlays. From Traditions.
Price: Uplander III Silver 12, 20 ga. **$2,699.00**
Price: Uplander V Silver 12, 20 ga. **$3,199.00**

TRISTAR ROTA MODEL 411 SIDE-BY-SIDE

Gauge: 12, 16, 20, 410, 3" chambers; 28, 2-3/4". **Barrel:** 12 ga., 26", 28"; 16, 20, 28 ga., 410-bore, 26"; 12 and 20 ga. have three choke tubes, 16, 28 (Imp. Cyl. & Mod.), 410 (Mod. & Full) fixed chokes. **Weight:** 6-1/2 to 7-1/4 lbs. **Stock:** 14-3/8" l.o.p. Standard walnut with pistol grip, splinter-style forend; hand checkered. **Features:** Engraved, color case-hardened boxlock action; double triggers, extractors; solid barrel rib. Introduced 1998. Imported from Italy by Tristar Sporting Arms, Ltd.
Price: **$849.00**

Tristar Rota Model 411D Side-by-Side

Similar to Model 411 except automatic ejectors, straight English-style stock, single trigger. Solid barrel rib with matted surface; chrome bores; color case-hardened frame; splinter forend. Introduced 1999. Imported from Italy by Tristar Sporting Arms, Ltd.
Price: **$1,110.00**

Tristar Rota Model 411R Coach Gun Side-by-Side

Similar to Model 411 except in 12 or 20 gauge only with 20" barrels and fixed chokes (Cyl. & Cyl.). Double triggers, extractors, choke tubes. Introduced 1999. Imported from Italy by Tristar Sporting Arms, Ltd.
Price: **$745.00**

Tristar Rota Model 411F Side-by-Side

Similar to Model 411 except silver, engraved receiver, ejectors, IC, M and F choke tubes, English-style stock, single gold trigger, cut checkering. Imported from Italy by Tristar Sporting Arms Ltd.
Price: **$1,608.00**

TRISTAR DERBY CLASSIC SIDE-BY-SIDE

Gauge: 12. **Barrel:** 28" Mod. & Full fixed chokes. **Features:** Sidelock action, engraved, double trigger, auto ejectors, English straight stock. Maide in Eruope for Tristar Sporting Arms Ltd.
Price: **$1,059.00**

WEATHERBY ATHENA SIDE-BY-SIDE

Gauge: 12, 20. **Barrel:** 26", 28". **Stock:** Turkish walnut, straight grip. **Sights:** Brass bead front. **Features:** Barrel selector independent of crossbolt safety. Integral multi-choke system, interchangeable screw-in Briley choke tubes (excepting 410 bored IC & Mod.). Receivers engraved with rose and scroll.
Price: **$1,599.00**

WEATHERBY ORION SIDE-BY-SIDE

Gauge: 12, 20, 28, 410. **Barrel:** 26", 28". **Stock:** Turkish walnut, half round pistol grip. **Sights:** Brass bead front. **Features:** Barrel selector independent of crossbolt safety. Integral multi-choke system, interchangeable screw-in Briley choke tubes (excepting 410 bored IC & Mod.). Receivers engraved with rose and scroll.
Price: **$1,149.00**

SHOTGUNS

Variety of designs for utility and sporting purposes, as well as for competitive shooting.

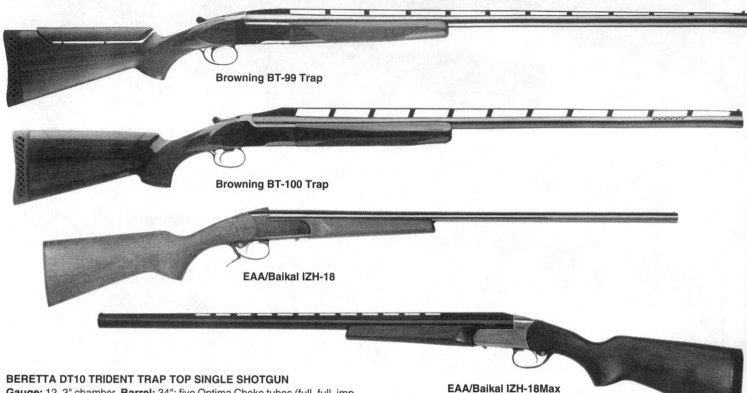

Browning BT-99 Trap

Browning BT-100 Trap

EAA/Baikal IZH-18

EAA/Baikal IZH-18Max

BERETTA DT10 TRIDENT TRAP TOP SINGLE SHOTGUN
Gauge: 12, 3" chamber. **Barrel:** 34"; five Optima Choke tubes (full, full, imp. modified, mod. and imp. cyl.). **Weight:** 8.8 lbs. **Stock:** High-grade walnut; adjustable. **Features:** Detachable, adjustable trigger group; Optima Bore for improved shot pattern and reduced recoil; slim Optima Choke tubes; raised and thickened receiver for long life. Introduced 2000. Imported from Italy by Beretta USA.
Price: **$8,500.00**

BRNO ZBK 100 SINGLE BARREL SHOTGUN
Gauge: 12 or 20. **Barrel:** 27.5". **Weight:** 5.5 lbs. **Length:** 44" overall. **Stock:** Beech. **Features:** Polished blue finish; sling swivels. Announced 1998. Imported from The Czech Republic by Euro-Imports.
Price: **$185.00**

BROWNING BT-99 TRAP SHOTGUN
Gauge: 12, 2-3/4" chamber. **Barrel:** 32" or 34"; Invector choke system (full choke tube only included); High Post Rib; back-bored. **Weight:** 8 lbs., 10 oz. (34" bbl.). **Length:** 50-1/2" overall (34" bbl.). **Stock:** Conventional or adjustable-comb. **Features:** Re-introduction of the BT-99 Trap Shotgun. Full beavertail forearm; checkered walnut stock; ejector; rubber butt pad. Re-introduced 2001. Imported by Browning.
Price: Conventional stock, 32" or 34" barrel **$1,216.00**
Price: Adj.-comb stock, 32" or 34" barrel **$1,449.00**

BROWNING BT-100 TRAP SHOTGUN
Gauge: 12, 2-3/4" chamber. **Barrel:** 32", 34" (Invector Plus); back-bored; also with fixed Full choke. **Weight:** 8 lbs., 10 oz. (34" bbl.). **Length:** 48-1/2" overall (32" barrel). **Stock:** 14-3/8"x1-9/16"x1-7/16x2" (Monte Carlo); 14-3/8"x1-3/4"x1-1/4"x2-1/8" (thumbhole). Walnut with high gloss finish; cut checkering. Wedge-shaped forend with finger groove. **Features:** Available in stainless steel or blue. Has drop-out trigger adjustable for weight of pull from 3-1/2 to 5-1/2 lbs., and for three length positions; Ejector-Selector allows ejection or extraction of shells. Available with adjustable comb stock and thumbhole style. Introduced 1995. Imported from Japan by Browning.
Price: Grade I, blue, Monte Carlo, Invector Plus **$2,222.00**
Price: Grade I, blue, adj. comb, Invector Plus **$2,455.00**
Price: Stainless steel, Monte Carlo, Invector Plus **$2,688.00**
Price: Stainless steel, adj. comb, Invector Plus **$2,923.00**

CHIPMUNK 410 YOUTH SHOTGUN
Gauge: 410. **Barrel:** 18-1/4" tapered, blue. **Weight:** 3.25 lbs. **Length:** 33". **Stock:** Walnut. **Features:** Manually cocking single shot bolt, blued receiver.
Price: **$225.95**

EAA/BAIKAL IZH-18 SINGLE BARREL SHOTGUN
Gauge: 12 (2-3/4" and 3" chambers), 20 (2-3/4" and 3"), 16 (2-3/4"), 410 (3"). **Barrel:** 26-1/2", 28-1/2"; modified or full choke (12 and 20 gauge); full only (16 gauge), improved cylinder (20 gauge) and full or improved modified (410). **Stock:** Walnut-stained hardwood; rubber recoil pad. **Features:** Hammer-forged steel barrel; machined receiver; cross-block safety; cocking lever with external cocking indicator; optional automatic ejector, screw-in chokes and rifle barrel. Imported by European American Armory.
Price: IZH-18 (12, 16, 20 or 410) **$95.00**
Price: IZH-18 (20 gauge with imp. cyl. or 410 with imp. mod.) . . . **$109.00**

EAA/BAIKAL IZH-18MAX SINGLE BARREL SHOTGUN
Gauge: 12, 3"; 20, 3"; 410, 3". **Barrel:** 24" (410), 26" (410 or 20 ga.) or 28" (12 ga.). **Weight:** 6.4 to 6.6 lbs. **Stock:** Walnut. **Features:** Polished nickel receiver; ventilated rib; I.C., Mod. and Full choke tubes; titanium-coated trigger; internal hammer; selectable ejector/extractor; rubber butt pad; de-cocking system. Imported by European American Armory.
Price: (12 or 20 ga., choke tubes) **$169.00**
Price: (410 ga., full choke only) **$189.00**
Price: Sporting, 12 ga., ported, Monte Carlo stock **$219.00**

FABARM MONOTRAP SHOTGUN
Caliber: 12; 2-3/4" chamber. **Barrel:** 30", 34". **Weight:** 6.7 to 6.9 lbs. **Length:** 48.5" overall (30" bbl.) **Stock:** Walnut; adjustable comb competition-style. **Sights:** Red front sight bar, mid-rib bead. **Features:** Built on 20-gauge receiver for quick handling. Silver receiver with blued barrel; special trap rib (micrometer adjustable); includes three choke tubes (M, IM, F). Introduced 2000.
Price: **$1,799.00**

Fabarm Monotrap

H&R 928 Ultra Slug Hunter Deluxe

H&R Tamer

H&R Topper

H&R Topper Deluxe

HARRINGTON & RICHARDSON NWTF SHOTGUNS
Gauge: 12, 3-1/2" chamber, fixed full choke; 20, 3" chamber, fixed modified choke. **Barrel:** 24" (12 ga.) or 22" (20 ga.) **Weight:** 5 to 6 lbs. **Stock:** Straight-grip camo laminate with recoil pad and sling swivel studs. **Sights:** Bead front. **Features:** Break-open single-shot action with side lever release; hand-checkered stock and forearm; includes trigger lock. Purchase supports National Wild Turkey Federation; NWTF logo on receiver.
Price: 12 ga. **$216.00**
Price: 20 ga. youth gun (12-1/2" length of pull, weighs 5 lbs.) . . . **$207.00**

HARRINGTON & RICHARDSON SB2-980 ULTRA SLUG
Gauge: 12, 20, 3" chamber. **Barrel:** 22" (20 ga. Youth) 24", fully rifled. **Weight:** 9 lbs. **Length:** NA. **Stock:** Walnut-stained hardwood. **Sights:** None furnished; comes with scope mount. **Features:** Uses the H&R 10 gauge action with heavy-wall barrel. Monte Carlo stock has sling swivels; comes with black nylon sling. Introduced 1995. Made in U.S. by H&R 1871, LLC.
Price: **$313.00**

Harrington & Richardson Model 928 Ultra Slug Hunter Deluxe
Similar to the SB2-980 Ultra Slug except uses 12 gauge action and 12 gauge barrel blank bored to 20 gauge, then fully rifled with 1:35" twist. Has hand-checkered camo laminate Monte Carlo stock and forend. Comes with Weaver-style scope base, offset hammer extension, ventilated recoil pad, sling swivels and nylon sling. Introduced 1997. Made in U.S. by H&R 1871 LLC.
Price: **$313.00**

HARRINGTON & RICHARDSON TAMER SHOTGUN
Gauge: 410, 3" chamber. **Barrel:** 20" (Full). **Weight:** 5-6 lbs. **Length:** 33" overall. **Stock:** Thumbhole grip of high density black polymer. **Features:** Uses H&R Topper action with matte electroless nickel finish. Stock holds four spare shotshells. Introduced 1994. From H&R 1871, LLC.
Price: **$161.00**

HARRINGTON & RICHARDSON TOPPER MODEL 098
Gauge: 12, 16, 20, 28 (2-3/4"), 410, 3" chamber. **Barrel:** 12 ga.—28" (Mod., Full); 16 ga.— 28" (Mod.); 20 ga.—26" (Mod.); 28 ga.—26" (Mod.); 410 bore— 26" (Full). **Weight:** 5-6 lbs. **Stock:** Black-finish hardwood with full pistol grip; semi-beavertail forend. **Sights:** Gold bead front. **Features:** Break-open action with side-lever release, automatic ejector. Satin nickel frame, blued barrel. Reintroduced 1992. From H&R 1871, LLC.
Price: **$143.00**
Price: Topper Junior 098 (as above except 22" barrel, 20 ga. (Mod.), 410-bore (Full), 12-1/2" length of pull) **$149.00**

Harrington & Richardson Topper Deluxe Model 098
Similar to the standard Topper 098 except 12 gauge only with 3-1/2" chamber, 28" barrel with choke tube (comes with Mod. tube, others optional). Satin nickel frame, blued barrel, black-finished wood. Introduced 1992. From H&R 1871, LLC.
Price: **$167.00**

Harrington & Richardson Topper Junior Classic Shotgun
Similar to the Topper Junior 098 except available in 20 gauge (3", Mod.), 410-bore (Full) with 3" chamber; 28 gauge, 2-3/4" chamber (Mod.); all have 22" barrel. Stock is American black walnut with cut-checkered pistol grip and forend. Ventilated rubber recoil pad with white line spacers. Blued barrel, blued frame. Introduced 1992. From H&R 1871, LLC.
Price: **$184.00**

SHOTGUNS

H&R Topper Junior

Ljutic Mono Gun

Mossberg 695 Slugster

Mossberg 695

NEW! ITHACA CLASSIC DOUBLES KNICKERBOCKER TRAP GUN

A reissue of the famous Ithaca Knickerbocker Trap Gun. Built on a custom basis only. Introduced 2003. Made in U.S.A. by Ithaca Classic Doubles.

Price: From **$9,000.00**

KRIEGHOFF K-80 SINGLE BARREL TRAP GUN

Gauge: 12, 2-3/4" chamber. **Barrel:** 32" or 34" Unsingle. Fixed Full or choke tubes. **Weight:** About 8-3/4 lbs. **Stock:** Four stock dimensions or adjustable stock available. All hand-checkered European walnut. **Features:** Satin nickel finish. Selective mechanical trigger adjustable for finger position. Tapered step vent. rib. Adjustable point of impact.

Price: Standard grade full Unsingle, from. **$7,950.00**

KRIEGHOFF KX-5 TRAP GUN

Gauge: 12, 2-3/4" chamber. **Barrel:** 34"; choke tubes. **Weight:** About 8-1/2 lbs. **Stock:** Factory adjustable stock. European walnut. **Features:** Ventilated tapered step rib. Adjustable position trigger, optional release trigger. fully adjustable rib shooter to adjust point of impact from 50%/50% to nearly 90%/ 10%. Satin gray electroless nickel receiver. Fitted aluminum case. Imported from Germany by Krieghoff International, Inc.

Price: **$4,200.00**

LJUTIC MONO GUN SINGLE BARREL

Gauge: 12 only. **Barrel:** 34", choked to customer specs; hollow-milled rib, 35-1/2" sight plane. **Weight:** Approx. 9 lbs. **Stock:** To customer specs. Oil finish, hand checkered. **Features:** Totally custom made. Pull or release trigger; removable trigger guard contains trigger and hammer mechanism; Ljutic pushbutton opener on front of trigger guard. From Ljutic Industries.

Price: With standard, medium or Olympic rib, custom 32"-34" bbls., and fixed choke. **$5,795.00**

Price: As above with screw-in choke barrel **$6,095.00**
Price: Stainless steel mono gun **$6,795.00**

Ljutic LTX PRO 3 Deluxe Mono Gun

Deluxe light weight version of the Mono Gun with high quality wood, upgrade checkering, special rib height, screw in chokes, ported and cased.

Price: **$8,995.00**
Price: Stainless steel model **$9,995.00**

MOSSBERG MODEL 695 SLUGSTER

Gauge: 12, 3" chamber. **Barrel:** 22"; fully rifled, ported. **Weight:** 7-1/2 lbs. **Stock:** Black synthetic, with swivel studs and rubber recoil pad. **Sights:** Blade front, folding rifle-style leaf rear; Fiber Optic. Comes with Weaver-style scope bases. **Features:** Matte metal finish; rotating thumb safety; detachable 2-shot magazine. Mossberg Cablelock. Made in U.S. by Mossberg. Introduced 1996.

Price: **$345.00**
Price: With Fiber Optic rifle sights **$367.00**
Price: With woodlands camo stock, Fiber Optic sights. **$397.00**

MOSSBERG SSi-ONE 12 GAUGE SLUG SHOTGUN

Gauge: 12, 3" chamber. **Barrel:** 24", fully rifled. **Weight:** 8 pounds. **Length:** 40" overall. **Stock:** Walnut, fluted and cut checkered; sling-swivel studs; drilled and tapped for scope base. **Sights:** None (scope base supplied). **Features:** Frame accepts interchangeable rifle barrels (see Mossberg SSi-One rifle listing); lever-opening, break-action design; ambidextrous, top-tang safety; internal eject/extract selector. Introduced 2000. From Mossberg.

Price: **$480.00**

Mossberg SSi-One Turkey Shotgun

Similar to SSi-One 12 gauge Slug Shotgun, but chambered for 12 ga., 3-1/2" loads. Includes Accu-Mag Turkey Tube. Introduced 2001. From Mossberg.

Price: **$459.00**

New England Firearms Camo Turkey

New England Firearms Tracker II

New England Firearms Special Purpose

New England Firearms Standard Pardner

NEW ENGLAND FIREARMS CAMO TURKEY SHOTGUNS

Gauge: 10, 3-1/2"; 12, 20, 3" chamber. **Barrel:** 24"; extra-full, screw-in choke tube (10 ga.); fixed full choke (12, 20). **Weight:** NA. **Stock:** American hardwood, green and black camouflage finish with sling swivels and ventilated recoil pad. **Sights:** Bead front. **Features:** Matte metal finish; stock counterweight to reduce recoil; patented transfer bar system for hammer-down safety; includes camo sling and trigger lock. Accepts other factory-fitted barrels. Introduced 2000. From New England Firearms.
Price: .... 10 ga. **$279.00**; 12 ga., **$177.00**
Price: 20 ga. youth model (22" bbl.) **$187.00**

NEW ENGLAND FIREARMS TRACKER II SLUG GUN

Gauge: 12, 20, 3" chamber. **Barrel:** 24" (Cyl.), rifle bore. **Weight:** 5-1/4 lbs. **Length:** 40" overall. **Stock:** Walnut-finished hardwood with full pistol grip, recoil pad. **Sights:** Blade front, fully adjustable rifle-type rear. **Features:** Break-open action with side-lever release; blued barrel, color case-hardened frame. Introduced 1992. From New England Firearms.
Price: Tracker II **$183.00**

NEW ENGLAND FIREARMS SPECIAL PURPOSE SHOTGUNS

Gauge: 10, 3-1/2" chamber. **Barrel:** 28" (Full), 32" (Mod.). **Weight:** 9.5 lbs. **Length:** 44" overall (28" barrel). **Stock:** American hardwood with walnut or matte camo finish; ventilated rubber recoil pad. **Sights:** Bead front. **Features:** Break-open action with side-lever release; ejector. Matte finish on metal. Introduced 1992. From New England Firearms.
Price: Walnut-finish wood sling and swivels **$212.00**
Price: Camo finish, sling and swivels **$268.00**
Price: Camo finish, 32", sling and swivels **$268.00**
Price: Black matte finish, 24", Turkey Full choke tube,
 sling and swivels **$247.00**

NEW ENGLAND FIREARMS SURVIVOR

Gauge: 12, 20, 410/45 Colt, 3" chamber. **Barrel:** 22" (Mod.); 20" (410/45 Colt, rifled barrel, choke tube). **Weight:** 6 lbs. **Length:** 36 overall. **Stock:** Black polymer with thumbhole/pistol grip, sling swivels; beavertail forend. **Sights:** Bead front. **Features:** Buttplate removes to expose storage for extra ammunition; forend also holds extra ammunition. Black or nickel finish. Introduced 1993. From New England Firearms.

Price: Black **$161.00**
Price: Nickel **$185.00**
Price: 410/45 Colt, black **$203.00**
Price: 410/45 Colt, nickel **$221.00**

NEW ENGLAND FIREARMS STANDARD PARDNER

Gauge: 12, 20, 410, 3" chamber; 16, 28, 2-3/4" chamber. **Barrel:** 12 ga.—28" (Full, Mod.), 32" (Full); 16 ga.—28" (Full), 32" (Full); 20 ga.—26" (Full, Mod.); 28 ga.—26" (Mod.); 410-bore—26" (Full). **Weight:** 5-6 lbs. **Length:** 43" overall (28" barrel). **Stock:** Walnut-finished hardwood with full pistol grip. **Sights:** Bead front. **Features:** Transfer bar ignition; break-open action with side-lever release. Introduced 1987. From New England Firearms.
Price: **$131.00**
Price: Youth model (12, 20, 28 ga., 410, 22" barrel, recoil pad). . **$140.00**
Price: 12 ga., 32" (Full) **$147.00**

ROSSI SINGLE-SHOT SHOTGUN

Gauge: 12, 20, 2-3/4" chamber; 410, 3" chamber. **Barrel:** 28" full, 22"Youth. **Weight:** 5 lbs. **Stock:** Stained hardwood. **Sights:** Bead. **Features:** Break-open, positive ejection, internal transfer bar, trigger block.
Price: **$101.00**

ROSSI MATCHED PAIR SINGLE-SHOT SHOTGUN/RIFLE

Gauge: 410, 20 or 12. **Barrel:** 22" (18.5"Youth), 28" (23"full). **Weight:** 4-6 lbs **Stock:** Hardwood (brown or black finish). **Sights:** Bead front. **Features:** Break-open internal transfer bar manual external safety; blued or stainless steel finish; sling-swivel studs; includes matched 22 LR or 22 Mag. barrel with fully adjustable front and rear sight. Trigger block system. Introduced 2001. Imported by BrazTech/Taurus.
Price: Blue **$139.95**
Price: Stainless steel **$169.95**

RUGER KTS-1234-BRE TRAP MODEL SINGLE-BARREL SHOTGUN

Gauge: 12, 2-3/4" chamber. **Barrel:** 34". **Weight:** 9 lbs. **Length:** 50-1/2" overall. **Stock:** Select walnut checkered; adjustable pull length 13"-15". **Features:** Fully adjustable rib for pattern position; adjustable stock comb cast for right- or left-handed shooters; straight grooves the length of barrel to keep wad from rotating for pattern improvement. Full and modified choke tubes supplied. Gold inlaid eagle and Ruger name on receiver. Introduced 2000. From Sturm Ruger & Co.
Price: **$2,850.00**

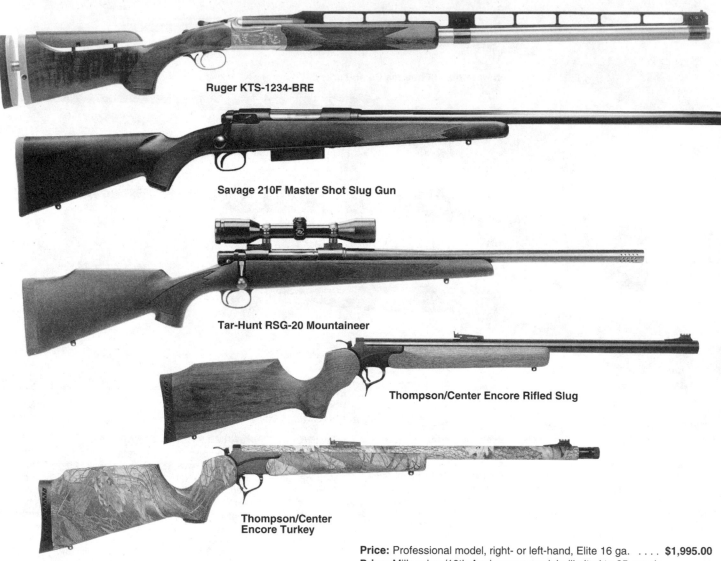

Ruger KTS-1234-BRE

Savage 210F Master Shot Slug Gun

Tar-Hunt RSG-20 Mountaineer

Thompson/Center Encore Rifled Slug

Thompson/Center Encore Turkey

SAVAGE MODEL 210F MASTER SHOT SLUG GUN
Gauge: 12, 3" chamber; 2-shot magazine. **Barrel:** 24" 1:35" rifling twist. **Weight:** 7-1/2 lbs. **Length:** 43.5" overall. **Stock:** Glass-filled polymer with positive checkering. **Features:** Based on the Savage Model 110 action; 60 bolt lift; controlled round feed; comes with scope mount. Introduced 1996. Made in U.S. by Savage Arms.
Price: **$440.00**
Price: (Camo) **$472.00**

STOEGER SINGLE-SHOT SHOTGUN
Gauge: 12, 20, 410, 2-3/4", 3" chambers. **Barrel:** 26", 28". **Weight:** 5.4 lbs. gth: 40-1/2" to 42-1/2" overall. **Sights:** Brass bead. **Features:** 410 ga. full fixed choke tubes, rest M, screw-in. 410 ga. 12 ga. hardwood pistol-grip stock and forend. 20 ga. 26" bbl., hardwood forend.
Price: Blue; Youth **$109.00**
Price: Youth with English stock **$119.00**

TAR-HUNT RSG-12 PROFESSIONAL RIFLED SLUG GUN
Gauge: 12, 16 & 20, 2-3/4" or 3" chamber, 1-shot magazine. **Barrel:** 21-1/2"; 23" fully rifled, with muzzle brake. **Weight:** 7-3/4 lbs. **Length:** 41-1/2" overall. **Stock:** Matte black McMillan fiberglass with Pachmayr Decelerator pad. **Sights:** None furnished; comes with Leupold windage or Weaver bases. **Features:** Uses rifle-style action with two locking lugs; two-position safety; Shaw barrel; single-stage, trigger; muzzle brake. Many options available. Right- and left-hand models at same prices. Introduced 1991. Made in U.S. by Tar-Hunt Custom Rifles, Inc.

Price: Professional model, right- or left-hand, Elite 16 ga. **$1,995.00**
Price: Millennium/10th Anniversary models (limited to 25 guns):
NP-3 nickel/Teflon metal finish, black McMillan
Fibergrain stock, Jewell adj. trigger **$2,300.00**

Tar-Hunt RSG-20 Mountaineer Slug Gun
Similar to the RSG-12 Professional except chambered for 20 gauge (2-3/4") shells; 21" Shaw rifled barrel, with muzzle brake; two-lug bolt; one-shot blind magazine; matte black finish; McMillan fiberglass stock with Pachmayr Decelerator pad; receiver drilled and tapped for Rem. 700 bases. Weighs 6-1/2 lbs. Introduced 1997. Made in U.S. by Tar-Hunt Custom Rifles, Inc.
Price: **$1,695.00**

THOMPSON/CENTER ENCORE RIFLED SLUG GUN
Gauge: 20, 3" chamber. **Barrel:** 26", fully rifled. **Weight:** About 7 pounds. **Length:** 40-1/2" overall. **Stock:** Walnut with walnut forearm. **Sights:** Steel, click-adjustable rear and ramp-style front, both with fiber optics. **Features:** Encore system features a variety of rifle, shotgun and muzzle-loading rifle barrels interchangeable with the same frame. Break-open design operates by pulling up and back on trigger guard spur. Composite stock and forearm available. Introduced 2000.
Price: **$665.00**

THOMPSON/CENTER ENCORE TURKEY GUN
Gauge: 12 ga. **Barrel:** 24". **Features:** Blued, high definition Realtree Hardwoods HD camo.
Price: **$726.00**

Designs for utility, suitable for and adaptable to competitions and other sporting purposes.

Benelli M3 Convertible

Benelli M1 Tactical

Benelli M1 Practical

Fabarm FP6

BENELLI M3 CONVERTIBLE SHOTGUN
Gauge: 12, 2-3/4", 3" chambers, 5-shot magazine. **Barrel:** 19-3/4" (Cyl.). **Weight:** 7 lbs., 4oz. **Length:** 41" overall. **Stock:** High-impact polymer with sling loop in side of butt; rubberized pistol grip on stock. **Sights:** Open rifle, fully adjustable. Ghost ring and rifle type. **Features:** Combination pump/auto action. Alloy receiver with inertia recoil rotating locking lug bolt; matte finish; automatic shell release lever. Introduced 1989. Imported by Benelli USA. Price with pistol grip, open rifle sights.
Price: With standard stock, open rifle sights. **$1,135.00**
Price: With ghost ring sight system, standard stock. **$1,185.00**
Price: With ghost ring sights, pistol grip stock **$1,200.00**

BENELLI M1 TACTICAL SHOTGUN
Gauge: 12, 2-3/4", 3" chambers, 5-shot magazine. **Barrel:** 18.5" IC, M, F choke tubes. **Weight:** 6.7 lbs. **Length:** 39.75" overall. **Stock:** Black polymer. **Sights:** Rifle type with ghost ring system, tritium night sights optional. **Features:** Semi-auto intertia recoil action. Cross-bolt safety; bolt release button; matte-finish metal. Introduced 1993. Imported from Italy by Benelli USA.
Price: With rifle sights, standard stock **$945.00**
Price: With ghost ring rifle sights, standard stock. **$1,015.00**
Price: With ghost ring sights, pistol grip stock **$1,030.00**
Price: With rifle sights, pistol grip stock **$960.00**
Price: MI Entry, 14" barrel (law enforcement only) . **$980.00 to $1,060.00**

Benelli M1 Practical
Similar to M1 Field Shotgun, Picatinny receiver rail for scope mounting, nine-round magazine, 26" compensated barrel and ghost ring sights. Designed for IPSC competition.
Price: **$1,265.00**

BERETTA MODEL 1201FP GHOST RING AUTO SHOTGUN
Gauge: 12, 3" chamber. **Barrel:** 18" (Cyl.). **Weight:** 6.3 lbs. **Stock:** Special strengthened technopolymer, matte black finish. **Stock:** Fixed rifle type. **Features:** Has 5-shot magazine. Adjustable Ghost Ring rear sight, tritium front. Introduced 1988. Imported from Italy by Beretta U.S.A.
Price: $890.00

CROSSFIRE SHOTGUN/RIFLE
Gauge/Caliber: 12, 2-3/4" Chamber: 4-shot/223 Rem. (5-shot). **Barrel:** 20" (shotgun), 18" (rifle). **Weight:** About 8.6 lbs. **Length:** 40" overall. **Stock:** Composite. **Sights:** Meprolight night sights. Integral Weaver-style scope rail. **Features:** Combination pump-action shotgun, rifle; single selector, single trigger; dual action bars for both upper and lower actions; ambidextrous selector and safety. Introduced 1997. Made in U.S. From Hesco.
Price: About $1,895.00
Price: With camo finish. $1,995.00

FABARM FP6 PUMP SHOTGUN
Gauge: 12, 3" chamber. **Barrel:** 20" (Cyl.); accepts choke tubes. **Weight:** 6.6 lbs. **Length:** 41.25" overall. **Stock:** Black polymer with textured grip, grooved slide handle. **Sights:** Blade front. **Features:** Twin action bars; anodized finish; free carrier for smooth reloading. Introduced 1998. New features include ghost-ring sighting system, low profile Picatinny rail, and pistol grip stock. Imported from Italy by Heckler & Koch, Inc.
Price: (Carbon fiber finish) $499.00
Price: With flip-up front sight, Picatinny rail with rear sight, oversize safety button $499.00

FABARM TACTICAL SEMI-AUTOMATIC SHOTGUN
Gauge: 12, 3" chamber. **Barrel:** 20". **Weight:** 6.6 lbs. **Length:** 41.2" overall. **Stock:** Polymer or folding. **Sights:** Ghost ring (tritium night sights optional). **Features:** Gas operated; matte receiver; twin forged action bars; oversized bolt handle and safety button; Picatinny rail; includes cylinder bore choke tube. New features include polymer pistol grip stock. Introduced 2001. Imported from Italy by Heckler & Koch Inc.
Price: $999.00

Fabarm Tactical

Mossberg Model 500 Persuader

Mossberg Model 500 Persuader

Mossberg Ghost Ring

Mossberg Model HS410

MOSSBERG MODEL 500 PERSUADER SECURITY SHOTGUNS

Gauge: 12, 20, 410, 3" chamber. **Barrel:** 18-1/2", 20" (Cyl.). **Weight:** 7 lbs. **Stock:** Walnut-finished hardwood or black synthetic. **Sights:** Metal bead front. **Features:** Available in 6- or 8-shot models. Top-mounted safety, double action slide bars, swivel studs, rubber recoil pad. Blue, Parkerized, Marinecote finishes. Mossberg Cablelock included. From Mossberg.

Price: 12 or 20 ga., 18-1/2", blue, wood or synthetic stock,
6-shot **$342.00**

Price: Cruiser, 12 or 20 ga., 18-1/2", blue, pistol grip, heat
shield **$347.00**

Price: As above, 410-bore **$335.00**

Mossberg Model 500, 590 Mariner Pump

Similar to the Model 500 or 590 Security except all metal parts finished with Marinecote metal finish to resist rust and corrosion. Synthetic field stock; pistol grip kit included. Mossberg Cablelock included.

Price: 6-shot, 18-1/2" barrel **$510.00**

Price: 9-shot, 20" barrel **$541.00**

Mossberg Model 500, 590 Ghost-Ring Shotguns

Similar to the Model 500 Security except has adjustable blade front, adjustable Ghost-Ring rear sight with protective "ears." Model 500 has 18.5" (Cyl.) barrel, 6-shot capacity; Model 590 has 20" (Cyl.) barrel,

9-shot capacity. Both have synthetic field stock. Mossberg Cablelock included. Introduced 1990. From Mossberg.

Price: 500 parkerized **$454.00**

Price: 590 parkerized **$463.00**

Price: Parkerized Speedfeed stock . . . . **$568.00 to $634.00**

Mossberg Model HS410 Shotgun

Similar to the Model 500 Security pump except chambered for 20 gauge or 410 with 3" chamber; has pistol grip forend, thick recoil pad, muzzle brake and has special spreader choke on the 18.5" barrel. Overall length is 37.5", weight is 6.25 lbs. Blue finish; synthetic field stock. Mossberg Cablelock and video included. Introduced 1990.

Price: HS 410 . . . . **$345.00**

MOSSBERG MODEL 590 SHOTGUN

Gauge: 12, 3" chamber. **Barrel:** 20" (Cyl.). **Weight:** 7-1/4 lbs. **Stock:** Synthetic field or Speedfeed. **Sights:** Metal bead front. **Features:** Top-mounted safety, double slide action bars. Comes with heat shield, bayonet lug, swivel studs, rubber recoil pad. Blue, Parkerized or Marinecote finish. Mossberg Cablelock included. From Mossberg.

Price: Blue, synthetic stock **$406.00**

Price: Parkerized, synthetic stock **$527.00**

Price: Parkerized, Speedfeed stock **$568.00**

Mossberg 590 DA

Tactical Response TR-870

Winchester Model 1300 Defender

Winchester Model 1300 Marine

Winchester Model 1300 Camp Defender®

Mossberg 590DA Double-Action Pump Shotgun

Similar to Model 590 except trigger requires a long stroke for each shot, duplicating the trigger pull of double-action-only pistols and revolvers. Available in 12 gauge only with black synthetic stock and parkerized finish with 14" (law enforcement only), 18-1/2" and 20" barrels. Six-shot magazine tube (nine-shot for 20" barrel). Front bead or ghost ring sights. Weighs 7 pounds (18-1/2" barrel). Introduced 2000. From Mossberg.

Price: Bead sight, 6-shot magazine	$510.00
Price: Ghost ring sights, 6-shot magazine	$558.00
Price: Bead sight, 9-shot magazine	$541.00
Price: Ghost ring sights, 9-shot magazine	$597.00

TACTICAL RESPONSE TR-870 STANDARD MODEL SHOTGUN

Gauge: 12, 3" chamber, 7-shot magazine. **Barrel:** 18" (Cyl.). **Weight:** 9 lbs. **Length:** 38" overall. **Stock:** Fiberglass-filled polypropolene with non-snag recoil absorbing butt pad. Nylon tactical forend houses flashlight. **Sights:** Trak-Lock ghost ring sight system. Front sight has tritium insert. **Features:** Highly modified Remington 870P with Parkerized finish. Comes with nylon three-way adjustable sling, high visibility non-binding follower, high performance magazine spring, Jumbo Head safety, and Side Saddle extended 6-shot shell carrier on left side of receiver. Introduced 1991. From Scattergun Technologies, Inc.

Price: Standard model	$815.00
Price: FBI model	$770.00
Price: Patrol model	$595.00
Price: Border Patrol model	$605.00

Price: K-9 model (Rem. 11-87 action)	$995.00
Price: Urban Sniper, Rem. 11-87 action	$1,290.00
Price: Louis Awerbuck model	$705.00
Price: Practical Turkey model	$725.00
Price: Expert model	$1,350.00
Price: Professional model	$815.00
Price: Entry model	$840.00
Price: Compact model	$635.00
Price: SWAT model	$1,195.00

WINCHESTER MODEL 1300 DEFENDER PUMP GUNS

Gauge: 12, 20, 3" chamber, 5- or 8-shot capacity. **Barrel:** 18" (Cyl.). **Weight:** 6-3/4 lbs. **Length:** 38-5/8" overall. **Stock:** Walnut-finished hardwood stock and ribbed forend, synthetic or pistol grip. **Sights:** Metal bead front or TRUGLO® fiber-optic. **Features:** Cross-bolt safety, front-locking rotary bolt, twin action slide bars. Black rubber butt pad. From U.S. Repeating Arms Co.

Price: 8-Shot (black synthetic stock, TRUGLO® sight)	$326.00
Price: 8-Shot Pistol Grip (pistol grip synthetic stock)	$326.00

Winchester Model 1300 Stainless Marine Pump Gun

Same as the Defender 8-Shot except has bright chrome finish, stainless steel barrel, bead front sight. Phosphate coated receiver for corrosion resistance.

Price:	$518.00

Winchester Model 1300 Camp Defender®

Same as the Defender 8-Shot except has hardwood stock and forearm, fully adjustable open sights and 22" barrel with WinChoke® choke tube system (cylinder choke tube included). Weighs 6-7/8 lbs. Introduced 2001. From U.S. Repeating Arms Co.

Price: Camp Defender®	$373.00

SHOTGUNS

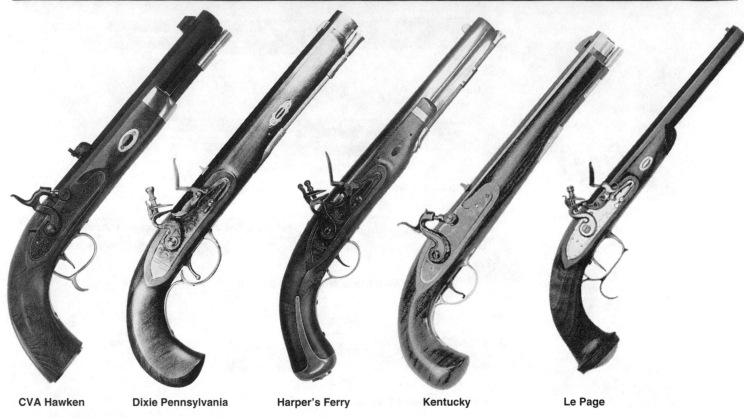

CVA Hawken   Dixie Pennsylvania   Harper's Ferry   Kentucky   Le Page

CVA HAWKEN PISTOL

Caliber: 50. **Barrel:** 9-3/4"; 15/16" flats. **Weight:** 50 oz. **Length:** 16-1/2" overall. **Stocks:** Select hardwood. **Sights:** Beaded blade front, fully adjustable open rear. **Features:** Color case-hardened lock, polished brass wedge plate, instep, ramrod thimble, trigger guard, grip cap. Imported by CVA.

Price: **$167.95**
Price: Kit **$127.95**

DIXIE PENNSYLVANIA PISTOL

Caliber: 44 (.430" round ball). **Barrel:** 10", (7/8" octagon). **Weight:** 2-1/2 labs. **Stocks:** Walnut-stained hardwood. **Sights:** Blade front, open rear drift-adjustable for windage; brass. **Features:** Available in flint only. Brass trigger guard, thimbles, instep, wedge plates; high-luster blue barrel. Imported from Italy by Dixie Gun Works.

Price: Finished **$215.00**
Price: Kit **$195.00**

FRENCH-STYLE DUELING PISTOL

Caliber: 44. **Barrel:** 10". **Weight:** 35 oz. **Length:** 15-3/4" overall. **Stocks:** Carved walnut. **Sights:** Fixed. **Features:** Comes with velvet-lined case and accessories. Imported by Mandall Shooting Supplies.

Price: **$295.00**

HARPER'S FERRY 1806 PISTOL

Caliber: 58 (.570" round ball). **Barrel:** 10". **Weight:** 40 oz. **Length:** 16" overall. **Stocks:** Walnut. **Sights:** Fixed. **Features:** Case-hardened lock, brass-mounted browned barrel. Replica of the first U.S. Gov't.-made flintlock pistol. Imported by Navy Arms, Dixie Gun Works.

Price: . . . . **$275.00 to $405.00**
Price: Kit (Dixie) **$249.00**

KENTUCKY FLINTLOCK PISTOL

Caliber: 44, 45. **Barrel:** 10-1/8". **Weight:** 32 oz. **Length:** 15-1/2" overall. **Stocks:** Walnut. **Sights:** Fixed. **Features:** Specifications, including caliber, weight and length may vary with importer. Case-hardened lock, blued barrel; available also as brass barrel flint Model 1821. Imported by Navy Arms, The Armoury, Dixie Gun Works.

Price: **$300.00**

Price: In kit form, from . . . . **$90.00 to $112.00**
Price: Single cased set (Navy Arms) **$360.00**
Price: Double cased set (Navy Arms) **$590.00**

Kentucky Percussion Pistol

Similar to flint version but percussion lock. Imported by The Armoury, Navy Arms, CVA (50-cal.).

Price: . . . . **$129.95 to $225.00**
Price: Blued steel barrel (CVA) **$167.95**
Price: Kit form (CVA) **$119.95**
Price: Steel barrel (Armoury) **$179.00**
Price: Single cased set (Navy Arms) **$355.00**
Price: Double cased set (Navy Arms) **$600.00**

LE PAGE PERCUSSION DUELING PISTOL

Caliber: 44. **Barrel:** 10", rifled. **Weight:** 40 oz. **Length:** 16" overall. **Stocks:** Walnut, fluted butt. **Sights:** Blade front, notch rear. **Features:** Double-set triggers. Blued barrel; trigger guard and buttcap are polished silver. Imported by Dixie Gun Works.

Price: **$450.00**

LYMAN PLAINS PISTOL

Caliber: 50 or 54. **Barrel:** 8"; 1:30" twist, both calibers. **Weight:** 50 oz. **Length:** 15" overall. **Stocks:** Walnut half-stock. **Sights:** Blade front, square notch rear adjustable for windage. **Features:** Polished brass trigger guard and ramrod tip, color case-hardened coil spring lock, spring-loaded trigger, stainless steel nipple, blackened iron furniture. Hooked patent breech, detachable belt hook. Introduced 1981. From Lyman Products.

Price: Finished **$244.95**
Price: Kit **$189.95**

PEDERSOLI MANG TARGET PISTOL

Caliber: 38. **Barrel:** 10.5", octagonal; 1:15" twist, **Weight:** 2.5 lbs. **Length:** 17.25" overall. **Stocks:** Walnut with fluted grip. **Sights:** Blade front, open rear adjustable for windage. **Features:** Browned barrel, polished breech plug, rest color case-hardened. Imported from Italy by Dixie Gun Works.

Price: **$895.00**

Lyman Plains Pistol   Pedersoli Mang   Queen Anne   Thompson/Center Encore   Traditions Pioneer   Traditions William Parker

QUEEN ANNE FLINTLOCK PISTOL
Caliber: 50 (.490" round ball). **Barrel:** 7-1/2", smoothbore. **Stocks:** Walnut. **Sights:** None. **Features:** Browned steel barrel, fluted brass trigger guard, brass mask on butt. Lockplate left in the white. Made by Pedersoli in Italy. Introduced 1983. Imported by Dixie Gun Works.
Price: **$245.00**
Price: Kit **$195.00**

THOMPSON/CENTER ENCORE 209x50 MAGNUM PISTOL
Caliber: 50. **Barrel:** 15"; 1:20" twist. **Weight:** About 4 lbs. Grips: American walnut grip and forend. **Sights:** Click-adjustable, steel rear, ramp front. **Features:** Uses 209 shotgun primer for closed-breech ignition; accepts charges up to 110 grains of FFg black powder or two, 50-grain Pyrodex pellets. Introduced 2000.
Price: **$611.00**
Price: (barrel only) **$325.00**

TRADITIONS BUCKHUNTER PRO IN-LINE PISTOL
Caliber: 50. **Barrel:** 9-1/2", round. **Weight:** 48 oz. **Length:** 14" overall. **Stocks:** Smooth walnut or black epoxy-coated hardwood grip and forend. **Sights:** Beaded blade front, folding adjustable rear. **Features:** Thumb safety; removable stainless steel breech plug; adjustable trigger, barrel drilled and tapped for scope mounting. From Traditions.
Price: With walnut grip **$229.00**
Price: Nickel with black grip **$239.00**
Price: With walnut grip and 12-1/2" barrel **$239.00**
Price: Nickel with black grip, muzzle brake and 14-3/4" fluted barrel. **$289.00**
Price: 45 cal. nickel w/bl. grip, muzzlebrake and 14-3/4" fluted bbl. **$289.00**

TRADITIONS KENTUCKY PISTOL
Caliber: 50. **Barrel:** 10"; octagon with 7/8" flats; 1:20" twist. **Weight:** 40 oz. **Length:** 15" overall. **Stocks:** Stained beech. **Sights:** Blade front, fixed rear. **Features:** Birds-head grip; brass thimbles; color case-hardened lock. Percussion only. Introduced 1995. From Traditions.
Price: Finished **$139.00**
Price: Kit **$109.00**

TRADITIONS PIONEER PISTOL
Caliber: 45. **Barrel:** 9-5/8"; 13/16" flats, 1:16" twist. **Weight:** 31 oz. **Length:** 15" overall. **Stocks:** Beech. **Sights:** Blade front, fixed rear. **Features:**

Traditions Buckhunter Pro

V-type mainspring. Single trigger. German silver furniture, blackened hardware. From Traditions.
Price: **$139.00**
Price: Kit **$119.00**

TRADITIONS TRAPPER PISTOL
Caliber: 50. **Barrel:** 9-3/4"; 7/8" flats; 1:20" twist. **Weight:** 2-3/4 lbs. **Length:** 16" overall. **Stocks:** Beech. **Sights:** Blade front, adjustable rear. **Features:** Double-set triggers; brass buttcap, trigger guard, wedge plate, forend tip, thimble. From Traditions.
Price: Percussion **$189.00**
Price: Flintlock **$209.00**
Price: Kit **$149.00**

TRADITIONS VEST-POCKET DERRINGER
Caliber: 31. **Barrel:** 2-1/4"; brass. **Weight:** 8 oz. **Length:** 4-3/4" overall. **Stocks:** Simulated ivory. **Sights:** Beed front. **Features:** Replica of riverboat gamblers' derringer; authentic spur trigger. From Traditions.
Price: **$109.00**

TRADITIONS WILLIAM PARKER PISTOL
Caliber: 50. **Barrel:** 10-3/8"; 15/16" flats; polished steel. **Weight:** 37 oz. **Length:** 17-1/2" overall. **Stocks:** Walnut with checkered grip. **Sights:** Brass blade front, fixed rear. **Features:** Replica dueling pistol with 1:20" twist, hooked breech. Brass wedge plate, trigger guard, cap guard; separate ramrod. Double-set triggers. Polished steel barrel, lock. Imported by Traditions.
Price: **$269.00**

Army 1860

Baby Dragoon 1848

Dixie Wyatt Earp

Le Mat Revolver

Navy Arms 1836 Paterson

ARMY 1860 PERCUSSION REVOLVER

Caliber: 44, 6-shot. **Barrel:** 8". **Weight:** 40 oz. **Length:** 13-5/8" overall. **Stocks:** Walnut. **Sights:** Fixed. **Features:** Engraved Navy scene on cylinder; brass trigger guard; case-hardened frame, loading lever and hammer. Some importers supply pistol cut for detachable shoulder stock, have accessory stock available. Imported by Cabela's (1860 Lawman), E.M.F., Navy Arms, The Armoury, Cimarron, Dixie Gun Works (half-fluted cylinder, not roll engraved), Euroarms of America (brass or steel model), Armsport, Traditions (brass or steel), Uberti U.S.A. Inc., United States Patent Fire-Arms.

Price: About **$190.00**
Price: Hartford model, steel frame, German silver trim,
cartouches (E.M.F.) **$215.00**
Price: Single cased set (Navy Arms) **$300.00**
Price: Double cased set (Navy Arms). **$490.00**
Price: 1861 Navy: Same as Army except 36-cal., 7-1/2" bbl., weighs 41 oz., cut for shoulder stock; round cylinder (fluted available), from Cabela's, CVA (brass frame, 44-cal.), United States Patent Fire-Arms
. . . . **$99.95 to $385.00**
Price: Steel frame kit (E.M.F., Euroarms). . . . . **$125.00 to $216.25**
Price: Colt Army Police, fluted cyl., 5-1/2", 36-cal. (Cabela's) . . . **$124.95**
Price: With nickeled frame, barrel and backstrap, gold-tone fluted cylinder, trigger and hammer, simulated ivory grips (Traditions) **$199.00**

BABY DRAGOON 1848, 1849 POCKET, WELLS FARGO

Caliber: 31. **Barrel:** 3", 4", 5", 6"; seven-groove; RH twist. **Weight:** About 21 oz. **Stocks:** Varnished walnut. **Sights:** Brass pin front, hammer notch rear. **Features:** No loading lever on Baby Dragoon or Wells Fargo models. Unfluted cylinder with stagecoach holdup scene; cupped cylinder pin; no grease grooves; one safety pin on cylinder and slot in hammer face; straight (flat) mainspring. From Armsport, Cimarron F.A. Co., Dixie Gun Works, Uberti U.S.A. Inc.

Price: 6" barrel, with loading lever (Dixie Gun Works) **$275.00**
Price: 4" (Uberti USA Inc.) **$335.00**

CABELA'S 1860 ARMY SNUBNOSE REVOLVER

NEW! **Caliber:** .44. **Barrel:** 3". **Weight:** 2 lbs., 3 oz. **Length:** 9" overall. **Grips:** Hardwood. **Sights:** Blade front, hammer notch near. **Features:** Shortened barrels sans loading lever. Separate brass loading tool included.
Price: . . . . **$149.99** (revolver only); **$189.99** (with starter kit).

CABELA'S 1862 POLICE SNUBNOSE REVOLVER

NEW! **Caliber:** .36. **Barrel:** 3". **Weight:** 2 lbs., 3 oz. **Length:** 8.5" overall. **Grips:** Hardwood. **Sights:** Blade front, hammer notch rear. **Features:** Shortened barrel, removed loading lever. Separate brass loading tool included.
Price: . . . . **$169.99** (revolver only); **$209.99** (with starter kit).

DIXIE WYATT EARP REVOLVER

Caliber: 44. **Barrel:** 12", octagon. **Weight:** 46 oz. **Length:** 18" overall. **Stocks:** Two-piece walnut. **Sights:** Fixed. **Features:** Highly polished brass frame, backstrap and trigger guard; blued barrel and cylinder; case-hardened hammer, trigger and loading lever. Navy-size shoulder stock ($45) will fit with minor fitting. From Dixie Gun Works.
Price: **$160.00**

LE MAT REVOLVER

Caliber: 44/65. **Barrel:** 6-3/4" (revolver); 4-7/8" (single shot). **Weight:** 3 lbs., 7 oz. **Stocks:** Hand-checkered walnut. **Sights:** Post front, hammer notch rear. **Features:** Exact reproduction with all-steel construction; 44-cal. 9-shot cylinder, 65-cal. single barrel; color case-hardened hammer with selector; spur trigger guard; ring at butt; lever-type barrel release. From Navy Arms.
Price: Cavalry model (lanyard ring, spur trigger guard) **$595.00**
Price: Army model (round trigger guard, pin-type barrel release) **$595.00**
Price: Naval-style (thumb selector on hammer) **$595.00**

NAVY ARMS NEW MODEL POCKET REVOLVER

Caliber: 31, 5-shot. **Barrel:** 3-1/2", octagon. **Weight:** 15 oz. **Length:** 7-3/4". **Stocks:** Two-piece walnut. **Sights:** Fixed. **Features:** Replica of the Remington New Model Pocket. Available with polisehd brass frame or nickel plated finish. Introduced 2000. Imported by Navy Arms.
Price: **$300.00**

NAVY ARMS 1836 PATERSON REVOLVER

Features: Hidden trigger, 36 cal., blued barrel, replica of 5-shooter, roll-engraved with stagecoach hold-up.
Price: . . . . **$340.00 to $499.00**

BLACKPOWDER REVOLVERS

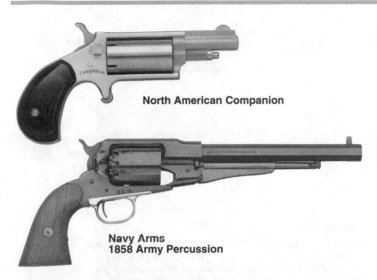

North American Companion

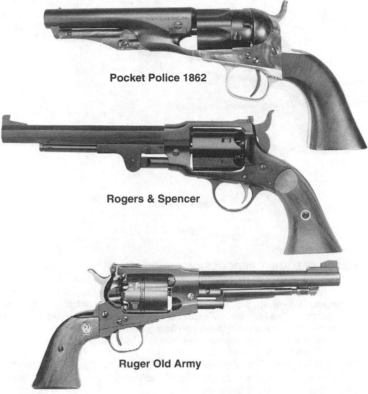

Pocket Police 1862

Rogers & Spencer

**Navy Arms
1858 Army Percussion**

Ruger Old Army

NAVY MODEL 1851 PERCUSSION REVOLVER

Caliber: 36, 44, 6-shot. **Barrel:** 7-1/2". **Weight:** 44 oz. **Length:** 13" overall. **Stocks:** Walnut finish. **Sights:** Post front, hammer notch rear. **Features:** Brass backstrap and trigger guard; some have 1st Model squareback trigger guard, engraved cylinder with navy battle scene; case-hardened frame, hammer, loading lever. Imported by The Armoury, Cabela's, Cimarron F.A. Co., Navy Arms, E.M.F., Dixie Gun Works, Euroarms of America, Armsport, CVA (44-cal. only), Traditions (44 only), Uberti U.S.A. Inc., United States Patent Fire-Arms.

Price: Brass frame . . . . $99.95 to $385.00
Price: Steel frame . . . . $130.00 to $285.00
Price: Kit form . . . . $110.00 to $123.95
Price: Engraved model (Dixie Gun Works) $182.50
Price: Single cased set, steel frame (Navy Arms) $280.00
Price: Double cased set, steel frame (Navy Arms) $455.00
Price: Confederate Navy (Cabela's) $89.99
Price: Hartford model, steel frame, German silver trim, cartouche (E.M.F.) $190.00

NEW MODEL 1858 ARMY PERCUSSION REVOLVER

Caliber: 36 or 44, 6-shot. **Barrel:** 6-1/2" or 8". **Weight:** 38 oz. **Length:** 13-1/2" overall. **Stocks:** Walnut. **Sights:** Blade front, groove-in-frame rear. **Features:** Replica of Remington Model 1858. Also available from some importers as Army Model Belt Revolver in 36-cal., a shortened and lightened version of the 44. Target Model (Uberti U.S.A. Inc., Navy Arms) has fully adjustable target rear sight, target front, 36 or 44. Imported by Cabela's, Cimarron F.A. Co., CVA (as 1858 Army, brass frame, 44 only), Dixie Gun Works, Navy Arms, The Armoury, E.M.F., Euroarms of America (engraved, stainless and plain), Armsport, Traditions (44 only), Uberti U.S.A. Inc.

Price: Steel frame, about . . . . $99.95 to $280.00
Price: Steel frame kit (Euroarms, Navy Arms) . . . . . . $115.95 to $150.00
Price: Single cased set (Navy Arms) $290.00
Price: Double cased set (Navy Arms) $480.00
Price: Stainless steel Model 1858 (Euroarms, Uberti U.S.A. Inc., Cabela's, Navy Arms, Armsport, Traditions) . . . . $169.95 to $380.00
Price: Target Model, adjustable rear sight (Cabela's, Euroarms, Uberti U.S.A. Inc., Stone Mountain Arms) . . . . $95.95 to $399.00
Price: Brass frame (CVA, Cabela's, Traditions, Navy Arms) . . . . $79.95 to $159.95
Price: As above, kit (Dixie Gun Works, Navy Arms) . . $145.00 to $188.95
Price: Buffalo model, 44-cal. (Cabela's) $119.99
Price: Hartford model, steel frame, German silver trim, cartouche (E.M.F.) $215.00

NORTH AMERICAN COMPANION PERCUSSION REVOLVER

Caliber: 22. **Barrel:** 1-1/8". **Weight:** 5.1 oz. **Length:** 4-5/10" overall. **Stocks:** Laminated wood. **Sights:** Blade front, notch fixed rear. **Features:**

All stainless steel construction. Uses standard #11 percussion caps. Comes with bullets, powder measure, bullet seater, leather clip holster, gun rug. Long Rifle or Magnum frame size. Introduced 1996. Made in U.S. by North American Arms.

Price: Long Rifle frame $156.00

North American Magnum Companion Percussion Revolver

Similar to the Companion except has larger frame. Weighs 7.2 oz., has 1-5/8" barrel, measures 5-7/16" overall. Comes with bullets, powder measure, bullet seater, leather clip holster, gun rag. Introduced 1996. Made in U.S. by North American Arms.

Price: $174.00

POCKET POLICE 1862 PERCUSSION REVOLVER

Caliber: 36, 5-shot. **Barrel:** 4-1/2", 5-1/2", 6-1/2", 7-1/2". **Weight:** 26 oz. **Length:** 12" overall (6-1/2" bbl.). **Stocks:** Walnut. **Sights:** Fixed. **Features:** Round tapered barrel; half-fluted and rebated cylinder; case-hardened frame, loading lever and hammer; silver or brass trigger guard and backstrap. Imported by Dixie Gun Works, Navy Arms (5-1/2" only), Uberti U.S.A. Inc. (5-1/2", 6-1/2" only), United States Patent Fire-Arms and Cimarron F.A. Co.

Price: About . . . . $139.95 to $335.00
Price: Single cased set with accessories (Navy Arms) $365.00
Price: Hartford model, steel frame, German silver trim, cartouche (E.M.F.) $215.00

ROGERS & SPENCER PERCUSSION REVOLVER

Caliber: 44. **Barrel:** 7-1/2". **Weight:** 47 oz. **Length:** 13-3/4" overall. **Stocks:** Walnut. **Sights:** Cone front, integral groove in frame for rear. **Features:** Accurate reproduction of a Civil War design. Solid frame; extra large nipple cut-out on rear of cylinder; loading lever and cylinder easily removed for cleaning. From Dixie Gun Works, Euroarms of America (standard blue, engraved, burnished, target models), Navy Arms.

Price: . . . . $160.00 to $299.95
Price: Nickel-plated $215.00
Price: Engraved (Euroarms) $287.00
Price: Kit version . . . . $245.00 to $252.00
Price: Target version (Euroarms) . . . . $239.00 to $270.00
Price: Burnished London Gray (Euroarms) . . . . $245.00 to $270.00

BLACKPOWDER

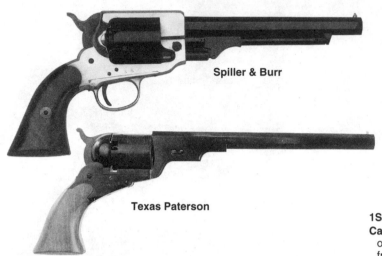

Spiller & Burr

Texas Paterson

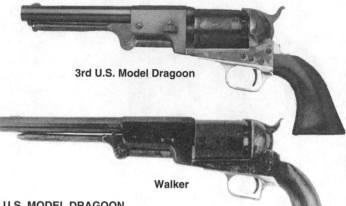

3rd U.S. Model Dragoon

Walker

RUGER OLD ARMY PERCUSSION REVOLVER

Caliber: 45, 6-shot. Uses .457" dia. lead bullets or 454 conical. **Barrel:** 7-1/2" (6-groove; 1:16" twist). **Weight:** 2-7/8 lbs. **Length:** 13-1/2" overall. **Stocks:** Rosewood. **Sights:** Ramp front, rear adjustable for windage and elevation; or fixed (groove). **Features:** Stainless steel; standard size nipples, chrome-moly steel cylinder and frame, same lockwork as original Super Blackhawk. Also stainless steel. Includes hard case and lock. Made in USA. From Sturm, Ruger & Co.
Price: Blued steel, fixed sight (Model BP-5F) **$499.00**
Price: Stainless steel, fixed sight (Model KBP-5F-I) **$576.00**
Price: Stainless steel (Model KBP-7) **$535.00**
Price: Blued steel (Model BP-7) **$499.00**
Price: Blued steel, fixed sight (BP-7F) **$499.00**
Price: Stainless steel, fixed sight (KBP-7F) **$535.00**

SHERIFF MODEL 1851 PERCUSSION REVOLVER

Caliber: 36, 44, 6-shot. **Barrel:** 5". **Weight:** 40 oz. **Length:** 10-1/2" overall. **Stocks:** Walnut. **Sights:** Fixed. **Features:** Brass backstrap and trigger guard; engraved navy scene; case-hardened frame, hammer, loading lever. Imported by E.M.F.
Price: Steel frame. **$169.95**
Price: Brass frame **$140.00**

SPILLER & BURR REVOLVER

Caliber: 36 (.375" round ball). **Barrel:** 7", octagon. **Weight:** 2-1/2 lbs. **Length:** 12-1/2" overall. **Stocks:** Two-piece walnut. **Sights:** Fixed. **Features:** Reproduction of the C.S.A. revolver. Brass frame and trigger guard. Also available as a kit. From Dixie Gun Works, Navy Arms.
Price: **$150.00**
Price: Kit form (Dixie) **$125.00**
Price: Single cased set (Navy Arms) **$270.00**
Price: Double cased set (Navy Arms). **$430.00**

TEXAS PATERSON 1836 REVOLVER

Caliber: 36 (.375" round ball). **Barrel:** 7-1/2". **Weight:** 42 oz. **Stocks:** One-piece walnut. **Sights:** Fixed. **Features:** Copy of Sam Colt's first commercially-made revolving pistol. Has no loading lever but comes with loading tool. From Cimarron F.A. Co., Dixie Gun Works, Navy Arms, Uberti U.S.A. Inc.
Price: About **$495.00**
Price: With loading lever (Uberti U.S.A. Inc.) **$450.00**
Price: Engraved (Navy Arms). **$485.00**

UBERTI 1861 NAVY PERCUSSION REVOLVER

Caliber: 36. **Barrel:** 7-1/2", round. **Weight:** 40-1/2 oz. **Stocks:** One-piece oiled American walnut. **Sights:** Brass pin front, hammer notch rear. **Features:** Rounded trigger guard, German silver blade front sight, "creeping" loading lever. Available with fluted or round cylinder. Imported by Uberti U.S.A. Inc.
Price: Steel backstrap, trigger guard, cut for stock. **$265.00**

1ST U.S. MODEL DRAGOON

Caliber: 44. **Barrel:** 7-1/2", part round, part octagon. **Weight:** 64 oz. **Stocks:** One-piece walnut. **Sights:** German silver blade front, hammer notch rear. **Features:** First model has oval bolt cuts in cylinder, square- back flared trigger guard, V-type mainspring, short trigger. Ranger and Indian scene roll-engraved on cylinder. Color case-hardened frame, loading lever, plunger and hammer; blue barrel, cylinder, trigger and wedge. Available with old-time charcoal blue or standard blue-black finish. Polished brass backstrap and trigger guard. From Cimarron F.A. Co., Dixie Gun Works, Uberti U.S.A. Inc., Navy Arms.
Price: . . . . **$295.00 to $435.00**

2nd U.S. Model Dragoon Revolver

Similar to the 1st Model except distinguished by rectangular bolt cuts in the cylinder. From Cimarron F.A. Co., Uberti U.S.A. Inc., United States Patent Fire-Arms, Navy Arms, Dixie Gunworks.
Price: . . . . **$295.00 to $435.00**

3rd U.S. Model Dragoon Revolver

Similar to the 2nd Model except for oval trigger guard, long trigger, modifications to the loading lever and latch. Imported by Cimarron F.A. Co., Uberti U.S.A. Inc., United States Patent Fire-Arms, Dixie Gunworks.
Price: Military model (frame cut for shoulder stock, steel backstrap) . . . . **$295.00 to $435.00**
Price: Civilian (brass backstrap, trigger guard) . . . . . **$295.00 to $325.00**

1862 POCKET NAVY PERCUSSION REVOLVER

Caliber: 36, 5-shot. **Barrel:** 5-1/2", 6-1/2", octagonal, 7-groove, LH twist. **Weight:** 27 oz. (5-1/2" barrel). **Length:** 10-1/2" overall (5-1/2" bbl.). **Stocks:** One-piece varnished walnut. **Sights:** Brass pin front, hammer notch rear. **Features:** Rebated cylinder, hinged loading lever, brass or silver-plated backstrap and trigger guard, color-cased frame, hammer, loading lever, plunger and latch, rest blued. Has original-type markings. From Cimarron F.A. Co., Uberti U.S.A. Inc., Dixie Gunworks.
Price: With brass backstrap, trigger guard . . . . **$260.00 to $310.00**

1861 Navy Percussion Revolver

Similar to Colt 1851 Navy except has round 7-1/2" barrel, rounded trigger guard, German silver blade front sight, "creeping" loading lever. Fluted or round cylinder. Imported by Cimarron F.A. Co., Uberti U.S.A. Inc., Dixie Gunworks.
Price: Steel backstrap, trigger guard, cut for stock. . . **$255.00 to $300.00**

WALKER 1847 PERCUSSION REVOLVER

Caliber: 44, 6-shot. **Barrel:** 9". **Weight:** 84 oz. **Length:** 15-1/2" overall. **Stocks:** Walnut. **Sights:** Fixed. **Features:** Case-hardened frame, loading lever and hammer; iron backstrap; brass trigger guard; engraved cylinder. Imported by Cabela's, Cimarron F.A. Co., Navy Arms, Dixie Gun Works, Uberti U.S.A. Inc., E.M.F., Cimarron, Traditions, United States Patent Fire-Arms.
Price: About . . . . **$225.00 to $445.00**
Price: Single cased set (Navy Arms) **$405.00**
Price: Deluxe Walker with French fitted case (Navy Arms) **$540.00**
Price: Hartford model, steel frame, German silver trim, cartouche (E.M.F.) **$295.00**

Austin & Halleck 420 LR In-Line

Austin & Halleck 320 LR In-Line

Austin & Halleck Mountain

Cabela's Blue Ridge

Cabela's Traditional Hawken

ARMOURY R140 HAWKEN RIFLE

Caliber: 45, 50 or 54. **Barrel:** 29". **Weight:** 8-3/4 to 9 lbs. **Length:** 45-3/4" overall. **Stock:** Walnut, with cheekpiece. **Sights:** Dovetail front, fully adjustable rear. **Features:** Octagon barrel, removable breech plug; double set triggers; blued barrel, brass stock fittings, color case-hardened percussion lock. From Armsport, The Armoury.
Price: .... $225.00 to $245.00

AUSTIN & HALLECK MODEL 420 LR IN-LINE RIFLE

Caliber: 50. **Barrel:** 26", 1" octagon to 3/4" round; 1:28" twist. **Weight:** 7-7/8 lbs. **Length:** 47-1/2" overall. **Stock:** Lightly figured maple in Classic or Monte Carlo style. **Sights:** Ramp front, fully adjustable rear. **Features:** Blue or electroless nickel finish; in-line percussion action with removable weather shroud; Timney adjustable target trigger with sear block safety. Introduced 1998. Made in U.S. by Austin & Halleck.
Price: Blue **$459.00**
Price: Stainless steel **$549.00**
Price: Blue, hand-select highly figured stock **$775.00**
Price: Blue, exhibition-grade Monte Carlo stock. **$1,322.00**
Price: Stainless steel, exhibition-grade Monte Carlo stock. **$1,422.00**

Austin & Halleck Model 320 LR In-Line Rifle

Similar to the Model 420 LR except has black resin synthetic stock with checkered grip and forend. Introduced 1998. Made in U.S. by Austin & Halleck.
Price: Blue **$380.00**
Price: Stainless steel **$447.00**

AUSTIN & HALLECK MOUNTAIN RIFLE

Caliber: 50. **Barrel:** 32"; 1:28" or 1:66" twist; 1" flats. **Weight:** 7-1/2 lbs. **Length:** 49" overall. **Stock:** Curly maple. **Sights:** Silver blade front, buckhorn rear. **Features:** Available in percussion or flintlock; double throw adjustable set triggers; rust brown finish. Made in U.S. by Austin & Halleck.
Price: Flintlock **$539.00**
Price: Percussion **$578.00**
Price: Percussion, fancy wood **$592.00**
Price: Percussion, select wood **$660.00**

BOSTONIAN PERCUSSION RIFLE

Caliber: 45. **Barrel:** 30", octagonal. **Weight:** 7-1/4 lbs. **Length:** 46" overall. **Stock:** Walnut. **Sights:** Blade front, fixed notch rear. **Features:** Color case-hardened lock, brass trigger guard, buttplate, patchbox. Imported from Italy by E.M.F.
Price: **$285.00**

CABELA'S BLUE RIDGE RIFLE

Caliber: 32, 36, 45, 50, .54. **Barrel:** 39", octagonal. **Weight:** About 7-3/4 lbs. **Length:** 55" overall. **Stock:** American black walnut. **Sights:** Blade front, rear drift adjustable for windage. **Features:** Color case-hardened lockplate and cock/hammer, brass trigger guard and buttplate, double set, double-phased triggers. From Cabela's.
Price: Percussion **$409.99**
Price: Flintlock **$429.99**

CABELA'S TRADITIONAL HAWKEN

Caliber: 50, 54. **Barrel:** 29". **Weight:** About 9 lbs. **Stock:** Walnut. **Sights:** Blade front, open adjustable rear. **Features:** Flintlock or percussion. Adjustable double-set triggers. Polished brass furniture, color case-hardened lock. Imported by Cabela's.
Price: Percussion, right-hand **$219.99**
Price: Percussion, left-hand **$219.99**
Price: Flintlock, right-hand **$249.99**

BLACKPOWDER MUSKETS & RIFLES

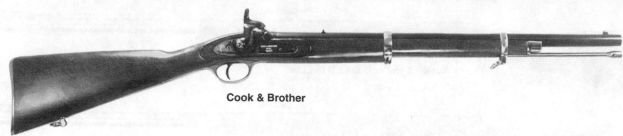

Cook & Brother

Cabela's Sporterized Hawken Hunter Rifle
Similar to the Traditional Hawken except has more modern stock style with rubber recoil pad, blued furniture, sling swivels. Percussion only, in 50- or 54-caliber.
Price: Carbine or rifle, right-hand **$229.99**

CABELA'S KODIAK EXPRESS DOUBLE RIFLE
Caliber: 50, 54, 58, 72. **Barrel:** Length n/a; 1:48" twist. **Weight:** 9.3 lbs. **Length:** 45-1/4" overall. **Stock:** European walnut, oil finish. **Sights:** Fully adjustable double folding-leaf rear, ramp front. **Features:** Percussion. Barrels regulated to point of aim at 75 yards; polished and engraved lock, top tang and trigger guard. From Cabela's.
Price: 50, 54, 58 calibers **$729.99**
Price: 72 caliber **$759.99**

COOK & BROTHER CONFEDERATE CARBINE
Caliber: 58. **Barrel:** 24". **Weight:** 7-1/2 lbs. **Length:** 40-1/2" overall. **Stock:** Select walnut. **Features:** Recreation of the 1861 New Orleans-made artillery carbine. Color case-hardened lock, browned barrel. Buttplate, trigger guard, barrel bands, sling swivels and nosecap of polished brass. From Euroarms of America.
Price: **$447.00**
Price: Cook & Brother rifle (33" barrel) **$480.00**

CVA YOUTH HUNTER RIFLE
Caliber: 50. **Barrel:** 24"; 1:48" twist, octagonal. **Weight:** 5 lbs. **Length:** 38" overall. **Stock:** Stained hardwood. **Sights:** Bead front, Williams adjustable rear. **Features:** Oversize trigger guard; wooden ramrod. From CVA.
Price: **$135.95**

CVA BOBCAT RIFLE
Caliber: 50 or 54. **Barrel:** 26"; 1:48" twist. **Weight:** 6 lbs. **Length:** 42" overall. **Stock:** Dura-Grip synthetic or wood. **Sights:** Blade front, open rear. **Features:** Oversize trigger guard; wood ramrod; matte black finish. From CVA.
Price: (wood stock, 50 cal. only). **$127.95**
Price: (black synthetic stock, 50 or 54 cal.) **$104.95**

CVA ECLIPSE 209 MAGNUM IN-LINE RIFLE
Caliber: 45, 50. **Barrel:** 24" round; 1:28" rifling. **Weight:** 7.3 lbs. **Length:** 42" overall. **Stock:** Black or Mossy Oak® Break-Up™ camo synthetic. **Sights:** Illuminator Fiber Optic Sight System; drilled and tapped for scope mounting. **Features:** In-line action uses modern trigger with automatic safety; stainless percussion bolt; swivel studs. Three-way ignition system (No. 11, musket or No. 209 shotgun primers). From CVA.
Price: Blue, black stock **$149.95**
Price: Blue, Break-Up™ camo stock **$179.95**

CVA Stag Horn 209 Magnum Rifle
Similar to the Eclipse except has light-gathering Solar Sights, manual safety, black synthetic stock and ramrod. From CVA.
Price: 50 cal. **$121.95**

CVA MOUNTAIN RIFLE
Caliber: 50. **Barrel:** 32"; 1:66" rifling. **Weight:** 8-1/2 lbs. **Length:** NA. **Stock:** American hard maple. **Sights:** Blade front, buckhorn rear. **Features:** Browned steel furniture; German silver wedge plates; patchbox. Made in U.S. From CVA.
Price: **$399.95**
Price: Hunter **$259.95**

CVA ST. LOUIS HAWKEN RIFLE
Caliber: 50, 54. **Barrel:** 28", octagon; 15/16" across flats; 1:48" twist. **Weight:** 8 lbs. **Length:** 44" overall. **Stock:** Select hardwood. **Sights:** Beaded blade front, fully adjustable open rear. **Features:** Fully adjustable double-set triggers; synthetic ramrod (kits have wood); brass patchbox, wedge plates, nosecap, thimbles, trigger guard and buttplate; blued barrel; color case-hardened, engraved lockplate. V-type mainspring. Button breech. Introduced 1981. From CVA.
Price: St. Louis Hawken, finished (50- , 54-cal.) **$229.95**
Price: Left-hand, percussion. **$274.95**

CVA Plainsman Rifle
Similar to the St. Louis Hawken except has 26" blued barrel, overall length of 42". Select hardwood stock. Weighs 6-1/2 lbs. From CVA.
Price: **$179.95**

CVA FIREBOLT MUSKETMAG BOLT-ACTION IN-LINE RIFLES
Caliber: 45 or 50. **Barrel:** 26". **Weight:** 7 lbs. **Length:** 44". **Stock:** Rubber-coated black or Mossy Oak® Break-Up™ camo synthetic. **Sights:** CVA Illuminator Fiber Optic Sight System. **Features:** Bolt-action, in-line ignition system handles up to 150 grains blackpowder or Pyrodex; Nickel or matte blue barrel; removable breech plug; trigger-block safety. Three-way ignition system. From CVA.
Price: FiberGrip/nickel, 50 cal. **$259.95**
Price: Breakup/nickel, 50 cal.. . . . . **$299.95**
Price: FiberGrip/nickel, 45 cal. **$259.95**
Price: Breakup/nickel, 45 cal.. . . . . **$299.95**
Price: FiberGrip/blue, 50 cal. **$239.95**
Price: Breakup/blue, 50 cal. **$279.95**
Price: FiberGrip/blue, 45 cal. **$239.95**
Price: Breakup/blue, 45 cal. **$279.95**

CVA HunterBolt 209 Magnum Rifle
Similar to the Firebolt except has 24" barrel and black or Mossy Oak® Break-Up™ synthetic stock. Three-way ignition system. Weighs 6 lbs. From CVA.
Price: 45 or 50 cal. . . . . **$189.95 to $239.95**

DIXIE EARLY AMERICAN JAEGER RIFLE
Caliber: 54. **Barrel:** 27-1/2" octagonal; 1:24" twist. **Weight:** 8-1/4 lbs. **Length:** 43-1/2" overall. **Stock:** American walnut; sliding wooden patchbox on on butt. **Sights:** Notch rear, blade front. **Features:** Flintlock or percussion. Browned steel furniture. Imported from Italy by Dixie Gun Works.
Price: Flintlock or percussion **$750.00**

DIXIE DELUXE CUB RIFLE
Caliber: 40. **Barrel:** 28". **Weight:** 6-1/2 lbs. **Stock:** Walnut. **Sights:** Fixed.**Features:** Short rifle for small game and beginning shooters. Brass patchbox and furniture. Flint or percussion. From Dixie Gun Works.
Price: Finished **$450.00**
Price: Kit. **$390.00**
Price: Super Cub (50-caliber). **$435.00**

DIXIE 1863 SPRINGFIELD MUSKET
Caliber: 58 (.570" patched ball or .575" Minie). **Barrel:** 50", rifled. **Stock:** Walnut stained. **Sights:** Blade front, adjustable ladder-type rear. **Features:** Bright-finish lock, barrel, furniture. Reproduction of the last of the regulation muzzleloaders. Imported from Japan by Dixie Gun Works.
Price: Finished **$595.00**
Price: Kit. **$525.00**

BLACKPOWDER MUSKETS & RIFLES

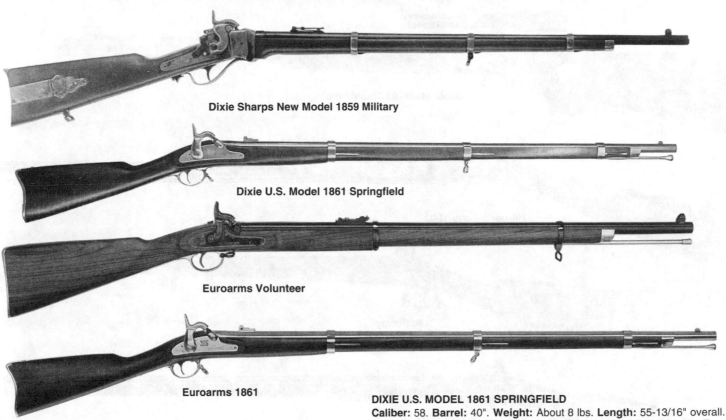

Dixie Sharps New Model 1859 Military

Dixie U.S. Model 1861 Springfield

Euroarms Volunteer

Euroarms 1861

DIXIE INLINE CARBINE
Caliber: 50, 54. **Barrel:** 24"; 1:32" twist. **Weight:** 6.5 lbs. **Length:** 41" overall. **Stock:** Walnut-finished hardwood with Monte Carlo comb. **Sights:** Ramp front with red insert, open fully adjustable rear. **Features:** Sliding "bolt" fully encloses cap and nipple. Fully adjustable trigger, automatic safety. Aluminum ramrod. Imported from Italy by Dixie Gun Works.
Price: $349.95

DIXIE PEDERSOLI 1857 MAUSER RIFLE
Caliber: 54. **Barrel:** 39-3/8". **Weight:** N/A. **Length:** 52" overall. **Stock:** European walnut with oil finish, sling swivels. **Sights:** Fully adjustable rear, lug front. **Features:** Percussion (musket caps). Armory bright finish with color case-hardened lock and barrel tang, engraved lockplate, steel ramrod. Introduced 2000. Imported from Italy by Dixie Gun Works.
Price: $950.00

DIXIE PEDERSOLI 1766 CHARLEVILLE MUSKET
Caliber: 69. **Barrel:** 44-3/4". **Weight:** 10-1/2 lbs. **Length:** 57-1/2" overall. **Stock:** European walnut with oil finish. **Sights:** Fixed rear, lug front. **Features:** Smoothbore flintlock. Armory bright finish with steel furniture and ramrod. Introduced 2000. Imported from Italy by Dixie Gun Works.
Price: $865.00

DIXIE SHARPS NEW MODEL 1859 MILITARY RIFLE
Caliber: 54. **Barrel:** 30", 6-groove; 1:48" twist. **Weight:** 9 lbs. **Length:** 45-1/2" overall. **Stock:** Oiled walnut. **Sights:** Blade front, ladder-style rear. **Features:** Blued barrel, color case-hardened barrel bands, receiver, hammer, nosecap, lever, patchbox cover and buttplate. Introduced 1995. Imported from Italy by Dixie Gun Works.
Price: $965.00

DIXIE U.S. MODEL 1816 FLINTLOCK MUSKET
Caliber: 69. **Barrel:** 42", smoothbore. **Weight:** 9.75 lbs. **Length:** 56.5" overall. **Stock:** Walnut with oil finish. **Sights:** Blade front. **Features:** All metal finished "National Armory Bright"; three barrel bands with springs; steel ramrod with button-shaped head. Imported by Dixie Gun Works.
Price: $825.00

DIXIE U.S. MODEL 1861 SPRINGFIELD
Caliber: 58. **Barrel:** 40". **Weight:** About 8 lbs. **Length:** 55-13/16" overall. **Stock:** Oil-finished walnut. **Sights:** Blade front, step adjustable rear. **Features:** Exact recreation of original rifle. Sling swivels attached to trigger guard bow and middle barrel band. Lockplate marked "1861" with eagle motif and "U.S. Springfield" in front of hammer; "U.S." stamped on top of buttplate. From Dixie Gun Works.
Price: Kit $525.00

E.M.F. 1863 SHARPS MILITARY CARBINE
Caliber: 54. **Barrel:** 22", round. **Weight:** 8 lbs. **Length:** 39" overall. **Stock:** Oiled walnut. **Sights:** Blade front, military ladder-type rear. **Features:** Color case-hardened lock, rest blued. Imported by E.M.F.
Price: $600.00

EUROARMS VOLUNTEER TARGET RIFLE
Caliber: .451. **Barrel:** 33" (two-band), 36" (three-band). **Weight:** 11 lbs. (two-band). **Length:** 48.75" overall (two-band). **Stock:** European walnut with checkered wrist and forend. **Sights:** Hooded bead front, adjustable rear with interchangeable leaves. **Features:** Alexander Henry-type rifling with 1:20" twist. Color case-hardened hammer and lockplate, brass trigger guard and nosecap, rest blued. Imported by Euroarms of America, Dixie Gun Works.
Price: Two-band . . . . (Two-band) $795.00 (Three-band) $845.00

EUROARMS 1861 SPRINGFIELD RIFLE
Caliber: 58. **Barrel:** 40". **Weight:** About 10 lbs. **Length:** 55.5" overall. **Stock:** European walnut. **Sights:** Blade front, three-leaf military rear. **Features:** Reproduction of the original three-band rifle. Lockplate marked "1861" with eagle and "U.S. Springfield." Metal left in the white. Imported by Euroarms of America.
Price: $530.00

GONIC MODEL 93 M/L RIFLE
Caliber: 45, 50. **Barrel:** 26"; 1:24" twist. **Weight:** 6-1/2 to 7 lbs. **Length:** 43" overall. **Stock:** American hardwood with black finish. **Sights:** Adjustable or aperture rear, hooded post front. **Features:** Adjustable trigger with side safety; unbreakable ram rod; comes with A. Z. scope bases installed. Introduced 1993. Made in U.S. by Gonic Arms, Inc.
Price: Model 93 Standard (blued barrel) $720.00
Price: Model 93 Standard (stainless brl., 50 cal. only) $782.00

BLACKPOWDER MUSKETS & RIFLES

Gonic Model 93 Thumbhole

Harper's Ferry 1803

J.P. Murray

Kentucky Flintlock

Gonic Model 93 Deluxe M/L Rifle
Similar to the Model 93 except has classic-style walnut or gray laminated wood stock. Introduced 1998. Made in U.S. by Gonic Arms, Inc.
Price: Blue barrel, sights, scope base, choice of stock **$902.00**
Price: Stainless barrel, sights, scope base, choice of stock
(50 cal. only) **$964.00**

Gonic Model 93 Mountain Thumbhole M/L Rifles
Similar to the Model 93 except has high-grade walnut or gray laminate stock with extensive hand-checkered panels, Monte Carlo cheekpiece and beavertail forend; integral muzzle brake. Introduced 1998. Made in U.S. by Gonic Arms, Inc.
Price: Blue or stainless **$2,700.00**

HARPER'S FERRY 1803 FLINTLOCK RIFLE
Caliber: 54 or 58. **Barrel:** 35". **Weight:** 9 lbs. **Length:** 59-1/2" overall. **Stock:** Walnut with cheekpiece. **Sights:** Brass blade front, fixed steel rear. **Features:** Brass trigger guard, sideplate, buttplate; steel patchbox. Imported by Euroarms of America, Navy Arms (54-cal. only), Cabela's, and Dixie Gun Works.
Price: . . . . **$495.95 to $729.00**
Price: 54-cal. (Navy Arms) **$625.00**
Price: 54-caliber (Cabela's) **$599.99**
Price: 54-caliber (Dixie Gun Works) **$795.00**

HAWKEN RIFLE
Caliber: 45, 50, 54 or 58. **Barrel:** 28", blued, 6-groove rifling. **Weight:** 8-3/4 lbs. **Length:** 44" overall. **Stock:** Walnut with cheekpiece. **Sights:** Blade front, fully adjustable rear. **Features:** Coil mainspring, double-set triggers, polished brass furniture. From Armsport and E.M.F.
Price: . . . . **$220.00 to $345.00**

J.P. MURRAY 1862-1864 CAVALRY CARBINE
Caliber: 58 (.577" Minie). **Barrel:** 23". **Weight:** 7 lbs., 9 oz. **Length:** 39" overall. **Stock:** Walnut. **Sights:** Blade front, rear drift adjustable for windage. **Features:** Browned barrel, color case-hardened lock, blued swivel and band springs, polished brass buttplate, trigger guard, barrel bands. From Euroarms of America.
Price: . . . . **$405.00 to $453.00**

J.P. HENRY TRADE RIFLE
Caliber: 54. **Barrel:** 34"; 1" flats. **Weight:** 8-1/2 lbs. **Length:** 45" overall. **Stock:** Premium curly maple. **Sights:** Silver blade front, fixed buckhorn rear. **Features:** Brass buttplate, side plate, trigger guard and nosecap; browned barrel and lock; L&R Large English percussion lock; single trigger. Made in U.S. by J.P. Gunstocks, Inc.
Price: **$965.50**

KENTUCKIAN RIFLE
Caliber: 44. **Barrel:** 35". **Weight:** 7 lbs. (Rifle), 5-1/2 lbs. (Carbine). **Length:** 51" overall (Rifle), 43" (Carbine). **Stock:** Walnut stain. **Sights:** Brass blade front, steel V-ramp rear. **Features:** Octagon barrel, case-hardened and engraved lockplates. Brass furniture. Imported by Dixie Gun Works.
Price: Flintlock or Percussion **$395.00**

KENTUCKY FLINTLOCK RIFLE
Caliber: 44, 45, or 50. **Barrel:** 35". **Weight:** 7 lbs. **Length:** 50" overall. **Stock:** Walnut stained, brass fittings. **Sights:** Fixed. **Features:** Available in carbine model also, 28" bbl. Some variations in detail, finish. Kits also available from some importers. Imported by The Armoury.
Price: About . . . . **$217.95 to $345.00**

Kentucky Percussion Rifle
Similar to flintlock except percussion lock. Finish and features vary with importer. Imported by The Armoury and CVA.
Price: About **$259.95**
Price: 45- or 50-cal. (Navy Arms) **$425.00**
Price: Kit, 50-cal. (CVA) **$189.95**

BLACKPOWDER

BLACKPOWDER MUSKETS & RIFLES

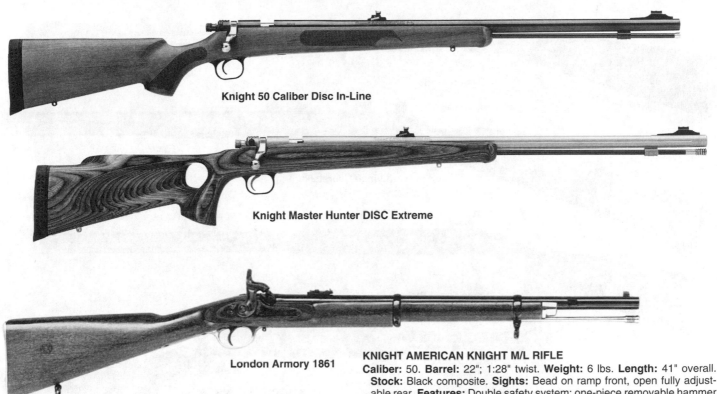

Knight 50 Caliber Disc In-Line

Knight Master Hunter DISC Extreme

London Armory 1861

KNIGHT 50 CALIBER DISC IN-LINE RIFLE
Caliber: 50. **Barrel:** 24", 26". **Weight:** 7 lbs., 14 oz. **Length:** 43" overall (24" barrel). **Stock:** Checkered synthetic with palm swell grip, rubber recoil pad, swivel studs; black, Advantage or Mossy Oak Break-Up camouflage. **Sights:** Bead on ramp front, fully adjustable open rear. **Features:** Bolt-action in-line system uses #209 shotshell primer for ignition; primer is held in plastic drop-in Primer Disc. Available in blued or stainless steel. Made in U.S. by Knight Rifles (Modern Muzzleloading).
Price: . . . . **$439.95 to $632.45**

Knight Master Hunter II DISC In-Line Rifle
Similar to Knight 50 caliber DISC rifle except features premier, wood laminated two-tone stock, gold-plated trigger and engraved trigger guard, jeweled bolt and fluted, air-gauged Green Mountain 26" barrel. Length 45" overall, weighs 7 lbs., 7 oz. Includes black composite thumbhole stock. Introduced 2000. Made in U.S. by Knight Rifles (Modern Muzzleloading).
Price: **$1,099.95**

KNIGHT MUZZLELOADER DISC EXTREME
Caliber: 45 fluted, 50. **Barrel:** 26". **Stock:** Stainless steel laminate, blued walnut, black composite thumbhole with blued or SS. **Sights:** Fully adjustable metallic. **Features:** New full plastic jacket ignition system.
Price: 50 SS laminate. **$703.95**
Price: 45 SS laminate. **$769.95**
Price: 50 blue walnut **$626.95**
Price: 45 blue walnut **$703.95**
Price: 50 blue composite **$549.95**
Price: 45 blue composite **$632.45**
Price: 50 SS composite **$632.45**
Price: 45 SS composite **$703.95**

Knight Master Hunter DISC Extreme
Similar to DISC Extreme except fluted barrel, two-tone laminated thumbhole Monte Carlo-style stock, black composite thumbhole field stock included. Jeweled bolt, adjustable premium trigger.
Price: 50 . . . . **$1,044.95**

KNIGHT AMERICAN KNIGHT M/L RIFLE
Caliber: 50. **Barrel:** 22"; 1:28" twist. **Weight:** 6 lbs. **Length:** 41" overall. **Stock:** Black composite. **Sights:** Bead on ramp front, open fully adjustable rear. **Features:** Double safety system; one-piece removable hammer assembly; drilled and tapped for scope mounting. Introduced 1998. Made in U.S. by Knight Rifles.
Price: blued, black comp **$197.95**
Price: blued, black comp VP **$225.45**

KNIGHT WOLVERINE 209
Caliber: 50. **Barrel:** 22". **Stock:** HD stock with SS barrel, break-up stock blued, black composite thumbhole with stainless steel, standard black composite with blued or SS. **Sights:** Metallic with fiber optic. **Features:** Double safety system, adjustable match grade trigger, left-hand model available. Full plastic jacket ignition system.
Price: Starting at **$302.45**

LONDON ARMORY 2-BAND 1858 ENFIELD
Caliber: .577" Minie, .575" round ball. **Barrel:** 33". **Weight:** 10 lbs. **Length:** 49" overall. **Stock:** Walnut. **Sights:** Folding leaf rear adjustable for elevation. **Features:** Blued barrel, color case-hardened lock and hammer, polished brass buttplate, trigger guard, nosecap. From Navy Arms, Euroarms of America, Dixie Gun Works.
Price: . . . . **$385.00 to $600.00**

LONDON ARMORY 1861 ENFIELD MUSKETOON
Caliber: 58, Minie ball. **Barrel:** 24", round. **Weight:** 7 - 7-1/2 lbs. **Length:** 40-1/2" overall. **Stock:** Walnut, with sling swivels. **Sights:** Blade front, graduated military-leaf rear. **Features:** Brass trigger guard, nosecap, buttplate; blued barrel, bands, lockplate, swivels. Imported by Euroarms of America, Navy Arms.
Price: . . . . **$300.00 to $515.00**
Price: Kit. . . . . **$365.00 to $373.00**

LONDON ARMORY 3-BAND 1853 ENFIELD
Caliber: 58 (.577" Minie, .575" round ball, .580" maxi ball). **Barrel:** 39". **Weight:** 9-1/2 lbs. **Length:** 54" overall. **Stock:** European walnut. **Sights:** Inverted "V" front, traditional Enfield folding ladder rear. **Features:** Recreation of the famed London Armory Company Pattern 1853 Enfield Musket. One-piece walnut stock, brass buttplate, trigger guard and nosecap. Lockplate marked "London Armoury Co." and with a British crown. Blued Baddeley barrel bands. From Dixie Gun Works, Euroarms of America, Navy Arms.
Price: About . . . . **$350.00 to $645.00**
Price: Assembled kit (Dixie, Euroarms of America) **$495.00**

BLACKPOWDER MUSKETS & RIFLES

Lyman Trade

Lyman Deerstalker

Lyman Great Plains

Markesbery KM Colorado

LYMAN TRADE RIFLE
Caliber: 50, 54. **Barrel:** 28" octagon;1:48" twist. **Weight:** 8-3/4 lbs. **Length:** 45" overall. **Stock:** European walnut. **Sights:** Blade front, open rear adjustable for windage or optional fixed sights. **Features:** Fast twist rifling for conical bullets. Polished brass furniture with blue steel parts, stainless steel nipple. Hook breech, single trigger, coil spring percussion lock. Steel barrel rib and ramrod ferrules. Introduced 1980. From Lyman.
Price: 50 cal. Percussion $581.80
Price: 50 cal. Flintlock $652.80
Price: 54 cal. Percussion $581.80
Price: 54 cal. Flintlock $652.80

LYMAN DEERSTALKER RIFLE
Caliber: 50, 54. **Barrel:** 24", octagonal; 1:48" rifling. **Weight:** 7-1/2 lbs. **Stock:** Walnut with black rubber buttpad. **Sights:** Lyman #37MA beaded front, fully adjustable fold-down Lyman #16A rear. **Features:** Stock has less drop for quick sighting. All metal parts are blackened, with color case-hardened lock; single trigger. Comes with sling and swivels. Available in flint or percussion. Introduced 1990. From Lyman.
Price: 50 cal. flintlock $652.80
Price: 50- or 54-cal., percussion, left-hand, carbine $695.40
Price: 50- or 54-cal., flintlock, left-hand $645.00
Price: 54 cal. flintlock $780.50
Price: 54 cal. percussion $821.80
Price: Stainless steel $959.80

LYMAN GREAT PLAINS RIFLE
Caliber: 50- or 54-cal. **Barrel:** 32"; 1:60" twist. **Weight:** 9 lbs. **Stock:** Walnut. **Sights:** Steel blade front, buckhorn rear adjustable for windage and elevation and fixed notch primitive sight included. **Features:** Blued steel furniture. Stainless steel nipple. Coil spring lock, Hawken-style trigger guard and double-set triggers. Round thimbles recessed and sweated into rib. Steel wedge plates and toe plate. Introduced 1979. From Lyman.
Price: Percussion $469.95
Price: Flintlock $494.95
Price: Percussion kit $359.95
Price: Flintlock kit $384.95
Price: Left-hand percussion $474.95
Price: Left-hand flintlock $499.95

Lyman Great Plains Hunter Rifle
Similar to Great Plains model except 1:32" twist shallow-groove barrel and comes drilled and tapped for Lyman 57GPR peep sight.
Price: $959.80

MARKESBERY KM BLACK BEAR M/L RIFLE
Caliber: 36, 45, 50, 54. **Barrel:** 24"; 1:26" twist. **Weight:** 6-1/2 lbs. **Length:** 38-1/2" overall. **Stock:** Two-piece American hardwood, walnut, black laminate, green laminate, black composition, X-Tra or Mossy Oak Break-Up camouflage. **Sights:** Bead front, open fully adjustable rear. **Features:** Interchangeable barrels; exposed hammer; Outer-Line Magnum ignition system uses small rifle primer or standard No. 11 cap and nipple. Blue, black matte, or stainless. Made in U.S. by Markesbery Muzzle Loaders.
Price: American hardwood walnut, blue finish $536.63
Price: American hardwood walnut, stainless $553.09
Price: Black laminate, blue finish $539.67
Price: Black laminate, stainless $556.27
Price: Camouflage stock, blue finish $556.46
Price: Camouflage stock, stainless $573.73
Price: Black composite, blue finish $532.65
Price: Black composite, stainless $549.93
Price: Green laminate, blue finish $539.00
Price: Green laminate, stainless $556.27

MARKESBERY KM COLORADO ROCKY MOUNTAIN M/L RIFLE
Caliber: 36, 45, 50, 54. **Barrel:** 24"; 1:26" twist. **Weight:** 6-1/2 lbs. **Length:** 38-1/2" overall. **Stock:** American hardwood walnut, green or black laminate. **Sights:** Firesight bead on ramp front, fully adjustable open rear. **Features:** Replicates Reed/Watson rifle of 1851. Straight grip stock with or without two barrel bands, rubber recoil pad, large-spur hammer. Made in U.S. by Markesbery Muzzle Loaders, Inc.
Price: American hardwood walnut, blue finish $545.92
Price: Black or green laminate, blue finish $548.30
Price: American hardwood walnut, stainless $563.17
Price: Black or green laminate, stainless $566.34

BLACKPOWDER

Mississippi 1841

Navy Arms Charleville

Navy Arms 1859 Sharps

Markesbery KM Brown Bear M/L Rifle

Similar to KM Black Bear except one-piece thumbhole stock with Monte Carlo comb. Stock in Crotch Walnut composite, green or black laminate, black composite or X-Tra or Mossy Oak Break-Up camouflage. Contact maker for complete price listing. Made in U.S. by Markesbery Muzzle Loaders, Inc.

Price: Black composite, blue finish **$658.83**
Price: Crotch Walnut, blue finish **$658.83**
Price: Camo composite, blue finish **$682.64**
Price: Walnut wood **$662.81**
Price: Black wood **$662.81**
Price: Black laminated wood **$662.81**
Price: Green laminated wood **$662.81**
Price: Camo wood **$684.69**
Price: Black composite, stainless **$676.11**
Price: Crotch Walnut composite, stainless **$676.11**
Price: Camo composite, stainless **$697.69**
Price: Walnut wood, stainless **$680.07**
Price: Black wood, stainless **$680.07**
Price: Black laminated wood, stainless **$680.07**
Price: Green laminate, stainless **$680.07**
Price: Camo wood, stainless **$702.76**

Markesbery KM Grizzly Bear M/L Rifle

Similar to KM Black Bear except thumbhole buttstock with Monte Carlo comb. Stock in Crotch Walnut composite, green or black laminate, black composite or X-Tra or Mossy Oak Break-Up camouflage. Contact maker for complete price listing. Made in U.S. by Markesbery Muzzle Loaders, Inc.

Price: Black composite, blue finish **$642.96**
Price: Crotch Walnut, blue finish **$642.96**
Price: Camo composite, blue finish **$666.67**
Price: Walnut wood **$646.93**
Price: Black wood **$646.93**
Price: Black laminate wood **$646.93**
Price: Green laminate wood **$646.93**
Price: Camo wood **$670.74**
Price: Black composite, stainless **$660.98**
Price: Crotch Walnut composite, stainless **$660.98**
Price: Black laminate wood, stainless **$664.20**
Price: Green laminate, stainless **$664.20**
Price: Camo wood, stainless **$685.74**
Price: Camo composite, stainless **$684.04**
Price: Walnut wood, stainless **$664.20**
Price: Black wood, stainless **$664.20**

Markesbery KM Polar Bear M/L Rifle

Similar to KM Black Bear except one-piece stock with Monte Carlo comb. Stock in American Hardwood walnut, green or black laminate, black composite, or X-Tra or Mossy Oak Break-Up camouflage. Interchangeable barrel system, Outer-Line ignition system, cross-bolt double safety. Available in 36, 45, 50, 54 caliber. Contact maker for full price listing. Made in U.S. by Markesbery Muzzle Loaders, Inc.

Price: American Hardwood walnut , blue finish **$539.01**
Price: Black composite, blue finish **$536.63**
Price: Black laminate, blue finish **$541.17**
Price: Green laminate, blue finish **$541.17**
Price: Camo, blue finish **$560.43**
Price: American Hardwood walnut, stainless **$556.27**
Price: Black composite, stainless **$556.04**
Price: Black laminate, stainless **$570.56**
Price: Green laminate, stainless **$570.56**
Price: Camo, stainless **$573.94**

MDM BUCKWACKA IN-LINE RIFLES

Caliber: 45, 50. **Barrel:** 23", 25". **Weight:** 7 to 7-3/4 lbs. **Stock:** Black, walnut, laminated and camouflage finishes. **Sights:** Williams Fire Sight blade front, Williams fully adjustable rear with ghost-ring peep aperture. **Features:** Break-open action; Incinerating Ignition System incorporates 209 shotshell primer directly into breech plug; 50-caliber models handle up to 150 grains of Pyrodex; synthetic ramrod; transfer bar safety; stainless or blued finish. Made in U.S. by Millennium Designed Muzzleloaders Ltd.

Price: 50 cal., blued finish **$309.95**
Price: 50 cal., stainless **$339.95**
Price: Camouflage stock . . . . **$359.95 to $389.95**

MDM M2K In-Line Rifle

Similar to Buckwacka except adjustable trigger and double-safety mechanism designed to prevent misfires. Made in U.S. by Millennium Designed Muzzleloaders Ltd.

Price: . . . . **$529.00 to $549.00**

Mississippi 1841 Percussion Rifle

Similar to Zouave rifle but patterned after U.S. Model 1841. **Caliber:** 54, 58. Imported by Dixie Gun Works, Euroarms of America, Navy Arms.

Price: About **$595.00**

NAVY ARMS 1763 CHARLEVILLE

Caliber: 69. **Barrel:** 44-5/8". **Weight:** 8 lbs., 12 oz. **Length:** 59-3/8" overall. **Stock:** Walnut. **Sights:** Brass blade front. **Features:** Replica of French musket used by American troops during the Revolution. Imported by Navy Arms.

Price: **$1,020.00**

NAVY ARMS PARKER-HALE VOLUNTEER RIFLE

Caliber: .451. **Barrel:** 32". **Weight:** 9-1/2 lbs. **Length:** 49" overall. **Stock:** Walnut, checkered wrist and forend. **Sights:** Globe front, adjustable ladder-type rear. **Features:** Recreation of the type of gun issued to volunteer regiments during the 1860s. Rigby-pattern rifling, patent breech, detented lock. Stock is glass bedded for accuracy. Imported by Navy Arms.

Price: **$905.00**

BLACKPOWDER MUSKETS & RIFLES

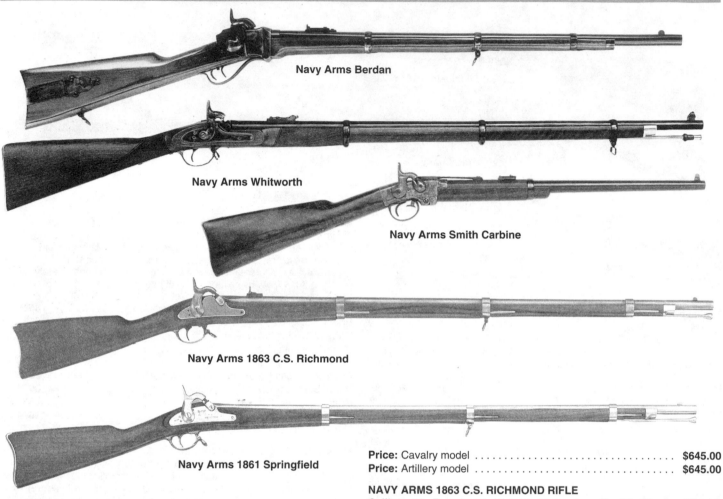

Navy Arms Berdan

Navy Arms Whitworth

Navy Arms Smith Carbine

Navy Arms 1863 C.S. Richmond

Navy Arms 1861 Springfield

NAVY ARMS 1859 SHARPS CAVALRY CARBINE
Caliber: 54. **Barrel:** 22". **Weight:** 7-3/4 lbs. **Length:** 39" overall. **Stock:** Walnut. **Sights:** Blade front, military ladder-type rear. **Features:** Color case-hardened action, blued barrel. Has saddle ring. Introduced 1991. Imported from Navy Arms.
Price: **$1,000.00**

NAVY ARMS BERDAN 1859 SHARPS RIFLE
Caliber: 54. **Barrel:** 30". **Weight:** 8 lbs., 8 oz. **Length:** 46-3/4" overall. **Stock:** Walnut. **Sights:** Blade front, folding military ladder-type rear. **Features:** Replica of the Union sniper rifle used by Berdan's 1st and 2nd Sharpshooter regiments. Color case-hardened receiver, patchbox, furniture. Double-set triggers. Imported by Navy Arms.
Price: **$1,165.00**
Price: 1859 Sharps Infantry Rifle (three-band) **$1,100.00**

NAVY ARMS PARKER-HALE WHITWORTH MILITARY TARGET RIFLE
Caliber: 45. **Barrel:** 36". **Weight:** 9-1/4 lbs. **Length:** 52-1/2" overall. **Stock:** Walnut. Checkered at wrist and forend. **Sights:** Hooded post front, open step-adjustable rear. **Features:** Faithful reproduction of Whitworth rifle, only bored for 45-cal. Trigger has detented lock, capable of being adjusted very finely without risk of the sear nose catching on the half-cock bent and damaging both parts. Introduced 1978. Imported by Navy Arms.
Price: **$930.00**

NAVY ARMS SMITH CARBINE
Caliber: 50. **Barrel:** 21-1/2". **Weight:** 7-3/4 lbs. **Length:** 39" overall. **Stock:** American walnut. **Sights:** Brass blade front, folding ladder-type rear. **Features:** Replica of breech-loading Civil War carbine. Color case-hardened receiver, rest blued. Cavalry model has saddle ring and bar, Artillery model has sling swivels. Imported by Navy Arms.

Price: Cavalry model **$645.00**
Price: Artillery model **$645.00**

NAVY ARMS 1863 C.S. RICHMOND RIFLE
Caliber: 58. **Barrel:** 40". **Weight:** 10 lbs. **Length:** NA. **Stocks:** Walnut. **Sights:** Blade front, adjustable rear. **Features:** Copy of three-band rifle musket made at Richmond Armory for the Confederacy. All steel polished bright. Imported by Navy Arms.
Price: **$590.00**

NAVY ARMS 1861 SPRINGFIELD RIFLE
Caliber: 58. **Barrel:** 40" **Weight:** 10 lbs., 4 oz. **Length:** 56" overall. **Stock:** Walnut. **Sights:** Blade front, military leaf rear. **Features:** Steel barrel, lock and all furniture have polished bright finish. Has 1855-style hammer. Imported by Navy Arms.
Price: **$590.00**

NAVY ARMS 1863 SPRINGFIELD
Caliber: 58, uses .575 Minie. **Barrel:** 40", rifled. **Weight:** 9-1/2 lbs. **Length:** 56" overall. **Stock:** Walnut. **Sights:** Open rear adjustable for elevation. **Features:** Full-size, three-band musket. Polished bright metal, including lock. From Navy Arms.
Price: Finished rifle. **$590.00**

BLACKPOWDER

BLACKPOWDER MUSKETS & RIFLES

New England Firearms Huntsman

Peifer TS-93

Remington Model 700 ML

NEW ENGLAND FIREARMS HUNTSMAN
Caliber: 50. **Barrel:** 24". **Weight:** 6-1/2 lbs. **Length:** 40". **Stock:** Walnut-finished American hardwood with pistol grip. **Sights:** Adjustable fiber optics open sights, tapped for scope base. **Features:** Break-open action, color case-hardened frame, black oxide barrel. Made in U.S.A. by New England Firearms.
Price: **$185.00**

New England Firearms "Stainless" Huntsman
Similar to Huntsman, but with matte nickel finish receiver. Introduced 2003. From New England Firearms.
Price: **$269.00**

PACIFIC RIFLE MODEL 1837 ZEPHYR
Caliber: 62. **Barrel:** 30", tapered octagon. **Weight:** 7-3/4 lbs. **Length:** NA. **Stock:** Oil-finished fancy walnut. **Sights:** German silver blade front, semi-buckhorn rear. Options available. **Features:** Improved underhammer action. First production rifle to offer Forsyth rifle, with narrow lands and shallow rifling with 1:144" pitch for high-velocity round balls. Metal finish is slow rust brown with nitre blue accents. Optional sights, finishes and integral muzzle brake available. Introduced 1995. Made in U.S. by Pacific Rifle Co.
Price: From **$995.00**

Pacific Rifle Big Bore, African Rifles
Similar to the 1837 Zephyr except in 72-caliber and 8-bore. The 72-caliber is available in standard form with 28" barrel, or as the African with flat buttplate, checkered upgraded wood; weight is 9 lbs. The 8-bore African has dual-cap ignition, 24" barrel, weighs 12 lbs., checkered English walnut, engraving, gold inlays. Introduced 1998. Made in U.S. by Pacific Rifle Co.
Price: 72-caliber, from **$1,150.00**
Price: 8-bore from **$2,500.00**

PEIFER MODEL TS-93 RIFLE
Caliber: 45, 50. **Barrel:** 24" Douglas premium; 1:20" twist in 45; 1:28" in 50. **Weight:** 7 lbs. **Length:** 43-1/4" overall. **Stock:** Bell & Carlson solid composite, with recoil pad, swivel studs. **Sights:** Williams bead front on ramp, fully adjustable open rear. Drilled and tapped for Weaver scope mounts with dovetail for rear peep. **Features:** In-line ignition uses #209 shotshell primer; extremely fast lock time; fully enclosed breech; adjustable trigger; automatic safety; removable primer holder. Blue or stainless. Made in U.S. by Peifer Rifle Co. Introduced 1996.
Price: Blue, black stock **$730.00**
Price: Blue, wood or camouflage composite stock, or stainless
with black composite stock **$803.00**
Price: Stainless, wood or camouflage composite stock **$876.00**

PRAIRIE RIVER ARMS PRA BULLPUP RIFLE
Caliber: 50, 54. **Barrel:** 28"; 1:28" twist. **Weight:** 7-1/2 lbs. **Length:** 31-1/2" overall. **Stock:** Hardwood or black all-weather. **Sights:** Blade front, open adjustable rear. **Features:** Bullpup design thumbhole stock. Patented internal percussion ignition system. Left-hand model available. Dovetailed for scope mount. Introduced 1995. Made in U.S. by Prairie River Arms, Ltd.
Price: 4140 alloy barrel, hardwood stock **$199.00**
Price: Stainless barrel, hardwood stock **$225.00**
Price: All Weather stock, alloy barrel **$205.00**
Price: All Weather stock, stainless barrel **$230.00**

REMINGTON MODEL 700 ML, MLS RIFLES
Caliber: 50, new 45 (MLS Magnum).**Barrel:** 24"; 1:28" twist, 26" (Magnum). **Weight:** 7-3/4 lbs. **Length:** 42"-44-1/2" overall. **Stock:** Black fiberglass-reinforced synthetic with checkered grip and forend; magnum-style buttpad. **Sights:** Ramped bead front, open fully adjustable rear. Drilled and tapped for scope mounts. **Features:** Uses the Remington 700 bolt action, stock design, safety and trigger mechanisms; removable stainless steel breech plug, No. 11 nipple; solid aluminum ramrod. Comes with cleaning tools and accessories; 3-way ignition.
Price: ML, blued, 50-caliber only **$415.00**
Price: MLS, stainless, 45 Magnum, 50-caliber **$533.00**
Price: MLS, stainless, Mossy Oak Break-Up camo stock **$569.00**

RICHMOND, C.S., 1863 MUSKET
Caliber: 58. **Barrel:** 40". **Weight:** 11 lbs. **Length:** 56-1/4" overall. **Stock:** European walnut with oil finish. **Sights:** Blade front, adjustable folding leaf rear. **Features:** Reproduction of the three-band Civil War musket. Sling swivels attached to trigger guard and middle barrel band. Lockplate marked "1863" and "C.S. Richmond." All metal left in white. Brass buttplate and forend cap. Imported by Euroarms of America, Navy Arms, and Dixie Gun Works.
Price: Euroarms **$530.00**
Price: Dixie Gun Works **$675.00**

RUGER 77/50 IN-LINE PERCUSSION RIFLE
Caliber: 50. **Barrel:** 22"; 1:28" twist. **Weight:** 6-1/2 lbs. **Length:** 41-1/2" overall. **Stock:** Birch with rubber buttpad and swivel studs. **Sights:** Gold bead front, folding leaf rear. Comes with Ruger scope mounts. **Features:** Shares design features with Ruger 77/22 rifle. Stainless steel bolt and nipple/breech plug; uses #11 caps, three-position safety, blued steel ramrod. Introduced 1997. Made in U.S. by Sturm, Ruger & Co.
Price: 77/50RS **$434.00**
Price: 77/50RSO Officer's (straight-grip checkered walnut stock,
blued) **$555.00**
Price: K77/50RSBBZ (stainless steel, black laminated stock) . . . **$601.00**
Price: K77/50RSP All-Weather (stainless steel, synthetic stock) . **$580.00**
Price: 77/50 RSP (blued, synthetic stock) **$434.00**

BLACKPOWDER MUSKETS & RIFLES

C.S. Richmond 1863

Ruger K77/50RSBBZ

Savage 10MLSS-IIXP

Second Model Brown Bess

T/C Firestorm

SAVAGE MODEL 10ML MUZZLELOADER RIFLE SERIES
Caliber: 50. **Barrel:** 24", 1:24 twist, blue or stainless. **Weight:** 7.75 lbs. **Stock:** Black synthetic, Realtree Hardwood JD Camo, brown laminate. **Sights:** Green adjustable rear, Red FiberOptic front. **Features:** XP Models scoped, no sights, smokeless powder, "easy to prime", #209 primer ignition. Removeable breech plut and vent liner.

Price: Model 10ML-II	$496.00
Price: Model 10ML-II Camo	$533.00
Price: Model 10MLSS-II Camo	$554.00
Price: Model 10MLBSS-II	$626.00
Price: Model 10ML-IIXP	$533.00
Price: Model 10MLSS-IIXP	$589.00

SECOND MODEL BROWN BESS MUSKET
Caliber: 75, uses .735" round ball. **Barrel:** 42", smoothbore. **Weight:** 9-1/2 lbs. **Length:** 59" overall. **Stock:** Walnut (Navy); walnut-stained hardwood (Dixie). **Sights:** Fixed. **Features:** Polished barrel and lock with brass trigger guard and buttplate. Bayonet and scabbard available. From Navy Arms, Dixie Gun Works, Cabela's.

Price: Finished	$475.00 to $850.00
Price: Kit (Dixie Gun Works, Navy Arms)	$575.00 to $625.00

Price: Carbine (Navy Arms)	$835.00
Price: Dixie Gun Works	$765.00

THOMPSON/CENTER FIRE STORM RIFLE
Caliber: 50. **Barrel:** 26"; 1:28" twist. **Weight:** 7 lbs. **Length:** 41-3/4" overall. **Stock:** Black synthetic with rubber recoil pad, swivel studs. **Sights:** Click-adjustable steel rear and ramp-style front, both with fiber optic inserts. **Features:** Side hammer lock is the first designed for up to three 50-grain Pyrodex pellets; patented Pyrodex Pyramid breech directs ignition fire 360 degrees around base of pellet. Quick Load Accurizor Muzzle System; aluminum ramrod. Flintlock only. Introduced 2000. Made in U.S. by Thomson/Center Arms.

Price: Blue finish, flintlock model with 1:48" twist for round balls, conicals.	$415.00
Price: SST, flintlock	$465.00

THOMPSON/CENTER ENCORE 209x50 MAGNUM
Caliber: 50. **Barrel:** 26"; interchangeable with centerfire calibers. **Weight:** 7 lbs. **Length:** 40-1/2" overall. **Stock:** American walnut butt and forend, or black composite. **Sights:** Tru-Glo Fiber Optic front, Tru-Glo Fiber Optic rear. **Features:** Blue or stainless steel. Uses the stock, frame and forend of the Encore centerfire pistol; break-open design using trigger guard spur; stainless steel universal breech plug; uses #209 shotshell primers. Introduced 1998. Made in U.S. by Thompson/Center Arms.

Price: Stainless wtih camo stock	$751.00
Price: Blue, walnut stock and forend	$640.00
Price: Blue, composite stock and forend	$613.00
Price: Stainless, composite stock and forend	$692.00

T/C Hawken

Traditions Deerhunter

Traditions Lightning

THOMPSON/CENTER BLACK DIAMOND RIFLE XR

Caliber: 50. **Barrel:** 26" with QLA; 1:28" twist. **Weight:** 6 lbs., 9 oz. **Length:** 41-1/2" overall. **Stock:** Black Rynite with moulded-in checkering and grip cap, or walnut. **Sights:** Tru-Glo Fiber Optic ramp-style front, Tru- Glo Fiber Optic open rear. **Features:** In-line ignition system for musket cap, No. 11 cap, or 209 shotshell primer; removable universal breech plug; stainless steel construction. Selected models available in .45 cal. Made in U.S. by Thompson/Center Arms.

Price: With composite stock, blued $335.00
Price: With walnut stock $405.00

THOMPSON/CENTER HAWKEN RIFLE

Caliber: 45, 50 or 54. **Barrel:** 28" octagon, hooked breech. **Stock:** American walnut. **Sights:** Blade front, rear adjustable for windage and elevation. **Features:** Solid brass furniture, double-set triggers, button rifled barrel, coil-type mainspring. From Thompson/Center Arms.

Price: Percussion model (45-, 50- or 54-cal.) $545.00
Price: Flintlock model (50-cal.) $570.00

TRADITIONS BUCKSKINNER CARBINE

Caliber: 50. **Barrel:** 21"; 15/16" flats, half octagon, half round; 1:20" or 1:66" twist. **Weight:** 6 lbs. **Length:** 37" overall. **Stock:** Beech or black laminated. **Sights:** Beaded blade front, fiber optic open rear click adjustable for windage and elevation or fiber optics. **Features:** Uses V-type mainspring, single trigger. Non-glare hardware; sling swivels. From Traditions.

Price: Flintlock $239.00
Price: Flintlock, laminated stock $309.00

TRADITIONS DEERHUNTER RIFLE SERIES

Caliber: 32, 50 or 54. **Barrel:** 24", octagonal; 15/16" flats; 1:48" or 1:66" twist. **Weight:** 6 lbs. **Length:** 40" overall. **Stock:** Stained hardwood or All-Weather composite with rubber buttpad, sling swivels. **Sights:** Lite Optic blade front, adjustable rear fiber optics. **Features:** Flint or percussion with color case-hardened lock. Hooked breech, oversized trigger guard, blackened furniture, PVC ramrod. All-Weather has composite stock and C-Nickel barrel. Drilled and tapped for scope mounting. Imported by Traditions, Inc.

Price: Percussion, 50; blued barrel; 1:48" twist $169.00
Price: Percussion, 54 . . . . $189.00
Price: Flintlock, 50 caliber only; 1:48" twist $199.00
Price: Flintlock, All-Weather, 50-cal. $179.00
Price: Redi-Pak, 50 cal. flintlock $219.00
New! **Price:** Flintlock, left-handed hardwood, 50 cal. $199.00
Price: Percussion, All-Weather, 50 or 54 cal. $159.00
Price: Percussion; 32 cal. $179.00

Traditions Panther Sidelock Rifle

Similar to Deerhunter rifle, but has blade front and windage-adjustable-only rear sight, black composite stock.
Price: $119.00

TRADITIONS E-BOLT 209 BOLT-ACTION RIFLES

Caliber: 45, 50. **Barrel:** 22" blued or C-Nickel finish, 1:20 and 1:28" twist. **Weight:** 6 lbs., 7 oz. **Length:** 41" overall. **Stock:** Black or Advantage Timber® composite. **Sights:** Lite Optic blade front, adjustable rear. **Features:** Thumb safety; quick-release bolt; covered breech; one-piece breech plug takes 209 shotshell primers; accepts 150 grains of Pyrodex pellets, receiver drilled and tapped for scope, sling swivel studs and rubber butt pad. From Traditions.

Price: Black composite stock with 22" blued barrel $169.00
Price: Black composite stock with 22" C-Nickel barrel $189.00
Price: Advantage Timber® stock with 22" C-Nickel barrel $229.00
Price: Redi-Pak with black stock/blued barrel and powder flask, capper, ball starter, other supplies $219.00
Price: Redi-Pak with Advantage Timber® stock/C-Nickel barrel and powder flask, capper, ball starter, other supplies $279.00
Price: Blue, Mossy Oak break-up $219.00
Price: 4X32 fixed scope $219.00
Price: Scoped w/Redi-Pak $269.00

TRADITIONS LIGHTNING MAG BOLT-ACTION MUZZLELOADER

Caliber: 50, 54. **Barrel:** 24" round; blued, stainless, C-Nickel or Ultra Coat. **Weight:** 6-1/2 to 7 lbs. 10 oz. **Length:** 43" overall. **Stock:** All-Weather composite, Advantage, or Break-Up camouflage. **Sights:** Fiber Optic blade front, fully adjustable open rear. **Features:** Field-removable stainless steel bolt; silent thumb safety; adjustable trigger; drilled and tapped for scope mounting. Lightning Fire Magnum System allows use of No. 11, musket caps or 209 shotgun primers. Imported by Traditions.

Price: All-Weather composite stock, blue finish $199.00
Price: All-Weather composite stock, blue finish, muzzle brake . . $229.00
Price: All-Weather composite, stainless steel $279.00
Price: Camouflage composite, stainless steel $309.00
Price: Camouflage composite $229.00
Price: Composite, with muzzle brake, stainless, fluted barrel . . . $329.00
Price: Walnut finish, synthetic stock $239.00

Traditions Lightning 45 LD Bolt-Action Rifles

Similar to Lightning Mag. but chambered for 45, 50 caliber with 26"fluted blued or C-Nickel barrel, 1:20", 1:28" twist. Black, synthetic break-up or Advantage Timber stock, fiber optic blade front, adjustable rear sights. Accepts 150 grains of Pyrodex. Weighs 7 lbs., 2 oz. Overal length 45". Introduced 2001. From Traditions.

Price: (black stock with blued barrel) $229.00
Price: (black stock with C-Nickel barrel) $239.00
Price: (Advantage Timber® stock with C-Nickel barrel) $289.00

Traditions Lightning Lightweight Magnum Bolt-Action Rifles

Similar to Lightning Mag except features 22" lightweight, fluted barrel and Spider Web-pattern black composite stock. Overall length 41", weighs 6 lb., 5 oz. Introduced 2000. From Traditions.

Price: Blued finish. $219.00
Price: C-Nickel finish. $229.00
Price: Nickel, camo stock $259.00

BLACKPOWDER

BLACKPOWDER MUSKETS & RIFLES

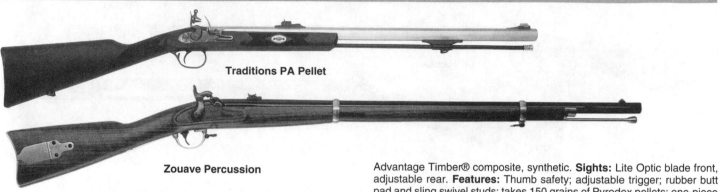

Traditions PA Pellet

Zouave Percussion

TRADITIONS PA PELLET FLINTLOCK
Caliber: 50. **Barrel:** 26", blued, nickel. **Weight:** 7 lbs. **Stock:** Hardwood, synthetic and synthetic break-up. **Sights:** FO. **Features:** Removeable breech plug, left-hand model with hardwood stock. 1:48" twist.
Price: Hardwood, blued $249.00
Price: Hardwood left, blued $269.00

TRADITIONS HAWKEN WOODSMAN RIFLE
Caliber: 50 and 54. **Barrel:** 28"; 15/16" flats. **Weight:** 7 lbs., 11 oz. **Length:** 44-1/2" overall. **Stock:** Walnut-stained hardwood. **Sights:** Beaded blade front, hunting-style open rear adjustable for windage and elevation. **Features:** Percussion only. Brass patchbox and furniture. Double triggers. From Traditions.
Price: 50 or 54 . . . . $239.00
Price: 50-cal., left-hand. $249.00
Price: 50-caliber, flintlock $279.00

TRADITIONS KENTUCKY RIFLE
Caliber: 50. **Barrel:** 33-1/2"; 7/8" flats; 1:66" twist. **Weight:** 7 lbs. **Length:** 49" overall. **Stock:** Beech; inletted toe plate. **Sights:** Blade front, fixed rear. **Features:** Full-length, two-piece stock; brass furniture; color case-hardened lock. From Traditions.
Price: $249.00

TRADITIONS PENNSYLVANIA RIFLE
Caliber: 50. **Barrel:** 40-1/4"; 7/8" flats; 1:66" twist, octagon. **Weight:** 9 lbs. **Length:** 57-1/2" overall. **Stock:** Walnut. **Sights:** Blade front, adjustable rear. **Features:** Brass patchbox and ornamentation. Double-set triggers. From Traditions.
Price: Flintlock $479.00
Price: Percussion $469.00

TRADITIONS SHENANDOAH RIFLE
Caliber: 36, 50. **Barrel:** 33-1/2" octagon; 1:66" twist. **Weight:** 7 lbs., 3 oz. **Length:** 49-1/2" overall. **Stock:** Walnut. **Sights:** Blade front, buckhorn rear. **Features:** V-type mainspring; double-set trigger; solid brass buttplate, patchbox, nosecap, thimbles, trigger guard. Introduced 1996. From Traditions.
Price: Flintlock $369.00
Price: Percussion $349.00
Price: 36 cal. Flintlock, 1:48"twist $399.00
Price: 36 cal. Percussion, 1:48"twist $389.00

TRADITIONS TENNESSEE RIFLE
Caliber: 50. **Barrel:** 24", octagon; 15/16" flats; 1:66" twist. **Weight:** 6 lbs. **Length:** 40-1/2" overall. **Stock:** Stained beech. **Sights:** Blade front, fixed rear. **Features:** One-piece stock has inletted brass furniture, cheekpiece; double-set trigger; V-type mainspring. Flint or percussion. From Traditions.
Price: Flintlock $299.00
Price: Percussion $279.00

TRADITIONS TRACKER 209 IN-LINE RIFLES
Caliber: 45, 50. **Barrel:** 22" blued or C-Nickel finish; 1:28" twist, 50 cal. 1:20" 45 cal. **Weight:** 6 lbs., 4 oz. **Length:** 41" overall. **Stock:** Black, Advantage Timber® composite, synthetic. **Sights:** Lite Optic blade front, adjustable rear. **Features:** Thumb safety; adjustable trigger; rubber butt pad and sling swivel studs; takes 150 grains of Pyrodex pellets; one-piece breech system takes 209 shotshell primers. Drilled and tapped for scope. From Traditions.
Price: (Black composite or synthetic stock, 22" blued barrel). . . . **$119.00**
Price: (Black composite or synthetic stock, 22" C-Nickel barrel) . **$129.00**
Price: (Advantage Timber® stock, 22" C-Nickel barrel) **$179.00**
Price: (Redi-Pak, black stock and blued barrel, powder flask,
capper, ball starter, other accessories) **$169.00**
Price: (Redi-Pak, synthetic stock and blued barrel, with scope) . **$229.00**

WHITE MODEL 97 WHITETAIL HUNTER RIFLE
Caliber: 45, 50. **Barrel:** 22", 1:20 twist (45 cal.); 1:24 twist (50 cal.). **Weight:** 7.7 lbs. **Length:** 40" overall. **Stock:** Black laminated or black composite. **Sights:** Marble TruGlo fully adjustable, steel rear with white diamond, red bead front with high-visibility inserts. **Features:** In-line ignition with FlashFire one-piece nipple and breech plug that uses standard or magnum No. 11 caps, fully adjustable trigger, double safety system, aluminum ramrod; drilled and tapped for scope. Hard gun case. Made in U.S.A. by Split Fire Sporting Goods.
Price: Whitetail w/laminated or composite stock **$449.95**
Price: Adventurer w/26" stainless barrel & thumbhole stock) . . . **$799.95**
Price: Odyssey w/24" carbon fiber wrapped
barrel & thumbhole stock **$1,199.95**

WHITE MODEL 98 ELITE HUNTER Rifle
Caliber: 45, 50. **Barrel:** 24", 1:24" twist (50 cal). **Weight:** 8.6 lbs. **Length:** 43-1/2" overall. **Stock:** Black laminate wtih swivel studs. **Sights:** TruGlo fully adjustable, steel rear with white diamond, red bead front with high-visibility inserts. **Features:** In-line ignition with FlashFire one-piece nipple and breech plug that uses standard or magnum No. 11 caps, fully adjustable trigger, double safety system, aluminum ramrod, drilled and taped for scope, hard gun case. Made in U.S.A. by Split Fire Sporting Goods.
Price: Composite or laminate wood stock **$599.95**

White Model Thunderbolt Rifle
Similar to the Elite Hunter but is designed to handle 209 shotgun primers only. Has 26" stainless steel barrel, weighs 9.3 lbs. and is 45-1/2" long. Composite or laminate stock.
Price: **$699.95**

WHITE MODEL 2000 BLACKTAIL HUNTER RIFLE
Caliber: 50. **Barrel:** 22", 1:24" twist (50 cal.). **Weight:** 7.6 lbs. **Length:** 39-7/8" overall. **Stock:** Black laminated with swivel studs with laser engraved deer or elk scene. **Sights:** TruGlo fully adjustable, steel rear with white diamond, red bead front with high-visibility inserts. **Features:** Teflon finished barrel, in-line ignition with FlashFire one-piece nipple and breech plug that uses standard or magnum No. 11 caps, fully adjustable trigger, double safety system, aluminum ramrod, drilled and tapped for scope. Hard gun case. Made in U.S.A. by Split Fire Sporting Goods.
Price: Laminate wood stock, w/laser engraved game scene . . . **$599.95**

ZOUAVE PERCUSSION RIFLE
Caliber: 58, 59. **Barrel:** 32-1/2". **Weight:** 9-1/2 lbs. **Length:** 48-1/2" overall. **Stock:** Walnut finish, brass patchbox and buttplate. **Sights:** Fixed front, rear adjustable for elevation. **Features:** Color case-hardened lockplate, blued barrel. From Navy Arms, Dixie Gun Works, E.M.F., Cabela's, Euroarms of America.
Price: About . . . . **$415.00 to $515.00**

BLACKPOWDER

Knight TK2000

Traditions Buckhunters Pro

CABELA'S BLACKPOWDER SHOTGUNS

Gauge: 10, 12, 20. **Barrel:** 10-ga., 30"; 12-ga., 28-1/2" (Extra-Full, Mod., Imp. Cyl. choke tubes); 20-ga., 27-1/2" (Imp. Cyl. & Mod. fixed chokes). **Weight:** 6-1/2 to 7 lbs. **Length:** 45" overall (28-1/2" barrel). **Stock:** American walnut with checkered grip; 12- and 20-gauge have straight stock, 10-gauge has pistol grip. **Features:** Blued barrels, engraved, color case-hardened locks and hammers, brass ramrod tip. From Cabela's.
Price: 10-gauge **$599.99**
Price: 12-gauge **$559.99**
Price: 20-gauge **$539.99**

CVA TRAPPER PERCUSSION SHOTGUN

Gauge: 12. **Barrel:** 28". **Weight:** 6 lbs. **Length:** 46" overall. **Stock:** English-style checkered straight grip of walnut-finished hardwood. **Sights:** Brass bead front. **Features:** Single-blued barrel; color case-hardened lockplate and hammer; screw adjustable sear engagements, V-type mainspring; brass wedge plates; color case-hardened and engraved trigger guard and tang. From CVA.
Price: Finished **$287.95**

DIXIE MAGNUM PERCUSSION SHOTGUN

Gauge: 10, 12, 20. **Barrel:** 30" (Imp. Cyl. & Mod.) in 10-gauge; 28" in 12-gauge. **Weight:** 6-1/4 lbs. **Length:** 45" overall. **Stock:** Hand-checkered walnut, 14" pull. **Features:** Double triggers; light hand engraving; case-hardened locks in 12-gauge, polished steel in 10-gauge; sling swivels. From Dixie Gun Works.
Price: Upland **$449.00**
Price: 12-ga. kit **$445.00**
Price: 20-ga. **$525.00**
Price: 10-ga. **$525.00**
Price: 10-ga. kit **$445.00**

KNIGHT TK2000 MUZZLELOADING SHOTGUN (209)

Gauge: 12. **Barrel:** 26", extra-full choke tube. **Weight:** 7 lbs., 9 oz. **Length:** 45" overall. **Stock:** Synthetic black or Advantage Timber HD; recoil pad; swivel studs. **Sights:** Fully adjustable rear, blade front with fiber optics. **Features:** Receiver drilled and tapped for scope mount; in-line ignition; adjustable trigger; removable breech plug; double safety system; imp. cyl. choke tube available. Made in U.S. by Knight Rifles.
Price: . . . . **$349.95 to $399.95**

KNIGHT VERSATILE TK2002

Gauge: 12. **Stock:** Black composite, blued, Advantage Timber HD finish. Both with sling swivel studs installed. **Sights:** Adjustable metallic TruGol fiber optic. **Features:** Full plastic jacket ignition system, screw-on choke tubes, load without removing choke tubes, incredible shot density with jug-chocked barrel design. Improved cylinder and modified choke tubes available.
Price: . . . . **$349.95 to $399.95**

NAVY ARMS STEEL SHOT MAGNUM SHOTGUN

Gauge: 10. **Barrel:** 28" (Cyl. & Cyl.). **Weight:** 7 lbs., 9 oz. **Length:** 45-1/2" overall. **Stock:** Walnut, with cheekpiece. **Features:** Designed specifically for steel shot. Engraved, polished locks; sling swivels; blued barrels. Imported by Navy Arms.
Price: **$605.00**

NAVY ARMS T&T SHOTGUN

Gauge: 12. **Barrel:** 28" (Full & Full). **Weight:** 7-1/2 lbs. **Stock:** Walnut. **Sights:** Bead front. **Features:** Color case-hardened locks, double triggers; blued steel furniture. From Navy Arms.
Price: **$580.00**

TRADITIONS BUCKHUNTER PRO SHOTGUN

Gauge: 12. **Barrel:** 24", choke tube. **Weight:** 6 lbs., 4 oz. **Length:** 43" overall. **Stock:** Composite matte black, Break-Up or Advantage camouflage. **Features:** In-line action with removable stainless steel breech plug; thumb safety; adjustable trigger; rubber buttpad. Introduced 1996. From Traditions.
Price: **$248.00**
Price: With Advantage, Shadow Branch, or Break-Up
camouflage stock **$292.00**

WHITE TOMINATOR SHOTGUN

Caliber: 12. **Barrel:** 25" blue, straight, tapered stainless steel. **Weight:** NA. **Length:** NA. **Stock:** Black laminated or black wood. **Sights:** Drilled and tapped for easy scope mounting. **Features:** Interchangeable choke tubes. Custom vent-rib with high visibility front bead. Double safeties. Fully adjustable custom trigger. Recoil pad and sling swivel studs.
Price: **$349.95**

BLACKPOWDER

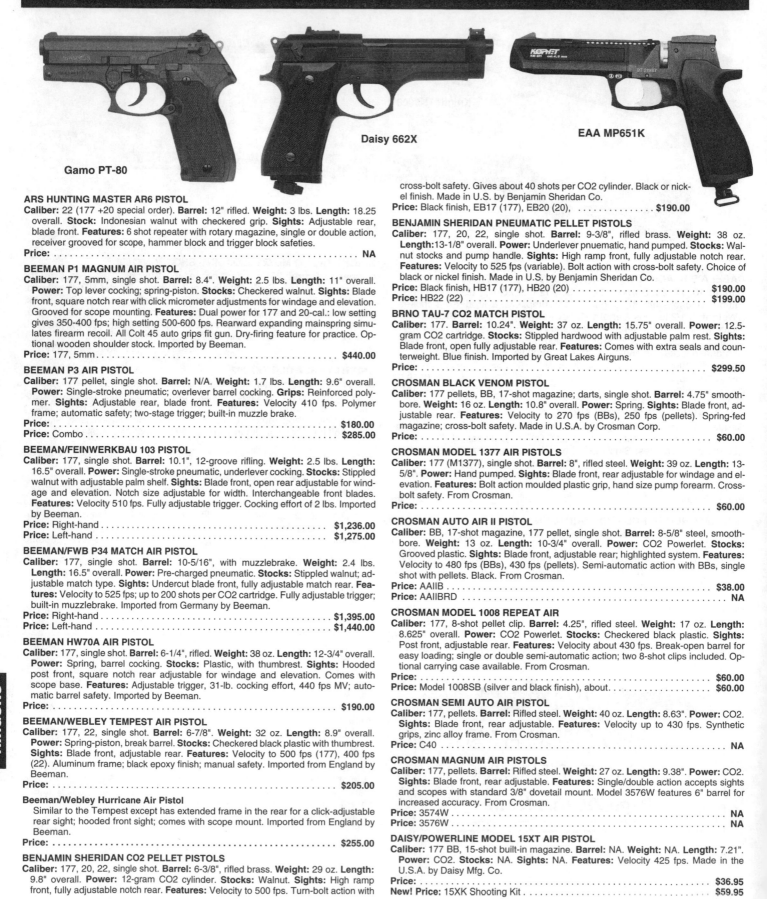

Gamo PT-80

Daisy 662X

EAA MP651K

ARS HUNTING MASTER AR6 PISTOL
Caliber: 22 (177 +20 special order). **Barrel:** 12" rifled. **Weight:** 3 lbs. **Length:** 18.25 overall. **Stock:** Indonesian walnut with checkered grip. **Sights:** Adjustable rear, blade front. **Features:** 6 shot repeater with rotary magazine, single or double action, receiver grooved for scope, hammer block and trigger block safeties.
Price: . . . . **NA**

BEEMAN P1 MAGNUM AIR PISTOL
Caliber: 177, 5mm, single shot. **Barrel:** 8.4". **Weight:** 2.5 lbs. **Length:** 11" overall. **Power:** Top lever cocking; spring-piston. **Stocks:** Checkered walnut. **Sights:** Blade front, square notch rear with click micrometer adjustments for windage and elevation. Grooved for scope mounting. **Features:** Dual power for 177 and 20-cal.: low setting gives 350-400 fps; high setting 500-600 fps. Rearward expanding mainspring simulates firearm recoil. All Colt 45 auto grips fit gun. Dry-firing feature for practice. Optional wooden shoulder stock. Imported by Beeman.
Price: 177, 5mm. **$440.00**

BEEMAN P3 AIR PISTOL
Caliber: 177 pellet, single shot. **Barrel:** N/A. **Weight:** 1.7 lbs. **Length:** 9.6" overall. **Power:** Single-stroke pneumatic; overlever barrel cocking. **Grips:** Reinforced polymer. **Sights:** Adjustable rear, blade front. **Features:** Velocity 410 fps. Polymer frame; automatic safety; two-stage trigger; built-in muzzle brake.
Price: **$180.00**
Price: Combo **$285.00**

BEEMAN/FEINWERKBAU 103 PISTOL
Caliber: 177, single shot. **Barrel:** 10.1", 12-groove rifling. **Weight:** 2.5 lbs. **Length:** 16.5" overall. **Power:** Single-stroke pneumatic, underlever cocking. **Stocks:** Stippled walnut with adjustable palm shelf. **Sights:** Blade front, open rear adjustable for windage and elevation. Notch size adjustable for width. Interchangeable front blades. **Features:** Velocity 510 fps. Fully adjustable trigger. Cocking effort of 2 lbs. Imported by Beeman.
Price: Right-hand **$1,236.00**
Price: Left-hand **$1,275.00**

BEEMAN/FWB P34 MATCH AIR PISTOL
Caliber: 177, single shot. **Barrel:** 10-5/16", with muzzlebrake. **Weight:** 2.4 lbs. **Length:** 16.5" overall. **Power:** Pre-charged pneumatic. **Stocks:** Stippled walnut; adjustable match type. **Sights:** Undercut blade front, fully adjustable match rear. **Features:** Velocity to 525 fps; up to 200 shots per CO2 cartridge. Fully adjustable trigger; built-in muzzlebrake. Imported from Germany by Beeman.
Price: Right-hand **$1,395.00**
Price: Left-hand **$1,440.00**

BEEMAN HW70A AIR PISTOL
Caliber: 177, single shot. **Barrel:** 6-1/4", rifled. **Weight:** 38 oz. **Length:** 12-3/4" overall. **Power:** Spring, barrel cocking. **Stocks:** Plastic, with thumbrest. **Sights:** Hooded post front, square notch rear adjustable for windage and elevation. Comes with scope base. **Features:** Adjustable trigger, 31-lb. cocking effort, 440 fps MV; automatic barrel safety. Imported by Beeman.
Price: **$190.00**

BEEMAN/WEBLEY TEMPEST AIR PISTOL
Caliber: 177, 22, single shot. **Barrel:** 6-7/8". **Weight:** 32 oz. **Length:** 8.9" overall. **Power:** Spring-piston, break barrel. **Stocks:** Checkered black plastic with thumbrest. **Sights:** Blade front, adjustable rear. **Features:** Velocity to 500 fps (177), 400 fps (22). Aluminum frame; black epoxy finish; manual safety. Imported from England by Beeman.
Price: **$205.00**

Beeman/Webley Hurricane Air Pistol
Similar to the Tempest except has extended frame in the rear for a click-adjustable rear sight; hooded front sight; comes with scope mount. Imported from England by Beeman.
Price: **$255.00**

BENJAMIN SHERIDAN CO2 PELLET PISTOLS
Caliber: 177, 20, 22, single shot. **Barrel:** 6-3/8", rifled brass. **Weight:** 29 oz. **Length:** 9.8" overall. **Power:** 12-gram CO2 cylinder. **Stocks:** Walnut. **Sights:** High ramp front, fully adjustable notch rear. **Features:** Velocity to 500 fps. Turn-bolt action with

cross-bolt safety. Gives about 40 shots per CO2 cylinder. Black or nickel finish. Made in U.S. by Benjamin Sheridan Co.
Price: Black finish, EB17 (177), EB20 (20), ... **$190.00**

BENJAMIN SHERIDAN PNEUMATIC PELLET PISTOLS
Caliber: 177, 20, 22, single shot. **Barrel:** 9-3/8", rifled brass. **Weight:** 38 oz. **Length:** 13-1/8" overall. **Power:** Underlever pnuematic, hand pumped. **Stocks:** Walnut stocks and pump handle. **Sights:** High ramp front, fully adjustable notch rear. **Features:** Velocity to 525 fps (variable). Bolt action with cross-bolt safety. Choice of black or nickel finish. Made in U.S. by Benjamin Sheridan Co.
Price: Black finish, HB17 (177), HB20 (20) **$190.00**
Price: HB22 (22) **$199.00**

BRNO TAU-7 CO2 MATCH PISTOL
Caliber: 177. **Barrel:** 10.24". **Weight:** 37 oz. **Length:** 15.75" overall. **Power:** 12.5-gram CO2 cartridge. **Stocks:** Stippled hardwood with adjustable palm rest. **Sights:** Blade front, open fully adjustable rear. **Features:** Comes with extra seals and counterweight. Blue finish. Imported by Great Lakes Airguns.
Price: **$299.50**

CROSMAN BLACK VENOM PISTOL
Caliber: 177 pellets, BB, 17-shot magazine; darts, single shot. **Barrel:** 4.75" smoothbore. **Weight:** 16 oz. **Length:** 10.8" overall. **Power:** Spring. **Sights:** Blade front, adjustable rear. **Features:** Velocity to 270 fps (BBs), 250 fps (pellets). Spring-fed magazine; cross-bolt safety. Made in U.S.A. by Crosman Corp.
Price: **$60.00**

CROSMAN MODEL 1377 AIR PISTOLS
Caliber: 177 (M1377), single shot. **Barrel:** 8", rifled steel. **Weight:** 39 oz. **Length:** 13-5/8". **Power:** Hand pumped. **Sights:** Blade front, rear adjustable for windage and elevation. **Features:** Bolt action moulded plastic grip, hand size pump forearm. Cross-bolt safety. From Crosman.
Price: **$60.00**

CROSMAN AUTO AIR II PISTOL
Caliber: BB, 17-shot magazine, 177 pellet, single shot. **Barrel:** 8-5/8" steel, smoothbore. **Weight:** 13 oz. **Length:** 10-3/4" overall. **Power:** CO2 Powerlet. **Stocks:** Grooved plastic. **Sights:** Blade front, adjustable rear; highlighted system. **Features:** Velocity to 480 fps (BBs), 430 fps (pellets). Semi-automatic action with BBs, single shot with pellets. Black. From Crosman.
Price: AAIIB **$38.00**
Price: AAIIBRD . . . . **NA**

CROSMAN MODEL 1008 REPEAT AIR
Caliber: 177, 8-shot pellet clip. **Barrel:** 4.25", rifled steel. **Weight:** 17 oz. **Length:** 8.625" overall. **Power:** CO2 Powerlet. **Stocks:** Checkered black plastic. **Sights:** Post front, adjustable rear. **Features:** Velocity about 430 fps. Break-open barrel for easy loading; single or double semi-automatic action; two 8-shot clips included. Optional carrying case available. From Crosman.
Price: **$60.00**
Price: Model 1008SB (silver and black finish), about. **$60.00**

CROSMAN SEMI AUTO AIR PISTOL
Caliber: 177, pellets. **Barrel:** Rifled steel. **Weight:** 40 oz. **Length:** 8.63". **Power:** CO2. **Sights:** Blade front, rear adjustable. **Features:** Velocity up to 430 fps. Synthetic grips, zinc alloy frame. From Crosman.
Price: C40 . . . . **NA**

CROSMAN MAGNUM AIR PISTOLS
Caliber: 177, pellets. **Barrel:** Rifled steel. **Weight:** 27 oz. **Length:** 9.38". **Power:** CO2. **Sights:** Blade front, rear adjustable. **Features:** Single/double action accepts sights and scopes with standard 3/8" dovetail mount. Model 3576W features 6" barrel for increased accuracy. From Crosman.
Price: 3574W . . . . **NA**
Price: 3576W . . . . **NA**

DAISY/POWERLINE MODEL 15XT AIR PISTOL
Caliber: 177 BB, 15-shot built-in magazine. **Barrel:** NA. **Weight:** NA. **Length:** 7.21". **Power:** CO2. **Stocks:** NA. **Sights:** NA. **Features:** Velocity 425 fps. Made in the U.S.A. by Daisy Mfg. Co.
Price: **$36.95**
New! Price: 15XK Shooting Kit **$59.95**

AIRGUNS—HANDGUNS

DAISY/POWERLINE 717 PELLET PISTOL
Caliber: 177, single shot. **Barrel:** 9.61". **Weight:** 2.25 lbs. **Length:** 13-1/2" overall. **Stocks:** Moulded wood-grain plastic, with thumbrest. **Sights:** Blade and ramp front, micro-adjustable notch rear. **Features:** Single pump pneumatic pistol. Rifled steel barrel. Cross-bolt trigger block. Muzzle velocity 385 fps. From Daisy Mfg. Co.
Price: **$71.95**

DAISY/POWERLINE 1270 CO2 AIR PISTOL
Caliber: BB, 60-shot magazine. **Barrel:** Smoothbore steel. **Weight:** 17 oz. **Length:** 11.1" overall. **Power:** CO2 pump action. **Stocks:** Moulded black polymer. **Sights:** Blade on ramp front, adjustable rear. **Features:** Velocity to 420 fps. Crossbolt trigger block safety; plated finish. Made in U.S. by Daisy Mfg. Co.
Price: **$39.95**

DAISY/POWERLINE 93 AIR PISTOL
Caliber: BB, 15-shot magazine. **Barrel:** Smoothbore steel. **Weight:** 1.1 lbs. **Length:** 7.9" overall. **Power:** CO2 powered semi-auto. **Stocks:** Moulded brown checkered. **Sights:** Blade on ramp front, fixed open rear. **Features:** Velocity to 400 fps. Manual trigger block. Made in U.S.A. by Daisy Mfg. Co.
Price: **$48.95**

Daisy/Powerline 693 Air Pistol
Similar to Model 93 except has velocity to 235 fps.
Price: **$52.95**

DAISY/POWERLINE 622X PELLETPISTOL
Caliber: 22 (5.5mm), 6-shot. **Barrel:** Rifled steel. **Weight:** 1.3 lbs. **Length:** 8.5". **Power:** CO2. **Grips:** Molded black checkered. **Sights:** Fiber optic front, fixed open rear. **Features:** Velocity 225 fps. Rotary hammer block. Made by Daisy Mfg. Co.
Price: **$69.95**

DAISY/POWERLINE 45 AIR PISTOL
Caliber: BB, 13-shot magazine. **Barrel:** Rifled steel. **Weight:** 1.25 lbs. **Length:** 8.5" overall. **Power:** CO2 powered semi-auto. **Stocks:** Moulded black checkered. **Sights:** TRUGLO® fiber optic front, fixed open rear. **Features:** Velocity to 224 fps. Manual trigger block. Made in U.S.A. by Daisy Mfg. Co.
Price: **$54.95**

Daisy/Powerline 645 Air Pistol
Similar to Model 93 except has distinctive black and nickel-finish.
Price: **$59.95**

EAA/BAIKAL IZH-M46 TARGET AIR PISTOL
Caliber: 177, single shot. **Barrel:** 10". **Weight:** 2.4 lbs. **Length:** 16.8" overall. **Power:** Underlever single-stroke pneumatic. **Grips:** Adjustable wooden target. **Sights:** Micrometer fully adjustable rear, blade front. **Features:** Velocity about 420 fps. Hammer-forged, rifled barrel. Imported from Russia by European American Armory.
Price **$319.00**

EAA/BAIKAL MP-651K AIR PISTOL/RIFLE
Caliber: 177 pellet (8-shot magazine); 177 BB (23-shot). **Barrel:** 5.9" (17.25" with rifle attachment). **Weight:** 1.54 lbs. (3.3 lbs. with rifle attachment). **Length:** 9.4" (31.3" with rifle attachment) **Power:** CO2 cartridge, semi-automatic. **Stock:** Plastic. **Sights:** Notch rear/blade front (pistol); periscopic sighting system (rifle). **Features:** Velocity 328 fps. Unique pistol/rifle combination allows the pistol to be inserted into the rifle shell. Imported from Russia by European American Armory.
Price: **$99.00**

GAMO AUTO 45
Caliber: .177 (12-shot). **Barrel:** 4.25". **Weight:** 1.10 lbs. **Length:** 7.50". **Power:** CO2 cartridge, semi-automatic, 410 fps. **Stock:** Plastic. **Sights:** Rear sights adjusts for windage. **Features:** Looking very much like a Glock cartridge pistol, it fires in the double-action mode and has a manual safety. Imported from Spain by Gamo.
Price: **$99.95**

GAMO COMPACT TARGET PISTOL
Caliber: .177, single shot. **Barrel:** 8.26". **Weight:** 1.95 lbs. **Length:** 12.60. **Power:** Spring-piston, 400 fps. **Stock:** Walnut. **Sights:** Micro-adjustable. **Features:** Rifle steel barrel, adjustable match trigger, recoil and vibration-free. Imported from Spain by Gamo.
Price: **$229.95**

GAMO P-23, P-23 LASER PISTOL
Caliber: .177 (12-shot). **Barrel:** 4.25". **Weight:** 1 lb. **Length:** 7.5". **Power:** CO2 cartridge, semi-automatic, 410 fps. **Stock:** Plastic. **Sights:** NA. **Features:** Style somewhat like a Walther PPK cartridge pistol, an optional laser allows fast sight acquisition. Imported from Spain by Gamo.
Price: .... **$89.95**, (with laser) **$129.95**

GAMO PT-80, PT-80 LASER PISTOL
Caliber: .177 (8-shot). **Barrel:** 4.25". **Weight:** 1.2 lbs. **Length:** 7.2". **Power:** CO2 cartridge, semi-automatic, 410 fps. **Stock:** Plastic. **Sights:** 3-dot. **Features:** Available with optional laser sight and wit optional walnut grips. Imported from Spain by Gamo.
Price: .... **$108.95,** (with laser) **$129.95**, (with walnut grip) **$119.95**

"GAT" AIR PISTOL
Caliber: 177, single shot. **Barrel:** 7-1/2" cocked, 9-1/2" extended. **Weight:** 22 oz. **Power:** Spring-piston. **Stocks:** Cast checkered metal. **Sights:** Fixed. **Features:** Shoots pellets, corks or darts. Matte black finish. Imported from England by Stone Enterprises, Inc.
Price: **$24.95**

HAMMERLI AP40 AIR PISTOL
Caliber: 177. **Barrel:** 10". **Stocks:** Adjustable orthopaedic. **Sights:** Fully adjustable micrometer. **Features:** Sleek, light, well balanced and accurate. Imported from Switzerland by Nygord Precision Products.
Price: **$1,195.00**

MARKSMAN 2000 REPEATER PISTOL
Caliber: 177, 18-shot BB repeater. **Barrel:** 2-1/2", smoothbore. **Weight:** 24 oz. **Length:** 8-1/4" overall. **Power:** Spring. **Features:** Velocity to 200 fps. Thumb safety. Uses BBs, darts, bolts or pellets. Repeats with BBs only. From Marksman Products.
Price: **$27.00**

MARKSMAN 2005 LASERHAWK SPECIAL EDITION AIR PISTOL
Caliber: 177, 24-shot magazine. **Barrel:** 3.8", smoothbore. **Weight:** 22 oz. **Length:** 10.3" overall. **Power:** Spring-air. **Stocks:** Checkered. **Sights:** Fixed fiber optic front sight. **Features:** Velocity to 300 fps with Hyper-Velocity pellets. Square trigger guard with skeletonized trigger; extended barrel for greater velocity and accuracy. Shoots BBs, pellets, darts or bolts. Made in the U.S. From Marksman Products.
Price: **$32.00**

MORINI 162E MATCH AIR PISTOL
Caliber: 177, single shot. **Barrel:** 9.4". **Weight:** 32 oz. **Length:** 16.1" overall. **Power:** Scuba air. **Stocks:** Adjustable match type. **Sights:** Interchangeable blade front, fully adjustable match-type rear. **Features:** Power mechanism shuts down when pressure drops to a pre-set level. Adjustable electronic trigger. Imported from Switzerland by Nygord Precision Products.
Price: **$825.00**
Price: 162 EI **$1,075.00**

MORINI SAM K-11 AIR PISTOL
Caliber: 177. **Barrel:** 10". **Weight:** 38 oz. **Stocks:** Fully adjustable. **Sights:** Fully adjustable. **Features:** Improved trigger, more angle adjustment on grip. Sophisticated counter balance system. Deluxe aluminum case, two cylinders and manometer. Imported from Switzerland by Nygord Precision Products.
Price: **$975.00**

PARDINI K58 MATCH AIR PISTOL
Caliber: 177, single shot. **Barrel:** 9". **Weight:** 37.7 oz. **Length:** 15.5" overall. **Power:** Pre-charged compressed air; single-stroke cocking. **Stocks:** Adjustable match type; stippled walnut. **Sights:** Interchangeable post front, fully adjustable match rear. **Features:** Fully adjustable trigger. Short version K-2 available. Imported from Italy by Nygord Precision Products.
Price: **$795.00**
Price: K2S model, precharged air pistol, introduced in 1998 .... **$945.00**

RWS 9B/9N AIR PISTOLS
Caliber: 177, single shot. **Grips:** Plastic with thumbrest. **Sights:** Adjustable. **Features:** Spring-piston powered; 550 fps. Black or nickel finish. Imported from Spain by Dynamit Nobel-RWS.
Price: 9B **$169.00**
Price: 9N **$185.00**

STEYR LP 5CP MATCH AIR PISTOL
Caliber: 177, 5-shot magazine. **Weight:** 40.7 oz. **Length:** 15.2" overall. **Power:** Pre-charged air cylinder. **Stocks:** Adjustable match type. **Sights:** Interchangeable blade front, fully adjustable match rear. **Features:** Adjustable sight radius; fully adjustable trigger. Barrel compensator. One-shot magazine available. Imported from Austria by Nygord Precision Products.
Price: **$1,100.00**

STEYR LP10P MATCH PISTOL
Caliber: 177, single shot. **Barrel:** 9". **Weight:** 38.7 oz. **Length:** 15.3" overall. **Power:** Scuba air. **Stocks:** Fully adjustable Morini match, palm shelf, stippled walnut. **Sights:** Interchangeable blade in 4mm, 4.5mm or 5mm widths, fully adjustable open rear, interchangeable 3.5mm or 4mm leaves. **Features:** Velocity about 500 fps. Adjustable trigger, adjustable sight radius from 12.4" to 13.2". With compensator. New "aborber" eliminates recoil. Imported from Austria by Nygord Precision Products.
Price: **$1,175.00**

TECH FORCE SS2 OLYMPIC COMPETITION AIR PISTOL
Caliber: 177 pellet, single shot. **Barrel:** 7.4". **Weight:** 2.8 lbs. **Length:** 16.5" overall. **Power:** Spring piston, sidelever. **Grips:** Hardwood. **Sights:** Extended adjustable rear, blade front accepts inserts. **Features:** Velocity 520 fps. Recoilless design; adjustments allow duplication of a firearm's feel. Match-grade, adjustable trigger; includes carrying case. Imported from China by Compasseco Inc.
Price: **$295.00**

TECH FORCE 35 AIR PISTOL
Caliber: 177 pellet, single shot. **Weight:** 2.86 lbs. **Length:** 14.9" overall. **Power:** Spring piston, underlever. **Grips:** Hardwood. **Sights:** Micrometer adjustable rear, blade front. **Features:** Velocity 400 fps. Grooved for scope mount; trigger safety. Imported from China by Compasseco Inc.
Price: **$39.95**

Tech Force 8 Air Pistol
Similar to Tech Force 35, but with break-barrel action, ambidextrous polymer grips.
Price: **$59.95**

Tech Force S2-1 Air Pistol
Similar to Tech Force 8, more basic grips and sights for plinking.
Price: **$29.95**

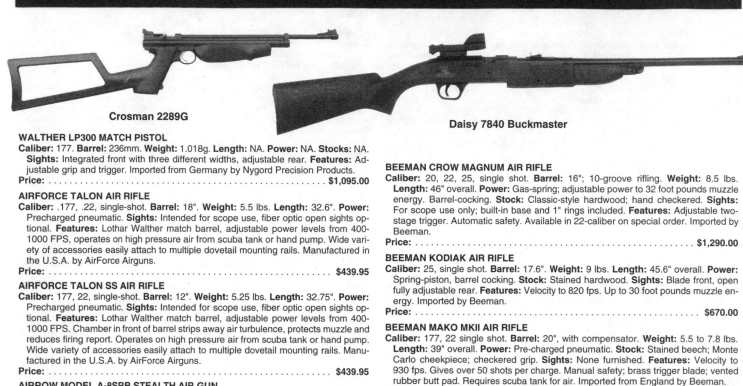

Crosman 2289G

Daisy 7840 Buckmaster

WALTHER LP300 MATCH PISTOL
Caliber: 177. **Barrel:** 236mm. **Weight:** 1.018g. **Length:** NA. **Power:** NA. **Stocks:** NA. **Sights:** Integrated front with three different widths, adjustable rear. **Features:** Adjustable grip and trigger. Imported from Germany by Nygord Precision Products.
Price: $1,095.00

AIRFORCE TALON AIR RIFLE
Caliber: .177, .22, single-shot. **Barrel:** 18". **Weight:** 5.5 lbs. **Length:** 32.6". **Power:** Precharged pneumatic. **Sights:** Intended for scope use, fiber optic open sights optional. **Features:** Lothar Walther match barrel, adjustable power levels from 400-1000 FPS, operates on high pressure air from scuba tank or hand pump. Wide variety of accessories easily attach to multiple dovetail mounting rails. Manufactured in the U.S.A. by AirForce Airguns.
Price: $439.95

AIRFORCE TALON SS AIR RIFLE
Caliber: 177, 22, single-shot. **Barrel:** 12". **Weight:** 5.25 lbs. **Length:** 32.75". **Power:** Precharged pneumatic. **Sights:** Intended for scope use, fiber optic open sights optional. **Features:** Lothar Walther match barrel, adjustable power levels from 400-1000 FPS. Chamber in front of barrel strips away air turbulence, protects muzzle and reduces firing report. Operates on high pressure air from scuba tank or hand pump. Wide variety of accessories easily attach to multiple dovetail mounting rails. Manufactured in the U.S.A. by AirForce Airguns.
Price: $439.95

AIRROW MODEL A-8SRB STEALTH AIR GUN
Caliber: 177, 22, 25, 9-shot. **Barrel:** 20"; rifled. **Weight:** 6 lbs. **Length:** 34" overall. **Power:** CO2 or compressed air; variable power. **Stock:** Telescoping CAR-15-type. **Sights:** Variable 3.5-10x scope. **Features:** Velocity 1100 fps in all calibers. Pneumatic air trigger. All aircraft aluminum and stainless steel construction. Mil-spec materials and finishes. From Swivel Machine Works, Inc.
Price: About $2,299.00

AIRROW MODEL A-8S1P STEALTH AIR GUN
Caliber: #2512 16" arrow. **Barrel:** 16". **Weight:** 4.4 lbs. **Length:** 30.1" overall. **Power:** CO2 or compressed air; variable power. **Stock:** Telescoping CAR-15-type. **Sights:** Scope rings only. 7 oz. rechargeable cylinder and valve. **Features:** Velocity to 650 fps with 260-grain arrow. Broadhead guard. All aircraft aluminum and stainless steel construction. Mil-spec materials and finishes. A-8S Models perform to 2,000 PSIG above or below water levels. Waterproof case. From Swivel Machine Works, Inc.
Price: $1,699.00

ARS HUNTING MASTER AR6 AIR RIFLE
Caliber: 22, 6-shot repeater. **Barrel:** 25-1/2". **Weight:** 7 lbs. **Length:** 41-1/4" overall. **Power:** Pre-compressed air from 3000 psi diving tank. **Stock:** Indonesian walnut with checkered grip; rubber buttpad. **Sights:** Blade front, adjustable peep rear. **Features:** Velocity over 1000 fps with 32-grain pellet. Receiver grooved for scope mounting. Has 6-shot rotary magazine. Imported by Air Rifle Specialists.
Price: $580.00

ARS/CAREER 707 AIR RIFLE
Caliber: 22, 6-shot repeater. **Barrel:** 23". **Weight:** 7.75 lbs. **Length:** 40.5" overall. **Power:** Pre-compressed air; variable power. **Stock:** Indonesian walnut with checkered grip, gloss finish. **Sights:** Hooded post front with interchangeable inserts, fully adjustable diopter rear. **Features:** Velocity to 1000 fps. Lever-action with straight feed magazine; pressure gauge in lower front air reservoir; scope mounting rail included. Imported from the Philippines by Air Rifle Specialists.
Price: $580.00

ANSCHUTZ 2002 MATCH AIR RIFLE
Caliber: 177, single shot. **Barrel:** 25.2". **Weight:** 10.4 lbs. **Length:** 44.5" overall. **Stock:** European walnut, blonde hardwood or colored laminated hardwood; stippled grip and forend. Also available with flat-forend walnut stock for benchrest shooting and aluminum. **Sights:** Optional sight set #6834. **Features:** Muzzle velocity 575 fps. Balance, weight match the 1907 ISU smallbore rifle. Uses #5021 match trigger. Recoil and vibration free. Fully adjustable cheekpiece and buttplate; accessory rail under forend. Available in Pneumatic and Compressed Air versions. Imported from Germany by Gunsmithing, Inc., Accuracy International, Champion's Choice.
Price: Right-hand, blonde hardwood stock, with sights $1,275.00
Price: Right-hand, walnut stock $1,275.00
Price: Right-hand, color laminate stock $1,300.00
Price: Right-hand, aluminum stock, butt plate $1,495.00
Price: Left-hand, color laminate stock $1,595.00
Price: Model 2002D-RT Running Target, right-hand, no sights $1,248.90
Price: #6834 Sight Set $227.10

BEEMAN CROW MAGNUM AIR RIFLE
Caliber: 20, 22, 25, single shot. **Barrel:** 16"; 10-groove rifling. **Weight:** 8.5 lbs. **Length:** 46" overall. **Power:** Gas-spring; adjustable power to 32 foot pounds muzzle energy. Barrel-cocking. **Stock:** Classic-style hardwood; hand checkered. **Sights:** For scope use only; built-in base and 1" rings included. **Features:** Adjustable two-stage trigger. Automatic safety. Available in 22-caliber on special order. Imported by Beeman.
Price: $1,290.00

BEEMAN KODIAK AIR RIFLE
Caliber: 25, single shot. **Barrel:** 17.6". **Weight:** 9 lbs. **Length:** 45.6" overall. **Power:** Spring-piston, barrel cocking. **Stock:** Stained hardwood. **Sights:** Blade front, open fully adjustable rear. **Features:** Velocity to 820 fps. Up to 30 foot pounds muzzle energy. Imported by Beeman.
Price: $670.00

BEEMAN MAKO MKII AIR RIFLE
Caliber: 177, 22 single shot. **Barrel:** 20", with compensator. **Weight:** 5.5 to 7.8 lbs. **Length:** 39" overall. **Power:** Pre-charged pneumatic. **Stock:** Stained beech; Monte Carlo cheekpiece; checkered grip. **Sights:** None furnished. **Features:** Velocity to 930 fps. Gives over 50 shots per charge. Manual safety; brass trigger blade; vented rubber butt pad. Requires scuba tank for air. Imported from England by Beeman.
Price: $999.00

BEEMAN R1 AIR RIFLE
Caliber: 177, 20 or 22, single shot. **Barrel:** 19.6", 12-groove rifling. **Weight:** 8.5 lbs. **Length:** 45.2" overall. **Power:** Spring-piston, barrel cocking. **Stock:** Walnut-stained beech; cut-checkered pistol grip; Monte Carlo comb and cheekpiece; rubber buttpad. **Sights:** Tunnel front with interchangeable inserts, open rear click-adjustable for windage and elevation. Grooved for scope mounting. **Features:** Velocity of 940-1000 fps (177), 860 fps (20), 800 fps (22). Non-drying nylon piston and breech seals. Adjustable metal trigger. Milled steel safety. Right- or left-hand stock. Adjustable cheekpiece and buttplate at extra cost. Custom and Super Laser versions available. Imported by Beeman.
Price: Right-hand, 177, 20, 22 . . . . $605.00
Price: Left-hand, 177, 20, 22 . . . . $680.00

BEEMAN R7 AIR RIFLE
Caliber: 177, 20, single shot. **Barrel:** 17". **Weight:** 6.1 lbs. **Length:** 40.2" overall. **Power:** Spring piston. **Stock:** Stained beech. **Sights:** Hooded front, fully adjustable micrometer click open rear. **Features:** Velocity to 700 fps (177), 620 fps (20). Receiver grooved for scope mounting; double-jointed cocking lever; fully adjustable trigger; checkered grip. Imported by Beeman.
Price: $330.00

BEEMAN R9 AIR RIFLE
Caliber: 177, 20, single shot. **Barrel:** NA. **Weight:** 7.3 lbs. **Length:** 43" overall. **Power:** Spring-piston, barrel cocking. **Stock:** Stained hardwood. **Sights:** Tunnel post front, fully adjustable open rear. **Features:** Velocity to 1000 fps (177), 800 fps (20). Adjustable Rekord trigger; automatic safety; receiver dovetailed for scope mounting. Imported from Germany by Beeman Precision Airguns.
Price: $360.00

Beeman R9 Deluxe Air Rifle
Same as R9 except has extended forend stock, checkered pistol grip, grip cap, carved Monte Carlo cheekpiece. Globe front sight with inserts. Imported by Beeman.
Price: $440.00

BEEMAN R11 MKII AIR RIFLE
Caliber: 177, single shot. **Barrel:** 19.6". **Weight:** 8.6 lbs. **Length:** 43.5" overall. **Power:** Spring-piston, barrel cocking. **Stock:** Walnut-stained beech; adjustable buttplate and cheekpiece. **Sights:** None furnished. Has dovetail for scope mounting. **Features:** Velocity 910-940 fps. All-steel barrel sleeve. Imported by Beeman.
Price: $620.00

BEEMAN SUPER 12 AIR RIFLE
Caliber: 22, 25, 12-shot magazine. **Barrel:** 19", 12-groove rifling. **Weight:** 7.8 lbs. **Length:** 41.7" overall. **Power:** Pre-charged pneumatic; external air reservoir. **Stock:** European walnut. **Sights:** None furnished; drilled and tapped for scope mounting; scope mount included. **Features:** Velocity to 850 fps (25-caliber). Adjustable power setting gives 30-70 shots per 400 cc air bottle. Requires scuba tank for air. Imported by Beeman.
Price: $1,940.00

BEEMAN RX-2 GAS-SPRING MAGNUM AIR RIFLE

Caliber: 177, 20, 22, 25, single shot. **Barrel:** 19.6", 12-groove rifling. **Weight:** 8.8 lbs. **Power:** Gas-spring piston air; single stroke barrel cocking. **Stock:** Walnut-finished hardwood, hand checkered, with cheekpiece. Adjustable cheekpiece and buttplate. **Sights:** Tunnel front, click-adjustable rear. **Features:** Velocity adjustable to about 1200 fps. Uses special sealed chamber of air as a mainspring. Gas-spring cannot take a set. Imported by Beeman.

Price: 177, 20, 22 or 25 regular, right-hand **$670.00**
Price: 177, 20, 22, 25, left-hand **$670.00**

BEEMAN R1 CARBINE

Caliber: 177, 20, 22, 25, single shot. **Barrel:** 16.1". **Weight:** 8.6 lbs. **Length:** 41.7" overall. **Power:** Spring-piston, barrel cocking. **Stock:** Stained beech; Monte Carlo comb and checkpiece; cut checkered pistol grip; rubber buttpad. **Sights:** Tunnel front with interchangeable inserts, open adjustable rear; receiver grooved for scope mounting. **Features:** Velocity up to 1000 fps (177). Non-drying nylon piston and breech seals. Adjustable metal trigger. Machined steel receiver end cap and safety. Right- or left-hand stock. Imported by Beeman.

Price: 177, 20, 22, 25, right-hand **$605.00**
Price: As above, left-hand **$680.00**

BEEMAN/FEINWERKBAU 603 AIR RIFLE

Caliber: 177, single shot. **Barrel:** 16.6". **Weight:** 10.8 lbs. **Length:** 43" overall. **Power:** Single stroke pneumatic. **Stock:** Special laminated hardwoods and hard rubber for stability. Multi-colored stock also available. **Sights:** Tunnel front with interchangeable inserts, click micrometer match aperture rear. **Features:** Velocity to 570 fps. Recoilless action; double supported barrel; special, short rifled area frees pellet form barrel faster so shooter's motion has minimum effect on accuracy. Fully adjustable match trigger with separately adjustable trigger and trigger slack weight. Trigger and sights blocked when loading latch is open. Imported by Beeman.

Price: Right-hand **$1,625.00**
Price: Left-hand **$1,775.00**
Price: Junior **$1,500.00**

BEEMAN/FEINWERKBAU 300-S AND 300 JUNIOR MINI-MATCH

Caliber: 177, single shot. **Barrel:** 17-1/8". **Weight:** 8.8 lbs. **Length:** 40" overall. **Power:** Spring-piston, single stroke sidelever cocking. **Stock:** Walnut. Stippled grip, adjustable buttplate. Scaled-down for youthful or slightly built shooters. **Sights:** Globe front with interchangeable inserts, micro. adjustable rear. Front and rear sights move as a single unit. **Features:** Recoilless, vibration free. Grooved for scope mounts. Steel piston ring. Cocking effort about 9-1/2 lbs. Barrel sleeve optional. Left-hand model available. Imported by Beeman.

Price: Right-hand **$1,680.00**
Price: Left-hand **$1,825.00**

BEEMAN/FEINWERKBAU P70 AND P70 JUNIOR AIR RIFLE

Caliber: 177, single shot. **Barrel:** 16.6". **Weight:** 10.6 lbs. **Length:** 42.6" overall. **Power:** Precharged pneumatic. **Stock:** Laminated hardwoods and hard rubber for stability. Multi-colored stock also available. **Sights:** Tunnel front with interchangeable inserts, click micormeter match aperture rear. **Features:** Velocity to 570 fps. Recoilless action; double supported barrel; special short rifled area frees pellet from barrel faster so shooter's motion has minimum effect on accuracy. Fully adjustable match trigger with separately adjustable trigger and trigger slack weight. Trigger and sights blocked when loading latch is open. Imported by Beeman.

Price: P70, pre-charged, right-hand **$1,600.00**
Price: P70, pre-charged, left-hand **$1,690.00**
Price: P70, pre-charged, Junior **$1,600.00**
Price: P70, pre-charged, right-hand, multi **$1,465.00**

BEEMAN/HW 97 AIR RIFLE

Caliber: 177, 20, single shot. **Barrel:** 17.75". **Weight:** 9.2 lbs. **Length:** 44.1" overall. **Power:** Spring-piston, underlever cocking. **Stock:** Walnut-stained beech; rubber buttpad. **Sights:** None. Receiver grooved for scope mounting. **Features:** Velocity 830 fps (177). Fixed barrel with fully opening, direct loading breech. Adjustable trigger. Imported by Beeman Precision Airguns.

Price: Right-hand only **$605.00**

BENJAMIN SHERIDAN PNEUMATIC (PUMP-UP) AIR RIFLES

Caliber: 177 or 22, single shot. **Barrel:** 19-3/8", rifled brass. **Weight:** 5-1/2 lbs. **Length:** 36-1/4" overall. **Power:** Underlever pneumatic, hand pumped. **Stock:** American walnut stock and forend. **Sights:** High ramp front, fully adjustable notch rear. **Features:** Variable velocity to 800 fps. Bolt action with ambidextrous push-pull safety. Black or nickel finish. Made in the U.S. by Benjamin Sheridan Co.

Price: Black finish, Model 397 (177), Model 392 (22) **$224.00**
Price: Nickel finish, Model S397 (177), Model S392 (22) **$245.00**

BENJAMIN SHERIDAN AIR RIFLE

Caliber: 177 single-shot. **Barrel:** 19-3/8", rifled brass. **Weight:** 5 lbs. **Length:** 36-1/2" overall. Power 12-gram CO2 cylinder. **Stocks:** American walnut with buttplate. **Sights:** High ramp front, fully adjustable notch rear. **Features:** Velocity to 680 fps (177). Bolt action with ambidextrous push-pull safety. Gives about 40 shots per cylinder. Black finish. Made in the U.S. by Benjamin Sheridan Co.

Price: Black finish, Model G397 (177) **$140.00**

BRNO TAU-200 AIR RIFLE

Caliber: 177, single shot. **Barrel:** 19", rifled. **Weight:** 7-1/2 lbs. **Length:** 42" overall. **Power:** 6-oz. CO2 cartridge. **Stock:** Wood match style with adjustable comb and buttplate. **Sights:** Globe front with interchangeable inserts, fully adjustable open rear. **Features:** Adjustable trigger. Comes with extra seals, large CO2 bottle, counterweight. Imported by Great Lakes Airguns. Available in Standard Universal, Deluxe Universal, International and Target Sporter versions.

Price: Standard Universal (ambidex. stock with buttstock extender, adj. cheekpiece).. . . . . **$349.50**
Price: Deluxe Universal (as above but with micro-adj. aperture sight) **$449.50**
Price: International (like Deluxe Universal but with right- or left-hand stock) **$454.50**
Price: Target Sporter (like Std. Universal but with 4X scope, no sights) **$412.50**

BSA MAGNUM SUPERSTAR™ MK2 MAGNUM AIR RIFLE, CARBINE

Caliber: 177, 22, 25, single shot. **Barrel:** 18-1/2". **Weight:** 8 lbs., 8 oz. **Length:** 43" overall. **Power:** Spring-air, underlever cocking. **Stock:** Oil-finished hardwood; Monte Carlo with cheekpiece, checkered at grip; recoil pad. **Sights:** Ramp front, micrometer adjustable rear. Maxi-Grip scope rail. **Features:** Velocity 950 fps (177), 750 fps (22), 600 fps (25). Patented rotating breech design. Maxi-Grip scope rail protects optics from recoil; automatic anti-beartrap plus manual safety. Imported from U.K. by Precision Sales International, Inc.

Price: **$349.95**
Price: MKII Carbine (14" barrel, 39-1/2" overall) **$349.95**

BSA MAGNUM SUPERSPORT™ AIR RIFLE

Caliber: 177, 22, 25, single shot. **Barrel:** 18-1/2". **Weight:** 6 lbs., 8 oz. **Length:** 41" overall. **Power:** Spring-air, barrel cocking. **Stock:** Oil-finished hardwood; Monte Carlo with cheekpiece, recoil pad. **Sights:** Ramp front, micrometer adjustable rear. Maxi-Grip scope rail. **Features:** Velocity 950 fps (177), 750 fps (22), 600 fps (25). Patented Maxi-Grip scope rail protects optics from recoil; automatic anti-beartrap plus manual tang safety. Muzzle brake standard. Imported for U.K. by Precision Sales International, Inc.

Price: **$194.95**
Price: Carbine, 14" barrel, muzzle brake **$214.95**

BSA MAGNUM GOLDSTAR MAGNUM AIR RIFLE

Caliber: 177, 22, 10-shot repeater. **Barrel:** 17-1/2". **Weight:** 8 lbs., 8 oz. **Length:** 42.5" overall. **Power:** Spring-air, underlever cocking. **Stock:** Oil-finished hardwood; Monte Carlo with cheekpiece, checkered at grip; recoil pad. **Sights:** Ramp front, micrometer adjustable rear; comes with Maxi-Grip scope rail. **Features:** Velocity 950 fps (177), 750 fps (22). Patented 10-shot indexing magazine; Maxi-Grip scope rail protects optics from recoil; automatic anti-beartrap plus manual safety; muzzlebrake standard. Imported from U.K. by Precision Sales International, Inc.

Price: **$499.95**

BSA MAGNUM SUPERTEN AIR RIFLE

Caliber: 177, 22 10-shot repeater. **Barrel:** 17-1/2". **Weight:** 7 lbs., 8 oz. **Length:** 37" overall. **Power:** Precharged pneumatic via buddy bottle. **Stock:** Oil-finished hardwood; Monte Carlo with cheekpiece, cut checkering at grip; adjustable recoil pad. **Sights:** No sights; intended for scope use. **Features:** Velocity 1000+ fps (177), 1000+ fps (22). Patented 10-shot indexing magazine, bolt-action loading. Left-hand version also available. Imported from U.K. by Precision Sales International, Inc.

Price: **$599.95**

BSA METEOR MK6 AIR RIFLE

Caliber: 177, 22, single shot. **Barrel:** 18-1/2". **Weight:** 6 lbs. **Length:** 41" overall. **Power:** Spring-air, barrel cocking. **Stock:** Oil-finished hardwood. **Sights:** Ramp front, micrometer adjustable rear. **Features:** Velocity 650 fps (177), 500 fps (22). Automatic anti-beartrap; manual tang safety. Receiver grooved for scope mounting. Imported from U.K. by Precision Sales International, Inc.

Price: Rifle **$144.95**
Price: Carbine **$164.95**

CROSMAN MODEL 66 POWERMASTER

Caliber: 177 (single shot pellet) or BB, 200-shot reservoir. **Barrel:** 20", rifled steel. **Weight:** 3 lbs. **Length:** 38-1/2" overall. **Power:** Pneumatic; hand pumped. **Stock:** Wood-grained ABS plastic; checkered pistol grip and forend. **Sights:** Ramp front, fully adjustable open rear. **Features:** Velocity about 645 fps. Bolt action, cross-bolt safety. From Crosman.

Price: Model 66BX **$60.00**
Price: Model 664X (as above, with 4x scope) **$70.00**
Price: Model 664SB (as above with silver and black finish), about **$75.00**
Price: Model 664GT (black and gold finish, 4x scope) about. **$73.00**

CROSMAN MODEL 760 PUMPMASTER

Caliber: 177 pellets (single shot) or BB (200-shot reservoir). **Barrel:** 19-1/2", rifled steel. **Weight:** 2 lbs., 12 oz. **Length:** 33.5" overall. **Power:** Pneumatic, hand pumped. **Stock:** Walnut-finished ABS plastic stock and forend. **Features:** Velocity to 590 fps (BBs, 10 pumps). Short stroke, power determined by number of strokes. Post front sight and adjustable rear sight. Cross-bolt safety. From Crosman.

Price: Model 760B **$40.00**
Price: Model 764SB (silver and black finish), about. **$55.00**
Price: Model 760SK . . . . . **NA**
Price: Model 760BRO . . . . . **NA**

CROSMAN MODEL 1077 REPEATAIR RIFLE
Caliber: 177 pellets, 12-shot clip. **Barrel:** 20.3", rifled steel. **Weight:** 3 lbs., 11 oz. **Length:** 38.8" overall. **Power:** CO2 Powerlet. **Stock:** Textured synthetic or American walnut. **Sights:** Blade front, fully adjustable rear. **Features:** Velocity 590 fps. Removable 12-shot clip. True semi-automatic action. From Crosman.
Price: $75.00
Price: 1077W (walnut stock) $110.00

CROSMAN 2260 AIR RIFLE
Caliber: 22, single shot. **Barrel:** 24". **Weight:** 4 lbs., 12 oz. **Length:** 39.75" overall. **Power:** CO2 Powerlet. **Stock:** Hardwood. **Sights:** Blade front, adjustable rear open or peep. **Features:** About 600 fps. Made in U.S. by Crosman Corp.
Price: .... NA

CROSMAN MODEL 2289 RIFLE
Caliber: .22, single shot. **Barrel:** 14.625", rifled steel. **Weight:** 2 lbs. 15 oz. **Length:** 30.25" overall. **Power:** Hand pumped, pneumatic. **Stock:** Composition, skeletal type. **Sights:** Fixed front, rear peep or open, fully adjustable. **Features:** Velocity to 495 fps. Synthetic stock. From Crosman.
Price: $73.00

CROSMAN MODEL 2100 CLASSIC AIR RIFLE
Caliber: 177 pellets (single shot), or BB (200-shot BB reservoir). **Barrel:** 21", rifled. **Weight:** 4 lbs., 13 oz. **Length:** 39-3/4" overall. **Power:** Pump-up, pneumatic. **Stock:** Wood-grained checkered ABS plastic. **Features:** Three pumps give about 450 fps, 10 pumps about 755 fps (BBs). Cross-bolt safety; concealed reservoir holds over 200 BBs. From Crosman.
Price: Model 2100B $75.00
Price: Model 2104GT (black and gold finish, 4x scope), about $95.00

CROSMAN MODEL 2200 MAGNUM AIR RIFLE
Caliber: 22, single shot. **Barrel:** 19", rifled steel. **Weight:** 4 lbs., 12 oz. **Length:** 39" overall. **Stock:** Full-size, wood-grained ABS plastic with checkered grip and forend or American walnut. **Sights:** Ramp front, open step-adjustable rear. **Features:** Variable pump power—three pumps give 395 fps, six pumps 530 fps, 10 pumps 595 fps (average). Full-size adult air rifle. Has white line spacers at pistol grip and buttplate. From Crosman.
Price: $75.00

DAISY 1938 RED RYDER 60th ANNIVERSARY CLASSIC
Caliber: BB, 650-shot repeating action. **Barrel:** Smoothbore steel with shroud. **Weight:** 2.2 lbs. **Length:** 35.4" overall. **Stock:** Walnut stock burned with Red Ryder lariat signature. **Sights:** Post front, adjustable V-slot rear. **Features:** Walnut forend. Saddle ring with leather thong. Lever cocking. Gravity feed. Controlled velocity. One of Daisy's most popular guns. From Daisy Mfg. Co.
Price: $39.95

DAISY MODEL 840 GRIZZLY
Caliber: 177 pellet single shot; or BB 350-shot. **Barrel:** 19", smoothbore, steel. **Weight:** 2.25 lbs. **Length:** 36.8" overall. **Power:** Pneumatic, single pump. **Stock:** Moulded wood-grain stock and forend. **Sights:** Ramp front, open, adjustable rear. **Features:** Muzzle velocity 320 fps (BB), 300 fps (pellet). Steel buttplate; straight pull bolt action; cross-bolt safety. Forend forms pump lever. From Daisy Mfg. Co.
Price: $32.95
Price: 840C Mossy Oak® Break Up™ camo $49.95

DAISY MODEL 7840 BUCKMASTER
Caliber: 177 pellets, or BB. **Barrel:** Smoothbore steel. **Weight:** 2.25 lbs. **Length:** 36.8" overall. **Power:** Single-pump pneumatic. **Stock:** Moulded with checkering and woodgrain. **Sights:** Ramp and blade front, adjustable open rear plus Electronic Point Sight. **Features:** Velocity to 320 fps (BB), 300fps (pellet). Cross-bolt trigger block safety. From Daisy Mfg. Co.
Price: $54.95

DAISY MODEL 105 BUCK
Caliber: 177 or BB. **Barrel:** Smoothbore steel. **Weight:** 1.6 lbs. **Length:** 29.8" overall. **Power:** Lever cocking, spring air. **Stock:** Stained solid wood. **Sights:** TRUGLO® Fiber Optic, open fixed rear. **Features:** Velocity to 275. Cross-bolt trigger block safety. From Daisy Mfg. Co.
Price: .... NA

Daisy Model 95 Timberwolf
Similar to the 105 Buck except velocity to 325 fps. Weighs 2.4 lbs, overall length 35.2".
Price: $38.95

DAISY/POWERLINE 853
Caliber: 177 pellets, single shot. **Barrel:** 20.9"; 12-groove rifling, high-grade solid steel by Lothar Walther®, precision crowned; bore size for precision match pellets. **Weight:** 5.08 lbs. **Length:** 38.9" overall. **Power:** Single-pump pneumatic. **Stock:** Full-length select American hardwood, stained and finished; black buttplate with white spacers. **Sights:** Globe front with four aperture inserts; precision micrometer adjustable rear peep sight mounted on a standard 3/8" dovetail receiver mount.
Price: $225.00

DAISY/POWERLINE 856 PUMP-UP AIRGUN
Caliber: 177 pellets (single shot) or BB (100-shot reservoir). **Barrel:** Rifled steel with shroud. **Weight:** 2.7 lbs. **Length:** 37.4" overall. **Power:** Pneumatic pump-up. **Stock:** Moulded wood-grain with Monte Carlo cheekpiece. **Sights:** Ramp and blade front, open rear adjustable for elevation. **Features:** Velocity from 315 fps (two pumps) to 650 fps (10 pumps). Shoots BBs or pellets. Heavy die-cast metal receiver. Cross-bolt trigger-block safety. From Daisy Mfg. Co.
Price: $39.95
Price: 856C $59.95

DAISY/POWERLINE 1170 PELLET RIFLE
Caliber: 177, single shot. **Barrel:** Rifled steel. **Weight:** 5.5 lbs. **Length:** 42.5" overall. **Power:** Spring-air, barrel cocking. **Stock:** Hardwood. **Sights:** Hooded post front, micrometer adjustable open rear. **Features:** Velocity to 800 fps. Monte Carlo comb. From Daisy Mfg. Co.
Price: $129.95
Price: Model 131 (velocity to 600 fps) $117.95
Price: Model 1150 (black copolymer stock, velocity to 600 fps) $77.95

DAISY/POWERLINE EAGLE 7856 PUMP-UP AIRGUN
Caliber: 177 (pellets), BB, 100-shot BB magazine. **Barrel:** Rifled steel with shroud. **Weight:** 3.3 lbs. **Length:** 37.4" overall. **Power:** Pneumatic pump-up. **Stock:** Moulded wood-grain plastic. **Sights:** Ramp and blade front, open rear adjustable for elevation. **Features:** Velocity from 315 fps (two pumps) to 650 fps (10 pumps). Finger grooved forend. Cross-bolt trigger-block safety. From Daisy Mfg. Co.
Price: With 4x scope, about $49.95

DAISY/POWERLINE 880
Caliber: 177 pellet or BB, 50-shot BB magazine, single shot for pellets. **Barrel:** Rifled steel. **Weight:** 3.7 lbs. **Length:** 37.6" overall. **Power:** Multi-pump pneumatic. **Stock:** Moulded wood grain; Monte Carlo comb. **Sights:** Hooded front, adjustable rear. **Features:** Velocity to 685 fps. (BB). Variable power (velocity, range) increase with pump strokes; resin receiver with dovetail scope mount. Made in U.S.A. by Daisy Mfg. Co.
Price: $50.95

DAISY/POWERLINE 1000 AIR RIFLE
Caliber: 177, single shot. **Barrel:** NA. **Weight:** 6.15 lbs. **Length:** 43" overall. **Power:** Spring-air, barrel cocking. **Stock:** Stained hardwood. **Sights:** Hooded blade front on ramp, fully adjustable micrometer rear. **Features:** Velocity to 1000 fps. Blued finish; trigger block safety. From Daisy Mfg. Co.
Price: $208.95

DAISY/YOUTHLINE MODEL 105 AIR RIFLE
Caliber: BB, 400-shot magazine. **Barrel:** 13-1/2". **Weight:** 1.6 lbs. **Length:** 29.8" overall. **Power:** Spring. **Stock:** Moulded woodgrain. **Sights:** Blade on ramp front, fixed rear. **Features:** Velocity to 275 fps. Blue finish. Cross-bolt trigger block safety. Made in U.S. by Daisy Mfg. Co.
Price: $28.95

DAISY/YOUTHLINE MODEL 95 AIR RIFLE
Caliber: BB, 700-shot magazine. **Barrel:** 18". **Weight:** 2.4 lbs. **Length:** 35.2" overall. **Power:** Spring. **Stock:** Stained hardwood. **Sights:** Blade on ramp front, open adjustable rear. **Features:** Velocity to 325 fps. Cross-bolt trigger block safety. Made in U.S. by Daisy Mfg. Co.
Price: $38.95

EAA/BAIKAL MP-512 AIR RIFLE
Caliber: 177, single shot. **Barrel:** 17.7". **Weight:** 6.2 lbs. **Length:** 41.3" overall. **Power:** Spring-piston, single stroke. **Stock:** Black synthetic. **Sights:** Adjustable rear, hooded front. **Features:** Velocity 490 fps. Hammer-forged, rifled barrel; automatic safety; scope mount rail. Imported from Russia by European American Armory.
Price: 177 caliber $50.00
Price: 512M (590 fps) .... $NA

EAA/BAIKAL IZH-61 AIR RIFLE
Caliber: 177 pellet, 5-shot magazine. **Barrel:** 17.8". **Weight:** 6.4 lbs. **Length:** 31" overall. **Power:** Spring piston, side-cocking lever. **Stock:** Black plastic. **Sights:** Adjustable rear, fully hooded front. **Features:** Velocity 490 fps. Futuristic design with adjustable stock. Imported from Russia by European American Armory.
Price: $99.00

EAA/BAIKAL IZHMP-532 AIR RIFLE
Caliber: 177 pellet, single shot. **Barrel:** 15.8". **Weight:** 9.3 lbs. **Length:** 46.1" overall. **Power:** Single-stroke pneumatic. **Stock:** One- or two-piece competition-style stock with adjustable butt pad, pistol grip. **Sights:** Fully adjustable rear, hooded front. **Features:** Velocity 460 fps. Five-way adjustable trigger. Imported from Russia by European American Armory.
Price: $599.00

GAMO DELTA AIR RIFLE
Caliber: 177. **Barrel:** 15.7". **Weight:** 4.2 lbs. **Length:** 37.8". **Power:** Single-stroke pneumatic, 525 fps. **Stock:** Synthetic. **Sights:** Truglo fiber optic.
Price: $89.95

GAMO YOUNG HUNTER AIR RIFLE
Caliber: 177. **Barrel:** 17.7". **Weight:** 5.5 lbs. **Length:** 41". **Power:** Single-stroke pneumatic, 640 fps. **Stock:** Wood. **Sights:** Truglo fiber optic adjustable. **Features:** Excellent for young adults, it has a rifled steel barrel, hooded front sight, grooved receiver for scope. Imported from Spain by Gamo.
Price: $129.95
Price: Combo packed with BSA 4x32 scope and rings $169.95

AIRGUNS

AIRGUNS—LONG GUNS

GAMO SPORTER AIR RIFLE
Caliber: 177. **Barrel:** NA **Weight:** 5.5 lbs. **Length:** 42.5". **Power:** Single-stroke pneumatic, 760 fps. **Stock:** Wood. **Sights:** Adjustable Truglo fiber optic. **Features:** Intended to bridge the gap between Gamo's Young Hunter model and the adult-sized Hunter 440. Imported from Spain by Gamo.
Price: **$159.95**

GAMO HUNTER 440 AIR RIFLE
Caliber: 177, 22. **Barrel:** NA. **Weight:** 6.6 lbs. **Length:** 43.3". **Power:** Single-stroke pneumatifc, 1,000 fps (177), 750 fps (22). **Stock:** Wood. **Sights:** Adjustable Truglo fiber optic. **Features:** Adjustable two-stage trigger, rifled barrel, raised scope ramp on receiver. Realtree camo model available.
Price: **$229.95**
Price: Hunter 440 Combo with BSA 4x32mm scope **$259.95**

HAMMERLI AR 50 AIR RIFLE
Caliber: 177. **Barrel:** 19.8". **Weight:** 10 lbs. **Length:** 43.2" overall. **Power:** Compressed air. **Stock:** Anatomically-shaped universal and right-hand; match style; multi-colored laminated wood. **Sights:** Interchangeable element tunnel front, fully adjustable Hammerli peep rear. **Features:** Vibration-free firing release; fully adjustable match trigger and trigger stop; stainless air tank, built-in pressure gauge. Gives 270 shots per filling. Imported from Switzerland by Sigarms, Inc.
Price: **$1,653.00**

HAMMERLI MODEL 450 MATCH AIR RIFLE
Caliber: 177, single shot. **Barrel:** 19.5". **Weight:** 9.8 lbs. **Length:** 43.3" overall. **Power:** Pneumatic. **Stock:** Match style with stippled grip, rubber buttpad. Beach or walnut. **Sights:** Match tunnel front, Hammerli diopter rear. **Features:** Velocity about 560 fps. Removable sights; forend sling rail; adjustable trigger; adjustable comb. Imported from Switzerland by Sigarms, Inc.
Price: Beech stock **$1,355.00**
Price: Walnut stock **$1,395.00**

MARKSMAN BB BUDDY AIR RIFLE
Caliber: 177, 20-shot magazine. **Barrel:** 10.5" smoothbore. **Weight:** 1.6 lbs. **Length:** 33" overall. **Power:** Spring-air. **Stock:** Moulded composition. **Sights:** Blade on ramp front, adjustable V-slot rear. **Features:** Velocity 275 fps. Positive feed; automatic safety. Youth-sized lightweight design. Made in U.S. From Marksman Products.
Price: **$27.95**

MARKSMAN 2015 LASERHAWK™ BB REPEATER AIR RIFLE
Caliber: 177 BB, 20-shot magazine. **Barrel:** 10.5" smoothbore. **Weight:** 1.6 lbs. **Length:** Adjustable to 33", 34" or 35" overall. **Power:** Spring-air. **Stock:** Moulded composition. **Sights:** Fixed fiber optic front sight, adjustable elevation V-slot rear. **Features:** Velocity about 275 fps. Positive feed; automatic safety. Adjustable stock. Made in the U.S. From Marksman Products.
Price: **$33.00**

RWS/DIANA MODEL 24 AIR RIFLE
Caliber: 177, 22, single shot. **Barrel:** 17", rifled. **Weight:** 6 lbs. **Length:** 42" overall. **Power:** Spring-air, barrel cocking. **Stock:** Beech. **Sights:** Hooded front, adjustable rear. **Features:** Velocity of 700 fps (177). Easy cocking effort; blue finish. Imported from Germany by Dynamit Nobel-RWS, Inc.
Price: 24, 24C **$215.00**

RWS/Diana Model 34 Air Rifle
Similar to the Model 24 except has 19" barrel, weighs 7.5 lbs. Gives velocity of 1000 fps (177), 800 fps (22). Adjustable trigger, synthetic seals. Comes with scope rail.
Price: 177 or 22 . . . . **$290.00**
Price: Model 34N (nickel-plated metal, black epoxy-coated wood stock) . . . **$350.00**
Price: Model 34BC (matte black metal, black stock, 4x32 scope, mounts) . . **$510.00**

RWS/DIANA MODEL 36 AIR RIFLE
Caliber: 177, 22, single shot. **Barrel:** 19", rifled. **Weight:** 8 lbs. **Length:** 45" overall. **Power:** Spring-air, barrel cocking. **Stock:** Beech. **Sights:** Hooded front (interchangeable inserts available), adjustable rear. **Features:** Velocity of 1000 fps (177-cal.). Comes with scope mount; two-stage adjustable trigger. Imported from Germany by Dynamit Nobel-RWS, Inc.
Price: 36, 36C **$435.00**

RWS/DIANA MODEL 52 AIR RIFLE
Caliber: 177, 22, 25, single shot. **Barrel:** 17", rifled. **Weight:** 8-1/2 lbs. **Length:** 43" overall. **Power:** Spring-air, sidelever cocking. **Stock:** Beech, with Monte Carlo, cheekpiece, checkered grip and forend. **Sights:** Ramp front, adjustable rear. **Features:** Velocity of 1100 fps (177). Blue finish. Solid rubber buttpad. Imported from Germany by Dynamit Nobel-RWS, Inc.
Price: 177, 22 . . . . **$565.00**
Price: 25 . . . . **$605.00**
Price: Model 52 Deluxe (177) **$810.00**
Price: Model 48B (as above except matte black metal, black stock) **$535.00**
Price: Model 48 (same as Model 52 except no Monte Carlo, cheekpiece or checkering) **$520.00**

RWS/DIANA MODEL 45 AIR RIFLE
Caliber: 177, single shot. **Weight:** 8 lbs. **Length:** 45" overall. **Power:** Spring-air, barrel cocking. **Stock:** Walnut-finished hardwood with rubber recoil pad. **Sights:** Globe front with interchangeable inserts, micro. click open rear with four-way blade. **Features:** Velocity of 820 fps. Dovetail base for either micrometer peep sight or scope mounting. Automatic safety. Imported from Germany by Dynamit Nobel-RWS, Inc.
Price: **$350.00**

RWS/DIANA MODEL 46 AIR RIFLE
Caliber: 177, 22, single shot. **Barrel:** 18". **Weight:** 8.2 lbs. **Length:** 45" overall. **Stock:** Hardwood Monte Carlo. **Sights:** Blade front, adjustable rear. **Features:** Underlever cocking spring-air (950 fps in 177, 780 fps in 22); extended scope rail, automatic safety, rubber buttpad, adjustable trigger. Imported from Germany by Dynamit Nobel-RWS Inc.
Price: **$470.00**
Price: Model 46E (as above except matte black metal, black stock) **$430.00**

RWS/DIANA MODEL 54 AIR RIFLE
Caliber: 177, 22, single shot. **Barrel:** 17". **Weight:** 9 lbs. **Length:** 43" overall. **Power:** Spring-air, sidelever cocking. **Stock:** Walnut with Monte Carlo cheekpiece, checkered grip and forend. **Sights:** Ramp front, fully adjustable rear. **Features:** Velocity to 1000 fps (177), 900 fps (22). Totally recoilless system; floating action absorbs recoil. Imported from Germany by Dynamit Nobel-RWS, Inc.
Price: **$785.00**

RWS/DIANA MODEL 92/93/94 AIR RIFLES
Caliber: 177, 22, single shot. **Barrel:** N/A. **Weight:** N/A. **Length:** N/A. **Stock:** Beechwood; Monte Carlo. **Sights:** Hooded front, fully adjustable rear. **Features:** Break-barrel, spring-air; receiver grooved for scope; adjustable trigger; lifetime warranty. Imported from Spain by Dynamit Nobel-RWS Inc.
Price: Model 92 (auto safety, 700 fps in 177) . . . . **NA**
Price: Model 93 (manual safety, 850 fps in 177) . . . . **NA**
Price: Model 94 (auto safety, 1,000 fps in 177) . . . . **NA**

RWS/DIANA MODEL 350 MAGNUM AIR RIFLE
Caliber: 177, 22, single shot. **Barrel:** 19-1/2". **Weight:** 8 lbs. **Length:** 48". **Stock:** Beechwood; Monte Carlo. **Sights:** Hooded front, fully adjustable rear. **Features:** Break-barrel, spring-air; 1,250 fps. Imported from Germany by Dynamit Nobel-RWS Inc.
Price: Model 350 . . . . **NA**

TECH FORCE BS4 OLYMPIC COMPETITION AIR RIFLE
Caliber: 177 pellet, single shot. **Barrel:** N/A. **Weight:** 10.8 lbs. **Length:** 43.3" overall. **Power:** Spring piston, sidelever action. **Stock:** Wood with semi-pistol grip, adjustable butt plate. **Sights:** Micro-adjustable competition rear, hooded front. **Features:** Velocity 640 fps. Recoilless action; adjustable trigger. Includes carrying case. Imported from China by Compasseco Inc.
Price: **$595.00**
Price: Optional diopter rear sight **$79.95**

TECH FORCE 6 AIR RIFLE
Caliber: 177 pellet, single shot. **Barrel:** 14". **Weight:** 6 lbs. **Length:** 35.5" overall. **Power:** Spring piston, sidelever action. **Stock:** Paratrooper-style folding, full pistol grip. **Sights:** Adjustable rear, hooded front. **Features:** Velocity 800 fps. All-metal construction; grooved for scope mounting. Imported from China by Compasseco Inc.
Price: **$69.95**

Tech Force 51 Air Rifle
Similar to Tech Force 6, but with break-barrel cocking mechanism and folding stock fitted with recoil pad. Overall length, 36". Weighs 6 lbs. From Compasseco Inc.
Price: **$69.95**

TECH FORCE 25 AIR RIFLE
Caliber: 177, 22 pellet, single shot. **Barrel:** N/A. **Weight:** 7.5 lbs. **Length:** 46.2" overall. **Power:** Spring piston, break-action barrel. **Stock:** Oil-finished wood; Monte Carlo stock with recoil pad. **Sights:** Adjustable rear, hooded front with insert. **Features:** Velocity 1,000 fps (177); grooved receiver and scope stop for scope mounting; adjustable trigger; trigger safety. Imported from China by Compasseco Inc.
Price: 177 or 22 caliber **$125.00**
Price: Includes rifle and Tech Force 96 red dot point sight **$164.95**

TECH FORCE 36 AIR RIFLE
Caliber: 177 pellet, single shot. **Barrel:** N/A. **Weight:** 7.4 lbs. **Length:** 43" overall. **Power:** Spring piston, underlever cocking. **Stock:** Monte Carlo hardwood stock; recoil pad. **Sights:** Adjustable rear, hooded front. **Features:** Velocity 900 fps; grooved receiver and scope stop for scope mounting; auto-reset safety. Imported from China by Compasseco Inc.
Price: **$89.95**

WHISCOMBE JW SERIES AIR RIFLES
Caliber: 177, 20, 22, 25, single shot. **Barrel:** 15", Lothar Walther. Polygonal rifling. **Weight:** 9 lbs., 8 oz. **Length:** 39" overall. **Power:** Dual spring-piston, multi-stroke; underlever cocking. **Stock:** Walnut with adjustable buttplate and cheekpiece. **Sights:** None furnished; grooved scope rail. **Features:** Velocity 660-1000 (JW80) fps (22-caliber, fixed barrel) depending upon model. Interchangeable barrels; automatic safety; muzzle weight; semi-floating action; twin opposed pistons with counter-wound springs; adjustable trigger. All models include H.O.T. System (Harmonic Optimization Tunable System). Imported from England by Pelaire Products.
Price: JW50, MKII fixed barrel only **$2,085.00**
Price: JW65, MKII **$2,085.00**
Price: JW80, MKII **$2,195.00**

AIRGUNS

A

A Zone Bullets, 2039 Walter Rd., Billings, MT 59105 / 800-252-3111; FAX: 406-248-1961

A&B Industries,Inc (See Top-Line USA Inc)

A&W Repair, 2930 Schneider Dr., Arnold, MO 63010 / 617-287-3725

A.A. Arms, Inc., 4811 Persimmont Ct., Monroe, NC 28110 / 704-289-5356; or 800-935-1119; FAX: 704-289-5859

A.B.S. III, 9238 St. Morritz Dr., Fern Creek, KY 40291

A.G. Russell Knives, Inc., 1920 North 26th Street, Springdale, AR 72764 / 479-751-7341; FAX: 479-751-4520 ag@agrussell.com agrussell.com

A.R.M.S., Inc., 230 W. Center St., West Bridgewater, MA 02379-1620 / 508-584-7816; FAX: 508-588-8045

A.W. Peterson Gun Shop, Inc., 4255 W. Old U.S. 441, Mt. Dora, FL 32757-3299 / 352-383-4258; FAX: 352-735-1001

AC Dyna-tite Corp., 155 Kelly St., P.O. Box 0984, Elk Grove Village, IL 60007 / 847-593-5566; FAX: 847-593-1304

Acadian Ballistic Specialties, P.O. Box 787, Folsom, LA 70437 / 504-796-0078 gunsmith@neasoft.com

Accuracy International, Foster, RR Box 111, Wilsall, MT 59086 / 406-587-7922; FAX: 406-585-9434

Accuracy Internationl Precision Rifles (See U.S.)

Accuracy Int'l. North America, Inc., PO Box 5267, Oak Ridge, TN 37831 / 423-482-0330; FAX: 423-482-0336

Accuracy Unlimited, 16036 N. 49 Ave., Glendale, AZ 85306 / 602-978-9089; FAX: 602-978-9089 fglenn@cox.net www.glenncustom.com

Accuracy Unlimited, 7479 S. DePew St., Littleton, CO 80123

Accura-Site (See All's, The Jim Tembelis Co., Inc.)

Accurate Arms Co., Inc., 5891 Hwy. 230 West, McEwen, TN 37101 / 931-729-4207; FAX: 931-729-4211 email@accuratecompanies.com www.accuratepowder.com

Accu-Tek, 4510 Carter Ct., Chino, CA 91710

Ace Custom 45's, Inc., 1880 1/2 Upper Turtle Creek Rd., Kerrville, TX 78028 / 830-257-4290; FAX: 830-257-5724 www.acecustom45.com

Ace Sportswear, Inc., 700 Quality Rd., Fayetteville, NC 28306 / 919-323-1223; FAX: 919-323-5392

Ackerman & Co., Box 133 US Highway Rt. 7, Pownal, VT 05261 / 802-823-9874 muskets@togsther.net

Ackerman, Bill (See Optical Services Co.)

Acra-Bond Laminates, 134 Zimmerman Rd., Kalispell, MT 59901 / 406-257-9003; FAX: 406-257-9003 merlins@digisys.net www.acrabondlaminates.com

Action Bullets & Alloy Inc., RR 1, P.O. Box 189, Quinter, KS 67752 / 785-754-3609; FAX: 785-754-3629 bullets@ruraltel.net

Action Direct, Inc., P.O. Box 770400, Miami, FL 33177 / 305-969-0056; FAX: 530-734-3760 www.action-direct.com

Action Products, Inc., 22 N. Mulberry St., Hagerstown, MD 21740 / 301-797-1414; FAX: 301-733-2073

Action Target, Inc., PO Box 636, Provo, UT 84603 / 801-377-8033; FAX: 801-377-8096

Actions by "T" Teddy Jacobson, 16315 Redwood Forest Ct., Sugar Land, TX 77478 / 281-277-4008; FAX: 281-277-9112 tjacobson@houston.rr.com www.actionsbyt.com

AcuSport Corporation, 1 Hunter Place, Bellefontaine, OH 43311-3001 / 513-593-7010; FAX: 513-592-5625

Ad Hominem, 3130 Gun Club Lane, RR #3, Orillia, ON L3V 6H3 CANADA / 705-689-5303; FAX: 705-689-5303

Adair Custom Shop, Bill, 2886 Westridge, Carrollton, TX 75006

ADCO Sales, Inc., 4 Draper St. #A, Woburn, MA 01801 / 781-935-1799; FAX: 781-935-1011

Adkins, Luther, 1292 E. McKay Rd., Shelbyville, IN 46176-8706 / 317-392-3795

Advance Car Mover Co., Rowell Div., P.O. Box 1, 240 N. Depot St., Juneau, WI 53039 / 414-386-4464; FAX: 414-386-4416

Adventure 16, Inc., 4620 Alvarado Canyon Rd., San Diego, CA 92120 / 619-283-6314

Adventure Game Calls, R.D. 1, Leonard Rd., Spencer, NY 14883 / 607-589-4611

Aero Peltor, 90 Mechanic St., Southbridge, MA 01550 / 508-764-5500; FAX: 508-764-0188

African Import Co., 22 Goodwin Rd, Plymouth, MA 02360 / 508-746-8552; FAX: 508-746-0404

AFSCO Ammunition, 731 W. Third St., P.O. Box L, Owen, WI 54460 / 715-229-2516

Ahlman Guns, 9525 W. 230th St., Morristown, MN 55052 / 507-685-4243; FAX: 507-685-4280 www.ahlmans.com

Ahrends, Kim (See Custom Firearms, Inc), Box 203, Clarion, IA 50525 / 515-532-3449; FAX: 515-532-3926

Aimtech Mount Systems, P.O. Box 223, Thomasville, GA 31799 / 229-226-4313; FAX: 229-227-0222 mail@aimtech-mounts.com www.aimtech-mounts.com

Air Arms, Hailsham Industrial Park, Diplocks Way, Hailsham, E. Sussex, BN27 3JF ENGLAND / 011-0323-845853

Air Rifle Specialists, P.O. Box 138, 130 Holden Rd., Pine City, NY 14871-0138 / 607-734-7340; FAX: 607-733-3261 ars@stny.rr.com www.air-rifles.com

Air Venture Airguns, 9752 E. Flower St., Bellflower, CA 90706 / 562-867-6355

AirForce Airguns, P.O. Box 2478, Fort Worth, TX 76113 / 817-451-8966; FAX: 817-451-1613 www.airforceairguns.com

Airrow, 11 Monitor Hill Rd., Newtown, CT 06470 / 203-270-6343

Aitor-Cuchilleria Del Norte S.A., Izelaieta, 17, 48260, Ermua, S SPAIN / 43-17-08-50 info@aitor.com www.ailor.com

Ajax Custom Grips, Inc., 9130 Viscount Row, Dallas, TX 75247 / 214-630-8893; FAX: 214-630-4942

Aker International, Inc., 2248 Main St., Suite 6, Chula Vista, CA 91911 / 619-423-5182; FAX: 619-423-1363 aker@akerleather.com www.akerleather.com

AKJ Concealco, P.O. Box 871596, Vancouver, WA 98687-1596 / 360-891-8222; FAX: 360-891-8221 Concealco@aol.com www.greatholsters.com

Al Lind Custom Guns, P.O. Box 97268, Tacoma, WA 98497 / 253-584-6361; FAX: 253-584-6361

Alana Cupp Custom Engraver, P.O. Box 207, Annabella, UT 84711 / 801-896-4834

Alaska Bullet Works, Inc., 9978 Crazy Horse Drive, Juneau, AK 99801 / 907-789-3834; FAX: 907-789-3433

Alaskan Silversmith, The, 2145 Wagner Hollow Rd., Fort Plain, NY 13339 / 518-993-3983 sidbell@capital.net www.sidbell.cizland.com

Aldis Gunsmithing & Shooting Supply, 502 S. Montezuma St., Prescott, AZ 86303 / 602-445-6723; FAX: 602-445-6763

Alessi Holsters, Inc., 2465 Niagara Falls Blvd., Amherst, NY 14228-3527 / 716-691-5615

Alex, Inc., 3420 Cameron Bridge Rd., Manhattan, MT 59741-8523 / 406-282-7396; FAX: 406-282-7396

Alfano, Sam, 36180 Henry Gaines Rd., Pearl River, LA 70452 / 504-863-3364; FAX: 504-863-7715

All American Lead Shot Corp., P.O. Box 224566, Dallas, TX 75062

All Rite Products, Inc., 9554 Wells Circle, Suite D, West Jordan, UT 84088-6226 / 800-771-8471; FAX: 801-280-8302 www.allriteproducts.com

Allard, Gary/Creek Side Metal & Woodcrafters, Fishers Hill, VA 22626 / 703-465-3903

Allen Co., Bob, 214 SW Jackson, P.O. Box 477, Des Moines, IA 50315 / 515-283-2191; or 800-685-7020; FAX: 515-283-0779

Allen Co., Inc., 525 Burbank St., Broomfield, CO 80020 / 303-469-1857; or 800-876-8600; FAX: 303-466-7437

Allen Firearm Engraving, P.O. Box 155, Camp Verde, AZ 86322 / 928-567-6711; FAX: 928-567-3901 rosebudmukco@aol.com

Allen Mfg., 6449 Hodgson Rd., Circle Pines, MN 55014 / 612-429-8231

Allen Sportswear, Bob (See Allen Co., Bob)

Alley Supply Co., PO Box 848, Gardnerville, NV 89410 / 775-782-3800; FAX: 775-782-3827 jetalley@aol.com www.alleysupplyco.com

Alliant Techsystems Smokeless Powder Group, P.O. Box 6, Rt. 114, Bldg. 229, Radford, VA 24141-0096 www.alliantpowder.com

Allred Bullet Co., 932 Evergreen Drive, Logan, UT 84321 / 435-752-6983; FAX: 435-752-6983

All's, The Jim J. Tembelis Co., Inc., 216 Loper Ct., Neenah, WI 54956 / 920-725-5251; FAX: 920-725-5251

Alpec Team, Inc., 201 Ricken Backer Cir., Livermore, CA 94550 / 510-606-8245; FAX: 510-606-4279

Alpha 1 Drop Zone, 2121 N. Tyler, Wichita, KS 67212 / 316-729-0800; FAX: 316-729-4262

Alpha LaFranck Enterprises, P.O. Box 81072, Lincoln, NE 68501 / 402-466-3193

Alpha Precision, Inc., 3238 Della Slaton Rd., Comer, GA 30629-2212 / 706-783-2131 jim@alphaprecisioninc.com www.alphaprecisioninc.com

Alpine Indoor Shooting Range, 2401 Government Way, Coeur d'Alene, ID 83814 / 208-676-8824; FAX: 208-676-8824

Altamont Co., 901 N. Church St., P.O. Box 309, Thomasboro, IL 61878 / 217-643-3125; or 800-626-5774; FAX: 217-643-7973

Alumna Sport by Dee Zee, 1572 NE 58th Ave., P.O. Box 3090, Des Moines, IA 50316 / 800-798-9899

Amadeo Rossi S.A., Rua: Amadeo Rossi, 143, Sao Leopoldo, RS 93030-220 BRAZIL / 051-592-5566

AmBr Software Group Ltd., P.O. Box 301, Reistertown, MD 21136-0301 / 800-888-1917; FAX: 410-526-7212

American Ammunition, 3545 NW 71st St., Miami, FL 33147 / 305-835-7400; FAX: 305-694-0037

American Derringer Corp., 127 N. Lacy Dr., Waco, TX 76705 / 800-642-7817 or 254-799-9111; FAX: 254-799-7935

American Display Co., 55 Cromwell St., Providence, RI 02907 / 401-331-2464; FAX: 401-421-1264

American Frontier Firearms Mfg., Inc, PO Box 744, Aguanga, CA 92536 / 909-763-0014; FAX: 909-763-0014

American Gas & Chemical Co., Ltd, 220 Pegasus Ave, Northvale, NJ 07647 / 201-767-7300

American Gripcraft, 3230 S Dodge 2, Tucson, AZ 85713 / 602-790-1222

American Gunsmithing Institute, 1325 Imola Ave #504, Napa, CA 94559 / 707-253-0462; FAX: 707-253-7149

American Handgunner Magazine, 591 Camino de la Reina, Ste. 200, San Diego, CA 92108 / 619-297-5350; FAX: 619-297-5353

American Pioneer Video, PO Box 50049, Bowling Green, KY 42102-2649 / 800-743-4675

American Products, Inc., 14729 Spring Valley Road, Morrison, IL 61270 / 815-772-3336; FAX: 815-772-8046

American Safe Arms, Inc., 1240 Riverview Dr., Garland, UT 84312 / 801-257-7472; FAX: 801-785-8156

American Security Products Co., 11925 Pacific Ave., Fontana, CA 92337 / 909-685-9680; or 800-421-6142; FAX: 909-685-9685

American Small Arms Academy, P.O. Box 12111, Prescott, AZ 86304 / 602-778-5623

American Target, 1328 S. Jason St., Denver, CO 80223 / 303-733-0433; FAX: 303-777-0311

American Target Knives, 1030 Brownwood NW, Grand Rapids, MI 49504 / 616-453-1998

Americase, P.O. Box 271, 1610 E. Main, Waxahachie, TX 75165 / 800-880-3629; FAX: 214-937-8373

Ames Metal Products, 4323 S. Western Blvd., Chicago, IL 60609 / 773-523-3230 or 800-255-6937; FAX: 773-523-3854

Amherst Arms, P.O. Box 1457, Englewood, FL 34295 / 941-475-2020; FAX: 941-473-1212

Ammo Load, Inc., 1560 E. Edinger, Suite G, Santa Ana, CA 92705 / 714-558-8858; FAX: 714-569-0319

Amrine's Gun Shop, 937 La Luna, Ojai, CA 93023 / 805-646-2376

Amsec, 11925 Pacific Ave., Fontana, CA 92337

Analog Devices, Box 9106, Norwood, MA 02062

Andela Tool & Machine, Inc., RD3, Box 246, Richfield Springs, NY 13439

Anderson Manufacturing Co., Inc., 22602 53rd Ave. SE, Bothell, WA 98021 / 206-481-1858; FAX: 206-481-7839

Andres & Dworsky KG, Bergstrasse 18, A-3822 Karlstein, Thaya, AUSTRIA / 0 28 44-285; FAX: 02844 28619 andres.dnorsky@wvnet.as

Angelo & Little Custom Gun Stock Blanks, P.O. Box 240046, Dell, MT 59724-0046

Answer Products Co., 1519 Westbury Drive, Davison, MI 48423 / 810-653-2911

Antique American Firearms, P.O. Box 71035, Dept. GD, Des Moines, IA 50325 / 515-224-6552

Antique Arms Co., 1110 Cleveland Ave., Monett, MO 65708 / 417-235-6501

AO Sight Systems, 2401 Ludelle St., Fort Worth, TX 76105 / 888-744-4880 or 817-536-0136; FAX: 817-536-3517

Apel GmbH, Ernst, Am Kirschberg 3, D-97218, Gerbrunn, GERMANY / 0 (931) 707192 info@eaw.de www.eaw.de

Aplan Antiques & Art, James O., James O., HC 80, Box 793-25, Piedmont, SD 57769 / 605-347-5016

AR-7 Industries, LLC, 998 N. Colony Rd., Meriden, CT 06450 / 203-630-3536; FAX: 203-630-3637

Arizona Ammunition, Inc., 21421 No. 14th Ave., Suite E, Phoenix, AZ 85027 / 623-516-9004; FAX: 623-516-9012 www.azammo.com

ArmaLite, Inc., P.O. Box 299, Geneseo, IL 61254 / 800-336-0184 or 309-944-6939; FAX: 309-944-6949

Armament Gunsmithing Co., Inc., 525 Rt. 22, Hillside, NJ 07205 / 908-686-0960; FAX: 718-738-5019 armamentgunsmithing@worldnet.att.net

Armas Garbi, S.A., 12-14 20.600 Urki, 12, Eibar (Guipuzcoa), / 943203873; FAX: 943203873 armosgarbi@euskalnet.n

Armas Kemen S. A. (See U.S. Importers)

Armfield Custom Bullets, 10584 County Road 100, Carthage, MO 64836 / 417-359-8480; FAX: 417-359-8497

Armi Perazzi S.p.A., Via Fontanelle 1/3, I-25080, Botticino Mattina, / 030-2692591; FAX: 030 2692594

Armi San Marco (See U.S. Importers-Taylor's & Co I

Armi San Paolo, 172-A, I-25062, via Europa, ITALY / 030-2751725

Armi Sport (See U.S. Importers-Cape Outfitters)

MANUFACTURER'S DIRECTORY

Armite Laboratories, 1560 Superior Ave., Costa Mesa, CA 92627 / 213-587-7768; FAX: 213-587-5075

Armoloy Co. of Ft. Worth, 204 E. Daggett St., Fort Worth, TX 76104 / 817-332-5604; FAX: 817-335-6517

Armor (See Buck Stop Lure Co., Inc.)

Armor Metal Products, P.O. Box 4609, Helena, MT 59604 / 406-442-5560; FAX: 406-442-5650

Armory Publications, 17171 Bothall Way NE, #276, Seattle, WA 98155 / 206-364-7653; FAX: 206-362-9413 armorypub@aol.com www.grocities.com/armorypub

Armoury, Inc., The, Rt. 202, Box 2340, New Preston, CT 06777 / 860-868-0001; FAX: 860-868-2919

Arms & Armour Press, Wellington House, 125 Strand, London, WC2R 0BB ENGLAND / 0171-420-5555; FAX: 0171-240-7265

Arms Corporation of the Philippines, Bo. Parang Marikina, Metro Manila, PHILIPPINES / 632-941-6243 or 632-941-6244; FAX: 632-942-0682

Arms Craft Gunsmithing, 1106 Linda Dr., Arroyo Grande, CA 93420 / 805-481-2830

Arms Ingenuity Co., P.O. Box 1, 51 Canal St., Weatogue, CT 06089 / 203-658-5624

Arms Software, 4851 SW Madrona St., Lake Oswego, OR 97035 / 800-366-5559 or 503-697-0533; FAX: 503-697-3337

Arms, Programming Solutions (See Arms Software)

Armscorp USA, Inc., 4424 John Ave., Baltimore, MD 21227 / 410-247-6200; FAX: 410-247-6205 info@armscorpusa.com www.armscorpusa.com

Arratoonian, Andy (See Horseshoe Leather Products)

Arrieta S.L., Morkaiko 5, 20870, Elgoibar, SPAIN / 34-43-743150; FAX: 34-43-743154

Art Jewel Enterprises Ltd., Eagle Business Ctr., 460 Randy Rd., Carol Stream, IL 60188 / 708-260-0400

Artistry in Wood, 134 Zimmerman Rd., Kalispell, MT 59901 / 406-257-9003; FAX: 406-257-9167 merlins@digisys.net www.acrabondlaminates.com

Art's Gun & Sport Shop, Inc., 6008 Hwy. Y, Hillsboro, MO 63050

Arundel Arms & Ammunition, Inc., A., 24A Defense St., Annapolis, MD 21401 / 410-224-8683

Arvo Ojala Holsters, P.O. Box 98, N. Hollywood, CA 91603 / 818-222-9700; FAX: 818-222-0401

Ashby, David. See: ASHBY TURKEY CALLS

Ashby Turkey Calls, David L. Ashby, P.O. Box 1653, Ozark, MO 65721-1653

Ashley Outdoors, Inc., 2401 Ludelle St., Fort Worth, TX 76105 / 888-744-4880; FAX: 800-734-7939

Aspen Outfitting Co., Jon Hollinger, 9 Dean St., Aspen, CO 81611 / 970-925-3406

A-Square Co., 205 Fairfield Ave., Jeffersonville, IN 47130 / 812-283-0577; FAX: 812-283-0375

Astra Sport, S.A., Apartado 3, 48300 Guernica, Espagne, SPAIN / 34-4-6250100; FAX: 34-4-6255186

Atamec-Bretton, 19 rue Victor Grignard, F-42026, St.-Etienne (Cedex 1, / 77-93-54-69; FAX: 33-77-93-57-98

Atlanta Cutlery Corp., 2143 Gees Mill Rd., Box 839 CIS, Conyers, GA 30207 / 800-883-0300; FAX: 404-388-0246

Atlantic Mills, Inc., 1295 Towbin Ave., Lakewood, NJ 08701-5934 / 800-242-7374

Atlantic Rose, Inc., P.O. Box 10717, Bradenton, FL 34282-0717

Atsko/Sno-Seal, Inc., 2664 Russell St., Orangeburg, SC 29115 / 803-531-1820; FAX: 803-531-2139 info@atsko.com www.atsko.com

Auguste Francotte & Cie S.A., rue du Trois Juin 109, 4400 Herstal-Liege, BELGIUM / 32-4-248-13-18; FAX: 32-4-948-11-79

Austin & Halleck, Inc., 2150 South 950 East, Provo, UT 84606-6285 / 801-374-3256; or 801-374-9990; FAX: 801-374-9998 www.austinhallek.com

Austin Sheridan USA, Inc., P.O. Box 577, 36 Haddam Quarter Rd., Durham, CT 06422 / 860-349-1772; FAX: 860-349-1771 swalzer@palm.net

Autauga Arms, Inc., Pratt Plaza Mall No. 13, Prattville, AL 36067 / 800-262-9563; FAX: 334-361-2961

Auto Arms, 738 Clearview, San Antonio, TX 78228 / 512-434-5450

Auto-Ordnance Corp., PO Box 220, Blauvelt, NY 10913 / 914-353-7770

Autumn Sales, Inc. (Blaser), 1320 Lake St., Fort Worth, TX 76102 / 817-335-1634; FAX: 817-338-0119

Avnda Otaola Norica, 16 Apartado 68, 20600, Eibar, SPAIN

AWC Systems Technology, P.O. Box 41938, Phoenix, AZ 85080-1938 / 602-780-1050; FAX: 602-780-2967

Axtell Rifle Co., 353 Mill Creek Road, Sheridan, MT 59749 / 406-842-5814

AYA (See U.S. Importer-New England Custom Gun Serv

B

B&D Trading Co., Inc., 3935 Fair Hill Rd., Fair Oaks, CA 95628 / 800-334-3790 or 916-967-9366; FAX: 916-967-4873

B&P America, 12321 Brittany Cir., Dallas, TX 75230 / 972-726-9069

B.A.C., 17101 Los Modelos St., Fountain Valley, CA 92708 / 435-586-3286

B.B. Walker Co., PO Box 1167, 414 E Dixie Dr, Asheboro, NC 27204 / 910-625-1380; FAX: 910-625-8125

B.C. Outdoors, Larry McGhee, PO Box 61497, Boulder City, NV 89006 / 702-294-3056; FAX: 702-294-0413 jdalton@pmcammo.com www.pmcammo.com

B.M.F. Activator, Inc., 12145 Mill Creek Run, Plantersville, TX 77363 / 936-894-2397; FAX: 936-894-2397

Badger Creek Studio, 1629 Via Monserate, Fallbrook, CA 92028 / 760-723-9279; or 619-728-2663

Badger Shooters Supply, Inc., P.O. Box 397, Owen, WI 54460 / 800-424-9069; FAX: 715-229-2332

Baekgaard Ltd., 1855 Janke Dr., Northbrook, IL 60062 / 708-498-3040; FAX: 708-493-3106

Baelder, Harry, Alte Goennebeker Strasse 5, 24635, Rickling, GERMANY / 04328-722732; FAX: 04328-722733

Baer Custom Inc., Les, 29601 34th Ave., Hillsdale, IL 61257 / 309-658-2716; FAX: 309-658-2610

Baer's Hollows, P.O. Box 284, Eads, CO 81036 / 719-438-5718

Bagmaster Mfg., Inc., 2731 Sutton Ave., St. Louis, MO 63143 / 314-781-8002; FAX: 314-781-3363

Bain & Davis, Inc., 307 E. Valley Blvd., San Gabriel, CA 91776-3522 / 626-573-4241 baindavis@aol.com

Baker, Stan. See: STAN BAKER SPORTS

Baker's Leather Goods, Roy, PO Box 893, Magnolia, AR 71754 / 870-234-0344 pholsters@ipa.net

Bald Eagle Precision Machine Co., 101-A Allison St., Lock Haven, PA 17745 / 570-748-6772; FAX: 570-748-4443

Balickie, Joe, 408 Trelawney Lane, Apex, NC 27502 / 919-362-5185

Ballard, Donald. See: BALLARD INDUSTRIES

Ballard Industries, Donald Ballard Sr., PO Box 2035, Arnold, CA 95223 / 408-996-0957; FAX: 408-257-6828

Ballard Rifle & Cartridge Co., LLC, 113 W. Yellowstone Ave., Cody, WY 82414 / 307-587-4914; FAX: 307-527-6097 ballard@wyoming.com www.ballardrifles.com

Ballistic Product, Inc., 20015 75th Ave. North, Corcoran, MN 55340-9456 / 763-494-9237; FAX: 763-494-9236 info@ballisticproducts.com www.ballisticproducts.com

Ballistic Research, 1108 W. May Ave., McHenry, IL 60050 / 815-385-0037

Ballisti-Cast, Inc., P.O. Box 1057, Minot, ND 58702-1057 / 701-497-3333; FAX: 701-497-3335

Bandcor Industries, Div. of Man-Sew Corp., 6108 Sherwin Dr., Port Richey, FL 34668 / 813-848-0432

Bang-Bang Boutique (See Holster Shop, The)

Banks, Ed, 2011 Alabama Ave., Savannah, GA 31404-2721 / 912-987-4665

Bansner's Ultimate Rifles, LLC, P.O. Box 839, 261 E. Main St., Adamstown, PA 19501 / 717-484-2370; FAX: 717-484-0523 bansner@aol.com www.bansnersrifle.com

Barbour, Inc., 55 Meadowbrook Dr., Milford, NH 03055 / 603-673-1313; FAX: 603-673-6510

Barnes, 4347 Tweed Dr., Eau Claire, WI 54703-6302

Barnes Bullets, Inc., P.O. Box 215, American Fork, UT 84003 / 801-756-4222 or 800-574-9200; FAX: 801-756-2465 email@barnesbullets.com www.barnesbullets.com

Baron Technology, 62 Spring Hill Rd., Trumbull, CT 06611 / 203-452-0515; FAX: 203-452-0663 dbaron@baronengraving.com www.baronengraving.com

Barraclough, John K., 55 Merit Park Dr., Gardena, CA 90247 / 310-324-2574

Barramundi Corp., P.O. Drawer 4259, Homosassa Springs, FL 32687 / 904-628-0200

Barrett Firearms Manufacturer, Inc., P.O. Box 1077, Murfreesboro, TN 37133 / 615-896-2938; FAX: 615-896-7313

Bar-Sto Precision Machine, 73377 Sullivan Rd., PO Box 1838, Twentynine Palms, CA 92277 / 760-367-2747; FAX: 760-367-2407 barsto@eee.org www.barsto.com

Barta's Gunsmithing, 10231 US Hwy. 10, Cato, WI 54230 / 920-732-4472

Barteaux Machete, 1916 SE 50th Ave., Portland, OR 97215-3238 / 503-233-5880

Bartlett Engineering, 40 South 200 East, Smithfield, UT 84335-1645 / 801-563-5910

Bates Engraving, Billy, 2302 Winthrop Dr. SW, Decatur, AL 35603 / 256-355-3690 bbrn@aol.com

Battenfeld Technologies, 5875 W. Van Horn Tavern Rd., Columbia, MO 65203 / 573-445-9200; FAX: 573-447-4158 battenfeldtechnologies.com

Bauer, Eddie, 15010 NE 36th St., Redmond, WA 98052

Baumgartner Bullets, 3011 S. Alane St., W. Valley City, UT 84120

Bauska Barrels, 105 9th Ave. W., Kalispell, MT 59901 / 406-752-7706

Bear Archery, RR 4, 4600 Southwest 41st Blvd., Gainesville, FL 32601 / 904-376-2327

Bear Arms, 374-A Carson Road, St. Mathews, SC 29135

Bear Mountain Gun & Tool, 120 N. Plymouth, New Plymouth, ID 83655 / 208-278-5221; FAX: 208-278-5221

Beartooth Bullets, PO Box 491, Dept. HLD, Dover, ID 83825-0491 / 208-448-1865 bullets@beartoothbullets.com beartoothbullets.com

Beaver Lodge (See Fellowes, Ted)

Beaver Park Product, Inc., 840 J St., Penrose, CO 81240 / 719-372-6744

BEC, Inc., 1227 W. Valley Blvd., Suite 204, Alhambra, CA 91803 / 626-281-5751; FAX: 626-293-7073

Beeks, Mike. See: GRAYBACK WILDCATS

Beeman Precision Airguns, 5454 Argosy Dr., Huntington Beach, CA 92649 / 714-890-4800; FAX: 714-890-4808

Behlert Precision, Inc., P.O. Box 288, 7067 Easton Rd., Pipersville, PA 18947 / 215-766-8681 or 215-766-7301; FAX: 215-766-8681

Beitzinger, George, 116-20 Atlantic Ave., Richmond Hill, NY 11419 / 718-847-7661

Belding's Custom Gun Shop, 10691 Sayers Rd., Munith, MI 49259 / 517-596-2388

Bell & Carlson, Inc., Dodge City Industrial Park, 101 Allen Rd., Dodge City, KS 67801 / 800-634-8586 or 620-225-6688; FAX: 620-225-6688 email@bellandcarlson.com www.bellandcarlson.com

Bell Reloading, Inc., 1725 Harlin Lane Rd., Villa Rica, GA 30180

Bell's Gun & Sport Shop, 3309-19 Mannheim Rd, Franklin Park, IL 60131

Bell's Legendary Country Wear, 22 Circle Dr., Bellmore, NY 11710 / 516-679-1158

Belltown Ltd., 11 Camps Rd., Kent, CT 06757 / 860-354-5750; FAX: 860-354-6764

Ben William's Gun Shop, 1151 S. Cedar Ridge, Duncanville, TX 75137 / 214-780-1807

Benchmark Knives (See Gerber Legendary Blades)

Benelli Armi S.p.A., Via della Stazione, 61029, Urbino, ITALY / 39-722-307-1; FAX: 39-722-327427

Benelli USA Corp, 17603 Indian Head Hwy, Accokeek, MD 20607 / 301-283-6981; FAX: 301-283-6988 benelliusa.com

Bengtson Arms Co., L., 6345-B E. Akron St., Mesa, AZ 85205 / 602-981-6375

Benjamin/Sheridan Co., Crosman, Rts. 5 and 20, E. Bloomfield, NY 14443 / 716-657-6161; FAX: 716-657-5405 www.crosman.com

Ben's Machines, 1151 S. Cedar Ridge, Duncanville, TX 75137 / 214-780-1807; FAX: 214-780-0316

Bentley, John, 128-D Watson Dr., Turtle Creek, PA 15145

Beomat of America, Inc., 300 Railway Ave., Campbell, CA 95008 / 408-379-4829

Beretta S.p.A., Pietro, Via Beretta, 18, 25063, Gardone Vae Trompia, ITALY / 39-30-8341-1 info@benetta.com www.benetta.com

Beretta U.S.A. Corp., 17601 Beretta Drive, Accokeek, MD 20607 / 301-283-2191; FAX: 301-283-0435

Berger Bullets Ltd., 5443 W. Westwind Dr., Glendale, AZ 85310 / 602-842-4001; FAX: 602-934-9083

Bernardelli, Vincenzo, P.O. Box 460243, Houston, TX 77056-8243 www.bernardelli.com

Bernardelli S.p.A., Vincenzo, 125 Via Matteotti, PO Box 74, Brescia, ITALY / 39-30-8912851-2-3; FAX: 39-30-8910249

Berry's Mfg., Inc., 401 North 3050 East St., St. George, UT 84770 / 435-634-1682; FAX: 435-634-1683 sales@berrysmfg.com www.berrysmfg.com

Bersa S.A., Benso Bonadimani, Magallanes 775 B1704 FLC, Ramos Mejia, ARGENTINA / 011-4656-2377; FAX: 011-4656-2093+ info@bersa-sa.com.dr www.bersa-sa.com.ar

Bert Johanssons Vapentillbehor, S-430 20 Veddige, SWEDEN,

Bertuzzi (See U.S. Importer-New England Arms Co)

Better Concepts Co., 663 New Castle Rd., Butler, PA 16001 / 412-285-9000

Beverly, Mary, 3201 Horseshoe Trail, Tallahassee, FL 32312

Bianchi International, Inc., 100 Calle Cortez, Temecula, CA 92590 / 909-676-5621; FAX: 909-676-6777

Big Bear Arms & Sporting Goods, Inc., 1112 Milam Way, Carrollton, TX 75006 / 972-416-8051 or 800-400-BEAR; FAX: 972-416-0771

MANUFACTURER'S DIRECTORY

Big Bore Bullets of Alaska, PO Box 521455, Big Lake, AK 99652 / 907-373-2673; FAX: 907-373-2673 doug@mtaonline.net ww.awloo.com/bbb/index.

Big Bore Express, 16345 Midway Rd., Nampa, ID 83651 / 208-466-9975; FAX: 208-466-6927 bigbore.com

Big Spring Enterprises "Bore Stores", P.O. Box 1115, Big Spring Rd., Yellville, AR 72687 / 870-449-5297; FAX: 870-449-4446

Bilal, Mustafa. See: TURK'S HEAD PRODUCTIONS

Bilinski, Bryan. See: FIELDSPORT LTD.

Bill Adair Custom Shop, 2886 Westridge, Carrollton, TX 75006 / 972-418-0950

Bill Austin's Calls, Box 284, Kaycee, WY 82639 / 307-738-2552

Bill Hanus Birdguns, P.O. Box 533, Newport, OR 97365 / 541-265-7433; FAX: 541-265-7400 www.billhanusbirdguns.com

Bill Russ Trading Post, William A. Russ, 23 William St., Addison, NY 14801-1326 / 607-359-3896

Bill Wiseman and Co., P.O. Box 3427, Bryan, TX 77805 / 409-690-3456; FAX: 409-690-0156

Billeb, Stephn. See: QUALITY CUSTOM FIREARMS

Billings Gunsmiths, 1841 Grand Ave., Billings, MT 59102 / 406-256-8390; FAX: 406-256-6530 blgsgunsmiths@msn.com www.billingsgunsmiths.net

Billingsley & Brownell, P.O. Box 25, Dayton, WY 82836 / 307-655-9344

Bill's Custom Cases, P.O. Box 2, Dunsmuir, CA 96025 / 530-235-0177; FAX: 530-235-4959 billscustomcases@mindspring.com

Bill's Gun Repair, 1007 Burlington St., Mendota, IL 61342 / 815-539-5786

Billy Bates Engraving, 2302 Winthrop Dr. SW, Decatur, AL 35603 / 256-355-3690 bbrn@aol.com

Birchwood Casey, 7900 Fuller Rd., Eden Prairie, MN 55344 / 800-328-6156 or 612-937-7933; FAX: 612-937-7979

Birdsong & Assoc., W. E., 1435 Monterey Rd, Florence, MS 39073-9748 / 601-366-8270

Bismuth Cartridge Co., 3500 Maple Ave., Suite 1650, Dallas, TX 75219 / 214-521-5880; FAX: 214-521-9035

Bison Studios, 1409 South Commerce St., Las Vegas, NV 89102 / 702-388-2891; FAX: 702-383-9967

Bitterroot Bullet Co., P.O. Box 412, 2001 Cedar Ave., Lewiston, ID 83501-0412 / 208-743-5635; FAX: 208-743-5635 brootbil@lewiston.com

BKL Technologies, PO Box 5237, Brownsville, TX 78523

Black Belt Bullets (See Big Bore Express)

Black Hills Ammunition, Inc., P.O. Box 3090, Rapid City, SD 57709-3090 / 605-348-5150; FAX: 605-348-9827

Black Hills Shooters Supply, P.O. Box 4220, Rapid City, SD 57709 / 800-289-2506

Black Powder Products, 67 Township Rd. 1411, Chesapeake, OH 45619 / 614-867-8047

Black Sheep Brand, 3220 W. Gentry Parkway, Tyler, TX 75702 / 903-592-3853; FAX: 903-592-0527

Blacksmith Corp., P.O. Box 280, North Hampton, OH 45349 / 800-531-2665; FAX: 937-969-8399 sales@blacksmith.com www.blacksmithcorp.com

BlackStar AccuMax Barrels, 11501 Brittmoore Park Drive, Houston, TX 77041 / 281-721-6040; FAX: 281-721-6041

BlackStar Barrel Accurizing (See BlackStar AccuMax)

Blacktail Mountain Books, 42 First Ave. W., Kalispell, MT 59901 / 406-257-5573

Blammo Ammo, P.O. Box 1677, Seneca, SC 29679 / 803-882-1768

Blaser Jagdwaffen GmbH, D-88316, Isny Im Allgau, GERMANY

Blount, Inc., Sporting Equipment Div., 2299 Snake River Ave., P.O. Box 856, Lewiston, ID 83501 / 800-627-3640 or 208-746-2351; FAX: 208-799-3904

Blount/Outers ATK, P..O Box 39, Onalaska, WI 54650 / 608-781-5800; FAX: 608-781-0368

Blue and Gray Products Inc. (See Ox-Yoke Originals)

Blue Book Publications, Inc., 8009 34th Ave. S., Ste. 175, Minneapolis, MN 55425 / 800-877-4867 or 612-854-5229; FAX: 612-853-1486 bluebook@bluebookinc.com www.bluebookinc.com

Blue Mountain Bullets, 64146 Quail Ln., Box 231, John Day, OR 97845 / 541-820-4594; FAX: 541-820-4594

Blue Ridge Machinery & Tools, Inc., P.O. Box 536-GD, Hurricane, WV 25526 / 800-872-6500; FAX: 304-562-5311 blueridgemachine@worldnet.att.net www.blueridgemachinery.com

BMC Supply, Inc., 26051 - 179th Ave. S.E., Kent, WA 98042

Bob Allen Co.214 SW Jackson, P.O. Box 477, Des Moines, IA 50315 / 800-685-7020; FAX: 515-283-0779

Bob Rogers Gunsmithing, P.O. Box 305, 344 S. Walnut St., Franklin Grove, IL 61031 / 815-456-2685; FAX: 815-456-2777

Bob's Gun Shop, P.O. Box 200, Royal, AR 71968 / 501-767-1970; FAX: 501-767-1970 gunparts@hsnp.com www.gun-parts.com

Bob's Tactical Indoor Shooting Range & Gun Shop, 90 Lafayette Rd., Salisbury, MA 01952 / 508-465-5561

Boessler, Erich, Am Vogeltal 3, 97702, Munnerstadt, GERMANY

Boker USA, Inc., 1550 Balsam Street, Lakewood, CO 80215 / 303-462-0662; FAX: 303-462-0668 sales@bokerusa.com bokerusa.com

Boltin, John M., P.O. Box 644, Estill, SC 29918 / 803-625-2185

Bo-Mar Tool & Mfg. Co., 6136 State Hwy. 300, Longview, TX 75604 / 903-759-4784; FAX: 903-759-9141 marykor@earthlink.net bo-mar.com

Bonadimani, Benso. See: BERSA S.A.

Bonanza (See Forster Products), 310 E. Lanark Ave., Lanark, IL 61046 / 815-493-6360; FAX: 815-493-2371

Bond Arms, Inc., P.O. Box 1296, Granbury, TX 76048 / 817-573-4445; FAX: 817-573-5636

Bond Custom Firearms, 8954 N. Lewis Ln., Bloomington, IN 47408 / 812-332-4519

Bondini Paolo, Via Sorrento 345, San Carlo di Cesena, ITALY / 0547-663-240; FAX: 0547-663-780

Boone Trading Co., Inc., PO Box 669, Brinnon, WA 98320 / 800-423-1945; or 360-796-4330; FAX: 360-796-4511 sales@boonetrading.com boonetrading.com

Boone's Custom Ivory Grips, Inc., 562 Coyote Rd., Brinnon, WA 98320 / 206-796-4330

Boonie Packer Products, P.O. Box 12517, Salem, OR 97309-0517 / 800-477-3244; or 503-581-3244; FAX: 503-581-3191 booniepacker@aol.com www.booniepacker.com

Borden Ridges Rimrock Stocks, RR 1 Box 250 BC, Springville, PA 18844 / 570-965-2505; FAX: 570-965-2328

Borden Rifles Inc., RD 1, Box 250BC, Springville, PA 18844 / 717-965-2505; FAX: 717-965-2328

Border Barrels Ltd., Riccarton Farm, Newcastleton, SCOTLAND UK

Borovnik KG, Ludwig, 9170 Ferlach, Bahnhofstrasse 7, AUSTRIA / 042 27 24 42; FAX: 042 26 43 49

Bosis (See U.S. Importer-New England Arms Co.)

Boss Manufacturing Co., 221 W. First St., Kewanee, IL 61443 / 309-852-2131; or 800-447-4581; FAX: 309-852-0848

Bostick Wildlife Calls, Inc., P.O. Box 728, Estill, SC 29918 / 803-625-2210; or 803-625-4512

Bowen Classic Arms Corp., PO Box 67, Louisville, TN 37777 / 865-984-3583 www.bowenclassicarms.com

Bowen Knife Co., Inc., P.O. Box 590, Blackshear, GA 31516 / 912-449-4794

Bowerly, Kent, 710 Golden Pheasant Dr., Redmond, OR 97756 / 541-923-3501 jkbowerly@aol.com

Boyds' Gunstock Industries, Inc., 25376 403 Rd. Ave., Mitchell, SD 57301 / 605-996-5011; FAX: 605-996-9878

Brace, Larry D., 771 Blackfoot Ave., Eugene, OR 97404 / 541-688-1278; FAX: 541-607-5833

Brass Eagle, Inc., 7050A Bramalea Rd., Unit 19, Mississauga,, ON L4Z 1C7 CANADA / 416-848-4844

Brauer Bros., 1520 Washington Avenue., St. Louis, MO 63103 / 314-231-2864; FAX: 314-249-4952 www.brauerbros.com

Break-Free, Inc., 1035 S. Linwood Ave., Santa Ana, CA 92705 / 714-953-1900; FAX: 714-953-0402

Brenneke GmbH, P.O. Box 1646, 30837 Langenhagen, Langenhagen, GERMANY / +49-511-97262-0; FAX: +49-511-97262-62 info@brenneke.de brenneke.com

Bridgeman Products, Harry Jaffin, 153 B Cross Slope Court, Englishtown, NJ 07726 / 732-536-3604; FAX: 732-972-1004

Bridgers Best, P.O. Box 1410, Berthoud, CO 80513

Briese Bullet Co., Inc., RR1, Box 108, Tappen, ND 58487 / 701-327-4578; FAX: 701-327-4579

Brigade Quartermasters, 1025 Cobb International Blvd., Dept. VH, Kennesaw, GA 30144-4300 / 404-428-1248; or 800-241-3125; FAX: 404-426-7726

Briganti, A.J., 512 Rt. 32, Highland Mills, NY 10930 / 914-928-9573

Briley Mfg. Inc., 1230 Lumpkin, Houston, TX 77043 / 800-331-5718; or 713-932-6995; FAX: 713-932-1043

Brill, R. See: ROYAL ARMS INTERNATIONAL

British Sporting Arms, RR1, Box 130, Millbrook, NY 12545 / 914-677-8303

Broad Creek Rifle Works, Ltd., 120 Horsey Ave., Laurel, DE 19956 / 302-875-5446; FAX: 302-875-1448 bcrw4guns@aol.com

Brockman's Custom Gunsmithing, P.O. Box 357, Gooding, ID 83330 / 208-934-5050

Brocock Ltd., 43 River Street, Digbeth, Birmingham, B5 5SA ENGLAND / 011-021-773-1200; FAX: 011-021-773-1211 sales@brocock.co.un www.brocock.co.uk

Broken Gun Ranch, 10739 126 Rd., Spearville, KS 67876 / 316-385-2587; FAX: 316-385-2597

Brooker, Dennis, Rt. 1, Box 12A, Derby, IA 50068 / 515-533-2103

Brooks Tactical Systems-Agrip, 279-C Shorewood Ct., Fox Island, WA 98333 / 253-549-2866 FAX: 253-549-2703 brooks@brookstactical.com www.brookstactical.com

Brown, H. R. (See Silhouette Leathers)

Brown Co., E. Arthur, 3404 Pawnee Dr., Alexandria, MN 56308 / 320-762-8847

Brown Dog Ent., 2200 Calle Camelia, 1000 Oaks, CA 91360 / 805-497-2318; FAX: 805-497-1618

Brown Precision, Inc., 7786 Molinos Ave., Los Molinos, CA 96055 / 530-384-2506; FAX: 916-384-1638 www.brownprecision.com

Brown Products, Inc., Ed, 43825 Muldrow Trail, Perry, MO 63462 / 573-565-3261; FAX: 573-565-2791 www.edbrown.com

Brownells, Inc., 200 S. Front St., Montezuma, IA 50171 / 641-623-5401; FAX: 641-623-3896 orderdesk@brownells.com www.brownells.com

Browning Arms Co., One Browning Place, Morgan, UT 84050 / 801-876-2711; FAX: 801-876-3331

Browning Arms Co. (Parts & Service), 3005 Arnold Tenbrook Rd., Arnold, MO 63010 / 617-287-6800; FAX: 617-287-9751

BRP, Inc. High Performance Cast Bullets, 1210 Alexander Rd., Colorado Springs, CO 80909 / 719-633-0658

Brunton U.S.A., 620 E. Monroe Ave., Riverton, WY 82501 / 307-856-6559; FAX: 307-856-1840

Bryan & Assoc., R D Sauls, PO Box 5772, Anderson, SC 29623-5772 / 864-261-6810 bryanandac@aol.com www.huntersweb.com/bryanandac

Brynin, Milton, P.O. Box 383, Yonkers, NY 10710 / 914-779-4333

BSA Guns Ltd., Armoury Rd. Small Heath, Birmingham B11 2PP, ENGLAND / 011-021-772-8543; FAX: 011-021-773-0845 sales@bsagun.com www.bsagun.com

BSA Optics, 3911 SW 47th Ave., Ste. 914, Ft. Lauderdale, FL 33314 / 954-581-2144; FAX: 954-581-3165 4info@basaoptics.com www.bsaoptics.com

B-Square Company, Inc., ; ;, P.O. Box 11281, 2708 St. Louis Ave., Ft. Worth, TX 76110 / 817-923-0964 or 800-433-2909; FAX: 817-926-7012

Buchsenmachermeister, Peter Hofer Jagdwaffen, Buchsenmachermeister, Kirchgasse 24 A-9170, Ferlach, AUSTRIA / 43 4227 3683; FAX: 43 4227 368330 peterhofer@hoferwaffen.com www.hoferwaffen.com

Buck Knives, Inc., 1900 Weld Blvd., P.O. Box 1267, El Cajon, CA 92020 / 619-449-1100; or 800-326-2825; FAX: 619-562-5774 8

Buck Stix-SOS Products Co., Box 3, Neenah, WI 54956

Buck Stop Lure Co., Inc., 3600 Grow Rd. NW, P.O. Box 636, Stanton, MI 48888 / 517-762-5091; FAX: 517-762-5124

Buckeye Custom Bullets, 6490 Stewart Rd., Elida, OH 45807 / 419-641-4463

Buckhorn Gun Works, 8109 Woodland Dr., Black Hawk, SD 57718 / 605-787-6472

Buckskin Bullet Co., P.O. Box 1893, Cedar City, UT 84721 / 435-586-3286

Budin, Dave, Main St., Margaretville, NY 12455 / 914-568-4103; FAX: 914-586-4105

Budin, Dave. See: DEL-SPORTS, INC.

Buenger Enterprises/Goldenrod Dehumidifier, 3600 S. Harbor Blvd., Oxnard, CA 93035 / 800-451-6797; or 805-985-5828; FAX: 805-985-1534

Buffalo Arms Co., 660 Vermeer Ct., Ponderay, ID 83852 / 208-263-6953; FAX: 208-265-2096 www.buffaloarms.com

Buffalo Bullet Co., Inc., 12637 Los Nietos Rd., Unit A, Santa Fe Springs, CA 90670 / 800-423-8069; FAX: 562-944-5054

Buffalo Gun Center, 3385 Harlem Rd., Buffalo, NY 14225 / 716-833-2581; FAX: 716-833-2265 www.buffaloguncenter.com

Buffalo Rock Shooters Supply, R.R. 1, Ottawa, IL 61350 / 815-433-2471

Buffer Technologies, P.O. Box 104930, Jefferson City, MO 65110 / 573-634-8529; FAX: 573-634-8522

Bull Mountain Rifle Co., 6327 Golden West Terrace, Billings, MT 59106 / 406-656-0778

Bullberry Barrel Works, Ltd., 2430 W. Bullberry Ln., Hurricane, UT 84737 / 435-635-9866; FAX: 435-635-0348 fred@bullberry.com www.bullberry.com

Bullet Metals, Bill Ferguson, P.O. Box 1238, Sierra Vista, AZ 85636 / 520-458-5321; FAX: 520-458-1421 info@theantimonyman.com www.bullet-metals.com

Bullet N Press, 1210 Jones St., Gastonia, NC 28052 / 704-853-0265 bnpress@quik.com www.nemaine.com/bnpress

Bullet Swaging Supply, Inc., P.O. Box 1056, 303 McMillan Rd., West Monroe, LA 71291 / 318-387-3266; FAX: 318-387-7779 leblackmon@colla.com

Bullseye Bullets, 1808 Turkey Creek Rd. #9, Plant City, FL 33567 / 800-741-6343 bbullets8100@aol.com

Bull-X, Inc., 411 E. Water St., Farmer City, IL 61842-1556 / 309-928-2574 or 800-248-3845; FAX: 309-928-2130

Burkhart Gunsmithing, Don, P.O. Box 852, Rawlins, WY 82301 / 307-324-6007

Burnham Bros., P.O. Box 1148, Menard, TX 78659 / 915-396-4572; FAX: 915-396-4574

Burris Co., Inc., PO Box 1747, 331 E. 8th St., Greeley, CO 80631 / 970-356-1670; FAX: 970-356-8702

Bushmaster Firearms, 999 Roosevelt Trail, Windham, ME 04062 / 800-998-7928; FAX: 207-892-8068 info@bushmaster.com www.bushmaster.com

Bushmaster Hunting & Fishing, 451 Alliance Ave., Toronto, ON M6N 2J1 CANADA / 416-763-4040; FAX: 416-763-0623

Bushnell Sports Optics Worldwide, 9200 Cody, Overland Park, KS 66214 / 913-752-3400 or 800-423-3537; FAX: 913-752-3550

Buster's Custom Knives, P.O. Box 214, Richfield, UT 84701 / 801-896-5319

Butler Creek Corp., 2100 S. Silverstone Way, Meridian, ID 83642-8151 / 800-423-8327 or 406-388-1356; FAX: 406-388-7204

Butler Enterprises, 834 Oberting Rd., Lawrenceburg, IN 47025 / 812-537-3584

Butterfield's, 220 San Bruno Ave., San Francisco, CA 94103 / 415-861-7500; FAX: 415-861-0183 arms@butterfields.com www.butterfields.com

Buzz Fletcher Custom Stockmaker, 117 Silver Road, P.O. Box 189, Taos, NM 87571 / 505-758-3486

C

C&D Special Products (See Claybuster Wads & Harvester Bullets)

C&H Research, 115 Sunnyside Dr., Box 351, Lewis, KS 67552 / 316-324-5445888-324-5445; FAX: 620-324-5984 info@mercuryrecoil.com www.mercuryrecoil.com

C. Palmer Manufacturing Co., Inc., P.O. Box 220, West Newton, PA 15089 / 412-872-8200; FAX: 412-872-8302

C. Sharps Arms Co. Inc./Montana Armory, 100 Centennial Dr., PO Box 885, Big Timber, MT 59011 / 406-932-4353; FAX: 406-932-4443

C.S. Van Gorden & Son, Inc., 1815 Main St., Bloomer, WI 54724 / 715-568-2612 vangorden@bloomer.net

C.W. Erickson's L.L.C., 530 Garrison Ave. NE, PO Box 522, Buffalo, MN 55313 / 763-682-3665; FAX: 763-682-4328 www.archerhunter.com

Cabanas (See U.S. Importer-Mandall Shooting Supply

Cabela's, One Cabela Drive, Sidney, NE 69160 / 308-254-5505; FAX: 308-254-8420

Cabinet Mtn. Outfitters Scents & Lures, P.O. Box 766, Plains, MT 59859 / 406-826-3970

Cache La Poudre Rifleworks, 140 N. College, Ft. Collins, CO 80524 / 920-482-6913

Cali'co Hardwoods, Inc., 3580 Westwind Blvd., Santa Rosa, CA 95403 / 707-546-4045; FAX: 707-546-4027 calicohardwoods@msn.com

Calico Light Weapon Systems, 1489 Greg St., Sparks, NV 89431

California Sights (See Fautheree, Andy)

Cambos Outdoorsman, 532 E. Idaho Ave., Ontario, OR 97914 / 541-889-3135; FAX: 541-889-2633

Cambos Outdoorsman, Fritz Hallberg, 532 E. Idaho Ave., Ontario, OR 97914 / 541-889-3135; FAX: 541-889-2633

Camdex, Inc., 2330 Alger, Troy, MI 48083 / 810-528-2300; FAX: 810-528-0989

Cameron's, 16690 W. 11th Ave., Golden, CO 80401 / 303-279-7365; FAX: 303-628-5413 ncnoremac@aol.com

Camillus Cutlery Co., 54 Main Ave., Camillus, NY 13031 / 315-672-8111; FAX: 315-672-8832

Campbell, Dick, 20000 Silver Ranch Rd., Conifer, CO 80433 / 303-697-0150; FAX: 303-697-0150 dicksknives@aol.com

Camp-Cap Products, P.O. Box 3805, Chesterfield, MO 63006 / 314-532-4340; FAX: 314-532-4340

Cannon Safe, Inc., 216 S. 2nd Ave. #BLD-932, San Bernardino, CA 92400 / 310-692-0636; or 800-242-1055; FAX: 310-692-7252

Canons Delcour, Rue J.B. Cools, B-4040, Herstal, BELGIUM / 32.(0)42.40.61.40; FAX: 32(0)42.40.22.88

Canyon Cartridge Corp., P.O. Box 152, Albertson, NY 11507 FAX: 516-294-8946

Cape Outfitters, 599 County Rd. 206, Cape Girardeau, MO 63701 / 573-335-4103; FAX: 573-335-1555

Caraville Manufacturing, P.O. Box 4545, Thousand Oaks, CA 91359 / 805-499-1234

Carbide Checkering Tools (See J&R Engineering)

Carhartt,Inc., P.O. Box 600, 3 Parklane Blvd., Dearborn, MI 48121 / 800-358-3825; or 313-271-8460; FAX: 313-271-3455

Carl Walther GmbH, B.P. 4325, D-89033, Ulm, GERMANY

Carl Zeiss Inc., 13005 N. Kingston Ave., Chester, VA 23836 / 800-441-3005; FAX: 804-530-8481

Carlson, Douglas R, Antique American Firearms, P.O. Box 71035, Dept GD, Des Moines, IA 50325 / 515-224-6552

Carolina Precision Rifles, 1200 Old Jackson Hwy., Jackson, SC 29831 / 803-827-2069

Carrell, William. See: CARRELL'S PRECISION FIREARMS

Carrell's Precision Firearms, William Carrell, 1952 W.Silver Falls Ct., Meridian, ID 83642-3837

Carry-Lite, Inc., P.O. Box 1587, Fort Smith, AR 72902 / 479-782-897 I; FAX: 479-783-0234

Carter's Gun Shop, 225 G St., Penrose, CO 81240 / 719-372-6240

Cartridge Transfer Group, Pete de Coux, HC 30 Box 932 G, Prescott, AZ 86305-7447 / 928-776-8285; FAX: 928-776-8276 pdbullets@commspeed.net

Cascade Bullet Co., Inc., 2355 South 6th St., Klamath Falls, OR 97601 / 503-884-9316

Cascade Shooters, 2155 N.W. 12th St., Redwood, OR 97756

Case & Sons Cutlery Co., W R, Owens Way, Bradford, PA 16701 / 814-368-4123; or 800-523-6350; FAX: 814-768-5369

Case Sorting System, 12695 Cobblestone Creek Rd., Poway, CA 92064 / 619-486-9340

Cash Mfg. Co., Inc., P.O. Box 130, 201 S. Klein Dr., Waunakee, WI 53597-0130 / 608-849-5664; FAX: 608-849-5664

Caspian Arms, Ltd., 14 North Main St., Hardwick, VT 05843 / 802-472-6454; FAX: 802-472-6709

Cast Performance Bullet Company, PO Box 153, Riverton, WY 82501 / 307-857-2940; FAX: 307-857-3132 castperform@wyoming.com castperformance.com

Casull Arms Corp., P.O. Box 1629, Afton, WY 83110 / 307-886-0200

Cathey Enterprises, Inc., P.O. Box 2202, Brownwood, TX 76804 / 915-643-2553; FAX: 915-643-3653

Cation, 2341 Alger St., Troy, MI 48083 / 810-689-0658; FAX: 810-689-7558

Caywood, Shane J., P.O. Box 321, Minocqua, WI 54548 / 715-277-3866

Caywood Gunmakers, 18 King's Hill Estates, Berryville, AR 72616 / 870-423-4741 www.caywoodguns.com

CBC, Avenida Humberto de Campos 3220, 09400-000, Ribeirao Pires, SP, BRAZIL / 55-11-742-7500; FAX: 55-11-459-7385

CBC-BRAZIL, 3 Cuckoo Lane, Honley, Yorkshire HD7 2BR, ENGLAND / 44-1484-661062; FAX: 44-1484-663709

CCG Enterprises, 5217 E. Belknap St., Halton City, TX 76117 / 800-819-7464

CCI Ammunition ATK, P.O. Box 856, Lewiston, ID 83501 / 208-746-2351 www.cci_ammunition.com

CCL Security Products, 199 Whiting St, New Britain, CT 06051 / 800-733-8588

Cedar Hill Game Calls, Inc., 238 Vic Allen Rd, Downsville, LA 71234 / 318-982-5632; FAX: 318-368-2245

Centaur Systems, Inc., 1602 Foothill Rd., Kalispell, MT 59901 / 406-755-8609; FAX: 406-755-8609

Center Lock Scope Rings, 9901 France Ct., Lakeville, MN 55044 / 612-461-2114

Central Specialties Ltd (See Trigger Lock Division

Century Gun Dist. Inc., 1467 Jason Rd., Greenfield, IN 46140 / 317-462-4524

Century International Arms, Inc., 1161 Holland Dr, Boca Raton, FL 33487

CFVentures, 509 Harvey Dr., Bloomington, IN 47403-1715 paladinwilltravel@yahoo.com

CH Tool & Die Co. (See 4-D Custom Die Co.), 711 N Sandusky St., P.O. Box 889, Mt. Vernon, OH 43050-0889 / 740-397-7214; FAX: 740-397-6600

Chace Leather Products, 507 Alden St., Fall River, MA 02722 / 508-678-7556; FAX: 508-675-9666

Chadick's Ltd., P.O. Box 100, Terrell, TX 75160 / 214-563-7577

Chambers Flintlocks Ltd., Jim, 116 Sams Branch Rd., Candler, NC 28715 / 828-667-8361; FAX: 828-665-0852 www.flintlocks.com

Champion Shooters' Supply, P.O. Box 303, New Albany, OH 43054 / 614-855-1603; FAX: 614-855-1209

Champion Target Co., 232 Industrial Parkway, Richmond, IN 47374 / 800-441-4971

Champion's Choice, Inc., 201 International Blvd., LaVergne, TN 37086 / 615-793-4066; FAX: 615-793-4070 champ.choice@earthlink.net www.champchoice.com

Champlin Firearms, Inc., P.O. Box 3191, Woodring Airport, Enid, OK 73701 / 580-237-7388; FAX: 580-242-6922 info@champlinarms.com www.champlinarms.com

Chapman Academy of Practical Shooting, 4350 Academy Rd., Hallsville, MO 65255 / 573-696-5544; FAX: 573-696-2266 ha@chapmanacademy.com

Chapman, J Ken. See: OLD WEST BULLET MOULDS

Chapman Manufacturing Co., 471 New Haven Rd., PO Box 250, Durham, CT 06422 / 860-349-9228; FAX: 860-349-0084 sales@chapmanmfg.com www.chapmanmfg.com

Chapuis Armes, 21 La Gravoux, BP15, 42380, St. Bonnet-le-Chatea, FRANCE / (33)77.50.06.96

Chapuis USA, 416 Business Park, Bedford, KY 40006

Charter 2000, 273 Canal St, Shelton, CT 06484 / 203-922-1652

Checkmate Refinishing, 370 Champion Dr., Brooksville, FL 34601 / 352-799-5774; FAX: 352-799-2986 checkmatecustom.com

Cheddite, France S.A., 99 Route de Lyon, F-26501, Bourg-les-Valence, FRANCE / 33-75-56-4545; FAX: 33-75-56-3587 export@cheddite.com

Chelsea Gun Club of New York City Inc., 237 Ovington Ave., Apt. D53, Brooklyn, NY 11209 / 718-836-9422; or 718-833-2704

Cherry Creek State Park Shooting Center, 12500 E. Belleview Ave., Englewood, CO 80111 / 303-693-1765

Chet Fulmer's Antique Firearms, P.O. Box 792, Rt. 2 Buffalo Lake, Detroit Lakes, MN 56501 / 218-847-7712

CheVron Bullets, RR1, Ottawa, IL 61350 / 815-433-2471

Cheyenne Pioneer Products, PO Box 28425, Kansas City, MO 64188 / 816-413-9196; FAX: 816-455-2859 cheyennepp@aol.com www.cartridgeboxes.com

Chicago Cutlery Co., 1536 Beech St., Terre Haute, IN 47804 / 800-457-2665

Chicasaw Gun Works, 4 Mi. Mkr., Pluto Rd., Box 868, Shady Spring, WV 25918-0868 / 304-763-2848; FAX: 304-763-3725

Chipmunk (See Oregon Arms, Inc.)

Choate Machine & Tool Co., Inc., P.O. Box 218, 116 Lovers Ln., Bald Knob, AR 72010 / 501-724-6193; or 800-972-6390; FAX: 501-724-5873

Christensen Arms, 192 East 100 North, Fayette, UT 84630 / 435-528-7999; FAX: 435-528-7494 www.christensenarms.com

Christie's East, 20 Rockefeller Plz., New York, NY 10020-1902 / 212-606-0406 christics.com

Chu Tani Ind., Inc., P.O. Box 2064, Cody, WY 82414-2064

Chuck's Gun Shop, P.O. Box 597, Waldo, FL 32694 / 904-468-2264

Chuilli, Stephen, 8895 N. Military Trl. Ste., Ste. 201E, Palm Beach Gardens, FL 33410

Churchill (See U.S. Importer-Ellett Bros.)

Churchill, Winston G., 2838 20 Mile Stream Rd., Proctorville, VT 05153 / 802-226-7772

Churchill Glove Co., James, PO Box 298, Centralia, WA 98531 / 360-736-2816; FAX: 360-330-0151

CIDCO, 21480 Pacific Blvd., Sterling, VA 22170 / 703-444-5353

Ciener Inc., Jonathan Arthur, 8700 Commerce St., Cape Canaveral, FL 32920 / 321-868-2200; FAX: 321-868-2201

Cimarron F.A. Co., P.O. Box 906, Fredericksburg, TX 78624-0906 / 830-997-9090; FAX: 830-997-0802 cimgraph@koc.com www.cimarron-firearms.com

Cincinnati Swaging, 2605 Marlington Ave., Cincinnati, OH 45208

Clark Custom Guns, Inc., 336 Shootout Lane, Princeton, LA 71067 / 318-949-9884; FAX: 318-949-9829

Clark Firearms Engraving, P.O. Box 80746, San Marino, CA 91118 / 818-287-1652

Clarkfield Enterprises, Inc., 1032 10th Ave., Clarkfield, MN 56223 / 612-669-7140

Claro Walnut Gunstock Co., 1235 Stanley Ave., Chico, CA 95928 / 530-342-5188; FAX: 530-342-5199 wally@clarowalnutgunstock.com www.clarowalnutgunstock.com

Classic Arms Company, Rt 1 Box 120F, Burnet, TX 78611 / 512-756-4001

Classic Arms Corp., P.O. Box 106, Dunsmuir, CA 96025-0106 / 530-235-2000

Classic Old West Styles, 1060 Doniphan Park Circle C, El Paso, TX 79936 / 915-587-0684

Claybuster Wads & Harvester Bullets, 309 Sequoya Dr., Hopkinsville, KY 42240 / 800-922-6287 or 800-284-1746; FAX: 502-885-8088 50

Clean Shot Technologies, 21218 St. Andrews Blvd. Ste 504, Boca Raton, FL 33433 / 888-866-2532

Clearview Mfg. Co., Inc., 413 S. Oakley St., Fordyce, AR 71742 / 501-352-8557; FAX: 501-352-7120

Clearview Products, 3021 N. Portland, Oklahoma City, OK 73107

Cleland's Outdoor World, Inc, 10306 Airport Hwy, Swanton, OH 43558 / 419-865-4713; FAX: 419-865-5865

Clements' Custom Leathercraft, Chas, 1741 Dallas St., Aurora, CO 80010-2018 / 303-364-0403; FAX: 303-739-9824 gryphons@home.com kuntaoslcat.com

Clenzoil Worldwide Corp, Jack Fitzgerald, 25670 1st St., Westlake, OH 44145-1430 / 440-899-0482; FAX: 440-899-0483

Clift Mfg., L. R., 3821 Hammonton Rd., Marysville, CA 95901 / 916-755-3390; FAX: 916-755-3393

Clymer Mfg. Co., 1645 W. Hamlin Rd., Rochester Hills, MI 48309-3312 / 248-853-5555; FAX: 248-853-1530

C-More Systems, P.O. Box 1750, 7553 Gary Rd., Manassas, VA 20108 / 703-361-2663; FAX: 703-361-5881

Cobalt Mfg., Inc., 4020 Mcewen Rd Ste 180, Dallas, TX 75244-5090 / 817-382-8986; FAX: 817-383-4281

Cobra Enterprises, Inc., 1960 S. Milestone Drive, Suite F, Salt Lake City, UT 84104 / 801-908-8301 www.cobrapistols@networld.com

Cobra Sport S.r.l., Via Caduti Nei Lager No. 1, 56020 San Romano, Montopoli v/Arno (Pi, ITALY / 0039-571-450490; FAX: 0039-571-450492

Coffin, Charles H., 3719 Scarlet Ave., Odessa, TX 79762 / 915-366-4729; FAX: 915-366-4729

Coffin, Jim (See Working Guns)

Coffin, Jim. See: WORKING GUNS

Cogar's Gunsmithing, 206 Redwine Dr., Houghton Lake, MI 48629 / 517-422-4591

Coghlan's Ltd., 121 Irene St., Winnipeg, MB R3T 4C7 CANADA / 204-284-9550; FAX: 204-475-4127

Cold Steel Inc., 3036 Seaborg Ave. Ste. A, Ventura, CA 93003 / 800-255-4716; or 800-624-2363; FAX: 805-642-9727

Cole-Grip, 16135 Cohasset St., Van Nuys, CA 91406 / 818-782-4424

Coleman Co., Inc., 250 N. St. Francis, Wichita, KS 67201

Cole's Gun Works, Old Bank Building, Rt. 4 Box 250, Moyock, NC 27958 / 919-435-2345

Collings, Ronald, 1006 Cielta Linda, Vista, CA 92083

Colonial Arms, Inc., P.O. Box 636, Selma, AL 36702-0636 / 334-872-9455; FAX: 334-872-9540 colonialarms@mindspring.com www.colonialarms.com

Colonial Repair, 47 Navarre St., Roslindale, MA 02131-4725 / 617-469-4951

Colorado Gunsmithing Academy, RR 3 Box 79B, El Campo, TX 77437 / 719-336-4099 or 800-754-2046; FAX: 719-336-9642

Colorado School of Trades, 1575 Hoyt St., Lakewood, CO 80215 / 800-234-4594; FAX: 303-233-4723

Colt Blackpowder Arms Co., 110 8th Street, Brooklyn, NY 11215 / 719-499-4678; FAX: 718-768-8056

Colt's Mfg. Co., Inc., PO Box 1868, Hartford, CT 06144-1868 / 800-962-COLT; or 860-236-6311; FAX: 860-244-1449

Compass Industries, Inc., 104 East 25th St., New York, NY 10010 / 212-473-2614 or 800-221-9904; FAX: 212-353-0826

Compasseco, Ltd., 151 Atkinson Hill Ave., Bardtown, KY 40004 / 502-349-0910

Competition Electronics, Inc., 3469 Precision Dr., Rockford, IL 61109 / 815-874-8001; FAX: 815-874-8181

Competitor Corp., Inc., Appleton Business Center, 30 Tricnit Road Unit 16, New Ipswich, NH 03071 / 603-878-3891; FAX: 603-878-3950

Component Concepts, Inc., 530 S Springbrook Road, Newberg, OR 97132 / 503-554-8095; FAX: 503-554-9370 cci@cybcon.com www.phantomonline.com

Concept Development Corp., 16610 E. Laser Drive, Suite 5, Fountain Hills, AZ 85268-6644

Conetrol Scope Mounts, 10225 Hwy. 123 S., Seguin, TX 78155 / 830-379-3030 or 800-CONETROL; FAX: 830-379-3030 email@conetrol.com www.conetrol.com

CONKKO, P.O. Box 40, Broomall, PA 19008 / 215-356-0711

Connecticut Shotgun Mfg. Co., P.O. Box 1692, 35 Woodland St., New Britain, CT 06051 / 860-225-6581; FAX: 860-832-8707

Connecticut Valley Classics (See CVC, BPI)

Conrad, C. A., 3964 Ebert St., Winston-Salem, NC 27127 / 919-788-5469

Cook Engineering Service, 891 Highbury Rd., Vict, 3133 AUSTRALIA

Cooper Arms, P.O. Box 114, Stevensville, MT 59870 / 406-777-0373; FAX: 406-777-5228

Cooper-Woodward, 3800 Pelican Rd., Helena, MT 59602 / 406-458-3800 dolymama@msn.com

Corbin Mfg. & Supply, Inc., 600 Industrial Circle, P.O. Box 2659, White City, OR 97503 / 541-826-5211; FAX: 541-826-8669 sales@corbins.com www.corbins.com

Cor-Bon Inc./Glaser LLC, P.O. Box 173, 1311 Industry Rd., Sturgis, SD 57785 / 605-347-4544 or 800-221-3489; FAX: 605-347-5055 email@corbon.com www.corbon.com

Corkys Gun Clinic, 4401 Hot Springs Dr., Greeley, CO 80634-9226 / 970-330-0516

Corry, John, 861 Princeton Ct., Neshanic Station, NJ 08853 / 908-369-8019

Cosmi Americo & Figlio s.n.c., Via Flaminia 307, Ancona, ITALY / 071-888208; FAX: 39-071-887008

Coulston Products, Inc., P.O. Box 30, 201 Ferry St. Suite 212, Easton, PA 18044-0030 / 215-253-0167; or 800-445-9927; FAX: 215-252-1511

Counter Assault, 120 Industrial Court, Kalispell, MT 59901 / 406-257-4740; FAX: 406-257-6674

Cousin Bob's Mountain Products, 7119 Ohio River Blvd., Ben Avon, PA 15202 / 412-766-5114; FAX: 412-766-5114

Cox, Ed. C., RD 2, Box 192, Prosperity, PA 15329 / 412-228-4984

CP Bullets, 1310 Industrial Hwy #5-6, South Hampton, PA 18966 / 215-953-7264; FAX: 215-953-7275

CQB Training, P.O. Box 1739, Manchester, MO 63011

Craftguard, 3624 Logan Ave., Waterloo, IA 50703 / 319-232-2959; FAX: 319-234-0804

Crandall Tool & Machine Co., 19163 21 Mile Rd., Tustin, MI 49688 / 616-829-4430

Creedmoor Sports, Inc., P.O. Box 1040, Oceanside, CA 92051 / 767-757-5529; FAX: 760-757-5558 shoot@creedmoorsports.com www.creedmoorsports.com

Creek Side Metal & Woodcrafters, Fishers Hill, VA 22626 / 703-465-3903

Creighton Audette, 19 Highland Circle, Springfield, VT 05156 / 802-885-2331

Crimson Trace Lasers, 8090 SW Cirrus Dr., Beverton, OR 97008 / 800-442-2406; FAX: 503-627-0166 www.crimsontrace.com

Crit'R Call (See Rocky Mountain Wildlife Products)

Crosman Airguns, Rts. 5 and 20, E. Bloomfield, NY 14443 / 716-657-6161; FAX: 716-657-5405

Crosman Blades (See Coleman Co., Inc.)

Crouse's Country Cover, P.O. Box 160, Storrs, CT 06268 / 860-423-8736

CRR, Inc./Marble's Inc., 420 Industrial Park, P.O. Box 111, Gladstone, MI 49837 / 906-428-3710; FAX: 906-428-3711

Crucelegui, Hermanos (See U.S. Importer-Mandall)

Cubic Shot Shell Co., Inc., 98 Fatima Dr., Campbell, OH 44405 / 330-755-0349

Cullity Restoration, 209 Old Country Rd., East Sandwich, MA 02537 / 508-888-1147

Cumberland Arms, 514 Shafer Road, Manchester, TN 37355 / 800-797-8414

Cumberland Mountain Arms, P.O. Box 710, Winchester, TN 37398 / 615-967-8414; FAX: 615-967-9199

Cummings Bullets, 1417 Esperanza Way, Escondido, CA 92027

Cupp, Alana, Custom Engraver, PO Box 207, Annabella, UT 84711 / 801-896-4834

Curly Maple Stock Blanks (See Tiger-Hunt)

Curtis Cast Bullets, 527 W. Babcock St., Bozeman, MT 59715 / 406-587-8117; FAX: 406-587-8117

Curtis Gun Shop (See Curtis Cast Bullets)

Custom Bullets by Hoffman, 2604 Peconic Ave., Seaford, NY 11783

Custom Calls, 607 N. 5th St., Burlington, IA 52601 / 319-752-4465

Custom Checkering Service, Kathy Forster, 2124 S.E. Yamhill St., Portland, OR 97214 / 503-236-5874

Custom Chronograph, Inc., 5305 Reese Hill Rd., Sumas, WA 98295 / 360-988-7801

Custom Firearms (See Ahrends, Kim)

Custom Gun Stocks, 3062 Turners Bend Rd, McMinnville, TN 37110 / 615-668-3912

Custom Products (See Jones Custom Products)

Custom Quality Products, Inc., 345 W. Girard Ave., P.O. Box 71129, Madison Heights, MI 48071 / 810-585-1616; FAX: 810-585-0644

Custom Riflestocks, Inc., Michael M. Kokolus, 7005 Herber Rd., New Tripoli, PA 18066 / 610-298-3013; FAX: 610-298-2431 mkokolus@prodigy.net

Custom Single Shot Rifles, 9651 Meadows Lane, Guthrie, OK 73044 / 405-282-3634

Custom Stocking, Mike Yee, 29927 56 Pl. S., Auburn, WA 98001 / 253-839-3991

Custom Tackle and Ammo, P.O. Box 1886, Farmington, NM 87499 / 505-632-3539

Cutco Cutlery, P.O. Box 810, Olean, NY 14760 / 716-372-3111

CVA, 5988 Peachtree Corners East, Norcross, GA 30071 / 770-449-4687; FAX: 770-242-8546 info@cva.com www.cva.com

Cylinder & Slide, Inc., William R. Laughridge, 245 E. 4th St., Fremont, NE 68025 / 402-721-4277; FAX: 402-721-0263 bill@cylinder-slide.com www.clinder-slide.com

CZ USA, PO Box 171073, Kansas City, KS 66117 / 913-321-1811; FAX: 913-321-4901

D

D&D Gunsmiths, Ltd., 363 E. Elmwood, Troy, MI 48083 / 810-583-1512; FAX: 810-583-1524

D&G Precision Duplicators (See Greene Precision)

D&H Precision Tooling, 7522 Barnard Mill Rd., Ringwood, IL 60072 / 815-653-4011

D&L Industries (See D.J. Marketing)

D&L Sports, P.O. Box 651, Gillette, WY 82717 / 307-686-4008

D.C.C. Enterprises, 259 Wynburn Ave., Athens, GA 30601

D.J. Marketing, 10602 Horton Ave., Downey, CA 90241 / 310-806-0891; FAX: 310-806-6231

Dade Screw Machine Products, 2319 NW 7th Ave., Miami, FL 33127 / 305-573-5050

Daewoo Precision Industries Ltd., 34-3 Yeoeuido-Dong, Yeongdeungoo-GU 15th Fl., Seoul, KOREA

Daisy Outdoor Products, P.O. Box 220, Rogers, AR 72757 / 479-636-1200; FAX: 479-636-0573 www.daisy.com

Dakota (See U.S. Importer-EMF Co., Inc.)

Dakota Arms, Inc., 130 Industry Road, Sturgis, SD 57785 / 605-347-4686; FAX: 605-347-4459 info@dakotaarms.com www.dakotaarms.com

Dakota Corp., 77 Wales St., P.O. Box 543, Rutland, VT 05701 / 802-775-6062; or 800-451-4167; FAX: 802-773-3919

Daly, Charles (See U.S. Importer), P.O. Box 6625, Harrisburg, PA 17112 / 717-540-8518 www.charlesdaly.com

Da-Mar Gunsmith's Inc., 102 1st St., Solvay, NY 13209

damascususa@inteliport.com, 149 Deans Farm Rd., Tyner, NC 27980 / 252-221-2010; FAX: 252-221-2010 damascususa@inteliport.com

Dan Wesson Firearms, 119 Kemper Lane, Norwich, NY 13815 / 607-336-1174; FAX: 607-336-2730

Danforth, Mikael. See: VEKTOR USA

Dangler, Homer L., 2870 Lee Marie Dr., Adrian, MI 49220 / 517-266-1997

Danner Shoe Mfg. Co., 12722 NE Airport Way, Portland, OR 97230 / 503-251-1100; or 800-345-0430; FAX: 503-251-1119

Dan's Whetstone Co., Inc., 130 Timbs Place, Hot Springs, AR 71913 / 501-767-1616; FAX: 501-767-9598 questions@danswhetstone.com www.danswhetstone.com

Danuser Machine Co., 550 E. Third St., P.O. Box 368, Fulton, MO 65251 / 573-642-2246; FAX: 573-642-2240 sales@danuser.com www.danuser.com

Dara-Nes, Inc. (See Nesci Enterprises, Inc.)

D'Arcy Echols & Co., PO Box 421, Millville, UT 84326 / 435-755-6842

Darlington Gun Works, Inc., P.O. Box 698, 516 S. 52 Bypass, Darlington, SC 29532 / 803-393-3931

Dart Bell/Brass (See MAST Technology)

Darwin Hensley Gunmaker, PO Box 329, Brightwood, OR 97011 / 503-622-5411

Data Tech Software Systems, 19312 East Eldorado Drive, Aurora, CO 80013

Dave Norin Schrank's Smoke & Gun, 2010 Washington St., Waukegan, IL 60085 / 708-662-4034

Dave's Gun Shop, P.O. Box 2824, Casper, WY 82602-2824 / 307-754-9724

David Clark Co., Inc., PO Box 15054, Worcester, MA 01615-0054 / 508-756-6216; FAX: 508-753-5827 sales@davidclark.com www.davidclark.com

David Condon, Inc., 109 E. Washington St., Middleburg, VA 22117 / 703-687-5642

David Miller Co., 3131 E Greenlee Rd, Tucson, AZ 85716 / 520-326-3117

David R. Chicoine, 1210 Jones Street, Gastonia, NC 28052 / 704-853-0265 bnpress@quik.com

David W. Schwartz Custom Guns, 2505 Waller St., Eau Claire, WI 54703 / 715-832-1735

Davide Pedersoli and Co., Via Artigiani 57, Gardone VT, Brescia 25063, ITALY / 030-8912402; or 030-8915000;

FAX: 030-8911019 info@davidepedersoli.com www.davide_pedersoli.com

Davis, Don, 1619 Heights, Katy, TX 77493 / 713-391-3090

Davis Industries (See Cobra Enterprises, Inc.)

Davis Products, Mike, 643 Loop Dr., Moses Lake, WA 98837 / 509-765-6178; or 509-766-7281

Daystate Ltd., Birch House Lanee, Cotes Heath Staffs, ST15.022, ENGLAND / 01782-791755; FAX: 01782-791617

Dayton Traister, 4778 N. Monkey Hill Rd., P.O. Box 593, Oak Harbor, WA 98277 / 360-679-4657; FAX: 360-675-1114

DBI Books Division of Krause Publications, 700 E. State St., Iola, WI 54990-0001 / 715-445-2214

D-Boone Ent., Inc., 5900 Colwyn Dr., Harrisburg, PA 17109

de Coux, Pete (See Cartridge Transfer Group)

Dead Eye's Sport Center, 76 Baer Rd., Shickshinny, PA 18655 / 570-256-7432 deadeyeprizz@aol.com

Deepeeka Exports Pvt. Ltd., D-78, Saket, Meerut-250-006, INDIA / 011-91-121-640363 or ; FAX: 011-91-121-640988 deepeeka@poboxes.com www.deepeeka.com

Defense Training International, Inc., 749 S. Lemay, Ste. A3-337, Ft. Collins, CO 80524 / 303-482-2520; FAX: 303-482-0548

Degen Inc. (See Aristocrat Knives)

deHaas Barrels, 20049 W. State Hwy. Z, Ridgeway, MO 64481 / 660-872-6308

Del Rey Products, P.O. Box 5134, Playa Del Rey, CA 90296-5134 / 213-823-0494

Delhi Gun House, 1374 Kashmere Gate, New Delhi 110 006, INDIA / 2940974; or 394-0974; FAX: 2917344 dgh@vsnl.com

Delorge, Ed, 6734 W. Main, Houma, LA 70360 / 985-223-0206

Del-Sports, Inc., Dave Budin, Box 685, 817 Main St., Margaretville, NY 12455 / 845-586-4103; FAX: 845-586-4105

Delta Arms Ltd., P.O. Box 1000, Delta, VT 84624-1000

Delta Enterprises, 284 Hagemann Drive, Livermore, CA 94550

Delta Frangible Ammunition LLC, P.O. Box 2350, Stafford, VA 22555-2350 / 540-720-5778 or 800-339-1933; FAX: 540-720-5667 dfa@dfanet.com www.dfanet.com

Dem-Bart Checkering Tools, Inc., 1825 Bickford Ave., Snohomish, WA 98290 / 360-568-7356 walt@dembartco.com www.dembartco.com

Denver Instrument Co., 6542 Fig St., Arvada, CO 80004 / 800-321-1135; or 303-431-7255; FAX: 303-423-4831

DeSantis Holster & Leather Goods, Inc., P.O. Box 2039, 149 Denton Ave., New Hyde Park, NY 11040-0701 / 516-354-8000; FAX: 516-354-7501

Desert Mountain Mfg., P.O. Box 130184, Coram, MT 59913 / 800-477-0762; or 406-387-5361; FAX: 406-387-5361

Detroit-Armor Corp., 720 Industrial Dr. No. 112, Cary, IL 60013 / 708-639-7666; FAX: 708-639-7694

DGR Custom Rifles, 4191 37th Ave. SE, Tappen, ND 58487 / 701-327-8135

DGS, Inc., Dale A. Storey, 1117 E. 12th, Casper, WY 82601 / 307-237-2414; FAX: 307-237-2414 dalest@trib.com www.dgsrifle.com

DHB Products, 336 River View Dr., Verona, VA 24482-2547 / 703-836-2648

Diamond Machining Technology, Inc. (See DMT)

Diamond Mfg. Co., P.O. Box 174, Wyoming, PA 18644 / 800-233-9601

Dibble, Derek A., 555 John Downey Dr., New Britain, CT 06051 / 203-224-2630

Dietz Gun Shop & Range, Inc., 421 Range Rd., New Braunfels, TX 78132 / 210-885-4662

Dilliott Gunsmithing, Inc., 657 Scarlett Rd., Dandridge, TN 37725 / 865-397-9204 gunsmithd@aol.com dilliottgunsmithing.com

Dillon Precision Products, Inc., 8009 East Dillon's Way, Scottsdale, AZ 85260 / 480-948-8009; or 800-762-3845; FAX: 480-998-2786 sales@dillonprecision.com www.dillonprecision.com

Dina Arms Corporation, P.O. Box 46, Royersford, PA 19468 / 610-287-0266; FAX: 610-287-0266

Dixie Gun Works, P.O. Box 130, Union City, TN 38281 / 731-885-0700; FAX: 731-885-0440 info@dixiegunworks.com www.dixiegunworks.com

Dixon Muzzleloading Shop, Inc., 9952 Kunkels Mill Rd., Kempton, PA 19529 / 610-756-6271 dixonmuzzleloading.com

DKT, Inc., 14623 Vera Drive, Union, MI 49130-9744 / 800-741-7083 orders; FAX: 616-641-2015

DLO Mfg., 10807 SE Foster Ave., Arcadia, FL 33821-7304

DMT--Diamond Machining Technology Inc., 85 Hayes Memorial Dr., Marlborough, MA 01752 FAX: 508-485-3924

Dohring Bullets, 100 W. 8 Mile Rd., Ferndale, MI 48220

Dolbare, Elizabeth, P.O. Box 502, Dubois, WY 82513-0502

Domino, PO Box 108, 20019 Settimo Milanese, Milano, ITALY / 1-39-2-33512040; FAX: 1-39-2-33511587

Donnelly, C. P., 405 Kubli Rd., Grants Pass, OR 97527 / 541-846-6604

Doskocil Mfg. Co., Inc., P.O. Box 1246, 4209 Barnett, Arlington, TX 76017 / 817-467-5116; FAX: 817-472-9810

Douglas Barrels, Inc., 5504 Big Tyler Rd., Charleston, WV 25313-1398 / 304-776-1341; FAX: 304-776-8560 www.benchrest.com/douglas

Downsizer Corp., P.O. Box 710316, Santee, CA 92072-0316 / 619-448-5510 www.downsizer.com

DPMS (Defense Procurement Manufacturing Services, Inc.), 13983 Industry Avenue, Becker, MN 55308 / 800-578-DPMS; or 763-261-5600 FAX: 763-261-5599

Dr. O's Products Ltd., P.O. Box 111, Niverville, NY 12130 / 518-784-3333; FAX: 518-784-2800

Drain, Mark, SE 3211 Kamilche Point Rd., Shelton, WA 98584 / 206-426-5452

Dremel Mfg. Co., 4915-21st St., Racine, WI 53406

Dri-Slide, Inc., 411 N. Darling, Fremont, MI 49412 / 616-924-3950

Dropkick, 1460 Washington Blvd., Williamsport, PA 17701 / 717-326-6561; FAX: 717-326-4950

DS Arms, Inc., P.O. Box 370, 27 West 990 Industrial Ave., Barrington, IL 60010 / 847-277-7258; FAX: 847-277-7259 www.dsarms.com

DTM International, Inc., 40 Joslyn Rd., P.O. Box 5, Lake Orion, MI 48362 / 313-693-6670

Duane A. Hobbie Gunsmithing, 2412 Pattie Ave, Wichita, KS 67216 / 316-264-8266

Duane's Gun Repair (See DGR Custom Rifles)

Dubber, Michael W., P.O. Box 312, Evansville, IN 47702 / 812-424-9000; FAX: 812-424-6551

Duck Call Specialists, P.O. Box 124, Jerseyville, IL 62052 / 618-498-9855

Duffy, Charles E (See Guns Antique & Modern DBA), Williams Lane, PO Box 2, West Hurley, NY 12491 / 914-679-2997

Du-Lite Corp., 171 River Rd., Middletown, CT 06457 / 203-347-2505; FAX: 203-347-9404

Dumoulin, Ernest, Rue Florent Boclinville 8-10, 13-4041, Votten, BELGIUM / 41 27 78 92

Duncan's Gun Works, Inc., 1619 Grand Ave., San Marcos, CA 92069 / 760-727-0515

DunLyon R&D Inc., 52151 E. US Hwy. 60, Miami, AZ 85539 / 928-473-9027

Duofold, Inc., RD 3 Rt. 309, Valley Square Mall, Tamaqua, PA 18252 / 717-386-2666; FAX: 717-386-3652

Dybala Gun Shop, P.O. Box 1024, FM 3156, Bay City, TX 77414 / 409-245-0866

Dykstra, Doug, 411 N. Darling, Fremont, MI 49412 / 616-924-3950

Dynalite Products, Inc., 215 S. Washington St., Greenfield, OH 45123 / 513-981-2124

Dynamit Nobel-RWS, Inc., 81 Ruckman Rd., Closter, NJ 07624 / 201-767-7971; FAX: 201-767-1589

E

E&L Mfg., Inc., 4177 Riddle By Pass Rd., Riddle, OR 97469 / 541-874-2137; FAX: 541-874-3107

E. Arthur Brown Co., 3404 Pawnee Dr., Alexandria, MN 56308 / 320-762-8847

E.A.A. Corp., P.O. Box 1299, Sharpes, FL 32959 / 407-639-4842; or 800-536-4442; FAX: 407-639-7006

Eagan, Donald V., P.O. Box 196, Benton, PA 17814 / 717-925-6134

Eagle Arms, Inc. (See ArmaLite, Inc.)

Eagle Grips, Eagle Business Center, 460 Randy Rd., Carol Stream, IL 60188 / 800-323-6144; or 708-260-0400; FAX: 708-260-0486

Eagle Imports, Inc., 1750 Brielle Ave., Unit B1, Wanamassa, NJ 07712 / 908-493-0333

E-A-R, Inc., Div. of Cabot Safety Corp., 5457 W. 79th St., Indianapolis, IN 46268 / 800-327-3431; FAX: 800-488-8007

EAW (See U.S. Importer-New England Custom Gun Serv

Eckelman Gunsmithing, 3125 133rd St. SW, Fort Ripley, MN 56449 / 218-829-3176

Eclectic Technologies, Inc., 45 Grandview Dr., Suite A, Farmington, CT 06034

Ed Brown Products, Inc., P.O. Box 492, Perry, MO 63462 / 573-565-3261; FAX: 573-565-2791 edbrown@edbrown.com www.edbrown.com

Edenpine, Inc. c/o Six Enterprises, Inc., 320 D Turtle Creek Ct., San Jose, CA 95125 / 408-999-0201; FAX: 408-999-0216

EdgeCraft Corp., S. Weiner, 825 Southwood Road, Avondale, PA 19311 / 610-268-0500; or 800-342-3255; FAX: 610-268-3545 www.edgecraft.com

Edmisten Co., P.O. Box 1293, Boone, NC 28607

Edmund Scientific Co., 101 E. Gloucester Pike, Barrington, NJ 08033 / 609-543-6250

Ednar, Inc., 2-4-8 Kayabacho, Nihonbashi Chuo-ku, Tokyo, JAPAN / 81(Japan)-3-3667-1651; FAX: 81-3-3661-8113

Ed's Gun House, Ed Kukowski, P.O. Box 62, Minnesota City, MN 55959 / 507-689-2925

Eezox, Inc., P.O. Box 772, Waterford, CT 06385-0772 / 800-462-3331; FAX: 860-447-3484

Effebi SNC-Dr. Franco Beretta, via Rossa, 4, 25062, ITALY / 030-2751955; FAX: 030-2180414

Efficient Machinery Co., 12878 N.E. 15th Pl., Bellevue, WA 98005 / 425-453-9318 or 800-375-8554; FAX: 425-453-9311 priemc@aol.com www.sturdybench.com

Eggleston, Jere D., 400 Saluda Ave., Columbia, SC 29205 / 803-799-3402

Eichelberger Bullets, Wm., 158 Crossfield Rd., King Of Prussia, PA 19406

Ekol Leather Care, P.O. Box 2652, West Lafayette, IN 47906 / 317-463-2250; FAX: 317-463-7004

El Paso Saddlery Co., P.O. Box 27194, El Paso, TX 79926 / 915-544-2233; FAX: 915-544-2535 epsaddlery.com www.epsaddlery.com

Electro Prismatic Collimators, Inc., 1441 Manatt St., Lincoln, NE 68521

Electronic Shooters Protection, Inc., 15290 Gadsden Ct., Brighton, CO 80603 / 800-797-7791; FAX: 303-659-8668

Electronic Trigger Systems, Inc., PO Box 13, 230 Main St. S., Hector, MN 55342 / 320-848-2760; FAX: 320-848-2760

Eley Ltd., P.O. Box 705, Witton, Birmingham, B6 7UT ENGLAND / 021-356-8899; FAX: 021-331-4173

Elite Ammunition, P.O. Box 3251, Oakbrook, IL 60522 / 708-366-9006

Ellett Bros., 267 Columbia Ave., P.O. Box 128, Chapin, SC 29036 / 803-345-3751; or 800-845-3711; FAX: 803-345-1820

Ellicott Arms, Inc. / Woods Pistolsmithing, 8390 Sunset Dr., Ellicott City, MD 21043 / 410-465-7979

Elliott Inc., G. W., 514 Burnside Ave, East Hartford, CT 06108 / 203-289-5741; FAX: 203-289-3137

EMAP USA, 6420 Wilshire Blvd., Los Angeles, CA 90048 / 213-782-2000; FAX: 213-782-2867

Emerging Technologies, Inc. (See Laseraim Technologies, Inc.)

EMF Co., Inc., 1900 E. Warner Ave., Suite 1-D, Santa Ana, CA 92705 / 949-261-6611; FAX: 949-756-0133

Empire Cutlery Corp., 12 Kruger Ct., Clifton, NJ 07013 / 201-472-5155; FAX: 201-779-0759

English, Inc., A.G., 708 S. 12th St., Broken Arrow, OK 74012 / 918-251-3399 agenglish@wedzone.net www.agenglish.com

Engraving Artistry, 36 Alto Rd., Burlington, CT 06013 / 203-673-6837 bobburt44@hotmail.com

Engraving Only, Box 55 Rabbit Gulch, Hill City, SD 57745 / 605-574-2239

Enguix Import-Export, Alpujarras 58, Alzira, Valencia, SPAIN / (96) 241 43 95; FAX: (96) 241 43 95

Enhanced Presentations, Inc., 5929 Market St., Wilmington, NC 28405 / 910-799-1622; FAX: 910-799-5004

Enlow, Charles, 895 Box, Beaver, OK 73932 / 405-625-4487

Entre`prise Arms, Inc., 15861 Business Center Dr., Irwindale, CA 91706

EPC, 1441 Manatt St., Lincoln, NE 68521 / 402-476-3946

Epps, Ellwood/Isabella, Box 341, Washago, ON L0K 2B0 CANADA / 705-689-5348

Erhardt, Dennis, 4508 N. Montana Ave., Helena, MT 59602 / 406-442-4533

Essex Arms, P.O. Box 363, Island Pond, VT 05846 / 802-723-6203; FAX: 802-723-6203

Estate Cartridge, Inc., 900 Bob Ehlen Dr., Anoka, MN 55303-7502 / 409-856-7277; FAX: 409-856-5486

Euber Bullets, No. Orwell Rd., Orwell, VT 05760 / 802-948-2621

Euroarms of America, Inc., P.O. Box 3277, Winchester, VA 22604 / 540-662-1863; FAX: 540-662-4464 www.euroarms.net

Euro-Imports, 905 W. Main St. E., El Cajon, CA 92020 / 619-442-7005; FAX: 619-442-7005

European American Armory Corp (See E.A.A. Corp)

Evans Engraving, Robert, 332 Vine St, Oregon City, OR 97045 / 503-656-5693 norbob-ore@msn.com

Eversull Co., Inc., 1 Tracemont, Boyce, LA 71409 / 318-793-8728; FAX: 318-793-5483 bestguns@aol.com

Evolution Gun Works Inc., 4050 B-8 Skyron Dr., Doylestown, PA 18901 / 215-348-9892; FAX: 215-348-1056 egw@pil.net www.egw-guns.com

MANUFACTURER'S DIRECTORY

Excalibur Electro Optics Inc., P.O. Box 400, Fogelsville, PA 18051-0400 / 610-391-9105; FAX: 610-391-9220

Excalibur Publications, P.O. Box 35369, Tucson, AZ 85740 / 520-575-9057 militarypubs@earthlink.net

Excel Industries Inc., 4510 Carter Ct., Chino, CA 91710 / 909-627-2404; FAX: 909-627-7817

Executive Protection Institute, P.O. Box 802, Berryville, VA 22611 / 540-554-2540 ruk.@creslink.net www.personalprotecion.com

Eze-Lap Diamond Prods., P.O. Box 2229, 15164 West State St., Westminster, CA 92683 / 714-847-1555; FAX: 714-897-0280

E-Z-Way Systems, PO Box 4310, Newark, OH 43058-4310 / 614-345-6645; or 800-848-2072; FAX: 614-345-6600

F

F.A.I.R., Via Gitti, 41, 25060 Marcheno (Bres, ITALY / 030/861162-8610344; FAX: 030/8610179 info@fair.it www.fair.it

F.I., Inc. - High Standard Mfg. Co., 5200 Mitchelldale St., Ste. E17, Houston, TX 77092-7222 / 713-462-4200; or 800-272-7816; FAX: 713-681-5665 info@highstandard.com www.highstandard.com

Fabarm S.p.A., Via Averolda 31, 25039 Travagliato, Brescia, ITALY / 030-6863629; FAX: 030-6863684 info@fabarm.com www.fabarm.com

Fagan & Co.Inc, 22952 15 Mile Rd, Clinton Township, MI 48035 / 810-465-4637; FAX: 810-792-6996

Faith Associates, PO Box 549, Flat Rock, NC 28731-0549 FAX: 828-697-6827

Faloon Industries, Inc., P.O. Box 1060, Tijeras, NM 87059 / 505-281-3783

Far North Outfitters, Box 1252, Bethel, AK 99559

Farm Form Decoys, Inc., 1602 Biovu, P.O. Box 748, Galveston, TX 77553 / 409-744-0762; or 409-765-6361; FAX: 409-765-8513

Farr Studio, Inc., 183 Hunters Rd., Washington, VA 22747-2001 / 615-638-8825

Farrar Tool Co., Inc., 11855 Cog Hill Dr., Whittier, CA 90601-1902 / 310-863-4367; FAX: 310-863-5123

Faulhaber Wildlocker, Dipl.-Ing. Norbert Wittasek, Seilergasse 2, A-1010 Wien, AUSTRIA / OM-43-1-5137001; FAX: 43-1-5137001 faulhaber1ut@net.at

Faulk's Game Call Co., Inc., 616 18th St., Lake Charles, LA 70601 / 318-436-9726; FAX: 318-494-7205

Faust Inc., T. G., 544 minor St, Reading, PA 19602 / 610-375-8549; FAX: 610-375-4488

Fautheree, Andy, P.O. Box 4607, Pagosa Springs, CO 81157 / 970-731-5003; FAX: 970-731-5009

Feather, Flex Decoys, 4500 Doniphan Dr., Neosho, MO 64850 / 318-746-8596; FAX: 318-742-4815

Federal Arms Corp. of America, 7928 University Ave., Fridley, MN 55432 / 612-780-8780; FAX: 612-780-8780

Federal Cartridge Co., 900 Ehlen Dr., Anoka, MN 55303 / 612-323-2300; FAX: 612-323-2506

Federal Champion Target Co., 232 Industrial Parkway, Richmond, IN 47374 / 800-441-4971; FAX: 317-966-7747

Federated-Fry (See Fry Metals)

FEG, Budapest, Soroksariut 158, H-1095, HUNGARY

Feinwerkbau Westinger & Altenburger, Neckarstrasse 43, 78727, Oberndorf a. N., GERMANY / 07423-814-0; FAX: 07423-814-200 info@feinwerkbau.de www.feinwerkbau.de

Feken, Dennis, Rt. 2, Box 124, Perry, OK 73077 / 405-336-5611

Felk Pistols Inc., 2121 Castlebridge Rd., Midlothian, VA 23113 / 804-794-3744; FAX: 208-988-4834

Fellowes, Ted, Beaver Lodge, 9245 16th Ave. SW, Seattle, WA 98106 / 206-763-1698

Ferguson, Bill, P.O. Box 1238, Sierra Vista, AZ 85636 / 520-458-5321; FAX: 520-458-9125

Ferguson, Bill. See: BULLET METALS

FERLIB, Via Parte 33 Marcheno/BS, Marcheno/BS, ITALY / 00390308610191; FAX: 00390308966882 info@ferlib.com www.ferlib.com

Ferris Firearms, 7110 F.M. 1863, Bulverde, TX 78163 / 210-980-4424

Fibron Products, Inc., P.O. Box 430, Buffalo, NY 14209-0430 / 716-886-2378; FAX: 716-886-2394

Fieldsport Ltd., Bryan Bilinski, 3313 W South Airport Rd., Traverse City, MI 49684 / 616-933-0767

Fiocchi Munizioni S.p.A. (See U.S. Importer-Fiocch

Fiocchi of America, Inc., 5030 Fremont Rd., Ozark, MO 65721 / 417-725-4118 or 800-721-2666; FAX: 417-725-1039

Firearms Co Ltd. / Alpine (See U.S. Importer-Mandall

Firearms Engraver's Guild of America, 332 Vine St., Oregon City, OR 97045 / 503-656-5693

Firearms International, 5709 Hartsdale, Houston, TX 77036 / 713-460-2447

First Inc., Jack, 1201 Turbine Dr., Rapid City, SD 57701 / 605-343-9544; FAX: 605-343-9420

Fisher, Jerry A., 631 Crane Mt. Rd., Big Fork, MT 59911 / 406-837-2722

Fisher Custom Firearms, 2199 S. Kittredge Way, Aurora, CO 80013 / 303-755-3710

Fitzgerald, Jack. See: CLENZOIL WORLDWIDE CORP

Flambeau Products Corp., 15981 Valplast Rd., Middlefield, OH 44062 / 216-632-1631; FAX: 216-632-1581

Flannery Engraving Co., Jeff W, 11034 Riddles Run Rd, Union, KY 41091 / 606-384-3127

Flayderman & Co., Inc., PO Box 2446, Ft Lauderdale, FL 33303 / 954-761-8855

Fleming Firearms, 7720 E 126th St. N, Collinsville, OK 74021-7016 / 918-665-3624

Fletcher-Bidwell, LLC., 305 E. Terhune St., Viroqua, WI 54665-1631 / 866-637-1860 fbguns@netscape.net

Flintlocks, Etc., 160 Rossiter Rd., P.O. Box 181, Richmond, MA 01254 / 413-698-3822; FAX: 413-698-3866 flintetc@berkshire.rr.com

Flitz International Ltd., 821 Mohr Ave., Waterford, WI 53185 / 414-534-5898; FAX: 414-534-2991

Fluoramics, Inc., 18 Industrial Ave., Mahwah, NJ 07430 / 800-922-0075; FAX: 201-825-7035

Flynn's Custom Guns, P.O. Box 7461, Alexandria, LA 71306 / 318-455-7130

FN Manufacturing, PO Box 24257, Columbia, SC 29224 / 803-736-0522

Folks, Donald E., 205 W. Lincoln St., Pontiac, IL 61764 / 815-844-7901

Foothills Video Productions, Inc., P.O. Box 651, Spartanburg, SC 29304 / 803-573-7023; or 800-782-5358

Foredom Electric Co., Rt. 6, 16 Stony Hill Rd., Bethel, CT 06801 / 203-792-8622

Forgett, Valmore. See: NAVY ARMS COMPANY

Forgreens Tool & Mfg., Inc., PO Box 955, Robert Lee, TX 76945 / 915-453-2800; FAX: 915-453-2460

Forkin, Ben (See Belt MTN Arms)

Forkin Arms, 205 10th Avenue S.W., White Sulphur Spring, MT 59645 / 406-547-2344

Forrest Inc., Tom, PO Box 326, Lakeside, CA 92040 / 619-561-5800; FAX: 619-561-0227

Forrest Tool Co., P.O. Box 768, 44380 Gordon Lane, Mendocino, CA 95460 / 707-937-2141; FAX: 717-937-1817

Forster, Kathy (See Custom Checkering)

Forster, Larry L., P.O. Box 212, 216 Highway 13 E., Gwinner, ND 58040-0212 / 701-678-2475

Forster Products, 310 E Lanark Ave, Lanark, IL 61046 / 815-493-6360; FAX: 815-493-2371

Fort Hill Gunstocks, 12807 Fort Hill Rd., Hillsboro, OH 45133 / 513-466-2763

Fort Knox Security Products, 1051 N. Industrial Park Rd., Orem, UT 84057 / 801-224-7233; or 800-821-5216; FAX: 801-226-5493

Fort Worth Firearms, 2006-B, Martin Luther King Fwy., Ft. Worth, TX 76104-6303 / 817-536-0718; FAX: 817-535-0290

Forthofer's Gunsmithing & Knifemaking, 5535 U.S. Hwy 93S, Whitefish, MT 59937-8411 / 406-862-2674

Fortune Products, Inc., 205 Hickory Creek Rd, Marble Falls, TX 78654 / 210-693-6111; FAX: 210-693-6394

Forty Five Ranch Enterprises, Box 1080, Miami, OK 74355-1080 / 918-542-5875

Foster, . See: ACCURACY INTERNATIONAL

Fountain Products, 492 Prospect Ave., West Springfield, MA 01089 / 413-781-4651; FAX: 413-733-8217

4-D Custom Die Co., 711 N. Sandusky St., PO Box 889, Mt. Vernon, OH 43050-0889 / 740-397-7214; FAX: 740-397-6600 info@ch4d.com ch4d.com

Fowler Bullets, 806 Dogwood Dr., Gastonia, NC 28054 / 704-867-3259

Fowler, Bob (See Black Powder Products)

Fox River Mills, Inc., P.O. Box 298, 227 Poplar St., Osage, IA 50461 / 515-732-3798; FAX: 515-732-5128

Foy Custom Bullets, 104 Wells Ave., Daleville, AL 36322

Francesca, Inc., 3115 Old Ranch Rd., San Antonio, TX 78217 / 512-826-2584; FAX: 512-826-8211

Franchi S.p.A., Via del Serpente 12, 25131, Brescia, ITALY / 030-3581833; FAX: 030-3581554

Francotte & Cie S.A. Auguste, rue de Trois Juin 109, 4400 Herstal-Liege, BELGIUM / 32-4-248-13-18; FAX: 32-4-948-11-79

Frank Knives, 13868 NW Keleka Pl., Seal Rock, OR 97376 / 541-563-3041; FAX: 541-563-3041

Frank Mittermeier, Inc., P.O. Box 2G, 3577 E. Tremont Ave., Bronx, NY 10465 / 718-828-3843

Franzen International,Inc (See U.S. Importer for)

Fred F. Wells/Wells Sport Store, 110 N Summit St., Prescott, AZ 86301 / 928-445-3655 www.wellssportstore.com

Freedom Arms, Inc., P.O. Box 150, Freedom, WY 83120 / 307-883-2468; FAX: 307-883-2005

Fremont Tool Works, 1214 Prairie, Ford, KS 67842 / 316-369-2327

French, Artistic Engraving, J. R., 1712 Creek Ridge Ct, Irving, TX 75060 / 214-254-2654

Front Sight Firearms Training Institute, P.O. Box 2619, Aptos, CA 95001 / 800-987-7719; FAX: 408-684-2137

Frontier, 2910 San Bernardo, Laredo, TX 78040 / 956-723-5409; FAX: 956-723-1774

Frontier Arms Co.,Inc., 401 W. Rio Santa Cruz, Green Valley, AZ 85614-3932

Frontier Products Co., 2401 Walker Rd, Roswell, NM 88201-8950 / 614-262-9357

Frontier Safe Co., 3201 S. Clinton St., Fort Wayne, IN 46806 / 219-744-7233; FAX: 219-744-6678

Frost Cutlery Co., P.O. Box 22636, Chattanooga, TN 37422 / 615-894-6079; FAX: 615-894-9576

Fry Metals, 4100 6th Ave., Altoona, PA 16602 / 814-946-1611

Fujinon, Inc., 10 High Point Dr., Wayne, NJ 07470 / 201-633-5600; FAX: 201-633-5216

Fullmer, Geo. M., 2499 Mavis St., Oakland, CA 94601 / 510-533-4193

Fulmer's Antique Firearms, Chet, PO Box 792, Rt 2 Buffalo Lake, Detroit Lakes, MN 56501 / 218-847-7712

Fulton Armory, 8725 Bollman Place No. 1, Savage, MD 20763 / 301-490-9485; FAX: 301-490-9547

Furr Arms, 91 N. 970 W., Orem, UT 84057 / 801-226-3877; FAX: 801-226-3877

G

G C Bullet Co. Inc., 40 Mokelumne River Dr., Lodi, CA 95240

G&H Decoys,Inc., P.O. Box 1208, Hwy. 75 North, Henryetta, OK 74437 / 918-652-3314; FAX: 918-652-3400

G.G. & G., 3602 E. 42nd Stravenue, Tucson, AZ 85713 / 520-748-7167; FAX: 520-748-7583 ggg&3@aol.com www.ggg&3.com

G.H. Enterprises Ltd., Bag 10, Okotoks, AB T0L 1T0 CANADA / 403-938-6070

G.U. Inc (See U.S. Importer for New SKB Arms Co.)

G.W. Elliott, Inc., 514 Burnside Ave., East Hartford, CT 06108 / 203-289-5741; FAX: 203-289-3137

G96 Products Co., Inc., 85 5th Ave, Bldg. #6, Paterson, NJ 07544 / 973-684-4050; FAX: 973-684-3848 g96prod@aol

Gage Manufacturing, 663 W. 7th St., A, San Pedro, CA 90731 / 310-832-3546

Gaillard Barrels, P.O. Box 21, Pathlow, SK S0K 3B0 CANADA / 306-752-3769; FAX: 306-752-5969

Gain Twist Barrel Co. Rifle Works and Armory, 707 12th Street, Cody, WY 82414 / 307-587-4919; FAX: 307-527-6097

Galati International, P.O. Box 10, 616 Burley Ridge Rd., Wesco, MO 65586 / 636-584-0785; FAX: 573-775-4308 support@galatiinternational.com www.galatiinternational.com

Galaxy Imports Ltd., Inc., P.O. Box 3361, Victoria, TX 77903 / 361-573-4867; FAX: 361-576-9622 galaxy@cox_internet.com

GALCO International Ltd., 2019 W. Quail Ave., Phoenix, AZ 85027 / 602-258-8295; or 800-874-2526; FAX: 602-582-6854

Galena Industries AMT, 5463 Diaz St, Irwindale, CA 91706 / 626-856-8883; FAX: 626-856-8878

Gamba S.p.A. Societa Armi Bresciane Srl, Renato, Via Artigiani 93, ITALY / 30-8911640; FAX: 30-8911648

Gamba, USA, P.O. Box 60452, Colorado Springs, CO 80960 / 719-578-1145; FAX: 719-444-0731

Game Haven Gunstocks, 13750 Shire Rd., Wolverine, MI 49799 / 616-525-8257

Gamebore Division, Polywad Inc., P.O. Box 7916, Macon, GA 31209 / 478-477-0669 or 800-998-0669

Gamo (See U.S. Importers-Arms United Corp, Daisy M

Gamo USA, Inc., 3911 SW 47th Ave., Suite 914, Ft. Lauderdale, FL 33314 / 954-581-5822; FAX: 954-581-3165 gamousa@gate.net www.gamo.com

Gander Mountain, Inc., 12400 Fox River Rd., Wilmont, WI 53192 / 414-862-6848

GAR, 590 McBride Avenue, West Paterson, NJ 07424 / 973-754-1114; FAX: 973-754-1114 garreloading@aol.com

Garcia National Gun Traders, Inc., 225 SW 22nd Ave., Miami, FL 33135 / 305-642-2355

Garrett Cartridges, Inc., P.O. Box 178, Chehalis, WA 98532 / 360-736-0702 www.garrettcartridges.com

Garthwaite Pistolsmith, Inc., Jim, 12130 State Route 405, Watsontown, PA 17777 / 570-538-1566; FAX: 570-538-2945 www.garthwaite.com

Gary Goudy Classic Stocks, 1512 S. 5th St., Dayton, WA 99328 / 509-382-2726 goudy@innw.net

Gary Reeder Custom Guns, 2601 7th Avenue East, Flagstaff, AZ 86004 / 928-526-3313; FAX: 928-527-0840 gary@reedercustomguns.com www.reedercustomguns.com

Gary Schneider Rifle Barrels Inc., 12202 N. 62nd Pl., Scottsdale, AZ 85254 / 602-948-2525

Gator Guns & Repair, 7952 Kenai Spur Hwy., Kenai, AK 99611-8311

Gaucher Armes, S.A., 46 rue Desjoyaux, 42000, Saint-Etienne, FRANCE / 04-77-33-38-92; FAX: 04-77-61-95-72

GDL Enterprises, 409 Le Gardeur, Slidell, LA 70460 / 504-649-0693

Gehmann, Walter (See Huntington Die Specialties)

Genco, P.O. Box 5704, Asheville, NC 28803

Genecco Gun Works, 10512 Lower Sacramento Rd., Stockton, CA 95210 / 209-951-0706; FAX: 209-931-3872

Gene's Custom Guns, P.O. Box 10534, White Bear Lake, MN 55110 / 651-429-5105; FAX: 651-429-7365

Gentex Corp., 5 Tinkham Ave., Derry, NH 03038 / 603-434-0311; FAX: 603-434-3002 sales@derry.gentexcorp.com www.derry.gentexcorp.com

Gentner Bullets, 109 Woodlawn Ave., Upper Darby, PA 19082 / 610-352-9396

Gentry Custom Gunmaker, David, 314 N Hoffman, Belgrade, MT 59714 / 406-388-GUNS davidgent@mcn.net www.gentrycustom.com

George & Roy's, PO Box 2125, Sisters, OR 97759-2125 / 503-228-5424; or 800-553-3022; FAX: 503-225-9409

George E. Mathews & Son, Inc., 10224 S. Paramount Blvd., Downey, CA 90241 / 562-862-6719; FAX: 562-862-6719

George Hoenig, Inc., 6521 Morton Dr., Boise, ID 83704 / 208-375-1116; FAX: 208-375-1116

George Ibberson (Sheffield) Ltd., 25-31 Allen St., Sheffield, S3 7AW ENGLAND / 0114-2766123; FAX: 0114-2738465 sales@ebbintongroupco.uk www.eggintongroup.co.uk

George Madis Winchester Consultants, George Madis, P.O. Box 545, Brownsboro, TX 75756 / 903-852-6480; FAX: 903-852-3045 gmadis@earthlink.com www.georgemadis.com

Gerald Pettinger Books (See Pettinger Books), 47827 300th Ave., Russell, IA 50238 / 641-535-2239 gpettinger@lisco.com

Gerber Legendary Blades, 14200 SW 72nd Ave., Portland, OR 97223 / 503-639-6161; or 800-950-6161; FAX: 503-684-7008

Gervais, Mike, 3804 S. Cruise Dr., Salt Lake City, UT 84109 / 801-277-7729

Getz Barrel Co., P.O. Box 88, Beavertown, PA 17813 / 717-658-7263

Giacomo Sporting USA, 6234 Stokes Lee Center Rd., Lee Center, NY 13363

Gibbs Rifle Co., Inc., 211 Lawn St., Martinsburg, WV 25401 / 304-262-1651; FAX: 304-262-1658

Gil Hebard Guns Inc., 125 Public Square, Knoxville, IL 61448 / 309-289-2700; FAX: 309-289-2233

Gilbert Equipment Co., Inc., 960 Downtowner Rd., Mobile, AL 36609 / 205-344-3322

Gillmann, Edwin, 33 Valley View Dr., Hanover, PA 17331 / 717-632-1662 gillmaned@super-pa.net

Gilman-Mayfield, Inc., 3279 E. Shields, Fresno, CA 93703 / 209-221-9415; FAX: 209-221-9419

Gilmore Sports Concepts, 5949 S. Garnett, Tulsa, OK 74146 / 918-250-3810; FAX: 918-250-3845 gilmore@webzone.net www.gilmoresports.com

Giron, Robert E., 12671 Cousins Rd.., Peosta, IA 52068 / 412-731-6041

Glacier Glove, 4890 Aircenter Circle, Suite 210, Reno, NV 89502 / 702-825-8225; FAX: 702-825-6544

Glaser LLC, P.O. Box 173, Sturgis, SD 57785 / 605-347-4544 or 800-221-3489; FAX: 605-347-5055 email@corbon.com www.safetyslug.com

Glaser Safety Slug, Inc., PO Box 8223, Foster City, CA 94404 / 800-221-3489; FAX: 510-785-6685 safetyslug.com

Glass, Herb, PO Box 25, Bullville, NY 10915 / 914-361-3021

Glimm, Jerome. See: GLIMM'S CUSTOM GUN ENGRAVING

Glimm's Custom Gun Engraving, Jerome C. Glimm, 19 S. Maryland, Conrad, MT 59425 / 406-278-3574 jandlglimm@mcn.net

Glock GmbH, P.O. Box 50, A-2232, Deutsch Wagram, AUSTRIA

Glock, Inc., PO Box 369, Smyrna, GA 30081 / 770-432-1202; FAX: 770-433-8719

Glynn Scobey Duck & Goose Calls, Rt. 3, Box 37, Newbern, TN 38059 / 731-643-6128

GML Products, Inc., 394 Laredo Dr., Birmingham, AL 35226 / 205-979-4867

Gner's Hard Cast Bullets, 1107 11th St., LaGrande, OR 97850 / 503-963-8796

Goens, Dale W., P.O. Box 224, Cedar Crest, NM 87008 / 505-281-5419

Goergen's Gun Shop, Inc., 17985 538th Ave., Austin, MN 55912 / 507-433-9280; FAX: 507-433-9280

GOEX, Inc., P.O. Box 659, Doyline, LA 71023-0659 / 318-382-9300; FAX: 318-382-9303 mfahringer@goexpowder.com www.goexpowder.com

Golden Age Arms Co., 115 E. High St., Ashley, OH 43003 / 614-747-2488

Golden Bear Bullets, 3065 Fairfax Ave., San Jose, CA 95148 / 408-238-9515

Gonic Arms/North American Arm, 134 Flagg Rd., Gonic, NH 03839 / 603-332-8456 or 603-332-8457

Goodling's Gunsmithing, 1950 Stoverstown Road, Spring Grove, PA 17362 / 717-225-3350

Goodwin, Fred. See: GOODWIN'S GUN SHOP

Goodwin's Gun Shop, Fred Goodwin, Sherman Mills, ME 04776 / 207-365-4451

Gotz Bullets, 11426 Edgemere Ter., Roscoe, IL 61073-8232

Gould & Goodrich, 709 E. McNeil, Lillington, NC 27546 / 910-893-2071; FAX: 910-893-4742

Gournet Artistic Engraving, Geoffroy Gournet, 820 Paxinosa Ave., Easton, PA 18042 / 610-559-0710 www.geoffroygournet.com

Gournet, Geoffroy. See: GOURNET ARTISTIC ENGRAVING

Grace, Charles E., 1006 Western Ave., Trinidad, CO 81082 / 719-846-9435

Grace Metal Products, P.O. Box 67, Elk Rapids, MI 49629 / 616-264-8133

Graf & Sons, 4050 S Clark St., Mexico, MO 65265 / 573-581-2266; FAX: 573-581-2875

Grand Slam Hunting Products, Box 121, 25454 Military Rd., Cascade, MD 21719 / 301-241-4900; FAX: 301-241-4900 rlj6call@aol.com

Granite Mountain Arms, Inc., 3145 W Hidden Acres Trail, Prescott, AZ 86305 / 520-541-9758; FAX: 520-445-6826

Grant, Howard V., Hiawatha 15, Woodruff, WI 54568 / 715-356-7146

Graphics Direct, P.O. Box 372421, Reseda, CA 91337-2421 / 818-344-9002

Graves Co., 1800 Andrews Ave., Pompano Beach, FL 33069 / 800-327-9103; FAX: 305-960-0301

Grayback Wildcats, Mike Beeks, 5306 Bryant Ave., Klamath Falls, OR 97603 / 541-884-1072

Graybill's Gun Shop, 1035 Ironville Pike, Columbia, PA 17512 / 717-684-2739

Great American Gunstock Co., 3420 Industrial Drive, Yuba City, CA 95993 / 800-784-4867; FAX: 530-671-3906 gunstox@oro.net www.gunstocks.com

Great Lakes Airguns, 6175 S. Park Ave., Hamburg, NY 14075 / 716-648-6666; FAX: 716-648-6666 www.greatlakesairguns.com

Green, Arthur S., 485 S. Robertson Blvd., Beverly Hills, CA 90211 / 310-274-1283

Green, Roger M., P.O. Box 984, 435 E. Birch, Glenrock, WY 82637 / 307-436-9804

Green Head Game Call Co., RR 1, Box 33, Lacon, IL 61540 / 309-246-2155

Green Mountain Rifle Barrel Co., Inc., P.O. Box 2670, 153 West Main St., Conway, NH 03818 / 603-447-1095; FAX: 603-447-1099

Greenwood Precision, P.O. Box 407, Rogersville, MO 65742 / 417-725-2330

Greg Gunsmithing Repair, 3732 26th Ave. North, Robbinsdale, MN 55422 / 612-529-8103

Greg's Superior Products, P.O. Box 46219, Seattle, WA 98146

Greider Precision, 431 Santa Marina Ct., Escondido, CA 92029 / 760-480-8892; FAX: 760-480-9800 greider@msn.com

Gremmel Enterprises, 2111 Carriage Drive, Eugene, OR 97408-7537 / 541-302-3000

Gre-Tan Rifles, 29742 W.C.R. 50, Kersey, CO 80644 / 970-353-6176; FAX: 970-356-5940 www.gtrtooling.com

Grier's Hard Cast Bullets, 1107 11th St., LaGrande, OR 97850 / 503-963-8796

Griffin & Howe, Inc., 36 W. 44th St., Suite 1011, New York, NY 10036 / 212-921-0980 info@griffinhowe.com www.griffinhowe.com

Griffin & Howe, Inc., 33 Claremont Rd., Bernardsville, NJ 07924 / 908-766-2287; FAX: 908-766-1068 info@griffinhowe.com www.griffinhowe.com

Griffin & Howe, Inc., 340 W Putnam Avenue, Greenwich, CT 06830 / 203-618-0270 info@griffinhowe.com www.griffinhowe.com

Grifon, Inc., 58 Guinam St., Waltham, MS 02154

Groenewold, John, P.O. Box 830, Mundelein, IL 60060 / 847-566-2365; FAX: 847-566-4065 jgairguns@direcway.com http://jwww.gairguns.aupal.com/augmpubl.

GRS / Glendo Corp., P.O. Box 1153, 900 Overlander St., Emporia, KS 66801 / 620-343-1084; or 800-836-3519; FAX: 620-343-9640 glendo@glendo.com www.glendo.com

Grulla Armes, Apartado 453, Avda Otaloa 12, Eiber, SPAIN

Gruning Precision Inc., 7101 Jurupa Ave., No. 12, Riverside, CA 92504 / 909-289-4371; FAX: 909-689-7791 gruningprecision@earthlink.net www.gruningprecision.com

GSI, Inc., 7661 Commerce Ln., Trussville, AL 35173 / 205-655-8299

GTB, 482 Comerwood Court, San Francisco, CA 94080 / 650-583-1550

Guarasi, Robert. See: WILCOX INDUSTRIES CORP.

Guardsman Products, 411 N. Darling, Fremont, MI 49412 / 616-924-3950

Gun City, 212 W. Main Ave., Bismarck, ND 58501 / 701-223-2304

Gun Hunter Books (See Gun Hunter Trading Co.), 5075 Heisig St., Beaumont, TX 77705 / 409-835-3006; FAX: 409-838-2266 gunhuntertrading@hotmail.com

Gun Hunter Trading Co., 5075 Heisig St., Beaumont, TX 77705 / 409-835-3006; FAX: 409-838-2266 gunhuntertrading@hotmail.com

Gun Leather Limited, 116 Lipscomb, Ft. Worth, TX 76104 / 817-334-0225; FAX: 800-247-0609

Gun List (See Krause Publications), 700 E State St., Iola, WI 54945 / 715-445-2214; FAX: 715-445-4087

Gun South, Inc. (See GSI, Inc.)

Gun Vault, 7339 E Acoma Dr., Ste. 7, Scottsdale, AZ 85260 / 602-951-6855

Gun-Alert, 1010 N. Maclay Ave., San Fernando, CA 91340 / 818-365-0864; FAX: 818-365-1308

Guncraft Books (See Guncraft Sports Inc.), 10737 Dutchtown Rd, Knoxville, TN 37932 / 865-966-4545; FAX: 865-966-4500 findit@guncraft.com www.usit.net/guncraft

Guncraft Sports Inc., 10737 Dutchtown Rd., Knoxville, TN 37932 / 865-966-4545; FAX: 865-966-4500 findit@guncraft.com www.usit.net/guncraft

Guncraft Sports, Inc., Marie C. Wiest, 10737 Dutchtown Rd., Knoxville, TN 37932 / 865-966-4545; FAX: 865-966-4500 www.guncraft.com

Gunfitters, P.O. Box 426, Cambridge, WI 53523-0426 / 608-764-8128 gunfitters@aol.com www.gunfitters.com

Gun-Ho Sports Cases, 110 E. 10th St., St. Paul, MN 55101 / 612-224-9491

Gunline Tools, 2950 Saturn St., "O", Brea, CA 92821 / 714-993-5100; FAX: 714-572-4128

Gunnerman Books, P.O. Box 81697, Rochester Hills, MI 48308 / 989-729-7018

Guns Antique & Modern DBA / Charles E. Duffy, Williams Lane, West Hurley, NY 12491 / 914-679-2997

Guns Div. of D.C. Engineering, Inc., 8633 Southfield Fwy., Detroit, MI 48228 / 313-271-7111 or 800-886-7623; FAX: 313-271-7112 guns@rifletech.com www.rifletech.com

GUNS Magazine, 591 Camino de la Reina, Suite 200, San Diego, CA 92108 / 619-297-5350; FAX: 619-297-5353

Gunsite Custom Shop, P.O. Box 451, Paulden, AZ 86334 / 520-636-4104; FAX: 520-636-1236

Gunsite Gunsmithy (See Gunsite Custom Shop)

Gunsite Training Center, P.O. Box 700, Paulden, AZ 86334 / 520-636-4565; FAX: 520-636-1236

Gunsmithing Ltd., 57 Unquowa Rd., Fairfield, CT 06430 / 203-254-0436; FAX: 203-254-1535

Gunsmithing, Inc., 30 West Buchanan St., Colorado Springs, CO 80907 / 719-632-3795; FAX: 719-632-3493

Gurney, F. R., Box 13, Sooke, BC V0S 1N0 CANADA / 604-642-5282; FAX: 604-642-7859

H

H&B Forge Co., Rt. 2, Geisinger Rd., Shiloh, OH 44878 / 419-895-1856

H&P Publishing, 7174 Hoffman Rd., San Angelo, TX 76905 / 915-655-5953

H&R 1871.LLC, 60 Industrial Rowe, Gardner, MA 01440 / 508-632-9393; FAX: 508-632-2300 hr1871@hr1871.com www.hr1871.com

H&S Liner Service, 515 E. 8th, Odessa, TX 79761 / 915-332-1021

H. Krieghoff Gun Co., Boschstrasse 22, D-89079, Ulm, GERMANY / 731-401820; FAX: 731-4018270

MANUFACTURER'S DIRECTORY

H.K.S. Products, 7841 Founion Dr., Florence, KY 41042 / 606-342-7841; or 800-354-9814; FAX: 606-342-5865

H.P. White Laboratory, Inc., 3114 Scarboro Rd., Street, MD 21154 / 410-838-6550; FAX: 410-838-2802

Hafner World Wide, Inc., PO Box 1987, Lake City, FL 32055 / 904-755-6481; FAX: 904-755-6595 hafner@isgroupe.net

Hakko Co. Ltd., 1-13-12, Narimasu, Itabashiku Tokyo, JAPAN / 03-5997-7870/2; FAX: 81-3-5997-7840

Half Moon Rifle Shop, 490 Halfmoon Rd., Columbia Falls, MT 59912 / 406-892-4409 halfmoonrs@centurytel.net

Hall Manufacturing, 142 CR 406, Clanton, AL 35045 / 205-755-4094

Hall Plastics, Inc., John, P.O. Box 1526, Alvin, TX 77512 / 713-489-8709

Hallberg, Fritz. See: CAMBOS OUTDOORSMAN

Hallowell & Co., P.O. Box 1445, Livingston, MT 59047 / 406-222-4770; FAX: 406-222-4792 morris@hallowellco.com www.hallowellco.com

Hally Caller, 443 Wells Rd., Doylestown, PA 18901 / 215-345-6354; FAX: 215-345-8892 info@hallycaller.com www.hallycaller.com

Hamilton, Alex B (See Ten-Ring Precision, Inc)

Hammans, Charles E., P.O. Box 788, 2022 McCracken, Stuttgart, AR 72160-0788 / 870-673-1388

Hammerli Ltd., Seonerstrasse 37, CH-5600, SWITZERLAND / 064-50 11 44; FAX: 064-51 38 27

Hammerli Service-Precision Mac, Rudolf Marent, 9711 Tiltree St., Houston, TX 77075 / 713-946-7028

Hammerli USA, 19296 Oak Grove Circle, Groveland, CA 95321 FAX: 209-962-5311

Hammond Custom Guns Ltd., 619 S. Pandora, Gilbert, AZ 85234 / 602-892-3437

HandCrafts Unltd (See Clements' Custom Leather), 1741 Dallas St, Aurora, CO 80010-2018 / 303-364-0403; FAX: 303-739-9824 gryphons@home.com kuntaoslcat.com

Handgun Press, P.O. Box 406, Glenview, IL 60025 / 847-657-6500; FAX: 847-724-8831 handgunpress@earth-link.net

Hank's Gun Shop, Box 370, 50 West 100 South, Monroe, UT 84754 / 801-527-4456

Hanned Precision (See The Hanned Line)

Hansen & Co., 244-246 Old Post Rd., Southport, CT 06490 / 203-259-6222; FAX: 203-254-3832

Hanson's Gun Center, Dick, 233 Everett Dr, Colorado Springs, CO 80911

Hanusin, John, 3306 Commercial, Northbrook, IL 60062 / 708-564-2706

Harford (See U.S. Importer-EMF Co. Inc.)

Harper's Custom Stocks, 928 Lombrano St., San Antonio, TX 78207 / 210-732-7174

Harrell's Precision, 5756 Hickory Dr., Salem, VA 24153 / 540-380-2683

Harrington & Richardson (See H&R 1871, Inc.)

Harris Engineering Inc., Dept GD54, Barlow, KY 42024 / 502-334-3633; FAX: 502-334-3000

Harris Enterprises, P.O. Box 105, Bly, OR 97622 / 503-353-2625

Harris Gunworks, 11240 N. Cave Creek Rd., Ste. 104, Phoenix, AZ 85020 / 602-582-9627; FAX: 602-582-5178

Harris Hand Engraving, Paul A., 113 Rusty Ln, Boerne, TX 78006-5746 / 512-391-5121

Harris Publications, 1115 Broadway, New York, NY 10010 / 212-807-7100; FAX: 212-627-4678

Harrison Bullets, 6437 E. Hobart St., Mesa, AZ 85205

Harry Lawson Co., 3328 N. Richey Blvd., Tucson, AZ 85716 / 520-326-1117

Hart & Son, Inc., Robert W., 401 Montgomery St., Nescopeck, PA 18635 / 717-752-3655; FAX: 717-752-1088

Hart Rifle Barrels,Inc., PO Box 182, 1690 Apulia Rd., Lafayette, NY 13084 / 315-677-9841; FAX: 315-677-9610 hartrb@aol.com hartbarrels.com

Hartford (See U.S. Importer-EMF Co. Inc.)

Hartmann & Weiss GmbH, Rahlstedter Bahnhofstr. 47, 22143, Hamburg, GERMANY / (40) 677 55 85; FAX: (40) 677 55 92 hartmannundweisst-online.de

Harvey, Frank, 218 Nightfall, Terrace, NV 89015 / 702-558-6998

Harwood, Jack O., 1191 S. Pendlebury Lane, Blackfoot, ID 83221 / 208-785-5368

Hastings, P.O. Box 224, Clay Center, KS 67432 / 785-632-3169; FAX: 785-632-6554

Hatfield Gun, 224 N. 4th St., St. Joseph, MO 64501

Hawk Laboratories, Inc. (See Hawk, Inc.), 849 Hawks Bridge Rd, Salem, NJ 08079 / 609-299-2700; FAX: 609-299-2800

Hawk, Inc., 849 Hawks Bridge Rd., Salem, NJ 08079 / 609-299-2700; FAX: 609-299-2800

Hawken Shop, The (See Dayton Traister)

Haydel's Game Calls, Inc., 5018 Hazel Jones Rd., Bossier City, LA 71111 / 318-746-3586; FAX: 318-746-3711

Haydon Shooters Supply, Russ, 15018 Goodrich Dr. NW, Gig Harbor, WA 98329-9738 / 253-857-7557; FAX: 253-857-7884

Heatbath Corp., P.O. Box 2978, Springfield, MA 01101 / 413-543-3381

Hecht, Hubert J, Waffen-Hecht, PO Box 2635, Fair Oaks, CA 95628 / 916-966-1020

Heckler & Koch GmbH, PO Box 1329, 78722 Oberndorf, Neckar, GERMANY / 49-7423179-0; FAX: 49-7423179-2406

Heckler & Koch, Inc., 21480 Pacific Blvd., Sterling, VA 20166-8900 / 703-450-1900; FAX: 703-450-8160 www.hecklerkoch-usa.com

Hege Jagd-u. Sporthandels GmbH, P.O. Box 101461, W-7770, Ueberlingen a. Boden, GERMANY

Heidenstrom Bullets, Dalghte 86-3660 Rjukan, 35091818, NORWAY, olau.joh@online.tuo

Heilmann, Stephen, P.O. Box 657, Grass Valley, CA 95945 / 530-272-8758; FAX: 530-274-0285 sheilmann@jps.net www.metalwood.com

Heinie Specialty Products, 301 Oak St., Quincy, IL 62301-2500 / 217-228-9500; FAX: 217-228-9502 rheinie@heinie.com www.heinie.com

Helwan (See U.S. Importer-Interarms)

Henigson & Associates, Steve, PO Box 2726, Culver City, CA 90231 / 310-305-8288; FAX: 310-305-1905

Henriksen Tool Co., Inc., 8515 Wagner Creek Rd., Talent, OR 97540 / 541-535-2309; FAX: 541-535-2309

Henry Repeating Arms Co., 110 8th St., Brooklyn, NY 11215 / 718-499-5600

Hensley, Gunmaker, Darwin, PO Box 329, Brightwood, OR 97011 / 503-622-5411

Heppler, Keith. See: KEITH'S CUSTOM GUNSTOCKS

Hercules, Inc. (See Alliant Techsystems, Smokeless)

Heritage Firearms (See Heritage Mfg., Inc.)

Heritage Manufacturing, Inc., 4600 NW 135th St., Opa Locka, FL 33054 or 305-685-5966; FAX: 305-687-6721 infohmi@heritagemfg.com www.heritagemfg.com

Heritage/VSP Gun Books, P.O. Box 887, McCall, ID 83638 / 208-634-4104; FAX: 208-634-3101

Herrett's Stocks, Inc., P.O. Box 741, Twin Falls, ID 83303 / 208-733-1498

Herter's Manufacturing Inc., 111 E. Burnett St., P.O. Box 518, Beaver Dam, WI 53916-1811 / 414-887-1765; FAX: 414-887-8444

Hesco-Meprolight, 2139 Greenville Rd., LaGrange, GA 30241 / 706-884-7967; FAX: 706-882-4683

Hesse Arms, Robert Hesse, 1126 70th Street E., Inver Grove Heights, MN 55077-2416 / 651-455-5760; FAX: 612-455-5760

Hesse, Robert. See: HESSE ARMS

Heydenberk, Warren R., 1059 W. Sawmill Rd., Quakertown, PA 18951 / 215-538-2682

Hickman, Jaclyn, Box 1900, Glenrock, WY 82637

Hidalgo, Tony, 12701 SW 9th Pl., Davie, FL 33325 / 954-476-7645

High Bridge Arms, Inc, 3185 Mission St., San Francisco, CA 94110 / 415-282-8358

High North Products, Inc., P.O. Box 2, Antigo, WI 54409 / 715-627-2331; FAX: 715-623-5451

High Performance International, 5734 W. Florist Ave., Milwaukee, WI 53218 / 414-466-9040

High Precision, Bud Welsh, 80 New Road, E. Amherst, NY 14051 / 716-688-6344; FAX: 716-688-0425 welsh5168@aol.com www.high-precision.com

High Tech Specialties, Inc., P.O. Box 839, 293 E Main St., Rear, Adamstown, PA 19501 / 717-484-0405; FAX: 717-484-0523 bansner@aol.com www.bansmersrifle.com/hightech

Highline Machine Co., Randall Thompson, 654 Lela Place, Grand Junction, CO 81504 / 970-434-4971

Highwood Special Products, 1531 E. Highwood, Pontiac, MI 48340

Hi-Grade Imports, 8655 Monterey Rd., Gilroy, CA 95021 / 408-842-9301; FAX: 408-842-2374

Hill, Loring F., 304 Cedar Rd., Elkins Park, PA 19027

Hill Speed Leather, Ernie, 4507 N 195th Ave, Litchfield Park, AZ 85340 / 602-853-9222; FAX: 602-853-9235

Hinman Outfitters, Bob, 107 N Sanderson Ave, Bartonville, IL 61607-1839 / 309-691-8132

Hi-Performance Ammunition Company, 484 State Route 366, Apollo, PA 15613 / 412-327-8100

HIP-GRIP Barami Corp., P.O. Box 252224, West Bloomfield, MI 48325-2224 / 248-738-0462; FAX: 248-738-2542 hipgripja@aol.com www.hipgrip.com

Hi-Point Firearms/MKS Supply, 8611-A North Dixie Dr., Dayton, OH 45414 / 877-425-4867; FAX: 937-454-0503 www.hi-pointfirearms.com

Hiptmayer, Armurier, RR 112 750, P.O. Box 136, Eastman, PQ J0E 1P0 CANADA / 514-297-2492

Hiptmayer, Heidemarie, RR 112 750, P.O. Box 136, Eastman, PQ J0E 1P0 CANADA / 514-297-2492

Hiptmayer, Klaus, RR 112 750, P.O. Box 136, Eastman, PQ J0E 1P0 CANADA / 514-297-2492

Hirtenberger AG, Leobersdorferstrasse 31, A-2552, Hirtenberg, / 43(0)2256 81184; FAX: 43(0)2256 81808 www.hirtenberger.ot

HiTek International, 484 El Camino Real, Redwood City, CA 94063 / 415-363-1404; or 800-54-NIGHT; FAX: 415-363-1408

Hiti-Schuch, Atelier Wilma, A-8863 Predlitz, Pirming, Y1 AUSTRIA / 0353418278

HJS Arms, Inc., P.O. Box 3711, Brownsville, TX 78523-3711 / 956-542-2767; FAX: 956-542-2767

Hoag, James W., 8523 Canoga Ave., Suite C, Canoga Park, CA 91304 / 818-998-1510

Hobson Precision Mfg. Co., 210 Big Oak Ln, Brent, AL 35034 / 205-926-4662; FAX: 205-926-3193 cahobbob@dbtech.net

Hodgdon Powder Co., 6231 Robinson, Shawnee Mission, KS 66202 / 913-362-9455; FAX: 913-362-1307

Hodgman, Inc., 1750 Orchard Rd., Montgomery, IL 60538 / 708-897-7555; FAX: 708-897-7558

Hodgson, Richard, 9081 Tahoe Lane, Boulder, CO 80301

Hoehn Sales, Inc., 2045 Kohn Road, Wright City, MO 63390 / 636-745-8144; FAX: 636-745-8144 hoehnsal@usmo.com

Hofer Jagdwaffen, P., Buchsenmachermeister, Kirchgasse 24, A-9170 Ferlach, AUSTRIA / 43 4227 3683; FAX: 43 4227 368330 peterhofer@hoferwaffen.com www.hoferwaffen.com

Hoffman New Ideas, 821 Northmoor Rd., Lake Forest, IL 60045 / 312-234-4075

Hogue Grips, P.O. Box 1138, Paso Robles, CA 93447 / 800-438-4747 or 805-239-1440; FAX: 805-239-2553

Holland & Holland Ltd., 33 Bruton St., London, ENGLAND / 44-171-499-4411; FAX: 44-171-408-7962

Holland's Gunsmithing, P.O. Box 69, Powers, OR 97466 / 541-439-5155; FAX: 541-439-5155

Hollinger, Jon. See: ASPEN OUTFITTING CO.

Hollywood Engineering, 10642 Arminta St., Sun Valley, CA 91352 / 818-842-8376; FAX: 818-504-4168

Homak, 5151 W. 73rd St., Chicago, IL 60638-6613 / 312-523-3100; FAX: 312-523-9455

Home Shop Machinist, The Village Press Publications, P.O. Box 1810, Traverse City, MI 49685 / 800-447-7367; FAX: 616-946-3289

Hondo Ind., 510 S. 52nd St., I04, Tempe, AZ 85281

Hoppe's Div. Penguin Industries, Inc., P.O. Box 1690, Oregon City, OR 97045-0690 / 610-384-6000

Horizons Unlimited, P.O. Box 426, Warm Springs, GA 31830 / 706-655-3603; FAX: 706-655-3603

Hornady Mfg. Co., P.O. Box 1848, Grand Island, NE 68802 / 800-338-3220 or 308-382-1390; FAX: 308-382-5761

Horseshoe Leather Products, Andy Arratoonian, The Cottage Sharow, Ripon U.K., ENGLAND U.K. / 44-1765-605858 andy@horseshoe.co.uk www.horseshoe.co.uk

House of Muskets, Inc., The, PO Box 4640, Pagosa Springs, CO 81157 / 970-731-2295

Houtz & Barwick, P.O. Box 435, W. Church St., Elizabeth City, NC 27909 / 800-775-0337; or 919-335-4191; FAX: 919-335-1152

Howa Machinery, Ltd., Sukaguchi, Shinkawa-cho Nishikasugai-gun, Aichi 452-8601, JAPAN / 81-52-408-1231; FAX: 81-52-409-4855 howa@howa.co.jp http://www.howa.cojpl

Howell Machine, 815 1/2 D St., Lewiston, ID 83501 / 208-743-7418

H-S Precision, Inc., 1301 Turbine Dr., Rapid City, SD 57701 / 605-341-3006; FAX: 605-342-8964

HT Bullets, 244 Belleville Rd., New Bedford, MA 02745 / 508-999-3338

Hubert J. Hecht Waffen-Hecht, P.O. Box 2635, Fair Oaks, CA 95628 / 916-966-1020

Huebner, Corey O., PO Box 564, Frenchtown, MT 59834 / 406-721-7168

Huey Gun Cases, 820 Indiana St., Lawrence, KS 66044-2645 / 816-444-1637; FAX: 816-444-1637 hueycases@aol.com www.hueycases.com

Hume, Don, P.O. Box 351, Miami, OK 74355 / 800-331-2686; FAX: 918-542-4340 info@donhume.com www.donhume.com

Hunkeler, A (See Buckskin Machine Works, 3235 S 358th St., Auburn, WA 98001 / 206-927-5412

Hunter Co., Inc., 3300 W. 71st Ave., Westminster, CO 80030 / 303-427-4626; FAX: 303-428-3980

Hunterjohn, PO Box 771457, St. Louis, MO 63177 / 314-531-7250

Hunter's Specialties Inc., 6000 Huntington Ct. NE, Cedar Rapids, IA 52402-1268 / 319-395-0321; FAX: 319-395-0326

Hunters Supply, Inc., P.O. Box 313, Tioga, TX 76271 / 940-437-2458; FAX: 940-437-2228 hunterssupply@hotmail.com www.hunterssupply.net

Huntington Die Specialties, 601 Oro Dam Blvd., Oroville, CA 95965 / 530-534-1210; FAX: 530-534-1212 buy@huntingtons.com www.huntingtons.com

Hutton Rifle Ranch, P.O. Box 170317, Boise, ID 83717 / 208-345-8781 www.martinbrevik@aol.com

Hydrosorbent Products, PO Box 437, Ashley Falls, MA 01222 / 800-448-7903; FAX: 413-229-8743 orders@dehumidify.com www.dehumidify.com

I

I.A.B. (See U.S. Importer-Taylor's & Co. Inc.)

I.D.S.A. Books, 1324 Stratford Drive, Piqua, OH 45356 / 937-773-4203; FAX: 937-778-1922

I.N.C. Inc (See Kickeez I.N.C., Inc.)

I.S.S., P.O. Box 185234, Ft. Worth, TX 76181 / 817-595-2090; FAX: 817-595-2090 iss@concentric.net

I.S.W., 106 E. Cairo Dr., Tempe, AZ 85282

IAR Inc., 33171 Camino Capistrano, San Juan Capistrano, CA 92675 / 949-443-3642; FAX: 949-443-3647 sales@iar-arms.com iar-arms.com

Ide, K. See: STURGEON VALLEY SPORTERS

IGA (See U.S. Importer-Stoeger Industries)

Ignacio Ugartechea S.A., Chonta 26, Eibar, 20600 SPAIN / 43-121257; FAX: 43-121669

Image Ind. Inc., 382 Balm Court, Wood Dale, IL 60191 / 630-766-2402; FAX: 630-766-7373

Impact Case & Container, Inc., P.O. Box 1129, Rathdrum, ID 83858 / 877-687-2452; FAX: 208-687-0632 bradk@icc-case.com www.icc-case.com

Imperial (See E-Z-Way Systems), PO Box 4310, Newark, OH 43058-4310 / 614-345-6645; FAX: 614-345-6600 ezway@infinet.com www.jcunald.com

Imperial Magnum Corp., P.O. Box 249, Oroville, WA 98844 / 604-495-3131; FAX: 604-495-2816

Imperial Miniature Armory, 10547 S. Post Oak Road, Houston, TX 77035-3305 / 713-729-8428; FAX: 713-729-2274 miniguns@aol.com www.1800miniature.com

Imperial Schrade Corp., 7 Schrade Ct., Box 7000, Ellenville, NY 12428 / 914-647-7601; FAX: 914-647-8701 csc@schradeknives.com www.schradeknives.com

Import Sports Inc., 1750 Brielle Ave., Unit B1, Wanamassa, NJ 07712 / 908-493-0302; FAX: 908-493-0301

IMR Powder Co., 1080 Military Turnpike, Suite 2, Plattsburgh, NY 12901 / 518-563-2253; FAX: 518-563-6916

Info-Arm, P.O. Box 1262, Champlain, NY 12919 / 514-955-0355; FAX: 514-955-0357

Ingle, Ralph W., Engraver, 112 Manchester Ct., Centerville, GA 31028 / 478-953-5824 riengraver@aol.com www.fega.com

Innovative Weaponry Inc., 2513 E. Loop 820 N., Fort Worth, TX 76118 / 817-284-0099 or 800-334-3573

INTEC International, Inc., P.O. Box 5708, Scottsdale, AZ 85261 / 602-483-1708

Inter Ordnance of America LP, 3305 Westwood Industrial Dr, Monroe, NC 28110-5204 / 704-821-8337; FAX: 704-821-8523

Intercontinental Distributors, Ltd., PO Box 815, Beulah, ND 58523

Intrac Arms International, 5005 Chapman Hwy., Knoxville, TN 37920

Ion Industries, Inc., 3508 E Allerton Ave., Cudahy, WI 53110 / 414-486-2007; FAX: 414-486-2017

Iosso Products, 1485 Lively Blvd., Elk Grove Village, IL 60007 / 847-437-8400; FAX: 847-437-8478

Iron Bench, 12619 Bailey Rd., Redding, CA 96003 / 916-241-4623

Ironside International Publishers, Inc., 3000 S. Eaos St., Arlington, VA 22202 / 703-684-6111; FAX: 703-683-5486

Ironsighter Co., P.O. Box 85070, Westland, MI 48185 / 734-326-8731; FAX: 734-326-3378 www.ironsighter.com

Irwin, Campbell H., 140 Hartland Blvd., East Hartland, CT 06027 / 203-653-3901

Island Pond Gun Shop, Cross St., Island Pond, VT 05846 / 802-723-4546

Israel Arms International, Inc., 1085 Gessner Rd., Ste. F, Houston, TX 77055 / 713-789-0745; FAX: 713-914-9515 iaipro@wt.net www.israelarms.com

Ithaca Classic Doubles, Stephen Lamboy, No. 5 Railroad St., Victor, NY 14564 / 716-924-2710; FAX: 716-924-2737 ithacadoubles.com

Ithaca Gun Company LLC, 901 Rt. 34 B, King Ferry, NY 13081 / 315-364-7171; FAX: 315-364-5134 info@ithacagun.com

Ivanoff, Thomas G. (See Tom's Gun Repair)

J

J J Roberts Firearm Engraver, 7808 Lake Dr, Manassas, VA 20111 / 703-330-0448; FAX: 703-264-8600 james..roberts@angelfire.com www.angelfire.com/va2/engraver

J&D Components, 75 East 350 North, Orem, UT 84057-4719 / 801-225-7007

J&J Products, Inc., 9240 Whitmore, El Monte, CA 91731 / 818-571-5228; FAX: 800-927-8361

J&J Sales, 1501 21st Ave. S., Great Falls, MT 59405 / 406-727-9789 www.j&jsales.us

J&L Superior Bullets (See Huntington Die Special)

J&R Engineering, P.O. Box 77, 200 Lyons Hill Rd., Athol, MA 01331 / 508-249-9241

J&R Enterprises, 4550 Scotts Valley Rd., Lakeport, CA 95453

J&S Heat Treat, 803 S. 16th St., Blue Springs, MO 64015 / 816-229-2149; FAX: 816-228-1135

J. Dewey Mfg. Co., Inc., P.O. Box 2014, Southbury, CT 06488 / 203-264-3064; FAX: 203-262-6907 deweyrods@worldnet.att.net www.deweyrods.com

J. Korzinek Riflesmith, RD 2, Box 73D, Canton, PA 17724 / 717-673-8512

J.A. Blades, Inc. (See Christopher Firearms Co.)

J.A. Henckels Zwillingswerk Inc., 9 Skyline Dr., Hawthorne, NY 10532 / 914-592-7370

J.G. Anschutz GmbH & Co. KG, Daimlerstr. 12, D-89079 Ulm, Ulm, GERMANY / 49 731 40120; FAX: 49 731 4012700 JGA-info@anschuetz-sport.com www.anschuetz-sport.com

J.G. Dapkus Co., Inc., Commerce Circle, P.O. Box 293, Durham, CT 06422 www.explodingtargets.com

J.I.T. Ltd., P.O. Box 230, Freedom, WY 83120 / 708-494-0937

J.J. Roberts / Engraver, 7808 Lake Dr., Manassas, VA 20111 / 703-330-0448 jjrengraver@aol.com www.angelfire.com/va2/engraver

J.P. Enterprises Inc., P.O. Box 378, Hugo, MN 55110 / 612-486-9064; FAX: 612-482-0970

J.R. Williams Bullet Co., 2008 Tucker Rd., Perry, GA 31069 / 912-987-0274

J.W. Morrison Custom Rifles, 4015 W. Sharon, Phoenix, AZ 85029 / 602-978-3754

J/B Adventures & Safaris Inc., 2275 E. Arapahoe Rd., Ste. 109, Littleton, CO 80122-1521 / 303-771-0977

Jack A. Rosenberg & Sons, 12229 Cox Ln., Dallas, TX 75234 / 214-241-6302

Jack Dever Co., 8520 NW 90th St., Oklahoma City, OK 73132 / 405-721-6393 jbdever1@home.com

Jack First, Inc., 1201 Turbine Dr., Rapid City, SD 57703 / 605-343-8481; FAX: 605-343-9420

Jack Jonas Appraisals & Taki, 13952 E. Marina Dr., #604, Aurora, CO 80014

Jackalope Gun Shop, 1048 S. 5th St., Douglas, WY 82633 / 307-358-3441

Jaffin, Harry. See: BRIDGEMAN PRODUCTS

Jagdwaffen, Peter. See: BUCHSENMACHERMEISTER

James Calhoon Mfg., Shambo Rte. 304, Havre, MT 59501 / 406-395-4079 www.jamescalhoon.com

James Calhoon Varmint Bullets, Shambo Rt., 304, Havre, MT 59501 / 406-395-4079 www.jamescalhoon.com

James Churchill Glove Co., PO Box 298, Centralia, WA 98531 / 360-736-2816; FAX: 360-330-0151 churchillglove@localaccess.com

James Wayne Firearms for Collectors and Investors, 2608 N. Laurent, Victoria, TX 77901 / 361-578-1258; FAX: 361-578-3559

Jamison International, Marc Jamison, 3551 Mayer Ave., Sturgis, SD 57785 / 605-347-5090; FAX: 605-347-4704 jbell2@masttechnology.com

Jamison, Marc. See: JAMISON INTERNATIONAL

Jamison's Forge Works, 4527 Rd. 6.5 NE, Moses Lake, WA 98837 / 509-762-2659

Jantz Supply, 309 West Main Dept HD, Davis, OK 73030-0584 / 580-369-2316; FAX: 580-369-3082 jantz@brightok.net www.knifemaking.com

Jarrett Rifles, Inc., 383 Brown Rd., Jackson, SC 29831 / 803-471-3616 www.jarrettrifles.com

Jarvis, Inc., 1123 Cherry Orchard Lane, Hamilton, MT 59840 / 406-961-4392

Javelina Lube Products, PO Box 337, San Bernardino, CA 92402 / 714-882-5847; FAX: 714-434-6937

Jay McCament Custom Gunmaker, Jay McCament, 1730-134th St. Ct. S., Tacoma, WA 98444 / 253-531-8832

JB Custom, P.O. Box 6912, Leawood, KS 66206 / 913-381-2329

Jeff W. Flannery Engraving Co., 11034 Riddles Run Rd., Union, KY 41091 / 606-384-3127 engraving@fuse.net http://home.fuse.net/engraving/

Jeffredo Gunsight, P.O. Box 669, San Marcos, CA 92079 / 760-728-2695

Jena Eur, PO Box 319, Dunmore, PA 18512

Jenco Sales, Inc., P.O. Box 1000, Manchaca, TX 78652 / 800-531-5301; FAX: 800-266-2373 jencosales@sbcglobal.net

Jenkins Recoil Pads, Inc., 5438 E. Frontage Ln., Olney, IL 62450 / 618-395-3416

Jensen Bullets, RR 1 Box 187, Arco, ID 83213 / 208-785-5590

Jensen's Custom Ammunition, 5146 E. Pima, Tucson, AZ 85712 / 602-325-3346; FAX: 602-322-5704

Jensen's Firearms Academy, 1280 W. Prince, Tucson, AZ 85705 / 602-293-8516

Jericho Tool & Die Co., Inc., 2917 St. Hwy. 7, Bainbridge, NY 13733 / 607-563-8222; FAX: 607-563-8560 jerichotool.com www.jerichotool.com

Jerry Phillips Optics, P.O. Box L632, Langhorne, PA 19047 / 215-757-5037; FAX: 215-757-7097

Jesse W. Smith Saddlery, 0499 County Road J, Pritchett, CO 81064 / 509-325-0622

Jester Bullets, Rt. 1 Box 27, Orienta, OK 73737

Jewell Triggers, Inc., 3620 Hwy. 123, San Marcos, TX 78666 / 512-353-2999; FAX: 512-392-0543

J-Gar Co., 183 Turnpike Rd., Dept. 3, Petersham, MA 01366-9604

JGS Precision Tool Mfg., LLC, 60819 Selander Rd., Coos Bay, OR 97420 / 541-267-4331; FAX: 541-267-5996 jgstools@harborside.com www.jgstools.com

Jim Blair Engraving, P.O. Box 64, Glenrock, WY 82637 / 307-436-8115 jblairengrav@msn.com

Jim Noble Co., 1305 Columbia St, Vancouver, WA 98660 / 360-695-1309; FAX: 360-695-6835 jnobleco@aol.com

Jim Norman Custom Gunstocks, 14281 Cane Rd., Valley Center, CA 92082 / 619-749-6252

Jim's Gun Shop (See Spradlin's)

Jim's Precision, Jim Ketchum, 1725 Moclips Dr., Petaluma, CA 94952 / 707-762-3014

JLK Bullets, 414 Turner Rd., Dover, AR 72837 / 501-331-4194

Johanssons Vapentillbehor, Bert, S-430 20, Veddige, SWEDEN

John Hall Plastics, Inc., P.O. Box 1526, Alvin, TX 77512 / 713-489-8709

John J. Adams & Son Engravers, 7040 VT Rt 113, Vershire, VT 05079 / 802-685-0019

John Masen Co. Inc., 1305 Jelmak, Grand Prairie, TX 75050 / 817-430-8732; FAX: 817-430-1715

John Norrell Arms, 2608 Grist Mill Rd, Little Rock, AR 72207 / 501-225-7864

John Partridge Sales Ltd., Trent Meadows Rugeley, Staffordshire, WS15 2HS ENGLAND

John Rigby & Co., 500 Linne Rd. Ste. D, Paso Robles, CA 93446 / 805-227-4236; FAX: 805-227-4723 jribgy@calinet www.johnrigbyandco.com

Johnny Stewart Game Calls, Inc., P.O. Box 7954, 5100 Fort Ave., Waco, TX 76714 / 817-772-3261; FAX: 817-772-3670

John's Custom Leather, 523 S. Liberty St., Blairsville, PA 15717 / 724-459-6802; FAX: 724-459-5996

Johnson Wood Products, 34897 Crystal Road, Strawberry Point, IA 52076 / 563-933-6504 johnsonwoodproducts@yahoo.com

Johnston Bros. (See C&T Corp. TA Johnson Brothers)

Jonad Corp., 2091 Lakeland Ave., Lakewood, OH 44107 / 216-226-3161

Jonathan Arthur Ciener, Inc., 8700 Commerce St., Cape Canaveral, FL 32920 / 321-868-2200; FAX: 321-868-2201

Jones Co., Dale, 680 Hoffman Draw, Kila, MT 59920 / 406-755-4684

Jones Custom Products, Neil A., 17217 Brookhouser Rd., Saegertown, PA 16433 / 814-763-2769; FAX: 814-763-4228

Jones, L. See: SSK INDUSTRIES

Jones Moulds, Paul, 4901 Telegraph Rd, Los Angeles, CA 90022 / 213-262-1510

JP Sales, Box 307, Anderson, TX 77830

JRP Custom Bullets, RR2 2233 Carlton Rd., Whitehall, NY 12887 / 518-282-0084 or 802-438-5548

JSL Ltd (See U.S. Importer-Specialty Shooters)

Juenke, Vern, 25 Bitterbush Rd., Reno, NV 89523 / 702-345-0225

MANUFACTURER'S DIRECTORY

Jungkind, Reeves C., 509 E. Granite St., Llano, TX 78643-3055 / 512-442-1094

Jurras, L. See: L. E. JURRAS & ASSOC.

Justin Phillippi Custom Bullets, P.O. Box 773, Ligonier, PA 15658 / 412-238-9671

K

K&M Industries, Inc., Box 66, 510 S. Main, Troy, ID 83871 / 208-835-2281; FAX: 208-835-5211

K&M Services, 5430 Salmon Run Rd., Dover, PA 17315 / 717-292-3175; FAX: 717-292-3175

K. Eversull Co., Inc., 1 Tracemont, Boyce, LA 71409 / 318-793-8728; FAX: 318-793-5483 bestguns@aol.com

K.B.I. Inc., P.O. Box 6625, Harrisburg, PA 17112 / 717-540-8518; FAX: 717-540-8567

K.L. Null Holsters Ltd., 161 School St. NW, Hill City Station, Resaca, GA 30735 / 706-625-5643; FAX: 706-625-9392 ken@klnullholsters.com www.klnullholsters.com

Ka Pu Kapili, P.O. Box 745, Honokaa, HI 96727 / 808-776-1644; FAX: 808-776-1731

KA-BAR Knives, 1125 E. State St., Olean, NY 14760 / 800-282-0130; FAX: 716-373-6245 info@ka-bar.com www.ka-bar.com

Kahles A. Swarovski Company, 2 Slater Rd., Cranston, RI 02920 / 401-946-2220; FAX: 401-946-2587

Kahr Arms, PO Box 220, 630 Route 303, Blauvelt, NY 10913 / 845-353-7770; FAX: 845-353-7833 www.kahr.com

Kailua Custom Guns Inc., 51 N. Dean Street, Coquille, OR 97423 / 541-396-5413 kailuacustom@aol.com www.kailuacustom.com

Kalispel Case Line, P.O. Box 267, Cusick, WA 99119 / 509-445-1121

Kamik Outdoor Footwear, 554 Montee de Liesse, Montreal, PQ H4T 1P1 CANADA / 514-341-3950; FAX: 514-341-1861

Kane, Edward, P.O. Box 385, Ukiah, CA 95482 / 707-462-2937

Kane Products, Inc., 5572 Brecksville Rd., Cleveland, OH 44131 / 216-524-9962

Kapro Mfg. Co. Inc. (See R.E.I.)

Kasenit Co., Inc., 13 Park Ave., Highland Mills, NY 10930 / 914-928-9595; FAX: 914-928-7292

Kaswer Custom, Inc., 13 Surrey Drive, Brookfield, CT 06804 / 203-775-0564; FAX: 203-775-6872

KDF, Inc., 2485 Hwy. 46 N., Seguin, TX 78155 / 830-379-8141; FAX: 830-379-5420

KeeCo Impressions, Inc., 346 Wood Ave., North Brunswick, NJ 08902 / 800-468-0546

Kehr, Roger, 2131 Agate Ct. SE, Lacy, WA 98503 / 360-491-0691

Keith's Bullets, 942 Twisted Oak, Algonquin, IL 60102 / 708-658-3520

Keith's Custom Gunstocks, Keith M. Heppler, 540 Banyan Circle, Walnut Creek, CA 94598 / 925-934-3509; FAX: 925-934-3143 kmheppler@hotmail.com

Kelbly, Inc., 7222 Dalton Fox Lake Rd., North Lawrence, OH 44666 / 216-683-4674; FAX: 216-683-7349

Kelley's, P.O. Box 125, Woburn, MA 01801-0125 / 800-879-7273; FAX: 781-272-7077 kels@star.net www.kelsmilitary.com

Kellogg's Professional Products, 325 Pearl St., Sandusky, OH 44870 / 419-625-6551; FAX: 419-625-6167 skwigton@aol.com

Kelly, Lance, 1723 Willow Oak Dr., Edgewater, FL 32132 / 904-423-4933

Kel-Tec CNC Industries, Inc., PO Box 236009, Cocoa, FL 32923 / 407-631-0068; FAX: 407-631-1169

Kemen America, 2550 Hwy. 23, Wrenshall, MN 55797 / 218-384-3670 patrickl@midwestshootingschool.com midwestshootingschool.com

Ken Eyster Heritage Gunsmiths, Inc., 6441 Bishop Rd., Centerburg, OH 43011 / 740-625-6131; FAX: 740-625-7811

Ken Starnes Gunmaker, 15940 SW Holly Hill Rd, Hillsboro, OR 97123-9033 / 503-628-0705; FAX: 503-443-2096 kstarnes@kdsa.com

Keng's Firearms Specialty, Inc./US Tactical Systems, 875 Wharton Dr., P.O. Box 44405, Atlanta, GA 30336-1405 / 404-691-7611; FAX: 404-505-8445

Kennebec Journal, 274 Western Ave., Augusta, ME 04330 / 207-622-6288

Kennedy Firearms, 10 N. Market St., Muncy, PA 17756 / 717-546-6695

Kenneth W. Warren Engraver, P.O. Box 2842, Wenatchee, WA 98807 / 509-663-6123; FAX: 509-665-6123

Ken's Kustom Kartridges, 331 Jacobs Rd., Hubbard, OH 44425 / 216-534-4595

Kent Cartridge America, Inc., PO Box 849, 1000 Zigor Rd., Kearneysville, WV 25430

Kent Cartridge Mfg. Co. Ltd., Unit 16 Branbridges Industrial Esta, Tonbridge, Kent, ENGLAND / 622-872255; FAX: 622-872645

Keowee Game Calls, 608 Hwy. 25 North, Travelers Rest, SC 29690 / 864-834-7204; FAX: 864-834-7831

Kershaw Knives, 25300 SW Parkway Ave., Wilsonville, OR 97070 / 503-682-1966; or 800-325-2891; FAX: 503-682-7168

Kesselring Gun Shop, 4024 Old Hwy. 99N, Burlington, WA 98233 / 360-724-3113; FAX: 360-724-7003 info@kesselrings.com www.kesselrings.com

Ketchum, Jim (See Jim's Precision)

Kickeez I.N.C., Inc., 301 Industrial Dr, Carl Junction, MO 64834-8806 / 419-649-2100; FAX: 417-649-2200 kickey@ipa.net

Kilham & Co., Main St., P.O. Box 37, Lyme, NH 03768 / 603-795-4112

Kim Ahrends Custom Firearms, Inc., Box 203, Clarion, IA 50525 / 515-532-3449; FAX: 515-532-3926

Kimar (See U.S. Importer-IAR,Inc)

Kimber of America, Inc., 1 Lawton St., Yonkers, NY 10705 / 800-880-2418; FAX: 914-964-9340

King & Co., P.O. Box 1242, Bloomington, IL 61702 / 309-473-3964; FAX: 309-473-2161

King's Gun Works, 1837 W. Glenoaks Blvd., Glendale, CA 91201 / 818-956-6010; FAX: 818-548-8606

Kingyon, Paul L. (See Custom Calls)

Kirkpatrick Leather Co., PO Box 677, Laredo, TX 78040 / 956-723-6631; FAX: 956-725-0672 mike@kirkpatrickleather.com www.kirkpatrickleather.com

KK Air International (See Impact Case & Container Co.)

KLA Enterprises, P.O. Box 2028, Eaton Park, FL 33840 / 941-682-2829; FAX: 941-682-2829

Kleen-Bore,Inc., 16 Industrial Pkwy., Easthampton, MA 01027 / 413-527-0300; FAX: 413-527-2522 info@kleen-bore.com www.kleen-bore.com

Klein Custom Guns, Don, 433 Murray Park Dr, Ripon, WI 54971 / 920-748-2931 daklein@charter.net

Kleinendorst, K. W., RR 1, Box 1500, Hop Bottom, PA 18824 / 717-289-4687

Klingler Woodcarving, P.O. Box 141, Thistle Hill, Cabot, VT 05647 / 802-426-3811

Knifeware, Inc., P.O. Box 3, Greenville, WV 24945 / 304-832-6878

Knight & Hale Game Calls, Box 468, Industrial Park, Cadiz, KY 42211 / 502-924-1755; FAX: 502-924-1763

Knight Rifles, 21852 Hwy. J46, P.O. Box 130, Centerville, IA 52544 / 515-856-2626; FAX: 515-856-2628

Knight Rifles (See Modern Muzzle Loading, Inc.)

Knight's Mfg. Co., 7750 Ninth St. SW, Vero Beach, FL 32968 / 561-562-5697; FAX: 561-569-2955 civiliansales@knightarmco.com

Knock on Wood Antiques, 355 Post Rd., Darien, CT 06820 / 203-655-9031

Knoell, Doug, 9737 McCardle Way, Santee, CA 92071 / 619-449-5189

Knopp, Gary. See: SUPER 6 LLC

KOGOT, 410 College, Trinidad, CO 81082 / 719-846-9406; FAX: 719-846-9406

Kokolus, Michael M. (See Custom Riflestocks In)

Kolar, 1925 Roosevelt Ave, Racine, WI 53406 / 414-554-0800; FAX: 414-554-9093

Kolpin Mfg., Inc., P.O. Box 107, 205 Depot St., Fox Lake, WI 53933 / 414-928-3118; FAX: 414-928-3687

Korth Germany GmbH, Robert Bosch Strasse, 11, D-23909, 23909 Ratzeburg, GERMANY / 4541-840363; FAX: 4541-84 05 35

Korth USA, 437R Chandler St., Tewksbury, MA 01876 / 978-851-8656; FAX: 978-851-9462 info@kortusa.com www.korthusa.com

Korzinek Riflesmith, J., RD 2 Box 73D, Canton, PA 17724 / 717-673-8512

Koval Knives, 5819 Zarley St., Suite A, New Albany, OH 43054 / 614-855-0777; FAX: 614-855-0945 koval@kovalknives.com www.kovalknives.com

Kowa Optimed, Inc., 20001 S. Vermont Ave., Torrance, CA 90502 / 310-327-1913; FAX: 310-327-4177

Kramer Designs, P.O. Box 129, Clancy, MT 59634 / 406-933-8658; FAX: 406-933-8658

Kramer Handgun Leather, P.O. Box 112154, Tacoma, WA 98411 / 800-510-2666; FAX: 253-564-1214 www.kramerleather.com

Krause Publications, Inc., 700 E. State St., Iola, WI 54990 / 715-445-2214; FAX: 715-445-4087

Krico Deutschland GmbH, Nurnbergerstrasse 6, D-90602, Pyrbaum, GERMANY / 09180-2780; FAX: 09180-2661

Krieger Barrels, Inc., 2024 Mayfield Rd, Richfield, WI 53076 / 262-628-8558; FAX: 262-628-8748

Krieghoff Gun Co., H., Boschstrasse 22, D-89079 Elm, GERMANY or 731-4018270

Krieghoff International,Inc., 7528 Easton Rd., Ottsville, PA 18942 / 610-847-5173; FAX: 610-847-8691

Kukowski, Ed. See: ED'S GUN HOUSE

Kulis Freeze Dry Taxidermy, 725 Broadway Ave., Bedford, OH 44146 / 216-232-8352; FAX: 216-232-7305 jkulis@kastaway.com kastaway.com

KVH Industries, Inc., 110 Enterprise Center, Middletown, RI 02842 / 401-847-3327; FAX: 401-849-0045

Kwik-Site Co., 5555 Treadwell St., Wayne, MI 48184 / 734-326-1500; FAX: 734-326-4120 kwiksiteco@aol.com

L

L&R Lock Co., 1137 Pocalla Rd., Sumter, SC 29150 / 803-775-6127; FAX: 803-775-5171

L&S Technologies Inc. (See Aimtech Mount Systems)

L. Bengtson Arms Co., 6345-B E. Akron St., Mesa, AZ 85205 / 602-981-6375

L. E. Jurras & Assoc., L. E. Jurras, P.O. Box 680, Washington, IN 47501 / 812-254-6170; FAX: 812-254-6170 jurasgun@rtcc.net

L.A.R. Mfg., Inc., 4133 W. Farm Rd., West Jordan, UT 84088 / 801-280-3505; FAX: 801-280-1972

L.B.T., Judy Smith, HCR 62, Box 145, Moyie Springs, ID 83845 / 208-267-3588

L.E. Wilson, Inc., Box 324, 404 Pioneer Ave., Cashmere, WA 98815 / 509-782-1328; FAX: 509-782-7200

L.L. Bean, Inc., Freeport, ME 04032 / 207-865-4761; FAX: 207-552-2802

L.P.A. Inc., Via Alfieri 26, Gardone V.T., Brescia, ITALY / 30-891-14-81; FAX: 30-891-09-51

L.R. Clift Mfg., 3821 Hammonton Rd., Marysville, CA 95901 / 916-755-3390; FAX: 916-755-3393

L.W. Seecamp Co., Inc., PO Box 255, New Haven, CT 06502 / 203-877-3429; FAX: 203-877-3429 seecamp@optonline.net

La Clinique du .45, 1432 Rougemont, Chambly,, PQ J3L 2L8 CANADA / 514-658-1144

Labanu, Inc., 2201-F Fifth Ave., Ronkonkoma, NY 11779 / 516-467-6197; FAX: 516-981-4112

LaBoone, Pat. See: THE MIDWEST SHOOTING SCHOOL

LaBounty Precision Reboring, Inc, 7968 Silver Lake Rd., PO Box 186, Maple Falls, WA 98266 / 360-599-2047; FAX: 360-599-3018

LaCrosse Footwear, Inc., 18550 NE Riverside Parkway, Portland, OR 97230 / 503-766-1010; or 800-323-2668; FAX: 503-766-1015

LaFrance Specialties, P.O. Box 87933, San Diego, CA 92138 / 619-293-3373; FAX: 619-293-7087 timlafrance@att.net

Lake Center Marina, PO Box 670, St. Charles, MO 63302 / 314-946-7500

Lakefield Arms Ltd. (See Savage Arms, Inc.)

Lakewood Products LLC, 275 June St., Berlin, WI 54923 / 800-872-8458; FAX: 920-361-7719 lakewood@dotnet.com www.lakewoodproducts.com

Lamboy, Stephen. See: ITHACA CLASSIC DOUBLES

Lampert, Ron, Rt. 1, 44857 Schoolcraft Trl., Guthrie, MN 56461 / 218-854-7345

Lamson & Goodnow Mfg. Co., 45 Conway St., Shelburne Falls, MA 03170 / 413-625-6564; or 800-872-6564; FAX: 413-625-9816 www.lamsonsharp.com

Lansky Levine, Arthur. See: LANSKY SHARPENERS

Lansky Sharpeners, Arthur Lansky Levine, P.O. Box 50830, Las Vegas, NV 89016 / 702-361-7511; FAX: 702-896-9511

LaPrade, PO Box 250, Ewing, VA 24248 / 423-733-2615

Lapua Ltd., P.O. Box 5, Lapua, FINLAND / 6-310111; FAX: 6-4388991

LaRocca Gun Works, 51 Union Place, Worcester, MA 01608 / 508-754-2887; FAX: 508-754-2887 www.laroccagunworks.com

Larry Lyons Gunworks, 110 Hamilton St., Dowagiac, MI 49047 / 616-782-9478

Laser Devices, Inc., 2 Harris Ct. A-4, Monterey, CA 93940 / 831-373-0701; FAX: 831-373-0903 sales@laserdevices.com www.laserdevices.com

Laseraim Technologies, Inc., P.O. Box 3548, Little Rock, AR 72203 / 501-375-2227

Laserlyte, 2201 Amapola Ct., Torrance, CA 90501

LaserMax, Inc., 3495 Winton Place, Bldg. B, Rochester, NY 14623-2807 / 800-527-3703; FAX: 716-272-5427 customerservice@lasermax-inc.com www.lasermax-inc.com

Lassen Community College, Gunsmithing Dept., P.O. Box 3000, Hwy. 139, Susanville, CA 96130 / 916-251-8800; FAX: 916-251-8838

Lathrop's, Inc., Inc., 5146 E. Pima, Tucson, AZ 85712 / 520-881-0266; or 800-875-4867; FAX: 520-322-5704

MANUFACTURER'S DIRECTORY

Laughridge, William R (See Cylinder & Slide Inc)

Laurel Mountain Forge, P.O. Box 52, Crown Point, IN 46308 / 219-548-2950; FAX: 219-548-2950

Laurona Armas Eibar, S.A.L., Avenida de Otaola 25, P.O. Box 260, Eibar 20600, SPAIN / 34-43-700600; FAX: 34-43-700616

Lawrence Brand Shot (See Precision Reloading)

Lawrence Leather Co., P.O. Box 1479, Lillington, NC 27546 / 910-893-2071; FAX: 910-893-4742

Lawson Co., Harry, 3328 N Richey Blvd., Tucson, AZ 85716 / 520-326-1117; FAX: 520-326-1117

Lawson, John. See: THE SIGHT SHOP

Lawson, John G (See Sight Shop, The)

Lazzeroni Arms Co., PO Box 26696, Tucson, AZ 85726 / 888-492-7247; FAX: 520-624-4250

Le Clear Industries (See E-Z-Way Systems), PO Box 4310, Newark, OH 43058-4310 / 614-345-6645; FAX: 614-345-6600

Lea Mfg. Co., 237 E. Aurora St., Waterbury, CT 06720 / 203-753-5116

Leapers, Inc., 7675 Five Mile Rd., Northville, MI 48167 / 248-486-1231; FAX: 248-486-1430

Leatherman Tool Group, Inc., 12106 NE Ainsworth Cir., P.O. Box 20595, Portland, OR 97294 / 503-253-7826; FAX: 503-253-7830

Lebeau-Courally, Rue St. Gilles, 386 4000, Liege, BELGIUM / 042-52-48-43; FAX: 32-4-252-2008 info@lebeau-courally.com www.lebeau-courally.com

Leckie Professional Gunsmithing, 546 Quarry Rd., Ottsville, PA 18942 / 215-847-8594

Ledbetter Airguns, Riley, 1804 E Sprague St, Winston Salem, NC 27107-3521 / 919-784-0676

Lee Precision, Inc., 4275 Hwy. U, Hartford, WI 53027 / 262-673-3075; FAX: 262-673-9273 info@leeprecision.com www.leeprecision.com

Lee Supplies, Mark, 9901 France Ct., Lakeville, MN 55044 / 612-461-2114

LeFever Arms Co., Inc., 6234 Stokes, Lee Center Rd., Lee Center, NY 13363 / 315-337-6722; FAX: 315-337-1543

Legacy Sports International, 206 S. Union St., Alexandria, VA 22314 / 703-548-4837 www.legacysports.com

Legend Products Corp., 21218 Saint Andrews Blvd., Boca Raton, FL 33433-2435

Leibowitz, Leonard, 1205 Murrayhill Ave., Pittsburgh, PA 15217 / 412-361-5455

Leica USA, Inc., 156 Ludlow Ave., Northvale, NJ 07647 / 201-767-7500; FAX: 201-767-8666

LEM Gun Specialties, Inc. The Lewis Lead Remover, P.O. Box 2855, Peachtree City, GA 30269-2024 / 770-487-0556

Leonard Day, 6 Linseed Rd Box 1, West Hatfield, MA 01088-7505 / 413-337-8369

Les Baer Custom,Inc., 29601 34th Ave., Hillsdale, IL 61257 / 309-658-2716; FAX: 309-658-2610

LesMerises, Felix. See: ROCKY MOUNTAIN ARMOURY

Lethal Force Institute (See Police Bookshelf), PO Box 122, Concord, NH 03301 / 603-224-6814; FAX: 603-226-3554

Lett Custom Grips, 672 Currier Rd., Hopkinton, NH 03229-2652 / 800-421-5388; FAX: 603-226-4580 info@lettgrips.com www.lettgrips.com

Leupold & Stevens, Inc., 14400 NW Greenbrier Pky., Beaverton, OR 97006 / 503-646-9171; FAX: 503-526-1455

Lever Arms Service Ltd., 2131 Burrard St., Vancouver, BC V6J 3H7 CANADA / 604-736-2711; FAX: 604-738-3503

Lew Horton Dist. Co., Inc., 15 Walkup Dr., Westboro, MA 01581 / 508-366-7400; FAX: 508-366-5332

Liberty Metals, 2233 East 16th St., Los Angeles, CA 90021 / 213-581-9171; FAX: 213-581-9351 libertymfgsolder@hotmail.com

Liberty Safe, 999 W. Utah Ave., Payson, UT 84651-1744 / 800-247-5625; FAX: 801-489-6409

Liberty Shooting Supplies, P.O. Box 357, Hillsboro, OR 97123 / 503-640-5518; FAX: 503-640-5518 info@libertyshootingsupplies.com www.libertyshootingsupplies.com

Lightning Performance Innovations, Inc., RD1 Box 555, Mohawk, NY 13407 / 315-866-8819; FAX: 315-867-5701

Lilja Precision Rifle Barrels, P.O. Box 372, Plains, MT 59859 / 406-826-3084; FAX: 406-826-3083 lilja@riflebarrels.com www.riflebarrels.com

Lincoln, Dean, Box 1886, Farmington, NM 87401

Linder Solingen Knives, 4401 Sentry Dr., Tucker, GA 30084 / 770-939-6915; FAX: 770-939-6738

Lindsay Engraving & Tools, Steve Lindsay, 3714 W. Cedar Hills, Kearney, NE 68845 / 308-236-7885 steve@lindsayengraving.com www.handgravers.com

Lindsay, Steve. See: LINDSAY ENGRAVING & TOOLS

Lindsley Arms Cartridge Co., P.O. Box 757, 20 College Hill Rd., Henniker, NH 03242 / 603-428-3127

Linebaugh Custom Sixguns, P.O. Box 455, Cody, WY 82414 / 307-645-3332 www.sitgunner.com

Lion Country Supply, P.O. Box 480, Port Matilda, PA 16870

List Precision Engineering, Unit 1 Ingley Works, 13 River Road, Barking, ENGLAND / 011-081-594-1686

Lithi Bee Bullet Lube, 1728 Carr Rd., Muskegon, MI 49442 / 616-788-4479

"Little John's" Antique Arms, 1740 W. Laveta, Orange, CA 92668

Little Trees Ramble (See Scott Pilkington)

Littler Sales Co., 20815 W. Chicago, Detroit, MI 48228 / 313-273-6888; FAX: 313-273-1099 littlerptg@aol.com

Littleton, J. F., 275 Pinedale Ave., Oroville, CA 95966 / 916-533-6084

Ljutic Industries, Inc., 732 N. 16th Ave., Suite 22, Yakima, WA 98902 / 509-248-0476; FAX: 509-576-8233 ljuticgun.net www.ljuticgun.com

Llama Gabilondo Y Cia, Apartado 290, E-01080, Victoria, spain, SPAIN

Loch Leven Industries/Convert-A-Pell, P.O. Box 2751, Santa Rosa, CA 95405 / 707-573-8735; FAX: 707-573-0369

Lock's Philadelphia Gun Exchange, 6700 Rowland Ave., Philadelphia, PA 19149 / 215-332-6225; FAX: 215-332-4800 locks.gunshop@verlzon.net

Lodewick, Walter H., 2816 NE Halsey St., Portland, OR 97232 / 503-284-2554

Lodgewood Mfg., P.O. Box 611, Whitewater, WI 53190 / 262-473-5444; FAX: 262-473-6448 lodgewd@idcnet.com lodgewood.com

Log Cabin Sport Shop, 8010 Lafayette Rd., Lodi, OH 44254 / 330-948-1082; FAX: 330-948-4307 logcabin@logcabinshop.com www.logcabinshop.com

Logan, Harry M., Box 745, Honokaa, HI 96727 / 808-776-1644

Logdewood Mfg., P.O. Box 611, Whitewater, WI 53190 / 262-473-5444; FAX: 262-473-6448 lodgewd@idcnet.com www.lodgewood.com

Lohman Mfg. Co., Inc., 4500 Doniphan Dr., P.O. Box 220, Neosho, MO 64850 / 417-451-4438; FAX: 417-451-2576

Lomont Precision Bullets, 278 Sandy Creek Rd, Salmon, ID 83467 / 208-756-6819; FAX: 208-756-6824 www.klomont.com

London Guns Ltd., Box 3750, Santa Barbara, CA 93130 / 805-683-4141; FAX: 805-683-1712

Lone Star Gunleather, 1301 Brushy Bend Dr., Round Rock, TX 78681 / 512-255-1805

Lone Star Rifle Company, 11231 Rose Road, Conroe, TX 77303 / 936-856-3363 dave@lonestar.com

Long, George F., 1500 Rogue River Hwy., Ste. F, Grants Pass, OR 97527 / 541-476-7552

Lortone Inc., 2856 NW Market St., Seattle, WA 98107

Lothar Walther Precision Tool Inc., 3425 Hutchinson Rd., Cumming, GA 30040 / 770-889-9998; FAX: 770-889-4919 lotharwalther@mindspring.com www.lothar-walther.com

LPS Laboratories, Inc., 4647 Hugh Howell Rd., P.O. Box 3050, Tucker, GA 30084 / 404-934-7800

Lucas, Edward E, 32 Garfield Ave., East Brunswick, NJ 08816 / 201-251-5526

Lupton, Keith. See: PAWLING MOUNTAIN CLUB

Lyman Instant Targets, Inc. (See Lyman Products)

Lyman Products Corp., 475 Smith Street, Middletown, CT 06457-1541 / 800-423-9704; FAX: 860-632-1699 lymansales@cshore.com www.lymanproducts.com

M

M. Thys (See U.S. Importer-Champlin Firearms Inc)

M.H. Canjar Co., 6510 Raleigh St., Arvada, CO 80003 / 303-295-2638; FAX: 303-295-2638

MA Systems, P.O. Box 894, Pryor, OK 74362-0894 / 918-479-6378

Mac-1 Airgun Distributors, 13974 Van Ness Ave., Gardena, CA 90249-2900 / 310-327-3581; FAX: 310-327-0238 mac1@mac1airgun.com www.mac1airgun.com

Madis Books, 2453 West Five Mile Pkwy., Dallas, TX 75233 / 214-330-7168

Madis, George. See: GEORGE MADIS WINCHESTER CONSULTANTS

MAG Instrument, Inc., 1635 S. Sacramento Ave., Ontario, CA 91761 / 909-947-1006; FAX: 909-947-3116

Magma Engineering Co., P.O. Box 161, 20955 E. Ocotillo Rd., Queen Creek, AZ 85242 / 602-987-9008; FAX: 602-987-0148

Mag-Na-Port International, Inc., 41302 Executive Dr., Harrison Twp., MI 48045-1306 / 586-469-6727; FAX: 586-469-0425 email@magnaport.com www.magnaport.com

Magnolia Sports,Inc., 211 W. Main, Magnolia, AR 71753 / 501-234-8410; or 800-530-7816; FAX: 501-234-8117

Magnum Power Products, Inc., P.O. Box 17768, Fountain Hills, AZ 85268

Magnum Research, Inc., 7110 University Ave. NE, Minneapolis, MN 55432 / 800-772-6168 or 763-574-1868; FAX: 763-574-0109 info@magnumresearch.com

Magnus Bullets, P.O. Box 239, Toney, AL 35773 / 256-420-8359; FAX: 256-420-8360

Mag-Pack Corp., P.O. Box 846, Chesterland, OH 44026 / 440-285-9480 magpack@hotmail.com

MagSafe Ammo Co., 4700 S US Highway 17/92, Casselberry, FL 32707-3814 / 407-834-9966; FAX: 407-834-8185 www.magsafeonline.com

Magtech Ammunition Co. Inc., 837 Boston Rd #12, Madison, CT 06443 / 203-245-8983; FAX: 203-245-2883 rfine@mactechammunition.com www.mactech.com.br

Mahony, Philip Bruce, 67 White Hollow Rd., Lime Rock, CT 06039-2418 / 203-435-9341 filbalony-redbeard@snet.net

Mahovsky's Metalife, R.D. 1, Box 149a Eureka Road, Grand Valley, PA 16420 / 814-436-7747

Maine Custom Bullets, RFD 1, Box 1755, Brooks, ME 04921

Maionchi-L.M.I., Via Di Coselli-Zona, Industriale Di Guamo 55060, Lucca, ITALY / 011 39-583 94291

Makinson, Nicholas, RR 3, Komoka, ON N0L 1R0 CANADA / 519-471-5462

Malcolm Enterprises, 1023 E. Prien Lake Rd., Lake Charles, LA 70601

Mallardtone Game Calls, 10406 96th St., Court West, Taylor Ridge, IL 61284 / 309-798-2481; FAX: 309-798-2501

Mandall Shooting Supplies Inc., 3616 N. Scottsdale Rd., Scottsdale, AZ 85251 / 480-945-2553; FAX: 480-949-0734

Marathon Rubber Prods. Co., Inc., 1009 3rd St, Wausau, WI 54403-4765 / 715-845-6255

Marble Arms (See CRR, Inc./Marble's Inc.)

Marchmon Bullets, 8191 Woodland Shore Dr., Brighton, MI 48116

Marent, Rudolf. See: HAMMERLI SERVICE-PRECISION MAC

Mark Lee Supplies, 9901 France Ct., Lakeville, MN 55044 / 952-461-2114; FAX: 952-461-2194 marklee55044@usfamily.net

Markell,Inc., 422 Larkfield Center 235, Santa Rosa, CA 95403 / 707-573-0792; FAX: 707-573-9867

Markesbery Muzzle Loaders, Inc., 7785 Foundation Dr., Ste. 6, Florence, KY 41042 / 606-342-5553 or 606-342-2380

Marksman Products, 5482 Argosy Dr., Huntington Beach, CA 92649 / 714-898-7535; or 800-822-8005; FAX: 714-891-0782

Marlin Firearms Co., 100 Kenna Dr., North Haven, CT 06473 / 203-239-5621; FAX: 203-234-7991

MarMik, Inc., 2116 S. Woodland Ave., Michigan City, IN 46360 / 219-872-7231; FAX: 219-872-7231

Marocchi F.lli S.p.A, Via Galileo Galilei 8, I-25068 Zanano, ITALY

Marquart Precision Co., P.O. Box 1740, Prescott, AZ 86302 / 520-445-5646

Marsh, Mike, Croft Cottage, Main St., Derbyshire, DE4 2BY ENGLAND / 01629 650 669

Marshall Enterprises, 792 Canyon Rd., Redwood City, CA 94062

Marshall Fish Mfg. Gunsmith Sptg. Co., Rd. Box 2439, Westport, NY 12993 / 518-962-4897; FAX: 518-962-4897

Martin B. Retting Inc., 11029 Washington, Culver City, CA 90232 / 213-837-2412

Martini & Hagn, 1264 Jimsmith Lake Rd, Cranbrook, BC V1C 6V6 CANADA / 250-417-2926; FAX: 250-417-2928

Martin's Gun Shop, 937 S. Sheridan Blvd., Lakewood, CO 80226 / 303-922-2184

Martz, John V., 8060 Lakeview Lane, Lincoln, CA 95648 FAX: 916-645-3815

Marvel, Alan, 3922 Madonna Rd., Jarretsville, MD 21084 / 301-557-6545

Marx, Harry (See U.S. Importer for FERLIB)

Maryland Paintball Supply, 8507 Harford Rd., Parkville, MD 21234 / 410-882-5607

MAST Technology, Inc., 14555 US Hwy. 95 S., P.O. Box 60969, Boulder City, NV 89006 / 702-293-6969; FAX: 702-293-7255 info@masttechnology.com www.bellammo.com

Master Lock Co., 2600 N. 32nd St., Milwaukee, WI 53245 / 414-444-2800

Match Prep-Doyle Gracey, P.O. Box 155, Tehachapi, CA 93581 / 661-822-5383; FAX: 661-823-8680

Mathews & Son, Inc., George E., 10224 S Paramount Blvd., Downey, CA 90241 / 562-862-6719; FAX: 562-862-6719

Matthews Cutlery, 4401 Sentry Dr., Tucker, GA 30084 / 770-939-6915

Mauser Werke Oberndorf Waffensysteme GmbH, Postfach 1349, 78722, Oberndorf/N., GERMANY

Maverick Arms, Inc., 7 Grasso Ave., P.O. Box 497, North Haven, CT 06473 / 203-230-5300; FAX: 203-230-5420

Maxi-Mount Inc., P.O. Box 291, Willoughby Hills, OH 44096-0291 / 440-944-9456; FAX: 440-944-9456 maximount454@yahoo.com

Mayville Engineering Co. (See MEC, Inc.)

Mazur Restoration, Pete, 13083 Drummer Way, Grass Valley, CA 95949 / 530-268-2412

McBros Rifle Co., P.O. Box 86549, Phoenix, AZ 85080 / 602-582-3713; FAX: 602-581-3825

McCament, Jay. See: JAY MCCAMENT CUSTOM GUNMAKER

McCann Industries, P.O. Box 641, Spanaway, WA 98387 / 253-537-6919; FAX: 253-537-6919 mccann.machine@worldnet.att.net www.mccannindustries.com

McCann's Machine & Gun Shop, P.O. Box 641, Spanaway, WA 98387 / 253-537-6919; FAX: 253-537-6993 mccann.machine@worldnet.att.net www.mccannindustries.com

McCann's Muzzle-Gun Works, 14 Walton Dr., New Hope, PA 18938 / 215-862-2728

McCluskey Precision Rifles, 10502 14th Ave. NW, Seattle, WA 98177 / 206-781-2776

McCombs, Leo, 1862 White Cemetery Rd., Patriot, OH 45658 / 740-256-1714

McCormick Corp., Chip, 1715 W. FM 1626 Ste. 105, Manchaca, TX 78652 / 800-328-CHIP; FAX: 512-462-0009

McDonald, Dennis, 8359 Brady St., Peosta, IA 52068 / 319-556-7940

McFarland, Stan, 2221 Idella Ct., Grand Junction, CO 81505 / 970-243-4704

McGhee, Larry. See: B.C. OUTDOORS

McGowen Rifle Barrels, 5961 Spruce Lane, St. Anne, IL 60964 / 815-937-9816; FAX: 815-937-4024

Mchalik, Gary. See: ROSSI FIREARMS

McKenzie, Lynton, 6940 N. Alvernon Way, Tucson, AZ 85718 / 520-299-5090

McMillan Fiberglass Stocks, Inc., 1638 W. Knudsen Dr. #102, Phoenix, AZ 85027 / 602-582-9635; FAX: 602-581-3825

McMillan Optical Gunsight Co., 28638 N. 42nd St., Cave Creek, AZ 85331 / 602-585-7868; FAX: 602-585-7872

McMillan Rifle Barrels, P.O. Box 3427, Bryan, TX 77805 / 409-690-3456; FAX: 409-690-0156

McMurdo, Lynn (See Specialty Gunsmithing), PO Box 404, Afton, WY 83110 / 307-886-5535

MCS, Inc., 166 Pocono Rd., Brookfield, CT 06804-2023 / 203-775-1013; FAX: 203-775-9462

McWelco Products, 6730 Santa Fe Ave., Hesperia, CA 92345 / 619-244-8876; FAX: 619-244-9398 products@mcwelco.com www.mawelco.com

MDS, P.O. Box 1441, Brandon, FL 33509-1441 / 813-653-1180; FAX: 813-684-5953

Measurement Group Inc., Box 27777, Raleigh, NC 27611

Measures, Leon. See: SHOOT WHERE YOU LOOK

MEC, Inc., 715 South St., Mayville, WI 53050 / 414-387-4500; FAX: 414-387-5802 reloaders@mayul.com www.mayvl.com

MEC-Gar S.R.L., Via Madonnina 64, Gardone V.T. Brescia, ITALY / 39-30-8912687; FAX: 39-30-8910065

MEC-Gar U.S.A., Inc., Hurley Farms Industr. Park, 115, Hurley Road 6G, Oxofrd, CT 06478 / 203-262-1525; FAX: 203-262-1719 mecgar@aol.com www.mec-gar.com

Mech-Tech Systems, Inc., 1602 Foothill Rd., Kalispell, MT 59901 / 406-755-8055

Meister Bullets (See Gander Mountain)

Mele, Frank, 201 S. Wellow Ave., Cookeville, TN 38501 / 615-526-4860

Menck, Gunsmith Inc., T.W., 5703 S 77th St, Ralston, NE 68127

Mendez, John A., P.O. Box 620984, Orlando, FL 32862 / 407-344-2791

Men-Metallwerk Elisenhuette GmbH, P.O. Box 1263, Nassau/Lahn, D-56372 GERMANY / 2604-7819

Meprolight (See Hesco-Meprolight)

Mercer Custom Guns, 216 S Whitewater Ave, Jefferson, WI 53549 / 920-674-3839

Merit Corp., PO Box 9044, Schenectady, NY 12309 / 518-346-1420 sales@meritcorporation.com www.meritcorporation.com

Merkel, Schutzenstrasse 26, D-98527 Suhl, Suhl, GERMANY FAX: 011-49-3681-854-203 www.merkel-waffen.de

Merkuria Ltd., Argentinska 38, 17005, Praha 7 CZECH, REPUBLIC / 422-875117; FAX: 422-809152

Metal Merchants, PO Box 186, Walled Lake, MI 48390-0186

Metalife Industries (See Mahovsky's Metalife)

Michael's Antiques, Box 591, Waldoboro, ME 04572

Michaels Of Oregon, Inc., P.O. Box 1690, Oregon City, OR 97045 www.michaels-oregon.com

Micro Sight Co., 242 Harbor Blvd., Belmont, CA 94002 / 415-591-0769; FAX: 415-591-7531

Microfusion Alfa S.A., Paseo San Andres N8, P.O. Box 271, Eibar, 20600 SPAIN / 34-43-11-89-16; FAX: 34-43-11-40-38

Mid-America Recreation, Inc., 1328 5th Ave., Moline, IL 61265 / 309-764-5089; FAX: 309-764-5089 fmilcusguns@aol.com www.midamericarecreation.com

Middlebrooks Custom Shop, 7366 Colonial Trail East, Surry, VA 23883 / 757-357-0881; FAX: 757-365-0442

Midway Arms, Inc., 5875 W. Van Horn Tavern Rd., Columbia, MO 65203 / 800-243-3220; or 573-445-6363; FAX: 573-446-1018

Midwest Gun Sport, 1108 Herbert Dr., Zebulon, NC 27597 / 919-269-5570

Midwest Sport Distributors, Box 129, Fayette, MO 65248

Mike Davis Products, 643 Loop Dr., Moses Lake, WA 98837 / 509-765-6178; or 509-766-7281

Military Armament Corp., P.O. Box 120, Mt. Zion Rd., Lingleville, TX 76461 / 817-965-3253

Millennium Designed Muzzleloaders, PO Box 536, Routes 11 & 25, Limington, ME 04049 / 207-637-2316

Miller Arms, Inc., P.O. Box 260 Purl St., St. Onge, SD 57779 / 605-642-5160; FAX: 605-642-5160

Miller Custom, 210 E. Julia, Clinton, IL 61727 / 217-935-9362

Miller Single Trigger Mfg. Co., 6680 Rt. 5-20, P.O. Box 471, Bloomfield, NY 14469 / 585-657-6338

Millett Sights, 7275 Murdy Circle, Adm. Office, Huntington Beach, CA 92647 / 714-842-5575 or 800-645-5388; FAX: 714-843-5707

Mills Jr., Hugh B., 3615 Canterbury Rd., New Bern, NC 28560 / 919-637-4631

Milstor Corp., 80-975 Indio Blvd., Indio, CA 92201 / 760-775-9998; FAX: 760-775-5229 milstor@webtv.net

Miltex, Inc, 700 S Lee St, Alexandria, VA 22314-4332 / 888-642-9123; FAX: 301-645-1430

Minute Man High Tech Industries, 10611 Canyon Rd. E., Suite 151, Puyallup, WA 98373 / 800-233-2734

Mirador Optical Corp., P.O. Box 11614, Marina Del Rey, CA 90295-7614 / 310-821-5587; FAX: 310-305-0386

Mitchell, Jack, c/o Geoff Gaebe, Addieville East Farm, 200 Pheasant Dr, Mapleville, RI 02839 / 401-568-3185

Mitchell Bullets, R.F., 430 Walnut St, Westernport, MD 21562

Mitchell Optics, Inc., 2072 CR 1100 N, Sidney, IL 61877 / 217-688-2219; or 217-621-3018; FAX: 217-688-2505 mitche1@attglobal.net

Mitchell's Accuracy Shop, 68 Greenridge Dr., Stafford, VA 22554 / 703-659-0165

MI-TE Bullets, 1396 Ave. K, Ellsworth, KS 67439 / 785-472-4575; FAX: 785-472-5579

Mittermeier, Inc., Frank, PO Box 2G, 3577 E Tremont Ave, Bronx, NY 10465 / 718-828-3843

Mixson Corp., 7635 W. 28th Ave., Hialeah, FL 33016 / 305-821-5190; or 800-327-0078; FAX: 305-558-9318

MJK Gunsmithing, Inc., 417 N. Huber Ct., E. Wenatchee, WA 98802 / 509-884-7683

MKS Supply, Inc. (See Hi-Point Firearms)

MMC, 5050 E. Belknap St., Haltom City, TX 76117 / 817-831-9557; FAX: 817-834-5508

MOA Corporation, 2451 Old Camden Pike, Eaton, OH 45320 / 937-456-3669 www.moaguns.com

Modern Gun Repair School, PO Box 846, Saint Albans, VT 05478 / 802-524-2223; FAX: 802-524-2053 jfwp@dlilearn.com www.mgsinfoadlifearn.com

Modern Muzzleloading, Inc., P.O. Box 130, Centerville, IA 52544 / 515-856-2626

Moeller, Steve, 1213 4th St., Fulton, IL 61252 / 815-589-2300

Mogul Co./Life Jacket, 500 N. Kimball Rd., Ste. 109, South Lake, TX 76092

Molin Industries, Tru-Nord Division, P.O. Box 365, 204 North 9th St., Brainerd, MN 56401 / 218-829-2870

Monell Custom Guns, 228 Red Mills Rd., Pine Bush, NY 12566 / 914-744-3021

Moneymaker Guncraft Corp., 1420 Military Ave., Omaha, NE 68131 / 402-556-0226

Montana Armory, Inc (See C. Sharps Arms Co. Inc.), 100 Centennial Dr., P.O. Box 885, Big Timber, MT 59011 / 406-932-4353; FAX: 406-932-4443

Montana Outfitters, Lewis E. Yearout, 308 Riverview Dr. E., Great Falls, MT 59404 / 406-761-0859

Montana Precision Swaging, P.O. Box 4746, Butte, MT 59702 / 406-494-0600; FAX: 406-494-0600

Montana Rifleman, Inc., 2593A Hwy. 2 East, Kalispell, MT 59901 / 406-755-4867

Montana Vintage Arms, 2354 Bear Canyon Rd., Bozeman, MT 59715

Montgomery Community College, PO Box 787-GD, Troy, NC 27371 / 910-576-6222; or 800-839-6222; FAX: 910-576-2176 hammondp@mcc.montgomery.cc.nc.us www.montgomery.cc.nc.us

Morini (See U.S. Importers-Mandall Shooting Supply)

Morrison Custom Rifles, J. W., 4015 W Sharon, Phoenix, AZ 85029 / 602-978-3754

Morrison Precision, 6719 Calle Mango, Hereford, AZ 85615 / 520-378-6207 morprec@c2i2.com

Morrow, Bud, 11 Hillside Lane, Sheridan, WY 82801-9729 / 307-674-8360

Morton Booth Co., P.O. Box 123, Joplin, MO 64802 / 417-673-1962; FAX: 417-673-3642

Mo's Competitor Supplies (See MCS, Inc.)

Moss Double Tone, Inc., P.O. Box 1112, 2101 S. Kentucky, Sedalia, MO 65301 / 816-827-0827

Mountain Plains Industries, 244 Glass Hollow Rd., Alton, VA 22920 / 800-687-3000; FAX: 540-456-8134

Mountain South, P.O. Box 381, Barnwell, SC 29812 / FAX: 803-259-3227

Mountain State Muzzleloading Supplies, Inc., Box 154-1, Rt. 2, Williamstown, WV 26187 / 304-375-7842; FAX: 304-375-3737

Mowrey Gun Works, P.O. Box 246, Waldron, IN 46182 / 317-525-6181; FAX: 317-525-9595

Mowrey's Guns & Gunsmithing, 119 Fredericks St., Canajoharie, NY 13317 / 518-673-3483

MPC, P.O. Box 450, McMinnville, TN 37110-0450 / 615-473-5513; FAX: 615-473-5516 thebox@blomand.net www.mpc-thebox.com

MPI Stocks, PO Box 83266, Portland, OR 97283 / 503-226-1215; FAX: 503-226-2661

MSR Targets, P.O. Box 1042, West Covina, CA 91793 / 818-331-7840

Mt. Alto Outdoor Products, Rt. 735, Howardsville, VA 24562

MTM Molded Products Co., Inc., 3370 Obco Ct., Dayton, OH 45414 / 937-890-7461; FAX: 937-890-1747

Mulberry House Publishing, P.O. Box 2180, Apache Junction, AZ 85217 / 888-738-1567; FAX: 480-671-1015

Mulhern, Rick, Rt. 5, Box 152, Rayville, LA 71269 / 318-728-2688

Mullins Ammunition, Rt. 2 Box 304N, Clintwood, VA 24228 / 540-926-6772; FAX: 540-926-6092 www.extremeshockusa

Mullis Guncraft, 3523 Lawyers Road E., Monroe, NC 28110 / 704-283-6683

Multiplex International, 26 S. Main St., Concord, NH 03301 FAX: 603-796-2223

Multipropulseurs, La Bertrandiere, 42580, FRANCE / 77 74 01 30; FAX: 77 93 19 34

Multi-Scale Charge Ltd., 3269 Niagara Falls Blvd., N. Tonawanda, NY 14120 / 905-566-1255; FAX: 905-276-6295

Mundy, Thomas A., 69 Robbins Road, Somerville, NJ 08876 / 201-722-2199

Murmur Corp., 2823 N. Westmoreland Ave., Dallas, TX 75222 / 214-630-5400

Murphy, R.R. Murphy Co., Inc. See: MURPHY, R.R. CO., INC.

Murphy, R.R. Co., Inc., R.R. Murphy Co., Inc. Murphy, P.O. Box 102, Ripley, TN 38063 / 901-635-4003; FAX: 901-635-2320

Murray State College, 1 Murray Campus St., Tishomingo, OK 73460 / 508-371-2371

Muscle Products Corp., 112 Fennell Dr., Butler, PA 16002 / 800-227-7049 or 724-283-0567; FAX: 724-283-8310 mpc@mpc_home.com www.mpc_home.com

Muzzleloaders Etcetera, Inc., 9901 Lyndale Ave. S., Bloomington, MN 55420 / 952-884-1161 www.muzzleloaders-etcetera.com

MWG Co., P.O. Box 971202, Miami, FL 33197 / 800-428-9394 or 305-253-8393; FAX: 305-232-1247

N

N.B.B., Inc., 24 Elliot Rd., Sterling, MA 01564 / 508-422-7538; or 800-942-9444

N.C. Ordnance Co., P.O. Box 3254, Wilson, NC 27895 / 919-237-2440; FAX: 919-243-9845

Nagel's Custom Bullets, 100 Scott St., Baytown, TX 77520-2849

Nalpak, 1937-C Friendship Drive, El Cajon, CA 92020 / 619-258-1200

Nastoff, Steve. See: NASTOFFS 45 SHOP, INC.

Nastoffs 45 Shop, Inc., Steve Nastoff, 1057 Laverne Dr., Youngstown, OH 44511

National Bullet Co., 1585 E. 361 St., Eastlake, OH 44095 / 216-951-1854; FAX: 216-951-7761

National Target Co., 4690 Wyaconda Rd., Rockville, MD 20852 / 800-827-7060 or 301-770-7060; FAX: 301-770-7892

Nationwide Airgun Repair, 2310 Windsor Forest Dr, Louisville, KY 40272 / 502-937-2614; FAX: 812-637-1463 airgunrepair@aol.com

Naval Ordnance Works, Rt. 2, Box 919, Sheperdstown, WV 25443 / 304-876-0998

Navy Arms Co., Inc., 219 Lawn St., Martinsburg, WV 25401 / 304-262-1651; FAX: 304-262-1658

Navy Arms Company, Valmore J. Forgett Jr., 815 22nd Street, Union City, NJ 07087 / 201-863-7100; FAX: 201-863-8770 info@navyarms.com www.navyarms.com

NCP Products, Inc., 3500 12th St. N.W., Canton, OH 44708 / 330-456-5130; FAX: 330-456-5234

Necessary Concepts, Inc., P.O. Box 571, Deer Park, NY 11729 / 516-667-8509; FAX: 516-667-8588

NEI Handtools, Inc., 51583 Columbia River Hwy., Scappoose, OR 97056 / 503-543-6776; FAX: 503-543-7865 nei@columbia-center.com www.neihandtools.com

Neil A. Jones Custom Products, 17217 Brookhouser Road, Saegertown, PA 16433 / 814-763-2769; FAX: 814-763-4228

Nelson, Gary K., 975 Terrace Dr., Oakdale, CA 95361 / 209-847-4590

Nelson, Stephen. See: NELSON'S CUSTOM GUNS, INC.

Nelson/Weather-Rite, Inc., 14760 Santa Fe Trail Dr., Lenexa, KS 66215 / 913-492-3200; FAX: 913-492-8749

Nelson's Custom Guns, Inc., Stephen Nelson, 7430 Valley View Dr. N.W., Corvallis, OR 97330 / 541-745-5232 nelsons-custom@attbi.com

Nesci Enterprises Inc., P.O. Box 119, Summit St., East Hampton, CT 06424 / 203-267-2588

Nesika Bay Precision, 22239 Big Valley Rd., Poulsbo, WA 98370 / 206-697-3830

Nettestad Gun Works, 38962 160th Avenue, Pelican Rapids, MN 56572 / 218-863-4301

Neumann GmbH, Am Galgenberg 6, 90575, GERMANY / 09101/8258; FAX: 09101/6356

Nevada Pistol Academy, Inc., 4610 Blue Diamond Rd., Las Vegas, NV 89139 / 702-897-1100

New England Ammunition Co., 1771 Post Rd. East, Suite 223, Westport, CT 06880 / 203-254-8048

New England Arms Co., Box 278, Lawrence Lane, Kittery Point, ME 03905 / 207-439-0593; FAX: 207-439-0525 info@newenglandarms.com www.newenglandarms.com

New England Custom Gun Service, 438 Willow Brook Rd., Plainfield, NH 03781 / 603-469-3450; FAX: 603-469-3471 bestguns@cyborportal.net www.newenglandcustom.com

New Orleans Jewelers Supply Co., 206 Charters St., New Orleans, LA 70130 / 504-523-3839; FAX: 504-523-3836

New SKB Arms Co., C.P.O. Box 1401, Tokyo, JAPAN / 81-3-3943-9550; FAX: 81-3-3943-0695

New Ultra Light Arms, LLC, 1024 Grafton Rd., Morgantown, WV 26508 / 304-292-0600; FAX: 304-292-9662 newultralightarm@cs.com www.NewUltraLightArm

Newark Electronics, 4801 N. Ravenswood Ave., Chicago, IL 60640

Newell, Robert H., 55 Coyote, Los Alamos, NM 87544 / 505-662-7135

Newman Gunshop, 2035 Chester Ave. #411, Ottumwa, IA 52501-3715 / 515-937-5775

Nicholson Custom, 17285 Thornlay Road, Hughesville, MO 65334 / 816-826-8746

Nickels, Paul R., 4328 Seville St., Las Vegas, NV 89121 / 702-435-5318

Nicklas, Ted, 5504 Hegel Rd., Goodrich, MI 48438 / 810-797-4493

Niemi Engineering, W. B., Box 126 Center Rd., Greensboro, VT 05841 / 802-533-7180; FAX: 802-533-7141

Nikon, Inc., 1300 Walt Whitman Rd., Melville, NY 11747 / 516-547-8623; FAX: 516-547-0309

Nitex Gun Shop, P.O. Box 1706, Uvalde, TX 78801 / 830-278-8843

Noreen, Peter H., 5075 Buena Vista Dr., Belgrade, MT 59714 / 406-586-7383

Norica, Avnda Otaola, 16 Apartado 68, Eibar, SPAIN

Norinco, 7A Yun Tan N, Beijing, CHINA

Norincoptics (See BEC, Inc.)

Norma Precision AB (See U.S. Importers-Dynamit)

Normark Corp., 10395 Yellow Circle Dr., Minnetonka, MN 55343-9101 / 612-933-7060; FAX: 612-933-0046

North American Arms, Inc., 2150 South 950 East, Provo, UT 84606-6285 / 800-821-5783; or 801-374-9990; FAX: 801-374-9998

North American Correspondence Schools The Gun Pro, Oak & Pawney St., Scranton, PA 18515 / 717-342-7701

North American Shooting Systems, P.O. Box 306, Osoyoos, BC V0H 1V0 CANADA / 604-495-3131; FAX: 604-495-2816

North Devon Firearms Services, 3 North St., Braunton, EX33 1AJ ENGLAND / 01271 813624; FAX: 01271 813624

North Mountain Pine Training Center (See Executive

North Specialty Products, 10091 Stageline St., Corona, CA 92883 / 714-524-1665

North Star West, P.O. Box 488, Glencoe, CA 95232 / 209-293-7010 northstarwest.com

Northern Precision Custom Swaged Bullets, 329 S. James St., Carthage, NY 13619 / 315-493-1711

Northlake Outdoor Footwear, P.O. Box 10, Franklin, TN 37065-0010 / 615-794-1556; FAX: 615-790-8005

Northside Gun Shop, 2725 NW 109th, Oklahoma City, OK 73120 / 405-840-2353

Northwest Arms, 26884 Pearl Rd., Parma, ID 83660 / 208-722-6771; FAX: 208-722-1062

No-Sho Mfg. Co., 10727 Glenfield Ct., Houston, TX 77096 / 713-723-5332

Nosler, Inc., P.O. Box 671, Bend, OR 97709 / 800-285-3701 or 541-382-3921; FAX: 541-388-4667

Novak's, Inc., 1206 1/2 30th St., P.O. Box 4045, Parkersburg, WV 26101 / 304-485-9295; FAX: 304-428-6722

Now Products, Inc., P.O. Box 27608, Tempe, AZ 85285 / 800-662-6063; FAX: 480-966-0890

Nowlin Mfg. Co., 20622 S 4092 Rd, Claremore, OK 74017 / 918-342-0689; FAX: 918-342-0624 nowlinguns@msn.com nowlinguns.com

NRI Gunsmith School, P.O. Box 182968, Columbus, OH 43218-2968

Nu-Line Guns,Inc., 1053 Caulks Hill Rd., Harvester, MO 63304 / 314-441-4500; or 314-447-4501; FAX: 314-447-5018

Null Holsters Ltd. K.L., 161 School St NW, Resaca, GA 30735 / 706-625-5643; FAX: 706-625-9392

Numrich Arms Corp., 203 Broadway, W. Hurley, NY 12491

Numrich Gun Parts Corporation, 226 Williams Lane, P.O. Box 299, West Hurley, NY 12491 / 866-686-7424; FAX: 877-GUNPART info@gunpartscorp.com www.@-gunparts.com

Nygord Precision Products, Inc., P.O. Box 12578, Prescott, AZ 86304 / 928-717-2315; FAX: 928-717-2198 nygords@northlink.com www.nygordprecision.com

O

O.F. Mossberg & Sons,Inc., 7 Grasso Ave., North Haven, CT 06473 / 203-230-5300; FAX: 203-230-5420

Oakman Turkey Calls, RD 1, Box 825, Harrisonville, PA 17228 / 717-485-4620

Obermeyer Rifled Barrels, 23122 60th St., Bristol, WI 53104 / 262-843-3537; FAX: 262-843-2129

October Country Muzzleloading, P.O. Box 969, Dept. GD, Hayden, ID 83835 / 208-772-2068; FAX: 208-772-9230 ocinfo@octobercountry.com www.octobercountry.com

Oehler Research,Inc., P.O. Box 9135, Austin, TX 78766 / 512-327-6900 or 800-531-5125; FAX: 512-327-6903 www.oehler-research.com

Oil Rod and Gun Shop, 69 Oak St., East Douglas, MA 01516 / 508-476-3687

Ojala Holsters, Arvo, PO Box 98, N Hollywood, CA 91603 / 503-669-1404

OK Weber, Inc., P.O. Box 7485, Eugene, OR 97401 / 541-747-0458; FAX: 541-747-5927 okweber@pacinfo www.okweber.com

Oker's Engraving, P.O. Box 126, Shawnee, CO 80475 / 303-838-6042

Oklahoma Ammunition Co., 3701A S. Harvard Ave., No. 367, Tulsa, OK 74135-2265 / 918-396-3187; FAX: 918-396-4270

Oklahoma Leather Products,Inc., 500 26th NW, Miami, OK 74354 / 918-542-6651; FAX: 918-542-6653

Olathe Gun Shop, 716-A South Rogers Road, Olathe, KS 66062 / 913-782-6900; FAX: 913-782-6902 info@olathegunshop.com www.olathegunshop.com

Old Wagon Bullets, 32 Old Wagon Rd., Wilton, CT 06897

Old West Bullet Moulds, J Ken Chapman, P.O. Box 519, Flora Vista, NM 87415 / 505-334-6970

Old West Reproductions,Inc. R.M. Bachman, 446 Florence S. Loop, Florence, MT 59833 / 406-273-2615; FAX: 406-273-2615 rick@oldwestreproductions.com www.oldwestreproduction.com

Old World Gunsmithing, 2901 SE 122nd St., Portland, OR 97236 / 503-760-7681

Old World Oil Products, 3827 Queen Ave. N., Minneapolis, MN 55412 / 612-522-5037

Ole Frontier Gunsmith Shop, 2617 Hwy. 29 S., Cantonment, FL 32533 / 904-477-8074

Olson, Myron, 989 W. Kemp, Watertown, SD 57201 / 605-886-9787

Olson, Vic, 5002 Countryside Dr., Imperial, MO 63052 / 314-296-8086

Olympic Arms Inc., 620-626 Old Pacific Hwy. SE, Olympia, WA 98513 / 360-456-3471; FAX: 360-491-3447 info@olyarms.com www.olyarms.com

Olympic Optical Co., P.O. Box 752377, Memphis, TN 38175-2377 / 901-794-3890; or 800-238-7120; FAX: 901-794-0676 80

Omark Industries, Div. of Blount, Inc., 2299 Snake River Ave., P.O. Box 856, Lewiston, ID 83501 / 800-627-3640 or 208-746-2351

Omega Sales, P.O. Box 1066, Mt. Clemens, MI 48043 / 810-469-7323; FAX: 810-469-0425

100 Straight Products, Inc., P.O. Box 6148, Omaha, NE 68106 / 402-556-1055; FAX: 402-556-1055

One Of A Kind, 15610 Purple Sage, San Antonio, TX 78255 / 512-695-3364

One Ragged Hole, P.O. Box 13624, Tallahassee, FL 32317-3624

Op-Tec, P.O. Box L632, Langhorn, PA 19047 / 215-757-5037

Optical Services Co., P.O. Box 1174, Santa Teresa, NM 88008-1174 / 505-589-3833

Orchard Park Enterprise, P.O. Box 563, Orchard Park, NY 14127 / 616-656-0356

Oregon Arms, Inc. (See Rogue Rifle Co., Inc.)

Oregon Trail Bullet Company, PO Box 529, Dept. P, Baker City, OR 97814 / 800-811-0548; FAX: 514-523-1803

Original Box, Inc., 700 Linden Ave., York, PA 17404 / 717-854-2897; FAX: 717-845-4276

Original Deer Formula Co., The., PO Box 1705, Dickson, TN 37056 / 800-874-6965; FAX: 615-446-0646 deerformula1@aol.com

Original Mink Oil, Inc., 10652 NE Holman, Portland, OR 97220 / 503-255-2814; or 800-547-5895; FAX: 503-255-2487

Orion Rifle Barrel Co., RR2, 137 Cobler Village, Kalispell, MT 59901 / 406-257-5649

Otis Technology, Inc., RR 1 Box 84, Boonville, NY 13309 / 315-942-3320

Ottmar, Maurice, Box 657, 113 E. Fir, Coulee City, WA 99115 / 509-632-5717

Outa-Site Gun Carriers, 219 Market St., Laredo, TX 78040 / 210-722-4678; or 800-880-9715; FAX: 210-726-4858

Outdoor Edge Cutlery Corp., 4699 Nautilus Ct. S. Ste. 503, Boulder, CO 80301-5310 / 303-652-8212; FAX: 303-652-8238

Outdoor Enthusiast, 3784 W. Woodland, Springfield, MO 65807 / 417-883-9841

Outdoor Sports Headquarters, Inc., 967 Watertower Ln., West Carrollton, OH 45449 / 513-865-5855; FAX: 513-865-5962

Outers Laboratories Div. of ATK, Route 2, P.O. Box 39, Onalaska, WI 54650 / 608-781-5800; FAX: 608-781-0368

Ox-Yoke Originals, Inc., 34 Main St., Milo, ME 04463 / 800-231-8313; or 207-943-7351; FAX: 207-943-2416

Ozark Gun Works, 11830 Cemetery Rd., Rogers, AR 72756 / 479-631-1024; FAX: 479-631-1024 ogw@hotmail.com www.eocities.com/ocarkgunworks

P

P&M Sales & Services, LLC, 4697 Tote Rd. Bldg. H-B, Comins, MI 48619 / 989-848-8364; FAX: 989-848-8364 info@pmsales-online.com

P.A.C.T., Inc., P.O. Box 531525, Grand Prairie, TX 75053 / 214-641-0049

P.S.M.G. Gun Co., 10 Park Ave., Arlington, MA 02174 / 617-646-8845; FAX: 617-646-2133

Pachmayr Div. Lyman Products, 475 Smith St., Middletown, CT 06457 / 860-632-2020; or 800-225-9626; FAX: 860-632-1699 lymansales@cshore.com www.pachmayr.com

Pacific Armament Corp, 4813 Enterprise Way, Unit K, Modesto, CA 95356 / 209-545-2800 gunsparts@att.net

Pacific Cartridge, Inc., 2425 Salashan Loop Road, Ferndale, WA 98248 / 360-366-4444; FAX: 360-366-4445

Pacific Rifle Co., PO Box 1473, Lake Oswego, OR 97035 / 503-538-7437

PAC-NOR Barreling, 99299 Overlook Rd., P.O. Box 6188, Brookings, OR 97415 / 503-469-7330; FAX: 503-469-7331 info@pac-nor.com www.pac-nor.com

Paco's (See Small Custom Mould & Bullet Co.

Page Custom Bullets, P.O. Box 25, Port Moresby, NEW GUINEA

Pagel Gun Works, Inc., 1407 4th St. NW, Grand Rapids, MN 55744 / 218-326-3003

Pager Pal, 200 W Pleasantview, Hurst, TX 76054 / 800-561-1603; FAX: 817-285-8769 www.pagerpal.com

Paintball Games International Magazine Aceville, Castle House 97 High St., Essex, ENGLAND / 011-44-206-564840

MANUFACTURER'S DIRECTORY

Palmer Security Products, 2930 N. Campbell Ave., Chicago, IL 60618 / 773-267-0200; FAX: 773-267-8080 info@palmersecurity.com www.palmersecurity.com

Palsa Outdoor Products, P.O. Box 81336, Lincoln, NE 68501 / 402-488-5288; FAX: 402-488-2321

Paragon Sales & Services, Inc., 2501 Theodore St, Crest Hill, IL 60435-1613 / 815-725-9212; FAX: 815-725-8974

Para-Ordnance Mfg., Inc., 980 Tapscott Rd., Scarborough, ON M1X 1E7 CANADA / 416-297-7855; FAX: 416-297-1289

Para-Ordnance, Inc., 1919 NE 45th St., Ste 215, Ft. Lauderdale, FL 33308 info@paraord.com www.paraord.com

Pardini Armi Srl, Via Italica 154, 55043, Lido Di Camaiore Lu, ITALY / 584-90121; FAX: 584-90122

Paris, Frank J., 17417 Pershing St., Livonia, MI 48152-3822

Parker & Sons Shooting Supply, 9337 Smoky Row Road, Strawberry Plains, TN 37871 / 865-933-3286; FAX: 865-932-8586

Parker Gun Finishes, 9337 Smokey Row Rd., Strawberry Plains, TN 37871 / 423-933-3286; FAX: 865-932-8586

Parker Reproductions, 114 Broad St., Flemington, NJ 11232 / 718-499-6220; FAX: 718-499-6143

Parsons Optical Mfg. Co., PO Box 192, Ross, OH 45061 / 513-867-0820; FAX: 513-867-8380 psscopes@concentric.net

Partridge Sales Ltd., John, Trent Meadows, Rugeley, ENGLAND

Pasadena Gun Center, 206 E. Shaw, Pasadena, TX 77506 / 713-472-0417; FAX: 713-472-1322

Passive Bullet Traps, Inc. (See Savage Range Systems, Inc.)

Paterson Gunsmithing, 438 Main St., Paterson, NJ 07502 / 201-345-4100

Pathfinder Sports Leather, 2920 E. Chambers St., Phoenix, AZ 85040 / 602-276-0016

Patrick W. Price Bullets, 16520 Worthley Drive, San Lorenzo, CA 94580 / 510-278-1547

Pattern Control, 114 N. Third St., P.O. Box 462105, Garland, TX 75046 / 214-494-3551; FAX: 214-272-8447

Paul A. Harris Hand Engraving, 113 Rusty Lane, Boerne, TX 78006-5746 / 512-391-5121

Paul and Sharon Dressel, 209 N. 92nd Ave., Yakima, WA 98908 / 509-966-9233; FAX: 509-966-3365 dressels@nwinfo.net www.dressels.com

Paul D. Hillmer Custom Gunstocks, 7251 Hudson Heights, Hudson, IA 50643 / 319-988-3941

Paul Jones Moulds, 4901 Telegraph Rd., Los Angeles, CA 90022 / 213-262-1510

Paulsen Gunstocks, Rt. 71, Box 11, Chinook, MT 59523 / 406-357-3403

Pawling Mountain Club, Keith Lupton, PO Box 573, Pawling, NY 12564 / 914-855-3825

Paxton Quigley's Personal Protection Strategies, 9903 Santa Monica Blvd., 300, Beverly Hills, CA 90212 / 310-281-1762 www.defend-net.com/paxton

Payne Photography, Robert, Robert, P.O. Box 141471, Austin, TX 78714 / 512-272-4554

Peacemaker Specialists, P.O. Box 157, Whitmore, CA 96096 / 530-472-3438 www.peacemakerspecialists.com

Pearce Grip, Inc., PO Box 40367, Fort Worth, TX 76140 / 206-485-5488; FAX: 206-488-9497

Pease Accuracy, Bob, P.O. Box 310787, New Braunfels, TX 78131 / 210-625-1342

PECAR Herbert Schwarz GmbH, Kreuzbergstrasse 6, 10965, Berlin, GERMANY / 004930-785-7383; FAX: 004930-785-1934 michael.schwart@pecar-berlin.de www.pecar-berlin.de

Pecatonica River Longrifle, 5205 Nottingham Dr., Rockford, IL 61111 / 815-968-1995; FAX: 815-968-1996

Pedersen, C. R., 2717 S. Pere Marquette Hwy., Ludington, MI 49431 / 231-843-2061; FAX: 231-845-7695 fega@fega.com

Pedersen, Rex C., 2717 S. Pere Marquette Hwy., Ludington, MI 49431 / 231-843-2061; FAX: 231-845-7695 fega@fega.com

Peifer Rifle Co., P.O. Box 192, Nokomis, IL 62075-0192 / 217-563-7050; FAX: 217-563-7060

Pejsa Ballistics, 1314 Marquette Ave., Apt 807, Minneapolis, MN 55403 / 612-374-3337; FAX: 612-374-5383

Pelaire Products, 5346 Bonky Ct., W. Palm Beach, FL 33415 / 561-439-0691; FAX: 561-967-0052

Peltor, Inc. (See Aero Peltor)

PEM's Mfg. Co., 5063 Waterloo Rd., Atwater, OH 44201 / 216-947-3721

Pence Precision Barrels, 7567 E. 900 S., S. Whitley, IN 46787 / 219-839-4745

Pendleton Royal, c/o Swingler Buckland Ltd., 4/7 Highgate St., Birmingham, ENGLAND / 44 121 440 3060; or 44 121 446 5898; FAX: 44 121 446 4165

Pendleton Woolen Mills, P.O. Box 3030, 220 N.W. Broadway, Portland, OR 97208 / 503-226-4801

Penn Bullets, P.O. Box 756, Indianola, PA 15051

Pennsylvania Gun Parts Inc, P.O. Box 665, 300 Third St, East Berlin, PA 17316-0665 / 717-259-8010; FAX: 717-259-0057

Pennsylvania Gunsmith School, 812 Ohio River Blvd., Avalon, Pittsburgh, PA 15202 / 412-766-1812; FAX: 412-766-0855 pgs@pagunsmith.com www.pagunsmith.com

Penrod Precision, 312 College Ave., PO Box 307, N. Manchester, IN 46962 / 260-982-8385; FAX: 260-982-1819

Pentax Corp., 35 Inverness Dr. E., Englewood, CO 80112 / 303-799-8000; FAX: 303-790-1131

Pentheny de Pentheny, 2352 Baggett Ct., Santa Rosa, CA 95401 / 707-573-1390; FAX: 707-573-1390

Perazone-Gunsmith, Brian, Cold Spring Rd., Roxbury, NY 12474 / 607-326-4088; FAX: 607-326-3140

Perazzi U.S.A. Inc., 1010 West Tenth, Azusa, CA 91702 / 626-334-1234; FAX: 626-334-0344 perazziusa@aol.com

Performance Specialists, 308 Eanes School Rd., Austin, TX 78746 / 512-327-0119

Perugini Visini & Co. S.r.l., Via Camprelle, 126, 25080 Nuvolera, ITALY / 30-6897535; FAX: 30-6897821 peruvisi@virgilia.it

Pete Mazur Restoration, 13083 Drummer Way, Grass Valley, CA 95949 / 530-268-2412; FAX: 530-268-2412

Pete Rickard, Inc., 115 Roy Walsh Rd, Cobleskill, NY 12043 / 518-234-2731; FAX: 518-234-2454 rickard@telenet.net www.peterickard.com

Peter Dyson & Son Ltd., 3 Cuckoo Lane, Honley Huddersfield, Yorkshire, HD7 2BR ENGLAND / 44-1484-661062; FAX: 44-1484-663709 info@peterdyson.co.uk www.peterdyson.com

Peter Hale/Engraver, 800 E. Canyon Rd., Spanish Fork, UT 84660 / 801-798-8215

Peters Stahl GmbH, Stettiner Strasse 42, D-33106, Paderborn, GERMANY / 05251-750025; FAX: 05251-75611

Petersen Publishing Co., 6420 Wilshire Blvd., Los Angeles, CA 90048 / 213-782-2000; FAX: 213-782-2867

Peterson Gun Shop, Inc., A.W., 4255 W. Old U.S. 441, Mt. Dora, FL 32757-3299 / 352-383-4258; FAX: 352-735-1001

Petro-Explo Inc., 7650 U.S. Hwy. 287, Suite 100, Arlington, TX 76017 / 817-478-8888

Pettinger Books, Gerald, 47827 300th Ave., Russell, IA 50238 / 641-535-2239 gpettinger@lisco.com

Pflumm Mfg. Co., 10662 Widmer Rd., Lenexa, KS 66215 / 800-888-4867; FAX: 913-451-7857

PFRB Co., P.O. Box 1242, Bloomington, IL 61702 / 309-473-3964 or 800-914-5464; FAX: 309-473-2161

Philip S. Olt Co., P.O. Box 550, 12662 Fifth St., Pekin, IL 61554 / 309-348-3633; FAX: 309-348-3300

Phillippi Custom Bullets, Justin, P.O. Box 773, Ligonier, PA 15658 / 724-238-2962; FAX: 724-238-9671 jrp@wpa.net http://www.wpa.net~jrphil

Phillips & Rogers, Inc., 100 Hilbig #C, Conroe, TX 77301 / 409-435-0011

Phoenix Arms, 1420 S. Archibald Ave., Ontario, CA 91761 / 909-947-4843; FAX: 909-947-6798

Photronic Systems Engineering Company, 6731 Via De La Reina, Bonsall, CA 92003 / 619-758-8000

Piedmont Community College, P.O. Box 1197, Roxboro, NC 27573 / 336-599-1181; FAX: 336-597-3817 www.piedmont.cc.nc.us

Pierce Pistols, 55 Sorrellwood Lane, Sharpsburg, GA 30277-9523 / 404-253-8192

Pietta (See U.S. Importers-Navy Arms Co, Taylor's

Pilgrim Pewter,Inc. (See Bell Originals Inc. Sid)

Pilkington, Scott (See Little Trees Ramble)

Pine Technical College, 1100 4th St., Pine City, MN 55063 / 800-521-7463; FAX: 612-629-6766

Pinetree Bullets, 133 Skeena St., Kitimat, BC V8C 1Z1 CANADA / 604-632-3768; FAX: 604-632-3768

Pioneer Arms Co., 355 Lawrence Rd., Broomall, PA 19008 / 215-356-5203

Piotti (See U.S. Importer-Moore & Co, Wm. Larkin)

Piquette, Paul. See: PIQUETTE'S CUSTOM ENGRAVING

Piquette's Custom Engraving, Paul R. Piquette, 80 Bradford Dr., Feeding Hills, MA 01030 / 413-789-4582; FAX: 413-786-8118 ppiquette@aol.com www.pistoldynamics.com

Plaza Cutlery, Inc., 3333 Bristol, 161 South Coast Plaza, Costa Mesa, CA 92626 / 714-549-3932

Plum City Ballistic Range, N2162 80th St., Plum City, WI 54761 / 715-647-2539

PlumFire Press, Inc., 30-A Grove Ave., Patchogue, NY 11772-4112 / 800-695-7246; FAX: 516-758-4071

PMC/Eldorado Cartridge Corp., P.O. Box 62508, 12801 U.S. Hwy. 95 S., Boulder City, NV 89005 / 702-294-0025; FAX: 702-294-0121 kbauer@pmcammo.com www.pmcammo.com

Poburka, Philip (See Bison Studios)

Pohl, Henry A. (See Great American Gun Co.

Pointing Dog Journal, Village Press Publications, P.O. Box 968, Dept. PGD, Traverse City, MI 49685 / 800-272-3246; FAX: 616-946-3289

Police Bookshelf, PO Box 122, Concord, NH 03301 / 603-224-6814; FAX: 603-226-3554

Polywad, Inc., P.O. Box 7916, Macon, GA 31209 / 478-477-0669; or 800-998-0669 polywadmpb@aol.com www.polywad.com

Ponsness/Warren, 768 Ohio St., Rathdrum, ID 83858 / 800-732-0706; FAX: 208-687-2233

Pony Express Reloaders, 608 E. Co. Rd. D, Suite 3, St. Paul, MN 55117 / 612-483-9406; FAX: 612-483-9884

Pony Express Sport Shop, 23404 Lyons Ave., PMB 448, Newhall, CA 91321-2511 / 818-895-1231

Potts, Wayne E., 912 Poplar St., Denver, CO 80220 / 303-355-5462

Powder Horn Ltd., PO Box 565, Glenview, IL 60025 / 305-565-6060

Powell & Son (Gunmakers) Ltd., William, 35-37 Carrs Lane, Birmingham, B4 7SX ENGLAND / 121-643-0689; FAX: 121-631-3504

Powell Agency, William, 22 Circle Dr., Bellmore, NY 11710 / 516-679-1158

Power Custom, Inc., 29739 Hwy. J, Gravois Mills, MO 65037 / 573-372-5684; FAX: 573-372-5799 rwpowers@laurie.net www.powercustom.com

Power Plus Enterprises, Inc., PO Box 38, Warm Springs, GA 31830 / 706-655-2132

Powley Computer (See Hutton Rifle Ranch)

Practical Tools, Inc., 7067 Easton Rd., P.O. Box 133, Pipersville, PA 18947 / 215-766-7301; FAX: 215-766-8681

Prairie Gun Works, 1-761 Marion St., Winnipeg, MB R2J 0K6 CANADA / 204-231-2976; FAX: 204-231-8566

Prairie River Arms, 1220 N. Sixth St., Princeton, IL 61356 / 815-875-1616 or 800-445-1541; FAX: 815-875-1402

Pranger, Ed G., 1414 7th St., Anacortes, WA 98221 / 206-293-3488

Precision Airgun Sales, Inc., 5247 Warrensville Ctr Rd., Maple Hts., OH 44137 / 216-587-5005; FAX: 216-587-5005

Precision Cast Bullets, 101 Mud Creek Lane, Ronan, MT 59864 / 406-676-5135

Precision Delta Corp., PO Box 128, Ruleville, MS 38771 / 662-756-2810; FAX: 662-756-2590

Precision Firearm Finishing, 25 N.W. 44th Avenue, Des Moines, IA 50313 / 515-288-8680; FAX: 515-244-3925

Precision Gun Works, 104 Sierra Rd.Dept. GD, Kerrville, TX 78028 / 830-367-4587

Precision Reloading, Inc., PO Box 122, Stafford Springs, CT 06076 / 860-684-7979; FAX: 860-684-6788 info@precisionreloading.com www.precisionreloading.com

Precision Sales International, Inc., PO Box 1776, Westfield, MA 01086 / 413-562-5055; FAX: 413-562-5056 precision-sales.com

Precision Shooting, Inc., 222 McKee St., Manchester, CT 06040 / 860-645-8776; FAX: 860-643-8215 www.precisionshooting.com

Precision Small Arms Inc., 9272 Jeronimo Rd, Ste 121, Irvine, CA 92618 / 800-554-5515; or 949-768-3530; FAX: 949-768-4808 www.tcbebe.com

Precision Specialties, 131 Hendom Dr., Feeding Hills, MA 01030 / 413-786-3365; FAX: 413-786-3365

Precision Sport Optics, 15571 Producer Lane, Unit G, Huntington Beach, CA 92649 / 714-891-1309; FAX: 714-892-6920

Premier Reticles, 920 Breckinridge Lane, Winchester, VA 22601-6707 / 540-722-0601; FAX: 540-722-3522

Prescott Projectile Co., 1808 Meadowbrook Road, Prescott, AZ 86303

Preslik's Gunstocks, 4245 Keith Ln., Chico, CA 95926 / 916-891-8236

Price Bullets, Patrick W., 16520 Worthley Dr., San Lorenzo, CA 94580 / 510-278-1547

Prime Reloading, 30 Chiswick End, Meldreth, ROYSTON UK / 0763-260636

Primos, Inc., P.O. Box 12785, Jackson, MS 39236-2785 / 601-366-1288; FAX: 601-362-3274

PRL Bullets, c/o Blackburn Enterprises, 114 Stuart Rd., Ste. 110, Cleveland, TN 37312 / 423-559-0340

Pro Load Ammunition, Inc., 5180 E. Seltice Way, Post Falls, ID 83854 / 208-773-9444; FAX: 208-773-9441

Professional Gunsmiths of America, Rt 1 Box 224, Lexington, MO 64067 / 660-259-2636

Professional Hunter Supplies (See Star Custom Bullets), PO Box 608, 468 Main St., Ferndale, CA 95536 / 707-786-9140; FAX: 707-786-9117 wmebride@humboldt.com

PrOlixr Lubricants, P.O. Box 1348, Victorville, CA 92393 / 760-243-3129; FAX: 760-241-0148 prolix@accex.net www.prolixlubricant.com

Pro-Mark Div. of Wells Lamont, 6640 W. Touhy, Chicago, IL 60648 / 312-647-8200

Proofmark Corp., P.O. Box 610, Burgess, VA 22432 / 804-453-4337; FAX: 804-453-4337 proofmark@rivnet.net

Pro-Port Ltd., 41302 Executive Dr., Harrison Twp., MI 48045-1306 / 586-469-6727; FAX: 586-469-0425 e-mail@magnaport.com www.magnaport.com

Pro-Shot Products, Inc., P.O. Box 763, Taylorville, IL 62568 / 217-824-9133; FAX: 217-824-8861

Protektor Model, 1-11 Bridge St., Galeton, PA 16922 / 814-435-2442 mail@protektormodel.com www.protektormodel.com

Prototech Industries, Inc., 10532 E Road, Delia, KS 66418 / 785-771-3571; prototec@grapevine.net

ProWare, Inc., 15847 NE Hancock St., Portland, OR 97230 / 503-239-0159

PWL Gunleather, P.O. Box 450432, Atlanta, GA 31145 / 800-960-4072; FAX: 770-822-1704 covert@pwlusa.com www.pwlusa.com

Pyramyd Stone Inter. Corp., 2447 Suffolk Lane, Pepper Pike, OH 44124-4540

Q

Quack Decoy & Sporting Clays, 4 Ann & Hope Way, P.O. Box 98, Cumberland, RI 02864 / 401-723-8202; FAX: 401-722-5910

Quaker Boy, Inc., 5455 Webster Rd., Orchard Parks, NY 14127 / 716-662-3979; FAX: 716-662-9426

Quality Arms, Inc., Box 19477, Dept. GD, Houston, TX 77224 / 281-870-8377; FAX: 281-870-8524 arrieta2@excite.com www.gunshop.com

Quality Custom Firearms, Stepehn Billeb, 22 Vista View Drive, Cody, WY 82414 / 307-587-4278; FAX: 307-587-4297 stevebilleb@wyoming.com

Que Industries, Inc., PO Box 2471, Everett, WA 98203 / 425-303-9088; FAX: 206-514-3266 queinfo@queindustries.com

Queen Cutlery Co., PO Box 500, Franklinville, NY 14737 / 800-222-5233; FAX: 800-299-2618

R

R&C Knives & Such, 2136 CANDY CANE WALK, Manteca, CA 95336-9501 / 209-239-3722; FAX: 209-825-6947

R&D Gun Repair, Kenny Howell, RR1 Box 283, Beloit, WI 53511

R&J Gun Shop, 337 S. Humbolt St., Canyon City, OR 97820 / 541-575-2130 rjgunshop@highdestertnet.com

R&S Industries Corp., 8255 Brentwood Industrial Dr., St. Louis, MO 63144 / 314-781-5169 ron@miraclepolishingcloth.com www.miraclepolishingcloth.com

R. Murphy Co., Inc., 13 Groton-Harvard Rd., P.O. Box 376, Ayer, MA 01432 / 617-772-3481

R.A. Wells Custom Gunsmith, 3452 1st Ave., Racine, WI 53402 / 414-639-5223

R.E. Seebeck Assoc., P.O. Box 59752, Dallas, TX 75229

R.E.I., P.O. Box 88, Tallevast, FL 34270 / 813-755-0085

R.E.T. Enterprises, 2608 S. Chestnut, Broken Arrow, OK 74012 / 918-251-GUNS; FAX: 918-251-0587

R.F. Mitchell Bullets, 430 Walnut St., Westernport, MD 21562

R.I.S. Co., Inc., 718 Timberlake Circle, Richardson, TX 75080 / 214-235-0933

R.T. Eastman Products, P.O. Box 1531, Jackson, WY 83001 / 307-733-3217; or 800-624-4311

Rabeno, Martin, 92 Spook Hole Rd., Ellenville, NY 12428 / 845-647-2129; FAX: 845-647-2129 fancygun@aol.com

Radack Photography, Lauren, 21140 Jib Court L-12, Aventura, FL 33180 / 305-931-3110

Radiator Specialty Co., 1900 Wilkinson Blvd., P.O. Box 34689, Charlotte, NC 28234 / 800-438-6947; FAX: 800-421-9525

Radical Concepts, P.O. Box 1473, Lake Grove, OR 97035 / 503-538-7437

Rainier Ballistics Corp., 4500 15th St. East, Tacoma, WA 98424 / 800-638-8722 or 206-922-7589; FAX: 206-922-7854

Ralph Bone Engraving, 718 N. Atlanta St., Owasso, OK 74055 / 918-272-9745

Ram-Line ATK, P.O. Box 39, Onalaska, WI 54650

Ramon B. Gonzalez Guns, P.O. Box 370, Monticello, NY 12701 / 914-794-4515

Rampart International, 2781 W. MacArthur Blvd., B-283, Santa Ana, CA 92704 / 800-976-7240 or 714-557-6405

Ranch Products, P.O. Box 145, Malinta, OH 43535 / 313-277-3118; FAX: 313-565-8536

Randall-Made Knives, P.O. Box 1988, Orlando, FL 32802 / 407-855-8075

Randco UK, 286 Gipsy Rd., Welling, DA16 1JJ ENGLAND / 44 81 303 4118

Randolph Engineering Inc., 26 Thomas Patten Dr., Randolph, MA 02368 / 781-961-6070; FAX: 781-961-0337

Randy Duane Custom Stocks, 7822 Church St., Middletown, VA 22645-9521

Range Brass Products Company, P.O. Box 218, Rockport, TX 78381

Ranger Shooting Glasses, 26 Thomas Patten Dr., Randolph, MA 02368 / 800-541-1405; FAX: 617-986-0337

Ransom International Corp., 1027 Spire Dr, Prescott, AZ 86302 / 520-778-7899; FAX: 520-778-7993 ransom@primenet.com www.ransom-intl.com

Rapine Bullet Mould Mfg. Co., 9503 Landis Lane, East Greenville, PA 18041 / 215-679-5413; FAX: 215-679-9795

Ravell Ltd., 289 Diputacion St., 08009, Barcelona, SPAIN / 34(3) 4874486; FAX: 34(3) 4881394

Ray Riling Arms Books Co., 6844 Gorsten St., Philadelphia, PA 19119 / 215-438-2456; FAX: 215-438-5395 sales@rayrilingarmsbooks.com www.rayrilingarmsbooks.com

Ray's Gunsmith Shop, 3199 Elm Ave., Grand Junction, CO 81504 / 970-434-6162; FAX: 970-434-6162

Raytech Div. of Lyman Products Corp., 475 Smith Street, Middletown, CT 06457-1541 / 860-632-2020 or 800-225-9626; FAX: 860-632-1699 lymansales@cshore.com www.lymanproducts.com

RCBS Operations/ATK, 605 Oro Dam Blvd., Oroville, CA 95965 / 530-533-5191 or 800-533-5000; FAX: 530-533-1647 www.rcbs.com

RCBS/ATK, 605 Oro Dam Blvd., Oroville, CA 95965 / 800-533-5000; FAX: 916-533-1647

Reagent Chemical & Research, Inc., 114 Broad St., Flemington, NJ 11232 / 718-499-6220; FAX: 718-499-6143

Reardon Products, P.O. Box 126, Morrison, IL 61270 / 815-772-3155

Red Diamond Dist. Co., 1304 Snowdon Dr., Knoxville, TN 37912

Redding Reloading Equipment, 1089 Starr Rd., Cortland, NY 13045 / 607-753-3331; FAX: 607-756-8445 techline@redding-reloading.com www.redding-reloading.com

Redfield Media Resource Center, 4607 N.E. Cedar Creek Rd., Woodland, WA 98674 / 360-225-5000; FAX: 360-225-7616

Redman's Rifling & Reboring, 189 Nichols Rd., Omak, WA 98841 / 509-826-5512

Redwood Bullet Works, 3559 Bay Rd., Redwood City, CA 94063 / 415-367-6741

Reed, Dave, Rt. 1, Box 374, Minnesota City, MN 55959 / 507-689-2944

Reimer Johannsen, Inc., 438 Willow Brook Rd., Plainfield, NH 03781 / 603-469-3450; FAX: 603-469-3471

Reiswig, Wallace E. (See Claro Walnut Gunstock

Reloaders Equipment Co., 4680 High St., Ecorse, MI 48229

Reloading Specialties, Inc., Box 1130, Pine Island, MN 55463 / 507-356-8500; FAX: 507-356-8800

Remington Arms Co., Inc., 870 Remington Drive, P.O. Box 700, Madison, NC 27025-0700 / 800-243-9700; FAX: 910-548-8700

Remington Double Shotguns, 7885 Cyd Dr., Denver, CO 80221 / 303-429-6947

Renato Gamba S.p.A.-Societa Armi Bresciane Srl., Via Artigiani 93, 25063 Gardone, Val Trompia (BS), ITALY / 30-8911640; FAX: 30-8911648

Renegade, PO Box 31546, Phoenix, AZ 85046 / 602-482-6777; FAX: 602-482-1952

Renfrew Guns & Supplies, R.R. 4, Renfrew, ON K7V 3Z7 CANADA / 613-432-7080

Reno, Wayne, 2808 Stagestop Road, Jefferson, CO 80456

Republic Arms, Inc. (See Cobra Enterprises, Inc.)

Retting, Inc., Martin B, 11029 Washington, Culver City, CA 90232 / 213-837-2412

RG-G, Inc., PO Box 935, Trinidad, CO 81082 / 719-845-1436

RH Machine & Consulting Inc, PO Box 394, Pacific, MO 63069 / 314-271-8465

Rhino, P.O. Box 787, Locust, NC 28097 / 704-753-2198

Rhodeside, Inc., 1704 Commerce Dr., Piqua, OH 45356 / 513-773-5781

Rice, Keith (See White Rock Tool & Die)

Richards Micro-Fit Stocks, 8331 N. San Fernando Ave., Sun Valley, CA 91352 / 818-767-6097; FAX: 818-767-7121

Ridgeline, Inc., Bruce Sheldon, P.O. Box 930, Dewey, AZ 86327-0930 / 800-632-5900; FAX: 520-632-5900

Ridgetop Sporting Goods, P.O. Box 306, 42907 Hilligoss Ln. East, Eatonville, WA 98328 / 360-832-6422; FAX: 360-832-6424

Ries, Chuck, 415 Ridgecrest Dr., Grants Pass, OR 97527 / 503-476-5623

Riggs, Jim, 206 Azalea, Boerne, TX 78006 / 210-249-8567

Riley Ledbetter Airguns, 1804 E. Sprague St., Winston Salem, NC 27107-3521 / 919-784-0676

Rim Pac Sports, Inc., 1034 N. Soldano Ave., Azusa, CA 91702-2135

Ringler Custom Leather Co., 31 Shining Mtn. Rd., Powell, WY 82435 / 307-645-3255

Ripley Rifles, 42 Fletcher Street, Ripley, Derbyshire, DE5 3LP ENGLAND / 011-0773-748353

Rizzini F.lli (See U.S. Importers-Moore & C England)

Rizzini SNC, Via 2 Giugno, 7/7Bis-25060, Marcheno (Brescia), ITALY

RLCM Enterprises, 110 Hill Crest Drive, Burleson, TX 76028

RMS Custom Gunsmithing, 4120 N. Bitterwell, Prescott Valley, AZ 86314 / 520-772-7626

Robert Evans Engraving, 332 Vine St., Oregon City, OR 97045 / 503-656-5693

Robert Valade Engraving, 931 3rd Ave., Seaside, OR 97138 / 503-738-7672

Robinett, R. G., P.O. Box 72, Madrid, IA 50156 / 515-795-2906

Robinson, Don, Pennsylvania Hse, 36 Fairfax Crescent, W Yorkshire, ENGLAND / 0422-364458

Robinson Armament Co., PO Box 16776, Salt Lake City, UT 84116 / 801-355-0401; FAX: 801-355-0402 zdf@robarm.com www.robarm.com

Robinson Firearms Mfg. Ltd., 1699 Blondeaux Crescent, Kelowna, BC V1Y 4J8 CANADA / 604-868-9596

Robinson H.V. Bullets, 3145 Church St., Zachary, LA 70791 / 504-654-4029

Rochester Lead Works, 76 Anderson Ave., Rochester, NY 14607 / 716-442-8500; FAX: 716-442-4712

Rock River Arms, 101 Noble St., Cleveland, IL 61241

Rockwood Corp., Speedwell Division, 136 Lincoln Blvd., Middlesex, NJ 08846 / 800-243-8274; FAX: 980-560-7475

Rocky Mountain Armoury, Mr. Felix LesMerises, 610 Main Street, P.O. Box 691, Frisco, CO 80443-0691 / 970-668-0136; FAX: 970-668-4484 felix@rockymountainarmoury.com

Rocky Mountain Arms, Inc., 1813 Sunset Pl, Unit D, Longmont, CO 80501 / 800-375-0846; FAX: 303-678-8766

Rocky Mountain Target Co., 3 Aloe Way, Leesburg, FL 34788 / 352-365-9598

Rocky Mountain Wildlife Products, P.O. Box 999, La Porte, CO 80535 / 970-484-2768; FAX: 970-484-0807 critrcall@earthlink.net www.critrcall.com

Rocky Shoes & Boots, 294 Harper St., Nelsonville, OH 45764 / 800-848-9452; or 614-753-1951; FAX: 614-753-4024

Rodgers & Sons Ltd., Joseph (See George Ibberson)

Rogue Rifle Co., Inc., P.O. Box 20, Prospect, OR 97536 / 541-560-4040; FAX: 541-560-4041

Rogue River Rifleworks, 500 Linne Road #D, Paso Robles, CA 93446 / 805-227-4706; FAX: 805-227-4723 rrrifles@calinet.com

Rohner, Hans, 1148 Twin Sisters Ranch Rd., Nederland, CO 80466-9600

Rohner, John, 186 Virginia Ave, Asheville, NC 28806 / 303-444-3841

Rohrbaugh, P.O. Box 785, Bayport, NY 11705 / 631-363-2843; FAX: 631-363-2681 API380@aol.com

Romain's Custom Guns, Inc., RD 1, Whetstone Rd., Brockport, PA 15823 / 814-265-1948 romwhetstone@penn.com

Ron Frank Custom Classic Arms, 7131 Richland Rd., Ft. Worth, TX 76118 / 817-284-9300; FAX: 817-284-9300 rfrank3974@aol.com

Rooster Laboratories, P.O. Box 414605, Kansas City, MO 64141 / 816-474-1622; FAX: 816-474-7622

Rorschach Precision Products, 417 Keats Cir., Irving, TX 75061 / 214-790-3487

Rosenberg & Son, Jack A, 12229 Cox Ln, Dallas, TX 75234 / 214-241-6302

Ross, Don, 12813 West 83 Terrace, Lenexa, KS 66215 / 913-492-6982

Rosser, Bob, 1824 29th Ave. So., Suite 214, Homewood, AL 35209 / 205-870-4422; FAX: 205-870-4421 www.hand-engravers.com

Manufacturer's Directory

Rossi Firearms, Gary Mchalik, 16175 NW 49th Ave, Miami, FL 33014-6314 / 305-474-0401; FAX: 305-623-7506

Rottweil Compe, 1330 Glassell, Orange, CA 92667

Roy Baker's Leather Goods, PO Box 893, Magnolia, AR 71754 / 870-234-0344

Royal Arms Gunstocks, 919 8th Ave. NW, Great Falls, MT 59404 / 406-453-1149 royalarms@lmt.net www.lmt.net/~royalarms

Royal Arms International, R J Brill, P.O. Box 6083, Woodland Hills, CA 91365 / 818-704-5110; FAX: 818-887-2059 royalarms.com

Roy's Custom Grips, 793 Mt. Olivet Church Rd, Lynchburg, VA 24504 / 434-993-3470

RPM, 15481 N. Twin Lakes Dr., Tucson, AZ 85739 / 520-825-1233; FAX: 520-825-3333

Rubright Bullets, 1008 S. Quince Rd., Walnutport, PA 18088 / 215-767-1339

Rucker Dist. Inc., P.O. Box 479, Terrell, TX 75160 / 214-563-2094

Ruger (See Sturm, Ruger & Co., Inc.)

Ruger, Chris. See: RUGER'S CUSTOM GUNS

Ruger's Custom Guns, Chris Ruger, 1050 Morton Blvd., Kingston, NY 12401 / 845-336-7106; FAX: 845-336-7106 rugerscustom@outdrs.net rugergunsmith.com

Rundell's Gun Shop, 6198 Frances Rd., Clio, MI 48420 / 313-687-0559

Runge, Robert P., 1120 Helderberg Trl. #1, Berne, NY 12023-2909

Rupert's Gun Shop, 2202 Dick Rd., Suite B, Fenwick, MI 48834 / 517-248-3252 17rupert@pathwaynet.com

Russ Haydon's Shooters' Supply, 15018 Goodrich Dr. NW, Gig Harbor, WA 98329 / 253-857-7557; FAX: 253-857-7884 www.shooters-supply.com

Russ, William. See: BILL RUSS TRADING POST

Rusteprufe Laboratories, 1319 Jefferson Ave., Sparta, WI 54656 / 608-269-4144; FAX: 608-366-1972 rusteprufe@centurytel.net www.rusteprufe.com

Rusty Duck Premium Gun Care Products, 7785 Foundation Dr., Suite 6, Florence, KY 41042 / 606-342-5553; FAX: 606-342-5556

Rutgers Book Center, 127 Raritan Ave., Highland Park, NJ 08904 / 732-545-4344; FAX: 732-545-6686 gunbooks@rutgersgunbooks.com www.rutgersgunbooks.com

Rutten (See U.S. Importer-Labanu Inc)

RWS (See US Importer-Dynamit Nobel-RWS, Inc.), 81 Ruckman Rd., Closter, NJ 07624 / 201-767-7971; FAX: 201-767-1589

S

S&K Scope Mounts, RD 2 Box 72E, Sugar Grove, PA 16350 / 814-489-3091; or 800-578-9862; FAX: 814-489-5466 comments@scopemounts.com www.scopemounts.com

S&S Firearms, 74-11 Myrtle Ave., Glendale, NY 11385 / 718-497-1100; FAX: 718-497-1105

S.A.R.L. G. Granger, 66 cours Fauriel, 42100, Saint Etienne, FRANCE / 04 77 25 14 73; FAX: 04 77 38 66 99

S.C.R.C., PO Box 660, Katy, TX 77492-0660 FAX: 713-578-2124

S.D. Meacham, 1070 Angel Ridge, Peck, ID 83545

S.G.S. Sporting Guns Srl., Via Della Resistenza, 37 20090, Buccinasco, ITALY / 2-45702446; FAX: 2-45702464

S.I.A.C.E. (See U.S. Importer-IAR Inc)

Sabatti SPA, Via A Volta 90, 25063 Gandome V.T.(BS), Brescia, ITALY / 030-8912207-831312; FAX: 030-8912059 info@sabatti.it www.sabatti.com

SAECO (See Redding Reloading Equipment)

Safari Arms/Schuetzen Pistol Works, 620-626 Old Pacific Hwy. SE, Olympia, WA 98513 / 360-459-3471; FAX: 360-491-3447 info@olyarms.com www.olyarms.com

Safari Press, Inc., 15621 Chemical Lane B, Huntington Beach, CA 92649 / 714-894-9080; FAX: 714-894-4949

Safariland Ltd., Inc., 3120 E. Mission Blvd., P.O. Box 51478, Ontario, CA 91761 / 909-923-7300; FAX: 909-923-7400

SAFE, PO Box 864, Post Falls, ID 83877 / 208-773-3624; FAX: 208-773-6819 staysafe@safe-llc.com www.safe-llc.com

Safety Speed Holster, Inc., 910 S. Vail Ave., Montebello, CA 90640 / 323-723-4140; FAX: 323-726-6973 e-mail@safetyspeedholster.com www.safetyspeedholster.com

Saf-T-Lok Corp., 18245 SE, Tesquesta, FL 33469 / 800-723-8565

Sako Ltd (See U.S. Importer-Stoeger Industries)

Sam Welch Gun Engraving, Sam Welch, HC 64 Box 2110, Moab, UT 84532 / 435-259-8131

Samco Global Arms, Inc., 6995 NW 43rd St., Miami, FL 33166 / 305-593-9782; FAX: 305-593-1014 samco@samcoglobal.com www.samcoglobal.com

Sampson, Roger, 2316 Mahogany St., Mora, MN 55051 / 612-679-4868

San Marco (See U.S. Importers-Cape Outfitters-EMF

Sandia Die & Cartridge Co., 37 Atancacio Rd. NE, Auquerque, NM 87123 / 505-298-5729

Sarco, Inc., 323 Union St., Stirling, NJ 07980 / 908-647-3800; FAX: 908-647-9413

Sarsilmaz Shotguns - Turkey (see B.C. Outdoors)

Sauer (See U.S. Importers-Paul Co., The, Sigarms I

Sauls, R. See: BRYAN & ASSOC.

Saunders Gun & Machine Shop, 145 Delhi Rd, Manchester, IA 52057 / 563-927-4026

Savage Arms (Canada), Inc., 248 Water St., P.O. Box 1240, Lakefield, ON K0L 2H0 CANADA / 705-652-8000; FAX: 705-652-8431

Savage Arms, Inc., 100 Springdale Rd., Westfield, MA 01085 / 413-568-7001; FAX: 413-562-7764

Savage Range Systems, Inc., 100 Springdale Rd., Westfield, MA 01085 / 413-568-7001; FAX: 413-562-1152

Saville Iron Co. (See Greenwood Precision)

Savino, Barbara J., P.O. Box 51, West Burke, VT 05871-0051

Scansport, Inc., P.O. Box 700, Enfield, NH 03748 / 603-632-7654

Sceery Game Calls, P.O. Box 6520, Sante Fe, NM 87502 / 505-471-9110; FAX: 505-471-3476

Schaefer Shooting Sports, P.O. Box 1515, Melville, NY 11747-0515 / 516-643-5466; FAX: 516-643-2426 robert@robertschaefer.com www.schaefershooting.com

Scharch Mfg., Inc.-Top Brass, 10325 Co. Rd. 120, Salida, CO 81201 / 719-539-7242; or 800-836-4683; FAX: 719-539-3021 scharch@chaffee.net www.topbraass.tv

Scherer, Liz. See: SCHERER SUPPLIES

Scherer Supplies, Liz Scherer, Box 250, Ewing, VA 24248 FAX: 423-733-2073

Schiffman, Curt, 3017 Kevin Cr., Idaho Falls, ID 83402 / 208-524-4684

Schiffman, Mike, 8233 S. Crystal Springs, McCammon, ID 83250 / 208-254-9114

Schmidt & Bender, Inc., P.O. Box 134, Meriden, NH 03770 / 603-469-3565; FAX: 603-469-3471 scopes@cyberportal.net www.schmidtbender.com

Schmidtke Group, 17050 W. Salentine Dr., New Berlin, WI 53151-7349

Schneider Bullets, 3655 West 214th St., Fairview Park, OH 44126

Schneider Rifle Barrels, Inc., Gary, 12202 N 62nd Pl., Scottsdale, AZ 85254 / 602-948-2525

Schroeder Bullets, 1421 Thermal Ave., San Diego, CA 92154 / 619-423-3523; FAX: 619-423-8124

Schulz Industries, 16247 Minnesota Ave., Paramount, CA 90723 / 213-439-5903

Schumakers Gun Shop, 512 Prouty Corner Lp. A, Colville, WA 99114 / 509-684-4848

Scope Control, Inc., 5775 Co. Rd. 23 SE, Alexandria, MN 56308 / 612-762-7295

Score High Gunsmithing, 9812-A, Cochiti SE, Albuquerque, NM 087123 / 800-326-5632 or 505-292-5532; FAX: 505-292-2592

Scot Powder, Rt.1 Box 167, McEwen, TN 37101 / 800-416-3006; FAX: 615-729-4211

Scott Fine Guns Inc., Thad, PO Box 412, Indianola, MS 38751 / 601-887-5929

Searcy Enterprises, PO Box 584, Boron, CA 93596 / 760-762-6771; FAX: 760-762-0191

Second Chance Body Armor, P.O. Box 578, Central Lake, MI 49622 / 616-544-5721; FAX: 616-544-9824

Seebeck Assoc., R.E., P. O. Box 59752, Dallas, TX 75229

Seecamp Co. Inc., L. W., PO Box 255, New Haven, CT 06502 / 203-877-3429; FAX: 203-877-3429

Segway Industries, P.O. Box 783, Suffern, NY 10901-0783 / 914-357-5510

Seligman Shooting Products, Box 133, Seligman, AZ 86337 / 602-422-3607 shootssp@yahoo.com

Sellier & Bellot, USA Inc., P.O. Box 27006, Shawnee Mission, KS 66225 / 913-685-0916; FAX: 913-685-0917

Selsi Co. Inc., P.O. Box 10, Midland Park, NJ 07432-0010 / 201-935-0388; FAX: 201-935-5851

Semmer, Charles (See Remington Double Shotguns), 7885 Cyd Dr, Denver, CO 80221 / 303-429-6947

Sentinel Arms, P.O. Box 57, Detroit, MI 48231 / 313-331-1951; FAX: 313-331-1456

Servus Footwear Co., 1136 2nd St., Rock Island, IL 61204 / 309-786-7741; FAX: 309-786-9808

Shappy Bullets, 76 Milldale Ave., Plantsville, CT 06479 / 203-621-3704

Sharp Shooter Supply, 4970 Lehman Road, Delphos, OH 45833 / 419-695-3179

Sharps Arms Co., Inc., C., 100 Centennial, Box 885, Big Timber, MT 59011 / 406-932-4353

Shaw, Inc., E. R. (See Small Arms Mfg. Co.)

Shay's Gunsmithing, 931 Marvin Ave., Lebanon, PA 17042

Sheffield Knifemakers Supply, Inc., PO Box 741107, Orange City, FL 32774-1107 / 386-775-6453; FAX: 386-774-5754

Sheldon, Bruce. See: RIDGELINE, INC.

Shepherd Enterprises, Inc., Box 189, Waterloo, NE 68069 / 402-779-2424; FAX: 402-779-4010 sshepherd@shepherdscopes.com www.shepherdscopes.com

Sherwood, George, 46 N. River Dr., Roseburg, OR 97470 / 541-672-3159

Shilen, Inc., 205 Metro Park Blvd., Ennis, TX 75119 / 972-875-5318; FAX: 972-875-5402

Shiloh Rifle Mfg., 201 Centennial Dr., Big Timber, MT 59011 / 406-932-4454; FAX: 406-932-5627 lucinda@shilohrifle.com www.shilohrifle.com

Shockley, Harold H., 204 E. Farmington Rd., Hanna City, IL 61536 / 309-565-4524

Shoot Where You Look, Leon Measures, Dept GD, 408 Fair, Livingston, TX 77351

Shooters Arms Manufacturing Inc., Rivergate Mall, Gen. Maxilom Ave., Cebu City 6000, PHILIPPINES / 6332-254-8478 www.shootersarms.com.ph

Shooter's Choice Gun Care, 15050 Berkshire Ind. Pky., Middlefield, OH 44062 / 440-834-8888; FAX: 440-834-3388 www.shooterschoice.com

Shooter's Edge Inc., 3313 Creekstone Dr., Fort Collins, CO 80525

Shooters Supply, 1120 Tieton Dr., Yakima, WA 98902 / 509-452-1181

Shooter's World, 3828 N. 28th Ave., Phoenix, AZ 85017 / 602-266-0170

Shooters, Inc., 5139 Stanart St., Norfolk, VA 23502 / 757-461-9152; FAX: 757-461-9155 gflocker@aol.com

Shootin' Shack, 357 Cypress Drive, No. 10, Tequesta, FL 33469 / 561-842-0990; FAX: 561-545-4861

Shooting Specialties (See Titus, Daniel)

Shooting Star, 1715 FM 1626 Ste 105, Manchaca, TX 78652 / 512-462-0009

Shoot-N-C Targets (See Birchwood Casey)

Shotgun Sports, P.O. Box 6810, Auburn, CA 95604 / 530-889-2220; FAX: 530-889-9106 custsrv@shotgunsportsmagazine.com shotgunsportsmagazine.com

Shotgun Sports Magazine, dba Shootin' Accessories Ltd., P.O. Box 6810, Auburn, CA 95604 / 916-889-2220 custsrv@shotgunsportsmagazine.com shotgunspotsmagazine.com

Shotguns Unlimited, 2307 Fon Du Lac Rd., Richmond, VA 23229 / 804-752-7115

Siegrist Gun Shop, 8752 Turtle Road, Whittemore, MI 48770 / 989-873-3929

Sierra Bullets, 1400 W. Henry St., Sedalia, MO 65301 / 816-827-6300; FAX: 816-827-6300

Sierra Specialty Prod. Co., 1344 Oakhurst Ave., Los Altos, CA 94024 / 415-965-1536

SIG, CH-8212 Neuhausen, SWITZERLAND

Sigarms, Inc., Corporate Park, Exeter, NH 03833 / 603-772-2302; FAX: 603-772-9082 www.sigarms.com

Sightron, Inc., 1672B Hwy. 96, Franklinton, NC 27525 / 919-528-8783; FAX: 919-528-0995 info@sightron.com www.sightron.com

Signet Metal Corp., 551 Stewart Ave., Brooklyn, NY 11222 / 718-384-5400; FAX: 718-388-7488

SIG-Sauer (See U.S. Importer-Sigarms Inc.)

Silencio/Safety Direct, 56 Coney Island Dr., Sparks, NV 89431 / 800-648-1812 or 702-354-4451; FAX: 702-359-1074

Silent Hunter, 1100 Newton Ave., W. Collingswood, NJ 08107 / 609-854-3276

Silhouette Leathers, P.O. Box 1161, Gunnison, CO 81230 / 303-641-6639 oldshooter@yahoo.com

Silver Eagle Machining, 18007 N. 69th Ave., Glendale, AZ 85308

Silver Ridge Gun Shop (See Goodwin, Fred)

Simmons, Jerry, 715 Middlebury St., Goshen, IN 46528-2717 / 574-533-8546

Simmons Gun Repair, Inc., 700 S. Rogers Rd., Olathe, KS 66062 / 913-782-3131; FAX: 913-782-4189

Simmons Outdoor Corp., 6001 Oak Canyon, Irvine, CA 92618 / 949-451-1450; FAX: 949-451-1460 www.meade.com

Sinclair International, Inc., 2330 Wayne Haven St., Fort Wayne, IN 46803 / 260-493-1858; FAX: 260-493-2530 sales@sinclairintl.com www.sinclairintl.com

Singletary, Kent, 4538 W Carol Ave., Glendale, AZ 85302 / 602-526-6836 kent@kscustom www.kscustom.com

Siskiyou Gun Works (See Donnelly, C. P.)

Six Enterprises, 320-D Turtle Creek Ct., San Jose, CA 95125 / 408-999-0201; FAX: 408-999-0216

SKB Shotguns, 4325 S. 120th St., Omaha, NE 68137 / 800-752-2767; FAX: 402-330-8040 skb@skbshotguns.com www.skbshotguns.com

Skeoch, Brian R., PO Box 279, Glenrock, WY 82637 / 307-436-9655 brianskeoch@aol.com

Skip's Machine, 364 29 Road, Grand Junction, CO 81501 / 303-245-5417

Sklany's Machine Shop, 566 Birch Grove Dr., Kalispell, MT 59901 / 406-755-4257

Slezak, Jerome F., 1290 Marlowe, Lakewood (Cleveland), OH 44107 / 216-221-1668

Slug Site, Ozark Wilds, 21300 Hwy. 5, Versailles, MO 65084 / 573-378-6430 john@ebeling.com john.ebeling.com

Small Arms Mfg. Co., 5312 Thoms Run Rd., Bridgeville, PA 15017 / 412-221-4343; FAX: 412-221-4303

Small Arms Specialists, 443 Firchburg Rd, Mason, NH 03048 / 603-878-0427; FAX: 603-878-3905 miniguns@empire.net miniguns.com

Small Custom Mould & Bullet Co., Box 17211, Tucson, AZ 85731

Smart Parts, 1203 Spring St., Latrobe, PA 15650 / 412-539-2660; FAX: 412-539-2298

Smires, C. L., 5222 Windmill Lane, Columbia, MD 21044-1328

Smith & Wesson, 2100 Roosevelt Ave., Springfield, MA 01104 / 413-781-8300; FAX: 413-731-8980

Smith, Art, 230 Main St. S., Hector, MN 55342 / 320-848-2760; FAX: 320-848-2760

Smith, Mark A., P.O. Box 182, Sinclair, WY 82334 / 307-324-7929

Smith, Michael, 2612 Ashmore Ave., Red Bank, TN 37415 / 615-267-8341

Smith, Ron, 5869 Straley, Ft. Worth, TX 76114 / 817-732-6768

Smith, Sharmon, 4545 Speas Rd., Fruitland, ID 83619 / 208-452-6329 sharmon@fmtc.com

Smith Abrasives, Inc., 1700 Sleepy Valley Rd., P.O. Box 5095, Hot Springs, AR 71902-5095 / 501-321-2244; FAX: 501-321-9232

Smith, Judy. See: L.B.T.

Smith Saddlery, Jesse W., 0499 County Road J, Pritchett, CO 81064 / 509-325-0622

Smokey Valley Rifles, E1976 Smokey Valley Rd, Scandinavia, WI 54977 / 715-467-2674

Snapp's Gunshop, 6911 E. Washington Rd., Clare, MI 48617 / 989-386-9226

Sno-Seal, Inc. (See Atsko/Sno-Seal, Inc.)

Societa Armi Bresciane Srl (See U.S. Importer-Cape

SOS Products Co. (See Buck Stix-SOS Products Co.), Box 3, Neenah, WI 54956

Sotheby's, 1334 York Ave. at 72nd St., New York, NY 10021 / 212-606-7260

Sound Technology, Box 391, Pelham, AL 35124 / 205-664-5860; or 907-486-2825 rem700P@sprintmail.com www.soundtechsilencers.com

South Bend Replicas, Inc., 61650 Oak Rd.., South Bend, IN 46614 / 219-289-4500

Southeastern Community College, 1015 S. Gear Ave., West Burlington, IA 52655 / 319-752-2731

Southern Ammunition Co., Inc., 4232 Meadow St., Loris, SC 29569-3124 / 803-756-3262; FAX: 803-756-3583

Southern Bloomer Mfg. Co., P.O. Box 1621, Bristol, TN 37620 / 615-878-6660; FAX: 615-878-8761

Southern Security, 1700 Oak Hills Dr., Kingston, TN 37763 / 423-376-6297; FAX: 800-251-9992

Sparks, Milt, 605 E. 44th St. No. 2, Boise, ID 83714-4800

Spartan-Realtree Products, Inc., 1390 Box Circle, Columbus, GA 31907 / 706-569-9101; FAX: 706-569-0042

Specialty Gunsmithing, Lynn McMurdo, P.O. Box 404, Afton, WY 83110 / 307-886-5535

Specialty Shooters Supply, Inc., 3325 Griffin Rd., Suite 9mm, Fort Lauderdale, FL 33317

Speer Bullets, PO Box 856, Lewiston, ID 83501 / 208-746-2351; www.speer-bullets.com

Spegel, Craig, P.O. Box 387, Nehalem, OR 97131 / 503-368-5653

Speiser, Fred D., 2229 Dearborn, Missoula, MT 59801 / 406-549-8133

Spencer Reblue Service, 1820 Tupelo Trail, Holt, MI 48842 / 517-694-7474

Spencer's Rifle Barrels, Inc., 4107 Jacobs Creek Dr, Scottsville, VA 24590 / 804-293-6836; FAX: 804-293-6836 www.spencerriflebarrels.com

SPG LLC, P.O. Box 1625, Cody, WY 82414 / 307-587-7621; FAX: 307-587-7695 spg@cody.wtp.net www.blackpowderspg.com

Sphinx Systems Ltd., Gesteigtstrasse 12, CH-3800, Matten, BRNE, SWITZERLAND

Splitfire Sporting Goods, L.L.C., P.O. Box 1044, Orem, UT 84059-1044 / 801-932-7950; FAX: 801-932-7959 www.splitfireguns.com

Spolar Power Load Inc., 17376 Filbert, Fontana, CA 92335 / 800-227-9667

Sport Flite Manufacturing Co., PO Box 1082, Bloomfield Hills, MI 48303 / 248-647-3747

Sporting Clays Of America, 9257 Bluckeye Rd, Sugar Grove, OH 43155-9632 / 740-746-8334; FAX: 740-746-8605

Sports Innovations Inc., P.O. Box 5181, 8505 Jacksboro Hwy., Wichita Falls, TX 76307 / 817-723-6015

Sportsman Safe Mfg. Co., 6309-6311 Paramount Blvd., Long Beach, CA 90805 / 800-266-7150; or 310-984-5445

Sportsman's Communicators, 588 Radcliffe Ave., Pacific Palisades, CA 90272 / 800-538-3752

Sportsmatch U.K. Ltd., 16 Summer St. Leighton,, Buzzard Beds, Bedfordshire, LU7 8HT ENGLAND / 01525-381638; FAX: 01525-851236 info@sportsmatch-uk.com www.sportsmatch-uk.com

Sportsmen's Exchange & Western Gun Traders, Inc., 560 S. C St., Oxnard, CA 93030 / 805-483-1917

Spradlin's, 457 Shannon Rd, Texas CreekCotopaxi, CO 81223 / 719-275-7105; FAX: 719-275-3852 spradlins@prodigy.net www.spradlins.net

Springfield Armory, 420 W. Main St, Geneseo, IL 61254 / 309-944-5631; FAX: 309-944-3676 sales@springfield-armory.com www.springfieldarmory.com

Springfield Sporters, Inc., RD 1, Penn Run, PA 15765 / 412-254-2626; FAX: 412-254-9173

Springfield, Inc., 420 W. Main St., Geneseo, IL 61254 / 309-944-5631; FAX: 309-944-3676

Spyderco, Inc., 20011 Golden Gate Canyon Rd., Golden, CO 80403 / 800-525-7770; or 800-525-7770; FAX: 303-278-2229 sales@spyderco.com www.spyderco.com

SSK Industries, J. D. Jones, 590 Woodvue Lane, Wintersville, OH 43953 / 740-264-0176; FAX: 740-264-2257 www.sskindustries.com

Stackpole Books, 5067 Ritter Rd., Mechanicsburg, PA 17055-6921 / 717-796-0411 or 800-732-3669; FAX: 717-796-0412 tmanney@stackpolebooks.com www.stackpolebooks.com

Stalker, Inc., P.O. Box 21, Fishermans Wharf Rd., Malakoff, TX 75148 / 903-489-1010

Stalwart Corporation, PO Box 46, Evanston, WY 82931 / 307-789-7687; FAX: 307-789-7688

Stan Baker Sports, Stan Baker, 10000 Lake City Way, Seattle, WA 98125 / 206-522-4575

Stan De Treville & Co., 4129 Normal St., San Diego, CA 92103 / 619-298-3393

Stanley Bullets, 2085 Heatheridge Ln., Reno, NV 89509

Star Ammunition, Inc., 5520 Rock Hampton Ct., Indianapolis, IN 46268 / 800-221-5927; FAX: 317-872-5847

Star Custom Bullets, PO Box 608, 468 Main St., Ferndale, CA 95536 / 707-786-9140; FAX: 707-786-9117 wmebridge@humboldt.com

Star Machine Works, PO Box 1872, Pioneer, CA 95666 / 209-295-5000

Starke Bullet Company, P.O. Box 400, 605 6th St. NW, Cooperstown, ND 58425 / 888-797-3431

Starkey Labs, 6700 Washington Ave. S., Eden Prairie, MN 55344

Starkey's Gun Shop, 9430 McCombs, El Paso, TX 79924 / 915-751-3030

Starlight Training Center, Inc., Rt. 1, P.O. Box 88, Bronaugh, MO 64728 / 417-843-3555

Starline, Inc., 1300 W. Henry St., Sedalia, MO 65301 / 660-827-6640; FAX: 660-827-6650 info@starlinebrass.com http://www.starlinebrass.com

Starr Trading Co., Jedediah, PO Box 2007, Farmington Hills, MI 48333 / 810-683-4343; FAX: 810-683-3282

Starrett Co., L. S., 121 Crescent St., Athol, MA 01331 / 978-249-3551; FAX: 978-249-8495

Steelman's Gun Shop, 10465 Beers Rd., Swartz Creek, MI 48473 / 810-735-4884

Steffens, Ron, 18396 Mariposa Creek Rd., Willits, CA 95490 / 707-485-0873

Stegall, James B., 26 Forest Rd., Wallkill, NY 12589

Steve Henigson & Associates, P.O. Box 2726, Culver City, CA 90231 / 310-305-8288; FAX: 310-305-1905

Steve Kamyk Engraver, 9 Grandview Dr., Westfield, MA 01085-1810 / 413-568-0457 stevek201@attbi

Steven Dodd Hughes, P.O. Box 545, Livingston, MT 59047 / 406-222-9377; FAX: 406-222-9377

Steves House of Guns, Rt. 1, Minnesota City, MN 55959 / 507-689-2573

Stewart Game Calls, Inc., Johnny, PO Box 7954, 5100 Fort Ave., Waco, TX 76714 / 817-772-3261; FAX: 817-772-3670

Stewart's Gunsmithing, P.O. Box 5854, Pietersburg North 0750, Transvaal, SOUTH AFRICA / 01521-89401

Steyr Mannlicher GmbH P Co AG, Mannlicherstrasse 1, 4400 Steyr, Steyr, AUSTRIA / 0043-7252-896-0; FAX: 0043-7252-78620 office@steyr-mannlicher.com www.steyr-mannlicher.com

STI International, 114 Halmar Cove, Georgetown, TX 78628 / 800-959-8201; FAX: 512-819-0465 www.stiguns.com

Stiles Custom Guns, 76 Cherry Run Rd., Box 1605, Homer City, PA 15748 / 712-479-9945

Stillwell, Robert, 421 Judith Ann Dr., Schertz, TX 78154

Stoeger Industries, 17603 Indian Head Hwy., Suite 200, Accokeek, MD 20607-2501 / 301-283-6300; FAX: 301-283-6986 www.stoegerindustries.com

Stoeger Publishing Co. (See Stoeger Industries)

Stone Enterprises Ltd., 426 Harveys Neck Rd., PO Box 335, Wicomico Church, VA 22579 / 804-580-5114; FAX: 804-580-8421

Stone Mountain Arms, 5988 Peachtree Corners E., Norcross, GA 30071 / 800-251-9412

Stoney Point Products, Inc., P.O. Box 234, 1822 N Minnesota St., New Ulm, MN 56073-0234 / 507-354-3360; FAX: 507-354-7236 stoney@newulmtel.net www.stoneypoint.com

Storm, Gary, P.O. Box 5211, Richardson, TX 75083 / 214-385-0862

Stott's Creek Armory, Inc., 2526 S. 475W, Morgantown, IN 46160 / 317-878-5489; FAX: 317-878-9489 sccalendar@aol.com www.sccalendar.com

Stratco, Inc., P.O. Box 2270, Kalispell, MT 59901 / 406-755-1221; FAX: 406-755-1226

Strayer, Sandy. See: STRAYER-VOIGT, INC.

Strayer-Voigt, Inc., Sandy Strayer, 3435 Ray Orr Blvd, Grand Prairie, TX 75050 / 972-513-0575

Streamlight, Inc., 1030 W. Germantown Pike, Norristown, PA 19403 / 215-631-0600; FAX: 610-631-0712

Strong Holster Co., 39 Grove St., Gloucester, MA 01930 / 508-281-3300; FAX: 508-281-6321

Strutz Rifle Barrels, Inc., W. C., P.O. Box 611, Eagle River, WI 54521 / 715-479-4766

Stuart, V. Pat, Rt.1, Box 447-S, Greenville, VA 24440 / 804-556-3845

Sturgeon Valley Sporters, K. Ide, P.O. Box 283, Vanderbilt, MI 49795 / 517-983-4338

Sturm Ruger & Co. Inc., 200 Ruger Rd., Prescott, AZ 86301 / 928-541-8820; FAX: 520-541-8850 www.ruger.com

Sullivan, David S .(See Westwind Rifles Inc.)

Summit Specialties, Inc., P.O. Box 786, Decatur, AL 35602 / 205-353-0634; FAX: 205-353-9818

Sun Welding Safe Co., 290 Easy St. No.3, Simi Valley, CA 93065 / 805-584-6678; or 800-729-SAFE; FAX: 805-584-6169 sunwelding.com

Sunny Hill Enterprises, Inc., W1790 Cty. HHH, Malone, WI 53049 / 920-795-4722; FAX: 920-795-4822

"Su-Press-On", Inc., P.O. Box 09161, Detroit, MI 48209 / 313-842-4222

Super 6 LLC, Gary Knopp, 3806 W. Lisbon Ave., Milwaukee, WI 53208 / 414-344-3343; FAX: 414-344-0304

Sure-Shot Game Calls, Inc., P.O. Box 816, 6835 Capitol, Groves, TX 77619 / 409-962-1636; FAX: 409-962-5465

Survival Arms, Inc., 273 Canal St., Shelton, CT 06484-3173 / 203-924-6533; FAX: 203-924-2581

Svon Corp., 2107 W. Blue Heron Blvd., Riviera Beach, FL 33404 / 508-881-8852

Swann, D. J., 5 Orsova Close, Eltham North Vic., 3095 AUSTRALIA / 03-431-0323

Swanndri New Zealand, 152 Elm Ave., Burlingame, CA 94010 / 415-347-6158

Swanson, Mark, 975 Heap Avenue, Prescott, AZ 86301 / 928-778-4423

Swarovski Optik North America Ltd., 2 Slater Rd., Cranston, RI 02920 / 401-946-2220; or 800-426-3089; FAX: 401-946-2587

Sweet Home, Inc., P.O. Box 900, Orrville, OH 44667-0900

Swenson's 45 Shop, A. D., 3839 Ladera Vista Rd, Fallbrook, CA 92028-9431

Swift Bullet Co., P.O. Box 27, 201 Main St., Quinter, KS 67752 / 913-754-3959; FAX: 913-754-2359

Swift Instruments, Inc., 952 Dorchester Ave., Boston, MA 02125 / 617-436-2960; FAX: 617-436-3232

Swift River Gunworks, 450 State St., Belchertown, MA 01007 / 413-323-4052

Szweda, Robert (See RMS Custom Gunsmithing)

T

T&S Industries, Inc., 1027 Skyview Dr., W. Carrollton, OH 45449 / 513-859-8414

T.F.C. S.p.A., Via G. Marconi 118, B, Villa Carcina 25069, ITALY / 030-881271; FAX: 030-881826

T.G. Faust, Inc., 544 Minor St., Reading, PA 19602 / 610-375-8549; FAX: 610-375-4488

T.H.U. Enterprises, Inc., P.O. Box 418, Lederach, PA 19450 / 215-256-1665; FAX: 215-256-9718

T.K. Lee Co., 1282 Branchwater Ln., Birmingham, AL 35216 / 205-913-5222 odonmich@aol.com www.scopedot.com

T.W. Menck Gunsmith Inc., 5703 S. 77th St., Ralston, NE 68127 guntools@cox.net http://llwww.members.cox.net/guntools

Tabler Marketing, 2554 Lincoln Blvd., Suite 555, Marina Del Rey, CA 90291 / 818-755-4565; FAX: 818-755-0972

Taconic Firearms Ltd., Perry Lane, PO Box 553, Cambridge, NY 12816 / 518-677-2704; FAX: 518-677-5974

Tactical Defense Institute, 2174 Bethany Ridges, West Union, OH 45693 / 937-544-7228; FAX: 937-544-2887

Talley, Dave, P.O. Box 821, Glenrock, WY 82637 / 307-436-8724; or 307-436-9315

Talmage, William G., 10208 N. County Rd. 425 W., Brazil, IN 47834 / 812-442-0804

Talon Industries Inc. (See Cobra Enterprises, Inc.)

Tamarack Products, Inc., PO Box 625, Wauconda, IL 60084 / 708-526-9333; FAX: 708-526-9353

Tanfoglio Fratelli S.r.l., via Valtrompia 39, 41, Brescia, ITALY / 30-8910361; FAX: 30-8910183

Tanglefree Industries, 1261 Heavenly Dr., Martinez, CA 94553 / 800-982-4868; FAX: 510-825-3874

Tank's Rifle Shop, P.O. Box 474, Fremont, NE 68026-0474 / 402-727-1317 jtank@tanksrifleshop.com www.tanksrifleshop.com

Tanner (See U.S. Importer-Mandall Shooting Supply)

Taracorp Industries, Inc., 1200 Sixteenth St., Granite City, IL 62040 / 618-451-4400

Target Shooting, Inc., PO Box 773, Watertown, SD 57201 / 605-882-6955; FAX: 605-882-8840

Tar-Hunt Custom Rifles, Inc., 101 Dogtown Rd., Bloomsburg, PA 17815 / 570-784-6368; FAX: 570-784-6368 www.tar-hunt.com

Tarnhelm Supply Co., Inc., 431 High St., Boscawen, NH 03303 / 603-796-2551; FAX: 603-796-2918 info@tarnhelm.com www.tarnhelm.com

Tasco Sales, Inc., 2889 Commerce Pky., Miramar, FL 33025

Taurus Firearms, Inc., 16175 NW 49th Ave., Miami, FL 33014 / 305-624-1115; FAX: 305-623-7506

Taurus International Firearms (See U.S. Importer)

Taurus S.A. Forjas, Avenida Do Forte 511, Porto Alegre, RS BRAZIL 91360 / 55-51-347-4050; FAX: 55-51-347-3065

Taylor & Robbins, P.O. Box 164, Rixford, PA 16745 / 814-966-3233

Taylor's & Co., Inc., 304 Lenoir Dr., Winchester, VA 22603 / 540-722-2017; FAX: 540-722-2018

TCCI, P.O. Box 302, Phoenix, AZ 85001 / 602-237-3823; FAX: 602-237-3858

TCSR, 3998 Hoffman Rd., White Bear Lake, MN 55110-4626 / 800-328-5323; FAX: 612-429-0526

TDP Industries, Inc., P.O. Box 249, Ottsville, PA 18942-0249 / 215-345-8687; FAX: 215-345-6057

Techno Arms (See U.S. Importer- Auto-Ordnance Corp

Tecnolegno S.p.A., Via A. Locatelli, 6 10, 24019 Zogno, I ITALY / 0345-55111; FAX: 0345-55155

Ted Blocker Holsters, Inc., 9396 S.W. Tigard St., Tigard, OR 97223 / 800-650-9742; FAX: 503-670-9692 www.tedblocker.com

Tele-Optics, 630 E. Rockland Rd., PO Box 6313, Libertyville, IL 60048 / 847-362-7757; FAX: 847-362-7757

Tennessee Valley Mfg., 14 County Road 521, Corinth, MS 38834 / 601-286-5014

Ten-Ring Precision, Inc., Alex B. Hamilton, 1449 Blue Crest Lane, San Antonio, TX 78232 / 210-494-3063; FAX: 210-494-3066

TEN-X Products Group, 1905 N Main St, Suite 133, Cleburne, TX 76031-1305 / 972-243-4016; or 800-433-2225; FAX: 972-243-4112

Tepeco, P.O. Box 342, Friendswood, TX 77546 / 713-482-2702

Terry K. Kopp Professional Gunsmithing, Rt 1 Box 224, Lexington, MO 64067 / 816-259-2636

Testing Systems, Inc., 220 Pegasus Ave., Northvale, NJ 07647

Tetra Gun Care, 8 Vreeland Rd., Florham Park, NJ 07932 / 973-443-0004; FAX: 973-443-0263

Tex Shoemaker & Sons, Inc., 714 W. Cienega Ave., San Dimas, CA 91773 / 909-592-2071; FAX: 909-592-2378 texshoemaker@texshoemaker.com www.texshoemaker.com

Texas Armory (See Bond Arms, Inc.)

Texas Platers Supply Co., 2453 W. Five Mile Parkway, Dallas, TX 75233 / 214-330-7168

Thad Rybka Custom Leather Equipment, 2050 Canoe Creek Rd., Springvale, AL 35146-6709

Thad Scott Fine Guns, Inc., P.O. Box 412, Indianola, MS 38751 / 601-887-5929

The A.W. Peterson Gun Shop, Inc., 4255 West Old U.S. 441, Mount Dora, FL 32757-3299 / 352-383-4258

The Accuracy Den, 25 Bitterbrush Rd., Reno, NV 89523 / 702-345-0225

The Ballistic Program Co., Inc., 2417 N. Patterson St., Thomasville, GA 31792 / 912-228-5739 or 800-368-0835

The BulletMakers Workshop, RFD 1 Box 1755, Brooks, ME 04921

The Competitive Pistol Shop, 5233 Palmer Dr., Ft. Worth, TX 76117-2433 / 817-834-8479

The Concealment Shop, Inc., 617 W. Kearney St., Ste. 205, Mesquite, TX 75149 / 972-289-8997; or 800-444-7090; FAX: 972-289-4410 concealmentshop@email.msn.com www.theconcealmentshop.com

The Country Armourer, P.O. Box 308, Ashby, MA 01431-0308 / 508-827-6797; FAX: 508-827-4845

The Creative Craftsman, Inc., 95 Highway 29 North, P.O. Box 331, Lawrenceville, GA 30246 / 404-963-2112; FAX: 404-513-9488

The Custom Shop, 890 Cochrane Crescent, Peterborough, ON K9H 5N3 CANADA / 705-742-6693

The Dutchman's Firearms, Inc., 4143 Taylor Blvd., Louisville, KY 40215 / 502-366-0555

The Ensign-Bickford Co., 660 Hopmeadow St., Simsbury, CT 06070

The Firearm Training Center, 9555 Blandville Rd., West Paducah, KY 42086 / 502-554-5886

The Fouling Shot, 6465 Parfet St., Arvada, CO 80004

The Gun Doctor, 435 East Maple, Roselle, IL 60172 / 708-894-0668

The Gun Room, 1121 Burlington, Muncie, IN 47302 / 765-282-9073; FAX: 765-282-5270 bshstleguns@aol.com

The Gun Room Press, 127 Raritan Ave., Highland Park, NJ 08904 / 732-545-4344; FAX: 732-545-6686 gunbooks@rutgersgunbooks.com www.rutgersgunbooks.com

The Gun Shop, 5550 S. 900 East, Salt Lake City, UT 84117 / 801-263-3633

The Gun Shop, 62778 Spring Creek Rd., Montrose, CO 81401

The Gun Works, 247 S. 2nd St., Springfield, OR 97477 / 541-741-4118; FAX: 541-988-1097 gunworks@worldnet.att.net www.thegunworks.com

The Gunsight, 1712 North Placentia Ave., Fullerton, CA 92631

The Gunsmith in Elk River, 14021 Victoria Lane, Elk River, MN 55330 / 612-441-7761

The Hanned Line, P.O. Box 2387, Cupertino, CA 95015-2387 smith@hanned.com www.hanned.com

The Hawken Shop, P.O. Box 593, Oak Harbor, WA 98277 / 206-679-4657; FAX: 206-675-1114

The Keller Co., P.O. Box 4057, Port Angeles, WA 98363-0997 / 214-770-8585

The Lewis Lead Remover (See LEM Gun Specialties)

The Midwest Shooting School, Pat LaBoone, 2550 Hwy. 23, Wrenshall, MN 55797 / 218-384-3670 shootingschool@starband.net

The NgraveR Co., 67 Wawecus Hill Rd., Bozrah, CT 06334 / 860-823-1533

The Ordnance Works, 2969 Pidgeon Point Road, Eureka, CA 95501 / 707-443-3252

The Orvis Co., Rt. 7, Manchester, VT 05254 / 802-362-3622; FAX: 802-362-3525

The Outdoor Connection, Inc., 7901 Panther Way, Waco, TX 76712-6556 / 800-533-6076 or 254-772-5575; FAX: 254-776-3553 floyd@outdoorconnection.com www.outdoorconnection.com

The Park Rifle Co., Ltd., Unit 6a Dartford Trade Park, Power Mill Lane, Dartford DA7 7NX, ENGLAND / 011-0322-222512

The Paul Co., 27385 Pressonville Rd., Wellsville, KS 66092 / 785-883-4444; FAX: 785-883-2525

The Protector Mfg. Co., Inc., 443 Ashwood Place, Boca Raton, FL 33431 / 407-394-6011

The Robar Co.'s, Inc., 21438 N. 7th Ave., Suite B, Phoenix, AZ 85027 / 623-581-2648 www.robarguns.com

The School of Gunsmithing, 6065 Roswell Rd., Atlanta, GA 30328 / 800-223-4542

The Shooting Gallery, 8070 Southern Blvd., Boardman, OH 44512 / 216-726-7788

The Sight Shop, John G. Lawson, 1802 E. Columbia Ave., Tacoma, WA 98404 / 253-474-5465 parahellum9@aol.com www.thesightshop.org

The Southern Armory, 25 Millstone Road, Woodlawn, VA 24381 / 703-238-1343; FAX: 703-238-1453

The Surecase Co., 233 Wilshire Blvd., Ste. 900, Santa Monica, CA 90401 / 800-92ARMLOC

The Swampfire Shop (See Peterson Gun Shop, Inc.)

The Wilson Arms Co., 63 Leetes Island Rd., Branford, CT 06405 / 203-488-7297; FAX: 203-488-0135

Theis, Terry, 21452 FM 2093, Harper, TX 78631 / 830-864-4438

Thiewes, George W., 14329 W. Parada Dr., Sun City West, AZ 85375

Things Unlimited, 235 N. Kimbau, Casper, WY 82601 / 307-234-5277

Thirion Gun Engraving, Denise, PO Box 408, Graton, CA 95444 / 707-829-1876

Thomas, Charles C., 2600 S. First St., Springfield, IL 62794 / 217-789-8980; FAX: 217-789-9130

Thompson Bullet Lube Co., P.O. Box 409, Wills Point, TX 75169 / 866-476-1500; FAX: 866-476-1500 thompsonbulletlube.com www.thompsonbulletlube.com

Thompson Precision, 110 Mary St., P.O. Box 251, Warren, IL 61087 / 815-745-3625

Thompson, Randall. See: HIGHLINE MACHINE CO.

Thompson Target Technology, 4804 Sherman Church Ave. S.W., Canton, OH 44710 / 330-484-6480; FAX: 330-491-1087 www.thompsontarget.com

Thompson Tool Mount, 1550 Solomon Rd., Santa Maria, CA 93455 / 805-934-1281 ttm@pronet.net www.thompsontoolmount.com

Thompson, Randall (See Highline Machine Co.)

Thompson/Center Arms, P.O. Box 5002, Rochester, NH 03866 / 603-332-2394; FAX: 603-332-5133 tech@tcarms.com www.tcarms.com

3-Ten Corp., P.O. Box 269, Feeding Hills, MA 01030 / 413-789-2086; FAX: 413-789-1549

Thunden Ranch, HCR 1, Box 53, Mt. Home, TX 78058 / 830-640-3138

Thurston Sports, Inc., RD 3 Donovan Rd., Auburn, NY 13021 / 315-253-0966

Tiger-Hunt Gunstocks, Box 379, Beaverdale, PA 15921 / 814-472-5161 tigerhunt4@aol.com www.gunstockwood.com

Tikka (See U.S. Importer-Stoeger Industries)

Time Precision, 4 Nicholas Sq., New Milford, CT 06776-3506 / 203-775-8343

Tinks & Ben Lee Hunting Products (See Wellington)

Tink's Safariland Hunting Corp., P.O. Box 244, 1140 Monticello Rd., Madison, GA 30650 / 706-342-4915; FAX: 706-342-7568

Tioga Engineering Co., Inc., P.O. Box 913, 13 Cone St., Wellsboro, PA 16901 / 570-724-3533; FAX: 570-724-3895 tiogaeng@epix.net

Tippman Pneumatics, Inc., 3518 Adams Center Rd., Fort Wayne, IN 46806 / 219-749-6022; FAX: 219-749-6619

Tirelli, Snc Di Tirelli Primo E.C., Via Matteotti No. 359, Gardone V.T. Brescia, I ITALY / 030-8912819; FAX: 030-832240

TM Stockworks, 6355 Maplecrest Rd., Fort Wayne, IN 46835 / 219-485-5389

TMI Products (See Haselbauer Products, Jerry)

Tom Forrest, Inc., P.O. Box 326, Lakeside, CA 92040 / 619-561-5800; FAX: 619-561-0227

Tombstone Smoke`n' Deals, PO Box 31298, Phoenix, AZ 85046 / 602-905-7013; FAX: 602-443-1998

Tom's Gun Repair, Thomas G. Ivanoff, 76-6 Rt. Southfork Rd., Cody, WY 82414 / 307-587-6949

Tom's Gunshop, 3601 Central Ave., Hot Springs, AR 71913 / 501-624-3856

Tonoloway Tack Drives, HCR 81, Box 100, Needmore, PA 17238

Torel, Inc., 1708 N. South St., P.O. Box 592, Yoakum, TX 77995 / 512-293-2341; FAX: 512-293-3413

TOZ (See U.S. Importer-Nygord Precision Products)

Track of the Wolf, Inc., 18308 Joplin St. NW, Elk River, MN 55330-1773 / 763-633-2500; FAX: 763-633-2550

Traditions Performance Firearms, P.O. Box 776, 1375 Boston Post Rd., Old Saybrook, CT 06475 / 860-388-4656; FAX: 860-388-4657 info@traditionsfirearms.com www.traditionsfirearms.com

Trafalgar Square, P.O. Box 257, N. Pomfret, VT 05053 / 802-457-1911

Trail Visions, 5800 N. Ames Terrace, Glendale, WI 53209 / 414-228-1328

Trax America, Inc., PO Box 898, 1150 Eldridge, Forrest City, AR 72335 / 870-633-0410; or 800-232-2327; FAX: 870-633-4788 trax@ipa.net www.traxamerica.com

Treadlok Gun Safe, Inc., 1764 Granby St. NE, Roanoke, VA 24012 / 800-729-8732; or 703-982-6881; FAX: 703-982-1059

Treemaster, P.O. Box 247, Guntersville, AL 35976 / 205-878-3597

Trevallion Gunstocks, 9 Old Mountain Rd., Cape Neddick, ME 03902 / 207-361-1130

Trico Plastics, 28061 Diaz Rd., Temecula, CA 92590 / 909-676-7714; FAX: 909-676-0267 ustinfo@ustplastics.com www.tricoplastics.com

Trigger Lock Division / Central Specialties Ltd., 220-D Exchange Dr., Crystal Lake, IL 60014 / 847-639-3900; FAX: 847-639-3972

Trijicon, Inc., 49385 Shafer Ave., P.O. Box 930059, Wixom, MI 48393-0059 / 248-960-7700 or 800-338-0563

Trilby Sport Shop, 1623 Hagley Rd., Toledo, OH 43612-2024 / 419-472-6222

Trilux, Inc., P.O. Box 24608, Winston-Salem, NC 27114 / 910-659-9438; FAX: 910-768-7720

Trinidad St. Jr. Col. Gunsmith Dept., 600 Prospect St., Trinidad, CO 81082 / 719-846-5631; FAX: 719-846-5667

Triple-K Mfg. Co., Inc., 2222 Commercial St., San Diego, CA 92113 / 619-232-2066; FAX: 619-232-7675 sales@triplek.com www.triplek.com

Tristar Sporting Arms, Ltd., 1814 Linn St. #16, N. Kansas City, MO 64116-3627 / 816-421-1400; FAX: 816-421-4182 tristar@blity-it.net www.tristarsportingarms

Trlus Traps, Inc., P.O. Box 25, 221 S. Miami Ave., Cleves, OH 45002 / 513-941-5682; FAX: 513-941-7970 triustraps@fuse.net www.triustraps.com

Trooper Walsh, 2393 N Edgewood St, Arlington, VA 22207

Trotman, Ken, 135 Ditton Walk, Unit 11, Cambridge, CB5 8PY ENGLAND / 01223-211030; FAX: 01223-212317 www.kentrolman.com

Tru-Balance Knife Co., P.O. Box 140555, Grand Rapids, MI 49514 / 616-647-1215

True Flight Bullet Co., 5581 Roosevelt St., Whitehall, PA 18052 / 610-262-7630; FAX: 610-262-7806

Truglo, Inc., P.O. Box 1612, McKinna, TX 75070 / 972-774-0300; FAX: 972-774-0323 www.truglosights.com

Trulock Tool, PO Box 530, Whigham, GA 31797 / 229-762-4678; FAX: 229-762-4050 trulockchokes@hotmail.com trulockchokes.com

Tru-Square Metal Products Inc., 640 First St. SW, P.O. Box 585, Auburn, WA 98071 / 253-833-2310; or 800-225-1017; FAX: 253-833-2349 t-tumbler@qwest.net

Tucker, James C., P.O. Box 1212, Paso Robles, CA 93447-1212

Tucson Mold, Inc., 930 S. Plumer Ave., Tucson, AZ 85719 / 520-792-1075; FAX: 520-792-1075

Turk's Head Productions, Mustafa Bilal, 908 NW 50th St., Seattle, WA 98107-3634 / 206-782-4164; FAX: 206-783-5677 info@turkshead.com www.turkshead.com

Turnbull Restoration, Doug, 6680 Rt. 5 & 20, P.O. Box 471, Bloomfield, NY 14469 / 585-657-6338; FAX: 585-657-6338 turnbullrest@mindspring.com www.turnbullrestoration.com

Tuttle, Dale, 4046 Russell Rd., Muskegon, MI 49445 / 616-766-2250

Tyler Manufacturing & Distributing, 3804 S. Eastern, Oklahoma City, OK 73129 / 405-677-1487; or 800-654-8415

U

U.S. Fire Arms Mfg. Co., Inc., 55 Van Dyke Ave., Hartford, CT 06106 / 877-227-6901; FAX: 800-644-7265 usfirearms.com

U.S. Importer-Wm. Larkin Moore, 8430 E. Raintree Ste. B-7, Scottsdale, AZ 85260

U.S. Repeating Arms Co., Inc., 275 Winchester Ave., Morgan, UT 84050-9333 / 801-876-3440; FAX: 801-876-3737

U.S. Tactical Systems (See Keng's Firearms Specialty)

Ugartechea S. A., Ignacio, Chonta 26, Eibar, SPAIN / 43-121257; FAX: 43-121669

Ultra Dot Distribution, P.O. Box 362, 6304 Riverside Dr., Yankeetown, FL 34498 / 352-447-2255; FAX: 352-447-2266

Ultralux (See U.S. Importer-Keng's Firearms)

UltraSport Arms, Inc., 1955 Norwood Ct., Racine, WI 53403 / 414-554-3237; FAX: 414-554-9731

Uncle Bud's, HCR 81, Box 100, Needmore, PA 17238 / 717-294-6000; FAX: 717-294-6005

Uncle Mike's (See Michaels of Oregon Co.)

Unertl Optical Co., Inc., 103 Grand Avenue, P.O. Box 895, Mars, PA 16046-0895 / 724-625-3810; FAX: 724-625-3819 unertl@nauticom.net www.unertloptics.net

Unique/M.A.P.F., 10 Les Allees, 64700, Hendaye, FRANCE / 33-59 20 71 93

UniTec, 1250 Bedford SW, Canton, OH 44710 / 216-452-4017

United Binocular Co., 9043 S. Western Ave., Chicago, IL 60620

United Cutlery Corp., 1425 United Blvd., Sevierville, TN 37876 / 865-428-2532; or 800-548-0835; FAX: 865-428-2267

United States Optics Technologies, Inc., 5900 Dale St., Buena Park, CA 90621 / 714-994-4901; FAX: 714-994-4904 www.usoptics.com

United States Products Co., 518 Melwood Ave., Pittsburgh, PA 15213-1136 / 412-621-2130; FAX: 412-621-8740 sales@us-products.com www.us-products.com

Universal Sports, PO Box 532, Vincennes, IN 47591 / 812-882-8680; FAX: 812-882-8680

Unmussig Bullets, D. L., 7862 Brentford Dr., Richmond, VA 23225 / 804-320-1165

Upper Missouri Trading Co., P.O. Box 100, 304 Harold St., Crofton, NE 68730-0100 / 402-388-4844

USAC, 4500-15th St. East, Tacoma, WA 98424 / 206-922-7589

Utica Cutlery Co., 820 Noyes St., Utica, NY 13503 / 315-733-4663; FAX: 315-733-6602

V

V.H. Blackinton & Co., Inc., 221 John L. Dietsch, Attleboro Falls, MA 02763-0300 / 508-699-4436; FAX: 508-695-5349

Valdada Enterprises, P.O. Box 773122, 31733 County Road 35, Steamboat Springs, CO 80477 / 970-879-2983; FAX: 970-879-0851 www.valdada.com

Valtro USA, Inc, 1281 Andersen Dr., San Rafael, CA 94901 / 415-256-2575; FAX: 415-256-2576

VAM Distribution Co. LLC, 1141-B Mechanicsburg Rd., Wooster, OH 44691 www.rex10.com

Van Gorden & Son Inc., C. S., 1815 Main St., Bloomer, WI 54724 / 715-568-2612

Van Horn, Gil, P.O. Box 207, Llano, CA 93544

Van Patten, J. W., P.O. Box 145, Foster Hill, Milford, PA 18337 / 717-296-7069

Vann Custom Bullets, 330 Grandview Ave., Novato, CA 94947

Van's Gunsmith Service, 224 Route 69-A, Parish, NY 13131 / 315-625-7251

Varmint Masters, LLC, Rick Vecqueray, PO Box 6724, Bend, OR 97708 / 541-318-7306; FAX: 541-318-7306 varmintmasters@bendcable.com www.varmintmasters.net

Vecqueray, Rick. See: VARMINT MASTERS, LLC

Vega Tool Co., c/o T.R. Ross, 4865 Tanglewood Ct., Boulder, CO 80301 / 303-530-0174 clanlaird@aol.com www.vegatool.com

Vektor USA, Mikael Danforth, 5139 Stanart St, Norfolk, VA 23502 / 888-740-0837; or 757-455-8895; FAX: 757-461-9155

Venco Industries, Inc. (See Shooter's Choice Gun Care)

Venus Industries, P.O. Box 246, Sialkot-1, PAKISTAN FAX: 92 432 85579

Verney-Carron, BP 72-54 Boulevard Thiers, 42002 St Etienne Cedex 1, St Etienne Cedex 1, FRANCE / 33-477791500; FAX: 33-477790702 email@verney-carron.com www.verney-carron.com

Vest, John, 1923 NE 7th St., Redmond, OR 97756 / 541-923-8898

VibraShine, Inc., PO Box 577, Taylorsville, MS 39168 / 601-785-9854; FAX: 601-785-9874

Vibra-Tek Co., 1844 Arroya Rd., Colorado Springs, CO 80906 / 719-634-8611; FAX: 719-634-6886

Vic's Gun Refinishing, 6 Pineview Dr., Dover, NH 03820-6422 / 603-742-0013

Victory Ammunition, PO Box 1022, Milford, PA 18337 / 717-296-5768; FAX: 717-296-9298

Victory USA, P.O. Box 1021, Pine Bush, NY 12566 / 914-744-2060; FAX: 914-744-5181

Vihtavuori Oy, FIN-41330 Vihtavuori, FINLAND, / 358-41-3779211; FAX: 358-41-3771643

Vihtavuori Oy/Kaltron-Pettibone, 1241 Ellis St., Bensenville, IL 60106 / 708-350-1116; FAX: 708-350-1606

Viking Video Productions, P.O. Box 251, Roseburg, OR 97470

Vincent's Shop, 210 Antoinette, Fairbanks, AK 99701

Vincenzo Bernardelli S.p.A., 125 Via Matteotti, P.O. Box 74, Gardone V.T., Bresci, 25063 ITALY / 39-30-8912851-2-3; FAX: 39-30-8910249

Vintage Arms, Inc., 6003 Saddle Horse, Fairfax, VA 22030 / 703-968-0779; FAX: 703-968-0780

Vintage Industries, Inc., 781 Big Tree Dr., Longwood, FL 32750 / 407-831-8949; FAX: 407-831-5346

Viper Bullet and Brass Works, 11 Brock St., Box 582, Norwich, ON N0J 1P0 CANADA

Viramontez Engraving, Ray Viramontez, 601 Springfield Dr., Albany, GA 31721 / 229-432-9683 sgtvira@aol.com

Viramontez, Ray. See: VIRAMONTEZ ENGRAVING

Virgin Valley Custom Guns, 450 E 800 N #20, Hurricane, UT 84737 / 435-635-8941; FAX: 435-635-8943 vvcguns@infowest.com www.virginvalleyguns.com

Visible Impact Targets, Rts. 5 & 20, E. Bloomfield, NY 14443 / 716-657-6161; FAX: 716-657-5405

Vitt/Boos, 1195 Buck Hill Rd., Townshend, VT 05353 / 802-365-9232

Voere-KGH GmbH, Untere Sparchen 56, A-6330 Kufstein, Tirol, AUSTRIA / 0043-5372-62547; FAX: 0043-5372-65752 voere@aon.com www.voere.com

Volquartsen Custom Ltd., 24276 240th Street, PO Box 397, Carroll, IA 51401 / 712-792-4238; FAX: 712-792-2542 vcl@netins.net www.volquartsen.com

Vorhes, David, 3042 Beecham St., Napa, CA 94558 / 707-226-9116; FAX: 707-253-7334

Vortek Products, Inc., P.O. Box 871181, Canton, MI 48187-6181 / 313-397-5656; FAX: 313-397-5656

VSP Publishers (See Heritage/VSP Gun Books), PO Box 887, McCall, ID 83638 / 208-634-4104; FAX: 208-634-3101

VTI Gun Parts, P.O. Box 509, Lakeville, CT 06039 / 860-435-8068; FAX: 860-435-8146 mail@vtigunparts.com www.vtigunparts.com

Vulpes Ventures, Inc. Fox Cartridge Division, P.O. Box 1363, Bolingbrook, IL 60440-7363 / 630-759-1229

W

W. Square Enterprises, 9826 Sagedale Dr., Houston, TX 77089 / 281-484-0935; FAX: 281-464-9940 lfdw@pdq.net www.loadammo.com

W. Waller & Son, Inc., 2221 Stoney Brook Rd., Grantham, NH 03753-7706 / 603-863-4177 www.wallerandson.com

W.B. Niemi Engineering, Box 126 Center Road, Greensboro, VT 05841 / 802-533-7180 or 802-533-7141

W.C. Wolff Co., PO Box 458, Newtown Square, PA 19073 / 610-359-9600; or 800-545-0077; mail@gunsprings.com www.gunsprings.com

W.E. Birdsong & Assoc., 1435 Monterey Rd., Florence, MS 39073-9748 / 601-366-8270

W.E. Brownell Checkering Tools, 9390 Twin Mountain Cir., San Diego, CA 92126 / 858-695-2479; FAX: 858-695-2479

W.J. Riebe Co., 3434 Tucker Rd., Boise, ID 83703

W.R. Case & Sons Cutlery Co., Owens Way, Bradford, PA 16701 / 814-368-4123; or 800-523-6350; FAX: 814-368-1736 jsullivan@wrcase.com www.wrcase.com

Wagoner, Vernon G., 2325 E. Encanto St., Mesa, AZ 85213-5917 / 480-835-1307

Wakina by Pic, 24813 Alderbrook Dr., Santa Clarita, CA 91321 / 800-295-8194

Waldron, Herman, Box 475, 80 N. 17th St., Pomeroy, WA 99347 / 509-843-1404

Walker Arms Co., Inc., 499 County Rd. 820, Selma, AL 36701 / 334-872-6231; FAX: 334-872-6262

Wallace, Terry, 385 San Marino, Vallejo, CA 94589 / 707-642-7041

Walls Industries, Inc., P.O. Box 98, 1905 N. Main, Cleburne, TX 76033 / 817-645-4366; FAX: 817-645-7946 www.wallsoutdoors.com

Walters Industries, 6226 Park Lane, Dallas, TX 75225 / 214-691-6973

Walters, John. See: WALTERS WADS

Walters Wads, John Walters, 500 N. Avery Dr., Moore, OK 73160 / 405-799-0376; FAX: 405-799-7727 www.tinwadman@cs.com

Walther America, PO Box 22, Springfield, MA 01102 / 413-747-3443 www.walther-usa.com

Walther GmbH, Carl, B.P. 4325, D-89033 Ulm, GERMANY

Walt's Custom Leather, Walt Whinnery, 1947 Meadow Creek Dr., Louisville, KY 40218 / 502-458-4361

WAMCO-New Mexico, P.O. Box 205, Peralta, NM 87042-0205 / 505-869-0826

Ward & Van Valkenburg, 114 32nd Ave. N., Fargo, ND 58102 / 701-232-2351

Ward Machine, 5620 Lexington Rd., Corpus Christi, TX 78412 / 512-992-1221

Wardell Precision Handguns Ltd., 48851 N. Fig Springs Rd., New River, AZ 85027-8513 / 602-465-7995

Warenski, Julie, 590 E. 500 N., Richfield, UT 84701 / 801-896-5319; FAX: 801-896-5319

Warne Manufacturing Co., 9057 SE Jannsen Rd., Clackamas, OR 97015 / 503-657-5590 or 800-683-5590; FAX: 503-657-5695 info@warnescopemounts.com www.warnescopemounts.com

Warren Muzzleloading Co., Inc., Hwy. 21 North, P.O. Box 100, Ozone, AR 72854 / 501-292-3268

Washita Mountain Whetstone Co., P.O. Box 378, Lake Hamilton, AR 71951 / 501-525-3914

Wasmundt, Jim, P.O. Box 511, Fossil, OR 97830

Watson Bros., 39 Redcross Way, SE1 1H6, London, ENGLAND FAX: 44-171-403-336

Watson Trophy Match Bullets, 467 Pine Loop, Frostproof, FL 33843 / 863-635-7948 or 864-244-7948 cbestbullet@aol.com

Wayne E. Schwartz Custom Guns, 970 E. Britton Rd., Morrice, MI 48857 / 517-625-4079

Wayne Firearms For Collectors & Investors

Wayne Specialty Services, 260 Waterford Drive, Florissant, MO 63033 / 413-831-7083

WD-40 Co., 1061 Cudahy Pl., San Diego, CA 92110 / 619-275-1400; FAX: 619-275-5823

Weatherby, Inc., 3100 El Camino Real, Atascadero, CA 93422 / 805-466-1767; FAX: 805-466-2527 www.weatherby.com

Weaver Products ATK, P.O. Box 39, Onalaska, WI 54650 / 800-648-9624 or 608-781-5800; FAX: 608-781-0368

Weaver Scope Repair Service, 1121 Larry Mahan Dr., Suite B, El Paso, TX 79925 / 915-593-1005

Webb, Bill, 6504 North Bellefontaine, Kansas City, MO 64119 / 816-453-7431

Weber & Markin Custom Gunsmiths, 4-1691 Powick Rd., Kelowna, BC V1X 4L1 CANADA / 250-762-7575; FAX: 250-861-3655 www.weberandmarkinguns.com

Weber Jr., Rudolf, P.O. Box 160106, D-5650, GERMANY / 0212-592136

Webley and Scott Ltd., Frankley Industrial Park, Tay Rd., Birmingham, B45 0PA ENGLAND / 011-021-453-1864; FAX: 0121-457-7846 guns@webley.co.uk www.webley.co.uk

Webster Scale Mfg. Co., P.O. Box 188, Sebring, FL 33870 / 813-385-6362

Weems, Cecil, 510 W Hubbard St., Mineral Wells, TX 76067-4847 / 817-325-1462

Weigand Combat Handguns, Inc., 1057 South Main Rd., Mountain Top, PA 18707 / 570-868-8358; FAX: 570-868-5218 sales@jackweigand.com www.scopemount.com

Weihrauch KG, Hermann, Industriestrasse 11, 8744 Mellrichstadt, Mellrichstadt, GERMANY

Welch, Sam. See: SAM WELCH GUN ENGRAVING

Wellington Outdoors, P.O. Box 244, 1140 Monticello Rd., Madison, GA 30650 / 706-342-4915; FAX: 706-342-7568

Wells, Rachel, 110 N. Summit St., Prescott, AZ 86301 / 928-445-3655 wellssportstore@aol.com

Wells Creek Knife & Gun Works, 32956 State Hwy. 38, Scottsburg, OR 97473 / 541-587-4202; FAX: 541-587-4223

Welsh, Bud. See: HIGH PRECISION

Wenger North America/Precise Int'l, 15 Corporate Dr., Orangeburg, NY 10962 / 800-431-2996; FAX: 914-425-4700

Wenig Custom Gunstocks, 103 N. Market St., PO Box 249, Lincoln, MO 65338 / 660-547-3334; FAX: 660-547-2881 gustock@wenig.com www.wenig.com

Werth, T. W., 1203 Woodlawn Rd., Lincoln, IL 62656 / 217-732-1300

Wescombe, Bill (See North Star West)

Wessinger Custom Guns & Engraving, 268 Limestone Rd., Chapin, SC 29036 / 803-345-5677

West, Jack L., 1220 W. Fifth, P.O. Box 427, Arlington, OR 97812

Western Cutlery (See Camillus Cutlery Co.)

Western Design (See Alpha Gunsmith Division)

Western Mfg. Co., 550 Valencia School Rd., Aptos, CA 95003 / 831-688-5884 lotsabears@eathlink.net

Western Missouri Shooters Alliance, PO Box 11144, Kansas City, MO 64119 / 816-597-3950; FAX: 816-229-7350

Western Nevada West Coast Bullets, PO BOX 2270, DAYTON, NV 89403-2270 / 702-246-3941; FAX: 702-246-0836

Westley Richards & Co., 40 Grange Rd., Birmingham, ENGLAND / 010-214722953

Westley Richards Agency USA (See U.S. Importer for

Westwind Rifles, Inc., David S. Sullivan, P.O. Box 261, 640 Briggs St., Erie, CO 80516 / 303-828-3823

Weyer International, 2740 Nebraska Ave., Toledo, OH 43607 / 419-534-2020; FAX: 419-534-2697

Whildin & Sons Ltd, E.H., RR 2 Box 119, Tamaqua, PA 18252 / 717-668-6743; FAX: 717-668-6745

Whinnery, Walt (See Walt's Custom Leather)

Whiscombe (See U.S. Importer-Pelaire Products)

White Barn Wor, 431 County Road, Broadlands, IL 61816

White Pine Photographic Services, Hwy. 60, General Delivery, Wilno, ON K0J 2N0 CANADA / 613-756-3452

White Rifles, Inc., 1464 W. 40 South, Linden, UT 84042 / 801-932-7950 www.whiterifles.com

White Rock Tool & Die, 6400 N. Brighton Ave., Kansas City, MO 64119 / 816-454-0478

Whitestone Lumber Corp., 148-02 14th Ave., Whitestone, NY 11357 / 718-746-4400; FAX: 718-767-1748

Wichita Arms, Inc., 923 E. Gilbert, P.O. Box 11371, Wichita, KS 67211 / 316-265-0661; FAX: 316-265-0760

Wick, David E., 1504 Michigan Ave., Columbus, IN 47201 / 812-376-6960

Widener's Reloading & Shooting Supply, Inc., P.O. Box 3009 CRS, Johnson City, TN 37602 / 615-282-6786; FAX: 615-282-6651

Wideview Scope Mount Corp., 13535 S. Hwy. 16, Rapid City, SD 57701 / 605-341-3220; FAX: 605-341-9142 wvdon@rapidnet.com www.jii.to

Wiebe, Duane, 5300 Merchant Cir. #2, Placerville, CA 95667 / 530-344-1357; FAX: 530-344-1357 wiebe@d-wdb.com

Wiest, Marie. See: GUNCRAFT SPORTS, INC.

Wilcox All-Pro Tools & Supply, 4880 147th St., Montezuma, IA 50171 / 515-623-3138; FAX: 515-623-3104

Wilcox Industries Corp., Robert F Guarasi, 53 Durham St., Portsmouth, NH 03801 / 603-431-1331; FAX: 603-431-1221

Wild Bill's Originals, P.O. Box 13037, Burton, WA 98013 / 206-463-5738; FAX: 206-465-5925 wildbill@haleyon.com

Wild West Guns, 7521 Old Seward Hwy., Unit A, Anchorage, AK 99515 / 800-992-4570 or 907-344-4500; FAX: 907-344-4005 wwguns@ak.net www.wildwestguns.com

Wilderness Sound Products Ltd., 4015 Main St. A, Springfield, OR 97478 / 800-47-0006; FAX: 541-741-0263

Wildey, Inc., 45 Angevine Rd, Warren, CT 06754-1818 / 203-355-9000; FAX: 203-354-7759

Wildlife Research Center, Inc., 1050 McKinley St., Anoka, MN 55303 / 612-427-3350; or 800-USE-LURE; FAX: 612-427-8354

Will-Burt Co., 169 S. Main, Orrville, OH 44667

William Fagan & Co., 22952 15 Mile Rd., Clinton Township, MI 48035 / 810-465-4637; FAX: 810-792-6996

William E. Phillips Firearms, 38 Avondale Rd., Wigston, Leicester, ENGLAND / 0116 2886334; FAX: 0116 2810644 wephillips@aol.com

William Powell & Son (Gunmakers) Ltd., 35-37 Carrs Lane, Birmingham, B4 7SX ENGLAND / 121-643-0689; FAX: 121-631-3504

William Powell Agency, 22 Circle Dr., Bellmore, NY 11710 / 516-679-1158

Williams Gun Sight Co., 7389 Lapeer Rd., Box 329, Davison, MI 48423 / 810-653-2131 or 800-530-9028; FAX: 810-658-2140 williamsgunsight.com

Williams Mfg. of Oregon, 110 East B St., Drain, OR 97435 / 503-836-7461; FAX: 503-836-7245

Williams Shootin' Iron Service, The Lynx-Line, Rt. 2 Box 223A, Mountain Grove, MO 65711 / 417-948-0902; FAX: 417-948-0902

Williamson Precision Gunsmithing, 117 W. Pipeline, Hurst, TX 76053 / 817-285-0064; FAX: 817-280-0044

Willow Bend, P.O. Box 203, Chelmsford, MA 01824 / 978-256-8508; FAX: 978-256-8508

Wilsom Combat, 2234 CR 719, Berryville, AR 72616-4573 / 800-955-4856; FAX: 870-545-3310

Wilson Case, Inc., PO Box 1106, Hastings, NE 68902-1106 / 800-322-5493; FAX: 402-463-5276 sales@wilsoncase.com www.wilsoncase.com

Wilson Combat, 2234 CR 719, Berryville, AR 72616-4573 / 800-955-4856

Winchester Div. Olin Corp., 427 N. Shamrock, E. Alton, IL 62024 / 618-258-3566; FAX: 618-258-3599

Winchester Sutler, Inc., The, 270 Shadow Brook Lane, Winchester, VA 22603 / 540-888-3595; FAX: 540-888-4632

Windish, Jim, 2510 Dawn Dr., Alexandria, VA 22306 / 703-765-1994

Wingshooting Adventures, 0-1845 W. Leonard, Grand Rapids, MI 49544 / 616-677-1980; FAX: 616-677-1986

Winkle Bullets, R.R. 1, Box 316, Heyworth, IL 61745

Winter, Robert M., P.O. Box 484, 42975-287th St., Menno, SD 57045 / 605-387-5322

Wise Custom Guns, 1402 Blanco Rd., San Antonio, TX 78212-2716 / 210-828-3388

Wise Guns, Dale, 1402 Blanco Rd., San Antonio, TX 78212 / 210-734-9999

Wiseman and Co., Bill, PO Box 3427, Bryan, TX 77805 / 409-690-3456; FAX: 409-690-0156

Wisners Inc/Twin Pine Armory, P.O. Box 58, Hwy. 6, Adna, WA 98522 / 360-748-4590; FAX: 360-748-1802

Wolf (See J.R. Distributing)

Wolf Performance Ammunition, 2201 E. Winston Rd. Ste. K, Anaheim, CA 92806-5537 / 702-837-8506; FAX: 702-837-9250

Wolfe Publishing Co., 6471 Airpark Dr., Prescott, AZ 86301 / 520-445-7810 or 800-899-7810; FAX: 520-778-5124

Wolf's Western Traders, 1250 Santa Cora Ave. #613, Chula Vista, CA 91913 / 619-482-1701 patwolf4570book@aol.com

Wolverine Footwear Group, 9341 Courtland Dr. NE, Rockford, MI 49351 / 616-866-5500; FAX: 616-866-5658

Wood, Frank (See Classic Guns, Inc.), 5305 Peachtree Ind. Blvd., Norcross, GA 30092 / 404-242-7944

Woodleigh (See Huntington Die Specialties)

Woods Wise Products, P.O. Box 681552, Franklin, TN 37068 / 800-735-8182; FAX: 615-726-2637

Woodstream, P.O. Box 327, Lititz, PA 17543 / 717-626-2125; FAX: 717-626-1912

Woodworker's Supply, 1108 North Glenn Rd., Casper, WY 82601 / 307-237-5354

Woolrich, Inc., Mill St., Woolrich, PA 17701 / 800-995-1299; FAX: 717-769-6234/6259

Working Guns, Jim Coffin, 1224 NW Fernwood Cir., Corvallis, OR 97330-2909 / 541-928-4391

World of Targets (See Birchwood Casey)

World Trek, Inc., 7170 Turkey Creek Rd., Pueblo, CO 81007-1046 / 719-546-2121; FAX: 719-543-6886

Worthy Products, Inc., RR 1, P.O. Box 213, Martville, NY 13111 / 315-324-5298

Wostenholm (See Ibberson [Sheffield] Ltd., George)

Wright's Gunstock Blanks, 8540 SE Kane Rd., Gresham, OR 97080 / 503-666-1705 doyal@wrightsguns.com www.wrightsguns.com

WTA Manufacturing, P.O. Box 164, Kit Carson, CO 80825 / 800-700-3054; FAX: 719-962-3570 wta@rebeltec.net http://www.members.aol.com/ductman249/wta.html

Wyant Bullets, Gen. Del., Swan Lake, MT 59911

Wyant's Outdoor Products, Inc., PO Box 9, Broadway, VA 22815

Wyoming Custom Bullets, 1626 21st St., Cody, WY 82414

Wyoming Knife Corp., 101 Commerce Dr., Ft. Collins, CO 80524 / 303-224-3454

X

X-Spand Target Systems, 26-10th St. SE, Medicine Hat, AB T1A 1P7 CANADA / 403-526-7997; FAX: 403-528-2362

Y

Yankee Gunsmith "Just Glocks", 2901 Deer Flat Dr., Copperas Cove, TX 76522 / 817-547-8433; FAX: 254-547-8887 ed@justglocks.com www.justglocks.com

Yavapai College, 1100 E. Sheldon St., Prescott, AZ 86301 / 520-776-2353; FAX: 520-776-2355

Yavapai Firearms Academy Ltd., P.O. Box 27290, Prescott Valley, AZ 86312 / 928-772-8262; FAX: 928-772-0062 info@yfainc.com www.yfainc.com

Yearout, Lewis E. (See Montana Outfitters), 308 Riverview Dr E, Great Falls, MT 59404 / 406-761-0859

Yee, Mike. See: CUSTOM STOCKING

Yellowstone Wilderness Supply, P.O. Box 129, W. Yellowstone, MT 59758 / 406-646-7613

Yesteryear Armory & Supply, P.O. Box 408, Carthage, TN 37030

York M-1 Conversions, 12145 Mill Creek Run, Plantersville, TX 77363 / 936-894-2397; FAX: 936-894-2397

Young Country Arms, William, 1409 Kuehner Dr. #13, Simi Valley, CA 93063-4478

Z

Zabala Hermanos S.A., P.O. Box 97, 20600 Elbar, Elgueta, Guipuzcoa, 20600 SPAIN / 943-768076; FAX: 943-768201

Zander's Sporting Goods, 7525 Hwy 154 West, Baldwin, IL 62217-9706 / 800-851-4373; FAX: 618-785-2320

Zanotti Armor, Inc., 123 W. Lone Tree Rd., Cedar Falls, IA 50613 / 319-232-9650

Zeeryp, Russ, 1601 Foard Dr., Lynn Ross Manor, Morristown, TN 37814 / 615-586-2357

Zero Ammunition Co., Inc., 1601 22nd St. SE, PO Box 1188, Cullman, AL 35056-1188 / 800-545-9376; FAX: 205-737-4683

Ziegel Engineering, 1390 E. Bunnett St. #I, Signal Hill, CA 90755 / 562-596-9481; FAX: 562-598-4734 ziegel@aol.com www.ziegeleng.com

Zim's, Inc., 4370 S. 3rd West, Salt Lake City, UT 84107 / 801-268-2505

Z-M Weapons, 203 South St., Bernardston, MA 01337 / 413-648-9501; FAX: 413-648-0219

Zufall, Joseph F., P.O. Box 304, Golden, CO 80402-0304